PACIFIC NORTHWEST CAMPING

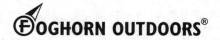

PACIFIC NORTHWEST CAMPING

The Complete Guide to Tent and RV Campgrounds in Oregon and Washington

EIGHTH EDITION

Tom Stienstra

AVALON
TRAVEL

FOGHORN OUTDOORS
PACIFIC NORTHWEST CAMPING
The Complete Guide to
Tent and RV Campgrounds in
Oregon and Washington

Eighth Edition

Tom Stienstra

Please send all feedback about this book to:

ⒻOGHORN OUTDOORS®
Pacific Northwest Camping
Avalon Travel Publishing
1400 65th Street, Suite 250
Emeryville, CA 94608, USA
email: atpfeedback@avalonpub.com
website: www.foghorn.com

Printing History
1st edition—1988
8th edition—May 2003
5 4 3 2 1

ISBN: 1-56691-631-3
ISSN: 1078-9588

Editor: Rebecca K. Browning
Series Manager: Marisa Solís
Senior Research Editor: Stephani Cruickshank
Research Editor: Pamela S. Padula
Copy Editor: Kimberly Marks
Proofreader: Erika Howsare
Graphics Coordinator: Susan Snyder
Illustrator: Bob Race
Production Coordinator: Jacob Goolkasian
Cover Designer: Jacob Goolkasian
Interior Designer: Darren Alessi
Layout: Alvaro Villanueva
Map Editor: Olivia Solís
Cartographers: Kat Kalamaras, Suzanne Service, Mike Morgenfeld, Landis Bennitt, CHK America
Indexers: Amy Scott, Marisa Solís

Front cover photo: © Chuck Mitchell

Printed in the United States of America by Worzalla

Distributed by Publishers Group West

About the Author

Tom Stienstra has made it his life's work to explore the West, traveling 150 days a year—camping, hiking, fishing, biking, boating, and flying—searching for the best of the outdoors and then writing about it. As an airplane owner and pilot, he is able to travel from the San Juan Islands to the Oregon border touring every destination in the Pacific Northwest.

Tom is the nation's top-selling author of outdoor guidebooks and has twice been awarded National Outdoor Writer of the Year, newspaper division, by the Outdoor Writers Association of America. Tom is also an outdoors columnist and his articles are distributed across the nation by the New York Times News Service.

His wife, Stephani Stienstra, has co-authored two books with him, including *Foghorn Outdoors Oregon Camping*. They live with their sons on an 80-acre ranch.

You can contact Tom directly via the website www.TomStienstra.com. His books are also available on his website, and include:

Foghorn Outdoors California Camping
Foghorn Outdoors California Fishing
Foghorn Outdoors California Hiking (with Ann Marie Brown)
Foghorn Outdoors California Recreational Lakes & Rivers
Foghorn Outdoors California Wildlife (with illustrator Paul Johnson)
Foghorn Outdoors Northern California Cabins & Cottages (with Stephani Stienstra)
Foghorn Outdoors Oregon Camping
Foghorn Outdoors Washington Camping (with Stephani Stienstra)

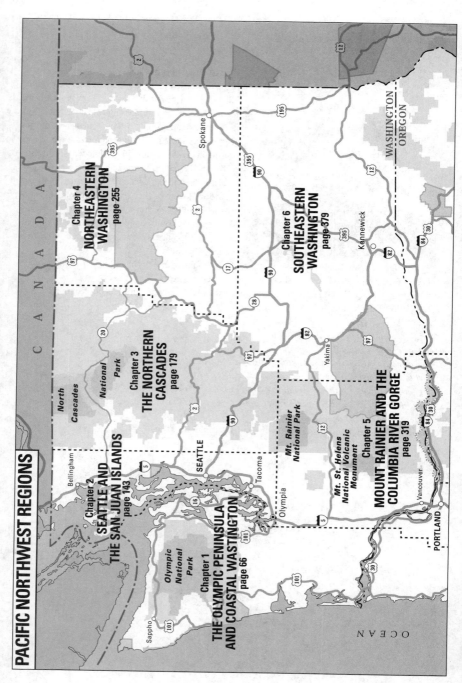

PACIFIC NORTHWEST REGIONS

Chapter 1
THE OLYMPIC PENINSULA
AND COASTAL WASHINGTON
page 66

Chapter 2
SEATTLE AND
THE SAN JUAN ISLANDS
page 143

Chapter 3
THE NORTHERN
CASCADES
page 179

Chapter 4
NORTHEASTERN
WASHINGTON
page 255

Chapter 5
MOUNT RAINIER AND THE
COLUMBIA RIVER GORGE
page 319

Chapter 6
SOUTHEASTERN
WASHINGTON
page 379

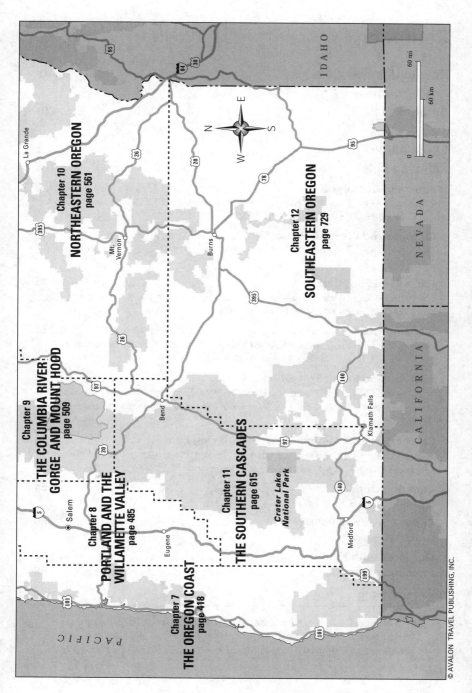

Chapter 7
THE OREGON COAST
page 418

Chapter 8
PORTLAND AND THE WILLAMETTE VALLEY
page 485

Chapter 9
THE COLUMBIA RIVER: GORGE AND MOUNT HOOD
page 509

Chapter 10
NORTHEASTERN OREGON
page 561

Chapter 11
THE SOUTHERN CASCADES
page 615

Chapter 12
SOUTHEASTERN OREGON
page 729

Crater Lake National Park

PACIFIC

IDAHO

NEVADA

CALIFORNIA

La Grande

Mt. Vernon

Burns

Salem

Eugene

Bend

Klamath Falls

Medford

60 mi
60 km

© AVALON TRAVEL PUBLISHING, INC.

Contents

Gorge Lake • Icicle Creek • Icicle River • Kachess Lake • Lake Chelan • Lake Easton • Lake Entiat • Lake Wapato • Lake Wenatchee • Little Greider Lake • Little Naches River • Little Wenatchee River • Loup Loup Ski Area • Lower Ashland Lake • Marble Creek • Methow River • Mt. Baker-Snoqualmie National Forest • Napequa River • Nooksack River • Pacific Crest Trail • Pasayten Wilderness • Pearrygin Lake • Penshastin Creek • Ross Lake National Recreation Area • Salmon Creek • Sauk River • Skagit River • Skykomish River • Snohomish • Snoqualmie River • Squire Creek • Stillaguamish River • Suiattle River • Swauk Creek • Sweat Creek • Taneum Creek • Teanaway River • Tiffany Lake • Tucquala Lake • Twin Falls Lake • Twin Lakes • Twisp River • Upper Ashland Lake • Wenatchee National Forest • Wenatchee River • White River • Yakima River

Including: Alta Lake • Banks Lake • Beaver Lake • Beth Lake • Big Meadow Lake • Blue Lake • Bonaparte Lake • Browns Lake • Chewelah • Chopaka Lake • Clear Lake • Cold Creek • Columbia River • Conconully Reservoir • Crawfish Lake • Curlew Lake • Davis Lake • East Portal Historical Site • Ferry Lake • Flodelle Creek • Franklin Roosevelt Lake • Grand Coulee Dam • Jump Off Joe Lake • Lake Chelan • Lake Ellen • Lake Gillette • Lake Leo • Lake Thomas • Leader Lake • Little Spokane River • Little Twin Lakes • Long Lake • Loon Lake • Lost Lake • Loup Loup Creek • Lyman Lake • Mill Creek • Mt. Spokane • Newport • Okanogan River • Osoyoos Lake • Palmer Lake • Park Lake • Pend Oreille River • Pierre Lake • Rock Creek • Rock Lake • Rocky Lake • Rufus Woods Lake • Sanpoil River • Sheep Creek • Sherman Pass • Sherry Lake • Silver Lake • South Skookum Lake • Spectacle Lake • Spokane River • Spokane • Starvation Lake • Sugarloaf Lake • Sullivan Lake • Sun Lakes State Park • Swan Lake • Toats Coulee Creek • Trout Lake • Twin Lakes Reservoir • Upper Conconully Reservoir • Waitts Lake • Wannacut Lake • West Medical Lake • Williams Lake

Including: Ahtanum Creek • Alder Lake • American River • Battle Ground Lake • Big Creek • Big Lava Bed • Bird Creek • Black Lake • Blue Lake • Bumping River • Carbon River • Cat Creek • Cedar Creek • Centralia • Chehalis • Cispus River • Clear Lake • Columbia River • Cowlitz River • Dalles Dam • Deep Lake • Dog Lake • Elbe • Evans Creek • Goat Rocks Wilderness • Goose Lake • Green River • Horseshoe Lake • Indian Heaven Wilderness • Kalama River • Leech Lake • Lewis River • Little Goose Creek • Little Naches River • Little White Salmon River • Mayfield Lake • Meadow Lake • Morrison Creek • Mount Adams Wilderness • Mount Adams • Mount Baker-Snoqualmie National Forest • Mount Rainier National Park • Mount St. Helens • Naches River • Newaukum River • Offut Lake • Ohanapecosh River • Olallie Lake • Olympia • Pacific Crest Trail • Packwood • Panther Creek •

Paradise Creek • Paradise Point State Park • Quartz Creek • Riffle Lake • Rimrock Lake • Rock Creek • Silver Lake • Spring Creek • Summit Creek • Takhlakh Lake • Tanwax Lake • Tieton River • Toutle River • Trout Lake • Trout Lake Creek • Walupt Lake • Washougal River • Wenatchee National Forest • White River • Wind River • Woodland • Yale Lake

Including: Ahtanum Creek • Colfax • Columbia River • George • Goldendale Observatory • Lake Bryan • Lake Sacajawea • Lake Umatilla • Lake Wallula • Lewis and Clark Trail • Lower Granite Lake • Moses Lake State Park • Naches River • Palouse River • Pasco • Potholes Reservoir • Puffer Butte • Ritzville • Snake River • Soap Lake • Sprague Lake • Tieton River • Umatilla National Forest • Wenaha-Tucannon Wilderness • Williams Lake • Yakima River • Yakima

Oregon

Including: Alder Lake • Alsea Bay • Alsea River • Beaver Creek • Bluebill Lake • Bullards Beach State Park • Canal Creek • Cape Arago State Park • Cape Creek • Cape Perpetua • Carter Lake • Chetco River • Cleowax Lake • Columbia River • Coos Bay • Coquille • Coquille River • Devil's Lake • Ecola State Park • Eel Lake • Elk Creek • Elk River • Fairview • Florence • Fort Stevens State Park • Gales Creek • Garibaldi • Gold Beach • Grants Pass • Hebo Lake • Jordan Creek • Knowles Creek • Laird Lake • Loon Lake • Mercer Lake • Myers Creek • Neawanna River • Nestucca River • Netarts Bay • North Bend • Oregon Dunes National Recreation Area • Pacific Ocean • Rock Creek • Rogue River • Saddle Mountain • Seal Rock State Park • Siletz Bay • Siltcoos Lake • Siltcoos River • Siuslaw National Forest • Siuslaw River • Sixes River • Squaw Lake • Sunset Bay • Sutton Lake • Tahkenitch Lake • Tenmile Creek • Tenmile Lake • Three Rivers • Tillamook Bay • Tillamook River • Tillamook State Forest • Umpqua River • Wilson River • Winchester Bay • Winchuck River • Woahink Lake • Yamhill River • Yaquina Bay

Including: Aurora • Clackamas River • Clear Creek • Columbia River • Cottage Grove Reservoir • Dexter Point Reservoir • Dorena Lake • Eugene • Fall Creek Reservoir State Recreation Area • Fern Ridge Reservoir • Foster Reservoir • Green Peter Reservoir • Little North Santiam River • Molalla River • North Santiam River • Quartzville Creek • Salem • Santiam River • Scappoose • Siuslaw River • South Santiam River • South Yamhill River • Tualatin • Willamette River

River • Fish Lake • Fourbit Creek • Fourmile Lake • Glendale • Gold Lake • Grants Pass • Hackleman Creek • Haystack Reservoir • Hemlock Lake • Hills Creek Reservoir • Horse Creek • Hosmer Lake • Howard Prairie Lake • Hyatt Lake • Illinois River • Indian Ford Creek • Irish Lake • Jackson Creek • Klamath Lake • Lake Selmac • Lake in the Woods • Lava Lake • Layng Cree • Lemolo Lake • Little Cultus Lake • Little Deschutes River • Little Lava Lake • Little River • Lost Creek Reservoir • Lost Creek • McKenzie River • Metolius River • Miller Lake • North Davis Creek • North Twin Lake • North Umpqua River • Odell Lake • Oregon Caves National Monument • Pacific Crest Trail • Parker Meadow • Paulina Creek • Quinn Creek • Rock Creek • Rogue River • Roseburg • Salmon Creek • Salt Creek • Santiam River • Scott Lake • Sharps Creek • Sky Lakes Wilderness • Smith Reservoir • Smith Rock State Park • South Rogue River • South Santiam River • South Twin Lake • South Umpqua River • Sparks Lake • Sprague River • Squaw Lake • Steamboat Creek • Suttle Lake • Taylor Lake • Three Creeks Lake • Three Sisters Wilderness • Timpanogas Lake • Tingley Lake • Todd Lake • Toketee Lake • Trailbridge Reservoir • Trout Creek Swamp • Twin Lakes • Umpqua River • Upper Deschutes River • Upper Klamath Lake • Upper Klamath River • Upper Rogue River • Waldo Lake • Whitefish Creek • Wickiup Reservoir • Willamette National Forest • Willamette River • Willow Lake • Winberry Creek • Winema National al Forest • Wood River • Woodruff Creek

Our Commitment

We are committed to making *Foghorn Outdoors Pacific Northwest Camping* the most accurate, thorough, and enjoyable camping guide to the region. With this eighth edition, you can rest assured that every camping spot in this book has been carefully reviewed and accompanied by the most up-to-date information available. It is possible in few cases, primarily at a small number of private RV parks, that some campground fees will be raised after we have gone to press. If you have a specific need or concern, it's a good idea to call the campground ahead of time.

If you would like to comment on the book, whether it's to suggest a tent or RV spot we overlooked, or to let us know about any noteworthy experience—good or bad—that occurred while using *Foghorn Outdoors Pacific Northwest Camping* as your guide, we would appreciate hearing from you. Please address correspondence to:

Foghorn Outdoors Pacific Northwest Camping, 8th Edition
Avalon Travel Publishing
1400 65th Street, Suite 250
Emeryville, CA 94608, U.S.A.

email: atpfeedback@avalonpub.com

How to Use This Book

Foghorn Outdoors Pacific Northwest Camping is divided into 12 chapters based on major geographic regions in the states. Each chapter begins with a map of the region, which is further broken down into detail maps. These detail maps show the location of all the campgrounds in that chapter.

This guide can be navigated easily in two ways:

1. If you know the name of the specific campground you want to use, or the name of the surrounding geographical area or nearby feature (town, national or state park, forest, mountain, lake, river, etc.), look it up in the index and turn to the corresponding page.

2. If you know the general area you want to visit, turn to the map at the beginning of the chapter that covers the area. Each chapter map is broken down into detail maps, which show by number all the campgrounds in that chapter. You can then determine which campsites are in or near your destination by their corresponding numbers. Campgrounds are listed sequentially in each chapter so you can turn to the page with the corresponding map number for the site you're interested in.

ABOUT THE CAMPGROUND PROFILES

Each campground in this book is listed in a consistent, easy-to-read format to help you choose the ideal camping spot. From a general overview of the setting to detailed driving directions, the profile will provide all the information you need. Here is an example:

Map number and campground name →

General location of the campground named by its proximity to the nearest major town or landmark →

Icons noting activities and facilities at or nearby the campground

Scenic rating, on a scale of 1–10

Map the campground can be found on, grid reference on map, and page number the map can be found on

1 SOMEWHERE USA CAMPGROUND

Rating: 10

South of Somewhere USA Lake.

Map 1.2, grid f6, page 4

Each campground in this book begins with a brief overview of its setting. The description typically covers ambience, information about the attractions, and activities popular at the campground.

Campsites, facilities: This section provides the number of campsites for both tents and RVs and whether hookups are available. Facilities such as restrooms, picnic areas, recreation areas, laundry, and dump stations will be addressed, as well as the availability of piped water, showers, playground, stores, and others amenities. The campground's pet policy is also mentioned here.

Reservations, fees: This section notes whether reservations are accepted, and the rates for tent sites and RV sites. If there are additional fees for parking or pets, or discounted weekly or seasonal rates, those will also be noted here.

Directions: This section provides mile-by-mile driving directions to the campground from the nearest major town.

Contact: This section provides an address, phone number, and Internet address, if available, for each campground.

ABOUT THE ICONS

The icons in this book are designed to provide at-a-glance information on activities, facilities, and services provided that are available on-site or within walking distance of each campground. The icons are not meant to represent every activity or service, but rather those that are most significant.

— Hiking trails are available.

— Biking trails or routes are available. This usually refers to mountain biking, although it may represent road cycling as well. Refer to the text for that campground for details.

— Swimming opportunities are available.

— Fishing opportunities are available.

— Boating opportunities are available. Various types of vessels apply under this umbrella activity, including motorboats and personal watercrafts (Jet Skis). Refer to the text for that campground for more details, including mph restrictions and boat ramp availability.

— Winter sports are available. This general category may include activities such as downhill skiing, cross-country skiing, snowshoeing, snowmobiling, snowboarding, and ice skating. Refer to the text for that campground for more details on which sports are available.

— Pets are permitted. Campgrounds that allow pets may require an additional fee or that pets be leashed. Campgrounds may also restrict pet size or behavior. Refer to the text for that campground for specific instructions or call in advance.

— A playground is available. A campground with a playground can be desirable for campers traveling with children.

— Wheelchair access is provided, as advertised by campground managers. However, concerned persons are advised to call the contact number of a campground to be certain that their specific needs will be met.

— RV sites are provided.

— Tent sites are provided.

Author's Note

If this book looks different from anything you have ever seen about the Pacific Northwest, that is because it is.

I have made it a personal mission to win your trust and put the best of Oregon and Washington's great outdoors right in the palms of your hands in this book.

The reason I wrote the book was simple: I never wanted to get stuck for the night without a spot again. So I searched them out, primarily for myself. In the end, that is the best public value of the book: you will never get stuck for the night. With this book, the days of being a prisoner of hope are over.

In this mission to make *Foghorn Outdoors Pacific Northwest Camping* your book of choice, I have incorporated what I have learned in the past 25 years of roaming around the West as a full-time outdoors writer. I then hired three research editors to fact-check my work and review it with resource specialists. Together we faxed hundreds of pages of galley proofs to more than 400 rangers and recreation specialists at field offices and to the owners of each privately operated park. In the process, each word of every page has been reviewed by three or four specialists, with hundreds of people involved in polishing the final product.

When we checked out the competition and compared the work with other books on the market, we discovered thousands of errors and listings that were outdated. We also discovered directions that were simply wrong or incoherent.

I have written every direction in the book so it is as if a person in the passenger seat is reading it to the person who is driving. Compare the directions and maps in this book with anything else out there and that alone will make it your book of choice.

Many of the most beautiful places on earth are in the Pacific Northwest, and when my family and friends heard I was writing this book, they all instantly hated me! They figured all of their favorite spots would be revealed to all. But after reviewing the manuscript, they don't hate me anymore (except for this one cousin). That is because they have discovered, as I have, that Oregon and Washington are filled with beautiful, little-used campgrounds that are perfect jump-off points for adventures—and they represent hundreds of outstanding destinations, in addition to their sprinkling of favorites.

Some of the highlights of this book include:

• 1344 campgrounds, featuring national forests, local, county, state and national parks, BLM land, land managed by the U.S. Army Corps of Engineers and Department of Forestry, and privately owned and operated parks.

• 96 updated maps.

• Directions that are the easiest-to-use (and fact-checked) of any outdoor book in the state.

• Detailed and fact-checked information about each camp's facilities, fees, reservation policies, and nearby recreation.

• Helpful and anecdotal information about how to put the fun into every trip, including tips on catching fish, dealing with bears, and finding the best camp tents, bags, food, water purifiers, and more.

• Icons that quickly identify activities at each camp, and if pets are allowed.

I get tons of emails and letters, and I read each one carefully. These have been of great benefit. In the process, I have incorporated dozen of suggestions from readers to make this the book they want it to be. Your comments are always welcome and appreciated.

As you might figure, this is not a hobby for me, as it is for some part-time writers who publish books. This is my full-time job. Because I spend 150 to 200 days a year in the field, I understand how seriously people take their fun, what they need to know to make their trips work, as well as their underlying fears that they might get stuck for the night without a spot.

My advice is to never go anywhere without this book sitting on your front seat. See you out there!

Tom Stienstra
website: www.TomStienstra.com

Introduction

Camping Tips

FOOD AND COOKING GEAR

It was a warm, crystal clear day, the kind of day when if you had ever wanted to go skydiving, you would go skydiving. That was exactly the case for my old pal Foonsky, who had never before tried the sport. But a funny thing happened after he jumped out of the plane and pulled on the rip cord: his parachute didn't open.

In total free fall, Foonsky watched the earth below getting closer and closer. Not one to panic, he calmly pulled the rip cord on the emergency parachute. Again nothing happened. No parachute, no nothing.

The ground was getting ever closer, and as he tried to search for a soft place to land, Foonsky detected a small object shooting up toward him, growing larger as it approached. It looked like a camper.

Figuring this was his last chance, Foonsky shouted as they passed in midair, "Hey, do you know anything about parachutes?"

The other fellow just yelled back as he headed off into space, "Do you know anything about lighting camping stoves?"

Well, Foonsky got lucky and his parachute opened. As for the other guy, well, he's probably in orbit like a NASA weather satellite. If you've ever had a mishap while lighting a camping stove, you know exactly what I'm talking about.

When it comes to camping, all gear is not created equal. Nothing is more important than lighting your stove easily and having it reach full heat without feeling as if you're playing with a short fuse to a miniature bomb. If your stove does not work right, your trip can turn into a disaster, regardless of how well you have planned the other elements. In addition, a bad stove will add an underlying sense of foreboding to your day. You will constantly have the inner suspicion that your darn stove is going to foul up again.

Camping Stoves

If you are buying a camping stove, remember this one critical rule: do not leave the store with a new stove unless you have been shown exactly how to use it.

Know what you are getting. Many stores that specialize in outdoor recreation equipment now provide experienced campers/employees who will demonstrate the use of every stove they sell and while they're at it, describe their respective strengths and weaknesses.

An innovation by Peak 1 is a two-burner backpacking stove that allows you to boil water and heat a pot of food simultaneously. While that has long been standard for car campers using Coleman's legendary camp stove, it was previously unheard of for wilderness campers in high-elevation areas.

A stove that has developed a cultlike following is the little Sierra, which burns small twigs and pinecones, then uses a tiny battery-driven fan to develop increased heat and cooking ability. It's an excellent alternative for long-distance backpacking trips, as it solves the problem of carrying a fuel bottle, especially on expeditions for which large quantities of fuel would otherwise be needed. Some tinkering with the flame (a very hot one) is required, and they are legal and functional only in the alpine zone where dry wood is available. Also note that in years with high fire danger, the U.S. Forest Service will enact rules prohibiting open flames, and fires are also often prohibited above an elevation of 10,000 feet.

For expeditions, I prefer a small, lightweight stove that uses white gas so I can closely gauge fuel consumption. My pal Foonsky uses one with a butane bottle because it lights so easily. We have contests to see who can boil a pot of water faster, and the difference is usually negligible. Thus, other factors are important when choosing a stove.

Of these, ease of cleaning the burner is the most important. If you camp often, especially with a smaller stove, the burner holes will eventually become clogged. Some stoves have a built-in cleaning needle; a quick twist of the knob and you're in business. Others require disassembly and a protracted session using special cleaning tools. If a stove is difficult to clean, you will tend to put off doing it, and your stove will sputter and pant while you feel humiliated watching the cold pot of water sitting there.

Before making a purchase, have the salesperson show you how to clean the burner head. Except in the case of large, multiburner family camping stoves, which rarely require cleaning, this test can do more to determine the long-term value of a stove than any other factor.

Fuels for Camping Stoves

White gas and butane have long been the most popular camp fuels, but a newly developed fuel could dramatically change that.

LPG (liquid petroleum gas) comes in cartridges for easy attachment to a stove or lantern. At room temperature, LPG is delivered in a combustible gaseous form. When you shake the cartridge, the contents sound liquid; that is because the gas liquefies under pressure, which is why it is so easy to use. Large amounts of fuel are compressed into small canisters.

While convenience has always been the calling card for LPG, recent innovations have allowed it to become a suitable choice for winter and high-altitude mountaineering expeditions,

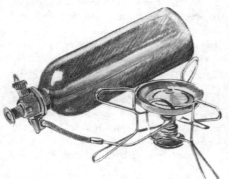

Stoves are available in many styles and burn a variety of fuels. These are three typical examples. Top: **White gas stoves** are the most popular because they are inexpensive and easy to find; they do require priming and can be explosive. Middle: **Gas canister stoves** burn propane, butane, isobutane, and mixtures of the three. These are the easiest to use but have two disadvantages: 1) Because the fuel is bottled, determining how much fuel is left can be difficult. 2) The fuel is limited to above-freezing conditions. Bottom: **Liquid fuel stoves** burn Coleman fuel, denatured alcohol, kerosene, and even gasoline; these fuels are economical and have a high heat output, but most must be primed.

coming close to matching white gas performance specs. For several years now, MSR, Epi (Coleman), Coleman, Primus, Camping Gaz, Markill, and other makers have been mixing propane, butane, and isobutane to improve performance capabilities.

Two important hurdles that stood in the way of LPG's popularity have been leaped. Coleman, working in cooperation with the U.S. Postal Service, has developed a program in which three-packs of 170-gram Coleman Max fuel cartridges can be shipped by mail to any address or post office in the 50 states and Puerto Rico. Also, each Coleman Max fuel cartridge is now made of aluminum and comes with a special device that allows the consumer to puncture the cartridge safely once the fuel is gone and then toss it into any aluminum recycling container.

The following details the benefits and drawbacks of other available fuels:

White gas: White gas is the most popular camp fuel because it is sold at most outdoor recreation stores and many supermarkets and is inexpensive and effective. It burns hot, has virtually no smell, and evaporates quickly when spilled. If you are caught in wet, miserable weather and can't get a fire going, you can use white gas as an emergency fire starter; however, if you do so, use it sparingly and never on an open flame.

During high fire danger the U.S. Forest Service will enact rules prohibiting open flames. Fires are also often prohibited above an elevation of 10,000 feet.

White gas is a popular fuel both for car campers, who use the large, two-burner stoves equipped with a fuel tank and a pump, and for hikers who carry a lightweight backpacking stove. On the latter, lighting can require priming with a gel called priming paste, which some people dislike. Another problem with white gas is that it can be extremely explosive.

As an example, I once almost burned my beard completely off in a mini-explosion while lighting one of the larger stoves designed for car camping. I was in the middle of cooking dinner when the flame suddenly shut down. Sure enough, the fuel tank was empty, and after refilling it, I pumped the tank 50 or 60 times to regain pressure. When I lit a match, the sucker ignited from three feet away. The resulting explosion was like a stick of dynamite going off, and immediately the smell of burning beard was in the air. In a flash, my once thick, dark beard had been reduced to a mass of little yellow burned curlicues.

My error? After filling the tank, I forgot to shut the fuel cock off while pumping up the pressure in the tank. As a result, the stove burners were slowly producing the gas/air mixture as I pumped the tank, filling the air above the stove. Then strike a match from even a few feet away and ka-boom!

Butane: The explosive problem can be solved by using stoves that burn bottled butane fuel. Butane requires no pouring, pumping, or priming, and butane stoves are the easiest to light. Just turn a knob and light—that's it. On the minus side, because it comes in bottles, you never know precisely how much fuel you have left. And when a bottle is empty, you have a potential piece of litter. (Never litter. Ever.)

The other problem with butane is that it just plain does not work well in cold weather or when there is little fuel left in the cartridge. Since you cannot predict mountain weather in spring or fall, you can wind up using more fuel than originally projected. That can be frustrating, particularly if your stove starts wheezing when there are still several days left to go. In addition, with most butane cartridges, if there is any chance of the temperature's falling below freezing, you often have to sleep with the cartridge to keep it warm or forget about using it come morning.

Coleman Max Performance Fuel: This new fuel offers a unique approach to solving the consistent burn challenge facing all pressurized gas cartridges: operating at temperatures at or below 0°F. Using a standard propane/butane blend for high-octane performance, Coleman gets around the drop-off in performance other cartridges experience by using a version of fuel injection. A hose inside the cartridge pulls liquid fuel into the stove, where it vaporizes—a switch from the standard approach of pulling only a gaseous form of the fuel into a stove. By drawing liquid out of the cartridge, Coleman gets around the tendency of propane to burn off first and allows each cartridge to deliver a consistent mix of propane and butane to the stove's burners throughout the cartridge's life.

Butane/Propane: This blend offers higher octane performance than butane alone, solving the cold temperature doldrums somewhat. However, propane burns off before butane, so there will be a performance drop as the fuel level in the cartridge lowers.

Propane: Now available for single-burner stoves using larger, heavier cartridges to accommodate higher pressures, propane offers the very best performance of any of the pressurized gas canister fuels.

Primus Tri-Blend: This blend is made up of 20 percent propane, 70 percent butane, and 10 percent isobutane and is designed to burn with more consistent heat and efficiency than standard propane/butane mixes.

Denatured alcohol: Though this fuel burns cleanly and quietly and is virtually explosion-proof, it generates much less heat than pressurized or liquid gas fuels.

Kerosene: Never buy a stove that uses kerosene for fuel. Kerosene is smelly and messy, generates low heat, needs priming, and is virtually obsolete as a camp fuel in the United States. As a test I once tried using a kerosene stove. I could scarcely boil a pot of water. In addition, some kerosene leaked out when the stove was packed, ruining everything it touched. The smell of kerosene never did go away. Kerosene remains popular in Europe only because most campers there haven't yet heard much about white gas. When they do, they will demand it.

Building Fires

One summer expedition took me to the Canadian wilderness in British Columbia for a 75-mile canoe trip on the Bowron Lake Circuit, a chain of 13 lakes, six rivers, and seven portages. It is one of the truly great canoe trips in the world, a loop that ends just a few hundred feet from its starting point. But at the first camp at Kibbee Lake, my stove developed a fuel leak at the base of the burner, and the nuclear-like blast that followed just about turned Canada into a giant crater.

As a result, the final 70 miles of the trip had to be completed without a stove, cooking done on open fires each night. The problem was compounded by the weather. It rained eight of the 10 days. Rain? In Canada, raindrops the size of silver dollars fall so hard they actually bounce on the lake surface. We had to stop paddling a few times to empty the rainwater out of the canoe. At the end of the day we'd make camp and then face the test: either make a fire or go to bed cold and hungry.

With an ax, at least we had a chance for success. As soaked as all the downed wood was, I was able to make my own fire-starting tinder from the chips of split logs; no matter how hard it rains, the inside of a log is always dry.

In miserable weather, matches don't stay lit long enough to get the tinder started. Instead we used either a candle or the little waxlike fire-starter cubes that remain lit for several minutes. From those we could get the tinder going. Then we added small, slender strips of wood that had been axed from the interior of the logs. When the flame reached a foot high, we added the logs, their dry interior facing in. By the time the inside of the logs had caught fire, the outside would be drying from the heat. It wasn't long before a royal blaze was brightening the rainy night.

Keep It Wild Tip 1: Campfires

1. Fire use can scar the backcountry. If a fire ring is not available, use a lightweight stove for cooking.
2. Where fires are permitted, use existing fire rings away from large rocks or overhangs.
3. Don't char rocks by building new rings.
4. Gather sticks from the ground that are no larger than the diameter of your wrist.
5. Don't snap branches of live, dead, or downed trees, which can cause personal injury and also scar the natural setting.
6. Put the fire "dead out" and make sure it's cold before departing. Remove all trash from the fire ring and sprinkle dirt over the site.
7. Remember that some forest fires can be started by a campfire that appears to be out. Hot embers burning deep in the pit can cause tree roots to catch fire and burn underground. If you ever see smoke rising from the ground, seemingly from nowhere, dig down and put the fire out.

That's a worst-case scenario, and I hope you will never face anything like it. Nevertheless, being able to build a good fire and cook on it can be one of the more satisfying elements of a camping trip. At times just looking into the flames can provide a special satisfaction at the end of a good day.

However, never expect to build a fire for every meal or in some cases even to build one at all. Many state and federal campgrounds have been picked clean of downed wood, or forest fire danger forces rangers to prohibit fires altogether during the fire season. In either case you must use your camp stove or go hungry.

But when you can build a fire and the resources for doing so are available, it will enhance the quality of your camping experience. Of the campgrounds listed in this book, those where you are permitted to build fires will usually have fire rings. In primitive areas where you can make your own fire, you should dig a ring eight inches deep, line the edges with rock, and clear all the needles and twigs in a five-foot radius. The next day, when the fire is dead, you can discard the rocks, fill over the black charcoal with dirt, and then scatter pine needles and twigs over it. Nobody will even know you camped there. That's the best way I know to keep a secret spot a real secret.

When you start to build a campfire, the first thing you will notice is that no matter how good your intentions, your fellow campers will not be able to resist moving the wood around. Watch. You'll be getting ready to add a key piece of wood at just the right spot, and your companion will stick his mitts in, confidently believing he has a better idea. He'll shift the fire around and undermine your best-thought-out plans.

So I enforce a rule on camping trips: one person makes the fire while everybody else stands clear or is involved with other camp tasks such as gathering wood, getting water, putting up tents, or planning dinner. Once the fire is going strong, then it's fair game; anyone adds logs at his or her discretion. But in the early, delicate stages of the campfire, it's best to leave the work to one person.

Before a match is ever struck, you should gather a complete pile of firewood. Then start small, with the tiniest twigs you can find, and slowly add larger twigs as you go, crisscrossing them like a miniature tepee. Eventually you will get to the big chunks that will produce high heat. The key is to get one piece of wood burning into another, which then burns into another, setting off what I call the chain of flame. Conversely, single pieces of wood set apart from each other will not burn.

On a dry summer evening at a campsite where plenty of wood is available, about the only way you can blow the deal is to get impatient and try to add the big pieces too quickly. Do that and you'll get smoke, not flames, and it won't be long before every one of your fellow campers is poking at your fire. It will drive you crazy, but they just won't be able to help it.

Cooking Gear

I like traveling light, and I've found that all I need for cooking is a pot, small frying pan, metal pot grabber, fork, knife, cup, and matches. If you want to keep the price of food low and also cook customized dinners each night, a small pressure cooker can be just the ticket. (See Keeping the Price Down on page 8.) I store all my gear in one small bag that fits into my pack. If I'm camping out of my four-wheel-drive rig, the little bag of cooking gear is easy to keep track of. Going simple, not complicated, is the key to keeping a camping trip on the right track.

You can get more elaborate by buying complete kits with plates, a coffeepot, large pots, and other cookware, but what really counts is having a single pot that makes you happy. It needs to be just the right size, not too big or small, and stable enough so it won't tip over, even if it is at a slight angle on a fire, full of water at a full boil. Mine is just 6 inches wide and 4.5 inches deep. It holds better than a quart of water and has served me well for several hundred camp dinners.

The rest of your cook kit is easy to complete. The frying pan should be small, light-gauge aluminum, and Teflon-coated, with a fold-in handle so it's no hassle to store. A pot grabber is a great addition. It's a little aluminum gadget that clamps to the edge of pots and allows you to lift them and pour water with total control without burning your fingers. For cleanup take a plastic scrubber and a small bottle filled with dish cleaner, and you're in business.

A sierra cup, a wide aluminum cup with a wire handle, is an ideal item to carry because you can eat out of it as well as use it for drinking. This means no plates to scrub after dinner, so cleanup is quick and easy. In addition, if you go for a hike, you can clip it to your belt with its handle.

If you want a more formal setup complete with plates, glasses, silverware, and the like, you can end up spending more time preparing and cleaning up from meals than you do enjoying the country you are exploring. In addition, the more equipment you bring, the more loose ends you will have to deal with, and loose ends can cause plenty of frustration. If you have a choice, go simple.

And remember what Thoreau said: "A man is rich in proportion to what he can do without."

Food and Cooking Tricks

On a trip to the Bob Marshall Wilderness in western Montana, I woke up one morning, yawned, and said, "What've we got for breakfast?"

The silence was ominous. "Well," finally came the response, "we don't have any food left."
"What!?"

"Well, I figured we'd catch trout for meals every other night."

On the return trip, we ended up eating wild berries, buds, and, yes, even roots (not too tasty). When we finally landed the next day at a suburban pizza parlor, we nearly ate the wooden tables.

Running out of food on a camping trip can do more to turn reasonable people into violent grumps than any other event. There's no excuse for it, not when a system for figuring meals can be outlined with precision and little effort. You should not go out and buy a bunch of food, throw it in your rig, and head off for yonder. That leaves too much to chance. And if you've ever been in the woods and real hungry, you'll know it's worth taking a little effort to make sure a day or two of starvation will not occur. Here's a three-step solution:

1. Draw up a general meal-by-meal plan and make sure your companions like what's on it.
2. Tell your companions to buy any specialty items (such as a special brand of coffee) on their own and not to expect you to take care of everything.
3. Put all the food on your living room floor and literally plan out every day of your trip, meal by meal, putting the food in plastic bags as you go. That way you will know exact food quotas and will not go hungry.

Fish for your dinner? There's one guarantee as far as that goes: if you expect to catch fish for meals, you will most certainly get skunked. If you don't expect to catch fish for meals, you will probably catch so many they'll be coming out of your ears. I've seen it a hundred times.

Keeping the Price Down

"There must be some mistake," I said with a laugh. "Whoever paid $750 for camp food?"

But the amount was as clear as the digital numbers on the cash register: $753.27.

"How is this possible?" I asked the clerk.

"Just add it up," she responded, irritated.

Then I started figuring. The freeze-dried backpack dinners cost $6 apiece. A small pack of beef jerky went for $2, the beef sticks for $.75, granola bars for $.50. Multiply it all by four hungry men, including Foonsky, for 21 days. This food was to sustain us on a major expedition—four guys hiking 250 miles over three weeks from Mt. Whitney to Yosemite Valley.

The dinners alone cost close to $500. Add in the usual goodies—jerky, granola bars, soup, dried fruit, oatmeal, Tang, candy, and coffee—and I felt as if an earthquake had struck when I saw the tab.

How to Make Beef Jerky in Your Own Kitchen

Start with a couple pieces of meat: lean top round, sirloin, or tri-tip. Cut it into 3/16-inch strips across the grain, trimming out the membrane, gristle, and fat. Marinate the strips for 24 hours in a glass dish. The fun begins in picking a marinade. Try two-thirds teriyaki sauce, one-third Worcestershire sauce. You can customize the recipe by adding pepper, ground mustard, bay leaf, red wine vinegar, garlic, and, for the brave, Tabasco sauce.

After a day or so, squeeze out each strip of meat with a rolling pin, lay them in rows on a cooling rack over a cookie sheet, and dry them in the oven at 125 degrees for 12 hours. Thicker pieces can take as long as 18 to 24 hours.

That's it. The hardest part is cleaning the cookie sheet when you're done. The easiest part is eating your own homemade jerky while sitting at a lookout on a mountain ridge. The do-it-yourself method for jerky may take a day or so, but it is cheaper and can taste better than any store-bought jerky.

A lot of campers have received similar shocks. In preparation for their trips, campers shop with enthusiasm. Then they pay the bill in horror.

Well, there are solutions, lots of them. You can eat gourmet style in the outback without having your wallet cleaned out. But it requires do-it-yourself cooking, more planning, and careful shopping. It also means transcending the push-button I-want-it-now attitude that so many people can't leave behind when they go to the mountains.

The secret is to bring along a small pressure cooker. A reader in San Francisco, Mike Bettinger, passed this tip on to me. Little pressure cookers weigh about two pounds, which may sound like a lot to backpackers and backcountry campers. But when three or four people are on a trip, it actually saves weight.

The key is that it allows campers to bring items that are difficult to cook at high altitudes, such as brown and white rice; red, black, pinto, and lima beans; and lentils. You pick one or more for a basic staple and then add a variety of freeze-dried ingredients to make a complete dish. Available are packets of meat, vegetables, onions, shallots, and garlic. Sun-dried tomatoes, for instance, reconstitute wonderfully in a pressure cooker. Add herbs, spices, and maybe a few rainbow trout and you will be eating better out of a backpack than most people do at home.

"In the morning, I have used the pressure cooker to turn dried apricots into apricot sauce to put on the pancakes we made with sourdough starter," Bettinger said. "The pressure cooker is also big enough for washing out cups and utensils. The days when backpacking meant eating terrible freeze-dried food are over. It doesn't take a gourmet cook to prepare these meals, only some thought beforehand."

Now when Foonsky, Mr. Furnai, Rambob, and I sit down to eat such a meal, we don't call it "eating." We call it "hodgepacking" or "time to pack your hodge." After a particularly long day on the trail, you can do some serious hodgepacking.

If your trip is a shorter one, say for a weekend, you can bring more fresh food to add some sizzle to the hodge. You can design a hot soup/stew mix that is good enough to eat at home.

Start by bringing a pot of water to a full boil, then adding pasta, ramen noodles, or macaroni. While it simmers, cut in a potato, carrot, onion, and garlic clove, and cook for about 10 minutes. When the vegetables have softened, add in a soup mix or two, maybe some cheese, and you are just about in business. But you can still ruin it and turn your hodge into sludge. Make sure you read the directions on the soup mix to determine cooking time. It can vary widely. In addition, make sure you stir the whole thing up; otherwise you will get these hidden dry clumps of soup mix that taste like garlic sawdust.

How do I know? Well, it was up near Kearsage Pass in the Sierra Nevada, where, feeling half-starved, I dug into our nightly hodge. I will never forget that first bite—I damn near gagged to death. Foonsky laughed at me, until he took his first bite (a nice big one) and then turned green.

Another way to trim food costs is to make your own beef jerky, the trademark staple of campers for more than 200 years. A tiny packet of beef jerky costs $2, and for that 250-mile expedition, I spent $150 on jerky alone. Never again. Now we make our own and get big strips of jerky that taste better than anything you can buy.

If all this still doesn't sound like your idea of a gourmet but low-cost camping meal, well, you are forgetting the main course: rainbow trout. Remember: if you don't plan on catching them for dinner, you'll probably snag more than you can finish in one night's hodgepacking.

Some campers go to great difficulties to cook their trout, bringing along frying pans, butter, grills, tinfoil, and more, but all you need is some seasoned salt and a campfire.

Rinse the gutted trout, and while it's still wet, sprinkle on a good dose of seasoned salt, both inside and out. Clear any burning logs to the side of the campfire, then lay the trout right on the coals, turning it once so both sides are cooked. Sound ridiculous? Sound like you are throwing the fish away? Sound like the fish will burn up? Sound like you will have to eat the campfire ash? Wrong on all counts. The fish cooks perfectly, the ash doesn't stick, and after cooking trout this way, you may never fry trout again.

But if you can't convince your buddies, who may insist the trout should be fried, then make sure you have butter to fry them in, not oil. Also make sure you cook them all the way through, so the meat strips off the backbone in two nice, clean fillets. The fish should end up looking like one that Sylvester the Cat just drew out of his mouth—only the head, tail, and a perfect skeleton.

You can supplement your eats with sweets, nuts, freeze-dried fruits, and drink mixes. In any case, make sure you keep the dinner menu varied. If you and your buddies look into your dinner cups and groan, "Ugh, not this again," you will soon start dreaming of cheeseburgers and french fries instead of hiking, fishing, and finding beautiful campsites.

If you are car camping and have a big ice chest, you can bring virtually anything to eat and drink. If you are on the trail and don't mind paying the price, the newest freeze-dried dinners provide another option.

Some of the biggest advances in the outdoors industry have come in the freeze-dried dinners now available to campers. Some of them are almost good enough to serve in restaurants. Sweet-and-sour pork over rice, tostadas, Burgundy chicken—it sure beats the poopy goop we used to eat, like the old soupy chili-mac dinners that tasted bad and looked so unlike food that consumption was near impossible, even for my dog, Rebel. Foonsky usually managed to get it down, but just barely.

To provide an idea of how to plan a menu, consider what my companions and I ate while hiking 250 miles on California's John Muir Trail:

- Breakfast: instant soup, oatmeal (never get plain), one beef or jerky stick, coffee or hot chocolate.
- Lunch: one beef stick, two jerky sticks, one granola bar, dried fruit, half cup of pistachio nuts, Tang, one small bag of M&Ms.
- Dinner: instant soup, one freeze-dried dinner, one milk bar, rainbow trout.

What was that last item? Rainbow trout? Right! Unless you plan on it, you can catch them every night.

CLOTHING AND WEATHER PROTECTION

What started as an innocent pursuit of a perfect campground evolved into one heck of a predicament for Foonsky and me.

We had parked at the end of a logging road and then bushwhacked our way down a canyon to a pristine trout stream. On my first cast—a little flip into the plunge pool of a waterfall—I caught a 16-inch rainbow trout, a real beauty that jumped three times. Magic stuff.

Then just across the stream, we saw it: The Perfect Camping Spot. On a sandbar on the edge of the forest, there lay a flat spot, high and dry above the river. Nearby was plenty of downed wood collected by past winter storms that we could use for firewood. And, of course, this beautiful trout stream was bubbling along just 40 yards from the site.

But nothing is perfect, right? To reach it, we had to wade across the river, although it didn't appear to be too difficult. The cold water tingled a bit, and the river came up surprisingly high, just above the belt. But it would be worth it to camp at The Perfect Spot.

Once across the river, we put on some dry clothes, set up camp, explored the woods, and fished the stream, catching several nice trout for dinner. But late that afternoon, it started raining. What?

Rain in the summertime? Nature makes its own rules. By the next morning, it was still raining, pouring like a Yosemite waterfall from a solid gray sky.

That's when we noticed The Perfect Spot wasn't so perfect. The rain had raised the river level too high for us to wade back across. We were marooned, wet, and hungry.

"Now we're in a heck of a predicament," said Foonsky, the water streaming off him.

Getting cold and wet on a camping trip with no way to warm up is not only unnecessary and uncomfortable, it can be a fast ticket to hypothermia, the number one killer of campers in the woods. By definition, hypothermia is a condition in which body temperature is lowered to the point that it causes illness. It is particularly dangerous because the afflicted are usually unaware it is setting in. The first sign is a sense of apathy, then a state of confusion, which can lead eventually to collapse (or what appears to be sleep), then death.

You must always have a way to get warm and dry in short order, regardless of any conditions you may face. If you have no way of getting dry, then you must take emergency steps to prevent hypothermia. (Those steps are detailed in First Aid and Insect Protection section on page 28.)

But you should never reach that point. For starters, always have spare sets of clothing tucked away so no matter how cold and wet you might get, you have something dry to put on. On hiking trips I always carry a second set of clothes, sealed to stay dry, in a plastic garbage bag. I keep a third set waiting back at the truck.

If you are car camping, your vehicle can cause an illusory sense of security. But with an extra set of dry clothes stashed safely away, there is no illusion. The security is real. And remember, no matter how hot the weather is when you start your trip, always be prepared for the worst. Foonsky and I learned the hard way.

So both of us were soaking wet on that sandbar, and with no other choice we tried holing up in the tent for the night. A sleeping bag with Quallofil or another polyester fiberfill can retain warmth even when wet, because the fill is hollow and retains its loft. So as miserable as it was, we made it through the night.

The rain stopped the next day and the river dropped a bit, but it was still rolling big and angry. Using a stick as a wading staff, Foonsky crossed about 80 percent of the stream before he was dumped, but he made a jump for it and managed to scramble to the riverbank. He waved for me to follow. "No problem," I thought.

It took me 20 minutes to reach nearly the same spot where Foonsky had been dumped. The heavy river current was above my belt and pushing hard. Then in the flash of an instant, my wading staff slipped on a rock. I teetered in the river current and was knocked over like a bowling pin. I became completely submerged. I went tumbling down the river, heading right toward the waterfall. While underwater I looked up at the surface, and I can remember how close it seemed yet how out of control I was. Right then this giant hand appeared, and I grabbed it. It was Foonsky. If it weren't for that hand, I would have sailed right over the waterfall.

My momentum drew Foonsky right into the river, and we scrambled in the current, but I suddenly sensed the river bottom under my knees. On all fours, the two of us clambered ashore. We were safe.

"Thanks, ol' buddy," I said.

"Man, we're wet," he responded. "Let's get to the rig and get some dry clothes on."

The Art of Layering

The most important element in enjoying the outdoor experience in any condition is to stay dry and warm. There is no substitute. You must stay dry and you must stay warm.

Thus comes the theory behind layering, which suggests that as your body temperature fluctuates or the weather shifts, you simply peel off or add available layers as needed—and have a waterproof shell available in case of rain.

The introduction of a new era of outdoor clothing has made it possible for campers to turn choosing clothes into an art form. Like art, it comes much more expensive than throwing on a pair of blue jeans, a T-shirt, and some flannel, but for many it is worth the price.

In putting together your ideal layering system, there are some general considerations. What you need to do is create a system that effectively combines elements of breathability, wicking, rapid drying, insulation, durability, wind resistance, and water repellence while still being lightweight and offering the necessary freedom of movement, all with just a few garments.

The basic intent of a base layer is to manage moisture. Your base layer will be the first article of clothing you put on and the last to come off. Since your own skin will be churning out the perspiration, the goal of this second skin is to manage the moisture and move it away from you. That is why the best base layer available is from bicomponent knits, that is, blends of polyester and cotton, which work to provide wicking and insulating properties in one layer.

The way it works is that the side facing your skin is water hating, while the side away from your skin is water loving; thus it pulls or "wicks" moisture through. You'll stay dry and happy, even with only one layer on, something not possible with old single-function weaves. The best include Thermax, Capilene, Driclime, Lifa, and Polartec 100. The only time that cotton should become a part of your base layer is if you wish to keep cool, not warm, such as in a hot desert climate where evaporative cooling becomes your friend, not your enemy.

Stretch fleece and microdenier pile also provide a good base layer, though they can be used as a second layer as well. Microdenier pile can be worn alone or layered under or over other pieces, and it has excellent wicking capability as well as more windproof potential.

The next layer should be a light cotton shirt or a long-sleeved cotton/wool shirt, or both, depending on the coolness of the day. For pants, many just wear blue jeans when camping, but blue jeans can be hot and tight, and once wet, they tend to stay that way. Putting on wet blue jeans on a cold morning is a torturous way to start the day. (I tell you this from experience, since I have suffered that fate a number of times.) A better choice is pants made from a cotton/canvas mix, which are available at outdoors stores. They are light, have a lot of give, and dry quickly. If the weather is quite warm, shorts that have some room to them can be the best choice.

Finally, you'll top the entire ensemble off with a thin windproof, water-resistant layer. You want this layer to breathe like crazy, yet not be so porous that rain runs through it like floodwaters through a leaking dike. Patagonia's Velocity shell is one of the best. Its outer fabric is DWR (durable water-repellent) treated, and the coating is by Gore. Patagonia calls it Pneumatic (Gore now calls it Activent, while Marmot, Moonstone, and North Face all offer their own versions). Though condensation will still build up inside, it manages to get rid of enough moisture.

It is critical to know the difference between "water-resistant" and "waterproof." (This is covered later in the chapter under the Rain Gear section.)

But hey, why does anybody need all this fancy stuff just to go camping? Fair question. Like the introduction of Gore-Tex years ago, all this fabric and fiber mumbo jumbo has its skeptics, including me. You don't have to opt for this aerobic-function fashion statement; it is unnecessary on many camping trips. But the fact is you must be ready for anything when you venture into the outdoors. And the truth is that the new era of outdoor clothing works, and it works better than anything that has come before.

Regardless of what you choose, weather should never be a nuisance or cause discomfort, regardless of what you experience. Instead it should provide a welcome change of pace.

About Hats

One final word of advice: always pack along a warm hat for those times when you need to seal in warmth. You lose a large percentage of heat through your head. I almost always wear a wide-brimmed hat, something like the legendary outlaws wore 150 years ago. There's actually logic behind it: my hat is made of kangaroo skin (waterproof), is rigged with a lariat (it can be cinched down when it's windy), and has a wide brim that keeps the tops of my ears from being sunburned (years ago they once were burned to a red crisp on a trip where I was wearing a baseball hat). But to be honest, I like how it looks, kind of like my pal Waylon Jennings.

Vests and Parkas

In cold weather you should take the layer system one step further with a warm vest and a parka jacket. Vests are especially useful because they provide warmth without the bulkiness of a parka. The warmest vests and parkas are either filled with down or Quallofil, or they are made with a cotton/wool mix. Each has its respective merits and problems. Down fill provides the most warmth for the amount of weight, but becomes useless when wet, closely resembling a wet dishrag. Quallofil keeps much of its heat-retaining quality even when wet, but it is expensive. Vests made of cotton/wool mixes are the most attractive and also are quite warm, but they can be as heavy as a ship's anchor when wet.

Sometimes the answer is combining the two. One of my best camping companions wears a good-looking cotton/wool vest and a parka filled with Quallofil. The vest never gets wet, so weight is not a factor.

Rain Gear

One of the most miserable nights I ever spent in my life was on a camping trip where I didn't bring my rain gear or a tent. Hey, it was early August, the temperature had been in the 90s for weeks, and if anybody had said it was going to rain, I would have told him to consult a brain doctor. But rain it did. And as I got wetter and wetter, I kept saying to myself, "Hey, it's summer, it's not supposed to rain." Then I remembered one of the 10 commandments of camping: forget your rain gear and you can guarantee it will rain.

To stay dry, you need some form of water-repellent shell. It can be as simple as a $5 poncho made out of plastic or as elaborate as a Gore-Tex rain jacket-and-pants set that costs $300. What counts is not how much you spend, but how dry you stay.

The most important thing to realize is that waterproof and water-resistant are completely different things. In addition, there is no such thing as rain gear that is both waterproof and breathable. The more waterproof a jacket is, the less it breathes. Conversely, the more breathable a jacket is, the less waterproof it becomes.

Waterproof: impervious to water. Though rain won't penetrate waterproof material, if you're at all mobile you'll soon find yourself wet from perspiration that can't evaporate. **Water-resistant: resistant but not impervious to water.** You'll stay dry using water-resistant material only if it isn't pouring.

If you wear water-resistant rain gear in a downpour, you'll get soaked. Water-resistant rain gear is appealing because it breathes and will keep you dry in the light stuff, such as mist, fog, even a little splash from a canoe paddle. But in rain? Forget it.

So what is the solution?

I've decided that the best approach is a set of fairly light but 100 percent-waterproof rain gear. I recently bought a hooded jacket and pants from Coleman, and my assessment is that it is the most cost-efficient rain gear I've ever had. All I can say is, hey, it works: I stay dry, it doesn't weigh much, and it didn't cost a fortune.

You can also stay dry with any of the waterproof plastics and even heavy-duty rubber-coated outfits made for commercial fishermen. But these are uncomfortable during anything but a heavy rain. Because they are heavy and don't breathe, you'll likely get soaked anyway (that is, from your own sweat), even if it isn't raining hard.

On backpacking trips, I still stash a super lightweight water-repellent slicker for day hikes, and a poncho, which I throw over my pack at night to keep it dry. But otherwise I never go any-where—*anywhere*—without my rain gear.

Some do just fine with a cheap poncho, and note that ponchos can serve other uses in addition to a raincoat. Ponchos can be used as a ground tarp, as a rain cover for supplies or a back-pack, or can be roped up to trees in a pinch to provide a quick storm ceiling if you don't have a tent. The problem with ponchos is that in a hard rain, you just don't stay dry. First your legs get wet, then they get soaked. Then your arms follow the same pattern. If you're wearing cotton, you'll find that once part of the garment gets wet, the water will spread until, alas, you are dripping wet, poncho and all. Before long you start to feel like a walking refrigerator.

One high-cost option is buying a Gore-Tex rain jacket and pants. Gore-Tex is actually not a fabric as is commonly believed, but a laminated film that coats a breathable fabric. The result is lightweight, water-repellent, breathable jackets and pants. They are perfect for campers, but they cost a fortune.

Some hiking buddies of mine have complained that the older Gore-Tex rain gear loses its water-repellent quality over time. However, manufacturers insist that this is the result of water seeping through seams, not leaks in the jacket. At each seam, tiny needles have pierced the fab-ric, and as tiny as the holes are, water will find a way through. An application of Seam Lock, especially at major seams around the shoulders of a jacket, can usually fix the problem.

If you don't want to spend the big bucks for Gore-Tex rain gear but want more rain protec-tion than a poncho affords, a coated nylon jacket is the compromise that many choose. They are inexpensive, have the highest water-repellency of any rain gear, and are warm, providing a good outer shell for your layers of clothing. But they are not without fault. These jackets don't breathe at all, and if you zip them up tight, you can sweat a river.

My brother Rambob gave me a nylon jacket before a mountain climbing expedition. I wore that $20 special all the way to the top with no complaints; it's warm and 100 percent waterproof. The one problem with nylon is when temperatures drop below freezing. It gets so stiff that it feels as if you are wearing a straitjacket. But at $20, it seems like a treasure, especially compared to a $180 Gore-Tex jacket.

There's one more jacket-construction term to know: DWR, or durable water-repellent finish. All of the top-quality jackets these days are DWR-treated. The DWR causes water to bead up on the shell. When the DWR wears off, even a once-waterproof jacket will feel like a wet dishrag.

Also note that ventilation is the key to coolness. The only ventilation on most shells is often the zipper. But waterproof jackets need additional openings. Look for mesh-backed pockets and underarm zippers, as well as cuffs, waists, and hems that can be adjusted to open wide. Storm flaps (the baffle over the zipper) that close with hook-and-loop material or snaps let you leave the zipper open for airflow into the jacket.

Other Gear—and a Few Tips

What are the three items most commonly forgotten on a camping trip? A hat, sunglasses, and lip balm.

A hat is crucial, especially when you are visiting high elevations. Without one you are constantly exposed to everything nature can give you. The sun will dehydrate you, sap your energy, sunburn your head, and in worst cases, cause sunstroke. Start with a comfortable hat. Then finish with sunglasses, lip balm, and sunscreen for additional protection. They will help protect you from extreme heat.

To guard against extreme cold, it's a good idea to keep a pair of thin ski gloves stashed away with your emergency clothes, along with a wool ski cap. The gloves should be thick enough to keep your fingers from stiffening up, but pliable enough to allow full movement so you don't have to take them off to complete simple tasks, like lighting a stove. An alternative to gloves is glovelets, which look like gloves with no fingers. In any case, just because the weather turns cold doesn't mean that your hands have to.

And if you fall into a river as Foonsky and I did—well, I hope you have a set of dry clothes waiting back at your rig. Oh, and a hand reaching out to you.

HIKING AND FOOT CARE

We had set up a nice little camp in the woods, and my buddy, Foonsky, was strapping on his hiking boots, sitting against a big Douglas fir.

"New boots," he said with a grin. "But they seem pretty stiff."

We decided to hoof it down the trail for a few hours, exploring the mountain wildlands that are said to hide Bigfoot and other strange creatures. After just a short while on the trail, a sense of peace and calm seemed to settle in. The forest provides the chance to be purified with clean air and the smell of trees, freeing you from all troubles.

But it wasn't long before a look of trouble was on Foonsky's face. And no, it wasn't from seeing Bigfoot.

"Got a hot spot on a toe," he said.

Immediately we stopped. He pulled off his right boot, then his socks, and inspected the left side of his big toe. Sure enough, a blister had bubbled up, filled with fluid, but hadn't popped. From his medical kit, Foonsky cut a small piece of moleskin to fit over the blister and taped it to hold it in place. In a few minutes we were back on the trail.

A half hour later, there was still no sign of Bigfoot. But Foonsky stopped again and pulled off his other boot. "Another hot spot." On the little toe of his left foot was another small blister, over which he taped a Band-Aid to keep it from further chafing against the inside of his new boot.

In just a few days, ol' Foonsky, a strong, 6-foot-5, 200-plus-pound guy, was walking around like a sore-hoofed horse that had been loaded with a month's worth of supplies and ridden over sharp rocks. Well, it wasn't the distance that had done Foonsky in; it was those blisters. He had them on eight of his 10 toes and was going through Band-Aids, moleskin, and tape like a walking emergency ward. If he used any more tape, he would've looked like a mummy from an Egyptian tomb.

If you've ever been in a similar predicament, you know the frustration of wanting to have a good time, wanting to hike and explore the area where you have set up a secluded camp, only to be held up by several blisters. No one is immune—all are created equal before the blister god. You can be forced to bow to it unless you get your act together.

That means wearing the right-style boots for what you have in mind and then protecting your feet with carefully selected socks. If you are still so unfortunate as to get a blister or two, it means knowing how to treat them fast so they don't turn your walk into a sore-footed endurance test.

What causes blisters? In almost all cases, it is the simple rubbing of a foot against the rugged interior of a boot. That can be worsened by several factors:

1. A very stiff boot or one in which your foot moves inside as you walk, instead of the boot flexing as if it were another layer of skin.
2. Thin, ragged, or dirty socks. This is the fastest route to blisters. Thin socks will allow your feet to move inside of your boots, ragged socks will allow your skin to chafe directly against the boot's interior, and dirty socks will wrinkle and fold, also rubbing against your feet instead of cushioning them.
3. Soft feet. By themselves, soft feet will not cause blisters, but in combination with a stiff boot or thin socks, they can cause terrible problems. The best way to toughen up your feet is to go barefoot. In fact, some of the biggest, toughest-looking guys you'll ever see, from Hell's Angels to pro football players, have feet that are as soft as a baby's butt. Why? Because they never go barefoot and don't hike much.

The Perfect Boot

Every hiker eventually conducts a search for the perfect boot in the mission for ideal foot comfort and to stay free of blisters. While there are many entries in this search, in fact, so many that it can be confusing, there is a way to find that perfect boot for you.

To stay blister-free, the most important factors are socks and the flexibility of a boot. If there is any foot slippage from a thin sock or a stiff boot, you can rub up a blister in minutes. For instance, I never wear stiff boots and I always wear two fresh sets of SmartWools ($13 a pop).

This search for the perfect boot included discussions with the nation's preeminent long-distance hikers, Brian Robinson of Mountain View (7,200 miles in 2001) and Ray Jardine of Oregon (2,700 miles of Pacific Crest Trail in three months). Both believe that the weight of a boot (or athletic shoe, as they often use) is the defining factor when selecting hiking footware. They both go as light as possible, believing that heavy boots will eventually wear you out by forcing you to pick up several pounds on your feet over and over again. A compatriot at the *San Francisco Chronicle,* outdoors writer Paul McHugh, offers the reminder that arch support may be even more vital, especially for people who hike less frequently and thus have not developed great foot strength as have Robinson and Jardine.

It is absolutely critical to stay away from very stiff boots and thin socks. Always wear the right-style boots for what you have in mind and then protect your feet with carefully selected socks. If you are still so unfortunate as to get a blister or two, it means knowing how to treat them fast so they don't turn your walk into a sore-footed endurance test.

What Causes Blisters

What causes blisters? In almost all cases, it is the simple rubbing of a foot against the rugged interior of a boot. That can be worsened by several factors:

1. A very stiff boot or one in which your foot moves inside as you walk, instead of the boot flexing as if it were another layer of skin.
2. Thin, ragged, or dirty socks. This is the fastest route to blisters. Thin socks will allow your feet to move inside your boots, ragged socks will allow your skin to chafe directly against the

boot's interior, and dirty socks will wrinkle and fold, also rubbing against your feet instead of cushioning them.

3. Soft feet. By themselves, soft feet will not cause blisters, but in combination with a stiff boot or thin socks, they can cause terrible problems. The best way to toughen up your feet is to go barefoot. In fact, some of the biggest, toughest-looking guys you'll ever see, from Hells Angels to pro football players, have feet that are as soft as a baby's butt. Why? Because they never go barefoot and don't hike much.

Selecting the Right Boots

When I hiked the John Muir Trail, I hiked 400 miles in three months, that is, 250 miles in three weeks from Mt. Whitney to Yosemite Valley, then another 150 miles in an earlier general training program. In that span I got just one blister, suffered on the fourth day of the 250-miler. I treated it immediately and suffered no more. One key is wearing the right boot, and for me, that means a boot that acts as a thick layer of skin that is flexible and pliable to my foot. I want my feet to fit snugly in them, with no interior movement.

There are four kinds of hiking footwear, most commonly known as: 1. Hiking boots; 2. Hunting boots; 3. Mountaineering boots; 4. Athletic shoes. Select the right one for you or pay the consequences.

One great trick when on a hiking vacation is to bring all four, and then for each hike, wear different footwear. This has many benefits. By changing boots, you change the points of stress for your feet and legs, greatly reducing soreness and the chance of creating a hot spot on a foot. It also allows you to go light on flat trails, and heavy on steep trails, where additional boot weight can help traction in downhill stretches.

Hiking Boots

Hiking boots can resemble low-cut leather/Gore-Tex hunting boots or Gore-Tex walking shoes, almost as if they were heavy athletic shoes. They are designed for day walks or short backpacking trips. Some of the newer models are like rugged athletic shoes, designed with a Gore-Tex top for lightness and a Vibram sole for traction. These are perfect for people who like to walk but rarely carry a heavy backpack. Because they are flexible, they are easy to break in, and with fresh socks they rarely cause blister problems. Because they are light, general hiking fatigue is greatly reduced.

On the negative side, because hiking boots are light, traction can be far from good on steep, slippery surfaces. In addition, they provide less than ideal ankle support, which can be a problem in rocky areas, such as along a stream where you might want to go trout fishing. Turn your ankle and your trip can be ruined.

For day-hiking, they are the footwear of choice for most.

Hunting Boots

Hunting boots are also called backpacking boots, super boots, or wilderness boots. They feature high ankle support, deep Vibram lug sole, built-in orthotics and arch support, and waterproof exterior.

Many larger backpackers prefer them because of the additional support they provide when carrying a heavy pack. They also can stand up to hundreds of miles of wilderness use, constantly being banged against rocks and walked through streams while supporting 200 pounds. On the negative side, they can be quite hot, weigh a ton, and if they get wet, take days to dry. Because they are heavy, they can wear you out. Often the extra weight can add days to long-distance expeditions, cutting into the number of miles a hiker is capable of on a daily basis.

Mountaineering Boots

Mountaineering boots are identified by midrange tops, laces that extend almost as far as the toe area, and ankle areas that are as stiff as a board. The lack of "give" is what endears them to mountaineers. Their stiffness is preferred when rock-climbing, walking off-trail on craggy surfaces, or hiking along the edge of streambeds where walking across small rocks can cause you to turn your ankle. Because these boots don't give on rugged, craggy terrain, they reduce ankle injuries and provide better traction.

The drawback to stiff boots is that if you don't have the proper socks and your foot starts slipping around in the boot, you will get a set of blisters that can have you using so much tape and moleskin that you can end up looking like a mummy. If you just want to go for a walk or a good tromp with a backpack, then hiking shoes or hunting boots will serve you better.

Athletic Shoes

Athletic shoes are built so well these days that they often can make good hiking footwear. They are often featherlight, so the long-term wear on your legs is minimal. For many short walks, they are ideal. For those with very strong feet and arches, they are popular even on multiday trips, where you carry a small pack.

But there can be many problems with such a shoe. On steep sections, you can lose your footing, slip, and fall. If you stub your toe, you have little protection, and it hurts like heck. If you try to carry a backpack and don't have a strong arch, your arch can collapse, or at the minimum, overstress your ankles and feet. In addition, heavy socks usually are not a good fit in these lightweight shoes; if you go with a thin cotton sock and if folds over, you can rub up a blister in minutes.

At the Store

There are a many styles, brands, and price ranges to choose from. If you wander about comparing all their many features, you will get as confused as a kid in a toy store.

Instead, go into the store with your mind clear about what you want, find it, and buy it. If you want the best, expect to spend $85–150 for hiking boots, $100–175 for hunting boots, $140–200 for mountaineering boots, and $50–90 for athletic shoes. If you go much cheaper, well, then you are getting cheap.

Yet you don't always get what you pay for. Once I spent $250 for hiking boots custom-made in Germany that I have worn for close to 2,000 miles, yet which weighed four pounds each! Another time, trying to go light, I spent $185 on some low-cut hiking boots; they turned out to be miserable blister makers. Even after a year of trying to get my money's worth, they never worked right on the trail and now occupy a dark place deep in my closet.

This is one area where you don't want to scrimp, so try not to yelp about the high cost.

Instead, walk out of the store believing you deserve the best, and that's exactly what you just paid for. Another trick I have learned is to stash several pairs of different-style hiking boots in my vehicle. Then, when out on adventures, I can pick the perfect boot for the type of terrain. I have seven sets of boots and constantly rotate them. Use heavy boots for steep trails with loose footing, lightweight models for flat routes with a hard surface. This works wonders to avoid blisters and muscle soreness because you are constantly changing the point of attack.

Keep It Wild Tip 2: Travel Lightly

1. Visit the backcountry in small groups.
2. Below tree line, always stay on designated trails.
3. Don't cut across switchbacks.
4. When traveling cross-country where no trails are available, follow animal trails or spread out with your group so no new routes are created.
5. Read your map and orient yourself with landmarks, a compass, and an altimeter. Avoid marking trails with rock cairns, tree scars, or ribbons.

If you plan to use the advice of a shoe salesperson, first look at what kind of boots he or she is wearing. If he or she isn't even wearing boots, then any advice the salesperson might tender may not be worth much. Most people I know who own quality boots, including salespeople, will wear them almost daily if their jobs allow, since boots are the best footwear available. However, even these well-meaning folks can offer sketchy advice. Every hiker I've ever met will tell you he wears the world's greatest boot! Instead of asking how great the boot is, ask, "How many blisters did you get when you hiked 12 miles a day for a week?"

Enter the store with a precise use and style in mind. Rather than fish for suggestions, tell the salesperson exactly what you want, try two or three brands of the same style, and always try on both boots in a pair simultaneously so you know exactly how they'll feel. If possible, walk up and down stairs with them. Are they too stiff? Are your feet snug yet comfortable, or do they slip? Do they have that "right" kind of feel when you walk?

If you get the right answers to those questions, then you're on your way to blister-free, pleasure-filled days of walking.

Socks

People can spend so much energy selecting the right kind of boot that they virtually overlook wearing the right kind of socks. One goes with the other.

Your socks should be thick enough to cushion your feet as well as fit snugly. Without good socks you might try to get the bootlaces too tight—and that's like putting a tourniquet on your feet. You should have plenty of clean socks on hand, or plan on washing what you have on your trip. As socks are worn, they become compressed, dirty, and damp. If they fold over, you'll rub up a blister in minutes.

My companions believe I go overboard when it comes to socks, that I bring too many and wear too many. But it works, so that's where the complaints stop. So how many do I wear? Well, it varies. On day hikes, I have found a sock called a SmartWool that makes my size 13s feel as if I'm walking on pillows. I always wear two of them, that is, two on each foot.

Do not wear cotton socks. Your foot can get damp and mix with dirt, which can cause a hot spot to start on your foot. Eventually you get blisters, lots of them.

SmartWool socks and other similar socks are a synthetic composite. They can partially wick moisture away from the skin.

The exterior sock can be wool or its equivalent. This will cushion your foot, provide that just-right snug fit in your boot, and give you some additional warmth and insulation in cold weather. It is critical to keep the sock clean. If you wear a dirty wool sock over and over again, it will compact and lose its cushion and start wrinkling while you hike, and then your feet will catch on fire from the blisters that start popping up. Of course, when wearing multiple socks, especially a wool composite, you will likely need to go up a boot size so they fit comfortably.

A Few More Tips

If you are like most folks—that is, the bottoms of your feet are rarely exposed and quite soft—you can take additional steps in their care. The best tip is keeping a fresh foot pad made of sponge rubber in your boot. But note that brand-new foot pads are often slippery for a few days, and that can cause blisters. They need to be broken in before an expedition, just as with new boots.

Another cure for soft feet is to get out and walk or jog on a regular basis before your camping trip. On one trip, I ran into the long-distance master Jardine, and he swore that going barefoot regularly is the best way to build up foot strength, arch support, and to toughen up the bottom of your feet.

If you plan to use a foot pad and wear two heavy socks, you will need to use these items when sizing boots. It is an unforgiving error to wear thin cotton socks when buying boots and later try to squeeze all this stuff, plus your feet, into them. There just won't be enough room.

Treating Blisters

The key to treating blisters is fast work at the first sign of a hot spot. If you feel a hot spot, never keep walking, figuring that the problem will go away or that you will work through it. Wrong! Stop immediately and go to work.

Before you remove your socks, check to see if the sock has a wrinkle in it, a likely cause of the problem. If so, either change socks or pull them tight, removing the tiny folds, after taking care of the blister.

To take care of the blister, cut a piece of moleskin to cover the offending toe, securing the moleskin with white medical tape. If moleskin is not available, small Band-Aids can do the job, but these have to be replaced daily, and sometimes with even more frequency. At night, clean your feet and sleep without socks. That will allow your feet to dry and heal.

Tips in the Field

Two other items that can help your walking are an Ace bandage and a pair of gaiters.

For sprained ankles and twisted knees, an Ace bandage can be like an insurance policy to get you back on the trail and out of trouble. In many cases a hiker with a twisted ankle or sprained knee has relied on a good wrap with a four-inch bandage for the added support to get home. Always buy the Ace bandages that come with the clips permanently attached, so you don't have to worry about losing them.

Gaiters are leggings made of Gore-Tex that fit from just below your knees, over your calves, and attach under your boots. They are of particular help when walking in damp areas or in places where rain is common. As your legs brush against ferns or low-lying plants, gaiters will deflect the moisture. Without them, your pants will be soaking wet in short order.

Should your boots become wet, a good tip is never to try to force-dry them. Some well-meaning folks will try to dry them quickly at the edge of a campfire or actually put the boots in an oven. While this may dry the boots, it can also loosen the glue that holds them together, ultimately weakening them until one day they fall apart in a heap.

A better bet is to treat the leather so the boots become water-repellent. Silicone-based liquids are the easiest to use and least greasy of the treatments available.

A final tip is to have another pair of lightweight shoes or moccasins that you can wear around camp and in the process give your feet the rest they deserve.

SLEEPING GEAR

One mountain night in the pines on an eve long ago, my dad, brother, and I had rolled out our sleeping bags and were bedded down for the night. After the pretrip excitement, a long drive, an evening of trout fishing, and a barbecue, we were like three tired doggies who had played too much.

But as I looked up at the stars, I was suddenly wide awake. This kid was still wired. A half hour later? No change—wide awake.

And as little kids can do, I had to wake up ol' dad to tell him about it. "Hey, Dad, I can't sleep."

"This is what you do," he said. "Watch the sky for a shooting star and tell yourself that you cannot go to sleep until you see at least one. As you wait and watch, you will start getting tired, and it will be difficult to keep your eyes open. But tell yourself you must keep watching. Then you'll start to really feel tired. When you finally see a shooting star, you'll go to sleep so fast you won't know what hit you."

Well, I tried it that night and I don't even remember seeing a shooting star, I went to sleep so fast.

It's a good trick, and along with having a good sleeping bag, ground insulation, maybe a tent, or a few tricks for bedding down in a pickup truck or motor home, you can get a good night's sleep on every camping trip.

More than 20 years after that camping episode with my dad and brother, we made a trip to the planetarium at the Academy of Sciences in San Francisco to see a show on Halley's Comet. The lights dimmed, and the ceiling turned into a night sky, filled with stars and a setting moon. A scientist began explaining phenomena of the heavens.

After a few minutes, I began to feel drowsy. Just then, a shooting star zipped across the planetarium ceiling. I went into a deep sleep so fast it was like I was in a coma. I didn't wake up until the show was over, the lights were turned back on, and the people were leaving.

Feeling drowsy, I turned to see if ol' Dad had liked the show. Oh yeah? Not only had he gone to sleep too, but he apparently had no intention of waking up, no matter what. Just like a camping trip.

Sleeping Bags

Question: What could be worse than trying to sleep in a cold, wet sleeping bag on a rainy night without a tent in the mountains?

Answer: Trying to sleep in a cold, wet sleeping bag on a rainy night without a tent in the mountains when your sleeping bag is filled with down.

Water will turn a down-filled sleeping bag into a mushy heap. Many campers do not like a high-tech approach, but the state-of-the-art polyfiber sleeping bags can keep you warm even when wet. That factor, along with temperature rating and weight, is key when selecting a sleeping bag.

A sleeping bag is a shell filled with heat-retaining insulation. By itself it is not warm. Your body provides the heat, and the sleeping bag's ability to retain that heat is what makes it warm or cold.

The old-style canvas bags are heavy, bulky, cold, and when wet, useless. With other options available, their use is limited. Anybody who sleeps outdoors or backpacks should choose otherwise.

Buy and use a sleeping bag filled with down or one of the quality poly-fills. Down is light, warm, and aesthetically pleasing to those who don't think camping and technology mix. If you choose a down bag, be sure to keep it double wrapped in plastic garbage bags on your trip to keep it dry. Once it's wet, you'll spend your nights howling at the moon.

The polyfiber-filled bags are not necessarily better than those filled with down, but they can be. Their one key advantage is that even when wet, some poly-fills can retain up to 85 percent of your body heat. This allows you to sleep and get valuable rest even in miserable conditions. And my camping experience is that no matter how lucky you may be, there comes a time when you will get caught in an unexpected, violent storm and everything you've got will get wet, including your sleeping bag. That's when a poly-fill bag becomes priceless. You either have one and can sleep, or you don't have one and suffer. It is that simple. Of the synthetic fills, Quallofil made by DuPont is the industry leader.

But just because a sleeping bag uses a high-tech poly-fill doesn't necessarily make it a better bag. There are other factors.

The most important are a bag's temperature rating and weight. The temperature rating of a sleeping bag refers to how cold it can get before you start actually feeling cold. Many campers make the mistake of thinking, "I only camp in the summer, so a bag rated at 30 or 40°F should be fine." Later they find out it isn't so fine, and all it takes is one cold night to convince them of that. When selecting the right temperature rating, visualize the coldest weather you might ever confront, and then get a bag rated for even colder weather.

For instance, if you are a summer camper, you may rarely experience a night in the low 30s or high 20s. A sleeping bag rated at 20°F would be appropriate, keeping you snug, warm, and asleep. For most campers, I advise bags rated at 0 or 10°F.

If you buy a poly-filled sleeping bag, never leave it squished in your stuff sack between camping trips. Instead, keep it on a hanger in a closet or use it as a blanket. One thing that can reduce a poly-filled bag's heat-retaining qualities is if you lose the loft out of the tiny hollow fibers that make up the fill. You can avoid this with proper storage.

The weight of a sleeping bag can also be a key factor, especially for backpackers. When you have to carry your gear on your back, every ounce becomes important. Sleeping bags that weigh just three pounds are available, although they are expensive. But if you hike much, it's worth the price to keep your weight to a minimum. For an overnighter, you can get away with a four- or 4.5-pound bag without much stress. However, bags weighing five pounds and up should be left back at the car.

I have two sleeping bags: a seven-pounder that feels like a giant sponge, and a little three-pounder. The heavy-duty model is for pickup truck camping in cold weather and doubles as a blanket at home. The lightweight bag is for hikes. Between the two, I'm set.

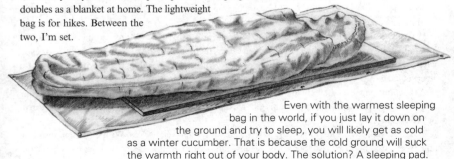

Even with the warmest sleeping bag in the world, if you just lay it down on the ground and try to sleep, you will likely get as cold as a winter cucumber. That is because the cold ground will suck the warmth right out of your body. The solution? A sleeping pad.

Insulation Pads

Even with the warmest sleeping bag in the world, if you just lay it down on the ground and try to sleep, you will likely get as cold as a winter cucumber. That is because the cold ground will suck the warmth right out of your body. The solution is to have a layer of insulation between you and the ground. For this you can use a thin Insulite pad, a lightweight Therm-a-Rest inflatable pad, a foam pad or mattress, air bed, or a cot. Here is a capsule summary of all three:

- **Insulite pads:** They are light, inexpensive, roll up quick for transport, and can double as a seat pad at your camp. The negative side is that in one night, they will compress, making you feel that you are sleeping on granite.
- **Therm-a-Rest pads:** These are a real luxury because they do everything an Insulite pad does, but also provide a cushion. The negative side is that they are expensive by comparison, and if they get a hole in them, they become worthless without a patch kit.
- **Air beds, foam mattresses, and cots:** These are excellent for car campers. The new line of air beds available are outstanding, especially the thicker ones, and inflate quickly with an electric motor inflator that plugs into a power plug or cigarette lighter in your vehicle. Foam mattresses are also excellent, in fact, the most comfortable of all, but their size precludes many from considering them. I've found that cots work great, too. I finally wore out an old wood one just before this book went to press; replaced it immediately with one of the new high-tech and light metal ones. For camping in the back of a pickup truck with a camper shell, the cots with three-inch legs are best, of course.

A Few Tricks

When surveying a camp area, the most important consideration should be to select a good spot to sleep. Everything else is secondary. Ideally, you want a flat spot that is wind-sheltered and on ground soft enough to drive stakes into. Yeah, and I want to win the lottery, too.

Sometimes that ground will have a slight slope to it. In that case, always sleep with your head on the uphill side. If you sleep parallel to the slope, every time you roll over, you'll find yourself rolling down the hill. If you sleep with your head on the downhill side, you'll get a headache that feels as if an ax is embedded in your brain.

When you've found a good spot, clear it of all branches, twigs, and rocks, of course. A good tip is to dig a slight indentation in the ground where your hip will fit. Since your body is not flat, but has curves and edges, it will not feel comfortable on flat ground. Some people even get severely bruised on the sides of their hips when sleeping on flat, hard ground. For that reason alone they learn to hate camping. What a shame, especially when the problem is solved easily with a Therm-a-Rest pad, foam insulation, air bed, or a cot.

After the ground is prepared, throw a ground cloth over the spot, which will keep much of the morning dew off you. In some areas, particularly where fog is a problem, morning dew can be heavy and get the outside of your sleeping bag quite wet. In that case, you need overhead protection, such as a tent or some kind of roof, like a poncho or tarp with its ends tied to trees.

Tents and Weather Protection

All it takes is to get caught in the rain once without a tent and you will never go anywhere without one again. A tent provides protection from rain, wind, and mosquito attacks. In exchange, you can lose a starry night's view, though some tents now even provide moon roofs.

A tent can be as complex as a four-season, tubular-jointed dome with a rain fly or as simple as two ponchos snapped together and roped up to a tree. They can be as cheap as a $10 tube tent, which is nothing more than a hollow piece of plastic, or as expensive as a $500 five-person deluxe expedition dome model. They vary greatly in size, price, and put-up time. If you plan on getting a good one, plan on doing plenty of shopping and asking lots of questions. With a little bit of homework, you can get the right answers to these questions:

Will It Keep Me Dry?

On many one-person and two-person tents, the rain fly does not extend far enough to keep water off the bottom sidewalls of the tent. In a driving rain, water can also drip from the rain fly and to the bottom sidewalls of the tent. Eventually the water can leak through to the inside, particularly through the seams where the tent has been sewn together.

You must be able to stake out your rain fly so it completely covers all of the tent. If you are tent shopping and this does not appear possible, then don't buy the tent. To prevent potential leaks, use a seam waterproofer such as Seam Lock, a gluelike substance, to close potential leak areas on tent seams. For large umbrella tents, keep a patch kit handy. Starting in 2003, note that Coleman tents are now guaranteed to keep campers dry.

Another way to keep water out of your tent is to store all wet garments outside the tent, under a poncho. Moisture from wet clothes stashed in the tent will condense on the interior tent walls. If you bring enough wet clothes into the tent, by the next morning you can feel as if you're camping in a duck blind.

How Hard Is It to Put Up?

If a tent is difficult to erect in full sunlight, you can just about forget it at night, especially the first night out. Some tents can go up in just a few minutes, without requiring help from another camper. This might be the kind of tent you want.

The way to compare put-up time of tents when shopping is to count the number of connecting points from the tent poles to the tent and the number of stakes required. The fewer the better. Think simple. My two-person-plus-a-dog tent has seven connecting points and, minus the rain fly, requires no stakes. It goes up in a few minutes. If you need a lot of stakes, it is a sure tip-off to a long put-up time. Try it at night or in the rain, and you'll be ready to cash your chips and go for broke. My bigger family tent, which has three rooms with walls, so we can keep our two kids, Jeremy and Kris, isolated on each side, takes about a half hour to put up. That's without anybody's help. With their help, add about 15 minutes, heh, heh.

Another factor is the tent poles themselves. Some small tents have poles that are broken into small sections that are connected by bungee cords. It takes only an instant to convert them to a complete pole.

Some outdoor shops have tents on display on their showroom floors. Before buying the tent, have the salesperson take the tent down and put it back up. If it takes him more than five minutes, or he says he doesn't have time, then keep looking.

Is It Roomy Enough?
Don't judge the size of a tent on floor space alone. Some tents small on floor space can give the illusion of roominess with a high ceiling. You can be quite comfortable in them and snug.

But remember that a one-person or two-person tent is just that. A two-person tent has room for two people plus gear. That's it. Don't buy a tent expecting it to hold more than it is intended to.

How Much Does It Weigh?
If you're a hiker, this becomes the preeminent question. If it's much more than six or seven pounds, forget it. A 12-pound tent is bad enough, but get it wet and it's like carrying a piano on your back. On the other hand, weight is scarcely a factor if you camp only where you can take your car. My dad, for instance, used to have this giant canvas umbrella tent that folded down to a neat little pack that weighed about 500 pounds.

Family Tents
It is always worth spending the time and money to buy a tent you and your family will be happy with.

Many excellent family tents are available for $125–175, particularly from Coleman, Cabela's, and Remington. Guide-approved expedition tents for groups cost higher, generally $350–600. Here is a synopsis of some of best tents available:

Coleman Weathermaster
800/835-3278
website: www.coleman.com
$150–200

The Weathermaster series features tents with multiple rooms, walls, and ample headroom, and they are guaranteed to keep rain out. The 17- by 9-foot model sleeps six to eight, has a 76-inch ceiling, and has zippered dividers. This is the tent I bought for my family. Since the dividers are removable, you can configure the tent in many designs. The frame is designed with poles that are not moved around yet are adjustable to three different heights to accommodate uneven ground.

Coleman Modified Dome
tel. 800/835-3278
website: www.coleman.com
$70–230

Coleman Modified Dome tents are available in six different single- and multi-room designs. The

A-frame style **tents** have gone the way of the dinosaur. With the world going high-tech, tents of today vary greatly in complexity, size, price, and put-up time. And they wouldn't be fit for this new millennium without offering options such as moon roofs, rain flies, and tent wings. Be sure to buy the one that's right for your needs.

pole structure is unique, with all four upright poles and one ridgepole shock-corded together for a integrated system that makes setup extremely fast and easy. Yet the tent has passed tests in high winds because of the engineering of the ridgepole. Mesh panels in the ceiling are a tremendous plus for ventilation.

Coleman Sundome
tel. 800/835-3278
website: www.coleman.com
$60–160

This tent is the traditional square and rectangular dome tents that are widely known for their simple setup with two-pole construction and roomy design. A standard feature is the tub floor, which wraps partially up the outer wall for increased water resistance. Mesh roof vents, D-shaped doors, shock-corded poles, and three-quarter-length rainflies are standard.

Cabela's Three-Room Cabin
tel. 800/237-4444
website: www.cabelas.com
$270

A beautiful three-room tent colored forest green and featuring a 10- by 20-foot floor available in different configurations with removable interior walls. Three doors mean everybody doesn't tromp through the center room for access to the side rooms. It will stand up to wind, rain, and frequent use.

Cabela's Alaskan Vestibule
tel. 800/237-4444
website: www.cabelas.com
$129–250

The new Alaskan Vestibule series for 2003 is based around a dome tent that can be connected by a tube to another dome tent. In use, it looks like a giant caterpillar, with dome tents that sleep four, or six to eight, on each end of a connector tube. It allows privacy without having to buy separate tents. A favorite for both family use and professionals.

Kelty Nirvana
tel. 800/423-2320
website: www.kelty.com
$325

The Nirvana is a top-of-the-line tent based on a sleek dome profile. This is a great package, with mesh sides, tops, and doors, along with a full awning fly and coverage for weather protection. Clip sleeves and rubber-tipped poles for easy slide during set-up are a nice bonus.

Bivouac Bags

If you like going solo and choose not to own a tent at all, a bivy bag, short for bivouac bag and pronounced "bivvy" as in dizzy, and not "bivy" as in ivy, can provide the extremely lightweight weather protection you require. A bivy bag is a water-repellent shell in which your sleeping bag fits. It is light and tough, and for some is the perfect alternative to a heavy tent. My own bivy weighs 31 ounces and cost me $240; it's made by OR (Outdoor Research), and I just plain love the thing on expeditions. On the downside, however, it can be a bit difficult getting settled just right in it, and some say they feel claustrophobic at the close quarters. Once you get used to a bivy, then spend a night in a tent, the tent feels like a room at the Mirage.

My biggest fear was the idea of riding out a storm. You can hear the rain hitting you, and sometimes even feel the pounding of the drops through the bivy bag. For some, it can be unsettling to try to sleep under such circumstances. On the other hand, I've always looked forward to it. In cold weather, a bivy also helps keep you warm. I've had just one miserable night in mine. That was when my sleeping bag was a bit wet when I started the night. By the middle of the night, the water was condensing from the sleeping bag on the interior walls of the bivy, and then soaking the bag, like a storm cycle. The night hit only about 45°F but I just about froze to death anyway. Otherwise, I've used it on multiweek expeditions with great results, with warm, dry nights and deep, restful sleeps by night, and a pack lightened without carrying a tent by day.

Pickup Truck Campers

If you own a pickup truck with a camper shell, you can turn it into a self-contained campground with a little work. This can be an ideal way to go: it's fast, portable, and you are guaranteed a dry environment.

But that does not necessarily mean it is a warm environment. In fact, without insulation from the metal truck bed, it can be like trying to sleep on an iceberg. That is because the metal truck bed will get as cold as the air temperature, which is often much colder than the ground temperature. Without insulation, it can be much colder in your camper shell than it would be on the open ground.

When I camp in my rig, I use a large piece of foam for a mattress and insulation. The foam measures four inches thick, 48 inches wide, and 76 inches long. It makes for a bed as comfortable as anything one might ask for. In fact, during the winter, if I don't go camping for a few weeks because of writing obligations, I sometimes will throw the foam on the floor, lay down the old sleeping bag, light a fire, and camp right in my living room. It's in my blood, I tell you. Air beds and cots are also extremely comfortable and I've used both many times. Whatever you choose, just make sure you have a comfortable sleeping unit. Good sleep makes for great camping trips.

RVs

The problems RVers encounter come from two primary sources: lack of privacy and light intrusion.

The lack of privacy stems from the natural restrictions of where a land yacht can go. Without careful use of the guide section of this book, motor-home owners can find themselves in parking lot settings, jammed in with plenty of neighbors. Because RVs often have large picture windows, you lose your privacy, causing some late nights; then, come daybreak, light intrusion forces an early wake up. The result is you get shorted on your sleep.

The answer is to carry inserts to fit over the inside of your windows. This closes off the outside and retains your privacy. And if you don't want to wake up with the sun at daybreak, you don't have to. It will still be dark.

FIRST AID AND INSECT PROTECTION

The mountain night could not have been more perfect, I thought as I lay in my sleeping bag.

The sky looked like a mass of jewels and the air tasted sweet and smelled of pines. A shooting star fireballed across the sky, and I remember thinking, "It just doesn't get any better."

Just then, as I was drifting into sleep, a mysterious buzz appeared from nowhere and deposited itself inside my left ear. Suddenly awake, I whacked my ear with the palm of my hand, hard enough to cause a minor concussion. The buzz disappeared. I pulled out my flashlight and shined it on my palm, and there, lit in the blackness of night, lay the squished intruder: a mosquito, dead amid a stain of blood.

Satisfied, I turned off the light, closed my eyes, and thought of the fishing trip planned for the next day. Then I heard them. It was a squadron of mosquitoes flying landing patterns around my head. I tried to grab them with an open hand, but they dodged the assault and flew off. Just 30 seconds later another landed in my left ear. I promptly dispatched the invader with a rip of the palm.

Now I was completely awake, so I got out of my sleeping bag to retrieve some mosquito repellent. But en route, several of the buggers swarmed and nailed me in the back and arms. After I applied the repellent and settled snugly again in my sleeping bag, the mosquitoes would buzz a few inches from my ear. After getting a whiff of the poison, they would fly off. It was like sleeping in a sawmill.

The next day, drowsy from little sleep, I set out to fish. I'd walked but 15 minutes when I brushed against a bush and felt this stinging sensation on the inside of my arm, just above the wrist. I looked down: a tick had his clamps in me. I ripped it out before he could embed his head into my skin.

After catching a few fish, I sat down against a tree to eat lunch and just watch the water go by. My dog, Rebel, sat down next to me and stared at the beef jerky I was munching as if it were a T-bone steak. I finished eating, gave him a small piece, patted him on the head, and said, "Good dog." Right then, I noticed an itch on my arm where a mosquito had drilled me. I unconsciously scratched it. Two days later, in that exact spot, some nasty red splotches started popping up. Poison oak. By petting my dog and then scratching my arm, I had transferred the oil residue of the poison oak leaves from Rebel's fur to my arm.

When I returned home, Foonsky asked me about the trip.

"Great," I said. "Mosquitoes, ticks, poison oak. Can hardly wait to go back."

"Sorry I missed out," he answered.

Mosquitoes, No-See-Ums, Gnats, and Horseflies

On a trip to Canada, Foonsky and I were fishing a small lake from the shore when suddenly a black horde of mosquitoes could be seen moving across the lake toward us. It was like when the French army looked across the Rhine and saw the Wehrmacht coming. There was a buzz in the air. We fought them off for a few minutes, then made a fast retreat to the truck and jumped in, content the buggers had been fooled. But in some way still unknown to us, the mosquitoes gained entry to the truck. In 10 minutes, we squished 15 of them as they attempted to plant their oil drills into our skins. Just outside the truck, the black horde waited for us to make a tactical error such as rolling down a window. It finally took a miraculous hailstorm to foil the attack.

When it comes to mosquitoes, no-see-ums, gnats, and horseflies, there are times when there is nothing you can do. However, in most situations you can muster a defense to repel the attack.

The first key with mosquitoes is to wear clothing too heavy for them to drill through. Expose a minimum of skin, wear a hat, and tie a bandanna around your neck, preferably one that has been sprayed with repellent. If you try to get by with just a cotton T-shirt, you will be declared a federal mosquito sanctuary.

So first your skin must be well covered, exposing only your hands and face. Second, you should have your companion spray your clothes with repellent. Third, you should dab liquid repellent directly on your skin.

At night, the easiest way to get a good sleep without mosquitoes buzzing in your ear is to sleep in a bug-proof tent. If the nights are warm and you want to see the stars, new tent models are available that have a skylight covered with mosquito netting. If you don't like tents on summer evenings, mosquito netting rigged with an air space at your head can solve the problem. Otherwise prepare to get bitten, even with the use of mosquito repellent.

Mosquito Repellent: Taking vitamin B1 and eating garlic are reputed to act as natural insect repellents, but I've met a lot of mosquitoes that are not convinced. A better bet is to examine the label of the repellent in question for N, N-diethylmetatoluamide, commonly known as DEET. That is the poison, and the percentage of it in the container must be listed and will indicate that brand's effectiveness. Inert ingredients are mainly fluids used to fill the bottles.

If your problems are with no-see-ums or biting horseflies, then you need a slightly different approach.

No-see-ums are tiny black insects that look like nothing more than a sliver of dirt on your skin. Then you notice something stinging, and when you rub the area, you scratch up a little no-see-um. The results are similar to mosquito bites, making your skin itch, splotch, and when you get them bad, swell. In addition to using the techniques described to repel mosquitoes, you should go one step further.

The problem is that no-see-ums are tricky little devils. Somehow they can actually get under your socks and around your ankles where they will bite to their hearts' content all night long while you sleep, itch, sleep, and itch some more. The best solution is to apply a liquid repellent to your ankles, then wear clean socks.

Horseflies are another story. They are rarely a problem, but when they get their dander up, they can cause trouble you'll never forget.

One such episode occurred when Foonsky and I were paddling a canoe along the shoreline of a large lake. This giant horsefly, about the size of a fingertip, started dive-bombing the canoe. After 20 minutes, it landed on Foonsky's thigh. He immediately slammed it with an open hand, then let out a blood-curdling "Yeeeee-ow!" that practically sent ripples across the lake. When Foonsky whacked it, the horsefly had somehow turned around and bit him on the hand, leaving a huge red welt.

In the next 10 minutes, that big fly strafed the canoe on more dive-bomb runs. I finally got my canoe paddle, swung it as if it were a baseball bat, and nailed that horsefly as if I'd hit a home run. It landed about 15 feet from the boat, still alive and buzzing in the water. While I was trying to figure what it would take to kill this bugger, a large rainbow trout surfaced and snatched it out of the water, finally avenging the assault.

If you have horsefly or yellow jacket problems, you'd best just leave the area. One, two, or a few can be dealt with. More than that and your fun camping trip will be about as fun as being roped to a tree and stung by an electric shock rod.

On most trips, you will spend time doing everything possible to keep from getting bitten by mosquitoes or no-see-ums. When that fails, you must know what to do next, and fast, if you are among those ill-fated campers who get big red lumps from a bite inflicted from even a microscopic mosquito.

A fluid called After Bite or a dab of ammonia should be applied immediately to the bite. To start the healing process, apply a first-aid gel (not a liquid), such as the one made by Campho-Phenique.

DEET Versus "Natural" Repellents

What is DEET? You're not likely to find the word DEET on any repellent label. That's because DEET stands for N,N diethyl-m-toluamide. If the label contains this scientific name, the repellent contains DEET. Despite fears of DEET-associated health risks and the increased attention given natural alternatives, DEET-based repellents are still acknowledged as by far the best option when serious insect protection is required.

What are the health risks associated with using DEET? A number of deaths and a number of medical problems have been attributed in the press to DEET in recent years—events that those in the DEET community vehemently deny as being specifically DEET-related, pointing to reams of scientific documentation as evidence. It does seem logical to assume that if DEET can peel paint, melt nylon, destroy plastic, wreck wood finishes, and damage fishing line, then it must be hell on the skin—perhaps worse.

On one trip, I had a small bottle of mosquito repellent in the same pocket as a Swiss army knife. Guess what happened? The mosquito repellent leaked a bit and literally melted the insignia right off the knife. DEET will also melt synthetic clothes. That is why in bad mosquito country, I'll expose a minimum of skin, just hands and face (with full beard), and apply the repellent only to my cheeks and the back of my hands, perhaps wear a bandanna sprinkled with a few drops as well. That does the trick, with a minimum of exposure to the repellent.

Although nothing definitive has been published, there is a belief among a growing number in the scientific community that repeated applications of products containing low percentages of DEET can be potentially dangerous. It is theorized that this actually puts consumers at a greater risk for absorbing high levels of DEET into the body than if they had just used one application of a 30–50 percent DEET product with an efficacy of four to six hours. Also being studied is the possibility that low levels of DEET, which might not otherwise be of toxicological concern, may become hazardous if they are formulated with solvents or dilutents (considered inert ingredients) that may enhance the absorption rate.

Are natural alternatives a safer choice? To imply that essential oils are completely safe because they are a natural product is not altogether accurate. Essential oils, while derived from plants that grow naturally, are chemicals too. Some are potentially hazardous if ingested, and most are downright painful if they find their way into the eyes or onto mucus membranes. For example, pennyroyal is perhaps the most toxic of the essential oils used to repel insects and can be deadly if taken internally. Other oils used include citronella (perhaps the most common, it's extracted from an aromatic grass indigenous to Southern Asia), eucalyptus, cedarwood, and peppermint.

Three citronella-based products, Buzz Away (manufactured by Quantum), Avon's Skin-So-Soft, and Natrapel (manufactured by Tender), have received EPA registration and approval for sale as repellents for use in controlling mosquitoes, flies, gnats, and midges.

How effective are natural repellents? While there are numerous studies cited by those on the DEET and citronella sides of the fence, the average effective repelling time of a citronella product appears to range from 1.5 to two hours. Tests conducted at Cambridge University, England, comparing Natrapel to DEET-based Skintastic (a low-percentage DEET product) found citronella to be just as effective in repelling mosquitoes. The key here is effectiveness and the amount of time until reapplication.

Citronella products work for up to two hours and then require reapplication (the same holds true for other natural formulations). Products using a low-percentage level of DEET also require reapplication every two hours to remain effective. So if you're going outside for only a short period in an environment where insect bites are more an irritant than a hazard, you would do just as well to go natural.

What other chemical alternatives are there? Another line of defense against insects is the chemical permethrin, used on clothing, not on skin. Permethrin-based products are designed to repel and kill arthropods or crawling insects, making them a preferred repellent for ticks. The currently available products will remain effective, repelling and killing mosquitoes, ticks, and chiggers, for two weeks and through two launderings.

Ticks
Ticks are nasty little vermin that will wait in ambush, jump on unsuspecting prey, and then crawl to a prime location before filling their bodies with their victim's blood.

Keep It Wild Tip 4: Sanitation

If no refuse facility is available:
1. Deposit human waste in "cat holes" dug six to eight inches deep. Cover and disguise the cat hole when finished.
2. Deposit human waste at least 75 paces (200 feet) from any water source or camp.
3. Use toilet paper sparingly. When finished, carefully burn it in the cat hole, then bury it.
4. If no appropriate burial locations are available, such as in popular wilderness camps above tree line in granite settings, then all human refuse should be double-bagged and packed out.
5. At boat-in campsites, chemical toilets are required. Chemical toilets can also solve the problem of larger groups camping for long stays at one location where no facilities are available.
6. To wash dishes or your body, carry water away from the source and use small amounts of biodegradable soap. Scatter dishwater after all food particles have been removed.
7. Scour your campsites for even the tiniest piece of trash and any other evidence of your stay. Pack out all the trash you can, even if it's not yours. Finding cigarette butts, for instance, provides special irritation for most campers. Pick them up and discard them properly.
8. Never litter. Never. Or you become the enemy of all others.

I call them Dracula bugs, but by any name they can be a terrible camp pest. Ticks rest on grass and low plants and attach themselves to those who brush against the vegetation (dogs are particularly vulnerable). Typically they are no more than 18 inches above ground, and if you stay on the trails, you can usually avoid them.

There are two common species of ticks. The common coastal tick is larger, brownish in color, and prefers to crawl around before putting its clamps on you. The latter habit can be creepy, but when you feel it crawling, you can just pick it off and dispatch it. The coastal tick's preferred destination is usually the back of your neck, just where the hairline starts. The other species, the wood tick, is small and black, and when he puts his clamps in, it's immediately painful. When a wood tick gets into a dog for a few days, it can cause a large red welt. In either case, ticks should be removed as soon as possible.

If you have hiked in areas infested with ticks, it is advisable to shower as soon as possible, washing your clothes immediately. If you just leave your clothes in a heap, a tick can crawl out and invade your home. They like warmth, and one way or another, they can end up in your bed. Waking up in the middle of the night with a tick crawling across your chest can really give you the creeps.

Once a tick has its clampers in you, you must decide how long it has been there. If it has been a short time, the most painless and effective method for removal is to take a pair of sharp tweezers and grasp the little devil, making certain to isolate the mouth area, then pull him out. Reader Johvin Perry sent in the suggestion to coat the tick with Vaseline, which will cut off its oxygen supply, after which it may voluntarily give up the hunt.

If the tick has been in longer, you may wish to have a doctor extract it. Some people will burn a tick with a cigarette, or poison it with lighter fluid, but this is not advisable. No matter how you do it, you must take care to remove all of it, especially its clawlike mouth.

The wound, however small, should then be cleansed and dressed. This is done by applying liquid peroxide, which cleans and sterilizes, and then applying a dressing coated with a first-aid gel such as First-Aid Cream, Campho-Phenique, or Neosporin.

Lyme disease, which can be transmitted by the bite of the deer tick, is rare but common enough to warrant some attention. To prevent tick bites, some people tuck their pant legs into their hiking socks and spray tick repellent, called Permamone, on their pants.

The first symptom of Lyme disease is that the bite area will develop a bright red, splotchy rash. Other possible early symptoms include headache, nausea, fever, and/or a stiff neck. If this happens, or if you have any doubts, you should see your doctor immediately. If you do get Lyme disease, don't panic. Doctors say it is easily treated in the early stages with simple antibiotics. If you are nervous about getting Lyme disease, carry a small plastic bag with you when you hike. If a tick manages to get his clampers into you, put it in the plastic bag after you pull it out. Then give it to your doctor for analysis to see if the tick is a carrier of the disease.

During the course of my hiking and camping career, I have removed ticks from my skin hundreds of times without any problems. However, if you are worried about ticks, you can buy a tick removal kit from any outdoors store. These kits allow you to remove ticks in such a way that their toxins are guaranteed not to enter your bloodstream.

If you are particularly wary of ticks or perhaps even have nightmares of them, wear long pants that are tucked into the socks, as well as a long-sleeved shirt tucked securely into the pants and held with a belt. Clothing should be light in color, making it easier to see ticks, and tightly woven so ticks have trouble hanging on. On one hike with my mom, Eleanor, I brushed more than 100 ticks off my blue jeans in less than an hour, while she did not pick up a single one on her polyester pants.

Perform tick checks regularly, especially on the back of the neck. The combination of DEET insect repellents applied to the skin and permethrin repellents applied directly to clothing is considered to be the most effective line of defense against ticks.

Poison Oak

After a nice afternoon hike, about a five-miler, I was concerned about possible exposure to poison oak, so I immediately showered and put on clean clothes. Then I settled into a chair with my favorite foamy elixir to watch the end of a baseball game. The game went 18 innings; meanwhile, my dog, tired from the hike, went to sleep on my bare ankles.

A few days later I had a case of poison oak. My feet looked as though they had been on fire and put out with an ice pick. The lesson? Don't always trust your dog, give him a bath as well, and beware of extra-inning ball games.

You can get poison oak only from direct contact with the oil residue from the leaves. It can be passed in a variety of ways, as direct as skin-to-leaf contact or as indirect as leaf to dog, dog to sofa, sofa to skin. Once you have it, there is little you can do but itch yourself to death. Applying Caladryl lotion or its equivalent can help because it contains antihistamines, which attack and dry the itch.

A tip that may sound crazy but seems to work is advised by my pal Furniss. You should expose the afflicted area to the hottest water you can stand, then suddenly immerse it in cold water. The hot water opens the skin pores and gets the "itch" out, and the cold water then quickly seals the pores.

Avoiding Poison Oak
Remember the old Boy Scout saying: "Leaves of three, let them be."

In any case, you're a lot better off if you don't get poison oak to begin with. Remember that poison oak can disguise itself. In the spring, it is green; then it gradually turns reddish in the summer. By fall, it becomes a bloody, ugly-looking red. In the winter, it loses its leaves altogether and appears to be nothing more than barren, brown sticks of a small plant. However, at any time and in any form, its contact with skin can quickly lead to infection.

Some people are more easily afflicted than others, but if you are one of the lucky few who aren't, don't cheer too loudly. While some people can be exposed to the oil residue of poison oak with little or no effect, the body's resistance can gradually be worn down with repeated exposure. At one time I could practically play in the stuff and the only symptom would be a few little bumps on the inside of my wrist. Now, more than 15 years later, my resistance has broken down. If I merely rub against poison oak now, in a few days the exposed area can look as if it were used for a track meet.

So regardless of whether you consider yourself vulnerable or not, you should take heed to reduce your exposure. That can be done by staying on trails when you hike and making sure your dog does the same. Remember, the worst stands of poison oak are usually brush-infested areas just off the trail. Protect yourself also by dressing so your skin is completely covered, wearing long-sleeved shirts, long pants, and boots. If you suspect you've been exposed, immediately wash your clothes and then wash yourself with aloe vera, rinsing with a cool shower.

And don't forget to give your dog a bath as well.

Sunburn

The most common injury suffered on camping trips is sunburn, yet some people wear it as a badge of honor, believing that it somehow enhances their virility. Well, it doesn't. Neither do suntans. And too much sun can lead to serious burns or sunstroke.

It is easy enough to avoid. Use a high-level sunscreen on your skin, apply lip balm with sunscreen, and wear sunglasses and a hat. If any area gets burned, apply first-aid cream, which will soothe and provide moisture for your parched, burned skin.

The best advice is not to get even a suntan. Those who do are involved in a practice that can be eventually ruinous to their skin and possibly lead to cancer.

A Word about Giardia and Cryptosporidium

You have just hiked in to your backwoods spot, you're thirsty and a bit tired, but you smile as you consider the prospects. Everything seems perfect—there's not a stranger in sight, and you have nothing to do but relax with your pals.

You toss down your gear, grab your cup, dip it into the stream, and take a long drink of that ice-cold mountain water. It seems crystal pure and sweeter than anything you've ever tasted. It's not till later that you find out it can be just like drinking a cup of poison.

Whether you camp in the wilderness or not, if you hike, you're going to get thirsty. And if your canteen runs dry, you'll start eyeing any water source. Stop! Do not pass Go. Do not drink.

By drinking what appears to be pure mountain water without first treating it, you can ingest a microscopic protozoan called *Giardia lamblia.* The pain of the ensuing abdominal cramps can make you feel that your stomach and intestinal tract are in a knot, ready to explode. With that comes long-term diarrhea that is worse than even a bear could imagine.

Treating Your Water Means Avoiding Diarrhea: The only sure way to beat giardia and other water-borne diseases is to filter or boil your water before drinking, eating, or brushing your teeth. And the best way to prevent the spread of giardia is to bury your waste products at least eight inches deep and 200 feet away from natural waters.

Doctors call the disease giardiasis, or giardia for short, but it is difficult to diagnose. One friend of mine who contracted giardia was told he might have stomach cancer before the proper diagnosis was made.

Drinking directly from a stream or lake does not mean you will get giardia, but you are taking a giant chance. There is no reason to assume such a risk, potentially ruining your trip and enduring weeks of misery.

A lot of people are taking that risk. I made a personal survey of campers in the Yosemite National Park wilderness, and found that roughly only one in 20 was equipped with some kind of water-purification system. The result, according to the Public Health Service, is that an average of 4 percent of all backpackers and campers suffer giardiasis. According to the Parasitic Diseases Division of the Center for Infectious Diseases, the rates range from 1 percent to 20 percent across the country.

But if you get giardia, you are not going to care about the statistics. "When I got giardia, I just about wanted to die," said Henry McCarthy, a California camper. "For about 10 days, it was the most terrible thing I have ever experienced. And through the whole thing, I kept thinking, 'I shouldn't have drunk that water, but it seemed all right at the time.'"

That is the mistake most campers make. The stream might be running free, gurgling over boulders in the high country, tumbling into deep, oxygenated pools. It looks pure. Then in a few days, the problems suddenly start. Drinking untreated water from mountain streams is a lot like playing Russian roulette. Sooner or later the gun goes off.

Filters

There's really no excuse for going without a water filter: handheld filters are getting more compact, lighter, easier to use, and often less expensive. Having to boil water or endure chemicals that leave a bad taste in the mouth has been all but eliminated.

With a filter, you just pump and drink. Filtering strains out microscopic contaminants, rendering the water clear and somewhat pure. How pure? That depends on the size of the filter's pores—what manufacturers call pore-size efficiency. A filter with a pore-size efficiency of one micron or smaller will remove protozoa such as *Giardia lamblia* and cryptosporidium, as well as parasitic eggs and larva, but it takes a pore-size efficiency of less than 0.4 microns to remove bacteria. All but one of the filters recommended here do that.

A good backcountry water filter weighs less than 20 ounces, is easy to grasp, simple to use, and a snap to clean and maintain. At the very least, buy one that will remove protozoa and bacteria. (A number of cheap, pocket-sized filters remove only *Giardia lamblia* and cryptosporidium. That, in my book, is risking your health to save money.) Consider the flow rate, too: a liter per minute is good.

All filters will eventually clog—it's a sign that they've been doing their job. If you force water through a filter that's becoming difficult to pump, you risk injecting a load of microbial nasties into your bottle. Some models can be backwashed, brushed, or, as with ceramic elements, scrubbed to extend their useful lives. And if the filter has a prefilter to screen out the big stuff, use it: it will give your filter a boost in mileage, which can then top out at about 100 gallons per disposable element. Any of

Water filters are a wise investment since all wilderness water should be considered contaminated. Make sure the filter can be easily cleaned or has a replaceable cartridge. The filter pores must be 0.4 microns or less to remove bacteria.

the filters reviewed here will serve well on an outing into the wilds, providing you always play by the manufacturer's rules. They cost about $35–75, up to more than $200, depending on the volume of water they are constructed to filter.

- **First Need Deluxe:** The 15-ounce First Need Deluxe from General Ecology does something no other handheld filter will do: it removes protozoa, bacteria, and viruses without using chemicals. Such effectiveness is the result of a fancy three-stage matrix system. Unfortunately, if you drop the filter and unknowingly crack the cartridge, all the little nasties can get through. General Ecology's solution is to include a bottle of blue dye that indicates breaks. The issue hasn't scared off too many folks, though: the First Need has been around since 1982. Additional cartridges cost $30. A final note: the filter pumps smoothly and puts out more than a liter per minute. A favorite of mine.

- **PentaPure Oasis:** The PentaPure Oasis Water Purification System from WTC/Ecomaster offers drinkable water with a twist: you squeeze and sip instead of pumping. Weighing 6.5 ounces, the system packages a three-stage filter inside a 21-ounce-capacity sport bottle with an angled and sealing drinking nozzle, ideal for mountain bikers. The filter removes and/or kills protozoa, bacteria, and viruses, so it's also suitable for world travel. It's certainly convenient: just fill the bottle with untreated water, screw on the cap, give it a firm squeeze (don't expect the easy flow of a normal sport bottle; there's more work being done), and sip. The Oasis only runs into trouble if the water source is shallow; you'll need a cup for scooping.

- **Basic Designs Ceramic:** The Basic Designs Ceramic Filter Pump weighs eight ounces and is as stripped-down a filter as you'll find. The pump is simple, easy to use, and quite reliable. The ceramic filter effectively removes protozoa and bacteria, making it ideal and cost effective for backpacking—but it won't protect against viruses. Also, the filter element is too bulbous to work directly from a shallow water source; like the PentaPure, you'll have to decontaminate a pot, cup, or bottle to transfer your unfiltered water. It's a great buy, though, for anyone worried only about *Giardia lamblia* and cryptosporidium.

- **SweetWater WalkAbout:** The WalkAbout is perfect for the day hiker or backpacker who obsesses on lightening the load. The filter weighs just 8.5 ounces, is easily cleaned in the field, and removes both protozoa and bacteria: a genuine bargain. There are some trade-offs, however, for its diminutiveness. Water delivery is a tad slow at just under a liter per minute, but redesigned filter cartridges ($12.50) are now good for up to 100 gallons.

- **MSR MiniWorks:** Like the WalkAbout, the bargain-priced MiniWorks has a bigger and more expensive water-filtering brother. But in this case the differences are harder to discern: the new 14.3-ounce MiniWorks looks similar to the $140 WaterWorks II, and like the WaterWorks is fully field-maintainable, while guarding against protozoa, bacteria, and chemicals. But the Mini is the best-executed, easiest-to-use ceramic filter on the market, and it attaches directly to a standard one-quart Nalgene water bottle. Too bad it takes 90 seconds to filter that quart.

- **PUR Explorer:** The Explorer offers protection from all the bad guys—viruses as well as protozoa and bacteria—by incorporating an iodine matrix into the filtration process. An optional carbon cartridge ($20) neutralizes the iodine's noxious taste. The Explorer is also considered a trusty veteran among water filters because of its smooth pumping action and nifty backwashing feature: with a quick twist, the device switches from filtering mode to self-cleaning mode. It may be on the heavy side (20 ounces) and somewhat pricey, but the Explorer works very well on iffy water anywhere.

- **Katadyn U.S.A. Mini Filter:** The Mini Filter is a much more compact version of Katadyn's venerable Pocket Filter. This one weighs just eight ounces, ideal for the minimalist backcountry traveler, and it effectively removes protozoa and bacteria. A palm-of-the-hand-size filter, however, makes it challenging to put any kind of power behind the pump's tiny handle, and the filtered water comes through at a paltry half-liter per minute. It also requires more cleaning than most filters—though the good news is that the element is made of long-lasting ceramic. Ironically, one option lets you buy the Mini Filter with a carbon element instead of the ceramic. The pumping is easier, the flow rate is better, and the price is way down ($99), but I'd only go that route if you'll be pumping from clear mountain streams.

- **MSR WaterWorks II Ceramic:** At 17.4 ounces the WaterWorks II isn't light, but for the same price as the Katadyn you get a better flow rate (90 seconds per liter), an easy pumping action, and—like the original Mini Filter—a long-lasting ceramic cartridge. This filter is a good match for the person who encounters a lot of dirty water—its three-stage filter weeds out protozoa, bacteria, and chemicals—and is mechanically inclined. The MSR can be completely disassembled afield for troubleshooting and cleaning. (If you're not so endowed, take the filter apart at home only, as the potential for confusion is somewhat high.) By the way, the company has corrected the clogging problem that plagued a previous version of the WaterWorks. The big drawback with filters is that if you pump water from a mucky lake, the filter can clog in a few days. Therein lies the weakness. Once plugged up, it is useless, and you have to replace it or take your chances.

One trick to extend the filter life is to fill your cook pot with water, let the sediment settle, then pump from there. As an insurance policy, always have a spare filter canister on hand.

Boiling Water

Except for water filtration, this is the only treatment that you can use with complete confidence. According to the federal Parasitic Diseases Division, it takes a few minutes at a rolling boil to be certain you've killed *Giardia lamblia.* At high elevations, boil for three to five minutes. A side benefit is that you'll also kill other dangerous bacteria that live undetected in natural waters.

But to be honest, boiling water is a thorn for most people on backcountry trips. For one thing, if you boil water on an open fire, what should taste like crystal-pure mountain water tastes instead like a mouthful of warm ashes. If you don't have a campfire, it wastes stove fuel. And if you are thirsty *now,* forget it. The water takes hours to cool.

The only time boiling always makes sense, however, is when you are preparing dinner. The ash taste will disappear in whatever freeze-dried dinner, soup, or hot drink you make.

Water-Purification Pills

Pills are the preference for most backcountry campers, and this can get them in trouble. At just $3–8 per bottle, which can figure up to just a few cents per canteen, they do come cheap. In addition, they kill most of the bacteria, regardless of whether you use iodine crystals or potable aqua iodine tablets.

The problem is they just don't always kill *Giardia lamblia,* and that is the one critter worth worrying about on your trip. That makes water-treatment pills unreliable and dangerous.

Another key element is the time factor. Depending on the water's temperature, organic content, and pH level, these pills can take a long time to do the job. A minimum wait of 20 minutes is advised. Most people don't like waiting that long, especially when they're hot and thirsty after a hike and thinking, "What the heck, the water looks fine."

And then there is the taste. On one trip, my water filter clogged and we had to use the iodine pills instead. It doesn't take long to get tired of the iodine-tinged taste of the water. Mountain water should be one of the greatest tasting beverages of the world, but the iodine kills that.

No Treatment

This is your last resort and, using extreme care, can be executed with success. One of my best hiking buddies, Michael Furniss, is a nationally renowned hydrologist, and on wilderness trips he has showed me the difference between safe and dangerous water sources.

Long ago, people believed that just finding water running over a rock was a guarantee of its purity. Imagine that. What we've learned is that the safe water sources are almost always small springs in high, craggy mountain areas. The key is making sure no one has been upstream from where you drink. We drink untreated water only when we can see the source, such as a spring.

Furniss mentioned that another potential problem in bypassing water treatment is that even in settings free of *Giardia lamblia,* you can still ingest other bacteria that cause stomach problems.

Hypothermia

No matter how well planned your trip might be, a sudden change in weather can turn it into a puzzle for which there are few answers. Bad weather or an accident can set in motion a dangerous chain of events.

Such a chain of episodes occurred for my brother Rambob and me on a fishing trip one fall day just below the snow line. The weather had suddenly turned very cold, and ice was forming along the shore of the lake. Suddenly, the canoe became terribly imbalanced, and just that quick it flipped. The little life vest seat cushions were useless, and using the canoe as a paddleboard, we tried to kick our way back to shore where my dad was going crazy at the thought of his two sons drowning before his eyes.

It took 17 minutes in that 38-degree water, but we finally made it to shore. When they pulled me out of the water, my legs were dead, not strong enough even to hold up my weight. In fact, I didn't feel so much cold as tired, and I just wanted to lie down and go to sleep.

I closed my eyes, and my brother-in-law, Lloyd Angal, slapped me in the face several times, then got me on my feet and pushed and pulled me about.

In the celebration over our making it to shore, only Lloyd had realized that hypothermia was setting in. Hypothermia is the condition in which the temperature of the body is lowered to the point that it causes poor reasoning, apathy, and collapse. It can look like the afflicted person is just tired and needs to sleep, but that sleep can be the first step toward a coma.

Ultimately my brother and I shared what little dry clothing remained. Then we began hiking around to get muscle movement, creating internal warmth. We ate whatever munchies were available because the body produces heat by digestion. But most important, we got our heads as dry as possible. More body heat is lost through wet hair than any other single factor.

A few hours later, we were in a pizza parlor replaying the incident, talking about how only a life vest can do the job of a life vest. We decided never again to rely on those little flotation seat cushions that disappear when the boat flips.

Almost by instinct we had done everything right to prevent hypothermia: don't go to sleep, start a physical activity, induce shivering, put dry clothes on, dry your head, and eat something. That's how you fight hypothermia. In a dangerous situation, whether you fall in a lake or a stream or get caught unprepared in a storm, that's how you can stay alive.

After being in that ice-bordered lake for almost 20 minutes and then finally pulling ourselves to the shoreline, we discovered a strange thing. My canoe was flipped right-side up and almost all of its contents were lost: tackle box, flotation cushions, and cooler. But remaining were one paddle and one fishing rod, the trout rod my grandfather had given me for my 12th birthday.

Lloyd gave me a smile. "This means that you are meant to paddle and fish again," he said with a laugh.

Getting Unlost

You could not have been more lost. But there I was, a guy who is supposed to know about these things, transfixed by confusion, snow, and hoofprints from a big deer.

I discovered it is actually quite easy to get lost. If you don't get your bearings, getting found is

To keep from getting lost (above tree line or in sparse vegetation), mark your route with **trail ducks,** small piles of rock which act as directional signs for the return trip.

the difficult part. This occurred on a wilderness trip where I'd hiked in to a remote lake and then set up a base camp for a deer hunt.

"There are some giant bucks up on that rim," confided Mr. Furnai, who lives near the area. "But it takes a mountain man to even get close to them."

That was a challenge I answered. After four-wheeling it to the trailhead, I tromped off with pack and rifle, gut-thumped it up 100 switchbacks over the rim, then followed a creek drainage up to a small but beautiful lake. The area was stark and nearly treeless, with bald granite broken only by large boulders. To keep from getting lost, I marked my route with piles of small rocks to act as directional signs for the return trip.

But at daybreak the next day, I stuck my head out of my tent and found eight inches of snow on the ground. I looked up into a gray sky filled by huge, cascading snowflakes. Visibility was about 50 yards, with fog on the mountain rim. "I better get out of here and get back to my truck," I said to myself. "If my truck gets buried at the trailhead, I'll never get out."

After packing quickly, I started down the mountain. But after 20 minutes, I began to get disoriented. You see, all the little piles of rocks I'd stacked to mark the way were now buried in snow, and I had only a smooth white blanket of snow to guide me. Everything looked the same, and it was snowing even harder now.

Five minutes later I started chewing on some jerky to keep warm, then suddenly stopped. Where was I? Where was the creek drainage? Isn't this where I was supposed to cross over a creek and start the switchbacks down the mountain?

Right then I looked down and saw the tracks of a huge deer, the kind Mr. Furnai had talked about. What a predicament: I was lost and snowed in and seeing big hoofprints in the snow. Part of me wanted to abandon all safety and go after that deer, but a little voice in the back of my head won out. "Treat this as an emergency," it said.

The first step in any predicament is to secure your present situation, that is, to make sure it does not get any worse. I unloaded my rifle (too easy to slip, fall, and have a misfire), took stock of my food (three days' worth), camp fuel (plenty), and clothes (rain gear keeping me dry). Then I wondered, "Where the hell am I?"

I took out my map, compass, and altimeter, then opened the map and laid it on the snow. It immediately began collecting snowflakes. I set the compass atop the map and oriented it to north. Because of the fog, there was no way to spot landmarks, such as prominent mountaintops, to verify my position. Then I checked the altimeter, which read 4,900 feet. Well, the elevation at my lake was 5,320 feet. That was critical information.

I scanned the elevation lines on the map and was able to trace the approximate area of my position, somewhere downstream from the lake, yet close to a 4,900-foot elevation. "Right here," I said, pointing to a spot on the map with a finger. "I should pick up the switchback trail down the mountain somewhere off to the left, maybe just 40 or 50 yards away."

Slowly and deliberately, I pushed through the light, powdered snow. In five minutes, I suddenly stopped. To the left, across a 10-foot depression in the snow, appeared a flat spot that veered off to the right. "That's it! That's the crossing."

In minutes, I was working down the switchbacks, on my way, no longer lost. I thought of the hoofprints I had seen, and now that I knew my position, I wanted to head back and spend the day hunting. Then I looked up at the sky, saw it filled with falling snowflakes, and envisioned my truck buried deep in snow. Alas, this time logic won out over dreams.

In a few hours, now trudging through more than a foot of snow, I was at my truck at a spot called Doe Flat, and next to it was a giant, all-terrain U.S. Forest Service vehicle and two rangers.

"Need any help?" I asked them.

They just laughed. "We're here to help you," one answered. "It's a good thing you filed a trip plan with our district office in Gasquet. We wouldn't have known you were out here."

"Winter has arrived," said the other. "If we don't get your truck out now, it will be stuck here until next spring. If we hadn't found you, you might have been here until the end of time."

They connected a chain from the rear axle of their giant rig to the front axle of my truck and started towing me out, back to civilization. On the way to pavement, I figured I had gotten some of the more important lessons of my life. Always file a trip plan and have plenty of food, fuel, and a camp stove you can rely on. Make sure your clothes, weather gear, sleeping bag, and tent will keep you dry and warm. Always carry a compass, altimeter, and map with elevation lines, and know how to use them, practicing in good weather to get the feel of it.

And if you get lost and see the hoofprints of a giant deer, well, there are times when it is best to pass them by.

CATCHING FISH, AVOIDING BEARS, AND HAVING FUN

Feet tired and hot, stomachs hungry, we stopped our hike for lunch beside a beautiful little river pool that was catching the flows from a long but gentle waterfall. My brother Rambob passed me a piece of jerky. I took my boots off, then slowly dunked my feet into the cool, foaming water.

I was gazing at a towering peak across a canyon when suddenly, Wham! There was a quick jolt at the heel of my right foot. I pulled my foot out of the water to find that, incredibly, a trout had bitten it.

My brother looked at me as if I had antlers growing out of my head. "Wow!" he exclaimed. "That trout almost caught himself an outdoors writer!"

It's true that in remote areas trout sometimes bite on almost anything, even feet. On one high-country trip I caught limits of trout using nothing but a bare hook. The only problem is that the fish will often hit the splitshot sinker instead of the hook. Of course, fishing isn't usually that easy. But it gives you an idea of what is possible.

America's wildlands are home to a remarkable abundance of fish and wildlife. Deer browse with little fear of man, bears keep an eye out for your food, and little critters such as squirrels and chipmunks are daily companions. Add in the fishing, and you've got yourself a camping trip.

Your camping adventures will evolve into premium outdoor experiences if you can work in a few good fishing trips, avoid bear problems, and occasionally add a little offbeat fun with some camp games.

Trout and Bass

He creeps up on the stream as quiet as an Indian scout, keeping his shadow off the water. With his little spinning rod he'll zip his lure within an inch or two of its desired mark, probing along rocks, the edges of riffles, pocket water, or wherever he can find a change in river habitat. Rambob is trout fishing, and he's a master at it.

In most cases he'll catch a trout on his first or second cast. After that it's time to move up the river, giving no spot much more than five minutes' due. Stick and move, stick and move, stalking the stream like a bobcat zeroing in on an unsuspecting rabbit. He might keep a few trout for dinner, but mostly he releases what he catches. Rambob doesn't necessarily fish for food. It's the feeling that comes with it.

Why We Fish: Fishing can give you a sense of exhilaration, like taking a hot shower after being coated with dust. On your walk back to camp, the steps come easy. You suddenly understand what John Muir meant when he talked of developing a oneness with nature, because you have it. That's what fishing can provide.

You don't need a million dollars' worth of fancy gear to catch fish. What you need is the right outlook, and that can be learned. That goes regardless of whether you are fishing for trout or bass, the two most popular fisheries in the United States. Your fishing tackle selection should be as simple and clutter free as possible.

At home I've got every piece of fishing tackle you might imagine, more than 30 rods and many tackle boxes, racks and cabinets filled with all kinds of stuff. I've got one lure that looks like a chipmunk and another that resembles a miniature can of beer with hooks. If I hear of something new, I want to try it and usually do. It's a result of my lifelong fascination with the sport.

But if you just want to catch fish, there's an easier way to go. And when I go fishing, I take that path. I don't try to bring everything. It would be impossible. Instead I bring a relatively small amount of gear. At home I will scan my tackle boxes for equipment and lures, make my selections, and bring just the essentials. Rod, reel, and tackle will fit into a side pocket of my backpack or a small carrying bag.

So what kind of rod should be used on an outdoor trip? For most camper/anglers, I suggest the use of a light, multipiece spinning rod that will break down to a small size. The lowest-priced, quality six-piece rod on the market is the Daiwa 6.5-foot pack rod, number 6752, which is made of a graphite/glass composite that gives it the quality of a much more expensive model. And it comes in a hard plastic carrying tube for protection. Other major rod manufacturers, such as Fenwick, offer similar premium rods. It's tough to miss with any of them.

The use of graphite/glass composites in fishing rods has made them lighter and more sensitive, yet stronger. The only downside to graphite as a rod material is that it can be brittle. If you rap your rod against something, it can crack or cause a weak spot. That weak spot can eventually snap under even light pressure, like setting a hook or casting. Of course, a bit of care will prevent that from ever occurring.

If you haven't bought a fishing reel in some time, you will be surprised at the quality and price of micro spinning reels on the market. The reels come tiny and strong, with rear-control drag systems. Sigma, Shimano, Cardinal, Abu, and others all make premium reels. They're worth it. With your purchase, you've just bought a reel that will last for years and years.

The one downside to spinning reels is that after long-term use, the bail spring will weaken. The result is that after casting and beginning to reel, the bail will sometimes not flip over and allow the reel to retrieve the line. Then you have to do it by hand. This can be incredibly frustrating, particularly when stream fishing, where instant line pickup is essential. The solution is to have a new bail spring installed every few years. This is a cheap, quick operation for a tackle expert.

You might own a giant tackle box filled with lures, but on your fishing trip you are better off to fit just the essentials into a small container. One of the best ways to do that is to use the Plano Micro-Magnum 3414, a tiny two-sided tackle box for trout anglers that fits into a shirt pocket. In mine, I can fit 20 lures in one side of the box and 20 flies, splitshot, and snap swivels in the other. For bass lures, which are bigger, you need a slightly larger box, but the same principle applies.

There are more fishing lures on the market than you can imagine, but a few special ones can do the job. I make sure these are in my box on every trip. For trout, I carry a small black Panther Martin spinner with yellow spots, a small gold Kastmaster, a yellow Roostertail, a gold Z-Ray with red spots, a Super Duper, and a Mepps Lightning spinner.

You can take it a step further using insider's wisdom. My old pal Ed "the Dunk" showed me his trick of taking a tiny Dardevle spoon, spray painting it flat black, and dabbing five tiny red dots on it. It's a real killer, particularly in tiny streams where the trout are spooky.

The best trout catcher I've ever used on rivers is a small metal lure called a Met-L Fly. On days when nothing else works, it can be like going to a shooting gallery. The problem is that the lure is nearly impossible to find. Rambob and I consider the few we have remaining so valuable that if the lure is snagged on a rock, a cold swim is deemed mandatory for its retrieval. These lures are as hard to find in tackle shops as trout can be to catch without one.

For bass, you can also fit all you need into a small plastic tackle box. I have fished with many bass pros, and all of them actually use just a few lures: a white spinner bait, a small jig called a Gits-It, a surface plug called a Zara Spook, and plastic worms. At times, as when the bass move into shoreline areas during the spring, shad minnow imitations like those made by Rebel or Rapala can be dynamite. My favorite is the one-inch, blue-silver Rapala. Every spring as the lakes begin to warm and the fish snap out of their winter doldrums, I like to float and paddle around in my small raft. I'll cast that little Rapala along the shoreline and catch and release hundreds of bass, bluegill, and sunfish. The fish are usually sitting close to the shoreline, awaiting my offering.

Fishing Tips

There's an old angler's joke about how you need to think like a fish. But if you're the one getting zilched, you may not think it's so funny.

The irony is that it is your mental approach, what you see and what you miss, that often determines your fishing luck. Some people will spend a lot of money on tackle, lures, and fishing clothes, and that done, just saunter up to a stream or lake, cast out, and wonder why they are not catching fish. The answer is their mental outlook. They are not attuning themselves to their surroundings.

You must live on nature's level, not your own. Try this and you will become aware of things you never believed even existed. Soon you will see things that will allow you to catch fish. You can get a head start by reading about fishing, but to get your degree in fishing, you must attend the University of Nature.

On every fishing trip, regardless what you fish for, try to follow three hard-and-fast rules:
1. Always approach the fishing spot so you will be undetected.
2. Present your lure, fly, or bait in a manner so it appears completely natural, as if no line was attached.
3. Stick and move, hitting one spot, working it the best you can, then move to the next.

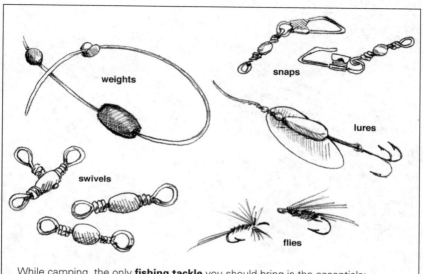

While camping, the only **fishing tackle** you should bring is the essentials: several varying weights, about 20 lures, and about 20 flies, splitshot, and snap swivels. These should all fit into a container just bigger than a deck of cards.

Approach

No one can just walk up to a stream or lake, cast out, and start catching fish as if someone had waved a magic wand. Instead, give the fish credit for being smart. After all, they live there.

Your approach must be completely undetected by the fish. Fish can sense your presence through sight and sound, though this is misinterpreted by most people. By sight, this rarely means the fish actually see you; more likely they will see your shadow on the water or the movement of your arm or rod while casting. By sound, it doesn't mean they hear you talking, but that they will detect the vibrations of your footsteps along the shore, kicking a rock, or the unnatural plunking sound of a heavy cast hitting the water. Any of these elements can spook them off the bite. In order to fish undetected, you must walk softly, keep your shadow off the water, and keep your casting motion low. All of these keys become easier at sunrise or sunset, when shadows are on the water. At midday a high sun causes a high level of light penetration in the water, which can make the fish skittish to any foreign presence.

Like hunting, you must stalk the spots. When my brother Rambob sneaks up on a fishing spot, he is like a burglar sneaking through an unlocked window.

Presentation

Your lure, fly, or bait must appear in the water as if no line were attached, so it looks as natural as possible. My pal Mo Furniss has skin-dived in rivers to watch what the fish see when somebody is fishing.

"You wouldn't believe it," he said. "When the lure hits the water, every trout within 40 feet,

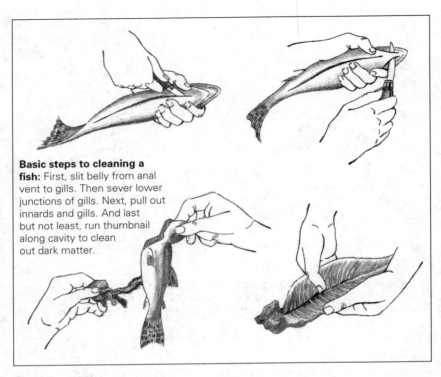

Basic steps to cleaning a fish: First, slit belly from anal vent to gills. Then sever lower junctions of gills. Next, pull out innards and gills. And last but not least, run thumbnail along cavity to clean out dark matter.

like 15, 20 trout, will do a little zigzag. They all see the lure and are aware something is going on. Meanwhile, onshore the guy casting doesn't get a bite and thinks there aren't any fish in the river."

If your offering is aimed at fooling a fish into striking, it must appear as part of its natural habitat, like an insect just hatched or a small fish looking for a spot to hide. That's where you come in.

After you have sneaked up on a fishing spot, you should zip your cast upstream and start your retrieval as soon as it hits the water. If you let the lure sink to the bottom and then start the retrieval, you have no chance. A minnow, for instance, does not sink to the bottom, then start swimming. On rivers, the retrieval should be more of a drift, as if the "minnow" is in trouble and the current is sweeping it downstream.

When fishing on trout streams, always hike and cast upriver and retrieve as the offering drifts downstream in the current. This is effective because trout will sit almost motionless, pointed upstream, finning against the current. This way they can see anything coming their direction, and if a potential food morsel arrives, all they need to do is move over a few inches, open their mouths, and they've got an easy lunch. Thus you must cast upstream.

Conversely, if you cast downstream, your retrieval will bring the lure from behind the fish, where he cannot see it approaching. And I've never seen a trout that had eyes in its tail. In addition, when retrieving a downstream lure, the river current will tend to sweep your lure inshore to the rocks.

The rule of the wild is that wildlife will congregate wherever there is a distinct change in habitat. To find where fish are hiding, look where a riffle pours into a small pond, where a rapid plunges into a deep hole and flattens, and around submerged trees, rock piles, and boulders in the middle of a long riffle.

Finding Spots

A lot of anglers don't catch fish, and a lot of hikers never see any wildlife. The key is where they are looking.

The rule of the wild is that fish and wildlife will congregate wherever there is a distinct change in the habitat. This is where you should begin your search. To find deer, for instance, forget probing a thick forest, but look for where it breaks into a meadow or a clear-cut has splayed a stand of trees. That's where the deer will be.

In a river, it can be where a riffle pours into a small pool, a rapid that plunges into a deep hole and flattens, a big boulder in the middle of a long riffle, a shoreline point, a rock pile, a submerged tree. Look for the changes. Conversely, long, straight stretches of shoreline will not hold fish—the habitat is lousy.

On rivers, the most productive areas are often where short riffles tumble into small oxygenated pools. After sneaking up from the downstream side and staying low, you should zip your cast so the lure plops gently into the white water just above the pool. Start your retrieval instantly; the lure will drift downstream and plunk into the pool. Bang! That's where the trout will hit. Take a few more casts and then head upstream to the next spot.

With a careful approach and lure presentation and by fishing in the right spots, you have the ticket to many exciting days on the water.

Of Bears and Food

The first time you come nose-to-nose with a bear can make your skin quiver.

Even the sight of mild-mannered black bears, the most common bear in America, can send shock waves through your body. They weigh 250–400 pounds and have large claws and teeth that are made to scare campers. When they bound, the muscles on their shoulders roll like ocean breakers.

Bears in camping areas are accustomed to sharing the mountains with hikers and campers. They have become specialists in the food-raiding business. As a result, you must be able to make a bear-proof food hang or be able to scare the fellow off. Many campgrounds provide bear- and raccoon-proof food lockers. You can also stash your food in your vehicle, but that limits the range of your trip.

If you are staying at one of the easy backpack sites listed in this book, there will be no food lockers available. Your car will not be there, either. The solution is to make a bear-proof food hang, suspending all of your food wrapped in a plastic garbage bag from a rope in midair, 10 feet from the trunk of a tree and 20 feet off the ground. (Counterbalancing two bags with a rope thrown over a tree limb is very effective, but finding an appropriate limb can be difficult.)

This is accomplished by tying a rock to a rope, then throwing it over a high but sturdy tree limb. Next, tie your food bag to the rope and hoist it in the air. When you are satisfied with the position of the food bag, tie off the end of the rope to another tree. In an area frequented by bears, a good food bag is a necessity—nothing else will do.

I've been there. On one trip my pal Foonsky and my brother Rambob left to fish, and I was stoking up an evening campfire when I felt the eyes of an intruder on my back. I turned around and saw a big bear heading straight for our camp. In the next half hour I scared the bear off twice, but then he got a whiff of something sweet in my brother's pack.

The bear rolled into camp like a truck, grabbed the pack, ripped it open, and plucked out the Tang and the Swiss Miss. The 350-pounder then sat astride a nearby log and lapped at the goodies like a thirsty dog drinking water.

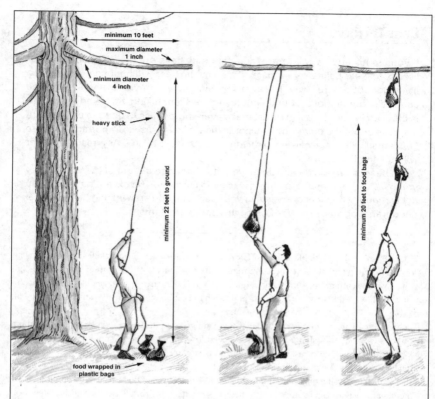

In an area frequented by bears, a good **bear-proof food hang** is a must. Food should be stored in a plastic bag 10 feet from the trunk of the tree and at least 20 feet from the ground.

Once a bear gets his mitts on your gear, he considers it his. I took two steps toward the pack, and that bear jumped off the log and galloped across the camp right at me. Scientists say a man can't outrun a bear, but they've never seen how fast I can go up a granite block with a bear on my tail.

Shortly thereafter, Foonsky returned to find me perched on top of the rock and demanded to know how I could let a bear get our Tang. It took all three of us, Foonsky, Rambob, and me, charging at once and shouting like madmen, to clear the bear out of camp and send him off over the ridge. We learned never to let food sit unattended.

The Grizzly

When it comes to grizzlies, well, my friends, you need what we call an attitude adjustment. Or that big ol' bear may just decide to adjust your attitude for you, making your stay at the park a short one.

Bear Territory

If you are hiking in a wilderness area that may have grizzlies, it becomes a necessity to wear bells on your pack. That way the bear will hear you coming and likely get out of your way. Keep talking, singing, or maybe even debating the country's foreign policy, but do not fall into a silent hiking vigil. And if a breeze is blowing in your face, you must make even more noise (a good excuse to rant and rave about the government's domestic affairs). Noise is important, because your smell will not be carried in the direction you are hiking. As a result the bear will not smell you coming.

If a bear can hear you and smell you, it will tend to get out of the way and let you pass without your knowing it was even close by. The exceptions are if you are carrying fish or lots of sweets in your pack or if you are wearing heavy, sweet deodorants or makeup. All of these are bear attractants.

Grizzlies are nothing like black bears. They are bigger, stronger, have little fear, and take what they want. Some people believe there are many different species of this critter, such as Alaskan brown, silvertip, cinnamon, and Kodiak, but the truth is they are all grizzlies. Any difference in appearance has to do with diet, habitat, and life habits, not speciation. By any name, they all come big.

The first thing you must do is determine if there are grizzlies in the area where you are camping (if you're in Oregon or Washington, there is no need to worry—grizzlies do not live in these states). That can usually be done by asking local rangers. If you are heading into Yellowstone or Glacier National Park, or the Bob Marshall Wilderness of Montana, well, you don't have to ask. They're out there, and they're the biggest and potentially most dangerous critters you could run into.

One general way to figure the size of a bear is from his footprint. Take the width of the footprint in inches, add one to it, and you'll have an estimated length of the bear in feet. For instance, a nine-inch footprint equals a 10-foot bear. Any bear that big is a grizzly, my friends. In fact, most grizzly footprints average about nine to 10 inches across, and black bears (though they may be brown in color) tend to have footprints only 4.5 to six inches across.

Most encounters with grizzlies occur when hikers fall into a silent march in the wilderness with the wind in their faces, and they walk around a corner and right into a big, unsuspecting grizzly. If you do this and see a big hump just behind its neck, well, don't think twice. It's a grizzly.

And then what should you do? Get up a tree, that's what. Grizzlies are so big that their claws cannot support their immense weight, and thus they cannot climb trees. And although their young can climb, they rarely want to get their mitts on you.

If you do get grabbed, every instinct in your body will tell you to fight back. Don't believe it. Play dead. Go limp. Let the bear throw you around a little, because after awhile you become unexciting play material and the bear will get bored. My grandmother was grabbed by a grizzly in Glacier National Park and after a few tosses and hugs, was finally left alone to escape.

Some say it's a good idea to tuck your head under his chin, since that way the bear will be unable to bite your head. I'll take a pass on that one. If you are taking action, any action, it's a signal that you are a force to be reckoned with, and he'll likely respond with more aggression. And bears don't lose many wrestling matches.

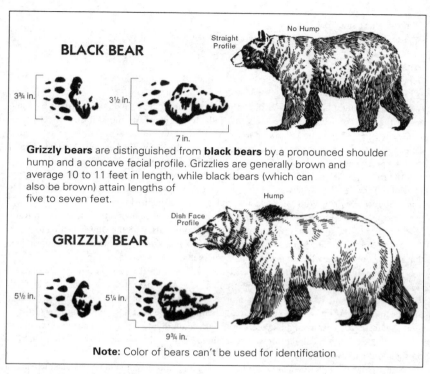

BLACK BEAR

3¾ in.   3½ in.

7 in.

Grizzly bears are distinguished from **black bears** by a pronounced shoulder hump and a concave facial profile. Grizzlies are generally brown and average 10 to 11 feet in length, while black bears (which can also be brown) attain lengths of five to seven feet.

Straight Profile

No Hump

GRIZZLY BEAR

Dish Face Profile

Hump

5½ in.   5¼ in.

9¾ in.

Note: Color of bears can't be used for identification

What grizzlies really like to do, believe it or not, is to pile a lot of sticks and leaves on you. Just let them, and keep perfectly still. Don't fight them; don't run. And when you have a 100 percent chance (not 98 or 99) to dash up a nearby tree, that's when you let fly. Once safely in a tree, you can hurl down insults and let your aggression out.

In a wilderness camp there are special precautions you should take. Always hang your food at least 100 yards downwind of camp and get it high; 30 feet is reasonable. In addition, circle your camp with rope and hang the bells from your pack on it. Thus, if a bear walks into your camp, he'll run into the rope, the bells will ring, and everybody will have a chance to get up a tree before ol' griz figures out what's going on. Often the unexpected ringing of bells is enough to send him off in search of a quieter environment.

You see, more often than not, grizzlies tend to clear the way for campers and hikers. So be smart, don't act like bear bait, and always have a plan if you are confronted by one.

My pal Foonsky had such a plan during a wilderness expedition in Montana's northern Rockies. On our second day of hiking, we started seeing scratch marks on the trees 13 to 14 feet off the ground.

"Mr. Griz made those," Foonsky said. "With spring here, the grizzlies are coming out of hibernation and using the trees like a cat uses a scratch board to stretch the muscles."

The next day, I noticed Foonsky had a pair of track shoes tied to the back of his pack. I just laughed.

"You're not going to outrun a griz," I said. "In fact, there's hardly any animal out here in the wilderness that man can outrun."

Foonsky just smiled.

"I don't have to outrun a griz," he said. "I just have to outrun you!"

Fun and Games

"Now what are we supposed to do?" the young boy asked his dad.

"Yeah, Dad, think of something," said another son.

Well, Dad thought hard. This was one of the first camping trips he'd taken with his sons and one of the first lessons he received was that kids don't appreciate the philosophic release of mountain quiet. They want action and lots of it. With a glint in his eye, Dad searched around the camp and picked up 15 twigs, breaking them so each was four inches long. He laid them in three separate rows, three twigs in one row, five twigs in another, and seven in the other.

"OK, this game is called 3-5-7," said Dad. "You each take turns picking up sticks. You are allowed to remove all or as few as one twig from a row, but here's the catch: you can pick only from one row per turn. Whoever picks up the last stick left is the loser."

I remember this episode well because those two little boys were my brother Bobby, as in Rambobby, and me. And to this day, we still play 3-5-7 on campouts, with the winner getting to watch the loser clean the dishes. What I have learned in the span of time since that original episode is that it does not matter what your age is: campers need options for camp fun.

Some evenings, after a long hike or ride, you are likely to feel too worn out to take on a serious romp downstream to fish, or a climb up to a ridge for a view. That is especially true if you have been in the outback for a week or more. At that point a lot of campers will spend their time resting and gazing at a map of the area, dreaming of the next day's adventure, or just take a seat against a rock, watching the colors of the sky and mountain panorama change minute by minute. But kids in the push-button video era, and a lot of adults too, want more. After all, "I'm on vacation; I want some fun."

There are several options, such as the 3-5-7 twig game, and they should be just as much a part of your trip planning as arranging your gear.

For kids, plan on games, the more physically challenging the competition, the better. One of the best games is to throw a chunk of wood into a lake and challenge the kids to hit it by throwing rocks. It wreaks havoc on the fishing, but it can keep kids totally absorbed for some time. Target practice with a wrist-rocket slingshot is also all consuming for kids, firing rocks away at small targets like pinecones set on a log.

You can also set kids off on little missions near camp, such as looking for the footprints of wildlife, searching out good places to have a "snipe hunt," picking up twigs to get the evening fire started, or having them take the water purifier to a stream to pump some drinking water into a canteen. The latter is an easy, fun, yet important task that will allow kids to feel a sense of equality they often don't get at home.

For adults, the appeal should be more to the intellect. A good example is star and planet identification, and while you are staring into space, you're bound to spot a few asteroids or shooting stars. A star chart can make it easy to find and identify many distinctive stars and constellations, such as Pleiades (the Seven Sisters), Orion, and others from the zodiac, depending on the time of year. With a little research, this can add a unique perspective to your trip. You could point to Polaris, one of the most easily identified of all stars, and note that navigators in the 1400s used it to find their way. Polaris, of course, is the North Star and is at the end of the handle of the Little Dipper. Pinpointing Polaris is quite easy. First find the Big Dipper and then find the outside stars of the ladle of the Big Dipper. They are called the "pointer stars" because they point right at Polaris.

A tree identification book can teach you a few things about your surroundings. It is also a good idea for one member of the party to research the history of the area you have chosen and another to research the geology. With shared knowledge, you end up with a deeper love of wild places.

Another way to add some recreation into your trip is to bring a board game, a number of which have been miniaturized for campers. The most popular are chess, checkers, and cribbage. The latter comes with an equally miniature set of playing cards. And if you bring those little cards, that opens a vast set of other possibilities. With kids along, for instance, just take three queens out of the deck and you can play Old Maid.

But there are more serious card games, and they come with high stakes. Such occurred on one high-country trip where Foonsky, Rambob, and I sat down for a late-afternoon game of poker. In a game of seven-card stud, I caught a straight on the sixth card and felt like a dog licking on a T-bone. Already I had bet several Skittles and peanut M&Ms on this promising hand.

Then I examined the cards Foonsky had face up. He was showing three sevens, and acting as happy as a grizzly with a pork chop—or a full house. He matched my bet of two peanut M&Ms, then raised me three SweetTarts, one Starburst, and one sour apple Jolly Rancher. Rambob folded, but I matched Foonsky's bet and hoped for the best as the seventh and final card was dealt.

Just after Foonsky glanced at that last card, I saw him sneak a look at my grape stick and beef jerky stash.

"I raise you a grape stick," he said.

Rambob and I both gasped. It was the highest bet ever made, equivalent to a million dollars laid down in Las Vegas. Cannons were going off in my chest. I looked hard at my cards. They looked good, but were they good enough?

Even with a great hand like I had, a grape stick was too much to gamble, my last one with 10 days of trail ahead of us. I shook my head and folded my cards. Foonsky smiled at his victory.

But I still had my grape stick.

Old Tricks Don't Always Work

Most people are born honest, but after a few camping trips, they usually get over it.

I remember some advice I got from Rambob, normally an honest soul, on one camping trip. A giant mosquito had landed on my arm and he alerted me to some expert advice.

Keep It Wild Tip 5: Keep the Wilderness Wild

1. Let nature's sound prevail. Avoid loud voices and noises.
2. Leave radios and tape players at home. At drive-in camping sites, never open car doors with music playing.
3. Careful guidance is necessary when choosing any games to bring for children. Most toys, especially any kind of gun toys with which children simulate shooting at each other, shouldn't be allowed on a camping trip.
4. Control pets at all times or leave them with a sitter at home.
5. Treat natural heritage with respect. Leave plants, rocks, and historical artifacts where you find them.

"Flex your arm muscles," he commanded, watching the mosquito fill with my blood. "He'll get stuck in your arm, then he'll explode."

For some reason, I believed him. We both proceeded to watch the mosquito drill countless holes in my arm.

Alas, the unknowing face sabotage from their most trusted companions on camping trips. It can arise at any time, usually in the form of advice from a friendly, honest-looking face, as if to say, "What? How can you doubt me?" After that mosquito episode, I was a little more skeptical of my dear old brother. Then the next day, when another mosquito was nailing me in the back of the neck, out came this gem:

"Hold your breath," he commanded. I instinctively obeyed. "That will freeze the mosquito," he said, "then you can squish him."

But in the time I wasted holding my breath, the little bugger was able to fly off without my having the satisfaction of squishing him. When he got home, he probably told his family, "What a dummy I got to drill today!"

Over the years, I have been duped numerous times with dubious advice:

On a grizzly bear attack: "If he grabs you, tuck your head under the grizzly's chin; then he won't be able to bite you in the head." This made sense to me until the first time I came face-to-face with a nine-foot grizzly 40 yards away. In seconds, I was at the top of a tree, which suddenly seemed to make the most sense.

On coping with animal bites: "If a bear bites you in the arm, don't try to jerk it away. That will just rip up your arm. Instead force your arm deeper into his mouth. He'll lose his grip and will have to open it to get a firmer hold, and right then you can get away." I was told this in the Boy Scouts, and when I was 14, I had a chance to try it out when a friend's dog bit me as I tried to pet it. What happened? When I shoved my arm deeper into his mouth, he bit me three more times.

On cooking breakfast: "The bacon will curl up every time in a camp frying pan. So make sure you have a bacon stretcher to keep it flat." As a 12-year-old Tenderfoot, I spent two hours looking for the bacon stretcher until I figured out the camp leader had forgotten it. It wasn't for several years that I learned that there is no such thing.

On preventing sore muscles: "If you haven't hiked for a long time and you are facing a rough climb, you can keep from getting sore muscles in your legs, back, and shoulders by practicing the 'Dead Man's Walk.' Simply let your entire body go slack, and then take slow, wobbling steps. This will clear your muscles of lactic acid, which causes them to be so sore after a rough hike." Foonsky pulled this one on me. Rambob and I both bought it and tried it while we were hiking up Mt. Whitney, which requires a 6,000-foot elevation gain in six miles. In one 45-minute period, about 30 other hikers passed us and looked at us as if we were suffering from some rare form of mental aberration.

Fish won't bite? No problem: "If the fish are not feeding or will not bite, persistent anglers can still catch dinner with little problem. Keep casting across the current, and eventually, as they hover in the stream, the line will feed across their open mouths. Keep reeling and you will hook the fish right in the side of the mouth. This technique is called 'lining.' Never worry if the fish will not bite, because you can always line 'em." Of course, heh, heh, heh, that explains why so many fish get hooked in the side of the mouth.

How to keep bears away: "To keep bears away, urinate around the borders of your campground. If there are a lot of bears in the area, it is advisable to go right on your sleeping bag." Yeah, surrrrrre.

What to do with trash: "Don't worry about packing out trash. Just bury it. It will regenerate into the earth and add valuable minerals." Bears, raccoons, skunks, and other critters will dig up your trash as soon as you depart, leaving one huge mess for the next camper. Always pack out everything.

Often the advice comes without warning. That was the case after a fishing trip with a female companion, when she outcaught me two to one, the third such trip in a row. I explained this to a shopkeeper, and he nodded, then explained why.

"The male fish are able to detect the female scent on the lure, and thus become aroused into striking."

Of course! That explains everything!

Getting Revenge

I was just a lad when Foonsky pulled the old snipe-hunt trick on me. It took nearly 30 years to get revenge.

You probably know about snipe hunting. The victim is led out at night in the woods by a group, and then is left holding a bag.

"Stay perfectly still and quiet," Foonsky explained. "You don't want to scare the snipe. The rest of us will go back to camp and let the woods settle down. Then when the snipe are least expecting it, we'll form a line and charge through the forest with sticks, beating bushes and trees, and we'll flush the snipe out right to you. Be ready with the bag. When we flush the snipe out, bag it. But until we start our charge, make sure you don't move or make a sound or you will spook the snipe and ruin everything."

I sat out there in the woods with my bag for hours, waiting for the charge. I waited, waited, and waited. Nothing happened. No charge, no snipe. It wasn't until well past midnight that I figured something was wrong. When I finally returned to camp, everybody was sleeping.

Well, I tell ya, don't get mad at your pals for the tricks they pull on you. Get revenge. About 25 years later, on the last day of a camping trip, the time finally came.

"Let's break camp early," Foonsky suggested to Mr. Furnai and me. "Get up before dawn, eat breakfast, pack up, and be on the ridge to watch the sun come up. It will be a fantastic way to end the trip."

"Sounds great to me," I replied. But when Foonsky wasn't looking, I turned his alarm clock ahead three hours. So when the alarm sounded at the appointed 4:30 A.M. wake-up time, Mr. Furnai and I knew it was actually only 1:30 A.M.

Foonsky clambered out of his sleeping bag and whistled with a grin. "Time to break camp."

"You go ahead," I answered. "I'll skip breakfast so I can get a little more sleep. At the first sign of dawn, wake me up, and I'll break camp."

"Me, too," said Mr. Furnai.

Foonsky then proceeded to make some coffee, cook a breakfast, and eat it, sitting on a log in the black darkness of the forest, waiting for the sun to come up. An hour later, with still no sign of dawn, he checked his clock. It now read 5:30 A.M. "Any minute now we should start seeing some light," he said.

He made another cup of coffee, packed his gear, and sat there in the middle of the night, looking up at the stars, waiting for dawn. "Anytime now," he said. He ended up sitting there all night long.

Revenge is sweet. Before a fishing trip at a lake, I took Foonsky aside and explained that the third member of the party, Jimbobo, was hard of hearing and very sensitive about it. "Don't mention it to him," I advised. "Just talk real loud."

Meanwhile, I had already told Jimbobo the same thing. "Foonsky just can't hear very good." We had fished less than 20 minutes when Foonsky got a nibble.

"GET A BITE?" shouted Jimbobo.

"YEAH!" yelled back Foonsky, smiling. "BUT I DIDN'T HOOK HIM!"

"MAYBE NEXT TIME!" shouted Jimbobo with a friendly grin.

Well, they spent the entire day yelling at each other from the distance of a few feet. They never did figure it out. Heh, heh, heh.

That is, I thought so, until we made a trip salmon fishing. I got a strike that almost knocked my fishing rod out of the boat. When I grabbed the rod, it felt as if Moby Dick were on the other end. "At least a 25-pounder," I said. "Maybe bigger."

The fish dove, ripped off line, and then bulldogged. "It's acting like a 40-pounder," I announced, "Huge, just huge. It's going deep. That's how the big ones fight."

Some 15 minutes later, I finally got the "salmon" to the surface. It turned out to be a coffee can that Foonsky had clipped on the line with a snap swivel. By maneuvering the boat, he made the coffee can fight like a big fish.

This all started with a little old snipe hunt years ago. You never know what your pals will try next. Don't get mad. Get revenge.

CAMPING OPTIONS
Boat-in Seclusion

Most campers would never think of trading in their cars, pickup trucks, or RVs for a boat, but people who go by boat on a camping trip enjoy virtually guaranteed seclusion and top-quality outdoor experiences.

Camping with a boat is a do-it-yourself venture in living under primitive circumstances. Yet at the same time you can bring along any luxury item you wish, from giant coolers, stoves, and lanterns to portable gasoline generators. Weight is almost never an issue.

Many outstanding boat-in campgrounds in beautiful surroundings are available in California. The best are on the shores of lakes accessible by canoe or skiff, and at offshore islands reached by saltwater cruisers. Several boat-in camps are detailed in this book.

If you want to take the adventure a step further and create your own boat-in camp, perhaps near a special fishing spot, this is a go-for-it deal that provides the best way possible to establish your own secret campsite. But most people who set out freelance style forget three critical items for boat-in camping: a shovel, a sunshade, and an ax. Here is why these items can make a key difference in your trip:

Shovel: Many lakes and virtually all reservoirs have steep, sloping banks. At reservoirs subject to drawdowns, what was lake bottom in the spring can be a campsite in late summer. If you want a flat area for a tent site, the only answer is to dig one out yourself. A shovel gives you that option.

Sunshade: The flattest spots to camp along lakes often have a tendency to support only sparse tree growth. As a result, a natural shield from sun and rain is rarely available. What? Rain in the summer? Oh yeah, don't get me started. A light tarp, set up with poles and staked ropes, solves the problem.

Ax: Unless you bring your own firewood, which is necessary at some sparsely wooded reservoirs, there is no substitute for a good, sharp ax. With an ax, you can almost always find dry firewood, since the interior of an otherwise wet log will be dry. When the weather turns bad is precisely when you will most want a fire. You may need an ax to get one going.

In the search to create your own personal boat-in campsite, you will find that the flattest areas are usually the tips of peninsulas and points, while the protected back ends of coves are often steeply sloped. At reservoirs, the flattest areas are usually near the mouths of the feeder streams and the points are quite steep. On rivers, there are usually sandbars on the inside of tight bends that make for ideal campsites.

Almost all boat-in campsites developed by government agencies are free of charge, but you are on your own. Only in extremely rare cases is piped water available.

Any way you go, by canoe, skiff, or power cruiser, you end up with a one-in-a-million campsite you can call your own.

Desert Outings

It was a cold, snowy day in Missouri when 10-year-old Rusty Ballinger started dreaming about the vast deserts of the West.

"My dad was reading aloud from a Zane Grey book called *Riders of the Purple Sage*," Ballinger said. "He would get animated when he got to the passages about the desert. It wasn't long before I started to have the same feelings."

That was in 1947. Ballinger, now in his 60s, has spent a good part of his life exploring the West, camping along the way. "The deserts are the best part. There's something about the uniqueness of each little area you see," Ballinger said. "You're constantly surprised. Just the time of day and the way the sun casts a different color. It's like the lady you care about. One time she smiles, the next time she's pensive. The desert is like that. If you love nature, you can love the desert. After awhile, you can't help but love it."

A desert adventure is not just an antidote for a case of cabin fever in the winter. Whether you go by RV, pickup truck, car, or on foot, it provides its own special qualities.

If you go camping in the desert, your approach has to be as unique as the setting. For starters,

Keep It Wild Tip 6: Respect Other Users

1. Horseback riders have priority over hikers. Step to the downhill side of the trail and talk softly when encountering horseback riders.
2. Hikers and horseback riders have priority over mountain bikers. When mountain bikers encounter other users even on wide trails, they should pass at an extremely slow speed. On very narrow trails they should dismount and get off to the side so hikers or horseback riders can pass without having their trip disrupted.
3. Mountain bikes aren't permitted on most single-track trails and are expressly prohibited in designated wilderness areas and all sections of the Pacific Crest Trail. Mountain bikers breaking these rules should be confronted and told to dismount and walk their bikes until they reach a legal area.
4. It's illegal for horseback riders to break off branches that may be in the path of wilderness trails.
5. Horseback riders on overnight trips are prohibited from camping in many areas and are usually required to keep stock animals in specific areas where they can do no damage to the landscape.

don't plan on any campfires, but bring a camp stove instead. And unlike in the mountains, do not camp near a water hole. That's because an animal such as a badger, coyote, or desert bighorn might be desperate for water, and if you set up camp in the animal's way, you may be forcing a confrontation.

In some areas, there is a danger of flash floods. An intense rain can fall in one area, collect in a pool, then suddenly burst through a narrow canyon. If you are in its path, you could be injured or drowned. The lesson? Never camp in a gully.

"Some people might wonder, 'What good is this place?'" Ballinger said. "The answer is that it is good for looking at. It is one of the world's unique places."

CAMP ETHICS AND POLITICS

The perfect place to set up a base camp turned out to be not so perfect. In fact, according to a letter from a reader, it did not even exist.

Doug Williams and his son, James, had driven deep into a national forest, prepared to set up camp and then explore the surrounding area on foot. But when they reached their destination, no campground existed.

"I wanted a primitive camp in a national forest where I could teach my son some basics," said the senior Williams. "But when we got there, there wasn't much left of the camp, and it had been closed. It was obvious that the area had been vandalized."

It turned out not to be an isolated incident. A lack of outdoor ethics practiced by a few people using the unsupervised campgrounds available on national forestland has caused the U.S. Forest Service to close a few of them and make extensive repairs to others.

"There have been sites closed" said David Flohr, regional campground coordinator for the U.S. Forest Service. "It's an urban type of thing, affecting forests near urban areas. They get a lot of urban users and they bring with them a lot of the same ethics they have in the city. They get drinking and they're not afraid to do things. They vandalize and run. Of course, it is a public facility, so they think nobody is getting hurt."

But while these occurances are isolated incidents, somebody is getting hurt, starting with the next person who wants to use the campground. And if the ranger district budget doesn't have enough money to pay for repairs—common in this era of budget cuts—the campground is then closed for the next arrivals. Just ask Doug and James Williams.

In an era of considerable fiscal restraint for the U.S. Forest Service, many more vandalized campgrounds could face closure instead of repair in the next few years. Williams had just a taste of it, but Flohr, as camping coordinator, gets a steady diet.

"It starts with behavior," Flohr said. "General rowdiness, drinking, partying, and then vandalism. It goes all the way from the felt-tip pen things (graffiti) to total destruction, blowing up toilet buildings with dynamite. I have seen toilets destroyed totally with shotguns. They burn up tables, burn barriers. They'll burn up signs for firewood, even the shingles right off the roofs of the bathrooms. They'll shoot anything, garbage cans, signs. It can get a little hairy. A favorite is to remove the stool out of a toilet building. We've had people fall in the open hole."

The National Park Service had a similar problem some years back, especially with rampant littering. Park Director Bill Mott responded by creating an interpretive program that attempts to teach visitors the wise use of natural areas, and to have all park workers set examples by picking up litter and reminding others to do the same.

The U.S. Forest Service has responded with a similar program, making brochures available that detail the wise use of national forests. The four most popular brochures are titled: "Rules for Visitors to the National Forest," "Recreation in the National Forests," "Is the Water Safe?" and "Backcountry Safety Tips." These include details on campfires, drinking water from lakes or streams, hypothermia, safety, and outdoor ethics. They are available free by writing to Public Affairs, U.S. Forest Service, Pacific Northwest Region 6, 333 S.W. 1st Ave. Portland, OR 97204-3440, or P.O. Box 3623, Portland, OR 97208-3623; www.fs.fed.us/r6.

Flohr said even experienced campers sometimes cross over the ethics line unintentionally. The most common example, he said, is when campers toss garbage into the outhouse toilet, rather than packing it out in a plastic garbage bag.

"They throw it in the vault toilet bowls, which just fills them up," Flohr said. "That creates an extremely high cost to pump it. You know why? Because some poor guy has to pick that stuff out piece by piece. It can't be pumped."

At most backcountry sites, the U.S. Forest Service has implemented a program called "Pack it in, pack it out," even posting signs that remind all visitors to do so. But a lot of people don't do it, and others may even uproot the sign and burn it for firewood.

Most people intuitively know the difference between right and wrong. When camping, draw the line and pick right over wrong.

Getting Along with Fellow Campers

The most important thing about a camping, fishing, or hunting trip is not where you go, how many fish you catch, or how many shots you fire. It often has little to do with how beautiful the view is, how easily the campfire lights, or how sunny the days are.

Oh yeah? Then what is the most important factor? The answer: the people you are with. It is that simple.

Who would you rather camp with? Your enemy at work or your dream mate in a good mood? Heh, heh. You get the idea. A camping trip is a fairly close-knit experience, and you can make lifetime friends or lifelong enemies in the process. That is why your choice of companions is so important. Your own behavior is equally consequential.

Yet most people spend more time putting together their camping gear than considering why they enjoy or hate the company of their chosen companions. Here are 10 rules of behavior for good camping mates:

Two Dogs: "There are two dogs inside of you," my dad once said, "a good one, and a bad one. The one you feed is the one that will grow. Always try to feed the good dog."

1. **No whining:** Nothing is more irritating than being around a whiner. It goes right to the heart of adventure, since often the only difference between a hardship and an escapade is simply whether or not an individual has the spirit for it. The people who do can turn a rugged day in the outdoors into a cherished memory. Those who don't can ruin it with their incessant sniveling.
2. **Activities must be agreed upon:** Always have a meeting of the minds with your companions over the general game plan. Then everybody will possess an equal stake in the outcome of the trip. This is absolutely critical. Otherwise they will feel like merely an addendum to your trip, not an equal participant, and a whiner will be born (see number one).
3. **Nobody's in charge:** It is impossible to be genuine friends if one person is always telling another what to do, especially if the orders involve simple camp tasks. You need to share the space on the same emotional plane, and the only way to do that is to have a semblance of equality, regardless of differences in experience. Just try ordering your mate around at home for a few days. You'll quickly see the results, and they aren't pretty.

4. **Equal chances at the fun stuff:** It's fun to build the fire, fun to get the first cast at the best fishing spot, and fun to hoist the bagged food for a bear-proof food hang. It is not fun to clean the dishes, collect firewood, or cook every night. So obviously there must be an equal distribution of the fun stuff and the not-fun stuff, and everybody on the trip must get a shot at the good and the bad.

5. **No heroes:** No awards are bestowed for achievement in the outdoors, yet some guys treat mountain peaks, big fish, and big game as if they are prizes in a trophy competition. Actually, nobody cares how wonderful you are, which is always a surprise to trophy chasers. What people care about is the heart of the adventure, the gut-level stuff.

6. **Agree on a wake-up time:** It is a good idea to agree on a general wake-up time before closing your eyes for the night, and that goes regardless of whether you want to sleep in late or get up at dawn. Then you can proceed on course regardless of what time you crawl out of your sleeping bag in the morning, without the risk of whining (see number one).

7. **Think of the other guy:** Be self-aware instead of self-absorbed. A good test is to count the number of times you say, "What do you think?" A lot of potential problems can be solved quickly by actually listening to the answer.

8. **Solo responsibilities:** There are a number of essential camp duties on all trips, and while they should be shared equally, most should be completed solo. That means that when it is time for you to cook, you don't have to worry about me changing the recipe on you. It means that when it is my turn to make the fire, you keep your mitts out of it.

9. **Don't let money get in the way:** Of course everybody should share equally in trip expenses, such as the cost of food, and it should be split up before you head out yonder. Don't let somebody pay extra, because that person will likely try to control the trip. Conversely, don't let somebody weasel out of paying a fair share.

10. **Accordance on the food plan:** Always have complete agreement on what you plan to eat each day. Don't figure that just because you like Steamboat's Sludge, everybody else will, too, especially youngsters. Always, always, always check for food allergies such as nuts, onions, or cheese, and make sure each person brings his or her own personal coffee brand. Some people drink only decaffeinated; others might gag on anything but Burma monkey beans.

Obviously, it is difficult to find companions who will agree on all of these elements. This is why many campers say that the best camping buddies they'll ever have are their mates, who know all about them and like them anyway.

OUTDOORS WITH KIDS

How do you get a boy or girl excited about the outdoors? How do you compete with the television and remote control? How do you prove to a kid that success comes from persistence, spirit, and logic, which the outdoors teaches, and not from pushing buttons?

The answer is in the **Ten Camping Commandments for Kids.** These are lessons that will get youngsters excited about the outdoors, and that will make sure adults help the process along, not kill it. I've put this list together with the help of my own kids, Jeremy and Kris, and their mother, Stephani. Some of the commandments are obvious, some are not, but all are important:

1. Take children to places where there is a guarantee of action. A good example is camping in a park where large numbers of wildlife can be viewed, such as squirrels, chipmunks, deer, and even bears. Other good choices are fishing at a small pond loaded with bluegill, or hunting in a spot where a kid can shoot a .22 at pinecones all day. Boys and girls want action, not solitude.

2. Enthusiasm is contagious. If you aren't excited about an adventure, you can't expect a child to be. Show a genuine zest for life in the outdoors, and point out everything as if it is the first time you have ever seen it.

3. Always, always, always be seated when talking to someone small. This allows the adult and child to be on the same level. That is why fishing in a small boat is perfect for adults and kids. Nothing is worse for youngsters than having a big person look down at them and give them orders. What fun is that?

4. Always *show* how to do something, whether it is gathering sticks for a campfire, cleaning a trout, or tying a knot. Never tell—always show. A button usually clicks to "off" when a kid is lectured. But kids can learn behavior patterns and outdoor skills by watching adults, even when the adults are not aware they are being watched.

5. Let kids be kids. Let the adventure happen, rather than trying to force it within some pre-conceived plan. If they get sidetracked watching pollywogs, chasing butterflies, or sneaking up on chipmunks, let them be. A youngster can have more fun turning over rocks and looking at different kinds of bugs than sitting in one spot, waiting for a fish to bite.

6. Expect short attention spans. Instead of getting frustrated about it, use it to your advantage. How? By bringing along a bag of candy and snacks. Where there is a lull in the camp activity, out comes the bag. Don't let them know what goodies await, so each one becomes a surprise.

7. Make absolutely certain the child's sleeping bag is clean, dry, and warm. Nothing is worse than discomfort when trying to sleep, but a refreshing sleep makes for a positive attitude the next day. In addition, kids can become quite scared of animals at night. A parent should not wait for any signs of this, but always play the part of the outdoor guardian, the one who will take care of everything.

8. Kids quickly relate to outdoor ethics. They will enjoy eating everything they kill, building a safe campfire, and picking up all their litter, and they will develop a sense of pride that goes with it. A good idea is to bring extra plastic garbage bags to pick up any trash you come across. Kids long remember when they do something right that somebody else has done wrong.

9. If you want youngsters hooked on the outdoors for life, take a close-up photograph of them holding up fish they have caught, blowing on the campfire, or completing other camp tasks. Young children can forget how much fun they had, but they never forget if they have a picture of it.

10. The least important word you can ever say to a kid is "I." Keep track of how often you are saying "Thank you" and "What do you think?" If you don't say them very often, you'll lose out. Finally, the most important words of all are: "I am proud of you."

PREDICTING WEATHER

Foonsky climbed out of his sleeping bag, glanced at the nearby meadow, and scowled hard.

"It doesn't look good," he said. "Doesn't look good at all."

I looked at my adventure companion of 20 years, noting his discontent. Then I looked at the meadow and immediately understood why: *"When the grass is dry at morning light, look for rain before the night."*

"How bad you figure?" I asked him.

"We'll know soon enough, I reckon," Foonsky answered. "Short notice, soon to pass. Long notice, long it will last."

Keep It Wild Tip 7: Plan Ahead and Prepare

1. Learn about the regulations and issues that apply to the area you're visiting.
2. Avoid heavy-use areas.
3. Obtain all maps and permits.
4. Bring extra garbage bags to pack out any refuse you come across.

When you are out in the wild, spending your days fishing and your nights camping, you learn to rely on yourself to predict the weather. It can make or break you. If a storm hits the unprepared, it can quash the trip and possibly endanger the participants. But if you are ready, a potential hardship can be an adventure.

You can't rely on TV weather forecasters, people who don't even know that when all the cows on a hill are facing north, it will rain that night for sure. God forbid if the cows are all sitting. But what do you expect from TV's talking heads?

Foonsky made a campfire, started boiling some water for coffee and soup, and we started to plan the day. In the process, I noticed the smoke of the campfire: it was sluggish, drifting and hovering.

"You notice the smoke?" I asked, chewing on a piece of homemade jerky.

"Not good," Foonsky said. "Not good." He knew that sluggish, hovering smoke indicates rain.

"You'd think we'd have been smart enough to know last night that this was coming," Foonsky said. "Did you take a look at the moon or the clouds?"

"I didn't look at either," I answered. "Too busy eating the trout we caught." You see, if the moon is clear and white, the weather will be good the next day. But if there is a ring around the moon, the number of stars you can count inside the ring equals the number of days until the next rain. As for clouds, the high, thin clouds called cirrus indicate a change in the weather.

We were quiet for a while, planning our strategy, but as we did so, some terrible things happened: a chipmunk scampered past with his tail high, a small flock of geese flew by very low, and a little sparrow perched on a tree limb quite close to the trunk.

"We're in for trouble," I told Foonsky.

"I know, I know," he answered. "I saw 'em, too. And come to think of it, no crickets were chirping last night either."

"Damn, that's right!"

These are all signs of an approaching storm. Foonsky pointed at the smoke of the campfire and shook his head as if he had just been condemned. Sure enough, now the smoke was blowing toward the north, a sign of a south wind. *"When the wind is from the south, the rain is in its mouth."*

"We'd best stay hunkered down until it passes," Foonsky said.

I nodded. "Let's gather as much firewood now as we can, get our gear covered up, then plan our meals."

"Then we'll get a poker game going."

As we accomplished these camp tasks, the sky clouded up, then darkened. Within an hour we had gathered enough firewood to make a large pile, enough wood to keep a fire going no matter how hard it rained. The day's meals had been separated out of the food bag so it wouldn't have to be retrieved during the storm. We buttoned two ponchos together, staked two of the corners with ropes to the ground, and tied the other two with ropes to different tree limbs to create a slanted roof/shelter.

As the first raindrop fell with that magic sound on our poncho roof, Foonsky was just starting to shuffle the cards.

"Cut for deal," he said.

Just as I did so, it started to rain a bit harder. I pulled out another piece of beef jerky and started chewing on it. It was just another day in paradise.

Weather lore can be valuable. Small signs provided by nature and wildlife can be translated to provide a variety of weather information. Here is the list I have compiled over the years:

When the grass is dry at morning light,
Look for rain before the night.

Short notice, soon to pass.
Long notice, long it will last.

When the wind is from the east,
'Tis fit for neither man nor beast.

When the wind is from the south,
The rain is in its mouth.

When the wind is from the west,
Then it is the very best.

Red sky at night, sailors' delight.
Red sky in the morning, sailors take warning.

When all the cows are pointed north,
Within a day rain will come forth.

Onion skins very thin, mild winter coming in.
Onion skins very tough, winter's going to be very rough.

When your boots make the squeak of snow,
Then very cold temperatures will surely show.

If a goose flies high, fair weather ahead.
If a goose flies low, foul weather will come instead.

A thick coat on a woolly caterpillar means a big, early snow is coming.
Chipmunks will run with their tails up before a rain.
Bees always stay near their hives before a rainstorm.
When the birds are perched on large limbs near tree trunks, an intense but short storm will arrive.
On the coast, if groups of seabirds are flying a mile inland, look for major winds.

If crickets are chirping very loud during the evening, the next day will be clear and warm.

If the smoke of a campfire at night rises in a thin spiral, good weather is assured for the next day.

If the smoke of a campfire at night is sluggish, drifting, and hovering, it will rain the next day.

If there is a ring around the moon, count the number of stars inside the ring, and that is how many days until the next rain.

If the moon is clear and white, the weather will be good the next day.

High, thin clouds, or cirrus, indicate a change in the weather.

Oval-shaped lenticular clouds indicate high winds.

Two levels of clouds moving in different directions indicate changing weather soon.

Huge, dark, billowing clouds, called cumulonimbus, suddenly forming on warm afternoons in the mountains mean that a short but intense thunderstorm with lightning can be expected.

When squirrels are busy gathering food for extended periods, it means good weather is ahead in the short term, but a hard winter is ahead in the long term.

And God forbid if all the cows are sitting down. . . .

© TOM STIENSTRA

Washington

Chapter 1
The Olympic Peninsula
and Coastal Washington

Chapter 1—
The Olympic Peninsula and
Coastal Washington

Vast, diverse, and beautiful, the Olympic Peninsula is like no other landscape in the world. Water borders the region on three sides: the Pacific Ocean to the west, the Strait of Juan de Fuca to the north, and the inlets of the Hood Canal to the east. At its center are Olympic National Park and Mt. Olympus, with rainforests on its slopes feeding rivers and lakes that make up the most dynamic river complex in America.

Only heavy rainfall for months on end from fall through spring and coastal fog in the summer have saved this area from a massive residential boom. At the same time, those conditions make it outstanding for getaways and virtually all forms of recreation. A series of stellar campgrounds ring the perimeter foothills of Mt. Olympus, both in Olympic National Park and at the state parks and areas managed by the Department of Natural Resources. Your campsite can be your launch pad for adventure—just be sure to bring your rain gear.

In winter, campers can explore the largest array of steelhead rivers anywhere—there is no better place in America to fish for steelhead. Almost every one of these rivers provides campsites, often within walking distance of prime fishing spots.

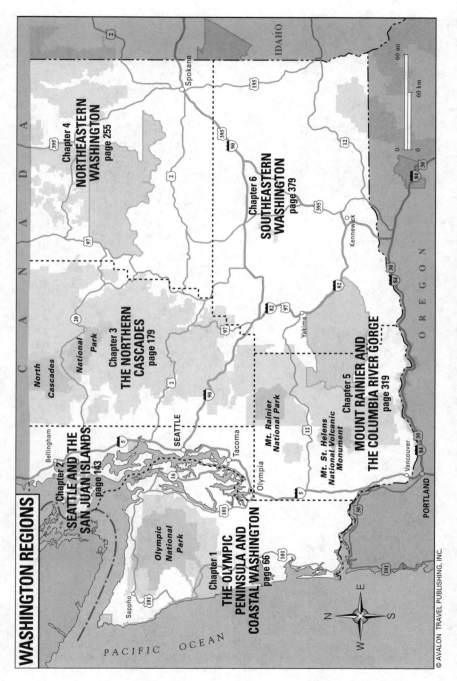

WASHINGTON REGIONS

Chapter 2
SEATTLE AND THE SAN JUAN ISLANDS
page 143

Chapter 1
THE OLYMPIC PENINSULA AND COASTAL WASHINGTON
page 66

Chapter 3
THE NORTHERN CASCADES
page 179

Chapter 4
NORTHEASTERN WASHINGTON
page 255

Chapter 6
SOUTHEASTERN WASHINGTON
page 379

Chapter 5
MOUNT RAINIER AND THE COLUMBIA RIVER GORGE
page 319

North Cascades National Park

Olympic National Park

Mt. Rainier National Park

Mt. St. Helens National Volcanic Monument

PACIFIC OCEAN

CANADA

IDAHO

OREGON

Bellingham
Sappho
Seattle
Tacoma
Olympia
Vancouver
PORTLAND
Spokane
Kennewick
Yakima

0   60 mi
0   60 km

© AVALON TRAVEL PUBLISHING, INC.

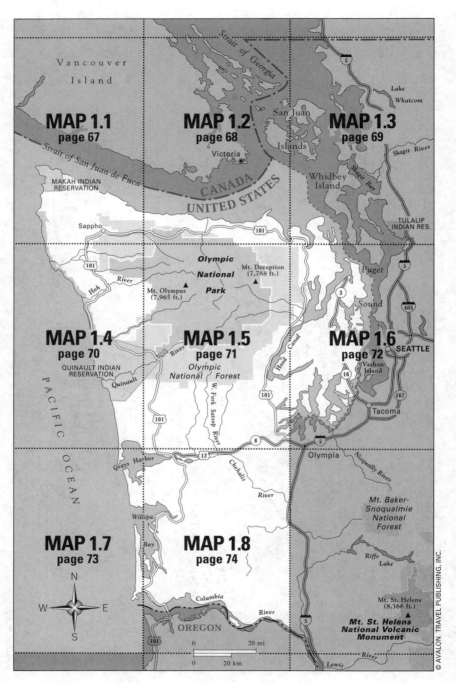

MAP 1.1
page 67

MAP 1.2
page 68

MAP 1.3
page 69

MAP 1.4
page 70

MAP 1.5
page 71

MAP 1.6
page 72

MAP 1.7
page 73

MAP 1.8
page 74

Vancouver
Island

Strait of San Juan de Fuca

MAKAH INDIAN
RESERVATION

Sappho

Olympic

National

Mt. Olympus
(7,965 ft.)

Park

Mt. Deception
(7,788 ft.)

Hoh

River

QUINAULT INDIAN
RESERVATION

Olympic

National   Forest

Quinault

W. Fork Satsop River

River

P A C I F I C

O C E A N

Grays Harbor

Chehalis

River

Willipa

Bay

OREGON

Columbia

River

Strait of Georgia

San Juan

Islands

Victoria

CANADA

UNITED STATES

Lake
Whatcom

Skagit   River

Whidbey
Island

Skagit Bay

TULALIP
INDIAN RES.

Puget

Sound

SEATTLE

Vashon
Island

Tacoma

Hood Canal

Olympia

Nisqually River

Mt. Baker-
Snoqualmie
National
Forest

Riffe
Lake

Mt. St. Helens
(8,366 ft.)

Mt. St. Helens
National Volcanic
Monument

Lewis

River

N

W   E

S

0   20 mi

0   20 km

© AVALON TRAVEL PUBLISHING, INC.

Map 1.1

Campgrounds 1–9
Pages 75–78

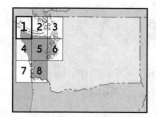

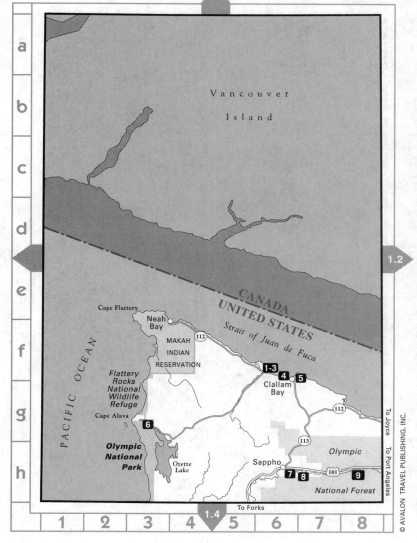

© AVALON TRAVEL PUBLISHING, INC.

Map 1.2

Campgrounds 10–27
Pages 79–86

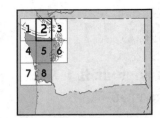

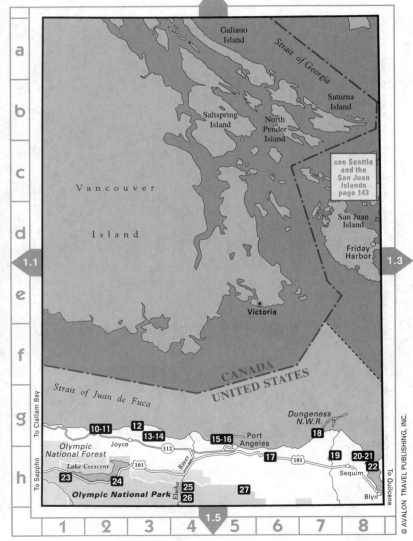

Galiano Island

Strait of Georgia

Saturna Island

Saltspring Island

North Pender Island

see Seattle and the San Juan Islands page 143

Vancouver

Island

San Juan Island

Friday Harbor

Victoria

CANADA
UNITED STATES

Strait of Juan de Fuca

To Clallam Bay

Dungeness N.W.R.

10-11   12
Joyce   13-14   (112)   15-16   Port Angeles   18

Olympic National Forest

To Sappho

Lake Crescent   (101)   River   17   (101)   19   20-21
                                                            22

23   24   25   Sequim   To Quilcene
                                              26   27
Olympic National Park   Elwha   Blyn

1.1   1.3

1.5

© AVALON TRAVEL PUBLISHING, INC.

a b c d e f g h

1 2 3 4 5 6 7 8

Map 1.3

Campgrounds 28–31
Pages 86–88

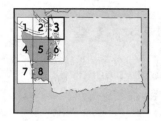

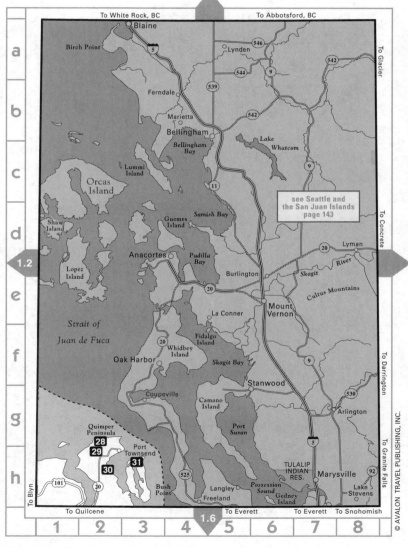

To White Rock, BC

To Abbotsford, BC

Blaine

Birch Point

Lynden   546

542

544   9

Ferndale   539

Marietta

Bellingham   542

Lake Whatcom

Bellingham Bay

Lummi Island   9

11

Orcas Island

see Seattle and the San Juan Islands page 143

Shaw Island

Samish Bay

Guemes Island

Anacortes   Padilla Bay   Lyman   20

Skagit River

Lopez Island   Burlington   Skagit   Cultus Mountains

20

La Conner   Mount Vernon

Strait of Juan de Fuca

Fidalgo Island   9

20   Whidbey Island

Oak Harbor   Skagit Bay

Stanwood   530

Coupeville

Camano Island   Arlington

Quimper Peninsula   Port Susan   5

28

Port Townsend   **29**

30   **31**

TULALIP INDIAN RES.   Marysville   92

101   20   525   Bush Point

Langley   Possession Sound   Gedney Island   Lake Stevens

Freeland

To Blyn

To Quilcene   To Everett   To Everett   To Snohomish

To Glacier

To Concrete

To Darrington

To Granite Falls

1.2

1.6

a b c d e f g h

1 2 3 4 5 6 7 8

© AVALON TRAVEL PUBLISHING, INC.

Map 1.4

Campgrounds 32–51
Pages 89–97

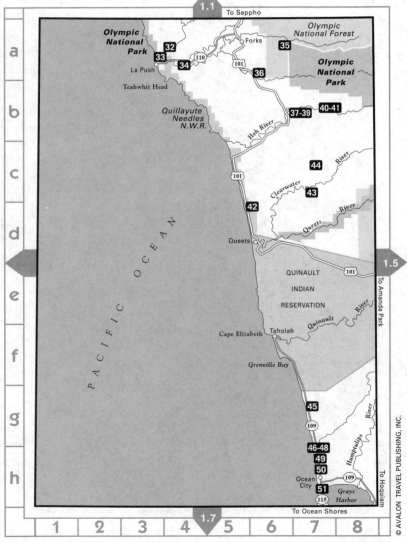

Map 1.5

Campgrounds 52–83
Pages 97–111

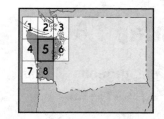

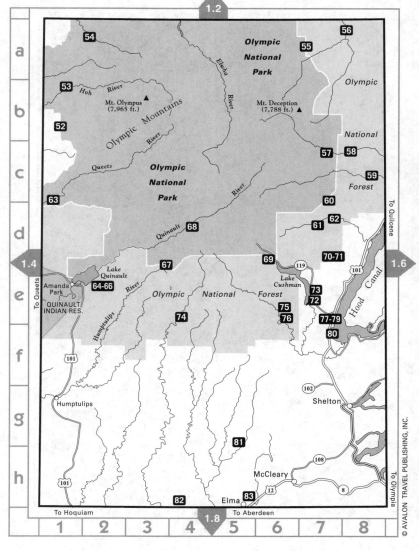

Map 1.6

Campgrounds 84–108
Pages 111–123

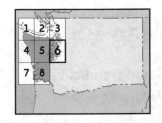

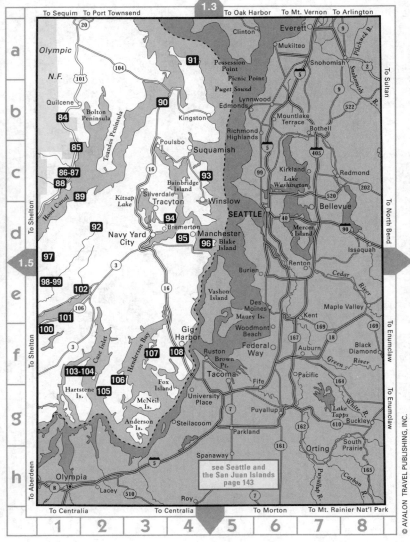

To Sequim   To Port Townsend   To Oak Harbor   To Mt. Vernon   To Arlington

1.3

a

Olympic

N.F.

20

104

101

91

Possession
Point

Picnic Point

Puget Sound

Clinton

Everett

Mukilteo

Snohomish

9

5

2

To Sultan

b

Quilcene

84

Bolton
Peninsula

85

90

Kingston

Lynnwood

Edmonds

Richmond
Highlands

Mountlake
Terrace

Bothell

522

Snohomish R.

9

Pilchuck R.

c

Toandos Peninsula

Poulsbo

86-87

88

89

Kitsap
Lake

Silverdale

Tracyton

Bainbridge
Island

Suquamish

93

Winslow

99

5

405

Kirkland

Lake
Washington

Redmond

520

202

To Shelton

Hood Canal

d

92

Navy Yard
City

16

94

Bremerton

95

Manchester

96

Blake
Island

SEATTLE

Bellevue

Mercer
Island

40

90

To North Bend

Issaquah

1.5

e

97

98-99

102

106

101

100

3

16

Burien

Vashon
Island

Des
Moines

Maury Is.

Renton

Kent

Cedar   River

Maple Valley

169

169

To Enumclaw

To Shelton

f

3

Case Inlet

Henderson Bay

107

108

Gig
Harbor

Ruston

Brown
Pt.

Tacoma

Fife

Woodmont
Beach

Federal
Way

167

Auburn

18

Green   River

Pacific

164

Black
Diamond

To Enumclaw

g

103-104

106

105

Hartstene
Is.

Fox
Island

McNeil
Is.

Anderson
Is.

University
Place

Steilacoom

Puyallup

7

162

Lake
Tapps

410

White R.

Buckley

South
Prairie

Orting

165

Carbon R.

Puyallup R.

© AVALON TRAVEL PUBLISHING, INC.

h

Olympia

Lacey

8

510

Spanaway

Roy

Parkland

161

see Seattle and
the San Juan Islands
page 143

To Aberdeen   To Centralia   To Centralia   To Morton   To Mt. Rainier Nat'l Park

1   2   3   4   5   6   7   8

Map 1.7

Campgrounds 109–133
Pages 123–134

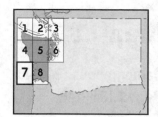

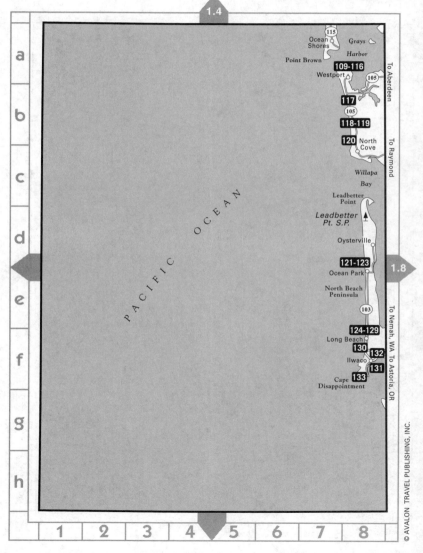

To Aberdeen

To Raymond

To Nemah, WA   To Astoria, OR

Ocean Shores

Grays Harbor

Point Brown

Westport

North Cove

Willapa Bay

Leadbetter Point

Leadbetter Pt. S.P.

Oysterville

Ocean Park

North Beach Peninsula

Long Beach

Ilwaco

Cape Disappointment

PACIFIC OCEAN

115

109-116

105

117

105

118-119

120

121-123

103

124-129

130

132

131

133

Map 1.8

Campgrounds 134–146
Pages 134–140

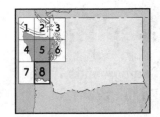

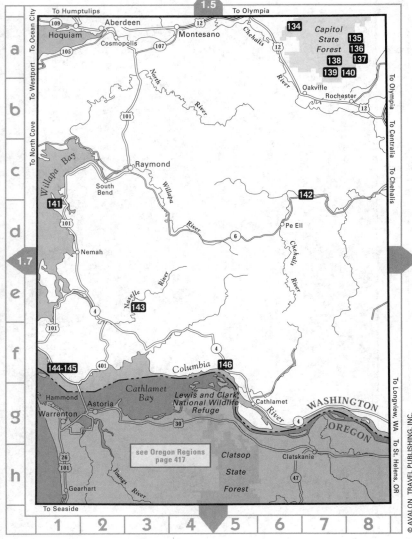

❶ VAN RIPER'S RESORT

🚶 🚴 🏊 ⛵ 🛶 🏕 🐕 ♿ 🚐 ⛺

Rating: 7

On Clallam Bay in Sekiu.
Map 1.1, grid f6, page 67

Part of this campground hugs the waterfront and the other part sits on a hill overlooking the Strait of Juan de Fuca. Most sites are graveled, many with views of the strait. Other sites are grassy, without views. Hiking, fishing, and boating are among the options here, with salmon fishing being the principal draw. The beaches in the area, a mixture of sand and gravel, provide diligent rock hounds with agates and fossils.

Campsites, facilities: There are 150 sites with full or partial hookups for tents or RVs of any length; 60 are drive-through sites. Other accommodations include two cabins, mobile homes, a house, and 12 motel rooms. Electricity, drinking water, and picnic tables are provided. An RV dump station, toilets, showers, and ice are available. A store, café, and laundry facilities are located within one mile. Firewood is available for a fee. Boat docks, launching facilities, and rentals are available in spring and summer. Leashed pets are permitted. No pets are allowed in cabins or other buildings. Some facilities are wheelchair accessible.

Reservations, fees: Reservations are not accepted for campsites. Sites are $11–18 per night. Open April–September. Major credit cards accepted.

Directions: From Aberdeen, drive north on U.S. 101 for 119 miles to Sappho and Highway 113. Turn north on Highway 113 and drive nine miles to Clallam Bay. Continue north on Highway 113/112 for two miles to Sekiu and Front Street. Turn right and drive one-quarter mile to the resort on the right.

Contact: Van Riper's Resort, P.O. Box 246, Sekiu, WA 98381, 360/963-2334, website: www.vanripersresort.com.

❷ OLSON'S RESORT

🚴 ⛵ 🛶 🏕 🐕 🚐 ⛺

Rating: 5

In Sekiu.
Map 1.1, grid f6, page 67

This full-service camp is large and private. The nearby marina is salmon fishing headquarters. In fact, the resort caters to anglers, offering all-day salmon fishing trips and boat moorage. Chartered trips can be arranged by reservation. A tackle shop, cabins, houses, and a motel are also available. See the description of Van Riper's for details on the Sekiu area.

Campsites, facilities: There are 100 sites for tents and RVs of any length , 64 sites for RVs with full hookups. Seven cabins, 14 motel rooms, and four houses are also available. Picnic tables, drinking water, an RV dump station, flush toilets, showers, a laundry room, a store, and ice are available. Boat docks, launching facilities, boat rentals, bait, tackle, a fish-cleaning station, gear storage, gas, and diesel fuel are also available on-site. Call for pet policy. A restaurant is located one mile away.

Reservations, fees: Reservations are not accepted. Sites are $12–16 per night, $2 per person per night for more than two people. Cabins and other lodging are $45–110 per night. Major credit cards accepted. Open year-round.

Directions: From Aberdeen, drive north on U.S. 101 and drive 119 miles to Sappho and Highway 113. Turn north on Highway 113 and drive nine miles to a fork with Highway 112. Continue straight on Highway 112 and continue to Sekiu and Front Street. Turn right and drive one block to the resort on the right.

Contact: Olson's Resort, P.O. Box 216, Sekiu, WA 98381, 360/963-2311, website: www.olsonsresort.com.

3 COHO RV PARK AND MARINA

Rating: 5

Near Sekiu.

Map 1.1, grid f6, page 67

Set across the highway from water, this camp features campsites that are entirely concrete-free. They are mainly gravel, and some have grass. Coho is one of several camps in the immediate area. A full-service marina nearby provides boating access. See the descriptions of Van Riper's Resort Hotel, Olson's Resort, and Surfside Resort for information on the area.

Campsites, facilities: There are 100 sites for tents and 108 for tents or RVs of any length; 60 are full-hookup sites and the remainder are partial hookups with electricity and water. Cable TV is available at a few sites. An RV dump station, toilets, coin-operated showers, a café, a restaurant, laundry facilities, and ice are available. A store is located within one mile. A full-service marina with docks, launching facilities, and gas is available. Leashed pets are permitted.

Reservations, fees: Reservations are not accepted. Sites are $14–18 per night, $1 per person per night for more than two people. No credit cards are accepted. Open April–September.

Directions: From Aberdeen, drive north on U.S. 101 for 119 miles to Sappho and Highway 113. Turn north on Highway 113 and drive nine miles to a junction with Highway 112. Continue straight on Highway 112 and continue toward Sekiu. The campground is located between Mileposts 15 and 16, about three-quarters of a mile before the town of Sekiu.

Contact: Coho Resort and Trailer Park, 15572 Hwy. 112, Sekiu, WA 98381, 360/963-2333.

4 SURFSIDE RESORT

Rating: 7

In Sekiu.

Map 1.1, grid f6, page 67

This park is smaller, less crowded, and more secluded than many in the area. Campers can enjoy the park's private beach and panoramic views of the Strait of Juan de Fuca and Vancouver Island to the north. Nearby recreation options include marked hiking and bike trails within 30 miles, beachcombing, a full-service marina, and the finest fishing for miles.

Campsites, facilities: There are 10 tent sites and 10 drive-through sites for RVs of any length. Fire rings, picnic tables, electricity, and sewer hookups are provided. Drinking water, toilets and showers, an RV dump station, and cable TV are available. Bottled gas, a store, a café, coin-operated laundry facilities, and ice are available within one mile. Boat docks, launching facilities, and rentals are located within one mile. Leashed pets are permitted.

Reservations, fees: Reservations recommended. Sites are $10–18 per night. No credit cards accepted. Open year-round.

Directions: From Aberdeen, drive north on U.S. 101 for 119 miles to Sappho and Highway 113. Turn north on Highway 113 and drive nine miles to a junction with Highway 112. Continue straight on Highway 112 and drive to Clallam Bay. Continue about one mile west; the campground is located on the left, halfway between the towns of Clallam Bay and Sekiu.

Contact: Surfside Resort, P.O. Box 39, Sekiu, WA 98381, 360/963-2723, website: www.oHighwaycom/wa/s/surfsidr.htm.

5 SAM'S TRAILER AND RV PARK

Rating: 5

On Clallam Bay.

Map 1.1, grid f7, page 67

New owners promise improvements here.

Sam's is an alternative to Van Riper's Resort, Olson's Resort, Surfside Resort, and Coho Resort and Trailer Park on Clallam Bay. It's a family-oriented park with grassy sites and many recreation options nearby. Beaches and shopping are within walking distance. Those wanting to visit Cape Flattery, Hoh Rain Forest, or Port Angeles will find this a good central location.

Campsites, facilities: There are four tent sites and 25 sites with full hookups for RVs of any length; 10 are drive-through sites. One RV rental is available. Picnic tables are provided. Restrooms, showers, an RV dump station, cable TV, and coin-operated laundry facilities are available. Bottled gas, a store, a café, and ice are located within one mile. Boat docks, launching facilities, and rentals are also located within one mile. Leashed pets are permitted.

Reservations, fees: Reservations accepted. Sites are $10–16 per night. Senior discount available. No credit cards accepted. Open year-round.

Directions: From Aberdeen, drive north on U.S. 101 for 119 miles to Sappho and Highway 113. Turn north on Highway 113 and drive nine miles to Clallam Bay and Highway 112. Continue straight on Highway 112 and drive into Clallam Bay. Just as you come into town, the campground is on the right at 17053 Highway 112.

Contact: Sam's Trailer and RV Park, P.O. Box 45, Clallam Bay, WA 98326, 360/963-2402.

6 OZETTE

Rating: 6

On Lake Ozette in Olympic National Park.

Map 1.1, grid g3, page 67

Many people visit this site located on the shore of Lake Ozette just a few miles from the Pacific Ocean. Set close to a trailhead road and ranger station, with multiple trailheads nearby, this camp is a favorite for both

hikers and boaters and is one of the first to fill in the park.

Campsites, facilities: There are 13 sites for tents or RVs up to 21 feet long. Drinking water, picnic tables, vault toilets, and fire grills are available. Leashed pets are permitted.

Reservations, fees: Reservations are not accepted. Sites are $10 per night, plus a $10 national park entrance fee per vehicle. Senior discount available. Open year-round.

Directions: From Port Angeles, drive west on U.S. 101 to the junction with Highway 112. Bear right on Highway 112 and drive to Hoko-Ozette Road. Turn left and drive 21 miles to the ranger station. The camp parking lot is across from the ranger station on the northwest corner of Lake Ozette.

Contact: Olympic National Park, 600 East Park Ave., Port Angeles, WA 98362, 360/565-3130, fax 360/565-3147.

7 BEAR CREEK MOTEL AND RV PARK
[icons]

Rating: 7

On Bear Creek.

Map 1.1, grid h6, page 67

This quiet little spot is set where Bear Creek empties into the Sol Duc River. It's private and developed, with a choice of sunny or shaded sites in a wooded setting. There are many recreation options in the area, including fishing, hunting, and nature and hiking trails leading to the ocean. Sol Duc Hot Springs is 25 miles north and well worth the trip. A restaurant next to the camp serves family-style meals.

Campsites, facilities: There are 12 drive-through sites for RVs of any length. Electricity, drinking water, sewer hookups, and picnic tables are provided. Restrooms, showers, an RV dump station, a café, coin-operated laundry, and firewood are available. A motel is also available on the premises. Boat-launching facilities are located within one-half mile. Leashed pets are permitted.

Reservations, fees: Reservations are not accepted. Sites are $15 per night. Major credit cards accepted. Open year-round.

Directions: From Aberdeen, drive north on U.S. 101 to Forks. Continue past Forks for 15 miles to Milepost 205 (just past Sappho) to the campground on the right at 205860 Highway 101 West.

Contact: Bear Creek Motel and RV Park, P.O. Box 236, Beaver, WA 98305, 360/327-3660, website: www.hungrybearcafemotel.com.

8 BEAR CREEK

Rating: 8

On the Sol Duc River.

Map 1.1, grid h7, page 67

Fishing for salmon and hiking along the Sol Duc River make this a good launch point for recreation. There are also good opportunities for wildlife viewing and photography, including a wheelchair-accessible viewing platform overlooking the Sol Duc River. This camp is also popular in the fall with hunters. Note: No drinking water.

Campsites, facilities: There are 10 tent sites. Vault toilets and fire pits are available, but there is no drinking water. Some facilities are wheelchair accessible. Leashed pets are permitted.

Reservations, fees: Reservations are not accepted. There is no fee for camping. Open year-round.

Directions: From Olympia on I-5, take Exit 104 and drive north on U.S. 101 to the Aberdeen/Highway 8 exit. Turn west on Highway 8 and drive 36 miles to Aberdeen. Continue through Aberdeen four miles to U.S. 101 and turn north and drive to Forks. Continue past Forks for 15 miles to Milepost 206 (two miles past Sappho) to the campground on the right.

Contact: Department of Natural Resources,

Olympic Region, 411 Tillicum Lane, Forks, WA 98331-9797, 360/374-6131, fax 360/374-5446.

9 KLAHOWYA

Rating: 9

On the Sol Duc River in Olympic National Forest.

Map 1.1, grid h8, page 67

Klahowya features great views of Lake Crescent and Mt. Olympus. It makes a good choice if you don't want to venture far from U.S. 101 yet want to retain the feel of being in the Olympic National Forest. Set along the Sol Duc River, this 32-acre camp is pretty and wooded, with hiking trails in the area. A favorite, the Kloshe Nanitch Lookout Trail, is across the river and leads up to a lookout on Snider Ridge overlooking Sol Duc Valley. The Pioneer Path Interpretive Trail starts in the camp, an easy 0.3-mile loop that is wheelchair-accessible. Fishing for salmon and steelhead, in season, can be good about one-quarter mile downstream from camp; always check regulations. This camp gets medium use.

Campsites, facilities: There are 54 sites for RVs up to 30 feet long and two walk-in sites requiring a 700-foot walk. Picnic tables are provided. Drinking water, vault and flush toilets, and wheelchair-accessible restrooms are available. An amphitheater with summer interpretive programs is also available. A boat ramp is nearby. Leashed pets are permitted.

Reservations, fees: Reservations are not accepted. Sites are $12 per night. The campground is open May–late September with full service. Limited service is available in the off-season. Senior discount available.

Directions: From I-5 at Olympia, turn north on U.S. 101 and drive about 122 miles to Port Angeles. Continue on U.S. 101 past Port Angeles for about 36 miles (nine miles west of Lake Crescent) to the campground on the right side of the road, close to Milepost 212.

(Coming from the other direction on U.S. 101, drive eight miles east of Sappho to the campground.)

Contact: Olympic National Forest, Pacific Ranger District, 437 Tillicum Ln., Forks, WA 98331, 360/374-6522, fax 360/374-1250.

10 LYRE RIVER

Rating: 7

On the Lyre River.
Map 1.2, grid g2, page 68

This prime spot is one of the rare free campgrounds on the Olympic Peninsula. Although quite primitive, it does offer drinking water and an even more precious commodity in these parts: privacy. The camp is set along the Lyre River, about 15 miles from where it enters the ocean. A popular camp for anglers, Lyre River offers good salmon fishing during fish migrations; always check regulations. A wheelchair-accessible fishing pier is available.

Campsites, facilities: There are 10 primitive tent sites. Picnic tables, fire grills, tent pads, vault toilets, and drinking water are provided. A roofed group shelter is available. Leashed pets are permitted.

Reservations, fees: Reservations are not accepted. There is no fee for camping. Open year-round.

Directions: From Olympia on I-5, take U.S. 101 and drive north 127 miles to a fork with Highway 112 (five miles past the town of Port Angeles). Turn right (west) on Highway 112 and drive about 15 miles to Milepost 46. Look to the right for a paved road between Mileposts 46 and 47; then turn north and drive four-tenths of a mile to the camp entrance road on the left.

Contact: Department of Natural Resources, Olympic Region, 411 Tillicum Ln., Forks, WA 98331-9797, 360/374-6131, fax 360/374-5446.

11 LYRE RIVER PARK

Rating: 9

Near the Lyre River.
Map 1.2, grid g2, page 68

With open space surrounding the park, this beautiful 23-acre camp is situated in a wooded area tucked between the Strait of Juan de Fuca and the Lyre River. Both freshwater and saltwater beaches lend the park a unique flavor. Kids can give their rods a try in the pond stocked with trout (a fee charged), while adult anglers can head for excellent fishing in the Lyre River (steelhead are tops during migrations) and along the nearby shoreline (for perch). Tubing down the river is popular here, and bike and hiking trails are available nearby.

Campsites, facilities: There are 97 sites for tents or RVs of any length; 55 have full hookups and 30 are drive-through sites. Picnic tables are provided and some sites have fire rings. Restrooms, bottled gas, an RV dump station, a store, a coin-operated laundry, and ice are available. Showers and firewood are available for a fee. Leashed pets are permitted.

Reservations, fees: Reservations accepted. Sites are $15–26 per night, $2 per person per night for more than two people. Group reservations welcome with an advance deposit. Major credit cards accepted. Open year-round.

Directions: From Olympia on I-5, take U.S. 101 and drive north 127 miles (five miles past the town of Port Angeles) to a fork with Highway 112. Turn west on Highway 112 and drive 15 miles to West Lyre River Road. Turn right and drive one-half mile to the park on the right.

Contact: Lyre River Park, 596 West Lyre River Rd., Port Angeles, WA 98363, 360/928-3436, website: www.lyreriverpark.com.

12 WHISKEY CREEK BEACH

Rating: 7

On the Strait of Juan de Fuca.

Map 1.2, grid g3, page 68

Located on the beach along the Strait of Juan de Fuca, this campground covers 30 acres and sits next to vast timberland. It is popular with rock hounds. Surf fishing for perch and other species draws anglers, and this is an excellent launch point for sea kayaking. The setting is rustic, with 1.25 miles of beach access. Olympic National Park is located five miles away and offers numerous recreation opportunities, including miles of stellar hiking trails. This camp is a good option if the national park camps are full, but note that almost one-half of the campground is permanently rented out.

Campsites, facilities: There are 30 sites for tents and RVs, including six with full hookups and five with partial hookups, plus seven cabins on the beach. Picnic tables and fire rings are provided. Drinking water and pit toilets are available. Launching facilities for small boats are on-site. A store, a gas station, and a coin-operated laundry are available within three miles. Leashed pets are permitted.

Reservations, fees: Reservations are accepted. The fee is $15 per night for tent sites, $18–25 per night for RV sites; pets $1 per night. No credit cards are accepted. Open May–late October; cabins available year-round.

Directions: From Olympia on I-5, take U.S. 101 and drive north 127 miles (five miles past the town of Port Angeles) to a fork with Highway 112. Turn right (west) on Highway 112 and drive 13 miles (three miles past Joyce) to Whiskey Creek Beach Road. Turn right and continue 1.5 miles to the campground on the right (well marked).

Contact: Whiskey Creek Beach, P.O. Box 130, Joyce, WA 98343, 360/928-3489, fax 360/928-3218, website: www.whiskey-creek-beach.com.

13 CRESCENT BEACH RV

Rating: 6

On the Strait of Juan de Fuca.

Map 1.2, grid g3, page 68

Set on a half-mile stretch of sandy beach, this campground makes a perfect weekend spot. Popular activities include swimming, fishing, surfing, sea kayaking, and beachcombing. It borders Salt Creek Recreation Area, with direct access available. Numerous attractions and recreation options are available in Port Angeles.

Campsites, facilities: There are 41 sites for tents or RVs with full or partial hookups, with a separate area for tent camping. Picnic tables and fire rings are provided. Restrooms, showers, a coin-operated laundry, a pay phone, a recreation field, and horseshoe pits are available. An RV dump station is nearby. Leashed pets are permitted.

Reservations, fees: Reservations recommended. Sites are $25–30 per night, $5 per person per night for more than two people, $5 per extra vehicle per night unless towed, and $5 per night per pet. Weekly and monthly rates available. Open year-round.

Directions: From Olympia on I-5, take U.S. 101 and drive north 127 miles (five miles past the town of Port Angeles) to a fork with Highway 112. Turn right (west) on Highway 112 and drive 10 miles to Camp Hayden Road (between Mileposts 53 and 54). Turn right on Camp Hayden Road and drive four miles to the campground on the left, on the beach.

Contact: Crescent Beach RV, 2860 Crescent Beach Rd., Port Angeles, WA 98363, 360/928-3344, website: www.olypen.com/crescent.

14 SALT CREEK RECREATION AREA

Rating: 8

Near the Strait of Juan de Fuca.

Map 1.2, grid g3, page 68

The former site of Camp Hayden, a World War II-era facility, Salt Creek Recreation Area is a great spot for gorgeous ocean views, fishing, and hiking near Striped Peak, which overlooks the campground. Only a small beach area is available because of the rugged coastline, but there is an exceptionally good spot for tidepool viewing on the park's west side. The park covers 192 acres and overlooks the Strait of Juan de Fuca. Recreation options include nearby hiking trails, swimming, fishing, horseshoes, and field sports. It's a good layover spot if you're planning to take the ferry out of Port Angeles to Victoria, British Columbia. Reservations are strongly advised, with the camp filling up quickly most summer weekends.

Campsites, facilities: There are 92 sites for tents or RVs of any length. Picnic tables are provided. A restroom, flush toilets, coin-operated showers, an RV dump station, and a playground are available. Firewood is available for a fee. Some facilities are wheelchair accessible. Leashed pets are permitted.

Reservations, fees: Reservations are not accepted. Sites are $10–12 per night, $3 per extra vehicle per night; six campers maximum per site. Open year-round.

Directions: From Olympia on I-5, take U.S. 101 and drive north 127 miles (five miles past the town of Port Angeles) to a fork with Highway 112. Turn right (west) on Highway 112 and drive six miles to Camp Hayden Road. Turn right (north) and drive 3.5 miles to the campground.

Contact: Salt Creek Recreation Area, Clallam County, 3506 Camp Hayden Rd., Port Angeles, WA 98363, 360/928-3441, website: www.clallam.net/park.

15 PEABODY CREEK RV PARK

Rating: 5

In Port Angeles.
Map 1.2, grid g5, page 68

This three-acre RV park is right in the middle of town but offers a wooded, streamside setting. Nearby recreation options include salmon fishing, an 18-hole golf course, marked biking trails, a full-service marina, and tennis courts. The park is within walking distance of shopping and ferry services.

Campsites, facilities: There are 36 sites with full hookups for RVs of any length, but note that 19 are permanent rentals. An RV dump station, restrooms with coin-operated showers, ice, and coin-operated laundry facilities are available. A cable TV hookup is available for $3 per night. A store and a café are located within one block. Boat docks, launching facilities, and boat rentals are located within 1.5 miles. Leashed pets are permitted.

Reservations, fees: Reservations accepted. Sites are $23 per night. No credit cards accepted. Open year-round.

Directions: From I-5 at Olympia, turn north on U.S. 101 and drive about 122 miles to Port Angeles and Lincoln Street. Bear left on Lincoln and drive one-half mile to Second Street and the park entrance on the right.

Contact: Peabody Creek RV Park, 127 South Lincoln, Port Angeles, WA 98362, 360/457-7092 (phone or fax) or 800/392-2361, website: www.members.tripod.peabodyrv.com.

16 AL'S RV PARK

Rating: 8

Near Port Angeles.
Map 1.2, grid g5, page 68

This adult-oriented campground is a good choice for RV owners. The campground is set in the country at about 1,000 feet elevation yet is centrally located and not far from the Strait of Juan de Fuca. Nearby recreation options include an 18-hole golf course and a full-service marina. Olympic National Park and the Victoria ferry are a short drive away.

Campsites, facilities: There are 31 sites with full hookups, including some drive-through, for RVs up to 40 feet long, 20 sites for tents, and one rental trailer for up to four people. No fires allowed. Picnic tables are provided.

Restrooms, drinking water, flush toilets, showers, cable TV, a clubhouse, and laundry facilities are available. Telephone service is available for all sites. A store, a café, bottled gas, and ice are located within one mile. Boat docks and launching facilities are located within two miles. Some facilities are wheelchair accessible. Leashed pets are permitted.

Reservations, fees: Reservations accepted at 360/457-9844 (preferred) or 800/357-1553. Sites are $15–25 per night, $2 per person per night for more than two people. Trailers are $25 per night. Weekly and monthly rates available. Major credit cards accepted. Open year-round.

Directions: From Port Angeles, take U.S. 101 west for two miles to North Brook Avenue. Turn right (north) on North Brook Avenue, then left (almost immediately) on Lees Creek Road, and drive one-half mile to the park on the right.

Contact: Al's RV Park, 521 North Lees Creek Rd., Port Angeles, WA 98362, 360/457-9844.

17 KOA PORT ANGELES-SEQUIM

Rating: 5

Near Port Angeles.

Map 1.2, grid h6, page 68

This is a private, developed camp covering 13 acres in a country setting. A pleasant park, it features the typical KOA offerings, including a pool, recreation hall, and playground. Horseshoe pits and a sports field are also available. Hayrides are available in summer. Nearby recreation options include miniature golf, an 18-hole golf course, marked hiking trails, and tennis courts, and nearby side trips feature Victoria, Butchart Gardens, and whale-watching tours.

Campsites, facilities: There are 90 sites with full and partial hookups, including 45 drive-through, for tents or RVs of any length and 12 cabins. Picnic tables are provided. Restrooms, drinking water, flush toilets, showers,

cable TV, bottled gas, firewood, an RV dump station, a store, a coin-operated laundry, ice, a playground, miniature golf, a recreation room, and a swimming pool are available. A café is located within two miles. Some facilities are wheelchair accessible. Leashed pets are permitted.

Reservations, fees: Reservations accepted at 800/562-7558. Sites are $21–35 per night, $4 per person per night for more than two people, and $5 per extra vehicle per night. Cabins are $44–60 per night. No charge for ages 5 and under. Major credit cards accepted. Open mid-March–mid-November.

Directions: From I-5 at Olympia, turn north on U.S. 101 and drive 116 miles to O'Brien Road, six miles southeast of Port Angeles. Turn left on O'Brien Road and drive half a block to the campground on the right.

Contact: KOA Port Angeles-Sequim, 80 O'Brien Rd., Port Angeles, WA 98362, 360/457-5916, fax 360/452-4248, website: www.koa.com.

18 DUNGENESS RECREATION AREA

Rating: 5

Near the Strait of Juan de Fuca.

Map 1.2, grid g7, page 68

This park overlooks the Strait of Juan de Fuca and is set near the Dungeness National Wildlife Refuge. Quite popular, it fills up on summer weekends. A highlight, the refuge sits on a seven-mile spit with a historic lighthouse at its end. Bird-watchers often spot bald eagles in the wildlife refuge. Nearby recreation options include marked hiking trails, fishing, and golfing. The toll ferry at Port Angeles can take you to Victoria, British Columbia.

Campsites, facilities: There are 65 sites, including five drive-through, for tents or RVs of any length. Picnic tables and fire grills are provided. Restrooms, drinking water, flush toilets, coin-operated showers, firewood, an RV dump station, and a playground are available. No hookups. Leashed pets are permitted.

Reservations, fees: Reservations are not accepted. Sites are $12 per night, $3 per extra vehicle per night. Open February–October, with facilities limited to day use in the winter. Entrance gates close at dusk year-round.

Directions: From Sequim, drive north on U.S. 101 for four miles to Kitchen-Dick Road. Turn right on Kitchen-Dick Road and drive four miles to the park on the left.

Contact: Dungeness Recreation Area, Clallam County, 554 Voice of America Rd., Sequim, WA 98382, 360/683-5847.

19 SEQUIM WEST INN & RV PARK

Rating: 5

Near the Dungeness River.
Map 1.2, grid h7, page 68

This two-acre camp is near the Dungeness River and within 10 miles of Dungeness Spit State Park. It's a pleasant spot with full facilities and an urban setting. An 18-hole golf course and a full-service marina at Sequim Bay are close by.

Campsites, facilities: There are 27 drive-through sites with full hookups for tents or RVs of any length, 17 cabins, and 21 motel rooms. Picnic tables are provided. Restrooms, drinking water, flush toilets, showers, cable TV, a coin-operated laundry, a pay phone, and ice are available. Bottled gas, a store, and a café are located within one mile. Leashed pets are permitted.

Reservations, fees: Reservations accepted. Sites are $24–27, $1 per person per night for more than two people (under 18 free). Major credit cards accepted. Open year-round.

Directions: From Sequim and U.S. 101, take the Washington Street exit and drive west on Washington Street for 2.7 miles to the park on the left.

Contact: Sequim West Inn & RV Park, 740 West Washington Ave., Sequim, WA 98382,

360/683-4144 or 800/528-4527, fax 360/683-6452, website: www.olypen.com/swi.

20 RAINBOW'S END RV PARK

Rating: 6

On Sequim Bay.
Map 1.2, grid h8, page 68

This park on Sequim Bay is pretty and clean and features a rainbow trout pond and a creek running through the campground. There is a weekly potluck dinner in the summer, with free hamburgers and hot dogs, and a special landscaped area available for reunions, weddings, and other gatherings. Nearby recreation opportunities include an 18-hole golf course, marked bike trails, a full-service marina, and tennis courts. New owners in 2002 plan long-term improvements.

Campsites, facilities: There are 39 sites with full hookups, including some drive-through sites, for RVs of any length and 10 tent sites. Telephone and cable TV hookups are provided at RV sites. Picnic tables and fire grills are provided at tent sites. Restrooms, drinking water, flush toilets, showers, an RV dump station, bottled gas, a coin-operated laundry, and a clubhouse are available. A store, a café, and ice are located within one mile. Firewood is available for a fee. Leashed pets are permitted.

Reservations, fees: Reservations are accepted. The fee is $16.50 per night for tent sites; $21–27 for RV sites; $2 per person per night for more than two people. Weekly and monthly rates are available. Major credit cards accepted. Open year-round.

Directions: From Sequim, drive west on U.S. 101 for one mile past the River Road exit to the park on the right (along the highway).

Contact: Rainbow's End RV Park, 261831 U.S. 101, Sequim, WA 98382, 360/683-3863, fax 360/683-2150.

21 SEQUIM BAY RESORT

Rating: 5

On Sequim Bay.

Map 1.2, grid h8, page 68

This is Sequim Bay headquarters for salmon anglers. The camp is set in a wooded, hilly area, close to many activity centers, and with an 18-hole golf course nearby.

Campsites, facilities: There are 43 sites with full hookups, including 34 drive-through, for RVs of any length and eight cabins. No tent camping. Restrooms, drinking water, flush toilets, showers, cable TV, and a coin-operated laundry are available. Boat docks and launching facilities are located across the street from the resort. Leashed pets are permitted.

Reservations, fees: Reservations recommended. Sites are $21.50 per night, $3 per person per night for more than two people. Cabins are $35–65 per night, and are rented by night with a two-night minimum May–September and by the month the rest of the year. Open year-round.

Directions: From Olympia on I-5, turn north on U.S. 101 and drive about 100 miles (near Sequim) to Whitefeather Way (located between Mileposts 267 and 268, 2.5 miles east of Sequim). Turn north on Whitefeather Way and drive one-half mile to West Sequim Bay Road. Turn left (west) and drive one block to the park on the left.

Contact: Sequim Bay Resort, 2634 West Sequim Bay Rd., Sequim, WA 98382, 360/681-3853, fax 360/681-3854.

22 SEQUIM BAY STATE PARK

Rating: 8

On Sequim Bay.

Map 1.2, grid h8, page 68

Sequim translates to "quiet waters," which is an appropriate description of this area. Set in the heart of Washington's rain show, a region with far less rainfall than the surrounding areas, Sequim averages only 17 inches of rainfall a year. The park features 4,909 feet of saltwater shoreline, and two natural overlapping sand bars protect the bay waters from the rough waves and currents of the Strait of Juan de Fuca. The park has only one mile of hiking trails. This 90-acre camp on Sequim Bay features an underwater park for scuba divers.

Campsites, facilities: There are 60 developed sites for tents or RVs, 16 sites with full hookups for RVs up to 30 feet long, and three primitive tent sites. Picnic tables and fire grills are provided. Restrooms, drinking water, flush toilets, showers, an RV dump station, a picnic area with kitchen shelters, an amphitheater, athletic fields, a basketball court, and a playground are available. Boat docks, launching facilities, and boat mooring are also available. Facilities are wheelchair-accessible. Leashed pets are permitted.

Reservations, fees: Reservations at 888/CAMP-OUT (888/226-7688), website: www.parks.wa.gov/reservations ($7 reservation fee). Sites are $16–22 per night, $6 per extra vehicle per night; boat mooring is $10–16 per night; $6 per night for bike-in sites. Major credit cards accepted. Senior discount available. Open year-round.

Directions: From Olympia on I-5, turn north on U.S. 101 and drive 100 miles (near Sequim) to the park entrance on the right (along the highway). The park is located four miles southeast of the town of Sequim.

Contact: Sequim Bay State Park, 360/683-4235; State Park information, 360/902-8844.

23 FAIRHOLM

Rating: 9

On Lake Crescent in Olympic National Park Bay.

Map 1.2, grid h1, page 68

This camp is set on the shore of Lake Crescent, a pretty lake situated within the boundary of Olympic National Park, at an elevation of 580 feet. The campsites lie along the western end of the lake, in a cove with a boat ramp. Located less than one mile off U.S. 101, Fairholm gets heavy use during tourist months; some highway noise is audible at some sites. A naturalist program is often available in the summer. Water skiing is permitted at Lake Crescent, but personal watercraft are prohibited.

Campsites, facilities: There are 88 sites for tents or RVs up to 21 feet long. Picnic tables and fire grills are provided. An RV dump station, restrooms, and drinking water are available. Some facilities are wheelchair accessible. A store and a café are located within one mile. Boat-launching facilities and rentals are nearby on Lake Crescent. Leashed pets are permitted.

Reservations, fees: Reservations are not accepted. Sites are $10 per night, plus a $10 national park entrance fee. Senior discount available. Open year-round, weather permitting.

Directions: From Port Angeles, drive west on U.S. 101 for about 26 miles and continue along Lake Crescent to North Shore Road. Turn right and drive one-half mile to the camp on North Shore Road on the right.

Contact: Olympic National Park, 600 East Park Ave., Port Angeles, WA 98362, 360/565-3130, fax 360/565-3147.

24 LOG CABIN RESORT

Rating: 10

On Lake Crescent in Olympic National Park Bay.

Map 1.2, grid h2, page 68

This pretty camp along the shore of Lake Crescent is a good spot for boaters as it features many sites near the water with excellent views. Fishing and swimming are two options at this family-oriented resort. It is home to a strain of Beardslee trout. Note the fishing became catch-and-release in 2000. Water skiing is permitted, but no personal watercraft are allowed. A marked hiking trail traces the lake's 22-mile shoreline. This camp is extremely popular in the summer months and you may need to make reservations 6–12 months in advance.

Campsites, facilities: There are 38 sites with full hookups for RVs of any length and 28 cabins. Picnic tables and fire barrels are provided. An RV dump station, restrooms, a store, a café, laundry facilities, ice, and a recreation field are available. Showers and firewood are also available for a fee. Boat docks, launching facilities, and boat rentals and hydrobikes are available nearby. Some facilities are wheelchair accessible. Leashed pets are permitted.

Reservations, fees: Reservations accepted. Sites are $20–31 per night, $12 per person per night for more than two people, and $12 per pet per night. Open April–October. Major credit cards accepted.

Directions: From I-5 at Olympia, turn north on U.S. 101 and drive about 122 miles to Port Angeles. Continue on U.S. 101 past Port Angeles for about 18 miles to East Beach Road. Turn right and drive three miles (along Lake Crescent) to the camp on the left.

Contact: Log Cabin Resort, 3183 East Beach Rd., Port Angeles, WA 98363, 360/928-3325, fax 360/928-2088, website: www.logcabin resort.net.

25 ELWHA

Rating: 7

On the Elwha River in Olympic National Park Bay.

Map 1.2, grid h4, page 68

The Elwha River is the backdrop for this popular camp with excellent hiking trails close by in Olympic National Park. The elevation is 390 feet. Check at one of the visitors centers for maps and backcountry information; also see the description of neighboring Altaire for more information.

Campsites, facilities: There are 41 sites for tents or RVs up to 21 feet long. Picnic tables and fire grills are provided. Restrooms and drinking water are available. Some facilities are wheelchair accessible. Leashed pets are permitted.

Reservations, fees: Reservations are not accepted. Sites are $10 per night, plus a $10 national park entrance fee per vehicle. Senior discount available. Open year-round.

Directions: From Port Angeles, drive west on U.S. 101 for about nine miles (just past Lake Aldwell) to the signed entrance road on the left. Turn left at the entrance road and drive three miles south along the Elwha River to the campground on the left.

Contact: Olympic National Park, 600 East Park Ave., Port Angeles, WA 98362, 360/565-3130, fax 360/565-3147.

26 ALTAIRE

Rating: 8

On the Elwha River in Olympic National Park Bay.

Map 1.2, grid h4, page 68

A pretty and well-treed camp with easy highway access, this camp is set on the Elwha River about one mile from Lake Mills. Fishing is good in season; check regulations. The elevation is 450 feet. Altaire also makes for a nice layover spot before taking the ferry at Port Angeles to Victoria, British Columbia.

Campsites, facilities: There are 30 sites for tents or RVs up to 21 feet long. Picnic tables and fire grills are provided. Restrooms and drinking water are available. Some facilities are wheelchair accessible. Leashed pets are permitted.

Reservations, fees: Reservations are not accepted. Sites are $10 per night, plus a $10 national park entrance fee per vehicle. Senior discount available. Open June–September.

Directions: From I-5 at Olympia, turn north on U.S. 101 and drive about 122 miles to Port Angeles. Continue on U.S. 101 past Port Angeles for about nine miles (just past Lake Aldwell). Turn left at the signed entrance road and drive four miles south along the Elwha River.

Contact: Olympic National Park, 600 East Park Ave., Port Angeles, WA 98362, 360/565-3130, fax 360/565-3147.

27 HEART O' THE HILLS

Rating: 9

In Olympic National Park Bay.

Map 1.2, grid h5, page 68

Heart O' the Hills is nestled on the northern edge of Olympic National Park at an elevation of 1,807 feet. You can drive into the park on Hurricane Ridge Road and take one of numerous hiking trails. Little Lake Dawn is less than one-half mile to the west, but note that most of the property around this lake is privately owned. Naturalist programs are available in summer months.

Campsites, facilities: There are 105 sites for tents or RVs up to 21 feet long. Picnic tables and fire grills are provided. Restrooms and drinking water are available. Some facilities are wheelchair accessible. Leashed pets are permitted.

Reservations, fees: Reservations are not accepted. Sites are $10 per night, plus a $10 national park entrance fee per vehicle. Senior discount available. Open year-round, weather permitting.

Directions: From I-5 at Olympia, turn north on U.S. 101 and drive about 122 miles to Port Angeles to Hurricane Ridge Road. Turn left and drive five miles to the camp on the left. (Access roads can be impassable in severe weather.)

Contact: Olympic National Park, 600 East Park Ave., Port Angeles, WA 98362, 360/565-3130, fax 360/565-3147.

28 FORT WORDEN STATE PARK

Rating: 9

Near Puget Sound.

Map 1.3, grid g2, page 69

This park is set on the northeastern tip of the Olympic Peninsula, at the northern end of Port

Townsend, on a high bluff overlooking Puget Sound. Highlights here include great lookouts and two miles of trails over the Strait of Juan de Fuca as it feeds into Puget Sound. The park covers 433 acres at historic Fort Worden (on which construction was begun in 1897 and decommissioned in 1953) and includes buildings from the turn of the 20th century. It has 11,020 feet of saltwater shoreline. Recreation options include 12 miles of marked hiking and biking trails, with five miles of wheelchair-accessible trails. The Coast Artillery Museum, Rothschild House, and the Marine Science Center are open during the summer season. A ferry at Port Townsend will take you across the strait to Whidbey Island. Special note on reservations: This is an extremely popular park and campground and reservations are required via the internet up to five months in advance or over the counter up to four months in advance.

Campsites, facilities: There are 80 sites with full or partial hookups, including some drive-through, for tents or RVs up to 60 feet long, and five primitive, hike-in or bike-in tent sites. Picnic tables and fire grills are provided. Restrooms, drinking water, flush toilets, coin-operated showers, a laundry room, a store, and firewood for sale are available. A restaurant, conference facilities, a sheltered amphitheater, athletic fields, and interpretive activities are available nearby. Boat docks, buoys, floats, and launching facilities are also nearby. Wheelchair-accessible facilities are available. Several golf courses are located nearby. Leashed pets are permitted.

Reservations, fees: Reservations available at website: www.fortworden.org — then click on on-line camping reservations. Sites are $6–22 per night, $6 per extra vehicle per night; moorage is $10–16 per night. Senior discount available. Open year-round.

Directions: From Olympia, turn north on U.S. 101 and drive 86 miles to Highway 20 (Port Townsend turnoff). Turn north on Highway 20 and drive 13 miles to Port Townsend. Continue through Port Townsend to Cherry Street.

Turn left at Cherry Street and drive 1.75 miles to the park entrance at the end of the road.

Contact: Fort Worden State Park, 200 Battery Way, Port Townsend, WA 98638, 360/344-4400, fax 360/385-7240.

29 POINT HUDSON RESORT & MARINA

Rating: 5

In Port Townsend.

Map 1.3, grid h2, page 69

Point Hudson Resort is located on the site of an old Coast Guard station near the beach in Port Townsend. The park features ocean views and 2,000 feet of beach frontage. Known for its Victorian architecture, Port Townsend is called Washington's Victorian seaport. Fishing and boating are popular here, and nearby recreation opportunities include an 18-hole municipal golf course, a full-service marina, Old Fort Townsend State Park, Fort Flagler State Park, and Fort Worden State Park. Note that the past concessionaire's lease with the Port of Port Townsend expired in spring of 2002 and changes are likely.

Campsites, facilities: There are 60 sites, most drive-through with full hookups, for RVs of any length. No tents are allowed. Restrooms, drinking water, flush toilets, showers, three restaurants, and a coin-operated laundry are available. A 100-plus slip marina is on-site. Leashed pets are permitted.

Reservations, fees: Reservations encouraged. Sites are $19–25 per night. Major credit cards accepted. Open year-round.

Directions: From Port Townsend on State Route 20, take the Water Street exit. Turn left (north) and continue (the road becomes Sims Way and then Water Street) to the end of Water Street at the marina. Turn left for registration.

Contact: Point Hudson Resort, 103 Hudson St., Port Townsend, WA 98368, 360/385-2828 or 800/228-2803, fax 360/385-7331, website: www.portofpt.com.

30 OLD FORT TOWNSEND STATE PARK

Rating: 10

Near Quilcene.

Map 1.3, grid h2, page 69

This 367-acre park features a thickly wooded landscape, nearly 4,000 feet of saltwater shoreline on Port Townsend Bay, and 6.5 miles of hiking trails. Built in 1856, the historic fort is one of the oldest remaining in the state. The scenic campground has access to a good clamming beach, and visitors can take a short self-guided walking tour. Note that the nearest boat ramps are at Port Townsend, Fort Flagler, and Hadlock. Mooring buoys are located one mile south of Glenn Cove on the west side of Port Townsend Bay.

Campsites, facilities: There are 40 sites for tents or RVs up to 40 feet long, three primitive tent sites, and one group site. Picnic tables and fire grills are provided. Restrooms, drinking water, flush toilets, coin-operated showers, a playground, boat buoys, firewood, an RV dump station, and a picnic area with a kitchen shelter are available. Leashed pets are permitted.

Reservations, fees: Reservations are not accepted for family sites. Group site reservations required at 360/344-4431. Sites are $7–15 per night, $2 per person for more than two people, and $6 per extra vehicle per night. Senior discount available. Open mid-April–mid-September.

Directions: From Port Townsend and State Route 20, drive south on State Route 20 for two miles to Old Fort Townsend Road. Turn left and drive one-half mile to the park entrance road.

Contact: Old Fort Townsend State Park, Rte. 1, Port Townsend, WA 98368, 360/385-3595; State Park information, 360/902-8844.

31 FORT FLAGLER STATE PARK

Rating: 10

Near Port Townsend.

Map 1.3, grid h3, page 69

This beautiful park sits on a high bluff overlooking Puget Sound with views of the Olympic and Cascade Mountains. The park covers 784 acres and is surrounded on three sides by 19,100 feet of saltwater shoreline. Highlights include five miles of trails for hiking and biking, an interpretive trail, and a military museum featuring gun batteries that is open in the summer. Historic Fort Flagler is a pretty and unique state park, set on Marrowstone Island east of Port Townsend. The RV sites are situated right on the beach. Anglers like this spot for year-round rockfish and salmon fishing, and crabbing and clamming are good in season. The park offers an underwater park, which attracts scuba divers. Fort Flagler, under construction on some level from 1897 until its closure in 1953, offers tours. There is a youth hostel in the park.

Campsites, facilities: There are 101 tent sites, 15 sites with partial hookups (water and electricity) for RVs up to 50 feet long, and two primitive tent sites. Picnic tables and fire grills are provided. Restrooms, drinking water, flush toilets, coin-operated showers, interpretive activities, an RV dump station, a store, a café, boat buoys, floats, and a launch are available. Facilities are wheelchair-accessible. Leashed pets are permitted.

Reservations, fees: Reserve at 888/CAMP-OUT (888/226-7688), website: www.parks.wa.gov/reservations ($7 reservation fee). Sites are $6–22 per night. Senior discount available. Major credit cards accepted. Open March–October, weather permitting.

Directions: From Port Townsend at Highway 20, drive east on Highway 20 for three miles to Ness' Corner Road (at the traffic light). Continue straight onto Highway 19 and go eight miles to Oak Bay Road/State Route

116. Turn left and drive two miles through Port Hadlock (turning left to stay on State Route 116). Continue about eight miles to the entrance.

Contact: Fort Flagler State Park, 360/385-1259, fax 360/379-1746; State Park information, 360/902-8844.

32 MORA

Rating: 8

Near the Pacific Ocean in Olympic National Park.

Map 1.4, grid a4, page 70

At an elevation of 50 feet, this is a good out-of-the-way choice near the Pacific Ocean and the Olympic Coast Marine Sanctuary. The Quillayute River feeds into the ocean near the camp, and upstream lies the Bogachiel, a prime steelhead river in winter months. A naturalist program is available during the summer. This camp includes eight sites, several of which are stellar, requiring short walks.

Campsites, facilities: There are 94 sites for tents or RVs up to 21 feet long, and 8 walk-in sites. Picnic tables and fire grills are provided. Restrooms, drinking water, and an RV dump station are available. Some facilities are wheelchair accessible. A naturalist program is available in summer months. Leashed pets are permitted.

Reservations, fees: Reservations are not accepted. Sites are $10 per night, plus a $10 national park entrance fee per vehicle. Senior discount available. Open year-round.

Directions: From Aberdeen, drive north on U.S. 101 for 108 miles to Forks. Continue past Forks for two miles to La Push Road (Highway 110). Turn left (west) and drive 12 miles to the campground on the left (well marked along the route).

Contact: Olympic National Park, 600 East Park Ave., Port Angeles, WA 98362, 360/565-3130, fax 360/565-3147.

33 LONESOME CREEK RV RESORT

Rating: 8

On the Pacific Ocean.

Map 1.4, grid a3, page 70

This private, developed park is set along the Pacific Ocean and the coastal Dungeness National Wildlife Refuge. It has some of the few ocean sites available in the area and offers such recreation options as fishing, beachcombing, boating, whale-watching, and sunbathing.

Campsites, facilities: There are 36 sites for RVs and 10 sites for tents. Picnic tables and fire rings are provided. Restrooms, coin-operated showers, a coin-operated laundry, gasoline and bottled gas, and a store with a deli and ice are available. Boat docks and launching facilities are located within one mile. Leashed pets are permitted.

Reservations, fees: Reservations accepted for RV sites and are recommended for oceanfront sites. Sites are $18 per night for tent sites and $30–34 for RV sites. Major credit cards accepted. Open year-round.

Directions: From Aberdeen, drive north on U.S. 101 for 108 miles to Forks. Continue past Forks for two miles to La Push Road/Highway 110. Turn left (west) and drive 14 miles to the campground on the left.

Contact: Lonesome Creek RV Resort, P.O. Box 130, La Push, WA 98350, 360/374-4338.

34 THREE RIVERS RESORT

Rating: 8

On the Quillayute River.

Map 1.4, grid a4, page 70

This small, private camp is set at the junction of three rivers—the Quillayute, Sol Duck, and Bogachiel. Situated above this confluence, about six miles upstream from the ocean, this pretty spot features wooded, spacious sites. Hiking and fishing are popular here. Salmon and steelhead migrate upstream, best on the Sol Duc and Bogachiel Rivers; anglers should check regulations. The coastal Dungeness National Wildlife Refuge and Pacific Ocean, which often offer good whale-watching in the spring, are a short drive to the west. Hoh Rain Forest, a worthwhile side trip, is about 45 minutes away.

Campsites, facilities: There are 10 sites for tents or RVs of any length, and 14 sites with full or partial hookups for RVs only, plus five rental cabins. Picnic tables are provided. Restrooms, coin-operated showers, a store, a café, a coin-operated laundry, and ice are available. Firewood is available for a fee. Leashed pets are permitted.

Reservations, fees: Reservations accepted. Sites are $8–12 per night, $5 per pet per night. Major credit cards accepted. Open year-round.

Directions: From Aberdeen, drive north on U.S. 101 for 108 miles to Forks. Continue past Forks for two miles to La Push Road/Highway 110. Turn left (west) and drive eight miles to the campground on the right.

Contact: Three Rivers Resort, 7764 La Push Rd., Forks, WA 98331, 360/374-5300, website: www.northolympic.com/threerivers.

35 KLAHANIE

Rating: 8

On the North Fork Klahanie River.
Map 1.4, grid a6, page 70

This camp was closed for several years because of vandalism. Forest Rangers said they may reopen the campground and try again in 2003. That means two things. One, Klahanie is a giant question mark, certainly not a destination worth counting on. Two, it is likely off the radar scope of many travelers, so it is worth checking in on. Sites nestle amid large, old-growth spruce and lots of ferns. It is quite pretty, set along a riparian zone on the North Fork Klahamie River, and features a hiking trail that hugs the river for one-quarter mile.

Campsites, facilities: There are 15 sites for tents or RVs of any length. Picnic tables and fire grills are provided. Drinking water and vault toilets are available. Garbage must be packed out. Some facilities are wheelchair accessible. Leashed pets are permitted.

Reservations, fees: Reservations are not accepted. The fee is $5 per site per night. Senior discount available. Open May–late September with facilities listed. Open with limited facilities in off-season.

Directions: From Aberdeen, drive north on U.S. 101 to Forks. Continue past Forks for one mile to Forest Road 29. Turn right (east) and drive five miles to the campground on the right.

Contact: Olympic National Forest, Pacific Ranger District, 437 Tillicum Ln., Forks, WA 98331, 360/374-6522, fax 360/374-1250.

36 BOGACHIEL STATE PARK

Rating: 6

On the Bogachiel River.
Map 1.4, grid a6, page 70

A good base camp for salmon or steelhead fishing trips, this 123-acre park is set on the Bogachiel River, with marked hiking trails in the area. It can be noisy at times because a logging mill is located directly across the river from the campground. Also note that there is highway noise, and you can see the highway from some campsites. A one-mile hiking trail is nearby. Hunting is popular in the adjacent national forest. This region is heavily forested, with lush vegetation fed by 140–160 inches of rain on the average each year.

Campsites, facilities: There is one primitive tent site, 36 developed tent sites, and six sites with water and electrical hookups for RVs up to 30 feet long. Picnic tables and fire grills are provided. Restrooms, drinking water, coin-operated showers, an RV dump station, and a picnic area are available. A store, ice, and firewood are located within one mile. A primitive boat ramp is nearby. Leashed pets are permitted.

Reservations, fees: Reservations are not ac-

cepted. Sites with hookups are $16–22 per night; tent sites are $6–8 per night, $6 per extra vehicle per night. Senior discount available. Open year-round.

Directions: From Olympia on I-5, take Exit 104 and drive north on U.S. 101 to the Aberdeen/Highway 8 exit. Turn west on Highway 8 and drive 36 miles to Aberdeen. Continue through Aberdeen four miles to U.S. 101. Turn north on U.S. 101 and drive 102 miles to the park (six miles south of Forks) on the left side of the road.

Contact: Bogachiel State Park, Northwest Region, 185983 U.S. 101, Forks, WA 98331, 360/374-6356; State Park information, 360/902-8844.

37 HOH RIVER RESORT

Rating: 6

On the Hoh River.
Map 1.4, grid b7, page 70

This camp along U.S. 101 features a choice of grassy or graveled, shady sites and is most popular as a fishing camp. Although the Hoh River is nearby, you cannot see the river from the campsites. Marked hiking trails are in the area. This pleasant little park offers steelhead and salmon fishing as well as elk hunting in the fall. Horseshoe pits and a recreation field are provided for campers.

Campsites, facilities: There are 23 sites for tents or RVs of any length, some with full hookups, some with electrical hookups only, and several cabins remodeled in 2002. Fire pits and picnic tables are provided. Restrooms, coin-operated showers, a coin-operated laundry, a store, a gas station, and ice are available. Firewood is available for a fee. A boat launch is available nearby. Leashed pets are permitted.

Reservations, fees: Reservations accepted. Sites are $10–18 per night, $3 per extra vehicle per night. No credit cards accepted. Open year-round.

Directions: From Aberdeen, drive north on U.S. 101 for 90 miles to the resort (15 miles south of Forks) on the left.

Contact: Hoh River Resort, 175443 U.S. 101 S, Forks, WA 98331, 360/374-5566.

38 COTTONWOOD

Rating: 8

On the Hoh River.
Map 1.4, grid b7, page 70

This primitive camp is set along the Hoh River, providing an alternative to Hoh Oxbow, Willoughby Creek, and Minnie Peterson campgrounds. Like Hoh Oxbow, Cottonwood offers the bonus of a boat launch. Its distance from the highway makes it quieter here.

Campsites, facilities: There are nine sites for tents or small trailers. Picnic tables, fire grills, and tent pads are provided. No drinking water is available. Vault toilets and a boat launch are available. Some facilities are wheelchair accessible. Leashed pets are permitted.

Reservations, fees: Reservations are not accepted. There is no fee for camping. Open year-round.

Directions: From Olympia on I-5, take Exit 104 and drive north on U.S. 101 to the Aberdeen/Highway 8 exit. Turn west on Highway 8 and drive 36 miles to Aberdeen. Continue through Aberdeen four miles to U.S. 101. Turn north on U.S. 101 and drive 92 miles to Oil City Road between Mileposts 177 and 178. Turn west on Oil City Road and drive 2.3 miles. Turn left on Road H4060 (gravel) and drive one mile to the camp at the end of the road.

Contact: Department of Natural Resources, Olympic Region, 411 Tillicum Ln., Forks, WA 98331-9797, 360/374-6131, fax 360/374-5446.

39 HOH OXBOW

Rating: 7

On the Hoh River.
Map 1.4, grid b7, page 70

This is the most popular of the five camps on the Hoh River. It's primitive and close to the highway, and the price is right. The adjacent boat launch makes this the camp of choice for anglers, best in fall and winter for salmon and steelhead; check regulations. It is also a popular hunter's camp in the fall. One downer: there is some highway noise within range of the campsites. You can't see the traffic, but you can hear it, which can be irritating for those who want perfect quiet.

Campsites, facilities: There are seven sites for tents or small trailers up to 16 feet. Picnic tables, fire grills, and tent pads are provided. Vault toilets and a hand boat launch are available, but there is no drinking water. Some facilities are wheelchair accessible. Leashed pets are permitted.

Reservations, fees: Reservations are not accepted. There is no fee for camping. Open year-round.

Directions: From Aberdeen, drive north on U.S. 101 for 90 miles to the campground (15 miles south of Forks). Exit between Mileposts 176 and 177 and look for the campground on the right, next to the river.

Contact: Department of Natural Resources, Olympic Region, 411 Tillicum Ln., Forks, WA 98331-9797, 360/374-6131, fax 360/374-5446.

40 WILLOUGHBY CREEK

Rating: 9

In Hoh Clearwater State Forest.

Map 1.4, grid b7, page 70

This little-known camp along Willoughby Creek and the Hoh River is tiny and rustic, with good fishing nearby for steelhead and salmon during peak migrations in season. The area gets heavy rainfall. Other campground options in the vicinity include Hoh Oxbow, Cottonwood, and Minnie Peterson.

Campsites, facilities: There are three campsites for tents or RVs up to 16 feet long. Picnic tables, fire grills, and tent pads are provided. Vault toilets are available, but there is no drinking water. Leashed pets are permitted.

Reservations, fees: Reservations are not accepted. There is no fee for camping. Open year-round.

Directions: From Olympia on I-5, take Exit 104 and drive north on U.S. 101 to the Aberdeen/Highway 8 exit. Turn west on Highway 8 and drive 36 miles to Aberdeen. Continue through Aberdeen four miles to U.S. 101. Turn north on U.S. 101 and drive about 90 miles. Exit between Mileposts 178 and 179. At Hoh Rain Forest Road/Upper Hoh Valley Road, turn east and drive 3.5 miles to the campground on the right.

Contact: Department of Natural Resources, Olympic Region, 411 Tillicum Ln., Forks, WA 98331-9797, 360/374-6131, fax 360/374-5446.

41 MINNIE PETERSON

Rating: 9

On the Hoh River.

Map 1.4, grid b7, page 70

Not many folks know about this primitive camp, set on the Hoh River on the edge of the Hoh Rain Forest. It's quite pretty, forested with Sitka spruce and western hemlock, and offers nice riverside sites. Bring your rain gear.

Campsites, facilities: There are eight campsites for tents or small RVs. Picnic tables, fire grills, and tent pads are provided. Vault toilets are available. No drinking water is available, and discharging firearms is prohibited. Some facilities are wheelchair accessible. Leashed pets are permitted.

Reservations, fees: Reservations are not accepted. There is no fee for camping. Open year-round.

Directions: From Olympia on I-5, take Exit 104 and drive north on U.S. 101 to the Aberdeen/Highway 8 exit. Turn west on Highway 8 and drive 36 miles to Aberdeen. Continue through Aberdeen four miles to U.S. 101. Turn north on U.S. 101 and drive about 90 miles. Exit between Mileposts 178 and 179. At Hoh Rain Forest Road/Upper Hoh Valley Road, turn east and drive 4.5 miles to the campground on the left.

Contact: Department of Natural Resources, Olympic Region, 411 Tillicum Ln., Forks, WA 98331-9797, 360/374-6131, fax 360/374-5446.

42 KALALOCH

Rating: 10

Near the Pacific Ocean in Olympic National Park.

Map 1.4, grid d6, page 70

This camp, located on a bluff above the beach, offers some wonderful ocean-view sites—which explains its popularity. It can fill quickly. Like other camps set on the coast of the Olympic Peninsula, heavy rain in winter and spring is common, and it's often foggy in the summer. A naturalist program is offered in the summer months. There are several good hiking trails in the area; check out the visitors center for maps and information.

Campsites, facilities: There are 175 sites for tents or RVs up to 21 feet long and one group site. Picnic tables and fire grills are provided. Restrooms, drinking water, wheelchair-accessible facilities, and an RV dump station are available. A store and a restaurant are located within one mile. Leashed pets are permitted in the campground.

Reservations, fees: Reservations for the group site only, phone 360/962-2271; individual sites are $12 per night, the group site is $20 per night plus $2 per person, plus a $10 national park entrance fee per vehicle. Senior discount available. Open year-round.

Directions: From Aberdeen, drive north on U.S. 101 for 83 miles to the campground on the left. It is located near the mouth of the Kalaloch River five miles north of the U.S. 101 bridge over the Queets River.

Contact: Olympic National Park, 600 East Park Ave., Port Angeles, WA 98362, 360/565-3130, fax 360/565-3147.

43 COPPERMINE BOTTOM

Rating: 9

On the Clearwater River.

Map 1.4, grid c7, page 70

Few tourists ever visit this primitive, hidden campground set on the Clearwater River, a tributary of the Queets River, which runs to the ocean. The river dory–launching facility is a bonus and makes this a perfect camp for anglers and river runners who want to avoid the usual U.S. 101 crowds. Salmon fishing is popular here during the migratory journey of the anadromous fish. Good news: The access road, once washed out in a flood, is again open.

Campsites, facilities: There are nine campsites for tents or RVs up to 16 feet long. Picnic tables, fire grills, and tent pads are provided. Vault toilets, a group shelter, and a hand boat launch are available, but there is no drinking water. Leashed pets are permitted.

Reservations, fees: Reservations are not accepted. There is no fee for camping. Open year-round.

Directions: From Olympia on I-5, take Exit 104 and drive north on U.S. 101 to the Aberdeen/Highway 8 exit. Turn west on Highway 8 and drive 36 miles to Aberdeen. Continue through Aberdeen four miles to U.S. 101. Turn north on U.S. 101 and drive about 60 miles to Milepost 147. Turn north on Clearwater Mainline Road and drive about 14 miles to C-3000 Road. Turn east on C-3000 Road (a gravel one-lane road) and drive two miles to C-1010 Road. Turn right on C-1010 Road and drive one mile. The camp is on the left.

Contact: Department of Natural Resources, Olympic Region, 411 Tillicum Ln., Forks, WA 98331-9797, 360/374-6131, fax 360/374-5446.

44 UPPER CLEARWATER

Rating: 8

On the Clearwater River.
Map 1.4, grid c7, page 70

One of the three primitive camps set along the Clearwater River, Upper Clearwater is a great camp: It's very pretty, is unused by most tourists, and has a boat ramp and other amenities. Best of all, it's free. Campsites sit amid a forest of western hemlock, red alder, and big leaf maple.

Campsites, facilities: There are seven sites for tents or RVs up to 16 feet long. Picnic tables, fire grills, tent pads, and vault toilets are provided, but there is no drinking water. There are unimproved boat-launching facilities for small crafts, such as river dories, rafts, canoes, and kayaks. Leashed pets are permitted.

Reservations, fees: Reservations are not accepted. There is no fee for camping. Open year-round.

Directions: From Olympia on I-5, take Exit 104 and drive north on U.S. 101 to the Aberdeen/Highway 8 exit. Turn west on Highway 8 and drive 36 miles to Aberdeen. Continue through Aberdeen four miles to U.S. 101. Turn north on U.S. 101 and drive about 60 miles to Milepost 147. Turn north on Hoh Clearwater Mainline Road and drive about 13 miles to C-3000 Road (a gravel one-lane road). Turn right and drive 3.3 miles to the camp entrance on the right.

Contact: Department of Natural Resources, Olympic Region, 411 Tillicum Ln., Forks, WA 98331-9797, 360/374-6131, fax 360/374-5446.

45 PACIFIC BEACH STATE PARK

Rating: 10

On the Pacific Ocean.
Map 1.4, grid g7, page 70

This is the only state park campground in Washington where you can see the ocean from your campsite. Set on just nine acres, within the town of Pacific Beach, it boasts 2,300 feet of beachfront. This spot is great for long beach walks, although it can be windy, especially in the spring and early summer. Because of those winds, this is a great place for kite flying. Clamming (for razor clams) is permitted only in season. Note that rangers advise against swimming or body surfing because of strong riptides. Vehicle traffic is allowed seasonally on the uppermost portions of the beach, but ATVs are not allowed in the park, on the beach, or on sand dunes. This camp is popular and often fills up quickly.

Campsites, facilities: There are 30 developed tent sites, 31 sites with partial hookups (electricity) for RVs up to 50 feet long, and two primitive tent sites. Picnic tables are provided. Restrooms, drinking water, flush toilets, coin-operated showers, an RV dump station, and a picnic area are available. No fires are permitted. Some facilities are wheelchair accessible. Leashed pets are permitted.

Reservations, fees: Reserve at 888/CAMP-OUT (888/226-7688), website: www.parks.wa.gov/reservations ($7 reservation fee). Sites are $16–22 per night, $6 per night for bike-in sites. Senior discount available. Major credit cards accepted. Open year-round.

Directions: From Hoquiam, drive north on State Route 109 for 37 miles to Pacific Beach and the park on the right.

Contact: Pacific Beach State Park, 148 Rte. 115, Hoquiam, WA 98550, 360/276-4297; State Park information, 360/902-8844.

46 DRIFTWOOD ACRES OCEAN CAMPGROUND

Rating: 7

In Copalis Beach.
Map 1.4, grid g7, page 70

Driftwood Acres spreads over some 150 acres and features secluded tent sites and large RV sites. It is located along a tidal river basin, out of the wind. Most find the camp, with its beach access, evergreens, and marked hiking trails, to be family friendly. A bundle of firewood is provided for each night's stay. Clamming is often good in the area. Additional facilities within five miles include an 18-hole golf course and a riding stable.

Campsites, facilities: There are 45 tent sites and 17 sites with partial hookups (water and electricity) for RVs of any length. Picnic tables and fire pits are provided. Restrooms, drinking water, flush toilets, coin-operated showers, a free bundle of firewood, a recreation hall, and an RV dump station are available. A clam-cleaning station is nearby. Bottled gas, a store, a café, and ice are located within one mile. Leashed pets are permitted, but no Rottweilers, pitbulls, Dobermans, or aggressive dogs of any type.

Reservations, fees: Reservations accepted. Sites are $25 per night in summer, $15 per night in winter, $5 per person for more than two adults and two children, and $5 per extra vehicle per night. Open year-round.

Directions: From Hoquiam, drive west on State Route 109 for 21 miles to Copalis Beach. Continue one-half mile north to the camp on the left, between Mileposts 21 and 22.

Contact: Driftwood Acres Ocean Campground, P.O. Box 216, 3209 Rte. 109, Copalis Beach, WA 98535, 360/289-3484.

47 SURF AND SAND RV PARK, COPALIS BEACH

Rating: 5

In Copalis Beach.
Map 1.4, grid h7, page 70

Although not particularly scenic, this five-acre park is a decent layover for an RV vacation and will do the job if you're tired and ready to get off U.S. 101. It does have beach access, possible with a 15-minute walk, but as of spring 2002, the creek had washed out the nearby road to the ocean, so check for status. The surrounding terrain is flat and grassy.

Campsites, facilities: There are 50 sites with full or partial hookups, including 20 drive-through, for RVs of any length and 16 tent sites. Picnic tables and fire grills are provided. Restrooms, drinking water, flush toilets, showers, cable TV hookups, a coin-operated laundry, a café, a recreation room with kitchen facilities, and ice are available. Bottled gas is available within one mile. Leashed pets are permitted.

Reservations, fees: Reservations accepted. Sites are $15–32, $4 per extra vehicle per night. Major credit cards accepted. Open year-round.

Directions: From Hoquiam, drive west on State Route 109 for 21 miles to Copalis Beach and Heath Road. Turn left (west) on Heath Road and drive two-tenths of a mile to the campground.

Contact: Surf and Sand RV Park, Copalis Beach, P.O. Box 208, No. 8 McCullough, Copalis Beach, WA 98535, 360/289-2707.

48 RIVERSIDE RV RESORT

Rating: 8

Near Copalis Beach.
Map 1.4, grid h7, page 70

River access is a bonus at this nice and clean six-acre park. Most sites have a river view. Salmon fishing can be good in the Copalis River, and a boat ramp is available nearby for anglers. Other options include swimming and beachcombing.

Campsites, facilities: There are 53 sites with full hookups, including 20 drive-through, for RVs of any length and 15 tent sites. Picnic tables and fire grills are provided. Restrooms, drinking water, flush toilets, showers, an RV dump station, a hot tub, firewood, and a recreation hall are available. A café is located within one mile. A boat dock and launching facilities are nearby. Leashed pets are permitted.

Reservations, fees: Reservations accepted. $15 per night for tent sites; $20 per night for RV sites; $2 per person per night for more than two people. Senior discount available. Major credit cards accepted. Open year-round.

Directions: From Hoquiam, drive west on State Route 109 for 22 miles to Copalis Beach. The park is off the highway on the left.

Contact: Riverside RV Resort, P.O. Box 307, No. 11 Condra Rd., Copalis Beach, WA 98535, 360/289-2111, website: www.riversidervresort.net.

49 TIDELANDS RESORT

Rating: 7

Near Copalis Beach.
Map 1.4, grid h7, page 70
This flat, wooded campground covers 47 acres and provides beach access and a great ocean view. It's primarily an RV park, and the sites are pleasant and grassy. Ten sites are set on sand dunes, while the remainder are in a wooded area. In the spring, azaleas and wildflowers abound. Horseshoe pits and a sports field offer recreation possibilities. Though more remote than at the other area sites, clamming is an option in season. Various festivals are held in the area from spring through fall. Remodeling is scheduled for 2002.

Campsites, facilities: There are 100 tent sites, 55 with full or partial hookups, including some drive-through, for RVs of any length, one three-bedroom trailer, and three two-bedroom cabins. Picnic tables and fire rings are provided. Restrooms, drinking water, flush toilets, coin-operated showers, an RV dump station, firewood, ice, cable TV, and a playground are available. Boat docks and a café are located within one mile. A golf course is located nearby. A casino and horseback riding are within five miles. Leashed pets are permitted.

Reservations, fees: Reservations accepted. Sites are $14–20 per night. Senior discount available. Major credit cards accepted. Open year-round.

Directions: From Hoquiam, drive west on State Route 109 for about 20 miles to the campground on the left. It is located between Mileposts 20 and 21, about one mile south of Copalis Beach.

Contact: Tidelands Resort, P.O. Box 36, Copalis Beach, WA 98535, 360/289-8963, website: www.tidelandsresort.com.

50 OCEAN MIST RESORT

Rating: 9

On Conners Creek.
Map 1.4, grid h7, page 70
Always call to determine whether space is available before planning a stay here. This is a membership resort RV campground, and members always come first. If space is available, they will rent sites to the public. Surf fishing is popular in the nearby Pacific Ocean, while the Capellis River offers salmon fishing and canoeing opportunities. It's about a one-block walk to the beach. There's a golf course within five miles.

Campsites, facilities: There are 120 sites, most with full hookups, for RVs, an area for dispersed camping for up to 20 tents, and three RVs. Picnic tables are provided. Restrooms, drinking water, flush toilets, showers, cable TV, an RV dump station, two community fire pits, a hot tub, and a coin-operated laundry are available. A grocery store is within one mile in Ocean City. Leashed pets are permitted.

Reservations, fees: Reservations required in the summer; phone 360/289-3656 or fax 360/289-2807. Sites are $20–30 per night, trailers are $60 per night. Major credit cards accepted. Open year-round.

Directions: From Hoquiam, drive west on State Route 109 for 19 miles to the campground on the left (one mile north of Ocean City)

Contact: Ocean Mist Resort, 2781 Rte. 109, Ocean City, WA 98569, 360/289-3656, fax 360/289-2807.

51 OCEAN CITY STATE PARK

Rating: 9

Near Hoquiam.

Map 1.4, grid h7, page 70

This 170-acre oceanfront camp, an excellent example of coastal wetlands and dune succession, features ocean beach, dunes, and dense thickets of pine surrounding freshwater marshes. The Ocean Shores Interpretive Center is located on the south end of Ocean Shores near the marina (open summer season only). This area is part of the Pacific Flyway, and the migratory route for gray whales and other marine mammals lies just offshore. Spring wildflowers are excellent and include lupine, buttercups, and wild strawberry. This is also a good area for surfing and kite flying, with springs typically windy. Beachcombing, clamming, and fishing are possibilities at this park. An 18-hole golf course is nearby.

Campsites, facilities: There are 149 standard sites for tents or RVs, 29 sites with full hookups, including some drive-through, for RVs up to 55 feet long, and three primitive tent sites. Picnic tables and fire rings are provided. Restrooms, drinking water, flush toilets, showers, an RV dump station, a sheltered picnic area, and firewood are available. Some facilities are wheelchair accessible. Leashed pets are permitted.

Reservations, fees: Reserve at 888/226-7688 (CAMP-OUT), website: www.parks.wa.gov/reservations ($7 reservation fee). Sites are $6–22 per night. Senior discount available. Open year-round.

Directions: From Hoquiam, drive northwest on State Route 109 for 16 miles to State Route 115. Turn left and drive 1.2 miles south to the park on the right (1.5 miles north of Ocean Shores).

Contact: Ocean City State Park, 148 Rte. 115, Hoquiam, WA 98550, 360/289-3553; State Park information, 360/902-8844.

52 SOUTH FORK HOH

Rating: 10

In Hoh Clearwater State Forest.

Map 1.5, grid b1, page 71

This rarely used, beautiful camp set along the cascading South Fork of the Hoh River is way out there. It's tiny and primitive but offers a guarantee of peace and quiet, something many U.S. 101 cruisers would cheerfully give a limb for after a few days of fighting crowds. Fishing for steelhead can be excellent; check regulations.

Campsites, facilities: There are three campsites for tents or small RVs. Picnic tables, fire grills, vault toilets, and tent pads are provided. No drinking water is available. Leashed pets are permitted.

Reservations, fees: Reservations are not accepted. There is no fee for camping. Open year-round.

Directions: From Olympia on I-5, take Exit 104 and drive north on U.S. 101 to the Aberdeen/Highway 8 exit. Turn west on Highway 8 and drive 36 miles to Aberdeen. Continue through Aberdeen four miles to U.S. 101. Turn north on U.S. 101 and drive about 94 miles. Exit at Milepost 176. At Hoh Mainline Road turn east and drive 6.5 miles. Turn left on Road H1000 and drive 7.5 miles to the campground on the right. Obtaining a Department of Natural Resources (DNR) map is advised.

Contact: Department of Natural Resources, Olympic Region, 411 Tillicum Ln., Forks, WA 98331-9797, 360/374-6131, fax 360/374-5446.

53 HOH

Rating: 10

In Olympic National Park.

Map 1.5, grid b1, page 71

This camp at a trailhead leading into the interior of Olympic National Park is located in the beautiful heart of a temperate, old-growth rainforest. Hoh Oxbow, Cottonwood, Willough-by Creek, and Minnie Peterson campgrounds are nearby, set downstream on the Hoh River, outside national park boundaries. In the summer, there are naturalist programs, and a visitors center is nearby. This is one of the most popular camps in the park. The elevation is 578 feet.

Campsites, facilities: There are 88 sites for tents or RVs up to 21 feet long. Picnic tables and fire grills are provided. Restrooms and drinking water are available, and an RV dump station is available nearby. Some facilities are wheelchair accessible. Leashed pets are permitted.

Reservations, fees: Reservations are not accepted. Sites are $10 per night, plus a $10 national park entrance fee per vehicle. Senior discount available. Open year-round.

Directions: From Aberdeen, drive north on U.S. 101 for about 90 miles to Milepost 176. Turn east on Hoh River Road and drive 19 miles to the campground on the right (near the end of the road).

Contact: Olympic National Park, 600 East Park Ave., Port Angeles, WA 98362, 360/565-3130, fax 360/565-3147.

54 SOL DUC

Rating: 10

On the Sol Duc River in Olympic National Park.
Map 1.5, grid a2, page 71

This site is a nice hideaway, with nearby Sol Duc Hot Springs a highlight. The problem is that this camp is very popular. It fills up quickly on weekends, and a fee is charged to use the hot springs, which have been fully developed since the early 1900s. The camp is set at 1,680 feet along the Sol Duc River. A naturalist program is available in the summer.

Campsites, facilities: There are 82 sites for tents or RVs up to 21 feet long, and one group site. Picnic tables and fire grills are provided. Restrooms and drinking water are available. Some

facilities are wheelchair accessible. An RV dump station is available nearby, and a store and a café are within one mile. Leashed pets are permitted.

Reservations, fees: Reservations for the group site only, phone 360/327-3534 from April 16 through October 31, phone 360/928-3380 from November 1 through April 15. Individual sites are $12 per night, group sites are $20 per night and $1 per person, plus a $10 national park entrance fee per vehicle. Senior discount available. Open from May–late October, with limited winter facilities.

Directions: From I-5 at Olympia, turn north on U.S. 101 and drive about 122 miles to Port Angeles. Continue on U.S. 101 past Port Angeles for 27 miles, just past Lake Crescent. Turn left at the Sol Duc turnoff and drive 12 miles to the camp.

Contact: Olympic National Park, 600 East Park Ave., Port Angeles, WA 98362, 360/565-3130, fax 360/565-3147.

55 DEER PARK

Rating: 9

Near Blue Mountain in Olympic National Park.
Map 1.5, grid a7, page 71

This camp is set in the Olympic Peninsula's high country at an elevation of 5,400 feet, just below 6,000-foot Blue Mountain. There are numerous trails in the area, including a major trailhead into the backcountry of Olympic National Park and the Buckhorn Wilderness.

Campsites, facilities: There are 14 tent sites. Picnic tables and fire grills are provided. Vault toilets and drinking water are available. Leashed pets are permitted.

Reservations, fees: Reservations are not accepted. Sites are $8 per night, $10 per vehicle park entrance fee. Senior discount available. Open mid-June–late September, with limited winter facilities.

Directions: From Port Angeles, drive east on

U.S. 101 for about five miles to Deer Park Road. Turn south and drive 18 miles to the campground at the end of the road. Note that the last six miles are gravel, steep and narrow, closed to RVs and trailers, and often closed to all vehicles in winter.

Contact: Olympic National Park, 600 East Park Ave., Port Angeles, WA 98362, 360/565-3132, fax 360/565-3147.

56 DUNGENESS FORKS

Rating: 7

On the Dungeness and Gray Wolf Rivers in Olympic National Forest.

Map 1.5, grid a8, page 71

This pretty, wooded spot is nestled at the confluence of the Dungeness and Gray Wolf Rivers at an elevation of 1,000 feet. It offers seclusion, yet easy access from the highway. The campsites are set in forest. If you want quiet, you'll often find it here. The Upper Dungeness Trailhead, located about seven miles south of camp, provides access to Buckhorn Wilderness and Olympic National Park. The trailhead for the Gray Wolf Trail is four miles from camp, but note that portions of this trail are closed due to slides; check with rangers before embarking on a long trip. The Gray Wolf River is closed to fishing year-around to protect salmon.

Campsites, facilities: There are 10 tent sites. Picnic tables and fire rings are provided. Drinking water and vault toilets are available. Garbage must be packed out. Leashed pets are permitted.

Reservations, fees: Reservations are not accepted. Sites are $10 per night. Open May–September.

Directions: From Olympia on I-5 at, turn north on U.S. 101 and drive approximately 100 miles to Palo Alto Road, located 1.5 miles north of Sequim Bay State Park and 3 miles southeast of Sequim. Turn left (south) on Palo Alto Road and drive about seven miles to Forest Road 2880. Turn right (west) and drive one mile

(after crossing Dungeness River Bridge) to the campground on the right. Obtaining a U.S. Forest Service map is advised. Trailers and RVs are not recommended because of the steep, narrow, and unpaved access road.

Contact: Olympic National Forest, Quilcene Ranger District, P.O. Box 280, Quilcene, WA 98376, 360/765-2200, fax 360/765-2202.

57 DOSEWALLIPS

Rating: 7

On the Dosewallips River in Olympic National Park.

Map 1.5, grid c7, page 71

This park was closed to vehicles due to a road washout. It is expected to reopen in 2003 or 2004. The washout occurred at Milepost 10, where you can still get to the campground on foot or mountain bike, but it requires a six-mile hike or bike ride. Dosewallips is a more remote option to Elkhorn and Collins. Set on the Dosewallips River at an elevation of 1,500 feet, the camp provides a major trailhead into the backcountry of Olympic National Park. The trail follows the Dosewallips River over Anderson Pass, proceeds along the Quinault River, and ultimately reaches Quinault Lake. Note that as of spring 2002, this trail was not accessible to Quinault Lake because of a bridge closure; check the status before departing. Other hiking trails are available nearby.

Campsites, facilities: There are 30 tent sites. Picnic tables and fire grills are provided. Restrooms, drinking water, and flush toilets are available. Some facilities are wheelchair accessible. Leashed pets are permitted.

Reservations, fees: Reservations are not accepted. Sites are $10 per night, $10 park entrance fee. Senior discount available. Open mid-May–late September.

Directions: From Olympia on I-5, drive north on U.S. 101 for 60 miles to a signed turnoff near Brinnon (located about one mile north of Dosewallips State Park) for Forest Road 2610 (County Road 2500). Turn west and drive 15 miles along the Dosewallips River to the camp at the end of the road. Note that the access road is not paved and is not recommended for RVs or trailers.

Contact: Olympic National Park, 600 East Park Ave., Port Angeles, WA 98362, 360/565-3132, fax 360/565-3147.

58 ELKHORN

Rating: 8

On the Dosewallips River in Olympic National Forest.

Map 1.5, grid c8, page 71

This eight-acre, wooded camp is set on the Dosewallips River at 600 feet elevation and has river access. Some campsites lie along the north bank of the river. The surrounding landscape features old-growth forest, with deer and a variety of birds often spotted. It's not far from Olympic National Park, which makes a good side trip. Note that this park was closed to vehicles due to a road washout. It is expected to reopen in 2003 or 2004. The washout occurred at Milepost 10, where you can still get past on foot or mountain bike, requiring a one-mile hike or bike ride to reach the campground.

Campsites, facilities: There are 20 sites for tents or RVs up to 21 feet long. Picnic tables and fire pits are provided. Drinking water and vault toilets are available. Leashed pets are permitted.

Reservations, fees: Reservations are not accepted. Sites are $10 per night. Senior discount available. Open mid-May–September.

Directions: From Olympia on I-5, drive north on U.S. 101 for 60 miles to a signed turnoff near Brinnon (about one mile north of Dosewallips State Park) for Forest Road 2610 (County Road 2500). Turn west and drive 10 miles along the Dosewallips River. Look for the camp on the left. Note that the last four miles of the road have a lot of potholes.

Contact: Olympic National Forest, Quilcene Ranger District, P.O. Box 280, Quilcene, WA 98376, 360/765-2200, fax 360/765-2202.

59 COLLINS

Rating: 7

On the Duckabush River in Olympic National Forest.

Map 1.5, grid c8, page 71

Most vacationers cruising U.S. 101 don't have a clue about this quiet spot set on a great launch point for adventure, yet it's only five or six miles from the highway. This four-acre camp is located on the Duckabush River at 200 feet elevation. It has small, shaded sites, river access nearby, and plenty of fishing and hiking; check fishing regulations. Just one mile from camp is the Duckabush Trail, which connects to trails in Olympic National Park. The Murhut Falls Trail starts about three miles from the campground, providing access to a 0.8-mile trail to the falls. It's a 1.5-mile drive to nearby Dosewallips State Park and a 30- to 35-minute drive to Olympic National Park.

Campsites, facilities: There are six tent sites and nine sites for RVs up to 21 feet long. Picnic tables and fire rings are provided. No drinking water. Vault toilets are available. Some facilities are wheelchair accessible. Leashed pets are permitted.

Reservations, fees: Reservations are not accepted. Sites are $10 per night. Senior discount available. Open mid-May–September.

Directions: From Olympia on I-5, drive north on U.S. 101 for 59 miles to Forest Road 2510 (near Duckabush). Turn left on Forest Road 2510 and drive five miles west to the camp on the left.

Contact: Olympic National Forest, Hood Canal Ranger District, Hoodsport Office, P.O. Box 68, Hoodsport, WA 98548, 360/877-5254.

60 LENA LAKE HIKE-IN

Rating: 8

Near the Hamma Hamma River in Olympic National Forest.

Map 1.5, grid c7, page 71

Lena Lake is one of the most popular lakes on the Olympic Peninsula. Though comparatively crowded in the summer, you can usually get a site. The 55-acre lake is nestled along the Hamma Hamma drainage, between rugged peaks and adjacent to the Brothers Wilderness. It takes a three-mile hike-in from the trailhead at Lena Creek to reach this camp. This adventure is suitable for the entire family—an outstanding way to turn youngsters onto backpacking. It's a lovely setting, too, with a pleasantly mild climate in summer. The lake is good for swimming and fishing for rainbow trout. The elevation is 1,800 feet.

Campsites, facilities: There are 29 primitive sites at this hike-in campground. There is no drinking water. Vault toilets are available. Leashed pets are permitted.

Reservations, fees: Reservations are not accepted. There is no fee for camping, but you must obtain a $30 annual Trail Park Pass or pay $3 per day to park at the trailhead. Open year-round, weather permitting.

Directions: From Olympia on I-5, turn north on U.S. 101 and drive about 37 miles to Hoodsport. Continue north on U.S. 101 from 14 miles to Forest Road 25. Turn west on Forest Road 25 and drive eight miles to the Lena Creek Camp and the trailhead. Hike 3.2 miles north to Lena Lake. Campsites are scattered around the lake.

Contact: Olympic National Forest, Hood Canal Ranger District, P.O. Box 68, Hoodsport, WA 98548, 360/877-5254, fax 360/352-2569.

61 LENA CREEK

Rating: 7

On the Hamma Hamma River in Olympic National Forest.

Map 1.5, grid d7, page 71

This seven-acre camp, set amid both conifers and hardwoods, is located where Lena Creek empties into the Hamma Hamma River. A popular trailhead camp, Lena Creek features a three-mile trail from camp to Lena Lake, with four additional miles to Upper Lena Lake. A map of Olympic National Forest details the trail and road system. The camp is rustic with some improvements.

Campsites, facilities: There are 14 sites for tents or RVs up to 21 feet long. Picnic tables and fire rings are provided. No drinking water. Vault toilets are available. Some facilities are wheelchair accessible. Leashed pets are permitted.

Reservations, fees: Reservations are not accepted. Sites are $10 per night. Senior discount available. Open mid-May–September.

Directions: From Olympia on I-5, turn north on U.S. 101 and drive about 37 miles to Hoodsport. Continue north on U.S. 101 for 14 miles to Forest Road 25. Turn west on Forest Road 25 and drive eight miles to the camp on the left.

Contact: Olympic National Forest, Hood Canal Ranger District, Hoodsport office, P.O. Box 68, Hoodsport, WA 98548, 360/877-5254, fax 360/352-2569.

62 HAMMA HAMMA

Rating: 7

On the Hamma Hamma River in Olympic National Forest.

Map 1.5, grid d7, page 71

This camp is set on the Hamma Hamma River at an elevation of 600 feet. It's small and primitive, but it can be preferable to some of the developed camps on the U.S. 101 circuit. The Civilian Conservation Corps is memorialized in a wheelchair-accessible interpretive trail that begins in the campground and leads one-quarter mile along the river. The camps are set among conifers and hardwoods.

Campsites, facilities: There are three tent sites and 12 sites for RVs up to 21 feet long. Picnic tables and fire rings are provided. Hand-pumped water and vault toilets are available. Some facilities are wheelchair accessible. Leashed pets are permitted.

Reservations, fees: Reservations are not accepted. Sites are $10 per night. Senior discount available. Open May–September.

Directions: From Olympia on I-5, turn north on U.S. 101 and drive 37 miles to Hoodsport. Continue on U.S. 101 for 14 miles north to Forest Road 25. Turn left on Forest Road 25 and drive 6.5 miles to the camp on the left side of the road.

Contact: Olympic National Forest, Hood Canal Ranger District, Hoodsport Office, P.O. Box 68, Hoodsport, WA 98548, 360/877-5254, fax 360/352-2569.

63 QUEETS

Rating: 6

On the Queets River in Olympic National Park.

Map 1.5, grid c1, page 71

This primitive camp on the shore of the Queets River is a gem if you don't mind bringing your own water or purifying river water. A trailhead leads into the interior of Olympic National Park. The elevation is 290 feet.

Campsites, facilities: There are 20 primitive tent sites. Picnic tables and fire grills are provided. Toilets are available, but there is no drinking water. Some facilities are wheelchair accessible. Leashed pets are permitted.

Reservations, fees: Reservations are not accepted. Sites are $8 per night, plus a $10 national park entrance fee per vehicle. Senior discount available. Open year-round.

Directions: From Aberdeen, drive north on

U.S. 101 for 38 miles to Lake Quinault, and continue for 19 miles to a signed turnoff for the campground. Turn right (northeast) on an unpaved road and drive 14 miles along the Queets River. The campground is at the end of the unpaved road, which is not recommended for RVs or trailers.

Contact: Olympic National Park, 600 East Park Ave., Port Angeles, WA 98362, 360/565-3130, fax 360/565-3147.

64 WILLABY

Rating: 8

On Lake Quinault in Olympic National Forest.

Map 1.5, grid e2, page 71

This pretty, 14-acre wooded camp is set on the shore of Lake Quinault at 200 feet elevation, adjacent to where Willaby Creek empties into the lake. Part of the Quinault Indian Reservation, the lake is closed to fishing. The campsites vary, with some open and featuring lake views, while others are more private, with no views. The tree cover consists of Douglas fir, western red cedar, western hemlock, and big leaf maple. The forest floor is covered with wall-to-wall greenery, with exceptional moss growth. The Quinault Rain Forest Nature Trail and the Quinault National Recreation Trail System are nearby. Lake Quinault covers about six square miles. This camp is concessionaire operated.

Campsites, facilities: There are 22 drive-in sites for tents or RVs up to 16 feet long. Picnic tables and fire pits are provided. Drinking water, flush toilets, and electricity in the restrooms are available. Some facilities are wheelchair accessible. Launching facilities and rentals are available at nearby Lake Quinault. Leashed pets are permitted.

Reservations, fees: Reservations are not accepted. Sites are $14 per night. Senior discount available. Open from Memorial Day weekend through September.

Directions: From Olympia on I-5, take Exit 104 and drive north on U.S. 101 to the Aberdeen/Highway 8 exit. Turn west on Highway 8 and drive 36 miles to Aberdeen. Continue through Aberdeen four miles to U.S. 101. Turn north on U.S. 101 and drive about 45 miles to the Lake Quinault turnoff and South Shore Road. Turn northeast on South Shore Road and drive 1.5 miles to the camp set on the southern shore of the lake.

Contact: Olympic National Forest, Pacific Ranger District, Quinault Office, P.O. Box 9, Quinault, WA 98575, 360/288-2525, fax 360/352-2676.

65 FALLS CREEK

Rating: 8

On Lake Quinault in Olympic National Forest.

Map 1.5, grid e2, page 71

This scenic, wooded three-acre camp is set where Falls Creek empties into Quinault Lake. A canopy of lush big leaf maple hangs over the campground. The campsites feature both drive-in and walk-in sites, with the latter requiring about a 125-yard walk. The Quinault Rain Forest Nature Trail and Quinault National Recreation Trail System are nearby. The camp is located adjacent to the Quinault Ranger Station and historic Lake Quinault Lodge at an elevation of 200 feet.

Campsites, facilities: There are 11 tent sites and 20 sites for RVs up to 16 feet long. Picnic tables and fire pits are provided. Drinking water, flush toilets, and electricity in the restrooms are available. A camp host has firewood for sale nearby. Some facilities are wheelchair accessible. Four picnic sites are available nearby. Launching facilities and boat rentals are available at Lake Quinault. Leashed pets are permitted.

Reservations, fees: Reservations are not accepted. Sites are $14 per night. Senior discount available. Open Memorial Day through Labor Day.

Directions: From Aberdeen, drive north on U.S. 101 for 38 miles to Quinault and South Shore Road. Turn right (northeast) and drive 2.5 miles to the camp on the southeast shore of Lake Quinault.

Contact: Olympic National Forest, Pacific Ranger District, Quinault Office, P.O. Box 9, Quinault, WA 98575, 360/288-2525, fax 360/352-2676.

66 GATTON CREEK WALK-IN

Rating: 9

On Lake Quinault in Olympic National Forest.

Map 1.5, grid e2, page 71

This five-acre wooded camp is set on the shore of Lake Quinault (elevation 200 feet), where Gatton Creek empties into it. Reaching the campsites requires about a 100-yard walk from the parking area. The camp features great views across the lake to the forested slopes of Olympic National Park. The lake is part of the Quinault Indian Nation, which has jurisdiction here. Rules allow a 24-mph speed limit on the lake, but no towing and no personal watercraft. Salmon fishing is catch-and-release only, and fishing opportunities can vary from year to year; always check regulations. Lake Quinault covers about six square miles. The Quinault Rain Forest Nature Trail and the Quinault National Recreation Trail System are nearby. About nine miles of loop trails are accessible here. This camp, like the others on the lake, is concessionaire operated.

Campsites, facilities: There are seven walk-in tent sites and eight overflow RV sites (in a parking area). Picnic tables and fire pits are provided. Pit toilets, firewood, and a picnic area are available. Some facilities are wheelchair accessible. Leashed pets are permitted.

Reservations, fees: Reservations are not accepted. Sites are $11 per night. There is no charge for picnicking. Open May–September.

Directions: From Aberdeen, drive north on U.S. 101 for 38 miles to the Lake Quinault turnoff and South Shore Road. Turn right (northeast) and drive 3.5 miles to the camp on the southeast shore of Lake Quinault.

Contact: Olympic National Forest, Pacific Ranger District, Quinault Office, P.O. Box 9, Quinault, WA 98575, 360/288-2525, fax 360/352-2676.

67 CAMPBELL TREE GROVE

Rating: 8

On the Humptulips River in Olympic National Forest.

Map 1.5, grid e3, page 71

This 14-acre camp is set amid dense, old-growth forest featuring stands of both conifers and hardwoods, with licorice ferns growing on the trunks and branches of the big leaf maples. The camp is a favorite for hikers, with trailheads nearby that provide access to the Colonel Bob Wilderness. One of the best, the 3,400-foot climb to the Colonel Bob Summit provides a four-mile round-trip accessible from camp, much of it a great butt kicker. The West Fork of the Humptulips River runs near the camp, and the Humptulips Trail provides access. Fishing is an option here as well; check state regulations.

Campsites, facilities: There are eight tent sites and three sites for RVs up to 16 feet long. Picnic tables are provided. Vault toilets and drinking water (well water) are available. Some facilities are wheelchair accessible. Leashed pets are permitted.

Reservations, fees: Reservations are not accepted. There is no fee for camping. The campground is open June–October.

Directions: From Aberdeen, drive north on U.S. 101 for 22 miles to Humptulips and continue for another five miles to Forest Road 22 (Donkey Creek Road). Turn right and drive eight miles to Forest Road 2204. Turn left (north) and drive 17 miles to the campground.

Contact: Olympic National Forest, Pacific Ranger District, Quinault Office, P.O. Box 9, Quinault, WA 98575, 360/288-2525, fax 360/352-2676.

68 GRAVES CREEK

Rating: 6

Near the Quinault River in Olympic National Park.

Map 1.5, grid d4, page 71

The road providing access to this campground was reopened in the summer of 2002. Drinking water is expected to be available again in 2003. This camp, located at an elevation of 540 feet, sits a short distance from a trailhead leading into the backcountry of Olympic National Park. See an Olympic National Park and U.S. Forest Service map for details. The East Fork Quinault River is nearby, and there are lakes in the area.

Campsites, facilities: There are 30 sites for tents or RVs up to 21 feet long. Picnic tables, fire grills, drinking water (confirm if critical to your trip), and restrooms are available. Some facilities are wheelchair accessible. Leashed pets are permitted.

Reservations, fees: Reservations are not accepted. There is a $10 per-night fee, plus a $10 national park entrance fee per vehicle. Senior discount available. Camp opening pending repairs to bridge on access road.

Directions: From Aberdeen, drive north on U.S. 101 for 38 miles to the Lake Quinault turnoff and South Shore Road. Turn east on South Shore Road and drive 15 miles (the road becomes unpaved) to the campground at the end of the road. The Graves Creek Ranger Station is located nearby.

Contact: Olympic National Park, 600 East Park Ave., Port Angeles, WA 98362, 360/565-3130, fax 360/565-3147.

69 STAIRCASE

Rating: 9

On the North Fork of the Skokomish River in Olympic National Park.

Map 1.5, grid d6, page 71

This camp is located near the Staircase Rapids

of the North Fork of the Skokomish River, about one mile from where it empties into Lake Cushman. The elevation is 765 feet. A major trailhead at the camp leads to the backcountry of Olympic National Park, and other trails are nearby. See an Olympic National Park and U.S. Forest Service map for details. A beautiful two-mile loop trail running along the river is closed as of spring 2002 due to a bridge closure. Call before planning this hike. Other trails are accessible nearby. Stock facilities are also available nearby.

Campsites, facilities: There are 56 sites for tents or RVs up to 21 feet long. Picnic tables and fire grills are provided. Restrooms and drinking water are available. Some facilities are wheelchair accessible. Leashed pets are permitted in camp.

Reservations, fees: Reservations are not accepted. There is a $10 per-night fee, plus a $10 national park entrance fee per vehicle. Senior discount available. Open year-round.

Directions: From Olympia on I-5, take U.S. 101 and drive north about 37 miles to the town of Hoodsport and Lake Cushman Road (County Road 119). Turn left (west) and drive 17 miles to the camp at the end of the road (set about one mile above the inlet of Lake Cushman). The last several miles of the road are unpaved.

Contact: Olympic National Park, 600 East Park Ave., Port Angeles, WA 98362, 360/565-3130, fax 360/565-3147.

70 LILLIWAUP CREEK

Rating: 7

On Lilliwaup Creek in Bert Cole State Forest.

Map 1.5, grid d7, page 71

This camp is set along Lilliwaup Creek, a quiet and primitive setting. Fishing for trout is available here, as well as at nearby Lake Cushman, Melbourne, and Prices lakes.

Campsites, facilities: There are 13 sites for tents

or small trailers. Picnic tables, fire grills, vault toilets, and tent pads are provided. No drinking water is available. Garbage must be packed out. Leashed pets are permitted.

Reservations, fees: Reservations are not accepted. There is no fee for camping. Open mid-April–October

Directions: From Olympia on I-5, turn north on U.S. 101 and drive 41 miles to Lilliwaup (four miles north of Hoodsport). Continue north on U.S. 101 for seven miles to Jorsted Creek Road (Forest Road 24). Turn left and drive 1.5 miles to a fork. Bear left at the fork (still Forest Road 24) and drive five miles to the camp.

Contact: Department of Natural Resources, South Puget Sound Region, 950 Farman Ave. N, Enumclaw, WA 98022, 360/825-1631, fax 360/825-1672.

71 MELBOURNE

Rating: 7

On Melbourne Lake in Hood Canal State Forest.

Map 1.5, grid d7, page 71

This primitive camp is on Melbourne Lake at about 1,000 feet in a little-known, rustic setting. Melbourne Lake, a small, lesser-known lake on the southeast flank of the Olympic Mountains in Hood Canal State Forest, provides bass and trout fishing. If you want quiet, and don't mind a lack of facilities, this is a good drive-to option.

Campsites, facilities: There are five sites for tents or small RVs. Picnic tables, fire grills, vault toilets, and tent pads are provided. No drinking water is available. Garbage must be packed out. Leashed pets are permitted.

Reservations, fees: Reservations are not accepted. There is no fee for camping. Open mid-April–September.

Directions: From Olympia on I-5, turn north on U.S. 101 and drive 41 miles to Lilliwaup (four miles north of Hoodsport). Continue north on U.S. 101 for seven miles to Jorsted Creek Road (Forest Road 24). Turn left and drive 1.5 miles to a fork. Bear left at the fork (still Forest Road 24) and drive four miles to a gravel road. Turn left on the gravel road and drive 1.7 miles to a T intersection. Turn left, and drive one mile to the camp at Melbourne Lake.

Contact: Department of Natural Resources, South Puget Sound Region, 950 Farman Ave. N, Enumclaw, WA 98022, 360/825-1631, fax 360/825-1672.

72 LAKE CUSHMAN STATE PARK

Rating: 10

On Lake Cushman.

Map 1.5, grid e7, page 71

Set in the foothills of the Olympic Mountains on the shore of Lake Cushman, this state park features a 10-mile-long blue-water mountain lake, eight miles of park shoreline, forested hillsides, and awesome views of snowcapped peaks. Beach access and good trout fishing are other highlights. The park has eight miles of hiking trails and five miles of bike trails. In fall, mushrooming is popular. Windsurfing, water-skiing, and swimming are all popular here. An 18-hole golf course is nearby.

Campsites, facilities: There are 50 tent sites, 30 with full hookups for RVs up to 60 feet long, and two primitive sites. Picnic tables and fire grills are provided. Restrooms, drinking water, flush toilets, showers, a picnic area, an amphitheater, horseshoe pits, volleyball, and firewood are available. A store, a restaurant, and ice are available within one mile. Boat docks and launching facilities are located at nearby Lake Cushman. Leashed pets are permitted.

Reservations, fees: Reserve at 888/CAMP-OUT (888/226-7688), website: www.parks.wa.gov/reservations ($7 reservation fee). Sites are $16–22 per night, $6 per extra vehicle per night. Senior discount available. Major credit cards accepted. Open April–October.

Directions: From Olympia on I-5, take the U.S. 101 exit and drive north 37 miles to Hoodsport and Highway 119 (Lake Cushman Road). Turn left (west) on Lake Cushman Road and drive seven miles to the park on the left.

Contact: Lake Cushman State Park, 360/877-5491; State Park information, 360/902-8844.

73 BIG CREEK

Rating: 7

Near Lake Cushman in Olympic National Forest.

Map 1.5, grid e7, page 71

Big Creek is an alternative to Staircase camp on the North Fork of Skokomish River and Lake Cushman State Park on Lake Cushman, both of which get heavier use. The sites here are large and well spaced for privacy over 30 acres, primarily of second-growth forest. Big Creek runs adjacent to the campground. A four-mile loop trail extends from camp and connects to the Mt. Eleanor Trail. A bonus: two walk-in sites (quarter-mile walk), which are located along the creek.

Campsites, facilities: There are 23 sites for tents or RVs up to 30 feet long, and two walk-in sites (requiring a quarter-mile walk). Picnic tables and fire grills are provided. Drinking water, vault toilets, and sheltered picnic tables are available. A boat dock and ramp are located at nearby Lake Cushman. Leashed pets are permitted.

Reservations, fees: Reservations are not accepted. Sites are $10 per night. Senior discount available. Open May–September.

Directions: From Olympia on I-5, take Exit 104 for U.S. 101/Highway 8. Drive north on U.S. 101 for 37 miles to Hoodsport and Lake Cushman Road (Highway 119). Turn left on Lake Cushman Road and drive nine miles (two miles north of Lake Cushman State Park) to the T intersection. Turn left and the campground is on the right.

Contact: Olympic National Forest, Hood Canal

Ranger District, Hoodsport Office, P.O. Box 68, Hoodsport, WA 94548, 360/877-5254, fax 360/352-2569.

74 COHO

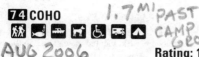

[handwritten: 1.7 MI PAST CAMP GROUND]

[handwritten: AUG 2006]

Rating: 10

On Wynoochee Lake in Olympic National Forest.

Map 1.5, grid e4, page 71

This eight-acre camp sits on the shore of Wynoochee Lake, which is 4.4 miles long and covers 1,140 acres. The camp is set at an elevation of 900 feet. The fishing season opens June 1 and closes October 31. Power boats, water-skiing, and personal watercraft are permitted. Points of interest include the Working Forest Trail, Wynoochee Dam Viewpoint and exhibits, and the 16-mile Wynoochee Lake Shore Trail, which circles the lake. This is one of the most idyllic drive-to settings you could hope to find.

Campsites, facilities: There are 58 sites for tents or RVs up to 36 feet long. Picnic tables are provided. Restrooms, flush toilets, and drinking water are available. There is an RV dump station nearby. Some facilities are wheelchair accessible. Boat docks and launching facilities are available at Wynoochee Lake. Leashed pets are permitted.

Reservations, fees: Reservations are not accepted. The fee is $12 per night for drive-in sites, $10 per night for walk-in sites. Senior discount available. Open May–September.

Directions: From Olympia on I-5, take Exit 104 and drive north on U.S. 101 to the Aberdeen/Highway 8 exit. Turn west on Highway 8 and drive 36 miles (it becomes Highway 12 at Elma) to Montesano. Continue two miles on Highway 12 to Wynoochee Valley Road. Turn north on Wynoochee Valley Road and drive 12 miles to Forest Road 22. Continue north on Forest Road 22 (a gravel road) to Wynoochee Lake. Just south of the lake, bear left and drive on Forest Road 2294 (which runs along the lake's northwest shore) for one mile to the camp on the west shore of Wynoochee Lake. Obtaining a U.S. Forest Service map is helpful.

Contact: Olympic National Forest, Hood Canal Ranger District, Hoodsport Office, P.O. Box 68, Hoodsport, WA 98548, 360/877-5254.

75 BROWN CREEK

Rating: 9

On Brown Creek in Olympic National Forest.

Map 1.5, grid e6, page 71

Brown Creek is little known among out-of-town visitors. While this camp is accessible to two-wheel-drive vehicles, the access road connects to a network of primitive, backcountry forest roads. The small campground (just six acres) is situated within the vast Olympic National Forest, which offers many opportunities for outdoor recreation. The wheelchair-accessible Brown Creek Nature Trail begins at the hand pump and makes a one-mile loop around the camp, featuring views of an active beaver pond. Obtain a U.S. Forest Service map to expand your trip. Note that in 2003 or 2004, this camp is scheduled to be moved out of the riparian area; check for possible short-term closures.

Campsites, facilities: There are seven tent sites and 12 sites for RVs up to 25 feet long. Picnic tables and fire rings are provided. Drinking water and vault toilets are available. Leashed pets are permitted.

Reservations, fees: Reservations are not accepted. Sites are $10 per night. Open year-round, with limited winter facilities.

Directions: From Olympia on I-5, take Exit 104 for U.S. 101/Highway 8. Drive north on U.S. 101 for 31 miles (about six miles past Shelton) to Skokomish Valley Road. Turn left and drive five miles (the road becomes Forest Road 23). Continue on Forest Road 23 for nine miles to Forest Road 2353. Bear right (cross the bridge) and drive to Forest Road 2340. Turn right and continue to the campground sign and drive three-quarters of a mile to the camp. Obtaining a U.S. Forest Service map is advisable.

Contact: Olympic National Forest, Hood Canal Ranger District, Hoodsport Office, P.O. Box 68, Hoodsport, WA 94548, 360/877-5254, fax 360/352-2569.

76 LEBAR HORSE CAMP

Rating: 9

In Olympic National Forest.
Map 1.5, grid e6, page 71

Campers with horses or pack animals, such as mules, mollies, llamas, and goats, are allowed to camp here. The camp provides access to the Lower South Fork Skokomish Trail, a 10.9-mile trip, one-way. The camp features beautiful old-growth forest, with western hemlock and Douglas fir.

Campsites, facilities: There are 13 sites for tents or RVs up to 21 feet long for the exclusive use of campers with pack animals. Picnic tables, fire grills, and hitching posts are provided. Drinking water and vault toilets are available. Garbage must be packed out. A day-use area with a picnic shelter is available nearby. Some facilities are wheelchair accessible. Leashed pets are permitted.

Reservations, fees: Reservations are not accepted. Sites are $10 per night. Senior discount available. Open May–September.

Directions: From Olympia on I-5, take Exit 104 for U.S. 101/Highway 8. Drive north on U.S. 101 for 31 miles (about six miles past Shelton) to Skokomish Valley Road. Turn left and drive five miles (the road becomes Forest Road 23). Continue on Forest Road 23 for nine miles (it becomes Forest Road 2353). When you cross the bridge, turn left. Stay on Forest Road 2353 (do not go straight to Forest Road 2340) and drive one mile to the campground on the right.

Contact: Olympic National Forest, Hood Canal Ranger District, P.O. Box 68, Hoodsport, WA 94548, 360/877-5254, fax 360/352-2569.

77 REST-A-WHILE RV PARK

Rating: 5

On the Hood Canal.
Map 1.5, grid e7, page 71

This seven-acre park, located at sea level on the Hood Canal, offers waterfront sites and a private beach for clamming and oyster gathering, not to mention plenty of opportunities to fish, boat, and scuba dive. It's an alternative to Potlatch State Park and Glen-Ayr RV Park.

Campsites, facilities: There are 80 sites with full hookups, including some drive-through, for RVs of any length and two tent sites. Picnic tables and fire rings are provided. Restrooms, drinking water, flush toilets, showers, bottled gas, firewood, a clubhouse, a store, a seafood market, a drive-in restaurant, laundry facilities, and ice are available. A café is within walking distance. Boat docks, launching facilities, a scuba diving shop, seasonal boat and kayak rentals, and a private beach for clamming and oyster gathering are also available. Leashed pets are permitted.

Reservations, fees: Reservations accepted. Sites are $20–28 per night, $2 per extra vehicle per night, and $4 per person per night for more than two people. Major credit cards accepted. Open year-round.

Directions: From Olympia on I-5, take Exit 104 for U.S. 101/Highway 8. Drive north on U.S. 101 for 37 miles to Hoodsport. Continue 2.5 miles north on U.S. 101 to the park located at Milepost 329.

Contact: Rest-a-While RV Park, North 27001 U.S. 101, Hoodsport, WA 98548, 360/877-9474, website: www.restawhile.com.

78 GLEN-AYR RV PARK & MOTEL

Rating: 5

On the Hood Canal.
Map 1.5, grid e7, page 71

This adults-only, fully developed, nine-acre park is located at sea level on the Hood Canal, where there are opportunities to fish and scuba dive. Salmon fishing is especially excellent. Swimming and boating round out the options. The park has a spa, moorage, horseshoe pits, a recreation field, and a motel.

Campsites, facilities: There are 40 sites with full hookups, including some drive-through, for RVs of any length, 14 motel rooms, and two suites with kitchens. Restrooms, drinking water, flush toilets, showers, picnic tables, bottled gas, a spa, a recreation hall, horseshoe pits, and a coin-operated laundry are available. A store, a café, and ice are within one mile. A boat dock is located across the street from the park. Leashed pets are permitted.

Reservations, fees: Campers must be 18 years of age or older. Reservations accepted. Sites are $27 per night, $4 per person per night for more than two people. Major credit cards accepted. Open year-round.

Directions: From Olympia on I-5, take Exit 104 for U.S. 101/Highway 8. Drive north on U.S. 101 for 37 miles to Hoodsport. Continue one mile north on U.S. 101 to the park on the left.

Contact: Glen-Ayr RV Park & Motel, 25381 North U.S. 101, Hoodsport, WA 98548, 800/367-9522 or 360/877-9522, fax 360/877-5177.

79 MINERVA BEACH RESORT

Rating: 5

On the Hood Canal.

Map 1.5, grid e7, page 71

This resort is on Hood Canal, a layover spot if you're cruising up or down U.S. 101. For the highly sensitive, road noise is discernible. While there are some permanent rentals here, they are located in a separate area, apart from the campground. Recreational opportunities at this park include salmon fishing, crabbing, and digging for oysters and clams in season; check regulations. A winery is located three miles to the north. Nearby Potlatch State Park provides a good side trip.

Campsites, facilities: There are 23 sites with

full hookups for RVs up to 50 feet long and 20 tent sites. Picnic tables and fire grills are provided. Restrooms, drinking water, flush toilets, coin-operated showers, cable TV, a public phone, a coin-operated laundry, limited groceries, ice, RV supplies, and LP gas are available. Horseshoe pits and a gift shop are nearby. Leashed pets are permitted.

Reservations, fees: Reservations recommended. Sites are $16–22 per night, $2 per person per night for more than two people. Major credit cards accepted. Open year-round.

Directions: From Tumwater/Olympia, take the U.S. 101 exit and drive north to Shelton. Continue north for 10 miles past Potlatch State Park to the resort entrance on the left.

Contact: Minerva Beach Resort, 21110 U.S. 101 N, Shelton, WA 98584, 360/877-5145 or 866/500-5145, website: http://home.att.net /minervabeach.

80 POTLATCH STATE PARK

Rating: 8

On the Hood Canal.

Map 1.5, grid f7, page 71

This state park features good shellfish harvesting in season and to celebrate it, hosts an annual "Shellfish Shindig" every April. The park has 9,570 feet of shoreline on the Hood Canal. There are 1.5 miles of trails for hiking and biking, but the shoreline and water bring people here for the good kayaking, windsurfing, scuba diving, clamming, and fishing. The park is named for the potlatch, which is a gift-giving ceremony of the Skokomish Indians. There are four major rivers, the Skokomish, Hamma Hamma, Duckabush, and Dosewallips, within a 30-mile radius of the park. The park receives an annual rainfall of 64 inches.

Campsites, facilities: There are 18 drive-through sites with full hookups for RVs up to 60 feet long, 17 developed tent sites, and two primitive tent sites. Picnic tables and fire grills are provided. Restrooms, drinking water, flush toilets, showers, an RV dump station, firewood, an amphitheater, a picnic area, and interpretive programs are available. A boat launch and five mooring buoys are located at the park, and boat docks are available nearby at the Hood Canal. Leashed pets are permitted.

Reservations, fees: Reservations are not accepted. Sites are $6–22 per night, $6 per extra vehicle per night, and $7–16 for mooring buoys. Winter and senior discounts available. Open April–October.

Directions: From Olympia on I-5, take Exit 104 for U.S. 101/Highway 8. Drive north on U.S. 101 for 22 miles to Shelton. Continue north on U.S. 101 for 12 miles to the park on the right (located along the shoreline of Annas Bay in the Hood Canal).

Contact: Potlatch State Park, 360/877-5361; State Park information, 360/902-8844.

81 SCHAFER STATE PARK

Rating: 8

On the Satsop River.

Map 1.5, grid g5, page 71

This unique destination boasts many interesting features, including buildings constructed from native stone. A heavily wooded, rural camp, Schafer State Park covers 119 acres along the East Fork of the Satsop River. The river is well known for fishing and rafting. Fish for sea-run cutthroat in summer, salmon in fall, and steelhead in late winter. There are good canoeing and kayaking spots, some with Class II and III rapids, along the Middle and West Forks of the Satsop. Two miles of hiking trails are also available. At one time, this park was the Schafer Logging Company Park and was used by employees and their families.

Campsites, facilities: There are 34 developed tent sites, six sites with partial hookups (water and electricity) for RVs up to 40 feet long, and two primitive tent sites. Picnic tables and fire grills are provided. Restrooms, drinking water, flush toilets, showers, a covered picnic shelter,

interpretive activities, an RV dump station, and a playground with horseshoe pits are available. Some facilities are wheelchair accessible. Leashed pets are permitted.

Reservations, fees: Reservations are not accepted. Sites are $6–22 per night, $6 per extra vehicle per night. Winter and senior discounts available. Open May–September.

Directions: From Olympia on I-5, take Exit 104 to U.S. 101. Drive west on U.S. 101 six miles to Highway 8. Turn west on Highway 8 to Elma (Highway 8 becomes Highway 12). Continue west on Highway 12 for seven miles to East Satsop Road (four miles east of Montesano). Turn right (north) and drive five miles to the park. The park is 12 miles north of Elma.

Contact: Schafer State Park, 360/482-3852; State Park information, 360/902-8844.

82 LAKE SYLVIA STATE PARK

Rating: 8

On Lake Sylvia.

Map 1.5, grid h4, page 71

This 234-acre state park on the shore of Lake Sylvia features nearly three miles of freshwater shoreline. The park is located in a former logging camp in a wooded area set midway between Olympia and the Pacific Ocean. Expect plenty of rustic charm, with displays of old logging gear, a giant ball carved out of wood from a single log, and some monstrous stumps. The lake is good for fishing and ideal for canoes, prams, or small boats with oars or electric motors; no gas motors are permitted. Five miles of hiking trails and a half-mile wheelchair-accessible trail meander through the park. Additional recreation options include trout fishing and swimming. If Lake Sylvia is full, nearby camps include East Crossing and Rainbow Cove.

Campsites, facilities: There are 35 sites for tents or self-contained RVs up to 30 feet long, two primitive tent sites, and one group site for up to 10 people. Picnic tables and fire grills are provided. Drinking water and vault toilets are available. Restrooms, drinking water, flush toilets, showers, an RV dump station, a store, fishing supplies, a boat launch, boat rentals, a picnic area, and a playground are available. A fee is charged for showers and firewood. Laundry facilities and ice are located within one mile. Some facilities are wheelchair accessible. Leashed pets are permitted.

Reservations, fees: Reservations are not accepted for family sites. Sites are $6–16 per night, $6 per extra vehicle per night, and the group site requires a $25 reservation fee plus $2 per person, with a 20-person minimum. Senior discount available. Open early April–early October.

Directions: From Olympia on I-5, take Exit 104 to U.S. 101. Drive west on U.S. 101 six miles to Highway 8. Turn west on Highway 8 and drive 26 miles to Montesano and the last exit, Highway 7. Take Highway 7 and drive to Pioneer (the only stoplight in town). Turn left on Pioneer and drive three blocks to Third Street. Turn right and drive two miles to the park entrance (route is well signed).

Contact: Lake Sylvia State Park, Montesano, WA 98563, 360/249-3621; State Park information, 360/902-8844.

83 TRAVEL INN RESORT

Rating: 7

On Lake Sylvia.
Map 1.5, grid h5, page 71

This is a membership campground, which means sites for RV travelers are available only if there is extra space. It can be difficult to get a spot May–September, but the park opens up significantly in the off-season. There are five major rivers or lakes within 15 minutes of this camp (Satsop, Chehalis, Wynoochee, Black River, and Lake Sylvia). Nearby Lake Sylvia State Park provides multiple marked hiking trails. Additional recreation options include trout fishing, swimming, and golf (three miles away).

Campsites, facilities: There are 144 sites with full or partial hookups for RVs of any length and 10 tent sites. Picnic tables and fire grills are provided. Restrooms, drinking water, flush toilets, showers, a public phone, a coin-operated laundry, two community fire pits, a gazebo, a heated swimming pool, a game room, cable TV, and a social hall are available. A grocery store and restaurant are available within one mile. Some facilities are wheelchair accessible. Leashed pets are permitted.

Reservations, fees: Reservations required May–September at 800/871-2888 (Washington and Oregon residents only) or 360/482-3877. Sites are $30 per night, plus $1 each for electricity or cable TV hookups. Open year-round.

Directions: From Olympia on I-5, take Exit 104 to U.S. 101. Drive west on U.S. 101 six miles to Highway 8. Turn west on Highway 8 and drive to Elma. Take the first Elma exit and at the stop sign at Highway 12, turn right. Drive about 200 yards to the end of the highway and a stop sign. Turn right and drive another 200 yards to the resort on the right.

Contact: Travel Inn Resort, 801 East Main St., Elma, WA 98541, 360/482-3877, website: www.kmresorts.com.

84 FALLS VIEW

Rating: 8

On the Big Quilcene River in Olympic National Forest.
Map 1.6, grid b1, page 72

A viewing area to a pretty waterfall on the Big Quilcene River, where you see a narrow, 100-foot cascade, is only a 150-foot walk from the campground. That explains why, despite the rustic setting, this spot on the edge of the Olympic National Forest has a host of facilities and is popular. Enjoy the setting of mixed conifers and rhododendrons along a one-mile scenic loop trail, which overlooks the river and provides views of the waterfall. A picnic area is also located near the waterfall.

Campsites, facilities: There are 30 sites for tents or RVs up to 21 feet long. Picnic tables are provided. Restrooms, drinking water, and flush toilets are available. Some facilities are wheelchair accessible. Leashed pets are permitted.
Reservations, fees: Reservations are not accepted. Sites are $10 per night. Senior discount available. Open May–mid-September.
Directions: From Olympia on I-5, turn north on U.S. 101 and drive approximately 70 miles to the campground entrance on the left (located about four miles south of Quilcene).
Contact: Olympic National Forest, Quilcene Ranger District, P.O. Box 280, Quilcene, WA 98376, 360/765-2200, fax 360/765-2202.

85 RAINBOW GROUP CAMP

Rating: 7

Near Quilcene in Olympic National Forest.
Map 1.6, grid c1, page 72

Rainbow Group Camp is in a rugged, primitive setting on the edge of Olympic National Forest. This area is heavily wooded with old-growth and new-growth forest, a variety of wildflowers, and spring-blooming rhododendrons. The Rainbow Canyon Trailhead, located at the far side of the campground, provides a short hike to the Big Quicene River and a waterfall. It is fairly steep, but not a butt kicker. Forest roads provide considerable backcountry access (obtaining a U.S. Forest Service map is advisable). The nearest is Forest Road 2730, just one-tenth of a mile away, which leads to spectacular scenery at the Mt. Walker Observation Area. Olympic National Park is also just a short drive away.
Campsites, facilities: There are nine sites for tents and small RVs that are reserved for groups up to 50 people. Picnic tables and fire grills are provided. Drinking water and vault toilets are available. A store, a café, a coin-operated laundry, and ice are within five miles. Leashed pets are permitted.

Reservations, fees: Reservations required at 360/765-2200. The group site is $50 per night.
Directions: From I-5 at Olympia, go north on U.S. 101 and drive approximately 69 miles to the campground (about six miles past Dosewallips State Park) on the left (near Walker Pass).
Contact: Olympic National Forest, Quilcene Ranger District, P.O. Box 280, Quilcene, WA 98376, 360/765-2200, fax 360/765-2202.

86 COVE RV PARK

Rating: 5

Near Dabob Bay.
Map 1.6, grid c1, page 72

This five-acre private camp enjoys a rural setting close to the shore of Dabob Bay, yet is fully developed. Sites are grassy and graveled with a few trees. Scuba diving is popular in this area, and the park sells air for scuba tanks. Dosewallips State Park is a short drive away and a possible side trip.
Campsites, facilities: There are 32 sites with full hookups (including cable TV) for RVs up to 40 feet long and six tent sites. Picnic tables and fire rings (in season) are provided. Restrooms, drinking water, flush toilets, coin-operated showers, bottled gas, an RV dump station, a store, a coin-operated laundry, and ice are available. Boat docks and launching facilities are on the Hood Canal 2.2 miles from the park. Leashed pets are permitted.
Reservations, fees: Reservations accepted. Sites are $14–20 per night, $3 per person per night for more than two people (over 12). Major credit cards accepted. Open year-round.
Directions: From Olympia on I-5, drive north on U.S. 101 for 60 miles to Brinnon (located about one mile north of Dosewallips State Park). Continue three miles north on U.S. 101 to the park on the right (before Milepost 303).
Contact: Cove RV Park, 303075 U.S. 101, Brinnon, WA 98320, 866/796-4723 or 360/796-4723, fax 360/796-3452.

87 SEAL ROCK

88 DOSEWALLIPS STATE PARK

Rating: 9

Rating: 8

On Dabob Bay in Olympic National Forest.
Map 1.6, grid c1, page 72

Seal Rock is a 30-acre camp set along the shore near the mouth of Dabob Bay. This is one of the few national forest campgrounds anywhere located on saltwater. It brings with it the opportunity to harvest oysters and clams in season, and an outstanding jumping-off point for scuba diving. Most campsites are set along the waterfront, spaced among trees. Carry-in boats, such as kayaks and canoes, can be launched from the north landing. The Native American Nature Trail and the Marine Biology Nature Trail begin at the day-use area. These are short walks, each less than one-half mile. This camp is extremely popular in the summer, often filling up quickly.

Campsites, facilities: There are 40 sites for tents or RVs up to 21 feet long. Picnic tables and fire rings are provided. Restrooms, drinking water, flush toilets, a picnic area, and a public telephone are available. Some facilities, including viewing areas and trails, are wheelchair-accessible. A camp host is on-site in summer. Boat docks and launching facilities are nearby on the Hood Canal and in Dabob Bay. Leashed pets are permitted.

Reservations, fees: Reservations are not accepted. Sites are $12 per night. Senior discount available. Open mid-April–September.

Directions: From Olympia on I-5, drive north on U.S. 101 for 60 miles to Brinnon (located about one mile north of Dosewallips State Park). Continue two miles north on U.S. 101 to Seal Rock and the camp on the right.

Contact: Olympic National Forest, Quilcene Ranger District, P.O. Box 280, Quilcene, WA 98376, 360/765-2200, fax 360/765-2202.

On Dosewallips Creek.
Map 1.6, grid c1, page 72

This 425-acre park is set on the shore of the Hood Canal at the mouth of Dosewallips River. It features 5,500 feet of saltwater shoreline on Hood Canal and 5,400 feet of shoreline on both sides of the Dosewallips River. All campsites are grassy and located in scenic, rustic settings. Mushrooming is available in season. Check regulations for fishing and clamming, which fluctuate according to time and season. This camp is popular because it's set right off a major highway; reservations or early arrival are advised. Access is not affected by the nearby slide area.

Campsites, facilities: There are 90 sites, including 40 with full hookups, for tents or RVs up to 60 feet long, and two primitive sites. Picnic tables and fire rings are provided. Restrooms, drinking water, flush toilets, coin-operated showers, a sheltered picnic area, interpretive activities, and a summer Junior Ranger Program are available. A wildlife-viewing platform, horseshoe pits, saltwater boat-launching facilities, a recreation hall, a store, a café, and laundry facilities are available nearby. Some facilities are wheelchair accessible. Leashed pets are permitted.

Reservations, fees: Reserve at 888/CAMP-OUT (888/226-7688), website: www.parks.wa.gov/reservations ($7 reservation fee). Sites are $6–22 per night, $6 per extra vehicle per night. Winter and senior discounts available. Major credit cards accepted. Open year-round.

Directions: From Olympia on I-5, drive north on U.S. 101 for 61 miles (one mile south of Brinnon) to the state park entrance on the right.

Contact: Dosewallips State Park, 360/796-4415; State Park information, 360/902-8844.

89 SCENIC BEACH STATE PARK

Rating: 10

On the Hood Canal.

Map 1.6, grid c2, page 72

Scenic Beach is an exceptionally beautiful state park with beach access and superb views of the Olympic Mountains. It features 1,500 feet of saltwater beachfront on Hood Canal. The park is also known for its wild rhododendrons in spring. Wheelchair-accessible paths lead to a country garden, gazebo, rustic bridge, and large trees. Many species of birds and wildlife can often be seen here. This camp is also close to Green Mountain Forest, where there is extensive hiking. A boat ramp is one-half mile east of the park, with dock and moorage available at Seabeck, one mile east of the park. A nice touch here is that park staff will check out volleyballs and horseshoes during the summer.

Campsites, facilities: There are 50 sites for tents or RVs up to 40 feet long. Picnic tables and fire grills are provided. Restrooms, drinking water, flush toilets, coin-operated showers, and an RV dump station are available. A sheltered picnic area, horseshoe pits, and volleyball fields (May–August) are available nearby. Some facilities are wheelchair accessible. Leashed pets are permitted.

Reservations, fees: Reserve at 888/CAMP-OUT (888/226-7688), website: www.parks .wa.gov/reservations ($7 reservation fee). Sites are $16 per night, $6 per extra vehicle per night. Senior discount available. Open April–mid-November.

Directions: From Tacoma at I-5, turn north on Highway 16 and drive 30 miles to Bremerton to the junction with Highway 3. Turn north on Highway 3 and drive about nine miles and take the first Silverdale exit (Newberry Hill Road). Turn left and drive approximately three miles to the end of the road. Turn right on Seabeck Highway and drive six miles to Scenic Beach Road. Turn right and drive one mile to the park.

Contact: Scenic Beach State Park, 360/830-5079; State Park information, 360/902-8844.

90 KITSAP MEMORIAL STATE PARK

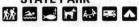

Rating: 10

On the Hood Canal.

Map 1.6, grid b3, page 72

Kitsap Memorial State Park is a beautiful spot for tent campers along the Hood Canal. The park covers only 58 acres but features sweeping views of Puget Sound and 1,797 feet of shoreline. The park has 1.5 miles of hiking trails and two open grassy fields for family play. Note that the nearest boat launch is four miles away, north on State Route 3 at Salisbury County Park. An 18-hole golf course and swimming, fishing, and hiking at nearby Anderson Lake Recreation Area are among the activities available. A short drive north will take you to historic Old Fort Townsend, which is an excellent day trip.

Campsites, facilities: There are 25 sites for tents or RVs up to 30 feet long, 18 sites with partial hookups (water and electricity) for RVs, and three primitive tent sites. Picnic tables and fire grills are provided. Restrooms, drinking water, flush toilets, showers, an RV dump station, a sheltered picnic area, firewood, and a playground are available. One boat buoy is available. Leashed pets are permitted.

Reservations, fees: Reservations are not accepted. Sites are $6–22 per night. Winter and senior discounts available. Open year-round.

Directions: From Tacoma on I-5, turn north on Highway 16 and drive 44 miles (Highway 16 turns into Highway 3). Continue north on Highway 3 and drive six miles to Park Street. Turn left and drive 200 yards to the park entrance on the right (well marked). The park is located four miles south of the Hood Canal Bridge.

Contact: Kitsap Memorial State Park, 202 N.E. Park St., Poulsbo, WA 98370, 360/779-3205; State Park information, 360/902-8844.

91 CAPTAIN'S LANDING

Rating: 8

In Hansville.

Map 1.6, grid a4, page 72

This camp overlooks Puget Sound and sits right next to the water. Admiralty Inlet offers a rural escape, and the Point-No-Point is within walking distance and offers tours on weekends. Trout fishing at Buck Lake is three miles away. Grassy, open sites make this a good choice for campers wanting an in-town location. An 18-hole golf course and a full-service marina are close by. A wildlife sanctuary is five miles away. No open fires are permitted.

Campsites, facilities: There are 22 drive-through sites with full hookups for self-contained trailers or RVs of any length and four cabins. No restrooms are available. No fires are allowed. A store and ice are available. Boat docks, launching facilities, and boat rentals are located within one mile. Leashed pets are permitted.

Reservations, fees: Reservations accepted. Sites are $28–35 per night. Open year-round.

Directions: From Bremerton, drive north on Highway 16 for 10 miles (Highway 16 turns into Highway 3) and continue north on Highway 3 for 11 miles to Port Gamble. Bear southeast toward Kingston (still on Highway 3) to Hansville Road (at George's Corner). Turn left on Hansville Road and drive eight miles. The park is on the right side, at the bottom of the hill.

Contact: Captain's Landing, 39118 Hansville Rd. NE, Hansville, WA 98340, 360/638-2257, fax 360/638-2015.

92 GREEN MOUNTAIN HIKE-IN & HORSE CAMP

Rating: 7

In Green Mountain State Forest.

Map 1.6, grid d2, page 72

This is a prime spot—primitive but with hand-pumped water provided. Operated by the Department of Natural Resources, the campground is located in Green Mountain State Forest. The Backcountry Horsemen of Washington hosts the camp, which features facilities for horses.

Campsites, facilities: There are 12 hike-in sites for tents only. Picnic tables, fire grills, and tent pads are provided. Vault toilets, hand-pumped drinking water, a group shelter, and facilities for horses, including horse corrals, are available. Garbage must be packed out.

Reservations, fees: Reservations are not accepted. There is no fee for camping. A gate limits vehicular access to the camp on weekends from April–September, 9 A.M.–6 P.M. A free map and brochure are available.

Directions: From Tacoma on I-5, turn north on Highway 16 and drive 30 miles to Bremerton and the junction with Highway 3. Turn north on Highway 3 and drive a short distance to the Seabeck Highway. Turn left and drive three miles to Holly Road. Turn left on Holly Road and drive four miles to Tahuya Lake Road. Turn left and drive one mile to Green Mountain Road and the Department of Natural Resources (DNR) parking lot and trailhead. Hike four miles.

Contact: Department of Natural Resources, South Puget Sound Region, 950 Farman Ave. N, Enumclaw, WA 98022, 360/825-1631, fax 360/825-1672.

93 FAY BAINBRIDGE STATE PARK

Rating: 10

On Bainbridge Island.

Map 1.6, grid c4, page 72

A beach park that offers beauty and great recreation, this camp is set on the edge of Puget Sound. The park covers just 17 acres but features 1,420 feet of saltwater shoreline on the northeast corner of the island. You can hike several miles along the beach at low tide; the water temperature is typically about 55°F in summer. The primitive walk-in sites are heavily wooded, and the developed sites have great views of the sound. On clear days, campers can enjoy views of Mt. Rainier and Mt. Baker to the east, and at night the park provides beautiful vistas of the lights of Seattle. Clamming, diving, picnicking, beachcombing, and kite flying are popular here. In the winter months, there is excellent salmon fishing just offshore of the park.

Campsites, facilities: There are 26 sites for tents or self-contained RVs up to 30 feet long and 13 primitive tent sites. Picnic tables and fire grills are provided. Restrooms, drinking water, flush toilets, coin-operated showers, an RV dump station, a sheltered picnic area, horseshoes, and a playground are available. A store and a café are located within one mile. Firewood can be obtained for a fee. Some facilities are wheelchair accessible. Boat docks, launching facilities, and mooring buoys are nearby. Leashed pets are permitted.

Reservations, fees: Reservations are not accepted. Sites are $6–16 per night, $22 for RVs with hookups, $6 per extra vehicle per night, and $7–16 for mooring buoys. Senior discount available. Open mid-April–early October.

Directions: From Tacoma at I-5, turn north on Highway 16 and drive 30 miles to Bremerton to the junction with Highway 3. Turn north on Highway 3 and drive 18 miles to Highway 305. Turn south on Highway 305 and drive over the bridge to Bainbridge Island and continue three miles to Phelps Road Northeast. Turn left (northeast), drive two miles to Port Madison, and continue east one mile to the park entrance (well marked).

Note: From Seattle, this camp can be more easily accessed by taking the Bainbridge Island ferry and then Highway 305 north to the northeast end of the island.

Contact: Fay Bainbridge State Park, 206/842-3931; State Park information, 360/902-8844.

94 ILLAHEE STATE PARK

Rating: 9

Near Bremerton.

Map 1.6, grid d4, page 72

This 75-acre park, named for the Native American word for "earth" or "country," features the last stand of old-growth forest in Kitsap County, including one of the largest yew trees in America. The park also features 1,785 feet of saltwater frontage. The campsites are located in a pretty, forested area, and some are grassy. The shoreline is fairly rocky, set on the shore of Port Orchard Bay, although there is a small sandy area for sunbathers. Clamming is popular here. A fishing pier is available for anglers. Note that large vessels can be difficult to launch at the ramp here.

Campsites, facilities: There are 25 sites for tents or self-contained RVs up to 30 feet long, eight primitive tent sites, and one group site for up to 40 people. Picnic tables and fire grills are provided. Restrooms, drinking water, flush toilets, showers, firewood, and a pier are available. Boat docks, launching facilities, 56 mooring buoys, and 356 feet of moorage float space are available. A sheltered picnic area, horseshoes, volleyball, a field, and a playground are available nearby. Some facilities are wheelchair accessible. A coin-operated laundry and ice are located within one mile. Leashed pets are permitted.

Reservations, fees: Reservations are not accepted for family sites. Sites are $6–16 per night, $22 for RVs with hookups, $6 per extra vehicle per night, and mooring buoys are $7–16 per night. The group site requires a $25 reservation plus $2 per person per night. Senior discount available. Open year-round.

Directions: On Highway 3, drive to Bremerton and the East Bremerton exit. Drive east for 7.5 miles to Sylvan Way. Turn left and drive 1.5 miles (on the bridge over Port Washington Narrows) to the park entrance road.

Contact: Illahee State Park, 360/478-6460; State Park information, 360/902-8844.

95 MANCHESTER STATE PARK

Rating: 9

On Puget Sound.

Map 1.6, grid d4, page 72

Manchester State Park is set on the edge of Point Orchard, providing excellent lookouts across Puget Sound. The park covers 111 acres, with 3,400 feet of saltwater shoreline on Rich Passage in Puget Sound. The landscape is filled with fir and maple, which are very pretty in the fall. There are 1.9 miles of hiking trails, including an interpretive trail. The camp gets relatively little use, especially in the off-season, so you're almost always guaranteed a spot. Group and day-use reservations are available. Note that the beach is closed to shellfish harvesting. In the early 1900s, this park site was used as a U.S. Coast Guard defense installation. A gun battery remains from the park's early days, along with two other buildings that are on the register of National Historical Monuments.

Campsites, facilities: There are 34 sites, including 15 with partial hookups (water and electricity) for tents or RVs up to 60 feet long, three primitive tent sites, and one group site. Picnic tables and fire grills are provided. Restrooms, drinking water, flush toilets, showers, an RV dump station, firewood, and a sheltered picnic area are available. Some facilities are wheelchair accessible. Leashed pets are permitted.

Reservations, fees: Reserve at 888/CAMP-OUT (888/226-7688), website: www.parks .wa.gov/reservations ($7 reservation fee). Sites are $6–22 per night, $6 per extra vehicle per night. Senior discount available. Major credit cards accepted. Open year-round, with limited winter facilities.

Directions: From Tacoma on I-5, turn north on Highway 16 and drive through Bethel and continue to the Sedgwick Road exit and Highway 160. Turn right (east) and drive one mile to Highway 166. Turn left and drive six miles on Highway 166 to Colby. Turn left and drive along the shore through Manchester, continuing for two miles to the park. The last part of the trip is well marked.

Contact: Manchester State Park, P.O. Box 36, Manchester, WA 98353, 800/233-0321 or 360/871-4065.

96 BLAKE ISLAND BOAT-IN STATE PARK

Rating: 10

Near Seattle.

Map 1.6, grid d5, page 72

Blake Island offers a boat-in camp on a small island in the middle of the massive Seattle metropolitan area. At night, it can seem almost surreal. The park covers 475 acres and features magnificent views of the Seattle skyline and Olympic Mountains. It boasts five miles of saltwater shoreline, a three-quarter-mile nature trail, and 15.5 miles of hiking and biking trails. Good bottom fishing is available off the reef. The tidelands make up an underwater park. Blake Island was an ancestral camping ground of the Suquamish Indian tribe, and according to legend, the renowned Chief Seattle was born here. Native American–style dinners and dancing are available at Tillicum Village, a concession on the island. A bonus: primitive sites on the west side of the island available only by canoe or kayak.

Campsites, facilities: There are 54 boat-in tent sites. Picnic tables and fire grills are provided. Drinking water, pit toilets, showers, firewood, 1,500 feet of mooring with 20 mooring buoys, and two picnic shelters with a fire pit are available. There are also interpretive activities, horseshoe pits, volleyball, and a field. Garbage must be packed out. Some facilities are wheelchair accessible. A store and restaurant are available nearby. Leashed pets are permitted.

Reservations, fees: Reservations are not accepted. Sites are $10–16 per night. Senior discount available. Open year-round.

Directions: This island is best reached by launching from Bremerton, Port Orchard, or Manchester. From Manchester it is a two-mile cruise east to the island (three miles west of Seattle). Then trace the shore around to the buoy floats. There are four main camping areas located between Vashon Island and Bainbridge Island, a distance of eight miles from Seattle. The park can also be reached by tour boat; call 206/443-1244 for information.

Contact: Blake Island Boat-In State Park, 360/731-0770; State Park information, 360/902-8844.

97 ALDRICH LAKE

Rating: 7

On Aldrich Lake in Tahuya State Forest.

Map 1.6, grid d1, page 72

This campground on Aldrich Lake is managed by the Department of Natural Resources and provides primitive camping and fishing. Nearby Robbins Lake has day-use facilities and a hand launch for small boats. To reach Robbins Lake, follow the directions below, but after turning left on Hohobas Lane and driving one-half mile, make another left and drive one mile to the lake.

Campsites, facilities: There are four primitive campsites for tents or small trailers. Picnic tables, fire grills, and tent pads are provided. Vault toilets and drinking water are available. A hand launch for small boats is located at the lake. Garbage must be packed out. Leashed pets are permitted.

Reservations, fees: Reservations are not accepted. There is no fee for camping. A free map and brochure are available. Open mid-April–mid-September.

Directions: From Tacoma on I-5, drive to the junction with Highway 16. Turn north

on Highway 16 and drive 30 miles to Bremerton and Highway 3. Turn west on Highway 3 and drive nine miles to Belfair and Highway 300. Turn west on Highway 300 and drive 12 miles to the town of Tahuya and Belfair-Tahuya Road. Turn right (north) on Belfair-Tahuya Road and drive four miles to Dewatto Road. Turn left on Dewatto Road and drive two miles to Hohobas Lane. Turn left on Hohobas Lane and drive one-half mile to a Y intersection. Bear right and drive seven-tenths of a mile to the campground entrance road. Turn right and drive 200 yards to the campground.

Contact: Department of Natural Resources, South Puget Sound Region, 950 Farman Ave. N, Enumclaw, WA 98022, 360/825-1631, fax 360/825-1672.

98 TWIN LAKES

Rating: 7

In Tahuya State Forest.

Map 1.6, grid e1, page 72

This wooded campground is in Tahuya State Forest and managed by the Department of Natural Resources. It's free and quiet. The fishing can be decent, and other highlights include privacy, shady sites, lake views, and a boat ramp. Hiking trails are nearby. Don't forget to bring water. One anomaly: Although it is called Twin Lakes, there is actually just one lake here.

Campsites, facilities: There are six primitive campsites for tents or small trailers. Picnic tables, fire grills, and tent pads are provided. Vault toilets are available, but there is no drinking water. Garbage must be packed out. A hand launch for small boats is available at the lake. Leashed pets are permitted.

Reservations, fees: Reservations are not accepted. There is no fee for camping. A free map and brochure are available. Open mid-April–mid-September.

Directions: From Tacoma on I-5, drive to the

junction with Highway 16. Turn north on Highway 16 and drive about 30 miles to Bremerton and Highway 3. Turn south on Highway 3 and drive eight miles southwest to the town of Belfair and Highway 300. Turn west on Highway 300 and drive four miles to Belfair-Tahuya Road. Turn right on Belfair-Tahuya Road and drive one-half mile to Elfendahl Pass Road. Turn right on Elfendahl Pass Road and drive 2.5 miles to Goat Ranch Road. Turn left and drive 1.7 miles to Twin Lakes Road. Turn right and drive one-half mile to the camp.

Contact: Department of Natural Resources, South Puget Sound Region, 950 Farman Ave. N, Enumclaw, WA 98022, 360/825-1631, fax 360/825-1672.

99 CAMP SPILLMAN

Rating: 7

On the Tahuya River in Tahuya State Forest.
Map 1.6, grid e1, page 72

Camp Spillman is one of four campgrounds (along with Tahuya River Horse Camp, Howell Lake, and Twin Lakes) set in the immediate vicinity of Tahuya State Forest. This one sits along the Tahuya River with wooded riverside sites and trails for hikers, horses, and motorbikes.

Campsites, facilities: There are six primitive campsites for tents or small trailers. Picnic tables, fire grills, and tent pads are provided. Vault toilets and drinking water are available. Garbage must be packed out. Leashed pets are permitted.

Reservations, fees: Reservations are not accepted. There is no fee for camping. A free map and brochure are available. Open mid-April–mid-October.

Directions: From Tacoma on I-5, drive to the junction with Highway 16. Turn north on Highway 16 and drive about 30 miles to Bremerton and Highway 3. Turn south on Highway 3 and drive eight miles southwest to the town of Belfair and Highway 300. Turn west on High-

way 300 and drive four miles to Belfair-Tahuya Road. Turn right on Belfair-Tahuya Road and drive one-half mile to Elfendahl Pass Road. Turn right on Elfendahl Pass Road and drive 2.5 miles to Goat Ranch Road. Turn left and drive two-thirds mile to the camp.

Contact: Department of Natural Resources, South Puget Sound Region, 950 Farman Ave. N, Enumclaw, WA 98022, 360/825-1631, fax 360/825-1672.

100 ROBIN HOOD VILLAGE

Rating: 5

Near the Hood Canal.
Map 1.6, grid f1, page 72

This wooded park is set near a state park, Olympic National Forest, Mason Lake and Lake Cushman, and Hood Canal. Nearby recreation options include an 18-hole golf course.

Campsites, facilities: There are 16 sites with full or partial hookups for RVs of any length, four tent sites, and four cabins. Picnic tables are provided. Restrooms, drinking water, flush toilets, showers, a restaurant, an espresso stand, a liquor store, a massage therapist, a sauna, and a coin-operated laundry are available. Bottled gas, an RV dump station, a store, and ice are available within one mile. Boat docks and launching facilities are located in the park. Leashed pets are permitted.

Reservations, fees: Reservations accepted. Sites are $14–22 per night, cabins $85–200 per night. Major credit cards accepted. Open year-round.

Directions: From Tacoma, drive northeast on Highway 16 for about 30 miles to Bremerton and Highway 3. Turn south on Highway 3 and drive eight miles southwest to the town of Belfair and Highway 106. Bear right (southwest) on Highway 106 and drive 13 miles to the campground along Hood Canal.

Contact: Robin Hood Village, East 6780 Hwy. 106, Union, WA 98592, 360/898-2163, fax 360/898-2164, website: www.robinhoodvillage.com.

101 TWANOH STATE PARK

🏃 🏊 ⛵ 🚣 🎣 🏕 ♿ 🚗 ⛰

Rating: 8

Near Union.

Map 1.6, grid e1, page 72

This state park is set on the shore of Hood Canal at one of the warmest saltwater bodies in Puget Sound and likely the warmest saltwater beach in the state. *Twanoh,* from the Native American word meaning "gathering place," covers 182 acres, with 3,167 feet of saltwater shoreline. Swimming and oyster and crab harvesting are popular here. No clamming is allowed. Winter smelting is also popular; check regulations. In late fall, the chum salmon can be seen heading up the small creek; fishing for them is prohibited. Most of the park buildings are made of brick, stone, and round logs. They were built by the Civilian Conservation Corps in the 1930s. You'll also see extensive evidence of logging from the 1890s. Amenities include a tennis court, horseshoe pits, and a concession stand.

Campsites, facilities: There are 17 tent sites and nine sites for RVs up to 35 feet long, 13 with full hookups and nine with partial hookups. Picnic tables and fire grills are provided. Flush toilets, a store, and a playground are available. Electricity, drinking water, sewer hookups, showers, and firewood can be obtained for a fee. Some facilities are wheelchair accessible. Leashed pets are permitted.

Reservations, fees: Reservations are not accepted. Sites are $6–22 per night. Open April–October.

Directions: From Bremerton, take Highway 3 southwest to Belfair and Highway 106. Turn west and drive eight miles to the park. If driving from U.S. 101, turn east on Highway 106 and drive 12 miles to the park.

Contact: Twanoh State Park, 360/275-2222; State Park information, 360/902-8844.

102 BELFAIR STATE PARK

🏃 🚴 🏊 🎣 🏕 🐕 🏕 ♿ 🚗 ⛰

Rating: 8

On the Hood Canal.

Map 1.6, grid e2, page 72

Belfair State Park is situated along the southern edge of the Hood Canal, spanning 65 acres with 3,720 feet of saltwater shoreline. This park is known for its saltwater tidal flats, wetlands, and wind-blown beach grasses. Beach walking and swimming are good. The camp is set primarily amid conifer forest and marshlands on the Hood Canal with nearby streams, tideland, and wetlands. A gravel-rimmed pool that is separate from the Hood Canal creates a unique swimming area. A children's Easter egg hunt is held here each spring. Note that the DNR Tahuya Multiple-Use Area is nearby with trails for motorcycles, mountain biking, hiking, horseback riding, and off-road vehicles. Big Mission Creek and Little Mission Creek, both located in the park, are habitat for chum salmon during spawning season in fall.

Campsites, facilities: There are 137 sites for tents and 47 sites with full hookups for RVs up to 75 feet long. Picnic tables and fire grills are provided. Restrooms, drinking water, flush toilets, coin-operated showers, a bathhouse, an RV dump station, a swimming lagoon, and a playground with horseshoe pits are available. A store and a restaurant are located within one mile. Some facilities are wheelchair accessible. Leashed pets are permitted.

Reservations, fees: Reserve at 888/CAMP-OUT (888/226-7688), website: www.parks.wa.gov/reservations ($7 reservation fee). Sites are $15–22 per night, $6 per extra vehicle per night. Senior discount available. Major credit cards accepted. Open year-round.

Directions: From Tacoma on I-5, drive to the Highway 16 west exit. Take Highway 16 northwest and drive about 27 miles toward Bremerton and Belfair (after the Port Orchard exits, note that the highway merges into three lanes). Get in the left lane for the Belfair/State

Route 3 south exit. Take that exit and turn left at the traffic signal. Take State Route 3 eight miles south to Belfair to State Route 300 (at the signal just after the Safeway). Turn right and drive three miles to the park entrance.

Contact: Belfair State Park, 360/275-0668; State Park information, 360/902-8844.

103 JARRELL COVE STATE PARK

Rating: 8

On Harstine Island.
Map 1.6, grid f1, page 72

Most visitors to this park arrive by boat. Campsites are near the docks, set on a rolling, grassy area. The park covers just 43 acres but boasts 3,500 feet on saltwater shoreline on the northeast end of Harstine Island in South Puget Sound. The park's dense forest presses nearly to the water's edge at high tides—a beautiful setting. At low tides, tideland mud flats are unveiled. The beach is rocky and muddy, not exactly Hawaii. Hiking and biking is limited to just one mile of trail.

Campsites, facilities: There are 21 sites for tents or RVs up to 30 feet long, one boat-in site, and a group camp for up to 64 people. Picnic tables and fire grills are provided. Restrooms, drinking water, flush toilets, and coin-operated showers are available. Some facilities are wheelchair accessible. Boat docks, a marine pump-out, and 14 mooring buoys are available. A picnic area and a horseshoe pit are nearby. Leashed pets are permitted.

Reservations, fees: Reserve at 888/CAMP-OUT (888/226-7688), website: www.parks.wa.gov/reservations ($7 reservation fee). Sites are $6–15 per night, $7 per extra vehicle per night, $10–16 mooring fee, and the group site requires a $25 reservation plus $2 per person with a 20-person minimum. Senior discount available. Open year-round.

Directions: From Olympia on I-5, turn north on U.S. 101 and drive 22 miles to Shelton and Highway 3. Turn north on Highway 3 and drive about eight miles to Pickering Road. Turn right and drive to the Harstine Bridge. Turn left, cross the bridge to Harstine Island, and continue to a stop sign at North Island Drive. Turn left and drive four miles to Wingert Road. Turn left and drive one-quarter mile to the park on the left.

Contact: Jarrell Cove State Park, 360/426-9226; State Park information, 360/902-8844.

104 JARRELL'S COVE MARINA

Rating: 6

Near Shelton.
Map 1.6, grid f1, page 72

The marina and nearby Puget Sound are the big draws here. This small camp features 1,000 feet of shoreline and one-half mile of public beach. Clamming is available in season.

Campsites, facilities: There are four sites with partial hookups (water and electricity) for RVs up to 40 feet long. Picnic tables and barbecues are provided. Restrooms, drinking water, flush toilets, showers, bottled gas, an RV dump station, a store, fishing licenses, bait and tackle, a laundry room, boat docks, and boat rentals are available. Leashed pets are permitted.

Reservations, fees: Reservations accepted. Sites are $27 per night. Major credit cards accepted. Open year-round.

Directions: From Olympia on I-5, turn north on U.S. 101 and drive 22 miles to Shelton and Highway 3. Turn east on Highway 3 and drive about eight miles to Pickering Road. Turn right and drive to the Harstine Island Bridge. Turn left, cross the bridge to Harstine Island, and continue to a stop sign at North Island Drive. Turn left on North Island Drive and drive 2.8 miles to Haskell Hill Road. Turn left (west) on Haskell Hill Road and drive one mile to the marina.

Contact: Jarrell's Cove Marina, 220 East Wilson Rd., Shelton, WA 98584, 360/426-8823.

105 JOEMMA BEACH STATE PARK

Rating: 8

On Puget Sound.

Map 1.6, grid g2, page 72

This beautiful camp set along the shore of the peninsula provides an alternative to nearby Penrose Point State Park. It covers 122 acres and features 3,000 feet of saltwater frontage on the Southeast Kitsap Peninsula. This area is often excellent for boating, fishing, and crabbing. It is a forested park with the bonus of a boat-in campsite. Hiking is limited to a trail that is less than a mile long.

Campsites, facilities: There are 19 sites for tents or RVs up to 35 feet long and three primitive tent sites. Picnic tables, fire grills, and tent pads are provided. Vault toilets, drinking water, boat-launching facilities, and a dock are available. Leashed pets are permitted.

Reservations, fees: Reserve at 888/CAMP-OUT (888/226-7688), website: www.parks.wa.gov/reservations ($7 reservation fee). Sites are $6–22, $6 per extra vehicle per night. Senior discount available. Open May–September.

Directions: From Tacoma, drive north on Highway 16 for about 10 miles to Highway 302/Key Peninsula Highway. Turn west and drive about five miles to Key Peninsula Highway. Turn south and drive about 15 miles to Whiteman Road. Turn right and drive four miles to Bay Road. Turn right and drive one mile to the park entrance (stay on the asphalt road when entering the park).

Contact: Joemma Beach State Park, 253/265-3606; State Park information, 360/902-8844.

106 PENROSE POINT STATE PARK

Rating: 8

On Puget Sound.

Map 1.6, grid f2, page 72

This park on Carr Inlet in Puget Sound, overlooking Lake Bay, has a remote feel, but it's actually not far from Tacoma. The park covers 152 acres, with two miles of saltwater frontage on Mayo Cove and Carr Inlet. The camp has impressive stands of fir and cedars nearby, along with ferns and rhododendrons, the park has 2.5 miles of trails for biking and hiking. Bay Lake is a popular fishing lake for trout and is located one mile away; a boat launch is available there. Penrose is known for its excellent fishing, crabbing, clamming, and oysters. The nearest boat launch to Puget Sound is located three miles away in the town of Home.

Campsites, facilities: There are 83 developed sites for tents or self-contained RVs up to 35 feet long and one primitive tent site. Picnic tables and fire grills are provided. Restrooms, drinking water, flush toilets, coin-operated showers, an RV dump station, horseshoe pits, a picnic area, and a beach are available. Some facilities are wheelchair accessible. Boat docks, a marine pump-out, and mooring buoys are nearby. Leashed pets are permitted.

Reservations, fees: Reserve at 888/CAMP-OUT (888/226-7688), website: www.parks.wa.gov/reservations ($7 reservation fee). Sites are $6–16 per night, $7 per extra vehicle per night, and boat mooring $10–16 per night. Senior discount available. Major credit cards accepted. Open April–August.

Directions: From Tacoma, drive north on Highway 16 for about 10 miles to Highway 302/Key Peninsula Highway. Turn west and drive about five miles to Key Peninsula Highway. Turn south and drive 9.2 miles through the towns of Key Center and Home to Cornwall Road KPS (second road after crossing the Home Bridge). Turn left and drive 1.25 miles to 158 Avenue KPS and the park entrance.

Contact: Penrose Point State Park, 253/884-2514; State Park information, 360/902-8844.

107 KOPACHUCK STATE PARK

Rating: 8

On Puget Sound.
Map 1.6, grid f3, page 72

This park is located on Henderson Bay on Puget Sound near Tacoma. Noteworthy are the scenic views and dramatic sunsets across the Puget Sound and Olympic Mountains. The park covers 109 acres, with 5,600 feet of saltwater shoreline. A unique element of this park is that it includes Cutts Island (also called Deadman's Island), located one-half mile from shore, and is accessible only by boat (no camping on the island). The park has sandy beaches, located about 250 yards down the hill from the camp. Two miles of hiking trails are available. Fishing access is available by boat only. A boat launch is located not far from camp.

Campsites, facilities: There are 41 developed sites for tents or self-contained RVs up to 35 feet long, one primitive boat-in site for kayakers (no motorized boats permitted), and one group site for up to 40 people. Picnic tables and fire grills are provided. Restrooms, drinking water, flush toilets, coin-operated showers, an RV dump station, a covered picnic area, a Junior Ranger Program, interpretive activities, and boat buoys are available. Some facilities are wheelchair accessible. Leashed pets are permitted.

Reservations, fees: Reservations are not accepted for family sites. Sites are $16 per night, $2 per person from the primitive boat-in site, and $25 reservation fee for the group site, plus $2 per person with a 20-person minimum. Senior discount available. Open mid-May–September.

Directions: From Tacoma on I-5, turn north on Highway 16. Drive seven miles north to the second Gig Harbor exit. Take that exit and look for the sign for Kopachuck State Park. At the sign, turn west and drive five miles (the road changes names several times) to the camp (well marked).

Contact: Kopachuck State Park, 253/265-3606; State Park information, 360/902-8844.

108 GIG HARBOR RV RESORT

Rating: 7

Near Tacoma.
Map 1.6, grid f4, page 72

This is a popular layover spot for folks heading up to Bremerton. Just a short jaunt off the highway, it's pleasant, clean, and friendly. An 18-hole golf course, a full-service marina, and tennis courts are located nearby. Look for the great view of Mt. Rainier from the end of the harbor.

Campsites, facilities: There are 93 sites, most with full or partial hookups, including 28 drive-through sites and some long-term rentals, for tents or RVs of any length and one cabin. Restrooms, drinking water, flush toilets, showers, bottled gas, an RV dump station, a club room, a coin-operated laundry, ice, a playground with horseshoe pits, a sports field, and a heated swimming pool are available. Leashed pets are permitted.

Reservations, fees: Reservations recommended in the summer. Sites are $20–38 per night. Senior discount available. Major credit cards accepted. Open year-round.

Directions: From Tacoma, drive northwest on Highway 16 for 12 miles to Burnham Drive/North Rosedale exit. Take that exit and drive a short distance to the yield sign at Burnham Drive NW. Bear right on Burnham Drive NW and drive one mile to the campground on the left.

Contact: Gig Harbor RV Resort, 9515 Burnham Dr. NW, Gig Harbor, WA 98332, 253/858-8138 or 800/526-8311, fax 253/858-8399.

109 JOLLY ROGERS RV PARK

Rating: 7

Near Westport Harbor.
Map 1.7, grid a8, page 73

A beachside RV park with concrete sites and nearby beach access, this camp covers one acre near Westport Harbor. It's a prime spot for watching ocean sunsets, and on a clear day, snow-capped Mount Rainier is visible. Westport Light and Westhaven State Parks are nearby and offer day-use facilities along the ocean.

Campsites, facilities: There are 25 sites with full hookups for tents or RVs of any length. Restrooms, drinking water, flush toilets, showers, cable TV, and boat docks are available. Bottled gas, a store, a café, and a laundry are located within one mile. Leashed pets are permitted.

Reservations, fees: Reservations accepted. Sites are $18–20 per night. Open year-round.

Directions: From Aberdeen, drive south on State Route 105 for 22 miles southwest to Westport and Neddie Rose Drive. Turn right (north) and drive a short distance to the park on the right (Westport Docks).

Contact: Jolly Rogers RV Park, P.O. Box 342, Westport, WA 98595, 360/268-0265, fax 360/268-0265.

110 GRIZZLY JOE'S RV PARK

Rating: 9

On Point Chehalis.

Map 1.7, grid a8, page 73

Grizzly Joe's is a landscaped, one-acre park with ocean views on three sides. Sites are graveled and level. Snow-capped Mount Rainier is visible, and the sunsets are spectacular. Westport Light and Westhaven State Parks are nearby with multiple recreational options.

Campsites, facilities: There are 35 sites with full hookups and drive-through for RVs of any length. Electricity, drinking water, sewer, and cable TV are provided. An RV dump station, flush toilets, showers, a patio/picnic area with fire pit, a fish-cleaning station, outdoor cooking facilities, and boat docks are available. Bottled gas, a store, a café, a laundry, firewood, and ice are located within one-quarter mile. Leashed pets and permitted.

Reservations, fees: Reservations recommended. Sites are $21 per night. Open year-round.

Directions: From Aberdeen, drive south on State Route 105 for 22 miles southwest to Westport and Neddie Rose Drive. Turn right and drive four blocks to the park at the end of the road.

Contact: Grizzly Joe's RV Park, P.O. Box 1755, 743 Neddie Rose Dr., Westport, WA 98595, 360/268-5555, fax 360/268-1212.

111 AMERICAN SUNSET RV RESORT

Rating: 8

Near Westport Harbor.

Map 1.7, grid a8, page 73

If location is everything, then this RV camp, set on a peninsula, right on the ocean, is a big winner. It covers 32 acres and has its own hiking and biking trails. The park is divided into two areas: one for campers, another for long-term rentals. Nearby are Westhaven and Westport Light State Parks, popular with hikers, rock hounds, scuba divers, and surf anglers. Swimming (but not off the docks), fishing, and crabbing off the docks are also options. Monthly rentals are available in summer.

Campsites, facilities: There are 120 sites with full hookups, including some drive-through, for RVs up to 50 feet long, 50 tent sites, and one trailer. Picnic tables and fire rings are provided. Restrooms, drinking water, flush toilets, showers, modem hookups (in office), an RV dump station, a coin-operated laundry, a grocery store, propane, a seasonal heated pool, horseshoe pits, a playground, a fish-cleaning station, and a 2,400-square-foot recreation hall are available. Hookups for phone and cable TV are available for extended stays only. A marina is located three blocks away. Leashed pets are permitted.

Reservations, fees: Reservations recommended during the summer; phone 800/JOY-CAMP (800/569-2267). Sites are $13–22.50 per night, $5 per extra vehicle per night. Senior discount available. Major credit cards accepted. Open year-round.

Directions: From Aberdeen, drive south on State Route 105 for 22 miles southwest to Westport and Montesano Street (the first exit in Westport). Turn right (northeast) on Montesano and drive three miles to the resort on the left.

Contact: American Sunset RV Resort, 1209 N. Montesano St., Westport, WA 98595, 360/268-0207 or 800/569-2267, website: www.americansunsetrv.com.

112 COHO RV PARK, MOTEL & CHARTER

Rating: 4

Near Westport Harbor.
Map 1.7, grid a8, page 73

Fishermen stake out this RV park as their base camp. Fishing is good nearby for salmon and rockfish. One of several parks in the immediate area, Coho covers two acres and has its own fishing and whale-watching charters. Nearby Westhaven and Westport Light State Parks are popular with rock hounds, scuba divers, and surf anglers. A full-service marina is within easy walking distance.

Campsites, facilities: There are 76 sites, including six drive-through, with full hookups for RVs of any length. No tents are permitted. No open campfires are allowed. Restrooms, drinking water, flush toilets, coin-operated showers, an RV dump station, cable TV, a coin-operated laundry, a meeting hall, ice, and fishing charters are available. Boat docks and launching facilities are located nearby. Bottled gas, a store, and a café are within one mile. Leashed pets are permitted.

Reservations, fees: Reservations accepted. Sites are $20–22 per night, $2 per person per night for more than two people. Major credit cards accepted. Monthly rentals available. Open year-round.

Directions: From Aberdeen, drive south on State Route 105 for 22 miles southwest to Westport and Montesano Street (the first exit in Westport). Turn right (northeast) and drive 3.5 miles to Nyhus Street. Turn left (northwest) and drive 2.5 blocks to the campground on the left.

Contact: Coho RV Park, 2501 North Nyhus St., Westport, WA 98595, 360/268-0111 or 800/572-0177, fax 360/268-9425, website: www.westportwa.com/coho.

113 TOTEM RV PARK

Rating: 8

In Westport.
Map 1.7, grid a8, page 73

This 3.2-acre park, remodeled in 2000, is set 300 yards from the ocean and features an expanse of sand dunes between the park and the ocean. It has large, grassy sites close to Westhaven State Park, which offers day-use facilities. The owner is a fishing guide and can provide detailed fishing information. The salmon fishing within 10 miles of this park is often excellent in summer. Marked biking trails and a full-service marina are within five miles of the campground. A golf course will be opened just one block away in 2003 or 2004.

Campsites, facilities: There are 76 sites, most drive-through with full or partial hookups, for tents or RVs of any length. Picnic tables are provided. Restrooms, drinking water, flush toilets, coin-operated showers, an RV dump station, a coin-operated laundry, and ice are available. A pavilion, barbecue facilities with kitchen, and a fish-cleaning station are also available. Bottled gas and a café are located next door. A store is located within one-half mile. Boat docks, launching facilities, and fishing charters are nearby. Leashed pets are permitted.

Reservations, fees: Reservations accepted. Sites are $16.50–18.50 per night. Major credit cards accepted. Open year-round.

Directions: From Aberdeen, drive southwest on State Route 105 for 18 miles to the turnoff for Westport. Turn right (north) on the State Route 105 spur and drive 4.3 miles to the docks and Nyhus Street. Turn left on Nyhus Street and drive two blocks to the park on the left.

Contact: Totem RV, P.O. Box 1166, 2421 North Nyhus St., Westport, WA 98595, 360/268-0025 or 888/TOTEM-RV (888/868-3678).

114 HOLAND CENTER

Rating: 6

In Westport.

Map 1.7, grid a8, page 73

This pleasant, 18-acre RV park is one of several in the immediate area. The sites are graveled or grassy with pine trees between and have ample space. There is no beach access from the park, but full recreational facilities are available nearby. About half of the sites are long-term rentals.

Campsites, facilities: There are 80 sites with full hookups for RVs up to 40 feet long. No tents are allowed. Picnic tables are provided. Restrooms, drinking water, flush toilets, coin-operated showers, a coin-operated laundry, and storage sheds are available. Bottled gas, a store, a café, and ice are located within one mile. Boat docks and launching facilities are nearby. Leashed pets are permitted.

Reservations, fees: Reservations accepted. Sites are $20 per night. Open year-round.

Directions: From Aberdeen, drive south on State Route 105 for 22 miles to Westport. Continue on State Route 105 to Wilson Street. The park is at the corner of State Route 105 and Wilson Street.

Contact: Holand Center, 201 Wilson St., Westport, WA 98595, 360/268-9582, fax 360/532-3818.

115 PACIFIC MOTEL AND RV PARK

Rating: 5

Near Twin Harbors.

Map 1.7, grid a8, page 73

This five-acre park has grassy, shaded sites in a wooded setting. It's near Twin Harbors and Westport Light State Parks, both of which have beach access. A full-service marina is located within two miles. About 25 percent of the sites are occupied with long-term rentals.

Campsites, facilities: There are 80 sites with full hookups, including some drive-through, for RVs of any length and five tent sites. Picnic tables and fire rings are provided. Restrooms, drinking water, flush toilets, coin-operated showers, an RV dump station, propane gas, a fish-cleaning station, a recreation hall with a kitchen, cable TV, a public phone and fax, laundry facilities, and a heated swimming pool (seasonal) are available. A store, a café, and ice are located within one mile. Boat-launching and boat docks are nearby in a full-service marina. Leashed pets are permitted.

Reservations, fees: Reservations accepted. Sites are $15–20 per night, $2 per person per night for more than two people. Major credit cards accepted. Open year-round.

Directions: From Aberdeen, drive south on State Route 105 for approximately 18 miles to the State Route 105 spur road to Westport. Turn right (north) and drive 1.7 miles to the park on the right.

Contact: Pacific Motel and RV Park, 330 South Forrest, Westport, WA 98595, 360/268-9325, fax 360/268-6227, website: www.pacificmotelandrv.com.

116 ISLANDER RV PARK & MOTEL

Rating: 8

On Grays Harbor.

Map 1.7, grid a8, page 73

This three-acre park is located on Grays Harbor, close to Westport Light and Westhaven

State Parks, which offer oceanfront day-use facilities. On-site amenities include a hair salon, a gift shop, a restaurant, a motel, live music, dancing, fishing charters, and whale-watching trips. No open campfires are permitted.

Campsites, facilities: There are 60 sites with full hookups, including 30 drive-through, for RVs up to 40 feet long. Restrooms, drinking water, flush toilets, showers, a coffee shop, a gift shop, a restaurant, a coin-operated laundry, ice, a heated swimming pool (in season), boat docks, and fishing charters are available. Bottled gas, an RV dump station, and a store are located within one mile. Leashed pets are permitted.

Reservations, fees: Reservations accepted. Sites are $20–25 per night. Major credit cards accepted. Open year-round.

Directions: From Aberdeen, drive south on State Route 105 for 22 miles to Westport and Montesano Street. Turn right and drive two miles (Montesano becomes Dock Street) to the docks and Westhaven Drive. Turn left and drive four blocks to Neddie Rose Avenue. Turn right and drive one block to the park on the right.

Contact: Islander RV Park & Motel, 421 East Neddie Rose, Westport, WA 98595, 360/268-9166 or 800/322-1740, fax 360/268-0902, website: www.westportislander.com.

117 TWIN HARBORS STATE PARK

Rating: 8

On the Pacific Ocean.

Map 1.7, grid b8, page 73

The park covers 172 acres and is located four miles south of Westhaven. It was a military training ground in the 1930s. The campsites are close together and often crammed to capacity in the summer. Highlights include beach access and marked hiking trails, including the Shifting Sands Nature Trail. The most popular recreation activities are surf fishing, surfing, beachcombing, and kite flying. Fishing boats can be chartered nearby in Westport.

Campsites, facilities: There are 253 sites, including 49 with full hookups, for tents or RVs up to 35 feet long, five primitive tent sites, and one group site for up to 75 people. Picnic tables and fire grills are provided. Restrooms, drinking water, flush toilets, coin-operated showers, an RV dump station, interpretive activities, a picnic area with a kitchen shelter and electricity, and a playground with horseshoe pits are available. A store, a café, and ice are available within one mile. Some facilities are wheelchair accessible. Leashed pets are permitted.

Reservations, fees: Reserve at 888/CAMP-OUT (888/226-7688), website: www.parks.wa.gov/reservations ($7 reservation fee). Sites are $6–22 per night, $6 per extra vehicle per night. Senior discount available. The group site requires a $25 reservation fee and $2 per person with a 20-person minimum. Major credit cards accepted. Open mid-February–October.

Directions: From Aberdeen, drive south on State Route 105 for 17 miles to the park entrance on the left (three miles south of Westport).

Contact: Twin Harbors State Park, Twin Harbors State Park, Westport, WA 98595, 360/268-9717; State Park information, 360/902-8844.

118 OCEAN GATE RESORT

Rating: 5

In Grayland.

Map 1.7, grid b8, page 73

This privately run, seven-acre park has beach access and offers an alternative to the publicly run Grayland Beach State Park. Fishing, beach biking, and beachcombing are highlights.

Campsites, facilities: There are 24 sites with full hookups, including 12 drive-through, for RVs of any length, 20 tent sites, and six cabins. Picnic tables and fire rings are provided. Restrooms, drinking water, flush toilets, showers, a covered picnic shelter with barbecue, and a playground are available. Bottled gas, a store, a café, a laundry, and ice are available within one mile. Leashed pets are permitted.

Reservations, fees: Reservations accepted. Sites are $14.50–22 per night, $5 per extra vehicle per night. Open year-round.

Directions: From Aberdeen, drive south on State Route 105 for 21 miles to a Y intersection. Take State Route 105 left toward Grayland. The park is in Grayland on the right between Mileposts 26 and 27.

Contact: Ocean Gate Resort, P.O. Box 67, 1939 Rte. 105 S, Grayland, WA 98547, 360/267-1956 or 800/473-1956, website: www.ocean gateresort.net.

119 WESTERN SHORES MOTEL AND RV PARK

Rating: 4

In Grayland.
Map 1.7, grid b8, page 73

This small, private park is designed for families. Beach access and golf are not far, and Twin Harbors and Grayland Beach State Parks are just a few minutes away. This is an excellent layover for tourists who want to get off U.S. 101. About one-third of the RV sites are filled with permanent rentals.

Campsites, facilities: There are 30 drive-through sites with full hookups for RVs of any length. Picnic tables are provided. Restrooms, drinking water, flush toilets, showers, a community fire pit, cable TV, ice, propane, firewood, a pay phone, snacks, and a playground are available. A store, restaurant, and a lounge are located next door. Leashed pets are permitted.

Reservations, fees: Reservations recommended. Sites are $15.50 per night. Major credit cards accepted. Open year-round.

Directions: From Aberdeen, drive south on State Route 105 for 19 miles to Westport. Continue south on State Route 105 to Grayland. The RV park is located in town, right along State Route 105 on the right.

Contact: BWestern Shores Motel and RV Park, 2193 Rte. 105, Grayland, WA 98547, 360/267-1611.

120 GRAYLAND BEACH STATE PARK

Rating: 8

On the Pacific Ocean.
Map 1.7, grid b8, page 73

This state park features 7,500 feet of beach frontage. All the campsites are within easy walking distance of the ocean, with the bonus of a quarter-mile self-guided interpretive trail that provides a route from the campground to the beach. The campsites are relatively spacious for a state park, but they are not especially private. This park is popular with out-of-towners, especially during summer. Recreation options include fishing, beachcombing, and kite flying. The best spot for surfing is five miles north at Westhaven State Park.

Campsites, facilities: There are 60 sites with full-hookup for RVs up to 40 feet long and three primitive tent sites. Picnic tables and fire grills are provided. Drinking water and vault toilets are available. Restrooms, drinking water, flush toilets, and coin-operated showers are available. Some facilities are wheelchair accessible. Leashed pets are permitted.

Reservations, fees: Reserve at 888/CAMP-OUT (888/226-7688), website: www.parks.wa.gov/reservations ($7 reservation fee). Sites are $6–22 per night, $6 per extra vehicle per night. Senior discount available. Open year-round.

Directions: From Aberdeen, drive south on State Route 105 for 22 miles to the park entrance. The park is just south of the town of Grayland on the right (west).

Contact: Grayland Beach State Park, 360/268-9717; State Park information, 360/902-8844.

121 OCEAN PARK RESORT

Rating: 5

On Willapa Bay.
Map 1.7, grid e8, page 73

This wooded, 10-acre campground is located

one-half mile from Willapa Bay. With grassy, shaded sites, it caters primarily to RVs. Fishing, crabbing, and clamming are popular in season. Ocean Park has several festivals during the summer season. During these festivals, this resort fills up. To the north, Leadbetter Point State Park provides a side-trip option.

Campsites, facilities: There are 70 sites with full hookups, including some drive-through, for RVs of any length, seven tent sites, and several cottages (park model trailers). Picnic tables are provided. Fire pits are provided at tent sites. Restrooms, drinking water, flush toilets, coin-operated showers, bottled gas, a recreation hall, a coin-operated laundry, ice, a playground, firewood, a hot tub, and a heated swimming pool (in season) are available. A store and a café are available within one mile. Boat docks and launching facilities are located nearby on Willapa Bay. Leashed pets are permitted.

Reservations, fees: Reservations accepted. Sites are $20–22 per night, $3 per person per night for more than two people; cottages are $70–110 per night. Major credit cards accepted. Open year-round.

Directions: From Kelso/Longview on I-5, turn west on Highway 4 and drive 63 miles to U.S. 101. Turn south on U.S. 101 and drive 13 miles to the junction with Highway 103. Turn right (north) on Highway 103 and drive 11 miles to the town of Ocean Park and 259th Street. Turn right (east) on 259th Street and drive two blocks to the resort at the end of the road.

Contact: Ocean Park Resort, P.O. Box 339, 25904 R St., Ocean Park, WA 98640, 360/665-4585 or 800/835-4634, website: www.opresort.com.

122 WESTGATE MOTEL AND TRAILER COURT

Rating: 9

Near Long Beach.

Map 1.7, grid e8, page 73

Highlights at this pretty and clean four-acre camp include beach access, oceanfront sites, and all the amenities. There are 28 miles of beach that can be driven on. Additional facilities within five miles of the campground include an 18-hole golf course.

Campsites, facilities: There are 39 sites with full hookups, including 15 drive-through, for RVs of any length and six cabins. Restrooms, drinking water, flush toilets, showers, cable TV, a recreation hall, and ice are available. A store, a café, and a coin-operated laundry are available about four miles away. Boat docks and launching facilities are located nearby on Willapa Bay. Leashed pets are permitted.

Reservations, fees: Reservations accepted. Sites are $23–24 per night, $1 per person per night for more than two people; cabins are $55–65 per night. Major credit cards accepted. Open year-round.

Directions: From Kelso/Longview on I-5, turn west on Highway 4 and drive 63 miles to U.S. 101. Turn south on U.S. 101 and drive 13 miles to the junction with Highway 103. Turn north on Highway 103 and drive 7.5 miles to the campground on the left (located at the south edge of the town of Ocean Park).

Contact: Westgate Motel and Trailer Court, 20803 Pacific Hwy., Ocean Park, WA 98640, 360/665-4211.

123 OCEAN AIRE RV PARK

Rating: 4

Near Willapa Bay.

Map 1.7, grid e8, page 73

This camp is located in town, one-half mile from the shore of Willapa Bay. Tennis courts are one-quarter mile away, and a golf course is three miles away. Leadbetter Point State Park, about eight miles north, is open for day use and provides footpaths for walking through the state-designated natural area and wildlife refuge. Two-thirds of sites are long-term rentals, making reservations essential for the remaining sites during summer.

Campsites, facilities: There are 46 sites with

full hookups, including eight drive-through, for RVs of any length. No tents are allowed. Restrooms, drinking water, flush toilets, showers, picnic tables, an RV dump station, a coin-operated laundry, and ice are available. A store and a café are available next door. Boat rentals are nearby on Willapa Bay. Leashed pets are permitted.

Reservations, fees: Reservations accepted. Sites are $16 per night, $3 per person per night for more than two people. Open year-round.

Directions: From Kelso/Longview on I-5, turn west on Highway 4 and drive 63 miles to U.S. 101. Turn south on U.S. 101 and drive 13 miles to the junction with Highway 103. Turn north on Highway 103 and drive 11 miles to the town of Ocean Park and 259th Street. Turn right on 259th Street and drive two blocks to the camp.

Contact: Ocean Aire, 25918 R St., Ocean Park, WA 98640, 360/665-4027, website: www.opchamber.com.

124 MA AND PA'S PACIFIC RV PARK

LOTS PAINTED IN GRASS

Rating: 7

Near Long Beach. *NO TREES*

Map 1.7, grid f8, page 73

We wanted to give them some kind of award for the name of this place, but we haven't figured out what to give them yet. This park covers six acres and features both beach access and spacious, grassy sites near the shore. Additional facilities found within five miles of the campground include an 18-hole golf course, marked bike trails, and a riding stable.

Campsites, facilities: There are 53 sites with full or partial hookups for RVs of any length and an area for dispersed tent camping. Restrooms, drinking water, flush toilets, coin-operated showers, picnic tables, a coin-operated laundry, a recreation room, and ice are available. Bottled gas, a store, and a café are available within one mile. Leashed pets are permitted.

Reservations, fees: Reservations recommend-
ed. Sites are $22–25 per night, $2 per person per night for more than two people, $5 per extra vehicle per night, $2 per pet per night. Major credit cards accepted. Open year-round.

Directions: From Kelso/Longview on I-5, turn west on Highway 4 and drive 63 miles to U.S. 101. Turn south on U.S. 101 and drive 13 miles to the junction with Highway 103. Turn north on Highway 103 and drive four miles to the park on the left.

Contact: Ma and Pa's Pacific RV Park, 10515 Pacific Hwy., Long Beach, WA 98631, 360/642-3253, fax 360/642-5039, website: www.maandpasrvpark.com.

125 ANDERSEN'S RV PARK ON THE OCEAN

Rating: 7

Near Long Beach.

Map 1.7, grid f8, page 73

Timing is everything here. When the dates are announced for the local festivals, reservations start pouring in and the sites at this park can be booked a year in advance. Located near Long Beach, this five-acre camp features a path through the dunes that will get you to the beach in a flash. It is set in a flat, sandy area with gravel sites. Recreation options include beach bonfires, beachcombing, surf fishing, and clamming (seasonal). Additional facilities found within five miles of the campground include marked dune trails, a nine-hole golf course, a riding stable, and tennis courts.

Campsites, facilities: There are 57 sites with full hookups for RVs of any length and 15 tent sites. Picnic tables are provided, but not at tent sites. Tent sites have water available only. Restrooms, drinking water, flush toilets, showers, a meeting hall, cable TV, modem hookups, an RV dump station, a coin-operated laundry, ice, propane, bottled gas, a fax machine, a horseshoe pit, and a playground are available. A store and a café are available within two miles. Leashed pets are permitted.

Reservations, fees: Reservations accepted. Sites are $20–25 per night, $2 per person per night for more than two people. Major credit cards accepted. Open year-round.

Directions: From Kelso/Longview on I-5, turn west on Highway 4 and drive 63 miles to U.S. 101. Turn south on U.S. 101 and drive 13 miles to the junction with Highway 103. Turn north on Highway 103 and drive five miles to the park on the left.

Contact: Andersen's RV Park on the Ocean, 1400 138th St., Long Beach, WA 98631, 360/642-2231 or 800/645-6795, website: www.andersensrv.com.

126 OCEANIC RV PARK

Rating: 3

In Long Beach.
Map 1.7, grid f8, page 73
This two-acre park is located in the heart of downtown, within walking distance of restaurants and stores. It is also within five miles of an 18-hole golf course, marked bike trails, and a full-service marina.

Campsites, facilities: There are 20 drive-through sites with full hookups for RVs of any length. No tents are allowed. Restrooms, drinking water, flush toilets, and showers are available. Bottled gas, an RV dump station, a store, a café, a coin-operated laundry, and ice are located within one mile. Boat docks, launching facilities, and boat rentals are nearby. Leashed pets are permitted.

Reservations, fees: Reservations accepted. Sites are $14–21 per night, $2 per person per night for more than two people. Major credit cards accepted. Open year-round.

Directions: From Kelso/Longview on I-5, turn west on Highway 4 and drive 63 miles to U.S. 101. Turn south on U.S. 101 and drive 13 miles to the junction with Highway 103. Turn north on Highway 103 and drive two miles to Long Beach. Continue to the campground at the south junction of Pacific Highway (Highway 103) and Fifth Avenue on the right.

Contact: Oceanic RV Park, P.O. Box 242, 504 South Pacific Ave., Long Beach, WA 98631, 360/642-3836.

127 SAND-LO MOTEL AND RV PARK

Rating: 3

Near Long Beach.
Map 1.7, grid f8, page 73
Situated along the highway, this tiny, three-acre park is within four blocks of the beach. It is also within five miles of an 18-hole golf course, a full-service marina, and a riding stable.

Campsites, facilities: There are 15 sites with full hookups for tents or RVs of any length. Restrooms, drinking water, flush toilets, showers, cable TV, an RV dump station, and a coin-operated laundry are available. A restaurant is next door. Bottled gas, a store, a café, and ice are located within one mile. Leashed pets are permitted.

Reservations, fees: Reservations accepted. Sites are $15–20, $1 per person per night for more than two people. Major credit cards accepted. Open year-round.

Directions: From Kelso/Longview on I-5, turn west on Highway 4 and drive 63 miles to U.S. 101. Turn south on U.S. 101 and drive 13 miles to the junction with Highway 103. Turn north on Highway 103 and drive three miles to the park on the right.

Contact: Sand-Lo Motel and RV Park, 1920 North Pacific Hwy., Long Beach, WA 98631, 360/642-2600.

128 DRIFTWOOD RV PARK

Rating: 2

Near Long Beach.
Map 1.7, grid f8, page 73
This two-acre park features grassy, shaded sites and beach access. A fenced pet area is a bonus. Additional facilities within five miles of the

campground include an 18-hole golf course and a full-service marina.

Campsites, facilities: There are 55 sites with full hookups, including some drive-through, for RVs of any length. No tents are allowed. Restrooms, drinking water, flush toilets, showers, picnic tables, a coin-operated laundry, cable TV, and a fenced pet area are available. Bottled gas, a store, and a café are available within one mile. Leashed pets are permitted.

Reservations, fees: Reservations accepted. Sites are $22 per night, $2 per person per night for more than two people. Major credit cards accepted. Open year-round.

Directions: From Kelso/Longview on I-5, turn west on Highway 4 and drive 63 miles to U.S. 101. Turn south on U.S. 101 and drive 13 miles to the junction with Highway 103. Turn north on Highway 103 and drive two miles to the park on the right, at 14th North and Pacific.

Contact: Driftwood RV Park, P.O. Box 296, 1512 North Pacific Ave., Long Beach, WA 98631, 360/642-2711 or 888/567-1902, website: www.driftwood-rvpark.com.

129 SAND CASTLE RV PARK

Rating: 3

In Long Beach.

Map 1.7, grid f8, page 73

This park is set across the highway from the ocean. Although not particularly scenic, it is clean and does provide nearby beach access. The park covers two acres and is one of several in the immediate area. Additional facilities found within five miles of the campground include a nine-hole golf course, marked bike trails, a full-service marina, and two riding stables. Note that 25 percent of the sites are permanent rentals.

Campsites, facilities: There are 38 sites with full hookups, including some drive-through, for RVs of any length. Tents are permitted only with RVs. Restrooms, drinking water, flush toilets, coin-operated showers, cable TV hookups,

picnic tables, an RV dump station, a coin-operated laundry, and a pay phone are available. Bottled gas, a store, ice, and a café are available within one mile. Boat docks, launching facilities, and rentals are within five miles. Leashed pets are permitted.

Reservations, fees: Reservations accepted. Sites are $20–27, $1 per person per night for more than two people. Senior discount available in off-season. Major credit cards accepted. Open year-round.

Directions: From Kelso/Longview on I-5, turn west on Highway 4 and drive 63 miles to U.S. 101. Turn south on U.S. 101 and drive 13 miles to the junction with Highway 103. Turn north on Highway 103 and drive two miles to the park on the right.

Contact: Sand Castle RV Park, 1100 North Pacific Hwy., Long Beach, WA 98631, 360/642-2174.

130 SOU'WESTER LODGE, CABINS AND TRAILER PARK

Rating: 7

In Seaview on the Long Beach Peninsula.

Map 1.7, grid f8, page 73

This one-of-a-kind place features a lodge that dates back to 1892, vintage trailers available for rent, and cottages. Various cultural events are held at the park throughout the year, including fireside evenings with theater and chamber music. The park covers three acres, provides beach access, and is one of the few sites in the immediate area that provides spots for tent camping. This park often attracts creative people such as musicians and artists, and some arrive for vacations in organized groups. It is definitely not for Howie and Ethel from Iowa. Fishing is a recreation option. The area features the Lewis and Clark Interpretive Center, a lighthouse, museums, fine dining, bicycle and boat rentals, bicycle and hiking trails, and bird sanctuaries. Additional facilities found within five miles of the campground include an 18-hole golf course, a full-service marina, and a riding stable. The lodge was originally built for U.S. Senator Henry Winslow Corbett.

Campsites, facilities: There are 60 sites with full hookups, some drive-through, for RVs of any length, 10 tent sites, a historic lodge, four cottages, and 12 1950s-style trailers in vintage condition. Restrooms, drinking water, flush toilets, showers, cable TV, a coin-operated laundry, a classic video library, a picnic area with pavilion, and community fire pits and grills are available. Bottled gas, an RV dump station, a store, a café, and ice are located within one mile. Boat-launching facilities are nearby. Leashed pets are permitted.

Reservations, fees: Reservations accepted. Sites are $23–33, $2 per person per night for more than two people. Off-season discounts. Major credit cards accepted. Open year-round.

Directions: From Kelso/Longview on I-5, turn west on Highway 4 and drive 63 miles to U.S. 101. Turn south on U.S. 101 and drive 13 miles to the junction with Highway 103 (flashing light). Turn left to stay on U.S. 101 and drive one block to Seaview Beach Access Road (38th Place). Turn left and drive toward the ocean. Look for the campground on the left.

Contact: Sou'Wester Lodge, Cabins Trailer Park, P.O. Box 102, Seaview, WA 98644, 360/642-2542 (phone or fax), website: www .souwesterlodge.com.

131 FISHERMAN'S COVE RV PARK

Rating: 7

Near Fort Canby State Park.
Map 1.7, grid f8, page 73

This five-acre park is located by the docks, near where the Pacific Ocean and the Columbia River meet. It has beach and fishing access nearby and caters to fishermen. Fish- and clam-cleaning facilities are available in the park. A maritime museum, hiking trails, a full-service marina, and a riding stable are located within

five miles of the park. About 15 percent of the sites are taken by full-time renters.

Campsites, facilities: There are 51 sites with full hookups, including some drive-through, for RVs of any length and some tent sites. Restrooms, drinking water, flush toilets, coin-operated showers, cable TV hookups, an RV dump station, and a coin-operated laundry are available. Bottled gas, a store, and a café are located within one mile. Boat docks, launching facilities, and rentals are nearby. Leashed pets are permitted.

Reservations, fees: Reservations accepted. Sites are $10 for tents and $20 for RVs per night. Open year-round.

Directions: From Kelso/Longview on I-5, turn west on Highway 4 and drive 63 miles to U.S. 101. Turn south on U.S. 101 and drive 13 miles to the junction with Highway 103. Turn north on Highway 103 and drive two miles to Highway 100. Turn right (south) and drive to Ilwaco. At the junction of Spruce Street SW and First Street, turn right (west) on Spruce Street and drive one block to Second Avenue SW. Turn left (south) on Second Avenue SW and drive four blocks south to the campground on the right.

Contact: Fisherman's Cove RV Park, P.O. Box 921, 411 Second Ave. SW, Ilwaco, WA 98624, 360/642-3689 or 877/268-3789.

132 ILWACO KOA

Rating: 5

Near Fort Canby State Park.
Map 1.7, grid f8, page 73

This 17-acre camp is about nine miles from the beach and includes a secluded area for tents. You'll find a boardwalk nearby, as well as the Lewis and Clark Museum, lighthouses, an amusement park, and fishing from a jetty or charter boats. Additional facilities found within five miles of the campground include a maritime museum, hiking trails, and a nine-hole golf course. In our experience, attempts to phone this park were frustrated by a busy signal, over and over, for weeks.

Campsites, facilities: There are 114 sites with full hookups, including some drive-through, for RVs of any length, a tent area for up to 50 tents, and four cabins. Restrooms, drinking water, flush toilets, showers, cable TV, bottled gas, an RV dump station, a recreation hall, a store, a laundry, ice, and a playground are available. Leashed pets are permitted.

Reservations, fees: Reservations accepted; phone 800/562-3258. Sites are $25–35 per night, $5 per person per night for more than two people, and $6.50 for extra vehicle. Major credit cards accepted. Open mid-May–mid-October.

Directions: From Kelso/Longview on I-5, turn west on Highway 4 and drive 63 miles to U.S. 101. Turn south on U.S. 101 and drive 13 miles to the junction with Highway 103. The campground is located at the junction.

Contact: Ilwaco KOA, P.O. Box 549, Ilwaco, WA 98624, 360/642-3292 (phone or fax), website: www.koa.com.

133 FORT CANBY STATE PARK

Rating: 10

On the Pacific Ocean.

Map 1.7, grid f8, page 73

This park covers 1,882 acres set on the Long Beach Peninsula and is fronted by the Pacific Ocean. There is access to 27 miles of ocean beach and two lighthouses. The park contains old-growth forest, lakes, both freshwater and saltwater marshes, streams, and tidelands. It is the choice spot in the area for tent campers. There are two places to camp: a general camping area and the Lake O'Neil area, which offers sites right on the water. Highlights at the park include hiking trails and opportunities for surf, jetty, and ocean fishing. An interpretive center highlights the Lewis and Clark expedition as well as maritime and military history. North Head Lighthouse is open for touring. Colbert House Museum is open during the summer.

Campsites, facilities: There are 152 sites, including 27 sites with partial hookups (water and electricity) for tents or RVs up to 45 feet long, three cabins, and seven yurts. Picnic tables and fire grills are provided. Restrooms, drinking water, flush toilets, coin-operated showers, an RV dump station, a picnic area, interpretive activities, a horseshoe pit, athletic fields, a small store, and firewood are available. Some facilities are wheelchair accessible. Leashed pets are permitted.

Reservations, fees: Reserve at 888/CAMP-OUT (888/226-7688), website: www.parks.wa.gov/reservations ($7 reservation fee). Sites are $16–22 per night. Cabins and yurts are $35 per night. Senior discount available. Major credit cards accepted. Open year-round.

Directions: From the junction of Highway 4 and Highway 103 (a flashing light, south of Nemah), turn west on Highway 103 (toward Ilwaco) and drive two miles to Ilwaco and Highway 100. Turn right and drive three miles to the park entrance on the right.

Contact: Fort Canby State Park, 360/642-3078; State Park information, 360/902-8844.

134 PORTER CREEK

Rating: 7

On Porter Creek in Capitol Forest.

Map 1.8, grid a6, page 74

This primitive, rustic campground is located about 30 miles from Olympia. It is set in the Capitol Forest along the shore of Porter Creek and is managed by the Department of Natural Resources. It offers trails for hiking, horseback riding, or motorbiking. The camp serves as a launch point for a variety of trips. A trail leaves from across the road and leads one-half mile to Porter Falls, a hike most make. Within three miles, you can also access trails that lead to a network of 87 miles of off-road vehicle trails and 84 miles of trails for nonmotorized use— mountain biking is popular here. With corrals and hitching posts available, this camp is popular among horseback riders.

Campsites, facilities: There are 16 primitive sites for tents or small trailers. Picnic tables, fire grills, and tent pads are provided. Vault toilets, drinking water, corrals, hitching posts, and horse-loading ramps are available. All-terrain vehicles are permitted. Leashed pets are permitted.

Reservations, fees: Reservations are not accepted. There is no fee for camping. Open April–October.

Directions: On I-5, drive to Exit 88 (10 miles north of Chehalis) and U.S. 12. Turn west on U.S. 12 and drive 21 miles to Porter and Porter Creek Road. Turn right (northeast) on Porter Creek Road and drive three miles (last half mile is gravel) to a junction. Bear left and drive one-half mile to the campground on the left.

Contact: Department of Natural Resources, Central Region, 1405 Rush Rd., Chehalis, WA 98532-8763, 360/748-2383, fax 360/748-2387.

135 MIDDLE WADDELL

Rating: 7

On Waddell Creek in Capitol Forest.
Map 1.8, grid a8, page 74

This wooded campground is nestled along Waddell Creek in Capitol Forest. The trails in the immediate vicinity are used primarily for all-terrain vehicles (ATVs), making for some noise. There is an extensive network of ATV trails in the area. Mountain bikers tend to prefer Fall Creek camp.

Campsites, facilities: There are 24 sites for tents or RVs of any length. Picnic tables, fire grills, and tent pads are provided. Drinking water and vault toilets are available. This camp provides a full-time campground host. Some facilities are wheelchair accessible. Leashed pets are permitted.

Reservations, fees: Reservations are not accepted. There is no fee for camping. Open April–October.

Directions: From Olympia on I-5, drive south for about 10 miles to Exit 95 and Highway 121.

Turn west on Highway 121 and drive four miles to Littlerock. Continue west for one mile to Waddell Creek Road. Turn right and drive three miles and look for the campground entrance road on the left.

Contact: Department of Natural Resources, Central Region, 1405 Rush Rd., Chehalis, WA 98532-8763, 360/748-2383, fax 360/748-2387.

136 FALL CREEK

Rating: 7

On Fall Creek in Capitol Forest.
Map 1.8, grid a8, page 74

With good access to an 84-mile network of trails for nonmotorized use, this camp is something of a mountain-biking headquarters. Although ATVs are allowed in the campground, they are not allowed on the adjacent trails. This wooded camp on Fall Creek in Capitol Forest also provides horse facilities.

Campsites, facilities: There are eight primitive campsites for tents or small trailers. Picnic tables, fire grills, and tent pads are provided. Vault toilets, drinking water, corrals, a hitching post, and a horse-loading ramp are available. A day-use staging area is also available. Some facilities are wheelchair accessible. Leashed pets are permitted.

Reservations, fees: Reservations are not accepted. There is no fee for camping. Open April–October.

Directions: From Olympia on I-5, turn north on U.S. 101 and drive four miles to the Mud Bay exit. Take that to Delphi Road and drive south for six miles to Waddell Creek Road (bear right at the junction). Continue straight on Waddell Creek Road for two miles to the Triangle (turns into Sherman Valley Road). Continue straight on Sherman Valley Road for one mile (pavement ends, becomes C-Line Road) and continue four miles to Road C-6000. Turn left and drive three miles to the campground on the right.

Contact: Department of Natural Resources,

Central Region, 1405 Rush Rd., Chehalis, WA 98532-8763, 360/748-2383, fax 360/748-2387.

137 MARGARET MCKENNY

Rating: 7

In Capitol Forest.

Map 1.8, grid a8, page 74

With trails linked to an extensive network of trails for nonmotorized use only, this camp is used primarily as a trailhead for horseback riders and mountain bikers. Most of the campsites are well away from the stream, but seven walk-in sites are available, where a 300- to 400-foot walk down a stairway takes you to pretty streamside campsites.

Campsites, facilities: There are 25 primitive sites for tents or small trailers; seven sites are walk-ins. Picnic tables, fire grills, and tent pads are provided. Drinking water, vault toilets, a campfire circle, and a horse-loading ramp are available. A campground host is on-site. Some facilities are wheelchair accessible. Leashed pets are permitted.

Reservations, fees: Reservations are not accepted. There is no fee for camping. Open April–October.

Directions: From Olympia on I-5, drive south for about 10 miles to Exit 95 and Highway 121. Turn west on Highway 121 and drive four miles to Littlerock. Continue west for one mile to Waddell Creek Road. Turn right and drive 2.5 miles and look for the campground entrance road on the left.

Contact: Department of Natural Resources, Central Region, 1405 Rush Rd., Chehalis, WA 98532-8763, 360/748-2383, fax 360/748-2387.

138 SHERMAN VALLEY

Rating: 8

On Cedar Creek in Capitol Forest.

Map 1.8, grid a7, page 74

One of several secluded camps located in the Capitol Forest, Sherman Valley is managed by the Department of Natural Resources. Its pleasant, shady campsites are set along the shore of Porter Creek. The forest here is primarily alder and fir trees. Hiking trails can be found nearby (see North Creek Camp). Like nearby North Creek Camp, this camp is also used by hunters in season.

Campsites, facilities: There are seven primitive sites for tents or small trailers and three walk-in sites. Picnic tables, fire grills, and tent pads are provided. Vault toilets and drinking water are available. Mountain bikes are permitted on the roads only; trails are reserved for hikers. Leashed pets are permitted.

Reservations, fees: Reservations are not accepted. There is no fee for camping. Open April–October.

Directions: From Olympia, drive south on I-5 for 16 miles to U.S. 12. Turn west on U.S. 12 and drive 12 miles to Oakville. Continue west on U.S. 12 for 2.5 miles to D-Line Road (Cedar Creek entrance). Turn right (east) and drive 6.5 miles to the camp on the right (one lane, but paved all the way).

Contact: Department of Natural Resources, Central Region, 1405 Rush Rd., Chehalis, WA 98532-8763, 360/748-2383, fax 360/748-2387.

139 NORTH CREEK

Rating: 8

On Cedar Creek.

Map 1.8, grid a7, page 74

This little-known, wooded campground managed by the Department of Natural Resources is set along Cedar Creek (fishing available). There are trails for hikers only (no horses, no mountain bikes). A four-mile loop trail leads to Sherman Valley (in spring 2002, a bridge was out on this trail, with a longer alternative route available; call before planning a hike). Hunters use this camp in the fall. For a side trip, visit the Chehalis River, a five-mile drive to the west. A canoe launch off U.S. 12 is available north of Oakville.

Campsites, facilities: There are five primitive sites for tents or small trailers. Fire grills and tent pads are provided. Vault toilets and drinking water are available. Some facilities are wheelchair accessible. Mountain bikes are permitted on the roads only; trails are reserved for hikers. Leashed pets are permitted.

Reservations, fees: Reservations are not accepted. There is no fee for camping. Open April–October.

Directions: From Olympia, drive south on I-5 for 16 miles to U.S. 12. Turn west on U.S. 12 and drive 12 miles to Oakville. Continue west on U.S. 12 for 2.5 miles to D-Line Road (Cedar Creek entrance). Turn right (east) and drive 4.5 miles to the camp on the right (one lane, but paved all the way).

Contact: Department of Natural Resources, Central Region, 1405 Rush Rd., Chehalis, WA 98532-8763, 360/748-2383, fax 360/748-2387.

140 MIMA FALLS TRAILHEAD

Rating: 10

Near Mima Falls.

Map 1.8, grid a8, page 74

The highlight here is the five-mile loop trail for hikers and horseback riders that leads to beautiful 90-foot Mima Falls. The campground is quiet and pretty. When combined with the drinking water, free admission, and the tromp out to the waterfall, this spot is a first-rate choice. One of the unique qualities of this campground is that it provides facilities for both wheelchair users and horseback riders. The trail is not wheelchair accessible, but the facilities provide wheelchair users with horses access to Mima Falls. The trail runs across the brink of the falls.

Campsites, facilities: There is a primitive, dispersed camping area for about five tents or small trailers. Picnic tables, fire grills, and tent pads are provided. Drinking water, vault toilets, and a horse-loading ramp are available. Some facilities are wheelchair accessible. Leashed pets are permitted.

Reservations, fees: Reservations are not accepted. There is no fee for camping. Open April–October.

Directions: From Olympia, drive south on I-5 for 10 miles to Highway 121. Turn west on Highway 121 and drive four miles west to Littlerock. Continue west for one mile to Mima Road. Turn left on Mima Road and drive 1.5 miles to Bordeaux Road. Turn right on Bordeaux Road and drive one-half mile to Marksman Road. Turn right and drive two-thirds of a mile to the campground access road on the left. Turn left and drive 200 yards to the campground.

Contact: Department of Natural Resources, Central Region, 1405 Rush Rd., Chehalis, WA 98532-8763, 360/748-2383, fax 360/748-2387.

141 BAY CENTER/WILLAPA BAY KOA

Rating: 7

On Willapa Bay.

Map 1.8, grid c1, page 74

This KOA is set on the shore of Willapa Bay, within walking distance of a beach that seems to stretch to infinity. A trail leads to the beach and from here you can walk for miles in either direction. The beach sand is mixed with agates, driftwood, and seaweed. Dungeness crabs, clams, and oysters all live within the nearshore vicinity. Another bonus is that herds of Roosevelt elk roam the nearby woods. Believe it or not, there are also black bear, although they are seldom seen here. The park covers 11 acres, and the campsites are graveled and shaded. New owners in 2002 promise good things in future years.

Campsites, facilities: There are 55 sites with full or partial hookups, including some drive-through, for RVs of any length, 22 tent sites, and two cabins. Picnic tables are provided. Restrooms, drinking water, flush toilets, showers, bottled gas, an RV dump station, cable TV, modem hookups, a recreation hall, a store, firewood, a coin-operated laundry, and ice are available.

There is a café nearby. Boat docks and launching facilities are about three miles from camp on Willapa Bay. Leashed pets are permitted.

Reservations, fees: Reservations accepted at 800/562-7810. Sites are $21–27 per night, $4 per person per night for more than two people. Major credit cards accepted. Open mid-March–late October.

Directions: From Nemah on U.S. 101, drive north for five miles to Bay Center/Dike exit (located between Mileposts 42 and 43, 16 miles south of Raymond). Turn west and drive three miles to the campground.

Contact: Bay Center/Willapa Bay KOA, Bay Center Dike Rd., Bay Center, WA 98527, 360/875-6344, website: www.koa.com.

142 RAINBOW FALLS STATE PARK

Rating: 8

On the Chehalis River Bay.

Map 1.8, grid c7, page 74

This 139-acre park is set on the Chehalis River and boasts 3,400 feet of shoreline. The camp features stands of old-growth cedar and fir and is named after a few small cascades with drops of about 10 feet. The park has 10 miles of hiking trails, including an interpretive trail, seven miles of bike trails, and seven miles of horse trails. A pool at the base of Rainbow Falls is excellent for swimming. Another attraction, a small fuchsia garden, has more than 40 varieties. There are also several log structures built by the Civilian Conservation Corps in 1935.

Campsites, facilities: There are 47 sites for tents or self-contained RVs up to 32 feet long, three primitive tent sites, three equestrian sites with hitching points and stock water, and one group site. Picnic tables and fire rings are provided. Restrooms, drinking water, flush toilets, coin-operated showers, an RV dump station, a picnic area, interpretive activities, a playground with horseshoe pits, and a softball field are available. Firewood is available just outside the park. Leashed pets are permitted.

Reservations, fees: Reservations are not accepted. Sites are $6–16 per night, $6 per extra vehicle per night. Senior discount available. Open April–September.

Directions: From Chehalis on I-5, take Exit 77 to Highway 6. Turn west and drive 16 miles to the park entrance on the right.

Contact: Rainbow Falls State Park, 4008 Hwy. 6, Chehalis, WA 98532, 360/291-3767; State Park information, 360/902-8844.

143 WESTERN LAKES

Rating: 9

Near Naselle.

Map 1.8, grid e3, page 74

You want quiet and solitude? You found it. This tiny, primitive jewel of a campground sits near two lakes—Snag Lake and Western Lake (the lower lake)—in a wooded area near Western Lakes, just outside of Naselle. Snag Lake, the area's feature, provides fishing for rainbow trout, brook trout, and cutthroat trout. No gas motors are permitted, so it is ideal for float tubes, prams, rowboats, or canoes (with electric motors permitted). There are some good hiking trails nearby, including a route that connects the two lakes. The lake and campground offer good views of Radar Ridge. A wheelchair-accessible trail is available around Snag Lake, and all campsites provide wheelchair access. It's a prime camp for travelers heading to the coast who want a day or two of privacy before they hit the crowds.

Campsites, facilities: There are five tent sites, all wheelchair-accessible. Picnic tables, fire grills, tent pads, and vault toilets are provided, but there is no drinking water. Garbage must be packed out. Leashed pets are permitted.

Reservations, fees: Reservations are not accepted. There is no fee for camping. Open year-round.

Directions: From Kelso/Longview on I-5, turn west on Highway 4 and drive 60 miles (near Naselle) to Milepost 3 and C-Line Road. Turn north on C-Line Road (one-lane gravel road, becomes C-4000) uphill, take the left fork at Naselle Youth Camp Entrance, and drive 2.9 miles to C-2600 (gravel one-lane road). Turn left on Road C-2600 and drive nine-tenths of a mile (after four-tenths of a mile it becomes C-Line Road) to C-2650. Turn right and drive 1.2 miles to the campground on the right at Western Lake. Or for Snag Lake: At Road C-2400, turn on Road C-2400 and drive six-tenths of a mile to the campground at Snag Lake.

Contact: Department of Natural Resources, Central Region, 1405 Rush Rd., Chehalis, WA 98532-8763, 360/748-2383.

144 RIVER'S END CAMPGROUND AND RV PARK

Rating: 6

Near Fort Columbia State Park.
Map 1.8, grid f1, page 74

This wooded campground spreads over five acres and has riverside access. Salmon fishing is available here. Additional facilities found within five miles of the campground include marked bike trails and a full-service marina. Also nearby is Fort Columbia State Park.

Campsites, facilities: There are 54 sites with full hookups, including some drive-through, for RVs of any length and 24 tent sites. Picnic tables are provided at RV sites. Fire pits are provided at tent sites. Restrooms, drinking water, flush toilets, coin-operated showers, an RV dump station, a recreation hall, a coin-operated laundry, firewood for a fee, a fish-cleaning station, ice, and a playground are available. Bottled gas, a store, and a café are located within one mile. Boat docks, launching facilities, and rentals are nearby on the Columbia River. Leashed pets permitted.

Reservations, fees: Reservations accepted. Sites are $14–20 per night, $1 per person per night for more than two people. Open April–late October.

Directions: From Kelso/Longview on I-5, turn

west on Highway 4 and drive 60 miles to Highway 401. Turn south on Highway 401 and drive 14 miles to the park entrance (just south of Chinook) on the left.

Contact: River's End Campground and RV Park, P.O. Box 280, 12 Bayview St., Chinook, WA 98614, 360/777-8317.

145 MAUCH'S SUNDOWN RV PARK, INC.

Rating: 5

Near Fort Columbia State Park.
Map 1.8, grid f1, page 74

This is an adults-only park with about 35 percent of the sites rented long-term, usually throughout the summer. The park covers four acres, has riverside access, and is in a wooded, hilly setting with grassy sites. Nearby fishing from shore is available. It's near Fort Columbia State Park.

Campsites, facilities: There are 50 sites with full and partial hookups for RVs of any length. No tents, children, or large pets are permitted. Small pets are permitted. Restrooms, drinking water, flush toilets, coin-operated showers, picnic tables, an RV dump station, cable TV, a coin-operated laundry, a store, propane gas, and ice are available. A café is located within three miles. Boat docks and launching facilities are nearby on the Columbia River.

Reservations, fees: Reservations accepted. Sites are $8–20 per night, $1.50 per person per night for more than two people, and $1.50 per extra vehicle per night. Open year-round.

Directions: From Kelso/Longview on I-5, turn west on Highway 4 and drive 60 miles to Highway 401. Turn south on Highway 401 and drive to U.S. 101. Take U.S. 101 to the right and continue for one-half mile (do not go over the bridge) to the park on the right.

Contact: Mauch's Sundown RV Park, 158 Rte. 101, Chinook, WA 98614, 360/777-8713.

146 SKAMOKAWA VISTA PARK

Rating: 7

Near the Columbia River.

Map 1.8, grid f5, page 74

This public camp covers 70 acres and features one-half mile of sandy beach and a Lewis and Clark interpretive site installed in 2002. A short hiking trail is nearby. The camp also has nearby access to the Columbia River, where recreational options include fishing, swimming, and boating. Additional facilities found within five miles of the campground include a full-service marina and additional tennis courts. This park is in a growth mode, and there is a good chance that additional campsites and yurts will be added by 2003. In Skamokawa, a River Life Interpretive Center stays open year-round.

Campsites, facilities: There are 21 sites with par-

tial hookups for RVs of any length, nine sites with no hookups for tents or RVs, and four tent sites. Picnic tables and fire grills are provided. Restrooms, drinking water, flush toilets, coin-operated showers, an RV dump station, firewood, tennis courts, basketball courts, and a playground are available. Bottled gas, a store, a café, and ice are located within one mile. Boat docks, launching facilities, and canoe and kayak rentals are nearby. Leashed pets are permitted.

Reservations, fees: Reservations accepted. Sites are $13–22 per night. Open year-round.

Directions: From Kelso/Longview on I-5, turn west on Highway 4 and drive 35 miles to Skamokawa. Continue west on Highway 4 for one-half mile to the park on the left.

Contact: Skamokawa Vista Park, Port of Wahkiakum No. 2, P.O. Box 220, 13 Vista Park Rd., Skamokawa, WA 98647, 360/795-8605, fax 360/795-8611.

© TOM STIENSTRA

Chapter 2
Seattle and the
San Juan Islands

Chapter 2—
Seattle and the San Juan Islands

N o metropolitan area in the world offers a wider array of recreation than Seattle-Tacoma and its sphere of influence. At the center are water, woods, and islands. One of our favorite views anywhere is from the top of Mt. Constitution on Orcas Island, where on a clear day you can look out over an infinity of sunswept charm. Take one look and you'll know this is why you came.

The scope of parks, campgrounds, and recreation on the islands in this region is preeminent. Even if you're traveling by car, you still have an array of excellent destinations, including many available by ferry transport. Many state parks offer gorgeous water-view campsites. Well-furnished RV parks along the I-5 corridor offer respite for vacationers in need of a layover, and hidden lakes, such as Cascade Lake on Orcas Island, will surprise you with their beauty.

But live here for even a short time and you will realize that you need some kind of boat to do it right. A power boat, sailboat, or kayak offers instant access to adventure, not to mention access to boat-in campsites. With a power boat, you get instant freedom from the traffic on the I-5 corridor, as well as near-unlimited access to destinations in Puget Sound and the linked inlets, bays, and canals. Fishing can be good, too. On calm days with light breezes, roaming the peaceful waters in a sailboat amid dozens of islands provides a segue to instant tranquility. With some 25 boat-in campsites available, often along calm, sheltered waters, there is no better place anywhere to sea kayak. With near-perfect destinations like these, this area is quickly becoming the sea kayaking capital of the world.

People who live here year-round, fighting the rat maze of traffic on I-5, can easily fall into the trap of tunnel vision, never seeing beyond the line of cars ahead of them. Escape that tunnel. Scan the maps and pages in this region, and in the process, reward yourself with the best water-based adventure anywhere.

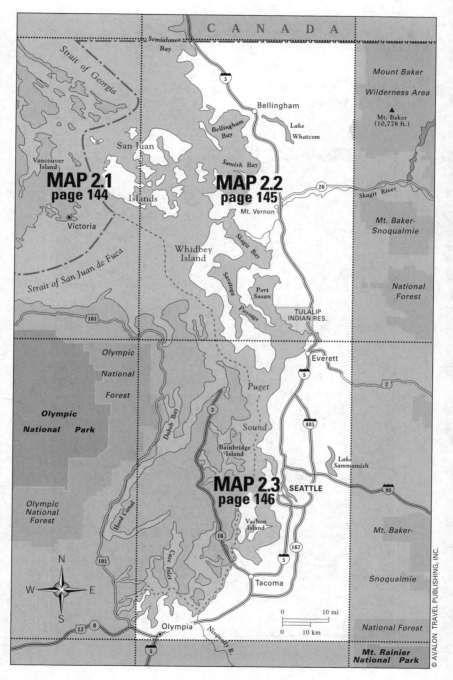

Map 2.1

Campgrounds 1–6
Pages 147–149

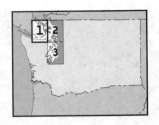

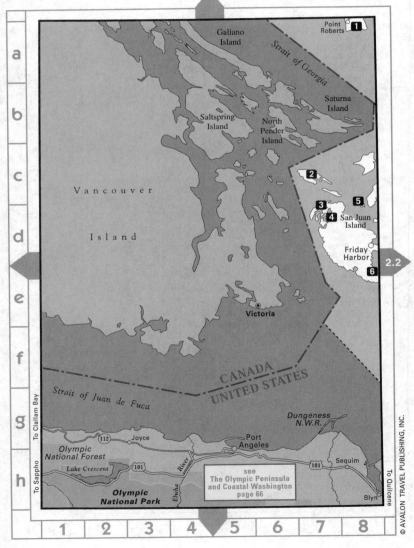

Map 2.2

Campgrounds 7–49
Pages 150–169

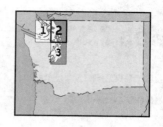

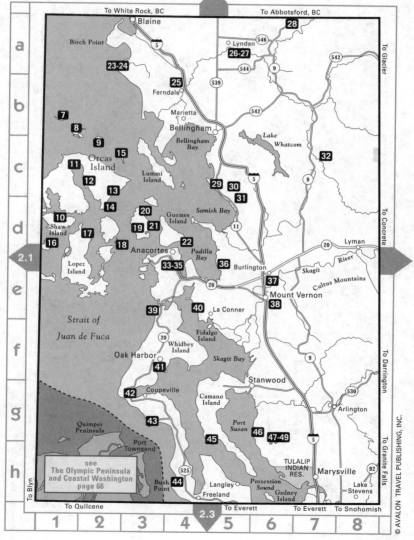

To White Rock, BC

To Abbotsford, BC

Blaine

28

Birch Point

Lynden

546

26-27

542

23-24

544

9

25

539

Ferndale

Marietta

542

Lake
Whatcom

Bellingham

Bellingham
Bay

7

8

9

15

Orcas
Island

11

Lummi
Island

32

12

5

13

9

14

29   30

31

20

Guemes
Island

Samish Bay

10

19   21

Shaw
Island

17

22

Padilla
Bay

11

16

18

Anacortes

20

Lyman

Lopez
Island

33-35

36   Burlington

Skagit   River

37

Cultus Mountains

20

Strait of
Juan de Fuca

39

40   La Conner

Mount Vernon

38

Fidalgo
Island

20

Whidbey
Island

9

Oak Harbor

Skagit Bay

41

Stanwood

42   Coupeville

Camano
Island

530

43

Arlington

Quimper
Peninsula

Port
Susan

46   47-49

5

45

Port
Townsend

see
The Olympic Peninsula
and Coastal Washington
page 66

TULALIP
INDIAN
RES.

Marysville

92

525

44

Langley
Freeland

Possession
Sound

Lake
Stevens

To Quilcene

To Everett

To Everett

To Snohomish

Bush
Point

Gedney
Island

To Blyn

2.1

2.3

To Glacier

To Concrete

To Darrington

To Granite Falls

© AVALON TRAVEL PUBLISHING, INC.

Map 2.3

Campgrounds 50–62
Pages 169–174

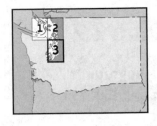

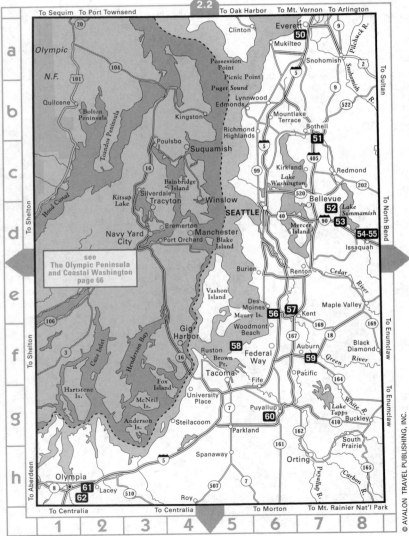

© AVALON TRAVEL PUBLISHING, INC.

❶ WHALEN'S RV PARK

🚶 🚐 🐕 🚗 ⛺

Rating: 6

On Point Roberts.

Map 2.1, grid a8, page 144

This RV park is located on Point Roberts, so remote you must drive through Canada and then return south into the United States to reach it. But don't hop on the bandwagon just yet. Take note that 80 percent of the campsites are booked for the entire summer. That makes reservations critical for anybody wishing to stay overnight. The park features a mix of woods and water, and has grassy sites and lots of trees. A recreation field is provided for campers. Nearby recreational options include an 18-hole golf course, a full-service marina, and tennis courts.

Campsites, facilities: There are 100 sites for tents and 50 sites with partial hookups (no sewer) for RVs of any length. Picnic tables and fire grills are provided. Restrooms, drinking water, flush toilets, coin-operated showers, an RV dump station, and firewood are available. A store, a café, a coin-operated laundry, and ice are located within one mile. Boat docks and launching facilities are nearby. Leashed pets are permitted.

Reservations, fees: Reservations accepted. Sites are $15–20 per night. Major credit cards accepted. Open May–late October.

Directions: From Bellingham, take I-5 north through Blaine and the border customs into Canada to Highway 99 North. Continue northwest on Highway BC 99N for 18 miles to BC 17. Turn and drive six miles to the town of Tsawwassen and 56th Street. Turn west and drive to Benson Road. Turn left on Benson Road and drive one mile to Boundary Bay Road. Turn left and drive one mile to Bay View Road. Turn left again and drive one-half mile to the park on the left.

Contact: Whalen's RV Park, Roosevelt and Derby, Point Roberts, WA 98281, 360/945-2874, fax 360/945-0934.

❷ STUART ISLAND MARINE STATE PARK BOAT-IN

🚶 🏊 🚐 🐕 ⛺

Rating: 9

Northwest of San Juan Island.

Map 2.1, grid c7, page 144

For most campers, this is really stalking the unknown. Stuart Island is a remote little spot on the edge of Canadian waters that covers 153 acres and has excellent harbors for mooring. It's the westernmost of the marine parks, making it a jumping-off point for Sucia Island, Orcas Island, and San Juan Island parks. There is good fishing at nearby Reid and Provost Harbors. On holiday weekends, it usually fills up; on summer weekends, it is typically about 70 percent filled; and on weekdays, it is about half filled. That makes it the second busiest park in the area, receiving about 70,000 visitors per year.

Campsites, facilities: There are 22 primitive boat-in campsites, including four reserved for non-motorized boats only. Picnic tables and fire rings are provided. Drinking water (summer season only) and composting toilets are available. There are also 22 buoys, and floats are available for overnight moorage. Garbage must be packed out. Leashed pets are permitted.

Reservations, fees: Reservations are not accepted. Sites are $6 per night, moorage is $10–16 per night, and buoys are $7 per night. Senior discount available. Open year-round, with limited facilities in winter.

Directions: The park is on the north side of Stuart Island and is accessible only by boat. Stuart Island is located northwest of San Juan Island.

Contact: San Juan Marine Area, Star Rte., Box 177, Olga, WA 98279, 360/378-2044; State Park information, 360/902-8844, fax 360/856-2150.

3 POSEY ISLAND STATE PARK BOAT-IN

Rating: 9

Near Roche Harbor.

Map 2.1, grid d7, page 144

If you want a beautiful little spot all to yourself, this can often be it. Imagine that, an island all to yourself. It's difficult to get here, however. You must arrive by non-motorized boat; that is, only kayak, canoe, or pelican sailboats. The best way is by sea kayak, paddling in from San Juan Island out of Roche Harbor. There are no docks or mooring buoys. Situated on a one-acre island, this is not only one of the smallest designated campgrounds in Washington, but also one of the most idyllic and beautiful to reach by small boat, with lots of wild flowers in spring, including chocolate lilies. In an attempt to keep it from being loved to death, no more than 16 people are permitted on the island at one time. There's not much here, and that's exactly why it is so well loved. Everything becomes simplified, so it feels as if you have the entire world to yourself. And on Posey Island, you do.

Campsites, facilities: There are two primitive boat-in campsites. Fire rings and a composting toilet are provided. No drinking water is available. Garbage must be packed out.

Reservations, fees: Reservations are not accepted. Sites are $6 per night. Senior discount available. Open year-round.

Directions: This little island is located just north of Roche Harbor (on San Juan Island) and is accessible only by small boat. From Roche Harbor, you head out Wescott Bay, turn right through Mosquito Pass, and cruise about two miles to Posey Island.

Contact: San Juan Marine Area, Star Rte., Box 177, Olga, WA 98279, 360/378-2044, fax 360/856-2150.

4 LAKEDALE RESORT FERRY-IN

Rating: 7

On San Juan Island.

Map 2.1, grid d7, page 144

This is a nice spot for visitors who want the solitude of an island camp, yet all the amenities of a privately run campground. Fishing, swimming, and boating are available at the Lakedale Lakes. A sand volleyball court, a half-court basketball area, and a grassy sports field are also on-site. Roche Harbor and Wescott Bay are nearby to the north, and Friday Harbor and its restaurants are nearby to the south.

Campsites, facilities: There are 102 sites for tents and 18 sites with partial hookups (no sewer) for tents or RVs up to 40 feet long. There are also six group sites, three tent cabins, six log cabins, and 10 luxury lodge rooms. Picnic tables and fire rings are provided. Restrooms, drinking water, flush toilets, showers, and firewood are available for a fee. A store and ice are available. Boat docks, three swimming beaches, and boat, bike, camping, and fishing gear rentals are available on-site. Leashed pets are permitted.

Reservations, fees: Reservations accepted. Sites are $28–31, discounts in off-season; $3.50–6 per person per night for more than two people, $7–8 per night per extra vehicle, and $1.50 per pet per night. Hike-in/bike-in sites are $5–9 per night per person. Major credit cards accepted. Open mid-March–mid-October for camping. Cabin rentals available year-round.

Directions: From Seattle on I-5, drive north to Burlington and Highway 20. Turn west on Highway 20 and drive 12 miles to the Highway 20 North spur, following signs to the San Juan Islands Ferry Terminal in Anacortes. Take the ferry to Friday Harbor on San Juan Island. From the ferry landing at Friday Harbor, drive two blocks on Spring Street to 2nd Street. Turn right (northwest) on 2nd Street and drive a one-half mile to Tucker Avenue (it becomes Roche Harbor Road). Turn right (north) and continue 4.5 miles to the campground on the left.

Contact: Lakedale Resort, 4313 Roche Harbor Rd., Friday Harbor, WA 98250, 360/378-2350 or 800/617-CAMP (800/617-2267), fax 360/378-0944, website: www.lakedale.com.

5 JONES ISLAND MARINE STATE PARK BOAT-IN

Rating: 9

Near Orcas Island.
Map 2.1, grid d8, page 144

This small island may seem like a hidden spot, but it is an easy boat ride out of Doe Harbor at Orcas. It gets among the heaviest use of all the island campgrounds in the region, even though only non-motorized craft are permitted (making it an ideal destination for sea kayakers). The campground is near the beach, so you don't have to carry your gear very far. The area offers good fishing and scuba diving. A note of caution: Raccoons have become pests and campers are advised to keep food well contained. Rangers here make a special request to please not feed the raccoons, deer, or other wildlife. Sunsets often provide breathtaking beauty from this island. In addition, it is set amid a national wildlife and migratory bird refuge. Another plus is that two big lawn areas make family and group camping ideal. Note that the docks are in place April–mid-October.

Campsites, facilities: There are 21 primitive boat-in campsites and a group site for up to 65 people. Picnic tables and fire rings are provided. Drinking water and vault, composting, and pit toilets (pick your favorite!) are available. Boat buoys and floats are available for overnight moorage. Leashed pets are permitted.

Reservations, fees: Reservations are not accepted for family sites. Reservations required for the group site. Sites are $6 per night, $10–16 for docking per night, $7 for a moorage buoy.

Senior discount available. The group site is $25, plus $2 per person per night. Open May–September.

Directions: The campground is on tiny Jones Island, located less than one mile off the southwest tip of Orcas Island. This camp is accessible only by boat. Look for the boat buoys just offshore from the campsites.

Contact: San Juan Marine Area, Star Rte., Box 177, Olga, WA 98279, 360/378-2044; State Park information, 360/902-8844, fax 360/856-2150.

6 GRIFFIN BAY BOAT-IN

Rating: 9

On San Juan Island.
Map 2.1, grid e8, page 144

This tiny, remote camp is ideal for husband-and-wife kayakers who want the place to themselves. It receives little use, yet it's located on one of the prettiest islands in the area and is a favorite among in-the-know kayakers. Only non-motorized boats are permitted to land. The island covers just four acres, and with one campsite and two mooring buoys, it is the smallest designated campground in Washington.

Campsites, facilities: There is one primitive boat-in campsite. A fire pit is provided. A pit toilet and three picnic sites are available. No drinking water is available. Garbage must be packed out. Two boat buoys are available for overnight moorage.

Reservations, fees: Reservations are not accepted. There is no fee for camping. Open year-round.

Directions: Griffin Bay is on the southeast side of San Juan Island (south of Friday Harbor), somewhat protected by Low Point. It's accessible only by boat.

Contact: Department of Natural Resources, Northwest Region, 919 North Township St., Sedro-Woolley, WA 98284-9395, 360/856-3500, fax 360/856-2150.

⑦ PATOS ISLAND STATE PARK BOAT-IN

🚶 🛶 🚤 🐕 ⛺

Rating: 9

Near Sucia Island.

Map 2.2, grid b1, page 145

If you're going to get stranded on an island, this is not a bad choice, provided you like your companion. There are good hiking trails and excellent fishing and clam-digging opportunities here. It's tiny, primitive, and used by few. Patos Lighthouse is a favorite attraction on this island. It also features great views of the Canadian islands, and sunsets are often drop-dead beautiful.

Campsites, facilities: There are seven primitive boat-in campsites. Fire rings are provided. Vault and pit toilets are available, but there is no drinking water. Boat buoys are available for overnight moorage. Garbage must be packed out. Leashed pets are permitted.

Reservations, fees: Reservations are not accepted. Sites are $6 per night, $7 per night for a mooring buoy. Senior discount available. Open year-round.

Directions: The park is on the east side of Patos Island, which is 2.5 miles northwest of Sucia Island and five miles northwest of Orcas Island. It's accessible only by boat and is the northernmost of the coastal islands.

Contact: San Juan Marine Area, Star Rte., Box 177, Olga, WA 98279, 360/378-2044; State Park information, 360/902-8844, fax 360/856-2150.

⑧ SUCIA ISLAND MARINE STATE PARK BOAT-IN

🚶 🛶 🚤 🐕 ⛺

Rating: 9

Near Orcas Island.

Map 2.2, grid b1, page 145

Here's a classic spot with rocky outcrops for lookout points and good beach and fishing areas. Sucia Island covers 562 acres and provides opportunities for hiking, clamming, crab-

bing, canoeing, and scuba diving. Although primitive, the campground is beautiful and well worth the trip, making it the busiest park in the chain of San Juan Islands. It also has the most moorage. This camp is full during summer, often even on weekdays.

Campsites, facilities: There are 55 primitive boat-in campsites and two group sites for up to 50 people each. Picnic tables and fire rings are provided. Drinking water is available in the summer season, and vault and composting toilets and two docks are also available. Boat buoys and floats are available for overnight moorage. Garbage must be packed out. Leashed pets are permitted.

Reservations, fees: Reservations are not accepted. Sites are $6 per night. Group sites are $2 per person per night. Senior discount available. Open year-round.

Directions: The park is on the north side of Sucia Island, which is located 2.5 miles north of Orcas Island. It's accessible only by boat.

Contact: San Juan Marine Area, Star Rte., Box 177, Olga, WA 98279, 360/378-2044; State Park information, 360/902-8844, fax 360/856-2150.

⑨ MATIA ISLAND STATE PARK BOAT-IN

🚶 🏊 🛶 🚤 🐕 ⛺

Rating: 9

Near Orcas Island.

Map 2.2, grid c2, page 145

Campsites here are located just a short walk from the docking facilities (available April–mid-October), a big plus since many of the other island campgrounds don't have docks. Otherwise the camp is primitive, so it gets lighter use than the other campgrounds set on islands in the area. A one-mile loop trail from the campground leads through an old-growth cedar forest. Other highlights include good fishing and beachcombing. Scuba diving is also popular.

Campsites, facilities: There are six primitive boat-in campsites. Fire rings and composting toilets are provided. No drinking water is available. There is a boat dock, and buoys and floats are available for overnight moorage. Note that docks are in place April–mid-October. Garbage must be packed out. Leashed pets are permitted.

Reservations, fees: Reservations are not accepted. Sites are $6 per night, dock moorage is $10–16 per night, and mooring buoys are $7 per night. Senior discount available. Open year-round, with extremely limited winter facilities.

Directions: The campground is located on the northeast side of Matia Island, which is 2.5 miles northeast of Orcas Island (located between Clark Island to the southeast, Sucia Island to the northwest, and Orcas Island to the south). It's accessible only by boat.

Contact: San Juan Marine Area, Star Rte., Box 177, Olga, WA 98279, 360/378-2044; State Park information, 360/902-8844, fax 360/856-2150.

10 BLIND ISLAND STATE PARK BOAT-IN

Rating: 9

Near Shaw Island.
Map 2.2, grid d1, page 145

This island has few trees and is known for its rocky shoreline. It's dangerous and ill advised to try beaching cruiser-style boats. Only non-motorized boats are permitted, and skilled kayakers will not have difficulty landing unless the water is rough. Blind Island State Park is a designated natural area and is committed to conserving a natural environment in a minimally developed state. This is not a place for large groups to throw big barbecues, but rather a quiet place for campers to enjoy the environment in its natural state.

Campsites, facilities: There are four primitive boat-in campsites. Fire rings are provided. Composting and pit toilets are available, but there is no drinking water. Boat buoys are available for overnight moorage. Leashed pets are permitted.

Reservations, fees: Reservations are not accepted. Sites are $6 per night, $7 for mooring buoys. Open year-round.

Directions: The campground is located just west of the Shaw Island ferry landing on little Blind Island in Blind Bay. The nearest boat ramps are at Obstruction Pass on Orcas Island or Odlin County Park on Lopez Island.

Contact: San Juan Marine Area, Star Rte., Box 177, Olga, WA 98279, 360/378-2044; State Park information, 360/902-8844, fax 360/856-2150.

11 WEST BEACH RESORT FERRY-IN

Rating: 9

On Orcas Island.
Map 2.2, grid c1, page 145

Right on the beach, this resort offers salmon fishing, boating, swimming, and an apple orchard. An excellent alternative to Moran State Park, which is often full, it offers the same recreation opportunities. The beaches at Orcas Island are prime spots for whale-watching and beautiful views, especially at sunrise and sunset.

Campsites, facilities: There are 62 sites with partial hookups (no sewer) for tents or RVs of any length. There are also 18 cabins. Restrooms, coin-operated showers (from April–October only), a public phone, a store, a playground, a coin-operated laundry, ice, bottled gas, and firewood are available. A hot tub is available for a fee. Also on-site are a boat ramp, a dock, a marina, and rentals. Leashed pets are permitted.

Reservations, fees: Reservations recommended. Sites are $25–35 per night for up to three people, $5 per extra vehicle per night, and $5 per pet per night. Major credit cards accepted. Open year-round.

Directions: From Seattle on I-5, drive north to Burlington and Highway 20. Turn west on Highway 20 and drive 12 miles to the Highway 20 North spur, following signs to the San Juan Islands Ferry Terminal in Anacortes. Take the ferry to Orcas Island. From the ferry landing, turn left and drive 11 miles on Horseshoe High-way/Orcas Road to the entrance of Eastsound. A green sign directs you left toward Moran State Park. Turn left (continuing on Orcas Road) and drive one-half mile to Enchanted Forest Road. Turn left and drive to the end of Enchanted Forest Road and the resort.

Contact: West Beach Resort, 190 Waterfront Way, Eastsound, WA 98245, 360/376-2240, fax 360/376-4746, website: www.westbeachresort.com.

12 MORAN STATE PARK FERRY-IN

Rating: 10

On Orcas Island.
Map 2.2, grid c2, page 145

This state park is drop-dead beautiful. It covers 5,252 acres, with surprise lakes, hiking trails, and the best mountaintop views anywhere in the chain of islands. There are actually four separate campgrounds plus a primitive area. You can drive to the summit of Mt. Constitution, which tops out at 2,409 feet, then climb up the steps to a stone observation tower (built in 1936 by the Civilian Conservation Corps) for sensational 360-degree views of Vancouver, Mt. Baker, the San Juan Islands, the Cascade Mountains, and several cities on the distant shores of mainland America and Canada. No RVs are allowed on the winding road to the top. There are five freshwater lakes with fishing for rainbow trout, cutthroat trout, and kokanee salmon, 33 miles of hiking trails, 11 miles of biking trails, and six miles of horse trails. The landscape features old-growth forest, primarily lodgepole pine, and several small waterfalls. Nearby recreation options include a nine-hole golf course.

Campsites, facilities: There are 136 developed sites, including some drive-through sites, for tents or RVs up to 45 feet long, 15 primitive hike-in/bike-in tent sites, and one cabin for up to 10 people. No hookups are available. Picnic tables and fire grills are provided. Rest-rooms, drinking water, flush toilets, coin-operated showers, an RV dump station, a picnic area with log kitchen shelter, and firewood are available. Boat docks, limited fishing supplies, launching facilities, and boat rentals are located at the concession stand in the park. Some facilities are wheelchair accessible. Leashed pets are permitted.

Reservations, fees: Reserve at 888/CAMP-OUT (888/226-7688), website: www.parks.wa.gov/reservations ($7 reservation fee); $6–16 for tent sites, $22 for RV sites, and $6 for bike-in/hike-in sites; $6 per extra vehicle per night. Reserve the cabin at 800/360-4240. Senior discount available. Major credit cards accepted. Open year-round.

Directions: From Seattle on I-5, drive north to Burlington and Highway 20. Turn west on Highway 20 and drive 12 miles to the Highway 20 North spur, following signs to the San Juan Islands Ferry Terminal in Anacortes. Take the ferry to Orcas Island. From the ferry landing, turn left on Horseshoe Highway/Oras Road and drive 13 miles to Moran State Park (well marked). Stop at the campground registration booth for directions to your site.

Contact: Moran State Park Ferry-In, 3572 Olga Rd., Olga, WA 98245, 360/376-2326; State Park information, 360/902-8844, fax 360/856-2150.

13 DOE ISLAND STATE PARK BOAT-IN

Rating: 9

Near Orcas Island.
Map 2.2, grid c2, page 145

Doe Island has a rocky shoreline, which makes an ideal fish habitat, and the scuba diving and fishing are exceptional. Doe Island State Park is a tiny, primitive park that receives little use. Docking is available April–mid-October.

Campsites, facilities: There are five primitive boat-in campsites. Fire rings and vault toilets are provided. No drinking water is available.

Docking and mooring buoys are available April–mid-October. Garbage must be packed out. Leashed pets are permitted.

Reservations, fees: Reservations are not accepted. Sites are $6 per night, docking is $10–16 per night, and mooring buoys are $7 per night. Senior discount available. Open year-round.

Directions: This small, secluded island is just off the southeastern shore of Orcas Island off Doe Bay. It's accessible only by boat.

Contact: San Juan Marine Area, Star Rte., Box 177, Olga, WA 98279, 360/378-2044; State Park information, 360/902-8844, fax 360/856-2150.

14 OBSTRUCTION PASS HIKE-IN

Rating: 8

On Orcas Island.
Map 2.2, grid d2, page 145

It takes a ferryboat ride, a tricky drive, and a half-mile walk to reach this campground, but that helps set it apart from others. Your journey will take you to a unique, primitive spot set in a forested area with good hiking near the shore of Orcas Island. The irony is that Obstruction Pass is so unique that it is often heavily used. Moran State Park, also on this island, is a more developed alternative with many recreation options.

Campsites, facilities: There are nine primitive, hike-in campsites. Picnic tables and fire grills are provided. Vault toilets are available. No drinking water is available. Garbage must be packed out. Two mooring buoys are available. Leashed pets are permitted.

Reservations, fees: Reservations are not accepted. There is no fee for camping. Open year-round.

Directions: From Seattle on I-5, drive north to Burlington and Highway 20. Turn west on Highway 20 and drive 12 miles to the Highway 20 North spur, following signs to the San Juan Islands Ferry Terminal in Anacortes. Take the ferry to Orcas Island. Then drive on

the Horseshoe Highway past Moran State Park and continue to the town of Olga and Doe Bay Road. Drive east on Doe Bay Road for one-half mile to Obstruction Pass Road. Turn right and drive seven-tenths of a mile to Trailhead Road. Bear right and drive straight for less than a mile to the parking area. Hike one-half mile to the campground.

Contact: Department of Natural Resources, Northwest Region, 919 North Township St., Sedro-Woolley, WA 98284-9395, 360/856-3500, fax 360/856-2150.

15 CLARK ISLAND STATE PARK BOAT-IN

Rating: 9

Northeast of Orcas Island.
Map 2.2, grid c2, page 145

Clark Island State Park offers beautiful beaches with opportunities for scuba diving, beachcombing, and sunbathing. It is a short boat trip from nearby Orcas Island. You can pretend you're on a deserted Caribbean island. Well, almost. From the campground there are excellent views of the other nearby islands. As of 2002, storm damage had temporarily closed six of the eight campsites; call for current status.

Campsites, facilities: There are eight primitive boat-in campsites. Vault toilets are available, but there is no drinking water. Fire rings are provided. Boat buoys for overnight moorage are available. Garbage must be packed out. Leashed pets are permitted.

Reservations, fees: Reservations are not accepted. Sites are $6 per night, $7 per night for mooring buoys. Open year-round.

Directions: The campground, accessible only by boat, is on tiny Clark Island, located northeast of Orcas Island. Look for the moorage floats set just offshore from the campsites.

Contact: San Juan Marine Area, Star Rte., Box 177, Olga, WA 98279, 360/378-2044; State Park information, 360/902-8844, fax 360/856-2150.

TURN ISLAND STATE PARK BOAT-IN

Rating: 10

Near Friday Harbor.

Map 2.2, grid d1, page 145

This spot is gorgeous, and while this is one of about 30 campgrounds in the area that can be reached only by boat, note that Turn Island State Park has no docks, only mooring buoys. This tiny island is just a long hop off San Juan Island's southern tip. Quiet, primitive, and beautiful, this spot offers good trails for tromping around and year-round angling for rockfish. There are pretty beaches for shell collectors. The island is set within the San Juan Islands National Wildlife Refuge.

Campsites, facilities: There are 12 primitive boat-in campsites. Picnic tables and fire rings are provided. Composting toilets are available. There is no drinking water. Boat buoys are available for overnight moorage. Garbage must be packed out. Leashed pets are permitted.

Reservations, fees: Reservations are not accepted. Sites are $6 per night, $7 per night for mooring buoys. Senior discount available. Open year-round.

Directions: Turn Island is located off the northeast tip of San Juan Island (in the San Juan Channel). It's accessible only by boat.

Contact: San Juan Marine Area, Star Rte., Box 177, Olga, WA 98279, 360/378-2044; State Park information, 360/902-8844, fax 360/856-2150.

17 **SPENCER SPIT STATE PARK FERRY-IN**

Rating: 9

On Lopez Island.

Map 2.2, grid d2, page 145

Spencer Spit State Park offers one of the few island campgrounds accessible to cars via ferry. It also features walk-in sites for privacy, which require anywhere from a 50-foot to a 200-yard

walk to the tent sites. A sand spit extends far into the water and provides both a lagoon and good access to prime clamming areas. The park covers 183 acres. Picnicking, beachcombing, and sunbathing are some pleasant activities for campers looking for relaxation.

Campsites, facilities: There are 25 sites for tents or self-contained RVs up to 20 feet long, nine walk-in sites, and one group site. No hookups are provided. Picnic tables and fire grills are provided. Restrooms, drinking water, flush toilets, a picnic area, and an RV dump station are available, and 16 mooring buoys are available on the Cascadia Marine Trail. Boat docks and a launch are within two miles. Some facilities are wheelchair accessible. Leashed pets are permitted.

Reservations, fees: Reserve at 888/CAMP-OUT (888/226-7688), website: www.parks.wa.gov/reservations ($7 reservation fee). Sites are $16 per night, $6 per extra vehicle per night, and $7 for mooring buoys per night. Senior discount available. Call for prices for the group site. Open March–October.

Directions: From Seattle on I-5, drive north to Burlington and Highway 20. Turn west on Highway 20 and drive 12 miles to the Highway 20 North spur, following signs to the San Juan Islands Ferry Terminal in Anacortes. Take the ferry to Lopez Island. The park is within four miles of the ferry terminal.

Contact: Spencer Spit State Park Ferry-In, 521A Bakerview Rd., Lopez, WA 98261, 360/468-2251; State Park information, 360/902-8844, fax 360/856-2150.

18 **JAMES ISLAND STATE PARK BOAT-IN**

Rating: 9

Near Decatur Island.

Map 2.2, grid d2, page 145

Small, hidden James Island provides good opportunities for hiking, fishing, and scuba diving. It's quiet and primitive, with lots of trees and a pretty beach for walking or sunbathing. Docks are in place April–mid-October.

Campsites, facilities: There are 12 primitive boat-in campsites and two designated sites for non-motorized boats. Fire rings are provided. Composting and pit toilets are available. Boat floats and buoys are available for moorage off the east side of the island. A moorage dock on the west side of the island is open April–mid-October. Leashed pets are permitted.

Reservations, fees: Reservations are not accepted. Sites are $6 per night, docking is $10–16 per night, and mooring buoys are $7 per night. Senior discount available. Open year-round.

Directions: This island is east of Decatur Island on Rosario Strait and is only accessible by boat. The campground is on the east side of the island.

Contact: San Juan Marine Area, Star Rte., Box 177, Olga, WA 98279, 360/378-2044; State Park information, 360/902-8844, fax 360/856-2150.

19 STRAWBERRY ISLAND BOAT-IN

Rating: 9

Near Cypress Island.

Map 2.2, grid d3, page 145

This campground is set on a small island and is used less often than the other islands nearby because of the hazards of landing here (see the directions below). Regardless, kayakers in the region have discovered it. If you can manage to land, you'll be rewarded with a pretty, forested camp and privacy.

Campsites, facilities: There are three primitive boat-in campsites. Picnic tables and fire grills are provided. Vault toilets are available. No drinking water is available. Garbage must be packed out.

Reservations, fees: Reservations are not accepted. There is no fee for camping. Open year-round.

Directions: This island is located off the west coast of Cypress Island and is accessible only by small boat. From Anacortes, cruise by boat west through Guemes Channel, continue around

the southern end of Cypress Island (Reef Point), and cruise north one mile to Strawberry Bay. Strawberry Island is located in Strawberry Bay. Note: The Department of Natural Resources cautions that strong currents and submerged rocks can make landing difficult.

Contact: Department of Natural Resources, Northwest Region, 919 North Township St., Sedro-Woolley, WA 98284-9395, 360/856-3500, fax 360/856-2150.

20 PELICAN BEACH BOAT-IN

Rating: 9

On Cypress Island.

Map 2.2, grid b1, page 145

This forested island campground offers a group shelter, beach access, and hiking trails. The 1.2-mile trail to Eagle Cliff is a must. Like Cypress Head, this scenic camp is set on the oceanfront in a well-treed area. Pelican Beach has become even more popular than Cypress Head, not only with individual kayakers, but also with commercial operations that work as outfitters who organize trips for small groups of kayakers.

Campsites, facilities: There are four primitive boat-in campsites. Picnic tables and fire grills are provided. Composting toilets and a group picnic shelter are available. No drinking water is available. Garbage must be packed out. Six mooring buoys are available nearby.

Reservations, fees: Reservations are not accepted. There is no fee for camping. Open year-round.

Directions: This camp is set on the east shore of Cypress Island and is accessible only by boat. Cypress Island can be accessed by boat from Anacortes. Cruise west through Guemes Channel to Bellingham Channel (located between Cypress Island and Guemes Island). Turn north in Bellingham Channel and cruise to the campground on the southeast side of Cypress Island, just north of Cypress Head.

Contact: Department of Natural Resources, Northwest Region, 919 North Township St.,

Sedro-Woolley, WA 98284-9395, 360/856-3500, fax 360/856-2150.

21 CYPRESS HEAD BOAT-IN

Rating: 9

On Cypress Island.
Map 2.2, grid d3, page 145
An alternative to Pelican Beach, this primitive but pretty camp is situated right on Puget Sound in a forested setting of primarily Douglas fir and madrone. This camp is popular and often gets heavy use from kayakers. A trail provides access to Cypress Island Natural Resource Conservation area.

Campsites, facilities: There are five primitive, boat-in campsites. Picnic tables and fire grills are provided. Vault toilets are available. No drinking water is available. Garbage must be packed out. Five mooring buoys are available nearby.

Reservations, fees: Reservations are not accepted. There is no fee for camping. Open year-round.

Directions: This camp is set on the east shore of Cypress Island and is accessible only by boat. Cypress Island can be accessed by boat from Anacortes. Cruise west through Guemes Channel to Bellingham Channel (located between Cypress Island and Guemes Island). Turn north in Bellingham Channel and cruise to the campground on the southeast side of Cypress Island in Deepwater Bay (just south of Pelican Beach Campground).

Contact: Department of Natural Resources, Northwest Region, 919 North Township St., Sedro-Woolley, WA 98284-9395, 360/856-3500, fax 360/856-2150.

22 SADDLEBAG ISLAND STATE PARK BOAT-IN

Rating: 9

Near Guemes Island.
Map 2.2, grid d4, page 145
Saddlebag Island State Park is a good cruise from Anacortes. The island is quiet and primitive, with a nice beach nearby for beachcombing and fine crabbing in the bay. Wildflowers are in bloom April–June. This island receives moderate use.

Campsites, facilities: There are five primitive boat-in campsites. Fire rings are provided. Vault and pit toilets are available, but there is no drinking water. Garbage must be packed out. Mooring buoys are available, but no docks. Leashed pets are permitted.

Reservations, fees: Reservations are not accepted. Sites are $6 per night, mooring buoys $7 per night. Senior discount available. Open year-round.

Directions: From Seattle on I-5, drive north to Burlington and Highway 20. Turn west on Highway 20 and drive 12 miles to the Highway 20 North spur, following signs to the San Juan Islands Ferry Terminal in Anacortes. Launch your boat and cruise northeast around the southeast tip of Guemes Island. As you approach, Hat Island will be to your right, Huckleberry Island to your left, and Saddlebag Island to your center in Padilla Bay. Continue to Saddlebag Island. The camp is accessible only by boat.

Contact: San Juan Marine Area, Star Rte., Box 177, Olga, WA 98279, 360/378-2044; State Park information, 360/902-8844, fax 360/856-2150.

23 BIRCH BAY STATE PARK

Rating: 8

On Birch Bay.
Map 2.2, grid a2, page 145
Birch Bay State Park covers 194 acres and features nearly two miles of beach as well as great views of the Canadian Gulf Islands and the Cascade Mountains. For water lovers it has the best of both worlds, with 8,255 feet of saltwater shoreline and 14,923 feet of freshwater shoreline on Terrell Creek. More than 100 different species of birds, many of which are migrating on the Pacific flyway, can be seen here.

The Terrell Creek Marsh Interpretive Trail extends one-half mile through both a forest of black birch trees and one of the few remaining saltwater/freshwater estuaries in northern Puget Sound. Bald eagles and great blue heron feed along the banks of Terrell Creek. Several 18-hole golf courses are located nearby. The campground is divided into two loops; hookups for RVs are in the North Loop.

Campsites, facilities: There are 146 sites for tents or self-contained RVs and 20 sites with full or partial hookups for RVs up to 60 feet. Picnic tables and fire grills are provided. Flush toilets, coin-operated showers, and an RV dump station are available. A boat ramp, launch facilities (for boats under 16 feet only), a picnic area with a sheltered kitchen with electricity, an amphitheater, basketball, interpretive activities, and a camp host are available. Some facilities are wheelchair accessible. A store, a restaurant, a coin-operated laundry, and ice are located within one mile. Leashed pets are permitted.

Reservations, fees: Reserve at 888/CAMP-OUT (888/226-7688), website: www.parks.wa.gov/reservations ($7 reservation fee). Sites are $7–22 per night, $6 per extra vehicle per night. Major credit cards accepted. Open year-round.

Directions: From Bellingham, drive north on I-5 to Exit 266. At Exit 266 take Grandview west and continue seven miles to Jackson Road. Turn right on Jackson Road and drive one mile to Helweg Road. Turn left and drive one-quarter mile to the reservation office.

Contact: Birch Bay State Park, 5105 Helweg Rd., Blaine, WA 98230, 360/371-2800, fax 360/371-0455; State Park information, 360/902-8844, fax 360/856-2150.

24 BEACHSIDE RV PARK

Rating: 8

On Birch Bay.
Map 2.2, grid a2, page 145
This pretty park comes with the opportunity to view a pair of nesting eagles. Evergreens and bay views surround the park. Hiking, fishing, mountain biking, and nearby golf are also options.

Campsites, facilities: There are 74 sites with full hookups, including some drive-through sites, for RVs and 12 sites for tents. Picnic tables are provided. Restrooms, drinking water, flush toilets, showers, a group fire pit, and a coin-operated laundry are available. A grocery store mini-mart and restaurant are located within one-half mile. Leashed pets are permitted.

Reservations, fees: Reservations recommended; phone 360/371-5962. Sites are $14–22 per night. Major credit cards accepted. Senior discount available. Open year-round.

Directions: From Bellingham, drive north on I-5 to Exit 270. Turn west on Birch Bay-Lynden Road and drive five miles to Birch Bay Drive. Turn left and drive one mile to the park on the left.

Contact: Beachside RV Park, 7630 Birch Bay Dr., Birch Bay, WA 98230, 360/371-5962 (phone or fax).

25 THE CEDARS RV RESORT

Rating: 5

In Ferndale.
Map 2.2, grid b4, page 145
This campground provides more direct access from I-5 than Windmill Inn and KOA Lynden, and note that you can usually get a site here. It's a nice, clean park covering 22 acres with spacious sites and trees. Horseshoe pits, a game room, and a recreation field provide possible activities for campers. Several golf courses are nearby.

Campsites, facilities: There are 127 sites with full or partial hookups, including drive-through sites, for tents or RVs of any length and a dispersed tent camping area on grass. Picnic tables and fire pits are provided. Restrooms, drinking water, flush toilets, showers, modem hookups (at 50 sites), two RV dump stations, a coin-operated laundry, a playground with horseshoes, badminton, volleyball, a recreation room, an arcade, a pool, a small store, and ice are available. Leashed pets are permitted.

Reservations, fees: Reservations accepted. Sites are $18.50–27.50 per night. Major credit cards accepted. Open year-round.

Directions: From Bellingham on I-5, drive north to Ferndale and Exit 263. Take Exit 263 and turn north on Portal Way. Drive less than one mile north to the campground on the left.

Contact: The Cedars RV Resort, 6335 Portal Way, Ferndale, WA 98248, 360/384-2622, fax 360/380-6365.

26 WINDMILL INN

Rating: 7

Near the Nooksack River.
Map 2.2, grid a5, page 145

This nice little spot, only 15 minutes from Puget Sound, is set near the Nooksack River and Wiser Lake. As the last stop before the U.S.-Canadian border, the camp serves primarily as a layover for people heading north. The quiet and pretty setting abounds with trees and flowers. Area attractions include Mt. Baker, the quaint little shops of Lynden, and the nearby Birch Bay area, which offers many recreation options.

Campsites, facilities: There are eight sites for tents or RVs of any length, and 15 motel rooms. Picnic tables are provided. Restrooms, drinking water, flush toilets, coin-operated showers, cable TV, phone hookups, and a park are available. A store, bottled gas, a café, a coin-operated laundry, and ice are available within one mile. Boat-launching facilities are located within 1.5 miles. Leashed pets are permitted.

Reservations, fees: Reservations accepted. Sites are $18 per night, $1 per person per night for more than two people. Major credit cards accepted. Open year-round.

Directions: In Bellingham on I-5, take Exit 256 for Highway 539 (called Meridian Street in Bellingham). Turn north on Highway 539 and drive 10

miles to Lynden. The campground is on the right side of the road as you enter Lynden.

Contact: Windmill Inn, 8022 Guide Meridian Rd., Lynden, WA 98264, 360/354-3424, fax 360/354-8138.

27 KOA LYNDEN

Rating: 9

In Lynden.
Map 2.2, grid a5, page 145

Lynden is a quaint Dutch town. The park features green lawns, flowers, and trees surrounding a miniature golf course and ponds, where you can fish for trout. This KOA stars as a unique layover spot for vacationers heading north to Canada via Highway 539 and Highway 546. Nearby recreational options include an 18-hole golf course.

Campsites, facilities: There are 80 tent sites, 100 sites with full or partial hookups, including 25 drive-through, for RVs of any length, and 12 cabins. Picnic tables are provided. Restrooms, drinking water, flush toilets, showers, bottled gas, an RV dump station, showers, firewood, a recreation hall, a store, a café (summer season only), an espresso bar, an ice cream parlor, laundry facilities, ice, a playground, miniature golf, and a swimming pool are available. Tackle and boat rentals are available. Leashed pets are permitted.

Reservations, fees: Reservations accepted at 800/562-4779. Sites are $25–33 per night for two campers, $4 for each additional person. Discounts with KOA card. Major credit cards accepted. Call the park for group rates. Open year-round.

Directions: From I-5 at Bellingham, take Exit 256 to Highway 539. Turn north on Highway 539 and drive 12 miles to Highway 546. Turn east on Highway 546 (Badger Road) and drive three miles to Line Road. Turn right (south) on Line Road and drive one-half mile to the campground on the right.

Contact: KOA Lynden, 8717 Line Rd.,

Lynden, WA 98264, 360/354-4772, fax 360/354-7050, website: www.koa.com.

28 SUMAS RV PARK

Rating: 5

In Sumas.

Map 2.2, grid a6, page 145

Located near the U.S.-Canadian border, this campground is a layover spot to spend American dollars before heading into British Columbia and making the conversion. The camp is set in the grassy flatlands; it has graveled sites and a few trees. Nearby recreation options include an 18-hole golf course and tennis courts.

Campsites, facilities: There are 24 tent sites and 50 sites with full or partial hookups, including 12 drive-through sites, for RVs of any length. Picnic tables and fire rings are provided. Restrooms, drinking water, flush toilets, showers, an RV dump station, firewood, and a ballpark are available. A store, a café, a coin-operated laundry, and ice are located within one mile. Leashed pets are permitted.

Reservations, fees: Reservations accepted. Sites are $1–20 per night. Open year-round.

Directions: From I-5 at Bellingham, take Exit 256 to Highway 539. Turn north on Highway 539 and drive 12 miles to Highway 546. Turn right (east) on Highway 546 (Badger Road) and drive 14 miles (the road becomes Highway 9) to Sumas and look for Cherry Street. Turn right (south) at Cherry Street (the road becomes Easterbrook Road) and drive two blocks to the park on the left.

Contact: Sumas RV Park, 9600 Easterbrook Rd., Sumas, WA 98295, 360/988-8875.

29 LARRABEE STATE PARK

Rating: 9

On Samish Bay.

Map 2.2, grid c5, page 145

This 2,683-acre state park sits on Samish Bay in Puget Sound and boasts 8,100 feet of saltwater shoreline. The park has two freshwater lakes, coves, and tidelands. Sunsets are often beautiful. The park has 13.7 miles of hiking trails and 11.7 miles of mountain-biking trails. The landscape is primarily forested with conifers, often with dense woodlands and vegetation, but also features marshlands, wetlands, streams, lakes, and Chuckanut Mountain. The area is known for Chuckanut sandstone. Fishing is available on Fragrance Lake and Lost Lake, which are hike-in lakes. Dating from 1915, this was the first state park established in Washington. The park lies on a beautiful stretch of coastline and offers prime spots for wildlife viewing. A relatively short drive south will take you to Anacortes, where you can catch a ferry to islands in the San Juan chain.

Campsites, facilities: There are 51 developed sites, including 26 with full hookups, for tents or RVs up to 60 feet long and eight primitive tent sites. Picnic tables and fire grills are provided. Restrooms, drinking water, flush toilets, coin-operated showers, an RV dump station, a picnic area with electricity and a covered shelter, and firewood are available. Boat-launching facilities are available nearby. Leashed pets are permitted.

Reservations, fees: Reserve at 888/CAMP-OUT (888/226-7688), website: www.parks.wa.gov/reservations ($7 reservation fee). Sites are $6–22 per night, $6 per extra vehicle per night. Senior discount available. Major credit cards accepted. Open year-round.

Directions: From Bellingham on I-5, take Exit 250 and turn on Fairhaven Parkway. Drive less than a mile to State Route 11/Chuckanut Drive (second stoplight). Turn left (stay left at the next stoplight) and drive six miles to the park entrance on the right.

Contact: Larrabee State Park, 245 Chuckanut, Bellingham, WA 98225, 360/676-2093; State Park information, 360/902-8844, fax 360/676-2061.

30 LIZARD LAKE HIKE-IN

Rating: 6

Near Bellingham.

Map 2.2, grid c5, page 145

Lizard Lake is located just two-tenths of a mile north by trail from Lily Lake, but this hike-in camp is even smaller and more isolated. It's set in a pretty, forested area. See the description of Lily Lake for more information.

Campsites, facilities: There are three primitive hike-in tent sites. Tent pads and fire grills are provided, and vault toilets are available. There is no drinking water. Garbage must be packed out. Leashed pets are permitted.

Reservations, fees: Reservations are not accepted. There is no fee for camping. Open year-round.

Directions: From Bellingham on I-5, drive south to Exit 240 to Samish Lake Road and drive one-half mile north to Barrel Springs Road. Turn left and drive one mile to Road SW-C-1000. Turn right and drive 1.5 miles to the Blanchard Hill Trailhead. Hike 3.2 miles, bear left, and continue three-quarters of a mile (just past Lily Lake) to the campground. A map is advisable.

Contact: Department of Natural Resources, Northwest Region, 919 North Township St., Sedro-Woolley, WA 98284-9395, 360/856-3500, fax 360/856-2150.

31 LILY LAKE HIKE-IN

Rating: 6

Near Bellingham.

Map 2.2, grid d5, page 145

This tiny, remote hike-in campground is one of those camps that few people ever go to or even know about. Set on little Lily Lake, it's completely secluded and primitive; you'll have to pack in everything you need and pack out everything that's left. This is a prime area for hiking, and hikers and horse packers alike use the nearby trails. Fishing is an option at Lily Lake. Nearby Lizard Lake provides an even smaller camp.

Campsites, facilities: There are six primitive hike-in tent sites. Tent pads and fire rings are provided. Drinking water and vault toilets are available. Garbage must be packed out. Leashed pets are allowed.

Reservations, fees: Reservations are not accepted. There is no fee for camping. Open year-round.

Directions: From Bellingham on I-5, drive south to Exit 240. On Samish Lake Road drive one-half mile north to Barrel Springs Road. Turn left and drive one mile to Road SW-C-1000. Turn right and drive 1.5 miles to the Blanchard Hill Trailhead. Hike 3.2 miles, bear left, and continue one-half mile to the campground. Obtaining a map is advisable.

Contact: Department of Natural Resources, Northwest Region, 919 North Township St., Sedro-Woolley, WA 98284-9395, 360/856-3500, fax 360/856-2150.

32 HUTCHINSON CREEK

Rating: 9

Near the South Fork of the Nooksack River.

Map 2.2, grid c7, page 145

This campground is set in the forest along Hutchinson Creek near the South Fork of the Nooksack River. Managed by the Department of Natural Resources, it's rustic, beautiful, and primitive. While wise locals know of this camp, out-of-town vacationers don't have much of a clue.

Campsites, facilities: There are 11 sites for tents or small trailers. Fire grills and tent pads are provided. Vault toilets are available. There is no drinking water. Garbage must be packed out. A store is located within three miles. Leashed pets are permitted.

Reservations, fees: Reservations are not accepted. There is no fee for camping. Open year-round.

Directions: From Seattle, drive north on I-5

to Burlington and Highway 20. Turn east on Highway 20 and drive seven miles to Highway 9. Turn north and drive 16 miles to Acme and Mosquito Lake Road (just north of the Nooksack River Bridge). Turn east on Mosquito Lake Road, drive 2.5 miles, and look for a gravel road on the right. Turn right on the gravel road and continue for one-half mile to the campground.

Contact: Department of Natural Resources, Northwest Region, 919 North Township St., Sedro-Woolley, WA 98284-9395, 360/856-3500, fax 360/856-2150.

33 PIONEER TRAILS RV RESORT & CAMPGROUND

Rating: 9

On Fidalgo Island, in the San Juan Islands.
Map 2.2, grid e4, page 145

This site offers resort camping in the beautiful San Juan Islands. Tall trees, breathtaking views, cascading waterfalls, and country hospitality can all be found here. Side trips include nearby Deception Pass State Park (eight minutes away) and ferries to Victoria, British Columbia, Friday Harbor, Orcas Island, and other nearby islands (it is imperative to arrive early at the ferry terminal). Nearby recreation activities include horseshoes, an 18-hole golf course, relaxing spas, and lake fishing.

Campsites, facilities: There are 80 sites with full or partial hookups, including some drive-through sites, for tents or RVs, plus 24 covered wagons and five cabins. Picnic tables and fire rings are provided. Restrooms, drinking water, flush toilets, showers, an RV dump station, cable TV, a public phone, and a coin-operated laundry are available. A recreation hall, a playground, and a sports field are available nearby. If RV camping, leashed pets are permitted.

Reservations, fees: Reservations recommended. A three-night minimum on holidays is required. Sites are $18–30 per night, $5 per extra

vehicle per night. One pet is free. Major credit cards accepted. Open year-round.

Directions: From Seattle on I-5, drive north to Burlington and take Exit 230 for Highway 20 West. Drive west on Highway 20 for 12 miles. At the traffic signal, turn left (still Highway 20, toward Oak Harbor/Deception Pass) and drive one-half mile to Miller Road. Turn right (west) on Miller Road, drive one-quarter mile, and look for the park on the right side of the road.

Contact: Pioneer Trails RV Resort & Campground, 7337 Miller Rd., Anacortes, WA 98221, 360/293-5355, 888/777-5355 or 360/299-2240, website: www.pioneertrails.com.

34 FIDALGO BAY RESORT

Rating: 4

On Fidalgo Bay.
Map 2.2, grid e4, page 145

This park is five minutes from Anacortes and right on Fidalgo Bay, providing easy access to boating, fishing, and swimming. A golf course is available two miles away. There are a few permanent rentals at this park.

Campsites, facilities: There are 187 sites with full hookups, including many drive-through sites and a few sites with phone hookups, for RVs and eight tent sites. Picnic tables are provided. Restrooms, drinking water, flush toilets, showers, modem access in the clubhouse, a large fire pit, a small boat launch, a grocery store, a dog run, and a coin-operated laundry are available. Leashed pets are permitted, but they must be kept quiet.

Reservations, fees: Reservations recommended at 800/727-5478. Sites are $25–40 per night, $2 per person per night for more than two people. Major credit cards accepted. Open year-round.

Directions: From Seattle on I-5, drive north to Burlington and Highway 20. Turn west on Highway 20 and drive about 14 miles to Fidalgo Bay Road. Turn right on Fidalgo Bay Road and drive one mile to the resort on the right.

Contact: Fidalgo Bay Resort, 4701 Fidalgo Bay Rd., Anacortes, WA 98211, 800/727-5478 or 360/293-5353, fax 360/299-3010, website: www.fidalgobay.com.

35 WASHINGTON PARK

🚶 🚲 🚙 🐴 🏕 🚐 ⛺

Rating: 6

In Washington Park.

Map 2.2, grid e4, page 145

This city park is set in the woods and features many hiking trails. A 2.3-mile paved loop route for vehicles, hikers, and bicyclists stretches around the perimeter of the park. The Washington State Ferry terminals are located one-half mile away, providing access to the San Juan Islands. This is a popular camp, and it's a good idea to arrive early to claim your spot.

Campsites, facilities: There are 70 sites, including 45 with partial hookups and some drive-through sites, for tents or RVs up to 40 feet long and one group tent site for up to 30 people. Restrooms, drinking water, flush toilets, coin-operated showers, a public phone, a playground, a recreation field, an RV dump station, and a coin-operated laundry are available. A day-use area is provided. A boat launch is also available. Leashed pets are permitted.

Reservations, fees: Reservations accepted for residents of Anacortes only. Sites are $12–15 per night; the group site is $50 per night. Open year-round.

Directions: From Seattle on I-5, drive north to Burlington and Highway 20. Turn west on Highway 20 and drive to Anacortes and Commercial Avenue. Turn right on Highway 20 and drive 24 blocks to 12th Street. Turn left and drive about four miles (west of the ferry landing; the road changes names several times) to Sunset Avenue. Drive straight across road to Sunset Avenue to the park entrance and campground.

Contact: Washington Park, City of Anacortes, P.O. Box 547, Anacortes, WA 98221, 360/293-1927 or 360/293-1918, website: www.cityofanacortes.org.

36 BAY VIEW STATE PARK

🏊 🚣 🏕 🚴 🚐 ⛺

Rating: 10

On Padilla Bay.

Map 2.2, grid e5, page 145

This campground set on Padilla Bay has a large, grassy area for kids, making it a good choice for families. Bordering 11,000 acres of Padilla Bay and the National Estuarine Sanctuary, this 25-acre park boasts 1,285 feet of saltwater shoreline. From the park, you can enjoy views of the San Juan Islands fronting Padilla Bay. On a clear day, you can see the Olympic Mountains to the west and Mt. Rainier to the south. Kayakers should note that Padilla Bay becomes a large mud flat during low tides. Windsurfing is becoming popular, but tracking tides and wind is required. Crabbing and clamming are best at other locations along Padilla Bay or Bellingham Bay. The Breazeale Padilla Bay Interpretive Center is located one-half mile north of the park. For a nice day trip, take the ferry at Anacortes to Lopez Island (there are several campgrounds there as well).

Campsites, facilities: There are 76 sites, some with full or partial hookups, for tents or self-contained RVs, nine sites with full hookups for RVs up to 60 feet long, three primitive sites, and one group tent site for up to 64 people. Picnic tables and fire rings are provided. Restrooms, drinking water, flush toilets, coin-operated showers, an RV dump station, and a picnic area with a beach shelter are available. A playground with horseshoes, volleyball, interpretive activities, windsurfing, water-skiing, swimming, clamming, crabbing, oyster gathering, and boating are available. A store and a coin-operated laundry are eight miles away in Burlington. Leashed pets are permitted. Note that some campsites are closed in winter months.

Reservations, fees: Reserve at 888/226-7688 (CAMP-OUT), website: www.parks.wa.gov/reservations ($7 reservation fee). Sites are $6–22 per night, $6 per extra vehicle per night. Senior discount available. Reservations required for the group camp: $25 reservation fee, plus $2 per person per night. Major credit cards accepted. Open year-round.

Directions: From Seattle on I-5, drive north to Burlington and Exit 230 for Highway 20. Turn west on Highway 20 and drive seven miles west (toward Anacortes) to Bay View-Edison Road. Turn right (north) on Bay View-Edison Road and drive four miles to the park on the right.

Contact: Bay View State Park, 1093 Bay View-Edison Rd., Brighton, WA 98273, 360/757-0227; State Park information, 360/902-8844, fax 360/676-2061.

37 BURLINGTON/ANACORTES KOA

Rating: 5

In Burlington.

Map 2.2, grid e6, page 145

This is a fine KOA campground, complete with all the amenities. The sites are spacious and comfortable. Possible side trips include tours of the Boeing plant, Victoria, Vancouver Island, and the San Juan Islands.

Campsites, facilities: There are 120 sites, most with full or partial hookups, some drive-through, for tents or RVs and nine cabins. Restrooms, drinking water, flush toilets, showers, an RV dump station, cable TV, a public phone, a coin-operated laundry, limited groceries, ice, LP gas, and a barbecue are available. There are also an indoor heated pool, a spa with sauna, a recreation hall, a game room, a playground, miniature golf, horseshoes, and a sports field. Leashed pets are permitted.

Reservations, fees: Reservations recommended in the summer, 800/562-9154. Sites are $23–32 per night, $2.50–4 per person per night for more than two people. Major credit cards accepted. Open year-round.

Directions: From Seattle on I-5, drive north to Exit 232/Cook Road in Burlington. Take that exit to Cook Road. Turn right on Cook Road and drive 100 feet to Old Highway 99. Turn left and drive 3.5 miles to the campground on the right.

Contact: Burlington/Anacortes KOA, 6397 North Green Rd., Burlington, WA 98233, 360/724-5511, website: www.koa.com.

38 RIVERBEND RV PARK

Rating: 5

On the Skagit River.

Map 2.2, grid e6, page 145

Riverbend RV Park is a pleasant layover spot for I-5 travelers. While not particularly scenic, it is clean and spacious. Access to the Skagit River here is a high point, with fishing for salmon, trout, and Dolly Varden in season; check regulations. Nearby recreational options include a casino and an 18-hole golf course.

Campsites, facilities: There are 90 drive-through sites with full hookups for RVs of any length and 25 tent sites. Picnic tables are provided at RV sites and fire pits are provided at tent sites. Restrooms, drinking water, flush toilets, coin-operated showers, an RV dump station, a coin-operated laundry, and a playground with horseshoe pits are available. A store, a café, ice, and a swimming pool are located within one-quarter mile. Leashed pets are permitted.

Reservations, fees: Reservations accepted. Sites are $10–21.50 per night, $2 per person for more than two people. Major credit cards accepted. Open year-round.

Directions: From Seattle on I-5, drive north to Mt. Vernon and the College Way exit. Take the College Way exit and drive one block west to Freeway Drive. Turn right (north) and drive one-quarter mile to the park.

Contact: Riverbend RV Park, 305 West Stewart Rd., Mt. Vernon, WA 98273, 360/428-4044.

39 DECEPTION PASS STATE PARK

🏃 🚴 🏊 🚣 🏄 🐕 ♿ 🚐 ⛰

Rating: 10

On Whidbey Island.

Map 2.2, grid e3, page 145

Located at beautiful Deception Pass on the west side of Whidbey Island, this state park encompasses 4,134 acres with almost 15 miles of saltwater shoreline and six miles of fresh-water shoreline on three lakes. The landscape ranges from old-growth forest to sand dunes. This diverse habitat has attracted 174 species of birds. An observation deck overlooks the Cranberry Lake wetlands. The park also features spectacular views of shoreline, mountains, and islands, often with dramatic sunsets. At one spot, rugged cliffs drop to the turbulent waters of Deception Pass. Recreation options include fishing and swimming at Pass Lake, a freshwater lake within the park. Fly-fishing for trout is a unique bonus for anglers. Note that each lake has different regulations for boating. Scuba diving is also popular. The park provides 38 miles of hiking trails, 1.2 miles of wheelchair-accessible trails, and six miles of biking trails. There are several historic Civilian Conservation Corps buildings near the campground.

Campsites, facilities: There are 246 developed sites, including some drive-through, for tents or self-contained RVs up to 50 feet long and five primitive tent sites. Picnic tables and fire rings are provided. Restrooms, drinking water, flush toilets, coin-operated showers, and an RV dump station are available. A concession stand, an amphitheater, interpretive activities, a picnic area with electricity and a kitchen shelter, a boat launch, boat rentals, and mooring buoys are available nearby. The facilities are wheelchair accessible. Leashed pets are permitted.

Reservations, fees: Reserve at 888/CAMP-OUT (888/226-7688), website: www.parks.wa.gov/reservations ($7 reservation fee). Sites are $6–22 per night, $6 per extra vehicle per night, and $7–16

for mooring buoys per night. Senior discount available. Major credit cards accepted. Open year-round, with limited winter services.

Directions: From Seattle on I-5, drive north to Burlington and Exit 230/Highway 20. Take that exit and drive west on Highway 20 for 12 miles to Highway 20 South. Turn south on Highway 20 South and drive six miles (across the bridge at Deception Pass) and continue to the park (three miles south of the bridge) on the right.

Contact: Deception Pass State Park, 360/675-2417, fax 360/675-3288; State Park information, 360/902-8844, fax 360/676-2061.

40 HOPE ISLAND STATE PARK BOAT-IN

🚣 🐕 ⛰

Rating: 8

In Skagit Bay.

Map 2.2, grid e4, page 145

Here's your chance to have an island all to yourself. This camp on the north side of Hope Island is lightly used and is a primitive alternative to the nearby and more developed drive-to sites. Located between Squaxin Island and Steamboat Island, it features a 106-acre county park set in Puget Sound and a landscape of old-growth forests and saltwater marshes. The park has a 1.5-mile beach, the top spot. The catch? You must have a boat to reach it. Solitude is your reward. A little-known option, a single campsite for kayakers was added in 2001 on the northeast tip of Skagit Island. Largely a secret, and with no mooring buoy, it's likely to remain that way.

Campsites, facilities: There are five primitive, boat-in campsites. Picnic tables and fire rings are provided. Pit toilets and three mooring buoys are available. No drinking water is available. Garbage must be packed out. Leashed pets are permitted.

Reservations, fees: Reservations are not accepted. Sites are $5 per night, $7–16 for mooring buoys. Senior discount available. Open year-round.

Directions: Hope Island is in Skagit Bay, directly between the Swinomish Indian Reservation on Fidalgo Island to the east and Whidbey Island to the west. After launching from the harbor at Cornet on Whidbey Island, cruise east out of Cornet Bay and turn south (Skagit Island will be on your left). Continue one mile to Hope Island. The boating access is on the north side of the island. It's accessible only by private boat.

Contact: Hope Island State Park, 360/675-2417, fax 360/675-3288; State Park information, 360/902-8844.

41 OAK HARBOR CITY BEACH PARK

Rating: 4

In Oak Harbor.

Map 2.2, grid f3, page 145

This popular park fills quickly on summer weekends. With graveled sites, it is geared toward RVers, but is also suitable for tent campers. Fishing, swimming, boating, and sunbathing are all options at Oak Harbor City Beach Park. A full-service marina is next door. Within a few miles are an 18-hole golf course and tennis courts. Fort Ebey and Fort Casey State Parks are both a short drive away and make excellent side trips.

Campsites, facilities: There are 56 sites with full hookups for RVs of any length. Restrooms, drinking water, flush toilets, showers, an RV dump station, coin-operated showers, and a playground are available. Bottled gas, a store, a café, a coin-operated laundry, and ice are available within one mile. Boat-launching facilities are available at Oak Harbor. Leashed pets are permitted.

Reservations, fees: Reservations are not accepted. Sites are $12–20 per night. Open year-round.

Directions: From Seattle on I-5, drive north to Burlington and Highway 20. Turn west on Highway 20 and drive 28 miles to the intersection

of Highway 20 and Pioneer Way in the town of Oak Harbor on Whidbey Island. Continue straight through the intersection onto Beeksma Drive and drive about one block to the park on the left.

Contact: Oak Harbor City Beach Park, 865 S.E. Berrington Dr., Oak Harbor, WA 98277, 360/679-5551, website: www.oakharbor.org.

42 FORT EBEY STATE PARK

Rating: 9

On Whidbey Island.

Map 2.2, grid g3, page 145

This park is situated on the west side of Whidbey Island at Point Partridge. It covers 645 acres and has access to a rocky beach that is good for exploring. There are also 28 miles of trails for hiking and biking. Fort Ebey is the site of a historic World War II bunker, where concrete platforms mark the locations of the historic gun batteries. Other options here include fishing and wildlife viewing. There is limited fishing available for smallmouth bass at Lake Pondilla, only about 100 yards away and a good place to see bald eagles. The saltwater shore access provides a good spot for surfing and paragliding.

Campsites, facilities: There are 50 developed campsites, including four sites with electricity, for tents or self-contained RVs up to 70 feet long and three primitive tent sites. Picnic tables and fire grills are provided. Restrooms, drinking water, flush toilets, coin-operated showers, a picnic area, and an RV dump station are available. Some facilities are wheelchair accessible. Leashed pets are permitted.

Reservations, fees: Reserve at 888/CAMP-OUT (888/226-7688), website: www.parks.wa.gov/reservations ($7 reservation fee). Sites are $6–22 per night, $6 per extra vehicle per night. Major credit cards accepted. Senior discount available. Open year-round.

Directions: From Seattle on I-5, drive north to Burlington and Exit 230/Highway 20. Turn west on Highway 20 and drive 23 miles (Whidbey Island) to Libbey Road (eight miles past Oak Harbor). Turn right and drive 1.5 miles to Hill Valley Drive. Turn left and enter the park.

Contact: Fort Ebey State Park, 395 North Fort Ebey Rd., Coupeville, WA 98239, 360/678-4636; State Park information, 360/902-8844.

43 FORT CASEY STATE PARK

Rating: 10

On Whidbey Island.

Map 2.2, grid g3, page 145

Fort Casey State Park features a lighthouse and sweeping views of Admiralty Inlet and the Strait of Juan de Fuca. The park has 10,180 feet of saltwater shoreline on Puget Sound at Admiralty Inlet and includes Keystone Spit, a two-mile stretch of land separating Admiralty Inlet and Crocket Lake. The park covers 467 acres, with just 1.8 miles of hiking trails, but as part of Eby's Landing National Historic Reserve, contains a coast artillery post featuring two historic guns on display. It is also a designated area for remote-control glider flying, with a parade field popular for kite flying. The lighthouse and interpretive center are open seasonally. Fishing is often good in this area, in season. Another highlight, the underwater park attracts divers. You can also take a ferry from here to Port Townsend on the Olympic Peninsula.

Campsites, facilities: There are 35 developed campsites for tents or self-contained RVs up to 40 feet long and three primitive tent sites. Picnic tables and fire grills are provided. Restrooms, drinking water, flush toilets, coin-operated showers, firewood, an interpretive center, a picnic area, and an amphitheater are available. Some facilities are wheelchair accessible. Boat-launching facilities are located in the park. Leashed pets are permitted.

Reservations, fees: Reservations are not accepted. Sites are $6–16 per night, $6 per extra vehicle per night. Senior discount available. Open year-round.

Directions: From Seattle on I-5, drive north to Burlington and Exit 230/Highway 20. Turn west on Highway 20 and drive 35 miles to Coupeville. Continue south on Highway 20 (adjacent to Whidbey Island Naval Air Station) and then turn right (still Highway 20, passing Crockett Lake and the Camp Casey barracks) to the park entrance.

Contact: Fort Casey State Park, 1280 Fort Casey, Coupeville, WA 98239, 360/678-4519; State Park information, 360/902-8844.

44 SOUTH WHIDBEY STATE PARK

Rating: 10

On Whidbey Island.

Map 2.2, grid h4, page 145

This park is located on the southwest end of Whidbey Island, covers 347 acres, and provides opportunities for hiking, scuba diving, picnicking, and beachcombing along a sandy beach. There are spectacular views of Puget Sound and the Olympic Mountains. The park features old-growth forest, tidelands for clamming and crabbing, and campsites set in the seclusion of a lush forest undergrowth. Shellfish harvesting is often plentiful; check regulations. The park has 4,500 feet of saltwater shoreline on Admiralty Inlet and 3.5 miles of hiking trails.

Campsites, facilities: There are 54 sites, some with partial hookups, for tents or RVs up to 45 feet long and six primitive tent sites. Picnic tables and fire grills are provided. Restrooms, drinking water, flush toilets, coin-operated showers, an RV dump station, a picnic area with a log kitchen shelter, an amphitheater, interpretive activities, a Junior Ranger program, and firewood are available. Some facilities are wheelchair accessible. Leashed pets are permitted.

Reservations, fees: Reserve at 888/CAMP-OUT (888/226-7688), website: www.parks.wa.gov/reservations ($7 reservation fee). Sites are $16–22 per night, $6 per night for primitive sites, $6 per extra vehicle per night. Senior discount available. Major credit cards accepted. Open late February–October.

Directions: From Seattle on I-5, drive north to Burlington and the Highway 20 exit. Take Highway 20 west and drive 28 miles (past Coupeville on Whidbey Island) to the Highway 525 cutoff. Turn south on Highway 525 and drive to Bush Point Road. Turn right (west) and drive to Smugglers Cove Road (the park access road, well marked). The park can also be reached easily with a ferry ride from Mulkilteo (located southeast of Everett) to Clinton (this also makes a great bike trip to the state park).

Contact: South Whidbey State Park, 360/331-4559, fax 360/331-7669; State Park information, 360/902-8844.

45 CAMANO ISLAND STATE PARK

Rating: 10

On Camano Island.

Map 2.2, grid g5, page 145

This park features panoramic views of Puget Sound, the Olympic Mountains, and Mt. Rainier. Set on the southwest point of Camano Island, near Lowell Point and Elger Bay along the Saratoga Passage, this wooded camp offers quiet and private campsites. The park covers 134 acres and features 6,700 feet of rocky shoreline and beach, three miles of hiking trails, and just one mile of bike trails. Good inshore angling for rockfish is available year-round, and salmon fishing is also good in season. Clamming is excellent during low tides in June. An underwater park is available for divers. There is also a self-guided nature trail.

Campsites, facilities: There are 87 developed campsites for tents or self-contained RVs up to 45 feet long, one primitive tent site, and one group camp for up to 200 people. Picnic tables and fire grills are provided. Restrooms, drinking water, flush toilets, coin-operated showers, firewood, an RV dump station, a playground, a sheltered picnic area with a

kitchen shelter, summer interpretive programs, an amphitheater, and a large field for ballgames in the day-use area are available. Boat-launching facilities are located in the park. Leashed pets are permitted. An 18-hole golf course is nearby.

Reservations, fees: Reservations are not accepted accepted for family camping. Reservations required for the group camp at 360/387-3031. Sites are $6–15 per night, $6 per extra vehicle per night. Senior discount available. The group reservation fee is $25, plus $2 per person per night. Open year-round.

Directions: From Seattle on I-5, drive north (17 miles north of Everett) to Exit 212. Take Exit 212 to Highway 532. Drive west on Highway 532 to Stanwood and continue three miles (to Camano Island) to a fork. Bear left at the fork and continue south on East Camano Drive (the road becomes Elger Bay Road) to Mountain View Road. Turn right and drive two miles (climbs a steep hill) and continue to Lowell Point Road. Turn left and continue to the park entrance of the road. (The park is 14 miles southwest of Stanwood).

Contact: Camano Island State Park, 360/387-3031; State Park information, 360/902-8844.

46 KAYAK POINT COUNTY PARK

Rating: 5

On Puget Sound.

Map 2.2, grid g6, page 145

This camp usually fills on summer weekends. Set on the shore of Puget Sound, this large, wooded county park covers 430 acres on Port Susan. It provides good windsurfing and whale-watching as well as an 18-hole golf course nearby. Good for crabbing and fishing, a 100-yard pier is also available. Four cabins at Flowing Lake are a nice plus.

Campsites, facilities: There are 34 sites with partial hookups (water and electricity), including some drive-through sites, for tents or RVs up to 32 feet long, 10 yurts with heat and electricity for up to five people, and four cabins. Picnic tables and fire rings are provided. Restrooms, drinking water, flush toilets, showers, firewood, a picnic area with covered shelter, and a 300-foot fishing pier are available. Boat docks and launching facilities are located in the park. Some facilities are wheelchair accessible. Leashed pets are permitted.

Reservations, fees: Reservations are not accepted for campsites. Reservations available for yurts. Sites are $12–17 per night. Yurts are $35 per night. Major credit cards accepted. Open year-round.

Directions: From Seattle on I-5, drive north past Everett to Exit 199 (Tulalip) at Marysville. Take Exit 199, bear left on Tulalip Road, and drive west for 13 miles (road name changes to Marine Drive) through the Tulalip Indian Reservation to the park entrance road on the left (marked for Kayak Point). Turn left and drive one-half mile to the park.

Contact: Kayak Point County Park, Snohomish County, 15422 Marine Dr., Stanwood, WA 98292, 425/388-6600 or 360/652-7992, fax 425/377-9509, website: www.co.snohomish.wa.us/parks.

47 WENBERG STATE PARK

Rating: 8

On Lake Goodwin.

Map 2.2, grid g6, page 145

This state park is set along the east shore of Lake Goodwin, where the trout fishing can be great. The park covers 46 acres with 1,140 feet of shoreline frontage on the lake. Power boats are allowed, and a seasonal concession stand provides food and fishing supplies. Lifeguards are on duty in the summer. Hiking is limited to a half-mile trail. This is a popular weekend spot for Seattle area residents.

Campsites, facilities: There are 46 developed tent sites and 30 sites with partial hookups (water and electricity), including some drive-through, for RVs up to 50 feet long. Picnic ta-

bles and fire grills are provided. Restrooms, drinking water, flush toilets, coin-operated showers, an RV dump station, a sheltered picnic area, a store, and a playground are available. Boat-launching facilities are located on Lake Goodwin. Leashed pets are permitted.

Reservations, fees: Reserve at 888/CAMP-OUT (888/226-7688), website: www.parks.wa.gov/reservations ($7 reservation fee). Sites are $16–22 per night, $6 per extra vehicle per night. Senior discount available. Major credit cards accepted. Open year-round.

Directions: From Seattle on I-5, drive north to Exit 206 (10 miles north of Everett). Take Exit 206/Smokey Point, turn west, and drive 2.4 miles to Highway 531. Bear right on Highway 531 and drive 2.7 miles to East Lake Goodwin Road. Turn left and drive 1.6 miles to the park entrance on the right.

Contact: Wenberg State Park, 360/652-7417; State Park information, 360/902-8844.

48 CEDAR GROVE SHORES RV PARK

Rating: 5

On Lake Goodwin.

Map 2.2, grid g6, page 145

This wooded resort is set on the shore of Lake Goodwin near Wenberg State Park. The camp is a busy place in summer, with highlights including trout fishing, water-skiing, and swimming. Tent campers should try Lake Goodwin Resort. An 18-hole golf course is nearby.

Campsites, facilities: There are 48 sites with full hookups, including some drive-through, for RVs. No tents are permitted. Restrooms, drinking water, flush toilets, coin-operated showers, a coin-operated laundry, an RV dump station, bottled gas, ice, a clubhouse, a recreation room, horseshoe pits, and firewood are available. A store and a café are located within one mile. Boat docks and launching facilities are available within 1,000 feet on Lake

Goodwin. Some facilities are wheelchair accessible. Leashed pets are permitted.

Reservations, fees: Reservations accepted. Sites are $20–28 per night, $4 per person (under 18 free) per night for more than two people. Major credit cards accepted. Open year-round.

Directions: From Seattle on I-5, drive north to Exit 206 (10 miles north of Everett). Take Exit 206/Smokey Point and drive west for 2.2 miles to Lakewood Road. Turn right and drive 3.2 miles to Westlake Goodwin Road. Turn left (the park is marked) and drive three-quarters of a mile to the park on the left.

Contact: Cedar Grove Shores RV Park, 16529 West Lake Goodwin Rd., Stanwood, WA 98292, 360/652-7083 or 866/342-4981.

49 LAKE GOODWIN RESORT

Rating: 5

On Lake Goodwin.
Map 2.2, grid g6, page 145

This private campground is set on Lake Goodwin, which is known for good trout fishing. Motorboats are permitted on the lake, and an 18-hole golf course is located nearby. Other activities include swimming in the lake, horseshoe pits, shuffleboard, and a recreation field. **Campsites, facilities:** There are 85 sites with full or partial hookups, including eight drive-through sites, for RVs of any length, 11 tent sites, and four cabins. Picnic tables and fire grills are provided. Restrooms, drinking water, flush toilets, coin-operated showers, bottled gas, an RV dump station, recreation equipment, a store, a coin-operated laundry, ice, a playground, and firewood are available. Boat moorage, a fishing pier, and boat rentals are located nearby on Lake Goodwin. Small leashed pets are permitted in RV sites only.

Reservations, fees: Reservations accepted; phone 800/242-8169. Sites are $18–40 per night. Major credit cards accepted. Open year-round.

Directions: From Seattle on I-5, drive north to Exit 206 (10 miles north of Everett). Take Exit

206/Smokey Point, turn west, and drive two miles to Highway 531. Bear right on Highway 531 and drive to a stop sign at Lakewood Road. Turn right at Lakewood Road and drive 3.5 miles to the park on the left.

Contact: Lake Goodwin Resort, 4726 Lakewood Rd., Stanwood, WA 98292, 360/652-8169, fax 360/652-4025.

50 LAKESIDE RV PARK

Rating: 6

In the town of Everett.
Map 2.3, grid a7, page 146

With 100 of the 150 RV spaces dedicated to permanent rentals, this camp can be a crapshoot for vacationers in summer; the remaining 50 spaces get filled nightly with vacationers all summer. The park is landscaped with annuals, roses, other perennials, and shrubs, which provide privacy and gardens for each site. There's an artificially constructed pond stocked with trout year-round, providing fishing for a fee. **Campsites, facilities:** There are 150 sites (50 non-permanent), including some drive-through, with full hookups for RVs and nine tent sites. Restrooms, drinking water, flush toilets, showers, a coin-operated laundry, propane gas, a playground, a modem hookup, and pay phones are available. Some facilities are wheelchair accessible. Leashed pets are permitted.

Reservations, fees: Reservations recommended at 800/468-7275. Sites are $31.31–34.79 per night. Senior discount available. Major credit cards accepted. Open year-round.

Directions: From Seattle on I-5, drive north to Everett and Exit 186. Take Exit 186 and turn west on 128th Street. Drive about two miles to Old Highway 99. Turn left (south) on Old Highway 99 and drive one-quarter mile to the park on the left.

Contact: Lakeside RV Park, 12321 Hwy. 99 S, Everett, WA 98204, 425/347-2970 or 800/468-7275, fax 206/347-9052.

51 LAKE PLEASANT RV PARK

Rating: 6

On Lake Pleasant.

Map 2.3, grid c7, page 146

A large, developed camp geared primarily toward RVers, this park is set on Lake Pleasant. The setting is pretty, with lakeside sites and plenty of trees. Just off the highway, it's a popular camp, so expect lots of company, especially in summer. This is a good spot for a little trout fishing. Note that half of the 196 sites are permanent rentals. All sites are paved.

Campsites, facilities: There are 196 sites with full hookups, including half available for overnight use and some drive-through sites, for RVs up to 42 feet long. Picnic tables are provided. Restrooms, drinking water, flush toilets, showers, cable TV, modem access, an RV dump station, a public phone, a coin-operated laundry, a playground, and LP gas are available. Some facilities are wheelchair accessible. Leashed pets are permitted.

Reservations, fees: Reservations recommended. Sites are $28 per night. Major credit cards accepted. Open year-round.

Directions: From the junction of I-5 and I-405 (just south of Seattle), take I-405 and drive to Exit 26. Take that exit to the Bothell/Everett Highway over the freeway and drive south for about one mile; look for the park on the left side. It's marked by a large sign.

Contact: Lake Pleasant RV Park, 24025 Bothell/Everett Hwy. SE, Bothell, WA 98021, 425/487-1785 or 800/742-0386.

52 TRAILER INNS RV PARK

Rating: 5

Near Lake Sammamish State Park.

Map 2.3, grid d7, page 146

This park features all the amenities for RV travelers. It's close to Lake Sammamish State Park as well. Nearby recreation options include an 18-hole golf course, hiking trails, marked bike trails, and tennis courts.

Campsites, facilities: There are 103 sites, including half that are permanently rented and some drive-through sites, with full or partial hookups for RVs of any length. Picnic tables are provided. Restrooms, drinking water, flush toilets, showers, bottled gas, a recreation hall, an indoor swimming pool, a laundry room, ice, and a playground are available. A spa and sauna, a store, and a café are available within one mile. Leashed pets are permitted.

Reservations, fees: Reservations accepted. Sites are $18–35 per night. Major credit cards accepted. Open year-round.

Directions: At the junction of I-405 and I-90 south of Seattle, turn east on I-90 and drive 1.5 miles to Exit 11A. Take Exit 11A (a two-avenue exit) and stay in the right lane for 150th Avenue SE. After the lanes split, stay in the left lane and drive to the intersection of 150th Avenue SE and 37th. Continue straight through the light and look for the park entrance at the fifth driveway on the right (about one mile from I-90).

Contact: Trailer Inns RV Park and Recreation Center, 15531 Southeast 37th St., Bellevue, WA 98006, 425/747-9181, 509/248-1142 or 800/659-4684, fax 425/747-0858.

53 VASA PARK RESORT

Rating: 5

On Lake Sammamish.

Map 2.3, grid d8, page 146

I was giving a seminar in Bellevue one evening when a distraught-looking couple walked in and pleaded, "Where can we camp tonight?" I answered, "Just look in the book," and they ended up staying at this camp. It was the easiest sale ever made. This is the most rustic of the parks in the immediate Seattle area. The resort is on the western shore of Lake Sammamish, and the state park is at the south end of the lake. An 18-hole golf course, hiking trails, and marked bike trails are close by. The park is within easy driving distance of Seattle.

Campsites, facilities: There are 16 sites with partial hookups (water and electricity) for tents or RVs and six sites with full hookups for RVs of any length. Picnic tables are provided. Restrooms, drinking water, flush toilets, coin-operated showers, an RV dump station, a playground, and a boat-launching facility are available. Bottled gas, firewood, a store, and a café are located within one mile. Leashed pets are permitted within the campsites only.

Reservations, fees: Reservations accepted. Sites are $20–25 per night, $3.25 per person per night for more than two people. Open mid-May–mid-October.

Directions: In Bellevue, drive east on I-90 to Exit 13. Take Exit 13 to West Lake Sammamish Parkway SE and drive north for one mile; the resort is on the right.

Contact: Vasa Park Resort, 3560 West Lake Sammamish Parkway SE, Bellevue, WA 98008, 425/746-3260, fax 425/746-0301.

54 ISSAQUAH VILLAGE RV PARK

Rating: 7

In Issaquah.
Map 2.3, grid d8, page 146

Although Issaquah Village RV Park doesn't allow tents, it's set in a beautiful environment ringed by the Cascade Mountains, making it a scenic alternative in the area. Lake Sammamish State Park is just a few miles north. Most of the sites are asphalt, and 20 percent are long-term rentals.

Campsites, facilities: There are 112 sites, including three drive-through sites, with full hookups for RVs of any length. No tents are allowed. Restrooms, drinking water, flush toilets, showers, cable TV, an RV dump station, a public phone, a coin-operated laundry, and LP gas are available. Picnic areas and a playground are also available. Some facilities are wheelchair accessible. Leashed pets are permitted.

Reservations, fees: Reservations recommended. Sites are $28–33 per night. Major credit cards accepted. Open year-round.

Directions: From Seattle on I-405 (preferred) or I-5, drive to the junction of I-90. Take I-90 east and drive 17 miles to Issaquah and Exit 17. Take Exit 17 for Front Street and turn left; drive under the freeway and look for the first right. Take the first right for a very short distance and keep bearing right on the frontage road that parallels the freeway. Drive one-quarter mile to the park on the left.

Contact: Issaquah Village RV Park, 650 First Ave. NE, Issaquah, WA 98027, 425/392-9233 or 800/258-9233.

55 BLUE SKY RV PARK

Rating: 5

Near Lake Sammamish State Park.
Map 2.3, grid d8, page 146

Blue Sky RV Park is situated in an urban setting just outside of Seattle. It provides a good off-the-beaten-path alternative to the more crowded metro area, yet is still only a short drive from the main attractions in the city. Nearby Lake Sammamish State Park provides more rustic recreation opportunities, including hiking and fishing. All sites are paved and level.

Campsites, facilities: There are 51 sites with full hookups, including some long-term rentals, for RVs. Restrooms, drinking water, flush toilets, showers, cable TV, a coin-operated laundry, and a covered picnic pavilion with barbecue are available. Leashed pets are permitted.

Reservations, fees: Reservations are not accepted. Sites are $30 per night, $5 per person per night for more than two people. Open year-round.

Directions: From Seattle on I-5, drive to the junction with Highway 90. Turn east on Highway 90 and drive 22 miles to Exit 22 (Preston/Falls City exit). Take that exit to SE 82nd Street. Turn right on SE 82nd Street and drive a very short distance to 302nd Avenue SE. Turn left and drive one-half mile to the campground entrance at the end of the road.

Contact: Blue Sky RV Park, 9002 302nd Ave. SE, Issaquah, WA 98027, 425/222-7910.

56 SALTWATER STATE PARK

Rating: 7

Near Seattle.
Map 2.3, grid e6, page 146

This state park is located halfway between Tacoma and Seattle. The cities jointly and literally buried a hatchet in the park to symbolize the end of their mutual competition. Campers still don't have it so peaceful, though. The camp is set on the flight path of Seattle-Tacoma International Airport, so it is often noisy from the jets. The park features tidepools and marine life, including salmon spawning in McSorley Creek in the fall. Scuba diving is good here with a nearby underwater reef. There are three trails for hiking and biking and four buildings from the 1930s built by the Civilian Conservation Corps. You'll find beautiful views of Maury and Vashon Islands and of the Olympic Mountains. Beaches offer clamming and picnic facilities.

Campsites, facilities: There are 52 sites for tents or self-contained RVs up to 50 feet long. Picnic tables and fire grills are provided. Restrooms, drinking water, flush toilets, showers, an RV dump station, a playground, a picnic area, horseshoe pits, volleyball, interpretive activities, and firewood are available. A store, a restaurant, and ice are located within one mile. Some facilities are wheelchair accessible. Boat buoys are nearby on Puget Sound. Leashed pets are permitted.

Reservations, fees: Reservations are not accepted. Sites are $15 per night, $6 per extra vehicle per night. Senior discount available. Open April–mid-September.

Directions: From the junction of I-5 and Highway 516 (located between Seattle and Tacoma

three miles south of SeaTac International Airport), take Highway 516 and drive west for two miles to Highway 509. Turn left and drive one mile to the park access road on the right. Turn right (well marked) and drive one-half mile to the park on the shore of Puget Sound.

Contact: Saltwater State Park, 253/661-4956, fax 206/8704294; State Park information, 360/902-8844.

57 SEATTLE/TACOMA KOA

Rating: 5

In Kent.
Map 2.3, grid e6, page 146

This is a popular urban campground, not far from the highway yet in a pleasant setting. The sites are spacious, all drive-through to accommodate large RVs. A public golf course is located nearby. During the summer, take a tour of Seattle from the campground. The tour highlights include the Space Needle, Pikes Place Market, Safeco Field, and Puget Sound.

Campsites, facilities: There are 134 drive-through sites, most with full hookups and the rest with partial hookups, for RVs, and 18 tent sites. Restrooms, drinking water, flush toilets, showers, an RV dump station, a public phone, a coin-operated laundry, limited groceries, bottled gas, ice, RV supplies, free movies, and a pancake breakfast are available. A large playground, a game room, a heated swimming pool, and a recreation hall are also available. Some facilities are wheelchair accessible. Leashed pets are permitted.

Reservations, fees: Reservations recommended. Sites are $28–45 per night, $3.50 per person per night for more than two people. Major credit cards accepted. Open year-round.

Directions: On I-5 in Seattle, take Exit 152 for 188th Street/Orillia. Drive east on Orillia for 2.5 miles (the road becomes 212th Street) to the campground on the right.

Contact: Seattle/Tacoma KOA, 5801 South

212th St., Kent, WA 98032, 253/872-8652 or 800/562-1892, fax 206/872-9221, website: www.koa.com.

58 DASH POINT STATE PARK

Rating: 8

Near Tacoma.

Map 2.3, grid f5, page 146

This urban state park set on Puget Sound features unobstructed water views. The park covers 398 acres, with 3,301 feet of saltwater shoreline and 11 miles of trails for hiking and biking. Fishing, windsurfing, swimming, boating, and mountain biking are all popular. Tacoma offers a variety of activities and attractions, including the Tacoma Art Museum (with a children's gallery); the Washington State Historical Society Museum; the Seymour Botanical Conservatory at Wrights Park; Point Defiance Park, Zoo, and Aquarium; the Western Washington Forest Industries Museum; and the Fort Lewis Military Museum.

Campsites, facilities: There are 110 tent sites and 28 sites for RVs up to 35 feet long. Picnic tables and fire grills are provided. Restrooms, drinking water, flush toilets, showers, an RV dump station, a playground, an amphitheater, interpretive activities, two sheltered picnic areas, and firewood are available. Leashed pets are permitted.

Reservations, fees: Reserve at 888/CAMP-OUT (888/226-7688), website: www.parks.wa.gov/reservations ($7 reservation fee). Sites are $6–16 per night, $6 per extra vehicle per night. Senior discount available. Open year-round.

Directions: On I-5, drive to Exit 143/320th Street. Take that exit and turn west on 320th Street and drive four miles to 47th Street (a T intersection). Turn right on 47th Street and drive to Highway 509 (another T intersection). Turn left on Highway 509/Dash Pint Road and drive two miles to the park. Note: The camping area is on the west side of the road; the day-use area is on the east side of the road.

Contact: Dash Point State Park, 253/661-4955, fax 253/838-2777; State Park information, 360/902-8844.

59 GAME FARM WILDERNESS PARK

Rating: 6

On the Stuck River in Auburn.

Map 2.3, grid f7, page 146

The Game Farm Wilderness Park is just minutes from downtown Auburn and a short drive from Mt. Rainier, the Seattle waterfront, and the Cascade Mountains. Located along the scenic Stuck River, it was demarcated with group outings in mind.

Campsites, facilities: There are six group campsites with partial hookups (water and electricity) for tents or RVs, with four sleeping units per site and a maximum of 16 people per site. Picnic tables and fire grills are provided. Restrooms, drinking water, flush toilets, a picnic shelter, and an RV dump station are available. Some facilities are wheelchair accessible. Leashed pets are permitted.

Reservations, fees: Reservations required in person at the Parks and Recreation Department. Group sites are $25 per night for city residents and $35 for nonresidents, with a two-week maximum. Open April–October.

Directions: On I-5 (north of Tacoma), drive to Exit 142 and Highway 18. Turn east on Highway 18 and drive to the Auburn/Enumclaw exit. Take that exit and drive to the light at Auburn Way. Turn left on Auburn Way South and drive one mile to Howard Road. Exit to the right on Howard Road and drive two-tenths of a mile to the stop sign at R Street. Turn right on R Street and drive 1.5 miles to Stuck River Drive SE (just over the river). Turn left and drive one-quarter mile upriver to the park on the left at 2401 Stuck River Drive.

Contact: City of Auburn Parks and Recreation Department, 25 West Main St., Auburn, WA 98001, 253/931-3043.

60 MAJESTIC MOBILE MANOR RV PARK

Rating: 7

On the Puyallup River.
Map 2.3, grid g6, page 146

This clean, pretty park along the Puyallup River and with views of Mt. Rainier caters to RVers. Nearby recreation options within 10 miles include an 18-hole golf course, a full-service marina, and tennis courts. For information on the attractions in Tacoma, see the description of Dash Point State Park.

Campsites, facilities: There are 118 sites with full hookups, including half reserved for long-term rentals, for RVs of any length and 12 tent sites available May–October only. Restrooms, drinking water, flush toilets, showers, bottled gas, an RV dump station, a recreation hall, a store, a coin-operated laundry, ice, and a swimming pool are available. Leashed pets are permitted.

Reservations, fees: Reservations accepted. Sites are $16–24 per night, $2 per person per night for more than two people. Open year-round.

Directions: From near Tacoma on I-5, take Exit 135 to Highway 167. Drive east on Highway 167 (River Road) for four miles to the park on the right.

Contact: Majestic Mobile Manor RV Park; 7022 River Rd., Puyallup, WA 98371, 253/845-3144 or 800/348-3144, fax 253/841-2248, website: www.majesticrvpark.com.

61 OLYMPIA CAMPGROUND

Rating: 7

Near Olympia.
Map 2.3, grid h1, page 146

This campground in a natural, wooded setting has all the comforts. Nearby recreation options include an 18-hole golf course, hiking trails, marked bike trails, and tennis courts.

Campsites, facilities: There are 95 sites with full or partial hookups, including 40 drive-through, for tents or RVs of any length and two cabins. Picnic tables are provided. Fire rings are provided at some sites. Restrooms, drinking water, flush toilets, showers, bottled gas, an RV dump station, a recreation hall, a store, a coin-operated laundry, ice, a playground, a heated swimming pool in the summer, and firewood are available. A gas station is nearby. A café is located within two miles. Leashed pets are permitted with permission.

Reservations, fees: Reservations accepted. Sites are $19–27 per night for two people, $4 per person per night for more than two people. Cabins are $39 per night for two people. Major credit cards accepted. Open year-round.

Directions: From Olympia on I-5, take Exit 101 to Airdustrial Way. Bear east for one-quarter mile to Center Street. Turn right on Center Street and drive one mile to 83rd Avenue. Turn right on 83rd Avenue and drive an eighth of a mile to the park on the left.

Contact: Olympia Campground, 1441 83rd Ave. SW, Olympia, WA 98512, 360/352-2551, website: www.olympiacampground.com.

62 NISQUALLY PLAZA RV PARK

Rating: 5

Near McAlister Creek.
Map 2.3, grid h1, page 146

This campground is located on McAlister Creek, where salmon fishing and boating are popular. Nearby recreation opportunities include an 18-hole golf course and the Nisqually National Wildlife Refuge, which offers seven miles of foot trails for viewing a great variety of flora and fauna.

Campsites, facilities: There are 51 sites with full hookups, including six drive-through, for RVs of any length. Picnic tables are provided. Restrooms, drinking water, flush toilets, coin-operated showers, a telephone, cable TV, a store, a café, a coin-operated laundry, ice, a playground, and a seasonal swimming pool are available. Some facilities are wheelchair accessible. Boat-launching facilities are nearby. Leashed pets are permitted.

Reservations, fees: Reservations accepted. Sites are $25 per night, $2 per person per night for more than two people. Open year-round.

Directions: In Olympia on I-5, take Exit 114 and drive a short distance to Martin Way. Turn right and drive a short distance to the first road (located between two gas stations), a private access road for the park. Turn right and drive to the park.

Contact: Nisqually Plaza RV Park, 10220 Martin Way E, Olympia, WA 98516, 360/491-3831.

© TOM STIENSTRA

Chapter 3
The Northern Cascades

Chapter 3—The Northern Cascades

Mt. Baker shines like a diamond in a field of coal. It is the centerpiece in a forested landscape with hundreds of lakes, rivers, and hidden campgrounds. The only limit here is weather. The Northern Cascades are deluged with the nation's highest snowfall in winter; Mt. Baker often receives a foot a day for weeks. While that shortens the recreation season to just a few months in summer, it has another effect as well. With so many recreation destinations available for such a short time—literally hundreds over the course of three or four months—many remain largely undiscovered.

The vast number of forests, lakes, and streams can make choosing your destination the most difficult decision of all. With so many stellar spots to choose from, newcomers will be well served starting at the state parks, which offer beautiful settings that are easy to reach. Many camps set along roads provide choice layover spots for vacationing travelers.

After awhile, though, searching for the lesser-known camps in the national forests becomes more appealing. Many beautiful spots are set alongside lakes and streams, often with trailheads for hikes into nearby wilderness. These areas are among the wildest in America, featuring abundant wildlife, good fishing, and great hiking.

It's true that anybody can get an overview of the area by cruising the highways and camping at the roadside spots we list. But you can take this one the extra mile. Your dream spot may be waiting out there.

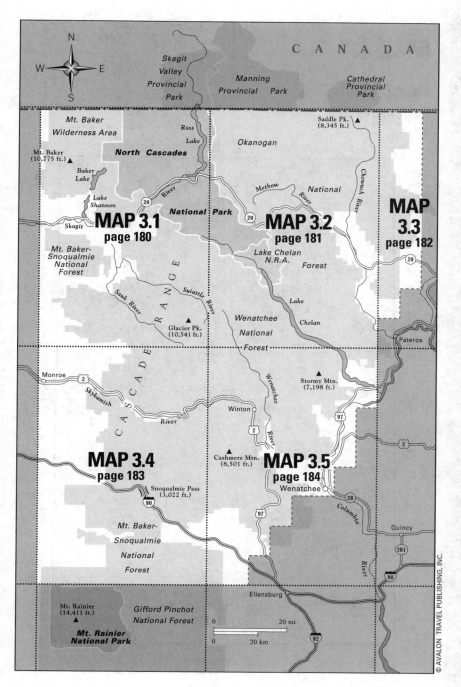

Map 3.1

Campgrounds 1–40
Pages 185–202

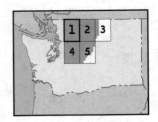

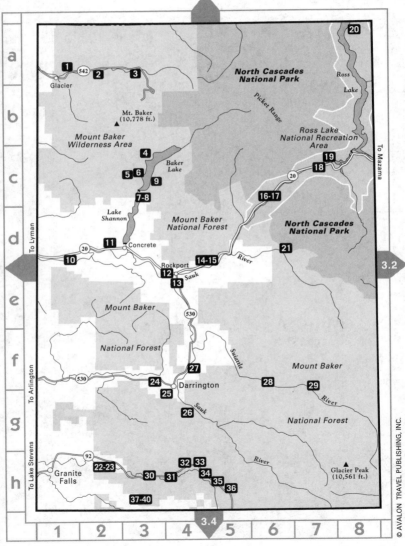

© AVALON TRAVEL PUBLISHING, INC.

Map 3.2

Campgrounds 41–74
Pages 202–217

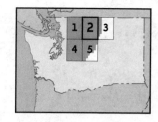

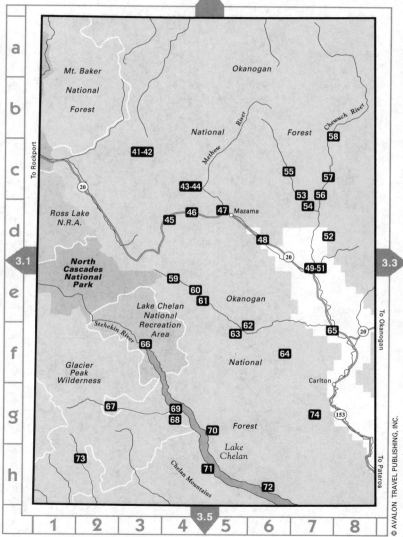

Map 3.3

Campgrounds 75–81
Pages 217–220

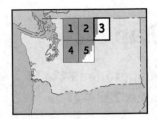

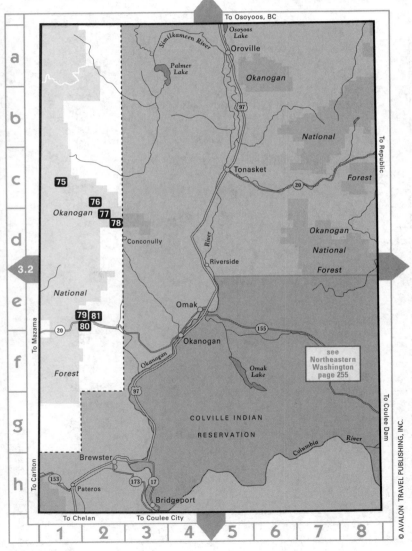

To Osoyoos, BC

Osoyoos Lake

Similkameen River

Oroville

Palmer Lake

Okanogan

97

National

Tonasket

20

Forest

75

76

77

78

Okanogan

Conconully

Okanogan

River

Riverside

National

3.2

Forest

National

Omak

79 81

80

155

20

To Mazama

Okanogan

Omak Lake

see Northeastern Washington page 255

Okanogan

97

COLVILLE INDIAN

RESERVATION

Forest

Columbia

River

To Coulee Dam

Brewster

To Carlton

153

Pateros

173

17

Bridgeport

To Chelan

To Coulee City

To Republic

1   2   3   4   5   6   7   8

© AVALON TRAVEL PUBLISHING, INC.

Map 3.4

Campgrounds 82–110
Pages 220–233

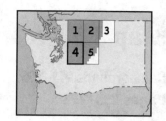

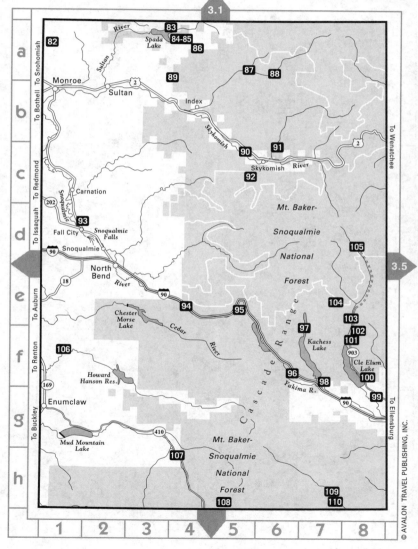

Map 3.5

Campgrounds 111–155
Pages 233–252

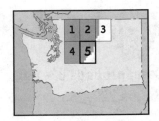

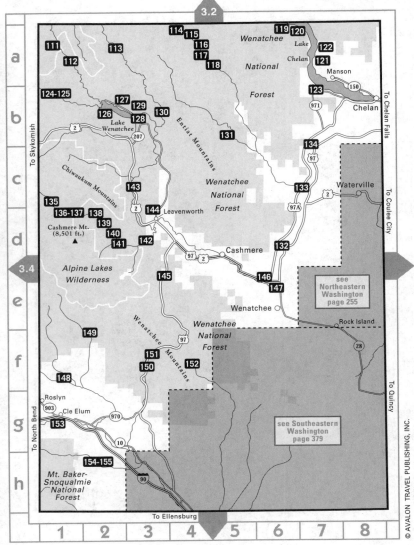

© AVALON TRAVEL PUBLISHING, INC.

❶ DOUGLAS FIR

🚶 🛶 🎣 🚐 ⛺

Rating: 10

On the Nooksack River in Mt. Baker-Snoqualmie National Forest.

Map 3.1, grid a1, page 180

Set along the Nooksack River, this camp features river views from some campsites. It is a beautiful camp, surrounded by old-growth Douglas fir, silver fir, and western hemlock. Trout fishing is available on the river, and there are hiking trails in the area, with a nearby trailhead at Silver Fir Camp.

Campsites, facilities: There are 30 sites for tents, trailers, or RVs up to 31 feet long. Picnic tables and fire grills are provided. Drinking water and vault toilets are available. A store, a café, a coin-operated laundry, and ice are located within five miles. Leashed pets are permitted.

Reservations, fees: Reservations recommended. Reserve at 877/444-6777 ($9 reservation fee) or website: www.ReserveUsa.com. Sites are $14 per night. Open May–September, with self-service access the remainder of the year.

Directions: From Bellingham on I-5, take the Highway 542 exit and drive 31 miles to Glacier. Continue two miles northeast on Highway 542 to the campground on the left.

Contact: Mt. Baker-Snoqualmie National Forest, Mt. Baker Ranger District, Sedro-Woolley, WA 98284, 360/856-5700, fax 360/856-1934.

❷ EXCELSIOR GROUP CAMP

🚶 🎣 ⛺

Rating: 6

Near the Nooksack River in Mt. Baker-Snoqualmie National Forest.

Map 3.1, grid a2, page 180

This campground is set near the Nooksack River less than one mile from Nooksack Falls and 1.5 miles from the site of the Excelsior Mine. The Excelsior Pass Trailhead is about five minutes away. There are numerous hiking

trails available within a 30-minute drive in the Mt. Baker Wilderness.

Campsites, facilities: There is one group site for up to 100 people. Picnic tables, vault toilets, and fire grills are provided, but there is no drinking water. Leashed pets are permitted.

Reservations, fees: Reservations required. Reserve at 877/444-6777 ($9 reservation fee) or website: www.ReserveUsa.com. The group site fee is $60–150 per night. Open May–September.

Directions: From Bellingham on I-5, take the Highway 542 exit and drive 37.5 miles (6.5 miles east of Glacier) to the camp on the right.

Contact: Mt. Baker-Snoqualmie National Forest, Mt. Baker Ranger District, Sedro-Woolley, WA 98284, 360/856-5700, fax 360/856-1934.

❸ SILVER FIR

🚶 🛶 ❄ 🎣 🚐 ⛺

Rating: 9

On the North Fork of the Nooksack River in Mt. Baker-Snoqualmie National Forest.

Map 3.1, grid a3, page 180

This campground is set on the North Fork of the Nooksack River. It is within 30 minutes of the Heather Meadows area, which provides some of the best hiking trails in the entire region. In addition, a one-mile round-trip to Artist Ridge promises views of Mt. Baker and Mt. Shuksan. The first part of the trail to the first viewpoint is wheelchair accessible. Fishing is available nearby, and in the winter the area offers cross-country skiing. You're strongly advised to obtain a U.S. Forest Service map in order to take maximum advantage of the recreational opportunities in the area.

Campsites, facilities: There are 20 sites for tents, trailers, or RVs up to 21 feet long. Picnic tables and barbecue grills are provided. Drinking water, vault toilets, and a group picnic shelter are available. Leashed pets are permitted.

Reservations, fees: Reservations accepted; phone 877/444-6777 or access the website: www.ReserveUsa.com ($9 reservation fee). Sites are $14 per night. Senior discount available. Open May–September.

Directions: From I-5 at Bellingham, turn east on Highway 542 and drive 31 miles to Glacier. Continue east on Highway 542 for 12.5 miles to the campground on the right.

Contact: Mt. Baker-Snoqualmie National Forest, Mt. Baker Ranger District, 810 Rte. 20, Sedro-Woolley, WA 98284, 360/856-5700, fax 360/856-1934.

4 PARK CREEK

Rating: 6

Near Baker Lake in Mt. Baker-Snoqualmie National Forest.

Map 3.1, grid c3, page 180

This pretty camp is set at an elevation of 800 feet on Park Creek amid a heavily wooded area comprising old-growth Douglas fir and western hemlock. Park Creek is a feeder stream to nearby Baker Lake. The camp is primitive and small but gets its fair share of use.

Campsites, facilities: There are 12 sites for tents or small RVs. Picnic tables are provided. Vault toilets are available, but there is no drinking water. Boat docks, launching facilities, and rentals are nearby on Baker Lake. Leashed pets are permitted.

Reservations, fees: Reservations required; phone 877/444-6777 or access the website: www.ReserveUsa.com ($9 reservation fee). Sites are $10 per night. Senior discount available. Open mid-May–early September.

Directions: From I-5 at Burlington, turn east on State Route 20 and drive approximately 24 miles to Milepost 82 and Baker Lake Highway (Forest Road 11). Turn north on Baker Lake Highway and drive about 19.5 miles to Forest Road 1144. Turn left (northwest) and drive about 200 yards to the campground on the left. Obtaining a U.S. Forest Service map is helpful.

Contact: Mt. Baker-Snoqualmie National Forest, Mt. Baker Ranger District, 810 Rte. 20,

Sedro-Woolley, WA 98284, 360/856-5700, fax 360/856-1934.

5 BOULDER CREEK

Rating: 8

Near Baker Lake in Mt. Baker-Snoqualmie National Forest.

Map 3.1, grid c3, page 180

This camp provides an alternative to Horseshoe Cove. It is set on Boulder Creek about one mile from the shore of Baker Lake. Fishing is fair here for rainbow trout, but typically far better at Baker Lake. A boat launch is located at Panorama Point, about 15 minutes away. Wild berries can be found in the area in season. The campground offers prime views of Mt. Baker.

Campsites, facilities: There are eight tent sites and two group sites. Picnic tables and fire grills are provided. Pit toilets are available, but there is no drinking water. Boat docks and launching facilities are nearby on Baker Lake. Leashed pets are permitted.

Reservations, fees: Reservations required for group sites and are available for some family sites; phone 877/444-6777 or access the website: www.ReserveUsa.com ($9 reservation fee). Family sites are $10 per night; group sites are $40–55 per night. Senior discount available. Open mid-May–early September.

Directions: From I-5 at Burlington, turn east on State Route 20 and drive approximately 24 miles to Milepost 82 and Baker Lake Highway (Forest Road 11). Turn north on Baker Lake Highway and drive 17.4 miles to the campground on the right.

Contact: Mt. Baker-Snoqualmie National Forest, Mt. Baker Ranger District, 810 Rte. 20, Sedro-Woolley, WA 98284, 360/856-5700, fax 360/856-1934.

6 PANORAMA POINT

Rating: 10

On Baker Lake in Mt. Baker-Snoqualmie National Forest.

Map 3.1, grid c3, page 180

With incredible scenic views of Mt. Baker, Mt. Shuk, Baker Lake, and Anderson Mountain, this camp is true to its name. Panorama Point is a well-maintained campground on the northwest shore of Baker Lake. The reservoir is one of the better fishing lakes in the area, often with good prospects for rainbow trout. Power boating and water-skiing are permitted. Hiking trails are nearby.

Campsites, facilities: There are 16 sites for tents, trailers, or RVs up to 21 feet long. Picnic tables are provided. Well water and vault toilets are available. A store and ice are located within one mile. A boat ramp is adjacent to the camp. Boat docks and rentals are nearby. Leashed pets are permitted.

Reservations, fees: Reservations accepted for some sites; phone 877/444-6777 or access the website: www.ReserveUsa.com ($9 reservation fee). Sites are $14 per night. Senior discount available. Open May–mid-September.

Directions: From I-5 at Burlington, turn east on State Route 20 and drive approximately 24 miles to Milepost 82 and Baker Lake Highway (Forest Road 11). Turn north on Baker Lake Highway and drive 18.7 miles to the campground entrance on the right on the shore of Baker.

Contact: Mt. Baker-Snoqualmie National Forest, Mt. Baker Ranger District, 810 Rte. 20 Sedro-Woolley, WA 98284, 360/856-5700, fax 360/856-1934.

7 HORSESHOE COVE

Rating: 9

On Baker Lake in Mt. Baker-Snoqualmie National Forest.

Map 3.1, grid c3, page 180

This camp is set along 5,000-acre Baker Lake. Anglers will often find good fishing for rainbow trout and kokanee salmon. Other highlights include swimming access from the campground and a boat ramp. Some hiking trails can be found nearby. The Baker Lake Basin has many trails, and the Mt. Baker National Recreation area is located within 30 minutes.

Campsites, facilities: There are eight sites for tents only, 34 sites for tents, trailers, or RVs up to 25 feet long, and three group sites. Picnic tables and fire grills are provided. Drinking water and flush toilets are available. A boat ramp and swimming beach are adjacent to camp. Leashed pets are permitted.

Reservations, fees: Reservations accepted for some sites; phone 877/444-6777 or access the website: www.ReserveUsa.com ($9 reservation fee). Sites are $14 per night. Senior discount available. Reservations required for group sites, $75 per night. Open May–September; one loop remains open through the off-season on a no-service, no-fee basis.

Directions: From I-5 at Burlington, turn east on State Route 20 and drive approximately 24 miles to Milepost 82 and the Baker Lake Highway (Forest Road 11). Turn north on Baker Lake Highway and drive about 14.8 miles to Forest Road 1118. Turn east on Forest Road 1118 and drive two miles to the campground. A U.S. Forest Service map is recommended.

Contact: Mt. Baker-Snoqualmie National Forest, Mt. Baker Ranger District, 810 Rte. 20, Sedro-Woolley, WA 98284, 360/856-5700, fax 360/856-1934.

8 BAY VIEW NORTH GROUP & SOUTH GROUP

🚶 🛶 ⛴ 🚐 🐕 🚌 ⛺

Rating: 9

On Baker Lake in Mt. Baker-Snoqualmie National Forest.

Map 3.1, grid c3, page 180

These are both group camps set along Baker Lake. They are located in forest, though not dense forest, and there is an open feel to the area here. Many sites are close to the water. Baker Lake covers 5,000 acres and offers fishing for rainbow trout and kokanee salmon.

Campsites, facilities: There are two group sites at separate camps for 25 people with tents, trailers, or RVs. Picnic tables and fire grills are provided. Vault toilets are available. No drinking water is available. A boat ramp is located nearby near Horseshoe Cove Camp. Leashed pets are permitted.

Reservations, fees: Reserve at 877/444-6777 ($9 reservation fee) or website: www.ReserveUsa.com. Sites are $75 per night. Major credit cards accepted. Open mid-May–mid-September, weather permitting.

Directions: From I-5 at Burlington, turn east on State Route 20 and drive approximately 24 miles to Milepost 82 and the Baker Lake Highway (Forest Road 11). Turn north on Baker Lake Highway and drive about 14.8 miles to Forest Road 1118. Turn east on Forest Road 1118 and drive two miles to the campground (adjacent to Horseshoe Cove). A U.S. Forest Service map is recommended.

Contact: Mt. Baker-Snoqualmie National Forest, Mt. Baker Ranger District, 810 Rte. 20, Sedro-Woolley, WA 98284, 360/856-5700, fax 360/856-1934.

9 MAPLE GROVE HIKE-IN, BOAT-IN

🚶 🛶 ⛴ 🛶 🐕 ⛺

Rating: 9

On Baker Lake in Mt. Baker-Snoqualmie National Forest.

Map 3.1, grid c3, page 180

Looking for a quiet spot on the edge of a popular lake? Here it is. This rustic campground on the shore of Baker Lake is hike-in or boat-in only. Many camps on this lake fill on summer weekends and boating activity, including fishing, power boating, and water-skiing, is high. Privacy and great mountain views are your reward for the extra effort, and it's all free.

Campsites, facilities: There are five primitive tent sites that are accessible only by boat or on foot. Picnic tables and fire grills are provided. Vault toilets are available. No drinking water is available. Boat-launching facilities are located nearby on Baker Lake. Leashed pets are permitted.

Reservations, fees: Reservations are not accepted. Northwest Forest Pass ($5 daily fee or $30 annual fee per parked vehicle) is required. Open year-round.

Directions: From I-5 at Burlington, turn east on State Route 20 and drive approximately 24 miles to Milepost 82 and Baker Lake Highway (Forest Road 11). Turn north on Baker Lake Highway and drive 13.3 miles to Forest Road 1106. Turn right (east) on Forest Road 1106 and drive across Baker Dam to Forest Road 1107. Turn left and drive one-half mile to the parking area and the trailhead on the left. To reach the camp by boat, launch at one of the campgrounds on the west side of the lake (Horseshoe Cove is the closest). Or take Trail 610/Baker Lake Trail (located on the east side of the lake, one-half mile north of the dam) and walk in four miles to the camp. Obtaining a U.S. Forest Service map is recommended.

Contact: Mt. Baker-Snoqualmie National Forest, Mt. Baker Ranger District, 810 Rte. 20, Sedro-Woolley, WA 98284, 360/856-5700, fax 360/856-1934.

10 RASAR STATE PARK

Rating: 8

On the Skagit River.
Map 3.1, grid d1, page 180

This park borders North Cascade National Park and is also near 10,778-foot Mt. Baker and the Baker River watershed. Fishing and hiking are the attractions here. The elevation is 4,000 feet.

Campsites, facilities: There are 39 sites, including 22 with full hookups for tents, trailers, and RVs, primitive hike-in/bike-in sites, and 10 walk-in sites at which there are three four-person Adirondack shelters available. Picnic tables and fire grills are provided. Restrooms, drinking water, flush toilets, coin-operated showers, and a kitchen shelter are available. Firewood gathering is prohibited. Leashed pets are permitted.

Reservations, fees: Reservations are not accepted. Sites are $6–22 per night, $6 per extra vehicle per night. Open year-round, weather permitting.

Directions: From Seattle, drive north on I-5 to Burlington and the Highway 20 exit. Turn east on Highway 20/North Cascade Highway and drive 20 miles to Lusk Road. Turn right on Lusk Road and drive three-quarters of a mile to Cape Horn Road. Turn left on Cape Horn Road and drive two miles to the park entrance.

Contact: Rasar State Park, 38730 Cape Horn Rd., Concrete, WA 98237, 360/826-3942; State Park information, 360/902-8844.

11 CREEKSIDE CAMPGROUND

Rating: 6

Near the Skagit River.
Map 3.1, grid d2, page 180

This pretty, wooded campground is centrally located to nearby recreational opportunities at Baker Lake and the Skagit River. Trout fishing is good here, and tackle is available nearby. Horseshoe pits and a recreation hall are also available.

Campsites, facilities: There are 29 sites for tents, trailers, or RVs up to 40 feet long. Picnic tables are provided. Restrooms, drinking water, flush toilets, showers, an RV dump station, a store, a laundry room, horseshoe pits, a recreation hall, and a playground are available. A café is located within one mile. Leashed pets are permitted.

Reservations, fees: Reservations recommended; $10 per night for tent sites, $22 per night for RV sites. Open year-round.

Directions: From Seattle, drive north on I-5 to Exit 232 (Cook Road). Take the exit up and over the highway to the flashing light and Cook Road. Turn left on Cook Road (Highway 20) and drive four miles to the light at Highway 20. Turn left at Highway 20 and drive 17 miles to Baker Lake Road (near Grasmere/Concrete). Turn left on Baker Lake Road and drive one-quarter mile to the camp.

Contact: Creekside Campground, 39602 Baker Lake Rd., Concrete, WA 98237, 360/826-3566.

12 ROCKPORT STATE PARK

Rating: 8

Near the Skagit River.
Map 3.1, grid e3, page 180

This state park covers 670 acres and is set at the foot of Sauk Mountain (5,400 feet). This area was never logged, creating a natural forest with a canopy so dense that minimal sunlight penetrates to the ground. The park features more than 600 acres of old-growth Douglas firs. There are five miles of hiking trails amid this forest. In addition, a steep but climbable trail extends three miles (one-way) to the top of Sauk Mountain. The summit offers good views of the Skagat Valley and the Northern Cascades. A bonus at this camp: four Adirondack shelters, which have three sides and a roof. The Skagit River, a good steelhead stream, runs nearby. Rafting and kayaking are allowed on the Skagit, with the put-in not at the park, but on nearby State Route 20.

Campsites, facilities: There are 50 sites with full hookups for RVs up to 45 feet long, three primitive tent sites, eight developed, walk-in tent sites, four Adirondack shelters, and one group tent site. Picnic tables and fire grills are provided. Restrooms, flush toilets, showers, and an RV dump station are available. Firewood is available for a fee. Some facilities are wheelchair accessible. A store, gas, and ice are located within one mile. Leashed pets are permitted.

Reservations, fees: Reservations required for the group site only; phone 360/853-8461. Sites are $16–22 per night, $6 per extra vehicle per night. Adirondack shelters are $21 per night. The group site is $40, plus $25 deposit, and $2 per person per night. Open April–late October.

Directions: From I-5 at Burlington, turn east on State Route 20 and drive 37 miles to Milepost 96. Look for the park entrance (one mile west of Rockport) on the right.

Contact: Rockport State Park, 5051 Rte. 20, Concrete, WA 98237, 360/853-8461; State Park information, 360/902-8844.

13 HOWARD MILLER STEELHEAD PARK

Rating: 5

On the Skagit River.

Map 3.1, grid e3, page 180

This Skagit County Park provides grassy sites and access to the Skagit River. The river is designated a Wild and Scenic River. The steelhead fishing is often good in season. Campsites at this spot are sunny and spacious. A bald eagle sanctuary is located at the east end of the park. November–January is the best time to see bald eagles here. This camp is most popular in July, August, and September, when the weather is best, but also attracts visitors in early winter who arrive primarily for bald eagle watching.

Campsites, facilities: There are 49 sites, including 18 with electrical and water hookups and 30 with electrical hookups, for tents, trailers, or RVs of any length and 10 sites for tents. Some sites can accommodate groups. Picnic tables and fire pits are provided. Restrooms, drinking water, flush toilets, showers, an RV dump station, a clubhouse, a picnic shelter, Adirondacks (three-sided, roofed shelters), and a playground with horseshoe pits are available. A store and ice are located within one mile. Boat-launching facilities are located on the Skagit River. Some facilities and sites are wheelchair-accessible. Leashed pets are permitted.

Reservations, fees: Reservations recommended ($2 reservation fee). Sites are $12–16 per night, $3 per extra vehicle per night. Major credit cards accepted. Call for group rates. Open year-round.

Directions: On I-5, drive to Exit 230/State Route 20 at Burlington. Turn east on State Route 20, and drive 44 miles to Rockport and Rockport-Darrington Road (Highway 530). Turn south and drive three blocks to the camp on the right.

Contact: Howard Miller Steelhead Park, P.O. Box 127, Rockport, WA 98283, 360/853-8808, fax 360/853-7315.

14 WILDERNESS VILLAGE AND RV PARK

Rating: 6

Near the Skagit River.

Map 3.1, grid d4, page 180

This RV park is located near the Skagit River. Cool and wooded, it offers nice, grassy sites and nearby access to the river and fishing. Horseshoe pits and a sports field provide recreation alternatives. Rockport State Park and hiking trails are nearby. Bald eagles can often be viewed on the Skagit River in December and January. A one-mile trail (round-trip) can be accessed along the river.

Campsites, facilities: There are 32 drive-through

sites with full hookups for RVs of any length and 20 tent sites. Picnic tables and fire rings are provided. Restrooms, flush toilets, coin-operated showers, cable TV, a recreation hall, and a coin-operated laundry are available. A café and ice are located within two miles. Leashed pets are permitted.

Reservations, fees: Reservations accepted. Sites are $11–17 per night. Open year-round.

Directions: From Burlington, drive east on State Route 20 for 44 miles to Rockport. Continue east on State Route 20 for five miles to the park. The park is between Mileposts 102 and 103 on the right.

Contact: Wilderness Village and RV Park, 57588 Rte. 20, Rockport, WA 98283, 360/873-2571.

15 SKAGIT RIVER RESORT

Rating: 9

On the Skagit River.

Map 3.1, grid d5, page 180

This beautiful camp is nestled in the trees along the Skagit River. The resort covers 125 acres, including 1.5 miles of river frontage. One feature, a restaurant called "The Eatery," has received awards for its pecan pie and is also known for its home-style meals. Fishing, river walks, and nearby hiking trails among the glaciers and waterfalls can be accessed close to the campground. There are also three hydroelectric plants nearby that offer tours. Recreational facilities include horseshoes and a sports field for volleyball, croquet, and badminton. This resort is popular from July–September, when reservations are often required to get a spot.

Campsites, facilities: There are 48 sites with full hookups, including some pull-through sites, for tents, trailers, and RVs, plus 34 cabins and mobile homes. Restrooms, drinking water, flush toilets, coin-operated showers, an RV dump station, a public phone, a coin-operated laundry, horseshoe pits, a sports field for volleyball, croquet, and badminton, and a restaurant are available. Leashed pets are permitted.

Reservations, fees: Reservations recommended. Sites are $10–20 per night. Major credit cards accepted. There is an added charge for pets in the cabins. Open year-round.

Directions: From Burlington, drive east on State Route 20 for 44 miles to Rockport. Continue east on State Route 20 for six miles to the campground on the left (between Mileposts 103 and 104).

Contact: Skagit River Resort, 58468 Clark Cabin Rd., Rockport, WA 98283, 800/273-2606, 360/873-2250, fax 360/873-4077, website: www.northcascades.com.

16 GOODELL CREEK & GOODELL CREEK GROUP

Rating: 7

On Goodell Creek and the Skagit River in Ross Lake National Recreation Area.

Map 3.1, grid c6, page 180

Goodell Creek Campground is an alternative to the nearby and larger Newhalem Creek Campground. This one is set at 500 feet elevation, where Goodell Creek pours into the Skagit River in the Ross Lake National Recreation Area. It's a popular put-in camp for raft trips downriver. That makes the group sites popular here. No firewood gathering is permitted.

Campsites, facilities: There are 21 campsites for tents or RVs up to 22 feet long and two group sites (Upper and Lower Goodell). Picnic tables and fire rings are provided. Vault toilets and a picnic shelter are available. Drinking water is available in the family sites, but not in the group sites. Leashed pets are permitted.

Reservations, fees: Reservations are not accepted for family sites. Reservations required for group sites only; phone 360/873-4590, ext. 17. Family sites are $10 per night, group sites $25 per night. Senior discount available. Open year-round, but there are no services (and no fees) in the winter.

Directions: On I-5, drive to Exit 230/State Route 20 at Burlington. Turn east on State

Route 20, and drive 46 miles to Marblemount. Continue on State Route 20 for 13 miles east to the campground entrance.

Contact: North Cascades National Park Headquarters, 810 Rte. 20, Sedro-Woolley, WA 98284, 360/856-5700, fax 360/856-1934.

17 NEWHALEM CREEK & NEWHALEM CREEK GROUP

Rating: 7

Near the Skagit River in Ross Lake National Recreation Area.

Map 3.1, grid c6, page 180

This spot is set along the Skagit River west of Newhalem at 500 feet elevation. Good hiking possibilities abound in the immediate area, and naturalist programs are available. Be sure to visit the North Cascades Visitor Center at the top of the hill from the campground. No firewood gathering is permitted here. If this camp is full, try Goodell Creek Campground, located just one mile west on State Route 20.

Campsites, facilities: There are 129 sites for tents or RVs up to 32 feet long and two group sites for up to 24 people each. Picnic tables and fire grills are provided. Flush toilets, drinking water, and an RV dump station are available. The group camp has a covered pavilion. Some facilities are wheelchair accessible. Leashed pets are permitted.

Reservations, fees: Reservations are not accepted for family sites. Reservations required for group camps at 360/873-4590, ext. 17. Family sites are $12 per night, group sites are $32 per night. Senior discount available. Open mid-May–mid-October.

Directions: On I-5, drive to Exit 230/State Route 20 at Burlington. Turn east on State Route 20, and drive 46 miles to Marblemount. Continue 14 miles east on State Route 20 to the camp.

Contact: North Cascades National Park Headquarters, 810 Rte. 20, Sedro-Woolley, WA 98284, 360/856-5700, fax 360/856-1934.

18 GORGE LAKE

Rating: 9

On Gorge Lake on Skagit River in Ross Lake National Recreation Area.

Map 3.1, grid c7, page 180

This small camp is set near the north shore of Gorge Lake, with lake views from many sites, and close to Colonial Creek and Goodell Creek. There is some tree cover. The elevation is 900 feet. Gorge Lake is very narrow and has trout fishing; check regulations. The camp is not well known and gets low use. One problem here is that the lake level can fluctuate (but not as much as Ross Lake), leaving the camps high and dry. No firewood gathering is permitted. There are two other lakes nearby on the Skagit River—Diablo Lake and Ross Lake.

Campsites, facilities: There are six sites for tents, trailers, or RVs up to 22 feet long. Picnic tables and fire grills are provided. Vault toilets are available. No drinking water is available. Garbage must be packed out. A boat ramp is nearby. Leashed pets are permitted.

Reservations, fees: Reservations are not accepted. There is no fee for camping. Open late May–October.

Directions: From I-5 near Burlington, take exit 230 for State Route 20. Turn east on State Route 20 and drive 46 miles to Marblemount. Continue east on State Route 20 for another 20 miles to the junction with Diablo Road. Bear left and drive six-tenths of a mile to the campground on the right.

Contact: North Cascades National Park Headquarters, 810 Rte. 20, Sedro-Woolley, WA 98284, 360/856-5700, fax 360/856-1934.

19 COLONIAL CREEK

Rating: 7

On Diablo Lake in Ross Lake National Recreation Area.

Map 3.1, grid c7, page 180

Colonial Creek Campground (elevation 1,200 feet) sits along the shore of Diablo Lake in the Ross Lake National Recreation Area. The five-mile-long lake offers many hiking and fishing opportunities. A naturalist program and guided walks are available during the summer months. No firewood gathering is permitted at this campsite.

Campsites, facilities: There are 164 campsites for tents or trailers, including a few walk-in tent sites; 18 lakefront sites remain open through the winter, but no services are available. Picnic tables and fire grills are provided. Flush toilets, drinking water, an RV dump station, three boat docks, and a boat ramp are available. Some facilities are wheelchair accessible. Leashed pets are permitted.

Reservations, fees: Reservations are not accepted. Sites are $12 per night. Senior discount available. Open mid-April–mid-October; 18 lakefront sites are open through the winter (no services provided).

Directions: From I-5 at Burlington, take Exit 230 and drive east to State Route 20. Turn east on State Route 20, drive 46 miles to Marblemount, and continue east on State Route 20 for 24 miles to the campground entrance.

Contact: North Cascades National Park Headquarters, 810 Rte. 20, Sedro-Woolley, WA 98284, 360/856-5700, fax 360/856-1934.

20 HOZOMEEN

Rating: 9

On Ross Lake in Ross Lake National Recreation Area.

Map 3.1, grid a8, page 180

Hozomeen campground, at 1,600 feet eleva-

tion, is just inside the U.S.-Canadian border at the northeast end of Ross Lake. It takes quite an effort to get here, which tends to weed out all but the most stalwart campers. This is good news for those few, for they will find a quiet, uncrowded camp in a beautiful setting. No firewood gathering is permitted here.

Campsites, facilities: There are 122 sites for tents or RVs up to 22 feet long. Picnic tables and fire grills are provided. Vault toilets are available. No drinking water is available. Garbage must be packed out. A boat launch on Ross Lake is available nearby. Leashed pets are permitted.

Reservations, fees: Reservations are not accepted. There is no fee for camping. Open late May–October.

Directions: This campground is accessible only through Canada. From the town of Hope, British Columbia, turn south on Silver-Skagit Road; it is a narrow dirt/gravel road, which is often rough. Drive south for 39 miles to the campground at the north end of Ross Lake.

Contact: North Cascades National Park Headquarters, 810 Rte. 20, Sedro-Woolley, WA 98284, 360/856-5700, fax 360/856-1934.

21 MARBLE CREEK

Rating: 7

On Marble Creek in Mt. Baker-Snoqualmie National Forest.

Map 3.1, grid d6, page 180

This primitive campground is set on Marble Creek amid old-growth Douglas fir and western hemlock. Fishing for rainbow trout is possible here. A trailhead to Hidden Lake just inside the boundary of North Cascades National Park can be found about five miles from camp at the end of Forest Road 1540. See a U.S. Forest Service map for details.

Campsites, facilities: There are 24 sites for tents, trailers, or RVs up to 22 feet long. Picnic tables and fire grills are provided. Vault toilets are available, but there is no drinking water. Leashed pets are permitted.

Reservations, fees: Reserve at 877/444-6777 ($9 reservation fee) or website: www.ReserveUsa.com. Sites are $20 per night. Senior discount available. Open mid-May–mid-September.

Directions: From I-5, drive to Exit 230/State Route 20 at Burlington. Turn east on State Route 20, and drive 46 miles to Marblemount and Forest Road 15 (Cascade River Road). Cross the bridge, turn east on Cascade River Road, and drive eight miles to Forest Road 1530. Turn south on Forest Road 1530 and drive one mile to the campground. Obtaining a U.S. Forest Service map is advised.

Contact: Mt. Baker-Snoqualmie National Forest, Mt. Baker Ranger District, 810 Rte. 20, Sedro-Woolley, WA 98284, 360/856-5700, fax 360/856-1934.

22 TURLO

Rating: 8

On the South Fork of the Stillaguamish River in Mt. Baker-Snoqualmie National Forest.
Map 3.1, grid h2, page 180

The westernmost camp on this stretch of Highway 92, Turlo is set at 900 feet elevation along the South Fork of the Stillaguamish River. A U.S. Forest Service Public Information Center is nearby. Riverside campsites are available, and the fishing can be good here. A few hiking trails can be found in the area; see a U.S. Forest Service map or consult the nearby information center for trail locations.

Campsites, facilities: There are 19 sites for tents or RVs up to 31 feet long. Picnic tables are provided. Vault toilets, drinking water, and firewood are available. Some facilities are wheelchair accessible. A store, a café, and ice are located one mile away. Leashed pets are permitted.

Reservations, fees: Reserve at 877/444-6777 ($9 reservation fee) or website: www.ReserveUsa.com. Sites are $14 per night, $7 per extra vehicle per night. Open mid-May–late September.

Directions: From Seattle, drive north on I-5 to Everett and U.S. 2. Turn east on U.S. 2 and drive five miles to Highway 9. Turn north and drive four miles to Highway 92. Turn east on Highway 92 and drive approximately 15 miles to the town of Granite Falls. Continue another 11 miles east on Highway 92 to the campground entrance on the right.

Contact: Mt. Baker-Snoqualmie National Forest, Darrington Ranger District, 1405 Emmens St., Darrington, WA 98241, 360/436-1155, fax 360/1309.

23 VERLOT

Rating: 9

On the South Fork of the Stillaguamish River in Mt. Baker-Snoqualmie National Forest.
Map 3.1, grid h2, page 180

This pretty campground is set along the South Fork of the Stillaguamish River. Some campsites provide river views. The camp is a short distance from the Lake Twenty-Two Research Natural Area and the Maid of the Woods Trail. A U.S. Forest Service map details back roads and hiking trails. Fishing is another recreation option.

Campsites, facilities: There are 26 sites for tents, trailers, or RVs up to 31 feet long. Picnic tables and fire rings are provided. Restrooms, drinking water, and flush toilets are available. A store, a café, and ice are located within one mile. Leashed pets are permitted.

Reservations, fees: Reservations accepted. Reserve at 877/444-6777 ($9 reservation fee) or website: www.ReserveUsa.com. Sites are $14 per night, $7 per extra vehicle per night. Open mid-May–late September.

Directions: From Seattle, drive north on I-5 to Everett and U.S. 2. Turn east on U.S. 2 and drive five miles to Highway 9. Turn north and drive four miles to Highway 92. Turn east on Highway 92 and drive approximately 15 miles to the town of Granite Falls, and continue another

11.6 miles east on Highway 92 to the campground entrance on the right.

Contact: Mt. Baker-Snoqualmie National Forest, Darrington Ranger District, 1405 Emmens St., Darrington, WA 98241, 360/436-1155, fax 360/1309.

24 SQUIRE CREEK COUNTY PARK

Rating: 7

On Squire Creek.

Map 3.1, grid f3, page 180

This pretty RV park is set amid old-growth forest, primarily Douglas fir and cedar, along Squire Creek. A family-oriented park, it often fills on summer weekends. The park covers 12.2 acres, and features several nearby trailheads. A trail from the park provides a 4.5-mile loop that heads toward White Horse Mountain. Other trailheads are located within five miles in nearby Snoqualmie-Mt. Baker National Forest, about three miles from the boundaries of the Boulder River Wilderness. No alcohol is permitted in this park.

Campsites, facilities: There are 34 drive-through sites for tents, trailers, or RVs up to 25 feet long and two sites for trailers up to 70 feet long. No hookups are provided. Picnic tables and fire rings are provided. Restrooms, drinking water, flush toilets, an RV dump station, and firewood are available. Some facilities are wheelchair accessible. A store is located three miles east in Darrington. Leashed pets are permitted.

Reservations, fees: Reservations are not accepted. Sites are $12 per night. Senior discount available. Open year-round.

Directions: From Seattle, drive north on I-5 to Exit 208 and the junction with Highway 530. Turn east on Highway 530 and drive 26 miles to the park on the left. The park is at Milepost 45.2.

Contact: Squire Creek County Park, 360/436-1283; Snohomish County Parks, 425/388-6600.

25 CASCADE KAMLOOPS TROUT FARM AND RV PARK

Rating: 5

In Darrington.

Map 3.1, grid g4, page 180

Campers will find a little bit of both worlds at this campground—a rustic quietness with all facilities available. A bonus is the trout pond, which is stocked year-round. No boats are allowed. Nearby recreation options include marked hiking trails, snowmobiling, cross-country skiing, river rafting, and tennis.

Campsites, facilities: There are 32 sites with full hookups for RVs of any length and four tent sites. Picnic tables and fire rings are provided. Restrooms, drinking water, flush toilets, showers, an RV dump station, firewood, a coin-operated laundry, a trout pond, and a recreation hall are available. Bottled gas, a store, a café, and ice are located within one mile. Leashed pets are permitted.

Reservations, fees: Reservations accepted. Sites are $14–18 per night, $2 per person per night for more than two people over 12. Open year-round.

Directions: From Seattle, drive north on I-5 to Exit 208 and the junction with Highway 530. Turn east on Highway 530 and drive 32 miles to Darrington and Madison Street. Turn right on Madison Street and drive about four blocks to Darrington Street. Turn right and drive two blocks to the park on the right.

Contact: Cascade Kamloops Trout Farm and RV Park, 1240 Darrington St., Darrington, WA 98241, 360/436-1003, website: www.glacier view.net/kamloops.

26 CLEAR CREEK

Rating: 8

On Clear Creek and the Sauk River in Mt. Baker-Snoqualmie National Forest.

Map 3.1, grid g4, page 180

This nice, secluded spot is set in old-growth fir

on the water but doesn't get heavy use. It's located at the confluence of Clear Creek and the Sauk River, a designated Wild and Scenic River. Fishing is available for rainbow trout, Dolly Varden trout, whitefish, and steelhead in season. A trail from camp leads about one mile up to Frog Pond.

Campsites, facilities: There are 13 sites for tents, trailers, or RVs up to 21 feet long. Picnic tables and fire grills are provided. Vault toilets and firewood are available. There is no drinking water. Some facilities are wheelchair accessible. A store, a café, a coin-operated laundry, and ice are located within four miles. Leashed pets are permitted.

Reservations, fees: Reserve at 877/444-6777 ($9 reservation fee) or website: www.ReserveUsa.com. Sites are $10 per night, $5 per extra vehicle. Senior discount available. Open late May–mid-October.

Directions: From Seattle, drive north on I-5 to Exit 208 and the junction with Highway 530. Turn east on Highway 530 and drive 32 miles to Darrington and Forest Road 20 (Mountain Loop Highway). Turn south on Forest Road 20 and drive 3.3 miles to the campground entrance on the left.

Contact: Mt. Baker-Snoqualmie National Forest, Darrington Ranger District, 1405 Emmens St., Darrington, WA 98241, 360/436-1155, fax 360/436-1309.

27 WILLIAM C. DEARINGER

Rating: 7

On the Sauk River.
Map 3.1, grid f4, page 180

This secluded campground sits on the Sauk River and is managed by the Department of Natural Resources. It may be difficult to reach, but that's why you'll probably be the only one here. It's pretty, with lots of trees and sites overlooking the river.

Campsites, facilities: There are 12 sites for tents or small trailers. Picnic tables, fire grills, and

tent pads are provided. Vault toilets and firewood are available, but there is no drinking water. Garbage must be packed out. Leashed pets are permitted.

Reservations, fees: Reservations are not accepted. There is no fee for camping. Open year-round.

Directions: From Seattle, drive north on I-5 to Exit 208 and the junction with Highway 530. Turn east on Highway 530 and drive 32 miles to Darrington. Continue on Highway 530 a third of a mile to Mountain Loop Road. Turn east on Mountain Loop Road and drive one-half mile; then continue straight for five miles to East Sauk Prairie Road. Turn left and drive two-thirds of a mile to Road SWD 5000. Bear right on Road SWD 5000 and drive 2.7 miles. Bear left for one mile to Road SWD 5400. Turn left on SWD 5400 and drive one-quarter mile to the campground.

Contact: Department of Natural Resources, Northwest Region, 919 North Township St., Sedro-Woolley, WA 98284-9395, 360/856-3500, fax 360/856-2150.

28 BUCK CREEK

Rating: 9

Near the Suiattle River in
Mt. Baker-Snoqualmie National Forest.
Map 3.1, grid f6, page 180

Quiet and remote, this primitive campground is set along Buck Creek near its confluence with the Suiattle River in the Glacier Peak Wilderness. An interpretive trail runs along Buck Creek and provides access to fishing on the stream for rainbow trout, Dolly Varden, whitefish, and steelhead in season. There's a large (18 feet by 18 feet) Adirondack shelter by the creek and stands of old-growth timber. A zigzagging trail routed into the Glacier Peak Wilderness is accessible about one mile west of camp. See a U.S. Forest Service map for specifics.

Campsites, facilities: There are 26 sites for tents, trailers, or RVs up to 30 feet long. Picnic tables and fire grills are provided. Vault toilets and firewood are available. No drinking water is available. Leashed pets are permitted.

Reservations, fees: Reserve at 877/444-6777 ($9 reservation fee) or website: www.ReserveUsa.com. Sites are $10 per night, $5 per extra vehicle. Senior discount available. Open June–early October.

Directions: From Seattle, drive north on I-5 to Exit 208 and the junction with Highway 530. Turn east on Highway 530 and drive 32 miles to Darrington. Continue 7.5 miles on Highway 530 to Forest Road 26 (Suiattle River Road). Turn right (southeast) on Forest Road 26 and drive 14 miles to the campground on the left. Obtaining a U.S. Forest Service map is essential.

Contact: Mt. Baker-Snoqualmie National Forest, Darrington Ranger District, 1405 Emmens St., Darrington, WA 98241, 360/436-1155, fax 360/436-1309.

29 SULPHUR CREEK

Rating: 8

On the Suiattle River in
Mt. Baker-Snoqualmie National Forest.
Map 3.1, grid f7, page 180

This camp is set near the Suiattle River near the border of the Glacier Peak Wilderness. The Suiattle gets a lot of silt from glacier melt, and most anglers prefer to fish the nearby creeks instead. The Suiattle River Trail provides streamside access. Sulphur Creek is also a good base camp for a wilderness expedition; a trailhead located about one-quarter mile south of the campground provides access to a route leading deep into the backcountry. The trail hooks up with the Pacific Crest Trail.

Campsites, facilities: There are 20 sites for tents, trailers, or RVs up to 15 feet long. Picnic tables and fire grills are provided. Downed wood can be gathered and used for firewood. Vault toilets are available. There is no drinking water. Leashed pets are permitted.

Reservations, fees: Reserve at 877/444-6777

($9 reservation fee) or website: www.ReserveUsa.com. Sites are $10 per night, $5 per extra vehicle. Senior discount available. Open June–September.

Directions: From Seattle, drive north on I-5 to Exit 208 and the junction with Highway 530. Turn east on Highway 530 and drive 32 miles to Darrington. Continue 7.5 miles to Forest Road 26 (Suiattle River Road), turn right, and drive 22 miles southeast on Forest Road 26 to the campground on the right.

Contact: Mt. Baker-Snoqualmie National Forest, Darrington Ranger District, 1405 Emmens St., Darrington, WA 98241, 360/436-1155, fax 360/436-1309.

30 GOLD BASIN

Rating: 9

On the South Fork of the Stillaguamish
River in Mt. Baker-Snoqualmie
National Forest.
Map 3.1, grid h3, page 180

This is the largest campground in Mt. Baker-Snoqualmie National Forest, and since it's loaded with facilities, it's a favorite with RVers. Set at 1,100 feet along the South Fork of the Stillaguamish River, the campground features riverside sites, easy access, and a wheelchair-accessible interpretive trail. This area once provided good fishing, but a slide upstream put clay silt into the water, and it has hurt the fishing. Rafting and hiking are options.

Campsites, facilities: There are 10 tent sites, 83 sites for tents, trailers, or RVs up to 60 feet long, and two group sites for up to 50 people. Picnic tables and fire rings are provided. Drinking water, restrooms, vault toilets, showers, and firewood are available. A store, a café, and ice are located within 2.5 miles. Some facilities are wheelchair accessible. Leashed pets are permitted.

Reservations, fees: Some sites can be reserved; phone 877/444-6777 or access the website: www.ReserveUsa.com ($9 reservation fee).

Sites are $16 per night, $7 per extra vehicle; group sites $75–100 per night. Open mid-May–early October.

Directions: From Seattle, drive north on I-5 to Everett and Highway 92. Turn east on Highway 92 and drive about 15 miles to the town of Granite Falls and Mountain Loop Highway (Forest Road 7). Continue east on Mountain Loop Highway for 13.5 miles to the campground entrance on the left.

Contact: Mt. Baker-Snoqualmie National Forest, Darrington Ranger District, 1405 Emmens St., Darrington, WA 98241, 360/436-1155, fax 360/436-1309.

31 ESSWINE GROUP CAMP

Rating: 6

In Mt. Baker-Snoqualmie National Forest.
Map 3.1, grid h4, page 180

This small, quiet camp is a great place for a restful group getaway. The only drawback? No drinking water. Fishing access is available nearby. The Boulder River Wilderness is located to the north; see a U.S. Forest Service map for trailhead locations.

Campsites, facilities: This is a specially designated group campground for tents or small RVs for up to 25 people. Picnic tables are provided. Vault toilets and firewood are available, but there is no drinking water. A store, a café, and ice are located within four miles. Leashed pets are permitted.

Reservations, fees: Reservations required; phone 877/444-6777 or access the website: www.ReserveUsa.com. The fee is $60 per night. Open mid-May–September.

Directions: From Seattle, drive north on I-5 to Everett and Highway 92. Turn east on Highway 92 and drive about 15 miles to the town of Granite Falls and Mountain Loop Highway (Forest Road 7). Continue northeast on Mountain Loop Highway for 16 miles to the campground entrance on the left.

Contact: Mt. Baker-Snoqualmie National For-

est, Darrington Ranger District, 1405 Emmens St., Darrington, WA 98241, 360/436-1155, fax 360/436-1309.

32 BOARDMAN CREEK

Rating: 7

On the South Fork of the Stillaguamish River in Mt. Baker-Snoqualmie National Forest.
Map 3.1, grid h4, page 180

Roomy sites and river access highlight this pretty riverside camp. The fishing near here can be excellent for rainbow trout, Dolly Varden, whitefish, and steelhead in season. Forest roads in the area will take you to several backcountry lakes, including Boardman Lake, Lake Evan, and Ashland Lakes. Get a U.S. Forest Service map, set up your camp, and go for it.

Campsites, facilities: There are eight sites for tents, trailers, or RVs of any length. Picnic tables and fire grills are provided. Vault toilets and firewood are available. No drinking water is available. Leashed pets are permitted.

Reservations, fees: Reservations are not accepted; sites are $8 per night, $4 per extra vehicle. Senior discount available. Open late May–early September.

Directions: From Seattle, drive north on I-5 to Everett and Highway 92. Turn east on Highway 92 and drive about 15 miles to the town of Granite Falls and Mountain Loop Highway (Forest Road 7). Continue northeast on Mountain Loop Highway for 16.5 miles to the campground entrance on the left.

Contact: Mt. Baker-Snoqualmie National Forest, Darrington Ranger District, 1405 Emmens St., Darrington, WA 98241, 360/436-1155, fax 360/436-1309.

33 BEDAL

On the Sauk River in Mt. Baker-Snoqualmie National Forest.

Map 3.1, grid h4, page 180

This campground is set at the confluence of the North and South Forks of the Sauk River. It offers shaded sites, river views, and good fishing. It's a bit primitive. North Fork Falls is about one mile up the North Fork from camp and worth the trip.

Campsites, facilities: There are 18 sites for tents, trailers, or RVs up to 21 feet long. Picnic tables and fire grills are provided. Vault toilets and a picnic shelter are available. No drinking water is available. Some facilities are wheelchair accessible. A U.S. Forest Service district office is located 17 miles from the campground, in Darrington.

Reservations, fees: Reserve at 877/444-6777 ($9 reservation fee) or website: www.ReserveUsa.com. Sites are $10 per night, $5 per extra vehicle. Senior discount available. Open May–early September.

Directions: From Seattle, drive north on I-5 to Exit 208 and the junction with Highway 530. Turn east on Highway 530 and drive 32 miles to Darrington and Forest Road 20 (Mountain Loop Highway). Turn right (south) on Forest Road 20 and drive 17 miles to the campground on the right. Obtaining a U.S. Forest Service map is advised.

Contact: Mt. Baker-Snoqualmie National Forest, Darrington Ranger District, 1405 Emmens St., Darrington, WA 98241, 360/436-1155, fax 360/436-1309.

34 RED BRIDGE

Rating: 9

On the South Fork of Stillaguamish River in Mt. Baker-Snoqualmie National Forest.

Map 3.1, grid h4, page 180

Red Bridge is another classic spot, one of several in the vicinity, and a good base camp for a backpacking expedition. The campground is set at 1,300 feet elevation on the South Fork of the Stillaguamish River near Mallardy Creek. It has pretty, riverside sites with old-growth fir. A trailhead two miles east of camp leads to Granite Pass in the Boulder River Wilderness.

Campsites, facilities: There are 14 sites for tents, trailers, or RVs up to 31 feet long. Picnic tables are provided. Vault toilets are available, but there is no drinking water. Some facilities are wheelchair accessible. Leashed pets are permitted.

Reservations, fees: Reserve at 877/444-6777 ($9 reservation fee) or website: www.ReserveUsa.com. Sites are $10 per night. Open late May–mid-September.

Directions: From Seattle, drive north on I-5 to Everett and Highway 92. Turn east on Highway 92 and drive about 15 miles to the town of Granite Falls and Mountain Loop Highway (Forest Road 7). Continue northeast on Mountain Loop Highway for 18 miles to the campground entrance on the right.

Contact: Mt. Baker-Snoqualmie National Forest, Darrington Ranger District, 1405 Emmens St., Darrington, WA 98241, 360/436-1155, fax 360/436-1309.

35 TULALIP MILLSITE GROUP CAMP

Rating: 7

On the South Fork of the Stillaguamish River in Mt. Baker-Snoqualmie National Forest.

Map 3.1, grid h5, page 180

This campground is set along the South Fork of the Stillaguamish River, close to several other camps: Turlo, Verlot, Gold Basin, Esswine, Boardman Creek, Coal Creek Bar, and Red Bridge. A trailhead about one mile east of camp leads north into the Boulder River Wilderness. Numerous creeks and streams crisscross this area, providing good fishing prospects.

Campsites, facilities: This is a designated group camp for up to 60 people. Picnic tables and fire grills are provided. Vault toilets are available, but there is no drinking water. Leashed pets are permitted.

Reservations, fees: Reserve at 877/444-6777 ($9 reservation fee) or website: www.ReserveUsa.com. Sites are $75 per night. Open mid-May–late September.

Directions: From Seattle, drive north on I-5 to Everett and Highway 92. Turn east on Highway 92 and drive about 15 miles to the town of Granite Falls and Mountain Loop Highway (Forest Road 7). Continue east on Mountain Loop Highway for 18.5 miles to the campground entrance on the right.

Contact: Mt. Baker-Snoqualmie National Forest, Darrington Ranger District, 1405 Emmens St., Darrington, WA 98241, 360/436-1155, fax 360/436-1309.

36 COAL CREEK GROUP CAMP

Rating: 8

On the South Fork of the Stillaguamish River in Mt. Baker-Snoqualmie National Forest.
Map 3.1, grid h5, page 180

A U.S. Forest Service map will unlock the beautiful country around this campground set along the South Fork of the Stillaguamish River. Fishing access is available for rainbow trout, Dolly Varden, whitefish, and steelhead in season. Nearby forest roads lead to Coal Lake and a trailhead that takes you to other backcountry lakes.

Campsites, facilities: There is one group site for tents or small RVs for up to 25 people. Picnic tables and fire grills are provided. Vault toilets and firewood are available. There is no drinking water. Leashed pets are permitted.

Reservations, fees: Reserve at 877/444-6777 ($9 reservation fee) or website: www.ReserveUsa.com. Sites are $60 per night for the entire camp. Open mid-May–late September.

Directions: From Seattle, drive north on I-5 to Everett and Highway 92. Turn east on Highway 92 and drive about 15 miles to the town

of Granite Falls and Mountain Loop Highway (Forest Road 7). Continue northeast on Mountain Loop Highway for 23.5 miles to the campground entrance on the left.

Contact: Mt. Baker-Snoqualmie National Forest, Darrington Ranger District, 1405 Emmens St., Darrington, WA 98241, 360/436-1155, fax 360/436-1309.

37 BEAVER PLANT LAKE HIKE-IN

Rating: 8

On Beaver Plant Lake.
Map 3.1, grid h3, page 180

This campground is on Beaver Plant Lake, one of four campgrounds detailed in the area (the others include Upper Ashland Lake, Lower Ashland Lake, and Twin Falls Lake camps). Excellent hiking trails are a highlight of the region. One hiking trail connects to all four lakes. From this trail, you can also access the Bald Mountain Trail, which then leads to the Cutthroat Trail. It's a nine-mile hike from Beaver Plant Lake to Cutthroat Lake.

Campsites, facilities: There are six tent sites. Fire grills are provided. A vault toilet and firewood are available. There is no drinking water. Garbage must be packed out. Leashed pets are permitted.

Reservations, fees: Reservations are not accepted. There is no fee for camping. Open mid-June–October.

Directions: From Seattle, drive north on I-5 to Everett and Highway 92. Turn east on Highway 92 and drive about 15 miles to the town of Granite Falls and Mountain Loop Highway (Forest Road 7). Continue east on Mountain Loop Highway for 15 miles to Forest Road 4020. Turn right (south) on Forest Road 4020 and drive 2.5 miles to Forest Road 4021. Turn right on Forest Road 4021 and drive two miles to the Ashland Lakes Trailhead. From the trailhead, hike 2.1 miles to the campground.

Contact: Department of Natural Resources, Northwest Region, 919 North Township St.,

Sedro-Woolley, WA 98284-9395, 360/856-3500, fax 360/856-2150.

38 UPPER ASHLAND LAKE HIKE-IN

Rating: 9

Near Upper Ashland Lake.
Map 3.1, grid h3, page 180

Reaching this primitive and beautiful camp requires a short hike that's well worth the effort. The site is little known, so you can expect quiet and privacy. Several good hiking trails can be found near camp. A map available from the Department of Natural Resources is helpful.

Campsites, facilities: There are six tent sites. Fire grills are provided. A vault toilet and firewood are available, but there is no drinking water. Garbage must be packed out. Leashed pets are permitted.

Reservations, fees: Reservations are not accepted. There is no fee for camping. Open mid-June–October.

Directions: From Seattle, drive north on I-5 to Everett and Highway 92. Turn east on Highway 92 and drive about 15 miles to the town of Granite Falls and Mountain Loop Highway. Turn north on Mountain Loop Highway and drive 15 miles to Forest Road 4020. Turn right (south) on Forest Road 4020 and drive 2.5 miles to Forest Road 4021. Turn right on Forest Road 4021 and drive 2.6 miles to the Ashland Lakes Trailhead. From the trailhead, hike two miles to the campground.

Contact: Department of Natural Resources, Northwest Region, 919 North Township St., Sedro-Woolley, WA 98284-9395, 360/856-3500, fax 360/856-2150.

39 LOWER ASHLAND LAKE HIKE-IN

Rating: 8

On Lower Ashland Lake.
Map 3.1, grid h3, page 180

This campground is on Lower Ashland Lake,

set adjacent to Upper Ashland Lake; see the description of Upper Ashland Lake for details.

Campsites, facilities: There are five tent sites. Fire rings are provided. A vault toilet and firewood are available, but there is no drinking water. Garbage must be packed out. Leashed pets are permitted.

Reservations, fees: Reservations are not accepted. There is no fee for camping. Open mid-June–October.

Directions: From Seattle, drive north on I-5 to Everett and Highway 92. Turn east on Highway 92 and drive about 15 miles to the town of Granite Falls and Mountain Loop Highway. Turn north on Mountain Loop Highway and drive 15 miles to Forest Road 4020. Turn right (south) on Forest Road 4020 and drive 2.5 miles to Forest Road 4021. Turn right on Forest Road 4021 and drive two miles to the Ashland Lakes Trailhead. From the trailhead, hike three miles to the campground.

Contact: Department of Natural Resources, Northwest Region, 919 North Township St., Sedro-Woolley, WA 98284-9395, 360/856-3500, fax 360/856-2150.

40 TWIN FALLS LAKE HIKE-IN

Rating: 10

On Twin Falls Lake.
Map 3.1, grid h3, page 180

This beautiful camp features some lake-view campsites as well as two nearby waterfalls. The first waterfall cascades 100 feet into the lake. You are advised to avoid the second waterfall (at the outlet), where wet, slippery rocks have caused falls and fatalities. People willing to grunt a little will find good hiking, backpacking, and trout fishing at this camp. It's a beautiful and secluded area, yet it's not a long drive from Seattle.

Campsites, facilities: There are five tent sites. Fire grills are provided and a vault toilet and firewood are available. No drinking water is available. Garbage must be packed out. Leashed pets are permitted.

Reservations, fees: Reservations are not accepted. There is no fee for camping. Open mid-June–October.

Directions: From Seattle, drive north on I-5 to Everett and Highway 92. Turn east on Highway 92 and drive about 15 miles to the town of Granite Falls and Mountain Loop Highway (Forest Road 20). Continue on Mountain Loop Highway for 15 miles to Forest Road 4020. Turn south on Forest Road 4020 and drive 2.5 miles to Forest Road 4021. Turn right on Forest Road 4021 and drive two miles to the Ashland Lakes Trailhead. Hike in 4.5 miles from the trailhead.

Contact: Department of Natural Resources, Northwest Region, 919 North Township St., Sedro-Woolley, WA 98284-9395, 360/856-3500, fax 360/856-2150.

41 HARTS PASS WALK-IN

Rating: 10

Near the Pasayten Wilderness in Okanogan and Wenatchee National Forests.

Map 3.2, grid c3, page 181

At 6,198 feet elevation, Harts Pass is one of the highest drive-through mountain passes in Washington. It features great panoramic views of Mt. Gardner, Silver Star, Tower, Golden Horn, Mt. Azurite, Ballard, Crater Mountain, Mt. Baker (on a clear day), Jack Mountain, the Pickets Range, Pasayten Peak, and Mt. Robinson. This pretty little campground is near the Pasayten Wilderness, which offers 500 miles of trails leading to alpine meadows and glacier-fed lakes and streams, and along ridges to spectacular mountain heights. The Pacific Crest Trail passes near the camp and offers a great view of the Northern Cascade Range. No trailers permitted on access road.

Campsites, facilities: There are five walk-in tent sites requiring a 50-foot walk. No RVs or trailers. Picnic tables and fire grills are provided. Vault toilets are available, but there is no drinking water. Garbage must be packed out. Leashed pets are permitted.

Reservations, fees: Reservations are not accepted. Sites are $5 per night. Senior discount available. Open mid-July–late September.

Directions: From Burlington, drive east on State Route 20 for 120 miles to Mazama Road. Turn left on Mazama Road and drive one-quarter mile to County Road 9140. Turn left and drive northwest for seven miles to Lost River, where the pavement ends and the road soon becomes Forest Road 5400. Continue on Forest Road 5400 for 12.5 miles northwest to the campground (across from a guard station). Note: Forest Road 5400 is a narrow, curving road with steep slide cliffs that is closed to trailers. Drive slowly and yield to trucks.

Contact: Okanogan and Wenatchee National Forests, Methow Valley Visitor Center, 24 West Chewuch Rd., Winthrop, WA 98862, 509/996-4000, fax 509/996-4051.

42 MEADOWS

Rating: 9

Near the Pacific Crest Trail in Okanogan and Wenatchee National Forests.

Map 3.2, grid c3, page 181

This campground is about one mile from Harts Pass and offers the same opportunities. It is set adjacent to the Pacific Crest Trail. With its plentiful spruce and subalpine fir, the camp is beautiful in summer; springtime brings an array of wildflowers. No trailers are permitted on the access road.

Campsites, facilities: There are 14 tent sites. Picnic tables and fire grills are provided. Vault toilets are available, but there is no drinking water or garbage service; pack out garbage. Leashed pets are permitted.

Reservations, fees: Reservations are not accepted. Sites are $5 per night. Senior discount available. Open mid-July–late September.

Directions: From Burlington, drive east on State Route 20 for 120 miles to Mazama Road. Turn left on Mazama Road and drive one-quarter mile to County Road 9140. Turn left and drive northwest for seven miles to Lost River, where the pavement ends and the road soon becomes Forest Road 5400. Continue on Forest Road 5400 for 12.5 miles to Forest Road 5400-500. Turn left (south) and drive one mile to the campground. Note: Forest Road 5400 is a narrow, curving road with steep slide cliffs that is closed to trailers. Drive slowly and yield to trucks.

Contact: Okanogan and Wenatchee National Forests, Methow Valley Visitor Center, 24 West Chewuch Rd., Winthrop, WA 98862, 509/996-4000, fax 509/996-4051.

43 BALLARD

Rating: 6

Near the Methow River in Okanogan and Wenatchee National Forests.

Map 3.2, grid c4, page 181

Ballard is set at an elevation of 2,521 feet, about one-half mile from River Bend. Numerous hiking trails can be found in the area, as well as access to the West Fork Methow and Los River Monument Creek trails. It is also possible to hike west and eventually hook up with the Pacific Crest Trail. See the description of Early Winters Campground for area information. Livestock are not permitted in the campground, but a hitching rail and stock truck dock are available at the Robinson Creek Trailhead near the campground, where there are several primitive sites.

Campsites, facilities: There are six sites for tents, trailers, or RVs up to 20 feet long. Picnic tables and fire grills are provided. Vault toilets are available, but there is no drinking water. Garbage must be packed out. Leashed pets are permitted. No livestock is permitted in camp.

Reservations, fees: Reservations are not accepted. Sites are $3 per night, $3 per extra vehicle per night. Senior discount available. Open June–October, weather permitting.

Directions: From Burlington, drive east on State Route 20 for 120 miles to Mazama Road. Turn left on Mazama Road and drive one-quar-

ter mile to County Road 9140. Turn left and drive northwest for seven miles to Lost River, where the pavement ends and the road soon becomes Forest Road 5400. Continue northwest on Forest Road 5400 for two miles to the campground on the left.

Contact: Okanogan and Wenatchee National Forests, Methow Valley Visitor Center, 24 West Chewuch Rd., Winthrop, WA 98862, 509/996-4000, fax 509/996-4051.

44 RIVER BEND

Rating: 6

On the Methow River in Okanogan and Wenatchee National Forests.

Map 3.2, grid c4, page 181

This campground is located along the Methow River at 2,600 feet elevation, about two miles from the boundary of the Pasayten Wilderness. Several trails near the camp provide access to the wilderness, and another trail follows the Methow River west for about eight miles before hooking up with the Pacific Crest Trail near Azurite Peak; a U.S. Forest Service map will show you the options. See trip notes for Ballard Camp for more information about the area.

Campsites, facilities: There are five sites for tents, trailers, or RVs up to 16 feet long. Picnic tables and fire grills are provided. Vault toilets are available. No drinking water is available. Garbage must be packed out. Leashed pets are permitted.

Reservations, fees: Reservations are not accepted. Sites are $3 per night, $3 per extra vehicle per night. Senior discount available. Open June–late September.

Directions: From Burlington, drive east on State Route 20 for 120 miles to Mazama Road. Turn left on Mazama Road and drive one-quarter mile to County Road 9140. Turn left and drive northwest for seven miles to Lost River, where the pavement ends and the road soon becomes Forest Road 5400. Continue northwest on Forest Road 5400 for two miles to Forest Road 5400-600. Bear left (west) on Forest Road 5400-600 and drive one-half mile to the campground on the left.

Contact: Okanogan and Wenatchee National Forests, Methow Valley Visitor Center, 24 West Chewuch Rd., Winthrop, WA 98862, 509/996-4000, fax 509/996-4051.

45 LONE FIR

🚶 🚴 🏊 🏕 🔥 ♿ 🚐 ⛺

Rating: 9

On Early Winters Creek in Okanogan and Wenatchee National Forests.
Map 3.2, grid d4, page 181

Lone Fir is set at 3,640 feet elevation along the banks of Early Winters Creek. The area has had some timber operations in the past, but there are no nearby clear-cuts. To the west, Washington Pass Overlook offers a spectacular view. Anglers can fish in the creek, and many hiking and biking trails crisscross the area, including the trailhead for Cutthroat Lake. A U.S. Forest Service map will provide details. A loop trail through the campground woods is wheelchair accessible for four-tenths of a mile. See the description of Early Winters Camp for more information.

Campsites, facilities: There are 27 sites for tents, trailers, or RVs up to 20 feet long. Picnic tables and fire grills are provided. Vault toilets are available. No drinking water is available. Garbage must be packed out. Leashed pets are permitted.

Reservations, fees: Reservations are not accepted. Sites are $6 per night, $6 per extra vehicle per night. Senior discount available. Open June–late September.

Directions: From Burlington, drive east on State Route 20 for 107 miles to the campground (11 miles west of Mazama) on the right.

Contact: Okanogan and Wenatchee National Forests, Methow Valley Visitor Center, 24 West Chewuch Rd., Winthrop, WA 98862, 509/996-4000, fax 509/996-4051.

46 KLIPCHUCK

🚶 🏕 ♿ 🚐 ⛺

Rating: 7

On Early Winters Creek in Okanogan and Wenatchee National Forests.
Map 3.2, grid d4, page 181

This camp is located at an elevation of 3,000 feet along Early Winters Creek. The camp area is set amid majestic trees, primarily Douglas fir and subalpine firs. Klipchuck provides hiking aplenty, but note that rattlesnakes are occasionally seen in this area. A short loop trail from the camp leads about five miles up and over Delancy Ridge to Driveway Butte and down to the creek. Another trail starts nearby on Forest Road 200 (Sandy Butte-Cedar Creek Road) and goes two miles up Cedar Creek to lovely Cedar Creek Falls. Still another option from the campground is a two-mile trail along Early Winters Creek. This region is best visited in the spring and fall, with summer hot and dry. See the description of Early Winters for more information.

Campsites, facilities: There are 46 sites for tents, trailers, or RVs up to 34 feet long. Sites can be combined to accommodate groups. Picnic tables and fire grills are provided. Drinking water and vault toilets are available. Some facilities are wheelchair accessible. Leashed pets are permitted.

Reservations, fees: Reservations are not accepted. Sites are $8 per night, $8 per extra vehicle per night. Senior discount available. Open June–late September.

Directions: From Burlington, drive east on State Route 20 for 115 miles to Forest Road 300. (If you reach the Methow River Valley, you have gone four miles past the turnoff.) Turn left (marked) and drive northwest one mile to the camp at the end of the road.

Contact: Okanogan and Wenatchee National Forests, Methow Valley Visitor Center, 24 West Chewuch Rd., Winthrop, WA 98862, 509/996-4000, fax 509/996-4051.

47 EARLY WINTERS

Rating: 6

On Early Winters Creek in Okanogan and Wenatchee National Forests.

Map 3.2, grid d5, page 181

Located on each side of the highway, this campground has an unusual configuration. The confluence of Early Winters Creek and the Methow River mark the site of this campground. The elevation is 2,160 feet. You'll find great views of Goat Wall here. Campsites are flat, and the open landscape, set in a sparse lodgepole pine forest, provides an arid feel to the area. Several hiking trails can be found within five miles, including one that leads south to Cedar Creek Falls. Other possible side trips include Goat Wall to the north and the town of Winthrop to the south, which boasts a historical museum, a state fish hatchery, and Pearrygin Lake State Park.

Campsites, facilities: There are 13 sites for tents, trailers, or RVs up to 24 feet long. Picnic tables and fire grills are provided. Drinking water and vault toilets are available. There is a small store and snack bar in Mazama, about two miles away. Leashed pets are permitted.

Reservations, fees: Reservations are not accepted. Sites are $6 per night, $6 per extra vehicle per night. Senior discount available. Open June–October, weather permitting.

Directions: From Burlington, drive east on State Route 20 for 116 miles to the campground (if you reach County Road 1163 near Mazama, you have gone two miles too far).

Contact: Okanogan and Wenatchee National Forests, Methow Valley Visitor Center, 24 West Chewuch Rd., Winthrop, WA 98862, 509/996-4000, fax 509/996-4051.

48 ROCKING HORSE RANCH

Rating: 7

In the Methow River Valley.

Map 3.2, grid d6, page 181

This ranch is good for campers with horses. Set in the lovely Methow River Valley, it's flanked on both sides by national forest. There are numerous trails nearby and a horse stable at the ranch. Owen Wister, who wrote the novel *The Virginian,* lived in the nearby town of Winthrop at the turn of the 20th century. Portions of the novel were based on his experiences in this area. Horse rentals and guided trips are available if you want to try to relive the stuff of legends.

Campsites, facilities: There are 25 tent sites and 10 drive-through sites with full or partial hookups for RVs of any length. Picnic tables are provided. Restrooms, flush toilets, showers, an RV dump station, a horse stable, corrals, horseshoe pits, volleyball, and firewood are available. Some facilities are wheelchair accessible. Leashed pets are permitted.

Reservations, fees: Reservations accepted. Sites are $12–18 per night. Open April–late October.

Directions: From Winthrop, drive west on State Route 20 for nine miles to the campground on the right.

Contact: Rocking Horse Ranch, Star Route, 18381 Rte. 20, Winthrop, WA 98862, 509/996-2768, website: www.rockinghorsewinthrop.com.

49 PINE-NEAR RV PARK

Rating: 7

On the Methow River.

Map 3.2, grid e7, page 181

This camp is an adequate layover spot for State Route 20 cruisers and a good alternative camp to the more crowded sites at Pearrygin Lake. The Methow River is nearby; see the description of KOA Methow River for information on the various activities available in the Winthrop area.

Campsites, facilities: There are 40 tent sites and 28 sites with full hookups, including 14 drive-through, for RVs of any length. Three mobile homes are for rent on a per-night basis. Picnic tables are provided. Restrooms, flush toilets, coin-operated showers, an RV dump station, and a coin-operated laundry are available. A store, bottled gas, and a café are located within one mile. Leashed pets are permitted.

Reservations, fees: Reservations accepted. Sites are $10–19 per night, $2 per person for more than two people, $2 per extra vehicle. Major credit cards accepted. Open year-round.

Directions: From Winthrop, drive east on State Route 20 one block north of Riverside Drive to Castle Avenue. Turn right (east) and drive three blocks to the park on the left.

Contact: Pine-Near RV Park, Rte. 1, P.O. Box 400-32, Winthrop, WA 98862, 509/996-2391.

50 KOA METHOW RIVER-WINTHROP

Rating: 7

On the Methow River.

Map 3.2, grid e7, page 181

Here's another campground set along the Methow River, which offers opportunities for fishing, boating, swimming, and rafting. The park has a free shuttle into Winthrop, an interesting town with many restored, early-1900s buildings lining the main street. One such building, the Shafer Museum, displays an array of period items. If you would like to observe wildlife, take a short, two-mile drive southeast out of Winthrop on County Road 9129 on the east side of the Methow River. Turn east on County Road 1631 into Davis Lake, and follow the signs to the Methow River Habitat Management Area Headquarters. Depending on the time of year, you may see mule deer, porcupine, bobcat, mountain lion, snowshoe hare, black bear, red squirrel, and many species of birds. If you're looking for something tamer, other nearby recreation options include an 18-hole golf course and tennis courts.

Campsites, facilities: There are 70 sites with full or partial hookups, including some drive-through sites, for RVs of any length and 35 tent sites. There are also 17 one- and two-room cabins. Picnic tables and fire grills are provided. Restrooms, drinking water, flush toilets, showers, firewood, an RV dump station, a recreation hall, modem hookups, bike and video rentals, a store, a laundry room, ice, a playground, and a swimming pool are available. Bottled gas and a café are located within one mile. There is a courtesy shuttle to and from Winthrop. Leashed pets are permitted.

Reservations, fees: Reservations accepted; phone 800/562-2158. Sites are $20–28 per night, $4 per person per night for more than two people, and $2 per child 5–17 per night. Major credit cards accepted. Open mid-April–November.

Directions: From Winthrop, drive east on State Route 20 for one mile to the camp on the left. The camp is between Mileposts 194 and 195.

Contact: KOA Methow River-Winthrop, 1114 Rte. 20, Winthrop, WA 98862, 509/996-2258, website: www.koa.com.

51 BIG TWIN LAKE CAMPGROUND

Rating: 5

On Twin Lakes.

Map 3.2, grid e7, page 181

As you might figure from the name, this campground is set along the shore of Twin Lakes. With its sweeping lawn and shade trees, the camp features views of the lake from all campsites. No gas motors are permitted on the lake. Flyfishing is good for rainbow trout, with special regulations in effect: one-fish limit, single barbless hook, artificials only. This is an ideal lake for a float tube, rowboat with a casting platform, or a pram. See the description of KOA Methow River for information on the various activities available in the Winthrop area.

Campsites, facilities: There are 50 sites with full or partial hookups, including 18 drive-through sites for RVs of any length, and 35 tent sites. Picnic tables and fire grills are provided. Restrooms, drinking water, flush toilets, coin-operated showers, an RV dump station, firewood, ice, and a playground are available. Boat docks, launching facilities, and rentals can be obtained on Big Twin Lake. Leashed pets are permitted.

Reservations, fees: Reservations accepted. Sites are $13–19 per night, $3 per extra vehicle per night. Senior discount available. Open April–late October.

Directions: From Winthrop, drive east on State Route 20 for three miles to Twin Lakes Road. Turn right (west) on Twin Lakes Road and drive two miles to the campground on the right.

Contact: Big Twin Lake Campground, Rte. 2, Box 705, Winthrop, WA 98862, 509/996-2650, website: www.methownet.com/bigtwin.

52 PEARRYGIN LAKE STATE PARK

Rating: 8

On Pearrygin Lake.

Map 3.2, grid d7, page 181

Pearrygin Lake is fed from underground springs and Pearrygin Creek, the lifeblood for this setting and the adjacent 578-acre state park. Located in the beautiful Methow Valley, it's ringed by the Northern Cascade Mountains. The park is known for its expansive green lawns, which lead to 8,200 feet of waterfront and sandy beaches. Old willows and ash provide shade. The camp is frequented by red-winged and yellow-headed blackbirds, as well as marmots. Wildflower and wildlife viewing are excellent in the spring. The campground has access to a sandy beach and facilities for swimming, boating, fishing, and hiking. The sites are set close together and don't offer much privacy, but they are spacious, and a variety of recreation options make it worth the crunch.

Campsites, facilities: There are 53 tent sites and 30 sites with full hookups for tents or RVs up to 60 feet in length. Picnic tables and fire grills are provided. Restrooms, drinking water, flush toilets, coin-operated showers, an RV dump station, and firewood for a fee are available. A store, a deli, and ice are located within one mile. Some facilities are wheelchair accessible. Boat-launching and dock facilities are available. Leashed pets are permitted.

Reservations, fees: Reserve at 888/CAMP-OUT (888/226-7688), website: www.parks.wa.gov/reservations ($7 reservation fee); reservations accepted from April 15. Sites are $6–22 per night, $6 per extra vehicle per night. Senior discount available. Major credit cards accepted. Open April–October.

Directions: From Winthrop and State Route 20, drive north through town (road changes to East Chewuch Road). Continue 1.5 miles north from town to Bear Creek Road. Turn right and drive 15 miles to the end of the pavement and look for the cattle guard and the park entrance on the right. Turn right, drive over the cattle guard, and continue to the campground.

Contact: Pearrygin Lake State Park, 509/996-2370, fax 509/996-2630; State Park information, 360/902-8844.

53 FLAT

Rating: 6

On Eightmile Creek in Okanogan and Wenatchee National Forests.

Map 3.2, grid c7, page 181

This campground is set along Eightmile Creek, two miles from where it empties into the Chewuch River. The elevation is 2,858 feet. Buck Lake is about three miles away. This is the closest of six camps to County Road 1213. Other options include Honeymoon, Nice, and Falls Creek.

Campsites, facilities: There are 12 sites for tents, trailers, or RVs up to 18 feet long. Picnic tables and fire grills are provided, but there is no drinking water. Vault toilets are available. Garbage must be packed out. Leashed pets are permitted.

Reservations, fees: Reservations are not accepted. Sites are $3 per night, $3 per extra vehicle per night. Senior discount available. Open June–late September.

Directions: From Burlington, drive east on State Route 20 for 134 miles to Winthrop and County Road 1213 (West Chewuch Road). Turn north on West Chewuch Road and drive 6.5 miles (the road becomes Forest Road 51). Continue on Forest Road 51 and drive three miles to Forest Road 5130 (Eightmile Creek Road). Turn left (northwest) and drive two miles to the campground on the left.

Contact: Okanogan and Wenatchee National Forests, Methow Valley Visitor Center, 24 West Chewuch Rd., Winthrop, WA 98862, 509/996-4000, fax 509/996-4051.

54 NICE

Rating: 6

On Eightmile Creek in Okanogan and Wenatchee National Forests.

Map 3.2, grid d7, page 181

Nice is situated along Eightmile Creek, about four miles from Buck Lake. Youngsters will enjoy exploring a nearby beaver pond. A trail leading into the Pasayten Wilderness can be found at the end of Forest Road 5130. Pearrygin Lake State Park is just a few miles to the south, near Winthrop. Note: There is no turnaround area for RVs.

Campsites, facilities: There are three tent sites. Picnic tables and fire grills are provided. Vault toilets are available, but there is no drinking water. Garbage must be packed out. Leashed pets are permitted.

Reservations, fees: Reservations are not accepted. Sites are $3 per night, $3 per extra vehicle per night. Senior discount available. Open June–late September.

Directions: From Burlington, drive east on State Route 20 for 134 miles to Winthrop and County Road 1213 (West Chewuch Road). Turn north on West Chewuch Road and drive

6.5 miles (the road becomes Forest Road 51.) Continue on Forest Road 51 and drive three miles to Forest Road 5130 (Eightmile Creek Road). Turn left (northwest) and drive four miles to the campground on the left.

Contact: Okanogan and Wenatchee National Forests, Methow Valley Visitor Center, 24 West Chewuch Rd., Winthrop, WA 98862, 509/996-4000, fax 509/996-4051.

55 HONEYMOON

Rating: 8

On Eightmile Creek in Okanogan and Wenatchee National Forests.

Map 3.2, grid c6, page 181

This small camp is set along Eightmile Creek at an elevation of 3,280 feet. If you continue north seven miles to the end of Forest Road 5130, you'll reach a trailhead that provides access to the Pasayten Wilderness. See a U.S. Forest Service map for details. Why is it named Honeymoon? Well, it seems that a forest ranger and his bride chose this quiet and secluded spot along the creek to spend their wedding night.

Campsites, facilities: There are six sites for tents, trailers, or small RVs up to 18 feet long. Picnic tables and fire grills are provided. Vault toilets are available, but there is no drinking water. Garbage must be packed out. Leashed pets are permitted.

Reservations, fees: Reservations are not accepted. Sites are $3 per vehicle. Senior discount available. Open June–late September.

Directions: From Burlington, drive east on State Route 20 for 134 miles to Winthrop and County Road 1213/West Chewuch Road. Turn north on County Road 1213/West Chewuch Road and drive 6.5 miles (where it merges with Forest Road 5130). Continue north on Forest Road 5130 for 10 miles to the campground on the right.

Contact: Okanogan and Wenatchee National Forests, Methow Valley Visitor Center, 24 West

Chewuch Rd., Winthrop, WA 98862, 509/996-4000, fax 509/996-4051.

56 FALLS CREEK

Rating: 7

On the Chewuch River in Okanogan and Wenatchee National Forests.

Map 3.2, grid c7, page 181

About a 20-minute drive out of Winthrop, Falls Creek is a quiet and pretty campground located at the confluence of its namesake, Falls Creek, and the Chewuch River. The elevation is 2,100 feet. Highlights include fishing access and a quarter-mile trail (wheelchair accessible) to a waterfall located across the road from the campground.

Campsites, facilities: There are seven sites for tents, trailers, or RVs up to 18 feet long. Picnic tables and fire grills are provided. Vault toilets are available. No drinking water is available. Some facilities are wheelchair accessible. Leashed pets are permitted.

Reservations, fees: Reservations are not accepted. Sites are $5 per night, $3 per extra vehicle per night. Senior discount available. Open June–late September.

Directions: From Burlington, drive east on State Route 20 for 134 miles to Winthrop and County Road 1213 (West Chewuch Road). Turn north on West Chewuch Road and drive 6.5 miles (becomes Forest Road 51.) Continue on Forest Road 51 and drive 5.2 miles to the campground on the right. Obtaining a U.S. Forest Service map is advised.

Contact: Okanogan and Wenatchee National Forests, Methow Valley Visitor Center, 24 West Chewuch Rd., Winthrop, WA 98862, 509/996-4000, fax 509/996-4051.

57 CHEWUCH

Rating: 6

On the Chewuch River in Okanogan and Wenatchee National Forests.

Map 3.2, grid c7, page 181

Chewuch Camp is set along the Chewuch River at an elevation of 2,278 feet and is surrounded by ponderosa pines. It is a small camp where catch-and-release fishing is a highlight. There are also hiking and biking trails in the area. By traveling north, you can access trailheads that lead into the Pasayten Wilderness. See a U.S. Forest Service map for specific locations. This camp provides an alternative to the more developed nearby Falls Creek Campground.

Campsites, facilities: There are four sites for tents, small trailers, and small self-contained RVs up to 16 feet long. Picnic tables and fire grills are provided. Vault toilets are available. No drinking water is available. Garbage must be packed out. Leashed pets are permitted.

Reservations, fees: Reservations are not accepted. Sites are $3 per vehicle. Senior discount available. Open June–late September.

Directions: From Burlington, drive east on State Route 20 for 134 miles to Winthrop and County Road 1213/West Chewuch Road. Turn north on County Road 1213/West Chewuch Road and drive 6.5 miles (where it merges with Forest Road 51). Continue north on Forest Road 51 for seven miles to the campground on the right.

Contact: Okanogan and Wenatchee National Forests, Methow Valley Visitor Center, 24 West Chewuch Rd., Winthrop, WA 98862, 509/996-4000, fax 509/996-4051.

58 CAMP 4

Rating: 6

On the Chewuch River in Okanogan and Wenatchee National Forests.

Map 3.2, grid b7, page 181

Camp 4 is the smallest and most primitive of

the three camps along the Chewuch River (the others are Chewuch and Falls Creek). It is set at an elevation of 2,400 feet. Trailers are not recommended. There are three trailheads five miles north of camp: two at Lake Creek and another at Andrews Creek. They all have corrals, hitching rails, truck docks, and water for the stock at the trailheads, but no livestock are permitted in the campground itself. Trails leading into the Pasayten Wilderness leave from both locations. Contact the U.S. Forest Service for details.

Campsites, facilities: There are three tent sites and two sites for tents, small trailers, or RVs up to 16 feet long. Fire grills are provided. Vault toilets are available, but there is no drinking water. Garbage must be packed out. Leashed pets are permitted, but no livestock are permitted in camp.

Reservations, fees: Reservations are not accepted. Sites are $3 per night. Senior discount available. Open June–late September.

Directions: From Burlington, drive east on State Route 20 for 134 miles to Winthrop and County Road 1213/West Chewuch Road. Turn north on County Road 1213/West Chewuch Road and drive 6.5 miles (where it merges with Forest Road 51). Continue north on Forest Road 51 for 11 miles to the campground on the right.

Contact: Okanogan and Wenatchee National Forests, Methow Valley Visitor Center, 24 West Chewuch Rd., Winthrop, WA 98862, 509/996-4000, fax 509/996-4051.

59 ROADS END

Rating: 8

On the Twisp River in Okanogan and Wenatchee National Forests.
Map 3.2, grid e4, page 181
This quiet trailhead camp is located at the end of Twisp River Road. Set at an elevation of 3,600 feet along the Twisp River, it features a major trailhead that provides fishing access and a chance to hike for mountain views and explore the Lake

Chelan-Sawtooth Wilderness. The trail intersects with the Copper Creek Trail and the Pacific Crest Trail about nine miles from the camp. A U.S. Forest Service map is essential. Note that this camp is closed in the off-season to protect bull trout, an endangered species.

Campsites, facilities: There are four sites for tents, small trailers, or RVs up to 16 feet long. Picnic tables and fire grills are provided. Vault toilets are available. No drinking water is available. Garbage must be packed out. Leashed pets are permitted.

Reservations, fees: Reservations are not accepted. Sites are $6 per night, $6 per extra vehicle per night. Senior discount available. Open late May–early September.

Directions: On I-5, drive to Exit 230/State Route 20 at Burlington. Turn east on State Route 20, and drive 145 miles to Twisp and County Road 9114 (Twisp River Road). Turn west on County Road 9114 and drive 11 miles (becomes Forest Road 44). Continue west for 13.5 miles to the campground. Obtaining a U.S. Forest Service map is advisable.

Contact: Okanogan and Wenatchee National Forests, Methow Valley Visitor Center, 24 West Chewuch Rd., Winthrop, WA 98862, 509/996-4000, fax 509/996-4051.

60 SOUTH CREEK

Rating: 6

On the Twisp River in Okanogan and Wenatchee National Forests.
Map 3.2, grid e4, page 181
Although small, quiet, and little known, South Creek Campground packs a wallop with good recreation options. It's set at the confluence of the Twisp River and South Creek at a major trailhead that accesses the Lake Chelan-Sawtooth Wilderness. The South Creek Trailhead provides a hike to Louis Lake. The elevation at the camp is 3,100 feet. See a U.S. Forest Service map for details.

Campsites, facilities: There are four sites for

tents or small trailers, plus a few sites with parking for RVs up to 30 feet in length. No drinking water is available. Picnic tables and fire grills are provided. A vault toilet is available. No garbage service; pack out refuse. Leashed pets are permitted.

Reservations, fees: Reservations are not accepted. Sites are $3 per night, $3 per extra vehicle per night. Senior discount available. Open late May–early September.

Directions: From Burlington, drive east on State Route 20 for 145 miles to Twisp and County Road 9114 (Twisp River Road). Turn west on County Road 9114 and drive 22 miles (becomes Forest Road 44). Continue west (becomes Forest Road 4440) to the campground on the left.

Contact: Okanogan and Wenatchee National Forests, Methow Valley Visitor Center, 24 West Chewuch Rd., Winthrop, WA 98862, 509/996-4000, fax 509/996-4051.

61 POPLAR FLAT

Rating: 7

On the Twisp River in Okanogan and Wenatchee National Forests.

Map 3.2, grid e4, page 181

This campground is set at 2,900 feet elevation along the Twisp River. This area provides many wildlife-viewing opportunities, including for deer, black bear, and many species of birds. Several trails in the area, including the Twisp River Trail, follow streams and some provide access to the Lake Chelan-Sawtooth Wilderness. Twisp River Horse Camp, across the river from the campground, has facilities for horses.

Campsites, facilities: There are 16 sites for tents, trailers, or RVs up to 22 feet long and one double site for up to 12 people. Picnic tables and fire grills are provided. Drinking water and vault toilets are available. A day-use picnic area with a shelter is nearby. Some facilities are wheelchair accessible. Leashed pets are permitted.

Reservations, fees: Reservations are not ac-

cepted. Sites are $6 per night, $3 per extra vehicle per night. Senior discount available. Open May–September.

Directions: From Burlington, drive east on State Route 20 for 145 miles to Twisp and County Road 9114 (Twisp River Road). Turn west on County Road 9114 and drive 11 miles (becomes Forest Road 44). Continue west for 9.5 miles to the campground on the left.

Contact: Okanogan and Wenatchee National Forests, Methow Valley Visitor Center, 24 West Chewuch Rd., Winthrop, WA 98862, 509/996-4000, fax 509/996-4051.

62 WAR CREEK

Rating: 6

On the Twisp River in Okanogan and Wenatchee National Forests.

Map 3.2, grid f5, page 181

This trailhead camp is set at 2,400 feet elevation and provides several routes into the Lake Chelan-Sawtooth Wilderness. The War Creek Trail, Eagle Creek Trail, and Oval Creek Trail all offer wilderness access and trout fishing. Backpackers can extend this trip into the Lake Chelan National Recreation Area, for a 15-mile trek that finishes off at the shore of Lake Chelan and the National Park Service outpost. Rattlesnakes are occasionally spotted in this region in the summer.

Campsites, facilities: There are 10 sites for tents, trailers, or RVs up to 22 feet long. Drinking water, fire grills, and picnic tables are provided. Vault toilets and firewood are available. Leashed pets are permitted.

Reservations, fees: Reservations are not accepted. Sites are $6 per night, $6 per extra vehicle per night. Senior discount available. Open May–September.

Directions: On I-5, drive to Exit 230/State Route 20 at Burlington. Turn east on State Route 20, and drive 145 miles to Twisp and County Road 9114 (Twisp River Road). Turn west on County Road 9114 and drive 11 miles (becomes Forest

Road 44). Continue west on Forest Road 44 for 3.5 miles to the campground on the left.

Contact: Okanogan and Wenatchee National Forests, Methow Valley Visitor Center, 24 West Chewuch Rd., Winthrop, WA 98862, 509/996-4000, fax 509/996-4051.

63 TWISP RIVER HORSE CAMP

Rating: 7

On Twisp River in Okanogan and Wenatchee National Forests.

Map 3.2, grid f5, page 181

This camp is only for horses and their owners. It is set on the Twisp River at an elevation of 3,000 feet. The camp features nearby access to trails, including the North Fork Twisp River Trail, which leads to Copper Pass, and the South Fork Twisp River Trail, which leads to Lake Chelan National Recreation Area and Twisp Pass. The South Creek Trail is also available and leads from the camp to Lake Chelan National Recreation Area.

Campsites, facilities: There are 12 sites for tents, trailers, or RVs up to 30 feet long. Picnic tables and fire grills are provided. Vault toilets are available. No drinking water is available. Garbage must be packed out. For horses, a loading ramp, hitching rails, and feed stations are available. Leashed pets are permitted.

Reservations, fees: Northwest Forest Pass ($5 daily fee or $30 annual fee per parked vehicle) is required. Senior discount available. Open May–September.

Directions: On I-5, drive to Exit 230/State Route 20 at Burlington. Turn east on State Route 20, and drive 145 miles to Twisp and County Road 9114 (Twisp River Road). Turn west on County Road 9114 and drive 11 miles (becomes Forest Road 44). Continue west on Forest Road 44 for 3.5 miles to War Creek Campground on the left. Continue 250 yards to Forest Road 4430. Turn left (drive over the bridge) and drive approximately nine miles to the campground on the right.

Contact: Okanogan and Wenatchee National Forests, Methow Valley Visitor Center, 24 West Chewuch Rd., Winthrop, WA 98862, 509/996-4000, fax 509/996-4051.

64 BLACKPINE LAKE

Rating: 7

On the Blackpine Lake in Okanogan and Wenatchee National Forests.

Map 3.2, grid f6, page 181

This campground features great views of some local peaks. About one-third of the campsites have views; the rest are set in a forest of Douglas fir and Ponderosa pine. This popular spot often fills up on summer weekends and occasionally even during the week. Fishing is available for stocked rainbow trout. Note that boating is permitted, but no gas motors are allowed, only electric motors. Less than one-quarter mile long, an interpretive trail leads around the north end of the lake.

Campsites, facilities: There are 23 sites for tents, trailers, or RVs. Picnic tables and fire grills are provided. Drinking water and vault toilets are available. A boat launch and two floating docks are available nearby. Some facilities are wheelchair accessible. Leashed pets are permitted.

Reservations, fees: Reservations are not accepted. Sites are $8 per night, $8 per extra vehicle per night. Senior discount available. Open May–September.

Directions: From Burlington, drive east on State Route 20 for 145 miles to Twisp and County Road 9114 (Twisp River Road). Turn west on County Road 9114 and drive 10 miles to County Road 1090. Turn left and drive over a bridge (becomes Forest Road 43) and continue eight miles to the campground on the right.

Contact: Okanogan and Wenatchee National Forests, Methow Valley Visitor Center, 24 West Chewuch Rd., Winthrop, WA 98862, 509/996-4000, fax 509/996-4051.

65 RIVER BEND RV PARK

Rating: 6

Near the Methow River.

Map 3.2, grid f7, page 181

The shore of the Methow River skirts this campground, and there is a nice separate area for tent campers set right along the river. Trout fishing, river rafting, and swimming are popular here. The description of KOA Methow River details the recreation possibilities available within 10 miles.

Campsites, facilities: There are 69 sites with full hookups, including 30 drive-through sites and 31 riverfront sites, for RVs and trailers of any length, 35 tent sites, and rental trailers. Picnic tables and fire pits are provided. Restrooms, flush toilets, coin-operated showers, an RV dump station, firewood, a store, a coin-operated laundry, ice, a playground with horseshoe pits, bottled gas, modem access, and RV storage are available. Leashed pets are permitted.

Reservations, fees: Reservations accepted. Sites are $15–21 per night, $2 per person per night for more than two people, $1 for children over 5. Major credit cards accepted. Open year-round.

Directions: From Twisp, drive west on State Route 20 for two miles to the campground on the right.

Contact: River Bend RV, 19961 Rte. 20, Twisp, WA 98856, 509/997-3500 or 800/686-4498, website: www.riverbendrv.com.

66 WEAVER POINT BOAT-IN

Rating: 7

On Lake Chelan in Lake Chelan National Recreation Area.

Map 3.2, grid f3, page 181

The largest campground in the Stehekin area, this boat-in campground on Lake Chelan gets high use on summer weekends. The only direct access to Stehekin is by boat or a four-mile hike to Stehekin Landing from the campground. It's a fairly easy tromp, with no steep grades.

Campsites, facilities: There are 22 sites accessible only by boat, ferry, or floatplane. Picnic tables and fire grills are provided. Drinking water and vault toilets are available. Garbage must be packed out. Food storage lockers are available and must be used. Two floating docks are available for boats.

Reservations, fees: Reservations are not accepted, no camping fee; $5 per day docking fee (or $40 annual pass). Open year-round, with limited facilities in winter.

Directions: From Wenatchee, drive on U.S. 97 about 40 miles to Chelan and the ferry. Take the ferry and proceed to Weaver Point. Note that this is not a scheduled stop; you must request this stop in advance. The campground is also directly accessible by floatplane. (Call Chelan Airways at 509/682-5555 for more information.)

Contact: North Cascades National Park Headquarters, 810 Rte. 20, Sedro-Woolley, WA 98284, 360/856-5700, ext. 515, fax 360/856-1934. Lake Chelan Boat Company, 509/682-2224, website: www.ladyofthelake.com.

67 HOLDEN BALLPARK FERRY-IN, HIKE-IN

Rating: 7

Near the Glacier Peak Wilderness in Wenatchee National Forest.

Map 3.2, grid g2, page 181

Getting here is half the fun; the Lake Chelan Boat Company provides ferryboat rides that emphasize fun and education along with transportation. Several trails to lakes in the Glacier Peak Wilderness are accessible from a trail next to the campground, which is set along Railroad Creek. Because this area is situated on the eastern slope of the Cascade Range, it's comparatively arid; however, there is no shortage of glacier-fed streams and lakes in the area. See a U.S. Forest Service map for details. Less than one mile from the campground is the Holden Mine site, which was Washington's largest copper and zinc mine until it closed in 1957. Many of the buildings from the mining town have been preserved, and Holden Village offers housing and meals for travelers as space allows.

Campsites, facilities: There are two primitive tent sites that are accessible only by boat or ferry, followed by a 12-mile hike or bus trip via Holden Village up the Railroad Creek Valley. Picnic tables and fire rings are provided. One Wallowa (non-enclosed platform) pit toilet is available, but there is no drinking water. Garbage must be packed out. Be prepared to protect food from bears; bear-proof food hangs or canisters are required. Leashed pets are permitted.

Reservations, fees: Reservations are not accepted. There is no fee for camping. For ferry rates, which vary according to boat and age of passenger, phone 509/682-2224; typically the fee is in the $25 range. Open May–September.

Directions: From Wenatchee, drive north on U.S. 97 about 40 miles to Chelan and the ferry. Take the ferry and proceed 41 miles northwest to Lucerne. In Lucerne, take the bus 12 miles west to Holden Village. The campground is at the end of the road.

Contact: Okanogan and Wenatchee National Forests, Chelan Ranger District, 428 West Woodin Ave., Chelan, WA 98816, 509/682-2576, fax 509/682-9004. Lake Chelan Boat Company, 509/682-2224, website: www.lady-ofthelake.com.

68 DOMKE LAKE FERRY-IN, HIKE-IN

Rating: 9

Near the Glacier Peak Wilderness in Wenatchee National Forest.

Map 3.2, grid g4, page 181

Little known and little used, this spot is a perfect jumping-off point for a wilderness backpacking trip. Domke Lake is about one mile

long and one-half mile wide and offers good fishing by boat. Trails continue past the lake into the Glacier Peak Wilderness. See a U.S. Forest Service map for details. It is set at 2,210 feet elevation and is one of three national forest campgrounds near Domke Lake.

Campsites, facilities: There are eight tent sites accessible only by boat, ferry, or floatplane. Picnic tables and fire rings are provided. Pit toilets are available, but there is no drinking water. Garbage must be packed out. Boat rentals are available nearby at Domke Lake Resort. Be prepared to protect food from bears; bear-proof food hangs or canisters are required. Leashed pets are permitted.

Reservations, fees: Reservations are not accepted; no camping fee. A $5 per-day docking fee is required at Lucerne or Refrigerator Harbor campgrounds. For ferry rates, which vary according to boat and age of passenger, phone 509/682-2224; typically the fee is in the $25 range. Open May–late October.

Directions: From Wenatchee, drive north on U.S. 97 for 40 miles to Chelan and the ferry. Take the ferry and proceed 41 miles to Lucerne. From Lucerne, hike, bike, or motorbike on Trail 1280 for 2.5 miles to Domke Lake and the campground. The campground is also directly accessible by floatplane. (Call Chelan Airways at 509/682-5555 for more information.)

Contact: Okanogan and Wenatchee National Forests, Chelan Ranger District, 428 West Woodin Ave., Chelan, WA 98816, 509/682-2576, fax 509/682-9004. Lake Chelan Boat Company, 509/682-2224, website: www.lady ofthelake.com.

69 LUCERNE

Rating: 10

On Lake Chelan in Wenatchee National Forest.

Map 3.2, grid g4, page 181

This camp was named after Lucerne, Switzerland because of the 8,000-foot mountains that flank each side of neighboring Lake Chelan. The third deepest lake in North America, 55-mile-long Lake Chelan reaches a depth of 1,500 feet. This park is one of 13 national forest campgrounds on Lake Chelan but the only national forest camp in the vicinity that offers drinking water. Fishing, hiking, and boating are among your options here. Refrigerator Harbor and Domke Falls campgrounds are nearby. See the description of Holden for information on the Holden Mine and Village, which are also nearby.

Campsites, facilities: There are two tent sites accessible only by boat, ferry, or floatplane. Picnic tables and fire rings are provided. Drinking water, pit toilets, and boat docks and basin are available. Garbage must be packed out. Leashed pets are permitted.

Reservations, fees: Reservations are not accepted; no camping fee; $5 per day docking charge. For ferry rates, which vary according to boat and age of passenger, phone 509/682-2224; typically the fee is in the $25 range. Open April–October.

Directions: From Wenatchee, drive north on U.S. 97 for 40 miles to Chelan and the ferry. Take the ferry and proceed to Lucerne, 41 miles northwest of the town of Chelan on the west shore of Lake Chelan. (This spectacular voyage costs about $25 round-trip. For more information, call 509/682-2224.)

Contact: Wenatchee National Forest, Chelan Ranger District, 428 West Woodin Ave., Chelan, WA 98816, 509/682-2576, fax 509/682-9004. Lake Chelan Boat Company, 509/682-2224, website: www.ladyofthelake.com.

70 PRINCE CREEK

Rating: 10

On Lake Chelan in Wenatchee National Forest.

Map 3.2, grid g5, page 181

This camp is set along the east shore of Lake Chelan at the mouth of Prince Creek, 18 miles south of Stehekin on Trail 1247. It's a busy camp on summer weekends. A trail from camp follows Prince Creek into the Lake Chelan-Sawtooth Wilderness and then connects to a network of other trails, all of which lead to various lakes and streams. A U.S. Forest Service map shows details. Be prepared to protect food from bears; bear-proof food hangs or canisters are required. The elevation is 1,100 feet.

Campsites, facilities: There are six tent sites accessible only by boat, ferry, or floatplane. Picnic tables and fire rings are provided. Pit toilets are available, but there is no drinking water. Garbage must be packed out. A floating dock can accommodate about three boats.

Reservations, fees: Reservations are not accepted, no camping fee; $5 per day docking fee (or $40 annual pass). Open May–mid-November.

Directions: From Wenatchee, drive on U.S. 97 about 40 miles to Chelan and the ferry. Take the ferry and proceed to Prince Creek, 35 miles from Chelan. Note that the ferry will not stop here if water level does not allow for safe landing. The campground is also directly accessible by floatplane. (Call Chelan Airways at 509/682-5555 for more information.)

Contact: Wenatchee National Forest, Chelan Ranger District, 428 West Woodin Ave., Chelan, WA 98816, 509/682-2576, fax 509/682-9004. Lake Chelan Boat Company, 509/682-2224, website: www.ladyofthelake.com.

71 GRAHAM HARBOR CREEK

Rating: 10

On Lake Chelan in Wenatchee National Forest.

Map 3.2, grid h5, page 181

This campground is located along the west side of Lake Chelan at the mouth of Graham Harbor Creek, and features one of the best boat moorings for winds out of the north. It's one of the more remote and primitive campgrounds on giant Lake Chelan. Fishing and boating are the main recreation attractions here. The elevation is 1,100 feet. Be prepared to protect food from bears; bear-proof food hangs or canisters are required.

Campsites, facilities: There are five tent sites accessible only by boat, ferry, or floatplane. Picnic tables and fire rings are provided. Pit toilets are available, but there is no drinking water. Garbage must be packed out. A floating dock can accommodate about 10 boats.

Reservations, fees: Reservations are not accepted, no camping fee; $5 docking fee per boat per day. Open year-round.

Directions: From Wenatchee, drive on U.S. 97 about 40 miles to Chelan and the ferry. Take the ferry and proceed to Graham Harbor Creek (the ferry does not schedule a stop at this campground, but will usually stop here if you request it in advance). The campground is also directly accessible by floatplane. (Call Chelan Airways at 509/682-5555 for more information.)

Contact: Okanogan and Wenatchee National Forests, Chelan Ranger District, 428 West Woodin Ave., Chelan, WA 98816, 509/682-2576, fax 509/682-9004. Lake Chelan Boat Company, 509/682-2224, website: www.lady ofthelake.com.

72 DEER POINT BOAT-IN

Rating: 9

On Lake Chelan in Wenatchee National Forest.
Map 3.2, grid h6, page 181

Here's another little-known spot set along the shore of Lake Chelan. If you want to camp on the remote east shore, this is one of eight camps. It provides good protection from down-lake winds, but is exposed to up-lake winds. Fishermen at Lake Chelan often use this spot as their boat-in camp headquarters. Be prepared to protect food from bears; bear-proof food hangs or canisters are required.

Campsites, facilities: There are five tent sites accessible only by boat, ferry, or floatplane. Picnic tables and fire rings are provided. Pit

toilets are available, but there is no drinking water. A floating dock can accommodate about eight boats.

Reservations, fees: Reservations are not accepted, no camping fee; $5 per day docking fee (or $40 annual pass). Open May–October.

Directions: From Wenatchee, drive north on U.S. 97 about 40 miles to Chelan and the ferry. Take the ferry and proceed to Deer Point (the ferry does not schedule a stop at this campground, but will usually stop here if you request it in advance).

Contact: Okanogan and Wenatchee National Forests, Chelan Ranger District, 428 West Woodin Ave., Chelan, WA 98816, 509/682-2576, fax 509/682-9004. Lake Chelan Boat Company, 509/682-2224, website: www.lady ofthelake.com.

73 PHELPS CREEK

Rating: 7

On the Chiwawa River in Wenatchee National Forest.
Map 3.2, grid h2, page 181

This campground is set at an elevation of 2,800 feet at the confluence of Phelps Creek and the Chiwawa River. There's a key trailhead for backpackers and horseback riders nearby that provides access to the Glacier Peak Wilderness and Spider Meadows. The Phelps Creek Trail is routed out to Spider Meadows, a five-mile hike one-way, and the Buck Creek Trail extends into the Glacier Peak Wilderness. The Chiwawa River is closed to fishing to protect endangered species. A U.S. Forest Service map is advisable.

Campsites, facilities: There are seven sites for tents or trailers less than 30 feet long. Picnic tables and fire grills are provided. Pit toilets are available, but there is no drinking water. Garbage must be packed out. Horse facilities including loading ramps and high lines are nearby. Leashed pets are permitted.

Reservations, fees: Northwest Forest Pass ($5

daily fee or $30 annual fee per parked vehicle) is required. Senior discount available. Open mid-June–mid-October.

Directions: From Seattle, drive north on I-5 to Everett and U.S. 2. Turn east on U.S. 2 and drive 87 miles to State Route 207. Turn north on State Route 207 and drive four miles to Chiwawa Loop Road. Turn right (east) on Chiwawa Loop Road and drive 1.4 miles to Chiwawa Valley Road (Forest Road 6200). Bear left (north) and continue for 23.6 miles to the campground.

Contact: Okanogan and Wenatchee National Forests, Lake Wenatchee and Leavenworth Ranger District, Lake Wenatchee Office, 22976 Rte. 207, Leavenworth, WA 98826, 509/763-3103, fax 509/763-3211.

74 FOGGY DEW

Rating: 6

On Foggy Dew Creek in Okanogan and Wenatchee National Forests.
Map 3.2, grid g7, page 181

This private, remote campground is set at the confluence of Foggy Dew Creek and the North Fork of Old Creek. The elevation is 2,400 feet. Several trails for hiking and horseback riding nearby provide access to various backcountry lakes and streams. To get to the trailheads, follow the forest roads near camp. Bicycles are allowed on Trails 417, 429, and 431. There is also access to a motorcycle-use area. See a U.S. Forest Service map for options.

Campsites, facilities: There are 13 sites for tents, trailers, or RVs. Picnic tables and fire grills are provided. Vault toilets are available. No drinking water is available. Garbage must be packed out. Leashed pets are permitted.

Reservations, fees: Reservations are not accepted. Sites are $5 per night, $5 per extra vehicle per night. Senior discount available. Open late May–early September.

Directions: From Burlington, drive east on State Route 20 for 145 miles to Twisp. Continue east

on State Route 20 for three miles to Highway 153. Turn south on Highway 153 and drive 12 miles to County Road 1029 (Gold Creek Road). Turn right (south) and drive one mile to Forest Road 4340. Turn right (west) and drive four miles to the campground on the left.

Contact: Okanogan and Wenatchee National Forests, Methow Valley Visitor Center, 24 West Chewuch Rd., Winthrop, WA 98862, 509/996-4000, fax 509/996-4051.

75 TIFFANY SPRINGS

Rating: 7

Near Tiffany Lake in Okanogan National Forest.
Map 3.3, grid c1, page 182

Set at an elevation of 6,800 feet, this camp is less than a mile hike from Tiffany Lake. Tiffany Mountain rises 8,200 feet in the distance. The lake provides fishing for rainbow trout and brook trout. There are also some good hiking trails in the area. The Tiffany Mountain area provides a network of 26 miles of hiking trails, accessed from either here at Tiffany Springs or at Tiffany Lake. No other campgrounds are in the vicinity, and it's advisable to obtain a U.S. Forest Service map of the area.

Campsites, facilities: There are six sites for tents or RVs up to 15 feet long. Picnic tables are provided. Vault toilets are available, but there is no drinking water. Garbage must be packed out. Leashed pets are permitted.

Reservations, fees: Reservations are not accepted. Sites are $5 per night, $5 per extra vehicle. Open July–late September.

Directions: From East Wenatchee, drive north on U.S. 97 for 88 miles to Okanogan and County Road 9229. Turn north and drive 17.5 miles northwest to Conconully and County Road 2017. Turn left on County Road 2017 and drive 1.5 miles to Forest Road 37. Turn right (northwest) and drive 21 miles to Forest Road 39. Turn right (northeast) on Forest Road 39 and proceed 7.5 miles to the campground on the left.

Contact: Okanogan and Wenatchee National Forests, Tonasket Ranger District, 1 West Winesap Ave., Tonasket, WA 98855, 509/486-2186, fax 509/486-5161.

76 SALMON MEADOWS

Rating: 6

On Salmon Creek in Okanogan National Forest.

Map 3.3, grid c2, page 182

This camp is located along Salmon Creek at an elevation of 4,500 feet. Come in the spring for a spectacular wildflower display in an adjacent meadow. The camp features a forest setting, mainly Douglas fir, spruce, and some western larch. Trails from the campground are routed out to Angel Pass, two miles one-way, for views of the Tiffany area.

Campsites, facilities: There are seven sites for tents, small trailers, or RVs. Picnic tables and fire grills are provided. Vault toilets are available, but there is no drinking water. Garbage must be packed out. Some facilities are wheelchair accessible. Leashed pets are permitted.

Reservations, fees: Reservations are not accepted. Sites are $5 per night, $5 per extra vehicle per night. Senior discount available. Open mid-May–mid-September.

Directions: From East Wenatchee, drive north on U.S. 97 for 88 miles to Okanogan and County Road 9229. Turn left (north) on County Road 9229 and drive 17.5 miles to Conconully and County Road 2361. Continue northwest on County Road 2361 and drive four miles (becomes Forest Road 38) to Kerr Campground. Continue past Kerr for four miles to the campground on the right.

Contact: Okanogan and Wenatchee National Forests, Tonasket Ranger District, 1 West Winesap Ave., Tonasket, WA 98855, 509/486-2186, fax 509/486-5161.

77 KERR

Rating: 6

On Salmon Creek in Okanogan National Forest.

Map 3.3, grid d2, page 182

This camp sits at an elevation of 3,100 feet along Salmon Creek, about four miles north of Conconully Reservoir, and is one of many campgrounds near the lake. Fishing prospects are marginal for trout here. There are numerous recreation options available at Conconully Reservoir, including far better fishing.

Campsites, facilities: There are 13 sites for tents, trailers, or RVs up to 21 feet long. Picnic tables and fire grills are provided. Vault toilets are available, but there is no drinking water. Garbage must be packed out. Some facilities are wheelchair accessible. Leashed pets are permitted.

Reservations, fees: Reservations are not accepted. Sites are $5 per night, $5 per extra vehicle per night. Senior discount available. Open mid-May–mid-September.

Directions: From East Wenatchee, drive north on U.S. 97 for 88 miles to Okanogan and County Road 9229. Turn left (north) on County Road 9229 and drive 17.5 miles to Conconully and County Road 2361. Continue northwest on County Road 2361 and drive four miles (becomes Forest Road 38) to the campground on the left.

Contact: Okanogan and Wenatchee National Forests, Tonasket Ranger District, 1 West Winesap Ave., Tonasket, WA 98855, 509/486-2186, fax 509/486-5161.

78 ORIOLE

Rating: 6

On Salmon Creek in Okanogan National Forest.

Map 3.3, grid d2, page 182

This camp is located at 2,900 feet elevation

along Salmon Creek and offers a creek view from some of the campsites. This forest setting features well-spaced campsites among Western larch and lodgepole pine. This is a primitive camp, similar to Kerr and Salmon Meadows, also set on Salmon Creek.

Campsites, facilities: There are 10 sites for tents or small RVs. Picnic tables and fire grills are provided. Vault toilets are available, but there is no drinking water. Garbage must be packed out. Some facilities are wheelchair accessible. Leashed pets are permitted.

Reservations, fees: Reservations are not accepted. Sites are $5 per night, $5 per extra vehicle per night. Senior discount available. Open mid-May–mid-September.

Directions: From East Wenatchee, drive north on U.S. 97 for 88 miles to Okanogan and County Road 9229. Turn left (north) on County Road 9229 and drive 17.5 miles to Conconully and County Road 2361. Continue northwest on County Road 2361 and drive 2.5 miles to Forest Road 025. Turn left and drive one-half mile (crossing the creek) to the campground on the left.

Contact: Okanogan and Wenatchee National Forests, Tonasket Ranger District, 1 West Winesap Ave., Tonasket, WA 98855, 509/486-2186, fax 509/486-5161.

79 LOUP LOUP

Rating: 6

Near Loup Loup Ski Area in Okanogan National Forest.

Map 3.3, grid e1, page 182

This camp provides a good setup for large groups of up to 100 people. It is located next to the Loup Loup Ski Area at 4,200 feet elevation. The camp features a setting of Western larch trees, along with good access to biking and hiking trails as well as the ski area.

Campsites, facilities: There are 25 sites for tents, trailers, or RVs up to 21 feet long. Picnic tables and fire rings are provided. Drink-

ing water, vault toilets, and an RV dump station are available. Leashed pets are permitted.

Reservations, fees: Reservations are not accepted. Sites are $6 per night, $6 per extra vehicle per night. Open May–September, weather permitting.

Directions: From East Wenatchee, drive north on U.S. 97 for 88 miles to Okanogan and Highway 20. Turn west and drive 21 miles to Forest Road 42. Turn right (north) on Forest Road 42 and drive one mile to the campground on the left.

Contact: Okanogan and Wenatchee National Forests, Methow Valley Visitor Center, 24 West Chewuch Rd., Winthrop, WA 98862, 509/997-4000, fax 509/996-4051.

80 JR

Rating: 7

On Frazier Creek in Okanogan National Forest.

Map 3.3, grid e2, page 182

This camp is located along Frazier Creek near the Loup Loup summit and ski area at an elevation of 3,900 feet. Some of the recreation possibilities in the surrounding area include fishing, hunting, cross-country skiing, snowmobiling, hiking, and bicycling. This is a small layover for travelers looking for a spot on Highway 20.

Campsites, facilities: There are six sites for tents, trailers, or RVs up to 25 feet long. Picnic tables and fire rings are provided. Drinking water, vault toilets, and an RV dump station are available. Leashed pets are permitted.

Reservations, fees: Reservations are not accepted. Sites are $5 per night. Senior discount available. Open late May–early September.

Directions: From East Wenatchee, drive north on U.S. 97 for 88 miles to Okanogan and Highway 20. Turn west and drive 22 miles to the campground on the right.

Contact: Okanogan and Wenatchee National

Forests, Methow Valley Visitor Center, 24 West Chewuch Rd., Winthrop, WA 98862, 509/997-4000, fax 509/996-4051.

81 SPORTSMAN'S CAMP

Rating: 6

On Sweat Creek, in Lower Loomis State Forest.

Map 3.3, grid e2, page 182

In season, this is a popular camp with hunters, who may bring horses; although there are no livestock facilities, they are allowed in the camp. The landscape is shady and grassy with a small stream. Some roads in the area can be used by hikers and bikers. Highway 20 east of I-5 is a designated scenic route.

Campsites, facilities: There are six pull-through sites for tents, trailers, or RVs up to 30 feet long and a small, dispersed area for tents. Picnic tables and fire pits are provided. Vault toilets are available, but there is no drinking water. Garbage must be packed out. A gazebo shelter with a fire pit is also available. Leashed pets are permitted.

Reservations, fees: Reservations are not accepted. There is no fee for camping. Open year-round, weather permitting.

Directions: From East Wenatchee, drive north on U.S. 97 for 88 miles to Okanogan and Highway 20. Turn west and drive 15 miles to Sweat Creek Road. Turn left on Sweat Creek Road and drive one mile to the campground on the right.

Contact: Department of Natural Resources, Northeast Region, P.O. Box 190, Colville, WA 99114-0190, 509/684-7474, fax 509/684-7484.

82 FLOWING LAKE COUNTY PARK

Rating: 6

Near Snohomish.

Map 3.4, grid a1, page 183

This campground has a little something for everyone, including swimming, power boating, water-skiing, and good fishing on Flowing Lake. The campsites are in a wooded setting (that is, no lake view), and it is a quarter-mile walk to the beach. A one-mile nature trail is nearby. Note the private homes on the lake; all visitors are asked to respect the privacy of the owners.

Campsites, facilities: There are 40 drive-through sites, most with partial hookups (water and electricity) for tents, trailers, or RVs up to 40 feet long. Picnic tables and fire grills are provided. Restrooms, drinking water, flush toilets, coin-operated showers, an RV dump station, and firewood are available. A picnic area with covered shelter, a fishing dock, boat docks, and launching facilities are available nearby. Some facilities are wheelchair accessible. Leashed pets are permitted.

Reservations, fees: Reservations are not accepted for family sites. Sites are $12–17 per night, $5 for a second tent. Reservations required at group site, $20 per night plus $1 per person. Open year-round with limited winter facilities.

Directions: From Seattle, drive north on I-5 to Everett and U.S. 2. Turn east on U.S. 2, drive to Milepost 10, and look for 100 Street SE (Westwick Road). Turn left and drive five miles (becomes 171st Street Southeast) to 48th Street Southeast. Turn right and drive about one-half mile into the park at the end of the road.

Contact: Flowing Lake County Park, Snohomish County, 360/568-2274 or 425/388-6600, website: www.co.snohomish.wa.us/parks.

83 CUTTHROAT LAKES HIKE-IN

Rating: 9

On Bald Mountain.

Map 3.4, grid a4, page 183

Reaching this spot is worth the effort. You'll find beautiful lakeside camps, trout fishing, hiking, and few other campers. The "lakes" are actually small ponds, but they're very pretty. Backpacking stoves are recommended for cooking. No firewood is available.

Campsites, facilities: There are five tent sites at this primitive, hike-in campground. Vault toilets are available, but there is no drinking water. Garbage must be packed out. Leashed pets are permitted.

Reservations, fees: Reservations are not accepted. There is no fee for camping. Open mid-June–October.

Directions: From Seattle, drive north on I-5 to Everett and Highway 92. Turn east on Highway 92 and drive about 15 miles to the town of Granite Falls and Mountain Loop Highway (Forest Road 7). Continue northeast on Mountain Loop for 18 miles to Forest Road 4030 (at the bridge). Turn south and drive for three miles to Forest Road 4032 (follow the Mallardy Ridge signs). Bear right and take Forest Road 4032 for one mile to the end, where the trailhead begins. Hike 4.5 miles to Cutthroat Lakes.

Contact: Department of Natural Resources, Northwest Region, 919 North Township St., Sedro-Woolley, WA 98284-9395, 360/856-3500, fax 360/852-2150.

84 LITTLE GREIDER LAKE HIKE-IN

Rating: 10

On Little Greider Lake.

Map 3.4, grid a4, page 183

This is prime country for hiking, backpacking, and trout fishing. The primitive, wooded campground is on Little Greider Lake. Similar to the Big Greider camp, pretty Little Greider gets more use. But hey, the truth is that in this area, Boulder Lake is the most desirable spot of all.

Campsites, facilities: There are nine tent sites at this primitive, hike-in campground. Fire grills and tent pads are provided. Vault toilets and firewood are available. There is no drinking water. Garbage must be packed out. Leashed pets are permitted.

Reservations, fees: Reservations are not accepted. There is no fee for camping. Open mid-June–October.

Directions: From Seattle, drive north on I-5 to Everett and U.S. 2. Turn east on U.S. 2 and drive 24 miles to Sultan. Continue one-half mile east to Sultan Basin Road. Turn north on Sultan Basin Road and drive 13.6 miles to a fork. Take the middle road (Road SLS 4000) and drive 8.5 miles to the Greider Lake Trailhead. From the trailhead, hike 2.5 miles to the campground.

Contact: Department of Natural Resources, Northwest Region, 919 North Township St., Sedro-Woolley, WA 98284-9395, 360/856-3500, fax 360/856-2150.

85 BIG GREIDER LAKE HIKE-IN

Rating: 10

On Big Greider Lake.

Map 3.4, grid a4, page 183

This primitive campground on Big Greider Lake is a hideaway in a gorgeous setting. Although campers are few, a lot of day hikers do make the three-mile tromp to the lake. The landscape features subalpine-type terrain. Fishing is an option. This camp provides an alternative to Little Greider Lake Campground, adjacent to Little Greider Lake.

Campsites, facilities: There are five tent sites at this primitive, hike-in campground. Fire grills and tent pads are provided. Vault toilets and firewood are available, but there is no drinking water. Garbage must be packed out. Leashed pets are permitted.

Reservations, fees: Reservations are not accepted. There is no fee for camping. Open mid-June–October.

Directions: From Seattle, drive north on I-5 to Everett and U.S. 2. Turn east on U.S. 2 and drive 24 miles to Sultan. Continue one-half mile east to Sultan Basin Road. Turn north on Sultan Basin Road and drive 13.6 miles to a fork. Take the middle road (Road SLS 4000)

and drive 8.5 miles to the Greider Lake Trailhead. From the trailhead, hike three miles to the campground.

Contact: Department of Natural Resources, Northwest Region, 919 North Township St., Sedro-Woolley, WA 98284-9395, 360/856-3500, fax 360/856-2150.

86 BOULDER LAKE HIKE-IN

Rating: 10

On Boulder Lake.
Map 3.4, grid a4, page 183
Boulder Lake features cobalt-blue water, which turns a brilliant azure on sunny days. It is the most desirable of the three hike-in camps in the immediate area: Little Greider Lake and Big Greider Lake are the other two. Yet this camp gets less use than the other two because, at just under four miles, the hike-in is a bit longer. It serves as a good base camp for enjoying the beautiful surrounds, hiking, and fishing.

Campsites, facilities: There are nine sites for tents at this primitive, hike-in campground. Fire grills and tent pads are provided. Vault toilets and firewood are available. There is no drinking water. Garbage must be packed out. Leashed pets are permitted.

Reservations, fees: Reservations are not accepted. There is no fee for camping. Open mid-June–October.

Directions: From Seattle, drive north on I-5 to Everett and U.S. 2. Turn east on U.S. 2 and drive 24 miles to Sultan. Continue one-half mile east to Sultan Basin Road. Turn north on Sultan Basin Road and drive 13.6 miles to a fork. Take the middle road (Road SLS 4000) and drive 8.5 miles to the Greider Lake Trailhead. Bear right on Road SLS 7000 and drive one mile to the Boulder Lake Trailhead. From the Boulder Lake Trailhead, hike 3.8 miles to the campground.

Contact: Department of Natural Resources, Northwest Region, 919 North Township St.,
Sedro-Woolley, WA 98284-9395, 360/856-3500, fax 360/856-2150.

87 TROUBLESOME CREEK

Rating: 9

On the North Fork of the Skykomish River in Mt. Baker-Snoqualmie National Forest.
Map 3.4, grid a5, page 183
This campground is set along the North Fork of the Skykomish River among old-growth pine and fir. Highlights include a half-mile nature trail adjacent to the camp as well as rafting and good fishing in the river. A must-do trip here is the hike out to Blanca Lake. The trailhead is a short drive; then hike 3.5 miles to the lake, which is drop-dead beautiful with blue-green water fed by glacier-melt.

Campsites, facilities: There are 24 sites for tents, trailers, or RVs up to 21 feet long and six walk-in tent sites requiring about a 100-foot walk. Picnic tables and fire rings are provided. Drinking water and vault toilets are available. Some facilities are wheelchair accessible. Leashed pets are permitted.

Reservations, fees: Some sites, including three that are wheelchair-accessible, may be reserved; phone 877/444-6777 or access the website: www.ReserveUsa.com ($9 reservation fee). Sites are $14 per night, $7 per extra vehicle per night. Senior discount available. Open Memorial Day through Labor Day.

Directions: From Seattle, drive north on I-5 to Everett and U.S. 2. Turn east on U.S. 2 and drive 36 miles to the town of Index and Forest Road 63 (Index-Galena Road). Turn left (northeast) on Forest Road 63 and drive 12 miles to the campground on the right.

Contact: Mt. Baker-Snoqualmie National Forest, Skykomish Ranger District, P.O. Box 305, Skykomish, WA 98288, 360/677-2414, fax 425/744-3265.

88 SAN JUAN

Rating: 7

On the North Fork of the Skykomish River in Mt. Baker-Snoqualmie National Forest.
Map 3.4, grid a6, page 183

This camp is highlighted by old-growth Douglas fir and cedar and the adjacent North Fork of the Skykomish River. Campsites vary in size. It is similar to nearby Troublesome Creek Campground; see that camp for more trip notes. Note that no fishing is permitted at the river.

Campsites, facilities: There are nine sites for tents, trailers, or RVs. Picnic tables and fire grills are provided. Vault toilets are available. No drinking water is available. Leashed pets are permitted.

Reservations, fees: Reservations are not accepted. Sites are $10 per night, $6 per extra vehicle per night. Senior discount available. Open May–October, weather permitting.

Directions: From Seattle, drive north on I-5 to Everett and U.S. 2. Turn east on U.S. 2 and drive 36 miles to the town of Index and Forest Road 63 (Index-Galena Road). Turn left (northeast) on Forest Road 63, drive 12 miles to Troublesome Creek Campground (on the right), and continue two miles to the campground on the right.

Contact: Mt. Baker-Snoqualmie National Forest, Skykomish Ranger District, P.O. Box 305, Skykomish, WA 98288, 360/677-2414, fax 425/744-3265.

89 WALLACE FALLS STATE PARK WALK-IN

Rating: 8

Near Gold Bar.
Map 3.4, grid b3, page 183

The Wallace Falls State Park Management Area is a 4,735-acre camping park with shoreline on the Wallace River, Wallace Lake, Jay Lake, Show Lake, and the Skykomish River. Features include a 265-foot waterfall, old-growth conifer forests, and fast-moving rivers and streams. Mountain lions have been spotted near Wallace Falls. Peregrine falcons inhabit the rock cliffs of the Index Town Wall, 12 miles east of Wallace Falls. Rock climbing is permitted here. The campground is located in a heavily treed area at the trailhead to the falls. The trail leads along the Wallace River and is a lovely hike. The park has 12 miles of hiking trails, including a quarter-mile interpretive trail, five miles of biking trails, and is extremely busy on summer days. Fishing, rafting, kayaking, canoeing, and swimming are popular at Big Eddy, a satellite park located five miles east. Fishing for trout and steelhead, in season, is a sidelight.

Campsites, facilities: There are six walk-in tent sites. Picnic tables and fire grills are provided. Flush toilets and drinking water are available. A picnic area with kitchen shelters is available nearby. Some facilities are wheelchair accessible. Leashed pets are permitted.

Reservations, fees: Reservations are not accepted. Sites are $15 per night, $6 per extra vehicle per night. Open year-round, but closed Mondays and Tuesdays October–April.

Directions: From Seattle, drive north on I-5 to Everett and U.S. 2. Turn east on U.S. 2, drive 28 miles to the town of Gold Bar, and look for the sign for Wallace Falls State Park. Turn northeast at the sign and drive two miles to the park.

Contact: Wallace Falls State Park, 360/793-0420 (phone or fax); State Park information, 360/902-8844.

90 MONEY CREEK CAMPGROUND

Rating: 5

On the Skykomish River in Mt. Baker-Snoqualmie National Forest.
Map 3.4, grid c5, page 183

You have a little surprise waiting for you here. Trains go by regularly day and night, and the first time it happens while you're in deep sleep, you might just launch a hole right through the top of your tent. The Burlington Northern rail runs along the western boundary of the campground. By now you've got the picture: This can be a noisy camp. Money Creek Campground is on the Skykomish River, with hiking trails a few miles away. The best of these is the Dorothy Lake Trail. This camp was renovated in 2002.

Campsites, facilities: There are 24 sites for tents, trailers, or RVs up to 21 feet long. Picnic tables are provided. Vault toilets and drinking water are available. A store, a café, and ice are located within 3.5 miles. Some facilities are wheelchair accessible. Leashed pets are permitted.

Reservations, fees: Some sites can be reserved; phone 877/444-6777 or access the website: www.ReserveUsa.com ($9 reservation fee). Sites are $14 per night, $7 per extra vehicle per night. Senior discount available. Open Memorial Day Weekend through Labor Day Weekend.

Directions: From Seattle, drive north on I-5 to Everett and U.S. 2. Turn east on U.S. 2 and drive 46 miles to Old Cascade Highway, 11 miles east of Index. Turn south on Old Cascade Highway and drive across the bridge to the campground.

Contact: Mt. Baker-Snoqualmie National Forest, Skykomish Ranger District, P.O. Box 305, Skykomish, WA 98288, 360/677-2414, fax 425/744-3265.

91 BECKLER RIVER

Rating: 7

On the Beckler River in
Mt. Baker-Snoqualmie National Forest.
Map 3.4, grid c6, page 183

Located on the Beckler River at an elevation of 900 feet, this camp has scenic riverside sites in second-growth timber, primarily Douglas fir, cedar, and big leaf maple. Fishing at the camp-

ground is poor; it's better well up the river. The Skykomish Ranger Station is just a couple of miles away; maps are available for sale.

Campsites, facilities: There are 27 sites for tents, trailers, or RVs up to 21 feet long. Picnic tables and fire grills are provided. Vault toilets and drinking water are available. A store, a café, and ice are located within two miles. Some sites and facilities are wheelchair accessible. Leashed pets are permitted.

Reservations, fees: Some sites can be reserved; phone 877/444-6777 or access the website: www.ReserveUsa.com ($9 reservation fee). Sites are $14 per night, $7 per extra vehicle per night. Senior discount available. Open Memorial Day through Labor Day.

Directions: From Seattle, drive north on I-5 to Everett and U.S. 2. Turn east on U.S. 2 and drive 49 miles to Skykomish. Continue east on U.S. 2 for one-half mile to Forest Road 65. Turn left (north) on Forest Road 65 and drive 1.6 miles to the camp on the left.

Contact: Mt. Baker-Snoqualmie National Forest, Skykomish Ranger District, P.O. Box 305, Skykomish, WA 98288, 360/677-2414, fax 425/744-3265.

92 MILLER RIVER GROUP

Rating: 8

Near the Alpine Lakes Wilderness in
Mt. Baker-Snoqualmie National Forest.
Map 3.4, grid c5, page 183

This campground is located along the Miller River, a short distance from the boundary of the Alpine Lakes Wilderness. If you continue another seven miles on Forest Road 6410, you'll get to a trailhead leading to Dorothy Lake, a 1.5-mile hike. This pretty lake is two miles long. The trail continues past the lake to many other backcountry lakes. The group limit in wilderness is 12 people. A U.S. Forest Service map is essential.

Campsites, facilities: This is a group camp with 18 sites for up to 100 people with tents, trailers, or RVs. Picnic tables and fire grills are provided. Vault toilets, drinking water, a group barbecue, and a 24-foot group table are available. Some facilities are wheelchair accessible. A store, a café, and ice are within five miles. Leashed pets are permitted.

Reservations, fees: Reservations required; phone 877/444-6777 or access the website: www.ReserveUsa.com ($9 reservation fee). Sites are $75 for the first 50 people, $125 for 51–75, and $150 for 76–100 campers. Open mid-May–late September.

Directions: From Seattle, drive north on I-5 to Everett and U.S. 2. Turn east on U.S. 2 and drive 46 miles to Old Cascade Highway, 11 miles east of Index. Turn south on Old Cascade Highway (across the bridge) and drive one mile to Forest Road 6410. Turn right (south) and drive two miles to the campground on the left.

Contact: Mt. Baker-Snoqualmie National Forest, Skykomish Ranger District, P.O. Box 305, Skykomish, WA 98288, 360/677-2414, fax 425/744-3265.

93 SNOQUALMIE RIVER CAMPGROUND & RV PARK

Rating: 7

On the Snoqualmie River.
Map 3.4, grid d1, page 183

If you're in the Seattle area and stuck for a place for the night, this pretty 10-acre park set along the Snoqualmie River may be a welcome option. Activities include fishing, swimming, road biking, and rafting. Nearby recreation options include several nine-hole golf courses. A worthwhile side trip is beautiful Snoqualmie Falls, 3.5 miles away in the famed Twin Peaks country.

Campsites, facilities: There are 50 sites, including 12 long-term rentals, for RVs of any length and about 50 tent sites. Picnic tables are provided. Restrooms, drinking water, flush toilets, showers, firewood, and a playground are available. Bottled gas, a store, a café, and

ice are located within two miles. Boat-launching facilities are located within one-half mile. Leashed pets are permitted.

Reservations, fees: Reservations accepted. Sites are $21–25 per night, $3.50 per person per night for more than two people, and $2.50 per pet per night. Open April–October.

Directions: From the junction of I-5 and I-90 south of Seattle, turn east on I-90. Drive east for 26 miles to Exit 22 (Preston-Fall City). Take that exit and turn north on Preston-Fall City Road and drive 4.5 miles to SE 44th Place. Turn east and drive one mile to the campground at the end of the road.

Contact: Snoqualmie River Campground & RV Park, 425/222-5545.

94 TINKHAM

Rating: 9

On the Snoqualmie River in Mt. Baker-Snoqualmie National Forest.
Map 3.4, grid e4, page 183

About half the campsites here face the Snoqualmie River, making this a pretty spot. Fishing can be good; check regulations. The camp is set at an elevation of 1,600 feet. The creek provides hiking options. This camp is often used as an overflow for Denny Creek Camp. Wilderness trails for the Alpines Lakes Wilderness are located 5–10 miles away from the camp.

Campsites, facilities: There are 48 sites for tents, trailers, or RVs up to 35 feet long. Picnic tables and fire pits are provided. Drinking water and vault toilets are available. Firewood is available for purchase. Some facilities are wheelchair accessible. Leashed pets are permitted.

Reservations, fees: Some sites can be reserved; phone 877/444-6777 or access the website: www.ReserveUsa.com ($9 reservation fee). Sites are $14 per night, $7 per extra vehicle per night. Open mid-May–mid-September.

Directions: In Seattle on I-5, turn east on I-90.

Drive east on I-90 to Exit 42. Take that exit and turn right on Tinkham Road (Forest Road 55), and drive southeast 1.5 miles to the campground on the left. Obtaining a U.S. Forest Service map is advisable.

Contact: Mt. Baker-Snoqualmie National Forest, Snoqualmie Ranger District, North Bend office, 42404 S.E. North Bend Way, North Bend, WA 98045, 425/888-1421, fax 425/888-1910.

95 DENNY CREEK

Rating: 9

On Denny Creek.
Map 3.4, grid e5, page 183
This camp is set at 1,900 feet elevation along Denny Creek, which is pretty and offers nearby recreation access. The campground is secluded in an area of Douglas fir, hemlock, and cedar, with hiking trails available in addition to swimming and rafting opportunities. The Denny Creek Trail starts from the campground and provides a 4.5-mile round-trip hike that features Keckwulee Falls and Denny Creek Waterslide. You can climb to Hemlock Pass and Melakwa Lake. There is access for backpackers into the Alpine Lakes Wilderness.

Campsites, facilities: There are 33 sites, some with electricity, for tents or trailers up to 35 feet long and one group site for up to 35 people. Picnic tables and fire grills are provided. Drinking water, vault toilets, and an RV dump station are available. Firewood is available for purchase. Some facilities are wheelchair accessible. Leashed pets are permitted.

Reservations, fees: Reserve at 877/444-6777 ($9 reservation fee) or website: www.ReserveUsa.com. Sites are $14–18 per night, $7 per extra vehicle per night. The group site is $75 per night. Senior discount available. Open late May–early October, weather permitting.

Directions: In Seattle on I-5, turn east on I-90. Drive east on I-90 to Exit 47. Take that exit, cross the freeway, and at the T intersection turn right and drive one-quarter mile to Denny Creek Road (Forest Road 58). Turn left on Denny Creek Road and drive two miles to the campground on the left.

Contact: Mt. Baker-Snoqualmie National Forest, Snoqualmie Ranger District, North Bend office, 42404 S.E. North Bend Way, North Bend, WA 98045, 425/888-1421, fax 425/888-1910.

96 CRYSTAL SPRINGS

Rating: 5

On Yakima River in Wenatchee National Forest.
Map 3.4, grid f6, page 183
This campground is just off I-90, and if you think that means lots of highway noise, well, you are correct. This camp is worth knowing as an overflow campground from the more desirable Kachess Campground. It is set at 2,400 feet elevation and features the Yakima River and some old-growth trees. It's a short drive to Kachess and Keechelus Lakes. Both lakes have boat ramps. The Pacific West Ski Area is at the north end of Keechelus Lake.

Campsites, facilities: There are 22 sites, including some drive-through sites, and two double sites for tents, trailers, or RVs up to 21 feet long. Picnic tables and fire grills are provided. Drinking water, vault toilets, and firewood are available. Leashed pets are permitted.

Reservations, fees: Reservations are not accepted. Sites are $12–24 per night, $10 per extra vehicle per night. Senior discount available. Open mid-May–mid-September.

Directions: In Seattle on I-5, turn east on I-90. Drive east on I-90 for 60 miles to Exit 62. Take that exit and turn right (south) on Forest Road 54, and drive one-half mile to the campground on the right.

Contact: Okanogan and Wenatchee National Forests, Cle Elum Ranger District, West Second St., Cle Elum, WA 98922, 509/674-4411, fax 509/674-1530.

97 KACHESS & KACHESS GROUP

Rating: 8

On Kachess Lake in Wenatchee
National Forest.

Map 3.4, grid e7, page 183

This is the only campground on the shore of Kachess Lake, but note that the water level can drop significantly in summer during low-rain years. It is the most popular campground in the local area, often filling in July and August, especially on weekends. Recreation opportunities include water-skiing, fishing, hiking, and bicycling. A trail from camp heads north into the Alpine Lakes Wilderness; see a U.S. Forest Service map for details. The elevation is 2,300 feet.

Campsites, facilities: There are 120 sites, including 30 double sites, for tents, trailers, or RVs up to 32 feet long. A group site is also available. Picnic tables and fire grills are provided. Drinking water and vault toilets are available. Restrooms and dump stations are located at Kachess Lake. Some facilities are wheelchair accessible. Leashed pets are permitted but aren't allowed in swimming areas.

Reservations, fees: Some sites can be reserved; reserve at 877/444-6777 ($9 reservation fee) or website: www.ReserveUsa.com. Sites are $13–26 per night, $10 per extra vehicle per night. The group fee is $80 per night. Senior discount available. Open late May–mid-September.

Directions: In Seattle on I-5, turn east on I-90. Drive east on I-90 for 59 miles to Exit 62. Take that exit to Forest Road 49 and turn northeast; drive 5.5 miles to the campground on the right at the end of the paved road.

Contact: Okanogan and Wenatchee National Forests, Cle Elum Ranger District, West Second St., Cle Elum, WA 98922, 509/674-4411, fax 509/674-1530.

98 LAKE EASTON STATE PARK

Rating: 8

On Lake Easton.

Map 3.4, grid f7, page 183

This campground offers many recreational opportunities. For starters, it's set along the shore of Lake Easton on the Yakima River in the Cascade foothills. The landscape features old-growth forest, dense vegetation, and freshwater marshes, and the park covers 516 acres of the best of it. Two miles of trails for hiking and biking are available. The park provides opportunities for both summer and winter recreation, including swimming, fishing, boating, cross-country skiing, and snowmobiling. Note that high-speed boating is not recommended because Lake Easton is a shallow reservoir with stumps often hidden just below the water surface. Nearby recreation options include an 18-hole golf course and hiking trails. Kachess Lake and Keechelus Lake are just a short drive away.

Campsites, facilities: There are 92 developed tent sites, 45 sites with hookups for RVs up to 60 feet long, and two primitive tent sites. Picnic tables and fire grills are provided. Restrooms, drinking water, flush toilets, showers, an RV dump station, an amphitheater, a playground with basketball and horseshoe pits, and firewood are available. A café and ice are located within one mile. Some facilities are wheelchair accessible. Boat-launching facilities and floats are located on Lake Easton. Leashed pets are permitted.

Reservations, fees: Reserve at 888/CAMP-OUT (888/226-7688), website: www.parks.wa.gov/reservations ($7 reservation fee). Sites are $6–22 per night, $6 per extra vehicle per night. Senior discount available. Major credit cards accepted. Open May–mid-October, with limited winter facilities.

Directions: From Seattle, drive east on I-90 for 68 miles to Exit 70; the park entrance is on the right (it is located one mile west of the town of Easton).

Contact: Lake Easton State Park, P.O. Box 26, Easton, WA 98925, 509/656-2586, fax 509/656-2294; State Park information, 360/902-8844.

99 CAYUSE HORSE CAMP

Rating: 6

On the Cle Elum River in Wenatchee National Forest.

Map 3.4, grid g8, page 183

This camp is for horse campers only. It's located along the Cle Elum River at major trailheads for horses and hikers and marked trails for bikers. The elevation is 2,400 feet. See Salmon La Sac Campground for further information.

Campsites, facilities: There are 13 sites, including three double sites, for tents, trailers, or RVs, with some sites 25 feet and some up to 40 feet long. Picnic tables and fire pits are provided. Drinking water and vault toilets are available. Stock facilities include corrals, troughs, and hitching posts. Bring your own stock feed. Leashed pets are permitted.

Reservations, fees: Some sites are available by reservation. Reserve at 877/444-6777 ($9 reservation fee) or website: www.ReserveUsa.com. Sites are $13 per night, $10 per night for each additional vehicle. Senior discount available. Open mid-May–mid-September, depending on weather.

Directions: In Seattle on I-5, turn east on I-90. Drive east on I-90 for 78 miles to Exit 80 (two miles before Cle Elum). Take that exit and turn north on Bullfrog Road; drive four miles to Highway 903. Continue north on Highway 903 for 18 miles to the campground on the right.

Contact: Okanogan and Wenatchee National Forests, Cle Elum Ranger District, West Second St., Cle Elum, WA 98922, 509/674-4411, fax 509/674-1530.

100 WISH POOSH

Rating: 7

On Cle Elum Lake in Wenatchee National Forest.

Map 3.4, grid f8, page 183

This popular camp is set on the shore of Cle Elum Lake. It fills up on summer weekends and holidays. It is great during midweek, when many sites are usually available. While the lake is near the camp, note that the lake level can lower significantly in low-rainfall years. Waterskiing, sailing, fishing, and swimming are among recreation possibilities. The camp sits at an elevation of 2,400 feet.

Campsites, facilities: There are 34 sites, including five double sites, for tents, trailers, or RVs up to 21 feet long. Picnic tables and fire grills are provided. Restrooms, drinking water, flush toilets, showers, and firewood are available. Boat-launching facilities are located on Cle Elum Lake. Restaurant and ice are available nearby. Leashed pets are permitted.

Reservations, fees: Reservations are not accepted. Sites are $13–26 per night, $10 per extra vehicle per night. Senior discount available. Open mid-May–mid-September.

Directions: In Seattle on I-5, turn east on I-90. Drive east on I-90 for 78 miles to Exit 80 (two miles before Cle Elum). Take that exit, turn north on Bullfrog Road, and drive four miles to Highway 903. Continue north on Highway 903 for nine miles to the campground on the left.

Contact: Okanogan and Wenatchee National Forests, Cle Elum Ranger District, West Second St., Cle Elum, WA 98922, 509/674-4411, fax 509/674-1530.

101 CLE ELUM RIVER & CLE ELUM GROUP

🚶 🚴 🛶 🐕 🚐 ⛺

Rating: 6

On the Cle Elum River in Wenatchee National Forest.

Map 3.4, grid f8, page 183

The gravel roads in the campground make this setting a bit more rustic than nearby Salmon La Sac. It serves as a valuable overflow campground for Salmon La Sac and is similar in setting and opportunities. The group site fills on most summer weekends. A nearby trailhead provides access into the Alpine Lakes Wilderness.

Campsites, facilities: There are 23 sites, including some pull-through, for tents, trailers, or RVs up to 21 feet long and a group site for up to 100 people. Picnic tables and fire grills are provided. Drinking water and vault toilets are available. Leashed pets are permitted.

Reservations, fees: Reservations are not accepted for family sites. Reservation required for group site: 877/444-6777 ($9 reservation fee) or website: www.ReserveUsa.com. Sites are $10–20 per night, $8 per extra vehicle per night. The group site is $100 per night. Senior discount available. Open late May–mid-September.

Directions: In Seattle on I-5, turn east on I-90. Drive east on I-90 for 78 miles to Exit 80 (two miles before Cle Elum). Take that exit, turn north on Bullfrog Road, and drive four miles to Highway 903. Continue north on Highway 903 for 17 miles to the campground on the left.

Contact: Okanogan and Wenatchee National Forests, Cle Elum Ranger District, West Second St., Cle Elum, WA 98922, 509/674-4411, fax 509/674-1530.

102 RED MOUNTAIN

🛶 🐕 🚐 ⛺

Rating: 6

On the Cle Elum River in Wenatchee National Forest.

Map 3.4, grid f8, page 183

This alternative to nearby Wish Poosh has two big differences: There is no drinking water, and it's not on Cle Elum Lake. The camp sits along the Cle Elum River one mile from the lake, just above where the river feeds into it. The elevation is 2,200 feet.

Campsites, facilities: There are 10 sites for tents and small RVs. Picnic tables and fire grills are provided. Pit toilets and firewood are available, but there is no drinking water. Leashed pets are permitted.

Reservations, fees: Reservations are not accepted. Sites are $7 per vehicle per night, $5 for extra vehicle with a two-vehicle maximum. Senior discount available. Open mid-May–late November.

Directions: In Seattle on I-5, turn east on I-90. Drive east on I-90 for 78 miles to Exit 80 (two miles before Cle Elum). Take that exit and turn north on Bullfrog Road; drive four miles to Highway 903. Continue north on Highway 903 for 19 miles to the campground on the left.

Contact: Okanogan and Wenatchee National Forests, Cle Elum Ranger District, West Second St., Cle Elum, WA 98922, 509/674-4411, fax 509/674-1530.

103 SALMON LA SAC

🚶 🚴 🛶 🐕 ♿ 🚐 ⛺

Rating: 6

On the Cle Elum River in Wenatchee National Forest.

Map 3.4, grid e8, page 183

This is a base camp for backpackers and day hikers and is also popular with kayakers. It's located along the Cle Elum River at 2,400 feet elevation, about one-quarter mile from a major trailhead, the Salmon La Sac Trailhead.

Hikers can follow creeks heading off in several directions, including into the Alpine Lakes Wilderness. A campground host is available for information.

Campsites, facilities: There are 99 sites, including 12 double sites, for tents, trailers, or RVs up to 21 feet long. Picnic tables and fire grills are provided. Drinking water and vault toilets are available. Leashed pets are permitted.

Reservations, fees: Some sites can be reserved: 877/444-6777 ($9 reservation fee) or website: www.ReserveUsa.com. Sites are $13–26 per night, $10 per extra vehicle per night. Senior discount available. Open late May–mid-September.

Directions: In Seattle on I-5, turn east on I-90. Drive east on I-90 for 78 miles to Exit 80 (two miles before Cle Elum). Take that exit, turn north on Bullfrog Road, and drive four miles to Highway 903. Continue north on Highway 903 for 21 miles to the campground on the left.

Contact: Okanogan and Wenatchee National Forests, Cle Elum Ranger District, West Second St., Cle Elum, WA 98922, 509/674-4411, fax 509/674-1530.

104 OWHI WALK-IN

Rating: 9

On Cooper Lake in Wenatchee National Forest.

Map 3.4, grid e7, page 183

This spot has everything you need for a drive-to wilderness experience. Well, everything but drinking water. It's located on the shore of Cooper Lake, near the boundary of the Alpine Lakes Wilderness. The campsites require a walk of 100–300 feet. Some sites have lake views, whereas others have lots of vegetation and provide privacy. The old-growth Douglas fir and western hemlock are highlights. A nearby trailhead provides access to several lakes in the wilderness and extends to the Pacific Crest Trail; see a U.S. Forest Service map for details. Fishing, swimming, and canoeing are all

popular at Cooper Lake. No motors, including electric motors, are permitted at the lake, making it ideal for canoes, float tubes, and prams. The campground is minimally developed. The elevation is 2,800 feet.

Campsites, facilities: There are 21 walk-in tent sites. Picnic tables and fire grills are provided. Vault toilets are available, but there is no drinking water. Primitive boat-launching facilities are nearby. Leashed pets are permitted.

Reservations, fees: Reservations are not accepted. Sites are $7 per vehicle per night, $5 for extra vehicle with a two-vehicle maximum. Senior discount available. Open mid-June–late September.

Directions: In Seattle on I-5, turn east on I-90. Drive east on I-90 for 78 miles to Exit 80 (two miles before Cle Elum). Turn north on Bullfrog Road and drive four miles to Highway 903. Turn left (north) on Highway 903 and drive 19 miles to Forest Road 46. Turn left (west) on Forest Road 46 and drive five miles to Forest Road 4616 (pavement ends). Turn right and drive less than one-half mile to the campground. Campsites are located 100–300 feet from the parking lot.

Contact: Okanogan and Wenatchee National Forests, Cle Elum Ranger District, West Second St., Cle Elum, WA 98922, 509/674-4411, fax 509/674-1530.

105 FISH LAKE WALK-IN

Rating: 10

On Tucquala Lake in Wenatchee National Forest.

Map 3.4, grid d8, page 183

This campground is way out there and just a short jaunt from the Alpine Lakes Wilderness. The camp is nestled along the shore of tiny Tucquala Lake, a jewel near the headwaters of the Cle Elum River. Fishing is available for trout. The campsites require a 100- to 300-foot walk. The elevation is 3,400 feet. There are numerous opportunities to access trails into the backcountry.

Campsites, facilities: There are five tent sites. Picnic tables and fire grills are provided. Vault toilets are available, but there is no drinking water. Garbage must be packed out. Leashed pets are permitted.

Reservations, fees: Reservations are not accepted. There is no fee for camping. Open July–September.

Directions: In Seattle on I-5, turn east on I-90 and drive 78 miles to Exit 80 (two miles before Cle Elum). Take Exit 80 and turn north on Bullfrog Road; drive four miles to Highway 903. Continue north on Highway 903 for 19 miles to Forest Road 4330. Bear right and drive 11 miles to the campground entrance on the right. Park and walk 100–300 feet to the sites. The access road is rough; no trailers are permitted.

Contact: Wenatchee National Forest, Cle Elum Ranger District, West Second St., Cle Elum, WA 98922, 509/674-4411, fax 509/674-1530.

106 KANASKAT-PALMER STATE PARK

Rating: 8

On the Green River.
Map 3.4, grid f1, page 183

This wooded campground offers private campsites along the Green River. The park covers 320 acres with two miles of river frontage. It is set on a small, low, forested plateau. In summer, the river is ideal for expert-level rafting and kayaking, and the park is used as a put-in spot for the rafting run down the Green River Gorge. This area has much mining history and coal mining continues, as does cinnabar mining (the base ore for mercury). Nearby Flaming Geyser gets its name from a coal seam. In winter, the river attracts a run of steelhead. The park has three miles of hiking trails.

Campsites, facilities: There are 31 tent sites and 19 drive-through sites with partial hookups (electricity) for RVs up to 50 feet long. Picnic tables are provided. Restrooms, drinking water,

flush toilets, showers, a sheltered picnic area, horseshoe pits, and an RV dump station are available. Some facilities are wheelchair accessible. Boat rentals can be found nearby on the Green River. Leashed pets are permitted.

Reservations, fees: Reserve at 888/CAMP-OUT (888/226-7688), website: www.parks.wa.gov/reservations ($7 reservation fee). Sites are $16–22 per night, $6 per extra vehicle per night. Senior discount available. Major credit cards accepted. Open year-round, with limited facilities in the winter.

Directions: From Puyallup at the junction of Highway 167 and Highway 410, turn southeast on Highway 410 and drive 25 miles to Enumclaw and Farman Road. Turn northeast on Farman Road and drive nine miles to the park on the left.

Contact: Kanaskat-Palmer State Park, 360/886-0148; State Park information, 360/902-8844.

107 DALLES

Rating: 10

In Mt. Baker-Snoqualmie National Forest.
Map 3.4, grid h7, page 183

This campground is set at the confluence of Minnehaha Creek and the White River. Aptly, its name means "rapids." A nature trail is nearby, and the White River entrance to Mt. Rainier National Park is about 14 miles south on Highway 410. The camp sits amid a grove of old-growth trees; a particular point of interest is a huge old Douglas fir that is 9.5 feet in diameter and more than 235 feet tall. This is one of the prettiest camps in the area. It gets moderate use in summer.

Campsites, facilities: There are 44 sites for tents, trailers, or RVs up to 21 feet long. Picnic tables and fire grills are provided. Vault toilets, drinking water, and firewood are available. There is a large shaded picnic area for day use. Leashed pets are permitted.

Reservations, fees: Reservations accepted for some sites; phone 877/444-6777 or access the website: www.ReserveUsa.com ($9 reservation fee). Sites are $12 per night, $6 per extra vehicle per night. Senior discount available. Open mid-May–late September.

Directions: From Enumclaw, drive east on Highway 410 for 25.5 miles to the campground (three miles inside the forest boundary) on the right.

Contact: Mt. Baker-Snoqualmie National Forest, White River Ranger District, 450 Roosevelt Ave. E, Enumclaw, WA 98022, 360/825-6585, fax 360/825-0660.

108 CORRAL PASS

Rating: 10

In Mt. Baker-Snoqualmie National Forest.
Map 3.4, grid h5, page 183

This is the most remote of the campgrounds in the area. Set at an elevation of 5,600 feet, it's primitive, quiet, and an ideal base camp for a hiking trip. Groups of horse-packers heading into the adjacent Norse Peak Wilderness frequent the camp. The best trip is the two-mile backpack up to Hidden Lake and then along a river canyon for four miles to Echo Lake. Several trails nearby lead to backcountry fishing lakes and streams. See a U.S. Forest Service map for details. In late summer and fall, visitors can find wild berries in the area.

Campsites, facilities: There are 20 tent sites. Picnic tables and fire grills are provided. Vault toilets and a horse-loading ramp are available, but there is no drinking water. Garbage must be packed out. Downed firewood can be gathered. Leashed pets are permitted.

Reservations, fees: Reservations are not accepted; Northwest Forest Pass ($5 daily fee or $30 annual fee per parked vehicle) is required. Open July–late September.

Directions: From Enumclaw, drive east on Highway 410 for 30 miles to Forest Road 7174 (near Silver Springs Camp). Turn left (east) and drive six miles to the camp on the right. This curvy dirt road is not suitable for RVs.

Contact: Mt. Baker-Snoqualmie National Forest, White River Ranger District, 450 Roosevelt Ave. E, Enumclaw, WA 98022, 360/825-6585, fax 360/825-0660.

109 CROW CREEK

Rating: 5

On the Little Naches River in Wenatchee National Forest.
Map 3.4, grid h7, page 183

This campground on the Little Naches River is popular with off-road bikers and four-wheel-drive cowboys and is similar to the following camp, Kaner Flat, except that there is no drinking water. It is set at 2,900 feet elevation. A trail heading out from the camp leads into the backcountry and then forks in several directions. One route leads to the American River, another follows West Quartz Creek, and another goes along Fife's Ridge into the Norse Peak Wilderness (where no motorized vehicles are permitted). See a U.S. Forest Service map for details. There is good seasonal hunting and fishing in this area.

Campsites, facilities: There are 15 sites for tents, trailers, or RVs up to 30 feet long. Picnic tables and fire grills are provided. Vault toilets are available, but there is no drinking water. Downed firewood may be gathered. Leashed pets are permitted.

Reservations, fees: Reservations are not accepted. Sites are $7 per night, $5 per extra vehicle per night. Senior discount available. Open mid-April–late November.

Directions: From Yakima, drive northwest on U.S. 12 for 18 miles to Highway 410. Bear northwest on Highway 410 and drive 24.5 miles to Forest Road 1900. Turn northwest and drive 2.5 miles to Forest Road 1902. Turn west and drive one-half mile to the campground on the right.

Contact: Okanogan and Wenatchee National Forests, Naches Ranger District, 10061 U.S. 12, Naches, WA 98937, 509/653-2205, fax 509/653-2638.

110 KANER FLAT

Rating: 7

Near the Little Naches River in Wenatchee National Forest.

Map 3.4, grid h7, page 183

This campground is set near the Little Naches River, at an elevation of 2,678 feet. It is located at the site of a wagon-train camp on the Old Naches Trail, a route used in the 1800s by wagon trains, Native Americans, and the U.S. Cavalry on their way to west side markets. The Naches Trail is now used by motorcyclists and narrow-clearance four-wheel-drive enthusiasts. This camp is popular among them, similar to Crow Creek campground. Kaner Flat is larger, though, so it handles more multiple user groups.

Campsites, facilities: There are 41 sites for tents, trailers, or RVs up to 30 feet long, including two wheelchair-accessible sites. Picnic tables and fire grills are provided. Drinking water and vault toilets are available. Some facilities are wheelchair accessible. Leashed pets are permitted.

Reservations, fees: Reservations are not accepted. Sites are $9 per night, $5 for each additional vehicle. Senior discount available. Open mid-May–late November.

Directions: From Yakima, drive northwest on U.S. 12 for 18 miles to Highway 410. Bear northwest on Highway 410 and drive 25 miles to Forest Road 1900. Turn northwest and drive 2.5 miles to the campground on the right.

Contact: Okanogan and Wenatchee National Forests, Naches Ranger District, 10061 U.S. 12, Naches, WA 98937, 509/653-2205, fax 509/653-2638.

111 WHITE RIVER FALLS

Rating: 9

On the White River in Wenatchee National Forest.

Map 3.5, grid a1, page 184

Although very primitive, this quiet and beautiful campground is a perfect spot for those seeking solitude in the wilderness. It's next to White River Falls on the White River and close to a major trailhead that connects to a network of hiking trails into the Glacier Peak Wilderness. There is no viewing platform or fence at White River Falls, and viewing can be dangerous. People have slipped here and fallen to their deaths. There is no trailer turnaround at the camp. The elevation is 2,100 feet.

Campsites, facilities: There are five tent sites. Picnic tables and fire grills are provided. Pit toilets are available, but there is no drinking water. Garbage must be packed out. Leashed pets are permitted.

Reservations, fees: Reservations are not accepted. There is no fee for camping. Open June–mid-October.

Directions: From Leavenworth, drive west on U.S. 2 for 14 miles to Coles Corner and State Route 207. Turn north and drive 10 miles to Forest Road 6400 (White River Road). Turn right and drive 9.9 miles to the campground on the left.

Contact: Okanogan and Wenatchee National Forests, Lake Wenatchee and Leavenworth Ranger District, Lake Wenatchee Office, 22976 Rte. 207, Leavenworth, WA 98826, 509/763-3103, fax 509/763-3211.

112 NAPEEQUA CROSSING

Rating: 8

On the White and Napequa Rivers in Wenatchee National Forest.

Map 3.5, grid a1, page 184

A trail across the road from this camp on the White River heads east for about 3.5 miles to Twin Lakes in the Glacier Peak Wilderness. It's definitely worth the hike, with scenic views and wildlife observation as your reward. But note that Twin Lakes is closed to fishing. Sightings of osprey, bald eagles, and golden eagles can brighten the trip. This is also an excellent spot for fall colors.

Campsites, facilities: There are five sites for tents, trailers, or RVs up to 30 feet long. Picnic tables and fire grills are provided. Pit toilets are available, but there is no drinking water. Garbage must be packed out. Leashed pets are permitted.

Reservations, fees: Reservations are not accepted. There is no fee for camping. Open year-round, weather and snow level permitting.

Directions: From Leavenworth, drive west on U.S. 2 for 14 miles to Coles Corner and State Route 207. Turn north and drive 10 miles to Forest Road 6400 (White River Road). Turn right and drive 5.9 miles to the campground on the left.

Contact: Okanogan and Wenatchee National Forests, Lake Wenatchee and Leavenworth Ranger District, Lake Wenatchee Office, 22976 Rte. 207, Leavenworth, WA 98826, 509/763-3103, fax 509/763-3211.

113 CHIWAWA HORSE CAMP
🚶 🚴 🛶 🐴 ♿ 🚐 ⛰️

Rating: 8

In Wenatchee National Forest.
Map 3.5, grid a2, page 184

This camp is not designated solely for horse campers, as many horse camps are. Rather, it's for all users, but features many facilities for horseback riding. It is seldom full, but is popular among equestrians. Two short trails that are specifically designed for physically challenged visitors lead around the campground, covering about a mile. A trailhead at the camp also provides access to a network of backcountry trails. The elevation is 2,000 feet.

Campsites, facilities: There are 21 sites, including seven drive-through sites, for tents, trailers, or RVs up to 30 feet long. Picnic tables and fire grills are provided. Drinking water and vault toilets are available. Garbage must be packed out. Horse facilities include mounting ramps, high lines, water troughs, and a loading ramp. Some facilities are wheelchair accessible. Leashed pets are permitted.

Reservations, fees: Northwest Forest Pass ($5 daily fee or $30 annual fee per parked vehicle) is required. Open year-round, weather and snow level permitting.

Directions: From Seattle, drive north on I-5 to Everett and U.S. 2. Turn east on U.S. 2 and drive 87 miles to State Route 207, one mile west of Winton. Turn north on State Route 207 and drive 4.5 miles to Chiwawa Loop Road. Turn right and drive two miles to Chiwawa Valley Road/Forest Road 6200. Turn left and drive 15 miles to the campground on the right.

Contact: Okanogan and Wenatchee National Forests, Lake Wenatchee and Leavenworth Ranger District, Lake Wenatchee Office, 22976 Rte. 207, Leavenworth, WA 98826, 509/763-3103, fax 509/763-3211.

114 COTTONWOOD
🚶 🚴 🛶 🐴 ♿ 🚐 ⛰️

Rating: 8

On the Entiat River in Wenatchee National Forest.
Map 3.5, grid a4, page 184

Cottonwood Camp is set along the Entiat River, adjacent to a major trailhead leading into the Glacier Peak Wilderness. Note that dirt bikes are allowed on four miles of trail, the Entiat River Trail to Myrtle Lake, but no motorcycles or mountain bikes are allowed inside the boundary of the Glacier Peak Wilderness; violators will be prosecuted by backcountry rangers. In other words, cool your jets. Let backpackers have some peace and quiet. A U.S. Forest Service map details the backcountry. A bonus near the camp is good berry picking in season. Trout fishing is another alternative. The camp is set at an elevation of 3,100 feet.

Campsites, facilities: There are 25 sites for tents or small RVs. Picnic tables and fire grills are provided. Drinking water and vault toilets are available. Some facilities are wheelchair accessible. A campground host is available in summer. Leashed pets are permitted.

Reservations, fees: Reservations are not accepted. Sites are $8 per vehicle per night. Senior discount available. Open June–mid-October.

Directions: From Seattle, drive north on I-5 to Everett and U.S. 2. Turn east on U.S. 2 and drive 120 miles to U.S. 97-A. Turn north on U.S. 97-A and drive 18.5 miles to Entiat River Road. Turn left (northwest) and drive 38 miles to the campground on the left.

Contact: Okanogan and Wenatchee National Forests, Entiat Ranger District, P.O. Box 476, Entiat, WA 98822, 509/784-1511, fax 509/784-1150.

115 NORTH FORK

Rating: 8

On the Entiat River in Wenatchee National Forest.

Map 3.5, grid a4, page 184

One of seven campgrounds nestled along the Entiat River, North Fork is located near the confluence of the Entiat and the North Fork of the Entiat River. Highlights of this pretty, shaded camp include river fishing access and Entiat Falls, which are located about one-half mile downstream. Note: No fishing is permitted in the vicinity of Entiat Falls to protect the bull trout; check regulations. The elevation is 2,500 feet.

Campsites, facilities: There are eight tent sites and one site for a small RV. Picnic tables and fire grills are provided. Drinking water and pit toilets are available. Leashed pets are permitted.

Reservations, fees: Reservations are not accepted. Sites are $7 per vehicle per night. Senior discount available. Open June–mid-October.

Directions: From Seattle, drive north on I-5 to Everett and U.S. 2. Turn east on U.S. 2 and drive 120 miles to U.S. 97-A. Turn north on U.S. 97-A and drive 18.5 miles to Entiat River Road. Turn northwest and drive 33 miles to the campground on the left.

Contact: Okanogan and Wenatchee National Forests, Entiat Ranger District, P.O. Box

476, Entiat, WA 98822, 509/784-1511, fax 509/784-1150.

116 SILVER FALLS

Rating: 10

On the Entiat River in Wenatchee National Forest.

Map 3.5, grid a4, page 184

This campground is set in an enchanted spot at the confluence of Silver Creek and the Entiat River. A trail from camp leads one-half mile to the base of beautiful Silver Falls. This trail continues in a loop for another mile past the falls, parallel to the river. Fishing is available above Entiat Falls, located two–three miles upriver from Silver Falls. The elevation at the camp is 2,400 feet.

Campsites, facilities: There are 30 sites for tents, trailers, or RVs up to 21 feet long, plus one group site for 30–50 people. Picnic tables and fire grills are provided. Drinking water and vault toilets are available. A camp host is available in summer. Some facilities are wheelchair accessible. Leashed pets are permitted.

Reservations, fees: Reservations required for groups only. Family sites are $9 per vehicle per night; the group site is $60 a night. Senior discount available. Open mid-May–mid-October.

Directions: From Seattle, drive north on I-5 to Everett and U.S. 2. Turn east on U.S. 2 and drive 120 miles to U.S. 97-A. Turn north on U.S. 97-A and drive 18.5 miles to Entiat River Road. Turn left (northwest) and drive 30 miles to the campground on the left.

Contact: Okanogan and Wenatchee National Forests, Entiat Ranger District, P.O. Box 476, Entiat, WA 98822, 509/784-1511, fax 509/784-1150.

117 LAKE CREEK/ENTIAT

🏃 🚴 ⛵ 🏕 ♿ ⛰

Rating: 7

On the Entiat River in Wenatchee National Forest.

Map 3.5, grid a4, page 184

This camp is located at the confluence of Lake Creek and the Entiat River, at a trail crossroads. It ties into the Mad Lake Trail System, where all-purpose trails are available for hiking and mountain biking. Another trail ties into a loop system that features the Devils Backbone to Ramona Park. There is also linkage available to a network of trails in the Lake Creek Basin in the Chelan Mountains, and several others head south and west into the Entiat Mountains. Consult a U.S. Forest Service map for more details on backcountry routes. No fishing is available in the vicinity of Entiat Falls. Note that there is another Lake Creek Camp in the Lake Wenatchee and Leavenworth Ranger District.

Campsites, facilities: There are 18 tent sites. Picnic tables and fire grills are provided. Drinking water and composting toilets are available. Some facilities are wheelchair accessible. Leashed pets are permitted.

Reservations, fees: Reservations are not accepted. Sites are $8 per night per vehicle. Senior discount available. Open May–mid-October.

Directions: From Seattle, drive north on I-5 to Everett and U.S. 2. Turn east on U.S. 2 and drive 120 miles to U.S. 97-A. Turn north on U.S. 97-A and drive 18.5 miles to Entiat River Road. Turn northwest and drive 28 miles to the campground on the left.

Contact: Okanogan and Wenatchee National Forests, Entiat Ranger District, P.O. Box 476, Entiat, WA 98822, 509/784-1511, fax 509/784-1150.

118 FOX CREEK

🏃 🚴 ⛵ ❄ 🏕 ⛰

Rating: 7

On the Entiat River in Wenatchee National Forest.

Map 3.5, grid a5, page 184

This camp is located along the Entiat River near Fox Creek. Fishing is prohibited in the vicinity of Entiat Falls; check regulations. This camp features several campsites that are closer to the river than nearby Lake Creek Campground is, making it the more popular of the two. The elevation is 2,100 feet. Contact the U.S. Forest Service for details.

Campsites, facilities: There are 16 tent sites. Picnic tables and fire grills are provided. Drinking water and composting toilets are available. Leashed pets are permitted.

Reservations, fees: Reservations are not accepted. Sites are $8 per night per vehicle. Senior discount available. Open May–mid-October.

Directions: From Seattle, drive north on I-5 to Everett and U.S. 2. Turn east on U.S. 2 and drive 120 miles to U.S. 97-A. Turn north on U.S. 97-A and drive 18.5 miles to Entiat River Road. Turn northwest and drive 27 miles to the campground on the left.

Contact: Okanogan and Wenatchee National Forests, Entiat Ranger District, P.O. Box 476, Entiat, WA 98822, 509/784-1511, fax 509/784-1150.

119 SNOWBERRY BOWL

🏃 ⛵ 🏕 ♿ 🚐 ⛰

Rating: 7

Near Lake Chelan in Wenatchee National Forest.

Map 3.5, grid a6, page 184

Snowberry Bowl is set less than four miles from Twenty-Five Mile Creek State Park and Lake Chelan. Nestled amid a forest of Douglas fir and Ponderosa pine, which provide privacy screening, it sits at an elevation of 2,000 feet. The camp is most often used as an overflow camp when the state park fills up. It opened in 2001 and is not well known.

Campsites, facilities: There are seven sites for tents, trailers, or RVs up to 40 feet long and two double sites for up to 15 people each. Picnic tables, fire grills, and tent pads on sand are provided. Drinking water and vault toilets are available. Some facilities are wheelchair accessible. Leashed pets are permitted.

Reservations, fees: Reservations are not accepted. Sites are $9 per night, $18 for double sites. Senior discount available. Open year-round, with limited winter facilities.

Directions: From Chelan, drive south on Highway 97A for three miles to South Lakeshore Road. Turn right and drive 13.5 miles (passing the state park) to Shady Pass Road. Turn left and drive 2.5 miles to a Y intersection with Slide Ridge Road. Bear left and drive one-half mile to the campground on the right.

Contact: Okanogan and Wenatchee National Forests, Chelan Ranger District, 428 West Woodin Ave., Chelan, WA 98816, 509/682-2576, fax 509/682-9004.

120 TWENTY-FIVE MILE CREEK STATE PARK

Rating: 8

Near Lake Chelan.
Map 3.5, grid a6, page 184

This campground is located on Twenty-Five Mile Creek near where it empties into Lake Chelan. A 235-acre marine camping park, it sits on the forested south shore of Lake Chelan. The park separates the mountain from the lake and is surrounded by spectacular scenery, featuring a rocky terrain with forested areas. It's known for its boat access. You can use this park as your launching point for exploring the up-lake wilderness portions of Lake Chelan. Fishing access for trout and salmon is close by. Fishing supplies, a dock, a modern marina, and boat moorage are available. There is also a small wading area for kids. Forest Road

5900, which heads west from the park, accesses several trailheads leading into the U.S. Forest Service lands of the Chelan Mountains. Obtain a U.S. Forest Service map of Wenatchee National Forest for details. Note that a ferry can take visitors to a roadless community at the head of the lake.

Campsites, facilities: There are 53 sites for tents and 21 sites with full or partial hookups for RVs up to 30 feet long. Picnic tables and fire grills are provided. Drinking water and vault toilets are available. an RV dump station, firewood for sale, a boat dock, a fishing pier, a marina, a boat ramp, boat moorage, a picnic area, gasoline, and a grocery store are available nearby.

Reservations, fees: Reserve at 888/CAMP-OUT (888/226-7688), website: www.parks.wa.gov/reservations ($7 reservation fee). Sites are $16–22 per night, $2 per person for more than four people, and $6 per extra vehicle. Senior discount available. Major credit cards accepted. Open April–October.

Directions: From Chelan, drive south on Highway 97A for three miles to South Lakeshore Road. Turn right and drive 15 miles to the park on the right.

Contact: Twenty-Five Mile Creek State Park, Rte. 1, P.O. Box 142A, Chelan, WA 98816, 509/687-3710; State Park information, 360/902-8844. Lake Chelan Boat Company, 509/682-2224, website: www.ladyofthelake.com.

121 KAMEI CAMPGROUND & RV PARK

Rating: 6

On Lake Wapato.
Map 3.5, grid a7, page 184

This resort is on Lake Wapato, about two miles from Lake Chelan. Note that this is a seasonal lake that closes midsummer. If you have an extra day, take the ferryboat ride on Lake Chelan.

Campsites, facilities: There are 50 sites, some

with partial hookups, for tents, trailers, or RVs of any length. Picnic tables are provided. Restrooms, drinking water, flush toilets, showers, and ice are available. Boat docks, launching facilities, and rentals are nearby. Leashed pets are permitted.

Reservations, fees: Reservations accepted beginning in January. Sites are $16–17 per night, $4 per person for more than four people. Open late April–July.

Directions: From Chelan, drive west on Highway 150 for seven miles to Wapato Lake Road. Turn north on Wapato Lake Road and drive three miles to the resort on Wapato Lake Road.

Contact: Kamei Resort, Wapato Lake Rd. Rte. 1, Manson, WA 98831, 509/687-3690.

122 MITCHELL CREEK BOAT-IN

Rating: 8

On Lake Chelan in Wenatchee National Forest.

Map 3.5, grid a7, page 184

This is one of 13 national forest campgrounds set on Lake Chelan. It can be reached only by boat, although with advance notice it's possible to arrange a ferry ride to this campsite; it is not a scheduled stop. Note that this camp was closed temporarily in the late summer of 2002 because of forest fires.

Campsites, facilities: There are six tent sites accessible only by boat, ferry, or floatplane. Picnic tables and fire rings are provided. Pit toilets and a group shelter are available, but there is no drinking water. Garbage must be packed out. An on-site floating dock has a 17-boat capacity.

Reservations, fees: Reservations are not accepted, no camping fee; $5 per-day docking fee. Open May–late October.

Directions: From Wenatchee, drive north on U.S. 97-A for 40 miles to the town of Chelan. Take the ferry to Mitchell Creek, 15 miles from Chelan. Note that the ferry will not stop here if the water level does not allow for safe land-

ing. The campground is also directly accessible by floatplane. (Call Chelan Airways at 509/682-5555 for more information.)

Contact: Okanogan and Wenatchee National Forests, Chelan Ranger District, 428 West Woodin Ave., Chelan, WA 98816, 509/682-2576, fax 509/682-9004. Lake Chelan Boat Company, 509/682-2224, website: www.lady ofthelake.com.

123 LAKE CHELAN STATE PARK

Rating: 10

On Lake Chelan.

Map 3.5, grid b7, page 184

This park is the recreation headquarters for Lake Chelan. It provides boat docks and concession stands on the shore of the 55-mile lake. The park covers 127 acres, featuring 6,000 feet of shoreline on the forested south shore. Summers tend to be hot and dry, but expansive lawns provide a fresh feel, especially in the early evenings, looking out on the lake. A daily ferry service provides access to the roadless community at the head of the lake. The word *chelan* is Native American and translates to both "lake" and "blue water." See the descriptions of Holden Ballpark, Domke Lake, Lucerne, Deer Point, Graham Harbor, and Prince Creek for some of the recreation options available. Water sports include fishing, swimming, scuba diving, and water-skiing.

Campsites, facilities: There are 109 developed tent sites, 35 sites with full or partial hookups for RVs up to 30 feet, and two primitive tent sites. Picnic tables and fire grills are provided. Restrooms, drinking water, flush toilets, showers, firewood, a picnic area with a kitchen shelter, an RV dump station, a store, a restaurant, ice, a playground, a beach area, a boat dock, and launching facilities and moorage are available. Some facilities are wheelchair accessible.

Reservations, fees: Reserve at 888/CAMP-OUT (888/226-7688), website: www.parks.wa.gov/

reservations ($7 reservation fee). Sites are $6–22 per night, $6 per extra vehicle per night. Major credit cards accepted. Senior discount available. Open mid-March–October.

Directions: From Wenatchee, drive north on U.S. 97-A for 27 miles to State Route 971 (Navarre Coulee Road). Turn left (north) and drive seven miles to the end of the highway at South Lakeshore Road. Turn right, then immediately look for the park entrance to the left.

Contact: Lake Chelan State Park, 509/687-3710; State Park information, 360/902-8844.

124 SODA SPRINGS

Rating: 7

On the Little Wenatchee River in Wenatchee National Forest.

Map 3.5, grid b1, page 184

This campground is set along Little Wenatchee River Road and is a small, quiet, closer-to-civilization alternative to Tumwater Camp. But note that it lacks both drinking water and a trailer turnaround. It's off the beaten path in a pleasant wooded area, at an elevation of 2,000 feet. A small, cold soda spring is located next to the campground. There are some excellent hiking trails nearby.

Campsites, facilities: There are five tent sites. Picnic tables and fire grills are provided. Pit toilets are available, but there is no drinking water. Garbage must be packed out. Leashed pets are permitted.

Reservations, fees: Reservations are not accepted. There is no fee for camping. Open May–late October, weather permitting.

Directions: From Seattle, drive north on I-5 to Everett and U.S. 2. Turn east on U.S. 2 and drive 87 miles to State Route 207. Turn north on State Route 207 and drive 11 miles to Forest Road 6500. Turn left (west) on Forest Road 6500 and drive seven miles to the campground on the left.

Contact: Okanogan and Wenatchee National Forests, Lake Wenatchee Ranger District, 22976

Rte. 207, Leavenworth, WA 98826, 509/763-3103, fax 509/763-3211.

125 LAKE CREEK/WENATCHEE

Rating: 6

On the Little Wenatchee River in Wenatchee National Forest.

Map 3.5, grid b1, page 184

Fishing for rainbow trout can be good at this camp, which is set in a remote and primitive spot along the Little Wenatchee River. Berry picking is a bonus in late summer. The elevation is 2,300 feet. Note that there is another Lake Creek Camp in the Entiat Ranger District.

Campsites, facilities: There are eight sites for tents, trailers, or RVs of any length. Picnic tables and fire grills are provided, but there is no drinking water. Pit toilets are available. Garbage must be packed out. Leashed pets are permitted.

Reservations, fees: Reservations are not accepted. There is no fee for camping. Open May–late October, weather permitting.

Directions: From Seattle, drive north on I-5 to Everett and U.S. 2. Turn east on U.S. 2 and drive 87 miles to State Route 207. Turn north on State Route 207 and drive 11 miles to Forest Road 6500. Turn left (west) on Forest Road 6500 and drive 9.5 miles to the campground on the left.

Contact: Okanogan and Wenatchee National Forests, Lake Wenatchee and Leavenworth Ranger District, Lake Wenatchee Office, 22976 Rte. 207, Leavenworth, WA 98826, 509/763-3103, fax 509/763-3211.

126 GLACIER VIEW

Rating: 9

On Lake Wenatchee in Wenatchee National Forest.

Map 3.5, grid b2, page 184

This popular campground is set on the southwestern shore of Lake Wenatchee, near the head of the lake. It's a happening spot for boating, swimming, fishing, and windsurfing, and it fills up on summer weekends. Fishing is average. There are also some good hiking trails in the area and a golf course within a 10-minute drive. The camp sits at an elevation of 1,900 feet. Insider's note: The walk-in sites are set on the lake's shore, requiring a walk of about 100 feet.

Campsites, facilities: There are 23 sites for tents and small RVs. Trailers are not recommended. Picnic tables and fire grills are provided. Drinking water and pit toilets are available. A primitive boat launch for small boats is available. Leashed pets are permitted.

Reservations, fees: Reservations are not accepted. Sites are $11 per night, $7 per extra vehicle. Senior discount available. Open June–September, weather permitting.

Directions: From Leavenworth, drive north on State Route 207 and drive 3.5 miles to Cedar Brae Road. Turn left (west) and drive 5.5 miles (becomes Forest Road 6607), and continue to the campground at the end of the road.

Contact: Okanogan and Wenatchee National Forests, Lake Wenatchee and Leavenworth Ranger District, Lake Wenatchee Office, 22976 Rte. 207, Leavenworth, WA 98826, 509/763-3103, fax 509/763-3211.

127 LAKE WENATCHEE STATE PARK

Rating: 8

On Lake Wenatchee.

Map 3.5, grid b3, page 184

Lake Wenatchee is the centerpiece for a 489-acre park with two miles of waterfront. Glaciers and the Wenatchee River feed Lake Wenatchee, and the river, which bisects the park, helps make it a natural wildlife area. Visitors should be aware of bears; all food must be stored in bear-proof facilities. Lake Wenatchee is set in a transition zone between the wet, western Washington woodlands and the

sparse pine and fir of the eastern Cascades. Thanks to a nice location and drive-in sites that are spaced just right, you can expect plenty of company at this campground. The secluded campsites are set at the southeast end of Lake Wenatchee, which offers plenty of recreation opportunities, with a boat ramp nearby. There are eight miles of hiking trails, seven miles of bike trails, five miles of horse trails in and around the park, plus a 1.1-mile interpretive snowshoe trail in winter. Note that no horse facilities are available right in the park. In winter, there are 11 miles of multiuse trails and 23 miles of cross-country skiing trails.

Campsites, facilities: There are 197 sites for tents or self-contained RVs and two primitive tent sites. Picnic tables and fire grills are provided. Restrooms, drinking water, flush toilets, showers, an RV dump station, a store, ice, firewood, a restaurant, a playground, and horse rentals are available. Some facilities are wheelchair accessible. Boat docks, launching facilities, rentals, and golf are nearby. Leashed pets are permitted.

Reservations, fees: Reserve at 888/CAMP-OUT (888/226-7688), website: www.parks.wa.gov/reservations ($7 reservation fee). Sites are $6–16 per night, $6 per extra vehicle per night. Senior discount available. Open year-round, with limited winter facilities.

Directions: From Leavenworth, drive west on U.S. 2 for 15 miles to State Route 207 at Coles Corner. Turn right (north) and drive three miles to the park entrance.

Contact: Lake Wenatchee State Park, Rte. 207, Leavenworth, WA 98826, 509/763-3101; State Park information, 360/902-8844.

128 NASON CREEK

Rating: 7

Near Lake Wenatchee in Wenatchee National Forest.

Map 3.5, grid b3, page 184

This campground is located on Nason Creek near Lake Wenatchee, bordering Lake

Wenatchee State Park. Recreation activities include swimming, fishing, and water-skiing. Boat rentals, horseback riding, and golfing are available nearby.

Campsites, facilities: There are 73 sites, including some drive-through, for tents, trailers, or RVs of any length. Picnic tables and fire grills are provided. Restrooms, drinking water, flush toilets, showers, and electricity are available. Some facilities are wheelchair accessible. Boat-launching facilities are nearby.

Reservations, fees: Reservations are not accepted. Sites are $12 per night, $9 per extra vehicle. Senior discount available. Open May–mid-October.

Directions: From Seattle, drive north on I-5 to Everett and U.S. 2. Turn east on U.S. 2 and drive 87 miles to State Route 207, one mile west of Winton. Turn north on State Route 207 and drive 3.5 miles to Cedar Brae Road. Turn west and drive 100 yards to the campground.

Contact: Okanogan and Wenatchee National Forests, Lake Wenatchee and Leavenworth Ranger District, Lake Wenatchee Office, 22976 Rte. 207, Leavenworth, WA 98826, 509/763-3103, fax 509/763-3211.

129 MIDWAY VILLAGE AND GROCERY

Rating: 5

Near Wenatchee River.
Map 3.5, grid b3, page 184

This private campground is located about one-quarter mile from the Wenatchee River, and one mile from Lake Wenatchee State Park and Fish Lake, which is noted for good fishing year-round. There is good hiking and mountain biking out of the camp. Nearby recreation options include boating, fishing, water-skiing, swimming, windsurfing, hiking, and bike riding. The average annual snowfall is 12 feet. There is a snowmobile trail across the road from Midway Village. Snowmobile races are held in winter months within one-quarter mile of the camp-

ground. Winter options include cross-country skiing, dogsledding (25 miles east of Stevens Pass Ski Area), snowshoeing, and ice fishing.

Campsites, facilities: There are 18 sites with full hookups for RVs up to 40 feet long. Picnic tables and barbecues are provided. Restrooms, flush toilets, showers, a store, firewood, a café, a coin-operated laundry, ice, bottled gas, and a playground with horseshoe pits and volleyball are available. A convenience store and gas are on-site. Boat docks, launching facilities, and rentals are nearby. Leashed pets are permitted.

Reservations, fees: Reservations accepted. Sites are $8–16.50 per night. Major credit cards accepted. Open year-round.

Directions: From Seattle, drive north on I-5 to Everett and U.S. 2. Turn east on U.S. 2 and drive 88 miles over Steven's Pass to Coles Corner at State Route 207. Turn left (north) on State Route 207 and drive four miles, crossing the bridge over the Wenatchee River to a Y intersection. Turn right at the Y and drive one-quarter mile to the park on the right.

Contact: Midway Village and Grocery, 14193 Chiwawa Loop Rd., Leavenworth, WA 98826, 509/763-3344, fax 509/763-3519.

130 GOOSE CREEK

Rating: 7

On Goose Creek in Wenatchee National Forest.
Map 3.5, grid b3, page 184

With trails for dirt bikes available directly from the camp, Goose Creek is used primarily by motorcycle riders. A main trail links to the Entiat off-road vehicle trail system, so this camp gets high use during the summer. The camp is set near a small creek.

Campsites, facilities: There are 29 sites for tents, trailers, or RVs of any length. Picnic tables and fire rings are provided. Drinking water and pit toilets are available. Leashed pets are permitted.

Reservations, fees: Reservations are not accepted. Sites are $7 per vehicle per night. Senior discount available. Open May–mid-October.
Directions: From Seattle, drive north on I-5 to Everett and U.S. 2. Turn east on U.S. 2 and drive 87 miles to State Route 207, one mile west of Winton. Turn north on State Route 207 and drive 4.5 miles to Chiwawa Loop Road. Turn right and drive two miles to Chiwawa Valley Road/Forest Road 6200. Turn left and drive three miles to Forest Road 6100. Turn right and drive one-quarter mile to the camp on the right.
Contact: Okanogan and Wenatchee National Forests, Lake Wenatchee and Leavenworth Ranger District, Lake Wenatchee Office, 22976 Rte. 207, Leavenworth, WA 98826, 509/763-3103, fax 509/763-3211.

131 PINE FLAT

Rating: 5

Near Entiat River, in Wenatchee National Forest.
Map 3.5, grid b5, page 184
This camp has ready access to the Mad River off-road vehicle (ORV) area and is popular with bikers and ORV enthusiasts. The area boasts more than 100 miles of trails, which are ideal for quads and dirt bikes. It ties into many loop trails. The elevation is 1,600 feet.
Campsites, facilities: There are seven tent sites and one group site, which can accommodate up to 50 campers. Picnic tables and fire grills are provided. Drinking water and vault toilets are available.
Reservations, fees: Reservations required only for the group site; phone 509/784-1511. Sites are $5 per night per vehicle; the group site is $60 per night. Senior discount available. Open late May–October, weather permitting.
Directions: From Wenatchee, drive north on U.S. 97-A for 18.5 miles to Entiat River Road. Turn left (northwest) on County Road 371/Entiat River Road and drive nine miles to For-

est Road 5700. Continue northwest on Forest Road 5700 for one mile to the campground on the left.
Contact: Wenatchee National Forest, Entiat Ranger District, P.O. Box 476, Entiat, WA 98822, 509/784-1511, fax 509/784-1150.

132 LINCOLN ROCK STATE PARK

Rating: 5

On Lake Entiat.
Map 3.5, grid d6, page 184
Lincoln Rock State Park is an 80-acre park set along the shore of Lake Entiat. The lake was created by the Rocky Reach Dam on the Columbia River. The park is named for a basalt outcropping that is said to resemble the profile of Abraham Lincoln. The park features lawns and shade trees amid an arid landscape. There are two miles of hiking and bike trails, paved and flat. Water sports include swimming, boating, and water-skiing. Beavers are occasionally visible in the Columbia River.
Campsites, facilities: There are 67 sites with partial or full hookups for RVs up to 65 feet long and 27 sites for tents or self-contained RVs. Picnic tables and fire grills are provided. Restrooms, drinking water, flush toilets, coin-operated showers, an RV dump station, a playground, an athletic fields, horseshoe pits, a swimming beach, an amphitheater, three picnic shelters with electricity, and firewood are available. Some facilities are wheelchair accessible. Boat docks, moorage, and launching facilities are located on Lake Entiat. Leashed pets are permitted.
Reservations, fees: Reserve at 888/CAMP-OUT (888/226-7688), website: www.parks.wa.gov/reservations ($7 reservation fee). Sites are $16–22 per night, $6 per extra vehicle per night. Senior discount available. Major credit cards accepted. Open March–mid-October.
Directions: From East Wenatchee, drive northeast on U.S. 2 for seven miles to the park on the left.

Contact: Lincoln Rock State Park, 509/884-8702; State Park information, 360/902-8844.

133 ENTIAT CITY PARK

Rating: 8

On the Columbia River.
Map 3.5, grid c7, page 184
If you're hurting for a spot for the night, you can usually find a campsite here. Lake Entiat is actually a dammed portion of the Columbia River. Access to nearby launching facilities makes this a good camping spot for boaters.
Campsites, facilities: There are 25 tent sites and 31 sites with partial hookups (water and electricity) for RVs of any length. Picnic tables are provided. Restrooms, drinking water, flush toilets, coin-operated showers, an RV dump station, a playground, bottled gas, a store, a café, a laundry room, and ice are available. Boat docks and launching facilities are nearby. No open fires, dogs, or alcohol are permitted.
Reservations, fees: Reservation available at 800/736-8428. Sites are $20 per night, $2 per extra vehicle per night. Open mid-April-mid-September.
Directions: From Wenatchee, drive north on U.S. 97-A for 16 miles to Entiat; the park entrance is on the right (Shearson Street is adjacent on the left). Turn right and drive to the park along the shore of Lake Entiat.
Contact: Entiat City Park, P.O. Box 228, Entiat, WA 98822, 800/736-8428, city offices, 509/784-1500.

134 DAROGA STATE PARK

Rating: 5

On the Columbia River.
Map 3.5, grid c7, page 184
This 90-acre state park is set along 1.5 miles of shoreline on the Columbia River. It sits on the elevated edge of the desert "scab-lands."

This camp fills up quickly on summer weekends. The Desert Canyon Golf Course is two miles away. Fishing, along with walking and biking trails, are available out of the camp.
Campsites, facilities: There are 28 sites with partial hookups (water and electricity), including eight drive-through sites, for tents, trailers, and RVs up to 45 feet long, 17 walk-in or boat-in sites (requiring a quarter-mile trip), and two group sites for 20–100 people. Picnic tables and fire pits are provided. Restrooms, drinking water, flush toilets (near RV sites) and vault toilets (near walk-in sites), showers, an RV dump station, a swimming beach, boat-launching facilities and docks, a playground with a baseball field, basketball courts, softball and soccer fields, and a picnic area with a kitchen shelter are available. Leashed pets are permitted.
Reservations, fees: Reservations are not accepted for family sites. Reservations for group sites only; reserve at 888/CAMP-OUT (888/226-7688), website: www.parks.wa.gov/reservations ($7 reservation fee). Sites are $6–22, $6 per extra vehicle per night; group sites are $25 plus $2 per person per night, $14 per RV per night. Senior discount available. Open mid-March–mid-October, weather permitting.
Directions: From East Wenatchee, drive north on Highway 97 (east side of Columbia River) for 18 miles to the camp. For boat-in camps, launch boats from the ramp at the park and drive one-quarter mile.
Contact: Daroga State Park, 509/664-6380; State Park information, 360/902-8844.

135 BLACKPINE CREEK HORSE CAMP

Rating: 8

Near the Alpine Lakes Wilderness in Wenatchee National Forest.
Map 3.5, grid c1, page 184
A base camp for horse pack trips, Blackpine Creek Horse Camp is for horse campers only. It is set on Black Pine Creek near Icicle Creek,

at a major trailhead leading into the Alpine Lakes Wilderness. It's one of seven rustic camps on the creek, with the distinction of being the only one with facilities for horses. The elevation is 3,000 feet.

Campsites, facilities: There are 10 drive-through sites for tents, trailers, or RVs up to 21 feet long. Picnic tables and fire grills are provided. Drinking water and vault toilets are available. Horse facilities, including a loading ramp, are also available. Leashed pets are permitted.

Reservations, fees: Reservations are not accepted. Sites are $10 per vehicle per night. Senior discount available. Open mid-May–late October.

Directions: From Seattle, drive north on I-5 to Everett and U.S. 2. Turn east on U.S. 2 and drive 103 miles to Leavenworth and County Road 76 (Icicle River Road). Turn south and drive 19.2 miles to the campground on the left.

Contact: Okanogan and Wenatchee National Forests, Leavenworth Ranger District, 600 Sherbourne, Leavenworth, WA 98826, 509/548-6977, fax 509/548-5817.

136 ROCK ISLAND

Rating: 8

Near the Alpine Lakes Wilderness in Wenatchee National Forest.

Map 3.5, grid d1, page 184

Rock Island is one of several campgrounds in the immediate area along Icicle Creek and is located about one mile from the trailhead that takes hikers into the Alpine Lakes Wilderness. This is a pretty spot with good fishing access. The elevation is 2,900 feet.

Campsites, facilities: There are 22 sites for tents, trailers, or RVs up to 21 feet long. Picnic tables and fire grills are provided. Drinking water and vault toilets are available. Some facilities are wheelchair accessible. Leashed pets are permitted.

Reservations, fees: Reservations are not accepted. Sites are $10 per vehicle per night, $7

per extra vehicle. Senior discount available. Open May–late October.

Directions: From Seattle, drive north on I-5 to Everett and U.S. 2. Turn east on U.S. 2 and drive 103 miles to Leavenworth and County Road 76 (Icicle River Road). Turn south and drive 17.7 miles to the campground.

Contact: Okanogan and Wenatchee National Forests, Leavenworth Ranger District, 600 Sherbourne, Leavenworth, WA 98826, 509/548-6977, fax 509/548-5817.

137 CHATTER CREEK

Rating: 8

Near the Alpine Lakes Wilderness in Wenatchee National Forest.

Map 3.5, grid d1, page 184

Icicle and Chatter Creeks are the backdrop for this creek-side campground. The elevation is 2,800 feet. Trails lead out in several directions from the camp into the Alpine Lakes Wilderness.

Campsites, facilities: There are 12 sites for tents, trailers, or RVs up to 21 feet long and one group site for up to 45 people. Picnic tables and fire grills are provided. Drinking water and vault toilets are available. Leashed pets are permitted.

Reservations, fees: Reservations required only for group sites; phone 800/274-6104 (reservation fee). Rates are $10 per night for single sites, $7 per extra vehicle, and $70 per night for group sites. Senior discount available. Open May–late October.

Directions: From Seattle, drive north on I-5 to Everett and U.S. 2. Turn east on U.S. 2 and drive 103 miles to Leavenworth and County Road 76 (Icicle River Road). Turn south and drive 16.1 miles to the campground on the right.

Contact: Okanogan and Wenatchee National Forests, Leavenworth Ranger District, 600 Sherbourne, Leavenworth, WA 98826, 509/548-6977, fax 509/548-5817.

138 IDA CREEK

Rating: 8

On Icicle Creek in Wenatchee National Forest.

Map 3.5, grid d2, page 184

This campground is one of several small, quiet camps along Icicle and Ida Creeks, with recreation options similar to Chatter Creek and Rock Island campgrounds.

Campsites, facilities: There are five tent sites and five sites for tents, trailers, or RVs up to 21 feet long. Picnic tables and fire grills are provided. Drinking water and vault toilets are available. Some facilities are wheelchair accessible. Leashed pets are permitted.

Reservations, fees: Reservations are not accepted. Sites are $10 per night, $7 per extra vehicle. Senior discount available. Open May–late October.

Directions: From Seattle, drive north on I-5 to Everett and U.S. 2. Turn east on U.S. 2 and drive 103 miles to Leavenworth and County Road 76 (Icicle River Road). Turn south and drive 14.2 miles to the campground on the left.

Contact: Okanogan and Wenatchee National Forests, Leavenworth Ranger District, 600 Sherbourne, Leavenworth, WA 98826, 509/548-6977, fax 509/548-5817.

139 JOHNNY CREEK

Rating: 8

On Icicle Creek in Wenatchee National Forest.

Map 3.5, grid d2, page 184

This campground is split into two parts, and sits on both sides of the road, along Icicle and Johnny Creeks. It is fairly popular. Upper Johnny has a forest setting, whereas Lower Johnny is set alongside the creek, with adjacent forest. The elevation is 2,300 feet. See Bridge Creek Camp for area information.

Campsites, facilities: There are 65 sites for tents, trailers, or RVs up to 30 feet long. Picnic tables and fire grills are provided. Drinking water and vault toilets are available. Some facilities are wheelchair accessible. Leashed pets are permitted.

Reservations, fees: Reservations are not accepted. Sites are $10–11 per night, $7–8 per extra vehicle. Senior discount available. Open May–late October.

Directions: From Seattle, drive north on I-5 to Everett and U.S. 2. Turn east on U.S. 2 and drive 103 miles to Leavenworth and County Road 76 (Icicle River Road). Turn south and drive 12.4 miles to the campground (with camps on each side of the road).

Contact: Okanogan and Wenatchee National Forests, Leavenworth Ranger District, 600 Sherbourne, Leavenworth, WA 98826, 509/548-6977, fax 509/548-5817.

140 BRIDGE CREEK

Rating: 8

On Icicle Creek in Wenatchee National Forest.

Map 3.5, grid d2, page 184

This camp is a small, quiet spot along Icicle and Bridge Creeks. The elevation is 1,800 feet. About two miles south of the camp at Eightmile Creek, a trail accesses the Alpine Lakes Wilderness. See a U.S. Forest Service map for details. Horseback-riding opportunities are within four miles and golf is within five miles.

Campsites, facilities: There are six tent sites and one group site for up to 100 people. Picnic tables and fire grills are provided. Drinking water and vault toilets are available. The group site does not have drinking water available. Leashed pets are permitted.

Reservations, fees: Reservations required only for groups; phone 800/274-6104. Single sites are $10 per vehicle per night and group sites are $70 per night. Senior discount available. Open mid-April–late October.

Directions: From Seattle, drive north on I-5 to Everett and U.S. 2. Turn east on U.S. 2 and drive 103 miles to Leavenworth and County Road 76 (Icicle River Road). Turn south and drive 9.4 miles to the campground on the left.

Contact: Okanogan and Wenatchee National Forests, Leavenworth Ranger District, 600 Sherbourne, Leavenworth, WA 98826, 509/548-6977, fax 509/548-5817.

141 EIGHTMILE

Rating: 8

Near the Alpine Lakes Wilderness in Wenatchee National Forest.

Map 3.5, grid d2, page 184

This camp is set in the vicinity of trout fishing and hiking. Trailheads are located within two miles of the campground along Icicle and Eightmile Creeks, providing access to fishing, as well as a backpacking route into the Alpine Lakes Wilderness. The elevation is 1,800 feet. Horseback-riding opportunities are within four miles and golf is within five miles.

Campsites, facilities: There are 45 sites for tents, trailers, or RVs up to 21 feet long and one group site for up to 70 people. Picnic tables and fire grills are provided. Drinking water and vault toilets are available. Some facilities are wheelchair accessible. Leashed pets are permitted.

Reservations, fees: Reservations required only for group sites; phone 800/274-6104 (reservation fee). Rates are $11 per night, $8 per extra vehicle, and $70 per night for group sites. Senior discount available. Open mid-April–late October.

Directions: From Seattle, drive north on I-5 to Everett and U.S. 2. Turn east on U.S. 2 and drive 103 miles to Leavenworth and County Road 76 (Icicle River Road). Turn south and drive eight miles to the campground on the left.

Contact: Okanogan and Wenatchee National Forests, Leavenworth Ranger District, 600 Sherbourne, Leavenworth, WA 98826, 509/548-6977, fax 509/548-5817.

142 ICICLE RIVER RV RESORT

Rating: 9

On Icicle River.

Map 3.5, grid d3, page 184

Icicle River RV Resort is one of three campgrounds in the immediate area. The others include Pine Village Resort and Chalet Trailer Park. Note that no tent camping is permitted here, but six cabins are available for rent. This pretty, wooded spot is set along the Icicle River, where fishing and swimming are available. The park is clean and scenic and even has its own putting green. An 18-hole golf course and hiking trails are nearby.

Campsites, facilities: There are 100 sites with full or partial hookups for RVs of any length and six rustic cabins. Picnic tables and fire pits (at some sites) are provided. Restrooms, drinking water, flush toilets, showers, modem access, a hot tub, and bottled gas are available. Firewood is available for a fee. A putting green, horseshoe pits, and two pavilions are available nearby. Leashed pets are permitted.

Reservations, fees: Reservations accepted. Sites are $25–30 per night, $4 per extra vehicle per night, $4 per person per night for more than two people. Major credit cards accepted. Open April–mid-December, weather permitting.

Directions: From Seattle, drive north on I-5 to Everett and U.S. 2. Turn east on U.S. 2 and drive 103 miles to Leavenworth and County Road 76 (Icicle River Road). Turn south and drive three miles to the park on the left.

Contact: Icicle River RV Resort, 7305 Icicle Rd., Leavenworth, WA 98826, 509/548-5420, fax 509/548-6207, website: www.icicleriverrv.com.

143 TUMWATER

Rating: 7

Near the Alpine Lakes Wilderness in Wenatchee National Forest.

Map 3.5, grid c3, page 184

This large, popular camp provides a little bit of both worlds. It provides a good layover spot for campers cruising U.S. 2. But it also features two nearby forest roads, each less than a mile long, which end at trailheads that provide access to the Alpine Lakes Wilderness. If you don't like to hike, no problem. The camp is on the Wenatchee River in Tumwater Canyon. This section of river is closed to fishing. The elevation is 2,050 feet.

Campsites, facilities: There are 84 sites for tents, trailers, or RVs up to 30 feet long and one group site for up to 75 people. Drinking water, fire grills, and picnic tables are provided. Flush toilets are available. Some facilities are wheelchair accessible. Leashed pets are permitted.

Reservations, fees: Reservations required only for the group site; phone 800/274-6104 (reservation fee). Rates are $12 per night, $9 per extra vehicle, and $80 for group sites. Senior discount available. Open May–mid-October.

Directions: From Seattle, drive north on I-5 to Everett and U.S. 2. Turn east on U.S. 2 and drive 93 miles to the campground (10 miles west of Leavenworth).

Contact: Okanogan and Wenatchee National Forests, 509/998-6972, fax 509/548-5817.

144 PINE VILLAGE KOA/ LEAVENWORTH

Rating: 8

Near the Wenatchee River.

Map 3.5, grid d3, page 184

This lovely resort is located near the "Bavarian village" of Leavenworth, to which the park provides a free shuttle in the summer. The spectacularly scenic area is surrounded by the Cascade Mountains and set among Ponderosa pines. The camp has access to the Wenatchee River, not to mention many luxurious extras, including a hot tub and a heated pool. The park allows campfires and has firewood available. Nearby recreation options include an 18-hole golf course and hiking trails. Make a point to spend a day in Leavenworth if possible; it offers authentic German food and architecture, along with music and art shows in the summer.

Campsites, facilities: There are 60 sites, including 22 drive-through, for RVs up to 40 feet long, 40 tent sites, 20 cabins, and two cottages. Picnic tables and fire grills are provided. Restrooms, drinking water, flush toilets, showers, an RV dump station, firewood, a recreation hall, cable TV, a store, a laundry room, ice, a playground with horseshoe pits and volleyball, a spa, a heated swimming pool, and a beach area are available. Some facilities are wheelchair accessible. Bottled gas and a café are located within one mile. Leashed pets are permitted.

Reservations, fees: Reservations are accepted at 800/562-5709. The fee is $21–38 per night, $5 per extra vehicle per night, and $4.50 per person per night for more than two people. Cabins and cottages are $45–59. Major credit cards accepted. Open April–November.

Directions: From Seattle, drive north on I-5 to Everett and U.S. 2. Turn east on U.S. 2 and drive 103 miles to Leavenworth. Continue east on U.S. 2 for one-quarter mile to River Bend Drive. Turn north and drive one-half mile to the campground on the right.

Contact: Pine Village KOA/Leavenworth, 11401 River Bend Dr., Leavenworth, WA 98826, 509/548-7709 (phone or fax), website: www.koa.com.

145 BLU SHASTIN RV PARK

Rating: 6

Near Penshastin Creek.

Map 3.5, grid e3, page 184

This park is set in a mountainous area near

Penshastin Creek. Gold panning in the river is a popular activity here, and during the gold rush, the Penshastin was the best-producing river in the state. The camp has sites on the riverbank and plenty of shade trees. A heated pool, a recreation field, and horseshoe pits provide possible activities in the park. Hiking trails and marked bike trails are nearby.

Campsites, facilities: There are 86 sites with full hookups, including four drive-through sites, for tents, trailers, or RVs of any length. Picnic tables and fire rings are provided. Restrooms, drinking water, flush toilets, showers, an RV dump station, a recreation hall, firewood, a coin-operated laundry, ice, a playground, horseshoes, badminton, volleyball, and a heated swimming pool are available. Bottled gas, a store, and a café are located within seven miles. Leashed pets are permitted.

Reservations, fees: Reservations recommended. Sites are $20–25 per night. Major credit cards accepted. Open year-round, weather permitting.

Directions: From Leavenworth, drive south on U.S. 2 for four miles to U.S. 97. Turn south on U.S. 97 and drive seven miles to the park on the right.

Contact: Blu Shastin RV Park, 3300 Hwy. 97, Penshastin, WA 98847, 509/548-4184 or 888/548-4184, website: www.blushastin.com.

146 WENATCHEE RIVER COUNTY PARK

Rating: 5

On Wenatchee River.
Map 3.5, grid e6, page 184

This camp is set along the Wenatchee River, situated between the highway and the river. Though not the greatest setting, with some highway noise, it is convenient for RV campers. You can usually get a tree-covered site in the campground, despite it being a small park. The adjacent river is fast moving and provides whitewater rafting, with a put-in spot at the park. Fishing is typically poor.

Campsites, facilities: There are 80 sites, including 40 with full hookups, 40 with partial hookups for tents, and some drive-through sites for RVs, and 17 tent sites. Picnic tables and fire grills are provided. Restrooms, drinking water, flush toilets, and showers are available. A store and a restaurant are within one mile. Leashed pets are permitted.

Reservations, fees: Reservations available at 509/667-7503. Sites are $15–22 per night, $5 per person for more than four people, and $5 per extra vehicle per night. Major credit cards accepted. Open April–September.

Directions: From Wenatchee and U.S. 2, drive west on U.S. 2 for 4.7 miles to the campground on the left.

Contact: Chelan County Commissioner, 350 Orondo Ave., Wenatchee, WA 98801, 509/667-7503 or 509/667-6215, fax 509/667-6599, website: www.chelancounty.com.

147 WENATCHEE CONFLUENCE STATE PARK

Rating: 10

On the Columbia River.
Map 3.5, grid e6, page 184

This 197-acre state park is set at the confluence of the Wenatchee and Columbia Rivers. The park features expansive lawns shaded by deciduous trees and fronted by the two rivers. Wenatchee Confluence has something of a dual personality: The north portion of the park is urban and recreational, while the southern section is a designated natural wetland area. There are 10.5 miles of paved trail for hiking, biking, and in-line skating. A pedestrian bridge crosses the Wenatchee River. An interpretive hiking trail is available in the Horan Natural Area. Other recreation possibilities include fishing, swimming, boating, and water-skiing. Sports enthusiasts will find playing fields as well as tennis and basketball courts. Daroga State Park and Lake Chelan to the north offer side trip possibilities.

Campsites, facilities: There are 51 sites with full hookups for RVs up to 65 feet long, eight developed tent sites, and a group site for tents for up to 300 people. Picnic tables and fire grills are provided. Restrooms, drinking water, flush toilets, coin-operated showers, a boat launch, an RV dump station, a swimming beach, a playground, and athletic fields are available. Some facilities are wheelchair accessible. Leashed pets are permitted.

Reservations, fees: Reserve at 888/CAMP-OUT (888/226-7688), website: www.parks.wa.gov/reservations ($7 reservation fee). Sites are $16–22 per night, $6 per extra vehicle per night. Major credit cards accepted mid-May–mid-September. Senior discount available. Open year-round.

Directions: From Wenatchee and U.S. 2, take the Easy Street exit and drive south to Penny Road. Turn left and drive a short distance to Chester Kimm Street. Turn right and drive to a T intersection and Old Station Road. Turn left on Old Station Road and drive past the railroad tracks to the park on the right. The park is 1.3 miles from U.S. 2.

Contact: Wenatchee Confluence State Park, 333 Olds Station Rd., Wenatchee, WA 98801, 509/664-6373, fax 509/662-0459; State Park information, 360/902-8844.

148 INDIAN HORSE CAMP

Rating: 6

On the Middle Fork of the Teanaway River.
Map 3.5, grid f1, page 184

This campground along the Middle Fork of the Teanaway River is located in a primitive setting with sunny, open sites along the water. Fishing for brook trout is best here in May and June. Quiet and solitude are highlights of this little-used camp. It's an easy drive from here to trailheads accessing the Mt. Stuart Range. Be sure to bring your own drinking water.

Campsites, facilities: There are 10 campsites for tents or small trailers. Picnic tables, fire grills, and tent pads are provided. Pit toilets are available, but there is no drinking water. Garbage must be packed out. Some saddle-stock facilities are available, including hitching posts and corrals. Some facilities are wheelchair accessible. Leashed pets are permitted.

Reservations, fees: Reservations are not accepted. There is no fee for camping. Open year-round, weather permitting (heavy snows are generally expected December–March).

Directions: From Seattle, drive east on I-90 for 80 miles to Cle Elum and Exit 85 and Highway 970. Turn east on Highway 970 and drive 6.9 miles to Teanaway Road. Turn left on Teanaway Road and drive 7.3 miles to West Fork Teenaway Road. Turn left and drive six-tenths of a mile to Middle Fork Teanaway Road. Turn right and drive 3.9 miles to the campground on the left.

Contact: Department of Natural Resources, Southeast Region, 713 Bowers Rd., Ellensburg, WA 98926-9301, 509/925-8510, fax 509/925-8522.

149 BEVERLY

Rating: 8

On the North Fork of the Teanaway River in Wenatchee National Forest.
Map 3.5, grid f2, page 184

This primitive campground is set on the North Fork of the Teanaway River, a scenic area of the river. It is primarily a hiker's camp, with several trails leading up nearby creeks and into the Alpine Lakes Wilderness. Self-issued permits are required for wilderness hiking. Fishing is poor for cutthroat trout. The elevation is 3,100 feet.

Campsites, facilities: There are 13 sites for tents, trailers, or RVs up to 21 feet long. Picnic tables and fire grills are provided. Vault toilets are available, but there is no drinking water. Garbage must be packed out. Leashed pets are permitted.

Reservations, fees: Reservations are not accepted.

Sites are $5 per night per vehicle. Open June–mid-November.

Directions: In Seattle on I-5, turn east on I-90. Drive east on I-90 for 80 miles to Cle Elum and Exit 86. Take Exit 86 to Highway 970. Turn east on Highway 970 and drive eight miles to Teanaway Road (County Road 970). Turn left (north) on Teanaway Road and drive 13 miles to the end of the paved road. Bear right (north) on Forest Road 9737 and drive four miles to the campground on the left.

Contact: Okanogan and Wenatchee National Forests, Cle Elum Ranger District, West Second St., Cle Elum, WA 98922, 509/674-4411, fax 509/674-1530.

150 MINERAL SPRINGS

Rating: 6

On Swauk Creek in Wenatchee National Forest.

Map 3.5, grid f3, page 184

This campground at the confluence of Medicine and Swauk Creeks is one of five campgrounds along U.S. 97. Note that this camp is set along a highway, so there is some highway noise. Fishing, berry picking, and hunting are good in season in this area. It is at an elevation of 7,700 feet. Most use the camp as a one-night layover spot.

Campsites, facilities: There are 12 sites for tents, trailers, or RVs up to 21 feet long. Picnic tables and fire rings are provided. Drinking water and vault toilets are available. Leashed pets are permitted. A restaurant is nearby.

Reservations, fees: Reservations are not accepted. Sites are $10 per night, $8 per extra vehicle per night. Senior discount available. Open mid-May–late September.

Directions: From Seattle, drive east on I-90 for 80 miles to Cle Elum and Exit 85 and Highway 970. Turn northeast on Highway 970 and drive 12 miles to U.S. 97. Continue northeast (the road becomes U.S. 97) and drive about seven miles to the campground on the left.

Contact: Okanogan and Wenatchee National Forests, Cle Elum Ranger District, 830 West Second St., Cle Elum, WA 98922, 509/674-4411, fax 509/674-1530.

151 SWAUK

Rating: 6

On Swauk Creek in Wenatchee National Forest.

Map 3.5, grid f3, page 184

Some decent hiking trails can be found at this campground along Swauk Creek. A short loop trail, about a one mile round-trip, is the most popular. Fishing is marginal, and there is some highway noise from U.S. 97. The elevation is 3,200 feet. Three miles east of the camp on Forest Road 9716 is the Swauk Forest Discovery Trail. This three-mile interpretive trail explains some of the effects of logging and U.S. Forest Service management of the forest habitat.

Campsites, facilities: There are 22 sites, including two double sites, for tents, trailers, or RVs. Fire grills and picnic tables are provided. Pit toilets and firewood are available, but there is no drinking water. Leashed pets are permitted.

Reservations, fees: Reservations are not accepted. Sites are $10–20 per night, $8 per extra vehicle per night. Senior discount available. Open mid-April–late September.

Directions: In Seattle on I-5, turn east on I-90. Drive east on I-90 for 80 miles to Cle Elum and Exit 86. Take Exit 86 to County Road 970. Turn east on County Road 970 and drive 12 miles to U.S. 97. Turn north on U.S. 97 and drive 10 miles to the campground on the right (near Swauk Pass).

Contact: Okanogan and Wenatchee National Forests, Cle Elum Ranger District, West Second St., Cle Elum, WA 98922, 509/674-4411, fax 509/674-1530.

152 KEN WILCOX HORSE CAMP

Rating: 8

Near Swauk Creek at Haney Meadows in Wenatchee National Forest.

Map 3.5, grid f4, page 184

First note that the last couple miles of road are pretty rough, suitable only for high-clearance vehicles or pickups. The camp is set at an elevation of 5,500 feet, at the launch point for an extensive trail system. This scenic camp near Haney Meadows has been adopted by a local equestrian association that helps maintain the horse trails. Mountain bikers also use this camp; note that when bikes and horses meet on a trail, bikes must give way, even if it involves dismounting the bike and carrying it off the trail.

Campsites, facilities: There are 25 sites for tents, trailers, or RVs up to 25 feet long. Fire pits and vault toilets are provided. No drinking water is available. Garbage must be packed out. Stock facilities include hitching equipment, including rails and rings for suspending a high line.

Reservations, fees: Northwest Forest Pass ($5 daily fee or $30 annual fee per parked vehicle) is required. Open early July–mid-October (the access road is not plowed).

Directions: In Seattle, turn east on I-90. Drive east on I-90 for 80 miles to Cle Elum and Exit 86. Take Exit 86 to County Road 970. Turn east on County Road 970 and drive 12 miles to U.S. 97. Turn north on U.S. 97 and drive 15 miles to the summit of Swauk Pass and Forest Road 9716. Turn right on Forest Road 9716 (gravel) and drive about four miles to Forest Road 9712. Turn left on Forest Road 9712 and drive about five miles to the camp on the left.

Contact: Okanogan and Wenatchee National Forests, Cle Elum Ranger District, West Second St., Cle Elum, WA 98922, 509/674-4411, fax 509/674-1530.

153 TRAILER CORRAL

Rating: 7

On the Yakima River.

Map 3.5, grid g1, page 184

This wooded campground along the Yakima River offers a choice of grassy or graveled sites. Nearby recreation options include an 18-hole golf course, marked hiking trails, and tennis courts. New owners took over this operation in 2002.

Campsites, facilities: There are 23 sites with full hookups for RVs of any length, three tent sites, and six cabins. Picnic tables are provided. Restrooms, flush toilets, showers, an RV dump station, firewood, and a coin-operated laundry are available. A store is located within one mile. Boat-launching facilities are nearby. Leashed pets are permitted.

Reservations, fees: Reservations accepted. Sites are $15–25 per night. Major credit cards accepted. Open year-round.

Directions: From Seattle, drive east on I-90 for 80 miles to Cle Elum and Exit 85 and Highway 970. Turn east on Highway 970 and drive 1.5 mile to the park on the left.

Contact: Trailer Corral, 2781 Hwy. 970, Cle Elum, WA 98922, 509/674-2433.

154 TANEUM

Rating: 7

On Taneum Creek in Wenatchee National Forest.

Map 3.5, grid h2, page 184

This rustic spot is set along Taneum Creek, with an elevation of 2,400 feet. It is located several miles away from the camps popular with the off-road vehicle crowd. This is more of a quiet getaway, not a base camp. Ponderosa pines add to the setting. Trout fishing is popular here in the summer. The camp receives moderate use.

Campsites, facilities: There are 13 sites for RVs up to 21 feet long and one double site. Picnic tables and fire rings are provided. Drinking water and firewood are available. Some facilities are wheelchair accessible. Leashed pets are permitted.

Reservations, fees: Reservations are not accepted. Rates are $10–20 per night for single sites, $8 for each additional vehicle. Senior discount available. Open May–late September.

Directions: From Ellensburg, drive northeast on U.S. 90 for about 12 miles to Thorp Prairie Road. Turn south on Thorp Prairie Road and drive four miles (crossing back over the freeway) to Taneum Road. Turn right and drive west for three miles (it becomes Forest Road 33). Continue west for three miles to the campground on the left.

Contact: Okanogan and Wenatchee National Forests, Cle Elum Ranger District, 830 West Second St., Cle Elum, CA 98922, 509/674-4411, fax 509/674-1530.

155 ICEWATER CREEK

Rating: 7

On Taneum Creek in Wenatchee National Forest.
Map 3.5, grid h2, page 184

Icewater Creek Camp is similar to Taneum Camp, except that the trees are smaller and the sites are a bit more open. It is most popular with off-road motorcyclists because there are two ORV trails leading from the camp, both of which network with an extensive system of off-road riding trails. The best route extends along the South Fork Taneium River area. Fishing is fair, primarily for six- to eight-inch cutthroat trout.

Campsites, facilities: There are 14 sites for tents or RVs up to 26 feet long. Picnic tables and fire rings are provided. Drinking water and firewood are available. Some facilities are wheelchair accessible. Leashed pets are permitted.

Reservations, fees: Reservations are not accepted. Rates are $8 for single sites, $16 for double site, and $6 for each additional vehicle. Senior discount available. Open May–late September.

Directions: From Ellensburg, drive northeast on U.S. 90 for about 12 miles to Thorp Prairie Road. Turn south on Thorp Prairie Road and drive four miles (crossing back over the freeway) to Taneum Road. Turn right and drive west for three miles (it becomes Forest Road 33). Continue west for 4.5 miles to the campground on the left.

Contact: Okanogan and Wenatchee National Forests, Cle Elum Ranger District, 830 West Second St., Cle Elum, CA 98922, 509/674-4411, fax 509/674-1530.

© TOM STIENSTRA

Chapter 4
Northeastern Washington

Chapter 4—Northeastern Washington

A lot of people call this area "God's country." You know why? Because nobody else could have thought of it. The vast number of lakes, streams, and national forests provides an unlimited land of adventure. You could spend a lifetime here—your days hiking, fishing, and exploring, your nights camping out and staring up at the stars.

And that's exactly what some people do, like our friend Rich Landers, the outdoors writer for the Spokane Spokesman-Review. People know they have it good here, living on the threshold of a fantastic land of adventure, but with a population base in Spokane that creates a financial center with career opportunities.

The landscape features a variety of settings. The national forests (Colville, Kaniksu, Wenatchee), set in the northern tier of the state, are ideal for a mountain hideaway. You'll find remote ridges and valleys with conifers, along with many small streams and lakes. In the valleys, the region is carved by the Pacific Northwest's largest river system, featuring the Columbia River, Franklin D. Roosevelt Lake, and the Spokane River. These waterways are best for campers interested in water views, boating, and full facilities.

While many well-known destinations are stellar, our favorites are the lesser-known sites. There are dozens of such camps in this area, often along the shore of a small lake, that provide good fishing and hiking. You could search across the land and not find a better region for outdoor adventure. This is a wilderness to enjoy.

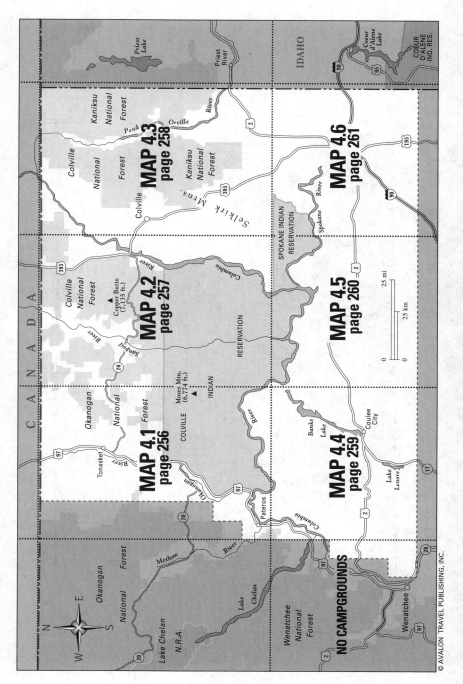

MAP 4.1
page 256

MAP 4.2
page 257

MAP 4.3
page 258

MAP 4.4
page 259

MAP 4.5
page 260

MAP 4.6
page 261

CANADA

IDAHO

Priest Lake

Priest River

Kaniksu National Forest

Colville National Forest

Pend Oreille River

Kaniksu National Forest

Coeur d'Alene Lake

COEUR D'ALENE IND. RES.

Selkirk Mtns.

Colville

Copper Butte (7,135 ft.)

Colville National Forest

Sanpoil River

Spokane River

SPOKANE INDIAN RESERVATION

Columbia River

Tonasket

Okanogan National Forest

Moses Mtn. (6,774 ft.)

COLVILLE INDIAN RESERVATION

Okanogan River

River

Banks Lake

Coulee City

Lake Lenore

Pateros

Columbia

Methow River

Lake Chelan

Lake Chelan N.R.A.

Okanogan National Forest

Wenatchee National Forest

Wenatchee

NO CAMPGROUNDS

25 mi

25 km

N W E S

© AVALON TRAVEL PUBLISHING, INC.

Map 4.1

Campgrounds 1–31
Pages 262–275

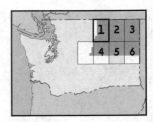

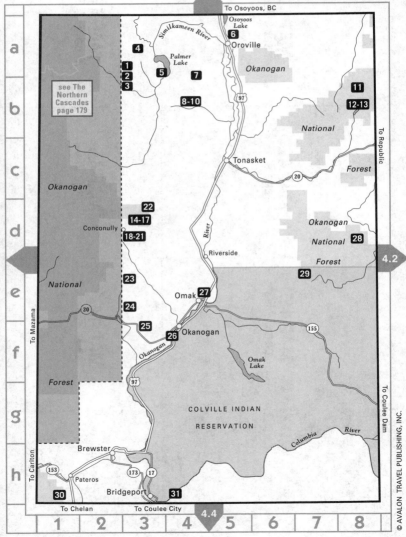

To Osoyoos, BC

Osoyoos Lake

Similkameen River

6 Oroville

Palmer Lake

4

1
2
3

see The Northern Cascades page 179

5

7

8-10

97

Okanogan

11

12-13

National

To Republic

Tonasket

20

Okanogan

River

22

14-17

Conconully

18-21

Forest

Okanogan

National

28

Riverside

Forest

29

4.2

23

Omak **27**

National

20

24

25

26 Okanogan

155

Okanogan

Omak Lake

Forest

97

To Mazama

COLVILLE INDIAN

RESERVATION

Columbia

River

To Coulee Dam

Brewster

153

Pateros

173 17

To Carlton

30

Bridgeport

31

To Chelan

To Coulee City

4.4

© AVALON TRAVEL PUBLISHING, INC.

1 2 3 4 5 6 7 8

a b c d e f g h

Map 4.2

Campgrounds 32–59
Pages 275–287

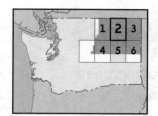

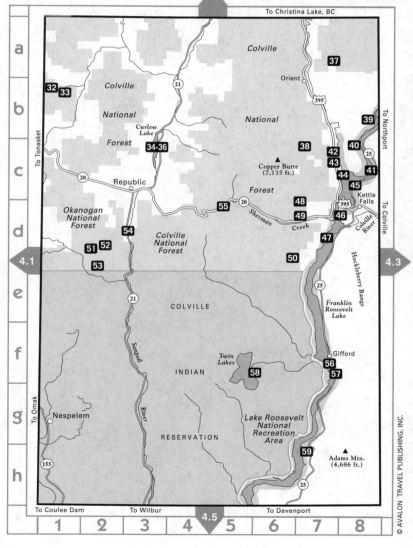

© AVALON TRAVEL PUBLISHING, INC.

Map 4.3

Campgrounds 60–94
Pages 287–302

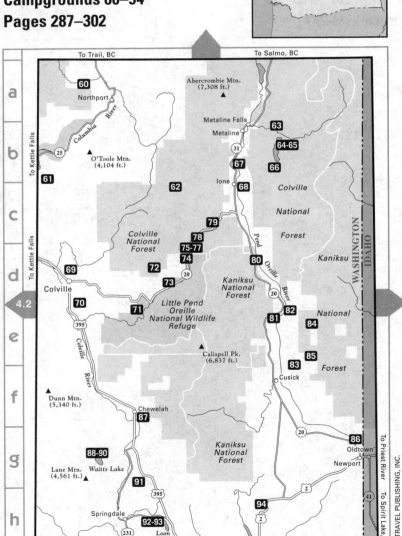

To Trail, BC To Salmo, BC

60 Northport

Abercrombie Mtn. (7,308 ft.) ▲

Metaline Falls
Metaline 63
31 64-65
67 66
61 O'Toole Mtn. (4,104 ft.) ▲
25
62 Ione 68

Colville
National
Forest

79 Kaniksu

78
75-77 Pend Oreille River
74
72 80
73 20

69 Colville
70 71 Kaniksu National Forest
Little Pend Oreille National Wildlife Refuge 20 82 National
81 84

WASHINGTON IDAHO

Calispell Pk. (6,837 ft.) ▲ 83 85 Forest
Cusick

Dunn Mtn. (5,340 ft.) ▲
Chewelah
87 86
88-90 Oldtown
Lane Mtn. (4,561 ft.) ▲ Waitts Lake Newport
91 395 2
Springdale 94
92-93 2 41
Loon Lake

To Reardan To Spokane To Country Homes

To Priest River To Spirit Lake, ID

© AVALON TRAVEL PUBLISHING, INC.

Map 4.4

Campgrounds 95–103
Pages 302–306

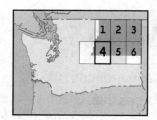

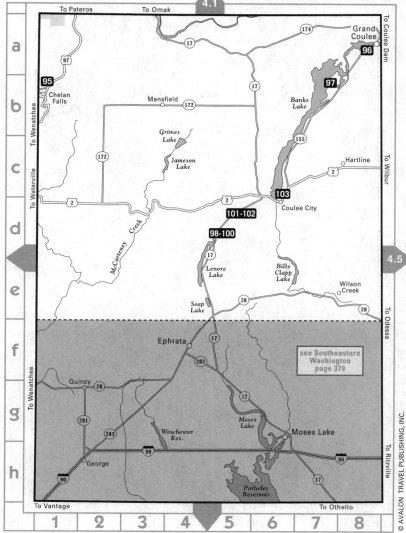

Map 4.5

Campgrounds 104–112
Pages 306–310

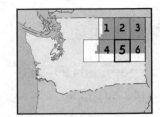

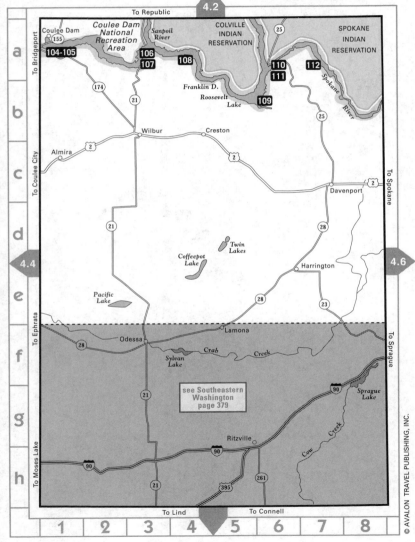

To Republic

4.2

Coulee Dam

Coulee Dam
National
Recreation
Area

Sanpoil
River

COLVILLE
INDIAN
RESERVATION

SPOKANE
INDIAN
RESERVATION

155

104-105

106
107

108

110
111

112

Spokane River

174

21

Franklin D.
Roosevelt
Lake

109

25

4.4

4.6

To Bridgeport

To Coulee City

To Ephrata

To Moses Lake

To Spokane

To Sprague

Wilbur

Creston

Almira

2

2

Davenport

2

21

28

Twin
Lakes

Coffeepot
Lake

Harrington

28

Pacific
Lake

28

23

Odessa

Lamona

28

Crab   Creek

Sylvan
Lake

see Southeastern
Washington
page 379

90

Sprague
Lake

21

Cow   Creek

Ritzville

90

90

21

395

261

To Lind

To Connell

© AVALON TRAVEL PUBLISHING, INC.

1 2 3 4 5 6 7 8

a b c d e f g h

Map 4.6

Campgrounds 113–123
Pages 310–315

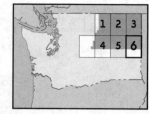

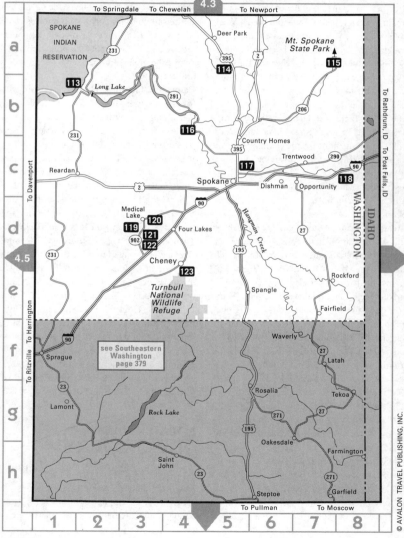

To Springdale   To Chewelah   4.3   To Newport

SPOKANE
INDIAN
RESERVATION

231

113 Long Lake

Deer Park

395   2

Mt. Spokane
State Park
115

291

231

116

206

Country Homes

395

Trentwood   290

Reardan

2

117

90

Spokane

Dishman   Opportunity   **118**

To Davenport

Medical
Lake
119 **120** Four Lakes
902 **121**
122

90

Hangman Creek

27

4.5   231

Cheney

123

195

Rockford

Turnbull
National
Wildlife
Refuge

Spangle

Fairfield

To Harrington

90

Waverly

27

To Ritzville

see Southeastern
Washington
page 379

Sprague

Latah

23

Rosalia

Tekoa

Lamont

Rock Lake

271

27

195

Oakesdale

Farmington

Saint
John

23

Steptoe

271

Garfield

To Pullman   To Moscow

WASHINGTON   IDAHO

To Rathdrum, ID   To Post Falls, ID

1   2   3   4   5   6   7   8

■ COLD SPRINGS

🏃 🚴 ❄ 🐎 🚐 ⛺

Rating: 8

Near Cold Creek.

Map 4.1, grid a3, page 256

It's quite a drive to get here, but you'll be happy you made the effort to reach this pretty forested camp. Campsites are located near a small stream amid a forest of lodgepole pine, Western larch, and several species of fir, including Douglas fir. Trails for horseback riding, hiking, and snowmobiling run through the area. Because the camp is little known and remote, it's advisable to obtain a map of the area from the Department of Natural Resources.

Campsites, facilities: There are nine campsites for tents or small RVs. Picnic tables, fire grills, and tent pads are provided. Vault toilets and drinking water are available. Leashed pets are permitted.

Reservations, fees: Reservations are not accepted. There is no fee for camping. Open year-round.

Directions: From Wenatchee, drive north on U.S. 97 for 120 miles to Tonasket and Forest Street. Turn left and drive two-tenths of a mile (crossing the Okanogan River) to Highway 7. Turn right (north) on Highway 7 (Loomis-Oroville Highway) and drive five miles. At the fork, continue on Loomis-Oroville Highway for about 12 miles to Toats Coulee Road, 2.1 miles north of Loomis. Turn left and drive 5.5 miles to the Toats Coulee Lower Site camp. Continue one-tenth of a mile to the upper site at the junction of roads. Take Road OM-T-1000 for 2.1 miles to Cold Creek Road. Turn right (gravel road) and drive four-tenths of a mile. Bear right and continue 1.8 miles. Bear left and drive 2.7 miles to the camp, past the picnic area.

Contact: Department of Natural Resources, Northeast Region, P.O. Box 190, Colville, WA 99114-0190, 360/902-1234 or 509/684-7474, fax 509/684-7484.

■ NORTH FORK NINE MILE

🚴 🛶 🐎 🚐 ⛺

Rating: 6

On the North Fork of Toats Coulee Creek.

Map 4.1, grid b3, page 256

Dear and black bears frequent this campground situated in the forest along the North Fork of Toats Coulee Creek and Nine Mile Creek. This camp is popular in the fall with hunters. Trout fishing is fair at Toats Coulee Creek; check regulations. It's advisable to obtain a map that details the area from the Department of Natural Resources.

Campsites, facilities: There are 11 campsites for tents or small RVs. Picnic tables, fire grills, and tent pads are provided. Vault toilets and drinking water are available. Leashed pets are permitted.

Reservations, fees: Reservations are not accepted. There is no fee for camping. Open year-round.

Directions: From Wenatchee, drive north on U.S. 97 for 120 miles to Tonasket and Forest Street. Turn left and drive two-tenths of a mile (crossing the Okanogan River) to Highway 7. Turn right (north) on Highway 7 (Loomis-Oroville Highway) and drive five miles. At the fork, continue on Loomis-Oroville Highway for about 12 miles to Toats Coulee Road, 2.1 miles north of Loomis. Turn left and drive 5.5 miles to the Toats Coulee Lower Site camp. Continue one-tenth of a mile to the upper site at the junction of roads. Take Road OM-T-1000 for 2.5 miles to the campground on the right.

Contact: Department of Natural Resources, Northeast Region, P.O. Box 190, Colville, WA 99114-0190, 360/902-1234 or 509/684-7474, fax 509/684-7484.

■ TOATS COULEE

🏃 🚴 🛶 ❄ 🐎 🚐 ⛺

Rating: 6

On Toats Coulee Creek.

Map 4.1, grid b3, page 256

Touts Coulee actually consists of two primitive campsites set a short distance apart. The camp is set in a wooded spot along Toats Coulee Creek. Trout fishing is available; check regulations. The best hiking is located 10 miles northwest in the Pasayten Wilderness (to reach this trailhead, continue driving up the campground road). These camps are popular in the fall with hunters. In the winter, a road for snowmobile use follows the South Fork of Toats Coulee Creek, swinging south and then heading east along Cecil Creek. Contact the Department of Natural Resources for details.

Campsites, facilities: There are nine sites for tents or small RVs. Picnic tables, fire grills, and tent pads are provided. Vault toilets are available. There is no drinking water. Garbage must be packed out. Leashed pets are permitted.

Reservations, fees: Reservations are not accepted. There is no fee for camping. Open year-round.

Directions: From Wenatchee, drive north on U.S. 97 for 120 miles to Tonasket and Forest Street. Turn left and drive two-tenths of a mile (crossing the Okanogan River) to Highway 7. Turn right (north) on Highway 7 (Loomis-Oroville Highway) and drive five miles. At the fork, continue on Loomis-Oroville Highway for about 12 miles to Toats Coulee Road, 2.1 miles north of Loomis. Turn left and drive 5.5 miles to the lower campsite on the left. Continue one-tenth of a mile to the upper campsite, located at the junction of Road OM-T-2000 and Road OM-T-1000.

Contact: Department of Natural Resources, Northeast Region, P.O. Box 190, Colville, WA 99114-0190, 360/902-1234 or 509/684-7474, fax 509/684-7484.

4 CHOPAKA LAKE

Rating: 8

On Chopaka Lake.
Map 4.1, grid a3, page 256

This campground provides a classic setting for the expert angler. It's nestled along the west-

ern shore of Chopaka Lake, which is extremely popular with trout anglers. No boat motors are permitted on the lake. That makes it a winner for flyfishers (barbless hooks required) using float tubes.

Campsites, facilities: There are 15 campsites for tents or small RVs. Picnic tables, fire grills, and tent pads are provided. Vault toilets, drinking water, a fishing platform, and primitive boat-launching and dock facilities are available. Some facilities are wheelchair accessible. Leashed pets are permitted.

Reservations, fees: Reservations are not accepted. There is no fee for camping. Open year-round.

Directions: From Wenatchee, drive north on U.S. 97 for 120 miles to Tonasket and Forest Street. Turn left and drive two-tenths of a mile (crossing the Okanogan River) to Highway 7. Turn right (north) on Highway 7 (Loomis-Oroville Highway) and drive five miles. At the fork, continue on Loomis-Oroville Highway for about 12 miles to Toats Coulee Road, 2.1 miles north of Loomis. Turn left and drive 1.5 miles. Turn right onto a steep, one-lane road and drive 3.4 miles. Bear left and drive 1.7 miles; turn right, and drive two miles to the campground.

Contact: Department of Natural Resources, Northeast Region, P.O. Box 190, Colville, WA 99114-0190, 360/902-1234 or 509/684-7474, fax 509/684-7484.

5 PALMER LAKE

Rating: 9

On Palmer Lake.
Map 4.1, grid b3, page 256

This shorefront camp is the only one at Palmer Lake. The campsites are set close to the lake's shore, which is very scenic. It fills up during the summer, even on weekdays, frequently with visitors from Canada. Fishing is often good for kokanee salmon and rainbow trout. Power boating and water-skiing are permitted. The winter range of the deer is in the Sinlahekin Valley to the south of Palmer Lake. There are numerous migration routes in the region. Wildlife that can be spotted includes the endangered bighorn sheep, cougar, bald and golden eagles, black bear, and grouse.

Campsites, facilities: There are six campsites for tents or small RVs. Picnic tables, fire grills, and tent pads are provided. Vault toilets and a fishing pier are available, but there is no drinking water. Garbage must be packed out. A primitive boat launch is located at the opposite end of the lake; four-wheel-drive is required. Leashed pets are permitted.

Reservations, fees: Reservations are not accepted. There is no fee for camping. Open year-round, weather permitting.

Directions: From Wenatchee, drive north on U.S. 97 for 120 miles to Tonasket and Forest Street. Turn left and drive two-tenths of a mile, crossing the Okanogan River, to Highway 7. Turn right (north) on Highway 7 (Loomis-Oroville Highway) and drive 18.5 miles, 8.5 miles past Loomis. Stay to the right and drive to the camp at the north end of the lake.

Contact: Department of Natural Resources, Northeast Region, P.O. Box 190, Colville, WA 99114-0190, 360/902-1234 or 509/684-7474, fax 509/684-7484.

6 OSOYOOS LAKE STATE PARK

Rating: 9

On Osoyoos Lake.

Map 4.1, grid a5, page 256

The park is set along the shore of Osoyoos Lake, a 14-mile-long lake created from the Okanogan River, located south of the Canadian Rockies. The park covers 47 acres and provides a base of operations for a fishing vacation. The lake has rainbow trout, kokanee salmon, smallmouth bass, crappie, and perch. Water sports are also popular in the summer, and in winter, it is an ideal location for ice

skating, ice fishing, and snow play. Expansive lawns lead down to the sandy shore of the lake. Osoyoos Lake is a winter nesting area for geese. The park also features a war veteran's memorial. A nine-hole golf course is located nearby. A history note: Many years ago, the area was the site of the annual *okanogan* (rendezvous) of the Washington and British Columbia Indians. They would gather and share supplies of fish and game for the year. Fishing gear and concessions are available at the park.

Campsites, facilities: There are 80 sites, including one site with full hookups, for tents or self-contained RVs up to 45 feet long and six primitive tent sites. Picnic tables and fire grills are provided. Restrooms, flush toilets, showers, an RV dump station, a store, a café, firewood, and a playground with horseshoes and volleyball are available. A coin-operated laundry facility and ice are located within one mile. Boat-launching and dock facilities are nearby. Leashed pets are permitted.

Reservations, fees: Reserve at 888/CAMP-OUT (888/226-7688), website: www.parks.wa.gov/reservations ($7 reservation fee). Sites are $6–22 per night, $6 per extra vehicle per night. Major credit cards accepted. Open year-round, with limited facilities in winter.

Directions: From Oroville, on U.S. 97 just south of the Canadian border, drive north on U.S. 97 for one mile to the park entrance on the right.

Contact: Osoyoos Lake State Park, 509/476-3321; State Park information, 360/902-8844.

7 SUN COVE RESORT

Rating: 9

On Wannacut Lake.

Map 4.1, grid b4, page 256

This beautiful resort is surrounded by trees and hills and set along the shore of Wannacut Lake, a spring-fed lake that doesn't get much traffic. The lake is approximately three miles long and 2.5 miles wide. An eight-mph speed limit is enforced for boats. Fishing, swimming, boating, and hiking are all summertime options. The park provides full facilities, including a heated pool, a playground, and a recreation hall. For the horsy set, a guided trail and overnight rides are available one mile from the resort.

Campsites, facilities: There are 22 tent sites, 26 drive-through sites with hookups for RVs of any length and two sites for RVs up to 38 feet long, two cottages, and 10 motel units with kitchens. Picnic tables are provided. Restrooms, flush toilets, showers (fee), an RV dump station, a recreation hall, a store, a café, a laundry room, ice, a playground, and a swimming pool are available. Some facilities are wheelchair accessible. Boat docks, launching facilities, and rentals are also available. Leashed pets are permitted.

Reservations, fees: Reservations accepted. Sites are $21 per night, $2 per person for more than four people. Major credit cards accepted. Open late April–October.

Directions: From Oroville (on U.S. 97 just south of the Canadian border), drive west on Ellemehan Mountain Road for about six miles to Wannacut Lake Road. Turn left (south) and drive five miles to the resort at the end of the road.

Contact: Sun Cove Resort, 93 East Wannacut Ln., Oroville, WA 98844, 509/476-2223 (phone or fax).

⑧ SPECTACLE LAKE RESORT

Rating: 7

On Spectacle Lake.
Map 4.1, grid b4, page 256
This pleasant resort on the shore of long, narrow Spectacle Lake has grassy, shaded sites. Space is usually available here, although reservations are accepted. Recreation options include boating, fishing, swimming, water-skiing, and hunting (in season).

Campsites, facilities: There are 40 sites with full hookups for tents or RVs of any length and 12 motel rooms with kitchenettes. Picnic tables are provided. Restrooms, flush toilets, showers, bottled gas, an RV dump station, a store, a coin-operated laundry, ice, a playground, a recreation hall, an exercise room, and a heated swimming pool are available. Boat docks, launching facilities, and rentals are also available nearby. Leashed pets are permitted.

Reservations, fees: Reservations accepted. Sites are $16.50 per night, $1.50 per person per night for more than two people. Major credit cards accepted. Open mid-April–late October.

Directions: In Tonasket on U.S. 97, turn west (left if arriving from south), cross the bridge, and continue to Highway 7. Turn right on Highway 7 and drive about 12 miles to Holmes Road. Turn left (south) on Holmes Road and drive one-half mile to McCammon Road. Turn right (west) and drive one block to the park at the end of the road.

Contact: Spectacle Lake Resort, 10 McCammon Rd., Tonasket, WA 98855, 509/223-3433, website: www.spectaclelakeresort.com.

⑨ RAINBOW RESORT

Rating: 7

On Spectacle Lake.
Map 4.1, grid b4, page 256
This resort on Spectacle Lake is an alternative to Spectacle Lake Resort. Major renovations were completed in late 2000. The camp features pretty lake views and full facilities. Nearby activities include swimming, fishing, hunting, tennis, and horseback riding, including overnight trail rides.

Campsites, facilities: There are 54 sites with full hookups for RVs of any length, including 34 drive-through sites, and 14 tent sites with electricity and water. Picnic tables and fire pits are provided. Restrooms, flush toilets, showers, ice, a recreation room, horseshoes, volleyball, boat docks, boat rentals, and launching facilities are available. Leashed pets are permitted.

Reservations, fees: Reservations accepted. Sites are $23 per night, $2 per person for more than four people. Major credit cards accepted. Senior discount available. Open April–October.

Directions: From Ellisford, turn west on Loomis Highway and drive 9.5 miles to the resort on the left.

Contact: Rainbow Resort, 761 Loomis Hwy., Tonasket, WA 98855, 509/223-3700 or 800/347-4375.

10 SPECTACLE FALLS RESORT

🏃 ≋ 🛶 � 🐕 🚐 🔺

Rating: 8

On Spectacle Lake.
Map 4.1, grid b4, page 256

Spectacle Falls Resort is set on the shore of Spectacle Lake. It is open only as long as fishing is available, which means an early closing in July. Be sure to phone ahead of time to verify that the resort is open. Nearby recreation options include hiking, swimming, fishing, tennis, and horseback riding, including guided trails and overnight rides. Rainbow Resort provides an alternative.

Campsites, facilities: There are 20 drive-through sites with full hookups for RVs of any length, 10 tent sites, and four mobile homes available for rent. Picnic tables are provided. Restrooms, flush toilets, showers, an RV dump station, ice, boat docks, launching facilities, and boat rentals are available. Leashed pets are permitted.

Reservations, fees: Reservations accepted. Sites are $16.50 per night, $2 per person per night for more than two people, $2 per extra vehicle per night. Open mid-April–late July.

Directions: From Tonasket on U.S. 97, turn northwest on Loomis Highway and drive 15 miles to the resort on the left.

Contact: Spectacle Falls Resort, 879 Loomis Hwy., Tonasket, WA 98855, 509/223-4141.

11 LOST LAKE

🏃 ≋ 🛶 🚏 🐕 🚐 🔺

Rating: 7

On Lost Lake in Okanogan National Forest.
Map 4.1, grid b8, page 256

This camp is set on the shore of Lost Lake at an elevation of 3,800 feet. It keeps visitors happy as a launch point for fishing, swimming, hiking, hunting, and horseback riding. Only electric motors are permitted on the lake (that is, no gas motors). The lake is similar to Beth and Beaver Lakes (see Beth Lake and Beaver Lake camp listings), but is rounder. The Big Tree Botanical Area is about one mile away. Note that the group site is often booked one year in advance.

Campsites, facilities: There are 18 single and double sites for tents or RVs up to 31 feet long. There is also one group unit available by reservation only. Picnic tables and fire rings are provided. Drinking water and vault toilets are available. Boat docks and launching facilities are nearby. Leashed pets are permitted.

Reservations, fees: Reservations required for the group site; phone 509/486-2186. Single and multiple sites are $8 per vehicle per night; group rates are $40 for up to 25 people, $60 for 26–50 people, and $80 for 51–100 people. Senior discount available. Open mid-May–mid-September.

Directions: From East Wenatchee, drive north on U.S. 97 for 20 miles to Tonasket and Highway 20. Turn east on Highway 20 and drive 20 miles to Bonaparte Lake Road (County Road 4953). Turn left (north) and drive six miles to Forest Road 32. Turn right (north) and drive three miles to Forest Road 33. Bear left (northwest) and drive three miles to a four-way intersection. Turn left on Forest Road 33-050 and drive three-tenths of a mile to the campground on the right.

Contact: Okanogan and Wenatchee National Forests, Tonasket Ranger District, 1 West Winesap Ave., Tonasket, WA 98855, 509/486-2186, fax 509/486-5161.

1.2 BONAPARTE LAKE

Rating: 7

On Bonaparte Lake in Okanogan
National Forest.

Map 4.1, grid b8, page 256

This campground is located on the southern shore of Bonaparte Lake at an elevation of 3,600 feet. The lake is stocked with rainbow trout, brook trout, and mackinaw trout. See the description of Bonaparte Lake Resort for lake recreation information. Several trails nearby provide access to Mt. Bonaparte Lookout. Consult a U.S. Forest Service map for details.

Campsites, facilities: There are 15 single and 10 multiple sites for tents or RVs up to 31 feet long, three bike-in/hike-in sites (require a walk of less than 100 feet), and one group site that can accommodate up to 30 people. Picnic tables and fire grills are provided. Drinking water and vault toilets are available. An RV dump station, a store, a café, and ice are available within one mile. Boat docks and launching facilities are also available. Some facilities are wheelchair accessible, including a wheelchair-accessible fishing dock. Leashed pets are permitted.

Reservations, fees: Reservations are not accepted. Sites are $8 per night, $8 per extra vehicle. Senior discount available. Open mid-May–mid-September.

Directions: From East Wenatchee, drive north on U.S. 97 for 20 miles to Tonasket and Highway 20. Turn east on Highway 20 and drive 20 miles to Bonaparte Lake Road (County Road 4953). Turn left (north) and drive six miles to Bonaparte Lake and Forest Road 32 and the campground on the left.

Contact: Okanogan and Wenatchee National Forests, Tonasket Ranger District, 1 West Winesap Ave., Tonasket, WA 98855, 509/486-2186, fax 509/486-5161.

1.3 BONAPARTE LAKE RESORT

Rating: 6

On Bonaparte Lake.

Map 4.1, grid b8, page 256

Fishing is popular at this resort, which is set on the southeast shore of Bonaparte Lake. A 10-mph speed limit keeps the lake quiet, ideal for fishing. Other recreational activities include hiking and hunting in the nearby U.S. Forest Service lands and snowmobiling and cross-country skiing in the winter.

Campsites, facilities: There are 35 sites, including many with full hookups and some drive-through sites, for RVs of any length, 10 tent sites, and 10 cabins. Picnic tables are provided. Restrooms, flush toilets, showers, bottled gas, an RV dump station, firewood, a recreation hall, a store, a restaurant, a laundry room, ice, a playground, boat docks, launching facilities, and boat rentals (licensed drivers only) are available. Leashed pets are permitted.

Reservations, fees: Reservations accepted. Sites are $10–18 per night. Open April–October.

Directions: From East Wenatchee, drive north on U.S. 97 for 20 miles to Tonasket and Highway 20. Turn east on Highway 20 and drive 20 miles to Bonaparte Lake Road (County Road 4953). Turn left (north) and drive six miles to Bonaparte Lake and the resort on the left.

Contact: Bonaparte Lake Resort, 615 Bonaparte Rd., Tonasket, WA 98855, 509/486-2828.

1.4 JACK'S RV PARK AND MOTEL

Rating: 5

Near Conconully Reservoir.

Map 4.1, grid d3, page 256

This park is in the town of Conconully, set between Conconully Reservoir and Conconully Lake. Horseshoe pits can be found in the park, and nearby recreation options include hiking trails, fishing, hunting (in season), and water sports (summer and winter) at the lake.

Campsites, facilities: There are 57 sites with full hookups, including 20 drive-through sites, for RVs of any length. Picnic tables are provided. Restrooms, flush toilets, showers, propane gas, a covered barbecue building, and a coin-operated laundry are available. A store, a café, and ice are located within two blocks. Boat docks, launching facilities, and rentals are nearby. A 5-hole putting green is adjacent. Leashed pets are permitted.

Reservations, fees: Reservations accepted. Sites are $18 per night, $2 per person per night for more than two people, and $3 per extra vehicle per night. Major credit cards accepted. Open mid-April–October, weather permitting.

Directions: From U.S. 97 in Okanogan, turn north (left if arriving from the south) on Pine Street/Conconully Highway and drive 17.5 miles northwest to Conconully and Broadway Street. Turn right (east) and drive one block to A Avenue. Turn left (north) on A Avenue and drive less than one block to the park on the right.

Contact: Jack's RV Park and Motel, P.O. Box 98, Conconully, WA 98819, 509/826-0132 or 800/893-5668.

15 LAZY DAZE RV PARK

Rating: 5

Near Conconully Reservoir.
Map 4.1, grid d3, page 256

This park is in downtown Conconully, a short distance from the lake. With its shaded grassy sites, the park is geared specifically toward RVs. Nearby recreational opportunities include hiking, fishing, swimming, boating—and in winter, snowmobiling.

Campsites, facilities: There are 43 drive-through sites with full hookups for RVs of any length. Picnic tables are provided. Restrooms, flush toilets, coin-operated showers, firewood, a coin-operated laundry, and ice are available. Bot-

tled gas, an RV dump station, a store, a café, and ice are located within two blocks. Boat docks, launching facilities, and rentals are nearby. Leashed pets are permitted.

Reservations, fees: Reservations accepted. Sites are $18 per night. Senior discount available. Open April–October, weather permitting.

Directions: From U.S. 97 in Okanogan, turn north (left if arriving from the south) on Pine Street/Conconully Highway and drive 17.5 miles northwest to Conconully and Silver Street. Turn right (east) and drive one block to A Avenue. Turn right (south) on A Avenue and drive about half a block to the park on the right.

Contact: Lazy Daze RV Park, P.O. Box 67, 209 A Ave., Conconully, WA 98819, 509/826-0326.

16 KOZY KABINS AND RV PARK

Rating: 7

Near Conconully Reservoir.
Map 4.1, grid d3, page 256

This quiet and private park in Conconully has a small creek running through it and plenty of greenery. A full-service marina is located close by. If you continue northeast of town on County Road 4015, the road will get a bit narrow for awhile, but will widen again when you enter the Sinlahekin Habitat Management Area, which is managed by the Department of Fish and Game. There are some primitive campsites in this valley, especially along the shores of the lakes in the area.

Campsites, facilities: There are 15 sites with full hookups for RVs up to 40 feet long, six tent sites, and eight cabins. Picnic tables and fire pits are provided. Restrooms, flush toilets, coin-operated showers, and firewood are available. Bottled gas, an RV dump station, a store, a café, a coin-operated laundry, and ice are located within one block. Boat docks, launching facilities, and boat rentals are nearby. Leashed pets are permitted.

Reservations, fees: Reservations accepted. Sites

are $8–16 per night, $2.75 per extra vehicle. Major credit cards accepted. Open year-round.

Directions: From U.S. 97 in Okanogan, turn north (left if arriving from the south) on Pine Street/Conconully Highway and drive 17.5 miles northwest to Conconully and Broadway Street. Turn right (east) and drive one block to A Avenue. The park is at the junction of A Avenue and Broadway.

Contact: Kozy Kabins and RV Park, P.O. Box 82, 111 East Broadway, Conconully, WA 98819, 509/826-6780 or 888/502-2246.

17 MAPLE FLATS RV PARK AND RESORT

Rating: 9

Near Conconully Reservoir.

Map 4.1, grid d3, page 256

This campground near Conconully Reservoir is in a beautiful setting, situated in a valley between two lakes. Nearby recreation options include hiking and biking on the many nature trails in the area, an 18-hole golf course (15 miles away), and trout fishing in the well-stocked Upper and Lower Conconully Reservoirs.

Campsites, facilities: There are 25 drive-through sites with full hookups for RVs of any length, a dispersed camping area with room for six tents, and one apartment with kitchen for rent. Picnic tables and fire pits are provided. Restrooms, flush toilets, showers, a coin-operated laundry, and a covered gazebo with electricity are available. Groceries, dining, dancing, and propane, as well as boat, snowmobile, and jet-ski rentals are located within two blocks. Boat docks and launching facilities are also nearby. Leashed pets are permitted.

Reservations, fees: Reservations accepted. Sites are $13–19 per night, $2 per person for more than two people. Open April–October.

Directions: From U.S. 97 in Okanogan, turn north (left if arriving from the south) on Pine Street/Conconully Highway and drive 17.5 miles

northwest to Conconully and Silver Street. Turn right (east) and drive one block to A Avenue. Turn left (north) on A Avenue and drive to the park on the right.

Contact: Maple Flats RV Park and Resort, P.O. Box 126, 310 A Ave., Conconully, WA 98819, 509/826-4231 (phone or fax) or 800/683-1180, website: www.conconully.com.

18 CONCONULLY STATE PARK

Rating: 9

On Conconully Reservoir.

Map 4.1, grid d3, page 256

This park is considered a fisherman's paradise, with trout, bass, and kokanee salmon. The park is set along Conconully Reservoir and covers 81 acres, with 5,400 feet of shoreline. A boat launch, beach access, swimming, and fishing provide all sorts of water sports possibilities. A half-mile nature trail is available. This park dates to 1910. A side-trip option is to Sinlahekin Habitat Management Area, which is accessible via County Road 4015. This route heads northeast along the shore of Conconully Reservoir on the other side of U.S. 97. The road is narrow at first, but then becomes wider as it enters the Habitat Management Area.

Campsites, facilities: There are 71 sites for tents or self-contained RVs up to 60 feet long and six primitive tent sites. Picnic tables and fire grills are provided. Restrooms, flush toilets, showers, an RV dump station, firewood, and a playground are available. A store, a café, a coin-operated laundry, and ice are located within one mile. Boat-launching and dock facilities are nearby. A picnic area with covered shelter and electricity, horseshoe pits, a baseball field, and interpretive activities are available nearby. Leashed pets are permitted.

Reservations, fees: Reservations are not accepted. Sites are $6–16 per night, $6 per extra vehicle per night. Senior discount available. Open April–September.

Directions: On U.S. 97 at Omak, take the North Omak exit. At the base of the hill, turn right and drive two miles until you reach Conconully Road. Turn right and drive 19 miles north to the park entrance.

Contact: Conconully State Park, P.O. Box 95, Conconully, WA 98819, 509/826-7408; State Park information, 360/902-8844.

19 CONCONULLY RESERVOIR RESORT

Rating: 6

On Upper Conconully Reservoir.
Map 4.1, grid d3, page 256

This resort is one of several set along the shore of Conconully Reservoir. Tents are permitted, but this is a prime vacation destination for RVers. Trout fishing, swimming, and boating are all options here.

Campsites, facilities: There are 11 sites with full hookups for RVs of any length, four cabins, and one apartment. Picnic tables are provided. Restrooms, flush toilets, coin-operated showers, and ice are available. Bottled gas, an RV dump station, a store with tackle, a café, and a coin-operated laundry are located within one mile. Boat docks, launching facilities, and a variety of boat rentals are available. Leashed pets are permitted.

Reservations, fees: Reservations accepted. Sites are $23 per night, $2 per person per night for more than two people. Major credit cards accepted. Open late April–late October.

Directions: From U.S. 97 in Okanogan, turn north (left if arriving from the south) on Pine Street/Conconully Highway and drive 17.5 miles northwest to Conconully and Lake Street. Turn right on Lake Street and drive one mile to the park on the right.

Contact: Conconully Reservoir Resort, P.O. Box 131, 102 Sinlahekin Rd., Conconully, WA 98819, 509/826-0813 or 800/850-0813, fax 509/826-1292, website: www.conconullylakeresort.com.

20 LIAR'S COVE RESORT

Rating: 6

On Conconully Reservoir.
Map 4.1, grid d3, page 256

Roomy sites for RVs can be found at this camp on the shore of Conconully Reservoir. Tents are allowed, too. Fishing, swimming, boating, and hiking opportunities are located nearby.

Campsites, facilities: There are 30 sites with full hookups, including 20 drive-through sites for tents or RVs up to 50 feet long, two cabins, one mobile home, and three motel rooms. Picnic tables and fire pits are provided. Restrooms, flush toilets, coin-operated showers, cable TV, and ice are available. Bottled gas, an RV dump station, a store, and a café are located within one mile. Boat docks, launching facilities, and boat rentals are available. Some facilities are wheelchair accessible. Leashed pets are permitted.

Reservations, fees: Reservations accepted. Sites are $20–21 per night, $2 per person per night for more than two people. Open April–October.

Directions: From U.S. 97 in Okanogan, turn north (left if arriving from the south) on Pine Street/Conconully Highway and drive 16.5 miles northwest to Conconully and look for the park on the left. It's located a quarter mile south of Conconully.

Contact: Liar's Cove Resort, P.O. Box 72, Conconully, WA 98819, 509/826-1288 or 800/830-1288, website: www.omakchronicle.com/liarscove.

21 SHADY PINES RESORT

Rating: 6

On Conconully Reservoir.
Map 4.1, grid d3, page 256

This camp is set on the western shore of Conconully Reservoir. It is near Conconully State Park and provides a possible option if the state park campground is full—a common occurrence in summer. But note that on summer weekends, this camp often fills as well. See the descriptions of Kozy Kabins and RV Park and Conconully State Park for area information.

Campsites, facilities: There are 23 sites for RVs of any length, including 21 sites with full hookups and 14 drive-through sites. Picnic tables and fire rings are provided. Restrooms, flush toilets, coin-operated showers, ice, and firewood are available. Bottled gas, an RV dump station, a store, a café, and a coin-operated laundry are located within one mile. Boat-launching facilities and boat rentals are available. Leashed pets are permitted.

Reservations, fees: Reservations accepted. Sites are $19–21 per night. Major credit cards accepted. Open mid-April–late October.

Directions: From U.S. 97 in Okanogan, turn north (left if arriving from the south) on Pine Street/Conconully Highway and drive 16.5 miles northwest to Conconully and Broadway Street. Turn left (west) and drive one mile. The park is on the west shore of the lake.

Contact: Shady Pines Resort, P.O. Box 44, 125 West Fork Rd., Conconully, WA 98819, 509/826-2287 or 800/552-2287, website: www.shady pinesresort.com.

22 SUGARLOAF

Rating: 6

On Sugarloaf Lake in Okanogan National Forest.
Map 4.1, grid d3, page 256

Sugarloaf Lake is a small lake, about 20 acres, and this small camp is set near its shore. It provides fishing for rainbow trout, but the lake level often drops during summer, so this camp gets little use in late summer and early fall. Conconully State Park and Information Center are nearby.

Campsites, facilities: There are five tent sites and one site for a tent, trailer, or RV up to 21 feet long. Picnic tables are provided, but there

is no drinking water. No garbage service is provided, so trash must be packed out. Vault toilets and firewood are available. Boat-launching facilities are available nearby. No boats with gas motors are permitted. Leashed pets are permitted.

Reservations, fees: Reservations are not accepted. Sites are $5 per night, $5 per extra vehicle per night. Senior discount available. Open mid-May–mid-September.

Directions: From East Wenatchee, drive north on U.S. 97 for 88 miles to Okanogan and County Road 9229. Turn north and drive about 17.5 miles northwest to Conconully and County Road 4015. Turn right (northwest) on County Road 4015 and drive 4.5 miles to the campground on the left.

Contact: Okanogan and Wenatchee National Forests, Tonasket Ranger District, 1 West Winesap Ave., Tonasket, WA 98855, 509/486-2186, fax 509/486-5161.

23 ROCK LAKES

Rating: 8

On Rock Lake.
Map 4.1, grid e3, page 256

This camp is set in a forested area along the shore of Rock Lake. Fishing for rainbow trout and brook trout is a plus at Rock Lake. A downer is that access for launching even cartop boats is difficult, requiring a quarter-mile hike. That makes it a better bet for float tubes. Note that the best fishing is early in the season and that the lake level often drops because of irrigation use. Some roads in the area are used by hikers and bikers. A good bet is to combine a trip here with nearby Leader Lake. Highway 20 east of I-5 is a designated scenic route.

Campsites, facilities: There are eight sites for tents or small RVs. Picnic tables and fire pits are provided. Vault toilets are available, but there is no drinking water. Leashed pets are permitted.

Reservations, fees: Reservations are not accepted. There is no fee for camping. Open year-round.

Directions: From East Wenatchee, drive north on U.S. 97 for 88 miles to Okanogan and Highway 20. Turn west and drive 10 miles to Loup Loup Canyon Road. Turn left on Loup Loup Canyon Road and drive 4.8 miles to Rock Lakes Road. Turn left on Rock Lakes Road and drive 5.8 miles to the campground entrance. Turn left and drive quarter mile to the campground.

Contact: Department of Natural Resources, Northeast Region, P.O. Box 190, Colville, WA 99114-0190, 509/684-7474, fax 509/684-7484.

24 ROCK CREEK

Rating: 6

On Rock Creek and Loup Loup Creek.
Map 4.1, grid e3, page 256

This wooded campground is situated at the confluence of Rock and Loup Loup Creeks. A group picnic shelter with a barbecue is available. The camp is used primarily in the fall as a base camp for hunters and occasionally during the summer, mostly on weekends. It's advisable to obtain a map detailing the area from the Department of Natural Resources.

Campsites, facilities: There are six sites for tents or RVs up to 30 feet long. Picnic tables and fire pits are provided. Vault toilets, a picnic area, and drinking water are available. Leashed pets are permitted.

Reservations, fees: Reservations are not accepted. There is no fee for camping. Open year-round.

Directions: From East Wenatchee, drive north on U.S. 97 for 88 miles to Okanogan and Highway 20. Turn west and drive 10 miles to Loup Loup Canyon Road. Turn left on Loup Loup Canyon Road and drive 3.9 miles to the camp on the left.

Contact: Department of Natural Resources, Northeast Region, P.O. Box 190, Colville, WA 99114-0190, 509/684-7474, fax 509/684-7484.

25 LEADER LAKE

Rating: 7

On Leader Lake.
Map 4.1, grid f3, page 256

This primitive but pretty camp is set along the shore of Leader Lake. It is just far enough off the beaten path to get missed by many travelers. The camp has forest cover. The boat ramp is a bonus, and trout fishing can be good in season. Note that the water level often drops in summer because of irrigation use.

Campsites, facilities: There are 16 sites for tents or small RVs. Picnic tables and fire pits are provided. Vault toilets, a boat ramp, and a fishing pier are available, but there is no drinking water. Boat-launching facilities are nearby. Leashed pets are permitted.

Reservations, fees: Reservations are not accepted. There is no fee for camping. Open year-round.

Directions: From East Wenatchee, drive north on U.S. 97 for 88 miles to Okanogan and Highway 20. Turn west and drive eight miles to Leader Lake Road. Turn left and drive four-tenths of a mile to the campground.

Contact: Department of Natural Resources, Northeast Region, P.O. Box 190, Colville, WA 99114-0190, 509/684-7474, fax 509/684-7484.

26 AMERICAN LEGION PARK

Rating: 6

On the Okanogan River.
Map 4.1, grid f4, page 256

This city park is located along the shore of the Okanogan River in an urban setting. The sites are graveled and sunny. Anglers may want to try their hand at the excellent bass fishing here. There is a historical museum at the park.

Campsites, facilities: There are 35 sites for tents or RVs of any length. No hookups. Picnic tables are provided. Restrooms, drinking water, flush toilets, and coin-operated showers are available. A store, a café, a coin-operated laundry, and ice are located within one mile. Leashed pets are permitted.

Reservations, fees: Reservations are not accepted. Sites are $3–5 per vehicle per night. Open May–October, weather permitting.

Directions: From East Wenatchee, drive north on U.S. 97 for 88 miles to Okanogan and Highway 215. Turn left (north) on Highway 215 and drive about three miles to the campground on the right.

Contact: Okanogan City Hall, P.O. Box 752, Okanogan, WA 98840, 509/422-3600, fax 509/422-0747.

27 EASTSIDE PARK AND CARL PRECHT MEMORIAL RV PARK

Rating: 6

On the Okanogan River.
Map 4.1, grid e4, page 256

This city park is in the town of Omak, along the shore of the Okanogan River. It covers about 10 acres and features campsites positioned on concrete pads surrounded by grass. Trout fishing is often good here, and there is a boat ramp near the campground. Nearby recreation options include an 18-hole golf course, a pool, and a sports field.

Campsites, facilities: There are 76 drive-through sites with full hookups for RVs of any length and 25 tent sites. Picnic tables are provided. Restrooms, flush toilets, coin-operated showers, an RV dump station, a swimming pool, a playground with horseshoe pits, a skateboarding park, and a fitness trail are available. A store, a café, a coin-operated laundry, and ice are located within one mile. Boat-launching facilities are nearby. Some facilities are wheelchair accessible. Leashed pets are permitted.

Reservations, fees: Reservations are not accepted. Sites are $14 per night. Open April–September, weather permitting.

Directions: From U.S. 97 in Omak, turn east (right, if coming from the south) on Highway

155 and drive three-tenths of a mile to the campground on the left.

Contact: City of Omak, P.O. Box 72, Omak, WA 98841, 509/826-1170, fax 509/826-6531.

28 LYMAN LAKE

Rating: 5

On Lyman Lake in Okanogan National Forest.
Map 4.1, grid d8, page 256

Little known and little used, this campground along the shore of Lyman Lake is an idyllic spot for those wanting solitude and quiet. The lake is quite small, just five acres at most, but fishing for stocked rainbow trout is an option.

Campsites, facilities: There are four sites for tents or RVs up to 31 feet long. Picnic tables and fire grills are provided. Vault toilets are available, but there is no drinking water. Garbage must be packed out. Leashed pets are permitted.

Reservations, fees: Reservations are not accepted. There is no fee for camping. Open mid-May–mid-September.

Directions: From East Wenatchee, drive north on U.S. 97 for 119 miles to Tonasket and Highway 20. Turn east on Highway 20 and drive 12.5 miles to County Road 9455. Turn right (southeast) on County Road 9455 and drive 13 miles to County Road 3785. Turn right (south) on County Road 3785 and drive 2.5 miles to the campground entrance on the right.

Contact: Okanogan and Wenatchee National Forests, 1 West Winesap Ave., Tonasket, WA 98855, 509/486-2186, fax 509/486-5161.

29 CRAWFISH LAKE

Rating: 8

On Crawfish Lake in Okanogan National Forest.
Map 4.1, grid e7, page 256

This pretty, remote, and primitive camp is set at 4,500 feet elevation along the shore of

Crawfish Lake. Crawdads were once abundant here, but overfishing has depleted their numbers. Swimming and fishing for trout are more popular.

Campsites, facilities: There are 19 sites for tents or RVs up to 31 feet long. Picnic tables and fire grills are provided. Vault toilets are available, but there is no drinking water. No garbage service is provided, so trash must be packed out. Boat-launching facilities are located on the lake. Leashed pets are permitted.

Reservations, fees: Reservations are not accepted. There is no fee for camping. Open mid-May–mid-September.

Directions: From East Wenatchee, drive north on U.S. 97 for 102 miles to Riverside and County Road 9320. Turn right (east) on County Road 9320 and drive 20 miles (becomes Forest Road 30) to Forest Road 30-100. Turn right and drive one-half mile to the campground on the right.

Contact: Okanogan and Wenatchee National Forests, Tonasket Ranger District, 1 West Winesap Ave., Tonasket, WA 98855, 509/486-2186, fax 509/486-5161.

30 ALTA LAKE STATE PARK

Rating: 8

On Alta Lake.
Map 4.1, grid h1, page 256

This state park is nestled among the pines along the shore of Alta Lake. The park covers 181 acres, and the lake is two miles long and one-half mile wide. Alta Lake brightens a region where the mountains and pines meet the desert and features good trout fishing in summer, along with a boat launch and a half-mile-long swimming beach. Windsurfing is often excellent on windy afternoons. Because of many hidden rocks just under the lake surface, it can be dangerous for water-skiing. An 18-hole golf course and a riding stable are close by, and a nice one-mile hiking trail leads up to a scenic lookout. Lake Chelan is about 30 minutes away.

Campsites, facilities: There are 157 developed tent sites, 32 sites with partial hookups (water and electricity) for RVs up to 40 feet long, and a group site for 20–88 people. Picnic tables and fire grills are provided. Restrooms, flush toilets, showers, electricity, firewood, and an RV dump station are available. A picnic area with a shelter is available nearby. A store, a café, and ice can be found within one mile. Some facilities are wheelchair accessible. Boat-launching facilities are nearby. Leashed pets are permitted.

Reservations, fees: Reservations are not accepted for family sites. Sites are $6–22 per night, $2 per person for more than two people, and $6 per extra vehicle per night. Senior discount available. Group reservations required at 509/923-2473; $25 reservation fee, $2 per person per night. Open April–October.

Directions: From East Wenatchee, drive north on U.S. 97 for 64 miles to Highway 153 (just south of Pateros). Turn left (northwest) on Highway 153 and drive two miles to Alta Lake Road. Turn left (southwest) and drive two miles to the park at the end of the road.

Contact: Alta Lake State Park, 509/923-2473; State Park information, 360/902-8844.

31 BRIDGEPORT STATE PARK

Rating: 8

On Rufus Woods Lake.
Map 4.1, grid h4, page 256

Bridgeport State Park is located along the shore of Rufus Woods Lake, a reservoir on the Columbia River above Chief Joseph Dam. It's a big place, covering 748 acres, including 7,500 feet of shoreline and 18 acres of lawn, with some shade amid the desert landscape. Highlights include beach access and a boat launch. A unique feature, the "haystacks," which are unusual volcanic formations that resemble their name, stand out as the park's most striking characteristic. Fishing is best by boat because shore fishing requires a Colville

Tribe Fishing License (for sale at the Bridgeport Hardware Store), in addition to a state fishing license. The lake has plenty of rainbow trout and walleye. A half-mile walking trail is available out of camp. Windsurfing in the afternoon wind and water-skiing are popular at the lake. Nearby recreation options include an 18-hole golf course.

Campsites, facilities: There are 14 sites for tents or self-contained RVs and 20 sites with water and electrical hookups for RVs up to 45 feet long. Picnic tables and fire grills are provided. Restrooms, flush toilets, coin-operated showers, firewood, a picnic area, and an RV dump station are available. A store, a café, and ice are located within two miles. Boat docks and launching facilities are nearby on both the upper and lower portions of the reservoir. Interpretive programs are available in summer. Leashed pets are permitted.

Reservations, fees: Reservations are not accepted. Sites are $16–22 per night. Reservations required for groups. Senior discount available. Open April–October.

Directions: From East Wenatchee, drive north on U.S. 97 for 71 miles to Highway 17. Turn south on Highway 17 and drive eight miles southeast to the park entrance on the left.

Contact: Bridgeport State Park, P.O. Box 846, Bridgeport, WA 98813, 509/686-7231; State Park information, 360/902-8844.

32 BETH LAKE

Rating: 7

On Beth Lake in Okanogan National Forest.
Map 4.2, grid b1, page 257

This campground is set between Beth Lake and Beaver Lake, both small, narrow lakes stocked with rainbow trout and brook trout. The elevation is 2,800 feet. A 1.9-mile-long hiking trail (one-way) connects the two lakes. Other side trips in the area include Lost Lake, Bonaparte Lake, and several hiking trails, one of which leads up to the Mt. Bonaparte Lookout.

Campsites, facilities: There are 15 sites for tents or RVs up to 31 feet long, plus one multiple site. Picnic tables and fire rings are provided. Drinking water and vault toilets are available. Boat-launching facilities are available nearby. Some facilities are wheelchair accessible. Leashed pets are permitted.

Reservations, fees: Reservations are not accepted. Sites are $6 per vehicle per night. Senior discount available. Open mid-May–mid-September.

Directions: From East Wenatchee, drive north on U.S. 97 for 20 miles to Tonasket and Highway 20. Turn east on Highway 20 and drive 20 miles to Bonaparte Lake Road (County Road 4953). Turn left (north) and drive six miles to Bonaparte Lake and Forest Road 32. Bear right (north) and drive six miles to County Road 9480. Turn left (northwest) and drive one mile to the campground on the left.

Contact: Okanogan and Wenatchee National Forests, Tonasket Ranger District, 1 West Winesap Ave., Tonasket, WA 98855, 509/486-2186, fax 509/486-5161.

33 BEAVER LAKE

Rating: 7

On Beaver Lake in Okanogan National Forest.
Map 4.2, grid b1, page 257

This camp calls the southeastern shore of long, narrow Beaver Lake home. Situated at 2,700 feet elevation, it is one of several lakes in this area. Beth Lake, the previous listing, is nearby and accessible with an hour-long hike. The lake is stocked with trout. Fishing, swimming, hunting, and hiking are all possibilities here. See the descriptions for Beth Lake, Lost Lake, and Bonaparte Lake for information on the other lakes in the area.

Campsites, facilities: There are nine single and two multiple sites for tents or RVs up to 21 feet long. Picnic tables are provided. Vault toilets are available. No drinking water is available. Boat-launching facilities are located within 100 yards of the campground. No boats with gas engines are permitted. Leashed pets are permitted.

Reservations, fees: Reservations are not accepted. Sites are $6 per vehicle per night. Senior discount available. Open mid-May–mid-September.

Directions: From East Wenatchee, drive north on U.S. 97 for 20 miles to Tonasket and Highway 20. Turn east on Highway 20 and drive 20 miles to Bonaparte Lake Road (County Road 4953). Turn left (north) and drive six miles to Bonaparte Lake and Forest Road 32. Bear right (north) and drive six miles to the campground on the left.

Contact: Okanogan and Wenatchee National Forests, Tonasket Ranger District, 1 West Winesap Ave., Tonasket, WA 98855, 509/486-2186, fax 509/486-5161.

34 CURLEW LAKE STATE PARK

Rating: 8

On Curlew Lake.

Map 4.2, grid c3, page 257

Boredom is banned at this park, which is set on the eastern shore of Curlew Lake. The park covers 123 acres, and the lake is 5.5 miles long. Fishing is often good for trout and large-mouth bass at the lake, and there are additional fishable lakes and streams in the immediate region. There is also beach access, swimming, water-skiing, and hiking, with two miles of hiking and biking trails in the park. The park is also used as a base for bicycle tour groups, with mountain biking available on a fairly steep trail that provides a view of the valley. An active osprey nest can be viewed from the park. Nearby recreation options include an 18-hole golf course. The park borders an air field and is located in the heart of a historic gold-mining district.

Campsites, facilities: There are 25 sites with full or partial hookups for RVs up to 40 feet long, 57 developed tent sites, and five primitive tent sites. Picnic tables are provided.

Restrooms, flush toilets, showers, an RV dump station, electricity, drinking water, sewer hookups, firewood, and boat-launching and dock facilities are available. Boat fuel is available at the marina. An amphitheater with interpretive activities is available nearby. Leashed pets are permitted.

Reservations, fees: Reservations are not accepted. Sites are $6–22 per night, $6 per extra vehicle per night. Senior discount available. Open April–October.

Directions: From Spokane on I-90, turn north on U.S. 395 and drive 87 miles to Colville and Highway 20. Turn west on Highway 20 and continue 34 miles to Highway 21 (two miles east of Republic). Turn north and drive 7.5 miles to the park entrance on the left.

Contact: Curlew Lake State Park, 509/775-3592; State Park information, 360/902-8844, fax 509/775-0822.

35 TIFFANYS RESORT

Rating: 7

On Curlew Lake.

Map 4.2, grid c3, page 257

Tiffanys Resort is located in a pretty, wooded setting along the western shore of Curlew Lake. This 6.5-mile-long lake is good for water-skiing. Fishing can be good for rainbow trout and largemouth bass. Most of the sites are fairly spacious. This is a smaller, more private alternative to Blacks Beach Resort.

Campsites, facilities: There are 15 sites with full hookups for RVs of any length and four tent sites. Picnic tables and fire pits are provided. Restrooms, flush toilets, showers, firewood, a store, a coin-operated laundry, ice, a playground, and a swimming beach are available. Boat docks, launching facilities, and rentals are available. Leashed pets are permitted.

Reservations, fees: Reservations accepted. Sites are $18–19 per night, $4 per person for more than two people. Major credit cards accepted. Open April–late October.

Directions: From Colville, drive west on Highway 20 for 36 miles into the town of Republic and Klondike Road. Turn right on Klondike Road and drive 10.2 miles (Klondike Road will turn into West Curlew Lake Road) to Tiffany Road. Turn right and drive one-half mile to the resort at the end of the road.

Contact: Tiffanys Resort, 58 Tiffany Rd., Republic, WA 99166, 509/775-3152, website: www.tiffanysresort.com.

36 BLACKS BEACH RESORT

Rating: 7

On Curlew Lake.
Map 4.2, grid c3, page 257

Here's another resort along Curlew Lake. This one is much larger, with beautiful waterfront sites and full facilities. Water-skiing, swimming, and fishing are all options.

Campsites, facilities: There are 120 sites with full hookups, including 60 drive-through sites, for RVs of any length, nine tent sites, and 13 lodging units. Picnic tables and fire pits are provided. Restrooms, flush toilets, coin-operated showers, an RV dump station, a store, a coin-operated laundry, ice, and a playground are available. Boat docks, launching facilities, and rentals are located at the resort. Leashed pets are permitted.

Reservations, fees: Reservations accepted. Sites are $15–19.50 per night, $3 per person for more than four people. Major credit cards accepted. Campground open April–October; two campsites and three cabins are available in winter.

Directions: From Colville, drive west on Highway 20 for 34 miles to Highway 21 (two miles east of Republic). Turn north and drive eight miles to West Curlew Lake Road. Turn right (north) on West Curlew Lake Road and continue for one mile to the resort on the lake.

Contact: Blacks Beach Resort, 80 Black Beach Rd., Republic, WA 99166, 509/775-3989 (phone or fax), website: www.blackbeachresort.com.

37 PIERRE LAKE

Rating: 8

On Pierre Lake in Colville National Forest.
Map 4.2, grid a7, page 257

Pierre Lake, just 105 acres, is a quiet jewel of a camp near the Canadian border. It's only a short drive from U.S. 395, yet the campground gets relatively little use. The camp is set on the west shore of the lake. It is popular and usually fills on summer weekends. The lake has fishing for rainbow trout, cutthroat trout, brook trout, crappie, bass, and catfish. While there is no speed limit, the lake is too small for big, fast boats.

Campsites, facilities: There are 15 sites for tents or RVs up to 24 feet long. Picnic tables and fire grills are provided. Vault toilets are available. No drinking water is available. Garbage must be packed out. Boat docks and launching facilities are available on-site. Some facilities are wheelchair accessible. A convenience store and ice are located within seven miles. Leashed pets are permitted.

Reservations, fees: Reservations are not accepted. Sites are $6 per night. Senior discount available. Open mid-April–mid-October.

Directions: From Spokane, drive north on U.S. 395 for 74 miles to Colville. Continue north on U.S. 395 for about 25 miles to Barstow and Pierre Lake Round (County Road 4013). Turn right (north) on Pierre Lake Road and drive nine miles to the campground on the west side of Pierre Lake.

Contact: Colville National Forest, Three Rivers Ranger District, 255 West 11th St., Kettle Falls, WA 99141, 509/738-6111, fax 509/738-7701.

38 DAVIS LAKE

Rating: 8

On Davis Lake, in Colville National Forest.
Map 4.2, grid c7, page 257

This tiny campground is set at 4,600 feet elevation at Little Davis Lake. It is a scenic spot, and the fishing for cutthroat trout is often good. Only small boats are permitted on the small, shallow lake, which covers just 17 acres. No gas motors are permitted, but it can be ideal for float tubes, canoes, and prams with electric motors or oars. A one-mile trail loops the lake.

Campsites, facilities: There are four sites for tents or small RVs. Picnic tables and fire grills are provided. Vault toilets are available. No drinking water is available. Garbage must be packed out. Some facilities are wheelchair accessible. Leashed pets are permitted.

Reservations, fees: Reservations are not accepted. There is no fee for camping. Open April–November, weather permitting.

Directions: From Spokane, drive north on U.S. 395 for 84 miles to Kettle Falls. Continue north on U.S. 395 for nine miles to Deadman Creek Road. Turn west on Deadman Creek Road and drive about three miles to County Road 465 (Jack Knife cutoff). Turn right and drive 2.5 miles. Bear right and drive about one-half mile to County Road 480. Turn left and drive about three miles to County Road 080. Turn right and drive about three miles to Davis Lake. Note: The access road is very rough; high-clearance vehicles are recommended.

Contact: Colville National Forest, Three Rivers Ranger District, Kettle Falls, 255 West 11th St., WA 99141, 509/738-6111, fax 509/738-7701.

39 NORTH GORGE

Rating: 7

On Franklin Roosevelt Lake in Lake Roosevelt National Recreation Area.
Map 4.2, grid b8, page 257
This is the first and northernmost of many campgrounds we discovered along the shore of 130-mile-long Franklin Roosevelt Lake, which was formed by damming the Columbia River at Coulee. This camp is set on the west shore, near the Coulee Dam National Recreation Area to the nearby south. Recreation

options include water-skiing and swimming, plus fishing for walleye, trout, bass, and sunfish. During the winter, the lake level lowers; for a unique trip, walk along the lake's barren edge. Note that this campground provides full facilities from May 1 through September 30, then limited facilities in the off-season. See the description of Spring Canyon for more recreation information.

Campsites, facilities: There are 10 sites for tents or RVs up to 26 feet long. Picnic tables and fire grills are provided. Drinking water, vault toilets, boat docks, and launching facilities are available. Some facilities are wheelchair accessible. Note that if the lake level drops below an elevation of 1,272 feet, there is no drinking water. Leashed pets are permitted.

Reservations, fees: Reservations are not accepted. Sites are $10 per night ($5 per night in off-season), and a $6 boat-launch fee. Senior discount available. Open year-round.

Directions: From Spokane on I-90, drive north on U.S. 395 for 84 miles to the town of Kettle Falls and Highway 25. Turn right (north) on Highway 25 and drive 20 miles to the campground entrance.

Contact: Lake Roosevelt National Recreation Area, 1008 Crest Dr., Coulee Dam, WA 99116-1259, 509/633-9441, fax 509/633-9332.

40 SNAG COVE

Rating: 8

On Franklin Roosevelt Lake in Lake Roosevelt National Recreation Area.
Map 4.2, grid c8, page 257
Snag Cove has a setting similar to North Gorge campground (see previous listing). It is set amid Ponderosa pines along the west shore of Franklin Roosevelt Lake, near the Coulee Dam National Recreation Area to the nearby north. This small camp has just nine sites, but the nearby boat launch makes it a find.

Campsites, facilities: There are nine sites for tents or RVs up to 26 feet long. Picnic tables and fire grills are provided. Vault toilets are available. When the lake level drops, there is no drinking water. Some facilities are wheelchair accessible. Boat-launching facilities and docks are nearby. Leashed pets are permitted.

Reservations, fees: Reservations are not accepted. Sites are $5–10 per night; there is a $6 boat-launch fee. Senior discount available. Open year-round, weather permitting.

Directions: From Spokane, turn north on U.S. 395 and drive 84 miles to the town of Kettle Falls. Continue north on U.S. 395 (crossing the Columbia River) for seven miles to the Hedlund Bridge turnoff. Turn right, cross Hedlund Bridge, and drive 7.5 miles to the campground on the right.

Contact: Lake Roosevelt National Recreation Area, 1008 Crest Dr., Coulee Dam, WA 99116-1259, 509/633-9441, fax 509/633-9332.

41 EVANS

Rating: 9

On Franklin Roosevelt Lake in Lake Roosevelt National Recreation Area.

Map 4.2, grid c8, page 257

This campground is another in a series set along the shore of Franklin Roosevelt Lake. This one sits along the eastern shoreline, just south of the town of Evans. Fishing, swimming, and water-skiing are among the activities here. See the description of Spring Canyon for more information.

Campsites, facilities: There are 46 sites for tents or RVs up to 26 feet long and one group site for up to 25 people. Picnic tables and fire grills are provided. Drinking water and flush toilets are available. A boat dock, launch facilities, an RV dump station, and a picnic area are available nearby. Some facilities are wheelchair accessible. Leashed pets are permitted.

Reservations, fees: Reservations are not accepted for family sites; reservations for group site required at 509/633-3860. Sites are $5–10

per night; there is a $6 launch fee. Open year-round, with limited facilities in the winter.

Directions: From Spokane on I-90, drive north on U.S. 395 for 84 miles to the town of Kettle Falls and Highway 25. Turn right (north) on Highway 25 and drive eight miles to the campground entrance on the left.

Contact: Lake Roosevelt National Recreation Area, 1008 Crest Dr., Coulee Dam, WA 99116-1259, 509/633-9441, fax 509/633-9332.

42 WHISPERING PINES RV RESORT & CAMPGROUND

Rating: 7

On Franklin Roosevelt Lake.

Map 4.2, grid c7, page 257

This campground is set along the long, narrow Kettle River Arm of Franklin Roosevelt Lake. A country resort, it is usually quiet and peaceful. A highlight is easy access to the lake. There is no steep walk like at so many other campgrounds at this lake. A one-mile loop nature trail is available along the lake shore, where wild turkeys and deer are often spotted. It's close to marked bike trails, a full-service marina, and tennis courts. Riding stables are available 20 miles away, and a golf course is within 15 miles. A good side trip is to Colville National Forest East Portal Interpretive Area, 10 miles away. (Drive south to the junction of Highway 20 and continue southwest for about six miles.) Highlights include a nature trail and the Bangs Mountain auto tour, a five-mile drive that takes you through old-growth forest to Bangs Mountain Vista overlooking the Roosevelt Lake-Kettle Falls area.

Campsites, facilities: There are 42 sites with full hookups, including 40 drive-through sites, for tents or RVs of any length, 15 tent sites, two cabins, three rental trailers, and two motel rooms with kitchens. An overflow camping area is also available. Picnic tables and fire grills are provided. Restrooms, drinking water, flush toilets, coin-operated showers, an RV dump station, a coin-operated laundry, a playground with horseshoe pits and volleyball, modem hookups, a store, and firewood are available. Lake swimming and fishing are onsite. Leashed pets are permitted. A restaurant is available within five miles.

Reservations, fees: Reservations accepted. Sites are $13–22 per night, $1 per person per night for more than four people. Weekly and monthly rates are available. Open year-round.

Directions: From Spokane, turn north on U.S. 395 and drive 84 miles to the town of Kettle Falls. Continue north on U.S. 395 for 6.5 miles (toward Canada) to the campground entrance road on the right. Turn east at the sign for the campground and drive 300 yards to the camp on the right.

Contact: Whispering Pines RV Resort and Campground, Roosevelt Rd., Kettle Falls, WA 99141, 509/738-2593 (phone or fax) or 800/597-4423.

43 KETTLE RIVER

Rating: 7

On Franklin Roosevelt Lake in Lake Roosevelt National Recreation Area.

Map 4.2, grid c7, page 257

This campground is set along the long, narrow Kettle River Arm of Franklin Roosevelt Lake, and features campsites amid Ponderosa pines. If the lake level drops below an elevation of 1,272 feet, there is no drinking water. The nearest boat launch is located at Napoleon Bridge.

Campsites, facilities: There are 13 sites for tents or RVs up to 16 feet long. Picnic tables and fire grills are provided. Vault toilets are available. When the lake level drops, there is no drinking water. Some facilities are wheelchair accessible. Boat docks are nearby. Leashed pets are permitted.

Reservations, fees: Reservations are not accepted. Sites are $5–10 per night. Senior discount available. Open year-round, weather permitting.

Directions: From Spokane, turn north on U.S. 395 and drive 84 miles to the town of Kettle Falls. Continue north on U.S. 395 (crossing the Columbia River) for seven miles to the campground on the right.

Contact: Lake Roosevelt National Recreation Area, 1008 Crest Dr., Coulee Dam, WA 99116-1259, 509/633-9441, fax 509/633-9332.

44 KAMLOOPS ISLAND

Rating: 10

On Franklin Roosevelt Lake in Lake Roosevelt National Recreation Area.

Map 4.2, grid c8, page 257

This is one of the more primitive campgrounds located along Franklin Roosevelt Lake. Located at Kamloops Island, an optimum area for water-skiing and fishing, it features unbelievably beautiful views of water and mountains. It is located near the mouth of the Kettle River Arm of the lake. While the scenic beauty merits a 10, note that the nearest boat launch is way across the lake at Kettle Falls and that if the lake level drops below an elevation of 1,272 feet, there is no drinking water.

Campsites, facilities: There are 17 tent sites. Picnic tables and fire grills are provided. Vault toilets are available. When the lake level drops, there is no drinking water. Some facilities are wheelchair accessible. Boat docks are nearby. Leashed pets are permitted.

Reservations, fees: Reservations are not accepted. Sites are $5–10 per night. Senior discount available. Open year-round, weather permitting.

Directions: From Spokane, turn north on U.S. 395 and drive 84 miles to the town of Kettle Falls. Continue north on U.S. 395 (crossing the Columbia River) for seven miles to the Hedlund Bridge turnoff. Turn right, cross Hedlund Bridge, and drive to the campground on the left.

Contact: Lake Roosevelt National Recreation Area, 1008 Crest Dr., Coulee Dam, WA 99116-1259, 509/633-9441, fax 509/633-9332.

45 MARCUS ISLAND

Rating: 8

**On Franklin Roosevelt Lake in Lake
Roosevelt National Recreation Area.**
Map 4.2, grid c8, page 257

This campground, located south of Evans camp on the eastern shore of Franklin Roosevelt Lake, is quite similar to that camp. Water-skiing, fishing, and swimming are the primary recreation options. See the description of Spring Canyon for information about the park and side-trip options in the area.

Campsites, facilities: There are 20 sites for tents or RVs up to 20 feet long. Picnic tables and fire grills are provided. Drinking water, vault toilets, and a picnic area are available. A boat launch and dock are available nearby. Some facilities are wheelchair accessible. Note that if the lake level drops below an elevation of 1,272 feet, there is no drinking water. A store is located within one mile. Leashed pets are permitted.

Reservations, fees: Reservations are not accepted. Sites are $5–10 per night; boat-launching is $6 per boat, good for seven days. Senior discount available. Open year-round, weather permitting.

Directions: From Spokane on I-90, drive north on U.S. 395 for 84 miles to the town of Kettle Falls and Highway 25. Turn right (north) on Highway 25 and drive four miles to the campground entrance on the left.

Contact: Lake Roosevelt National Recreation Area, 1008 Crest Dr., Coulee Dam, WA 99116-1259, 509/633-9441, fax 509/633-9332.

46 KETTLE FALLS

Rating: 8

**On Franklin Roosevelt Lake in Lake
Roosevelt National Recreation Area.**
Map 4.2, grid d7, page 257

This campground only fills occasionally. It's located along the eastern shore of Roosevelt Lake, about two miles south of the highway bridge near West Kettle Falls. In the summer, the rangers offer campfire programs in the evenings. Water-skiing, swimming, and fishing are all options. Local side trips include St. Paul's Mission in Kettle Falls, which was built in 1846 and is one of the oldest churches in Washington.

Campsites, facilities: There are 77 sites for tents or RVs up to 26 feet long and two group sites, one for up to 50 people and one for up to 75 people. Picnic tables and fire grills are provided. Restrooms, drinking water, flush toilets, showers, an RV dump station, firewood, a small marina with a store, and a playground are available. A store is located within one mile. Some facilities are wheelchair accessible. Boat docks, fuel, and launching facilities are available. Leashed pets are permitted.

Reservations, fees: Reservations are not accepted for family sites; reservations required for group sites at 509/633-3860. Sites are $5–10 per night; there is a $6 boat-launch fee. Senior discount available. Major credit cards accepted. Open year-round, with limited facilities in winter.

Directions: From Spokane, drive north on U.S. 395 for 84 miles to the town of Kettle Falls. Continue on U.S. 395 for three miles to Kettle Park Road on the left. Turn left and drive two miles to the campground on the right.

Contact: Lake Roosevelt National Recreation Area, 1008 Crest Dr., Coulee Dam, WA 99116-1259, 509/633-9441, fax 509/633-9332.

47 HAAG COVE

Rating: 8

**On Franklin Roosevelt Lake in Lake
Roosevelt National Recreation Area.**
Map 4.2, grid d7, page 257

This campground is tucked away in a cove along the western shore of Franklin Roosevelt Lake (Columbia River), about two miles south of Highway 20. A good side trip is to the Sherman Creek Habitat Management Area, located just north of camp. It's rugged and steep, but a good place to see and photograph wildlife, including bald eagles, golden eagles, and 200 other species of birds, along with the occasional black bear, cougar, and moose. Note that no boat launch is available at this camp, but boat ramps are available at Kettle Falls and French Rock. Also note that no drinking water is available if the lake level drops below an elevation of 1,275 feet.

Campsites, facilities: There are 18 sites for tents or RVs up to 26 feet long. Picnic tables and fire grills are provided. Drinking water and vault toilets are available. Boat docks are available nearby. Leashed pets are permitted.

Reservations, fees: Reservations are not accepted. Sites are $5–10 per night. Senior discount available. Open year-round, weather permitting.

Directions: From Spokane, drive north on U.S. 395 for 84 miles to the town of Kettle Falls and Highway 20. Continue on Highway 20 and drive 7.5 miles to Kettle Falls Road. Turn left (south) and drive two miles to the campground on the right.

Contact: Lake Roosevelt National Recreation Area, 1008 Crest Dr., Coulee Dam, WA 99116-1259, 509/633-9441, fax 509/633-9332.

48 TROUT LAKE

Rating: 8

On Trout Lake in Colville National Forest.
Map 4.2, grid d7, page 257

Trout Lake is a little lake, just eight acres, and is set at an elevation of 3,100 feet. It provides fishing for rainbow trout, with prospects similar to that of Davis Lake. No gas motors are permitted, but electric motors are allowed on small boats. The nearby, five-mile-long Hoodoo Canyon Trail, accessible for hiking or biking, offers spectacular views.

Campsites, facilities: There are four tent sites.

Picnic tables and fire pits are provided. Vault toilets are available. No drinking water is available. Garbage must be packed out. Some facilities are wheelchair accessible. Leashed pets are permitted.

Reservations, fees: Reservations are not accepted. There is no fee for camping. Open April–November, weather permitting.

Directions: From Spokane, turn north on U.S. 395 and drive 87 miles to Colville and Highway 20. Turn west on Highway 20 and drive 15 miles (crossing the Columbia River) to Trout Lake Road (Forest Road 020). Turn right on Trout Lake Road and drive five miles to the campground at the end of the road.

Contact: Colville National Forest, Three Rivers Ranger District, 255 West 11th St., Kettle Falls, WA 99141, 509/738-6111, fax 509/738-7701.

49 CANYON CREEK

Rating: 7

Near the East Portal Historical Site in Colville National Forest.
Map 4.2, grid d7, page 257

The campground is located four-tenths of a mile from the highway, just far enough to keep it from road noise. It's a popular spot among campers looking for a layover spot, with the bonus of trout fishing in the nearby creek. Canyon Creek lies within hiking distance of the East Portal Historical Site. The camp is set in a pretty area not far from the Columbia River, which offers a myriad of recreation options. A side trip is to the Bangs Mountain Auto Tour, featuring a scenic route with mountain vistas.

Campsites, facilities: There are 12 sites for tents or RVs up to 30 feet long. Picnic tables and fire grills are provided. Vault toilets are available. No drinking water is available. Garbage must be packed out. Some facilities are wheelchair accessible. Leashed pets are permitted.

Reservations, fees: Reservations are not accepted. Sites are $6 per night. Open late May–early September.

Directions: From Spokane, drive north on U.S. 395 for 87 miles to Highway 20. Turn west on Highway 20 and drive 18 miles (crossing the Columbia River) to Forest Road 136. Turn left and drive south for a third of a mile to the campground on the left.

Contact: Colville National Forest, Three Rivers, Ranger District, 255 West 11th St., Kettle Falls, WA 99141, 509/738-6111, fax 509/738-7701.

50 LAKE ELLEN & LAKE ELLEN WEST

Rating: 7

On Lake Ellen in Colville National Forest.
Map 4.2, grid d6, page 257

This 82-acre lake is a favorite for power boating (with no speed limit) and fishing for rainbow trout, which are a good size and plentiful early in the season. There are two small camps available here. The boat launch is located at the west end of the lake. It is located about three miles west of the Columbia River and the Lake Roosevelt National Recreation Area. See a U.S. Forest Service map for details.

Campsites, facilities: There are 11 sites at Lake Ellen and five sites at Lake Ellen West for tents or RVs up to 22 feet long. Picnic tables are provided, but there is no drinking water. Vault toilets and boat docks are available. Garbage must be packed out. Some facilities are wheelchair accessible. Leashed pets are permitted.

Reservations, fees: Reservations are not accepted. Sites are $6 per night. Senior discount available. Open mid-April–mid-October.

Directions: From Spokane, drive north on U.S. 395 for 87 miles to Colville and Highway 20. Turn west on Highway 20 and drive 14 miles (crossing the Columbia River) to County Road 3. Turn left and drive south for 4.5 miles to County Road 412. Turn right on County Road 412 and drive five miles to the Lake Ellen Campground or continue another seven-tenths of a mile to Lake Ellen West Campground.

Contact: Colville National Forest, Three Rivers Ranger District, 255 West 11th St., Kettle Falls, WA 99141, 509/738-6111, fax 509/738-7701.

51 SWAN LAKE

Rating: 8

On Swan Lake in Colville National Forest.
Map 4.2, grid d2, page 257

Scenic views greet visitors on the drive to Swan Lake and at the campground as well. The camp is set on the shore of Swan Lake, at an elevation of 3,700 feet. The Swan Lake Trail, a beautiful hiking trail, circles the lake. Fishing for rainbow trout is an option. Swimming, boating (gas motors prohibited), mountain biking, and hiking are some of the possibilities here. This is a good out-of-the-way spot for RV cruisers seeking a rustic setting. It commonly fills on summer weekends.

Campsites, facilities: There are 25 sites for tents or RVs up to 31 feet long. Picnic tables and fire grills are provided. Drinking water and vault toilets are available. A picnic shelter with barbecue, firewood, a boat dock, and launching facilities are available nearby. Gas motors are prohibited on the lake. Leashed pets are permitted.

Reservations, fees: Reservations are not accepted. Sites are $12 per night, $2 per extra vehicle per night. Senior discount available. Open May–September.

Directions: From Spokane on I-90, turn north on U.S. 395 and drive 87 miles to Highway 20. Turn west on Highway 20 and drive 36 miles to the town of Republic and Highway 21. Turn south on Highway 21 and drive seven miles to Forest Road 53 (Scatter Creek Road). Turn right (southwest) on Forest Road 53 and drive eight miles to the campground at the end of the road.

Contact: Colville National Forest, Republic Ranger District, Republic, WA 99166, 509/775-3305, fax 509/775-7401.

52 FERRY LAKE

Rating: 7

On Ferry Lake in Colville National Forest.
Map 4.2, grid d2, page 257
Ferry Lake is one of three fishing lakes within a four-square-mile area. The others include Swan Lake and Long Lake. Gas motors are prohibited on the lake. For more information, see the descriptions of the other two campgrounds.

Campsites, facilities: There are nine sites for tents or RVs up to 20 feet long. Fire grills and picnic tables are provided. Vault toilets and firewood are available. No drinking water is available. Garbage must be packed out. Launching facilities are nearby. Leashed pets are permitted.

Reservations, fees: Reservations are not accepted. Sites are $8 per night, $2 per extra vehicle per night. Senior discount available. Open May–September, weather permitting.

Directions: From Spokane on I-90, turn north on U.S. 395 and drive 87 miles to Highway 20. Turn west on Highway 20 and drive 36 miles to the town of Republic and Highway 21. Turn south on Highway 21 and drive seven miles to Forest Road 53 (Scatter Creek Road). Turn right (southwest) on Forest Road 53 and drive about seven miles to Forest Road 5330. Turn right (north) on Forest Road 5330 and drive one mile to Forest Road 100. Turn right (north) and drive one mile to the campground on the left.

Contact: Colville National Forest, Republic Ranger District, 180 North Jefferson, Republic, WA 99166, 509/775-3305, fax 509/775-7401.

53 LONG LAKE

Rating: 9

On Long Lake in Colville National Forest.
Map 4.2, grid e2, page 257
Long Lake is the third and smallest of the three lakes in this area (the others are Swan

Lake and Ferry Lake). Expert fly fishermen can get a quality experience here angling for cutthroat trout. No gas motors are allowed on the lake, and fishing is restricted (flyfishing only), but it's ideal for a float tube or a pram. The lake is set adjacent to little Fish Lake, and a half-mile trail runs between the two. The drive on Highway 21 south of Republic is particularly beautiful, with views of the Sanpoil River.

Campsites, facilities: There are 12 sites for tents or RVs up to 21 feet long. Picnic tables and fire grills are provided. Drinking water and vault toilets are available. Garbage must be packed out. Primitive launching facilities are nearby. Leashed pets are permitted.

Reservations, fees: Reservations are not accepted. Sites are $10 per night, $2 per extra vehicle per night. Open May–September.

Directions: From Spokane on I-90, turn north on U.S. 395 and drive 87 miles to Highway 20. Turn west on Highway 20 and drive 36 miles to the town of Republic and Highway 21. Turn south on Highway 21 and drive seven miles to Forest Road 53 (Scatter Creek Road). Turn right (southwest) on Forest Road 53 and drive seven miles to Forest Road 400. Turn south and drive 1.5 miles to the camp on the right.

Contact: Colville National Forest, Republic Ranger District, 180 North Jefferson, Republic, WA 99166, 509/775-3305, fax 509/775-7401.

54 TEN MILE

Rating: 7

On the Sanpoil River in Colville National Forest.
Map 4.2, grid d3, page 257
This spot is secluded and primitive. Located about nine miles from Swan Lake, Ferry Lake, and Long Lake, this campground along the Sanpoil River is a good choice for a multi-day trip visiting each of the lakes. The Sanpoil River provides fishing for rainbow trout, and a hiking trail leads west from camp for about 2.5 miles.

Campsites, facilities: There are nine sites for tents or RVs up to 21 feet long. Picnic tables and fire rings are provided. Vault toilets are available. No drinking water is available. Garbage must be packed out. Leashed pets are permitted.

Reservations, fees: Reservations are not accepted. Sites are $8 per night, $2 per extra vehicle per night. Senior discount available. Open mid-May–mid-October.

Directions: From Spokane on I-90, turn north on U.S. 395 and drive 87 miles to Highway 20. Turn west on Highway 20 and drive 40 miles to Republic and Highway 21. Turn south on Highway 21 and drive 10 miles to the campground entrance on the left.

Contact: Colville National Forest, Republic Ranger District, 180 North Jefferson, Republic, WA 99166, 509/775-3305, fax 509/775-7401.

55 SHERMAN PASS OVERLOOK

Rating: 6

At Sherman Pass in Colville National Forest.
Map 4.2, grid d5, page 257

Sherman Pass Scenic Byway (Highway 20) runs through here, so the camp does have some road noise. This roadside campground is located near Sherman Pass (5,575 feet elevation), one of the few high-elevation mountain passes maintained open year-round in Washington. Several nearby trails provide access to various peaks and vistas in the area. One of the best is the Kettle Crest National Recreation Trail, with the trailhead located one mile from camp. This trail extends for 45 miles, generally running north to south, and provides spectacular views of the Cascades on clear days. No other campgrounds are in the immediate vicinity.

Campsites, facilities: There are nine sites for tents or RVs up to 24 feet long. Picnic tables and fire grills are provided. Vault toilets are available. No drinking water is available. Garbage must be packed out. Some facilities are wheelchair accessible. Leashed pets are permitted.

Reservations, fees: Reservations are not ac-

cepted. Sites are $6 per night. Senior discount available. Open mid-May–late September.

Directions: From Spokane on I-90, turn north on U.S. 395 and drive 87 miles to Highway 20. Turn west on Highway 20 and drive 19.5 miles to the campground on the right.

Contact: Colville National Forest, Three Rivers Ranger District, 255 West 11th St., Kettle Falls, WA 99141, 509/738-6111, fax 509/738-7701.

56 CLOVERLEAF

Rating: 8

On Franklin Roosevelt Lake in Lake Roosevelt National Recreation Area.
Map 4.2, grid f7, page 257

This small and primitive camp is located on the east shore of Roosevelt Lake, just south of the town of Gifford. Nearby Gifford Camp to the south provides an alternative option. In this particular area of Roosevelt Lake, waterskiing and other high-speed boating is not advised because of submerged hazards, but fishing is fine. The tree cover in the area consists primarily of Ponderosa pine. See the descriptions of Springs Canyon and North Gorge for recreation details. Note that no drinking water is available if the lake level drops below 1,282 feet elevation.

Campsites, facilities: There are eight tent sites. Picnic tables and fire grills are provided. Drinking water and vault toilets are available. Boat-launching facilities and a picnic area are nearby. Some facilities are wheelchair accessible. Leashed pets are permitted.

Reservations, fees: Reservations are not accepted. Sites are $5–10 per night; there is a $6 launch fee. Open year-round, with limited winter facilities.

Directions: From Spokane on I-90, drive west for four miles to U.S. 2. Turn west on U.S. 2 and drive 34 miles to Highway 25. Turn right (north) on Highway 25 and drive 61 miles to Davenport and the campground (located about two miles south of Gifford).

Contact: Lake Roosevelt National Recreation Area, 1008 Crest Dr., Coulee Dam, WA 99116-1259, 509/633-9441, fax 509/633-9332.

57 GIFFORD

Rating: 7

On Franklin Roosevelt Lake in Lake Roosevelt National Recreation Area.
Map 4.2, grid f8, page 257

Fishing and water-skiing are two of the draws at this camp on the eastern shore of Franklin Roosevelt Lake (Columbia River). The nearby boat ramp is a big plus.

Campsites, facilities: There are 47 sites for tents or RVs up to 20 feet long and one group site for up to 50 people. Picnic tables and fire grills are provided. Drinking water and vault toilets are available. Boat docks and launching facilities, an RV dump station, and a picnic area are nearby. Some facilities are wheelchair accessible. Leashed pets are permitted.

Reservations, fees: Reservations are not accepted for family sites. Reservations for the group site required at 509/633-3860. Sites are $5–10 per night; $6 boat-launch fee. Senior discount available. Open year-round, with limited winter facilities.

Directions: From Spokane on I-90, drive west for four miles to U.S. 2. Turn west on U.S. 2 and drive 34 miles to Davenport and Highway 25. Turn right (north) on Highway 25 and drive 60 miles to the campground (located about three miles south of Gifford) on the left.

Contact: Lake Roosevelt National Recreation Area, 1008 Crest Dr., Coulee Dam, WA 99116-1259, 509/633-9441, fax 509/633-9332.

58 RAINBOW BEACH RESORT

Rating: 8

On Twin Lakes Reservoir.
Map 4.2, grid f5, page 257

This quality resort is set along the shore of Twin Lakes Reservoir in the Colville Indian Reservation. Busy in summer, the camp fills up virtually every day in July and August. Nearby recreation options include hiking trails, marked bike trails, a full-service marina, and tennis courts.

Campsites, facilities: There are 14 sites with full hookups, including five drive-through sites for RVs of any length, seven tent sites, and 26 cabins. Picnic tables are provided. Restrooms, drinking water, flush toilets, coin-operated showers, bottled gas, an RV dump station, firewood, a recreation hall, a store, a laundry room, ice, boat rentals, docks and launching facilities, and a playground with volleyball and horseshoe pits are available. Leashed pets are permitted.

Reservations, fees: Reservations recommended. Sites are $7–17 per night, with an extra charge for RV campers with tents. Pets are $10 per entire stay. Major credit cards accepted. Campsites are available April–October; cabins are available year-round.

Directions: From Spokane, drive north on U.S. 395 for 84 miles to the town of Kettle Falls and Highway 20. Turn east on Highway 20 and drive five miles to the turnoff for Inchelium Highway. Turn left (south) and drive about 20 miles to Inchelium and Bridge Creek-Twin Lakes County Road. Turn right (west) and drive two miles to Stranger Creek Road. Turn left and drive a quarter mile to the resort on the right.

Contact: Rainbow Beach Resort, 18 North Twin Lakes Rd., Inchelium, WA 99138, 509/722-5901, fax 509/722-7080.

59 HUNTERS PARK

Rating: 8

On Franklin Roosevelt Lake in Lake Roosevelt National Recreation Area.
Map 4.2, grid h7, page 257

This campground, on a shoreline point along Franklin Roosevelt Lake (Columbia River), offers good swimming, fishing, and water-skiing.

It is located on the east shore of the lake, adjacent to the mouth of Hunters Creek and near the town of Hunters. Note: No drinking water is available if the lake level drops below an elevation of 1,245 feet.

Campsites, facilities: There are 42 sites for tents or RVs up to 26 feet long and three group sites for up to 25 people each. Picnic tables and fire grills are provided. Drinking water and vault toilets are available. Restrooms, drinking water, flush toilets, an RV dump station, and a picnic area are available. Some facilities are wheelchair accessible. A store and ice are available within one mile. Boat docks and launching facilities are nearby. Leashed pets are permitted.

Reservations, fees: Reservations are not accepted for family sites. Reservations required for group sites at 509/633-3860. Sites are $5–10 per night; $6 launch fee. Senior discount available. Open year-round, with limited winter facilities.

Directions: From Spokane on I-90, drive west for four miles to U.S. 2. Turn west on U.S. 2 and drive 34 miles to Davenport and Highway 25. Turn north on Highway 25 and drive 47 miles to Hunters and the campground access road on the left side (west side) of the road (well marked). Turn left at the access road and drive two miles to the campground at the end of the road.

Contact: Lake Roosevelt National Recreation Area, 1008 Crest Dr., Coulee Dam, WA 99116-1259, 509/633-9441, fax 509/633-9332.

60 SHEEP CREEK

Rating: 8

On Sheep Creek.

Map 4.3, grid a2, page 258

This campground is in a forested area along Sheep Creek, about four miles from the Columbia River and close to the Canadian border. Although a primitive camp, it has drinking water and is crowded with locals on the Fourth of July weekend. Sheep Creek provides trout fishing. Huckleberry picking is good in August.

Campsites, facilities: There are 11 sites for tents or small RVs. Picnic tables, fire grills, and tent pads are provided. Vault toilets, drinking water, a wheelchair-accessible fishing platform, and a group picnic shelter with barbecues are available. Restaurants and stores are located within five miles. Some facilities are wheelchair accessible. Leashed pets are permitted.

Reservations, fees: Reservations are not accepted. There is no fee for camping. Open mid-April–November, weather permitting.

Directions: From Spokane, drive north on U.S. 395 for 84 miles to Kettle Falls and Highway 25. Turn north on Highway 25 and drive 33 miles to Northport. Continue north on Highway 25 for three-quarters of a mile to Sheep Creek Road (across the Columbia River Bridge). Turn left on Sheep Creek Road and drive 4.3 miles (on a gravel road) to the campground entrance on the right.

Contact: Department of Natural Resources, Northeast Region, P.O. Box 190, Colville, WA 99114-0190, 509/684-7474, fax 509/684-7484.

61 WILLIAMS LAKE

Rating: 9

On Williams Lake.

Map 4.3, grid b1, page 258

This camp is set along the shore of Williams Lake, providing some of the campsites with great views. With so many vacationers heading to nearby Franklin Roosevelt Lake, this secluded spot in a pretty, forested setting presents an alternative that is overlooked by nearly all out-of-towners. The landscape features lots of Douglas firs. This is a swimming lake, and with no motorized boats permitted, it can be ideal for canoes, kayaks, and rafts. There is a boat launch one-half mile from the camp. Only ice fishing is permitted here; check regulations.

Campsites, facilities: There are eight sites for tents or small RVs. Picnic tables, fire grills, and tent pads are provided. Vault toilets, drinking water, and a boat launch are available.

Some facilities are wheelchair accessible. Leashed pets are permitted.

Reservations, fees: Reservations are not accepted. There is no fee for camping. Open mid-April–November.

Directions: From Spokane, drive north for 74 miles to Colville. Continue north on U.S. 395 for two miles to Williams Lake Road. Turn north on Williams Lake Road and drive 13.7 miles to the campground entrance road on the left.

Contact: Department of Natural Resources, Northeast Region, P.O. Box 190, Colville, WA 99114-0190, 509/684-7474, fax 509/684-7484.

62 BIG MEADOW LAKE

Rating: 8

On Big Meadow Lake in Colville National Forest.

Map 4.3, grid c4, page 258

Big Meadow Lake is set at 3,400 feet elevation and has 71 surface acres. The camp, located in a scenic area, is quiet, remote, and relatively unknown, and the lake provides trout fishing. The U.S. Forest Service has built a wildlife-viewing platform, where osprey, ducks, geese, and occasionally even moose, elk, and cougar may be spotted. An environmental education lab is located near the campground.

Campsites, facilities: There are 16 sites for tents or RVs up to 32 feet long. Fire grills, picnic tables, and vault toilets are provided, but there is no drinking water. A boat launch, restrooms, and a wheelchair-accessible nature trail and fishing pier are available. Leashed pets are permitted.

Reservations, fees: Reservations are not accepted. There is no fee for camping. Open May–November, weather permitting.

Directions: From Spokane, drive north on U.S. 395 for 74 miles to Colville and Highway 20. Turn east on Highway 20 and drive one mile to Colville-Aladdin Northpoint Road (County Road 9435). Turn north and drive 20 miles

to Meadow Creek Road. Turn right (east) and drive six miles to the campground on the right. Note: The surface of the access road changes dramatically depending on the season.

Contact: Colville National Forest, Three Rivers Ranger District, Colville Office, 755 South Main St., Colville, WA 99114, 509/684-7000 or 509/684-7010, fax 509/684-7280.

63 MILL POND

Rating: 6

Near Sullivan Lake in Colville National Forest.

Map 4.3, grid b6, page 258

Mill Pond campground, located along the shore of a small reservoir just north of Sullivan Lake, offers a good base camp for backpackers. Note that boat size is limited to crafts that can be carried and hand launched; about a 50-foot walk from the parking area to the lake is necessary. A 1.5-mile hiking trail (no bikes) circles Mill Pond and ties into a historical and wheelchair-accessible interpretive trail (located at the opposite end of the lake). For more ambitious hikes, the nearby Hall Mountain Trail and Elk Creek Trail provide beautiful valley and mountain views. Nearby Sullivan Lake is well known for giant but elusive brown trout and produced the state record. There are also rainbow trout in the lake. All amenities are a short drive away in Metaline Falls. See the descriptions of East and West Sullivan Lakes for other information about the area.

Campsites, facilities: There are 10 sites for tents or RVs up to 25 feet long. Picnic tables and fire grills are provided. Hand-pumped water and vault toilets are available. An RV dump station is located within one mile. Boats can be hand launched after a 50-foot walk; no gas motors are permitted. Leashed pets are permitted.

Reservations, fees: Reservations are not accepted. Sites are $10 per night, $5 per night extra vehicle fee. Open late May–early September.

Directions: From Spokane, drive north on U.S.

395 for six miles to U.S. 2. Turn northeast on U.S. 2 and drive 30 miles to the Metaline turnoff and Highway 211 West. Turn northwest on Highway 211 West and drive 15 miles to Usk and Highway 20. Turn left(northwest) and drive 34 miles to Tiger and Highway 31. Turn left (north) on Highway 31 and drive 15 miles to the town of Metaline Falls and continue 2.5 miles Sullivan Lake Road (County Road 9345). Turn right (east) on Sullivan Lake Road and drive 7.5 miles to the campground on the east end of Mill Pond.

Contact: Colville National Forest, Sullivan Lake Ranger District, 12641 Sullivan Lake Rd., Metaline Falls, WA 99153-9701, 509/446-7500, fax 509/446-7580.

64 SULLIVAN LAKE EAST

Rating: 7

On Sullivan Lake in Colville National Forest.
Map 4.3, grid b6, page 258

This campground is the largest one on Sullivan Lake and by far the most popular. It fills up in summer. The camp is located on the lake's north shore. Some come here to try to catch the giant brown trout or the smaller, more plentiful rainbow trout. The boating and hiking are also good. The beautiful Salmo-Priest Wilderness is located just three miles to the east. It gets light use, which means quiet, private trails. This is a prime place to view wildlife, so carry binoculars while hiking for a chance to spot the rare Woodland caribou and Rocky Mountain bighorn sheep. A nearby grass airstrip provides an opportunity for fly-in camping, but pilots should note that there are chuck holes present and holes from lots of ground squirrels. Only planes suited for primitive landing conditions should be flown in; check FAA guide to airports.

Campsites, facilities: There are 38 sites, including some drive-through sites, for tents or RVs up to 45 feet long. Picnic tables and fire grills are provided. Drinking water and vault

toilets are available. A boat dock, launching facilities, a picnic area, a swimming platform, a camp host, and an RV dump station are nearby. Some facilities are wheelchair accessible. Leashed pets are permitted.

Reservations, fees: Reserve at 877/444-6777 ($9 reservation fee) or website: www.ReserveUsa.com. Sites are $10 per night, $5 per night extra vehicle fee, and the group site is $60 per night. Senior discount available. Open late May through August.

Directions: From Spokane, drive north on U.S. 395 for six miles to U.S. 2. Turn northeast on U.S. 2 and drive 30 miles to the Metaline turnoff and Highway 211 West. Turn northwest on Highway 211 West and drive 15 miles to Usk and Highway 20. Turn left (northwest) and drive 34 miles to Tiger and Highway 31. Turn left (north) on Highway 31 and drive 15 miles to the town of Metaline Falls (Highway 31 is also known as Lehigh Avenue in town); continue 2.5 miles to Sullivan Lake Road (County Road 9345). Turn right (east) on Sullivan Lake Road and drive eight miles to Sullivan Creek Road. Turn left (east) and drive one-quarter mile to the campground on the right.

Contact: Colville National Forest, Sullivan Lake Ranger District, 12641 Sullivan Lake Rd., Metaline Falls, WA 99153-9701, 509/446-7500, fax 509/446-7580.

65 SULLIVAN LAKE WEST

Rating: 7

On Sullivan Lake in Colville National Forest.
Map 4.3, grid b6, page 258

This small campground is set along the northwestern shore of Sullivan Lake and is a popular destination for boating, fishing, swimming, sailing, water-skiing, and hiking. See the previous listing for Sullivan Lake East for recreation and local details.

Campsites, facilities: There are seven sites for tents or RVs up to 30 feet long. Picnic tables and fire grills are provided. Drinking water and vault toilets, a picnic shelter, a boat launch, a developed swimming beach, a floating swim platform, and a camp host are available. Some facilities are wheelchair accessible. Leashed pets are permitted.

Reservations, fees: Reserve at 877/444-6777 ($9 reservation fee) or website: www.ReserveUsa.com. Sites are $10 per night, $5 per extra vehicle per night. Senior discount available. Open late May–August.

Directions: From Spokane, drive north on U.S. 395 for six miles to U.S. 2. Turn northeast on U.S. 2 and drive 30 miles to the Metaline turnoff and Highway 211 West. Turn northwest on Highway 211 West and drive 15 miles to Usk and Highway 20. Turn left (northwest) and drive 34 miles to Tiger and Highway 31. Turn left (north) on Highway 31 and drive 15 miles to the town of Metaline Falls (Highway 31 is also known as Lehigh Avenue in town); continue 2.5 miles to Sullivan Lake Road (County Road 9345). Turn right (east) on Sullivan Lake Road and drive 8.1 miles to the campground on the left (set at the foot of Sullivan Lake, just across the road from the Sullivan Lake Ranger Station).

Contact: Colville National Forest, Sullivan Lake Ranger District, 12641 Sullivan Lake Rd., Metaline Falls, WA 99153-9701, 509/446-7500, fax 509/446-7580.

66 NOISY CREEK & NOISY CREEK GROUP

Rating: 7

On Sullivan Lake in Colville National Forest.
Map 4.3, grid b6, page 258

This campground is situated on the southeast end of Sullivan Lake, adjacent to where Noisy Creek pours into Sullivan Lake. Note that the lake level can be drawn down for irrigation, leaving this camp well above the lake. The Noisy Creek Trail near camp heads east along Noisy Creek and then north up to Hall Mountain (elevation 6,323 feet), a distance of 5.3 miles; this is bighorn sheep country. The

Lakeshore Trailhead is located at the nearby day-use area. Water-skiing is allowed on the 3.5-mile-long lake, and the boat ramp near the camp provides a good launch point.

Campsites, facilities: There are 19 sites for RVs up to 45 feet long and one group camp for up to 30 people. If the group camp is not reserved, it is available as an overflow area. Picnic tables and fire grills are provided. Drinking water and vault toilets are available. Boat-launching facilities and a picnic area are nearby. Leashed pets are permitted.

Reservations, fees: Reserve at 877/444-6777 ($9 reservation fee) or website: www.ReserveUsa.com. Sites are $10 per night, $5 extra vehicle fee. Senior discount available. Group site is $60 per night. Open late May–early September.

Directions: From Spokane, drive north on U.S. 395 for six miles to U.S. 2. Turn northeast on U.S. 2 and drive 30 miles to the Metaline turnoff and Highway 211 West. Turn northwest on Highway 211 West and drive 15 miles to Usk and Highway 20. Turn left (northwest) and drive 34 miles to Tiger and Highway 31. Turn north on Highway 31 and drive 15 miles to the town of Metaline Falls (Highway 31 is known as Lehigh Avenue in town); continue 2.5 miles to Sullivan Lake Road (County Road 9345). Turn right (east) on Sullivan Lake Road and drive eight miles to the campground on the right (on the south end of Sullivan Lake).

Contact: Colville National Forest, Sullivan Lake Ranger District, 12641 Sullivan Lake Rd., Metaline Falls, WA 99153, 509/446-7500, fax 509/446-7580.

67 EDGEWATER

Rating: 6

On the Pend Oreille River in Colville National Forest.
Map 4.3, grid b5, page 258

Edgewater Camp is set on the shore of the Pend Oreille River about two miles upstream from the Box Canyon Dam. Although not far out of Ione, the camp has a primitive feel to it. Fishing for largemouth bass, rainbow trout, and brown trout is popular here, while suckers and squawfish present somewhat of a problem.

Campsites, facilities: There are 21 sites for tents or RVs up to 40 feet long. Picnic tables and fire grills are provided. Drinking water and vault toilets are available. A boat launch and six picnic sites for day use are available nearby. Leashed pets are permitted.

Reservations, fees: Reservations are not accepted. Sites are $10 per night, $5 per extra vehicle per night. Senior discount available. Open late May–early September.

Directions: From Spokane, drive north on U.S. 395 for six miles to U.S. 2. Turn northeast on U.S. 2 and drive 30 miles to the Metaline turnoff and Highway 211 West. Turn northwest on Highway 211 West and drive 15 miles to Usk and Highway 20. Turn left (northwest) and drive 34 miles to Tiger and Highway 31. Turn north on Highway 31 and drive 15 miles to the town of Metaline Falls (Highway 31 is known as Lehigh Avenue in town); continue 2.5 miles to Sullivan Lake Road (County Road 9345). Turn right (east) on Sullivan Lake Road and drive one-quarter mile to County Road 3669. Turn left (north) on County Road 3669 and drive two miles to the campground entrance road on the left. Turn left and drive one-quarter mile to the campground.

Contact: Colville National Forest, Sullivan Lake Ranger District, 12641 Sullivan Lake Rd., Metaline Falls, WA 99153-9701, 509/446-7500, fax 509/446-7580.

68 IONE RV PARK AND MOTEL

Rating: 8

On the Pend Oreille River.
Map 4.3, grid c5, page 258

This camp is a good layover spot for campers with RVs or trailers who want to stay in town. The park sits on the shore of the Pend Oreille River, which offers fishing, swimming, several bike trails, and boating. In the winter, bighorn sheep may be spotted north of town.

Campsites, facilities: There are 19 sites with full hookups for RVs of any length, seven tent sites, and 11 motel rooms. Picnic tables are provided. Restrooms, drinking water, flush toilets, showers, an RV dump station, and a coin-operated laundry are available. A store, a café, and ice are located within one mile. Boat docks, launching facilities, and a playground are nearby. Leashed pets are permitted.

Reservations, fees: Reservations accepted. Sites are $5–18 per night. Major credit cards accepted. Open year-round.

Directions: From Spokane, drive north on U.S. 2 for 48 miles to the junction with Highway 211 at the Washington/Idaho border. Turn west on Highway 211 and drive 48 miles northwest to Tiger and Highway 31. Turn north on Highway 31 and drive four miles to Ione. Cross a spillway (it looks like a bridge) on Highway 31 and continue to the campground on the right.

Contact: Ione RV Park and Motel, P.O. Box 730, Ione, WA 99139, 509/442-3213.

69 DOUGLAS FALLS

Rating: 8

On Mill Creek.
Map 4.3, grid d1, page 258

This campground in a wooded area along Mill Creek features Douglas Falls and is just outside of town. A 0.2-mile walk from the campground takes you to a beautiful overlook of a waterfall. Another unique highlight, a cabled free-span bridge is available. And best of all, this camp is free!

Campsites, facilities: There are 18 sites for tents or small RVs. Picnic tables, fire grills, and tent pads are provided. Vault toilets and drinking water are available. A barrier-free vault toilet, trails, and group picnic shelter with barbecue are also available. A baseball field is nearby. Leashed pets are permitted.

Reservations, fees: Reservations are not accepted. There is no fee for camping. Open Memorial Day weekend through November.

Directions: From Spokane, drive north on U.S. 395 for 74 miles to Colville and Highway 20. Turn east on Highway 20 and drive 1.1 miles to Aladdin Road. Turn left (north) and drive two miles to Douglas Falls Road. Turn left and drive three miles to the campground on the left.

Contact: Department of Natural Resources, Northeast Region, P.O. Box 190, Colville, WA 99114-0190, 509/684-7474, fax 509/684-7484.

70 ROCKY LAKE

Rating: 6

On Rocky Lake.

Map 4.3, grid e2, page 258

The campground is set on Rocky Lake, a shallow, weedy pond lined with a lot of rocks. This camp is good for overnight camping, but not for a long-term stay; for that, go to Douglas Falls. Fishing for rainbow trout is an option. If you backtrack about 10 miles on Rocky Lake Road, you'll see the entrance signs for the Little Pend Oreille Wildlife Refuge, a premium area for hiking, fishing, hunting, and wildlife photography.

Campsites, facilities: There are seven sites for tents or small RVs. Picnic tables, fire grills, and tent pads are provided. Vault toilets, drinking water, and a boat launch are available. Leashed pets are permitted.

Reservations, fees: Reservations are not accepted. There is no fee for camping. Open to overnight camping from mid-April–May and from Labor Day weekend through November. The interim period, June–early September, is open to day-use only.

Directions: From Spokane, drive north on U.S. 395 for 74 miles to Colville and Highway 20. Turn east on Highway 20 and drive six miles to Artman-Gibson Road. Turn right on Artman-Gibson Road and drive 3.2 miles to

a one-lane gravel road. Turn right on the gravel road (unnamed) and drive about one-half mile. Bear left and continue another two miles to the campground.

Contact: Department of Natural Resources, Northeast Region, P.O. Box 190, Colville, WA 99114-0190, 509/684-7474, fax 509/684-7484.

71 STARVATION LAKE

Rating: 8

On Starvation Lake.

Map 4.3, grid e3, page 258

Starvation Lake is only 15 feet deep and has a weed problem, so it's okay for trout fishing but not for swimming. Drowning is possible here if you get your feet tangled in the weeds. Osprey and bald eagles frequent the area. It's advisable to obtain a detailed map of the area. The camp is used extensively by locals during the early fishing season (end of April–early June) but is uncrowded thereafter, when the fishing becomes catch-and-release; check regulations. Boats must not exceed 16 feet.

Campsites, facilities: There are eight sites for tents or small RVs; six are pull-through sites. Picnic tables and fire grills are provided. Vault toilets, drinking water, and a barrier-free fishing dock are available. Some facilities are wheelchair accessible. Leashed pets are permitted.

Reservations, fees: Reservations are not accepted. There is no fee for camping. Open mid-April–November, weather permitting.

Directions: From Spokane, drive north on U.S. 395 for 74 miles to Colville and Highway 20. Turn east on Highway 20 and drive 10.5 miles to a gravel road (sign says Starvation Lake). Turn right on the gravel road and drive a third of a mile to the intersection. Turn left and drive one-half mile to the campground on the right.

Contact: Department of Natural Resources, Northeast Region, P.O. Box 190, Colville, WA 99114-0190, 509/684-7474, fax 509/684-7484.

72 LITTLE TWIN LAKES

Rating: 6

On Little Twin Lakes in Colville National Forest.

Map 4.3, grid d3, page 258

This campground was temporarily closed in 2002 because of tree blowdowns. Call before planning a trip here. Sites at this pretty, wooded campground on the shore of Little Twin Lakes have lake views and are free. Fishing is best here for cutthroat trout. See the description of North Gorge for more information.

Campsites, facilities: There are 20 sites for tents or RVs up to 16 feet long. Fire grills and picnic tables are provided. There is no drinking water. Pit toilets and firewood are available. Boat docks and launching facilities are located nearby. Leashed pets are permitted.

Reservations, fees: Reservations are not accepted. There is no fee for camping. Open May–mid-November, weather permitting.

Directions: From Spokane, drive north on U.S. 395 for 74 miles to Colville and Highway 20. Turn east on Highway 20 and drive 12.5 miles to County Road 4915. Turn northeast and drive 1.5 miles to Forest Road 4939. Turn right (north) and drive 4.5 miles to the campground on the right.

Contact: Colville National Forest, Three Rivers Ranger District, Colville Office, 755 South Main St., Colville, WA 99114, 509/684-7000 or 509/684-7010, fax 509/684-7280.

73 FLODELLE CREEK

Rating: 8

On Flodelle Creek.

Map 4.3, grid d4, page 258

This campground is set where hiking, hunting, and fishing are quite good. It's advisable to obtain a detailed map of the area. Off-road vehicle trails are available at this camp (see listing for Sherry Creek campground), and they are often in use, so don't count on a particularly quiet camping experience. This spot can provide good fishing, best for brook trout. Wildlife includes black bears, moose, mosquitoes, and black gnats, the latter occasionally so prevalent that they are considered wildlife. Be prepared.

Campsites, facilities: There are eight sites for tents or small RVs. Picnic tables, fire grills, and tent pads are provided. Vault toilets and drinking water are available. Leashed pets are permitted.

Reservations, fees: Reservations are not accepted. There is no fee for camping. Open May–November, weather permitting.

Directions: From Spokane, drive north on U.S. 395 for 74 miles to Colville and Highway 20. Turn east on Highway 20 and drive 19.4 miles to an unnamed two-lane gravel road on the right. Turn right on that road and drive one-quarter mile to the campground entrance road on the left.

Contact: Department of Natural Resources, Northeast Region, P.O. Box 190, Colville, WA 99114-0190, 509/684-7474, fax 509/684-7484.

74 SHERRY CREEK

Rating: 6

Near Sherry Lake.

Map 4.3, grid d4, page 258

This old fire camp is set near the off-road vehicle (ORV) trail network of the Pend Orielle Lake system. It is located on Sherry Creek, about three miles from Sherry Lake and is basically a fishing camp, with lots of brook trout and a few rainbow trout. It's advisable to obtain a detailed map of the area. Biking and hiking on the ORV trails is an option. It covers a network of 75 miles of ORV trails and can be accessed from this campground. This country has good numbers of black bear and even some moose, and because it is set next to a wetland, there can be tons of mosquitoes in summer.

Campsites, facilities: There are three sites for tents or small RVs. Picnic tables and fire pits are provided. Vault toilets are available, but there is no drinking water or garbage service. Leashed pets are permitted.

Reservations, fees: Reservations are not accepted. There is no fee for camping. Open May–November, weather permitting.

Directions: From Spokane, drive north on U.S. 395 for 74 miles to Colville and Highway 20. Turn east on Highway 20 and drive 23.8 miles to a gravel road. Turn right and drive about one-half mile to the campground.

Contact: Department of Natural Resources, Northeast Region, P.O. Box 190, Colville, WA 99114-0190, 509/684-7474, fax 509/684-7484.

75 LAKE GILLETTE

Rating: 8

On Lake Gillette in Colville National Forest.
Map 4.3, grid d4, page 258

This pretty and popular camp is situated right on the shore of Lake Gillette. Like neighboring East Gillette Campground, it fills up quickly in the summer with off-road motorcyclists. The camp is popular with off-road vehicle (ORV) users. An ORV system can't be accessed directly from the campground, but is close. Fishing at Lake Gillette is best for cutthroat trout.

Campsites, facilities: There are 14 sites for tents or RVs up to 31 feet long. Drinking water, fire grills, and picnic tables are provided. Vault toilets, an RV dump station, and an amphitheater are available. A store and ice are located within one mile. Some facilities are wheelchair accessible. Boat docks, launching facilities, and rentals are nearby. Leashed pets are permitted.

Reservations, fees: Reservations are not accepted. Sites are $10–14 per night. Senior discount available. Open mid-May–late September.

Directions: From Spokane, drive north on U.S. 395 for 74 miles to Colville and Highway

20. Turn east on Highway 20 and drive 20 miles to County Road 4987 (Lake Gillette Road). Turn right (east) on Lake Gillette Road and drive one-half mile to the campground on the right.

Contact: Colville National Forest, Three Rivers Ranger District, Colville Office, 755 South Main St., Colville, WA 99114, 509/684-7000 or 509/684-7010, fax 509/684-7280.

76 GILLETTE

Rating: 7

Near Lake Gillette in Colville National Forest.
Map 4.3, grid d4, page 258

This beautiful and extremely popular campground, just south of Beaver Lodge Resort and Lake Thomas, is near Lake Gillette, one in a chain of seven lakes. There are a few hiking trails in the area. See the description of Beaver Lodge Resort for other recreation information. Be sure to make reservations early.

Campsites, facilities: There are 30 sites for tents or RVs up to 31 feet long. Picnic tables and fire grills are provided. Drinking water, vault toilets, and an RV dump station are available. A store and ice are located within one mile. Some facilities are wheelchair accessible. Boat docks, launching facilities, and rentals are nearby. Leashed pets are permitted.

Reservations, fees: Reservations are not accepted. Sites are $8 per night. Senior discount available. Open mid-May–late September.

Directions: From Spokane, drive north on U.S. 395 for 74 miles to Colville and Highway 20. Turn east on Highway 20 and drive 20 miles to County Road 4987 (Lake Gillette Road). Turn right (east) on Lake Gillette Road and drive one-half mile to the campground on the left.

Contact: Colville National Forest, Three Rivers Ranger District, Colville Office, 755 South Main St., Colville, WA 99114, 509/684-7000 or 509/684-7010, fax 509/684-7280.

77 BEAVER LODGE RESORT

Rating: 9

On Lake Thomas.

Map 4.3, grid d4, page 258

This developed camp is set along the shore of Lake Gillette, one in a chain of four lakes. A highlight in this area: the numerous opportunities for off-road vehicles (ORVs), with a network of ORV trails. In addition, hiking trails and marked bike trails are close to the camp. In winter, downhill and cross-country skiing is available.

Campsites, facilities: There are 18 sites for tents or RVs up to 40 feet long, a separate tent camping area, and seven cabins. Picnic tables and fire grills are provided. Restrooms, drinking water, flush toilets, showers, gasoline, bottled gas, firewood, a recreation hall, a store, a café, ice, boat rentals, and a playground are available. An RV dump station is located within one mile. Boat docks and launching facilities are nearby. Leashed pets are permitted.

Reservations, fees: Reservations accepted. Sites are $10–16 per night; cabins are $45–65 per night. Major credit cards accepted. Open year-round.

Directions: From Spokane, drive north on U.S. 395 for 74 miles to Colville and Highway 20. Turn east on Highway 20 and drive 25 miles to the lodge on the right.

Contact: Beaver Lodge Resort, 2430 Hwy. 20 E, Colville, WA 99114, 509/684-5657 or 509/685-9426.

78 LAKE THOMAS

Rating: 6

On Lake Thomas in Colville National Forest.

Map 4.3, grid c4, page 258

This camp on the shore of Lake Thomas offers a less crowded alternative to the campgrounds at Lake Gillette. The lake provides fishing for cutthroat trout. Other nearby options include Lake Gillette and Beaver Lodge Resort; see these listings for recreation information.

Campsites, facilities: There are 15 sites for tents and small RVs. Picnic tables, fire grills, and tent pads are provided. Drinking water, vault toilets, and firewood are available. An RV dump station is located within one mile. Boat docks, launching facilities, and rentals are nearby. Leashed pets are permitted.

Reservations, fees: Reservations are not accepted. Sites are $10 per night. Senior discount available. Open mid-May–late September.

Directions: From Spokane, drive north on U.S. 395 for 74 miles to Colville and Highway 20. Turn east on Highway 20 and drive 20 miles to County Road 4987 (Lake Gillette Road). Turn right (east) on Lake Gillette Road and drive one mile to the campground on the left.

Contact: Colville National Forest, Three Rivers Ranger District, Colville Office, 755 South Main St., Colville, WA 99114, 509/684-7000 or 509/684-7010, fax 509/684-7280.

79 LAKE LEO

Rating: 6

On Lake Leo in Colville National Forest.

Map 4.3, grid c5, page 258

Lake Leo is the northernmost and quietest camp on the chain of lakes in the immediate vicinity. This lake provides fishing for cutthroat trout. Frater and Nile Lakes, both fairly small, are located one mile north. In winter, a Nordic ski trail starts adjacent to the camp. Fishing and boating are two recreation options here.

Campsites, facilities: There are eight sites for tents or RVs up to 15 feet long. Picnic tables and fire grills are provided. Vault toilets are available. No drinking water is available. A boat ramp and launching facilities are nearby. Leashed pets are permitted.

Reservations, fees: Reservations are not accepted. Sites are $10 per night. Senior discount available. Open mid-May–mid-September.

Directions: From Spokane on I-90, drive north on U.S. 395 for 74 miles to Colville and Highway 20. Turn east on Highway 20 and drive 23 miles to the campground entrance on the right.
Contact: Colville National Forest, Three Rivers Ranger District, Colville Office, 755 South Main St., Colville, WA 99114, 509/684-7000 or 509/684-7010, fax 509/684-7280.

80 BLUESLIDE RESORT

Rating: 7

On the Pend Oreille River.
Map 4.3, grid d6, page 258
This resort is situated along the western shore of the Pend Oreille River. It offers a head-quarters for fishermen and vacationers. Four to five bass tournaments are held each spring during May and June, and the river is stocked with both rainbow trout and bass. The resort offers full facilities for anglers, including tack-le, boat rentals, and a marina with the only boat gas for 53 miles. The park is lovely, with grassy, shaded sites, and is located along the waterfowl migratory path. Lots of groups camp here in the summer. Recreation options in-clude bicycling nearby. The only other camp-ground in the vicinity is the Outpost Resort (see next listing).

Campsites, facilities: There are 44 sites with full or partial hookups, including four drive-through sites, for tents or RVs of any length, seven tent sites, four motel units, and five cab-ins. Picnic tables and fire pits are provided. Restrooms, drinking water, flush toilets, show-ers, an RV dump station, a meeting hall, sev-eral sports fields, a store, propane, a laundry room, ice, firewood, a playground with bas-ketball, tetherball, volleyball, and horseshoe pits, a heated swimming pool, boat docks, launching facilities, and boat fuel are available. Leashed pets are permitted.

Reservations, fees: Reservations recommend-ed. Sites are $14–18 per night, $2 per person per night for more than two people. Cabins

are $47–65 per night. Major credit cards ac-cepted. Open year-round, but only cabins are available in the winter.
Directions: From Spokane, drive north on U.S. 395 for six miles to U.S. 2. Turn north on U.S. 2 and drive 26 miles northeast to Highway 211. Turn left and drive 18 miles to Highway 20. Turn left and drive 22 miles to the park (lo-cated on the right at Milepost 400).
Contact: Blueslide Resort, 400041 Rte. 20, Cu-sick, WA 99119, 509/445-1327.

81 OUTPOST RESORT

Rating: 8

On the Pend Oreille River.
Map 4.3, grid e6, page 258
This comfortable campground in a pretty set-ting along the west shore of the Pend Oreille River has fairly spacious sites and views of snow-capped mountains. If you're cruising Highway 20, Blueslide Resort is located about five miles north, the nearest alternative if this camp is full.

Campsites, facilities: There are 12 tent sites, 12 drive-through sites with full hookups for RVs of any length, and four cabins. Picnic tables are provided. Flush toilets, an RV dump station, a store, a café, ice, electricity, drinking water, sewer hookups, showers, a swimming area, boat rentals, boat docks, and launching facilities are available. Leashed pets are permitted.

Reservations, fees: Reservations accepted. Sites are $10–15 per night; $5 fee for boat launch for day-use (free for campers). Major credit cards accepted. Open year-round, with limit-ed winter facilities.
Directions: From Spokane, drive north on U.S. 395 for six miles to U.S. 2. Turn north on U.S. 2 and drive 34 miles to Highway 211. Turn left and drive 18 miles to Highway 20. Turn left and drive 17 miles to the park (located between Mileposts 405 and 406) on the right.
Contact: Outpost Resort, 405351 Hwy. 20, Cu-sick, WA 99119, 509/445-1317 or 888/888-9064.

82 PANHANDLE

Rating: 9

On the Pend Oreille River in Colville
National Forest.
Map 4.3, grid e6, page 258

In the tall trees and with views of the river,
here's a scenic spot to set up camp along the
eastern shore of the Pend Oreille River. This
camp makes a good base for a fishing or
water-skiing trip. Fishing for largemouth and
smallmouth bass is the most popular, with
an annual bass tournament held every summer in the area. The campground is located
in an area of mature trees directly across the
river from the Outpost Resort. A network of
hiking trails can be accessed by taking Forest Roads to the east. See a U.S. Forest Service map for details.

Campsites, facilities: There are 13 sites for tents
or RVs up to 32 feet long. Picnic tables and
fire grills are provided. Drinking water and
vault toilets are available. A small boat launch
is nearby. Some facilities are wheelchair accessible. Leashed pets are permitted.

Reservations, fees: Reserve at 877/444-6777
($9 reservation fee) or website: www.Re-
serveUsa.com. Sites are $10 per night, $5 per
extra vehicle per night. Senior discount available. Open late May–late September.

Directions: From Spokane, drive north on U.S.
395 for six miles to U.S. 2. Turn north on U.S.
2 and drive 30 miles to the Metaline turnoff
and Highway 211 West. Take Highway 211 West
and drive for 15 miles to the junction of Highway 20. Cross Highway 20, driving through
the town of Usk. Continue across the Pend
Oreille River to Le Clerk Road. Turn left and
drive 15 miles north on Le Clerk Road to the
campground on the left.

Contact: Colville National Forest, Newport
Ranger District, 315 North Warren Ave.,
Newport, WA 99156, 509/447-7300, fax
509/447-7301.

83 SKOOKUM CREEK

Rating: 5

Near the Pend Oreille River.
Map 4.3, grid e6, page 258

This campground is set in a wooded area along
Skookum Creek, about 1.5 miles from where
it empties into the Pend Oreille River. It's a
good canoeing spot, has drinking water, and
gets little attention. And you can't beat the
price of admission—free.

Campsites, facilities: There are 10 sites for tents
or small RVs. Picnic tables, fire grills, and tent
pads are provided. Drinking water and vault
toilets are available. A group picnic shelter
with a barbecue is available nearby. Leashed
pets are permitted.

Reservations, fees: Reservations are not accepted. There is no fee for camping. Open mid-
April–October, weather permitting.

Directions: From Spokane, drive north on U.S.
395 for six miles to U.S. 2. Turn north on U.S.
2 and drive 48 miles to Newport and Highway
20. Turn west on Highway 20 and drive 16
miles northwest to the town of Usk. Continue east across the bridge for nine-tenths of a
mile to Le Clerc Road. Turn right on Le Clerc
Road and drive 2.2 miles to a one-lane gravel
road. Turn left and drive a short distance to
another gravel road. Turn left and drive one-
quarter mile to the campground.

Contact: Department of Natural Resources,
Northeast Region, P.O. Box 190, Colville, WA
99114-0190, 509/684-7474, fax 509/684-7484.

84 BROWNS LAKE

Rating: 8

On Browns Lake in Colville National Forest.
Map 4.3, grid e7, page 258

This campground is set along the shore of
Browns Lake, with lakeside sites bordering old-
growth hemlock and cedar. No motorized boats
are permitted on the lake, and only flyfishing

is allowed, so it can be ideal for float tubes, canoes, and prams. A 1.25-mile-long hiking trail leaves the campground and ties into a wheelchair-accessible interpretive trail with beautiful views along the way. At the end of the trail sits a fishing viewing platform in the creek (Browns Creek) that feeds into the lake. South Skookum Lake is about five miles away.

Campsites, facilities: There are 18 sites for tents or RVs up to 21 feet long. Picnic tables and fire grills are provided. Vault toilets are available. No drinking water is available. A primitive boat launch is available for small boats, such as canoes, rowboats, and inflatables. Some facilities are wheelchair accessible. Leashed pets are permitted.

Reservations, fees: Reservations are not accepted. Sites are $8 per night, $4 per extra vehicle per night. Senior discount available. Open late May–late September.

Directions: From Spokane, drive north on U.S. 395 for six miles to U.S. 2. Turn north on U.S. 2 and drive 30 miles to the Metaline turnoff and Highway 211 West. Turn northwest on Highway 211 West and drive 15 miles to Usk and Highway 20. Drive north on Highway 20 a short distance to County Road 3389. Turn right (east) on County Road 3389 and drive (over the Pend Oreille River) four miles to a fork with Forest Road 5030. Bear north and drive four miles to the campground at the end of the road.

Contact: Colville National Forest, Newport Ranger District, 315 North Warren Ave., Newport, WA 99156, 509/447-7300, fax 509/447-7301.

85 SOUTH SKOOKUM LAKE

Rating: 7

On South Skookum Lake in Colville National Forest.

Map 4.3, grid e7, page 258

This camp is situated on the western shore of South Skookum Lake, at the foot of Kings Mountain (elevation 4,383 feet). This is a good fishing lake, stocked with cutthroat trout, and

is popular with families. A 1.3-mile-long hiking trail circles the water, and a spur trail leads to South Baldy Lookout.

Campsites, facilities: There are 25 sites for tents or RVs up to 30 feet long. Picnic tables and fire rings are provided. Drinking water and vault toilets are available. A boat ramp for small boats, two docks, and a wheelchair-accessible fishing dock are available nearby. Leashed pets are permitted.

Reservations, fees: Reservations are not accepted. Sites are $10 per night, $5 per extra vehicle per night. Senior discount available. Open late May–late September.

Directions: From Spokane, drive north on U.S. 395 for six miles to U.S. 2. Turn north on U.S. 2 and drive 30 miles to the Metaline turnoff and Highway 211 West. Turn northwest on Highway 211 West and drive 15 miles to Usk and Highway 20. Drive north on Highway 20 a short distance to Kings Lake Road (County Road 3389). Turn right (east) on Kings Lake Road (County Road 3389) and drive eight miles (over the Pend Oreille River) to the campground entrance road on the right. Turn right and drive one-quarter mile to the campground.

Contact: Colville National Forest, Newport Ranger District, 315 North Warren Ave., Newport, WA 99156, 509/447-7300, fax 509/447-7301.

86 PIONEER PARK

Rating: 8

On the Pend Oreille River in Colville National Forest.

Map 4.3, grid g8, page 258

Pioneer Park Campground is set along the shore of Box Canyon Reservoir on the Pend Oreille River near Newport. The launch and adjoining parking area are suitable for larger boats. Water-skiing and water sports are popular here. There is a wheelchair-accessible interpretive trail with a boardwalk and beautiful views of the river. Signs along the way explain the history of the Kalispel tribe.

Campsites, facilities: There are 17 sites for tents or RVs up to 32 feet long. Picnic tables and fire rings are provided. Drinking water, vault toilets, and a picnic area are available. Some facilities are wheelchair accessible. Boat docks, launching facilities, and rentals are nearby. Leashed pets are permitted.

Reservations, fees: Reserve at 877/444-6777 ($9 reservation fee) or website: www.ReserveUsa.com. Sites are $10 per night, $5 per extra vehicle per night. Senior discount available. Open May–late September, weather permitting.

Directions: From Spokane, drive north on U.S. 395 for six miles to U.S. 2. Turn north on U.S. 2 and drive 41 miles to Newport. Continue across the Pend Oreille River to Le Clerc Road (County Road 9305). Turn left on Le Clerc Road and drive two miles to the campground on the left.

Contact: Colville National Forest, Newport Ranger District, 315 North Warren Ave., Newport, WA 99156, 509/447-7300, fax 509/447-7301.

87 THE 49ER MOTEL AND RV PARK

Rating: 6

Near Chewelah.

Map 4.3, grid f3, page 258

This region is the heart of mining country. The park is located in a mountainous setting next to a motel and has grassy sites. Nearby recreation options include a 27-hole golf course, hiking trails, and marked bike trails. This park is a good deal for RV cruisers—a rustic setting right in town. In winter, note that the 49 Degrees Ski & Snowboard Parks is located 12 miles to the east.

Campsites, facilities: There are 27 sites with full hookups, including mostly drive-through sites, for tents or RVs up to 30 feet long and 13 motel rooms. Picnic tables are provided. Restrooms, drinking water, flush toilets, showers, an RV dump station, cable TV, a spa, a recreation hall, picnic tables, and an indoor heated swimming pool are available. Bottled gas, a store, a café, ice, and a coin-operated laundry are located within one mile. Leashed pets are permitted.

Reservations, fees: Reservations accepted. Sites are $12–17.75 per night, with weekly and monthly rates available, $5 per person for more than four people, and $4 per pet per night. Major credit cards accepted. Open year-round.

Directions: From Spokane, drive north on U.S. 395 and go 44 miles to Chewelah; the park is on the right (on U.S. 395 at the south edge of town, well marked).

Contact: The 49er Motel and RV Park, South 311 Park St., Chewelah, WA 99109, 509/935-8613 or 888/412-1994, fax 509/935-8705; www.the officenet.com/5˜49er.

88 WINONA BEACH RESORT AND RV PARK

Rating: 9

On Waitts Lake.

Map 4.3, grid g2, page 258

This beautiful and comfortable resort on the shore of Waitts Lake has spacious sites and friendly folks. The park fills up in July and August, and note that cabins here are available during this time by the week, not the night. In the spring, fishing for brown trout and rainbow trout can be quite good. The trout head to deeper water in the summer, and bluegill and perch are easier to catch then. Water-skiing and windsurfing are also popular.

Campsites, facilities: There are 54 sites with full hookups, including 20 lakeside sites and two drive-through sites, for tents or RVs up to 40 feet, seven tent sites, and seven cabins. Picnic tables and fire rings are provided. Restrooms, drinking water, flush toilets, coin-operated showers, an RV dump station, firewood, a snack bar, a general store, a playground with volleyball, horseshoe pits, basketball, a swimming beach, an antique store, and ice are available. Boat docks, launching facilities, and rentals are on-site. Leashed pets are permitted.

Reservations, fees: Reservations accepted. Sites are $15–22 per night, $2 per extra vehicle per night, and $3 per pet per night. Major credit cards accepted. Open April–September.

Directions: From Spokane, drive north on U.S. 395 for 42 miles to the Valley-Waitts Lake exit. Turn left (west) at that exit and drive one mile to Highway 231. Turn right (north) on Highway 231 and drive 1.5 miles to the town of Valley and Valley-Waitts Lake Road. Turn left and drive three miles to Winona Beach Road. Turn left and drive one-quarter mile to the resort at the end of the road.

Contact: Winona Beach Resort and RV Park, 33022 Winona Beach Rd., Valley, WA 99181, 509/937-2231, fax 509/937-2215, website: www.go campingamerica.com/winona.

89 SILVER BEACH RESORT

Rating: 6

On Waitts Lake.
Map 4.3, grid g2, page 258

Silver Beach Resort offers grassy sites on the shore of Waitts Lake, where fishing and water-skiing are popular. See the previous description of Winona Beach Resort and RV Park for information about the lake.

Campsites, facilities: There are 53 sites with full hookups, including four drive-through sites, for RVs up to 40 feet long and seven cabins. Picnic tables and fire pits are provided. Restrooms, drinking water, flush toilets, coin-operated showers, bottled gas, an RV dump station, a store, a restaurant, a coin-operated laundry, ice, a playground, boat docks, launching facilities, and boat rentals are available. Leashed pets are permitted.

Reservations, fees: Reservations accepted. Sites are $19.75 per night, $2 per person per night for more than two people, and a $2.50 per pet per night. Senior discount available. Major credit cards accepted. Open late April–September.

Directions: From Spokane, drive north on U.S.

395 for 42 miles to the Valley-Waitts Lake exit. Turn left (west) at that exit and drive six miles to Waitts Lake and the resort on the left-hand side near the shore of the lake.

Contact: Silver Beach Resort, 3323 Waitts Lake Rd., Valley, WA 99181, 509/937-2811, fax 509/937-2816.

90 WAITTS LAKE RESORT

Rating: 7

On Waitts Lake.
Map 4.3, grid g2, page 258

The shore of Waitts Lake is home to this clean, comfortable resort, where lake views are available and ice fishing is popular in the winter. See the previous description of Winona Beach Resort and RV Park for information about the lake.

Campsites, facilities: There are 13 sites with full hookups for tents or RVs up to 40 feet long. Picnic tables and fire rings are provided. Restrooms, drinking water, flush toilets, showers, a store, a year-round restaurant, firewood, boat docks, boat rentals, launching facilities, and ice are available. Leashed pets are allowed.

Reservations, fees: Reservations recommended. Sites are $19.50 per night, $5 per person for more than four people, and a $5 per pet per night. Major credit cards accepted. Open early April–late October.

Directions: From Spokane, drive north on U.S. 395 for 42 miles to the Valley-Waitts Lake exit. Turn left (west) at that exit and drive one mile to Highway 231. Turn right (north) on Highway 231 and drive 1.5 miles to the town of Valley and Valley-Waitts Lake Road. Turn left and drive three miles to the resort on the left.

Contact: Waitts Lake Resort, 3365 Waitts Lake Rd., Valley, WA 99181, 509/937-2400.

91 JUMP OFF JOE LAKE RESORT

Rating: 7

On Jump Off Joe Lake.
Map 4.3, grid g3, page 258

Located on the edge of Jump Off Joe Lake, this wooded campground offers lake views and easy boating access. Recreational activities include boating, fishing, and swimming. Spokane and Grand Coulee Dam are both within a short drive and provide excellent side-trip options. Within 10 miles to the north are an 18-hole golf course and casino.

Campsites, facilities: There are 20 sites for tents, 20 sites with full hookups, including one drive-through site, for tents or RVs, and five cabins. Picnic tables and fire rings are provided. Restrooms, drinking water, flush toilets, showers, a pay phone, horseshoe pits, a recreation field, a store, a swimming beach, and a barbecue are available. The camp also rents boats and has a boat ramp and dock. Some facilities are wheelchair accessible. Leashed pets are permitted.

Reservations, fees: Reservations recommended. Sites are $16.50–18.50 per night. A pet fee of $2.50 per night is charged. Major credit cards accepted. Open April–October.

Directions: From Spokane, drive north on U.S. 395 for about 40 miles (three miles south of the town of Valley) to the Jump Off Joe Road exit (Milepost 198). Take that exit, turn west, and drive 1.2 miles to the campground on the right.

Contact: Jump Off Joe Lake Resort, 3290 East Jump Off Joe Rd., Valley, WA 99181, 509/937-2133.

92 SHORE ACRES

Rating: 8

On Loon Lake.
Map 4.3, grid h3, page 258

Located along the shore of Loon Lake at 2,400 feet elevation, this family-oriented campground has a long expanse of beach and offers an alternative to Granite Point Park across the lake. See the description of Granite Point Park for details about the fishing opportunities.

Campsites, facilities: There are 30 sites with full hookups for tents or RVs up to 40 feet long and 10 cabins. Picnic tables are provided. Restrooms, drinking water, flush toilets, showers, an RV dump station, cable TV, a general store, firewood, propane, ice, a playground, a swimming area, boat docks, boat rentals, and launching facilities are available. Leashed pets are permitted.

Reservations, fees: Reservations recommended. Sites are $25 per night, pets $2.50 per night. Cabins are $480–615 per week in July and August, $80–100 per night the rest of the year. Major credit cards accepted. Open mid-April–September.

Directions: From Spokane, drive north on U.S. 395 for 30 miles to Highway 292. Turn west on Highway 292 and drive two miles to Shore Acres Road. Turn left and drive another two miles to the park.

Contact: Shore Acres, 41987 Shore Acres Rd., Loon Lake, WA 99148, 800/900-2474 or 509/233-2474, fax 509/233-9259, website: www.shoreacresresort.com.

93 GRANITE POINT PARK

Rating: 8

On Loon Lake.
Map 4.3, grid h3, page 258

This camp is located on the shore of Loon Lake, a clear, clean, spring-fed lake that covers 1,200 acres and features a sandy beach and swimming area. The campground features grass sites, no concrete. In the spring, the mackinaw trout range from 4–30 pounds and can be taken by deepwater trolling (downriggers suggested). Easier to catch are the kokanee salmon and rainbow trout in the 12- to 14-inch class. A sprinkling of perch, sunfish, and bass come out of their hiding places when the weather heats up. Water-skiing and windsurfing are popular in summer months.

Campsites, facilities: There are 80 sites with full hookups for RVs up to 40 feet long and 25 cottages with kitchens. Picnic tables and barbecues are provided. Restrooms, drinking water, flush toilets, showers, a recreation hall, a store, a café, a coin-operated laundry, ice, a playground with basketball, volleyball, and horseshoe pits, three swimming areas with a three-quarter-mile beach, two swimming docks, boat docks, boat rentals, and launching facilities are available. Bottled gas is located within one mile. Pets are not permitted.

Reservations, fees: Reservations accepted. Sites are $22 per night, $2 per person per night for more than two people. Open mid-April–mid-September.

Directions: From Spokane, drive north on U.S. 395 for 26 miles (eight miles past the town of Deer Park) to the campground on the left.

Contact: Granite Point Park, 41000 Granite Point Rd., Loon Lake, WA 99148, 509/233-2100, website: www.granitepointpark.com.

94 PEND OREILLE COUNTY PARK

Rating: 6

Near Newport.
Map 4.3, grid h6, page 258

This 440-acre park is wooded and features hiking trails throughout. There is some road noise from U.S. 2, but it's not intolerable. Pend Oreille is the only campground around, and it's not a bad choice if you're looking for a layover spot. It's a good alternative to the often-crowded Mt. Spokane State Park. Nearby activities include fishing and hunting.

Campsites, facilities: There are 34 sites for tents and two sites for RVs up to 30 feet long. No hookups are available. Picnic tables and barbecues are provided. Restrooms, drinking water, flush toilets, and showers are available. Leashed pets are permitted.

Reservations, fees: Reservations at 509/447-4821. Sites are $10–13 per night. Open Memorial Day Weekend to Labor Day Weekend.

Directions: From Spokane, drive north on U.S. 395 for six miles to U.S. 2. Turn north on U.S. 2 and drive 31 miles to the county park entrance on the left (west side). Or from Newport: Drive east on U.S 2 for 13 miles (past County Road 211) to the park entrance on the right.

Contact: Pend Oreille County Department of Parks and Recreation, P.O. Box 5067, Newport, WA 99156, 509/447-4821, website: www.pendoreillecounty.org.

95 LAKESHORE RV PARK AND MARINA

Rating: 7

On Lake Chelan.
Map 4.4, grid b1, page 259

This municipal park and marina on Lake Chelan is a popular family camp, with fishing, swimming, boating, and hiking among the available activities. The camp fills up in the summer, including on weekdays in July and August. This RV park covers 22 acres, featuring a large marina and a 15-acre day-use area. An 18-hole championship golf course and putting green, lighted tennis courts, and a visitors center are nearby. A trip worth taking, the ferry ride goes to several landings on the lake; the ferry terminal is one-half mile from the park.

Campsites, facilities: There are 167 sites with full hookups for tents or RVs of any length. Picnic tables are provided. Restrooms, flush toilets, coin-operated showers, an RV dump station, and a covered picnic area with a shelter are available. A store, a café, a coin-operated laundry, ice, a playground, and bottled gas are available within one mile. Boat docks and launching facilities are on-site.

Reservations, fees: Reservations accepted for each year beginning January 2. Sites are $11–33 per night, $5 per person for more than four people, $6 per extra vehicle per night. Major credit cards accepted. Open year-round.

Directions: From East Wenatchee, drive north on Highway 97-A for 40 miles to Chelan (after crossing the Dan Gordon Bridge, the road name changes to Saunders Street). Continue for one-tenth of a mile to Johnson Street. Turn left and drive two-tenths of a mile (becomes Highway 150/Manson Highway) to the campground on the left.

Contact: City of Chelan, P.O. Box 1669, Chelan, WA 98816, 509/682-8024, fax 509/682-8248, website: www.chelancityparks.com.

96 COULEE PLAYLAND RESORT

Rating: 7

Near the Grand Coulee Dam.
Map 4.4, grid a8, page 259

This park on North Banks Lake, south of the Grand Coulee Dam, is pretty and well treed, with spacious sites for both tents and RVs. The Grand Coulee Laser Light Show is just two miles away and is well worth a visit. Boating, fishing for many species, and water-skiing are all popular. In addition, hiking trails, marked bike trails, a full-service marina, and tennis courts are close by.

Campsites, facilities: There are 65 sites for tents or RVs of any length, and one yurt, which sleeps five. Picnic tables and fire grills are provided. Restrooms, flush toilets, coin-operated showers, an RV dump station, a store, a coin-operated laundry, firewood, ice, a playground, boat docks, launching facilities, boat rentals, gas, and a bait and tackle shop are available. Bottled gas and a café are located within one mile. Pets are permitted.

Reservations, fees: Reservations accepted. Sites are $18–21 per night, $10 per extra vehicle per night. Major credit cards accepted. Open year-round, with limited winter facilities.

Directions: From the junction of Highway 17 and U.S. 2 (north of Ephrata), drive east on U.S. 2 for five miles to Highway 155. Turn left (north) and drive 26 miles to Grand Coulee

and Electric City. The campground is just off the highway on the left.

Contact: Coulee Playland Resort, P.O. Box 457, 401 Coulee Blvd., Electric City, WA 99123, 509/633-2671, fax 509/633-2133, website: www.couleeplayland.com.

97 STEAMBOAT ROCK STATE PARK

Rating: 10

On Banks Lake.
Map 4.4, grid b7, page 259

Steamboat Rock State Park is an oasis in desert surroundings. The park covers 3,522 acres and features nine miles of shoreline along Banks Lake, a reservoir created by the Grand Coulee Dam. Dominating the landscape is the columnar basaltic rock, with a surface area of 600 acres, that rises 800 feet above the lake. Two campground areas and a large day-use area are set on green lawns sheltered by tall poplars. The park has 13 miles of hiking and biking trails, as well as 10 miles of horse trails. There is also a swimming beach. Fishing and water-skiing are popular; so is rock climbing. A hiking trail leads to Northrup Lake. Horse trails are available in nearby Northrup Canyon. Note that the one downer is mosquitoes, which are very prevalent in early summer. During the winter, the park is used by snowmobilers, cross-country skiers, and ice anglers.

Campsites, facilities: There are 100 sites with full hookups for RVs up to 50 feet long, 26 sites for tents or self-contained RVs, and 92 primitive campsites. Picnic tables and fire grills are provided. Restrooms, flush toilets, an RV dump station, a café, and a playground with volleyball are available. Some facilities are wheelchair accessible. Boat-launching facilities, docks, and a marine dump station are nearby. Leashed pets are permitted.

Reservations, fees: Reserve at 888/CAMP-OUT (888/226-7688), website: www.parks.wa.gov/reservations ($7 reservation fee). Sites are $16–22 per

night, $6 per extra vehicle per night. Senior discount available. Major credit cards accepted. Open year-round, with limited winter facilities. **Directions:** From East Wenatchee, drive north U.S. 2 for 70 miles to Highway 155 (five miles east of Coulee City). Turn north and drive 18 miles to the park on the left.
Contact: Steamboat Rock State Park, P.O. Box 352, Electric City, WA 99123, 509/633-1304, fax 509/633-1294. State Park information, 360/902-8844.

98 BLUE LAKE RESORT

Rating: 6

On Blue Lake.
Map 4.4, grid d5, page 259
Blue Lake Resort is set in a desert-like area along the shore of Blue Lake between Sun Lakes State Park and Lake Lenore Caves State Park. Both parks make excellent side trips. Activities at Blue Lake include trout fishing, swimming, and boating. Tackle and boat rentals are available at the resort.
Campsites, facilities: There are 56 sites with full or partial hookups, including six drive-through sites, for RVs of any length, 30 tent sites, and 10 cabins that sleep up to four people. Picnic tables and fire pits are provided. Restrooms, flush toilets, showers, an RV dump station, firewood, a store, ice, a roped swimming area, volleyball, a playground, boat docks, launching facilities, and boat rentals are available. Leashed pets are permitted.
Reservations, fees: Reservations are accepted. The fee is $15.50 per night, $2 per person for more than four people. Major credit cards accepted. Open April–September.
Directions: From the junction of I-90 and Highway 17 (just south of Moses Lake), drive north on Highway 17 for 36 miles to the park on the right.
Contact: Blue Lake Resort, 31199 Hwy. 17 N, Coulee City, WA 99115, 509/632-5364 or 509/632-5388.

99 SUN VILLAGE RESORT

Rating: 6

On Blue Lake.
Map 4.4, grid d5, page 259
Like Blue Lake Resort, this campground is situated along the shore of Blue Lake. The hot desert setting is perfect for swimming and fishing. Late July and early August are the busiest times of the year here. See the following description of Sun Lakes State Park for information on the nearby state parks and other recreation options.
Campsites, facilities: There are 95 sites, including 40 drive-through and most with full hookups, for RVs of any length and four tent sites. Picnic tables are provided. Restrooms, flush toilets, coin-operated showers, group fire pits, bottled gas, an RV dump station, a coin-operated laundry, a store, a café, bait and tackle, ice, a playground, boat docks, launching facilities, and boat rentals are available. Firewood can be obtained for a fee. Leashed pets are permitted.
Reservations, fees: Reservations accepted. Sites are $18.50 per night, $4 per extra vehicle per night, and $3 per pet per night. Major credit cards accepted. Open late April–late September.
Directions: From the junction of I-90 and Highway 17 (just south of Moses Lake), drive north on Highway 17 for 36 miles to Blue Lake and Park Lake Road. Turn right (east) on Park Lake Road (the south entrance) and drive one-half mile to the resort on the right.
Contact: Sun Village Resort, 33575 Park Lake Rd. NE, Coulee City, WA 99115, 509/632-5664 or 888/632-5664, 509/632-5360.

100 COULEE LODGE RESORT

Rating: 8

On Blue Lake.
Map 4.4, grid d5, page 259
This camp is set at Blue Lake, which often pro-

vides outstanding fishing for a mix of stocked rainbow trout and brown trout in early spring. It is one of five camps in the general area and one of three in the immediate vicinity. Blue Lake offers plenty of summertime recreation options, including a swimming beach. See the following description of Sun Lakes State Park for details.

Campsites, facilities: There are 22 sites with full hookups, including seven drive-through sites, for RVs up to 35 feet long and 14 tent sites. Picnic tables and fire pits are provided. Restrooms, flush toilets, coin-operated showers, bottled gas, an RV dump station, a store, firewood, a coin-operated laundry, boat docks, boat and personal watercraft rentals, launching facilities, and ice are available. A café is located within five miles. Some facilities are wheelchair accessible. Leashed pets are permitted.

Reservations, fees: Reservations accepted. Sites are $16–20 per night, $3 per person for more than two people, $3 per extra vehicle per night, and $2 per pet per night. Major credit cards accepted. Open mid-April–October.

Directions: From the junction of I-90 and Highway 17 (just south of Moses Lake), drive north on Highway 17 for 39 miles to the north end of Blue Lake.

Contact: Coulee Lodge Resort, 33017 Park Lake Rd. NE, Coulee City, WA, 509/632-5565, fax 509/632-8607, website: www.couleelodge resort.com.

101 SUN LAKES STATE PARK

Rating: 10

On Park Lake.
Map 4.4, grid d5, page 259

Sun Lakes State Park is situated on the shore of Park Lake, which is used primarily by anglers, boaters, and water-skiers. This 4,027-acre park near the foot of Dry Falls features 12 miles of shoreline. Dry Falls, a former waterfall, is now a stark 400-foot-high climb, 3.5 miles wide. During the Ice Age floods, this waterfall was

10 times the size of Niagara Falls. An interpretive center at Dry Falls is open May–September. Now, back to the present: There are nine lakes in the park. A trail at the north end of Lake Lenore leads to the Lake Lenore Caves. Nearby recreation possibilities include a nine-hole golf course and miniature golf.

Campsites, facilities: There are 162 sites for tents or self-contained RVs, 18 sites with full hookups for RVs up to 50 feet long, and one group campsite for up to 40 people. Picnic tables and fire pits are provided. Restrooms, flush toilets, coin-operated showers, an RV dump station, a café, a coin-operated laundry, ice, electricity, drinking water, sewer hookups, and firewood for sale are available. A store is located within one mile. Some facilities are wheelchair accessible. Boat docks, launching facilities, and rentals are nearby. Leashed pets are permitted.

Reservations, fees: Reserve at 888/CAMP-OUT (888/226-7688), website: www.parks.wa.gov/reservations ($7 reservation fee). Sites are $16–22 per night. Senior discount available. Major credit cards accepted. Open year-round.

Directions: From Ephrata, drive northeast on Highway 28 to Soap Lake and Highway 17. Turn north on Highway 17 and drive 17 miles to the park on the right.

Contact: Sun Lakes State Park, 509/632-5583, fax 509/632-5971; State Park information, 360/902-8844.

102 SUN LAKES PARK RESORT

Rating: 6

Sun Lakes State Park.
Map 4.4, grid d5, page 259

Run by the concessionaire that operates within Sun Lakes State Park, this camp offers full facilities and is a slightly more developed alternative to the state campground. See the description of Sun Lakes State Park.

Campsites, facilities: There are 110 sites with full hookups, including 64 drive-through for tents or RVs of any length. Picnic tables and fire grills are provided. Restrooms, flush toilets, coin-operated showers, bottled gas, an RV dump station, a store, firewood, a snack bar, a coin-operated laundry, ice, a playground, boat rentals, and a swimming pool are available. Boat docks and launching facilities are nearby. Some facilities are wheelchair accessible. Leashed pets are permitted.

Reservations, fees: Reservations accepted. Sites are $25–27 per night, $6 per extra vehicle per night. Open mid-April–mid-October, weather permitting.

Directions: From Ephrata, drive northeast on Highway 28 to Soap Lake and Highway 17. Turn north on Highway 17 and drive 17 miles to the Sun Lakes Park on the right. Enter the park and drive to the resort (well marked).

Contact: Sun Lakes Park Resort, 34228 Park Lake Rd. NE, Coulee City, WA 99115, 509/632-5291, fax 509/754-6240, website: www.sunlakesparkresort.com.

103 COULEE CITY PARK

Rating: 6

On Banks Lake.
Map 4.4, grid c6, page 259
Coulee City Park is a well-maintained park located in shade trees on the southern shore of 30-mile-long Banks Lake. You can see the highway from the park, and there is some highway noise. Campsites are usually available. The busiest time of the year is Memorial Day weekend because of the local rodeo. Boating, fishing, and water-skiing are popular. An 18-hole golf course is close by.

Campsites, facilities: There are 100 tent sites and 55 sites for RVs up to 35 feet long, including 32 drive-through sites with full hookups. Picnic tables and fire rings are provided. Restrooms, flush toilets, showers, group fire pits, an RV dump station, and a playground are available. Bottled gas, firewood, a store, a restaurant, a café, a coin-operated laundry, and

ice are located within one mile. Some facilities are wheelchair accessible. Boat docks and launching facilities are on-site.

Reservations, fees: Reservations are not accepted. Sites are $12–17 per night, $2 per extra vehicle. Open April–late October, weather permitting.

Directions: From Coulee City, drive east on U.S. 2 for one-half mile to the park on the left.

Contact: Coulee City Park, P.O. Box 398, Coulee City, WA 99115, 509/632-5331.

104 SPRING CANYON

Rating: 6

On Franklin Roosevelt Lake in Lake Roosevelt National Recreation Area.
Map 4.5, grid a1, page 260
This large, developed campground is a popular vacation destination. Fishing for bass, walleye, trout, and sunfish is popular at Franklin Roosevelt Lake, as is water-skiing. The campground is not far from Grand Coulee Dam. Lake Roosevelt National Recreation Area offers numerous recreation options, such as free programs conducted by rangers that include guided canoe trips, historical tours, campfire talks, and guided hikes. This lake is known as a prime location to view bald eagles, especially in winter. Side-trip options include visiting the Colville Tribal Museum in the town of Coulee Dam and touring the Grand Coulee Dam Visitor Center. Almost one mile long and twice as high as Niagara Falls, the dam is one of the largest concrete structures ever built. It is open for self-guided tours.

Campsites, facilities: There are 87 sites for tents or self-contained RVs up to 26 feet long and one group site for up to 25 people. Picnic tables and fire grills are provided. Restrooms, flush toilets, an RV dump station, a café, a picnic area, a public telephone, and a playground are available. Some facilities are wheelchair accessible. Boat docks, launching facilities, marine fuel, and a marine dump station are available nearby. Leashed pets are permitted.

Reservations, fees: Reservations are not accepted for family sites. Sites are $5–10 per night; $6 launch fee. Senior discount available. Reservations required for the group site at 509/633-3830. Open year-round, weather permitting.

Directions: From the junction of I-90 and Highway 17 (just south of Moses Lake), drive north on Highway 17 for 45 miles to U.S. 2. Turn east on U.S. 2 and drive five miles to Highway 155. Turn left (north) and drive 26 miles to Grand Coulee and Highway 174. Turn right (east) on Highway 174 and drive three miles to the campground entrance on the left.

Contact: Lake Roosevelt National Recreation Area, 1008 Crest Dr., Coulee Dam, WA 99116-1259, 509/633-9441, fax 509/633-5125.

105 LAKEVIEW TERRACE MOBILE AND RV PARK

Rating: 6

Near Franklin Roosevelt Lake.
Map 4.5, grid a1, page 260

This pleasant resort is situated near Franklin Roosevelt Lake, which was created by Grand Coulee Dam. It provides a slightly less crowded alternative to the national park camps in the vicinity. See the description of Spring Canyon for water recreation options. A full-service marina and tennis courts are nearby.

Campsites, facilities: There are 20 drive-through sites with full hookups for RVs of any length, 20 tent sites, and a group camp for up to 100 tents. Picnic tables and fire pits are provided. Restrooms, flush toilets, coin-operated showers, a coin-operated laundry, and a playground are available. Boat docks, launching facilities, and rentals are nearby. Leashed pets are permitted.

Reservations, fees: Reservations accepted. Sites are $15–18 per night, with an additional fee

for more than four people. The group site is $13 per tent. Senior discount available. Major credit cards accepted. Open year-round.

Directions: From Grand Coulee, drive east on Highway 174 for 3.5 miles east to the park entrance on the left.

Contact: Lakeview Terrace Mobile and RV Park, 44900 Rte. 174 N, Grand Coulee, WA 99133, 509/633-2169, website: www.lakeviewsterracepark.com.

106 KELLER FERRY

Rating: 7

On Franklin Roosevelt Lake in Lake Roosevelt National Recreation Area.
Map 4.5, grid a3, page 260

This camp is set along the shore of Franklin Roosevelt Lake, a large reservoir created by Grand Coulee Dam, which sits about 15 miles west of camp. Franklin Roosevelt Lake is known for its walleye fishing; although more than 30 species live in this lake, 90 percent of those caught are walleye. They average one–four pounds and always travel in schools. Trout and salmon often swim below the bluffs near Keller Ferry. Water-skiing, fishing, and swimming are all recreation options here.

Campsites, facilities: There are 50 sites for tents or RVs up to 16 feet long and two group sites for up to 50 people each. Picnic tables and fire grills are provided. Drinking water and vault toilets are available. An RV dump station, ice, a picnic area, a public telephone, and a playground are available nearby. Boat docks, launching facilities, fuel, and a marine dump station are also available. Some facilities are wheelchair accessible. Leashed pets are permitted.

Reservations, fees: Reservations are not accepted for family sites. Sites are $5–10 per night; there is a $6 launch fee. Reservations required for group sites, 509/633-3830. Senior discount available. Open year-round, weather permitting.

Directions: From Spokane on U.S. 90, turn

west on U.S. 2 and drive 71 miles to Wilbur and Highway 21. Turn north and drive 14 miles to the campground on the left.

Contact: Lake Roosevelt National Recreation Area, 1008 Crest Dr., Coulee Dam, WA 99116-1259, 509/633-9441, fax 509/633-9332.

107 RIVER RUE RV PARK

Rating: 7

Near the Columbia River.
Map 4.5, grid a3, page 260

This camp is located in high desert terrain yet is surrounded by lots of trees. Several hiking trails leave from the campground. You can fish, swim, water-ski, or rent a houseboat at Lake Roosevelt, which is one mile away. Another nearby side trip is to the Grand Coulee Dam. A nine-hole golf course is available in Wilbur.

Campsites, facilities: There are 86 sites for tents or RVs of any length, including some with full hookups, some with partial hookups, and some drive-through sites. Picnic tables and fire rings are provided. Restrooms, showers, an RV dump station, a pay phone, limited groceries, ice, a snack bar, RV supplies, fishing tackle, and LP gas are available. Recreational facilities include a playground, volleyball, and horseshoe pits. Some facilities are wheelchair accessible. Leashed pets are permitted.

Reservations, fees: Reservations recommended. Sites are $15–22 per night, $2 per person per night for more than two people. Major credit cards accepted. Open April–October.

Directions: On U.S. 2 at Wilbur, drive west on U.S. 2 for one mile to Highway 174. Turn north on Highway 174 and drive one-quarter mile to Highway 21. Turn right (north) on Highway 21 and drive 13 miles to the park on the right.

Contact: River Rue RV Park, 44892 Rte. 21 N, Wilbur, WA 99185, 509/647-2647, website: www.riverrue.com.

108 JONES BAY

Rating: 6

On Franklin Roosevelt Lake in Lake Roosevelt National Recreation Area.
Map 4.5, grid a4, page 260

This small and primitive campground is set on Jones Bay on Franklin Roosevelt Lake. Well known by locals, it gets high use on summer weekends. The camp is located at the bottom of a canyon in a cove with some Ponderosa pine and is quiet most weekdays. Fishing for bass, walleye, trout, and sunfish is popular at the Franklin Roosevelt Lake.

Campsites, facilities: There are nine sites for tents or self-contained RVs up to 16 feet long. Picnic tables and fire grills are provided. Vault toilets are available. No drinking water is available. A boat launch and dock is nearby. Some facilities are wheelchair accessible. Leashed pets are permitted.

Reservations, fees: Reservations are not accepted. Sites are $5–10 per night; $6 launch fee. Senior discount available. Open year-round, weather permitting.

Directions: From Spokane on U.S. 90, turn west on U.S. 2 and drive 71 miles to Wilbur and Highway 21. Turn north on Highway 21 and drive seven miles to Jones Bay Road (dirt road, marked). Turn right and drive eight miles to the campground entrance road on the right. A high-clearance vehicle is recommended.

Contact: Lake Roosevelt National Recreation Area, 1008 Crest Dr., Coulee Dam, WA 99116-1259, 509/633-9441, fax 509/633-9332.

109 HAWK CREEK

Rating: 8

On Franklin Roosevelt Lake in Lake Roosevelt National Recreation Area.
Map 4.5, grid b6, page 260

This pleasant camping spot is located along the shore of Roosevelt Lake (Columbia River), adjacent to the mouth of Hawk Creek. This is often a good fishing spot for walleye, trout, and bass. Note that there is no drinking water if the lake level drops below an elevation of 1,265 feet.

Campsites, facilities: There are 20 sites for tents or RVs up to 16 feet long. Picnic tables and fire grills are provided. Drinking water and vault toilets are available. Boat docks and launching facilities are nearby. Some facilities are wheelchair accessible. Leashed pets are permitted.

Reservations, fees: Reservations are not accepted. Sites are $5–10 per night; there is a $6 launch fee. Senior discount available. Open year-round, with limited winter facilities.

Directions: From Spokane on I-90, drive west for four miles to U.S. 2. Turn west on U.S. 2 and drive 34 miles to Davenport and Highway 25. Turn right (north) on Highway 25 and drive 23 miles to Miles-Creston Road. Turn left (northwest) and drive 10 miles to the campground at the mouth of Hawk Creek on the left.

Contact: Lake Roosevelt National Recreation Area, 1008 Crest Dr., Coulee Dam, WA 99116-1259, 509/633-9441, fax 509/633-9332.

110 SEVEN BAYS RESORT AND MARINA

Rating: 6

On Franklin Roosevelt Lake.

Map 4.5, grid a6, page 260

Friendly folks run this resort on the shore of Roosevelt Lake, where the highlights include manicured, grassy, lakeside sites among deciduous trees. This camp is an alternative to Fort Spokane and Hawk Creek. A full-service marina sets this spot apart from the others.

Campsites, facilities: There are 48 sites with full hookups, including two drive-through sites, for RVs up to 50 feet long and 24 tent sites. Picnic tables are provided. Restrooms, drink-

ing water, flush toilets, coin-operated showers, bottled gas, an RV dump station, a store, a café, a coin-operated laundry, and ice are available. Boat rentals, docks, and launching facilities are located at the resort. Leashed pets are permitted.

Reservations, fees: Reservations accepted. Sites are $10–15 per night. Major credit cards accepted. Open year-round.

Directions: From Spokane on I-90, drive west for four miles to U.S. 2. Turn west on U.S. 2 and drive 34 miles to Highway 25. Turn north on Highway 25 and drive 23 miles to Miles-Creston Road. Turn left and drive five miles to the resort on the right.

Contact: Seven Bays Resort, Rte. 1, 1250 Marina Dr., Seven Bays, WA 99122, 509/725-1676.

111 FORT SPOKANE

Rating: 8

On Franklin Roosevelt Lake in Lake Roosevelt National Recreation Area.

Map 4.5, grid a6, page 260

Rangers offer evening campfire programs and guided daytime activities at this modern campground on the shore of Roosevelt Lake. This park also hosts living-history demonstrations. Fort Spokane is one of 28 campgrounds on the 130-mile-long lake. A 190-mile scenic vehicle route encircles most of the lake.

Campsites, facilities: There are 67 sites for tents or RVs up to 26 feet long and two group sites for up to 30 people each. Picnic tables and fire grills are provided. Restrooms, drinking water, flush toilets, an RV dump station, and a playground are available. A picnic area and a public telephone are nearby. A store and ice are located within one mile. Some facilities are wheelchair accessible. Boat docks, launching facilities, and a marine dump station are nearby. Leashed pets are permitted.

Reservations, fees: Reservations are not accepted for family sites. Reservations required for group sites at 509/633-3830. Sites are $5–10 per night; there is a $6 launch fee. Senior discount available. Open year-round, with limited winter facilities.

Directions: From Spokane on I-90, drive west for four miles to U.S. 2. Turn west on U.S. 2 and drive 34 miles to Davenport and Highway 25. Turn right (north) on Highway 25 and drive 22 miles to the campground entrance on the right.

Contact: Lake Roosevelt National Recreation Area, 1008 Crest Dr., Coulee Dam, WA 99116-1259, 509/633-9441, fax 509/633-9332.

112 PORCUPINE BAY

Rating: 8

On Franklin Roosevelt Lake in Lake Roosevelt National Recreation Area.

Map 4.5, grid a7, page 260

This camp is extremely popular, and the sites are filled most of the summer. Its proximity to a nearby dock and launch makes it an especially good spot for campers with boats. A swimming beach is located adjacent to the campground.

Campsites, facilities: There are 31 sites for tents or RVs up to 20 feet long. Picnic tables and fire grills are provided. Drinking water and vault toilets are available. Restrooms, drinking water, flush toilets, an RV dump station, a picnic area, a public telephone, and a playground are available. Boat docks and launching facilities are nearby. Some facilities are wheelchair accessible. Leashed pets are permitted.

Reservations, fees: Reservations are not accepted. Sites are $5–10 per night; $6 boat-launch fee. Senior discount available. Open year-round, weather permitting.

Directions: From Spokane on I-90, drive west for four miles to U.S. 2. Turn west on U.S. 2 and drive 34 miles to Davenport and Highway 25. Turn right (north) on Highway 25 and drive 19 miles to Porcupine Bay Road. Turn right (east) and drive 4.3 miles to the campground at the end of the road.

Contact: Lake Roosevelt National Recreation

Area, 1008 Crest Dr., Coulee Dam, WA 99116-1259, 509/633-9441, fax 509/633-9332.

113 LONG LAKE CAMP AND PICNIC AREA

Rating: 8

On the Spokane River.

Map 4.6, grid b1, page 261

This campground is located about 45 minutes from Spokane. The camp is set on a terrace above Long Lake (Spokane River), where fishing can be good for rainbow trout and occasional brown trout. This area is also popular for power boating, water-skiing, and personal watercraft. Crowded in summer, it gets a lot of use from residents of the Spokane area.

Campsites, facilities: There are 12 sites for tents or small RVs. Picnic tables, fire grills, and tent pads are provided. Drinking water and vault toilets are available. A boat launch, a dock, a swimming beach, and a day-use area are nearby. Most of the facilities are wheelchair accessible.

Reservations, fees: Reservations are not accepted. There is no fee for camping. Open April–September.

Directions: From Spokane on I-90, drive west for four miles to U.S. 2. Turn west on U.S. 2 and drive 21 miles to Reardan and Highway 231. Turn north on Highway 231 and drive 14.2 miles to Long Lake Dam Road (Highway 291). Turn right and drive 4.7 miles to the campground entrance on the right.

Contact: Department of Natural Resources, Northeast Region, P.O. Box 190, Colville, WA 99114-0190, 509/684-7474, fax 509/684-7484.

114 DRAGOON CREEK

Rating: 5

Near the Little Spokane River.

Map 4.6, grid a5, page 261

This spot is frequented by locals but is often missed by out-of-town vacationers. The camp is set along Dragoon Creek, a tributary to the Little Spokane River. Its campsites are situated in a forest of Ponderosa pine and Douglas fir. Although fairly close to U.S. 395, it remains quiet and rustic. The Department of Natural Resources offers a map that details the region.

Campsites, facilities: There are 22 sites for tents or small RVs. Picnic tables, fire grills, and tent pads are provided. Vault toilets and drinking water are available. Leashed pets are permitted.

Reservations, fees: Reservations are not accepted. There is no fee for camping. Open April–September.

Directions: From Spokane, drive north on U.S. 395 for 10.2 miles to Dragoon Creek Road. Turn left on Dragoon Creek Road and drive four-tenths of a mile to the campground entrance at the end of the road.

Contact: Department of Natural Resources, Northeast Region, P.O. Box 190, Colville, WA 99114-0190, 509/684-7474, fax 509/684-7484.

115 MT. SPOKANE STATE PARK

Rating: 8

On Mt. Spokane.

Map 4.6, grid a7, page 261

This state park provides one of the better short trips available out of Spokane. It is set on the slopes of Mt. Spokane (5,883 feet), and little brother, Mt. Kit Carson (5,180 feet), sits alongside it. The park covers 13,643 acres in the Selkirk Mountains and features a stunning view from the top of Mt. Spokane. The lookout takes in Washington, Idaho, Montana, and Canada. The park has 86 miles of hiking trails, occasionally routed into old-growth forest and amid granite outcroppings. The Mt. Spokane Ski Resort operates here in winter. The park receives an average of 300 inches of snow annually.

Campsites, facilities: There are 12 sites for tents or self-contained RVs up to 30 feet long. Picnic tables and fire grills are provided. Restrooms, drinking water, and flush toilets are

available. A picnic area with a kitchen shelter, interpretive activities, and a café are available nearby, and a coin-operated laundry is within one mile. Leashed pets are permitted.

Reservations, fees: Reservations are not accepted. Sites are $16 per night, $6 per extra vehicle per night. Open June–September, weather permitting.

Directions: From Spokane, drive north on U.S. 395 for six miles to U.S. 2. Turn north on U.S. 2 and drive six miles to Highway 206. Turn northeast on Highway 206 and drive 15 miles north to the park.

Contact: Mt. Spokane State Park, 509/238-4258; State Park information, 360/902-8844.

116 RIVERSIDE STATE PARK

Rating: 8

Near Spokane.

Map 4.6, grid b4, page 261

This 10,000-acre park is set along the Spokane and Little Spokane Rivers and features freshwater marshes and a beautiful countryside. There are many recreation options, including fishing for bass, crappie, and perch. There are 55 miles of hiking and biking trails, featuring the 37-mile Centennial Trail, and 25 miles of trails for horseback riding, as well as riding stables nearby. The park also has a 600-acre riding area for dirt bikes in summer and snowmobiles in winter. An 18-hole golf course is located nearby. A local point of interest is the unique Bowl and Pitcher Lava Formation in the river.

Campsites, facilities: There are 22 tent sites, 17 sites with partial hookups for tents or RVs up to 45 feet long, three primitive tent sites, and two large group sites. Picnic tables and fire grills are provided. Restrooms, drinking water, flush toilets, showers, a picnic area with a kitchen shelter and electricity, an RV dump station, interpretive programs, and firewood are available. A store, a restaurant, and ice are located within three miles. Group camping can be accommodated. Boat-launching facilities and a dock are located on-site. Leashed pets are permitted.

Reservations, fees: Reservations are not accepted for family sites. Sites are $6–22 per night, $6 per extra vehicle per night. Senior discount available. Group site reservations required at least two weeks in advance at 509/465-5064. Open year-round.

Directions: In Spokane on I-90, take Exit 280/Maple Street North (cross the Maple Street Bridge), and drive north 1.1 miles to Maxwell Street (becomes Pettit Street). Turn left (west) and drive 1.9 miles, bearing left along the Spokane River to the park entrance. From the park entrance, continue for 1.5 miles on Aubrey L. White Parkway to the campground.

Contact: Riverside State Park, 9711 West Charles Rd., Nine Mile Falls, WA 99026, 509/465-5064; State Park information, 360/902-8844.

117 TRAILER INNS RV PARK

Rating: 5

In Spokane.
Map 4.6, grid c5, page 261

This large RV park makes a perfect layover spot on the way to Idaho. It's as close to a hotel as an RV park can get. Nearby recreation options include an 18-hole golf course, a racquet club, and tennis courts.

Campsites, facilities: There are 97 sites with full hookups, including 30 drive-through sites, for tents or RVs of any length. Picnic tables are provided. Restrooms, drinking water, flush toilets, showers, bottled gas, cable TV, a TV room, a coin-operated laundry, ice, and a playground are available. An RV dump station, a store, and a café are within one mile. Leashed pets are permitted.

Reservations, fees: Reservations accepted. Sites are $15–23 per night, two vehicles per site. Major credit cards accepted. Open year-round.

Directions: Note that your route will depend on your direction: In Spokane eastbound on I-90, take Exit 285 (Sprague Avenue/Eastern Road) to Eastern Road. Drive one-tenth of a mile on Eastern Road to Fourth Avenue. Turn right (west) on Fourth Avenue and drive two blocks to the campground. In Spokane westbound on I-90, take Exit 284 (Havana Street). Drive one block south on Havana Street to Fourth Avenue. Turn left (east) on Fourth Avenue and drive one mile to the park.

Contact: Trailer Inns RV Park, 6021 East Fourth Ave., Spokane, WA 99212, 509/535-1811 or 800/659-4864.

118 KOA SPOKANE

Rating: 5

On the Spokane River.
Map 4.6, grid c8, page 261

This KOA campground is located close to the shore of the Spokane River. Also nearby you'll find the Centennial Trail, as well as an 18-hole golf course and tennis courts.

Campsites, facilities: There are 150 sites with full hookups, including 109 drive-through sites, for RVs of any length, 50 tent sites, and three cabins. Picnic tables are provided. Restrooms, drinking water, flush toilets, showers, cable TV, an RV dump station, showers, a recreation hall, a playground, a store, a laundry room, ice, modem access, and a swimming pool are available. Some facilities are wheelchair accessible. A café is located within two miles. Leashed pets are permitted.

Reservations, fees: Reservations accepted at 800/562-3309. Sites are $24–30 per night. Major credit cards accepted. Open year-round.

Directions: From Spokane, drive east on I-90 for 13 miles to Exit 293. Take that exit to Barker Road. Turn north on Barker Road and drive 1.5 miles to the campground on the left.

Contact: KOA Spokane, 3025 North Barker,

Otis Orchards, WA 99027, 509/924-4722 or 800/562-3309, website: www.koa.com.

119 WEST MEDICAL LAKE RESORT

Rating: 7

On West Medical Lake.
Map 4.6, grid d3, page 261
This resort functions primarily as a fish camp for anglers. There are actually two lakes: West Medical is the larger of the two and has better fishing, with boat rentals available; Medical Lake is just one-quarter-mile wide and one-half-mile long, and boating is restricted to rowboats, canoes, kayaks, and sailboats. The lakes got their names from the wondrous medical powers once attributed to their waters. This family-operated shorefront resort, one of several campgrounds on Medical Lake, is a popular spot for Spokane locals.
Campsites, facilities: There are 20 tent sites and 20 sites with full hookups for RVs. At tent sites, fire pits are provided. Picnic tables, restrooms, drinking water, flush toilets, showers, a café, bait, tackle, and ice are available. Boat and fishing docks, launching facilities, a fish-cleaning station, and boat and barge rentals are nearby. Leashed pets are permitted.
Reservations, fees: Reservations recommended; $15 per night. Open late April–September.
Directions: In Spokane on I-90, drive west to Exit 264 and Salnave Road. Take that exit and turn north on Salnave Road; drive six miles to Fancher Road. Turn right (west) and drive 200 yards. Bear left on Fancher Road and drive 200 yards to the campground.
Contact: West Medical Lake Resort, 1432 West Fancher Rd., Medical Lake, WA 99022, 509/299-3921.

120 PICNIC PINES ON SILVER LAKE

Rating: 8

On Silver Lake.
Map 4.6, grid d3, page 261
This shorefront resort on Silver Lake caters primarily to RVers, although tent campers are welcome. Fishing can be excellent here. Nearby recreation options include marked bike trails, a full-service marina, and tennis courts. New owners took over this operation in April of 2002. See the description of West Medical Lake Resort for further details.
Campsites, facilities: There are 18 sites, six with full hookups and 12 with electricity, for RVs up to 35 feet in length and 13 tent sites. Hookups are available only from mid-March–mid-October. Picnic tables and fire pits are provided. Restrooms, drinking water, flush toilets, showers, a store, a restaurant, a lounge, a bait shop, boat docks, boat rentals, launching facilities, ice, and a swimming beach are available. Bottled gas and a coin-operated laundry are located within two miles. Leashed pets are permitted.
Reservations, fees: Reservations accepted. Sites are $15–19 per night. Major credit cards accepted. Open year-round.
Directions: In Spokane on I-90, drive west to Exit 270 and Medical Lake Road. Take that exit and turn west on Medical Lake Road; drive three miles to Silver Lake Road. Turn left and drive one-half mile to the park on the left.
Contact: Picnic Pines on Silver Lake, South 9212 Silver Lake Rd., Medical Lake, WA 99022, 509/299-6902.

121 MALLARD BAY RESORT

Rating: 8

On Clear Lake.
Map 4.6, grid d3, page 261
This resort is on the shore of Clear Lake, which is two miles long, a half-mile wide, and used

for water-skiing, windsurfing, and sailing. Most of the campsites are lakeshore sites on a 20-acre peninsula. Marked bike trails and tennis courts are nearby.

Campsites, facilities: There are 50 sites with partial hookups (water and electricity) for tents or RVs of any length, plus two cabins. Picnic tables and fire pits are provided. Restrooms, drinking water, flush toilets, showers, bottled gas, an RV dump station, a store, a tackle shop, ice, swimming facilities with a diving board, a playground, a basketball court, boat docks, launching facilities, a fishing pier, fish-cleaning stations, and boat rentals are available. Leashed pets are permitted.

Reservations, fees: Reservations accepted. Sites are $16 per night, $3 per person for more than four people, and $3 per extra vehicle per night. Cabins are $39 per night. Open mid-April to Labor Day Weekend.

Directions: In Spokane on I-90, drive west to Exit 264 and Salnave Road. Take that exit and turn north on Salnave Road; drive 1.5 miles to a junction signed by Mallard Bay Resort. Turn right at that sign and drive one-half mile on a dirt road to the resort at the end of the road.

Contact: Mallard Bay Resort, 14601 Salnave Rd., Cheney, WA 99004, 509/299-3830.

122 RAINBOW COVE RV AND FISHING RESORT

🏃 🚴 🏊 🏕 🐕 🚐 ⛺

Rating: 7

On Clear Lake.

Map 4.6, grid d3, page 261

This resort at Clear Lake features a 300-foot dock with benches that can be used for fishing. If you figured that most people here are anglers, well, that is correct. Fishing can be good for rainbow trout, brown trout, largemouth bass, crappie, bullhead, and catfish. Most of the campsites are at least partially shaded. Summer weekends are often busy.

Campsites, facilities: There are 16 sites with partial hookups (water and electricity) for RVs up to 40 feet long, four tent sites, and two rustic cabins. Picnic tables and fire pits are provided. Restrooms, drinking water, flush toilets, showers, a café, ice, bait and tackle, boat docks, boat rentals, and launching facilities and moorage are available. Leashed pets are permitted.

Reservations, fees: Reservations accepted. Sites are $17–20 per night, $3 per person per night for more than two people. Fee for extra vehicles. Open mid-April–mid-September.

Directions: In Spokane on I-90, drive west to Exit 264 and Salnave Road. Take that exit and turn right (north) on Salnave Road; drive a short distance to Clear Lake Road. Turn right (north) on Clear Lake Road and drive three miles to the resort on the left (well signed).

Contact: Rainbow Cove RV and Fishing Resort, 12514 South Clear Lake Rd., Medical Lake, WA 99022, 509/299-3717.

123 YOGI BEAR'S CAMP RESORT

🏊 🐕 🏕 ♿ 🚐 ⛺

Rating: 6

West of Spokane.

Map 4.6, grid e4, page 261

This resort is located 10 minutes from downtown Spokane, yet provides a wooded, rural setting. It features towering Ponderosa pines. Highlights include an 18-hole golf course next door and several other courses within 20 minutes of the resort.

Campsites, facilities: There are 168 sites with full hookups, including 63 drive-through sites, for tents or RVs up to 70 feet long, five cabins, and six bungalows. Restrooms, drinking water, flush toilets, showers, cable TV, modem-friendly phone service, an RV dump station, propane, a coin-operated laundry, an RV wash station, and three playgrounds are available. Other facilities include a camp store, an activity center with an indoor pool, a spa, an exercise room, a game room, a snack shack, a dog walk, and various sports facilities (volleyball, basketball, badminton, miniature golf, and daily, organized recreational activities). Some facilities are wheelchair accessible. Leashed pets are permitted.

Reservations, fees: Reservations accepted. Tent sites are $18 per night; RV sites are $40 per night, with discounts on weekdays and off-season; $10 per person for more than four people. Major credit cards accepted. Open year-round.

Directions: In Spokane on I-90, drive to Exit 272 and Westbow Road. Take that exit, turn east on Westbow Road, and drive to Thomas Mallen Road. Turn right (south) on Thomas Mallen Road and drive one-half mile to the campground on the right.

Contact: Yogi Bear's Camp Resort, 7520 South Thomas Mallen Rd., Cheney, WA 99004, 509/747-9415 or 800/494-7275, fax 509/459-0148, website: www.jellystonewa.com.

© TOM STIENSTRA

Chapter 5
Mount Rainier and the
Columbia River Gorge

Chapter 5—
Mount Rainier and
the Columbia River Gorge

As you stand at the rim of the Mount St. Helens volcano, the greatest natural spectacle anywhere on the planet is at your boot tips. The top 1,300 feet of the old mountain, along with the entire north flank, has been blown clean off. The half-moon crater walls drop almost 2,100 feet straight down to a lava plug dome, a mile across and still building, where a wisp of smoke emerges from its center. At its edges, the rising plumes of dust from continuous rock falls can be deceptive—you may think a small eruption is in progress. It's like looking inside the bowels of the earth.

The plug dome gives way to the blast zone, where the mountain has completely blown out its side and spreads out across 230 square miles of devastation. From here, it's largely a moonscape but for Spirit Lake on the northeast flank, where thousands of trees are still floating, log-jammed from the eruption in May 1980. Beyond this scene rises 14,411-foot Mount Rainier to the north, 12,276-foot Mount Adams to the northeast, and 11,235-foot Mount Hood to the south, all pristine jewels in contrast to the nearby remains.

We've hiked most of the Pacific Crest Trail and climbed most of the West's highest mountains, but no view compares to this. You could explore this sweeping panorama of a land for years. The most famous spots in this region are St. Helens, Rainier, and Adams; the latter are two of the three most beautiful mountains in the Cascade Range (Mount Shasta in Northern California is the third). All of them offer outstanding touring and hiking, with excellent camps of all kinds available around their perimeters. St. Helens provides the most eye-popping views and most developed visitor centers, Rainier the most pristine wilderness, and Adams some of the best lakeside camps, with trout fishing sometimes within casting range of your tent.

That's just the beginning. The Western Cascades span down river canyons and up mountain subridges, both filled with streams and lakes. There are camps throughout. At the same time, the I-5 corridor and its network of linked highways also provide many privately developed RV parks fully furnished with everything a vacationer could desire.

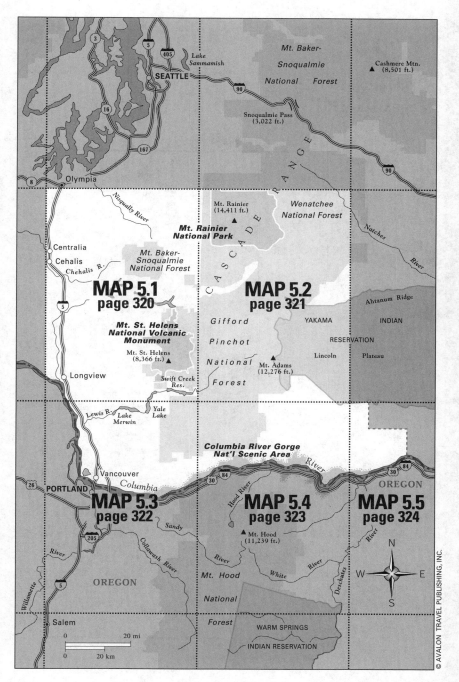

MAP 5.1
page 320

MAP 5.2
page 321

MAP 5.3
page 322

MAP 5.4
page 323

MAP 5.5
page 324

Lake Sammamish

SEATTLE

Mt. Baker-
Snoqualmie

National Forest

Cashmere Mtn.
(8,501 ft.)

Snoqualmie Pass
(3,022 ft.)

Olympia

Nisqually River

Mt. Rainier
(14,411 ft.)

Wenatchee
National Forest

Natches River

Mt. Rainier
National Park

C A S C A D E   R A N G E

Centralia

Cehalis

Chehalis R.

Mt. Baker-
Snoqualmie
National Forest

Gifford

Ahtanum Ridge

YAKAMA

INDIAN

Mt. St. Helens
National Volcanic
Monument

Pinchot

RESERVATION

Mt. St. Helens
(8,366 ft.)

National

Mt. Adams
(12,276 ft.)

Lincoln

Plateau

Longview

Forest

Swift Creek
Res.

Lewis R.

Lake
Merwin

Yale
Lake

Columbia River Gorge
Nat'l Scenic Area

River

Vancouver

Columbia

PORTLAND

OREGON

Hood River

Sandy

Mt. Hood
(11,239 ft.)

White

River

Deschutes

Clackamas River

River

River

N
W   E
S

OREGON

Mt. Hood

National

Willamette

Salem

Forest

WARM SPRINGS

INDIAN RESERVATION

0   20 mi
0   20 km

© AVALON TRAVEL PUBLISHING, INC.

Map 5.1

Campgrounds 1–25
Pages 325–336

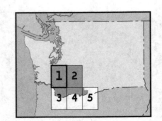

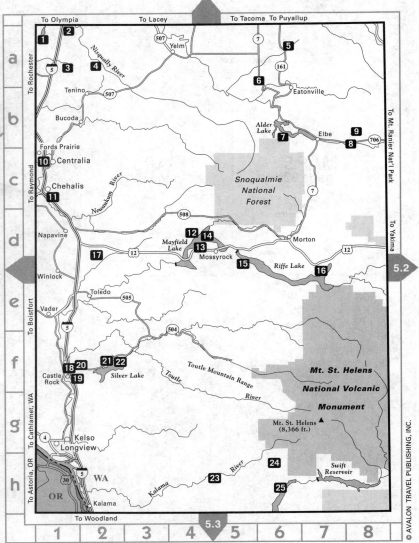

To Olympia   To Lacey   To Tacoma To Puyallup

1
2
To Rochester
3
4
507
Yelm
7
5
5
161
Nisqually River
6
Tenino
507
Eatonville
Bucoda
Alder Lake
9
Fords Prairie
7
Elbe
706
To Raymond
10 Centralia
8
To Mt. Ranier Nat'l Park
Chehalis
11
Newaukum River
Snoqualmie National Forest
7
508
Napavine
12 **14**
Morton
To Boistfort
17
12
Mayfield Lake
13
12
To Yakima
Winlock
Mossyrock
15
Riffe Lake
16
5.2
Toledo
505
Vader
5
504
18 **20**
21 **22**
Toutle Mountain Range
Mt. St. Helens
Castle Rock
19
Silver Lake
Toutle
National Volcanic
To Cathlamet, WA
River
Monument
To Kelso
4
Longview
Mt. St. Helens
(8,366 ft.)
To Astoria, OR
24
Swift Reservoir
5
WA
23
River
OR
Kalama
25
Kalama
To Woodland
5.3

© AVALON TRAVEL PUBLISHING, INC.

Map 5.2

Campgrounds 26–85
Pages 336–363

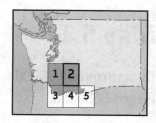

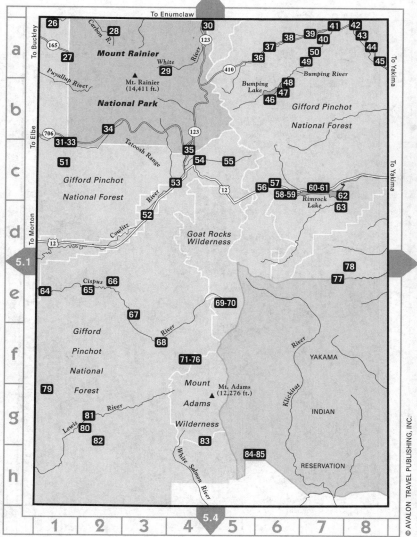

Map 5.3

Campgrounds 86–96
Pages 363–368

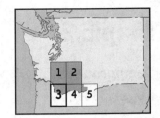

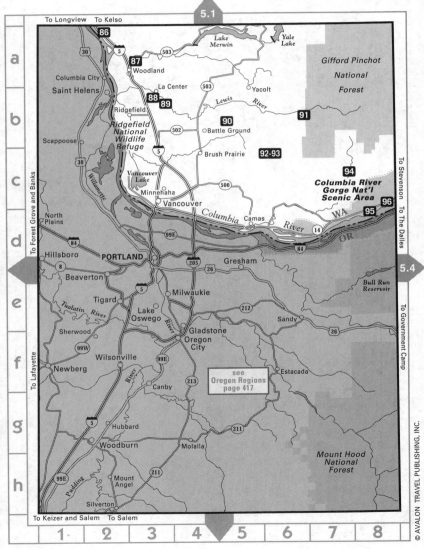

To Longview To Kelso

86

30 5

87 Woodland

503 Lake Merwin Yale Lake

Columbia City

Saint Helens

La Center 503 Yacolt

88 89

Ridgefield

Lewis River

Ridgefield National Wildlife Refuge

Scappoose 502 Battle Ground

90

Brush Prairie

92-93

Gifford Pinchot National Forest

91

94

Columbia River Gorge Nat'l Scenic Area

Vancouver Lake

Minnehaha

Vancouver

500

Columbia Camas River WA OR

96

95

14

84

North Plains

84

Hillsboro PORTLAND

8

Beaverton

Gresham

26

Bull Run Reservoir

5.4

Tigard 5

Milwaukie

Lake Oswego

212

Sandy

Tualatin River

Sherwood

Gladstone Oregon City

26

99W

Wilsonville 99E

Newberg

Estacada

Canby 213

see Oregon Regions page 417

5

Hubbard

211

Woodburn

Molalla

Mount Hood National Forest

99E

Mount Angel

211

Silverton

To Keizer and Salem To Salem

To Forest Grove and Banks

To Lafayette

To Stevenson To The Dalles

To Government Camp

© AVALON TRAVEL PUBLISHING, INC.

5.1

1 2 3 4 5 6 7 8

a b c d e f g h

Map 5.4

Campgrounds 97–110
Pages 368–374

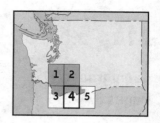

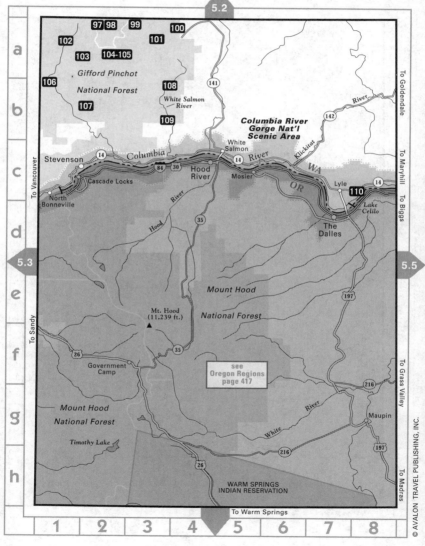

Map 5.5

Campground 111
Pages 374–375

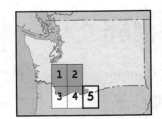

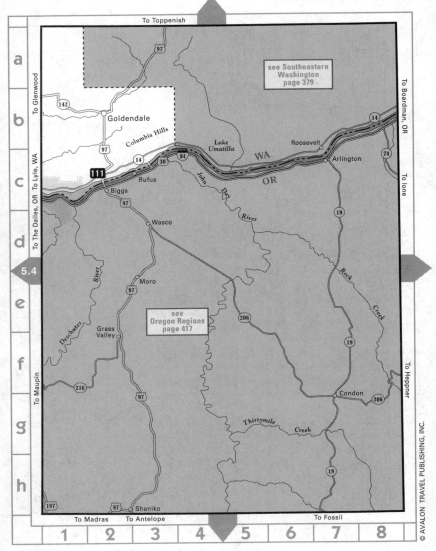

To Toppenish

see Southeastern
Washington
page 379

To Glenwood

142

To Boardman, OR

14

Goldendale

97

Columbia Hills

Lake
Umatilla

Roosevelt

WA

74

To Lyle, WA

97

14

30

84

Arlington

To Ione

111

Rufus

John

OR

To The Dalles, OR

Biggs

Day

19

97

Wasco

River

River

Rock

19

Moro

97

5.4

see
Oregon Regions
page 417

Deschutes

Grass
Valley

206

Creek

19

To Maupin

To Heppner

216

97

Condon

206

Thirtymile

Creek

19

197

97

Shaniko

To Madras   To Antelope

To Fossil

© AVALON TRAVEL PUBLISHING, INC.

1 COLUMBUS PARK

Rating: 7

On Black Lake.

Map 5.1, grid a1, page 320

This spot along the shore of Black Lake is pretty enough for special events, such as weddings and reunions. The campsites are wooded and a stream (no fishing) runs through the campground. Black Lake is good for fishing. An 18-hole golf course is nearby.

Campsites, facilities: There are 23 sites with partial hookups for RVs up to 40 feet long. Picnic tables are provided. Restrooms, drinking water, flush toilets, showers, an RV dump station, a coin-operated laundry, ice, firewood, a playground with volleyball and horseshoe pits, boat docks, and launching facilities are available. A picnic area for special events is nearby. Some facilities are wheelchair accessible. Bottled gas, ice, and a store are located within one mile; there is a restaurant within three miles. Leashed pets are permitted.

Reservations, fees: Reservations recommended during summer. Sites are $16.20 per night. Open year-round.

Directions: From I-5 in Olympia, take the U.S. 101 exit and drive 1.7 miles northwest to Black Lake Boulevard. Turn south on Black Lake Boulevard and drive 3.5 miles to the park on the left.

Contact: Columbus Park, 5700 Black Lake Blvd. SW, Olympia, WA 98502, 360/786-9460 or 800/848-9460.

2 AMERICAN HERITAGE CAMPGROUND

Rating: 6

Near Olympia.

Map 5.1, grid a1, page 320

This spacious, wooded campground situated just one-half mile off the highway is close to many activities, including an 18-hole golf course, hiking trails, marked bike trails, and tennis courts. The park features novelty cycle rentals, free wagon rides, and free nightly movies. It's exceptionally clean and pretty, making for a pleasant layover on your way up or down I-5. The park has a 5,000-square-foot pavilion for special events or groups.

Campsites, facilities: There are 72 sites with full or partial hookups for tents or RVs of any length, 23 tent sites, and one cabin. Picnic tables and fire rings are provided. Restrooms, drinking water, flush toilets, showers, bottled gas, an RV dump station, a recreation hall, a group pavilion, recreation programs, a store, a coin-operated laundry, ice, a playground, a heated swimming pool, and firewood are available. Leashed pets are permitted.

Reservations, fees: Reservations accepted. Sites are $20–28 per night for two people, $4 per person per night for more than two adults and two children. Major credit cards accepted. Open Memorial Day through Labor Day weekend.

Directions: From Olympia, drive five miles south on I-5 to Exit 99. Take that exit and drive one-quarter mile east to Kimmie Street. Turn right (south) on Kimmie Street and drive one-quarter mile to the end of the road to the campground on the left.

Contact: American Heritage Campground, 9610 Kimmie St. SW, Olympia, WA 98512, 360/943-8778, website: www.americanheritage campground.com.

3 MILLERSYLVANIA STATE PARK

Rating: 8

On Deep Lake.

Map 5.1, grid a1, page 320

This state park is set on the shore of Deep Lake and features 3,300 feet of waterfront. The park has many trails amid an abundance of old-growth cedar and fir trees, 8.6 miles of hiking trails, and 7.6 miles of bike trails. Boating at Deep Lake is restricted to hand-launched boats, with a five-mph speed limit. A fishing dock is available at the boat-launch area. Another highlight: a one-mile fitness trail. Remnants of a narrow-gauge railroad and several skid trails used in the 1800s by the logging industry are still present on park roads.

Campsites, facilities: There are 135 developed tent sites, 52 sites for RVs up to 45 feet long, and four primitive tent sites. Picnic tables and fire grills are provided. Restrooms, drinking water, flush toilets, coin-operated showers, an RV dump station, a playground, boat docks and launching facilities, and firewood are available. A picnic area, summer interpretive activities, and horseshoe pits are also nearby. A store, a restaurant, and ice are located within one mile. Some facilities are wheelchair accessible. Leashed pets are permitted.

Reservations, fees: Reserve at 888/CAMP-OUT (888/226-7688), website: www.parks.wa.gov/reservations ($7 reservation fee). Sites are $6–22 per night, $6 per extra vehicle per night. Senior discount available. Major credit cards accepted. Open year-round.

Directions: From Olympia, drive south on I-5 for 10 miles to Exit 95 and Highway 121. Turn east on Maytown Road (Highway 121) and drive 2.7 miles to Tilley Road. Turn left (north) and drive 1.3 miles to the park.

Contact: Millersylvania State Park, 360/753-1519; State Park information, 360/902-8844.

4 OFFUT LAKE RESORT

Rating: 8

On Offut Lake.

Map 5.1, grid a2, page 320

This wooded campground is set on Offut Lake, just enough off the beaten track to provide a bit of seclusion. Fishing, swimming, and boating are favorite activities here. Anglers will find everything they need, including tackle and boat rentals, at the resort. Boating is restricted to a five-mph speed limit, and no gas motors are permitted on the lake. Several fishing derbies are held here every year.

Campsites, facilities: There are 51 sites with full or partial hookups for RVs up to 40 feet in length, 25 tent sites, and 10 cabins. Picnic tables and fire rings are provided. Restrooms, drinking water, flush toilets, coin-operated showers, a picnic shelter, an RV dump station, firewood, a store, bait and tackle, propane gas, a laundry room, ice, and a playground with basketball and horseshoe pits are available. Boat rentals and docks are available; no gas motors permitted. Some facilities are wheelchair accessible. Leashed pets are permitted.

Reservations, fees: Reservations accepted. Sites are $17–24 per night, $5 per person per night for more than two adults and two children, $2 per extra vehicle per night, and a $1–2 per pet. Major credit cards accepted. Open year-round.

Directions: From Olympia, drive south on I-5 for seven miles to Exit 99. Take that exit and turn east on 93rd Avenue; drive four miles to Old Highway 99. Turn south and drive four miles to Offut Lake Road. Turn left (east) and drive 1.5 miles to the resort.

Contact: Offut Lake Resort, 4005 120th Ave. SE, Tenino, WA 98589, 360/264-2438, website: www.offutlakeresort.com.

5 RAINBOW RESORT

Rating: 8

On Tanwax Lake.

Map 5.1, grid a6, page 320

This wooded park along the shore of Tanwax Lake has spacious, shady sites with views of mountains, forest, and lake. Highlights include good fishing, a seasonal fishpond, and a nearby riding stable. Power boating and water-skiing are popular on hot summer weekends.

Campsites, facilities: There are about 50 sites with full hookups for tents or RVs up to 40 feet long. Picnic tables are provided. Restrooms, drinking water, flush toilets, coin-operated showers, bottled gas, a recreation hall, a store, a coin-operated laundry, a café, ice, cable TV, boat docks, boat rentals, and launching facilities are available. Leashed pets are permitted.

Reservations, fees: Reservations accepted. Sites are $21 per night, $3 per person per night for more than two people, and $3 per pet. Senior discount available. Major credit cards accepted. Open year-round.

Directions: From Tacoma, drive south on I-5 to Exit 127 and Highway 512. Turn east on Highway 512 and drive to Highway 161. Turn south on Highway 161 and drive to Tanwax Drive. Turn left (east) on Tanwax Drive and drive 200 yards to the resort.

Contact: Rainbow Resort, 34217 Tanwax Court E, Eatonville, WA 98328, 360/879-5115, fax 360/879-5116.

6 HENLEY'S SILVER LAKE RESORT

Rating: 8

On Silver Lake.

Map 5.1, grid a6, page 320

Silver Lake is a 150-acre spring-fed lake that can provide good trout fishing. This full-facility resort is set up as family vacation destination. A rarity, this private campground caters both to tent campers and RVers. Silver Lake is beautiful and stocked with trout. Highlights include a 250-foot fishing dock and 50 rental rowboats.

Campsites, facilities: There are 36 sites with full or partial hookups, including two drive-through, for RVs, a very large area for dispersed tent camping, and six cabins. Restrooms, drinking water, flush toilets, a public phone, snacks, boat rentals, a boat ramp, and a dock are available. Leashed pets are permitted except in the cabins.

Reservations, fees: Reservations accepted. Sites are $10–15 per night. Open the first day of fishing season in April–October, weather permitting.

Directions: From Tacoma, drive south on I-5 for five miles to Exit 127 and Highway 512.

Turn east of Highway 512 and drive two miles to Highway 7. Turn south on Highway 7 and drive 19 miles (two miles straight beyond the blinking light) to Silver Lake Road on the right (well marked). Turn right and drive one-quarter mile to the resort entrance on the left.

Contact: Henley's Silver Lake Resort, 40718 South Silver Lake Rd. E, Eatonville, WA 98328, 360/832-3580, website: www.washingtonlakes.com.

7 ALDER LAKE RECREATION AREA

Rating: 6

On Alder Lake.

Map 5.1, grid b6, page 320

This recreation area at Alder Lake features three camping areas: Rocky Point, Alder Lake Park, and Boathouse. Alder Lake is a 3,065-acre lake (7.5 miles long) often with good fishing for kokanee salmon, rainbow trout, and cutthroat trout. Rocky Point features a sunny beach and is set near the mouth of feeder streams, often the best fishing spots on the lake. At the west end of the lake, anglers can catch catfish, perch, and crappie. The campsites are set near the water with lots of trees and shrubbery. On clear, warm summer weekends, these camps can get crowded. The camps are always booked full for summer holiday weekends as soon as reservations are available in January. Another potential downer, the water level fluctuates here. Power boating, water-skiing, and personal watercraft are allowed at this lake. Mount Rainier Scenic Railroad leaves from Elbe regularly and makes its way through the forests to Mineral Lake. It features open deck cars, live music, and restored passenger cars.

Campsites, facilities: There are three camping areas with approximately 125 sites with full or partial hookups for RVs of any length, 100 tent sites, and one group site with full hookups for up to 20 RVs. Alder Lake Camp is the largest and most developed; Rocky Point is a nearby overflow camp for RVs, with no tent sites available; and Boathouse Camp is smaller (24 sites), primarily for tents, with some electricity hookups for self-contained RVs. Picnic tables and fire grills are provided. Drinking water and vault toilets are available. Boat docks and launching facilities are available nearby. A swimming beach, a day-use picnic area, a fishing dock, a small convenience store, and an RV dump station are also available nearby. Some facilities are wheelchair accessible. Leashed pets are permitted.

Reservations, fees: Reservations recommended, available in person or through mail; applications can be downloaded at internet site; $19–20 per night, $6 per extra vehicle per night. Senior discount available. The group camp is $20 per night per site. Major credit cards accepted. Open year-round, excluding December 20 through January 2.

Directions: From Chehalis, drive south on I-5 for 10 miles to U.S. 12. Turn east and drive 31 miles to Morton and Highway 7. Turn north on Highway 7 and drive 17 miles to Elbe. Bear left on Highway 7 and drive to the park entrance road on the left (on the east shore of Alder Lake). Turn left and drive two-tenths of a mile to the park entrance gate.

Contact: Alder Lake Park, Tacoma Power at 50324 School Rd., Eatonville, WA 98328, 360/569-2778, fax 253/502-8631, website: www.tacomapower.com.

8 SAHARA CREEK HORSE CAMP

Rating: 6

Near Elbe.
Map 5.1, grid c8, page 320

While this camp is called a "horse camp," it is actually a multiple-use camp, open to campers without horses. This pretty camp is set near the foot of Mount Rainier and features multiple trailheads and a camp host on-site. It is popular among equestrians.

Campsites, facilities: There are 18 tent sites.

Picnic tables and fire pits are provided. A covered pavilion, vault toilets, high lines, and hitching posts are available, but there is no drinking water. Garbage must be packed out. Leashed pets are permitted.

Reservations, fees: Reservations are not accepted. There is no fee for camping. Open year-round.

Directions: From Chehalis, drive south on I-5 for 10 miles to U.S. 12. Turn east and drive 31 miles to Morton and Highway 7. Turn north on Highway 7 and drive 17 miles to Elbe and Highway 706. Turn right (east) and drive five miles to the campground on the left.

Contact: Department of Natural Resources, South Puget Sound Region, 950 Farman Ave. N, Enumclaw, WA 98022, 360/825-1631, fax 360/825-1672.

9 ELBE HILLS

Rating: 6

Near Elbe.
Map 5.1, grid b8, page 320

Elbe Hills is not an official, designated campground, but rather a trailhead with room for three campsites for four-wheelers. The Department of Natural Resources manages this wooded campground and provides eight miles of trails for short-wheelbase four-wheel-drive vehicles. The area features a technical obstacle course. In some places, you must have a winch to make it through the course. Note: the area is always gated. You must obtain the key from the camp host at Sahara Creek Campground, located one mile away.

Campsites, facilities: There are three primitive sites for tents or small RVs. Picnic tables and fire grills are provided. Vault toilets and a group shelter are available. No drinking water is available. Garbage must be packed out. Leashed pets are permitted.

Reservations, fees: Reservations are not accepted. There is no fee for camping. Open year-round, weather permitting.

Directions: From Chehalis, drive south on I-5

for 10 miles to U.S. 12. Turn east and drive 31 miles to Morton and Highway 7. Turn north on Highway 7 and drive 17 miles to Elbe and Highway 706. Turn right (east) and drive six miles to Stoner Road (a Department of Natural Resources access road). Turn left and drive 2.5 miles to The 9 Road. Bear right on The 9 Road and drive one mile; look for a spur road on the left. Turn left and drive about 100 yards to the four-wheel-drive trailhead.

Contact: Department of Natural Resources, South Puget Sound Region, 950 Farman Ave. N, Enumclaw, WA 98022-0068, 360/825-1631, fax 360/825-1672.

10 PEPPERTREE WEST MOTOR INN & RV PARK

Rating: 5

In Centralia.

Map 5.1, grid c1, page 320

If you're driving I-5 and looking for a stopover, this spot is a good choice for tent campers and RVers. Surrounded by Chehalis Valley farmland, it's near an 18-hole golf course, hiking trails, and tennis courts.

Campsites, facilities: There are 42 sites with full or partial hookups, including mostly drive-through, for RVs of any length and 20 tent sites. Restrooms, drinking water, flush toilets, coin-operated showers, cable TV, an RV dump station, a recreation hall, a coin-operated laundry, and ice are available. Boat-launching facilities are nearby. A store, propane, and a café are also nearby. Leashed pets are permitted.

Reservations, fees: Reservations accepted. Sites are $16–20 per night. Senior discount available. Major credit cards accepted. Open year-round.

Directions: From Centralia on I-5, take Exit 81 to Melon Street. Turn west and then take the first left to the park (located in the southeast corner of Centralia).

Contact: Peppertree West Motor Inn & RV Park, 1208 Alder St., Centralia, WA 98531, 360/736-1124, fax 360/807-9779.

11 STAN HEDWALL PARK

Rating: 5

On the Newaukum River.

Map 5.1, grid c1, page 320

This park is set along the Newaukum River, and its proximity to I-5 makes it a good layover spot for vacation travelers. Recreational opportunities include fishing, hiking, and golf (an 18-hole course and hiking trails are nearby).

Campsites, facilities: There are 29 sites with partial hookups (water and electricity) for RVs of any length. Picnic tables are provided. Restrooms, drinking water, flush toilets, coin-operated showers, an RV dump station, cable TV, and a playground are available. Bottled gas, a store, a café, and a coin-operated laundry are located within one mile. Leashed pets are permitted.

Reservations, fees: Reservations accepted two weeks or more in advance. Sites are $15 per night. Open March–November, weather permitting.

Directions: Near Chehalis on I-5, take Exit 76 to Rice Road. Turn south and drive one-eighth mile to the park.

Contact: Stan Hedwall Park, City of Chehalis, P.O. Box 871, Chehalis, WA 98532, 360/748-0271, fax 360/748-6993.

12 IKE KINSWA STATE PARK

Rating: 8

At Mayfield Lake.

Map 5.1, grid d4, page 320

This state park is set alongside the north shore of Mayfield Lake. The park features 8.5 miles of shore, forested campsites, 2.5 miles of hiking trails, and two miles of bike trails. Mayfield Lake is a treasure trove of recreational possibilities. Fishing is a year-round affair here, with trout and tiger muskie often good. Boating, water-skiing, swimming, and driftwood collecting are all popular. The park is named after a prominent Cowlitz Indian, Ike Kinswa. Two fish hatcheries are located nearby. A spectacular view of Mount St. Helens can be found at a vista point 11 miles east. This popular campground often fills on summer weekends. Be sure to reserve well in advance.

Campsites, facilities: There are 60 developed tent sites, 41 sites for RVs up to 60 feet long, and two primitive tent sites. Picnic tables and fire grills are provided. Restrooms, drinking water, flush toilets, showers, an RV dump station, a store, a café, a playground, a picnic area, horseshoe pits, and firewood are available. Some facilities are wheelchair accessible. Boat docks and launching facilities are nearby. Leashed pets are permitted.

Reservations, fees: Reserve at 888/CAMP-OUT (888/226-7688), website: www.parks.wa.gov/reservations ($7 reservation fee). Sites are $8–22 per night, $6 per extra vehicle per night. Senior discount available. Major credit cards accepted. Open year-round.

Directions: From Longview, drive north on I-5 to Exit 68 and U.S. 12. Turn east on U.S. 12 and drive 14 miles to Silver Creek Road (State Route 122). Turn north and drive 1.9 miles to a Y intersection. Bear right on State Route 111/Harmony Road and drive 1.6 miles to the park entrance.

Contact: Ike Kinswa State Park, 873 Harmony Rd., Silver Lake, WA 98585, 360/983-3402, fax 360/983-3332; State Park information, 360/902-8844.

13 MAYFIELD LAKE PARK

Rating: 7

On Mayfield Lake.
Map 5.1, grid d4, page 320

Mayfield Lake is the centerpiece of this 50-acre park. Insider's tip: Campsites 42–54 are set along the lake's shoreline. The camp has a relaxing atmosphere and comfortable, wooded sites. Fishing is primarily for trout, bass, and silver salmon. Other recreational activities include water-skiing, swimming, and boating. For a great side trip, tour nearby Mount St. Helens. Note that this camp was managed for years as a county park. Tacoma Power first established new management in spring 2002.

Campsites, facilities: There are 54 sites for tents or self-contained RVs. Picnic tables and fire grills are provided. Restrooms, drinking water, flush toilets, coin-operated showers, a public phone, and a barbecue are available. An RV dump station is located within one-half mile. Some facilities are wheelchair accessible. Leashed pets are permitted.

Reservations, fees: Reservations recommended. Sites are $15–19 per night, $4 per person for more than four people, and $6 per extra vehicle per night. Open mid-April–mid-October.

Directions: From Longview, drive north on I-5 to Exit 68 and U.S. 12. Turn east on U.S. 12 and drive 11 miles. Look for the campground entrance signs on the left.

Contact: Mayfield Lake Park, 360/985-2364, fax 360/985-7825, website: www.tacomapower.com.

14 HARMONY LAKESIDE RV PARK

Rating: 6

Near Mayfield Lake.
Map 5.1, grid d4, page 320

This park fills up on weekends in July and August. It is set on Mayfield Lake, a ten-mile-long lake with numerous recreational activities, including fishing, boating, and water-skiing. Some sites feature lake views. Ike Kinswa State Park is a nearby side-trip option.

Campsites, facilities: There are 80 sites with full or partial hookups for tents or RVs of any length. Picnic tables and fire grills are provided. Restrooms, drinking water, flush toilets, coin-operated showers, an RV dump station, ice, firewood, a pay phone, boat docks, and launching facilities are available. Group facilities, including a banquet and meeting room, are also available. Leashed pets are permitted.

Reservations, fees: Reservations recommended. Sites are $24–29 per night, $3 per person for more than four people, and $2 per pet per night. Monthly rates available. Major credit cards accepted. Open year-round.

Directions: From Longview, drive north on I-5 to Exit 68 and U.S. 12. Turn east on U.S. 12 and drive 21 miles to Mossyrock (Highway 122). Turn left (north) and drive 2.3 miles to the park on the left.

Contact: Harmony Lakeside RV Park, 563 Rte. 122, Silver Creek, WA 98585, 360/983-3804, fax 360/983-8345, website: www.mayfield lake.com.

15 MOSSYROCK PARK

Rating: 8

At Riffe Lake.

Map 5.1, grid d5, page 320

This park is located along the southwest shore of Riffe Lake. It is an extremely popular campground for several reasons. For anglers, it provides the best of both worlds: a boat launch on Riffe Lake, which offers coho salmon, rainbow trout, and bass, and nearby Swofford Pond, a 240-acre pond stocked with rainbow trout, brown trout, bass, catfish, and bluegill. Swofford Pond is located south of Mossyrock on Swofford Road; no gas motors are permitted. This campground provides access to a half-mile loop nature trail. Bald eagles and osprey nest on the north side of the lake in the 14,000-acre Cowlitz Wildlife Area.

Campsites, facilities: There are 141 sites, including 77 with full hookups, for tents or RVs, 12 walk-in sites, one group camp with 60 sites, and a primitive group camp with 10 sites. Picnic tables and fire rings are provided. Restrooms, drinking water, flush toilets, showers, an RV dump station, a fishing bridge, fish-cleaning stations, a boat launch, a playground, a swimming area, a horseshoe pit, a volleyball net, and interpretive displays are available. In summer, a camp host is available.

Some facilities are wheelchair accessible. Leashed pets are permitted.

Reservations, fees: Reservations recommended at 360/983-3900. Sites are $10–19 per night, $6 per extra vehicle per night. Senior discount available. Call for group site prices. Major credit cards accepted in summer. Open year-round, excluding December 20 through January 20.

Directions: On I-5, drive to Exit 68 and Highway 12 East. Take Highway 12 East and drive 21 miles to Williams Street (flashing yellow light). Turn right and drive several blocks in the town of Mossyrock to a T intersection with State Street. Turn left and drive 3.5 miles (becomes Mossyrock Road East, then Ajlure Road) to the park. Ajlure Roads lead right into the park.

Contact: Taidnapam Park, Tacoma Power, 50324 School Rd., Eatonville, WA 98328, 360/983-3900, fax 360/983-3906, website: www.tacomapower.com.

16 TAIDNAPAM PARK

Rating: 8

At Riffe Lake.

Map 5.1, grid e7, page 320

This 50-acre park is located at the east end of Riffe Lake. Nestled in the cover of Douglas fir and maple, it is surrounded by thousands of acres of undeveloped greenbelt. Fishing is open year-round at the lake, with coho salmon, rainbow trout, and bass available. This camp was named after the Upper Cowlitz Indians, also known as "Taidnapam." Since it often fills in summer, the walk-in sites are an outstanding option.

Campsites, facilities: There are 52 sites with full or partial hookups for tents or RVs, 16 walk-in sites, and one group camp with 22 sites and a kitchen shelter. Picnic tables and fire rings are provided. Restrooms, drinking water, flush toilets, showers, an RV dump station, a fishing bridge, fish-cleaning stations, a boat launch, a playground, a swimming area, a horseshoe pit, a volleyball net, and interpretive displays are available. Some facilities are wheelchair accessible. Leashed pets are permitted.

Reservations, fees: Reservations recommended at 360/497-7707. Sites are $10–19 per night, $6 per extra vehicle per night. Senior discount available. Call for group site prices. Major credit cards accepted in summer season. Open year-round, excluding December 20 through January 20.

Directions: On I-5, drive to Exit 68 and Highway 12 East. Take Highway 12 East and drive 37 miles (five miles past Morton) to Kosmos Road. Turn right and drive 200 yards to No. 100 Chapion Haul Road (a gravel road). Turn left and drive four miles to the park.

Contact: Taidnapam Park, Tacoma Power, 50324 School Rd., Eatonville, WA 98328, 360/497-7707, fax 360/497-7708, website: www.tacomapower.com.

17 LEWIS AND CLARK STATE PARK

Rating: 8

Near Chehalis.
Map 5.1, grid d2, page 320

The highlight of this state park is an immense old-growth forest that contains some good hiking trails and a half-mile nature trail. This famous grove lost half of its old-growth trees along the highway when they were blown down in the legendary 1962 Columbus Day storm. This was a cataclysmic event for what is one of the last major stands of old-growth forest in the state. The park covers 621 acres and features primarily Douglas fir and red cedar, wetlands, and dense vegetation. There are eight miles of hiking trails and five miles of horse trails. June is Youth Fishing Month, when youngsters age 14 and younger can fish the creek. Jackhouse tours, in which visitors can see a pioneer home built in 1845 north of the Columbia River, are available year-round by appointment.

Campsites, facilities: There are 25 sites for tents

or self-contained RVs and two group camps for up to 50 people each. Picnic tables and fire grills are provided. Restrooms, drinking water, flush toilets, coin-operated showers, firewood, a picnic area, an amphitheater, horseshoe pits, volleyball, and badminton are available. Leashed pets are permitted.

Reservations, fees: Reservations are not accepted for family sites. Sites are $15 per night, $6 per extra vehicle per night. Senior discount available. Group sites require $25 reservation, plus $2 per person with a 20-person minimum. Open April–September.

Directions: From Chehalis, drive south on I-5 to Exit 68 and U.S. 12. Drive east on U.S. 12 for three miles to Jackson Highway. Turn right and drive three miles to the park entrance on the right.

Contact: Lewis and Clark State Park, 4583 Jackson Hwy., Winlock, WA 98596, 360/864-2643, fax 360/864-2515; State Park information, 360/902-8844.

18 RIVER OAKS RV PARK & CAMPGROUND

Rating: 8

On the Cowlitz River.
Map 5.1, grid f1, page 320

This camp is set right on the Cowlitz River, with opportunities for swimming, boating, and fishing—and nearby access to Mount St. Helens. In most years in the spring, the river is the site of a big smelt run, and they come thick. Using a dip net, you can sometimes fill a five-gallon bucket with just a couple of dips. Don't swim in smelting area.

Campsites, facilities: There are 50 tent sites and 24 sites with full hookups, including 12 long-term rentals and 15 drive-through, for RVs. Restrooms, drinking water, flush toilets, showers, picnic tables, fire rings, firewood, and a laundry room are available. Bottled gas, a store, bait and tackle, and a café are located within one mile. Boat-launching facilities, mooring buoys, and a fishing shelter are nearby. Leashed pets are permitted.

Reservations, fees: Reservations accepted. Sites are $15–22 per night, $3 per person for more than four people. Senior discount available. Open year-round.

Directions: From Castle Rock on I-5, take Exit 59 for Highway 506. Turn west on Highway 506 and drive three-tenths of a mile to the park on the left.

Contact: River Oaks RV Park & Campground, 491 Hwy. 506, Toledo, WA 98591, 360/864-2895.

19 PARADISE COVE RESORT & RV PARK

Rating: 7

Near the Toutle River.

Map 5.1, grid f1, page 320

This wooded park is situated about 400 yards from the Toutle River and one-half mile from the Cowlitz River. Take your pick: Seaquest State Park and Silver Lake to the east provide two excellent, activity-filled side-trip options. This is a major stopover for visits to Mount St. Helens.

Campsites, facilities: There are 52 sites with full hookups, including many drive-through, for RVs of any length, and a large dispersed tent camping area. Picnic tables are provided. Restrooms, drinking water, flush toilets, showers, propane, a coin-operated laundry, a store with video rentals, and ice are available. Boat-launching facilities are nearby. Leashed pets are permitted.

Reservations, fees: Reservations accepted. Sites are $16–22 per night. Senior discount available. Major credit cards accepted. Open year-round.

Directions: From Longview, drive 10 miles north on I-5 to Castle Rock and Exit 52. Take Exit 52 and look for the park on Frontage Road, just off the freeway (within view of the freeway).

Contact: Paradise Cove Resort & RV Park, 112 Burma Rd., Castle Rock, WA 98611, 360/274-6785.

20 MOUNT ST. HELENS RV PARK

Rating: 6

Near Silver Lake.

Map 5.1, grid f2, page 320

This RV park is located just outside Castle Rock, only three miles from the Mount St. Helens Visitor Center. It is close to the highway. Fishing and boating are available nearby on Silver Lake.

Campsites, facilities: There are 90 sites with full or partial hookups for tents or RVs. Restrooms, drinking water, flush toilets, coin-operated showers, cable TV, propane, a coin-operated laundry, an RV dump station, a public phone, and ice are available. Horseshoes, a recreation hall, and a playground are also provided. Some facilities are wheelchair accessible. Leashed pets are permitted.

Reservations, fees: Reservations recommended in the summer; phone 360/274-8522. Sites are $20–22 per night, $1 per person per night for more than two people. Major credit cards accepted. Open year-round.

Directions: From Longview, drive 10 miles north on I-5 to Castle Rock and Exit 49 and Highway 504. Take Exit 49 and drive east on Highway 504 for two miles to Schaffran Road. Turn left (well signed) and drive to the park at the top of the hill.

Contact: Mount St. Helens RV Park, 167 Schaffran Rd., Castle Rock, WA 98611, 360/274-8522, fax 360/274-4529.

21 SEAQUEST STATE PARK

Rating: 6

Near Silver Lake.

Map 5.1, grid f2, page 320

This camp fills nightly because it is set along the paved road to the awesome Johnston Ridge

Observatory, the premier lookout of Mount St. Helens. This state park is located adjacent to Silver Lake, one of western Washington's finest fishing lakes for bass and trout. But that's not all. The Mount St. Helens Visitor Center, which opened in 2000, is located across the road from the park entrance. This 425-acre park features more than one mile of lake shoreline and a heavily forested park with eight miles of trails for hiking and biking. The irony of the place is that some out-of-towners on vacation think that this park is located on the ocean because of its name, Seaquest. The park has nothing to do with the ocean, of course. It is named after Alfred L. Seaquest, who donated the property to the state for parkland. one interesting fact: He stipulated in his will that if liquor were ever sold on the property that the land would be transferred to Willamette University. The park is popular for day use as well as camping.

Campsites, facilities: There are 92 sites, including 16 with full hookups, for tents or self-contained RVs and four primitive tent sites. Picnic tables and fire grills are provided. Restrooms, drinking water, flush toilets, showers, a picnic area, a playground, six horseshoe pits, a ball field, an RV dump station, and firewood are available. A store is within one mile. Some facilities are wheelchair accessible. Leashed pets are permitted.

Reservations, fees: Reserve at 888/CAMP-OUT (888/226-7688), website: www.parks.wa.gov/reservations ($7 reservation fee). Sites are $6–22 per night, $6 per extra vehicle per night. Senior discount available. Major credit cards accepted. Open year-round.

Directions: From Longview, drive 10 miles north on I-5 to Castle Rock and Exit 49 and Highway 504. Take Exit 49 and drive east on Highway 504 for six miles to the park.

Contact: Seaquest State Park, 360/274-8633, fax 360/274-9285; State Park information, 360/902-8844.

22 SILVER LAKE MOTEL AND RESORT

Rating: 8

On Silver Lake.

Map 5.1, grid f2, page 320

This park is set near the shore of Silver Lake and features a view of Mount St. Helens. One of Washington's better lakes for largemouth bass and trout, it also has perch, crappie, and bluegill. Power boating and water-skiing are popular. This spot is considered a great fisherman's camp. The sites are set along a horseshoe-shaped driveway on grassy sites. Access is quick to Mount St. Helens, which is located to the nearby east.

Campsites, facilities: There are 22 sites with partial hookups (water and electricity) for RVs of any length, 13 tent sites, five cabins, and six motel rooms. Picnic tables and fire grills are provided. Restrooms, drinking water, flush toilets, coin-operated showers, a store, showers, ice, boat docks, boat rentals, launching facilities, and a playground are available. An RV dump station is within one mile, and a café is within four miles. Leashed pets are permitted.

Reservations, fees: Reservations accepted. Sites are $16–24 per night, $2 per person for more than four people, and $5 per extra vehicle per night. Major credit cards accepted. Open year-round.

Directions: From Longview, drive 10 miles north on I-5 to Castle Rock and Exit 49 and Highway 504. Take Exit 49 and drive east on Highway 504 for 6.5 miles to the park on the right.

Contact: Silver Lake Motel and Resort, 3201 Spirit Lake Hwy., Silver Lake, WA 98645, 360/274-6141, fax 360/274-2183, website: www.silverlake-resort.com.

23 KALAMA HORSE CAMP

Rating: 8

Near Mount St. Helens.
Map 5.1, grid h5, page 320

The most popular horse camp in the area, Kalama Horse Camp receives the enthusiastic volunteer support of local equestrians. The camp fills on weekends partly because of a network of 53 miles of horse trails accessible from camp. It is located very near Mount St. Helens.

Campsites, facilities: There are 27 sites for tents or RVs and three group sites. Picnic tables and fire grills are provided. Vault toilets are available. No drinking water is provided. Garbage must be packed out. Horse facilities include 10-by-10-foot corrals, a staging and mounting assist area, stock water, a stock loading ramp, and hitching rails. A 24-by-36-foot log cabin shelter with a picnic table and a picnic area with horseshoe pits are also available. Boat-launching facilities are located on Lake Merrill. Leashed pets are permitted.

Reservations, fees: Northwest Forest Pass ($5 daily fee or $30 annual fee per parked vehicle) is required. Open April–mid-December, weather permitting.

Directions: From Woodland on I-5, take Exit 21 for Highway 503. Drive east on Highway 503 and go 23 miles to the Highway 503 spur. Continue northeast on Highway 503 spur to Forest Road 81 (at Yale Lake, one mile south of Cougar). Turn left on Forest Road 81 and drive about eight miles to the camp on the right.

Contact: Gifford Pinchot National Forest, Mount St. Helens National Volcanic Monument, 42218 NE Yale Bridge Rd., Amboy, WA 98601-0369, 360/247-3900, fax 360/247-3901.

24 LAKE MERRILL

Rating: 7

Near Mount St. Helens.
Map 5.1, grid h6, page 320

Campers seeking a quiet setting will enjoy this site. The campground is nestled in old-growth Douglas fir on the shore of Lake Merrill, very near Mount St. Helens. It's free and provides an alternative to the more developed parks in the area, especially those along the main access roads to viewing areas of the volcano. The lake provides fishing for brown trout and cutthroat trout, but is restricted to fly-fishing only, with only nonmotorized boats permitted. These restrictions make it ideal for fly fishers with prams or float tubes.

Campsites, facilities: There are seven tent sites. Picnic tables, fire grills, and tent pads are provided. Vault toilets and hand-pumped drinking water are available. Some facilities are wheelchair accessible. Boat-launching facilities are located on Lake Merrill. Leashed pets are permitted.

Reservations, fees: Reservations are not accepted. There is no fee for camping. Open May–November, weather permitting.

Directions: From Woodland on I-5, take Exit 21 for Highway 503. Drive east on Highway 503 for 23 miles to Highway 503 spur. Drive northeast on Highway 503 spur to Forest Road 81. Turn left on Forest Road 81 and drive 4.5 miles. Turn left on the access road and continue to the campground.

Contact: Department of Natural Resources, Southwest Region, P.O. Box 280, Castle Rock, WA 98611-0280, 360/577-2025 or 360/274-4196, 360/274-2055.

25 LONE FIR RESORT

Rating: 4

Near Yale Lake.
Map 5.1, grid h6, page 320

This private campground is located near Yale

Lake (the smallest of four lakes in the area) and, with grassy sites and plenty of shade trees, is designed primarily for RV use. Mount St. Helens provides a side-trip option. The trailhead for the summit climb is located nearby at Climber's Bivouac on the south flank of the volcano; a primitive campground with dispersed sites for hikers only is available here. Note: This trailhead is the only one available for the summit climb.

Campsites, facilities: There are 17 sites with full hookups, including three drive-through, for RVs of any length and eight tent sites. Picnic tables are provided. Fire pits are provided at tent sites. Restrooms, drinking water, flush toilets, showers, a laundry room, coin-operated showers, ice, a snack bar, and a swimming pool in summer are available. Bottled gas, a store, and a restaurant are within one mile. Boat docks and launching facilities are nearby. Pets and motorbikes are permitted.

Reservations, fees: Reservations accepted. Sites are $14–20 per night, $2 per person per night for more than two people. Senior discount available if paying cash. Major credit cards accepted. Open year-round.

Directions: In Woodland on I-5, take Exit 21 for Highway 503. Drive east on Highway 503 for 29 miles to Cougar and the resort turnoff (marked, in town, with the park visible from the road) on the left.

Contact: Lone Fir Resort, 16806 Lewis River Rd., Cougar, WA 98616, 360/238-5210.

26 EVANS CREEK

Rating: 7

On Evans Creek in Mount Baker-Snoqualmie National Forest.
Map 5.2, grid a1, page 321

This primitive campground is located close to Evans Creek in an off-road-vehicle area near the northwestern corner of Mount Rainier National Park. If you're looking for a quiet, secluded spot, this isn't it. The two nearby roads

that lead into the park are secondary or gravel roads and provide access to several other primitive campgrounds and backcountry trails in the park. A national forest map details the back roads and hiking trails.

Campsites, facilities: There are 27 tent sites. Picnic tables and fire grills are provided. Drinking water and vault toilets are available. Downed wood can be gathered for campfires. Garbage must be packed out. Leashed pets are permitted.

Reservations, fees: Northwest Forest Pass ($5 daily fee or $30 annual fee per parked vehicle) is required. Open mid-June–late September.

Directions: From Tacoma on I-5, turn east on Highway 167 and drive nine miles to Highway 410. Continue 11 miles east on Highway 410 to the town of Buckley and Highway 165. Turn south on Highway 165 and drive 11 miles to Forest Road 7920. Turn left and drive 1.5 miles to the campground on the right.

Contact: Mount Baker-Snoqualmie National Forest, White River Ranger District, 450 Roosevelt Ave. E, Enumclaw, WA 98022, 360/825-6585, fax 360/825-0660.

27 MOWICH LAKE WALK-IN

Rating: 8

Near the Carbon River in Mount Rainier National Park.
Map 5.2, grid a1, page 321

This walk-in camp features campsites set adjacent to and above Mowich Lake, with a lake view from some of the sites. A 200-yard walk is required to reach the campsites. Some backpackers use the camp as a launch point for trips into the Mount Rainier Wilderness. The Wonderland Trail can be accessed at this campground. Fishing is poor for trout at Mowich Lake because it is not stocked and lacks a habitat for natural spawning.

Campsites, facilities: There are 30 walk-in tent sites. Picnic tables are available at some sites. Pit toilets are available. No drinking water is provided. No campfires are permitted; use a backpacking stove. Leashed pets are permitted in camp, but not on trails.

Reservations, fees: Reservations are not accepted; there is a $10 park entrance fee. Open June–October, weather permitting.

Directions: From Puyallup, drive east on Highway 167 to Highway 410. Turn east on Highway 410 and drive 11 miles to the town of Buckley and Highway 165. Turn south on Highway 165 and drive to a fork with Carbon River Park Road. Bear right and stay on Highway 165 for eight miles to the campground at the end of the road. High-clearance vehicles only are recommended for this access road.

Contact: Mount Rainier National Park, Tahoma Woods, Star Rte., Ashford, WA 98304, 360/569-2211, fax 360/569-2187.

28 IPSUT CREEK

Rating: 8

Near the Carbon River in Mount Rainier National Park.
Map 5.2, grid a2, page 321

This camp, set at the end of Carbon River Road, functions primarily as a trailhead camp for hikers heading into the backcountry of Mount Rainier National Park, past lakes, glaciers, waterfalls, and many other wonders. For day-hikers, the seven-mile Carbon Glacier Trail (round-trip) is accessible from the campground. The trail follows the Carbon River through the forest to the snout of the glacier; watch for falling rocks. In addition, the Carbon River Rain Forest Nature Trail begins at the Carbon River entrance to the park. This 0.3-mile loop trail explores the only inland rainforest at Mount Rainier National Park. Note that fishing is prohibited on Isput Creek above the campground at the water supply intake. Also note that in 2002, a problem occurred with the availability of drinking water. The elevation is 2,300 feet.

Campsites, facilities: There are 31 sites for tents

and two group camps for up to 40 people. Picnic tables and fire rings are provided. Vault toilets are available. No drinking water is available. Leashed pets are permitted in camp, but not on trails.

Reservations, fees: Reservations are not accepted. Sites are $9 per night, $5 per extra vehicle per night, plus $10 park entrance fee. Group sites are $40 per night. Senior discount available. Open year-round, weather permitting.

Directions: From Puyallup, drive east on Highway 167 to Highway 410. Turn east on Highway 410 and drive 11 miles to the town of Buckley and Highway 165. Turn south on Highway 165 and drive to a fork with Carbon River Park Road. Bear left and drive five miles to the campground on the left. Note: The access road is subject to flooding and closure after heavy rains.

Contact: Mount Rainier National Park, Tahoma Woods, Star Rte., Ashford, WA 98304, 360/569-2211, fax 360/569-2187.

29 WHITE RIVER

Rating: 7

On the White River in Mount Rainier National Park.
Map 5.2, grid a3, page 321

This campground is set on the White River at 4,400 feet elevation. The Glacier Basin Trail, a seven-mile round-trip, starts at the campground and leads along the Emmons Moraine to a view of the Emmons Glacier, the largest glacier in the continental United States. It is sometimes possible to spot mountain goats, as well as mountain climbers, on the surrounding mountain slopes. Note that another trail near camp leads a short distance (but vertically, for a rise of 2,200 feet) to the Sunrise Visitor Center. Local rangers recommend that trailers be left at the White River Campground and the 11-mile road trip to Sunrise be made by car. From there, you can take several trails that lead to backcountry lakes and glaciers.

Climbers planning to summit Mount Rainier often use White River as their base camp. Also note that this campground is located in what is considered to be a geo-hazard zone, where there is risk of a mudflow. It's never happened, but minor incidents have occurred up-slope from the camp.

Campsites, facilities: There are 112 sites for tents or RVs up to 20 feet long. Picnic tables and fire grills are provided. Flush toilets and drinking water are available. A small amphitheater is nearby. Some facilities are wheelchair accessible. Leashed pets are permitted in camp, but not on trails or in the wilderness.

Reservations, fees: Reservations are not accepted. Sites are $12 per night. Major credit cards accepted. Open mid-June–mid-September.

Directions: From Enumclaw, drive southeast on Highway 410 to the entrance of Mount Rainier National Park and White River Road. Turn right and drive seven miles to the campground on the left.

Contact: Mount Rainier National Park, Tahoma Woods, Star Rte., Ashford, WA 98304, 360/569-2211, fax 360/569-2187.

30 SILVER SPRINGS

Rating: 9

In Mount Baker-Snoqualmie National Forest.
Map 5.2, grid a4, page 321

This campground along the White River on the northeastern border of Mount Rainier National Park offers a good alternative to the more crowded camps in the park. It's located in a beautiful section of old-growth forest, primarily with Douglas fir, cedar, and hemlock, and is very scenic. Recreational options are limited to hiking. A U.S. Forest Service information center is located one mile away from the campground entrance on Highway 410.

Campsites, facilities: There are 55 sites for tents or RVs up to 21 feet long and one group site for up to 50 people. Picnic tables and fire grills are provided. Flush toilets, drinking water, and downed firewood for gathering are available. The group site has a picnic shelter. Some facilities are wheelchair accessible. Leashed pets are permitted.

Reservations, fees: Reservations accepted for some sites; phone 877/444-6777 or access the website: www.ReserveUsa.com ($9 reservation fee). Sites are $14 per night; $6 extra vehicle fee. Senior discount available. The group site is $75 per night. Open mid-May–late September.

Directions: From Enumclaw, drive east on Highway 410 for 31 miles (one mile south of the turnoff for Corral Pass) to the campground entrance on the right.

Contact: Mount Baker-Snoqualmie National Forest, White River Ranger District, 450 Roosevelt Ave. E, Enumclaw, WA 98022, 360/825-6585, fax 360/825-0660.

31 GATEWAY INN AND RV PARK

Rating: 8

Near Mount Rainier National Park.
Map 5.2, grid c1, page 321

This park is located fewer than 100 feet from the southwestern entrance to Mount Rainier National Park. In turn, it can provide a launching point for your vacation. One option: Enter the park at the Nisqually (southwestern) entrance to Mount Rainier National Park, then drive on Nisqually Paradise Road for about five miles to Longmire Museum; general park information and exhibits about the plants and geology of the area are available. If you then continue into the park for 10 more miles, you'll arrive at the Jackson Visitor Center in Paradise, which has more exhibits and an observation deck. This road is the only one into the park that's open year-round. Winter activities in the park include cross-country skiing, snowshoeing, and inner-tube sledding down slopes.

Campsites, facilities: There are 16 sites with full hookups for RVs of any length, a dispersed area for up to seven tents, and nine cabins. Picnic tables are provided. Drinking water and portable toilets are available. A restaurant, a gift shop, and a mini-mart are nearby. Leashed pets are permitted.

Reservations, fees: Reservations accepted. Sites are $12–22 per night. Cabins are $69–89 per night, $10 per person per night for more than two people. Senior discount available. Major credit cards accepted. Open April–September.

Directions: From Chehalis, drive south on I-5 for 10 miles to U.S. 12. Turn east and drive 31 miles to Morton and Highway 7. Turn north on Highway 7 and drive 17 miles to Elbe and Highway 706. Turn east on Highway 706 and drive 13 miles to the campground on the right.

Contact: Gateway Inn and RV Park, 38820 Hwy. 706 E, Ashford, WA 98304, 360/569-2506, website: www.gatewaytomtrainier.com.

32 MOUNTHAVEN RESORT

Rating: 6

Near Mount Rainier National Park.
Map 5.2, grid c1, page 321

This campground is located within one-half mile of the Nisqually entrance to Mount Rainier National Park. See the previous description of Gateway Inn and RV Park for information about the national park. A creek runs through this wooded camp.

Campsites, facilities: There are 17 sites with full hookups for RVs of any length, one tent site, and 11 furnished cabins. Picnic tables and fire grills are provided. Restrooms, drinking water, flush toilets, one shower, a coin-operated laundry, firewood, and a playground are available. A restaurant and a store are within one mile. Leashed pets are permitted.

Reservations, fees: Reservations at 800/456-9380. Sites are $15–20 per night. Cabins are $69–199 per night. Major credit cards accepted. Open year-round.

Directions: From Chehalis, drive south on I-5 for 10 miles to U.S. 12. Turn east and drive 31 miles to Morton and Highway 7. Turn north

on Highway 7 and drive 17 miles to Elbe and Highway 706. Turn east on Highway 706 and drive to Ashford; continue for six miles to the campground on the right.

Contact: Mounthaven Resort, 38210 Hwy. 706 E, Ashford, WA 98304, 360/569-2594, fax 360/569-2949, website: www.mounthaven.com.

33 SUNSHINE POINT

Rating: 7

In Mount Rainier National Park.
Map 5.2, grid c1, page 321

This campground is one of several in Mount Rainier National Park located near the Nisqually entrance. The others include Ipsut Creek, Cougar Rock, White River, Mounthaven, Gateway, and Ohanapecosh. The elevation is 2,000 feet. See the previous description of Gateway Inn and RV Park for information about nearby sights and facilities.

Campsites, facilities: There are 18 sites for tents or RVs up to 25 feet long. Picnic tables and fire rings are provided. Drinking water and pit toilets are available. Some facilities are wheelchair accessible. Leashed pets are permitted in the camp, but not on trails or in the wilderness.

Reservations, fees: Reservations accepted. Sites are $10 per night, $5 per extra vehicle per night, plus a $10 park entrance fee. Senior discount available. Major credit cards accepted. Open year-round.

Directions: From Chehalis, drive south on I-5 for 10 miles to U.S. 12. Turn east and drive 31 miles to Morton and Highway 7. Turn north on Highway 7 and drive 17 miles to Elbe and Highway 706. Turn east on Highway 706 and drive 12 miles to the park entrance. The campground is just inside the park entrance on the right.

Contact: Mount Rainier National Park, Tahoma Woods, Star Rte., Ashford, WA 98304, 360/569-2211, fax 360/569-2187.

34 COUGAR ROCK

🚶 🛶 ❄ 🐕 ♿ 🚐 ⛺

Rating: 9

In Mount Rainier National Park.

Map 5.2, grid b2, page 321

Cougar Rock is a national park campground set at 3,180 feet elevation at the foot of awesome Mount Rainier. To the east lies Paradise, a beautiful 1.2-mile loop trail. It begins at the visitors center and provides stellar views of Mount Rainier and the Nisqually Glacier. Fishing tends to be marginal. As in all national parks, no trout are stocked, and lakes without natural fisheries provide zilch. See previous listing for Gateway Inn and RV Park for information on the nearby park sights and visitors centers.

Campsites, facilities: There are 173 sites for tents or RVs up to 30 feet long and five group sites for up to 24–40 people each. Picnic tables and fire rings are provided. Restrooms, drinking water, flush toilets, an RV dump station, and an amphitheater are available. A camp store is located two miles away. Some facilities are wheelchair accessible. Leashed pets are permitted.

Reservations, fees: Reserve at 800/365-CAMP (800/365-2267) or website: http://reservations.nps.gov/. Sites are $15 per night, plus a $10 park entrance fee, and $6 per extra vehicle per night; $2 surcharge on holidays and summer weekends. Senior discount available. Group sites are $40–64 per night. Major credit cards accepted. Open mid-May–mid-October.

Directions: From Tacoma, drive south on I-5 for five miles to Highway 512. Turn east of Highway 512 and drive two miles to Highway 7. Turn south on Highway 7 and drive to Elbe and Highway 706. Continue east on Highway 706 and drive 12 miles to the park entrance. Continue 11 miles to the campground entrance on the left (about two miles past the Longmire developed area).

Contact: Mount Rainier National Park, Tahoma Woods, Star Rte., Ashford, WA 98304, 360/569-2211, fax 360/569-2187.

35 OHANAPECOSH

🚶 🛶 ❄ 🐕 ♿ 🚐 ⛺

Rating: 8

On the Ohanapecosh River in Mount Rainier National Park.

Map 5.2, grid c4, page 321

This camp is set at an elevation of 1,914 feet at the foot of North America's most beautiful volcano, 14,410-foot Mount Rainier. It is also set along the Ohanapecosh River, near the Ohanapecosh Visitor Center, which features exhibits on the history of the forest, plus visitor information. A half-mile loop trail leads from the campground, behind the visitors center, to Ohanapecosh Hot Springs. The Silver Falls Trail, a three-mile loop trail, follows the Ohanapecosh River to 75-foot Silver Falls. Warning: Do not climb on the wet rocks near the waterfall; they are wet and slippery. Note that Stevens Canyon Road heading west and Highway 123 heading north are closed by snowfall in winter.

Campsites, facilities: There are 188 sites for tents or RVs up to 30 feet long and one group site for up to 25 people. Picnic tables are provided. Flush toilets, drinking water, and an RV dump station are available. An amphitheater is nearby. Some facilities are wheelchair accessible. Leashed pets are permitted in camp, but not on trails.

Reservations, fees: Reservations accepted up to five months in advance for the late June–early September season; phone 800/365-CAMP (800/365-2267) or access the website: www.reservations.nps.gov. Sites are $15 per night, plus a $10 per vehicle park entrance fee. Senior discount available. The group site is $40 per night. Major credit cards accepted. Open mid-May–September.

Directions: On I-5, drive to Exit 68 (south of Chehalis) and U.S. 12. Turn east on U.S. 12 and drive 72 miles (seven miles past Packwood) to Highway 123. Turn north and drive five miles to the Ohanapecosh entrance to the park. As you enter the park, the camp is on the left, next to the visitors center.

Contact: Mount Rainier National Park, Tahoma Woods, Ashford, WA 98304, 360/569-2211, fax 360/569-2187.

36 LODGEPOLE

Rating: 6

On the American River in Wenatchee National Forest; .

Map 5.2, grid a5, page 321

This campground is set at an elevation of 3,500 feet along the American River, just eight miles east of the boundary of Mount Rainier National Park. See the previous description of Gateway Inn and RV Park for information on Mount Rainier. Fishing access is available nearby. The campground was remodeled in 2001.

Campsites, facilities: There are 33 sites for tents or RVs up to 20 feet long. Picnic tables and fire grills are provided. Drinking water, vault toilets, garbage service, and firewood are available. Leashed pets are permitted.

Reservations, fees: Reservations are not accepted. Sites are $13–15 per night, $5 for each additional vehicle, and $2 surcharge on holidays and summer weekends. Senior discount available. Open late May–late October.

Directions: From Yakima, drive northwest on U.S. 12 for 18 miles to Highway 410. Bear northwest on Highway 410 and drive 40.5 miles (eight miles east of the national park boundary) to the campground on the right.

Contact: Okanogan and Wenatchee National Forests, Naches Ranger District, 10061 U.S. 12, Naches, WA 98937, 509/653-2205, fax 509/653-2638.

37 PLEASANT VALLEY

Rating: 7

On the American River in Wenatchee National Forest.

Map 5.2, grid a6, page 321

This campground, set at an elevation of 3,300

feet, provides a good base camp for a hiking or fishing trip. A trail from the camp follows Kettle Creek up to the American Ridge and Kettle Lake in the William O. Douglas Wilderness. It joins another trail that follows the ridge and then drops down to Bumping Lake. A U.S. Forest Service map is essential. You can fish here for whitefish, steelhead, trout, and salmon in season; check regulations. In the winter, the area is popular with cross-country skiers. The campground was remodeled in 2001.

Campsites, facilities: There are 16 sites for tents or RVs up to 32 feet long. Picnic tables and fire grills are provided. Drinking water, garbage service, vault toilets, and a picnic shelter are available. Downed firewood may be gathered. Some facilities are wheelchair accessible. Leashed pets are permitted.

Reservations, fees: Reservations are not accepted. Rates are $13–15 per night for single sites, $26 per night for double sites, and $5 for each additional vehicle; $2 surcharge on holidays and summer weekends. Senior discount available. Open mid-May–mid-November.

Directions: From Yakima, drive northwest on U.S. 12 for 18 miles to Highway 410. Bear northwest on Highway 410 and drive 37 miles to the campground on the left.

Contact: Okanogan and Wenatchee National Forests, Naches Ranger District, 10061 U.S. 12, Naches, WA 98937, 509/653-2205, fax 509/653-2638.

38 HELLS CROSSING

Rating: 7

On the American River in Wenatchee National Forest.

Map 5.2, grid a6, page 321

This campground lies along the American River at an elevation of 3,250 feet. A steep trail from the camp leads up to Goat Peak and follows the American Ridge in the William O. Douglas Wilderness. Other trails join the ridgeline trail and connect with lakes and streams. A

U.S. Forest Service map details the backcountry. Fishing here is for trout, steelhead, salmon, and whitefish in season; check regulations.

Campsites, facilities: There are 18 sites for tents or RVs up to 20 feet long. Picnic tables and fire grills are provided. Drinking water (at the west end of camp) and vault toilets are available. Downed firewood may be gathered. Leashed pets are permitted.

Reservations, fees: Reservations are not accepted. Rates are $13–15 per night for single sites, $26 per night for double sites, and $5 for each additional vehicle; $2 surcharge on holidays and summer weekends. Senior discount available. Open late May–late November.

Directions: From Yakima, drive northwest on U.S. 12 for 18 miles to Highway 410. Bear northwest on Highway 410 and drive 33.5 miles northwest on Highway 410 to the campground on the right.

Contact: Okanogan and Wenatchee National Forests, Naches Ranger District, 10061 U.S. 12, Naches, WA 98937, 509/653-2205, fax 509/653-2638.

39 PINE NEEDLE GROUP CAMP

Rating: 7

On the American River in Wenatchee National Forest.

Map 5.2, grid a7, page 321

This reservations-only group campground sits on the edge of the William O. Douglas Wilderness along the American River at an elevation of 3,000 feet. There are trails leading south into the backcountry at nearby camps; see a U.S. Forest Service map. The camp is easy to reach, rustic, and beautiful. Fishing access is available for whitefish, trout, steelhead, and salmon in season. For a side trip, visit Bumping Lake to the south, where recreation options include boating, fishing, and swimming.

Campsites, facilities: There are six group sites for tents or RVs up to 21 feet long, with a maximum capacity of 60 campers and eight vehicles. Picnic tables and fire grills are provided. Pit toilets are available, but there is no drinking water. Note that drinking water is available 2.5 miles west at Hells Crossing Campground (see previous listing). Garbage must be packed out. Downed firewood may be gathered. Leashed pets are permitted.

Reservations, fees: Reservations required. Sites are $20 per night on weekdays and $40 per night on weekends. Discounts are available for three or more consecutive days. Open mid-May–late October.

Directions: From Yakima, drive northwest on U.S. 12 for 18 miles to Highway 410. Bear northwest on Highway 410 and drive 30.5 miles to the campground on the left.

Contact: Okanogan and Wenatchee National Forests, Naches Ranger District, 10061 U.S. 12, Naches, WA 98937, 509/653-2205, fax 509/653-2638.

40 CEDAR SPRINGS

Rating: 6

On the Bumping River in Wenatchee National Forest.

Map 5.2, grid a7, page 321

The Bumping River runs alongside this camp, set an elevation of 2,800 feet. Fishing here follows the seasons for trout, steelhead, and whitefish; check regulations. If you continue driving southwest for 11 miles on Forest Road 1800/Bumping River Road, you'll reach Bumping Lake, where recreation options abound.

Campsites, facilities: There are 15 sites for tents or RVs up to 22 feet long, including two multifamily sites. Picnic tables and fire grills are provided. Drinking water, vault toilets, and firewood are available. Leashed pets are permitted.

Reservations, fees: Reservations are not accepted. Rates are $13–15 per night for single sites, $26 per night for double sites, and $5 for each additional vehicle; $2 surcharge on holidays and summer weekends. Senior discount available. Open late May–late November.

Directions: From Yakima, drive northwest on U.S. 12 for 18 miles to Highway 410. Bear northwest on Highway 410 and drive 28.5 miles to the campground access road (Forest Road 1800/Bumping River Road). Turn southwest and drive one-half mile to the campground on the left.

Contact: Okanogan and Wenatchee National Forests, Naches Ranger District, 10061 U.S. 12, Naches, WA 98937, 509/653-2205, fax 509/653-2638.

41 INDIAN FLAT GROUP CAMP

Rating: 7

On the American River in Wenatchee National Forest.

Map 5.2, grid a7, page 321

This reservations-only group campground is set along the American River at an elevation of 2,600 feet. Fishing access is available for trout, steelhead, and whitefish in season; check regulations. A trail that starts just across the road from camp leads into the back-country, west along Fife's Ridge, and farther north to the West Quartz Creek drainage. A U.S. Forest Service map details the adventure possibilities.

Campsites, facilities: There are group sites for tents or RVs up to 30 feet long, with a maximum capacity of 65 campers and 22 vehicles. Picnic tables and fire grills are provided. Drinking water, vault toilets, and firewood are available. Garbage must be packed out. Leashed pets are permitted.

Reservations, fees: Reservations required. Sites are $45 per night on week days and $125 per night on weekends. Discounts are available for three or more consecutive days. Open late May–late October.

Directions: From Yakima, drive northwest on U.S. 12 for 18 miles to Highway 410. Bear northwest on Highway 410 and drive 27 miles to the campground on the left.

Contact: Okanogan and Wenatchee National Forests, Naches Ranger District, 10061 U.S. 12, Naches, WA 98937, 509/653-2205, fax 509/653-2638.

42 LITTLE NACHES

Rating: 5

On the Little Naches River in Wenatchee National Forest.

Map 5.2, grid a8, page 321

This campground on the Little Naches River near the American River is just one-tenth of a mile off the road and 24 miles from Mount Rainier. The easy access is a major attraction for highway cruisers, but the location also means you can hear highway noise, and at four sites, you can see highway vehicles. Trees act as a buffer between the highway and the campground at other sites. This camp is a destination for off-road motorcyclists and jeep campers because of a 200-mile network of off-road trails. It is possible, for instance, to reach Cle Elum from here without driving on asphalt. Fishing access is available from camp. The elevation is 2,562 feet.

Campsites, facilities: There are 21 sites for tents or RVs up to 20 feet long, with several sites accessible for RVs up to 32 feet long and two multi-family sites. Picnic tables and fire grills are provided. Drinking water, vault toilets, and garbage service are available. Some facilities are wheelchair accessible. Leashed pets are permitted.

Reservations, fees: Reservations are not accepted. Rates are $13–15 per night for single sites, $5 for each additional vehicle; $2 surcharge on holidays and summer weekends. Senior discount available. Open late May–late November.

Directions: From Yakima, drive northwest on U.S. 12 for 18 miles to Highway 410. Bear northwest on Highway 410 and drive 25 miles to the campground access road (Forest Road 1900). Turn left and drive 100 yards to the campground on the left.

Contact: Okanogan and Wenatchee National

Forests, Naches Ranger District, 10061 U.S. 12, Naches, WA 98937, 509/653-2205, fax 509/653-2638.

43 COTTONWOOD

Rating: 7

On the Naches River in Wenatchee National Forest.

Map 5.2, grid a8, page 321

Pretty, shaded sites and river views are the main draw at this camp along the Naches River. Sawmill Flat, Little Naches, Crow Creek, Kaner Flat, and Halfway Flat campgrounds provide nearby alternatives. The elevation here is 2,300 feet. The fishing is similar to that of the other camps.

Campsites, facilities: There are 16 sites for tents or RVs up to 22 feet long. Picnic tables and fire grills are provided. Drinking water, vault toilets, and garbage service are available. A store, a café, and ice are available nearby. Some facilities are wheelchair accessible. Leashed pets are permitted.

Reservations, fees: Reservations are not accepted. Sites are $13–15 per night, $5 for each additional vehicle; $2 surcharge on holidays and summer weekends. Senior discount available. Open April–November.

Directions: From Yakima, drive northwest on U.S. 12 for 18 miles to Highway 410. Turn left (northwest) on Highway 410 and drive 17.5 miles to the campground on the left.

Contact: Okanogan and Wenatchee National Forests, Naches Ranger District, 10061 U.S. 12, Naches, WA 98937, 509/653-2205, fax 509/653-2638.

44 SAWMILL FLAT

Rating: 6

On the Naches River in Wenatchee National Forest.

Map 5.2, grid a8, page 321

This campground on the Naches River near Halfway Flat is used more by off-road motorcyclists than others. It offers fishing access and a hiking trail that leads west from Halfway Flat Campground for several miles into the backcountry; note that you must wade across the river to reach Halfway Flat from Sawmill Flat. Fishing is primarily for trout in summer, whitefish in winter; check regulations. Another trailhead is located at Boulder Cave to the south. See a U.S. Forest Service map for details.

Campsites, facilities: There are 24 sites for tents or RVs up to 24 feet long. Picnic tables and fire grills are provided. Drinking water, vault toilets, an RV dump station, and an Adirondack group shelter are available. Downed firewood may be gathered. Some facilities are wheelchair accessible, including one campsite. A camp host is available in summer. Leashed pets are permitted.

Reservations, fees: Reservations are not accepted. Rates are $13–15 per night for single sites, $5 for each additional vehicle; $2 surcharge on holidays and summer weekends. Senior discount available. Open April–November.

Directions: From Yakima, drive northwest on U.S. 12 for 18 miles to Highway 410. Bear northwest on Highway 410 and drive 23.5 miles to the campground on the left.

Contact: Okanogan and Wenatchee National Forests, Naches Ranger District, 10061 U.S. 12, Naches, WA 98937, 509/653-2205, fax 509/653-2638.

45 HALFWAY FLAT

Rating: 7

On the Naches River in Wenatchee National Forest.

Map 5.2, grid a8, page 321

Fishing, hiking, and off-road vehicle (ORV) opportunities abound at this campground along the Naches River. A motorcycle trail leads from the campground into the backcountry adjacent to the William O. Douglas Wilderness; no motorized vehicles are permitted in the wilderness itself, however. Do not expect peace and quiet. This campground is something of a chameleon; that is, sometimes primarily a family campground, but at other times dominated by ORV users. It was remodeled in 2001.

Campsites, facilities: There are nine sites for tents or RVs up to 27 feet long. Picnic tables and fire grills are provided. Drinking water, vault toilets, garbage service, and firewood are available. Leashed pets are permitted.

Reservations, fees: Reservations are not accepted. Sites are $7 per night. Senior discount available. Open April–late November.

Directions: From Yakima, drive northwest on U.S. 12 for 18 miles to Highway 410. Turn left (northwest) on Highway 410 and drive 17 miles to the campground on the left.

Contact: Okanogan and Wenatchee National Forests, Naches Ranger District, 10061 U.S. 12, Naches, WA 98937, 509/653-2205, fax 509/653-2638.

46 LOWER BUMPING LAKE

Rating: 7

On Bumping Lake in Wenatchee National Forest.

Map 5.2, grid b6, page 321

This camp is set at an elevation of 3,200 feet near Bumping Lake amid a forest of primarily lodgepole pine. This popular campground features a variety of water activities at Bumping Lake, including water-skiing, fishing (salmon and trout), and swimming. A boat ramp is available near the camp. There are also several hiking trails that go into the William O. Douglas Wilderness surrounding the lake.

Campsites, facilities: There are 23 sites for tents or RVs up to 50 feet long. Picnic tables and fire grills are provided. Drinking water, vault toilets, and an RV dump station are available. Some facilities are wheelchair accessible. Boat-launching facilities are located nearby at Upper Bumping Lake Campground. Leashed pets are permitted.

Reservations, fees: Reservations are not accepted. Sites are $13–15 per night, $26 for a

double site, and $5 for each additional vehicle; $2 surcharge on holidays and summer weekends. Senior discount available. Open mid-May–late November, weather permitting.

Directions: From Yakima, drive northwest on U.S. 12 for 18 miles to Highway 410. Turn left (northwest) on Highway 410 and drive 28.5 miles to Forest Road 1800. Turn left (southwest) and drive 11 miles (along the Bumping River); look for the campground entrance road on the right (now paved all the way).

Contact: Wenatchee National Forest, Naches Ranger District, 10061 Hwy. 12, Naches, WA 98937, 509/653-2205, fax 509/653-2638.

47 UPPER BUMPING LAKE

Rating: 7

On Bumping Lake in Wenatchee National Forest.

Map 5.2, grid b6, page 321

Woods and water—this spot has them both. The cold lake is stocked with trout, and the nearby boat launch makes it a winner for campers with boats. This popular camp fills up quickly on summer weekends. A variety of water activities are allowed at Bumping Lake, including water-skiing, fishing (salmon and trout), and swimming. Six picnic sites are situated adjacent to the boat facilities. In addition, several hiking trails lead into the William O. Douglas Wilderness surrounding the lake. One of the more developed camps in the area, this camp was remodeled in 2001.

Campsites, facilities: There are 45 sites for tents or RVs up to 30 feet long. Picnic tables and fire grills are provided. Drinking water, vault toilets, and firewood are available. Boat docks, launching facilities, rentals, and an RV dump station are nearby. Leashed pets are permitted.

Reservations, fees: Reservations are not accepted. Sites are $13–15 per night, $5 for each additional vehicle; $2 surcharge on holidays and summer weekends. Senior discount available. Open mid-May–late November.

Directions: From Yakima, drive northwest on U.S. 12 for 18 miles to Highway 410. Turn left (northwest) on Highway 410 and drive 28.5 miles to Forest Road 1800. Turn left (southwest) and drive 11 miles (along the Bumping River) to the end of the pavement; look for the campground entrance road on the right.

Contact: Okanogan and Wenatchee National Forests, Naches Ranger District, 10061 U.S. 12, Naches, WA 98937, 509/653-2205, fax 509/653-2638.

48 BUMPING CROSSING

Rating: 5

On the Bumping River in Wenatchee National Forest.

Map 5.2, grid b6, page 321

This campground is set on the Bumping River about one mile from the boat landing at Bumping Lake. It provides a more primitive alternative to Bumping Lake and Boat Landing. Although a good spot for a weekend trip, it doesn't have drinking water. Fishing and boating are often good. The elevation is 3,200 feet.

Campsites, facilities: There are 12 sites for tents or RVs up to 15 feet long. Picnic tables and fire grills are provided. Vault toilets are available, but there is no drinking water. A store, a café, and ice are located within one mile. Boat docks, launching facilities, and rentals are nearby on Bumping Lake. Leashed pets are permitted.

Reservations, fees: Reservations are not accepted. There is no fee for camping. For boat launching, Northwest Forest Pass ($5 daily fee or $30 annual fee per parked vehicle) is required. Open late May–late November.

Directions: From Yakima, drive northwest on U.S. 12 for 18 miles to Highway 410. Turn left (northwest) on Highway 410 and drive 28.5 miles to Forest Road 1800. Turn left (southwest) and drive 10 miles (along the Bumping River) to the campground on the right.

Contact: Okanogan and Wenatchee National Forests, Naches Ranger District, 10061 U.S.

12, Naches, WA 98937, 509/653-2205, fax 509/653-2638.

49 COUGAR FLAT

Rating: 5

On the Bumping River in Wenatchee National Forest.

Map 5.2, grid a7, page 321

One of several camps in the immediate vicinity, this spot along the Bumping River is close to good fishing; a trail from the camp follows the river and then heads up the tributaries. The elevation is 3,100 feet. See the chapter map for nearby camping options.

Campsites, facilities: There are 12 sites for tents or RVs up to 20 feet long. Picnic tables and fire grills are provided. Drinking water and vault toilets are available. Some facilities are wheelchair accessible. Leashed pets are permitted.

Reservations, fees: Reservations are not accepted. Sites are $13–15 per night, $5 for each additional vehicle; $2 surcharge on holidays and summer weekends. Senior discount available. Open late May–mid-September.

Directions: From Yakima, drive northwest on U.S. 12 for 18 miles to Highway 410. Turn left (northwest) on Highway 410 and drive 28.5 miles to Forest Road 1800. Turn left (southwest) and drive six miles (along the Bumping River) to the campground on the left.

Contact: Okanogan and Wenatchee National Forests, Naches Ranger District, 10061 U.S. 12, Naches, WA 98937, 509/653-2205, fax 509/653-2638.

50 SODA SPRINGS

Rating: 6

On the Bumping River in Wenatchee National Forest.

Map 5.2, grid a7, page 321

Highlights at this camp along Bumping Creek

include natural mineral springs and a nature trail. The mineral spring is located next to a trail across the river from the campground, where the water bubbles up out of the ground. This cold-water spring is popular with some campers for soaking and drinking. Many campers use this camp for access to nearby Bumping Lake. Fishing access is available. A sheltered picnic area is provided.

Campsites, facilities: There are 26 sites for tents or RVs up to 30 feet in length. Picnic tables and fire grills are provided. Drinking water, vault toilets, an RV dump station, firewood, several picnic shelters with fireplaces, and garbage service are available. Some facilities are wheelchair accessible. Leashed pets are permitted.

Reservations, fees: Reservations are not accepted. Sites are $13–15 per night, $5 for each additional vehicle; $2 surcharge on holidays and summer weekends. Senior discount available. Open May–late November.

Directions: From Yakima, drive northwest on U.S. 12 for 18 miles to Highway 410. Turn left (northwest) on Highway 410 and drive 28.5 miles to Forest Road 1800. Turn left (southwest) and drive five miles (along the Bumping River) to the campground on the left.

Contact: Okanogan and Wenatchee National Forests, Naches Ranger District, 10061 U.S. 12, Naches, WA 98937, 509/653-2205, fax 509/653-2638.

51 BIG CREEK

Rating: 8

On Big Creek in Gifford Pinchot National Forest.

Map 5.2, grid c1, page 321

This camp is useful as an overflow spot for Mount Rainier and Puget Sound area campers. It is set along a stream next to a rural residential area in a forest setting made up of Douglas fir, western hemlock, western red cedar, and big leaf and vine maple. RV drivers should note that the required turning radius is fairly tight.

Campsites, facilities: There are 28 sites for tents or RVs up to 25 feet long. Picnic tables and fire rings are provided. Drinking water and vault toilets are available. Leashed pets are permitted.

Reservations, fees: Reservations recommended; phone 877/444-6777 or access the website: www.ReserveUsa.com ($9 reservation fee). Sites are $13 for a single, $26 for a double site per night, and $5 for each additional vehicle. Senior discount available. Open late May–mid-September.

Directions: On I-5, drive to Exit 68 (south of Chehalis) and U.S. 12. Turn east on U.S. 12 and drive 62 miles to Packwood and Forest Road 52/Skate Creek Road. Turn left (northwest) and drive 23 miles to the campground on the left.

Contact: Gifford Pinchot National Forest, Cowlitz Valley Ranger District, P.O. Box 670, Randle, WA 98377-0670, 360/497-1100, fax 360/497-1102.

52 PACKWOOD TRAILER AND RV PARK

Rating: 6

In Packwood.

Map 5.2, grid d3, page 321

This is a pleasant campground, especially in the fall when the maples turn color. Groups are welcome. Mount Rainier National Park is located just 25 miles north, and this camp provides a good alternative if the park is full. Nearby recreation options include a riding stable and tennis courts.

Campsites, facilities: There are 88 sites, most with full hookups, for RVs of any length and 15 tent sites. Picnic tables are provided. Restrooms, flush toilets, showers, an RV dump station, a store, cable TV, and a coin-operated laundry are available. A café and bottled gas are available within walking distance. Leashed pets are permitted.

Reservations, fees: Reservations accepted. Sites are $11–20 per night, $3 per person for more than two people. Major credit cards accepted. Open year-round.

Directions: On I-5, drive to Exit 68 (south of Chehalis) and U.S. 12. Turn east on U.S. 12 and drive 65 miles to Packwood. The park is on the north side of the highway in town at 19285 U.S. Highway 12.

Contact: Packwood Trailer and RV Park, P.O. Box 309, Packwood, WA 98361, 360/494-5145.

53 LA WIS WIS

Rating: 9

On the Cowlitz River in Gifford Pinchot National Forest.

Map 5.2, grid c4, page 321

This camp is ideally located for day trips to Mount Rainier and Mount St. Helens. It's set at an elevation of 1,400 feet along the Clear Fork of the Cowlitz River, near the confluence with the Ohanapecosh River. Trout fishing is an option. The landscape features an old-growth forest, a mix of Douglas fir, western hemlock, western red cedar, and Pacific yew, with an undergrowth of big leaf maple. A 200-yard trail provides access to the Blue Hole on the Ohanapecosh River, a deep pool designated by an observation point and interpretive signs. Another trail leads less than one-quarter mile to Purcell Falls. The entrance to Mount Rainier National Park is about seven miles south of the camp.

Campsites, facilities: There are 115 sites for tents or RVs up to 24 feet long. Picnic tables and fire rings are provided. Flush and vault toilets, drinking water, and firewood are available. Some facilities are wheelchair accessible. Leashed pets are permitted.

Reservations, fees: Reserve at 877/444-6777 ($9 reservation fee) or website: www.ReserveUsa.com. Sites are $14–28 per night, $5

per extra vehicle per night. Senior discount available. The maximum stay is 14 days. Open mid-May–late September.

Directions: On I-5, drive to Exit 68 (south of Chehalis) and U.S. 12. Turn east on U.S. 12 and drive 69 miles (about six miles past Packwood) to Forest Road 1272. Turn left and drive one-half mile to the campground on the left.

Contact: Gifford Pinchot National Forest, Cowlitz Valley Ranger District, P.O. Box 670, Randle, WA 98377-0670, 360/497-1100, fax 360/497-1102.

54 SUMMIT CREEK

Rating: 5

On Summit Creek in Gifford Pinchot National Forest.

Map 5.2, grid c4, page 321

This primitive campground nestles in the trees along Summit Creek at an elevation of 2,400 feet. It is another good base camp for trips into the Cascade Range backcountry. See the following description of Soda Springs.

Campsites, facilities: There are six primitive tent sites. Picnic tables and fire rings are provided. A vault toilet is available, but there is no drinking water. Garbage must be packed out. Leashed pets are permitted.

Reservations, fees: Reservations are not accepted. Northwest Forest Pass ($5 daily fee or $30 annual fee per parked vehicle) is required. Open mid-June–early September.

Directions: On I-5, drive to Exit 68 (south of Chehalis) and U.S. 12. Turn east on U.S. 12 and drive 75 miles (two miles past the Highway 123 turnoff) to Forest Road 45. Turn left and drive three miles (becomes Forest Road 4510) to the campground.

Contact: Gifford Pinchot National Forest, Cowlitz Valley Ranger District, P.O. Box 670, Randle, WA 98377-0670, 360/497-1100, fax 360/497-1102.

55 SODA SPRINGS

Rating: 6

On Summit Creek in Gifford Pinchot National Forest.

Map 5.2, grid c5, page 321

Soda Springs is set at an elevation of 3,200 feet along Summit Creek and the border of the William O. Douglas Wilderness. This primitive camp is ideal as a jumping-off base camp for a backpacking expedition or daily hiking trips in the Cascade Range. One trail out of camp leads three miles up to Jug Lake in the Douglas Wilderness. There are several trails and lakes to choose as destinations. Obtain a U.S. Forest Service map for details.

Campsites, facilities: There are six primitive tent sites. Picnic tables and fire rings are provided. A vault toilet is available, but there is no drinking water. Garbage must be packed out. Leashed pets are permitted.

Reservations, fees: Northwest Forest Pass ($5 daily fee or $30 annual fee per parked vehicle) is required. Open early-June–late October.

Directions: On I-5, drive to Exit 68 (south of Chehalis) and U.S. 12. Turn east on U.S. 12 and drive 75 miles (two miles past the Highway 123 turnoff) to Forest Road 45. Turn left and drive one mile (becomes Forest Road 4510) to the camp on the right.

Contact: Gifford Pinchot National Forest, Cowlitz Valley Ranger District, P.O. Box 670, Randle, WA 98377-0670, 360/497-1100, fax 360/497-1102.

56 WHITE PASS

Rating: 7

On Leech Lake in Wenatchee National Forest.

Map 5.2, grid c6, page 321

This campground on the shore of Leech Lake sits at an elevation of 4,500 feet and boasts nearby trails leading into the Goat Rocks Wilderness to the south and the William O. Douglas Wilderness to the north. A trailhead for the Pacific Crest Trail is also nearby. Beautiful Leech Lake is popular for fly-fishing for rainbow trout. Note that this is the only type of fishing allowed here; check regulations. White Pass Ski Area is located across the highway, less than one-quarter mile away. No gas motors are permitted on Leech Lake.

Campsites, facilities: There are 16 sites for tents or RVs up to 20 feet long. Picnic tables and fire grills are provided. Vault toilets and firewood are available, but there is no drinking water. A store, a café, a coin-operated laundry, and ice are located within one mile. Boat-launching facilities are nearby. No gas motors on boats are allowed; electric motors are permitted. Leashed pets are permitted.

Reservations, fees: Reservations are not accepted. Sites are $7 per night, $5 per extra vehicle per night. Senior discount available. Open late May–late October.

Directions: On I-5, drive to Exit 68 (south of Chehalis) and U.S. 12. Turn east on U.S. 12 and drive 84 miles (three miles past the White Pass Ski Area) to the campground entrance road on the left side. Turn north and drive 200 yards to Leech Lake and the campground.

Contact: Okanogan and Wenatchee National Forests, Naches Ranger District, 10061 U.S. 12, Naches, WA 98937, 509/653-2205, fax 509/653-2638.

57 DOG LAKE

Rating: 5

On Dog Lake in Wenatchee National Forest.

Map 5.2, grid c6, page 321

This campground is set on the shore of Dog Lake at 3,400 feet elevation. Fishing can be good for native rainbow trout, and the lake is good for hand-launched boats, such as canoes and prams. Nearby trails lead into the William O. Douglas Wilderness. See a U.S. Forest Service map for details.

Campsites, facilities: There are 11 sites for tents or RVs up to 20 feet long. Picnic tables and fire grills are provided. Vault toilets are available, but there is no drinking water. Leashed pets are permitted. No horses are allowed in the campground.

Reservations, fees: Reservations are not accepted. Sites are $7 per night, $5 per extra vehicle per night. Senior discount available. Open late May–late November.

Directions: On I-5, drive to Exit 68 (south of Chehalis) and U.S. 12. Turn east on U.S. 12 and drive 87 miles (six miles past the White Pass Ski Area) to the campground entrance road on the left side.

Contact: Okanogan and Wenatchee National Forests, Naches Ranger District, 10061 U.S. 12, Naches, WA 98937, 509/653-2205, fax 509/653-2638.

58 CLEAR LAKE NORTH

Rating: 7

On Clear Lake in Wenatchee National Forest.

Map 5.2, grid c6, page 321

This primitive campground is set along the shore of Clear Lake at an elevation of 3,100 feet and gets relatively little use. A five-mph speed limit keeps the lake quiet and ideal for fishing, often good for rainbow trout. It is stocked regularly in the summer. Clear lake is the forebay for Rimrock Lake. Swimming is allowed.

Campsites, facilities: There are 33 sites for tents or RVs up to 22 feet long. Picnic tables and fire grills are provided. Vault toilets and garbage service are available. There is no drinking water at Clear Lake North, but there is drinking water at Clear Lake South Campground. Some facilities are wheelchair accessible. Boat docks, launching facilities, and rentals are nearby. Leashed pets are permitted.

Reservations, fees: Reservations are not accepted. Sites are $10 per night, $5 per extra

vehicle per night. Senior discount available. Open mid-April–late November.

Directions: From Yakima, drive northwest on I-12 for 17 miles to the junction with Highway 410. Turn west on U.S. 12 and drive 31 miles to Forest Road 1200. Turn left (south) and drive one-quarter mile to Forest Road 1200-740. Continue south for one-half mile to the campground.

Contact: Okanogan and Wenatchee National Forests, Naches Ranger District, 10061 U.S. 12, Naches, WA 98937, 509/653-2205, fax 509/653-2638.

59 CLEAR LAKE SOUTH

Rating: 7

In Wenatchee National Forest.

Map 5.2, grid c6, page 321

This campground (elevation 3,100 feet) is located near the east shore of Clear Lake, which is the forebay for Rimrock Lake. Fishing and swimming are recreation options. For winter travelers, several Sno-Parks in the area offer snowmobiling and cross-country skiing. Many hiking trails lie to the north; see a U.S. Forest Service map.

Campsites, facilities: There are 23 sites for tents or RVs up to 22 feet long. Picnic tables and fire grills are provided. Drinking water and vault toilets are available. Downed firewood may be gathered. Boat-launching facilities are nearby. Leashed pets are permitted.

Reservations, fees: Reservations are not accepted. Sites are $10 per night, $5 per extra vehicle per night. Open mid-April–late November.

Directions: From Yakima, drive northwest on I-82 for 17 miles to the junction with Highway 410. Turn west on U.S. 12 and drive 31 miles to Forest Road 1200. Turn left (south) and drive one mile to Forest Road 1200-740. Continue south and drive one-quarter mile to the campground.

Contact: Okanogan and Wenatchee National Forests, Naches Ranger District, 10061 U.S.

12, Naches, WA 98937, 509/653-2205, fax 509/653-2638.

60 SILVER BEACH RESORT

Rating: 8

On Rimrock Lake.

Map 5.2, grid c7, page 321

This resort along the shore of Rimrock Lake is one of several camps in the immediate area. It's very scenic, with beautiful lakefront sites. Hiking trails, marked bike trails, a full-service marina, and a riding stable are close by.

Campsites, facilities: There are 97 sites, most with full hookups, for tents or RVs up to 40 feet long, three cabins with kitchens, and 16 motel rooms. Picnic tables and fire pits are provided. A restroom, coin-operated showers, a café, a store, an RV dump station, bait and tackle, bottled gas, propane, ice, a playground, a hot tub, boat docks, launching facilities, and boat and personal watercraft rentals are available. Leashed pets are permitted.

Reservations, fees: Reservations accepted. Sites are $13–18 per night, $5 per extra vehicle per night; cabins are $75 per night. Major credit cards accepted. Open year-round, with limited winter facilities.

Directions: From Yakima, drive northwest on U.S. 12 for 40 miles to the resort on the left.

Contact: Silver Beach Resort, 40350 Hwy. 12, Rimrock, WA 98937, 509/672-2500.

61 INDIAN CREEK AUG. 2004

Rating: 7

On Rimrock Lake in Wenatchee National Forest.

Map 5.2, grid c7, page 321

Fishing, swimming, and water-skiing are among the activities at this shorefront campground on Rimrock Lake (elevation 3,000 feet). The camp is adjacent to Rimrock Lake Marina and Silver Beach Resort. This is a developed lake and an extremely popular campground, often filling on summer weekends. Fishing is often good for rainbow trout. Many excellent hiking trails to the north, about 5–10 miles from the campground, lead into the William O. Douglas Wilderness, including the treasured Indian Creek Trail.

Campsites, facilities: There are 39 sites for tents or RVs up to 32 feet long. Picnic tables and fire grills are provided. Drinking water and vault toilets are available. Downed firewood may be gathered. A café, a store, ice, boat docks, launching facilities, and rentals are nearby. Leashed pets are permitted.

Reservations, fees: Reservations are not accepted. Sites are $13–15 per night, $5 per extra vehicle per night; $2 surcharge on holidays and summer weekends. Open late May–mid-September.

Directions: From Yakima, drive northwest on I-82 for 17 miles to the junction with Highway 410. Turn west on U.S. 12 and drive 20 miles to Rimrock Lake and the campground entrance at the lake.

Contact: Okanogan and Wenatchee National Forests, Naches Ranger District, 10061 U.S. 12, Naches, WA 98937, 509/653-2205, fax 509/653-2638.

62 PENINSULA

Rating: 7

On Rimrock Lake in Wenatchee National Forest.

Map 5.2, grid c7, page 321

Fishing for silvers and rainbow trout, swimming, and water-skiing are all allowed at Rimrock Lake (elevation 3,000 feet), where this shorefront recreation area and camp are located. The lake is stocked regularly in summer and is popular, in part because of the nearby vicinity of a boat ramp. This camp is one of several on the lake. A point of interest, the nearby emergency airstrip here features a grass landing runway. A nearby Sno-Park offers wintertime fun, including cross-country skiing and snowmobiling.

Campsites, facilities: There is a dispersed camping area for tents or RVs up to 20 feet long. Vault toilets and picnic tables are available, but there is no drinking water. Boat docks and launching facilities are nearby. Leashed pets are permitted.

Reservations, fees: Northwest Forest Pass ($5 daily fee or $30 annual fee per parked vehicle) is required. Senior discount available. Open mid-April–late November.

Directions: From Yakima, drive northwest on I-82 for 17 miles to the junction with Highway 410. Turn west on U.S. 12 and drive 22 miles to Forest Road 1200. Turn left (south) and drive three miles (across the cattle guard) to Forest Road 711. Turn right (west) and drive a short distance to the campground.

Contact: Okanogan and Wenatchee National Forests, Naches Ranger District, 10061 U.S. 12, Naches, WA 98937, 509/653-2205, fax 509/653-2638.

63 SOUTH FORK

Rating: 8

On the South Fork of the Tieton River in Wenatchee National Forest.

Map 5.2, grid d7, page 321

This campground (at 3,000 feet elevation) is set along the South Fork of the Tieton River, less than one mile from where it empties into Rimrock Lake. Note that fishing is prohibited to protect the bull trout. By traveling a bit farther south on Tieton River Road, you can see the huge Blue Slide, an enormous prehistoric rock and earth slide that has a curious blue tinge to it.

Campsites, facilities: There are nine sites for tents or RVs up to 20 feet long. Picnic tables and fire grills are provided. Vault toilets and garbage service are available, but there is no drinking water. Leashed pets are permitted.

Reservations, fees: Reservations are not accepted. Sites are $7 per night, $5 per extra vehicle per night. Open late May–mid-October.

Directions: From Yakima, drive northwest on I-82 for 17 miles to the junction with Highway 410. Turn west on U.S. 12 and drive 22 miles to Forest Road 1200. Turn left (south) and drive four miles to Forest Road 1203. Bear left and drive three-quarters of a mile to Forest Road 1203-517. Turn right and drive 200 feet to the campground.

Contact: Okanogan and Wenatchee National Forests, Naches Ranger District, 10061 U.S. 12, Naches, WA 98937, 509/653-2205, fax 509/653-2638.

64 IRON CREEK

Rating: 7

On the Cispus River in Gifford Pinchot National Forest.

Map 5.2, grid e1, page 321

This popular U.S. Forest Service campground is set along the Cispus River near its confluence with Iron Creek. Trout fishing is available. The landscape features primarily Douglas fir, western red cedar, and old-growth forest on fairly flat terrain. The camp is also located along the access route that leads to the best viewing areas on the eastern flank for Mount St. Helens. Take a 25-mile drive to Windy Ridge Vista Point for a breathtaking view of Spirit Lake and the blast zone of the volcano.

Campsites, facilities: There are 98 sites for tents or RVs. Picnic tables and fire rings are provided. Drinking water, vault toilets, and firewood are available. Some facilities are wheelchair accessible. Leashed pets are permitted.

Reservations, fees: Reserve at 877/444-6777 ($9 reservation fee) or website: www.ReserveUsa.com. Rates are $14–16 per night, $28 per night for a double site, $5 per extra vehicle per night. Senior discount available. Open mid-May–late September.

Directions: From Olympia, drive south on I-

5 to Exit 68 and U.S. 12. Turn east on U.S. 12 and drive 48 miles to Randle and Highway 131. Turn south on Highway 131 and drive one mile (becomes Forest Road 25). Continue south on Forest Road 25 and drive nine miles to a fork. Bear left at the fork, continue across the bridge, turn left, and drive two miles to the campground entrance on the left (along the south shore of the Cispus River).

Contact: Gifford Pinchot National Forest, Cowlitz Valley Ranger District, P.O. Box 670, Randle, WA 98377-0670, 360/497-1100, fax 360/497-1102.

65 TOWER ROCK

Rating: 5

On the Cispus River in Gifford Pinchot National Forest.

Map 5.2, grid e2, page 321

This campground along the Cispus River is an alternative to nearby Iron Creek and North Fork. It has shaded and sunny sites, with lots of trees and plenty of room. The camp is set fairly close to the river, and some sites feature river frontage. It is also fairly flat and forested with Douglas fir, western hemlock, red cedar, and big leaf maple. Fishing for trout is popular here.

Campsites, facilities: There are 22 sites for tents or RVs up to 21 feet long. Picnic tables and fire grills are provided. Drinking water, vault toilets, and firewood are available. A small store and a trout pond are nearby. Leashed pets are permitted.

Reservations, fees: Reserve at 877/444-6777 ($9 reservation fee) or website: www.ReserveUsa.com. Sites are $14–16 per night, $5 per extra vehicle per night. Senior discount available. Open mid-May–late September.

Directions: From Olympia, drive south on I-5 to Exit 68 and U.S. 12. Turn east on U.S. 12 and drive 48 miles to Randle and Highway 131. Turn south on Highway 131 and drive one mile to Forest Road 23. Turn left on Forest

Road 23 and drive eight miles to the campground entrance road on the right.

Contact: Gifford Pinchot National Forest, Cowlitz Valley Ranger District, P.O. Box 670, Randle, WA 98377-0670, 360/497-1100, fax 360/497-1102.

66 NORTH FORK & NORTH FORK GROUP

Rating: 6

On the Cispus River in Gifford Pinchot National Forest.

Map 5.2, grid e2, page 321

This campground set along the North Cispus River offers single sites, double sites, and a group camp, along with a river flowing between the sites for individual and group use. The elevation is 1,500 feet. The campsites are set back from the river in a well-forested area. A national forest map details the backcountry access to the Valley Trail, which is routed up the Cispus River Valley for about 15 miles. This trailhead provides access for hikers, bikers, all-terrain vehicles, and horses. Note that if you explore Road 2300-083 for 15 miles west you will find Layser Cave, a Native American archeological site that is open to the public.

Campsites, facilities: There are 33 sites for tents or RVs up to 31 feet long and an adjacent group camp with three sites. Picnic tables and fire grills are provided. Drinking water, vault toilets, and firewood are available. Leashed pets are permitted.

Reservations, fees: Reserve at 877/444-6777 ($9 reservation fee) or website: www.ReserveUsa.com. Sites are $14–16 per night, $5 per extra vehicle per night, and $71–89 for group sites. Senior discount available. Open mid-May–late September.

Directions: From Olympia, drive south on I-5 to Exit 68 and U.S. 12. Turn east on U.S. 12 and drive 48 miles to Randle and Highway 131. Turn south on Highway 131 and drive one mile to Forest Road 23. Bear left and drive 11 miles to the campground on the left.

Contact: Gifford Pinchot National Forest, Cowlitz Ranger District, P.O. Box 670, Randle, WA 98377, 360/497-1100, fax 360/497-1102.

67 BLUE LAKE CREEK

Rating: 7

Near Blue Lake in Gifford Pinchot National Forest.

Map 5.2, grid e3, page 321

This camp is set at an elevation of 1,900 feet along Blue Lake Creek. With access to a network of all-terrain vehicle (ATV) trails, it is a significant camp for ATV owners. There is nearby access to the Valley Trail, which features 25–30 miles of trail. This camp is also near the launch point for the 3.5-mile hike to Blue Lake; the trailhead lies about one-half mile from camp.

Campsites, facilities: There are 11 sites for tents or RVs up to 31 feet long. Picnic tables and fire rings are provided. Drinking water and vault toilets are available. Firewood can be gathered outside of the campground area. Leashed pets are permitted.

Reservations, fees: Reserve at 877/444-6777 ($9 reservation fee) or website: www.ReserveUsa.com. Sites are $12 per night, $5 per extra vehicle per night. Senior discount available. Open mid-May–late September.

Directions: From Olympia, drive south on I-5 to Exit 68 and U.S. 12. Turn east on U.S. 12 and drive 48 miles to Randle and Highway 131. Turn south on Highway 131 and drive one mile to Forest Road 23. Turn south and drive about 10 miles to the campground on the left.

Contact: Gifford Pinchot National Forest, Cowlitz Ranger District, P.O. Box 670, Randle, WA 98377, 360/497-1100, fax 360/497-1102.

68 ADAMS FORK

Rating: 7

On the Cispus River in Gifford Pinchot National Forest.

Map 5.2, grid f3, page 321

This campground is set at 2,600 feet elevation along the Upper Cispus River near Adams Creek and is popular with off-road vehicle (ORV) enthusiasts. There are many miles of trails designed for use by ORVs. A trail that is just one-half mile away leads north to Blue Lake, which is about a five-mile hike (one-way) from the camp. Most of the campsites are small, but a few are large enough for comfortable RV use. The area has many towering trees. The Cispus River provides trout fishing.

Campsites, facilities: There are 24 sites for tents or RVs up to 21 feet long. Picnic tables and fire grills are provided. Drinking water and vault toilets are available. Firewood may be gathered outside the campground area. Some facilities are wheelchair accessible. Leashed pets are permitted.

Reservations, fees: Reservations accepted; phone 877/444-6777 or access the website: www.ReserveUsa.com ($9 reservation fee). Rates are $14 per night for single sites, $28 per night for double sites, and group sites are $35 per night; $5 per extra vehicle per night. Senior discount available. Open May–late October.

Directions: On I-5, drive to Exit 68 (south of Chehalis) and U.S. 12. Turn east on U.S. 12 and drive 48 miles to Randle and U.S. 131. Turn right (south) and drive one mile to Forest Road 23. Turn left (southeast) and drive 18 miles to Forest Road 21. Turn left (southeast) on Forest Road 21 and drive five miles to Forest Road 56. Turn right on Forest Road 56 and drive 200 yards to the campground on the left.

Contact: Gifford Pinchot National Forest, Cowlitz Valley Ranger District, P.O. Box 670, Randle, WA 98377, 360/497-1100, fax 360/497-1102.

69 WALUPT LAKE

Rating: 8

On Walupt Lake in Gifford Pinchot National Forest.

Map 5.2, grid e5, page 321

This popular spot, set at 3,900 feet elevation along the shore of Walupt Lake, is a good base camp for a multi-day vacation. The trout fishing is often good here; check regulations. But note that only small boats are advisable here because the launch area at the lake is shallow and it can take a four-wheel-drive vehicle to get a boat in and out. A swimming beach is nearby. In addition, several nearby trails lead into the backcountry and to other smaller alpine lakes. One trail out of the campground leads to the upper end of the lake, then launches off to the Goat Rocks Wilderness, which is an outstanding hike. The trail is also excellent for horseback rides. See a U.S. Forest Service map for details.

Campsites, facilities: There are 44 sites for tents or RVs up to 22 feet long. Picnic tables are provided. Drinking water and vault toilets are available. Fire rings are located next to the campground. There is primitive boat access with a 10-mph speed limit; no water-skiing is allowed. Leashed pets are permitted.

Reservations, fees: Reservations accepted; phone 877/444-6777 or access the website: www.ReserveUsa.com ($9 reservation fee). Sites are $14–28 per night, $5 for each additional vehicle. Senior discount available. Open mid-June–mid-September.

Directions: On I-5, drive to Exit 68 (south of Chehalis) and U.S. 12. Turn east on U.S. 12 and drive 62 miles to Forest Road 21 (2.5 miles southwest of Packwood). Turn right (southeast) and drive 20 miles to Forest Road 2160. Turn left (east) and drive 4.5 miles to the campground.

Contact: Gifford Pinchot National Forest, Cowlitz Valley Ranger District, P.O. Box 670, Randle, WA 98377-0670, 360/497-1100, fax 360/497-1102.

70 WALUPT HORSE CAMP

Rating: 7

Near the Goat Rocks Wilderness in Gifford Pinchot National Forest.

Map 5.2, grid e5, page 321

This camp is for horse campers only and is set about one mile from Walupt Lake, which is good for trout fishing. Several trails lead from the lake into the backcountry of the southern Goat Rocks Wilderness, which has 50 miles of trails that can be used by horses, while other trails meander outside of the wilderness boundary. If you have planned a multi-day horse packing trip, you should bring in your own feed for the horses. Feed must be pellets or processed grain only. Hay is not permitted in the wilderness. The lake has a 10-mph speed limit for boats.

Campsites, facilities: There are nine sites for equestrians in tents or RVs up to 18 feet long. Picnic tables and fire grills are provided. Drinking water, vault toilets, and firewood are available. Garbage must be packed out. A horse ramp, high lines, and tethering areas are available. Leashed pets are permitted.

Reservations, fees: Northwest Forest Pass ($5 daily fee or $30 annual fee per parked vehicle) is required. Senior discount available. Open June–October, weather permitting.

Directions: On I-5, drive to Exit 68 (south of Chehalis) and U.S. 12. Turn east on U.S. 12 and drive 62 miles to Forest Road 21 (2.5 miles southwest of Packwood). Turn right (southeast) and drive 16.5 miles to Forest Road 2160. Turn left (east) and drive 3.5 miles to the campground on the right.

Contact: Gifford Pinchot National Forest, Cowlitz Valley Ranger District, Randle, WA 98377-0678, 360/497-1100, fax 360/497-1102.

71 OLALLIE LAKE

Rating: 9

On Olallie Lake in Gifford Pinchot National Forest.

Map 5.2, grid f4, page 321

This campground is located at 4,200 feet elevation on the shore of Olallie Lake, one of several small alpine lakes in the area fed by streams coming off the glaciers on nearby Mount Adams (elevation 12,276 feet). Trout fishing is good here in early summer. The campsites are situated close to the lake and feature gorgeous views of Mount Adams across the lake. Several of the campsites are small, in one larger area with room for RVs. A word to the wise: Mosquitoes can be a problem in the spring and early summer.

Campsites, facilities: There are five sites for tents or RVs up to 21 feet long. Picnic tables and fire rings are provided. Pit toilets are available, but there is no drinking water. Firewood may be gathered outside the campground area. Boat-launching facilities are nearby, but all gasoline motors are prohibited on the lake. Leashed pets are permitted.

Reservations, fees: Reservations are not accepted. Sites are $10 per night. Senior discount available. Open July–late September.

Directions: From Chehalis, drive south on I-5 for 10 miles to Exit 68 and U.S. 12. Turn east on U.S. 12 and drive 48 miles to Randle and U.S. 131. Turn south and drive one mile to Forest Road 23. Turn left (southeast) and drive 29 miles to Forest Road 2329. Turn left (northeast) and drive one mile to a junction with Forest Road 5601. Bear left and drive one-half mile to the campground on the right.

Contact: Gifford Pinchot National Forest, Cowlitz Valley Ranger District, P.O. Box 670, Randle, WA 98377-0670, 360/497-1100, fax 360/497-1102.

72 TAKHLAKH LAKE

Rating: 9

On Takhlakh Lake in Gifford Pinchot National Forest.

Map 5.2, grid f4, page 321

This campground is situated along the shore of Takhlakh Lake, one of five lakes in the area, all accessible by car. It's a beautiful place, set at 4,500 feet elevation, but alas, mosquitoes abound until late July. A viewing area (Mount Adams is visible across the lake) is available for visitors, while the more ambitious can go berry picking, fishing, and hiking. This lake is much better than nearby Horseshoe Lake, and in turn, the fishing is much better, especially for trout early in the season. The Takhlakh Meadow Loop Trail, a barrier-free trail, provides a 1.5-mile hike.

Campsites, facilities: There are 54 sites for tents or RVs up to 21 feet long. Drinking water and picnic tables are provided. Vault toilets are available. Firewood may be gathered outside the campground area. Boat-launching facilities are available in the day-use area, but all gasoline motors are prohibited on the lake. Some facilities are wheelchair accessible. Leashed pets are permitted.

Reservations, fees: Reservations accepted; phone 877/444-6777 or access the website: www.ReserveUsa.com ($9 reservation fee). Sites are $14–16 per night, $5 for each additional vehicle. Senior discount available. Open mid-June–late September.

Directions: From Chehalis, drive south on I-5 for 10 miles to Exit 68 and U.S. 12. Turn east on U.S. 12 and drive 48 miles to Randle and U.S. 131. Turn south and drive one mile to Forest Road 23. Turn left (southeast) and drive 29 miles to Forest Road 2329. Turn left (northeast) and drive 1.5 miles to the campground entrance road on the right.

Contact: Gifford Pinchot National Forest, Cowlitz Valley Ranger District, P.O. Box 670, Randle, WA 98377-0670, 360/497-1100, fax 360/497-1102.

73 CAT CREEK

Rating: 5

On Cat Creek and the Cispus River in Gifford Pinchot National Forest.

Map 5.2, grid f4, page 321

This small, rustic camp is set along Cat Creek at its confluence with the Cispus River about 10 miles from the summit of Mount Adams. The camp, which features a forested setting, gets a lot of all-terrain vehicle (ATV) use. A trail starts less than one mile from camp and leads up along Blue Lake Ridge to Blue Lake. See trip notes for Adams Fork camp. Obtaining a U.S. Forest Service map is advised.

Campsites, facilities: There are five sites for tents or RVs up to 15 feet long. Picnic tables and fire grills are provided. Pit toilets and firewood are available, but there is no drinking water. Garbage must be packed out. Firewood may be gathered outside the campground area. Leashed pets are permitted.

Reservations, fees: Northwest Forest Pass ($5 daily fee or $30 annual fee per parked vehicle) is required. Open mid-May–late October.

Directions: On I-5, drive to Exit 68 (south of Chehalis) and U.S. 12. Turn east on U.S. 12 and drive 48 miles to Randle and U.S. 131. Turn right (south) and drive one mile to Forest Road 23. Turn left (southeast) and drive 18 miles to Forest Road 21. Turn left (southeast) on Forest Road 21 and drive six miles to the campground.

Contact: Gifford Pinchot National Forest, Cowlitz Valley Ranger District, P.O. Box 670, Randle, WA 98377, 360/497-1100, fax 360/497-1102.

74 HORSESHOE LAKE

Rating: 9

On Horseshoe Lake in Gifford Pinchot National Forest.

Map 5.2, grid f4, page 321

This camp is set on the shore of picturesque Horseshoe Lake, a 10-acre lake. The camp-
sites are poorly defined, more like camping areas, though some are close to the lake. A trail runs partway around the lake and is open to mountain bikes and horse riders (which occasionally come from another nearby camp). Fishing for trout is just fair in the lake, which is stocked infrequently. The water is too cold for swimming. A trail from the camp, about a three-mile round-trip, goes up to nearby Green Mountain (elevation 5,000 feet). This is a multiuse trail, but it does tie into the High Lakes Trail system. Another trail heads up the north flank of Mount Adams. See a U.S. Forest Service map for details. Berry picking is an option in the late summer months.

Campsites, facilities: There are 11 sites for tents or RVs up to 16 feet long. Picnic tables are provided. Vault toilets are available, but there is no drinking water. Firewood may be gathered outside the campground area. Primitive launching facilities are located on the lake, but all gasoline motors are prohibited on the water. Leashed pets are permitted.

Reservations, fees: Northwest Forest Pass ($5 daily fee or $30 annual fee per parked vehicle) is required. Open mid-June–late September.

Directions: From Chehalis, drive south on I-5 for 10 miles to Exit 68 and U.S. 12. Turn east on U.S. 12 and drive 48 miles to Randle and U.S. 131. Turn south and drive one mile to Forest Road 23. Turn left (southeast) and drive 29 miles to Forest Road 2329. Turn left (northeast) and drive seven miles (bearing right at the junction with Forest Road 5601) to Forest Road 078. Turn left on Forest Road 078 and drive 1.5 miles to the campground on the left.

Contact: Gifford Pinchot National Forest, Cowlitz Valley Ranger District, P.O. Box 670, Randle, WA 98377-0670, 360/497-1100, fax 360/497-1102.

75 KEENE'S HORSE CAMP

Rating: 7

On the South Fork of Spring Creek in Gifford Pinchot National Forest.

Map 5.2, grid f4, page 321

This equestrians-only camp is set at 4,200 feet elevation along the South Fork of Spring Creek on the northwest flank of Mount Adams (elevation 12,276 feet). The Pacific Crest Trail passes within a couple miles of the camp. Several trails lead from here into the backcountry and to several alpine meadows. The meadows are fragile, so walk along their outer edges. See notes for Walupt Horse Camp. In summer 2002, a portion of campground was moved out of a riparian area.

Campsites, facilities: There are 12 sites in two areas for tents or RVs up to 21 feet long. Picnic tables and fire grills are provided. Pit toilets, water troughs, a mounting ramp, corrals, manure bins, and hitching facilities (high lines) are available, but there is no drinking water. Some facilities are wheelchair accessible. Firewood may be gathered outside the campground area. Leashed pets are permitted.

Reservations, fees: Northwest Forest Pass ($5 daily fee or $30 annual fee per parked vehicle) is required. Open July–late September.

Directions: On I-5, drive to Exit 68 (south of Chehalis) and U.S. 12. Turn east on U.S. 12 and drive 48 miles to Randle and U.S. 131. Turn right (south) and drive one mile to Forest Road 23. Turn left (southeast) and drive 18 miles to Forest Road 21. Turn left (southeast) on Forest Road 21 and drive five miles to Forest Road 56. Turn right on Forest Road 56 and drive five miles to Forest Road 5603. Turn right and drive five miles to Forest Road 2329. Turn right and drive two miles to the camp on the right.

Contact: Gifford Pinchot National Forest, Cowlitz Valley Ranger District, P.O. Box 670, Randle, WA 98377-0670, 360/497-1100, fax 360/497-1102.

76 KILLEN CREEK

Rating: 7

Near Mount Adams in Gifford Pinchot National Forest.

Map 5.2, grid f4, page 321

This wilderness trailhead camp is ideal as a launch point for backpackers. The campground, set along Killen Creek at the foot of Mount Adams (elevation 12,276 feet), marks the start of a three-mile trail that leads up the mountain and connects with the Pacific Crest Trail. It's worth the effort. The Killen Trail goes up to secondary ridges and shoulders of Mount Adams for stunning views. Berry picking is another summertime option.

Campsites, facilities: There are eight sites for tents or RVs up to 21 feet long. Picnic tables and fire are provided. Pit toilets are available, but there is no drinking water. Garbage must be packed out. Firewood may be gathered outside the campground area. Leashed pets are permitted.

Reservations, fees: Northwest Forest Pass ($5 daily fee or $30 annual fee per parked vehicle) is required. Open July–late September.

Directions: On I-5, drive to Exit 68 (south of Chehalis) and U.S. 12. Turn east on U.S. 12 and drive 48 miles to Randle and U.S. 131. Turn right (south) and drive one mile to Forest Road 23. Turn left (southeast) and drive 29 miles to Forest Road 2329. Turn left (northeast) and drive six miles to Forest Road 073. Turn left (west) and drive 200 yards to the campground.

Contact: Gifford Pinchot National Forest, Cowlitz Valley Ranger District, P.O. Box 670, Randle, WA 98377-0670, 360/497-1100, fax 360/497-1102.

77 CLOVER FLATS

Rating: 8

Near the Goat Rocks Wilderness.

Map 5.2, grid e7, page 321

This campground is located in the subalpine

zone on the slope of Darland Mountain, which peaks at 6,982 feet. Trails connect the area with the Goat Rocks Wilderness, six miles to the west. Contact the Department of Natural Resources or Wenatchee National Forest for details.

Campsites, facilities: There are nine campsites for tents or small RVs. Picnic tables, fire grills, and tent pads are provided. Pit toilets and drinking water are available. Garbage must be packed out. Leashed pets are permitted.

Reservations, fees: Reservations are not accepted. There is no fee for camping. Open year-round, weather permitting (heavy snows are generally expected from mid-November–early April).

Directions: From Yakima, drive south on I-82 for two miles to Union Gap and Ahtanum Road. Turn right (west) and drive 20 miles to Tampico and Road A-3000 (North Fork Road). Turn right (west) and drive 9.5 miles to the Ahtaman Camp. Continue to a junction with A-2000 (Middle Fork Road). Bear left and drive nine miles to the camp on the left. Note: The last few miles of Road A-2000 are very steep, with a 12 percent grade. High-clearance vehicles only are recommended.

Contact: Department of Natural Resources, Southeast Region, 713 Bowers Rd., Ellensburg, WA 98926-9301, 509/925-8510, fax 509/925-8522.

78 TREE PHONES

Rating: 7

On the Middle Fork of Ahtanum Creek.
Map 5.2, grid e8, page 321

This forested campground is set along the Middle Fork of Ahtanum Creek at an elevation of 4,800 feet. It is close to hiking, motorbiking, and horseback-riding trails. A shelter with a wood stove is available year-round for picnics. During summer, there are beautiful wildflower displays.

Campsites, facilities: There are 14 campsites for tents or small RVs. Picnic tables, fire grills, and tent pads are provided. Drinking water and vault toilets are available. A 20-by-40-foot snow shelter and saddle-stock facilities are also available. Some facilities are wheelchair accessible. Leashed pets are permitted.

Reservations, fees: Reservations are not accepted. There is no fee for camping. Open year-round, weather permitting (heavy snows are expected from late November–March).

Directions: From Yakima, drive south on I-82 for two miles to Union Gap and Ahtanum Road. Turn right (west) and drive 20 miles to Tampico and Road A-3000 (North Fork Road). Turn right (west) and drive 9.5 miles to the Ahtaman Camp. Continue to a junction with A-2000 (Middle Fork Road). Bear left and drive six miles to the camp. Note: High-clearance vehicles only are recommended.

Contact: Department of Natural Resources, Southeast Region, 713 Bowers Rd., Ellensburg, WA 98926-9301, 509/925-8510, fax 509/925-8522.

79 GREEN RIVER HORSE CAMP

Rating: 8

Near Green River in Gifford Pinchot National Forest.
Map 5.2, grid g1, page 321

First, note that access was cut off in 2002—likely temporarily—with a road closure at Ryan Lake. Call before planning a trip to this premier equestrians-only horse camp. It is set on the Green River near an area of beautiful, old-growth timber, but the campsites themselves are in a reforested clear-cut area with trees about 20–30 feet tall. The camp features access to great trails into the Mount St. Helens blast area. The lookout from Windy Ridge is one of the most drop-dead awesome views in North America, spanning Spirit Lake, the blast zone, and the open crater of Mount St. Helens. The campground features high lines at each site, and the access is designed for easy turning and parking with horse trailers.

Campsites, facilities: There are eight sites for up to two trailer rigs or three vehicles each. Picnic tables, fire grills, and high lines are provided. Vault toilets are available. No drinking water is provided. Stock water facilities are available starting 2002; call for confirmation. Garbage must be packed out. Drinking water is available five miles north at Norway Pass Trailhead. Leashed pets are permitted.

Reservations, fees: Northwest Forest Pass ($5 daily fee or $30 annual fee per parked vehicle) is required. Open mid-May–November, weather permitting.

Directions: From Olympia, drive south on I-5 to Exit 68 and U.S. 12. Turn east on U.S. 12 and drive 48 miles to Randle and Highway 131. Turn right (south) and drive one mile (becomes Forest Road 25). Continue south and drive 19 miles to Forest Road 99. Turn right (west, toward Windy Ridge) and drive 8.5 miles to Forest Road 26. Turn right (north) and drive five miles to Forest Road 2612 (gravel). Turn left (west) and drive about two miles to the campground entrance on the left. Note: Due to past flooding events, Forest Road 26 has deteriorated. For the last seven miles, high-clearance, four-wheel-drive vehicles are recommended.

Contact: Gifford Pinchot National Forest, Mount St. Helens National Volcanic Monument, 42218 N.E. Yale Bridge Rd., Amboy, WA 98601, 360/247-3900, fax 360/247-3901.

80 LOWER FALLS

Rating: 10

On the Lewis River in Gifford Pinchot National Forest.
Map 5.2, grid g2, page 321

This camp is set at 1,400 feet elevation in the primary viewing area for six major waterfalls on the Lewis River. The spectacular Lewis River Trail is available for hiking or horseback riding, and it features a wheelchair-accessible loop. Several other hiking trails in the area branch off along backcountry streams. The sites are paved and set among large fir trees on gently sloping ground; access roads were designed for easy RV parking. Note that above the falls, the calm water in the river looks safe, but it is not! Stay out. In addition, the trail goes along cliffs, providing beautiful views but potentially dangerous hiking.

Campsites, facilities: There are 42 sites for tents or RVs up to 35 feet long and two group sites for up to 20 people each. Picnic tables and fire grills are provided. Drinking water and composting toilets are available. Leashed pets are permitted.

Reservations, fees: Reservations are not accepted. Sites are $14 per night for single sites, $28 per night for double sites, and $5 per extra vehicle per night. Senior discount available. Group sites are $33 per night. Open May–September.

Directions: From Woodland on I-5, take Exit 21 for Highway 503. Drive east on Highway 503 for 23 miles to Highway 503 spur. Drive northeast on Highway 503 spur for seven miles (becomes Forest Road 90). Continue east on Forest Road 90 for 21 miles to the campground (along the Lewis River) on the right.

Contact: Gifford Pinchot National Forest, Mount St. Helens National Volcanic Monument, 42218 N.E. Yale Bridge Rd., Amboy, WA 98601-0369, 360/247-3900, fax 360/247-3901.

81 LEWIS RIVER HORSE CAMP

Rating: 7

Near the Lewis River and Quartz Creek in Gifford Pinchot National Forest.
Map 5.2, grid g2, page 321

During summer, this camp caters to equestrians only. The camp is not particularly scenic, but the area around it is. There are six waterfalls nearby on the Lewis River, for example. There are also many trails, all of which are open to mountain bikers and some to motorcycles. The spectacular Lewis River Trail is available for hiking, mountain biking, or horseback riding, and there is a wheelchair-accessible loop. Several other hiking trails in the area branch off along backcountry streams. See a U.S. Forest Service map for details.

Campsites, facilities: There are nine sites for tents or RVs. Picnic tables and fire rings are provided. A composting toilet is available. No drinking water is provided. Garbage must be packed out. Horse facilities include high lines, stock water, and three corrals. Leashed pets are permitted.

Reservations, fees: Northwest Forest Pass ($5 daily fee or $30 annual fee per parked vehicle) is required. Open May–November, weather permitting.

Directions: From Woodland on I-5, take Exit 21 for Highway 503. Drive east on Highway 503 and drive 23 miles to Highway 503 spur. Drive northeast on Highway 503 spur for seven miles (becomes Forest Road 90). Continue east on Forest Road 90 for 27 miles to Forest Road 93. Turn left and drive one mile to the campground (along the Lewis River) on the right.

Contact: Gifford Pinchot National Forest, Mount St. Helens National Volcanic Monument, 42218 N.E. Yale Bridge Rd., Amboy, WA 98601-0369, 360/247-3900, fax 360/449-7801.

82 TILLICUM & SADDLE

Rating: 8

Near Meadow Lake in Gifford Pinchot National Forest.

Map 5.2, grid g2, page 321

These two pretty camps are primitive but well forested and within walking distance of several recreation options. A 4.5-mile trail from the Tillicum camp leads southwest past little Meadow Lake to Squaw Butte, then over to Big Creek. It's a nice hike, as well as an excellent ride for mountain bikers. This area is premium for picking huckleberries in August and early September. The Lone Butte area about five miles to the south provides a side trip. Nearby Saddle camp, located one mile to the east, receives little use. There are two lakes nearby, Big and Little Mosquito Lakes, which are fed by Mosquito Creek. So, while we're on the subject, mosquito attacks in late spring and early summer can be like squadrons of World War II bombers moving in. The Pacific Crest Trail passes right by camp.

Campsites, facilities: There are eight sites for tents only and 37 sites for tents or RVs up to 18 feet long. Picnic tables and fire grills are provided. Drinking water, pit toilets, and firewood are available. Garbage must be packed out. Leashed pets are permitted.

Reservations, fees: No reservation, no fee at Saddle Campground. Northwest Forest Pass ($5 daily fee or $30 annual fee per parked vehicle) is required at Tillucum Campground. Open mid-June–late September.

Directions: From Vancouver (Washington) on I-205, take Highway 14 and drive east for 66 miles to Highway 141. Turn north on Highway 141 and drive 25 miles to Trout Lake and County Road 141 (Forest Road 24). Turn left (west) and drive two miles to a fork. Bear left at the fork and drive 20 miles (becomes Forest Road 24) to the campground on the left.

Contact: Gifford Pinchot National Forest, Mount St. Helens National Volcanic Monument, 42218 N.E. Yale Bridge Rd., Amboy, WA 98601, 360/247-3900, fax 360/247-3901.

83 MORRISON CREEK

Rating: 7

On Morrison Creek in Gifford Pinchot National Forest.

Map 5.2, grid g4, page 321

Here's a prime yet little-known spot. This camp is located along Morrison Creek at an elevation of 4,600 feet near the southern slopes of Mount Adams (12,276 feet). Nearby trails will take you to the snowfields and alpine meadows of the Mount Adams Wilderness. In particular, the Shorthorn Trail is accessible from this campground.

Campsites, facilities: There are 12 tent sites. Picnic tables and fire rings are provided in some sites. Vault toilets are available, but there is no drinking water. Garbage must be packed out. Leashed pets are permitted.

Reservations, fees: Northwest Forest Pass ($5 daily fee or $30 annual fee per parked vehicle) is required. Open July–late September.

Directions: From Hood River, Oregon, drive north on Highway 35 (over the Columbia River) to Highway 14. Turn left and drive two miles to Highway 141. Turn right (north) on Highway 141 and drive 20 miles to County Road 17 (just 200 yards east of the town of Trout Lake). Turn right (north) and drive two miles to Forest Road 80. Turn right (north) and drive 3.5 miles to Forest Road 8040. Bear left (north) and drive six miles to the campground on the left. The access road is rough and not recommended for RVs.

Contact: Gifford Pinchot National Forest, Mount Adams Ranger District, 2455 Hwy. 141, Trout Lake, WA 98650, 509/395-3400, fax 509/395-3424.

84 ISLAND CAMP
🏃 🛶 ❄ 🐕 🚐 ⛺

Rating: 8

On Bird Creek.

Map 5.2, grid h5, page 321

This campground in a forested area along Bird Creek is close to lava tubes and blowholes. It's about a three-quarter-mile walk to see the strange one-foot-wide slit in the ground (too small to climb into and explore). Bird Creek provides a chance to fish for brook trout in late spring. In the winter, the roads are used for snowmobiling. A snowmobile shelter with a wood stove is available year-round for picnics.

Campsites, facilities: There are six campsites for tents or small RVs. Picnic tables, fire grills, and tent pads are provided. Vault toilets are available, but there is no drinking water. Garbage must be packed out. Leashed pets are permitted.

Reservations, fees: Reservations are not accepted. There is no fee for camping. Open year-round.

Directions: From Yakima, drive south on I-82 for 15 miles to U.S. 97. Turn south and drive 49 miles to Goldendale and Highway 142. Turn right (west) and drive 10 miles to Counts Road. Turn right (northwest) and drive 26 miles to Glenwood; continue for one-quarter mile to Bird Creek Road. Turn right and drive nine-tenths of a mile to K-3000 Road (still Bird Creek Road). Turn left, drive over the cattle guard, and drive 1.2 miles to Road S-4000. Turn right and drive 1.3 miles to Road K-4000. Turn left and drive 3.4 miles to Road K-4200. Turn left and drive 1.1 miles to the campground entrance on the left. Turn left and drive one-quarter mile to the campground.

Contact: Department of Natural Resources, Southeast Region, 713 Bowers Rd., Ellensburg, WA 98926-9301, 509/925-8510, fax 509/925-8522.

85 BIRD CREEK
🏃 🚲 🛶 🐕 ♿ 🚐 ⛺

Rating: 7

Near the Mount Adams Wilderness.

Map 5.2, grid h6, page 321

This campground is set in a forested area of old-growth Douglas fir and Ponderosa pine along Bird Creek. It is one of two camps in the immediate area. (The other, also a primitive site, is Island Camp.) This spot lies just east of the Mount Adams Wilderness and is within three miles of Island Camp, where there are snowmobile trails.

Campsites, facilities: There are 12 campsites for tents or small RVs. Picnic tables, fire grills, and tent pads are provided. Pit and vault toilets are available, but there is no drinking water. Garbage must be packed out. Some facilities are wheelchair accessible. Leashed pets are permitted.

Reservations, fees: Reservations are not accepted. There is no fee for camping. Open May–mid-October, weather permitting.

Directions: From Yakima, drive south on I-82 for 15 miles to U.S. 97. Turn south and drive 49 miles to Goldendale and Highway 142. Turn right (west) and drive 10 miles to Counts Road. Turn right (northwest) and drive 26 miles to Glenwood. From the post office in Glenwood, continue one-quarter mile to Bird Creek Road. Turn right and drive nine-tenths of a mile. Turn left (still Bird Creek Road), cross the cattle guard to Road K-3000, and drive 1.2 miles to Road S-4000 (gravel). Turn right and drive 1.3 miles to Road K-4000. Turn left and drive two miles to the campground on the left.

Contact: Department of Natural Resources, Southeast Region, 713 Bowers Rd., Ellensburg, WA 98926-9301, 509/925-8510, fax 509/925-8522.

86 CAMP KALAMA RV AND CAMPGROUND

Rating: 6

On the Kalama River.
Map 5.3, grid a2, page 322

This alternative to Louis Rasmussen RV Park has a more rustic setting, with open and wooded areas and some accommodations for tent campers. It's set along the Kalama River, where salmon and steelhead fishing is popular. A full-service marina is nearby.

Campsites, facilities: There are 118 sites with full or partial hookups, including drive-through, for RVs of any length and 50 tent sites. Picnic tables are provided. Restrooms, drinking water, flush toilets, coin-operated showers, fire pits, cable TV, bottled gas, an RV dump

station, a store, a café, a beauty shop, a banquet room, firewood, a coin-operated laundry, ice, boat-launching facilities, a beach area, and a playground are available. Some facilities are wheelchair accessible. Leashed pets are permitted.

Reservations, fees: Reservations accepted. Sites are $17–28 per night, $1.50 per person per night for more than two adults, and $1 per pet. Senior discount available. Major credit cards accepted. Open year-round.

Directions: From near Kalama (between Kelso and Woodland) on I-5, take Exit 32 and drive south on the frontage road for one block to the campground.

Contact: Camp Kalama RV and Campground, 5055 North Meeker Dr., Kalama, WA 98625, 360/673-2456 or 800/750-2456, fax 360/673-2324.

87 WOODLAND

Rating: 7

Near Woodland.
Map 5.3, grid a3, page 322

Woodland is an optimum spot for people who are touring Washington on I-5 but want a quiet setting along the way. The campground is nestled in an area of evergreen and deciduous trees (maple and red alder), so it's private. It is about three miles off the highway. A popular side trip is a visit to the Hulda Klager Lilac Gardens, which is best visited in spring when the lilacs are blooming, a few miles away in Woodland.

Campsites, facilities: There are 10 sites for tents or small RVs. Picnic tables, fire grills, and tent pads are provided. Vault toilets, drinking water, horseshoe pits, volleyball and basketball courts, and a playground are available. Some facilities are wheelchair accessible. Leashed pets are permitted.

Reservations, fees: Reservations are not accepted. There is no fee for camping. Open May–September.

Directions: From Woodland on I-5, take Exit

21 and drive east for 100 yards to East CC Street. Turn right and drive across the Lewis River to just south of the bridge to County Road 1. Turn right on County Road 1 and drive one-quarter mile to 389th Street. Turn left on 389th Street and drive 2.5 miles to the campground on the left.

Contact: Department of Natural Resources, Southwest Region, P.O. Box 280, Castle Rock, WA 98611-0280, 360/577-2025 or 360/274-4196.

88 PARADISE POINT STATE PARK

Rating: 8

On the East Fork of the Lewis River.
Map 5.3, grid b3, page 322

This park is named for the serenity that once blessed this area. Alas, it has lost much of that peacefulness since the freeway went in next to the park. To reduce traffic noise, stay at one of the wooded sites in the small apple orchard. The sites in the grassy areas have little noise buffer. This park covers 88 acres and features 1,680 feet of river frontage. The two-mile hiking trail is good for families and children. Note that the dirt boat ramp is primitive and nonfunctional when the water level drops, and is recommended for car-top boats only. Fishing on the East Fork of the Lewis River is a bonus.

Campsites, facilities: There are nine primitive tent sites and 70 sites for tents or self-contained RVs up to 40 feet long. Picnic tables and fire grills are provided. Restrooms, drinking water, flush toilets, showers, an RV dump station, firewood, an amphitheater, and summer interpretive programs are available. A primitive, dirt boat-launching area is located nearby on the East Fork of the Lewis River. Leashed pets are permitted.

Reservations, fees: Reserve at 888/CAMP-OUT (888/226-7688), website: www.parks.wa.gov/reservations ($7 reservation fee). Sites are $6–16, $6 per extra vehicle per night.

Major credit cards accepted. Open mid-May–September.

Directions: From Vancouver (Washington), drive north on I-5 for 15 miles to Exit 16 (La Center/Paradise Point State Park exit). Take that exit and turn right, then almost immediately at Paradise Park Road, turn left and drive one mile to the park.

Contact: Paradise Point State Park, 360/263-2350; State Park information, 360/902-8844.

89 BIG FIR CAMPGROUND AND RV PARK

Rating: 6

Near Paradise Point State Park.
Map 5.3, grid b3, page 322

This campground is set in a heavily wooded, rural area not far from Paradise Point State Park. It's nestled among hills and features shaded gravel sites and wild berries. See the previous description of Paradise Point State Park for details on the area.

Campsites, facilities: There are 37 sites with full hookups, including three drive-through, for RVs of any length and 33 tent sites. Picnic tables are provided. Restrooms, drinking water, flush toilets, coin-operated showers, volleyball, croquet, a horseshoe pit, board games, a store, and ice are available. Boat-launching facilities are located within 1.5 miles. Leashed pets are permitted.

Reservations, fees: Reservations accepted. Sites are $16–22 per night, $2 per person for more than for more than two adults and three children. Major credit cards accepted. Open year-round.

Directions: From Vancouver (Washington), drive north on I-5 to Exit 14 (Ridgefield exit). Take that exit to Highway 269. Drive east on Highway 269 (the road changes names several times) for two miles to 10th Avenue. Turn right and drive to the first intersection at 259th Street. Turn left and drive two miles to the park on the right (route is well marked).

Contact: Big Fir Campground and RV Park, 5515 NE 259th St., Ridgefield, WA 98642, 360/887-8970 or 800/532-4397.

90 BATTLE GROUND LAKE STATE PARK

Rating: 8

On Battle Ground Lake.
Map 5.3, grid b5, page 322

The centerpiece of this state park is Battle Ground Lake, a spring-fed lake that is stocked with trout but is popular for bass and catfish fishing as well. The lake is of volcanic origin, fed by water from underground lava tubes, and is considered a smaller version of Crater Lake in Oregon. The park covers 280 acres, primarily forested with conifers, in the foothills of the Cascade Mountains. There are 10 miles of trails for hiking and biking, including a trail around the lake, and five miles of trails for horses; a primitive equestrian camp is also available. The lake is good for swimming and fishing, and it has a nice beach area; no motorized boats are allowed. If you're traveling on I-5 and looking for a layover, this camp, just 15 minutes from the highway, is ideal. In July and August, the area hosts several fairs and celebrations. Like many of the easy-access state parks on I-5, this one fills up quickly on weekends. The average annual rainfall is 35 inches.

Campsites, facilities: There are 35 sites for tents or self-contained RVs up to 50 feet long and 15 primitive tent sites. Picnic tables and fire grills are provided. Restrooms, drinking water, flush toilets, showers, an RV dump station, a store, firewood, a restaurant, a sheltered picnic area, an amphitheater, summer interpretive programs, a playground with horseshoe pits, and an athletic field are available. Some facilities are wheelchair accessible. Boat-launching facilities and rentals are nearby. Leashed pets are permitted.

Reservations, fees: Reserve at 888/CAMP-OUT

(888/226-7688), website: www.parks.wa.gov/reservations ($7 reservation fee). Sites are $6–16 per night. Major credit cards accepted. Senior discount available. Open year-round.

Directions from I-5 southbound: On I-5, take Exit 14 and drive to the city of Battle Ground (well marked); continue to the east end of town to Grace Avenue. Turn left and drive three miles (a marked route) to the park.

Directions from I-5 northbound: On I-5, take Exit 9 and drive to the city of Battle Ground (well marked); continue to the east end of town to Grace Avenue. Turn left and drive three miles (a marked route) to the park.

Contact: Battle Ground Lake State Park, 360/687-4621 (phone or fax); State Park information, 360/902-8844.

91 SUNSET

Rating: 9

On the East Fork of the Lewis River in Gifford Pinchot National Forest.
Map 5.3, grid b6, page 322

This campground is located at an elevation of 1,000 feet along the East Fork of the Lewis River. Fishing, hiking, and huckleberry and mushroom picking are some of the favored pursuits of visitors. Scenic Sunset Falls is located just upstream of the campground. A barrier-free viewing trail leads to an overlook.

Campsites, facilities: There are 10 sites for tents or RVs up to 22 feet long and six walk-in sites. Picnic tables and fire grills are provided. Drinking water (well water) and vault toilets are available. Leashed pets are permitted.

Reservations, fees: Reservations are not accepted. Sites are $14 per night, $5 per extra vehicle per night. Open year-round.

Directions: From Vancouver (Washington), drive north on I-5 about seven miles to County Road 502. Turn east on Highway 502 and drive six miles to Highway 503. Turn left and drive north for five miles to Lucia Falls Road. Turn right and drive eight miles to Moulton

Falls and Old County Road 12. Turn right on Old County Road 12 and drive seven miles to the Forest Boundary and the campground entrance on the right.

Contact: Gifford Pinchot National Forest, Mount St. Helens National Volcanic Monument, 42218 N.E. Yale Bridge Rd., Amboy, WA 98601, 360/247-3900, fax 360/449-7801.

92 COLD CREEK

Rating: 6

On Cedar Creek.
Map 5.3, grid c5, page 322

First, don't expect to find a "cold creek" here. There just is no such thing. And second, the directions are complicated. Hey, Waylon Jennings once told me that few things worth remembering come easy, right? Well, sometimes. This campground is set in a forested area with plenty of trails nearby for hiking and horseback riding. The camp gets minimal use. A large shelter is available at the day-use area.

Campsites, facilities: There are six campsites for tents or small RVs. Picnic tables, fire grills, and tent pads are provided. Vault toilets are available. No drinking water is provided. Some facilities are wheelchair accessible. Leashed pets are permitted.

Reservations, fees: Reservations are not accepted. There is no fee for camping. Open May–September.

Directions: From Vancouver (Washington), drive north on I-5 to Exit 9 and NE 179th Street. Turn east and drive 5.5 miles to Highway 503. Turn right and drive 1.5 miles to NE 159th Street. Turn left on NE 159th Street and drive three miles to 182nd Avenue. Turn right and drive one mile to NE 139th (Road L-1400). Turn left and drive eight miles to Road L-1000. Turn left and drive three miles. Turn left at the campground entrance road and drive one mile to the camp.

Contact: Department of Natural Resources,
Southwest Region, P.O. Box 280, Castle Rock, WA 98611-0280, 360/577-2025 or 360/274-4196.

93 ROCK CREEK CAMPGROUND AND HORSE CAMP

Rating: 6

On Rock Creek.
Map 5.3, grid c5, page 322

This camp is located in a wooded area along Rock Creek. It is popular among equestrians, especially on weekends, because of the Tarbell Trail, a 25-mile loop trail that is accessible from the campground and goes to the top of Larch Mountain.

Campsites, facilities: There are 19 campsites for tents or small RVs. Picnic tables, fire grills, and tent pads are provided. Vault toilets, drinking water, a horse-loading ramp, and corrals are available. Some facilities are wheelchair accessible. There is a campground host on-site. Leashed pets are permitted.

Reservations, fees: Reservations are not accepted. There is no fee for camping. Open year-round, weather permitting.

Directions: From Vancouver (Washington), drive on I-5 to Exit 9 and NE 179th Street. Turn east and drive 5.5 miles to Highway 503. Turn right and drive 1.5 miles to NE 159th Street. Turn left on NE 159th Street and drive three miles to 182nd Avenue. Turn right and drive one mile to NE 139th (Road L-1400). Turn left and drive eight miles to Road L-1000. Turn left and drive 3.5 miles (passing Cold Creek Campground after three miles) to Road L-1200. Turn left and drive 200 yards to the campground on your right.

Contact: Department of Natural Resources, Southwest Region, P.O. Box 280, Castle Rock, WA 98611-0280, 360/577-2025 or 360/274-4196.

94 DOUGAN CREEK

Rating: 7

Near the Washougal River.
Map 5.3, grid c7, page 322

Located on Dougan Creek where it empties into the Washougal River, this campground is small and remote. Heavily forested with second-growth Douglas fir, it features pretty sites with river views.

Campsites, facilities: There are seven campsites for tents or small RVs. Picnic tables, fire grills, and tent pads are provided. Vault toilets are available. No drinking water is provided. Some facilities are wheelchair accessible. Leashed pets are permitted.

Reservations, fees: Reservations are not accepted. There is no fee for camping. Open mid-May–mid-September.

Directions: From Vancouver (Washington) on I-205, take Highway 14 and drive east for 20 miles to Highway 140. Turn north on Highway 140 and drive five miles to Washougal River Road. Turn right on Washougal River Road and drive about seven miles until you come to the end of the pavement and pass the picnic area on the left. The campground is just beyond the picnic area.

Contact: Department of Natural Resources, Southwest Region, P.O. Box 280, Castle Rock, WA 98611-0280, 360/577-2025 or 360/274-4196.

95 BEACON ROCK RESORT

Rating: 7

On the Columbia River.
Map 5.3, grid d8, page 322

This trailer park is set along the Columbia River, a short distance from Beacon Rock State Park. See the following description of the state park for details. Nearby recreation options include a nine-hole golf course four miles away and two 18-hole golf courses, eight and 12 miles away, respectively.

Campsites, facilities: There are 20 sites with full hookups, including three drive-through, for RVs up to 45 feet and a grassy area for tents. Picnic tables and fire rings are provided. Restrooms, drinking water, flush toilets, coin-operated showers, bottled gas, firewood, a store, a recreation hall, a coin-operated laundry, and ice are available. Boat-launching facilities are located within one-quarter mile on the Columbia River. Leashed pets are permitted.

Reservations, fees: Reservations accepted with a deposit. Sites are $12–17 per night, $2 per person per night for more than two people. Open year-round.

Directions: From Vancouver (Washington) on I-205, take Highway 14 and drive east for 27 miles to Skamania. Look for the park along Highway 14 on the right at the corner of Moorage Road.

Contact: Beacon Rock Resort, 62 Moorage Rd., Skamania, WA 98648, 509/427-8473.

96 BEACON ROCK STATE PARK

Rating: 8

On the Columbia River.
Map 5.3, grid c8, page 322

This state park features Beacon Rock, the second largest monolith in the world, which overlooks the Columbia River Gorge. The park is located in the heart of the Columbia River Gorge National Scenic Area. The Beacon Rock Summit Trail, a 1.8-mile round-trip hike, provides panoramic views of the gorge. The rock is also excellent for rock climbing, with the climbing season running from mid-July–January. Lewis and Clark gave Beacon Rock its name on their expedition to the Pacific Ocean in 1805. The park covers nearly 5,000 acres and includes 9,500 feet of shoreline along the Columbia River and more then 20 miles of nearby roads open for hiking, mountain biking, and horseback riding. An eight-mile loop trail to Hamilton Mountain (2,300 feet elevation) is one of the best hikes, featuring even better views than from Beacon Rock. Fishing for sturgeon, salmon, steelhead, smallmouth bass (often excellent), and walleye is available on the Lower Columbia River below Bonneville Dam, in season; check regulations.

Campsites, facilities: There are 29 developed sites for tents or self-contained RVs up to 40 feet long, one hike-in/bike-in site, and one group site for up to 200 people. Picnic tables and fire grills are provided. Restrooms, drinking water, flush toilets, coin-operated showers, a picnic area with a kitchen shelter and electricity, and a playground are available. Some facilities are wheelchair accessible. Boat docks and launching facilities are on-site. Leashed pets are permitted.

Reservations, fees: Reservations are not accepted for family sites. Reservations required for group camp. Reserve at 888/CAMP-OUT (888/226-7688), website: www.parks.wa.gov/reservations ($25 reservation fee). Sites are $16 per night, $6 per extra vehicle; $5 launch fee, $10–16 for boat mooring. Senior discount available. Group site requires $25 reservation fee plus $2 per person with a 20-person minimum. Open April–October.

Directions: From Vancouver (Washington) on I-205, take Highway 14 and drive east for 35 miles. The park straddles the highway; follow the signs to the campground.

Contact: Beacon Rock State Park, 34841 Rte. 14, Skamania, WA 98648, 509/427-8265, fax 509/427-4471; State Park information, 360/902-8844.

97 CULTUS CREEK

Rating: 7

Near the Indian Heaven Wilderness in Gifford Pinchot National Forest.

Map 5.4, grid a2, page 323

This camp is set at an elevation of 4,000 feet along Cultus Creek on the edge of the Indian Heaven Wilderness. It offers nearby access to trails that will take you into the backcountry, which has numerous small meadows and lakes among old-growth stands of fir and pine. Horse trails are available as well. Access to the Pacific Crest Trail requires a two-mile climb. This camp is popular during the fall huckleberry season, when picking is good here, but gets light use the rest of the year. Situated amid gentle terrain, the sites are graveled and level.

Campsites, facilities: There are 43 sites for tents or RVs up to 32 feet long. Picnic tables and fire grills are provided. Drinking water, vault toilets, and firewood are available. Garbage must be packed out. Some facilities are wheelchair accessible. Leashed pets are permitted.

Reservations, fees: Reservations are not accepted. Northwest Forest Pass ($5 daily fee or $30 annual fee per parked vehicle) is required. Open June–September.

Directions: From Vancouver (Washington) on I-205, take Highway 14 east and drive 66 miles to State Route 141. Turn north on State Route 141 and drive 28 miles (becomes Forest Road 24); continue two miles to a junction. Turn right (staying on Forest Road 24) and drive 13.5 miles to the campground.

Contact: Gifford Pinchot National Forest, Mount Adams Ranger District, 2455 Hwy. 141, Trout Lake, WA 98650, 509/395-3400, fax 509/395-3424.

98 SMOKEY CREEK

Rating: 7

Near the Indian Heaven Wilderness in Gifford Pinchot National Forest.

Map 5.4, grid a2, page 323

This primitive, little-used campground is set in an area of old-growth Douglas fir along Smokey Creek. A trail leading into the Indian Heaven Wilderness passes near the camp. Berry picking can be good here in summer and early fall. The elevation is 3,700 feet. See the description of Tillicum and Saddle, Walupt Horse Camp, and Morrison Creek for details on more recreation options in the immediate area.

Campsites, facilities: There are three sites for RVs up to 22 feet long. Picnic tables and fire rings are provided. Pit toilets are available, but there is no drinking water. Garbage must be packed out. Leashed pets are permitted.

Reservations, fees: Reservations are not accepted. Northwest Forest Pass ($5 daily fee or $30 annual fee per parked vehicle) is required. Open late June–late September.

Directions: From Vancouver (Washington) on I-205, take Highway 14 east and drive 66 miles to State Route 141. Turn north on State Route 141 and drive 28 miles (becomes Forest Road 24); continue two miles to a junction. Turn right (staying on Forest Road 24) and drive seven miles to the campground.

Contact: Gifford Pinchot National Forest, Mount Adams Ranger District, 2455 Hwy. 141, Trout Lake, WA 98650, 509/395-3400, fax 509/395-3424.

99 LITTLE GOOSE & LITTLE GOOSE HORSE CAMP

Rating: 5

On Little Goose Creek in Gifford Pinchot National Forest.

Map 5.4, grid a3, page 323

This campground is near Little Goose Creek (located between Smokey and Cultus campgrounds). Huckleberry picking is quite good in August and early September. The camp sits close to the road and is sometimes dusty. Note that the access road is paved but is rough and not recommended for RVs or trailers. Campers with horse trailers must drive slowly. This camp has sites ranging from good to poor and is lightly used in fall. Several trails are available leading out from the campground. The elevation is 4,000 feet. See the description of Tillicum and Saddle, Walupt Horse Camp, and Morrison Creek camps for more details of the area.

Campsites, facilities: There are 10 sites for tents or RVs up to 18 feet long and one site for campers with stock animals. Picnic tables and

fire grills are provided. Pit toilets are available. No drinking water is available. Garbage must be packed out. Leashed pets are permitted.

Reservations, fees: Reservations are not accepted. Northwest Forest Pass ($5 daily fee or $30 annual fee per parked vehicle) is required. Open June–late September.

Directions: From Vancouver (Washington) on I-205, take Highway 14 east and drive 66 miles to State Route 141. Turn north on State Route 141 and drive 28 miles (becomes Forest Road 24); continue two miles to a junction. Turn right (staying on Forest Road 24) and drive eight miles (one mile past Smokey Creek) to the campground.

Contact: Gifford Pinchot National Forest, Mount Adams Ranger District, 2455 Hwy. 141, Trout Lake, WA 98650, 509/395-3400, fax 509/395-3424.

100 TROUT LAKE CREEK

Rating: 7

On Trout Lake Creek in Gifford Pinchot National Forest.

Map 5.4, grid a3, page 323

This spot makes a popular base camp for folks fishing at Trout Lake (five miles away). During the day, many anglers will fish at the lake, where fishing is good for stocked rainbow trout, then return to this camp for the night. Some bonus brook trout are occasionally caught at Trout Lake. The camp is set along a creek in a forest of Douglas fir. In season, berry picking can be good here.

Campsites, facilities: There are 17 sites for tents or RVs up to 32 feet long. Picnic tables and fire rings are provided. Pits toilets are available. Garbage must be packed out. Leashed pets are permitted.

Reservations, fees: Northwest Forest Pass ($5 daily fee or $30 annual fee per parked vehicle) is required. Senior discount available. Open May–September.

Directions: From Hood River, Oregon, drive

north on Highway 35 (over the Columbia River) to Highway 14. Turn left and drive two miles to Highway 141. Turn right (north) on Highway 141 and drive 25 miles north to Forest Road 88. Turn right and drive four miles to Forest Road 8810. Turn right and drive 1.5 miles to Forest Road 8810-010. Turn right and drive one-quarter mile to the campground on the right.

Contact: Gifford Pinchot National Forest, Mount Adams Ranger District, 2455 Hwy. 141, Trout Lake, WA 98650, 509/395-3400, fax 509/395-3424.

101 PETERSON PRAIRIE & PETERSON PRAIRIE GROUP

Rating: 8

Near the town of Trout Lake in Gifford Pinchot National Forest.

Map 5.4, grid a3, page 323

Here's a good base camp if you want to have a short ride to town as well as access to the nearby wilderness areas. Peterson Prairie is a prime spot for huckleberry picking in the fall. A trail from the camp leads about one mile to nearby ice caves; a stairway into the caves provides access to a variety of ice formations. An area Sno-Park with snowmobiling and cross-country skiing trails is open for winter recreation. The elevation is 2,800 feet.

Campsites, facilities: There are 23 sites for tents or RVs up to 32 feet long, one group site for up to 50 people, and one historic cabin. Picnic tables and fire grills are provided. Drinking water, vault toilets, and firewood are available. A camp host is available in summer. Some facilities are wheelchair accessible. Leashed pets are permitted.

Reservations, fees: Reservations required for the group site only; phone 877/444-6777 or access the website: www.ReserveUsa.com ($9 reservation fee). Rates are $13–26 per night for individual and double sites, $5 per extra vehicle per night; $32–67 per night for the group site. Senior discount available. Open May–late September.

Directions: From Hood River, Oregon, drive north on Highway 35 (over the Columbia River) to Highway 14. Turn left and drive two miles to Highway 141. Turn right (north) on Highway 141 and drive 25.5 miles to Forest Road 24 (5.5 miles beyond and southwest of the town of Trout Lake). Bear right (west) and drive 2.5 miles to the campground on the left.

Contact: Gifford Pinchot National Forest, Mount Adams Ranger District, 2455 Hwy. 141, Trout Lake, WA 98650, 509/395-3400, fax 509/395-3424.

102 PARADISE CREEK

Rating: 9

On Paradise Creek and the Wind River in Gifford Pinchot National Forest.

Map 5.4, grid a1, page 323

This camp is located deep in Gifford Pinchot National Forest among old-growth woods, primarily Douglas fir, cedar, and western hemlock, at the confluence of Paradise Creek and the Wind River. It gets light use despite easy access and easy RV parking. The campsites are well shaded. Lava Butte, located a short distance from the camp, is accessible by trail; the 1.2-mile round-trip hike from the campground provides a good view of the valley. Fishing is closed here. The elevation is 1,500 feet.

Campsites, facilities: There are 42 sites for tents or RVs up to 25 feet long. Picnic tables and fire grills are provided. Drinking water and vault toilets are available. Some facilities are wheelchair accessible. Leashed pets are permitted.

Reservations, fees: Reserve at 877/444-6777 ($9 reservation fee) or website: www.ReserveUsa.com. Sites are $13 per night, $5 per extra vehicle per night. Open mid-May–mid-November.

Directions: From Vancouver (Washington),

take Highway 14 east and drive 50 miles to Carson and the Wind River Highway (County Road 30). Turn north on the Wind River Highway and drive 20 miles to the camp on the right.

Contact: Gifford Pinchot National Forest, Wind River Work Center, 1262 Hemlock Rd., Carson, WA 98610, 509/427-3200, fax 509/427-3215.

103 FALLS CREEK HORSE CAMP

Rating: 5

Near the Pacific Crest Trail in Gifford Pinchot National Forest.

Map 5.4, grid a1, page 323

This camp sits at the threshold of a great launch point for hiking, horseback riding, and mountain biking. There are 90 miles of trail for horses and hiking and 40 miles for mountain bikes. The camp is set along the Race Track Trail, adjacent to the western border of Indian Heaven Wilderness. A wilderness trailhead is available right at the camp. While this is a multiple-use campground, note that the sites are small and the turnaround is tight for RVs.

Campsites, facilities: There are six sites for tents or RVs up to 15 feet long. Picnic tables and fire grills are provided. Pit toilets are available, but there is no drinking water. Garbage must be packed out. Leashed pets are permitted.

Reservations, fees: Northwest Forest Pass ($5 daily fee or $30 annual fee per parked vehicle) is required. Open mid-June–November.

Directions: From Vancouver (Washington) on I-205, take Highway 14 and drive east for 50 miles to Carson and the Wind River Highway (County Road 30). Turn north on the Wind River Highway and drive six miles to Forest Road 65. Turn left (north) and drive 15 miles to the campground on the left.

Contact: Gifford Pinchot National Forest, Mt. Adams Ranger District, 2455 Hwy. 141, Trout Lake, CA 98650, 509/395-3400, fax 509/395-3424.

104 CREST HORSE CAMP

Rating: 6

Bordering Big Lava Bed in Gifford Pinchot National Forest.

Map 5.4, grid a2, page 323

This small, primitive, multiple-use camp is set near the Pacific Crest Trail, adjacent to the eastern boundary of the Indian Heaven Wilderness. It is an excellent jumping-off spot for wilderness treks with horses or other stock animals. The camp features a forested setting, primarily second-growth Douglas fir.

Campsites, facilities: There are three sites for tents or RVs. Picnic tables and fire pits are provided. A vault toilet and high lines (for horses) are available. No drinking water is provided. Garbage must be packed out. Leashed pets are permitted.

Reservations, fees: Reservations are not accepted. Northwest Forest Pass ($5 daily fee or $30 annual fee per parked vehicle) is required. Open mid-May–mid-November, weather permitting.

Directions: From Vancouver (Washington), take Highway 14 east and drive 50 miles to Carson and the Wind River Highway (County Road 30). Turn north and drive nine miles to Forest Road 6517. Turn right (east) on Forest Road 6517 and drive 1.5 miles to Forest Road 65. Turn left (north) on Forest Road 65 and drive about 10 miles to Forest Road 60. Turn right and drive two miles to the camp on the right.

Contact: Gifford Pinchot National Forest, Mt. Adams Ranger District, 2455 Hwy. 141, Trout Lake, CA 98650, 509/395-3400, fax 509/395-3424.

105 GOOSE LAKE

Rating: 9

On Goose Lake in Gifford Pinchot National Forest.

Map 5.4, grid a3, page 323

This campground is set along the shore of

beautiful Goose Lake at an elevation of 3,200 feet. It can be crowded in summer. Trout fishing and berry picking are available. The northern edge of Big Lava Bed is adjacent to the camp. While the lake is quite pretty, the camp itself is set well above the lake and is not as nice as the lake. A five-mph speed limit is enforced on the lake.

Campsites, facilities: There are 25 tent sites and one site for RVs up to 18 feet long. Picnic tables and fire rings are provided. Vault toilets and firewood for sale are available, but there is no drinking water. A camp host is on-site. A boat ramp is nearby. Leashed pets are permitted.

Reservations, fees: Reserve at 877/444-6777 ($9 reservation fee) or website: www.ReserveUsa.com. Sites are $13–15 per night, $5 per extra vehicle per night. Senior discount available. Open mid-June–mid-September.

Directions: From Vancouver (Washington) on I-205, take Highway 14 east and drive 46 miles to County Road 30/Wind River Road. Turn left and drive six miles to Panther Creek Road and Forest Road 65. Turn right and drive 10 miles to a four-way intersection called Four Corners. Turn right on Forest Road 60 and drive 10 miles to the campground on the left.

Contact: Gifford Pinchot National Forest, Mount Adams Ranger District, 2455 Hwy. 141, Trout Lake, WA 98650, 509/395-3400, fax 509/395-3424.

106 BEAVER

Rating: 7

On the Wind River in Gifford Pinchot National Forest.

Map 5.4, grid b1, page 323

This campground is the closest one north of Stevenson in the Columbia Gorge. Set along the Wind River at an elevation of 1,100 feet, it features pretty, shaded sites. No fishing is permitted. The campsites are paved, and a large grassy day-use area is nearby. Hiking highlights include two nearby trailheads. Two

miles north lies the trailhead for the Trapper Creek Wilderness, with 30 miles of trails, including a loop possibility. Three miles north is the Falls Creek Trail.

Campsites, facilities: There are 26 sites for tents or RVs up to 25 feet long and one group site for up to 40 campers. Picnic tables and fire grills are provided. Drinking water and pit toilets are available. Some facilities are wheelchair accessible. Leashed pets are permitted.

Reservations, fees: Reservations accepted for family sites and required for the group site. Reserve at 877/444-6777 ($9 reservation fee) or website: www.ReserveUsa.com. Sites are $13–26 per night, $5 per extra vehicle per night. Senior discount available. The group site is $91 per night. Open mid-April–late September.

Directions: From Vancouver (Washington), take Highway 14 east and drive 50 miles to Carson and the Wind River Highway (County Road 80). Turn left (north) and drive 12 miles to the campground entrance (three miles past Stabler) on the left.

Contact: Gifford Pinchot National Forest, Wind River Work Center, 1262 Hemlock Rd., Carson, WA 98610, 509/427-3200, fax 509/427-4633.

107 PANTHER CREEK & PANTHER CREEK HORSE CAMP

Rating: 8

On Panther Creek in Gifford Pinchot National Forest.

Map 5.4, grid b2, page 323

This campground is set along Panther Creek in a second-growth forest of Douglas fir and western hemlock, adjacent to an old-growth forest. The sites are well-defined, and despite a paved road to the campground and easy parking and access, it gets light use. The camp lies 3.5 miles from the Wind River, an option for those who enjoy fishing, hiking, and horseback riding. The Pacific Crest Trail is accessible from the adjacent Panther Creek Horse Camp. The elevation is 1,000 feet.

Campsites, facilities: There are 33 sites for tents or RVs up to 25 feet long, and at the adjacent horse camp, one equestrian site, with a stock loading ramp. Picnic tables and fire rings are provided. Drinking water and pits toilets are available. Garbage must be packed out. Leashed pets are permitted.

Reservations, fees: Reserve at 877/444-6777 ($9 reservation fee) or website: www.ReserveUsa.com. Sites are $13–26 per night, $5 per extra vehicle per night. Senior discount available. Open mid-May–mid-September.

Directions: From Vancouver (Washington), take Highway 14 east and drive 50 miles to Carson and the Wind River Highway (County Road 30). Turn north and drive nine miles to Forest Road 6517 (just past Stabler). Turn right (east) on Forest Road 6517 and drive 1.5 miles to the campground entrance road on the right.

Contact: Gifford Pinchot National Forest, Wind River Work Center, 1262 Hemlock Rd., Carson, WA 98610, 509/427-3200, fax 509/427-4633.

108 OKLAHOMA

Rating: 7

On the Little White Salmon River in Gifford Pinchot National Forest.

Map 5.4, grid b3, page 323

This pretty campground is set along Little White Salmon River at an elevation of 1,700 feet. Fishing can be excellent in this area. The river is stocked in the spring with rainbow trout. The camp gets light use. It features some open meadow, but is generally flat. Close to the Columbia River Gorge, it features paved road all the way into the campground and easy RV parking. As to why they named the camp "Oklahoma," who knows? If you do, drop me a line.

Campsites, facilities: There are 23 sites for tents or RVs up to 22 feet long. Drinking water, fire rings, and picnic tables are provided. Vault toilets are available. Some facilities are wheelchair accessible. Leashed pets are permitted.

Reservations, fees: Reservations accepted; phone 877/444-6777 or access the website: www.ReserveUsa.com ($9 reservation fee). Sites are $13 per night, $5 for each additional vehicle. Senior discount available. Open mid-May–mid-September.

Directions: From Hood River, Oregon, drive north on Highway 35 for one mile over the Columbia River to Highway 14. Turn left on Highway 14 and drive about five miles to Cook and County Road 1800. Turn right (north) and drive 14 miles (becomes Cook-Underwood Road, then Willard Road, then Oklahoma Road) to the campground entrance at the end of the paved road.

Contact: Gifford Pinchot National Forest, Mt. Adams Ranger District, 2455 Hwy. 141, Trout Lake, CA 98650, 509/395-3400, fax 509/395-3424.

109 MOSS CREEK

Rating: 7

On the Little White Salmon River in Gifford Pinchot National Forest.

Map 5.4, grid b3, page 323

This campground is set at 1,400 feet elevation, about one mile from the Little White Salmon River. Although a short distance from Willard and Big Cedars County Park, the camp gets light use. The river provides good fishing prospects for trout in the spring, usually with few other people around. The sites are generally small but are shaded and still functional for most RVs. The road is paved all the way to the campground.

Campsites, facilities: There are 17 sites for tents or RVs up to 32 feet long. Picnic tables and fire grills are provided. Drinking water and vault toilets are available. Some facilities are wheelchair accessible. A camp host is available in the summer. Leashed pets are permitted.

Reservations, fees: Reservations accepted; phone 877/444-6777 or access the website: www.ReserveUsa.com ($9 reservation fee). Sites are

$13 per night; $5 for each additional vehicle. Senior discount available. Open mid-May–mid-September.

Directions: From Hood River, Oregon, drive north on Highway 35 for one mile over the Columbia River to Highway 14. Turn left on Highway 14 and drive about five miles to Cook and County Road 1800. Turn right (north) and drive 10 miles (becomes Cook-Underwood Road, then Willard road, then Oklahoma Road) to the campground entrance on the right.

Contact: Gifford Pinchot National Forest, Mt. Adams Ranger District, 2455 Hwy. 141, Trout Lake, CA 98650, 509/395-3400, fax 509/395-3424.

110 HORSETHIEF LAKE STATE PARK

Rating: 10

Near Dalles Dam.

Map 5.4, grid c8, page 323

This 338-acre park boasts 7,500 feet of Columbia River shoreline. It also adjoins the 3,000-acre Dalles Mountain Ranch State Park. Horsethief Butte, set adjacent to the lake, dominates the skyline. Horsethief Lake, created by The Dalles Dam, covers approximately 90 acres and is part of the Columbia River. Lupine and balsam root bloom in mid-April and create spectacular fields of purple and gold. Rock-climbing in the park is popular, but the river canyon is often windy, especially in late spring and early summer. Most people find the place as a spot camp while driving along the Columbia River Highway. There are hiking trails and access to both the lake and the Columbia River. Non-powered boats are allowed, and anglers can try for trout and bass. Guided tours on weekends feature pictographs and petroglyphs; reservations required at 509/767-1159. See the following description of Maryhill State Park for information on other recreation options in the region.

Campsites, facilities: There are 12 sites, most with partial hookups, for tents or self-contained RVs up to 30 feet long and two primitive tent sites. Picnic tables and fire grills are provided. Drinking water, flush toilets, firewood, an RV dump station, a horseshoe pit, and a picnic area are available. A store and a café are located within two miles. Boat-launching facilities are located on both the lake and the river. Leashed pets are permitted.

Reservations, fees: Reservations are not accepted. Sites are $6–22 per night, $6 per extra vehicle per night. Senior discount available. Open April–late October.

Directions: From The Dalles in Oregon, turn north on Highway 197, cross over the Columbia River, and drive four miles to Highway 14. Turn right (east) and drive two miles to Milepost 85 and the park entrance on the right.

Contact: Horsethief Lake State Park, 509/767-1159, fax 509/767-4304; State Park information, 360/902-8844.

111 MARYHILL STATE PARK

Rating: 8

On the Columbia River.

Map 5.5, grid c2, page 324

This 99-acre park has 4,700 feet of frontage along the Columbia River. Fishing, water-skiing, and windsurfing are among the recreation possibilities. The climate here is pleasant from March–mid-November. Two interesting places can be found near Maryhill: One is a full-scale replica of Stonehenge, located on a bluff overlooking the Columbia River, about one mile from the park. The other is the historic Mary Hill home, which is open to the public; Mary Hill's husband, Sam Hill, constructed the Stonehenge replica.

Campsites, facilities: There are 50 sites with full hookups for RVs up to 50 feet long and 20 tent sites, including three primitive sites. Picnic tables and fire pits are provided. Restrooms, flush toilets, showers, an RV dump station, a store, and a picnic area with covered shelters are available. A café is within one mile. Some facilities are wheelchair accessible. Boat docks and launching facilities are nearby. Leashed pets are permitted.

Reservations, fees: Reservations are not accepted. Sites are $16–22 per night, $6 per extra vehicle per night. Senior discount available.

Major credit cards accepted. Call 360/902-8844 for group camping information. Open year-round.

Directions: From Goldendale and U.S. 97, drive 12 miles south to the park on the left.

Contact: Maryhill State Park, 509/773-5007, fax 509/773-6337; State Park information, 360/902-8844.

© U.S. FISH AND WILDLIFE SERVICE

Chapter 6
Southeastern Washington

Chapter 6—Southeastern Washington

The expansive domain of southeastern Washington is a surprise for many newcomers. Instead of the high mountains of the Cascades, there are rolling hills. Instead of forests, there are miles of wheat fields (Washington's second-largest export crop behind lumber). Instead of a multitude of streams, there are giant rivers—the Columbia and Snake. Just one pocket of mountains and a somewhat sparse forest sit in the southeast corner of the state, in a remote sector of Umatilla National Forest.

The Lewis and Clark expedition was routed through this area some two hundred years ago, and today, several major highways, including I-82 and U.S. 395, bring out-of-town visitors through the region en route to other destinations. A network of camps is set along these highways, including RV parks created to serve the needs of travelers. Of the 16 area parks, the 13 state parks offer the best campgrounds. The prettiest picture you will find is of Palouse Falls, where a gorgeous fountain of water pours through a desert gorge.

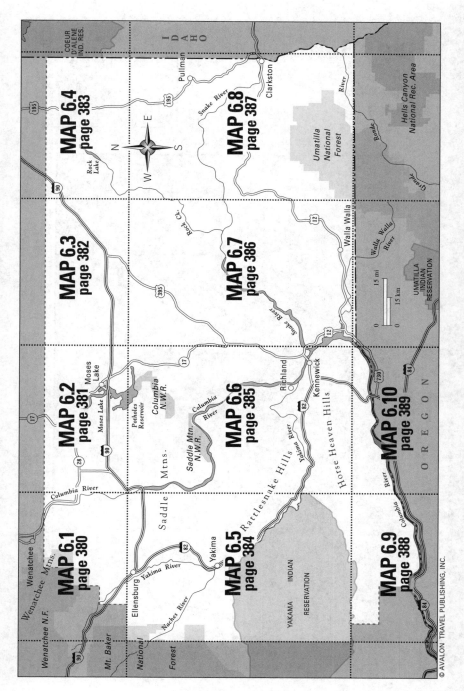

MAP 6.4
page 383

MAP 6.3
page 382

MAP 6.2
page 381

MAP 6.1
page 380

MAP 6.8
page 387

MAP 6.7
page 386

MAP 6.6
page 385

MAP 6.5
page 384

MAP 6.10
page 389

MAP 6.9
page 388

COEUR
D'ALENE
IND. RES.

I
D
A
H
O

OREGON

Pullman

Clarkston

Snake River

Rock Lake

Rock Ck.

Umatilla
National
Forest

Hells Canyon
National Rec. Area

Ronde

Grande River

Walla Walla

Walla Walla
River

Snake River

Richland

Kennewick

Horse Heaven Hills

Yakima River

Columbia
River

Saddle Mtn.
N.W.R.

Columbia
N.W.R.

Potholes
Reservoir

Moses Lake

Moses
Lake

Saddle   Mtns.

Columbia River

Rattlesnake Hills

Yakima

Yakima River

Ellensburg

Naches River

Wenatchee

Wenatchee N.F.

Wenatchee Mtns.

Mt. Baker

National   Forest

YAKAMA
INDIAN
RESERVATION

Columbia   River

UMATILLA
INDIAN
RESERVATION

N
W   E
S

15 mi
15 km
0
0

© AVALON TRAVEL PUBLISHING, INC.

Map 6.1

**Campground 1
Page 390**

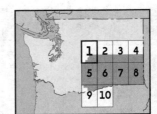

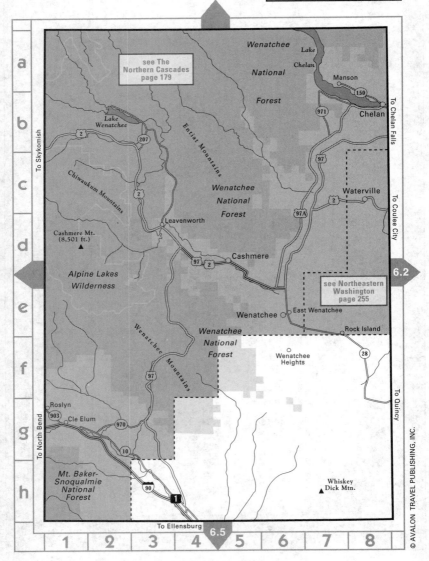

Map 6.2

Campgrounds 2–5
Pages 390–392

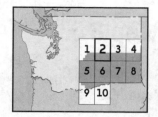

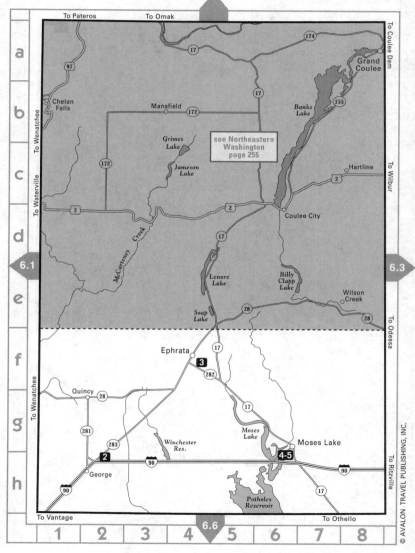

Map 6.3

Campground 6
Page 392

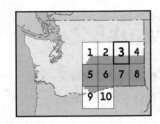

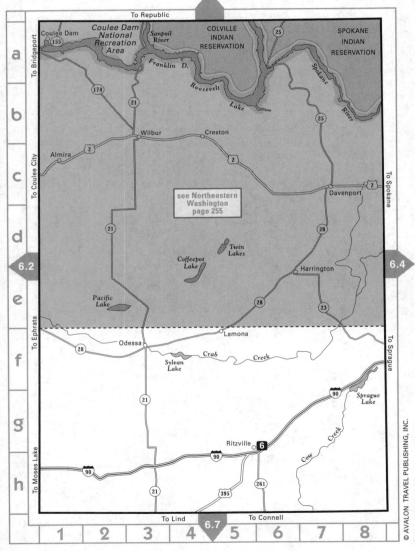

To Republic

Coulee Dam

Coulee Dam National Recreation Area

Sanpoil River

COLVILLE INDIAN RESERVATION

SPOKANE INDIAN RESERVATION

To Bridgeport

Franklin D. Roosevelt Lake

Spokane River

To Coulee City

Wilbur

Creston

Almira

Davenport

To Spokane

see Northeastern Washington page 255

Twin Lakes

Coffeepot Lake

Harrington

Pacific Lake

To Ephrata

Lamona

Odessa

Crab Creek

Sylvan Lake

To Sprague

Sprague Lake

Ritzville

Cow Creek

To Moses Lake

To Lind

To Connell

© AVALON TRAVEL PUBLISHING, INC.

Map 6.4

Campgrounds 7–10
Pages 392–394

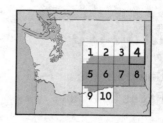

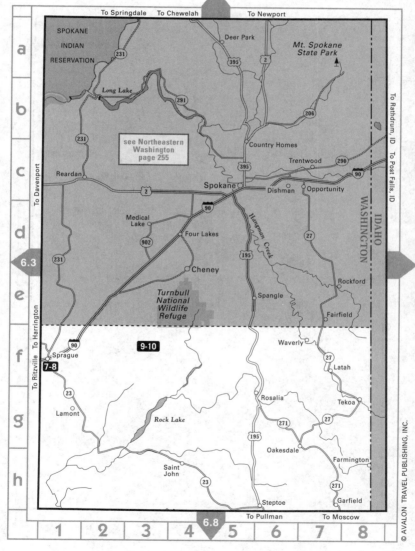

© AVALON TRAVEL PUBLISHING, INC.

Map 6.5

Campgrounds 11–21
Pages 394–398

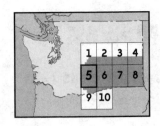

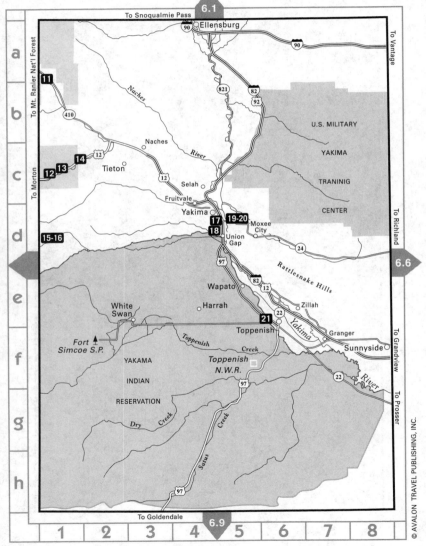

To Snoqualmie Pass   6.1

To Mt. Ranier Nat'l Forest

Ellensburg

90

To Vantage

821

82

92

a

11

410

b

U.S. MILITARY

YAKIMA

To Morton

Naches

Naches

River

TRANINIG

12

14

CENTER

12   13

c

Tieton

12

Selah

Fruitvale

Yakima

17   19-20

Moxee
City

d

15-16

18   Union
Gap

24

To Richland

97

Rattlesnake Hills   6.6

82

Wapato

12

e

White
Swan

Harrah

Zillah

22

21

Yakima

Toppenish

Granger

To Grandview

22

Fort
Simcoe S.P.

Toppenish

Creek

Sunnyside

To Prosser

f

YAKAMA

INDIAN

Toppenish
N.W.R.

97

River

22

RESERVATION

Dry

Creek

Satus   Creek

g

97

h

To Goldendale   6.9

1   2   3   4   5   6   7   8

© AVALON TRAVEL PUBLISHING, INC.

Map 6.6

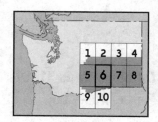

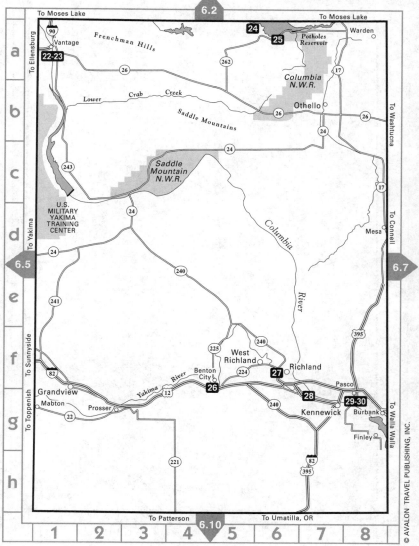

Map 6.7

Campgrounds 31–37
Pages 403–406

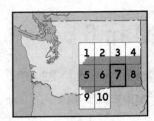

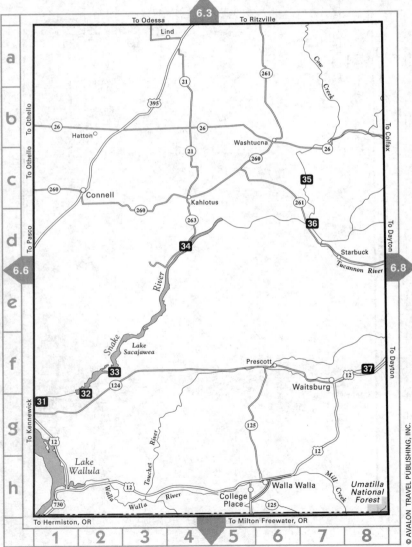

Map 6.8

Campgrounds 38–48
Pages 406–411

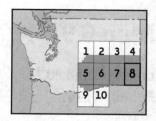

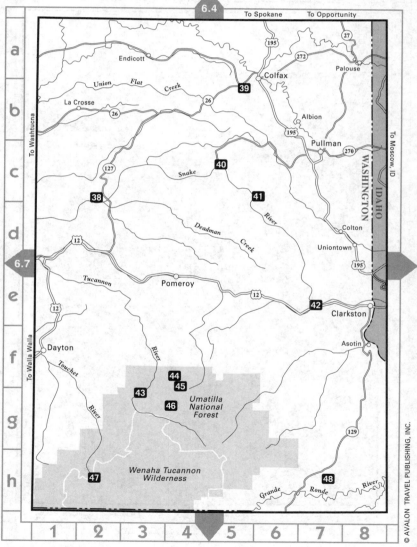

To Spokane   To Opportunity

6.4

195
27

a

Endicott

272

Palouse

Colfax
39

Union   Flat   Creek

26

La Crosse

26

b

Albion

195

Pullman

270

To Moscow, ID

127

Snake

40

c

41

River

38

WASHINGTON

IDAHO

Deadman   Creek

12

Colton

d

Uniontown

195

6.7

Tucannon

Pomeroy

12

e

42

Clarkston

12

To Walla Walla

Dayton

Asotin

Touchet

f

River

44
45

43

River

Umatilla
National
Forest

46

g

129

47

Wenaha Tucannon
Wilderness

48

h

Grande   Ronde   River

© AVALON TRAVEL PUBLISHING, INC.

1   2   3   4   5   6   7   8

Map 6.9

Campground 49
Pages 411–412

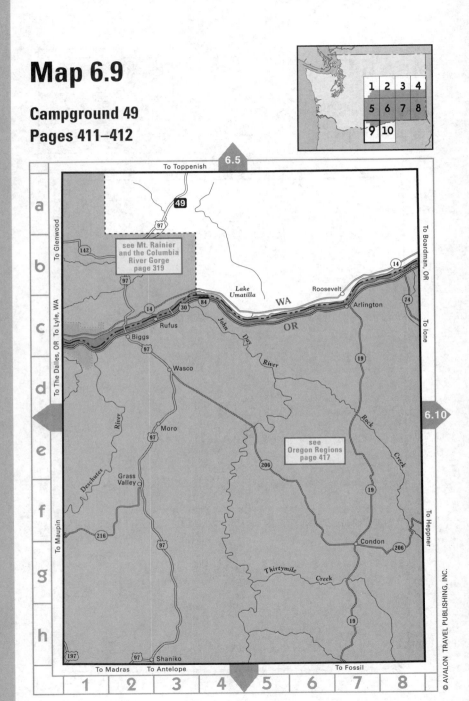

Map 6.10

Campgrounds 50–51
Pages 412–413

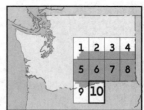

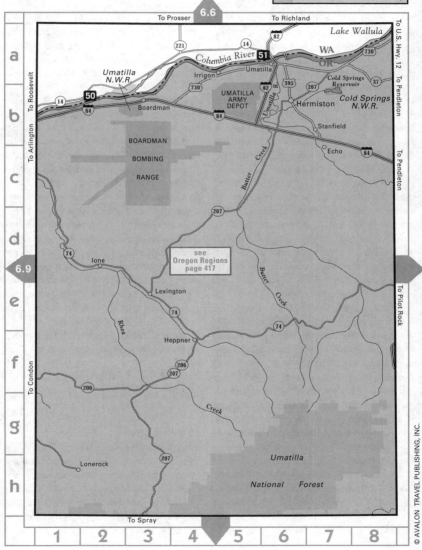

■ ELLENSBURG KOA

Rating: 8

On the Yakima River.

Map 6.1, grid h4, page 380

This KOA is one of the few campgrounds in a 25-mile radius. Exceptionally clean and scenic, it offers well-maintained, shaded campsites along the Yakima River. Rafting and fly-fishing on the nearby Yakima River are also popular. Other nearby recreation options include an 18-hole golf course, tennis courts, and horseback-riding rentals. The Kittitas County Historical Museum is in town at Third and Pine Streets.

Campsites, facilities: There are 100 sites for RVs of any length, including 48 drive-through sites, some with full hookups and the rest with water and electricity, and 25 tent sites. Picnic tables are provided. Restrooms, flush toilets, showers, an RV dump station, a video arcade, a store, a coin-operated laundry, ice, a playground, video rentals, a horseshoe pit, volleyball, a seasonal wading pool, and a heated swimming pool are available. Bottled gas and a café are located within one mile. Extra parking is available for horse trailers, vans, and boats. Leashed pets are permitted.

Reservations, fees: Reservations at 800/562-7616. Sites are $20–35 per night, $3 per person per night for more than two people, and $3 per extra vehicle per night. Major credit cards accepted. Open year-round.

Directions: From Seattle, drive east on I-90 for 106 miles to Exit 106 (near Ellensburg). Take that exit and continue one-quarter mile to Thorp Highway. Turn right at Thorp Highway and drive a short distance to the KOA entrance (well marked).

Contact: Ellensburg KOA, 32 Thorp Hwy. S, Ellensburg, WA 98926, 509/925-9319, fax 509/925-3607, website: www.koa.com.

■ SHADY TREE RV PARK

Rating: 8

Near George.

Map 6.2, grid h2, page 381

With shade trees and grassy sites, this camp is an oasis in a desert-like area. A natural outdoor amphitheater just eight miles away seats 2,000 and is the scene of major concerts from June–September. Within one mile of Moses Lake State Park and about 30 miles from here, the small and public Martha Lake provides another recreation option.

Campsites, facilities: There are 30 tent sites and 41 sites with full hookups for RVs of any length; four are drive-through sites. Picnic tables are provided. A restroom with flush toilets, showers, an RV dump station, a horseshoe pit, and a coin-operated laundry are available. Leashed pets are permitted.

Reservations, fees: Reservations are not accepted; $22 per night for RV sites are, $10 per night for tent sites, and $5 per person per night for more than two people over age 12. Open year-round.

Directions: From Spokane, drive west on I-90 to Exit 151 (two miles east of George). Take that exit and bear right to the campground right at the corner (just off the highway at the intersection of Highways 281 and 283).

Contact: Shady Tree RV Park, 1099 Hwy. 283 N, Quincy, WA 98848, 509/785-2851.

■ OASIS RV PARK AND GOLF

Rating: 5

Near Soap Lake.

Map 6.2, grid f4, page 381

This area can be extremely warm and arid during the summer months, but, fortunately, Oasis RV Park offers shaded sites. There are two fishing ponds at the resort: One has crappie, while the other is for kids and has trout and bass. There is also a nine-hole golf course at the park. Mineral baths are located just a few miles north.

Campsites, facilities: There are 38 tent sites and 68 sites with full hookups for RVs of any length; 10 are drive-through sites. Picnic tables are provided. A restroom with flush toilets and coin-operated showers is available. A nine-hole golf course, an RV dump station, a store, propane gas, a coin-operated laundry, ice, a swimming pool, and a fishing pond for children are available. A café is located within one mile. Leashed pets are permitted.

Reservations, fees: Reservations recommended. Sites are $15–20 per night, $2 per person for more than four people, and $2 per extra vehicle. Major credit cards accepted. Senior discount available. Open year-round, with limited winter facilities.

Directions: From Spokane, drive west on I-90 to the Moses Lake exit and Highway 17. Turn northeast and drive 17 miles to the Y junction with Highway 282. Take Highway 282 and drive four miles to Highway 281/283 (a stoplight). Turn left and drive 1.25 miles to the park on the right (just before reaching the town of Ephrata).

Contact: Oasis RV Park and Golf, 2541 Basin St. SW, Ephrata, WA 98823, 509/754-5102 or 877/754-5102.

❹ BIG SUN RESORT

Rating: 5

Near Moses Lake State Park.
Map 6.2, grid h6, page 381

This park sits a short distance from Moses Lake State Park, which is open for day-use only. The primary appeal is Moses Lake, where you will find shady picnic spots with tables and fire grills, beach access, and moorage floats. Water-skiing is allowed on the lake. New owners are anticipated for this resort in 2003.

Campsites, facilities: There are 10 tent sites and 42 sites with full hookups for RVs of any length; 13 are drive-through sites. Picnic tables

and fire pits are provided. A restroom with flush toilets and pay showers is available. A coin-operated laundry, ice, cable TV, rowboat rentals and launch facilities, and a playground are available. An RV dump station, a store, and a restaurant are located within one mile. Boat docks, launching facilities, and rentals are nearby. Leashed pets are permitted.

Reservations, fees: Reservations accepted. Sites are $13.50–22 per night, $2 per person ($1 per child) per night for more than two people. Major credit cards accepted. Open March–October.

Directions: From Spokane, drive west on I-90 to Moses Lake and Exit 176. Take that exit to Broadway and drive one-half mile to Burress Avenue. Turn west on Burress Avenue and drive one block to the park.

Contact: Big Sun Resort, 2300 West Marina, Moses Lake, WA 98837, 509/765-8294.

❺ WILLOWS TRAILER VILLAGE

Rating: 5

Near Moses Lake State Park.
Map 6.2, grid h6, page 381

One of two campgrounds in the area, this one has grassy, shaded sites, horseshoe pits, barbecues, and a recreation field. See the description of Big Sun Resort for information on recreation spots in the vicinity. Note that there are some permanent site rentals at this RV park, but a landscape barrier separates them from the other sites.

Campsites, facilities: There are 20 tent sites and 65 drive-through sites, most with full hookups, for RVs of any length. Electricity, drinking water, and picnic tables are provided. A restroom with flush toilets, coin-operated showers, bottled gas, a store, ice, a coin-operated laundry, and a playground with a horseshoe pit are available. There is also a hair salon on-site. Leashed pets are permitted.

Reservations, fees: Reservations accepted with deposits. Sites are $14.50–20.50 per night, $3 per person per night for more than two people. Open year-round.

Directions: From Spokane, drive west on I-90 to Moses Lake and Exit 179 and Highway 17. Turn south and drive 2.5 miles to Road M. Turn right (west) and drive one-quarter mile to the park on the left.

Contact: Willows Trailer Village, 1347 Road M SE, Moses Lake, WA 98837, 509/765-7531 (phone or fax).

6 LA QUINTA INN & RV

Rating: 7

In Ritzville.

Map 6.3, grid h6, page 382

If all you have is a tent, well, this is the only site to stake it on within a radius of 25 miles. The nearest fishing is at Sprague Lake, 22 miles north on U.S. 395. Burroughs Historical Museum is a possible side trip in town. An 18-hole golf course and tennis courts are nearby, just across the street. This RV park changed ownership and name in 2003. Some may remember it under its former name, "Best Inn Suites & RV."

Campsites, facilities: There are 39 drive-through sites with full hookups for tents or RVs of any length. Picnic tables and cable TV hookups are provided. Restrooms, flush toilets, showers, an RV dump station, a coin-operated laundry, modem hookups, ice, a playground, a hot tub, and a seasonal swimming pool are available. Some facilities are wheelchair accessible. Bottled gas, a store, a gift shop, a café, and a restaurant are located within one mile. Leashed pets are permitted.

Reservations, fees: Reservations accepted. Sites are $10–25 per night. Senior discount available. Major credit cards accepted. Open mid-April–mid-October.

Directions: From Pasco, take U.S. 395 and drive 85 miles north to Ritzville and I-90. Take I-90 east and drive one-half mile to Exit 221. Take that exit and drive one-quarter mile to

Smitty's Boulevard. Turn right and drive a short distance to the hotel/RV check-in on the left.

Contact: La Quinta Inn & RV, 1513 Smitty's Blvd., Ritzville, WA 99169, 509/659-1007, fax 509/659-1025.

7 FOUR SEASONS CAMPGROUND & RESORT

Rating: 7

On Sprague Lake.

Map 6.4, grid f1, page 383

This campground along the shore of Sprague Lake, one of the top fishing waters in the state, has spacious sites with plenty of vegetation. The fishing for rainbow trout is best in May and June, with some bass in spring and fall. Because there is an abundance of natural feed in the lake, the fish reach larger sizes here than in neighboring lakes. Walleye up to 11 pounds are taken here. Perch, crappie, blue gill, and catfish are also abundant. In late July–August, a fair algae bloom is a turnoff for swimmers and water-skiers.

Campsites, facilities: There are 38 sites with full or partial hookups, including some drive-through sites, for RVs, 25 tent sites, and four furnished cabins for up to six people. Picnic tables and fire grills are provided. Restrooms, drinking water, flush toilets, coin-operated showers, an RV dump station, firewood, ice, a store with fishing tackle, a fish-cleaning station, a small basketball court, and a swimming pool are available. Boat and fishing docks, launching facilities, and rentals are nearby. Leashed pets are permitted.

Reservations, fees: Reservations accepted. Sites are $16–21 per night, $2 per person for more than four people, and $1 per pet per night. Open March–October, weather permitting.

Directions: From Spokane, drive west on I-90 for about 40 miles to Exit 245. Take Exit 245 and drive south to Fourth Street. Turn right and drive one block to B Street. Turn left and drive two blocks to First Street. Turn

right and drive one-half mile to a Y intersection. Bear right to Doerschlag Road and
drive one mile to Lake Road. Turn left and
drive four miles to Bob Lee Road. Turn left
and drive one mile to the campground at the
end of the road.

Contact: Four Seasons Campground & Resort,
2384 North Bob Lee Rd., Sprague, WA 99032,
509/257-2332, website: www.fourseasons
campground.com.

8 SPRAGUE LAKE RESORT

Rating: 5

On Sprague Lake.

Map 6.4, grid f1, page 383

This developed campground is located on the
shore of Sprague Lake, about 35 miles from
Spokane. It offers a pleasant, grassy setting
with about 100 cottonwood and native trees
on the property. See listing for Four Seasons
Campground and Resort for more information about Sprague Lake.

Campsites, facilities: There are 30 drive-
through sites with full or partial hookups for
RVs of any length and 50 tent sites. Picnic
tables and fire grills are provided. Restrooms,
drinking water, flush toilets, coin-operated
showers, an RV dump station, a small store,
a coin-operated laundry, ice, firewood for
sale, a playground, boat docks, launching facilities, and rentals are available. Leashed
pets are permitted.

Reservations, fees: Reservations accepted. Sites
are $15-19 per night, $1 per person per night
for more than two people. Open April-October.

Directions: In Spokane, drive west on I-90 to
the Sprague Business Center exit. Take that
exit to Sprague Lake Road and drive two miles
to the resort on the left (well signed).

Contact: Sprague Lake Resort, 1999 Sprague
Lake Resort Rd., Sprague, WA 99032, 509/257-
2864, website: www.spraguelakeresort.com

9 KLINK'S WILLIAMS LAKE RESORT

Rating: 6

On Williams Lake.

Map 6.4, grid f3, page 383

This family-oriented resort is set on the shore
of Williams Lake, which is less than three
miles long and is popular for swimming and
water-skiing. The resort has a swimming area
with a floating dock and diving board. This
lake is also one of the top fishing lakes in
the region for rainbow trout and cutthroat
trout. Rocky cliffs border the lake in some
areas. Note that about 100 permanent residents live at the resort. See the description
of Peaceful Pines Campground for information on nearby Turnbull National Wildlife Refuge.

Campsites, facilities: There are 60 sites with
full or partial hookups, including one drive-
through site, for RVs of any length, 15 tent
sites, and three log cabins. Picnic tables are
provided. Restrooms, drinking water, flush toilets, coin-operated showers, bottled gas, an RV
dump station, firewood, a store, a café, a restaurant, ice, a playground, boat docks, launching
facilities, and boat rentals are available. Leashed
pets are permitted.

Reservations, fees: Reservations accepted. Sites
are $17-20 per night, $2 per person for more
than two adults and two children, and $1.50
per pet per night. Major credit cards accepted. Open mid-April-October.

Directions: From Spokane, drive west on I-90
for 10 miles to Exit 270 and Highway 904.
Turn south on Highway 904 and drive four
miles to Cheney and Cheney Plaza Road. Turn
left (south) on Cheney Plaza Road and drive
11.2 miles to Williams Lake Road. Turn right
(west) and drive 2.2 miles to the campground
on the left.

Contact: Klink's Williams Lake Resort, 18617
West Williams Lake Rd., Cheney, WA 99004,
509/235-2391, website: www.klinksrsort.com.

10 BUNKER'S RESORT

Rating: 8

On Williams Lake.

Map 6.4, grid f3, page 383

This campground is set on the shore of Williams Lake. See the description of Klink's Williams Lake Resort for information on the lake.

Campsites, facilities: There are 10 drive-through sites with full or partial hookups for RVs of any length, 10 sites for tents, and four furnished cabins. Fire pits are provided at tent sites. Picnic tables, restrooms, drinking water, flush toilets, showers, bottled gas, an RV dump station, a restaurant, a store, ice, boat and fishing docks, launching facilities, and rentals are available. Leashed pets are permitted.

Reservations, fees: Reservations accepted. Sites are $15–24.50 per night. Major credit cards accepted. Open mid-April–September.

Directions: From Spokane, drive west on I-90 for 10 miles to Exit 270 and Highway 904. Turn south on Highway 904 and drive six miles to Cheney and Mullinex Road. Turn left (south) on Mullinex Road and drive 12 miles to the resort.

Contact: Bunker's Resort, 36402 South Bunker Landing Rd., Cheney, WA 99004, 509/235-5212, 509/235-8707.

11 SQUAW ROCK RESORT

Rating: 8

On the Naches River.

Map 6.5, grid b1, page 384

This park, situated in a stand of old-growth fir and pine on the Naches River, is close to a host of activities, including trout fishing, hiking trails, marked bike trails, and a riding stable. The park has a pool and hot tub. The nearby town of Naches, located southeast of the campground on State Route 410, offers all services.

Campsites, facilities: There are 65 sites, most with full hookups, for RVs of any length, 25 tent sites, five cabins, and four motel rooms. Picnic tables are provided. Restrooms, flush toilets, showers, bottled gas, an RV dump station, cable TV, a recreation hall, a store, a café, ice, a playground, a hot tub, and a swimming pool are available. Leashed pets are permitted.

Reservations, fees: Reservations accepted. Sites are $15–23 per night, $2 per person per night for more than two people. Major credit cards accepted. Open year-round.

Directions: From Yakima, drive northwest on U.S. 12 for 18 miles to State Route 410. Continue straight on State Route 410 and drive 15 miles to the campground on the left.

Contact: Squaw Rock Resort, 15070 Rte. 410, Naches, WA 98937, 509/658-2926, fax 509/658-2927, website: www.mountainairinc.micrompcweb.com.

12 HAUSE CREEK

Rating: 7

On the Tieton River in Wenatchee National Forest.

Map 6.5, grid c1, page 384

Several creeks converge at this campground along the Tieton River (elevation 2,500 feet). The Tieton Dam, which creates Rimrock Lake, is located just upstream. Hause Creek is one of the larger, more developed camps in the area. Willows provides a primitive alternative.

Campsites, facilities: There are 42 sites for tents or RVs up to 30 feet long. Picnic tables and fire grills are provided. Drinking water and flush toilets are available. Some facilities are wheelchair accessible. Boat docks, launching facilities, and rentals are located on Rimrock Lake. Leashed pets are permitted.

Reservations, fees: Reservations accepted; phone 877/444-6777 or access the website: www.ReserveUsa.com ($9 reservation fee).

Sites are $13–15 per night, $26 for double sites, and $5 per extra vehicle per night. Senior discount available. Open late May–late November.

Directions: From Yakima, drive northwest on I-82 for 17 miles to the junction with Highway 410. Turn west on U.S. 12 and drive 22 miles to the campground on the left.

Contact: Okanogan and Wenatchee National Forests, Naches Ranger District, 10061 U.S. 12, Naches, WA 98937, 509/653-2205, fax 509/653-2638.

13 WILLOWS

Rating: 5

On the Tieton River in Wenatchee National Forest.

Map 6.5, grid c1, page 384

This primitive, beautiful, and easily accessible camp can be found on the Tieton River at 2,400 feet elevation. Rimrock Lake to the west provides many recreation options, and hiking trails leading into the William O. Douglas Wilderness are within driving distance.

Campsites, facilities: There are 15 sites for tents or RVs up to 20 feet long. Picnic tables and fire grills are provided. Drinking water, vault toilets, and garbage service are available. Leashed pets are permitted.

Reservations, fees: Reservations are not accepted. Sites are $13–15 per night, $5 per extra vehicle per night. Senior discount available. Open April–late November.

Directions: From Yakima, drive northwest on I-82 for 17 miles to the junction with Highway 410. Turn west on U.S. 12 and drive 16 miles to the campground on the left.

Contact: Okanogan and Wenatchee National Forests, Naches Ranger District, 10061 U.S. 12, Naches, WA 98937, 509/653-2205, fax 509/653-2638.

14 WINDY POINT

Rating: 5

On the Tieton River in Wenatchee National Forest.

Map 6.5, grid c1, page 384

This campground, located along the Tieton River at an elevation of 2,000 feet, is more isolated than the camps set westward toward Rimrock Lake. Drinking water is a bonus. Fishing access is available.

Campsites, facilities: There are 15 sites for tents or RVs up to 22 feet long. Picnic tables and fire grills are provided. Drinking water and vault toilets are available. Garbage service and firewood are available nearby. Leashed pets are permitted.

Reservations, fees: Reservations are not accepted. Sites are $13–15 per night, $5 per extra vehicle per night. Senior discount available. Open April–late November.

Directions: From Yakima, drive northwest on I-82 for 17 miles to the junction with Highway 410. Turn west on U.S. 12 and drive nine miles to the campground on the left.

Contact: Okanogan and Wenatchee National Forests, Naches Ranger District, 10061 U.S. 12, Naches, WA 98937, 509/653-2205, fax 509/653-2638.

15 SNOW CABIN

Rating: 7

On the North Fork of Ahtanum Creek.

Map 6.5, grid d1, page 384

Located in an area of old-growth timber, this place is popular with horse campers, who use it to access old logging roads. There are cutthroat trout in Ahtanum Creek, and fishing is permitted. The landscape features primarily Douglas fir. Those who have visited this camp may remember that saddle-stock facilities were once available. They have been removed.

Campsites, facilities: There are eight sites for

tents or small RVs. Picnic tables, fire grills, and tent pads are provided. Pit toilets are available, but there is no drinking water. Garbage must be packed out. Leashed pets are permitted.

Reservations, fees: Reservations are not accepted. There is no fee for camping. Open year-round, weather permitting.

Directions: From Yakima, drive south on I-82 for two miles to Union Gap and Ahtanum Road. Turn right (west) and drive 20 miles to Tampico and Road A-3000 (North Fork Road). Turn right (west) and drive 9.5 miles to Road A-3000 (North Fork Ahtanum Road). Turn right (west) and drive 5.6 miles (bearing left for the last mile) to the Gray Rock Trailhead. From Gray Rock, continue 1.5 miles to the campground on the left. Note: High-clearance vehicles only are recommended.

Contact: Department of Natural Resources, Southeast Region, 713 Bowers Rd., Ellensburg, WA 98926-9301, 509/925-8510, fax 509/925-8522.

16 AHTANUM & AHTANUM MEADOWS

Rating: 7

On Ahtanum Creek.

Map 6.5, grid d1, page 384

Ahtanum Creek separates these two campgrounds, but they are both primitive sites that have the same limited facilities. For a good side trip, drive 14 miles to the Darland Mountain viewpoint (6,900 feet elevation). The road gets very steep near the lookout and is not suitable for RVs or trailers. In the winter, this area offers 60 miles of groomed trails for snowmobilers. Tree Phones Campground provides a snow shelter. Contact the Department of Natural Resources for a map.

Campsites, facilities: There are 11 campsites for tents or small RVs at Ahtanum Meadows and nine sites at Ahtanum. Picnic tables, fire grills, and tent pads are provided. Vault and pit toilets and drinking water are available. Some facilities are wheelchair accessible. Leashed pets are permitted.

Reservations, fees: No reservation; no fee. Open year-round, weather permitting.

Directions: From Yakima, drive south on I-82 for two miles to Union Gap and Ahtanum Road. Turn right (west) and drive 20 miles to Tampico and Road A-3000 (North Fork Road). Turn right (west) and drive nine miles to the Ahtanum Meadows campground entrance on the left. To reach Antanum, continue one-half mile to the campground on the left. Note: High-clearance vehicles only are recommended.

Contact: Department of Natural Resources, Southeast Region, 713 Bowers Rd., Ellensburg, WA 98926-9301, 509/925-8510, fax 509/925-8522.

17 CIRCLE H RV RANCH

Rating: 8

In Yakima.

Map 6.5, grid d4, page 384

This pleasant, centrally located, and clean park with a Western flavor has comfortable, spacious sites among ornamental trees and roses. Nearby recreation options include an 18-hole golf course, hiking trails, marked bike trails, and a riding stable. See the description of KOA Yakima for information on points of interest in Yakima.

Campsites, facilities: There are 64 sites with full hookups for RVs of any length, including 16 drive-through sites, and 12 tent sites. Picnic tables are provided. Restrooms, flush toilets, showers, two recreation halls, a coin-operated laundry, a hot tub, modem hookups, two playgrounds with horseshoes, a tennis court, volleyball and basketball, a video arcade, a mini-golf course, and a swimming pool are available. Bottled gas, a store, a café, and ice are located within one mile. Mini-storage units are available for a fee. Leashed pets are permitted.

Reservations, fees: Reservations accepted. Sites

are $17–21 per night, $3 per person per night for more than two people. Major credit cards accepted. Open year-round.

Directions: In Yakima on I-82, take Exit 34 and drive one block to South 18th Street. Turn right (north) and drive one-quarter mile to the campground on the right.

Contact: Circle H RV Ranch, 1107 South 18th St., Yakima, WA 98901, 509/457-3683 (phone or fax), website: http://circlehrv park.uswestdex.com.

18 TRAILER INN RV PARK

Rating: 7

In Yakima.

Map 6.5, grid d4, page 384

Like the Trailer Inn RV Park in Spokane, this spot has many of the luxuries you'd find in a hotel, including a pool, a hot tub, a sauna, on-site security, and a large-screen TV. An 18-hole golf course, hiking trails, marked bike trails, and tennis courts are close by. It's especially pretty in the fall when the sycamores turn color. See the description of KOA Yakima for information on some of the points of interest in Yakima.

Campsites, facilities: There are 152 sites with full hookups for tents or RVs of any length; 30 are drive-through sites. Picnic tables are provided. Restrooms, flush toilets, showers, bottled gas, an RV dump station, a recreation hall, a coin-operated laundry, ice, an indoor heated swimming pool, a whirlpool, a TV room with a 52-inch screen, a dog walk, an enclosed barbecue (no open fires permitted), and a playground are available. A store and a café are located within one block. Leashed pets are permitted.

Reservations, fees: Reservations accepted. Sites are $17–25 per night, $5 per person per night for more than two people, and $5 per extra vehicle per night. Major credit cards accepted. Open year-round.

Directions: In Yakima on I-82, take Exit 31

and drive south for one block on North First Street to the park on the right (west side of the road).

Contact: Trailer Inn RV Park, 1610 North First St., Yakima, WA 98901, 509/452-9561, website: www.trailerinnrv.uswestdex.com.

19 YAKIMA SPORTSMAN STATE PARK

Rating: 8

On the Yakima River.

Map 6.5, grid d5, page 384

This park is located on the flood plain of the Yakima River and is an irrigated area in an otherwise desert landscape. Several deciduous trees shade the camping and picnic areas. More than 140 bird species have been identified in the park. It is a popular layover spot for visitors attending events in the Yakima area. There is a fishing pond for children (no anglers over age 15 are allowed). Hiking is permitted along two miles of unpaved roadway on the river dike. Kayaking and rafting are possible at this park on the Yakima River. No swimming is allowed. Nearby recreation options include an 18-hole golf course and hiking trails. See the description of KOA Yakima for information on other points of interest in Yakima.

Campsites, facilities: There are two primitive tent sites, 28 sites for tents or self-contained RVs, and 37 drive-through sites with full hookups for RVs up to 60 feet in length. Picnic tables and fire grills are provided. Flush toilets, an RV dump station, and a playground are available. Showers and firewood are available for an extra fee. Some facilities are wheelchair accessible. A store and ice are within one mile. Leashed pets are permitted.

Reservations, fees: Reservations accepted. Sites are $6–22 per night, $6 per extra vehicle per night. Major credit cards accepted. Senior discount available. Open year-round.

Directions: In Yakima, drive on I-82 to Milepost 34 and the Highway 24 exit. Turn east on

Highway 24 and drive one mile to Keys Road. Turn left and drive one mile to the park entrance on the left.

Contact: Yakima Sportsman State Park, 509/575-2774, fax 509/454-4114; State Park information, 360/902-8844.

20 KOA YAKIMA

🥾 🚴 ⛵ 🎣 🚂 🐕 🚶 🚙 ⛺

Rating: 6

On the Yakima River.
Map 6.5, grid d5, page 384

This campground along the Yakima River offers well-maintained, shaded sites and fishing access. Some points of interest in Yakima are the Yakima Valley Museum and the Yakima Trolley Lines, which offer rides on restored trolley cars originally built in 1906. Indian Rock Paintings State Park is located five miles west of Yakima on U.S. 12. Nearby recreation options include an 18-hole golf course, hiking trails, marked bike trails, and tennis courts. A casino is located 15 miles to the east.

Campsites, facilities: There are 120 sites, some with full hookups, the rest with water and electricity for RVs of any length, 40 tent sites, and seven cabins. Picnic tables are provided. Restrooms, flush toilets, showers, bottled gas, an RV dump station, a recreation hall, a store, a coin-operated laundry, ice, a pool, a playground with horseshoes, a basketball court, fishing ponds, firewood, bike rentals, and boat rentals including paddleboats are available. A café is located within one mile. Leashed pets permitted.

Reservations, fees: Reservations at 800/562-5773. Sites are $21–28 per night, $3 per person per night for more than two people. Major credit cards accepted. Open year-round.

Directions: In Yakima, drive on I-82 to Milepost 34 and the Highway 24 exit. Turn east on Highway 24 and drive one mile to Keys Road. Turn north on Keys Road and drive 300 yards to the campground on the left.

Contact: KOA Yakima, 1500 Keys Rd., Yakima, WA 98901, 509/248-5882, fax 509/469-3986, website: www.koa.com.

21 YAKAMA NATION RV RESORT

🚴 ⛵ 🐕 🚶 🚙 ⛺

Rating: 3

Near the Yakima River.
Map 6.5, grid e6, page 384

The park is set within the Yakama Indian Reservation (the tribe spells its name differently from the river and town), close to a casino and movie theater. The Toppenish National Wildlife Refuge, the best side trip, is almost always a good spot to see a large variety of birds. For information, phone 509/545-8588. Nearby Toppenish, a historic Old West town with a museum, is also worth a side trip.

Campsites, facilities: There are 125 sites with full hookups for RVs of any length, one tent site, and 14 teepees for up to 10 people each. Picnic tables and fire pits are provided. Restrooms, flush toilets, showers, modem hookups, an RV dump station, garbage service, a playground, a recreation room, an exercise room, a jogging track, ball courts, bicycle rentals, a heated pool, and a coin-operated laundry are available. A picnic shelter with drinking water, propane, and a sink is available in the tent area. A restaurant and grocery store are located within 1.5 miles. Leashed pets are permitted.

Reservations, fees: Reservations recommended; phone 800/874-3087. Sites are $20–26 per night, $2 per person per night for more than two people. Teepees are $30 per night for five campers, plus $5 each additional person. Major credit cards accepted. Open year-round.

Directions: From Yakima, drive south on U.S. 97 for 16 miles to the resort on the right.

Contact: Yakama Nation RV Resort, 280 Buster Rd., Toppenish, WA 98948, 509/865-2000 or 800/874-3087, website: www.yakamanation.com.

22 GINKGO-WANAPUM STATE PARK

Rating: 7

On the Columbia River and Wanapum Lake.
Map 6.6, grid a1, page 385

Ginkgo Petrified Forest State Park is one of the most unusual fossil forests in the world, and it is registered as a national natural landmark. Although a completely separate park, it is linked to Wanapum State Recreation Area. Camping is permitted only at Wanapum, which is seven miles south of the main entrance at Ginkgo. The site of an ancient petrified forest, the park features an interpretive center and trail. The petrified forest is open weekends and holidays from November–March. Ginkgo is set along Wanapum Lake in the course of the Columbia River. This is a huge recreation area, covering 7,740 acres and surrounding the 27,000 acres of Wanapum Lake. Recreation options include hiking (three miles of trails), swimming, boating, water-skiing, and fishing. There are also several historical Civilian Conservation Corps structures from the 1930s. The campground at Wanapum is set up primarily for RVs, with full hookups, restrooms, and showers. Note that the park always fills up during the Gorge concert season.

Campsites, facilities: There are 50 sites with full hookups for RVs up to 60 feet long. Picnic tables, fire grills, and flush toilets are provided. Showers and firewood are available for an extra fee. Boat docks, launching facilities, and a picnic area are nearby. Leashed pets are permitted.

Reservations, fees: Reserve at 888/CAMP-OUT (888/226-7688), website: www.parks.wa .gov/reservations ($7 reservation fee). Sites are $22 per night, $6 per extra vehicle per night. Senior discount available. Open April–October.

Directions: From Spokane, drive west on I-90 to the Vantage Highway/Huntzinger Road (Exit 136). Take that exit, turn south on Vantage Highway/Huntzinger Road, and drive three miles south to the park on the right.

Contact: Ginkgo-Wanapum State Park, Vantage, WA 98950, 360/902-8844; State Park information, 509/856-2700.

23 VANTAGE RIVERSTONE RESORT

Rating: 6

On the Columbia River.
Map 6.6, grid a1, page 385

This campground offers pleasant, grassy sites overlooking the Columbia River, which lies a short distance from the state park (see Ginkgo-Wanapum State Park). This campground is the only one in the immediate area that provides space for tent camping. The next closest camp is 12 miles away at Shady Tree RV Park in George.

Campsites, facilities: There are 50-plus tent sites and 50 sites with full hookups for RVs of any length. Picnic tables, a restroom with flush toilets, showers, an RV dump station, a recreation hall, a coin-operated laundry, ice, a playground, and a heated indoor swimming pool are available. A store and a café are located next to the resort. Boat docks and launching facilities are nearby. Leashed pets are permitted.

Reservations, fees: Reservations accepted. Sites are $19–23 per night, $9 per person for more than two people. Major credit cards accepted. Open year-round.

Directions: From Spokane, drive west on I-90 to Vantage and the Vantage Highway (Exit 136). Take that exit, turn north, and drive north for three blocks to the resort on the left.

Contact: Vantage Riverstone Resort, P.O. Box 1101, Vantage, WA 98950, 509/856-2230, fax 509/856-2800, website: www.vantagewa.com.

24 POTHOLES STATE PARK

Rating: 8

On Potholes Reservoir.

Map 6.6, grid a5, page 385

This park is set on Potholes Reservoir, also known as O'Sullivan Reservoir (because of the O'Sullivan Dam), where fishing is the highlight. Trout, walleye, crappie, and perch are among the species taken here. Water-skiing and hiking (three miles of hiking trails) are two other recreation options. There is a sand beach near the campground. The surrounding terrain is desert-like with freshwater marshes. A side trip to the Columbia Wildlife Refuge, located two miles east of the park, is recommended. Note that Potholes Reservoir is often confused with the Potholes Lakes, which are a 30- to 45-minute drive from the park.

Campsites, facilities: There are 121 sites for tents or RVs up to 50 feet long; 60 have full hookups. Picnic tables and fire grills are provided. Flush toilets, an RV dump station, a store, a playground, and a picnic area with a shelter are available. Showers and firewood are available for a fee. Boat-launching facilities and rentals are nearby. Leashed pets are permitted.

Reservations, fees: Reserve at 888/CAMP-OUT (888/226-7688), website: www.parks.wa.gov/reservations ($7 reservation fee). Sites are $8–22 per night, $6 per extra vehicle per night. Senior discount available. Open year-round.

Directions: From I-90 at Moses Lake, take Exit 179 and Highway 17. Turn south and drive nine miles to Highway 262/O'Sullivan Dam Road. Turn right (west) and drive 11 miles to the resort on the southern shore of Potholes Reservoir (well signed).

Contact: Potholes State Park, 6762 Hwy. 262 E, Othello, WA 99344, 509/346-2759, fax 509/346-1732; State Park information, 360/902-8844.

25 MAR DON RESORT

Rating: 7

Near Potholes Reservoir.

Map 6.6, grid a6, page 385

This resort is located on Potholes Reservoir and provides opportunities for fishing, swimming, and boating. A marina, tackle, and boat rentals are all available. Hiking trails and marked bike trails are close by. There are also a 25-unit motel and two rental homes at the resort. Many visitors find the café and cocktail lounge a nice bonus. The Columbia National Wildlife Refuge is located to the nearby south and provides exceptional bird-watching, with pelicans and kingfishers common and bald eagles and migratory sandhill cranes often seen.

Campsites, facilities: There are 275 sites for tents or RVs of any length, including 187 with full or partial hookups and seven with drive-through sites. Electricity, drinking water, and picnic tables are provided. A restroom with flush toilets, coin-operated showers, bottled gas, an RV dump station, a game room, a store, a coin-operated laundry, ice, a playground, boat moorage, boat rentals, and launching facilities are available. Some facilities are wheelchair accessible. Leashed pets are permitted.

Reservations, fees: Reservations at 800/416-2736. Sites are $18–23 per night, $3 per person for more than four people, $5 per extra vehicle per night, and $3 per pet per night. Major credit cards accepted. Open year-round.

Directions: From Spokane, drive west on I-90 to Moses Lake and Exit 179 and Highway 17. Turn south and drive nine miles to Highway 262. Turn west and drive 10 miles to the resort on the southern shore of Potholes Reservoir.

Contact: Mar Don Resort, 8198 Hwy. 262 SE, Othello, WA 99344, 509/346-2651, fax 509/346-9493, website: www.mardonresort.com.

26 BEACH RV PARK

Rating: 8

On the Yakima River.

Map 6.6, grid f5, page 385

If it's getting late, you'd best stop here because it's the only option for a long stretch. This park along the shore of the Yakima River is a pleasant spot with spacious RV sites, a large grassy area, and poplar trees and shrubs that provide privacy between sites. Nearby recreation options include an 18-hole golf course, a full-service marina, and tennis courts. The park was bought in 2000, and the new owner installed a deck overlooking the river.

Campsites, facilities: There are 39 sites with full hookups for tents or RVs of any length; five are drive-through sites. Electricity, drinking water, sewer hookups, and cable TV are provided. Flush toilets, showers, a coin-operated laundry, and ice are available. Bottled gas, an RV dump station, a store, and a café are located within one mile. Boat-launching facilities are nearby. Leashed pets are permitted.

Reservations, fees: Reservations accepted. Sites are $24 per night. Open year-round.

Directions: From Pasco, drive west on U.S. 12 past Richland and continue eight miles to Exit 96 and the Benton City/West Richland exit. Take that exit and drive one block north to Abby Avenue. Turn left (west) and drive 1.5 blocks to the park on the left.

Contact: Beach RV Park, 113 Abby Ave., Benton City, WA 99320, 509/588-5959 (phone or fax), website: www.angelfire.com/wa2 /beachrvpark.

27 DESERT GOLD RV PARK AND MOTEL

Rating: 6

Near the Columbia River.

Map 6.6, grid f6, page 385

Desert Gold is a nice RV park located about one mile from the Columbia River. Nearby recreation options include an 18-hole golf course, hiking trails, a full-service marina, and tennis courts. You can also visit the Department of Energy public information center at the Hanford Science Center. The RV park has a pool and spa if you just want to relax without going anywhere.

Campsites, facilities: There are 90 sites with full hookups for RVs of any length, including 15 drive-through sites, and 29 motel rooms, including 19 with kitchenettes. Picnic tables and cable TV are provided. Flush toilets, showers, bottled gas, an RV dump station, a store, a coin-operated laundry, ice, a game/meeting room, video rentals, and a seasonal hot tub and swimming pool are available. A café is located within one mile. Boat docks and launching facilities are nearby on the Columbia River. Leashed pets are permitted.

Reservations, fees: Reservations accepted. Sites are $20 per night, $1.50 per person per night for more than two people. Major credit cards accepted. Open year-round.

Directions: In Richland on I-182, take Exit 3 (Queensgate). Turn right and drive to Columbia Park Trail (the first left). Turn left and drive about two miles to the park.

Contact: Desert Gold RV Park and Motel, 611 Columbia Park Trail, Richland, WA 99352, 509/627-1000 or 800/788-GOLD (800/788-4653), fax 509/627-3467.

28 COLUMBIA PARK

Rating: 7

On the Columbia River.

Map 6.6, grid g7, page 385

This campground is set in a grassy suburban area on the Columbia River, adjacent to 605-acre Columbia Park. Nearby activities include water-skiing on the Columbia River, an 18-hole golf course, hiking trails, marked bike trails, tennis courts, and Frisbee golf. The sun can feel like a branding iron during the summer here.

Campsites, facilities: There are 58 sites, including 30 with partial hookups (water and electricity), for tents or RVs; 14 are drive-through. Picnic tables and fire grills are provided. Drinking water, restrooms, flush toilets, showers, an RV dump station, ice, and a playground with horseshoes are available. Firewood can be obtained for a fee. Group picnic shelters, a snack bar, and a public telephone are available nearby. Some facilities are wheelchair accessible. A store and a café are located within one mile. Boat docks and launching facilities are nearby. Leashed pets are permitted.

Reservations, fees: Reservations accepted at 509/585-4529. Sites are $7–11 per night. Major credit cards accepted. Open year-round.

Directions: In Kennewick on U.S. 395/Highway 240, drive west toward the Columbia River to the first exit, signed Columbia Park. Take that exit and continue to the campground along the highway. The campground is located adjacent to Columbia Park.

Contact: Columbia Park Campground, 6515 Columbia Park Trail, Kennewick, WA 99336, 509/585-4529.

29 GREENTREE RV PARK

Rating: 6

In Pasco.

Map 6.6, grid g8, page 385

This shady park in urban Pasco is close to an 18-hole golf course, hiking trails, a full-service marina, and tennis courts. The Franklin County Historical Museum, which is located in town, and the Sacajawea State Park Museum and Interpretive Center, located three miles southeast of town, both offer extensive collections of Native American artifacts. One bonus here: Parking is available for extra vehicles. Also note that about 15 site rentals are permanent.

Campsites, facilities: There are 40 sites with full hookups for RVs of any length. A coin-operated laundry and coin-operated showers are available. Bottled gas, a store, a café, and ice

are located within one mile. Boat docks, launching facilities, and rentals are nearby. Leashed pets are permitted.

Reservations, fees: Reservations accepted. Sites are $20 per night; call for weekly and monthly rates. Open year-round.

Directions: In Pasco on I-182, take Exit 13 onto Fourth Avenue and continue a short distance to the park entrance driveway on the right. Turn right and enter the park.

Contact: Greentree RV Park, 2103 North Fifth Ave., No. 69, Pasco, WA 99301, 509/547-6220 (phone or fax).

30 ARROWHEAD RV PARK

Rating: 5

Near the Columbia River.

Map 6.6, grid g8, page 385

Arrowhead provides a decent layover spot in Pasco. Nearby recreation options include an 18-hole golf course, a full-service marina, and tennis courts.

Campsites, facilities: There are 35 tent sites and 80 sites with full hookups for RVs of any length; 33 are drive-through sites. Electricity (30 amp), drinking water, sewer hookups, and picnic tables are provided. Flush toilets, showers, a pay phone, and a coin-operated laundry are available. A store and a café are located within walking distance. Small pets are permitted.

Reservations, fees: Reservations accepted. Sites are $20–30 per night for two people, $5 per person and $3 per child per night for more than two people, and $1 per pet per night. Open year-round.

Directions: In Pasco on U.S. 395 North, take the Hillsboro Street exit, turn east, and drive a short distance to Commercial Avenue. Turn right (south) and drive one-quarter mile to the park entrance on the right.

Contact: Arrowhead RV Park, 3120 Commercial Ave., Pasco, WA 99301, 509/545-8206.

31 HOOD PARK

Rating: 6

On Lake Wallula.

Map 6.7, grid g1, page 386

This 99-acre park is set on Lake Wallula. All the campsites at the main campground are paved; an overflow camping area and boat camping are also available. This park is a more developed, nearby alternative to Columbia Park Campground and provides access for swimming and boating. There are hiking trails throughout the park, along with two stocked fishing ponds. Other recreation options include basketball and horseshoes. McNary Wildlife Refuge is right next door, and Sacajawea State Park is within four miles.

Campsites, facilities: There are 69 sites for tents or RVs up to 60 feet long, including 25 pull-through sites, and an overflow camping area with 90 sites. Picnic tables and fire grills are provided. Drinking water, restrooms, flush toilets, showers, an RV dump station, a playground, horseshoe pits, a basketball court, a swimming beach, a covered picnic area, public phones, and an amphitheater are available. Summer programs are also available. A restaurant and convenience store are located within two miles. Some facilities are wheelchair accessible. Boat docks and launching facilities are nearby. Leashed pets are permitted.

Reservations, fees: Reservations accepted; phone 877/444-6777 or access the website: www.ReserveUsa.com ($9 reservation fee). Sites are $16 per night and $7 per night in the overflow area and for boat camping. Senior discount available. Open April–September. The gates are locked from 10 P.M.–6 A.M.

Directions: In Pasco, drive southeast on U.S. 12 for three miles to the junction with Highway 124. Turn left (east) on Highway 124 and drive an extremely short distance to the park entrance on the right.

Contact: U.S. Army Corps of Engineers, 2763 Monument Dr., Burbank, WA 99323, 509/547-7781, fax 509/543-3201.

32 CHARBONNEAU PARK

Rating: 6

On the Snake River.

Map 6.7, grid f2, page 386

This shorefront camp is the centerpiece of a 244-acre park that is set along the Snake River just above Ice Harbor Dam. It is a good spot for fishing, boating, swimming, and water-skiing. An overflow camping area provides an insurance policy if the numbered sites are full. At Lake Sacajawea, the dam's visitors center (open daily from April–October) features exhibits and a view through Lucite glass of a salmon fish ladder.

Campsites, facilities: There are 54 sites for tents or RVs up to 60 feet long, including 18 pull-through sites with full hookups, and an overflow camping area. Picnic tables and fire grills are provided. Flush toilets, showers, tent pads, an RV dump station, a public telephone, a playground with a volleyball net, and summer campground programs are available. Some facilities are wheelchair accessible. A marina with boat docks, launching facilities, a marine dump station, a swimming beach, a store, ice, and group shelters with electricity are nearby. Leashed pets are permitted.

Reservations, fees: Reservations accepted; phone 877/444-6777 or access the website: www.ReserveUsa.com ($9 reservation fee). Sites are $16–18 per night. Overflow and boat camping are $7 per night. Senior discount available. Open April–October with full facilities and gate closure from 10 P.M.–6 A.M.; there are limited facilities and no fee the rest of the year.

Directions: In Pasco, drive southeast on U.S. 12 for five miles to Highway 124. Turn east and drive eight miles to Sun Harbor Road. Turn north and drive two miles to the park.

Contact: U.S. Army Corps of Engineers, Rte. 6, Box 693, Pasco, WA 99301-9165, 509/547-7781.

33 FISHHOOK PARK

Rating: 6

On the Snake River.

Map 6.7, grid f2, page 386

If you're driving along Highway 124 and you need a spot for the night, make the turn on Fishhook Park Road and check out this wooded camp along the Snake River. It is a nice spot within a 46-acre park set on Lake Sacajawea. The park provides some lawn area, along with places to swim, fish, and water-ski. A one-mile walk along railroad tracks will take you to a fishing pond. This park is popular on summer weekends.

Campsites, facilities: There are 20 tent sites and 41 sites with partial hookups (electricity and water) for tents or RVs up to 45 feet long; eight are drive-through sites. Picnic tables and fire grills are provided. Drinking water, flush toilets, showers, an RV dump station, a public telephone, and a playground are available. Some facilities are wheelchair accessible. Campground programs are available in the summer. Boat docks, launching facilities, a swimming beach, and group shelters with electricity are nearby. Leashed pets are permitted.

Reservations, fees: Reservations accepted; phone 877/444-6777 or access the website: www.ReserveUsa.com ($9 reservation fee). Sites are $12–18 per night, and boat camping is $7 per night. Senior discount available. Open April–September. Park gates are locked from 10 P.M.–6 A.M.

Directions: In Pasco, drive southeast on U.S. 12 for five miles to Highway 124. Turn east and drive 18 miles to Fishhook Park Road. Turn left on Fishhook Park Road and drive four miles to the park.

Contact: U.S. Army Corps of Engineers, 2763 Monument Dr., Burbank, WA 99323, 509/547-7781, fax 509/543-3201.

34 WINDUST

Rating: 6

On Lake Sacajawea.

Map 6.7, grid d4, page 386

With no other campgrounds within a 20-mile radius, Windust is the only game in town. The camp is located along the shore of Lake Sacajawea near the Lower Monumental Dam on the Snake River. The park covers 54 acres. Swimming, water-skiing, and fishing are popular.

Campsites, facilities: Open camping areas at both ends of the park provide space for 24 tents or RVs. Picnic tables and fire grills are provided. Vault toilets and garbage bins are available year-round. Flush toilets are available from April–September. Drinking water, a playground and horseshoe pit, a swimming beach, covered sun shelters, and a public telephone are available nearby. Some facilities are wheelchair accessible. Boat docks and launching facilities are nearby. Leashed pets are permitted.

Reservations, fees: Reservations accepted; phone 877/444-6777 or access the website: www.ReserveUsa.com ($9 reservation fee). Sites are $10 per night, and boat camping is $7 per night. Senior discount available. Open year-round, with limited facilities and no fee from October–March.

Directions: From Pasco, drive east on U.S. 12 for four miles to Pasco/Kahlotus Highway. Turn east and drive 28 miles to Burr Canyon Road. Turn right on Burr Canyon Road and drive 5.2 miles to the park (from the north, Burr Canyon Road becomes Highway 263).

Contact: U.S. Army Corps of Engineers, 2763 Monument Dr., Burbank, WA 99323, 509/547-7781, fax 509/543-3201.

35 PALOUSE FALLS STATE PARK

Rating: 10

On the Snake and Palouse Rivers.

Map 6.7, grid c7, page 386

This remote state park is well worth the trip.

Spectacular 198-foot Palouse Falls is a sight not to miss. A quarter-mile wheelchair-accessible trail leads to a waterfall overlook. The park is set at the confluence of the Snake and Palouse Rivers, and it does not receive heavy use, even in summer. The park covers 1,282 acres and features a waterfall observation shelter, shaded picnic facilities, historical displays, and an abundance of wildlife.

Campsites, facilities: There are 10 primitive campsites for tents or self-contained RVs up to 40 feet long. Picnic tables and fire grills are provided. Pit toilets, a picnic area, and an RV dump station are available. Some facilities are wheelchair accessible. Leashed pets are permitted.

Reservations, fees: Reservations are not accepted. Sites are $8 per night, $6 per extra vehicle per night. Senior discount available. Open April–late September, weather permitting.

Directions: From Starbuck, drive northwest on Highway 261 for 16.4 miles (crossing the river) to the park entrance and Palouse Falls Road. Turn right and drive to the park.

Contact: Palouse Falls State Park, 509/646-3252, fax 509/646-3297; State Park information, 360/902-8844.

36 LYON'S FERRY STATE PARK

Rating: 8

On the Snake River.

Map 6.7, grid d7, page 386

This state park covers 1,282 acres, is located at the confluence of the Snake and Palouse Rivers. Although not a high-destination park, it is loaded with activities. A three-quarter-mile trail leads to a lookout point with interpretive plaques. In addition, another short hike from camp can take you to the Marmes Rock Shelter, where the Marmes Man—the oldest human remains ever found in the Western hemisphere—was unearthed in 1968. Many other recreation options include boating, fishing, swimming, and waterskiing. Note that high winds can occur suddenly and surprise many boaters. Another feature is the nearby terrain. The park is part of hundreds of square miles of "peeled ground," which span west from Spokane to the Cascades and south to the Snake River and which some geologists call "the strangest landscape this side of Mars." A good side trip is a visit to beautiful 198-foot Palouse Falls, located 10 miles north. Note that because of state budget problems, there were discussions in early 2003 of closing this campground; call for status.

Campsites, facilities: There are 49 sites, including 12 pull-through sites with full hookups, for tents or RVs up to 45 feet long and two primitive tent sites. Picnic tables and fire grills are provided. Restrooms, flush toilets, coin-operated showers, and an RV dump station are available. A bathhouse, a sheltered picnic area, a snack bar, a boat dock, and a boat launch and moorage are available nearby. Some facilities are wheelchair accessible. Leashed pets are permitted.

Reservations, fees: Reservations are not accepted. Sites are $15 per night, $6 per extra vehicle per night. The moorage fee is $7–16 per night. Senior discount available. Open April–September.

Directions: From Starbuck, drive northwest on Highway 261 for 14.2 miles (crossing the river) to the park entrance (just north of the river on the right). Turn right and drive to the park.

Contact: Lyon's Ferry State Park, 509/646-3252, fax 509/646-3297; State Park information, 360/902-8844.

37 LEWIS AND CLARK TRAIL STATE PARK

Rating: 8

On the Lewis and Clark Trail.

Map 6.7, grid f8, page 386

Fishing for rainbow trout and brown trout can be excellent here. The park is set on 37 acres with frontage along the Touchet River. The landscape is an unusual mixture of old-growth forest and riparian habitat, featuring long-leafed Ponderosa pine and cottonwood amid the surrounding arid prairie grasslands. An interpretive display explains much of it, as well as the history of the area. A Saturday evening living-history program depicts the story of Lewis and Clark and the site's history here on the original Lewis and Clark Trail. Also note: If it's getting late and you need to stop, consider this camp because it's the only one within 20 miles. In winter, cross-country skiing and snow-shoeing are good here.

Campsites, facilities: There are 25 sites for tents or self-contained RVs up to 28 feet long and four primitive tent sites. Picnic tables and fire grills are provided. Restrooms, flush toilets, showers, firewood, and an RV dump station are available. Two fire circles, an amphitheater, a picnic area, badminton, a baseball field, and a volleyball court are available nearby. A store, a café, and ice are located within one mile. Leashed pets are permitted.

Reservations, fees: Reservations are not accepted. Sites are $6–15 per night, $6 per extra vehicle per night. Open year-round, with limited winter facilities.

Directions: From Walla Walla, drive east on U.S. 12 for 22 miles to Waitsburg. Bear right on U.S. 12 and drive east for 4.5 miles to the park entrance on the left.

Contact: Lewis and Clark Trail State Park, Rte. 1, P.O. Box 90, Dayton, WA 99328, 509/337-6457; State Park information, 360/902-8844.

38 CENTRAL FERRY STATE PARK

Rating: 8

On the Snake River.
Map 6.8, grid c2, page 387

This campground is the only one within a 20-mile radius, yet it's a great spot to hunker down and enjoy the world. This 185-acre park is set on 10,000-acre Lake Bryan, a reservoir situated on the Snake River and created by Little Goose Dam. With summer daytime temperatures in the 90s and even 100s occasionally, boating is popular at the desert lake. Despite the lake, the surrounding terrain is dry, courtesy of just eight inches of average rainfall per year, as well as basaltic lava flows, according to geologic evidence. The park is named after a ferry that once operated in this area. A beach, swimming, boating, water-skiing, swimming, and fishing for bass and catfish are all options here. Navigational locks are on the lake. Note that because of state budget problems, there were discussions in early 2003 of closing this campground; call for status.

Campsites, facilities: There are eight primitive tent sites and 60 sites with full hookups for RVs up to 45 feet long. There is also one group camp accommodating up to 100 people. Picnic tables and fire grills are provided. Restrooms, flush toilets, coin-operated showers, an RV dump station, a group fire ring, a day-use picnic area with a covered kitchen shelter, a swimming beach and bathhouse, beachside shade structures, volleyball courts, and three horseshoe pit areas are available. A store and a restaurant are within five miles. Some facilities are wheelchair accessible. Boat docks, launching facilities, and a fishing pier are within the park. Leashed pets are permitted.

Reservations, fees: Reserve at 888/CAMP-OUT (888/226-7688), website: www.parks.wa.gov/reservations ($7 reservation fee). Sites are $8–22 per night, $6 per extra vehicle per night. Senior discount available. For group camp reservations, phone 509/549-3551; group sites are $25 per night plus $2 per night per camper and $13 per night per RV. Major credit cards accepted. Open mid-March–mid-November.

Directions: From Spokane, drive south on U.S. 195 for 59 miles to Highway 26. Turn west on Highway 26 and drive 17 miles southwest to the town of Dusty and Highway 127. Turn south on Highway 127 and drive 17 miles to the park entrance on the right (set on the north shore of the Snake River).

Contact: Central Ferry State Park, 10152 Rte. 127, Pomeroy, WA 99347, 509/549-3551, 509/549-3645; State Park information, 360/902-8844.

39 PALOUSE EMPIRE FAIRGROUNDS & HORSE CAMP

Rating: 6

West of Colfax, Whitman County.
Map 6.8, grid b5, page 387

The camp consists primarily of a large lawn area with shade trees and is set just off the road. The highway noise, surprisingly, is relatively limited. All sites are on grass. The park covers 47 acres, with paved trails available around the adjacent fairgrounds. This area is agricultural, with rolling hills, and it is considered the "Lentil Capital of the World." With wash racks, corrals, arenas, and water troughs, the camp encourages horse campers to stay here. It fills up for the Whitman County Fair in mid-September. They turn back the clock every Labor Day weekend with the annual "Threshing Bee," where there are demonstrations of historical farming practices dating back to the early 1900s, including the use of draft horses.

Campsites, facilities: There are 60 sites with partial hookups (water and electricity) for tents or RVs of any length. Large groups can be accommodated. Picnic tables are provided. Restrooms, drinking water, flush toilets, showers, and an RV dump station are available. Some facilities are wheelchair accessible. Restaurants, gas, and supplies are available 4.5 miles away in Colfax. Leashed pets are permitted.

Reservations, fees: Reservations are not accepted. Sites are $15 per night, horse stalls $10 per night. Open year-round with limited winter facilities.

Directions: From Colfax and Highway 26, drive west on Highway 26 for 4.5 miles to the fairgrounds on the right.

Contact: Palouse Empire Fairgrounds & Horse Camp, Whitman County, North 310 Main, Colfax, WA 99111, 509/397-6238, 509/397-3753, website: www.whitmancounty.org.

40 BOYER PARK AND MARINA

Rating: 7

On Lake Bryan on the Snake River.
Map 6.8, grid c5, page 387

This 99-acre park on the north shore of Lake Bryan is located two miles from the Lower Granite Dam. It features 3.5 miles of trails for hiking and biking, and the lake is popular for water-skiing and fishing for sturgeon, steelhead, and salmon. The camp features shade trees; all campsites are paved and bordered by a grassy day-use area. The landscape is flat and open, and it gets hot here in summer. The camp is well above the water level, typically about 100 feet above the lakeshore. The camp commonly fills on summer weekends.

Campsites, facilities: There are 28 sites, including 12 with full hookups and 16 with partial hookups (no sewer) for tents or RVs up to 40 feet long. Picnic tables and fire grills are provided. Restrooms, drinking water, flush toilets, showers, and an RV dump station are available. Some facilities are wheelchair accessible. A coin-operated laundry, covered shelters, a swimming area, a snack bar, a store, ice, gas, and public phones are available. A restaurant, a marina, boat docks, a boat launch, and a marine dump station are nearby. Leashed pets are permitted.

Reservations, fees: Reservations at 509/397-3208; sites are $10–22 per night, $2 per person for more than four people, and $5 per tent for more than two tents. Senior discount available. Major credit cards accepted. Open year-round, with limited winter facilities.

Directions: From U.S. 195 at Colfax, turn southwest on Almota Road and drive 17 miles to the park and campground.

Contact: Port of Whitman County, West 105 Island St., Colfax, WA 99111, 509/397-3208 or 509/397-3791, fax 509/397-6569, website: www.boyerpark.com.

41 WAWAWAI COUNTY PARK

Rating: 7

On Lower Granite Lake, Whitman County.
Map 6.8, grid c6, page 387

This park covers just 49 acres but is set near the inlet to Lower Granite Lake, about one-quarter mile from the lake. The camp itself is situated on a hillside, and all sites are paved. Some sites have views of a bay, but not the entire lake. Tree cover is a plus. So is a half-mile loop trail that leads to a bird-viewing platform, and a diverse mix of wildlife and geology, making interpretive hikes with naturalists often popular. One strange note: An underground house built in 1980 has been converted to a ranger's residence. This camp often fills on summer weekends.

Campsites, facilities: There are nine sites for tents or self-contained RVs up to 24 feet long. No hookups are available. Picnic tables and fire grills are provided. Drinking water and vault toilets are available. A playground with a volleyball net and a group covered shelter is available nearby. Some facilities are wheelchair accessible. Leashed pets are permitted.

Reservations, fees: Reservations are not accepted; sites are $10 per night, $5 per extra vehicle. Open year-round, with limited winter facilities and no fee from mid-October–mid-April.

Directions: From Colfax, drive south on U.S. 195 for 16 miles to Wawawai-Pullman Road (located just west of Pullman). Turn right (west) and drive about 10 miles to Wawawai Road. Turn right on Wawawai Road (signed) and drive to the park on Lower Granite Lake.

Contact: Wawawai County Park, Whitman County, North 310 Main, Colfax, WA 99111, 509/397-6238, website: www.whitmancounty.org.

42 CHIEF TIMOTHY STATE PARK

Rating: 8

On the Snake River.
Map 6.8, grid e7, page 387

This unusual state park is set on a bridged island in the Snake River and is accessible by car. The park covers 282 acres with two miles of shoreline. It features a desert landscape, and the park is set on an island composed of glacial tills. There are 2.5 miles of hiking trails, water sports, including fishing, swimming, boating, water-skiing, and sailing, plus docks for boating campers, a beach area, and an interpretive center focusing on the Lewis and Clark expedition. Outfitters in Clarkston will take you sightseeing up the Grand Canyon of the Snake River. Call the Clarkston Chamber of Commerce at 509/758-7712 for details. Note that because of state budget problems, there were discussions in early 2003 of closing this campground; call for status.

Campsites, facilities: There are 58 sites, including 25 with full hookups and eight with partial hookups (water and electricity) for tents or RVs up to 60 feet long and two primitive tent sites. Picnic tables and fire grills are provided. Restrooms, flush toilets, showers, an RV dump station, a picnic area, a small store, and a playground with volleyball courts and horseshoe pits are available. Firewood can be obtained for a fee. Some facilities are wheelchair accessible. Boat docks and launching facilities are nearby. Leashed pets are permitted.

Reservations, fees: Reserve at 888/CAMP-OUT (888/226-7688), website: www.parks.wa.gov/reservations ($7 reservation fee). Sites are $6–22 per night, $6 per extra vehicle per night. Senior discount available. Major credit cards accepted. Open year-round, with limited winter facilities.

Directions: From Clarkston on the Washington/Idaho border, drive west on U.S. 12 for seven miles to the signed park entrance road

on the right. Turn north and drive one mile to
the park, which is set on a bridged island in
the Snake River.

Contact: Chief Timothy State Park, Hwy. 12,
Clarkston, WA 99403, 509/758-9580; State
Park information, 360/902-8844.

43 TUCANNON

Rating: 8

In Umatilla National Forest.
Map 6.8, grid f3, page 387

For people willing to rough it, this backcountry camp in Umatilla National Forest is the
place, with plenty of hiking, fishing, and hunting, all in a rugged setting. The camp is set
along the Tucannon River, which offers a myriad of recreation options for vacationers. It is
popular from early spring (best time for fishing) through fall (when it makes a good hunting camp). In summer, several nearby ponds
are stocked with trout, making it a good family destination. There is some tree cover. The
elevation is 2,600 feet.

Campsites, facilities: There are 13 sites for tents
or RVs up to 21 feet long. Picnic tables and
fire grills are provided. Vault toilets are available, but there is no drinking water. Garbage
must be packed out. Two covered shelters are
available nearby. Leashed pets are permitted.

Reservations, fees: Reservations are not accepted. There is no fee for camping. Open year-
round, weather permitting.

Directions: From Clarkston, drive west on U.S.
12 for 37 miles to Pomeroy. Continue west for
five miles to Tatman Mountain Road (signed
for Camp Wooten). Turn left (south) and drive
19 miles (becomes Forest Road 47). Once inside the national forest boundary, continue
southwest on Forest Road 47 for four miles
to the campground on the left.

Contact: Umatilla National Forest, Pomeroy
Ranger District, 71 West Main St., Pomeroy,
WA 99347, 509/843-1891, fax 509/843-4621.

44 ALDER THICKET

Rating: 7

In Umatilla National Forest.
Map 6.8, grid f4, page 387

This is probably the first time you've heard of
this place. Hardly anybody knows about it, including people who live relatively nearby in
Walla Walla. It is set at an elevation of 5,100
feet, making it a prime base camp for a backcountry hiking adventure in summer or a jumping-off point for a hunting trip in the fall. This
is a primitive camp, but it's great if you're looking for quiet and solitude. Note: During summer, drinking water is available six miles away
at the Clearwater Guard Station.

Campsites, facilities: There are five sites for
tents or RVs up to 21 feet long. Picnic tables
and fire grills are provided. Vault toilets are
available, but there is no drinking water. Garbage
must be packed out. Some facilities are wheelchair accessible. Leashed pets are permitted.

Reservations, fees: Reservations are not accepted. There is no fee for camping. Open mid-
May–mid-November, weather permitting.

Directions: From Clarkston, drive west on U.S.
12 for 37 miles to Pomeroy and Highway 128.
Turn south and drive seven miles to a fork. At
the fork, continue straight to Forest Road 40
(15 miles from Pomeroy to the national forest
boundary) and drive 3.5 miles to the campground on the right.

Contact: Umatilla National Forest, Pomeroy
Ranger District, 71 West Main St., Pomeroy,
WA 99347, 509/843-1891, fax 509/843-4621.

45 BIG SPRINGS

Rating: 8

In Umatilla National Forest.
Map 6.8, grid f4, page 387

This camp is set at an elevation of 5,000 feet.
In the fall, primarily hunters use Big Springs,
while come summer, this nice, cool site becomes

a possible base camp for backpacking trips. Although quite primitive with little in the way of activity options, this is a perfect spot to get away from it all. It's advisable to obtain a U.S. Forest Service map. During summer, drinking water is available at the Clearwater Guard Station, located three miles to the southwest on Forest Road 42.

Campsites, facilities: There are eight tent sites. Picnic tables are provided. Vault toilets are available, but there is no drinking water. Some facilities are wheelchair accessible. Leashed pets are permitted.

Reservations, fees: Reservations are not accepted. There is no fee for camping. Open mid-May–early December, weather permitting.

Directions: From Clarkston, drive west on U.S. 12 for 37 miles to Pomeroy and Highway 128. Turn south and drive 25 miles to Forest Road 42 (to the Clearwater Lookout Tower). Turn left and continue on Forest Road 42 for five miles to the campground entrance road (Forest Road 4225). Turn left and drive to the campground at the end of the road.

Contact: Umatilla National Forest, Pomeroy Ranger District, 71 West Main St., Pomeroy, WA 99347, 509/843-1891, fax 509/843-4621.

46 TEAL SPRING

Rating: 8

In Umatilla National Forest.
Map 6.8, grid g4, page 387

The views of the Tucannun drainage and the Wenaha-Tucannon Wilderness are astonishing from the nearby lookout. Teal Springs Camp is set at 5,600 feet elevation and is one of several small, primitive camps in the area. Trails in the immediate area provide a variety of good day-hiking options. A U.S. Forest Service map details the backcountry roads, trails, and streams. Hunting is popular in the fall.

Campsites, facilities: There are five sites for tents or RVs up to 26 feet long. Vault toilets are available, but there is no drinking water.

Picnic tables and fire grills are provided. Garbage must be packed out. Some facilities are wheelchair accessible. Leashed pets are permitted.

Reservations, fees: Reservations are not accepted. There is no fee for camping. Open June–early December, weather permitting.

Directions: From Clarkston, drive west on U.S. 12 for 37 miles to Pomeroy and Highway 128. Turn south and drive 25 miles to Forest Road 42 (to the Clearwater Lookout Tower). Turn left and continue on Forest Road 42; drive one mile to the campground entrance road. Turn right and drive 200 yards to the campground.

Contact: Umatilla National Forest, Pomeroy Ranger District, 71 West Main St., Pomeroy, WA 99347, 509/843-1891, fax 509/843-4621.

47 GODMAN

Rating: 8

Near the Wenaha-Tucannon Wilderness in Umatilla National Forest.
Map 6.8, grid h2, page 387

This tiny, little-known spot bordering a wilderness area is set at 6,050 feet elevation and features drop-dead gorgeous views at sunset, as well as a wilderness trailhead. It is primarily used as a base camp for backcountry expeditions. A trailhead provides access to the Wenaha-Tucannon Wilderness for both hikers and horseback riders. Horse facilities are available less than one-quarter mile away. There are also opportunities for mountain biking, but note that bikes are forbidden past the wilderness boundary. A bonus here is a primitive cabin available year-round, including in winter when it's accessible only by snowmobile.

Campsites, facilities: There are eight sites for tents or RVs up to 15 feet long, plus one cabin that can accommodate up to eight people. Picnic tables and fire grills are provided. Vault toilets are available, but there is no drinking water. Garbage must be packed out. Some facilities are wheelchair accessible. Facilities, including hitching rails and a spring, are available nearby for up to six people with horses, with an additional fee for more than six. Leashed pets are permitted.

Reservations, fees: Reservations are not accepted. There is no fee for the campsites, but cabins are $30 a night plus $5 per person. Open mid-June–late October; cabin is available year-round.

Directions: From Walla Walla, drive northeast on U.S. 12 for 32 miles to Dayton and North Fork Touchet River Road. Turn right on North Fork Touchet River Road and drive 14 miles southeast to the national forest boundary; continue to Kendall Skyline Road. Turn left (south) and drive 11 miles to the campground on the left.

Contact: Umatilla National Forest, Pomeroy Ranger District, 71 West Main St., Pomeroy, WA 99347, 509/843-1891, fax 509/843-4621.

48 FIELDS SPRING STATE PARK

Rating: 8

Near Puffer Butte.
Map 6.8, grid h7, page 387

This 792-acre state park is located in the Blue Mountains and is set in a forested landscape atop Puffer Butte, offering a spectacular view of three states and the Grande Ronde River. A hiking trail leads up to Puffer Butte at 4,500 feet elevation, providing a panoramic view of the Snake River Canyon, the Wallowa Mountains, and Idaho, Oregon, and Washington. This park is noted for its variety of bird life and wildflowers. There are seven miles of mountain-biking trails, along with three miles of hiking trails. In winter, recreation opportunities include cross-country skiing, snowmobiling, snowshoeing, and general snow play. Basalt dominates the landscape. Not many people know about this spot, yet it's a good one, tucked away in the southeast corner of the state. It also has a designated environmental learning center. Two day-use areas with boat launches, managed by the Department of Fish and Game, are within about 25 miles of the park. One is the Snake River Access, 22.5 miles south of Asotin on Snake River Road; the other is the Grande Ronde River Access, 24 miles south of Asotin on the same road.

Campsites, facilities: There are 20 sites for tents or self-contained RVs up to 30 feet long, four primitive tent site and teepees. Picnic tables and fire grills are provided. Restrooms, drinking water, flush toilets, an RV dump station, two picnic shelters with electricity, two sheltered fire circles, a playground with horseshoe pits, a softball field, and volleyball courts are available. Showers and firewood are available for a fee. A store, a restaurant, and ice are located within one mile. Some facilities are wheelchair accessible. Leashed pets are permitted.

Reservations, fees: Reservations are not accepted. Sites are $6–16 per night, $6 per extra vehicle per night. Senior discount available. Open year-round, with limited winter facilities.

Directions: From Clarkston, turn south on Highway 129 and drive 28.5 miles (just south of Rattlesnake Pass) to the park entrance on the left (east) side of the road.

Contact: Fields Spring State Park, P.O. Box 86, Anatone, WA 99401, 509/256-3332; State Park information, 360/902-8844.

49 BROOKS MEMORIAL STATE PARK

Rating: 7

Near the Goldendale Observatory.
Map 6.9, grid a3, page 388

This 700-acre park is located between the barren hills of the South Yakima Valley and the lodgepole pine forests of the Simcoe Mountains. It is set at an elevation of nearly 3,000 feet. Highlights include nine miles of hiking trails, a 1.5-mile-long nature trail that runs along the Little Klickitat River, and occasionally excellent fishing for trout. You can extend your trip into the mountains, where you'll find open meadows with a panoramic view of Mt. Hood. The environmental learning center provides nature talks. Other activities near the park include stargazing at the Goldendale Observatory, visiting the Maryhill Museum, viewing the replica of Stonehenge on State Route 14, and driving the historic Columbia Highway in nearby Oregon. The Yakima Indian Nation is located two miles north of the park.

Campsites, facilities: There are 22 developed sites for tents or self-contained RVs, 23 sites with water and electrical hookups for RVs up to 50 feet long, and two primitive tent sites. Picnic tables and fire grills are provided. Restrooms, flush toilets, an RV dump station, and a playground are available. Showers are available for a fee. A picnic area with covered shelters and electricity and a ball field are nearby. A store is located within one mile. Leashed pets are permitted.

Reservations, fees: Reservations are not accepted. Sites are $6–22 per night, $6 per extra vehicle per night. Open year-round, with limited winter facilities.

Directions: From Toppenish, drive south on U.S. 97 for 40 miles to the park on the right (well signed).

Contact: Brooks Memorial State Park, 509/773-4611; State Park information, 360/902-8844.

50 CROW BUTTE STATE PARK

Rating: 8

On the Columbia River.
Map 6.10, grid b2, page 389

How would you like to be stranded on a romantic island? Well, this park offers that possibility. This state park is set on an island in the Columbia River and is the only campground in a 25-mile radius. Sometimes referred to as "The Maui of the Columbia," the park covers 1,312 acres and has several miles of shoreline.

It is set on the Lewis and Clark Trail, with the camp situated in a partially protected bay. The highlight of 3.5 miles of hiking trails is a mile-long path that leads to the top of a butte, where you can see Mt. Hood, Mt. Adams, and the Columbia River Valley. Water-skiing, sailboarding, fishing, swimming, and hiking are among the possibilities here. One downer: Keep an eye out for rattlesnakes, which are occasionally spotted. The Umatilla National Wildlife Refuge is adjacent to the park and allows fishing and hunting in specified areas. Note that because of state budget problems, there were discussions in early 2003 of closing this campground; call for status.

Campsites, facilities: There are two primitive tent sites and 50 sites with full hookups for tents or RVs up to 60 feet long, including 24 pull-through sites, and one group camp. Fire grills and picnic tables are provided. Restrooms, flush toilets, coin-operated showers, a sheltered picnic area, a swimming beach, and an RV dump station are available. Some facilities are wheelchair accessible. Boat-launching and moorage facilities are nearby. A store is open on weekends. Leashed pets are permitted.

Reservations, fees: Reserve at 888/CAMP-OUT (888/226-7688), website: www.parks.wa.gov/reservations ($7 reservation fee); $15–16 per night for tent sites; $21–22 per night for RV sites, $6 per extra vehicle per night. The group site is $35 plus $10 per person. Moorage fees are $7–16 per night. Senior discount available. Open year-round, with limited winter facilities.

Directions: From the junction of I-82/U.S. 395 and Highway 20 at Plymouth, just north of the Columbia River, turn west on Highway 14. Drive to Paterson and continue west for 13 miles to the park entrance road at Milepost 155 on the right. Turn right and drive one mile (across the bridge) to the park on the island.

Contact: Crow Butte State Park, 509/875-2644; State Park information, 360/902-8844.

51 PLYMOUTH PARK

Rating: 7

On Lake Umatilla, Benton County.
Map 6.10, grid a6, page 389

Plymouth Park is a family and RV-style campground set on Lake Umatilla on the Columbia River. The 112-acre park is not located on the shore of the lake, rather about a quarter-mile drive from the water. The camp has tree cover, which is a nice plus, and it fills up on most summer weekends. Each campsite has a tent pad.

Campsites, facilities: There are 32 sites, including 28 pull-through sites and 16 with partial hookups (no sewer), for tents or RVs up to 40 feet long. Picnic tables and fire grills are provided. Restrooms, drinking water, flush toilets, showers, an RV dump station, and a coin-operated laundry are available. A boat dock, boat launch, swimming areas, and covered shelters are available nearby. A store and a restaurant are within two miles. Some facilities are wheelchair accessible. Leashed pets are permitted.

Reservations, fees: Reserve at 877/444-6777 ($9 reservation fee) or website: www.ReserveUsa.com. Sites are $16–18 per night. Senior discount available. Major credit cards accepted. Open April–October.

Directions: From Richland and I-82, drive south on I-82 for about 30 miles to Highway 14. Turn west on Highway 14 and drive two miles to the Plymouth exit. Take that exit and drive to Christy Road; continue for 200 yards to the park entrance on the left.

Contact: U.S. Army Corps of Engineers, Portland District, 509/783-1270 or 541/506-7818.

Oregon

Chapter 7
The Oregon Coast

Chapter 7—The Oregon Coast

If you want to treat yourself to vacation memories you'll treasure forever, take a drive (and then set up camp) along U.S. 101 on the Oregon Coast. Here you'll see some of the most dramatic coastal frontage in North America: tidewater rock gardens, cliff-top views that seem to stretch to forever, vast sand dunes, protected bays, beautiful streams with giant salmon and steelhead (in fall and winter), and three major national forests. I prefer cruising north to south, in the right lane close to the coastline and with the wind behind me; it often seems I'm on the edge of never-never land.

On the way, you'll cross the Columbia River on the border of Oregon and Washington. The river is so wide here that it looks like an inland sea. I find that the best way to appreciate this massive waterway is to get off the main highway and explore the many coastal streams by two-lane road. There are numerous routes, from tiny Highway 15 on the Little Nestucca River, to well-known Highway 38 along the beautiful Umpqua.

The most spectacular region on the coast may be the Oregon Dunes National Recreation Area, which spans roughly from Coos Bay north past Florence to near the mouth of the Siuslaw River. Whenever I visit, I feel like I'm instantly transported to another universe. I have a photo of the dunes in my office. While I'm writing, I often look at the image of a lone raptor soaring past a pyramid of sand—it's my window to this wonderful otherworld.

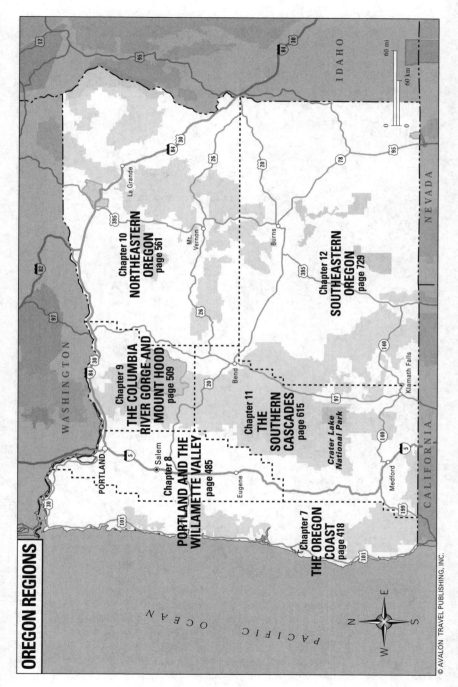

OREGON REGIONS

WASHINGTON

PACIFIC OCEAN

PORTLAND

Salem

Eugene

Medford

Chapter 8
PORTLAND AND THE
WILLAMETTE VALLEY
page 485

Chapter 9
THE COLUMBIA
RIVER GORGE AND
MOUNT HOOD:
page 509

Chapter 10
NORTHEASTERN
OREGON
page 561

La Grande

Mt.
Vernon

Burns

Chapter 11
THE
SOUTHERN
CASCADES
page 615

Crater Lake
National Park

Chapter 12
SOUTHEASTERN
OREGON
page 729

Klamath Falls

Chapter 7
THE OREGON
COAST
page 418

IDAHO

NEVADA

CALIFORNIA

0   60 mi

0   60 km

N
W   E
S

© AVALON TRAVEL PUBLISHING, INC.

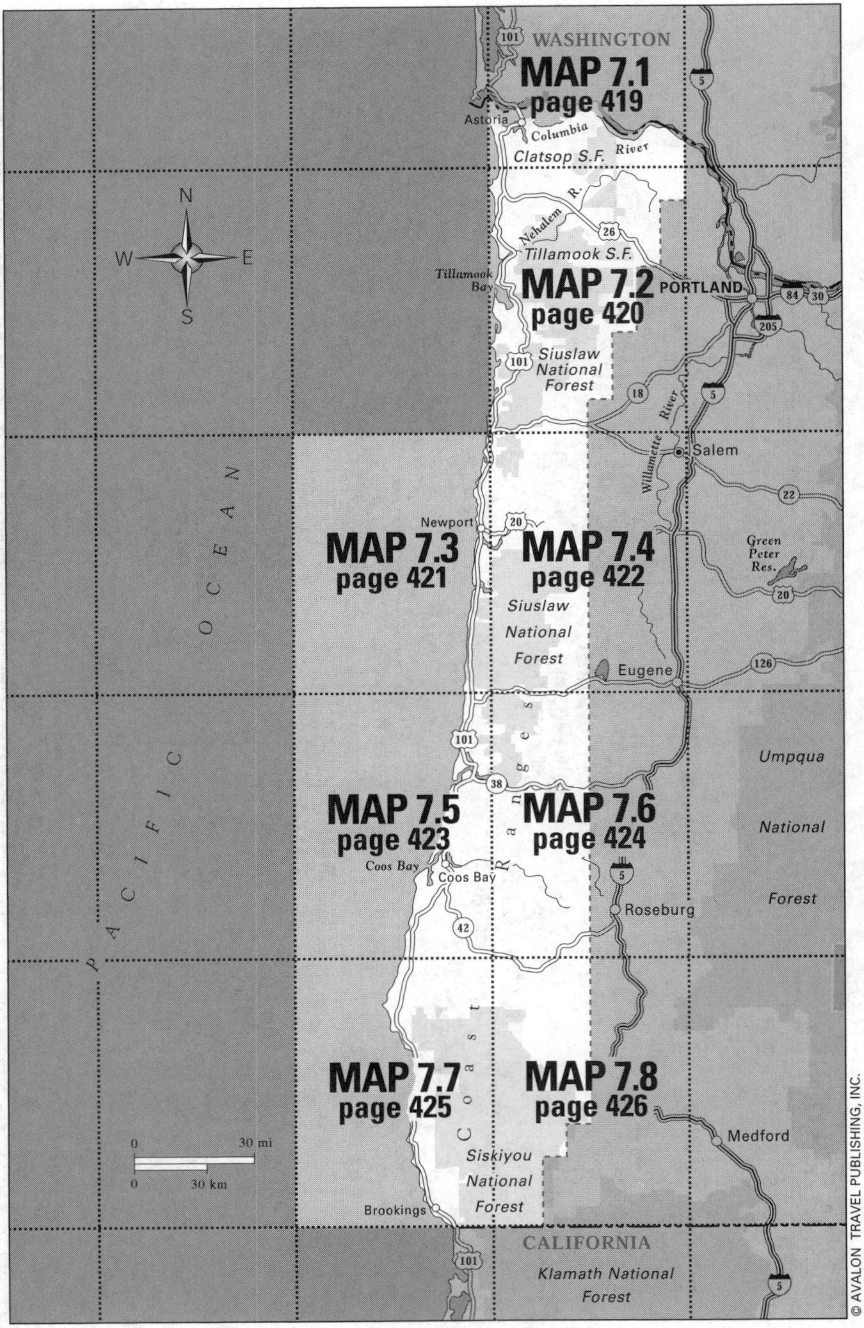
WASHINGTON
MAP 7.1
page 419
Astoria
Columbia River
Clatsop S.F.
Nehalem R.
Tillamook S.F.
Tillamook Bay
MAP 7.2
page 420
PORTLAND
Siuslaw National Forest
Willamette River
Salem
N
S
W
E
PACIFIC OCEAN
Newport
MAP 7.3
page 421
MAP 7.4
page 422
Green Peter Res.
Siuslaw National Forest
Eugene
Coast Ranges
Umpqua National Forest
MAP 7.5
page 423
MAP 7.6
page 424
Coos Bay
Coos Bay
Roseburg
MAP 7.7
page 425
MAP 7.8
page 426
Medford
0
30 mi
0
30 km
Siskiyou National Forest
Brookings
CALIFORNIA
Klamath National Forest
© AVALON TRAVEL PUBLISHING, INC.

Map 7.1

Campgrounds 1–3
Pages 427–428

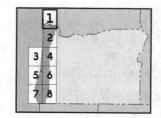

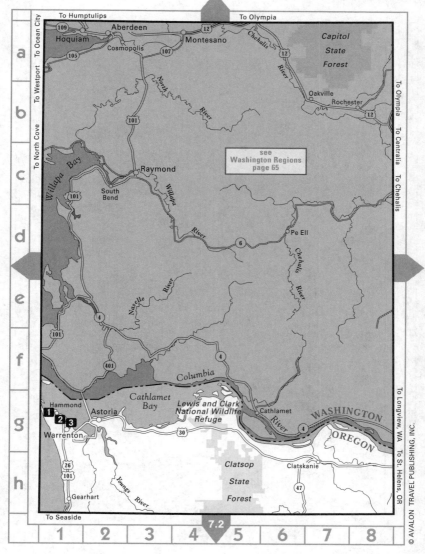

To Humptulips
To Olympia
To Ocean City
To Westport
To North Cove

To Humptulips

Aberdeen
Hoquiam
Cosmopolis
Montesano
Chehalis
River

Capitol
State
Forest

Oakville
Rochester

To Olympia
To Centralia
To Chehalis

North
River

Raymond

Willapa Bay

South
Bend

Willapa
River

see
Washington Regions
page 65

Pe Ell

Chehalis
River

Naselle
River

Columbia

Cathlamet
Bay

Lewis and Clark
National Wildlife
Refuge

Cathlamet

WASHINGTON

Hammond
Astoria
Warrenton

OREGON

To Longview, WA To St. Helens, OR

Clatskanie

Clatsop

State

Forest

Gearhart

Youngs River

To Seaside

7.2

© AVALON TRAVEL PUBLISHING, INC.

Map 7.2

Campgrounds 4–31
Pages 428–439

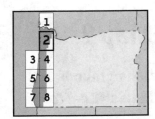

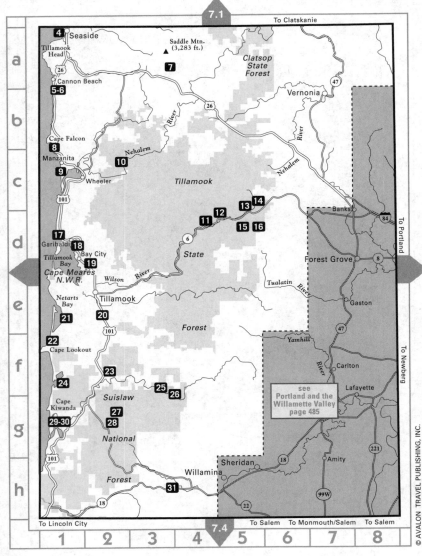

© AVALON TRAVEL PUBLISHING, INC.

Map 7.3

Campgrounds 32–54
Pages 439–448

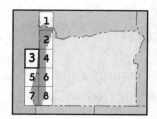

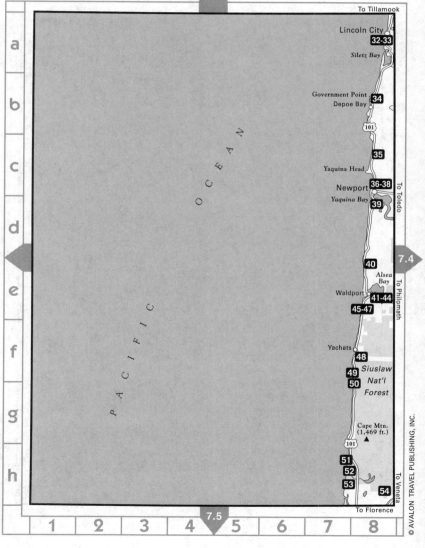

To Tillamook

Lincoln City
32-33

Siletz Bay

Government Point **34**
Depoe Bay

101

35

Yaquina Head

Newport **36-38**
Yaquina Bay **39**

To Toledo

7.4

40
Alsea Bay

Waldport **41-44**

To Philomath

45-47

Yachats

48

49 *Siuslaw*
50 *Nat'l Forest*

Cape Mtn.
(1,469 ft.)
101 ▲

To Veneta

51
52
53 **54**

To Florence

7.5

© AVALON TRAVEL PUBLISHING, INC.

OCEAN

PACIFIC

Map 7.4

Campgrounds 55–59
Pages 448–450

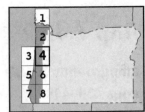

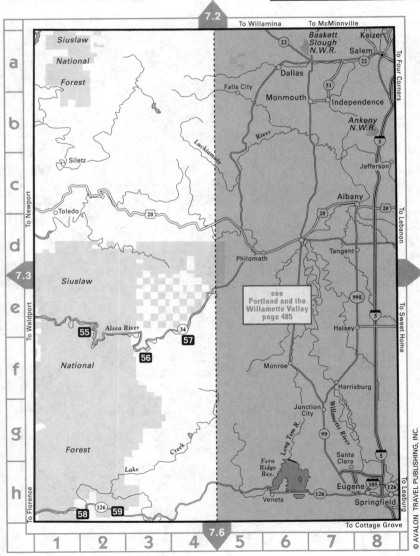

To Willamina   To McMinnville

7.2

Siuslaw National Forest

Baskett Slough N.W.R.

Keizer

Salem

22

Dallas

51

Falls City

Monmouth

Independence

Siletz

Ankeny N.W.R.

Luckiamute River

Jefferson

5

Toledo

20

Albany

To Newport

20

20

To Lebanon

Philomath

Tangent

Siuslaw

7.3

see Portland and the Willamette Valley page 485

99E

To Waldport

55   Alsea River   34

57

56

Halsey

5

To Sweet Home

National

Monroe

Forest

Harrisburg

Junction City

99

Willamette River

Creek

Long Tom R.

Santa Clara

5

Lake

Fern Ridge Res.

Eugene

105   126

To Florence

58   126   59

Veneta

126

Springfield

To Leaburg

To Cottage Grove

7.6

1   2   3   4   5   6   7   8

© AVALON TRAVEL PUBLISHING, INC.

Map 7.5

Campgrounds 60–94
Pages 450–465

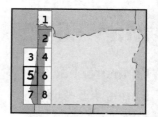

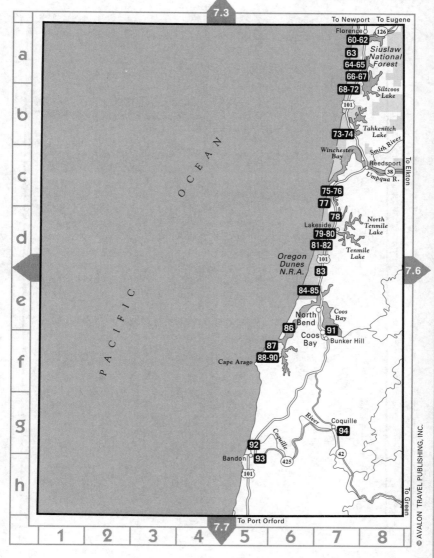

© AVALON TRAVEL PUBLISHING, INC.

Map 7.6

Campgrounds 95–98
Pages 465–466

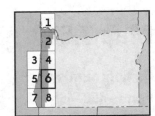

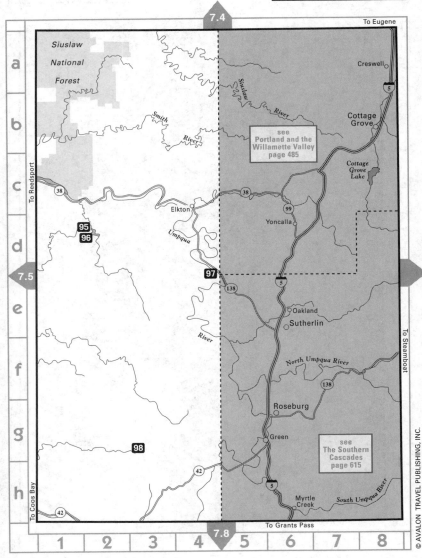

Map 7.7

Campgrounds 99–132
Pages 466–480

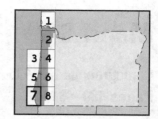

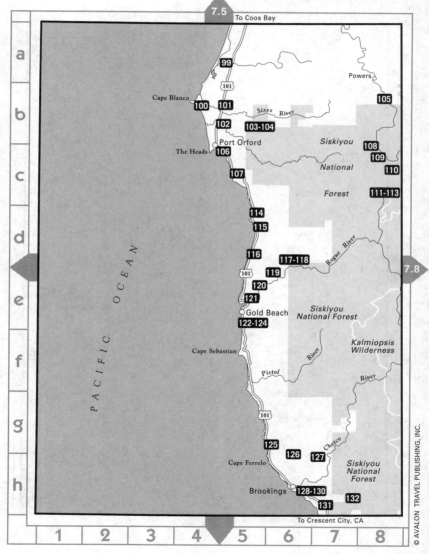

7.5

To Coos Bay

99

101

Powers

Cape Blanco

100 101

Sixes River

105

102

103-104

Siskiyou

108

Port Orford

109

The Heads 106

National

110

107

Forest

111-113

114

115

116

117-118

101

119

Rogue River

7.8

120

121

Gold Beach

Siskiyou
National Forest

122-124

Kalmiopsis
Wilderness

Cape Sebastian

Pistol

River

River

101

125

Chetco

126

127

Siskiyou
National
Forest

Cape Ferrelo

Brookings

128-130

132

131

To Crescent City, CA

PACIFIC OCEAN

Map 7.8

Campgrounds 133–135
Pages 480–481

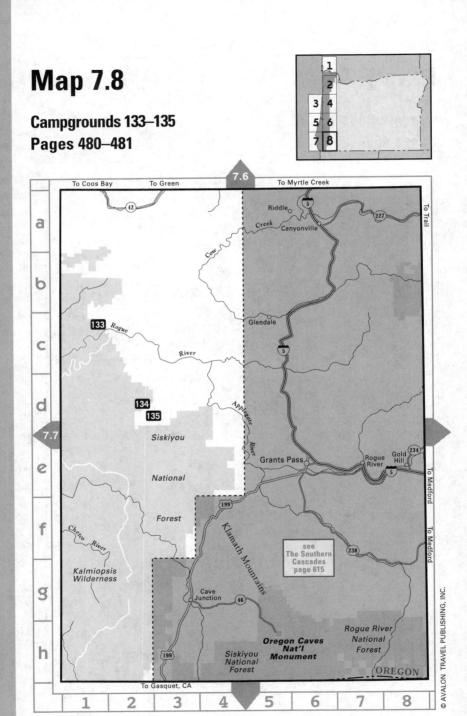

© AVALON TRAVEL PUBLISHING, INC.

1 FORT STEVENS STATE PARK

Rating: 8

At the mouth of the Columbia River.

Map 7.1, grid g1, page 419

This classic spot is set at the northern tip of Oregon, right where the Columbia River enters the Pacific Ocean. A historic military area, freshwater lake, swimming, beachcombing, trails, wildlife viewing, and a historic shipwreck site make Fort Stevens a uniquely diversified park. Covering 3,700 acres, the park has nine miles of bike trails and six miles of hiking trails, providing exploration through spruce and hemlock forests, wetlands, dunes, and shore pines. The trailhead for the Oregon Coast Trail is here as well. History buffs will find a museum, tours of the fort and artillery batteries, and the remains of the Peter Iredale shipwreck.

Campsites, facilities: There are 40 tent sites, 170 sites with full hookups and 320 sites with partial hookups for RVs up to 50 feet long, and a special camping area for hikers and bicyclists; 15 yurts and four group tent areas are also available. Picnic tables and fire grills are provided. Drinking water, flush toilets, an RV dump station, a transfer and recycling station, showers, firewood, and a playground are available. Some facilities are wheelchair accessible. Boat docks and launching facilities are nearby. Leashed pets are permitted.

Reservations, fees: Reservations at 800/452-5687 or website: www.OregonStateParks.org ($7 reservation fee). Sites are $18–22 per night, $4 for hikers/bikers, and group tent areas are $60 per night. Yurts are $28 per night. Major credit cards accepted. Open year-round.

Directions: From Portland, turn west on U.S. 26 and drive 73 miles to the junction with U.S. 101. Turn right (north) on U.S. 101 and drive about 15 miles (about one-quarter mile past the Camp Rilea Army Base). Turn west on Perkins Road/Highway 104 at the sign for Fort Stevens State Park and drive about one mile to Ocean View Cemetery Road. Turn left and drive about 2.5 miles (Ocean View Cemetery Road becomes Ridge Road) to the park entrance.

Contact: Fort Stevens State Park, Ridge Rd., Hammond, OR 97121, 800/551-6949 or 503/861-1671.

2 ASTORIA/WARRENTON SEASIDE KOA

Rating: 3

Near Fort Stevens State Park.

Map 7.1, grid g1, page 419

This campground is nestled in a wooded area adjacent to Fort Stevens State Park, and tours of that historical military site can be arranged. This camp provides an excellent alternative if the state park campground is full. A host of activities are available in the immediate area, including bicycling, hiking, deep-sea fishing, and beachcombing. Horse stables are within 10 miles. See the description of Fort Stevens State Park for further details about the area.

Campsites, facilities: There are 311 sites for tents or RVs up to 80 feet long and 54 one- and two-bedroom cabins. Cable TV, restrooms, showers, security, a public phone, a laundry room, limited groceries, ice, snacks, RV supplies, LP gas, and a barbecue are available. Recreational facilities include a playground, a game room, a recreation field, horseshoes, a spa, and a heated swimming pool. Some facilities are wheelchair accessible. Leashed pets are permitted.

Reservations, fees: Reservations at 800/562-8506. Sites are $23–50 per night, $3.50–4.50 per person for more than two people. Major credit cards accepted. Open year-round.

Directions: From Portland, turn west on U.S. 26 and drive 73 miles to the junction with U.S. 101. Turn right (north) on U.S. 101 and drive about 15 miles (about one-quarter mile past the Camp Rilea Army Base). Turn west on Perkins Road/Highway 104 at the sign for Fort Stevens State Park and drive about one mile to Ocean View Cemetery Road. Turn left and drive about 2.5 miles (Ocean View Cemetery Road becomes Ridge Road) to the campground directly across from the state park.

Contact: Astoria/Warrenton Seaside KOA, 1100 Ridge Rd., Hammond, OR 97121; or 503/861-2606, fax 503/861-3209, website: www.koa.com.

3 KAMPERS WEST CAMPGROUND

Rating: 7

Near Fort Stevens State Park.
Map 7.1, grid g1, page 419

Just four miles from Fort Stevens State Park, this privately run camp offers full RV services. Nearby recreation possibilities include an 18-hole golf course, hiking trails, marked bike trails, and a riding stable.

Campsites, facilities: There are 180 sites for RVs of any length, including a small area for tents only, and three park-model cabins. Electricity, drinking water, and picnic tables are provided. Flush toilets, bottled gas, an RV dump station, showers, laundry facilities, and ice are available. A store and a café are within one mile. Leashed pets are permitted.

Reservations, fees: Reservations accepted. Sites are $20–27.50 per night. Major credit cards accepted. Open year-round.

Directions: From Portland, turn west on U.S. 30 and drive 105 miles north and west to Astoria and the junction of U.S. 101. Turn south and drive 6.5 miles to the Warrenton/Hammond Junction. Turn west on Warrenton and drive 1.5 miles to the campground on the right.

Contact: Kampers West Campground, 1140 N.W. Warrenton Dr., Warrenton, OR 97146, 503/861-1814, fax 503/861-3620, website: www.kamperswest.com.

4 VENICE RV PARK

Rating: 3

On the Neawanna River.
Map 7.2, grid a1, page 420

This park along the Neawanna River—one of two rivers running through Seaside—is less than a mile from the beach. A great bonus: Crab pot rentals are available. Seaside offers beautiful ocean beaches for fishing and surfing, moped and bike rentals, shops, and a theater. The city provides swings and volleyball nets on the beach. An 18-hole golf course is nearby.

Campsites, facilities: There are 31 sites, including 13 drive-through, for RVs of any length and two tent sites. Electricity, drinking water, sewer, cable TV, and picnic tables are provided. Flush toilets, showers, a laundry room, and ice are available. A store and a café are within one mile. Leashed pets are permitted.

Reservations, fees: Reservations preferred. RV sites are $21 per night; tent sites are $12 per night; $2 per person for more than two people, $2 per extra vehicle, one-time $2 pet charge. Major credit cards accepted. Open year-round.

Directions: From Portland on I-5, turn west on U.S. 26 and drive 73 miles to the junction with U.S. 101. Turn north on U.S. 101 and drive four miles to Seaside. Continue to the north end of town and turn left (west) on 24th Avenue. The campground is on the corner at 1032 24th Avenue.

Contact: Venice RV Park, 1032 24th Ave., Seaside, OR 97138, 503/738-8851.

5 SEA RANCH RV PARK

Rating: 9

Near the Pacific Ocean.
Map 7.2, grid a1, page 420

This resort is set in a wooded area with nearby access to the beach. Activities at the camp include stream fishing, horseback riding, and swimming on the seashore. A golf course is six miles away, and the historic Lewis and Clark Trail is nearby. Elk hunters camp here in season. The beach and the town of Cannon Beach are within walking distance of the resort.

Campsites, facilities: There are 80 sites for tents or RVs and three cabins with fireplace and porch that sleep four each. Restrooms, showers, an RV dump station, and a public phone are available. Supplies are available within two miles. Leashed pets are permitted.

Reservations, fees: Reservations recommended. Sites are $19–24 per night, $2 per person for more than two people, $3 per extra vehicle, and $2 per pet per night. Major credit cards accepted. Open year-round.

Directions: From Portland on I-5, turn west on U.S. 26 and drive 73 miles to the junction with U.S. 101. Turn south on U.S. 101 and drive three miles to the Cannon Beach exit. The park is south three-tenths of a mile on the left.

Contact: Sea Ranch RV Park, P.O. Box 214, 415 Fir St., Cannon Beach, OR 97110, 503/436-2815, website: www.cannon-beach.net/searanch.

6 RV RESORT AT CANNON BEACH

Rating: 9

Near Ecola State Park.

Map 7.2, grid a1, page 420

This private resort is located about seven blocks from one of the nicest beaches in the region and about two miles from Ecola State Park. From the town of Cannon Beach you can walk for miles in either direction. Nearby recreational facilities include marked bike trails, a riding stable, and tennis courts. The city shuttle service stops here.

Campsites, facilities: There are 100 sites for RVs of any length; 11 are drive-through sites. Electricity, drinking water, sewer hookups, and picnic tables are provided. Flush toilets, bottled gas, showers, firewood, a recreation hall, a store, a spa, a laundry room, ice, a playground, and a swimming pool are available. Leashed pets are permitted.

Reservations, fees: Reservations at 800/847-2231. Sites are $24–36 per night. Major credit cards accepted. Open year-round.

Directions: From Portland on I-5, turn west on U.S. 26 and drive 73 miles to the junction with U.S. 101. Turn south on U.S. 101 and drive four miles to the Cannon Beach exit at Milepost 29.5. Turn left (east) and drive 200 feet to the campground.

Contact: RV Resort at Cannon Beach, P.O. Box 1037, 345 Elk Creek Rd., Cannon Beach, OR 97110, 503/436-2231, fax 503/436-1527; www.cbrvresort.com.

7 SADDLE MOUNTAIN STATE PARK

Rating: 7

On Saddle Mountain.

Map 7.2, grid a3, page 420

This inland camp offers a good alternative to the many beachfront parks. A 2.5-mile trail climbs to the top of Saddle Mountain, a great lookout on clear days. The park is a real find for the naturalist interested in rare and unusual varieties of plants, many of which have established themselves along the slopes of this isolated mountain.

Campsites, facilities: There are 10 primitive tent sites. Drinking water, garbage bins, picnic tables, and fire grills are provided. Flush toilets and firewood are available. Leashed pets are permitted.

Reservations, fees: Reservations are not accepted. Sites are $7–10 per night, $7 per extra vehicle. Open March–October.

Directions: From Portland turn west on U.S. 26 and drive about 63 miles to Necanicum Junction and Saddle Mountain Road. Turn north on Saddle Mountain Road and drive seven miles to the park. The road dead-ends at the park.

Contact: Saddle Mountain State Park, c/o Ecola State Park, P.O. Box 681, Cannon Beach, OR 97110, 800/551-6949 or 503/436-2844 (this phone number reaches Ecola State Park, which manages Saddle Mountain).

8 OSWALD WEST STATE PARK

Rating: 8

On the Pacific Ocean.

Map 7.2, grid b1, page 420

This state park is set along a dramatic section of the Oregon coast with rugged cliffs rising high above the ocean. You can't see the beach from the campsites, but you can hear the ocean. The park offers 15 miles of hiking trails, including the Oregon Coast Trail and a trail to the point of Cape Falcon, where campers can enjoy scenic views. A small beach attracts windsurfers and boogie boarders, and several fishing streams are nearby. The park is in a beautiful rainforest setting with gigantic spruce and cedar trees.

Campsites, facilities: There are 30 primitive walk-in tent sites. Wheelbarrows are available for campers to transport their supplies. Picnic tables and fire grills are provided. Drinking water, flush toilets, garbage bins, and firewood are available. Leashed pets are permitted.

Reservations, fees: Reservations are not accepted. Sites are $10–14 per night, $7 per extra vehicle. Open March–October.

Directions: From Portland, turn west on U.S. 26 and drive 73 miles to the junction with U.S. 101. Turn south on U.S. 101 and drive four miles to Cannon Beach. Continue 10 miles south on U.S. 101 to the parking area. Walk one-quarter mile to the campground.

Contact: Oswald West State Park, 9500 Sandpiper Ln., P.O. Box 366, Nehalem, OR 97131, 800/551-6949 or 503/368-5943.

9 NEHALEM BAY STATE PARK

Rating: 7

On the Pacific Ocean.

Map 7.2, grid c1, page 420

This state park on a sandy point separating the Pacific Ocean from Nehalem Bay features six miles of beach frontage. Crabbing and fishing on the bay are popular. The neighboring towns of Manzanita and Nehalem offer fine dining and shopping. The Oregon Coast Trail passes through the park. A horse camp with corrals and a 7.5-mile equestrian trail are available. There is also a 1.75-mile bike trail. An airport is adjacent to the park, and there are airstrip fly-in campsites.

Campsites, facilities: There are 277 sites for RVs up to 60 feet long, a special camping area for hikers and bicyclists, and six primitive fly-in sites next to the airport. There are also 16 yurts and 17 sites with stock corrals. Electricity, drinking water, picnic tables, and fire grills are provided. Flush toilets, an RV dump station, showers, and firewood are available. Some facilities are wheelchair accessible. Boat-launching facilities are nearby on Nehalem Bay, and an airstrip is adjacent to the park. Leashed pets are permitted.

Reservations, fees: Reservations at 800/452-5687 or website: www.OregonStateParks.org ($7 reservation fee). Sites are $16–19 per night, $7 per extra vehicle, and $4 per person per night for hikers/bikers. Yurts are $27 per night; horse sites are $10–14 per night and $1.50 per horse per night. Fly-in sites are $10–14 per night, not including tie-down. Major credit cards accepted. Open year-round.

Directions: From Portland, drive west on U.S. 26 for 73 miles to the junction with U.S. 101. Turn south on U.S. 101 and drive 19 miles to Manzanita. Turn right (west) on the park entrance road and drive 1.5 miles to the campground.

Contact: Nehalem Bay State Park, 9500 Sandpiper Ln., Nehalem, OR 97131, 800/551-6949 or 503/368-5154.

10 NEHALEM FALLS

Rating: 10

In Tillamook State Forest.

Map 7.2, grid c2, page 420

This beautiful campground, amid old-growth hemlock and spruce, is located within a two-minute walk of lovely Nehalem Falls. A half-mile loop trail follows the adjacent Nehalem River, where fishing and swimming are options.

Campsites, facilities: There are 14 sites for tents or RVs up to 40 feet long, four walk-in tent sites, and one group site. Drinking water, picnic tables, garbage dumpsters, fire grills, and vault toilets are available. Some facilities are wheelchair accessible. Leashed pets are permitted.

Reservations, fees: Reservations are not accepted. Sites are $10 per night, $2 per extra vehicle. Walk-in sites are $5 per night. Reservations required for the group site at 503/842-2545; $25 per night. Open Memorial Day weekend through October.

Directions: From Tillamook on U.S. 101 northbound, drive 22 miles to Highway 53. Turn right (east) and drive 1.3 miles to Miami Foley Road. Turn right (south) and drive one mile to Foss Road (narrow and rough). Turn left and drive seven miles to the campground on the left.

Contact: Tillamook State Forest, Tillamook District, 5005 E. 3rd St., Tillamook, OR 97141, 503/842-2545, fax 503/842-3143, website: www.odf.state.or.us.

11 JONES CREEK

Rating: 7

On the Wilson River in Tillamook State Forest.
Map 7.2, grid d4, page 420

Set in a forest of fir, hemlock, spruce, and alder, campsites here are spacious and private. The adjacent Wilson River provides opportunities for steelhead and salmon fishing (artificial lures only). A scenic 3.8-mile trail runs along the riverfront. The camp fills up on holiday weekends.

Campsites, facilities: There are 28 sites for tents or RVs (27 are 50 feet long and one is 72 feet long and pull-through), nine walk-in tent sites, and one group site. A camp host is on-site, and drinking water, picnic tables, fire grills, vault toilets, garbage dumpsters, and a horseshoe pit are available. Some facilities are wheelchair accessible. Leashed pets are permitted.

Reservations, fees: Reservations are not accepted. Sites are $10 per night, $2 per extra vehicle. Walk-in sites are $5 per night. Reservations required for the group site at 503/842-2545; $25 per night. Open Memorial Day weekend through October.

Directions: From Portland, turn west on U.S. 26 and drive 24 miles to Highway 6. Turn on Highway 6 and drive 28 miles to Milepost 22.7 and North Fork Road. Turn right and drive one-quarter mile to the campground on the left.

Contact: Tillamook State Forest, Tillamook District, 5005 E. 3rd St., Tillamook, OR 97141, 503/842-2545, fax 503/842-3143, website: www.odf.state.or.us.

12 ELK CREEK WALK-IN

Rating: 7

On Elk Creek in Tillamook State Forest.
Map 7.2, grid d5, page 420

This small campground is set among fir, alder, and maple on Elk Creek and borders the Wilson River. Elk Creek is closed to fishing. For fishing information on Wilson River, call first as regulations often change here.

Campsites, facilities: There are 15 walk-in tent sites. Drinking water, picnic tables, fire grills, and vault toilets are available. Pack out all garbage. Some facilities are wheelchair accessible. Leashed pets are permitted.

Reservations, fees: Reservations are not accepted. Sites are $5 per night, $2 per extra vehicle. Open Memorial Day weekend through October.

Directions: From Portland, turn west on U.S. 26 and drive 24 miles to Highway 6. Turn west on Highway 6 and drive 23 miles to Milepost 28 and the campground entrance road on the

right. Turn right on Elk Creek Road and drive one-half mile to the campground on the left.
Contact: Tillamook State Forest, Forest Grove District, 801 Gales Creek Rd., Forest Grove, OR 97116, 503/357-2191, website: www.odf.state.or.us

13 JORDAN CREEK OHV STAGING AREA

Rating: 6

Near Jordan Creek in Tillamook State Forest.
Map 7.2, grid c5, page 420

This off-highway vehicle (OHV) camp is set at the bottom of a scenic, steep canyon next to Jordan Creek. Wooded campsites are clustered around a central parking area, and the park caters to OHV campers. There are almost 40 miles of OHV trails, varying from moderate to difficult. There's no fishing in Jordan Creek.
Campsites, facilities: There are six sites for tents or RVs of any length. No drinking water, but picnic tables, fire grills, garbage bins, and vault toilets are available. Some facilities are wheelchair accessible. Leashed pets are permitted.
Reservations, fees: Reservations are not accepted. Sites are $5 per night, $2 per extra vehicle. Open March–November.
Directions: From Tillamook on U.S. 101, turn east on Highway 6 and drive 17.9 miles to Jordan Creek Road. Turn right and drive 2.2 miles to the campground on the right.
Contact: Tillamook State Forest, Tillamook District, 5005 E. 3rd St., Tillamook, OR 97141, 503/842-2545, fax 503/842-3143, website: www.odf.state.or.us.

14 GALES CREEK

Rating: 7

On Gales Creek in Tillamook State Forest.
Map 7.2, grid c5, page 420
Gales Creek runs through this heavily forest-

ed camp. The Gales Creek Trailhead is accessible from camp, providing hiking and mountain biking opportunities. A day-use picnic area is also available.
Campsites, facilities: There are 19 sites for tents or RVs up to 35 feet long and four walk-in tent sites. Drinking water, picnic tables, fire grills, garbage bins, and vault toilets are available. Some facilities are wheelchair accessible. Leashed pets are permitted.
Reservations, fees: Reservations are not accepted. Family sites are $10 per night; walk-in sites are $5 per night; an additional vehicle is $2 per night. Open Memorial Day weekend through October.
Directions: From Portland, turn west on U.S. 26 and drive 24 miles to Highway 6. Turn west on Highway 6 and drive 17 miles to the campground entrance road (Rogers Road) on the right at Milepost 35. Turn right on Rogers Road and drive one mile to the campground.
Contact: Tillamook State Forest, Forest Grove District, 801 Gales Creek Rd., Forest Grove, OR 97116, 503/357-2191, website: www.odf.state.or.us.

15 STAGECOACH HORSE CAMP

Rating: 6

In Tillamook State Forest.
Map 7.2, grid d5, page 420
This camp is for horse camping only. A small seasonal stream runs through the camp. Two-hour and four-hour loop trails are accessible from the camp.
Campsites, facilities: There are 11 sites for tents or RVs up to 30 feet long. No drinking water, but picnic tables, fire grills, a picnic shelter, and vault toilets are available. Pack out all garbage. Stock facilities include corrals at each site and stock water. Some facilities are wheelchair accessible. Leashed pets are permitted.
Reservations, fees: Reservations are not accepted. Sites are $5 per night, $2 per extra vehicle. Open year-round.

Directions: From Portland, turn west on U.S. 26 and drive 24 miles to Highway 6. Turn west on Highway 6 and drive 19 miles to Beaver Dam Road. Turn left (south) and drive one mile to University Falls Road. Turn right and drive 3.5 miles to Rutherford Road. Turn right again and drive a short distance to the first gravel road on the left. Turn left and drive one-half mile to the campground on the left.

Contact: Tillamook State Forest, Forest Grove District, 801 Gales Creek Rd., Forest Grove, OR 97116, 503/357-2191, website: www.odf .state.or.us.

16 BROWNS CAMP

Rating: 6

In Tillamook State Forest.
Map 7.2, grid d5, page 420

This camp is located next to the Devil's Lake Fork of the Wilson River and has sites with and without tree cover. Surrounded by miles of OHV trails, it caters to off-highway vehicle campers. Don't expect peace and quiet. No fishing is allowed here.

Campsites, facilities: There are 29 sites for tents or RVs up to 45 feet long. Drinking water, picnic tables, fire grills, garbage bins, and vault toilets are available. Some facilities are wheelchair accessible. Leashed pets are permitted.

Reservations, fees: Reservations are not accepted. Sites are $10 per night, $2 per extra vehicle. Open March–November.

Directions: From Portland, turn west on U.S. 26 and drive 24 miles to Highway 6. Turn west on Highway 6 and drive 19 miles to Beaver Dam Road. Turn left (south) and drive 2.5 miles to Scoggins Road. Turn left (southeast) and drive one-half mile to the campground.

Contact: Tillamook State Forest, Forest Grove District, 801 Gales Creek Rd., Forest Grove, OR 97116, 503/357-2191, website: www.odf .state.or.us.

17 BARVIEW JETTY COUNTY PARK

Rating: 7

Near Garibaldi.
Map 7.2, grid d1, page 420

This Tillamook County park covers 160 acres and is set near the beach, in a wooded area adjacent to Tillamook Bay. The sites are set on grassy hills. Nearby recreation options include an 18-hole golf course, hiking trails, bike trails, surf and scuba fishing, and a full-service marina.

Campsites, facilities: There are 249 sites, including 60 with full hookups, for tents or RVs of any length and five group sites. Electricity, drinking water, sewer hookups, and picnic tables are provided. Flush toilets, an RV dump station, showers, and a playground are available. Bottled gas, a store, a café, and ice are within one mile. Leashed pets are permitted.

Reservations, fees: Reservations accepted for some sites. Sites are $15–20 per night, plus $5 for each additional vehicle or tent, $2 dump station fee, $2 shower fee for non-registered guests (free for registered campers), and $5 for firewood; $25–30 for group sites. Major credit cards accepted. Open year-round.

Directions: From Portland on I-5, turn west on U.S. 26 and drive 24 miles to Highway 6. Turn left on Highway 6 and drive 44 miles to Tillamook. Turn north on U.S. 101 and drive 12 miles to the park on the left (two miles north of the town of Garibaldi).

Contact: Barview Jetty County Park, P.O. Box 633, Garibaldi, OR 97118, 503/322-3522, website: www.co.tillamook.or.us.

18 BIAK-BY-THE-SEA RV PARK

Rating: 7

On Tillamook Bay.
Map 7.2, grid d1, page 420

This park along the shore of Tillamook Bay is a prime retreat for deep-sea fishing, crabbing, clamming, surf fishing, scuba diving, and beachcombing. The nearby town of Tillamook is home to a cheese factory and a historical museum. A good side trip is to Cape Meares State Park, where you can hike through the national wildlife preserve and see how the seabirds nest along the cliffs. There is also a golf course nearby. Note that about 30 of the sites are monthly rentals.

Campsites, facilities: There are 45 drive-through sites for RVs of any length. Electricity, drinking water, sewer hookups, and cable TV are provided. Flush toilets, coin-operated showers, and laundry facilities are available. Bottled gas, a store, a café, and ice are within one mile. Boat docks, launching facilities, and rentals are nearby. Leashed pets are permitted.

Reservations, fees: Reservations recommended. Sites are $20 per night, $1 per pet per night. Major credit cards accepted. Open year-round.

Directions: From Portland, turn west on U.S. 26 and drive 24 miles to Highway 6. Turn west on Highway 6 and drive 44 miles to Tillamook and U.S. 101. Turn north and drive 10 miles to 7th Street. Turn left on 7th Street and drive to the park on the left (just over the tracks).

Contact: Biak-by-the-Sea RV Park, P.O. Box 396, Garibaldi, OR 97118, 503/322-2111.

19 PACIFIC CAMPGROUND

Rating: 6

On Tillamook Bay.
Map 7.2, grid d2, page 420

This campground is located at the southern end of Tillamook Bay, not far from the Wilson River. The Tillamook Cheese Factory—the place for cheese tours—is just south of the park. An 18-hole golf course is also nearby. See the description of Biak-by-the-Sea RV Park for more information about the area.

Campsites, facilities: There are 20 tent sites and 31 drive-through sites for RVs of any length. Electricity, drinking water, sewer hookups, and picnic tables are provided. Flush toilets, cable TV, showers, firewood, and ice are available. A store and a café are within one mile. Leashed pets (except in the tent area) and motorbikes are permitted.

Reservations, fees: Reservations accepted. Sites are $13–22 per night for two people, $1 per person for more than two people, and $1 per extra vehicle. Open year-round.

Directions: From Portland, turn west on U.S. 26 and drive 24 miles to Highway 6. Turn west on Highway 6 and drive 44 miles to Tillamook. Turn north on U.S. 101 and drive 1.5 miles to the campground entrance across from the Tillamook Cheese Factory.

Contact: Pacific Campground, 1950 Suppress Rd. N, Tillamook, OR 97141, 503/842-5201, fax 503/842-0588.

20 PLEASANT VALLEY RV PARK

Rating: 8

On the Tillamook River.
Map 7.2, grid e2, page 420

This campground along the Tillamook River is very clean and features many recreation options in the immediate area.

Campsites, facilities: There are 10 tent sites and 74 sites for RVs of any length, plus two cabins. Drinking water and picnic tables are provided. Flush toilets, bottled gas, an RV dump station, showers, firewood, a recreation hall, electricity, sewer hookups, cable TV, a store, a laundry room, ice, and a playground are available. Boat-launching facilities are nearby. Leashed pets are permitted.

Reservations, fees: Reservations accepted. Sites are $16–21.50 per night, $2 per person for more than two people; cabins are $27 per night. Senior discount available. Major credit cards accepted. Open year-round.

Directions: From Portland, turn west on U.S. 26 and drive 24 miles to Highway 6. Turn west on Highway 6 and drive 44 miles to Tillamook and U.S. 101. Turn south on U.S. 101 and drive six miles to the campground entrance on the right.

Contact: Pleasant Valley RV Park, 11880 U.S. 101 S, Tillamook, OR 97141, 503/842-4779, fax 503/842-2293.

21 NETARTS BAY RV PARK & MARINA

Rating: 8

On Netarts Bay.

Map 7.2, grid e1, page 420

This camp is one of three on the east shore of Netarts Bay. A golf course is eight miles away. Sunsets and wildlife viewing are notable here. Some sites are filled with rentals for the summer season. No tent campers permitted. This RV park was formerly known as Bay Shore RV Park.

Campsites, facilities: There are 53 sites for RVs of any length; 11 are drive-through sites. Electricity, drinking water, sewer hookups, and picnic tables are provided. Flush toilets, bottled gas, coin-operated showers, a meeting room, a laundry room, crab-cooking facilities, crab bait, and ice are available. Boat docks, launching facilities, and rentals are available on-site. A store and a café are within one mile. Leashed pets are permitted.

Reservations, fees: Reservations recommended. Sites are $24–27 per night. Major credit cards accepted. Monthly rentals available. Open year-round.

Directions: From Portland, turn west on U.S. 26 and drive 24 miles to Highway 6. Turn west on Highway 6 and drive 44 miles to Tillamook and Netarts Highway. Turn west on Netarts Highway and drive six miles to the campground entrance.

Contact: Netarts Bay RV Park & Marina, 2260 Bilyeu, P.O. Box 218, Netarts, OR 97413, 503/842-7774, website: www.netartsbay.com.

22 CAPE LOOKOUT STATE PARK

Rating: 8

Near Netarts Bay.

Map 7.2, grid f1, page 420

The park is set on a sand spit between Netarts Bay and the ocean. Cape Lookout has more than eight miles of hiking and walking trails that wind through old-growth forest. The Cape Lookout Trail follows the headland for more than two miles. Another walk will take you out through a variety of estuarine habitats along the five-mile sand spit that extends between the ocean and Netarts Bay. With many species to view, this area is a paradise for bird-watchers. You might also catch the local hang gliders and para gliders that frequent the park. Fishing is another option here.

Campsites, facilities: There are 177 tent sites, 35 sites with full or partial hookups for RVs up to 60 feet long, a special tent camping area for hikers and bicyclists, four group sites for up to 25 people each, three cabins, and 10 yurts. Picnic tables and fire grills are provided. Flush toilets, an RV dump station, showers, garbage bins, and firewood are available. A restaurant is within one mile. Some facilities are wheelchair accessible. Leashed pets are permitted.

Reservations, fees: Reservations at 800/452-5687 or website: www.OregonStateParks.org ($7 reservation fee). Sites are $12–20 per night, $7 per extra vehicle, $4 per person per night for hikers/bikers, $40–60 for group sites, $45–65 for cabins, and $27 per night for yurts. Major credit cards accepted. Open year-round.

Directions: From Portland, turn west on U.S. 26 and drive 24 miles to Highway 6. Turn west on Highway 6 and drive 44 miles to Tillamook. Turn southwest on Netarts Road and drive 11 miles to the park entrance on the right.

Contact: Cape Lookout State Park, 13000 Whiskey Creek Rd. W, Tillamook, OR 97141, 503/842-4981.

23 CAMPER COVE RV PARK AND CAMPGROUND

Rating: 6

On Beaver Creek.

Map 7.2, grid f2, page 420

This small, wooded campground along Beaver Creek is set just far enough off the highway to provide quiet. The park can be used as a base camp for anglers, with seasonal steelhead and salmon fishing in the nearby Nestucca River. It gets crowded here, especially in the summer, so be sure to make a reservation whenever possible. Ocean beaches are four miles away.

Campsites, facilities: There are 17 sites for RVs up to 40 feet long, five tent sites, and three cabins. Electricity, drinking water, sewer hookups, and picnic tables are provided. Flush toilets, fire pits, an RV dump station, showers, firewood, a recreation hall, laundry facilities, and ice are available. Leashed pets are permitted.

Reservations, fees: Reservations accepted. RV sites are $20 per night; tent sites are $15 per night, $3 per person for more than two people; and cabin rentals are $30–40 per night. Senior discount available. Open year-round.

Directions: From Portland, turn west on U.S. 26 and drive 24 miles to Highway 6. Turn west on Highway 6 and drive 44 miles to Tillamook and U.S. 101. Turn south on U.S. 101 and drive 11.5 miles to the park entrance on the right (2.5 miles north of Beaver).

Contact: Camper Cove RV Park and Campground, P.O. Box 42, Beaver, OR 97108, 503/398-5334, website: www.amadevice.com/campercove.

24 SAND BEACH

Rating: 5

In Siuslaw National Forest.

Map 7.2, grid f1, page 420

This area is known for its beaches with large sand dunes, which are popular with off-road vehicle enthusiasts. It's noisy and can be windy. The campground is set along the shore of Sand Lake, which is actually more like an estuary than a lake since the ocean is just around the bend. This is the only coastal U.S. Forest Service campground for many miles, and it's quite popular. If you're planning a trip for midsummer, be sure to reserve far in advance. Entry permits are required for three-day holiday weekends.

Campsites, facilities: There are 101 sites for tents or RVs up to 30 feet long. (If full, the east and west parking lots provide additional sites for RVs.) Picnic tables and fire pits are provided. Drinking water, garbage bins, and flush toilets are available. Leashed pets are permitted.

Reservations, fees: Reservations at 877/444-6777 or website: www.ReserveUsa.com ($9 reservation fee). Sites are $16 per night, $68 per extra vehicle. The east and west parking lots are $10 per night. Senior discount available. Open late April–late September.

Directions: From Tillamook on U.S. 101, drive south for 11 miles to County Road 8. Turn west on County Road 8 and follow the signs to the campground.

Contact: Siuslaw National Forest, Hebo Ranger District, 31525 Hwy. 22, Hebo, OR 97122, 503/392-3161, fax 503/392-4203.

25 ROCKY BEND

Rating: 5

On the Nestucca River in Siuslaw National Forest.

Map 7.2, grid f3, page 420

This campground along the Nestucca River is a little-known, secluded spot that provides guaranteed peace and quiet. There isn't much in the way of recreational activities out here, but hiking, fishing, clamming, and swimming are available along the coast, a relatively short drive away.

Campsites, facilities: There are six tent sites. Picnic tables and fire pits are provided, but there is no drinking water. Vault toilets are available. No garbage service is provided, so you must pack out what you bring in. Leashed pets are permitted.

Reservations, fees: Reservations are not accepted. There is no fee for camping. Open year-round.

Directions: On U.S. 101 southwest of Portland, drive to the tiny town of Beaver and Blaine Road. Turn east on Blaine Road (keep right; Blaine Road turns into Nestucca River Access Road) and drive 15.5 miles to the campground.

Contact: Siuslaw National Forest, Hebo Ranger District, 31525 Hwy. 22, Hebo, OR 97122, 503/392-3161, fax 503/392-4203.

26 DOVRE, FAN CREEK, ALDER GLEN

Rating: 5

On the Nestucca River.
Map 7.2, grid g3, page 420

This is a series of three BLM campgrounds set along the Nestucca River. The camps, separated by alder trees and shrubs, are near the river, and some have river views. Tourists don't know about these spots. The Nestucca is a gentle river, with the water not deep enough for swimming.

Campsites, facilities: Dovre has nine sites; Fan Creek has 11 sites; and Alder Glen has 10 sites for tents or small RVs. Picnic tables and fire grills are provided. Drinking water and vault toilets are available. Garbage must be packed out. Some facilities, including a fishing pier at Alder Glen, are wheelchair accessible. Leashed pets are permitted.

Reservations, fees: Reservations are not accepted. Sites are $6 per night, $4 per extra vehicle with a limit of two vehicles per site. Senior discount available. Open year-round.

Directions: On U.S. 101 southwest of Portland, drive to the tiny town of Beaver and Blaine Road. Turn east on Blaine Road (keep right; Blaine Road turns into Nestucca River Access Road) and drive 17.5 miles to Alder Glen. Continue

east for seven more miles to reach Fan Creek and nine more miles to reach Dovre.

Contact: Bureau of Land Management, Salem District, 1717 Fabry Rd. SE, Salem, OR 97306, 503/375-5646, fax 503/375-5622.

27 HEBO LAKE

Rating: 7

On Hebo Lake in Siuslaw National Forest.
Map 7.2, grid g2, page 420

This U.S. Forest Service campground along the shore of Hebo Lake is a secluded spot with sites nestled under trees. The trailhead for the eight-mile-long Pioneer-Indian Trail is located in the campground. The trail around the lake is wheelchair accessible.

Campsites, facilities: There are 15 sites for tents or RVs up to 18 feet long. Picnic tables and fire pits are provided. Drinking water, garbage bins, and vault toilets are available. Boats without motors are allowed on the lake. Some facilities are wheelchair accessible. Leashed pets are permitted.

Reservations, fees: Reservations are not accepted. Sites are $10 per night, $5 per extra vehicle. Senior discount available. Open May–mid-October.

Directions: On U.S. 101 southwest of Portland, drive to the town of Hebo and Highway 22. Turn east on Highway 22 and drive one-quarter mile to Forest Road 14. Turn left (east) and drive five miles to the campground.

Contact: Siuslaw National Forest, Hebo Ranger District, 31525 Hwy. 22, Hebo, OR 97122, 503/392-3161, fax 503/392-4203.

28 CASTLE ROCK

Rating: 4

On Three Rivers in Siuslaw National Forest.
Map 7.2, grid g2, page 420

This tiny spot along Three Rivers provides tent campers with an inland alternative to the large beachfront RV parks popular on the Oregon coast. Fishing can be good here. Though primitive, this camp is located along the edge of the highway and can fill up quickly.

Campsites, facilities: There are four tent sites. Drinking water, picnic tables, garbage bins, and a vault toilet are provided. Leashed pets are permitted.

Reservations, fees: Reservations are not accepted. There is no fee for camping. Open year-round.

Directions: On U.S. 101 southwest of Portland, drive to the town of Hebo and Highway 22. Turn east on Highway 22 and drive five miles to the campground.

Contact: Siuslaw National Forest, Hebo Ranger District, 31525 Hwy. 22, Hebo, OR 97122, 503/392-3161, fax 503/392-4203.

29 CAPE KIWANDA RV PARK

Rating: 8

On the Pacific Ocean.

Map 7.2, grid g1, page 420

This park is set a short distance from Cape Kiwanda State Park, which is open for day use only. Highlights at the park include a boat launch and hiking trails that lead out to the cape. Four miles south at Nestucca Spit, there is another day-use park, providing additional recreational options. The point extends about three miles and is a good spot for bird-watching. The campsites do not have ocean views.

Campsites, facilities: There are 150 sites for RVs of any length, 25 tent sites, and three camping cabins. Electricity, drinking water, sewer hookups, and picnic tables are provided. Flush toilets, an RV dump station, showers, firewood, a recreation hall, laundry facilities, propane, a seafood market, a gift shop, an automatic teller machine, and a playground are available. Bottled gas, a store, a café, and ice are within one mile. Boat docks, launching facilities, and rentals are nearby. Leashed pets are permitted.

Reservations, fees: Reservations accepted.

Sites are $17–26.50 per night, $2 per person for more than two people, and $1.50 per extra vehicle. Major credit cards accepted. Open year-round.

Directions: From Portland, turn west on U.S. 26 and drive 24 miles to Highway 6. Turn west on Highway 6 and drive 44 miles to Tillamook and U.S. 101. Turn south on U.S. 101 and drive 25 miles to the Pacific City exit and Brooten Road. Turn right and drive three miles toward Pacific City and Three Capes Drive. Turn left, cross the bridge, and bear right on Three Capes Drive. Continue one mile north to the park on the right.

Contact: Cape Kiwanda RV Park, P.O. Box 129, 33315, Cape Kiwanda Dr., Pacific City, OR 97135, 503/965-6230, fax 503/965-6235, website: www.capekiwandarvpark.com.

30 WEBB PARK

Rating: 7

Near the Pacific Ocean.

Map 7.2, grid g1, page 420

This public campground provides an excellent alternative to the more crowded commercial RV parks off U.S. 101. Although not as developed, it offers a quiet, private setting and access to the ocean. Fishing and swimming are among your options here. The camp is just behind the new inn at Cape Kiwanda.

Campsites, facilities: There are 30 sites for tents or RVs; six have partial hookups. Drinking water, an RV dump station, showers, flush toilets, and beach launching are available. Leashed pets are permitted.

Reservations, fees: Reservations at 503/965-5001 ($5 reservation fee). Sites are $14–16 per night. Open year-round.

Directions: From Portland, turn west on U.S. 26 and drive 24 miles to Highway 6. Turn west on Highway 6 and drive 44 miles to Tillamook and U.S. 101. Turn south on U.S. 101 and drive about 25 miles to the Pacific City exit and Highway 30. From Pacific City, turn right (north) and drive to the four-way stop at McPhillips Drive. Turn left and drive one-half mile to Cape Kiwanda and the park on the right.

Contact: Webb Park, Tillamook County Parks, P.O. Box 572, Pacific City, OR 97135, 503/965-5001, fax 503/842-2721, website: www.co.tilla mook.or.us.

31 WANDERING SPIRIT RV PARK

Rating: 6

On the Yamhill River.
Map 7.2, grid h3, page 420

The major draw here is the nearby casino, but there is the added benefit of shaded sites next to the Yamhill River, which provides fishing and swimming options. Fishing is good for steelhead and salmon in season. Golf courses and wineries are available within 10 miles. There is a combination of both monthly rentals and overnighters at this park.

Campsites, facilities: There are 105 sites for RVs up to 45 feet long and 10 tent sites. Drinking water, electricity, sewer hookups, cable TV, telephone service, restrooms, showers, an RV dump station, laundry facilities, and a small store are available. Propane, a clubhouse, a basketball hoop, an exercise room, and a game room are also available on-site. A 24-hour free bus shuttles campers to and from the Spirit Mountain Casino, restaurants, and shops less than two miles away. Some facilities are wheelchair accessible. Leashed pets are permitted.

Reservations, fees: Reservations at 800/390-6980. Sites are $12 for tents per night, $22 for RVs per night, and $2 per person for more than two people. Monthly rates available. Major credit cards accepted. Open year-round.

Directions: From Salem, drive west on Highway 22 about 25 miles to Highway 18. Turn west on Highway 18 and drive about nine miles to the park on the left.

Contact: Wandering Spirit RV Park, 28800

Salmon River Hwy., Grand Ronde, OR 97347, 503/879-5700, fax 503/879-5171, website: www.onlinemac.com/business/wander.

32 DEVIL'S LAKE STATE PARK

Rating: 7

On Devil's Lake.
Map 7.3, grid a8, page 421

Oregon's only coastal camp in the midst of a city, Devil's Lake is the center of summertime activity. A take-your-pick deal: You can boat, canoe, kayak, fish, or water-ski. For something different, head west and explore the seven miles of beaches. Lincoln City also has a number of arts and crafts galleries. East Devil's Lake is two miles east and offers a boat ramp and picnic facilities.

Campsites, facilities: There are 54 tent sites and 31 sites with full hookups for RVs up to 60 feet long. There are also 10 yurts and a separate area for hikers and bikers. Picnic tables and fire grills are provided. Drinking water, garbage bins, flush toilets, showers, and firewood are available. Some facilities are wheelchair accessible. Boat docks and launching facilities are nearby. Leashed pets are permitted.

Reservations, fees: Reservations at 800/452-5687 or website: www.OregonStateParks.org ($7 reservation fee). Sites are $17–22 per night, $7 per extra vehicle, $4 per person per night for hikers/bikers, and yurts are $27 per night. Boat mooring is $7 per night. Major credit cards accepted. Open year-round.

Directions: From Portland, drive south on Highway 99 to Highway 18. Turn west on Highway 18 and drive 47 miles to U.S. 101. Turn south on U.S. 101 and drive five miles to Lincoln City. Follow the signs to the park.

Contact: Devil's Lake State Park, 1452 N.E. 6th St., Lincoln City, OR 97367, 503/994-2002.

33 KOA LINCOLN CITY

Rating: 7

Near the Pacific Ocean.
Map 7.3, grid a8, page 421

This area offers opportunities for beachcombing, tidepool viewing, and fishing along a seven-mile stretch of beach. Two stops to consider if you're going into Lincoln City for supplies: the Premier Market, which has smoked salmon, and the Colonial Bakery, which carries the best pastries west of Paris. Nearby recreation options include an 18-hole golf course and tennis courts.

Campsites, facilities: There are 15 tent sites and 52 sites for RVs up to 60 feet long; 13 are drive-through sites. There are also one-room camping cabins. Electricity, drinking water, cable TV, modem access, flush toilets, an RV dump station, public phones, showers, a store, a café, a gift shop, LP gas, ice, RV supplies, video rentals, a game room, coin-operated laundry facilities, and a playground are available. Firewood is available for purchase. Leashed pets are permitted.

Reservations, fees: Reservations at 800/562-2791. Sites are $21–27 per night, $3 per person for more than two people, and $5 per extra vehicle. Major credit cards accepted. Open year-round.

Directions: From Portland, drive south on Highway 99 West to Highway 18. Turn west on Highway 18 and drive 47 miles to U.S. 101. Turn south on U.S. 101 and drive 1.5 miles to East Devil's Lake Road. Turn east on East Devil's Lake Road and drive one mile to the park.

Contact: KOA Lincoln City, 5298 N.E. Park Ln., Otis, OR 97368, 541/994-2961, fax 541/994-9454, website: www.koa.com.

34 SEA AND SAND RV PARK

Rating: 9

Near Siletz Bay.
Map 7.3, grid b8, page 421

Beachcombing for fossils and agates is popu-

lar at this oceanfront park near Gleneden Beach on Siletz Bay. The sites have ocean views and pleasant terraces. The Siletz River and numerous small creeks are in the area. The park is located 3.5 miles north of Depoe Bay.

Campsites, facilities: There are 85 sites for RVs up to 35 feet long. Electricity, drinking water, sewer hookups, cable TV, and picnic tables are provided. Flush toilets, showers, an RV dump station, firewood, and a laundry room are available. A store, a café, and ice are within one mile. Leashed pets are permitted.

Reservations, fees: Reservations accepted. Sites are $22–25 per night, $2 per person for more than two people, and $5 per extra vehicle unless towed. Open year-round.

Directions: From Portland, turn south on Highway 99 West and drive southwest to Highway 18. Turn west on Highway 18 and drive 47 miles to U.S. 101. Turn south on U.S. 101 and drive five miles to Lincoln City. Continue another nine miles south on U.S. 101 to the campground entrance (on the beach side of the highway).

Contact: Sea and Sand RV Park, 4985 U.S. 101 N, Depoe Bay, OR 97341, 541/764-2313.

35 BEVERLY BEACH STATE PARK

Rating: 7

On the Pacific Ocean.
Map 7.3, grid c8, page 421

This beautiful campground is set in a wooded, grassy area on the east side of U.S. 101. Giant, wind-sculpted trees surround the campsites along Spencer Creek. Like magic, you walk through a tunnel under the roadway and emerge on a beach that extends from Yaquna Head to the headlands of Otter Rock and from which a lighthouse is visible. A one-mile hiking trail is available. Just a mile to the north lies a small day-use state park called Devil's Punchbowl, named for an unusual bowl-shaped rock formation with caverns under it where the waves rumble about. For some great ocean views, head north one more mile to the Otter Crest Wayside. The Oregon Coast Aquarium is within a few minutes' drive.

Campsites, facilities: There are 129 tent sites, 129 sites with full or partial hookups for RVs of any length, a special camping area for hikers and bicyclists, and a reserved group area. There is also a village of 21 yurts. Picnic tables and fire grills are provided. Drinking water, flush toilets, showers, garbage bins, and an RV dump station are available. Some facilities are wheelchair accessible. Leashed pets are permitted.

Reservations, fees: Reservations at 800/452-5687 or website: www.OregonStateParks.org ($7 reservation fee). Sites are $11–21 per night, $7 per extra vehicle, $4 per person per night for hikers/bikers, $27 per night for yurts, and $43–60 for group sites. Major credit cards accepted. Open year-round.

Directions: From I-5 at Albany, turn west on U.S. 20 and drive 66 miles to Newport and U.S. 101. Turn north on U.S. 101 and drive seven miles to the park entrance.

Contact: Beverly Beach State Park, 198 N.E. 123rd St., Newport, OR 97365, 800/551-6949 or 541/265-9278.

36 AGATE BEACH RV PARK

Rating: 6

Near the Pacific Ocean.

Map 7.3, grid c8, page 421

This park is located a short distance from Agate Beach Wayside, a small state park with beach access. Agate hunting can be good. Sometimes a layer of sand covers the agates, and you have to dig a bit. But other times wave action will clear the sand, unveiling the agates at low tides. Beverly Beach State Park is 4.5 miles north. About half of the sites are filled with monthly rentals.

Campsites, facilities: There are 32 sites for RVs up to 40 feet long. Electricity, drinking water, sewer hookups, cable TV, and picnic tables are provided. Flush toilets, an RV dump station, showers, and a laundry room are available. A store and ice are within one mile. Leashed pets are permitted, with some species restricted.

Reservations, fees: Reservations accepted. Sites are $21.50–22.50 per night, $1 per person for more than two people, and $1 per extra vehicle. Major credit cards accepted. Open year-round.

Directions: From Albany, drive west on U.S. 20 for 66 miles to Newport and U.S. 101. Turn north on U.S. 101 and drive three miles to the park on the north end of town.

Contact: Agate Beach RV Park, 6138 N. Coast Hwy., Newport, OR 97365, 541/265-7670.

37 HARBOR VILLAGE RV PARK

Rating: 6

On Yaquina Bay.

Map 7.3, grid c8, page 421

This wooded and landscaped park is set near the shore of Yaquina Bay. See the description of Port of Newport Marina and RV Park for information on attractions in Newport. Nearby recreation options include clamming, crabbing, deep-sea fishing, an 18-hole golf course, hiking trails, and a full-service marina. No tent campers are permitted.

Campsites, facilities: There are 40 sites for RVs. Electricity, drinking water, sewer hookups, cable TV, and picnic tables are provided. Flush toilets, showers, and a laundry room are available. Bottled gas, a store, and a café are within one mile. Boat docks, launching facilities, and rentals are nearby. One leashed pet per site is permitted.

Reservations, fees: Reservations accepted. Sites are $20 per night, $3 per person for more than two people. Major credit cards accepted. Open year-round.

Directions: From Albany, drive west on U.S. 20 for 65.5 miles into Newport and John Moore Road (lighted intersection). Turn left (south) on John Moore Road and drive one-half mile

to the bay and Bay Boulevard. Bear left and drive a short distance to the park entrance on the left.
Contact: Harbor Village RV Park, 923 S.E. Bay Blvd., Newport, OR 97365, 541/265-5088, fax 541/265-5895.

38 PORT OF NEWPORT MARINA AND RV PARK

Rating: 7

On Yaquina Bay.
Map 7.3, grid c8, page 421
This public park is set along the shore of Yaquina Bay near Newport, a resort town that offers a variety of attractions. Among them are ocean fishing, a museum and aquarium at the nearby Hatfield Marine Science Center, the Undersea Garden, the Waxworks, Ripley's Believe It or Not, and the Lincoln County Historical Society Museum. Nearby recreation options include an 18-hole golf course, hiking trails, and a full-service marina.
Campsites, facilities: There are 115 sites for RVs. Electricity, drinking water, and sewer hookups are provided. Flush toilets, showers, cable TV, a store, a laundry room, and ice are available. A marina with boat docks and launching facilities is available on-site. Leashed pets are permitted.
Reservations, fees: Reservations at 541/867-3321. Sites are $23.54 per night, $1 per person for more than two people. Major credit cards accepted. Open year-round.
Directions: From Albany, drive west on U.S. 20 for 66 miles to Newport and U.S. 101. Turn south on U.S. 101 and drive one-half mile (over the bridge) to Marine Science Drive. Turn right (east) and drive one-half mile to the park entrance on the left.
Contact: Port of Newport Marina and RV Park, 600 S.E. Bay Blvd., Newport, OR 97365 (physical address: 2301 S.E. O.S.U. Dr., Newport, OR 97365), 541/867-3321, fax 541/867-3352, website: www.portofnewport.com.

39 SOUTH BEACH STATE PARK

Rating: 7

On the Pacific Ocean.
Map 7.3, grid d8, page 421
This park along the beach offers opportunities for beachcombing, fishing, crabbing, windsurfing, boating, and hiking. In fact, the Oregon Coast Trail passes right through the park. A primitive hike-in campground is also available. The park is within walking distance of Oregon Aquarium. A nice plus: An on-duty full-time naturalist provides campground talks. For information on attractions in Newport, see the description of Port of Newport Marina and RV Park
Campsites, facilities: There are 244 sites for RVs of any length and an area of six primitive tent sites for hikers and bicyclists. There are also three group sites and 22 yurts. Picnic tables, electricity, and fire grills are provided. Drinking water, restrooms with flush toilets and showers, garbage bins, recycling, an RV dump station, and firewood are available. Some facilities are wheelchair accessible. Leashed pets are permitted.
Reservations, fees: Reservations at 800/452-5687 or website: www.OregonStateParks.org ($7 reservation fee). Sites are $9–21 per night, $7 per extra vehicle, $4 per person per night for hikers/bicyclists, and $64 for group sites. Major credit cards accepted. Open year-round.
Directions: From Albany, drive west on U.S. 20 for 66 miles to Newport and U.S. 101. Turn south and drive three miles to the park entrance on the right.
Contact: South Beach State Park, 5580 S. Coast Hwy., South Beach, OR 97366, 541/867-4715.

40 SEAL ROCK'S RV COVE

Rating: 8

Near Seal Rock State Park.
Map 7.3, grid e8, page 421
This RV park is situated on the rugged coast-

line near Seal Rock State Park (open for day use only), where you may find seals, sea lions, and a variety of birds. The ocean views are stunning.

Campsites, facilities: There are 26 sites for RVs of any length—two are drive-through sites—and 15 tent sites. Electricity, drinking water, sewer hookups, picnic tables, and fire rings are provided. Flush toilets, showers, and firewood are available. A store, a café, and ice are within one mile. Leashed pets are permitted.

Reservations, fees: Reservations accepted. Sites are $15–31 per night, $1–3 per person for more than two people, $2 per extra vehicle unless towed. Senior discount available. Open year-round.

Directions: From Albany, drive west on U.S. 20 for 66 miles to Newport and U.S. 101. Turn south and drive 10 miles to the town of Seal Rock. Continue south on U.S. 101 for one-quarter mile to the park entrance on the left.

Contact: Seal Rock Rock's RV Cove, 1276 N.W. Cross St., P.O. Box 71, Seal Rock, OR 97376, 541/563-3955.

41 DRIFT CREEK LANDING

Rating: 6

On the Alsea River.

Map 7.3, grid e8, page 421

This campground is set along the shore of the Alsea River in a heavily treed and mountainous area. The Oregon Coast Aquarium is 15 miles away, and an 18-hole golf course is nearby. There are 10 mobile homes on this property with long-term renters. For more information on the area, see the description of Waldport/Newport KOA.

Campsites, facilities: There are 49 sites for RVs of any length and an area for tent camping. Electricity, drinking water, and sewer hookups are provided. Flush toilets, private telephone service, cable TV, bottled gas, showers, a recreation hall, a store, a café, a laundry room, boat

docks, boat rentals, and launching facilities are available. Leashed pets are permitted.

Reservations, fees: Reservations accepted. Sites are $22 per night, $2 per person for more than two people, and $5 per extra vehicle. Open year-round.

Directions: From Albany, drive west on U.S. 20 for 66 miles to Newport and U.S. 101. Turn south and drive 14 miles to Waldport and Highway 34. Turn east on Highway 34 and drive 3.5 miles to the campground.

Contact: Drift Creek Landing, 3851 Hwy. 34, Waldport, OR 97394, 541/563-3610, fax 541/563-5234.

42 FISHIN' HOLE RV PARK & MARINA

Rating: 6

On the Alsea River.

Map 7.3, grid e8, page 421

This campground is one of several along the shore of the Alsea River. About half of the sites here are filled with monthly rentals. For information on the area, see the description of Waldport/Newport KOA.

Campsites, facilities: There are 16 tent sites, 20 sites for RVs of any length, and one cabin. Electricity, drinking water, sewer hookups (10 sites only), picnic tables, flush toilets, showers, a laundry room, boat docks, boat rentals, and launching facilities are available. Leashed pets are permitted.

Reservations, fees: Reservations at 877/770-6137. Tent sites are $10 per night, and RV sites are $15–18; $2 per person for more than two people, with $1 additional fee per night for cable TV. Open year-round.

Directions: From Albany, drive west on U.S. 20 for 66 miles to Newport and U.S. 101. Turn south and drive 14 miles to Waldport and Highway 34. Turn east on Highway 34 and drive four miles to the entrance on the left.

Contact: Fishin' Hole RV Park & Marina, 3911 Hwy. 34, Waldport, OR 97394, 541/563-3401.

43 CHINOOK RV PARK

Rating: 7

On the Alsea River.

Map 7.3, grid e8, page 421

This trailer park is set along the shore of the Alsea River, about 3.5 miles from the ocean. The park is filled primarily with monthly rentals. Campsites are rented on a space-available basis. As a result, RV sites with hookups are almost never available; sites without hookups can almost always be found here as an emergency backup spot. For more information on the area, see the description of Waldport/Newport KOA.

Campsites, facilities: There are six sites for tents and 22 sites with full hookups for RVs of any length. Electricity, drinking water, cable TV, sewer hookups, flush toilets, showers, and a laundry room are available. A store, a café, and ice are within one mile. Boat docks are nearby. Bottled gas is available 3.5 miles away. Leashed pets are permitted.

Reservations, fees: Reservations accepted. Sites are $10–16 per night, $2 per person for more than two people. Open year-round.

Directions: From Albany, drive west on U.S. 20 for 66 miles to Newport and U.S. 101. Turn south and drive 14 miles to Waldport and Highway 34. Turn east on Highway 34 and drive 3.5 miles to the park entrance.

Contact: Chinook RV Park, 3299 Highway 34, Waldport, OR 97394, 541/563-3485.

44 TAYLOR'S LANDING

Rating: 9

On the Alsea River.

Map 7.3, grid e8, page 421

This campground is set along the Alsea River. Fall, when the salmon fishing is best, is the prime time here and the park often fills. For more information on the area, see the description of Waldport/Newport KOA.

Campsites, facilities: There are six tent sites and 28 sites for RVs. Electricity, drinking water, cable TV, sewer hookups, and picnic tables are provided. Flush toilets, bottled gas, showers, a café, and a laundry room are available. Boat docks, launching facilities, and rentals are nearby. Leashed pets are permitted.

Reservations, fees: Reservations accepted. Sites are $19–22 per night, $1 per person for more than two people. Monthly rates available. Open year-round.

Directions: From Albany, drive west on U.S. 20 for 66 miles to Newport and U.S. 101. Turn south and drive 14 miles to Waldport and Highway 34. Turn east on Highway 34 and drive seven miles to the entrance on the right.

Contact: Taylor's Landing, 7164 Alsea Hwy. 34, Waldport, OR 97394, 541/528-3388 (telephone and fax).

45 WALDPORT/NEWPORT KOA

Rating: 8

On Alsea Bay.

Map 7.3, grid e8, page 421

This pretty park, set amid some of the oldest pine trees in Oregon, is located within walking distance of the beach, the bay, and downtown Waldport—and to top it off, the campsites have beautiful ocean views. Alsea Bay's sandy and rocky shoreline makes this area a favorite with anglers. The crabbing and clamming can also be quite good. South Beach State Park, about five miles north on U.S. 101, offers more fishing and a boat ramp along Beaver Creek. It's open for day use only. Other nearby recreation options include hiking trails, marked bike trails, the Oregon Coast Aquarium, and a marina.

Campsites, facilities: There are 12 tent sites and 75 sites for RVs of any length, plus 15 cabins. Electricity, drinking water, cable TV, and sewer hookups are provided. Flush toilets, showers, and a recreation hall are available. Bottled gas, an RV dump station, a store, a café, a coin laundry, and ice are within one mile. Boat docks, launching facilities, and boat rentals are nearby. Leashed pets are permitted.

Reservations, fees: Reservations at 800/562-3443. Sites are $18–34 per night, $2–5 per person for more than two people. Major credit cards accepted. Open year-round.

Directions: From Albany, drive west on U.S. 20 for 66 miles to Newport and U.S. 101. Turn south and drive to Milepost 155 at the north end of the Alsea Bay Bridge. The park is on the west side of the bridge.

Contact: Waldport/Newport KOA, 1330 N.W. Pacific Coast Hwy., P.O. Box 397, Waldport, OR 97394, 541/563-2250, fax 541/563-4098, website: www.koa.com.

46 BEACHSIDE STATE PARK

Rating: 7

Near Alsea Bay.

Map 7.3, grid e8, page 421

This state park offers about nine miles of beach and is not far from Alsea Bay and the Alsea River. Every site is seconds from the beach. This is a popular winter camping park. Within 30 miles in either direction, you'll find visitor centers, tidepools, hiking and driving tours, three lighthouses, crabbing, clamming, fishing, an aquarium, and science centers. See the description of Waldport/Newport KOA for more information on the fishing opportunities in the area.

Campsites, facilities: There are 28 sites for tents, 33 sites with water and electrical hookups for RVs up to 30 feet long, two yurts, and a special camping area for hikers and bicyclists. Picnic tables and fire grills are provided. Drinking water, garbage bins, flush toilets, showers, recycling, and firewood are available. A horseshoe pit is available nearby. Some facilities are wheelchair accessible. Leashed pets are permitted.

Reservations, fees: Reservations at 800/452-5687 or website: www.OregonStateParks.org ($7 reservation fee). Sites are $13–20 per night,

$7 per extra vehicle, and $4 per person per night for hikers/bicyclists; yurts are $27 per night. Major credit cards accepted. Open mid-March–October, weather permitting.

Directions: From Albany, drive west on U.S. 20 for 66 miles to Newport and U.S. 101. Turn south on U.S. 101 and drive 16 miles to Waldport. Continue south on U.S. 101 for four miles to the park entrance.

Contact: Beachside State Park, P.O. Box 693, Waldport, OR 97394, 541/563-3220, fax 541/563-3657.

47 TILLICUM BEACH

Rating: 8

On the Pacific Ocean in Siuslaw National Forest.

Map 7.3, grid e8, page 421

Ocean-view campsites are a big draw at this campground just south of Beachside State Park. Nearby forest roads provide access to streams in the mountains east of the beach area. A U.S. Forest Service map details the possibilities. Since it's just off the highway and along the water, this camp fills up very quickly in the summer, so expect crowds.

Campsites, facilities: There are 61 sites for tents or RVs up to 40 feet long. Picnic tables and fire grills are provided. Flush toilets, garbage bins, and drinking water are available. Leashed pets are permitted.

Reservations, fees: Reservations are not accepted. Sites are $15 per night, $5 per extra vehicle. Senior discount available. Open year-round.

Directions: From Albany, drive west on U.S. 20 for 66 miles to Newport and U.S. 101. Turn south on U.S. 101 and drive 14 miles to Waldport. Continue south on U.S. 101 for 4.5 miles to the campground entrance on the right.

Contact: Siuslaw National Forest, Waldport Ranger District, P.O. Box 400, 1049 S.W. Pacific Coast Hwy., Waldport, OR 97394, 541/563-3211, fax 541/563-3124; concessionaire, 541/547-3679.

48 CAPE PERPETUA
🚶 🛶 🛏 🚐 ⛺

Rating: 8

On Cape Creek in Siuslaw National Forest.
Map 7.3, grid f8, page 421

This U.S. Forest Service campground is set along Cape Creek in the Cape Perpetua Scenic Area. The visitor information center provides hiking and driving maps to guide you through this spectacular region, and you can also watch a movie about the area. Maps highlight the tidepool and picnic spots. The coastal cliffs are perfect for whale-watching from December–March. Neptune State Park is just south and offers additional rugged coastline vistas.

Campsites, facilities: There are 37 sites for tents or RVs up to 22 feet long, plus one group site that can accommodate 100 campers. Picnic tables and fire grills are provided. Flush toilets, drinking water, and garbage bins are available. Leashed pets are permitted.

Reservations, fees: Reservations are not accepted for family sites. Sites are $15 per night, $5 per extra vehicle. Reservations required for the group site at 877/444-6777 or website: www.ReserveUsa.com ($9 reservation fee); $125 per night. Senior discount available. Open year-round.

Directions: From Albany, drive west on U.S. 20 for 66 miles to Newport and U.S. 101. Turn south and drive 23 miles to Yachats. Continue three miles south on U.S. 101 to the entrance on the left.

Contact: Siuslaw National Forest, Waldport Ranger District, 1049 S.W. Pacific Coast Hwy., P.O. Box 400, Waldport, OR 97394, 541/563-3211, fax 541/563-3124; concessionaire, 541/822-3799.

49 SEA PERCH
🚶 🛶 🛏 🚐

Rating: 8

Near Cape Perpetua.
Map 7.3, grid f8, page 421

Sea Perch sits right in the middle of one of the most scenic areas on the Oregon coast. This private camp just south of Cape Perpetua has sites on the beach and in lawn areas, plus its own shell museum and gift shop. Big rigs are welcome here. No tent camping is permitted. For more information on the area, see the description of Cape Perpetua.

Campsites, facilities: There are 18 back-up sites with full hookups and 17 pull-through sites for RVs of any length. Electricity, drinking water, sewer hookups, and picnic tables are provided. Flush toilets, an RV dump station, showers, firewood, a recreation hall, a laundry room, ice, a store, modem hookups, and a beach are available. Leashed pets are permitted.

Reservations, fees: Reservations accepted. Sites are $28–32 per night June–October, $24 in the off-season, and $2 per person for more than two people. Major credit cards accepted. Open year-round.

Directions: From Albany, drive west on U.S. 20 for 66 miles to Newport and U.S. 101. Turn south and drive 23 miles to Yachats. Continue south on U.S. 101 for 6.5 miles to the campground at Milepost 171 on the right.

Contact: Sea Perch Campground, 95480 U.S. 101, Yachats, OR 97498, 541/547-3505.

50 ROCK CREEK
🛶 🛏 🚐 ⛺

Rating: 7

On Rock Creek in Siuslaw National Forest.
Map 7.3, grid f8, page 421

This little campground is set along Rock Creek just one-quarter mile from the ocean. It's a premium spot for coastal-highway travelers, although it can get packed very quickly. An excellent side trip is to Cape Perpetua, a designated scenic area a few miles up the coast. The cape offers beautiful ocean views and a visitor center that will supply you with information on nature trails, picnic spots, tidepools, and where to find the best viewpoints in the area.

Campsites, facilities: There are 16 sites for tents or RVs up to 22 feet long. Fire grills and picnic tables are provided. Flush toilets, garbage bins, and drinking water are available. Leashed pets are permitted.

Reservations, fees: Reservations are not accepted. Sites are $15 per night, $5 per extra vehicle. Senior discount available. Open year-round.

Directions: From Albany, drive west on U.S. 20 for 66 miles to Newport and U.S. 101. Turn south and drive 23 miles to Yachats. Continue south on U.S. 101 for 10 miles to the campground entrance on the left.

Contact: Siuslaw National Forest, Waldport Ranger District, 1049 S.W. Pacific Coast Hwy., P.O. Box 400, Waldport, OR 97394, 541/563-3211, fax 541/563-3124; concessionaire, 541/547-3679.

51 CARL G. WASHBURNE STATE PARK

Rating: 7

On the Pacific Ocean.
Map 7.3, grid h8, page 421

These spacious campsites feature a buffer of native plants between you and the highway. At night you can hear the pounding surf. A creek runs through the campground, and elk have been known to wander through. Short hikes lead from the campground to a two-mile-long beach, extensive tidepools along the base of the cliffs, and a three-mile trail to Heceta Head Lighthouse. Just three miles south of the park are the Sea Lion Caves, where an elevator takes visitors down into a cavern for an insider's view of the life of a sea lion.

Campsites, facilities: There are seven primitive walk-in sites, 58 sites with full hookups for RVs up to 45 feet long, and two yurts. A special area is available for hikers and bicyclists. Drinking water, garbage bins, an RV dump station, and picnic tables are provided. Flush toilets, showers, and firewood are available. Leashed pets are permitted.

Reservations, fees: Reservations are not accepted. Sites are $13–19 per night, $7 per extra vehicle, and $4 per person per night for hikers/bicyclists; $27 per night for yurts. Major credit cards accepted. Open year-round.

Directions: From Eugene, drive west on Highway 126 for 61 miles to Florence and U.S. 101. Turn north on U.S. 101 and drive 12.5 miles to the park entrance road (well signed, 10 miles south of the town of Yachats). Turn west and drive a short distance to the park.

Contact: Carl G. Washburne State Park, 93111 U.S. 101 N, Florence, OR 97439, 800/551-6949 or 541/547-3416.

52 ALDER DUNE

Rating: 7

Near Alder Lake in Siuslaw National Forest.
Map 7.3, grid h8, page 421

This wooded campground is situated near four lakes–Alder Lake, Sutton Lake, Dune Lake, and Mercer Lake (the largest). A boat launch is available at Sutton Lake. An recreation option is to explore the expansive sand dunes in the area by foot. There is no off-road-vehicle access here. See the description of Harbor Vista Park for other information on the area.

Campsites, facilities: There are 39 sites for tents or RVs up to 30 feet long. Picnic tables and fire grills are provided. Flush toilets, garbage bins, and drinking water are available. Leashed pets are permitted.

Reservations, fees: Reservations are not accepted. Sites are $15 per night, $7 per extra vehicle. Senior discount available. Open mid-May–mid-September.

Directions: From Eugene, drive west on Highway 126 for 61 miles to Florence and U.S. 101. Turn north on U.S. 101 and drive eight miles to the campground on the left.

Contact: Siuslaw National Forest, Mapleton Ranger District, 4480 U.S. 101, Building G, Florence, OR 97439, 541/902-8526, fax 541/902-6946.

53 SUTTON

Rating: 7

Near Sutton Lake in Siuslaw National Forest.
Map 7.3, grid h8, page 421

This campground is located adjacent to Sutton Creek, not far from Sutton Lake. Vegetation provides some privacy between sites. Holman Vista on Sutton Beach Road provides a beautiful view of the dunes and ocean. Wading and fishing are both popular. A hiking trail system leads from the camp out to the dunes. There is no off-road-vehicle access here. An alternative camp is Alder Dune to the north.

Campsites, facilities: There are 80 sites, 20 with partial hookups, for tents or RVs up to 30 feet long and two group sites. Picnic tables and fire grills are provided. Flush toilets, garbage bins, and drinking water are available. A boat ramp is nearby. Leashed pets are permitted.

Reservations, fees: Reservations at 877/444-6777 or website: www.ReserveUsa.com ($9 reservation fee). Sites are $15–17 per night, $7 per extra vehicle, and $75–120 for group sites. Senior discount available. Open year-round.

Directions: From Eugene, drive west on Highway 126 for 61 miles to Florence and U.S. 101. Turn north on U.S. 101 and drive six miles to Sutton Beach Road (Forest Road 794). Turn northwest and drive 1.5 miles to the campground entrance.

Contact: Siuslaw National Forest, Mapleton Ranger District, 4480 U.S. 101, Building G, Florence, OR 97439, 541/902-8526, fax 541/902-6946.

54 NORTH FORK SIUSLAW

Rating: 6

On the North Fork of the Siuslaw River in Siuslaw National Forest.
Map 7.3, grid h8, page 421

Little known and little used, this wooded camp along the North Fork of the Siuslaw River is the ideal hideaway. This campground was once more developed, but it is now a primitive site, with toilets, fir grills, picnic tables, and garbage containers removed. A dirt road opposite the camp follows Wilhelm Creek for about two miles. A newly constructed trail through old-growth forest is nearby. See a U.S. Forest Service map for other side-trip possibilities.

Campsites, facilities: There are six tent sites. There is no drinking water. Garbage must be packed out. Leashed pets are permitted.

Reservations, fees: Reservations are not accepted. There is no fee for camping. Open May–October.

Directions: From Eugene, drive west on Highway 126 for 50 miles to County Road 5070/North Fork (one mile east of Florence). Turn right and drive 12 miles northeast to the campground.

Contact: Siuslaw National Forest, Mapleton Ranger District, 4480 U.S. 101, Building G, Florence, OR 97439, 541/902-8526, fax 541/902-6946.

55 CANAL CREEK

Rating: 5

On Canal Creek in Siuslaw National Forest.
Map 7.4, grid e1, page 422

This pleasant little campground is just off the beaten path in a large, wooded, open area along Canal Creek. It feels remote because of the creek that runs through the campground and the historic homesites nearby, with old fruit trees on the grounds. Yet it has easy access and is close to the coast and all the amenities. The climate here is relatively mild, but on the other hand, there is the rain in winter—lots of it.

Campsites, facilities: There are 11 sites for tents and 10 sites for tents or small RVs, plus a group area for up to 100 people. Picnic tables and fire grills are provided. Drinking water, garbage bins, and vault toilets are available. The group site has a picnic shelter and a play area. Leashed pets are permitted.

Reservations, fees: Reservations are not ac-

cepted for family sites. Sites are $10 per night, $5 per extra vehicle. Senior discount available. Group reservations at 877/444-6777 or website: www.ReserveUsa.com ($9 reservation fee); $95–125 per night. Open year-round.

Directions: From Albany, drive west on U.S. 20 for 15 miles to Philomath and Highway 34. Turn south on Highway 34 and drive 52 miles to Forest Road 3462. Turn south and drive four miles to the camp.

Contact: Siuslaw National Forest, Waldport Ranger District, 1049 S.W. Pacific Coast Hwy., P.O. Box 400, Waldport, OR 97394, 541/563-3211, fax 541/563-3124.

56 BLACKBERRY

Rating: 7

On the Alsea River in Siuslaw National Forest.
Map 7.4, grid f3, page 422

Blackberry makes a good base camp for a fishing trip on the Alsea River. The U.S. Forest Service provides boat launches and picnic areas at several spots along this stretch of river. Often there is a camp host, who can give you inside information on nearby recreational opportunities. Large fir trees and lawn separate the sites.

Campsites, facilities: There are 32 sites for tents or RVs. Picnic tables and fire grills are provided. Drinking water, garbage bins, and flush toilets are available. There is no firewood. A boat ramp is on-site. Leashed pets are permitted.

Reservations, fees: Reservations are not accepted. Sites are $10 per night, $5 per extra vehicle. Senior discount available. Open year-round.

Directions: From Albany, drive west on U.S. 20 for 15 miles to Philomath and Highway 34. Turn south on Highway 34 and drive 41 miles to the campground entrance.

Contact: Siuslaw National Forest, Waldport Ranger District, 1049 S.W. Pacific Coast Hwy., P.O. Box 400, Waldport, OR 97394, 541/563-3211, fax 541/563-3124.

57 ALSEA FALLS

Rating: 8

Adjacent to the South Fork of the Alsea River.
Map 7.4, grid f4, page 422

Enjoy the beautiful surroundings of Alsea Falls by exploring the trails that wander through this park and lead to a picnic area by the falls. Trails to McBee Park and Green Peak Falls are accessible from the campground along the South Fork of the river. The campsites are situated in a 40-year-old forest of Douglas fir and vine maple. On a warm day, Alsea Falls offers cool relief along the river. The area was named after its original inhabitants, the Alsea Indians.

Campsites, facilities: There are 22 sites for tents or RVs up to 30 feet long. Fire pits are provided. Drinking water, vault toilets, garbage bins, and fireplaces for wood and charcoal are available. Leashed pets are permitted.

Reservations, fees: Reservations are not accepted. Sites are $6 per night, $4 per extra vehicle. Senior discount available. Open mid-May–late September.

Directions: From Albany, drive west on U.S. 20 for nine miles to Corvallis. Turn left (south) onto Highway 99 and drive 15 miles to County Road 45120. Turn right (west) and drive five miles to Alpine Junction. Continue along the South Fork Alsea Access Road for nine miles to the campground on the right.

Contact: Bureau of Land Management, Salem District Office, 1717 Fabry Rd. SE, Salem, OR 97306, 503/375-5646, fax 503/375-5622.

58 MAPLE LANE TRAILER PARK-MARINA

Rating: 5

On the Siuslaw River.
Map 7.4, grid h2, page 422

This park along the shore of the Siuslaw River in Mapleton is close to hiking trails. The general area is surrounded by Siuslaw National

Forest land. A U.S. Forest Service map details nearby backcountry side-trip options. Fall is the most popular time of the year here, as it's prime time for salmon fishing on Siuslaw.

Campsites, facilities: There are two tent sites and 46 sites with full hookups for RVs up to 35 feet long. Electricity, drinking water, and sewer hookups are provided. Flush toilets, bottled gas, an RV dump station, and showers are available. A store, a café, and ice are behind the park. A bait and tackle shop is open during the fishing season. Boat docks and launching facilities are on-site. Small pets (under 15 pounds) are permitted.

Reservations, fees: Reservations accepted. Sites are $7–14 per night, $1.50 per person for more than two people, and $2 per extra vehicle. Open year-round.

Directions: From Eugene, drive west on Highway 126 for 47 miles to Mapleton. Continue on Highway 126 for one-quarter mile past the business district to the park entrance on the left.

Contact: Maple Lane Trailer Park-Marina, 10730 Hwy.126, Mapleton, OR 97453, 541/268-4822.

59 ARCHIE KNOWLES

Rating: 6

On Knowles Creek in Siuslaw National Forest.
Map 7.4, grid h2, page 422

This little campground along Knowles Creek about three miles east of Mapleton is rustic with a mix of forested and lawn areas, yet it offers easy proximity to the highway.

Campsites, facilities: There are nine sites for tents or RVs up to 16 feet long. Picnic tables and fire grills are provided. Chemical toilets, garbage bins, and drinking water are available. Leashed pets are permitted.

Reservations, fees: Reservations are not accepted. Sites are $10 per night, $7 per extra vehicle. Senior discount available. Open May–late September.

Directions: From Eugene, drive west on Highway 126 for 44 miles to the campground entrance (three miles east of Mapleton).

Contact: Siuslaw National Forest, Mapleton Ranger District, 4480 U.S. 101, Building G, Florence, OR 97439, 541/902-8526, fax 541/902-6946.

60 HARBOR VISTA COUNTY PARK

Rating: 6

Near Florence.
Map 7.5, grid a7, page 423

This county park out among the dunes near the entrance to the harbor offers a great lookout point from its observation deck. A number of side trips are available, including to the Sea Lion Caves, Darlington State Park, Jessie M. Honeyman Memorial State Park (see the description of Jessie M. Honeyman), and the Indian Forest, just four miles north. Florence also has displays of Native American dwellings and crafts.

Campsites, facilities: There are 38 sites for tents or RVs up to 60 feet long. Picnic tables and garbage bins are provided. Electricity, flush toilets, fire rings, an RV dump station, coin-operated showers, drinking water, a pay phone, and a playground are available. Leashed pets are permitted.

Reservations, fees: Reservations at 541/997-5987 ($10 reservation fee). Sites are $16 per night, $5 per night for a third vehicle. Open year-round.

Directions: From Eugene, drive west on Highway 126 for 61 miles to Florence and U.S. 101. Turn right (north) and drive four miles to 35th Street. Turn left and drive to where it dead-ends into Rhododendron Drive. Turn right and drive 1.4 miles to North Jetty Road. Turn left and drive half a block to Harbor Vista Road. Turn left and continue to the campground at 87658 Harbor Vista Road.

Note: Follow these exact directions. Previous visitors to this park taking a different route will discover that part of Harbor Vista Road is now gated.

Contact: Harbor Vista County Park, 87658 Harbor Vista Rd., Florence, OR 97439, 541/997-5987, website: www.co.lane.or.us/park.

61 B AND E WAYSIDE MOBILE HOME AND RV PARK

Rating: 5

Near Florence.
Map 7.5, grid a8, page 423
This landscaped park is beautifully maintained, clean, and quiet. The property features a 28-unit mobile home park that is adjacent to this RV park. Some sites at the RV park are taken by monthly rentals. No tent camping. See the descriptions of Lane County Harbor Vista Park and Port of Siuslaw RV and Marina for side-trip ideas. Nearby recreation options include two golf courses and a riding stable (two miles away).
Campsites, facilities: There are 24 sites for RVs of any length. Electricity, drinking water, sewer hookups, and picnic tables are provided. Flush toilets, an RV dump station, showers, and a laundry room are available. Bottled gas, a store, ice, a café, and a restaurant are within two miles. Boat-launching facilities are nearby. Small leashed pets are permitted.
Reservations, fees: Reservations accepted. Sites are $20 per night, $2 per person for more than two people. Open year-round.
Directions: From Eugene, drive west on Highway 126 for 61 miles to Florence and U.S. 101. Turn north on U.S. 101 and drive 1.8 miles to the park on the right.
Contact: B and E Wayside Mobile Home and RV Park, 3760 U.S. 101 N, Florence, OR 97439, 541/997-6451.

62 PORT OF SIUSLAW RV PARK AND MARINA

Rating: 8

On the Siuslaw River.
Map 7.5, grid a8, page 423
This public resort can be found along the Siuslaw River in a grassy, urban setting. Anglers with boats will find that the U.S. 101 bridge support pilings make good spots for crabbing as well as fishing for perch and flounder. A new set of docks with drinking water, electricity, gasoline, security, and a fish-cleaning station are available. The sea lion caves and estuary are a bonus for wildlife lovers, and nearby lakes make swimming and water-skiing a possibility. Golf is within driving distance, and horses can be rented about nine miles away.
Campsites, facilities: There are 84 sites for tents or RVs of any length. Electricity, drinking water, sewer hookups, cable TV and picnic tables are provided. Flush toilets, an RV dump station, showers, a laundry room, and boat docks are available. A café and ice are within one mile. Leashed pets are permitted.
Reservations, fees: Reservations at 541/997-3040. Sites are $20–22 per night. Major credit cards accepted. Open year-round.
Directions: From Eugene, drive west on Highway 126 for 61 miles to Florence and U.S. 101. Turn south on U.S. 101 and drive to Harbor Street. Turn left (east) on Harbor Street and drive about three blocks to the park and marina.
Contact: Port of Siuslaw RV Park and Marina, 080 Harbor St., P.O. Box 1638, Florence, OR 97439, 541/997-3040.

63 JESSIE M. HONEYMAN MEMORIAL STATE PARK

Rating: 7

Near Cleowax Lake.
Map 7.5, grid a8, page 423
This popular state park is within walking distance of the shore of Cleowax Lake and adjacent to the dunes of the Oregon Dunes National Recreation Area. Dunes stretch for two miles between the park and the ocean. The dunes here are quite impressive, with some reaching to 500 feet. In the winter, the area is open to OHV use. For thrill seekers, sand boards (for sand-boarding on the dunes) are available to rent in nearby Florence. The two lakes in the

park offer facilities for boating, fishing, and swimming. A one-mile hiking trail with access to the dunes is available in the park and off-road vehicle trails are nearby in the sand dunes.

Campsites, facilities: There are 237 sites for tents and 141 sites for RVs up to 60 feet long (with full or partial hookups), a special camping area for hikers and bicyclists, six group tent areas, and 10 yurts. Picnic tables, garbage bins, and fire grills are provided. Drinking water, flush toilets, an RV dump station, showers, evening interpretive programs and events, and firewood are available. Some facilities are wheelchair accessible. Boat docks and launching facilities are nearby. Leashed pets are permitted.

Reservations, fees: Reservations at 800/452-5687 or website: www.OregonStateParks.org ($7 reservation fee). Sites are $13–19 per night, $7 per extra vehicle, $4 per person per night for hikers/bicyclists, $27 per night for yurts, and $64 per night for group sites. Open year-round.

Directions: From Eugene, drive west on Highway 126 for 61 miles to Florence and U.S. 101. Turn south on U.S. 101 and drive three miles to the park entrance.

Contact: Jessie M. Honeyman Memorial State Park, 84505 U.S. 101, Florence, OR 97439, 800/551-6949 or 541/997-3641.

64 LAKESHORE RV PARK

Rating: 5

On Woahink Lake.

Map 7.5, grid a8, page 423

Here's a prime area for vacationers. This park is set along the shore of Woahink Lake, a popular spot to fish for trout, perch, catfish, crappie, bluegill, and bass. It's adjacent to Jessie M. Honeyman Memorial State Park and the Oregon Dunes National Recreation Area. Off-road-vehicle access to the dunes is four miles northeast of the park. Hiking trails through the dunes can be found at Honeyman Memo-

rial State Park. If you set out across the dunes off the trail, note your path. People hiking off-trail commonly get lost here. Six of the 20 sites are reserved for use by overnighters. The rest are usually filled by monthly rentals. No tent camping.

Campsites, facilities: There are 20 sites for RVs of any length; six are drive-through sites. Electricity, drinking water, cable TV, and sewer hookups are provided. Flush toilets, showers, and a laundry room are available. A café is within three miles. Boat docks are nearby. Leashed pets are permitted.

Reservations, fees: Reservations accepted. Sites are $20 per night, $2 per person for more than two people. Monthly rentals available. Open year-round.

Directions: From Eugene, drive west on Highway 126 for 61 miles to Florence and U.S. 101. Turn south on U.S. 101 and drive four miles to Milepost 195 and the park on the left.

Contact: Lakeshore RV Park, 83763 U.S. 101, Florence, OR 97439, 541/997-2741, website: www.lakeshorerv.com.

65 WOAHINK LAKE RV RESORT

Rating: 7

On Woahink Lake.

Map 7.5, grid a8, page 423

One of several RV parks in the Florence area, this quiet, clean camp is across from Woahink Lake, where trout fishing is an option. Nearby Oregon Dunes National Recreation Area makes a good side trip.

Campsites, facilities: There are 76 sites for RVs of any length and one cabin. No tent camping is allowed. Electricity, drinking water, sewer hookups, restrooms, showers, cable TV, a public phone, and a laundry room are available. Recreational facilities include horseshoe pits, a recreation hall, a game room, and a boat dock. One large or two small leashed pets per site are permitted.

Reservations, fees: Reservations recommended. Sites are $23.50 per night, $2 per person for more than two people, and $6 per extra vehicle. Senior discount available. Open year-round.

Directions: From Eugene, drive west on Highway 126 for 61 miles to Florence and U.S. 101. Turn south on U.S. 101 and drive 5.1 miles to the camp on the right.

Contact: Woahink Lake RV Resort, 83570 U.S. 101 S, Florence, OR 97439, 541/997-6454, reservations 800/659-6454, fax 541/902-0481, website: www.ohwy.com/or/w/woahlkrv.htm.

66 MERCER LAKE RESORT

Rating: 7

On Mercer Lake.
Map 7.5, grid a8, page 423

This resort is set along the shore of Mercer Lake, one of a number of lakes that have formed among the ancient dunes in this area.

Campsites, facilities: There are 13 sites, four drive-through, for RVs of any length and 10 cabins. Electricity, drinking water, cable TV, sewer hookups, and picnic tables are provided. Flush toilets, an RV dump station, showers, a store, a laundry room, and ice are available. Boat docks, launching facilities, and fishing boat rentals are on-site. Leashed pets are permitted.

Reservations, fees: Reservations at 800/355-3633. Sites are $16–20 per night, $2 per person for more than two people, and $2 per extra vehicle. Major credit cards accepted. Open year-round.

Directions: From Eugene, drive west on Highway 126 for 61 miles to Florence and U.S. 101. Turn north on U.S. 101 and drive five miles to Mercer Lake Road. Turn east and drive just under one mile to Bay Berry Lane. Turn left and drive to the campground.

Contact: Mercer Lake Resort, 88875 Bay Berry Ln., Florence, OR 97439, 541/997-3633, fax 541/997-5096, website: www.mlroregon.com.

67 CARTER LAKE

Rating: 9

On Carter Lake in Oregon Dunes National Recreation Area.
Map 7.5, grid a8, page 423

This campground sits on the north shore of Carter Lake, and you can fish almost right from your campsite. Boating, swimming, and fishing are permitted on this long, narrow lake, which is set among dunes overgrown with vegetation. The nearby Taylor Dunes Trail is an easy half-mile wheelchair-accessible trail to the dunes past Taylor Lake. Hiking is allowed in the dunes, but there is no off-road-vehicle access here. If you want off-road access, head north one mile to Siltcoos Road, turn west, and drive 1.3 miles to Driftwood II.

Campsites, facilities: There are 23 sites for tents or RVs up to 35 feet long. Picnic tables, garbage service, and fire grills are provided. Drinking water and flush toilets are available. Leashed pets are permitted.

Reservations, fees: Reservations at 877/444-6777 or website: www.ReserveUsa.com ($9 reservation fee). Sites are $15 per night, $7 per extra vehicle. Senior discount available. Open April–September.

Directions: From Eugene, drive west on Highway 126 for 61 miles to Florence and U.S. 101. Turn south on U.S. 101 and drive 8.5 miles to Forest Road 1084. Turn right on Forest Road 1084 and drive west 200 yards to the camp.

Contact: Oregon Dunes National Recreation Area, Visitor Center, 855 U.S. 101, Reedsport, OR 97467, 541/271-3611, fax 541/750-7244.

68 DRIFTWOOD II

Rating: 6

Near Siltcoos Lake in Oregon Dunes National Recreation Area.
Map 7.5, grid b7, page 423

Primarily a campground for off-road vehicles,

Driftwood II is set near the ocean, but without an ocean view, in the Oregon Dunes National Recreation Area. It has off-road-vehicle access. Several small lakes, the Siltcoos River, and Siltcoos Lake are nearby. Note that ATV use is prohibited between 10 P.M. and 6 A.M.

Campsites, facilities: There are 69 sites for tents or RVs up to 50 feet long. Picnic tables, garbage service, and fire grills are provided. Drinking water and flush and vault toilets are available. An RV dump station is within five miles. Some facilities are wheelchair accessible. Boat docks, launching facilities, and rentals can be found about four miles away on Siltcoos Lake. Leashed pets are permitted.

Reservations, fees: Reservations at 877/444-6777 or website: www.ReserveUsa.com ($9 reservation fee). Sites are $15 per night, $7 per night for each additional vehicle. Senior discount available. Open year-round.

Directions: From Eugene, drive west on Highway 126 for 61 miles to Florence and U.S. 101. Turn south on U.S. 101 and drive seven miles to Siltcoos Beach Road. Turn right and drive 1.5 miles west to the campground.

Contact: Oregon Dunes National Recreation Area, Visitor Center, 855 U.S. 101, Reedsport, OR 97467, 541/271-3611, fax 541/750-7244.

69 LAGOON

Rating: 9

Near Siltcoos Lake in Oregon Dunes National Recreation Area.

Map 7.5, grid b7, page 423

One of several campgrounds in the area, this camp is located along the lagoon, about one mile from Siltcoos Lake, and set one-half mile inland. The Lagoon Trail offers prime wildlife viewing for marine birds and other aquatic species.

Campsites, facilities: There are 39 sites for tents or RVs up to 35 feet long. Picnic tables, garbage service, and fire grills are provided. Drinking water and flush and vault toilets are available.

A telephone and an RV dump station are within five miles. Boat docks, launching facilities, and rentals are nearby on Siltcoos Lake. Leashed pets are permitted.

Reservations, fees: Reservations are not accepted. Sites are $15 per night, $7 per extra vehicle. Senior discount available. Open year-round.

Directions: From Eugene, drive west on Highway 126 for 61 miles to Florence and U.S. 101. Turn south on U.S. 101 and drive seven miles to Siltcoos Beach Road. Turn right on Siltcoos Beach Road and drive west for 1.2 miles to the campground.

Contact: Oregon Dunes National Recreation Area, 855 U.S. 101, Reedsport, OR 97467, 541/271-3611, fax 541/750-7244.

70 DARLINGS RESORT

Rating: 7

On Siltcoos Lake.

Map 7.5, grid b7, page 423

This park, in a rural area along the north shore of Siltcoos Lake, is adjacent to the extensive Oregon Dunes National Recreation Area. Sites are right on the lake; fish from your picnic table. An access point to the dunes for hikers and off-road vehicles is just across the highway. The lake has a full-service marina. About half the sites are taken by monthly rentals. No tent camping.

Campsites, facilities: There are 42 sites, 18 with full hookups, for RVs of any length. Electricity, cable TV, drinking water, sewer hookups, and picnic tables are provided. Flush toilets, showers, firewood, a store, a tavern, a deli, boat docks, boat rentals, launching facilities, and a laundry room are available. Leashed pets are permitted.

Reservations, fees: Reservations accepted. Sites are $22.50 per night, $5 per extra vehicle. Major credit cards accepted. Open year-round.

Directions: From Eugene, drive west on Highway 126 for 61 miles to Florence and U.S. 101.

Turn south on U.S. 101 and drive five miles to North Beach Road. Turn east and drive one-half mile to the resort.

Contact: Darlings Resort, 4879 Darling Loop, Florence, OR 97439, 541/997-2841, website: www.darlingsresort.com.

71 TYEE

Rating: 6

On the Siltcoos River in Oregon Dunes National Recreation Area.

Map 7.5, grid b7, page 423

This wooded campground along the shore of the Siltcoos River provides an alternative to Driftwood II and Lagoon. Swimming, fishing, and water-skiing are permitted at the nearby lake, where there is a canoe portage trail and a boat ramp. Off-road-vehicle access to the dunes is available from Driftwood II, and there are hiking trails in the area.

Campsites, facilities: There are 16 sites for tents or RVs up to 30 feet long. Picnic tables, garbage service, and fire grills are provided. Drinking water, vault toilets, and a day-use area (with horseshoe pits, electricity, and 10 tables) are available. A store, boat docks, launching facilities, and rentals are nearby. Some facilities are wheelchair accessible. Leashed pets are permitted.

Reservations, fees: Reservations at 877/444-6777 or website: www.ReserveUsa.com ($9 reservation fee). Sites are $15 per night, $7 per extra vehicle. Senior discount available. Open year-round.

Directions: From Eugene, drive west on Highway 126 for 61 miles to Florence and U.S. 101. Turn south on U.S. 101 and drive six miles to the Westlake turnoff. Turn and you'll see the campground.

Contact: Oregon Dunes National Recreation Area, Visitor Center, 855 U.S. 101, Reedsport, OR 97467, 541/271-3611, fax 541/750-7244.

72 WAXMYRTLE

Rating: 7

Near Siltcoos Lake in Oregon Dunes National Recreation Area.

Map 7.5, grid b7, page 423

One of three camps in the immediate vicinity, Waxmyrtle is adjacent to Lagoon and less than a mile from Driftwood II. The camp is near the Siltcoos River and a couple of miles from Siltcoos Lake, a good-sized lake with boating facilities where you can water-ski, fish, and swim. A pleasant hiking trail here meanders through the dunes and along the estuary.

Campsites, facilities: There are 54 sites for tents or RVs up to 35 feet long. Picnic tables, garbage service, and fire grills are provided. Drinking water and flush toilets are available. Boat docks, launching facilities, and rentals are nearby on Siltcoos Lake. Leashed pets are permitted.

Reservations, fees: Reservations are not accepted. Sites are $15 per night, $7 per extra vehicle. Senior discount available. Open late May–mid-October.

Directions: From Eugene, drive west on Highway 126 for 61 miles to Florence and U.S. 101. Turn south on U.S. 101 and drive seven miles to Siltcoos Beach Road. Turn right and drive 1.3 miles west to the campground.

Contact: Oregon Dunes National Recreation Area, 855 U.S. 101, Reedsport, OR 97467, 541/271-3611, fax 541/750-7244.

73 TAHKENITCH LANDING

Rating: 6

Near Tahkenitch Lake in Oregon Dunes National Recreation Area.

Map 7.5, grid b7, page 423

This camp overlooking Tahkenitch Lake has easy access for fishing and swimming. Fishing is excellent on Tahkenitch, which means "a lake with many fingers." There is no drinking water here, but water, a boat ramp, and a dock are available nearby at the lake.

Campsites, facilities: There are 27 sites for tents or RVs up to 30 feet long. Picnic tables and garbage service are provided. Vault toilets, boat-launching facilities, and a floating dock are available, but there is no drinking water. Leashed pets are permitted.

Reservations, fees: Reservations are not accepted. Sites are $15 per night, $7 per extra vehicle. Senior discount available. Open year-round.

Directions: From Eugene, drive west on Highway 126 for 61 miles to Florence and U.S. 101. Turn south on U.S. 101 and drive 14 miles to the campground on the east side of the road.

Contact: Oregon Dunes National Recreation Area, 855 U.S. 101, Reedsport, OR 97467, 541/271-3611, fax 541/750-7244.

74 TAHKENITCH

Rating: 7

Near Tahkenitch Lake in Oregon Dunes National Recreation Area.

Map 7.5, grid b7, page 423

This very pretty campground is set in a wooded area across the highway from Tahkenitch Lake, which has numerous coves and backwater areas for fishing and swimming. A hiking trail close to the camp goes through the dunes out to the beach, as well as to Threemile Lake. If this camp is full, Tahkenitch Landing provides space nearby.

Campsites, facilities: There are 25 sites for tents or RVs up to 30 feet long. Picnic tables, garbage service, and fire grills are provided. Drinking water and flush and vault toilets are available. Boat docks and launching facilities are on the lake across the highway. Leashed pets are permitted.

Reservations, fees: Reservations accepted ($8.65 reservation fee). Sites are $15 per night, $7 per extra vehicle. Senior discount available. Open mid-May through Labor Day weekend.

Directions: From Eugene, drive west on Highway 126 for 61 miles to Florence and U.S. 101. Turn south on U.S. 101 and drive 14 miles. The campground entrance is on the right.

Contact: Oregon Dunes National Recreation Area, Visitor Center, 855 U.S. 101, Reedsport, OR 97467, 541/271-3611, fax 541/750-7244.

75 DISCOVERY POINT RESORT & RV PARK

Rating: 7

On Winchester Bay.

Map 7.5, grid c7, page 423

This resort sits on the shore of Winchester Bay in a fishing village near the mouth of the Umpqua River, adjacent to sandy dunes. This park was designed around motor sports, and ATVs are available for rent. It is somewhat noisy, but that's what most people come for here. For details on more nearby recreation options, see the description of Surfwood Campground and RV Park.

Campsites, facilities: There are 12 tent sites, 50 sites, 14 drive-through, for RVs of any length, and eight cabins. Electricity, drinking water, sewer hookups, and picnic tables are provided. Flush toilets, showers, a store, a laundry room, and ice are available. An RV dump station and bottled gas are within one mile. Boat docks and launching facilities are nearby. Leashed pets are permitted.

Reservations, fees: Reservations are accepted. The fee is $15 for tent sites, $22–27 for RV sites. Major credit cards accepted. Open year-round.

Directions: From Eugene, drive south on I-5 for about 35 miles to Exit 162 and Highway 38. Turn west on Highway 38 and drive 64 miles to Reedsport and U.S. 101. Turn south on U.S. 101 and drive three miles to the Windy Cove exit near Winchester Bay. Take that exit and drive west 1.5 miles to the resort.

Contact: Discovery Point Resort & RV Park, 242 Discovery Point Ln., Reedsport, OR 97467, 541/271-3443, fax 541/271-9285.

76 WINDY COVE COUNTY PARK

Rating: 7

On the Pacific Ocean.
Map 7.5, grid c7, page 423

This Douglas County park actually comprises two parks, Windy Cove A and B. Set near ocean beaches and sand dunes, both offer a variety of additional recreational opportunities, including an 18-hole golf course, hiking trails, and a lighthouse.

Campsites, facilities: There are 29 tent sites, 63 sites with full hookups for RVs up to 60 feet long, and four sites with partial hookups. Electricity, drinking water, sewer hookups, and picnic tables are provided. Flush toilets, showers, and cable TV are available. Bottled gas, an RV dump station, a store, a café, a coin laundry, and ice are within one mile. Boat docks, launching facilities, boat charters, and rentals are nearby. Leashed pets are permitted.

Reservations, fees: Reservations at 541/440-4500. Sites are $12–15 per night, $3 per extra vehicle. Major credit cards accepted. Senior discount available for residents of Douglas County. Open year-round.

Directions: From Eugene, drive south on I-5 to Exit 162 and Highway 38. Turn west on Highway 38 and drive 64 miles to Reedsport and U.S. 101. Turn south on U.S. 101 and drive three miles to the Windy Cove exit near Winchester Bay. Take that exit and drive west to the park on the left.

Contact: Windy Cove County Park, 684 Salmon Harbor Dr., Reedsport, OR 97467, 541/271-5634 or 541/271-4138, website: www.co.douglas.or.us/parks.

77 UMPQUA LIGHTHOUSE STATE PARK

Rating: 7

On the Umpqua River.
Map 7.5, grid c7, page 423

This park is located near Lake Marie and less than a mile from Salmon Harbor on Winchester Bay. Near the mouth of the Umpqua River, this unusual area features dunes as high as 500 feet. Hiking trails lead out of the park and into the Oregon Dunes National Recreation Area. The park offers more than two miles of beach access on the ocean and one-half mile along the Umpqua River. The adjacent lighthouse is still in operation and tours are available during the summer season.

Campsites, facilities: There are 24 tent sites, 20 sites with full hookups for RVs up to 45 feet long, two cabins, and six deluxe yurts. Drinking water, garbage bins, and picnic tables are provided. Flush toilets, showers, and firewood are available. Boat docks and launching facilities are on the Umpqua River. Leashed pets are permitted.

Reservations, fees: Reservations at 800/452-5687 or website: www.OregonStateParks.org ($7 reservation fee). Sites are $11–17 per night, $7 per night for an extra vehicle, $4 per person per night for hikers/bikers, $35 for cabins, and $27–65 for yurts. Major credit cards accepted. Open year-round.

Directions: From Eugene, drive south on I-5 to Exit 162 and Highway 38. Turn west on Highway 38 and drive 64 miles to Reedsport and U.S. 101. Turn south on U.S. 101 and drive six miles to Umpqua Lighthouse Road. Turn right and drive one mile to the park.

Contact: Umpqua Lighthouse State Park, 460 Lighthouse Rd., Reedsport, OR 97467, 800/551-6949 or 541/271-4118.

78 WILLIAM M. TUGMAN STATE PARK

Rating: 7

On Eel Lake.
Map 7.5, grid d7, page 423

This campground is set along the shore of Eel Lake, which offers almost five miles of shoreline for swimming, fishing, boating, and sailing. It's perfect for bass fishing. A boat ramp is available, but there is a 10 mph speed limit for boats. Oregon Dunes National Recreation Area is across the highway. Hiking is available just a few miles north at Umpqua Lighthouse State Park. A trail along the south end of the lake allows hikers to get away from the developed areas of the park and explore the lake's many outlets. This camp has gone from three to 13 yurts, and they are almost always booked.

Campsites, facilities: There are 99 sites with water and electrical hookups for RVs up to 50 feet long, a special camping area for hikers, and 13 yurts. Electricity, drinking water, and picnic tables are provided. Flush toilets, an RV dump station, showers, firewood, and a picnic shelter are available. Some facilities are wheelchair accessible. Boat docks and launching facilities are nearby. Leashed pets are permitted.

Reservations, fees: Reservations at 800/452-5687 or website: www.OregonStateParks.org ($7 reservation fee). Sites are $15 per night, $7 per extra vehicle, $4 per person per night for hikers/bicyclists, and $27 per night for yurts. Major credit cards accepted. Open year-round.

Directions: From Eugene, drive south on I-5 to Exit 162 and Highway 38. Turn west on Highway 38 and drive 64 miles to Reedsport and U.S. 101. Turn south on U.S. 101 and drive eight miles to the park entrance on the left.

Contact: Sunset Bay State Park, 89814 Cape Arago Hwy., Coos Bay, OR 97420, 541/759-3604 or 800/551-6949.

79 NORTH LAKE RESORT AND MARINA

Rating: 8

On Tenmile Lake.

Map 7.5, grid d7, page 423

This 40-acre resort along the shore of Tenmile Lake is wooded and secluded, with a private beach, and makes the perfect layover spot for U.S. 101 travelers. The lake has a full-service marina, and bass fishing can be good here.

About 25 percent of the sites are taken by summer season rentals.

Campsites, facilities: There are 40 tent sites and 60 RV sites, some with full hookups. Picnic tables are provided. Flush toilets, an RV dump station, showers, firewood, a store, ice, electricity, phone/modem hookups, cable TV, drinking water, coin-operated laundry facilities, horseshoe pits, a volleyball court, and sewer hookups are available. A café, boat docks, launching facilities, and rentals are nearby. Leashed pets are permitted.

Reservations, fees: Reservations accepted. Tent sites are $18 per night; RV sites are $23 per night. Major credit cards accepted. Open April–October.

Directions: From Eugene, drive south on I-5 to Exit 162 and Highway 38. Turn west on Highway 38 and drive 64 miles to Reedsport and U.S. 101. Turn south on U.S. 101 and drive 11 miles to the Lakeside exit. Take that exit and drive east on North Lake Avenue for three-quarters of a mile, then continue on North Lake Road for one-half mile to the resort on the left.

Contact: North Lake Resort and Marina, 2090 North Lake Rd., Lakeside, OR 97449, 541/759-3515, fax 541/759-3326.

80 OSPREY POINT RV RESORT

Rating: 7

On Tenmile Lake.

Map 7.5, grid d7, page 423

Tenmile is one of Oregon's premier bass fishing lakes and yet is located only three miles from the ocean. The resort is situated in a large, open area adjacent to Tenmile Lake and one-half mile from North Lake. A navigable canal connects the lakes. The Oregon Dunes National Recreation Area provides nearby hiking trails, and Elliot State Forest offers wooded trails. With weekend barbecues and occasional live entertainment, Osprey Point is more a destination resort than an overnight stop.

Campsites, facilities: There are 20 tent sites and 132 sites for tents or RVs of any size. RV sites have electricity, drinking water, sewer, picnic tables, fire pits, phone, and cable TV provided. The park is also modem-friendly. Drinking water, restrooms with flush toilets and showers, garbage bins, an RV dump station, coin-operated laundry facilities, a restaurant, a cocktail lounge, a grocery store, a full service marina with boat docks, a launch, a fishing pier, a fish-cleaning station, horseshoe pits, volleyball, tether ball, a recreation hall, a video arcade, beauty and barber shops, and a pizza parlor are available. Leashed pets are permitted.

Reservations, fees: Reservations accepted. RV sites are $23–33 per night; tent sites are $18 per night; $2.50–3.50 per person for more than two people, $2.50 per extra vehicle. Major credit cards accepted. Open year-round.

Directions: From Coos Bay, drive north on U.S. 101 for 13 miles to the Lakeside exit. Take that exit east into town (across the railroad tracks) to North Lake Road. Turn left (north) on North Lake Road and drive one-half mile to the resort on the right.

Contact: Osprey Point RV Resort, 1505 North Lake Rd., Lakeside, OR 97449, 541/759-2801, fax 541/759-3198, website: www.ospreypoint.net.

81 EEL CREEK

Rating: 8

Near Eel Lake in Oregon Dunes National Recreation Area.

Map 7.5, grid d7, page 423

This campground along Eel Creek is located near both Eel and Tenmile Lakes. While Tenmile Lake allows water-skiing, Eel Lake does not. Nearby trails offer access to the Umpqua Dunes Scenic Area, where you'll find spectacular scenery in an area closed to off-road vehicles. Off-road access is available at Spinreel.

Campsites, facilities: There are 52 sites for tents or RVs up to 35 feet long. Picnic tables, garbage service, and fire grills are provided. Drinking water and flush and vault toilets are available. Boat docks, launching facilities, and rentals are nearby. Leashed pets are permitted.

Reservations, fees: Reservations at 877/444-6777 or website: www.ReserveUsa.com ($9 reservation fee). Sites are $15 per night, $7 per extra vehicle. Senior discount available. Open year-round.

Directions: From Eugene, drive south on I-5 to Exit 162 and Highway 38. Turn west on Highway 38 and drive 64 miles to Reedsport and U.S. 101. Turn south on U.S. 101 and drive 10.5 miles to the park entrance.

Contact: Oregon Dunes National Recreation Area, Visitor Center, 855 U.S. 101, Reedsport, OR 97467, 541/271-3611, fax 541/750-7244.

82 SPINREEL

Rating: 6

On Tenmile Creek in Oregon Dunes National Recreation Area.

Map 7.5, grid d7, page 423

This campground, primarily for off-road-vehicle enthusiasts, is set several miles inland at the outlet of Tenmile Lake in the Oregon Dunes National Recreation Area. A boat launch is near the camp. Other recreational opportunities include hiking trails and off-road-vehicle access to the dunes. Off-road-vehicle rentals are available adjacent to the camp.

Campsites, facilities: There are 36 sites for tents or RVs up to 40 feet long. Drinking water, garbage service, and flush toilets are available. Picnic tables and fire grills are provided. Firewood, a store, and a coin-operated laundry are nearby. Boat docks, launching facilities, and rentals are on Tenmile Lake. Leashed pets are permitted.

Reservations, fees: Reservations at 877/444-6777 or website: www.ReserveUsa.com ($9 reservation fee). Sites are $15 per night, $7 per extra vehicle. Senior discount available. Open year-round.

Directions: From Coos Bay, drive north on U.S. 101 for 10 miles to the campground entrance road (well signed). Turn northwest and drive one mile to the campground.

Contact: Oregon Dunes National Recreation Area, Visitor Center, 855 U.S. 101, Reedsport, OR 97467, 541/271-3611, fax 541/750-7244.

83 OREGON DUNES KOA

Rating: 5

Six miles north of North Bend, next to the Oregon Dunes National Recreation Area.
Map 7.5, grid d7, page 423

This ATV-friendly park has direct access to Oregon Dunes National Recreation Area, which offers miles of ATV trails. This fairly open campground features a landscape of grass, young trees, and a small lake. The ocean is a 15-minute drive away. Mill Casino is about six miles south on U.S. 101. Freshwater and ocean fishing are nearby. A golf course is about five miles away.

Campsites, facilities: There are 10 tent sites, 63 sites for tents or RVs of any size, and three cabins. RV sites have electricity, drinking water, sewer, picnic tables, fire pits, and satellite TV provided. There is a data port on-site for computers. Drinking water, restrooms with flush toilets and showers, garbage bins, wheelchair facilities, a coin-operated laundry, a small store, horseshoe pits, volleyball, and a picnic shelter with electricity, a sink, and electric cooktops are available. ORV rentals are nearby. Leashed pets are permitted, except in cabins.

Reservations, fees: Reservations at 800/562-4236. Sites are $20–34 per night, $.50–3.50 per person for more than two people, and $4.50 per extra vehicle. Major credit cards accepted. Open year-round.

Directions: From Coos Bay, drive north on U.S. 101 past North Bend for six miles to Milepost 229 and the campground entrance road on the left.

Contact: Oregon Dunes KOA, 68632 U.S. 101,

North Bend, OR 97459, 541/756-4851, fax 541/756-8838, website: www.koa.com.

84 WILD MARE HORSE CAMP

Rating: 7

Oregon Dunes National Recreation Area.
Map 7.5, grid e6, page 423

This horse camp has paved parking, with single and double corrals. No off-road vehicles are allowed within the campground. Horses can be ridden straight out into the dunes—they cannot be ridden on the developed trails. The heavily treed shoreline gives rise to treed sites with some bushes.

Campsites, facilities: There are 12 horse campsites for tents or RVs up to 50 feet long. There is a maximum of two vehicles per site. Picnic tables and fire pits are provided. Drinking water, vault toilets, and garbage bins are available. Leashed pets are permitted.

Reservations, fees: Reservations at 877/444-6777 or website: www.ReserveUsa.com ($9 reservation fee). Sites are $15 per night, $7 per extra vehicle. Major credit cards accepted. Senior discount available. Open year-round.

Directions: From Coos Bay, drive north on U.S. 101 for 1.5 miles to Horsfall Dunes and Beach Access Road. Turn left and drive west for one mile to the campground access road. Turn right and drive three-quarters of a mile to the campground on the left.

Contact: Oregon Dunes National Recreation Area, Visitor Center, 855 U.S. 101, Reedsport, OR 97467, 541/271-3611, fax 541/750-7244.

85 BLUEBILL

Rating: 6

On Bluebill Lake in Oregon Dunes National Recreation Area.
Map 7.5, grid e6, page 423

This campground gets very little camping pressure although there are some good hiking trails available. It's located next to little Bluebill Lake, which sometimes dries up during the summer. A one-mile trail goes around the lake bed. The camp is a short distance from Horsfall Lake, which is surrounded by private property. If you continue west on the forest road, you'll come to a picnicking and parking area near the beach. This spot provides off-road-vehicle access to the dunes at the Horsfall day-use area and Horsfall Beach.

Campsites, facilities: There are 18 sites for tents or RVs up to 30 feet long. Picnic tables, garbage service, and fire grills are provided. Flush toilets and drinking water are available. Leashed pets are permitted.

Reservations, fees: Reservations are not accepted. Sites are $15 per night, and $7 per night for each additional vehicle. Senior discount available. Open May–November.

Directions: From Coos Bay, drive north on U.S. 101 for 1.5 miles north to Horsfall Dunes and Beach Access Road. Turn west and drive one mile to Horsfall Road. Turn northwest and drive two miles to the campground entrance.

Contact: Oregon Dunes National Recreation Area, Visitor Center, 855 U.S. 101, Reedsport, OR 97467, 541/271-3611, fax 541/750-7244.

86 HORSFALL

Rating: 4

In Oregon Dunes National Recreation Area.
Map 7.5, grid e6, page 423

This campground is actually a nice, large paved area for parking RVs. It's the staging area for off-road-vehicle access into the southern section of Oregon Dunes National Recreation Area. If Horsfall is full, try nearby Horsfall Beach, an overflow area with 34 tent and RV sites.

Campsites, facilities: There are 70 sites for RVs up to 50 feet in length. Drinking water, garbage service, coin-operated showers, a pay phone, and flush toilets are available. Leashed pets are permitted.

Reservations, fees: Reservations at 877/444-6777 or website: www.ReserveUsa.com ($9 reservation fee). Sites are $15 per night, $7 per extra vehicle. Senior discount available. Open year-round.

Directions: From Coos Bay, drive north on U.S. 101 for 1.5 miles to Horsfall Road. Turn west on Horsfall Road and drive about one mile to the campground access road. Turn on the campground access road (well signed) and drive one-half mile to the campground.

Contact: Oregon Dunes National Recreation Area, Visitor Center, 855 U.S. 101, Reedsport, OR 97467, 541/271-3611, fax 541/750-7244.

87 SUNSET BAY STATE PARK

Rating: 8

Near Sunset Bay.
Map 7.5, grid f5, page 423

Situated in one of the most scenic areas on the Oregon Coast, this park features beautiful, sandy beaches protected by towering sea cliffs. A network of hiking trails connects Sunset Bay with nearby Shore Acres and Cape Arago Parks. Swimming, boating, fishing, clamming, and golfing are some of the recreation options here.

Campsites, facilities: There are 66 sites for tents or self-contained RVs, 29 sites with full hookups for RVs up to 47 feet long, a separate area for hikers and bicyclists, eight yurts, and two group camps for more than 25 people. Drinking water, picnic tables, garbage bins, and fire grills are provided. Flush toilets, showers, a meeting hall, a boat ramp, and firewood are available. A restaurant is within three miles. Some facilities are wheelchair accessible. Leashed pets are permitted.

Reservations, fees: Reservations at 800/452-5687 or website: www.OregonStateParks.org ($7 reservation fee). Sites are $13–20 per night, $7 per extra vehicle, $4 per person per night for hikers/bicyclists, $27 for yurts, and $60 for group camps. Major credit cards accepted. Open year-round.

Directions: In Coos Bay, take the Charleston Ocean Beaches exit to Newmark Avenue and drive west for three miles to Cape Arago Highway. Turn left and drive about five miles south to Charleston and cross the South Slough Bridge. Continue on Cape Arago Highway about three miles to the park entrance on the left.

Contact: Sunset Bay State Park, 89814 Cape Arago Hwy., Coos Bay, OR 97420, 541/888-4902.

88 BASTENDORFF BEACH PARK

Rating: 8

Near Cape Arago State Park.
Map 7.5, grid f5, page 423

This campground provides access to the ocean and a small lake. Nearby activities include sand-dune buggy riding, golfing, clamming, crabbing, fishing, swimming, whale-watching, and boating. Horses may be rented near Bandon. A nice side trip is to Shore Acres State Park and Botanical Gardens, about 2.5 miles away.

Campsites, facilities: There are 25 tent sites, 56 sites with partial hookups for RVs, and two cabins. Drinking water, picnic tables, restrooms, coin-operated showers, an RV dump station, a public phone, and a fireplace are provided. A fish-cleaning station, horseshoe pits, a playground, basketball courts, and a picnic area with a shelter and barbecue are also available. Some facilities are wheelchair accessible. Leashed pets are permitted.

Reservations, fees: Reservations are not accepted. Sites are $15-18 per night, $10-14 in the off-season, $5 per extra vehicle. Senior discount available. Major credit cards accepted. Reservations for the shelter and cabins at 541/396-3121, ext. 354. Open year-round.

Directions: In Coos Bay, take the Charleston Ocean Beaches exit to Newmark Avenue and drive west for three miles to Cape Arago Highway. Turn left and drive about five miles south to Charleston and cross the South Slough

Bridge. Continue on Cape Arago Highway about two miles to the park entrance.

Contact: Coos County Parks, Coos County Courthouse, 250 N. Baxter St., Coquille, OR 97423, or Bastendorff Beach Park, 4250 Bastendorff Beach Road, Coos Bay, OR 97420, 541/888-5353, website: www.cooscounty parks.com.

89 CHARLESTON MARINA RV PARK

Rating: 7

On Coos Bay.
Map 7.5, grid f5, page 423

This large, developed public park and marina is located near Charleston on the Pacific Ocean. Recreational activities in and near the campground include hiking, swimming, clamming, crabbing, boating, huckleberry and blackberry picking, and fishing for tuna, salmon, and halibut.

Campsites, facilities: There are 108 sites for tents or RVs up to 50 feet long and two yurts. Drinking water, cable TV, restrooms, showers, an RV dump station, a public phone, a laundry room, a playground, and LP gas are available. A marina with a boarding dock and launch ramp are on-site. Some facilities are wheelchair accessible. Leashed pets are permitted.

Reservations, fees: Reservations advised. Sites are $10-19 per night, $30 per night for yurts. Major credit cards accepted. Open year-round.

Directions: In Coos Bay, take the Charleston Ocean Beaches exit to Newmark Avenue and drive west for three miles to Cape Arago Highway. Turn left and drive about five miles south to Charleston and cross the South Slough Bridge; continue to Boat Basin Drive. Turn right and drive one-quarter mile to Kingfisher Drive. Turn right and drive 200 feet to the campground on the left.

Contact: Charleston Marina RV Park, P.O. Box 5409, Charleston, OR 97420-0607, 541/888-9512, fax 541/888-6111, website: www.charleston marina.com.

90 OCEANSIDE RV PARK

Rating: 7

Near the Pacific Ocean.

Map 7.5, grid f5, page 423

One of several private, developed parks in the Charleston area, this park is within walking distance of the Pacific Ocean, with opportunities for swimming, fishing, clamming, crabbing, and boating. A marina is 1.5 miles away.

Campsites, facilities: There are 10 tent sites and 70 full-hookup sites (30- or 50-amp) for RVs. Restrooms, showers, a public phone, modem hookups, a fish-cleaning station, and LP gas are available. Equipment for crabbing and clamming is also available. Some facilities are wheelchair accessible. Leashed pets are permitted.

Reservations, fees: Reservations at 800/570-2598. Tent sites are $15 per night; RV sites are $22 per night; $5 for an extra vehicle or tent. Senior discount available. Senior discount available. Major credit cards accepted. Open year-round.

Directions: In Coos Bay, take the Charleston Ocean Beaches exit to Newmark Avenue and drive west for three miles to Cape Arago Highway. Turn left and drive about five miles south to Charleston and cross the South Slough Bridge. Continue on Cape Arago Highway for 1.8 miles to the park entrance on the right.

Contact: Oceanside RV Park, 90281 Cape Arago Hwy., Charleston, OR 97420, 541/888-2598 or 800/570-2598, website: www.harborside.com/~oceanside.

91 KELLEY'S RV PARK

Rating: 5

Near Coos Bay.

Map 7.5, grid f7, page 423

This clean, well-maintained RV park is situated in the town of Coos Bay, well known for its rockfish and salmon fishing and for its lumber industry. A shaded picnic area here overlooks the bay. A full-service marina is a giant plus. More than half of the sites are filled with monthly rentals.

Campsites, facilities: There are 38 sites for tents or RVs of any length; three are drive-through sites. Electricity, drinking water, sewer hookups, and picnic tables are provided. Flush toilets and a laundry room are available. Boat docks and launching facilities are nearby. Bottled gas, a store, and a café are available within a mile. Leashed pets are permitted.

Reservations, fees: Reservations accepted. Sites are $15–16 per night, $2 per person for more than two people. Major credit cards accepted. Monthly rentals available. Open year-round.

Directions: In Coos Bay on U.S. 101, drive to the Charleston exit. Take that exit to South Empire Boulevard and drive 4.5 miles to the park at 555 South Empire Boulevard.

Contact: Kelley's RV Park, 555 S. Empire Blvd., Coos Bay, OR 97420, 541/888-6531, website: www.rverschoice.com.

92 BULLARDS BEACH STATE PARK

Rating: 7

On the Coquille River.

Map 7.5, grid g5, page 423

The Coquille River, which has good fishing in season for both boaters and crabbers, is the centerpiece of this park with four miles of shore access. If fishing is not your thing, the park also has several hiking trails. The Coquille River Lighthouse is at the end of the road that wanders through the park. During the summer there are tours to the tower. Equestrians can explore the seven-mile horse trail.

Campsites, facilities: There are 185 sites with full or partial hookups for RVs up to 64 feet long; 13 yurts are also available, including three that are wheelchair accessible. Each yurt can sleep five people. A special area for horses and an area reserved for hikers and bicyclists are also available. Drinking water, garbage bins, picnic tables, and fire grills are provided. Flush toilets, an RV dump station, showers, firewood, a yurt meeting hall, and a loading ramp for horses are available. Some facilities are wheelchair accessible. Boat docks and launching facilities are in the park on the Coquille River. Leashed pets are permitted.

Reservations, fees: Reservations at 800/452-5687 or website: www.OregonStateParks.org ($7 reservation fee). Sites are $16–20 per night, $7 per extra vehicle, $4 per person per night for hikers/bicyclists, and $27 per night for yurts. Horse camping is $10–14 per night. Major credit cards accepted. Open year-round.

Directions: In Coos Bay, drive south on U.S. 101 for about 22 miles to the park on the right (two miles north of Bandon).

Contact: Bullards Beach State Park, P.O. Box 569, Bandon, OR 97411, 541/347-2209.

93 BANDON RV PARK

Rating: 6

Near Bullards Beach State Park.

Map 7.5, grid h5, page 423

This in-town RV park is a good base for many adventures. Some sites are filled with rentals, primarily fishermen, for the summer season. Rock hounds will enjoy combing for agates and other semiprecious stones hidden along the beaches, while kids can explore the West Coast Game Park Walk-Through Safari petting zoo seven miles south of town. Bandon State Park, four miles south of town, has a nice wading spot in the creek at the north end of the park. Nearby recreation opportunities include two 18-hole golf courses, a riding stable, and tennis courts. Bullards Beach is about 2.5 miles north. Nice folks run this place.

Campsites, facilities: There are 44 sites for RVs of any length; some are drive-through sites. Electricity, drinking water, cable TV, and sewer hookups are provided. Flush toilets, an RV dump station, showers, and a laundry room are available. Bottled gas and a store are with-

in two blocks. Boat docks and launching facilities are nearby. Leashed pets are permitted.

Reservations, fees: Reservations at 800/393-4122. Sites are $18–20 per night, $2 per person for more than two people. Major credit cards accepted. Open year-round.

Directions: From Coos Bay, drive south on U.S. 101 for 26 miles to Bandon and the Highway 42S junction. Continue south on U.S. 101 for one block to the park.

Contact: Bandon RV Park, 935 2nd St. SE, Bandon, OR 97411, 541/347-4122.

94 LAVERNE COUNTY PARK

Rating: 9

In Fairview on the North Fork of the Coquille River.

Map 7.5, grid g7, page 423

This beautiful park sits on a river with a small waterfall and many trees, including a myrtle grove and old-growth Douglas fir. Mountain bikers can take an old wagon road, and golfers can enjoy any of several courses. There are a few hiking trails and a very popular swimming hole. Fishing includes salmon, steelhead, and trout, and the wildlife includes deer, elk, bear, raccoons, and cougar. You can take a side trip to the museums at Myrtle Point and Coos Bay, which display local Indian items, or an old stagecoach house in Dora.

Campsites, facilities: There are 76 sites for tents or RVs of any size. There is also a large group site at West Laverne B with 22 RV hookups. One cabin is also available. Drinking water, electricity, picnic tables, and fire pits are provided. Restrooms with flush toilets and showers (two barrier-free), garbage bins, an RV dump station, a playground, four cooking shelters with barbecues, a swimming hole (unsupervised), horseshoe pits, and volleyball and baseball areas are available. Ice and a restaurant are within 1.5 miles. Propane, bottled gas, a store, and gasoline are within five miles. Leashed pets are permitted, and there is a pet area.

Reservations, fees: Reservations are not accepted for family sites. Sites are $10–15 per night, $5 per extra vehicle. Reservations for the group site and cabin ($5 reservation fee) at 541/396-3121, ext. 354; the group site is $130 per night for the first six camping units, then $15 per unit. The cabin is $30 per night. Senior discount available for Coos County residents. Major credit cards accepted. Open year-round.

Directions: From Coos Bay, drive south on U.S. 101 for six miles to the junction with Highway 42. Turn east and drive 11 miles to Coquille and West Central. Turn left and drive one-half mile to Fairview McKinley Road. Turn right and drive eight miles to the Fairview Store. Continue east another five miles (past the store) to the park on the right.

Contact: Laverne County Park, Coos County, 61217 Fairview McKinley Rd., Coquille, OR 97423, 541/396-2344, website: www.co.coos.or.us.

95 LOON LAKE RECREATION AREA

Rating: 8

On Loon Lake.
Map 7.6, grid d2, page 424

Loon Lake was created 1,400 years ago when a nearby mountain crumbled and slid downhill, damming the creek with house-sized boulders. Today the lake is one-half mile wide and nearly two miles long, covers 260 acres, and is more than 100 feet deep in places. Its ideal location provides a warm, wind-sheltered summer climate for various water activities. A nature trail leads to a waterfall about one-half mile away. Evening interpretive programs are held during summer weekends.

Campsites, facilities: There are 61 sites for tents or RVs of any size. There are also five group sites for up to 15 people per site. Picnic tables and fire pits are provided. Drinking water, restrooms with flush toilets and showers, garbage bins, an RV dump station, a sand beach, a boat ramp and moorings,

and gasoline are available. Leashed pets are permitted.

Reservations, fees: Reservations are not accepted for family sites. Sites are $12–13 per night, $7 per extra vehicle. Senior discount available. Reservations required for group sites ($6 reservation fee) at 888/242-4256; $35 per night. Open late May–mid-September, weather permitting.

Directions: From Eugene, drive south on I-5 to Exit 162 and Highway 38. Turn west on Highway 38 and drive 43 miles to Milepost 13.5 and the County Road 3 exit. Turn south and drive 7.5 miles to the campground.

Contact: Bureau of Land Management, Coos Bay District Office, 1300 Airport Ln., North Bend, OR 97459, 541/756-0100, fax 541/751-4303.

96 LOON LAKE LODGE RESORT

Rating: 8

On Loon Lake.
Map 7.6, grid d2, page 424

This resort boasts one mile of lake frontage and nestles among the tall trees on pretty Loon Lake. It's not a long drive from either U.S. 101 or I-5, making it an ideal layover spot for travelers eager to get off the highway. The lake offers good bass fishing, swimming, boating, and water-skiing.

Campsites, facilities: There are 100 sites, 50 with partial hookups, for tents or RVs up to 32 feet long, group sites, cabins, and a motel. Electricity, drinking water, a public phone, security, a game room, a restaurant, a bar, a grocery store, ice, gas, and a beach are available. A boat ramp, dock, marina, and rentals are also available. No pets are permitted.

Reservations, fees: Reservations recommended. Sites are $16–19 per night, $4 per person for more than two people, and $8 per extra vehicle. Major credit cards accepted. Open year-round.

Directions: From Eugene, drive south on I-5 to Exit 162 and Highway 38. Turn west on Highway 38 and drive 43 miles to Milepost

13.5 and the County Road 3 exit. Turn south and drive 8.2 miles to the resort on the right. **Contact:** Loon Lake Lodge Resort, 9011 Loon Lake Rd., Reedsport, OR 97467, 541/599-2244, fax 541/599-2274.

97 TYEE

Rating: 7

On the Umpqua River.
Map 7.6, grid d4, page 424

Here's a classic spot set along the Umpqua River, which has great steelhead, salmon, and small mouth bass fishing in season. Boat launches are available a few miles upstream and downstream of the campground. The camp isn't far from I-5, and it's the only campground in the immediate vicinity. Another plus: This campground was renovated in 2001. Because Tyee has become popular, another camp will be constructed one mile down the road, likely available starting 2004.

Campsites, facilities: There are 15 sites for tents or RVs up to 25 feet long. Drinking water, garbage service, fire grills, and picnic tables are provided. Vault toilets, a day-use area with horseshoe pits, and a pavilion with a barbecue, water, electricity, and 10 tables are available. A camp host is on-site. A store is within one mile. Some facilities are wheelchair accessible. Leashed pets are permitted.

Reservations, fees: Reservations are not accepted. Sites are $8 per night, $3 for each additional vehicle. Senior discount available. Open year-round.

Directions: From Roseburg, drive north on I-5 to Exit 136 and Highway 138. Take that exit and drive west on Highway 138 for 12 miles. Cross Bullock Bridge and continue to County Road 57. Turn right and drive one-half mile to the campground entrance.

Contact: Bureau of Land Management, Roseburg District, 777 N.W. Garden Valley Blvd., Roseburg, OR 97470, 541/440-4930, fax 541/440-4948.

98 PARK CREEK

Rating: 7

Near Coquille.
Map 7.6, grid g3, page 424

Want to be by yourself? You came to the right place. This pretty little campground offers peaceful, shady campsites under an old-growth canopy of Douglas fir, western hemlock, red cedar, and myrtle. Relax and enjoy nearby Park Creek and Middle Creek.

Campsites, facilities: There are 15 sites for tents or small RVs. Picnic tables and fire grills are provided. Vault toilets and garbage bins are available. There is no drinking water. Leashed pets are permitted.

Reservations, fees: Reservations are not accepted. There is no fee, but the stay limit is 14 days. Open year-round.

Directions: From Coos Bay, drive south on U.S. 101 for six miles to the junction with Highway 42. Turn east and drive 11 miles to Coquille and Coquille Fairview Road. Turn east on Coquille Fairview Road and drive 7.5 miles to Fairview and Coos Bay Wagon Road. Turn right and drive four miles to Middle Creek Access Road. Turn left (east) and drive nine miles to the campground.

Contact: Bureau of Land Management, Coos Bay District, 1300 Airport Ln., North Bend, OR 97459, 541/756-0100, fax 541/751-4303.

99 KOA BANDON-PORT ORFORD

Rating: 7

Near the Elk River.
Map 7.7, grid a5, page 425

This spot is considered to be just a layover camp, but it offers large, secluded sites nestled among big trees and coastal ferns. A new pool and spa are now open. The Elk and Sixes Rivers, where the fishing can be good, are minutes away, and Cape Blanco State Park is just a few miles down the road.

Campsites, facilities: There are 46 tent sites and 26 drive-through sites for RVs of any length. Six cabins are also available. Picnic tables are provided. Flush toilets, bottled gas, an RV dump station, showers, firewood, a recreation hall, a store, a laundry room, ice, a playground, electricity, drinking water, and sewer hookups are available. Leashed pets are permitted.

Reservations, fees: Reservations at 800/562-3298. Sites are $22–28 per night, $3 per person for more than two people, and $5 per extra vehicle. Major credit cards accepted. Open year-round.

Directions: From Coos Bay, drive south on U.S. 101 for 50 miles to the campground at Milepost 286 near Langlois, on the west side of the highway.

Contact: KOA Bandon-Port Orford, 46612 U.S. 101, Langlois, OR 97450, 541/348-2358, website: www.koa.com.

100 CAPE BLANCO STATE PARK

Rating: 8

Between the Sixes and Elk Rivers.

Map 7.7, grid b4, page 425

This large park is named for the white (*blanco*) chalk appearance of the sea cliffs here, which rise 200 feet above the ocean. Sea lions inhabit the offshore rocks, and trails and a road lead to the black sand beach below the cliffs. Another highlight is the good access to the Sixes River, which runs for more than two miles through the meadows and forests of the park. Trails for horseback riding are also available; more than eight miles of trails lead through woodland and wetland settings and feature spectacular ocean vistas. Lighthouse and historic Hughes House tours are nearby.

Campsites, facilities: There are 54 sites with water and electrical hookups for tents or RVs up to 65 feet long. Other options are a special camp for horses, a camping area reserved for hikers and bicyclists, four cabins, and one primitive group site that can accommodate

25 people. Garbage bins, picnic tables, drinking water, electrical hookups, and fire grills are provided. Firewood, flush toilets, showers, and an RV dump station are available. Some facilities are wheelchair accessible. Leashed pets are permitted.

Reservations, fees: No reservation for single sites. Sites are $18 per night, $7 per extra vehicles, and $4 per person per night for hikers/bikers. Reservations for cabins, group site, and horse camp at 800/452-5687 or website: www.OregonStateParks.org ($7 reservation fee). The group site is $60 for the first 25 people, then $2.40 per person. Major credit cards accepted. Open year-round.

Directions: From Coos Bay, turn south on U.S. 101 and drive approximately 46 miles (south of Sixes, five miles north of Port Orford) to Cape Blanco Road. Turn right (northwest) and drive five miles to the campground on the left.

Contact: Humbug Mountain State Park, P.O. Box 1345, Port Orford, OR 97465, 541/332-6774. (This park is under the same management as Humbug Mountain State Park.)

101 SIXES RIVER

Rating: 6

On the Sixes River.

Map 7.7, grid b5, page 425

Set along the banks of the Sixes River at an elevation of 4,303 feet, this camp is a favorite of miners, fishermen, and nature lovers. There are opportunities to pan or sluice for gold year-round or through a special limited permit. Dredging is permitted from July 15 through September. The camp roads are paved.

Campsites, facilities: There are 19 sites for tents or RVs up to 30 feet long. Picnic tables, garbage service, and fire grills are provided. Drinking water and vault toilets are available. Leashed pets are permitted.

Reservations, fees: Reservations are not accepted. Sites are $5 per night, plus $3 for each additional vehicle, with a 14-day stay limit. Senior discount available. Open year-round.

Directions: From Coos Bay, drive south on U.S. 101 for 40 miles to Sixes and Sixes River Road. Turn left (east) on Sixes River Road and drive 12 miles to the campground. The last one-half mile is an unpaved road.

Contact: Bureau of Land Management, Coos Bay District, 1300 Airport Ln., North Bend, OR 97459, 541/756-0100, fax 541/751-4303.

102 ELK RIVER CAMPGROUND

Rating: 7

Near the Elk River.
Map 7.7, grid b5, page 425

This quiet and restful camp makes an excellent base for fall and winter fishing on the Elk River, which is known for its premier salmon fishing. A one-mile private access road goes to the river, so guests get their personal fishing holes. About half of the sites are taken by monthly rentals.

Campsites, facilities: There are 50 sites for tents or RVs up to 40 feet long, all with full hookups. Picnic tables are provided. Drinking water, restrooms, showers, an RV dump station, a public phone, modem hookups, cable TV, and a laundry room are available. Recreational facilities include a sports field, horseshoes, a recreation hall, and a boat ramp. Some facilities are wheelchair accessible. Leashed pets are permitted.

Reservations, fees: Reservations recommended. Sites are $11–15 per night, $1 per person for more than two people. Weekly and monthly rates are available. Open year-round.

Directions: From Port Orford, drive north on U.S. 101 for 1.5 miles to Elk River Road (Milepost 297). Turn right (east) on Elk River Road and drive 1.8 miles to the campground on the left.

Contact: Elk River Campground, 93363 Elk River Rd., Port Orford, OR 97465, 541/332-2255.

103 LAIRD LAKE

Rating: 8

On Laird Lake in Siskiyou National Forest.
Map 7.7, grid b5, page 425

This secluded campground is set at 1,600 feet elevation, along the shore of pretty Laird Lake (six feet at its deepest point) in a very private and scenic spot. Some old-growth cedar logs are in the lake. Most campers have no idea such a place exists in the area. This can be just what you're looking for if you're tired of fighting the crowds at the more developed camps along U.S. 101.

Campsites, facilities: There are four tent sites, with additional dispersed space for camping. There is no drinking water, and all garbage must be packed out. Leashed pets are permitted.

Reservations, fees: Reservations are not accepted. There is no fee for camping. Open year-round.

Directions: From Port Orford, drive north on U.S. 101 for three miles to County Road 208. Turn right and drive 7.5 miles southeast to Forest Road 5325. Turn southeast and drive 15.5 miles to the campground. The road is paved for 11 miles and rock surfaced for the last 4.5 miles to the campground.

Contact: Siskiyou National Forest, Powers Ranger District, 42861 Hwy. 242, Powers, OR 97466, 541/439-6200, fax 541/439-6217.

104 BUTLER BAR

Rating: 6

On the Elk River in Siskiyou National Forest.
Map 7.7, grid b5, page 425

This campground at an elevation of 800 feet is set back from the shore of the Elk River and surrounded by old-growth and hardwood forest, with some reforested areas nearby. Across the river is the Grassy Knob Wilderness, which has no trails and is generally too rugged to hike. No fishing for steelhead or salmon is permitted here on the Elk River.

Campsites, facilities: There are seven sites for tents. Picnic tables and fire grills are provided. Drinking water and pit toilets are available, but all garbage must be packed out. Leashed pets are permitted.

Reservations, fees: Reservations are not accepted. There is no fee for camping. Open year-round.

Directions: From Port Orford, drive north on U.S. 101 for three miles to County Road 208. Turn right and drive 7.5 miles southeast to Forest Road 5325. Turn southeast and drive 11 miles to the campground. The road is paved.

Contact: Siskiyou National Forest, Powers Ranger District, 42861 Highway 242, Powers, OR 97466, 541/439-6200, fax 541/439-6217.

105 POWERS COUNTY PARK

Rating: 9

Near the South Fork of the Coquille River.

Map 7.7, grid b8, page 425

This private and secluded public park in a wooded, mountainous area is a great stop for travelers going between I-5 and the coast. A small lake at the park provides a spot for visitors to boat, swim, and fish for trout. Only nonmotorized boats allowed. On display at the park are an old steam donkey and a hand-carved totem pole. This park is reputed to have the biggest cedar tree in Oregon.

Campsites, facilities: There are 40 sites for tents or RVs. One cabin is also available. Drinking water, restrooms, showers, an RV dump station, and a public phone are provided. Other facilities include a boat ramp, horseshoes, a playground, three large picnic shelters, tennis courts, and a recreation field. Supplies are available within one mile. Some facilities are wheelchair accessible. Leashed pets are permitted.

Reservations, fees: Reservations at 541/439-2791. Sites are $10–15 per night. Senior discount available. Major credit cards accepted. Open year-round.

Directions: From Coos Bay, drive south on U.S. 101 for six miles to the junction with Highway 42. Turn east and drive 20 miles to Myrtle Point. Continue on Highway 42 to the Powers Highway (Highway 242) exit. Turn right (southwest) and drive 19 miles to the park on the right.

Contact: Powers County Park, P.O. Box 12, Powers, OR 97466-0012, 541/396-3121, website: www.co.coos.or.us.

106 PORT ORFORD RV VILLAGE

Rating: 5

Near the Elk and Sixes Rivers.

Map 7.7, grid c5, page 425

The hosts make you feel at home at this friendly mom-and-pop campground in Port Orford. An informal group campfire and happy hour are scheduled each evening. Other nice touches include a small gazebo where you can get coffee each morning and a patio where you can sit. Fishing is good during the fall and winter on the nearby Elk and Sixes Rivers, and the campground has a smokehouse, a freezer, and a cleaning table. Some sites here are taken by summer season rentals, and some are taken by permanent residents.

Campsites, facilities: There are 49 sites for RVs of any length, and seven tent sites. Electricity, drinking water, sewer hookups, and picnic tables are provided. Flush toilets, bottled gas, an RV dump station, showers, a recreation hall, and a laundry room are available. Boat docks and launching facilities are nearby. Lake, river, and ocean are all within 1.5 miles. Leashed pets are permitted.

Reservations, fees: Reservations accepted. Sites are $20 per night, $1 per person for more than two people. Senior discount available. Open year-round.

Directions: In Port Orford on U.S. 101, drive to Madrona Avenue. Turn east and drive one block to Port Orford Loop. Turn north and drive one-half mile to the camp on the left side.

Contact: Port Orford RV Village, 2855 Port

Orford Loop Rd., P.O. Box 697, Port Orford, OR 97465, 541/332-1041.

107 HUMBUG MOUNTAIN STATE PARK

Rating: 7

Near the Pacific Ocean.
Map 7.7, grid c5, page 425

This park and campground are dominated by Humbug Mountain (1,756 feet elevation) and surrounded by forested hills. The campground enjoys some of the warmest weather on the Oregon coast. Windsurfing and scuba diving are popular, as is hiking the three-mile trail to Humbug Peak. Both ocean and freshwater fishing are accessible nearby.

Campsites, facilities: There are 63 tent sites and 35 sites with full hookups for RVs up to 55 feet long. A special camping area is provided for hikers and bicyclists. Fire grills, picnic tables, garbage bins, and drinking water are provided. Flush toilets, showers, and firewood are available. Leashed pets are permitted.

Reservations, fees: Reservations are not accepted. Sites are $16–18 per night, $7 per extra vehicles, and $4 per person per night for hikers/bicyclists. Major credit cards accepted. Open year-round.

Directions: From Port Orford, drive south on U.S. 101 for six miles to the park entrance on the left.

Contact: Humbug Mountain State Park, P.O. Box 1345, Port Orford, OR 97465, 541/332-6774 or 800/551-6949,

108 DAPHNE GROVE

Rating: 7

On the South Fork of the Coquille River in Siskiyou National Forest.
Map 7.7, grid c8, page 425

This prime spot (at 1,000 feet elevation) along the South Fork of the Coquille River, sur-

rounded by old-growth Douglas fir, cedar, and maple, is far enough out of the way to attract little attention. No fishing is allowed. The road is paved all the way to, and in, the campground, a plus for RVs and "city cars."

Campsites, facilities: There are 15 sites for tents or RVs up to 35 feet long. Picnic tables, garbage bins, and fire grills are provided. Vault toilets and drinking water are available. Some facilities are wheelchair accessible. Leashed pets are permitted.

Reservations, fees: Reservations are not accepted. Sites are $8 per night from late May–late September, senior discount available; free the rest of the year, $3 per extra vehicle. Open year-round, with limited winter facilities.

Directions: From Coos Bay, drive south on U.S. 101 for six miles to the junction with Highway 42. Turn east and drive 20 miles to Myrtle Point. Continue on Highway 42 to Powers Highway (Highway 242). Turn right (southwest) and drive 18 miles to Powers and County Road 90. Turn south and drive 4.3 miles to Forest Road 33. Turn south and drive 10.5 miles to the campground entrance.

Contact: Siskiyou National Forest, Powers Ranger District, 42861 Hwy. 242, Powers, OR 97466, 541/439-6200, fax 541/439-6217.

109 MYRTLE GROVE

Rating: 6

On the South Fork of the Coquille River in Siskiyou National Forest.
Map 7.7, grid c8, page 425

This U.S. Forest Service campground is located along the South Fork of the Coquille River, a little downstream from Daphne Grove, at an elevation of 500 feet. No fishing is allowed. Campsites are set under a canopy of big leaf maple and Douglas fir in a narrow, steep canyon. The Big Tree Recreation Site, home to a huge Port Orford cedar, is a few miles away. The trail that runs adjacent to Elk Creek provides a prime hike. (The road to Big Tree may be closed because of slides, so be sure to check with the ranger district in advance.)

Campsites, facilities: There are five tent sites. Picnic tables and fire grills are provided. Pit toilets are available. There is no drinking water, and all garbage must be packed out. Leashed pets are permitted.

Reservations, fees: Reservations are not accepted. There is no fee for camping. Open year-round.

Directions: From Coos Bay, drive south on U.S. 101 for six miles to the junction with Highway 42. Turn east and drive 20 miles to Myrtle Point. Continue on Highway 42 to Powers Highway (Highway 242). Turn right (southwest) and drive 18 miles to Powers and County Road 90. Turn south and drive 4.3 miles to Forest Road 33. Turn south to the camp. The road is paved all the way to the camp.

Contact: Siskiyou National Forest, Powers Ranger District, 42861 Hwy. 242, Powers, OR 96466, 541/439-6200, 541/439-6217.

110 SQUAW LAKE

Rating: 8

On Squaw Lake in Siskiyou National Forest.
Map 7.7, grid c8, page 425

This campground (at 2,200 feet elevation) along the shore of one-acre Squaw Lake is set in rich, old-growth forest. Squaw is more of a pond than a lake, but it is stocked with trout in the spring. Get there early; the fish are generally gone by midsummer. The trailheads for the Panther Ridge Trail and Coquille River Falls Trail are a 10-minute drive from the campground. It's strongly advised that you obtain a U.S. Forest Service map detailing the backcountry roads and trails.

Campsites, facilities: There are seven partially developed sites for tents or RVs up to 21 feet long. Picnic tables and fire rings are provided. Pit toilets are available. There is no drinking water, and all garbage must be packed out. Leashed pets are permitted.

Reservations, fees: Reservations are not accepted. There is no fee for camping. Open year-round.

Directions: From Coos Bay, drive south on U.S. 101 for six miles to the junction with Highway 42. Turn east and drive 20 miles to Myrtle Point. Continue on Highway 42 to Powers Highway (Highway 242). Turn right (southwest) and drive 18 miles to Powers and County Road 90. Turn south and drive 4.3 miles to Forest Road 33. Turn south and drive 12.5 miles to Forest Road 3348. Turn southeast and drive 4.5 miles to the campground entrance road. Turn east and drive one mile to the campground. The road is paved for all but the last one-half mile.

Contact: Siskiyou National Forest, Powers Ranger District, 42861 Hwy. 242, Powers, OR 97466, 541/439-6200, fax 541/439-6217.

111 ROCK CREEK

Rating: 6

Near the South Fork of the Coquille River in Siskiyou National Forest.
Map 7.7, grid c8, page 425

This little-known camp (elevation 1,400 feet) in a tree-shaded canyon is surrounded by old-growth forest and some reforested areas. It is set near Rock Creek, just upstream from its confluence with the South Fork of the Coquille River. No fishing is allowed. For a good side trip, take the one-mile climb to Azalea Lake, which is stocked with trout. There are some hike-in campsites at the lake, but no drinking water is provided. In July, the azaleas are spectacular.

Campsites, facilities: There are seven sites for tents or RVs. Picnic tables, drinking water, and fire grills are provided; all garbage must be packed out. Vault toilets and firewood are available. Leashed pets are permitted.

Reservations, fees: Reservations are not accepted. Sites are $8 per night from late May–late September, free the rest of the year, $3 per extra vehicle. Senior discount available. Open year-round, with limited winter facilities.

Directions: From Coos Bay, drive south on U.S. 101 for six miles to the junction with Highway 42. Turn east and drive 20 miles to Myrtle Point.

Continue on Highway 42 to Powers Highway (Highway 242). Turn right (southwest) and drive 18 miles to Powers and County Road 90. Turn south and drive 4.3 miles to Forest Road 33. Turn south and drive for 13 miles to the campground entrance road. Turn southwest and drive 1.5 miles to the campground. The road is paved all the way.

Contact: Siskiyou National Forest, Powers Ranger District, 42861 Hwy. 242, Powers, OR 97466, 541/439-6200, fax 541/439-6217.

112 ILLAHE

Rating: 7

On the Rogue River in Siskiyou National Forest.

Map 7.7, grid c8, page 425

This quiet and isolated camping area has great hiking opportunities, beginning at the nearby Upper Rogue River Trail. Boating and fishing are just a mile away at Foster Bar Campground. This pretty spot offers privacy between sites and is hidden from the majority of tourists. Deer are in abundance here.

Campsites, facilities: There are 14 sites for tents or RVs up to 21 feet long. Drinking water, fire rings, garbage bins, and picnic tables are provided. Flush toilets are available. A store is within five miles. Boat docks are nearby. Leashed pets are permitted.

Reservations, fees: Reservations are not accepted. Sites are $5 per night, plus $3 for each additional vehicle. Senior discount available. Open mid-May–mid-October.

Directions: From Gold Beach on U.S. 101, turn east on County Road 595. Drive east for 35 miles (it becomes Forest Road 33) to a junction for Illahe, Illahe Campground, and Foster Bar. Turn right on County Road 375 and drive five miles to the campground.

Contact: Siskiyou National Forest, Gold Beach Ranger District, 29279 Ellensburg Ave., Gold Beach, OR 97444, 541/247-3600, fax 541/247-3617.

113 FOSTER BAR

Rating: 5

On the Rogue River in Siskiyou National Forest.

Map 7.7, grid d8, page 425

This camping area is set on the banks of the Rogue River. At the nearby Rogue River Trail, there's a takeout point for rafters. Hiking opportunities are good and you can also fish from the river bar. Illahe Campground and Agness RV Park provide nearby camping alternatives.

Campsites, facilities: There are several dispersed sites for tents or RVs up to 16 feet long, though access is difficult for RVs and trailers. Flush toilets, garbage bins, and boat-launching facilities are available, but there is no drinking water. Leashed pets are permitted.

Reservations, fees: Reservations are not accepted. There is no fee for camping. Open year-round.

Directions: From Gold Beach on U.S. 101, turn east on County Road 595 and drive 35 miles (it becomes Forest Road 33) to the junction for Illahe, Illahe Campground, and Foster Bar. Turn right on County Road 375 and drive five miles to the campground.

Contact: Siskiyou National Forest, Gold Beach Ranger District, 29279 Ellensburg Ave., Gold Beach, OR 97444, 541/247-3600, fax 541/247-3617.

114 ARIZONA BEACH CAMPGROUND

Rating: 7

Near Gold Beach.

Map 7.7, grid d5, page 425

This pleasant campground offers grassy, tree-lined sites along one-half mile of ocean beach frontage. Many of the RV sites are located along the beach frontage. A creek runs through the campground, and you can swim at the mouth of it in the summer. Elk and deer roam nearby. A small lake is available for fishing.

Campsites, facilities: There are 78 sites for RVs

of any length, including seven drive-through, 48 tent sites, and furnished trailer rentals. Electricity, drinking water, sewer hookups, and picnic tables are provided. Flush toilets, bottled gas, an RV dump station, showers, firewood, a store, a laundry room, a recreation room, gold panning, and a playground are available. Leashed pets are permitted.

Reservations, fees: Reservations accepted. Tent sites are $16 per night and RV sites are $23–26 per night; $3 per person for more than two people, $5 for an extra vehicle. Senior discount available. Major credit cards accepted. Monthly rates available. Open year-round.

Directions: From Gold Beach, drive north on U.S. 101 for 14 miles to the campground on the right.

Contact: Arizona Beach Campground, 36939 Arizona Ranch Rd., Port Orford, OR 97465, 541/332-6491, website: www.arizonabeachrv.com.

115 HONEYBEAR CAMPGROUND

Rating: 10

Near Gold Beach.

Map 7.7, grid d5, page 425

This campground offers wooded sites with ocean views. The owners have built a huge, authentic chalet, which contains a German deli, a recreation area, and a big dance floor. On summer nights, they hold dances with live music. A restaurant is available on-site with authentic German food.

Campsites, facilities: There are 20 tent sites and 65 sites for RVs of any length; 30 are drive-through sites with full hookups, 15 with patios. Picnic tables are provided. Flush toilets, electricity, drinking water, cable TV, an RV dump station, showers, firewood, a recreation hall, a restaurant, a store, a laundry room, ice, and a playground are available. Leashed pets are permitted.

Reservations, fees: Reservations at 800/822-4444. Sites are $14.95–25 per night, $2 per person for more than two people, and $1 per extra vehicle. Open year-round, weather permitting.

Directions: From Gold Beach, drive north on U.S. 101 for nine miles to Ophir Road near Milepost 321. Turn north and drive two miles to the campground on the right side of the road.

Contact: Honeybear Campground, 34161 Ophir Rd., P.O. Box 97, Ophir, OR 97464, 541/247-2765, website: www.honeybearrv.com.

116 NESIKA BEACH RV PARK

Rating: 7

Near Gold Beach.

Map 7.7, grid d5, page 425

This campground next to Nesika Beach is a good layover spot for U.S. 101 cruisers. An 18-hole golf course is close by. There are many long-term rentals here.

Campsites, facilities: There are six tent sites and 32 sites for RVs of any length. Electricity, drinking water, cable TV, sewer hookups, and picnic tables are provided. Flush toilets, an RV dump station, showers, a store, a laundry room, and ice are available. Leashed pets are permitted.

Reservations, fees: Reservations accepted. Sites are $12–19 per night, $1 per person for more than two people. Senior discount available. Monthly rates available. Open year-round.

Directions: From Gold Beach, drive north on U.S. 101 for six miles to Nesika Road. Turn left and drive three-quarters of a mile west to the campground on the right.

Contact: Nesika Beach RV Park, 32887 Nesika Rd., Gold Beach, OR 97444, 541/247-6077.

117 QUOSATANA

Rating: 6

On the Rogue River in Siskiyou National Forest.

Map 7.7, grid e6, page 425

This campground is set along the banks of the Rogue River, upstream from the much smaller Lobster Creek Campground. The campground features a large, grassy area and a barrier-free trail with interpretive signs. Ocean access is just a short drive away, and the quaint town of Gold Beach offers a decent side trip. Nearby Otter Point State Park (day use only) has further recreation options. The Shrader Old-Growth Trail and Myrtle Tree Trail provide nearby hiking opportunities. Quosatana makes a good base camp for a hiking or fishing trip.

Campsites, facilities: There are 42 sites for tents or RVs up to 32 feet long. Drinking water, fire grills, garbage bins, and picnic tables are provided. Flush toilets, an RV dump station, a fish-cleaning station, and a boat ramp are available. Some facilities are wheelchair accessible. Leashed pets are permitted.

Reservations, fees: Reservations are not accepted. Sites are $10 per night, plus $3 for each additional vehicle. Senior discount available. Open year-round.

Directions: From Gold Beach on U.S. 101, turn east on County Road 595 and drive 13 miles (it becomes Forest Road 33) to the campground on the left.

Contact: Siskiyou National Forest, Gold Beach Ranger District, 29279 Ellensburg Ave., Gold Beach, OR 97444, 541/247-3600, fax 541/247-3617.

118 LOBSTER CREEK

Rating: 6

On the Rogue River in Siskiyou National Forest.

Map 7.7, grid e6, page 425

This small campground on a river bar along the Rogue River is about a 15-minute drive from Gold Beach, and it makes a good base for a fishing trip. The area is heavily forested with myrtle and Douglas fir, and the Shrader Old-Growth Trail and Myrtle Tree Trail are nearby.

Campsites, facilities: There are six sites for tents or RVs up to 21 feet long. Fire rings

and picnic tables are provided. Flush toilets are available, but there is no drinking water and all garbage must be packed out. A boat launch is also available. Leashed pets are permitted.

Reservations, fees: Reservations are not accepted. Sites are $5 per night, plus $3 for each additional vehicle. Camping is also permitted on a gravel bar area for $3 per night. Senior discount available. Open mid-May–mid-October.

Directions: From Gold Beach on U.S. 101, turn east on County Road 595 and drive 10 miles (it becomes Forest Road 33) to the campground on the left.

Contact: Siskiyou National Forest, Gold Beach Ranger District, 29279 Ellensburg Ave., Gold Beach, OR 97444, 541/247-3600, fax 541/247-3617.

119 KIMBALL CREEK BEND RV RESORT

Rating: 6

On the Rogue River.

Map 7.7, grid e5, page 425

This campground on the scenic Rogue River is just far enough from the coast to provide quiet and its own distinct character. Nearby recreation options include an 18-hole golf course, hiking trails, and boating facilities. Note than 17 of the sites are year-round rentals.

Campsites, facilities: There are 56 sites, 18 drive-through, for RVs of any length, 13 tent sites, two park-model cabins, and three motel rooms. Electricity, drinking water, sewer hookups, and picnic tables are provided. Flush toilets, bottled gas, an RV dump station, showers, a recreation hall, a store, a laundry room, ice, and a playground are available. Boat docks and launching facilities are nearby. Leashed pets are permitted.

Reservations, fees: Reservations at 888/814-0633. Sites are $23–32 per night for RVs, $20 per night for tents, and $1–3 per person for more than two people. Major credit cards accepted. Open year-round.

Directions: From Gold Beach, drive north on U.S. 101 for one mile (on the north side of the Rogue River) to Rogue River Road. Turn east and drive about eight miles to the campground.

Contact: Kimball Creek Bend RV Resort, 97136 North Bank Rogue, Gold Beach, OR 97444, 541/247-7580.

120 LUCKY LODGE RV PARK

Rating: 6

On the Rogue River.
Map 7.7, grid e5, page 425

Lucky Lodge is a good layover spot for U.S. 101 travelers who want to get off the highway circuit. Set on the shore of the Rogue River, it offers opportunities for fishing, boating, and swimming. Most sites have a view of the river. Nearby recreation options include hiking trails. This park has a few long-term rentals.

Campsites, facilities: There are 32 sites with full-hookups, most drive-through, for RVs of any length, four tent sites, and two cabins. Electricity, drinking water, sewer hookups, and picnic tables are provided. Flush toilets, bottled gas, an RV dump station, showers, firewood, a recreation hall, and a laundry room are available. Boat docks and rentals are within eight miles. Leashed pets are permitted.

Reservations, fees: Reservations accepted. Sites are $19–22 per night for RVs, $15 per night for tents, and $3 per person for more than two people. Open year-round.

Directions: From Gold Beach, drive north on U.S. 101 for four miles (on the north side of the Rogue River) to Rogue River Road. Turn east and drive one-quarter mile to the campground.

Contact: Lucky Lodge RV Park, 32040 Watson Ln., Gold Beach, OR 97444, 541/247-7618.

121 INDIAN CREEK RV PARK

Rating: 7

On the Rogue River.
Map 7.7, grid e5, page 425

This campground is set along the Rogue River on the outskirts of the town of Gold Beach. Nearby recreation options include a riding stable, riding trails, and boat trips on the Rogue.

Campsites, facilities: There are 25 tent sites and 100 sites for RVs of any length. Electricity, drinking water, sewer and cable TV hookups, and picnic tables are provided. Flush toilets, showers, firewood, a recreation hall, a store, a sauna, a café, a laundry room, ice, and a playground are available. Bottled gas is within two miles. Boat docks, launching facilities, and rentals are nearby. Leashed pets are permitted.

Reservations, fees: Reservations accepted. Sites are $15–25 per night, $1 per person for more than two people. Major credit cards accepted. Senior discount available. Open year-round, with limited winter facilities.

Directions: On U.S. 101, drive to the northern end of Gold Beach to Jerry's Flat Road (just south of the Patterson Bridge). Turn east on Jerry's Flat Road and drive one-half mile to the campground.

Contact: Indian Creek RV Park, 94680 Jerry's Flat Rd., Gold Beach, OR 97444, 541/247-7704, website: www.harborside.com/~indiancreek/.

122 IRELAND'S OCEAN VIEW RV PARK

Rating: 8

On the Pacific Ocean.
Map 7.7, grid e5, page 425

One of the newest RV parks in the area, this spot is situated on the beach in the quaint little town of Gold Beach, only one mile from the famous Rogue River. This park is very clean and features blacktop roads and grass beside each site. Recreation options include beachcombing, fishing, and boating. Great ocean views are possible from the observatory/lighthouse.

Campsites, facilities: There are 33 sites for RVs up to 40 feet long. Tent camping is permitted only in combination with an RV. Cable TV, phones, showers, restrooms, a laundry room, a recreation room, horseshoe pits, and picnic areas are available. Leashed pets are permitted.

Reservations, fees: Reservations recommended. Sites are $15–22 per night, $1 per person for more than two people. Monthly rates available. Open year-round.

Directions: On U.S. 101, drive to the southern end of Gold Beach (U.S. 101 becomes Ellensburg Avenue) and look for the camp at 20272 Ellensburg Avenue (across from the U.S. Forest Service office).

Contact: Ireland's Ocean View RV Park, 29272 Ellensburg Ave., P.O. Box 727, Gold Beach, OR 97444, 541/247-0148, website: www.ireland srvpark.com.

123 OCEANSIDE RV PARK

Rating: 5

On the Pacific Ocean.

Map 7.7, grid e5, page 425

Set 100 yards from the ocean, this park is close to beachcombing terrain, marked bike trails, and boating facilities. The park is also adjacent to the mouth of the Rogue River, in the Port of Gold Beach. No tent camping.

Campsites, facilities: There are 80 sites, 20 drive-through, for RVs of any length and two yurts. Electricity, drinking water, sewer hookups, and picnic tables are provided. Flush toilets, showers, a coin-operated laundry, cable TV, a small store, and ice are available. Bottled gas, an RV dump station, a store, and a café are within two miles. Boat docks, launching facilities, and rentals are nearby. Leashed pets are permitted.

Reservations, fees: Reservations recommended. Sites are $13–22, $1 per person for more

than two people, and $30 per night for yurts. Major credit cards accepted. Open year-round.

Directions: On U.S. 101, drive to central Gold Beach and the intersection with Moore Street. Turn west and drive two blocks to Airport Way. Turn right and drive three blocks to South Jetty Road. Turn left and look for the park on the left.

Contact: Oceanside RV Park, P.O. Box 1107, Gold Beach, OR 97444, 541/247-2301.

124 AGNESS RV PARK

Rating: 6

On the Rogue River.

Map 7.7, grid e5, page 425

Agness RV Park is a destination campground on the scenic Rogue River in the middle of the Siskiyou National Forest. Fishing is the main focus here. Boating is sharply limited because the nearest pullout is 12 miles downstream. It's advisable to obtain a U.S. Forest Service map detailing the backcountry. Note that more than half of the sites are taken by summer season rentals. There are also some year-round rentals. Tent camping is permitted at RV sites.

Campsites, facilities: There are 81 sites, 43 drive-through, for RVs of any length and one RV rental. Electricity, drinking water, sewer hookups, and picnic tables are provided. Flush toilets, an RV dump station, showers, and a laundry room are available. A store, a café, bottled gas, and ice are within 100 yards. Boat-launching facilities are nearby. Pets are permitted.

Reservations, fees: Reservations accepted. Sites are $17 per night, $2 per person for more than two people. Major credit cards accepted. Monthly rates available. Open year-round.

Directions: In Gold Beach, drive on U.S. 101 to the southern end of the Rogue River Bridge and Jerry's Flat Road. Turn east on Jerry's Flat Road and you'll see the entrance to the campground on the left.

Contact: Agness RV Park, 4215 Agness Rd., Agness, OR 97406, 541/247-2813, website: www.agnessrv.com.

125 WHALESHEAD BEACH RESORT

Rating: 7

Near the Pacific Ocean.

Map 7.7, grid h6, page 425

This resort, about one-quarter mile from the beach, is set in a forested area with a small stream nearby. Activities at and around the camp include ocean and river fishing, jet boat trips, whale-watching excursions, and a golf course (13 miles away). Each campsite has a deck, and all cabins have an ocean view. One unique feature, a tunnel connects the campground to a trail to the beach.

Campsites, facilities: There are 115 sites for tents or RVs of any length and 15 cabins. Cable TV, restrooms, showers, drinking water, a public phone, a laundry room, limited groceries, ice, snacks, RV supplies, LP gas, horseshoe pits, and a restaurant are available. An RV dump station is six miles away. Some facilities are wheelchair accessible. Leashed pets are permitted.

Reservations, fees: Reservations recommended. RV sites are $22–25 per night; tent sites are $18 per night; $2 per person for more than two people. Major credit cards accepted. Open year-round.

Directions: From Brookings, drive 6.5 miles north on U.S. 101 to Milepost 349.5 and look for the park on the right.

Contact: Whaleshead Beach Resort, 19921 Whaleshead Rd., Brookings, OR 97415, 541/469-7446, fax 541/469-7447, website: www.whalesheadresort.com.

126 LOEB STATE PARK

Rating: 8

Near the Chetco River.

Map 7.7, grid h7, page 425

This park is set in a canyon formed by the Chetco River. The campsites are nestled in a beautiful old myrtle grove. A three-quarter-mile self-guided River View Trail adjacent to the Chetco River leads to the northernmost redwood grove in the United States. Nature programs and interpretive tours are available.

Campsites, facilities: There are 50 sites with partial hookups (water and electricity) for tents or RVs up to 50 feet long and three log cabins. Picnic tables, drinking water, garbage bins, and fire grills are provided. Flush toilets and firewood are available. Leashed pets are permitted.

Reservations, fees: Reservations at 800/452-5687 or website: www.OregonStateParks.org ($7 reservation fee). Sites are $12–16 per night, $7 for extra vehicles, and $35 per night for cabins. Major credit cards accepted. Open year-round.

Directions: On U.S. 101, drive to south Brookings and County Road 784 (North Bank Chetco River Road). Turn northeast and drive 10 miles northeast on North Bank Road to the park entrance on the right.

Contact: Harris Beach State Park, 1655 U.S. 101, Brookings, OR 97415, 541/469-2021 or 800/551-6949.

127 LITTLE REDWOOD

Rating: 7

On the Chetco River in Siskiyou National Forest.

Map 7.7, grid h7, page 425

This campground is set among old-growth fir trees near the banks of the Chetco River. An official put-in spot for rafting and river boats, the camp is also on the main western access route to the Kalmiopsis Wilderness, which is about 20 miles away. Campsites are fairly private, though close together.

Campsites, facilities: There are 11 sites for tents or RVs up to 16 feet long. Picnic tables, garbage containers, and fire grills are provided. Drinking water and vault toilets are available. Leashed pets are permitted.

Reservations, fees: Reservations are not accepted. Sites are $10 per night, $3 for an extra vehicle; towed vehicles free. Senior discount available. Open late May–mid-September.

Directions: On U.S. 101, drive to south Brookings and County Road 784 (North Bank Chetco River Road). Turn northeast on North Bank Chetco River Road and drive 13.5 miles (the road becomes Forest Road 1376) to the campground.

Contact: Siskiyou National Forest, Chetco Ranger District, 539 Chetco Ave., P.O. Box 4580, Brookings, OR 97415, 541/412-6000, fax 541/412-6025.

128 HARRIS BEACH STATE PARK

Rating: 8

On the Pacific Ocean.
Map 7.7, grid h6, page 425

The park boasts the largest island off the Oregon coast. Bird Island (also called Goat Island) is a breeding site for such rare birds as the tufted puffin. This park has sandy beaches interspersed with eroded sea stacks. The park's beauty changes with the seasons. Wildlife viewing opportunities are abundant (gray whales, harbor seals, and sea lions). In the fall and winter, the nearby Chetco River attracts good runs of salmon and steelhead, respectively.

Campsites, facilities: There are 63 sites for tents or self-contained RVs and 86 sites with full or partial hookups for RVs up to 50 feet long. There are six yurts, each accommodating five people, and a special camping area for hikers and bicyclists. Picnic tables, garbage bins, and fire grills are provided. Electricity, drinking water, sewer and cable TV hookups, flush toilets, an RV dump station, showers, a laundry room, and firewood are available. Some facilities are wheelchair accessible. Leashed pets are permitted.

Reservations, fees: Reservations at 800/452-5687 or website: www.OregonStateParks.org ($7 reservation fee). Sites are $13–19 per night, $7 per night for an extra vehicle, $4 per night per person for hikers/bikers, and $27 per night for yurts. Major credit cards accepted. Open year-round.

Directions: From Brookings, drive north on U.S. 101 for two miles to the park entrance on the left.

Contact: Harris Beach State Park, 1655 U.S. 101, Brookings, OR 97415, 541/469-2021.

129 PORT OF BROOKINGS HARBOR BEACHFRONT RV PARK

Rating: 8

On the Pacific Ocean.
Map 7.7, grid h6, page 425

This park, located just past the Oregon/California border on the Pacific Ocean, makes a great layover spot. Oceanfront sites are available, and recreational activities include boating, fishing, and swimming. Nearby Harris Beach State Park, with its beach access and hiking trails, makes a good side trip.

Campsites, facilities: There are 25 tent sites and 138 spaces for RVs of any length. Restrooms, showers, an RV dump station, a public phone, a laundry room, ice, and a marina with a boat ramp, a boat dock, and snacks are available nearby. Some facilities are wheelchair accessible. Leashed pets are permitted.

Reservations, fees: Reservations recommended. Sites are $14–28 per night, $2 per person for more than two people. Major credit cards accepted. Open year-round.

Directions: From Brookings, drive south on U.S. 101 for 2.5 miles to Benham Lane. Turn west on Benham Lane and drive one-half mile (it becomes Lower Harbor Road) to Boat Basin Road. Turn left and drive two blocks to the park on the right.

Contact: Port of Brookings Harbor Beachfront RV Park, 16035 Boat Basin Rd., Brookings, OR 97415, 541/469-5867 or 800/441-0856 in Oregon, website: www.port/brookings /harbor.org.

130 ATRIVERS EDGE RV RESORT

Rating: 7

On the Chetco River.

Map 7.7, grid h6, page 425

This campground lies along the banks of the Chetco River, just upstream from Brookings Harbor. A favorite spot for fishermen, it features salmon and steelhead trips on the Chetco in the fall and winter. Deep-sea trips for salmon or rockfish are available nearby in the summer. This resort looks like the Rhine Valley in Germany, a pretty canyon between the trees and the river. A golf course is nearby.

Campsites, facilities: There are 110 sites, including 15 drive-through, for RVs of any length and five cabins. Electricity, drinking water, and sewer hookups are provided. Flush toilets, bottled gas, an RV dump station, showers, a recreation hall with exercise equipment, a laundry room, a recycling station, a small boat launch, and cable TV are available. Leashed pets are permitted.

Reservations, fees: Reservations recommended at 888/295-1441. RV sites are $22–30 per night, $16 per night for tent sites, and $3 per person for more than two people. Open year-round.

Directions: On U.S. 101, drive to the southern end of Brookings (harbor side) and to South Bank Chetco River Road (a cloverleaf exit). Turn east on South Bank Chetco River Road and drive 1.5 miles to the park entrance on the left (a slanted left turn, through the pillars, well signed).

Contact: AtRivers Edge RV Resort, 98203 South Bank Chetco Rd., Brookings, OR 97415, 541/469-3356, website: www.atriversedge.com.

131 SEA BIRD RV PARK

Rating: 5

On the Pacific Ocean.

Map 7.7, grid h6, page 425

This is one of several campgrounds in the area. Nearby recreation options include marked bike trails, a full-service marina, and tennis courts. A nice, neat park, it features paved roads and granite sites. There is also a beach for surfing near the park. In summer, most of the sites are reserved for the season. No tent camping.

Campsites, facilities: There are 60 sites for RVs of any length; nine are drive-through sites. Electricity, drinking water, sewer hookups, and picnic tables are provided. Flush toilets, an RV dump station, showers, a recreation hall, and a laundry room are available. Boat docks, launching facilities, and rentals are nearby. Leashed pets are permitted.

Reservations, fees: Reservations accepted. Sites are $16 per night, $1 per person for more than two people. Senior discount available. Open year-round.

Directions: In Brookings, drive south on U.S. 101 to the Chetco River Bridge. Continue one-quarter mile south on U.S. 101 to the park entrance on the left.

Contact: Sea Bird RV Park, 16429 U.S. 101 S, P.O. Box 1026, Brookings, OR 97415, 541/469-3512.

132 WINCHUCK

Rating: 6

On the Winchuck River in Siskiyou National Forest.

Map 7.7, grid h7, page 425

This forested campground hugs the banks of the Winchuck River, an out-of-the-way stream that out-of-towners don't know exists. It's quiet, remote, and not that far from the coast, although it feels like an inland spot. If this camp is full, Ludlum Campground is about two miles away on Forest Road 1108.

Campsites, facilities: There are 15 sites for tents or RVs up to 30 feet long. Picnic tables, garbage bins, and fire grills are provided. Vault toilets and drinking water are available. Leashed pets are permitted.

Reservations, fees: Reservations are not accepted. Sites are $10 per night, plus $3 for each additional non-towed vehicle. Senior discount available. Open late May–mid-September.

Directions: From Brookings, drive south on U.S. 101 for 5.5 miles to County Road 896. Turn east and drive six miles to Forest Road 1107. Turn east and drive one mile to the campground.

Contact: Siskiyou National Forest, Chetco Ranger District, 539 Chetco Ave., P.O. Box 4580, Brookings, OR 97415, 541/412-6000, fax 541/412-6025.

133 TUCKER FLAT

Rating: 7

On the Rogue River.

Map 7.8, grid c2, page 426

Above the clear waters of Mule Creek, this campground borders the Wild Rogue Wilderness. Tucker Flat offers a trailhead into the Wild Rogue Wilderness and lots of evidence of historic mining. Mosquitoes can be a problem, and bears occasionally wander through. The historic Rogue River Ranch is just one-quarter mile away, and the museum and other buildings are open during the summer. The Rogue River Ranch is on the National Register of Historic Places. There are also scenic bridges along Mule Creek. Tucker Flat campground can also be reached by hiking the Rogue River Trail or by floating the Rogue River and hiking up past the Rogue River Ranch. Campers and hikers are advised to stop by the Medford BLM office for maps.

Campsites, facilities: There are eight primitive tent sites. Picnic tables and fire grills are provided. Vault toilets and bear-proof trash cans are available. There is no drinking water. Leashed pets are permitted.

Reservations, fees: Reservations are not accepted. There is no fee for camping. Open year-round, weather permitting.

Directions: From Grants Pass, drive one mile north on I-5 to Exit 61. Take that exit and drive west on Merlin-Galice Access Road for 20 miles to the Grave Creek Bridge (the second bridge over the Rogue River). Cross the bridge and drive a short distance to BLM Road 34-8-1. Turn left and drive 16 miles to BLM Road 32-8-31. Turn left and drive seven miles to BLM Road 32-9-14.2. Turn left and drive 15 miles to the campground (around the bend from the Rogue River Ranch).

Contact: Bureau of Land Management, Medford District, 3040 Biddle Rd., Medford, OR 97504, 541/618-2200, fax 541/618-2400.

134 BIG PINE

Rating: 4

On Myers Creek in Siskiyou National Forest.

Map 7.8, grid d2, page 426

This little campground (elevation 2,400 feet) is set near the banks of Myers Creek in a valley of large pine and Douglas fir. Many sites are right on the creek, and all are shaded. One of the world's tallest ponderosa pine trees grows near the campground. A 1.1-mile barrier-free interpretive trail starts at the campground and a day-use area is available. Note that this campground was used as a staging area for fire fighters in the catastrophic Biscuit Fire in 2002. Although the fire did not burn the campground, it did burn nearby areas.

Campsites, facilities: There are 14 tent sites. Picnic tables and fire grills are provided. Vault toilets, drinking water, and garbage bins are available. Some facilities are wheelchair accessible. Leashed pets are permitted.

Reservations, fees: Reservations are not accepted. Sites are $5 per night, $2 per extra vehicle. Senior discount available. Open late May–mid-October.

Directions: From Grants Pass, drive north on I-5 for 3.5 miles to Exit 61 (Merlin-Galice Road). Take that exit and drive northwest for

12.5 miles to Forest Road 25. Turn left on Forest Road 25 and head southwest for 12.8 miles to the campground on the right.

Contact: Siskiyou National Forest, Galice Ranger District, 200 N.E. Greenfield Rd., Grants Pass, OR 97526, 541/471-6500, fax 541/471-6514.

135 SAM BROWN AND SAM BROWN HORSE CAMP

Rating: 4

Near Grants Pass in Siskiyou National Forest.

Map 7.8, grid d2, page 426

This campground is located in an isolated area near Grants Pass along Briggs Creek in a valley of pine and Douglas fir. It is set at an elevation of 2,500 feet. Many sites lie in the shade of trees, and a creek runs along one side of the campground. Taylor Creek Trail, Briggs Creek Trail, and Dutchy Creek Trail are nearby and are popular for hiking and horseback riding. An amphitheater is available for small group presentations. Although the campground was spared, the Biscuit Fire of 2002 did burn nearby areas.

Campsites, facilities: There are 37 sites for tents or RVs of any length at Sam Brown and seven equestrian tent sites with small corrals across the road at Sam Brown Horse Camp. At Sam Brown, picnic tables and fire rings or grills are provided and drinking water and vault toilets are available. A picnic shelter, solar shower, and an amphitheater are available. Some facilities are wheelchair accessible.

Reservations, fees: Reservations are not accepted. Sites are $5 per night, $2 for an extra vehicle. Senior discount available. Open late May–mid-October.

Directions: From Grants Pass, drive north on I-5 for 3.5 miles to Exit 61 (Merlin-Galice Road). Take that exit and drive northwest for 12.5 miles to Forest Road 25. Turn left on Forest Road 25 and head southwest for 13.5 miles to the campground.

Contact: Siskiyou National Forest, Galice Ranger District, 200 N.E. Greenfield Road, Grants Pass, OR 97526, 541/471-6500, fax 541/471-6514.

COURTESY OF OREGON TOURISM COMMISSION

Chapter 8
Portland and the
Willamette Valley

Chapter 8—
Portland and the Willamette Valley

For most tourists, Oregon is little more than a stretch of Interstate 5 from Portland to Cottage Grove. While there are some interesting things about this area—it's Oregon's business center and most of my relatives and pals live there—the glimpse provided from I-5 doesn't capture the beauty of much of the state. Residents, however, know the secret: Not only can you earn a good living here, it's also a great jump-off point to adventure.

To discover what the locals know, venture east to west on the slow two-lane highways that bordering the streams. Among the most notable are Highway 26 along the Nacanticum River, little Highway 6 along the Wilson, little Highway 22 along Three Rivers, tiny Highway 15 on the Little Nestucca, Highway 18 on the Salmon River, Highway 34 on the Alsea, Highway 126 on the Siuslaw, and Highway 38 on the Umpqua (my favorite). These roads provide routes to reach the coast, and can be used to create beautiful loop trips, with many hidden campgrounds to choose from while en route.

There are also parks and a number of lakes set in the foothills set along dammed rivers. The highlight is Silver Falls State Park, Oregon's largest state park, with a seven-mile hike that is routed past 10 awesome waterfalls, some falling more than 100 feet from their brinks. Lakes are plentiful, too, including Green Peter Reservoir on the Santiam River, Cottage Grove Reservoir, Dorena Lake, and Fall Creek Reservoir.

Portland is a great hub for finding recreation in the region. To the east is the Columbia River corridor and Mount Hood and its surrounding wilderness and national forest. To the south is Eugene, which leads to the McKenzie and Willamette Rivers and offers a good launch station to the Three Sisters in the east.

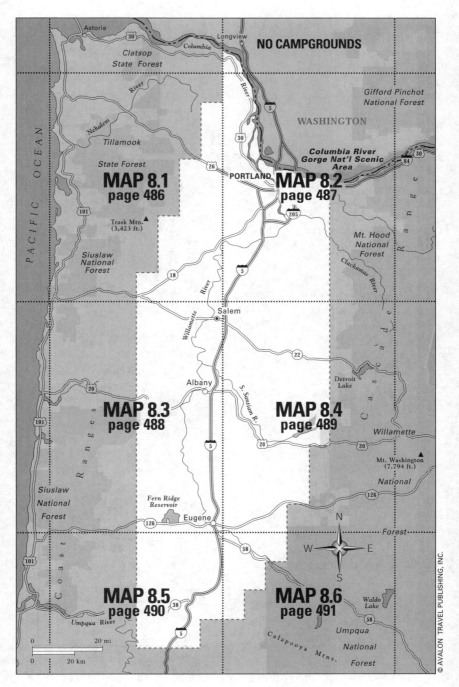

Map 8.1

**Campground 1
Page 492**

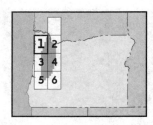

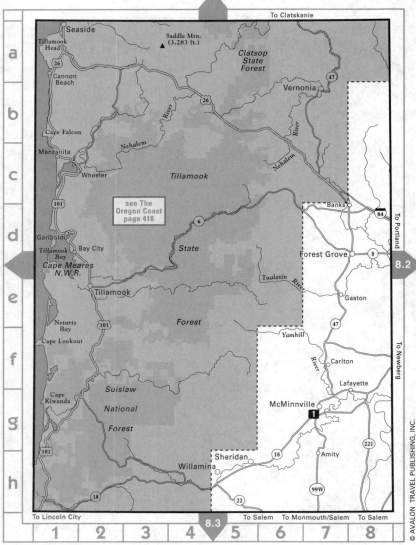

Map 8.2

Campgrounds 2–9
Pages 492–495

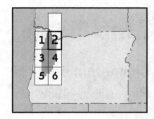

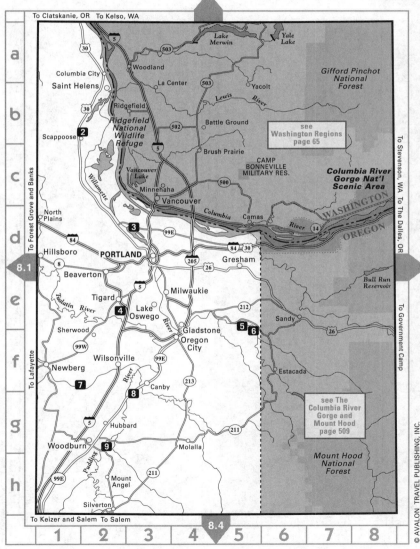

see
Washington Regions
page 65

see The
Columbia River
Gorge and
Mount Hood
page 509

© AVALON TRAVEL PUBLISHING, INC.

Map 8.3

Campgrounds 10–12
Pages 495–496

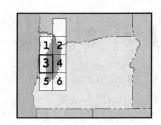

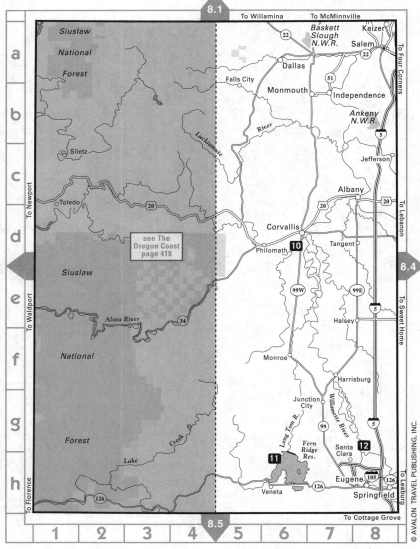

Map 8.4

Campgrounds 13–23
Pages 496–501

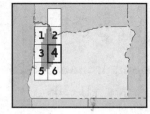

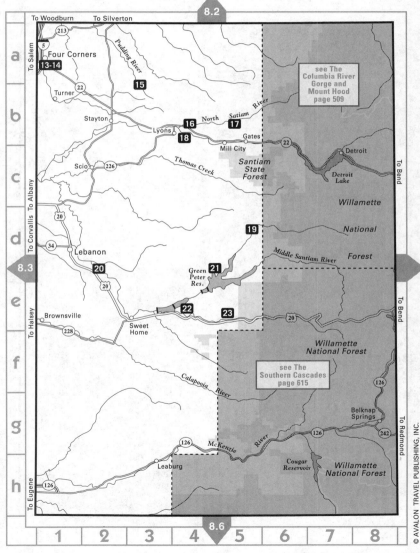

To Woodburn   To Silverton

8.2

a
To Salem
213
5
Four Corners
13-14
Turner
22
15
Stayton
Pudding River

b
North Santiam River
16
17
Lyons
18
Gates
Mill City
22
Detroit
see The
Columbia River
Gorge and
Mount Hood
page 509

c
Scio
226
Thomas Creek
Santiam
State
Forest
Detroit
Lake
Willamette
To Bend

d
To Corvallis To Albany
20
34
Lebanon
19
National
Middle Santiam River
Forest

8.3
20
20
21
Green
Peter
Res.

e
To Halsey
Brownsville
228
Sweet
Home
22
23
20
Willamette
National Forest
To Bend

f
Calapooia River
see The
Southern Cascades
page 615
126

g
126
McKenzie River
126
Belknap
Springs
126
242
To Redmond

h
To Eugene
126
Leaburg
Cougar
Reservoir
Willamette
National Forest

1   2   3   4   5   6   7   8

8.6

© AVALON TRAVEL PUBLISHING, INC.

Map 8.5

Campgrounds 24–29
Pages 501–503

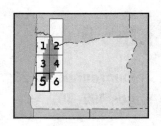

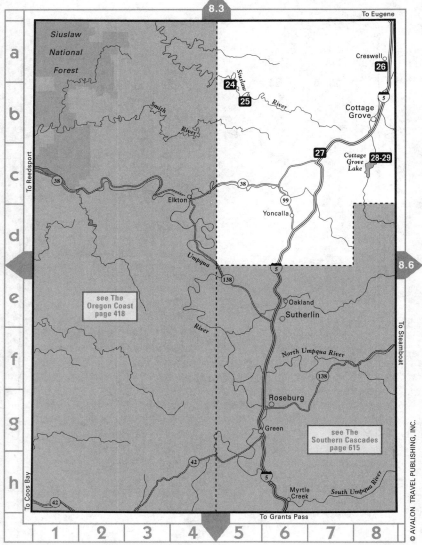

8.3

To Eugene

Siuslaw

National

Forest

Creswell

26

Siuslaw River

24

25

Cottage
Grove

Smith River

27

Cottage
Grove
Lake

28-29

To Reedsport

38

38

5

Elkton

99

Yoncalla

Umpqua

8.6

138

see The
Oregon Coast
page 418

Oakland

Sutherlin

River

North Umpqua River

To Steamboat

138

Roseburg

g

see The
Southern Cascades
page 615

Green

42

5

To Coos Bay

42

Myrtle
Creek

South Umpqua River

To Grants Pass

a b c d e f g h

1 2 3 4 5 6 7 8

© AVALON TRAVEL PUBLISHING, INC.

Map 8.6

Campgrounds 30–33
Pages 503–505

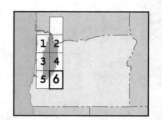

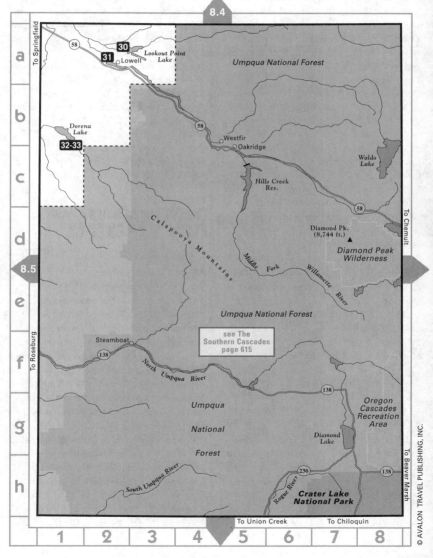

1 MULKEY RV PARK

⬛ 🐕 🚣 🚐 ⛺

Rating: 7

Near the South Yamhill River.

Map 8.1, grid g7, page 486

If you're in the area and looking for a camping spot, you'd best stop here—there are no other campgrounds within 30 miles. This wooded park is set near the South Yamhill River. Nearby recreation options include an 18-hole golf course, tennis courts, and the Western Deer Park and Arboretum, which has a playground.

Campsites, facilities: There are 70 sites for tents or RVs of any length. Electricity, drinking water, sewer hookups, and picnic tables are provided. Flush toilets, showers, a store, bottled gas, and a laundry are available. Leashed pets are permitted.

Reservations, fees: Reservations at 877/472-2475. Sites are $15–20 per night, $3 per person for more than two people. Monthly rates available. Major credit cards accepted. Open year-round.

Directions: From Portland, turn south on Highway 99 and drive about 31 miles to McMinnville and Highway 18. Turn southwest on Highway 18 and drive 3.5 miles to the park entrance.

Contact: Mulkey RV Park, 14325 S.W. Hwy. 18, McMinnville, OR 97128, 503/472-2475, fax 503/472-0718.

2 SCAPPOOSE RV PARK

🐕 🚣 ♿ 🚐 ⛺

Rating: 6

In Scappoose.

Map 8.2, grid b1, page 487

This county-operated RV park is set next to the rural Scappoose airport, making it a convenient spot for private pilots. The sites are partially shaded with spruce, oak, and maple trees. Set on the edge of a dike, it is less than a mile from the Columbia River and about a 30-minute drive from Portland.

Campsites, facilities: There are several tent sites in dispersed areas and seven sites for RVs, six with full hookups. Picnic tables and fire grills are provided. Drinking water, a restroom with flush toilets and showers, an RV dump station, firewood, and a playground with equipment and horseshoe pits are available. Leashed pets are permitted.

Reservations, fees: Reservations at 503/397-2353. Sites are $12–18 per night, $7 for each additional vehicle. Senior discount available. Open year-round.

Directions: From Portland, turn west on U.S. 30 and drive to Scappoose. Continue one mile north on U.S. 30 to West Lane Road. Turn right (east) and drive three-quarters of a mile to Honeyman Road. Turn left and drive one block to the park on the right.

Contact: Columbia County Forest, Parks and Recreation, 503/397-2353; Scappoose RV Park, 34038 N. Honeyman Rd., Scappoose, OR 97056, 503/543-3225.

3 JANTZEN BEACH RV PARK

🏃 ⛳ 🚲 🚣 🚤 🏠 🐕 🚣 🚐

Rating: 6

Near the Columbia River.

Map 8.2, grid d3, page 487

This RV campground is set near the banks of the Columbia River on the outskirts of Portland. Recreation options include seasonal swimming. An 18-hole golf course and tennis courts are close by. Many recreation opportunities are available in the Portland area. Numerous marinas on the Willamette and Columbia Rivers offer boat trips and rentals, and the city parks and nearby state parks have hiking, bicycling, and horseback riding possibilities. The Columbia River Highway (U.S. 30) is a scenic drive. If golf is your game, Portland has 18 public golf courses. The winter ski areas at Mount Hood are within an hour's drive.

Campsites, facilities: There are 169 sites for RVs of any length. No tents. Electricity, drinking water, sewer hookups, cable TV, modem access, and picnic tables are provided. Flush toilets, showers, a recreation hall, a laundry room, a playground, and a swimming pool (seasonal) are available. Bottled gas, a store, ice, and a café are within one mile. Boat docks, launching facilities, and rentals are nearby. Leashed pets are permitted.

Reservations, fees: Reservations at 800/443-7248. Sites are $26 per night, $1 per person for more than two people. Senior discount available. Major credit cards accepted. Weekly and monthly rates available. Open year-round.

Directions: From Portland on I-5, drive four miles north to the Jantzen Beach exit (Exit 308) and take Hayden Island Drive. Turn west on Hayden Island Drive and drive one-half mile to the park on the right.

Contact: Jantzen Beach RV Park, 1503 N. Hayden Island Dr., Portland, OR 97217, 503/289-7626.

▣ RV PARK OF PORTLAND

Rating: 6

In Tualatin.

Map 8.2, grid e2, page 487

This park, just south of Portland in a wooded setting, has spacious sites, all with access to lawn areas. More than half of the sites are taken by monthly and long-term rentals.

Campsites, facilities: There are 100 sites, most of them drive-through sites for RVs of any length. No tents. Electricity, drinking water, sewer hookups, and picnic tables are provided. Flush toilets, showers, an RV dump station, a laundry room, and a playground are available. Bottled gas, a store, a café, and ice are within one mile. Leashed pets are permitted.

Reservations, fees: Reservations at 800/856-2066. Sites are $20–23 per night, $1.60 per person for more than two people. Major credit cards accepted. Open year-round.

Directions: From Portland, drive south on I-5

to Tualatin and Exit 289. Take Exit 289, turn east on Highway 212, and drive one-half mile to the campground on the left.

Contact: RV Park of Portland, 6645 S.W. Nyberg Rd., Tualatin, OR 97062, 503/692-0225, website: www.rvparkofportland.com.

▣ BARTON PARK

Rating: 6

Near the Clackamas River.

Map 8.2, grid e5, page 487

Getting here may seem a bit of a maze, but the trip is well worth it. This camp is set on the Clackamas River and is surrounded by woods and tall trees. The nearby Clackamas River can provide good salmon fishing.

Campsites, facilities: There are 99 sites for tents or RVs of any length. Restrooms, showers, an RV dump station, a public phone, and a barbecue are available. Recreational facilities include horseshoe pits, a playground, volleyball, baseball, and a boat ramp. Supplies are available within one mile. Leashed pets are permitted.

Reservations, fees: Reservations recommended. Sites are $12–16 per night. Major credit cards accepted for reservations. Open May–October.

Directions: From Portland, drive south on I-5 to I-205. Turn east and drive about 20 miles to the Clackamas/Estacada exit (Highway 212). Turn east on Highway 212 and drive about five miles to the Carver exit (Highway 224). Turn right on Highway 224 and drive about 6.5 miles to the town of Barton and Baker's Ferry Road. Turn right and drive one-quarter mile to Barton Park Road. Turn left and drive to the park on the left.

Contact: Clackamas County Parks Department, 9101 S.E. Sunnybrook Blvd., Clackamas, OR 97015, 503/353-4414, fax 503/353-4420, website: www.co.clackamas.or.us.

6 METZLER PARK

🧍🏊🚣🐕🏕️🚐⛺

Rating: 8

On Clear Creek.

Map 8.2, grid f5, page 487

This county campground on a small stream not far from the Clackamas River is a hot spot for fishing, swimming, and picnicking. Be sure to make your reservation early at this very popular park.

Campsites, facilities: There are 70 sites for tents or RVs. Electricity, restrooms, showers, an RV dump station, a public phone, a playground, and a recreation field with basketball, volleyball, and baseball are available. Propane, ice, and laundry facilities are within five miles. Leashed pets are permitted.

Reservations, fees: Reservations recommended. Sites are $12–16 per night. Major credit cards accepted with reservations. Open May–September.

Directions: From Portland, drive east on U.S. 26 from Gresham 11 miles to Sandy and Highway 211. Turn right (south) and drive six miles to a junction. Turn south (still Highway 211) and drive over the bridge to South Springwater Road. Turn right on South Springwater Road and drive about one-quarter mile to Metzler Park Road. Turn left on Metzler Park Road and drive three-quarters of a mile to the park.

Contact: Clackamas County Parks Department, 9101 S.E. Sunnybrook Blvd., Clackamas, OR 97015, 503/353-4414, fax 503/353-4420, website: www.co.clackamas.or.us.

7 CHAMPOEG STATE HERITAGE AREA

🧍🚴🚣🚐🐕♿🚐⛺

Rating: 7

On the Willamette River.

Map 8.2, grid f1, page 487

Situated on the south bank of the Willamette River, this state park features an interpretive center, a botanical garden with native plants, and hiking and bike trails. In July, a pageant reenacting the early history of the area is staged in the evening, Thursday–Sunday. Also worth a tour: a log cabin museum, the historic Newell House, and a visitor center.

Campsites, facilities: There are six tent sites and 84 sites for RVs up to 50 feet long, eight with full hookups, the rest with partial hookups. There are also three group areas that accommodate a maximum of 25 people each, six walk-in sites, six cabins, six yurts, a hiker/biker camp, an RV group area with 10 sites with electric hookups only. Picnic tables and fire grills are provided. Drinking water, garbage bins, flush toilets, an RV dump station, showers, a group recreation hall for up to 55 people, and firewood are available. Some facilities are wheelchair accessible. Boat docking facilities are nearby. Leashed pets are permitted.

Reservations, fees: Reservations at 800/452-5687 ($6 reservation fee), website: www.oregonstateparks.org. Sites are $15–20 per night, $4 per person per night for hiker/biker sites; the group camp area is $80 for up to 10 camping units, then $8 per additional unit; yurts are $27 per night, and cabins are $35 per night; $7 per night for an additional vehicle. Major credit cards accepted. Open year-round, with limited winter facilities in day-use areas.

Directions: From Portland, drive south on I-5 to Exit 278, the Donald/Aurora exit. Take that exit and turn right (west) on Ehlen Road and drive three miles to Case Road. Turn north and drive 5.5 miles (the road becomes Champoeg Road) to the park on the right.

Contact: Champoeg State Heritage Area, 7679 Champoeg Rd. NE, Saint Paul, OR 97137, 503/678-1251.

8 ISBERG RV PARK

🏊🐕🚐

Rating: 7

Near Aurora.

Map 8.2, grid g3, page 487

This RV campground is located in a rural area

just off the main highway. The setting is very pretty, thanks to lots of evergreen trees that shelter the camp from the highway. Portland and Salem are just 20 minutes away.

Campsites, facilities: There are 148 sites for RVs of any length. Electricity, drinking water, and sewer hookups are provided. Flush toilets, bottled gas, showers, a recreation hall, cable TV, a store, a swimming pool, a laundry room, and ice are available. Leashed pets are permitted.

Reservations, fees: Reservations accepted. Sites are $25 per night. Major credit cards accepted. Weekly and monthly rates available. Open year-round.

Directions: From Portland, drive south on I-5 to Exit 278, the Donald/Aurora exit. Take that exit and turn left (east) on Ehlen Road and drive to Dolores Way. Turn right on Dolores Way and drive one-quarter mile to the park on the right.

Contact: Isberg RV Park, 21599 Dolores Way NE, Aurora, OR 97002, 503/678-2646, fax 503/678-2724.

9 FEYRER MEMORIAL PARK

Rating: 5

On the Molalla River.

Map 8.2, grid g2, page 487

On the scenic Molalla River, this county park offers swimming and excellent salmon fishing. A superb option for weary I-5 cruisers, the park is only 30 minutes off the highway and provides a peaceful, serene environment.

Campsites, facilities: There are 19 sites for tents or RVs. Electricity, drinking water, restrooms, showers, an RV dump station, and a public phone are provided. There are also a playground and recreation field. Some facilities are wheelchair accessible. Supplies are available within three miles. Leashed pets are permitted.

Reservations, fees: Reservations recommended. Sites are $12–16 per night. Major credit cards accepted with reservations. Open May–September.

Directions: From Portland, drive south on I-5 to Woodburn and Exit 271. Take that exit and drive east on Highway 214; continue (the road changes to Highway 211 at the crossing with Highway 99E) to Molalla and Feyrer Park Road. Turn right and drive three miles to the park on the left.

Contact: Clackamas County Parks Department, 9101 S.E. Sunnybrook Blvd., Clackamas, OR 97015, 503/353-4414, fax 503/353-4420, website: www.co.clackamas.or.us.

10 WILLAMETTE CITY PARK

Rating: 8

On the Willamette River.

Map 8.3, grid d6, page 488

This 40-acre city park sits on the banks of the Willamette River, just outside Corvallis. The camping area is actually a large clearing near the entrance to the park, which has been left in its natural state. There are trails leading down to the river, and the bird-watching is good here.

Campsites, facilities: There are 13 sites for tents or RVs of any length. Vault toilets, drinking water, a covered outdoor kitchen area, picnic tables, and a small playground are available. Bottled gas, a store, a café, a coin-operated laundry, and ice are within one mile. Boat docks and launching facilities are also within one mile. An RV dump station is in town, three miles away. Leashed pets are permitted.

Reservations, fees: Reservations are not accepted. Sites are $9 per night, $5 per extra vehicle. Open April–October; open November–March to self-contained RVs.

Directions: On I-5, take Exit 228 (five miles south of Albany) to Highway 34. Turn west and drive nine miles to Corvallis and Highway 99S. Turn left (south) and drive 1.3 mile to Southeast Goodnight Road. Turn left (east) and drive one mile to the park.

Contact: Corvallis Department of Parks and Recreation, 1310 SW Avery Park Dr., Corvallis,

OR 97333, 541/766-6918, fax 541/754-1701, website: www.ci.corvallis.or.us/pr/prhome.html.

11 RICHARDSON PARK

Rating: 7

On Fern Ridge Reservoir.

Map 8.3, grid h6, page 488

This pretty Lane County park is a favorite for sailing and sailboards, as the wind is consistent. Boating and water-skiing are also popular. A walking trail around the reservoir doubles as a bike trail. Additional activities include swimming, fishing, and wildlife viewing. The Corps of Engineers has wildlife areas nearby. A kiosk display in the park features the historic Applegate Trail.

Campsites, facilities: There are 88 partial hookup sites for tents or RVs up to 60 feet long. Electricity, drinking water, picnic tables, and fire pits are provided. Restrooms with flush toilets, sinks, hot showers, an RV dump station, and garbage bins are available. Some facilities are wheelchair accessible. Group sites are double campsites. A part-time attended marina with minimal supplies—including ice, a boat launch and transient boat docks—unsupervised swimming, and a playground are available in the park. There is a small town within 10 miles. Leashed pets are permitted.

Reservations, fees: Reservations required at least two weeks before visit; phone 541/935-2005 ($10 reservation fee). Sites are $16 per night, with a charge of $5 per additional vehicle. Maximum stay is 14 days in a 30-day period. Open mid-April–mid-October.

Directions: In Eugene on I-5, drive to Exit 195B and Belt Line Road. Turn west on Belt Line Road and drive 6.5 miles to Junction City Airport exit and Highway 99. Turn right on Highway 99 and drive north for two blocks to Clear Lake Road. Turn left and drive 8.5 miles to the campground on the left.

Contact: Richardson Park, 25950 Richardson Park Rd., Junction City, OR 97448, 541/935-2005, website: www.co.lane.or.us/parks.

12 EUGENE KAMPING WORLD

Rating: 5

Near the Willamette River.

Map 8.3, grid g8, page 488

Eugene is one of Oregon's major cities, but it offers many riverside parks and hiking opportunities. Both the Willamette and McKenzie Rivers run right through town. The McKenzie, in particular, can provide good trout fishing. A golf course is nearby.

Campsites, facilities: There are 30 tent sites and 114 drive-through sites for RVs of any length. Electricity, drinking water, sewer hookups, and picnic tables are provided. Flush toilets, bottled gas, an RV dump station, showers, a recreation hall, cable TV, a miniature golf course, a store, a laundry room, ice, and a playground are available. A café is within one mile. Small, leashed pets are permitted.

Reservations, fees: Reservations at 800/343-3008. Sites are $16–22 per night, $1.50 per person for more than two people, and $1 for an additional vehicle. Major credit cards accepted. Open year-round.

Directions: From Eugene, drive north on I-5 for seven miles to Coburg and Exit 199. Take that exit and drive west for one-quarter mile to South Stewart Way (the campground access road). Turn left and drive up the driveway.

Contact: Eugene Kamping World, 90932 S. Stewart Way, Coburg, OR 97408, 541/343-4832, fax 541/343-3313.

13 FOREST GLEN RV RESORT

Rating: 6

South of Salem.

Map 8.4, grid a1, page 489

This RV resort is set directly behind ThrillVille USA, an amusement park with rides, miniature golf, go-karts, waterslides, and a snack bar. ThrillVille is open during the summer. Another bonus: The campground has a fishing pond with bass and trout, along with paddle-boats. A winery tour at Willamette Vineyards is available just one mile south via I-5, and a golf course is located one mile to the north. Campsites here are often more private and shaded than in many RV parks. The park also hosts weekly activities, including Bingo and meals served on weekends. A big plus for overnighters: There are no monthly rentals.

Campsites, facilities: There are 70 sites for RVs of any length, some with picnic tables and fire pits. Electricity, drinking water, and sewer hookups are provided. Flush toilets, showers, and a laundry room are available. A clubhouse with exercise equipment and games and a playground are available nearby. A store, a café, and ice are within two miles. Leashed pets are permitted. Some facilities are wheelchair accessible.

Reservations, fees: Reservations are not accepted. Sites are $25.50 per night. Open year-round.

Directions: From Salem, drive south on I-5 for one mile to Exit 248. Take that exit and turn left on Delaney Road and drive 100 yards to Enchanted Way. Turn right and drive one-quarter mile to the park on the left.

Contact: Forest Glen RV Resort, 8372 Enchanted Way, Turner, OR 97392, 503/363-7616.

14 SALEM CAMPGROUND AND RVS

Rating: 5

In Salem.

Map 8.4, grid a1, page 489

This park with shaded sites is located just off I-5 in Salem. A picnic area and a lake for swimming are within walking distance, and a nine-hole golf course, hiking trails, a riding stable, and tennis courts are nearby.

Campsites, facilities: There are 30 tent sites and 190 sites with full hookups for RVs of any length, most of which are drive-through sites. Picnic tables are provided. Flush toilets, bottled gas, an RV dump station, showers, a recre-

ation hall with a game room, a store, a laundry room, ice, a playground, electricity, drinking water, and sewer hookups are available. A café is within one mile. Leashed pets are permitted; no pit bulls or Rottweillers.

Reservations, fees: Reservations at 800/826-9605. Sites are $14–23 per night, $2 per person for more than two people. Major credit cards accepted. Open year-round.

Directions: From Salem on I-5, take Exit 253 to Highway 22. Turn east and drive one-quarter mile to Lancaster Drive. Turn right on Lancaster Drive and drive to Hagers Grove Road. Turn right on Hagers Grove Road and drive to the park.

Contact: Salem Campground and RVs, 3700 Hagers Grove Rd. SE, Salem, OR 97301, 503/581-6736, fax 888/827-9605, website: www.salemrv.com.

15 SILVER FALLS STATE PARK

Rating: 8

Near Salem.

Map 8.4, grid b3, page 489

Oregon's largest state park, Silver Falls covers more than 8,700 acres. Numerous trails criss-cross the area. One of which, a seven-mile jaunt, meanders past 10 majestic waterfalls (some more than 100 feet high) in the rainforest of Silver Creek Canyon. Four of these falls have an amphitheater-like surrounding where you can walk behind the falls and feel the misty spray. A horse camp and a 14-mile equestrian trail are available in the park. Fitness-conscious campers can check out the three-mile jogging trail or the four-mile bike trail. There are also a rustic nature lodge and group lodging facilities.

Campsites, facilities: There are 51 tent sites and 54 sites with water and electrical hookups for RVs up to 60 feet long, three group sites, a horse camp, and 14 cabins. Picnic tables and fire grills are provided. Drinking water, garbage bins, flush toilets, showers, an RV dump station, firewood, and a playground are available.

Some facilities are wheelchair accessible. Leashed pets are permitted.

Reservations, fees: Reservations at 800/452-5687 or website: www.oregonstateparks.org. Sites are $13–20 per night; the tent group site is $60 per night; the RV group site is $80 per night for the first 10 units and then $8 per additional unit; horse campsites are $16 per night with a $1.50 fee per horse; the group horse camp is $39 per night for a maximum of 12 horses. There is a $7 per night charge for an additional vehicle. Major credit cards accepted. Open year-round.

Directions: From Salem on I-5, take Exit 253 to Highway 22. Turn east and drive five miles to Highway 214. Turn left (east) and drive 15 miles to the park.

Contact: Silver Falls State Park, 20024 Silver Falls Hwy. SE, Sublimity, OR 97385, 503/873-8681, 800/551-6949, fax 503/873-8925.

16 FISHERMEN'S BEND

Rating: 7

On the North Santiam River.

Map 8.4, grid b4, page 489

Fishermen's Bend is a popular site for anglers of all ages, and the sites are spacious. A barrier-free fishing and river viewing area and a network of trails provide access to more than a mile of river. There's a one-mile, self-guided nature trail, and the nature center has a variety of displays. The amphitheater has films and activities on weekends. The front gate closes at 10 P.M.

Campsites, facilities: There are 39 sites for tents or RVs; 21 are pull-through with water hookups, and 18 are tent/camper sites with water spigots nearby. There are also three group sites available for up to 60 people each and two cabins. Drinking water, picnic tables, and fire pits are provided. Restrooms with flush toilets, sinks, and hot showers, wheelchair facilities, an RV dump station, and garbage containers are available. A boat ramp, a day-use area with playgrounds, baseball, volleyball, and basketball courts and fields, horseshoe pits, firewood for sale, and a picnic shelter are also available. Leashed pets are permitted.

Reservations, fees: Reservations at 888/242-4256 ($7 reservation fee). Sites are $12–18 per night for up to two vehicles. Group sites are $60–90 per night. Cabins are $35 per night. Senior discount available. Open mid-May–mid-October.

Directions: From Salem on I-5, take Exit 253 to Highway 22. Turn east and drive 32 miles to the campground on the right.

Contact: Bureau of Land Management, Salem District Office, 1717 Fabry Rd. SE, Salem, OR 97306, 503/375-5646; reservations 888/242-4256, fax 503/375-5622, website: www.or.blm.gov/salem.

17 ELKHORN VALLEY

Rating: 7

On the Little North Santiam River.

Map 8.4, grid b5, page 489

This pretty campground along the Little North Santiam River, not far from the North Fork of the Santiam River, has easy access, an on-site host, and is only a short drive away from a major metropolitan area. The front gate is locked 10 P.M.–7 a.m. daily. This is an alternative to Shady Cove, which is about 10 miles to the east.

Campsites, facilities: There are 24 sites for tents or RVs up to 18 feet long. Picnic tables, garbage bins, fire grills, vault toilets, and drinking water are available. Firewood is available for purchase. Leashed pets are permitted.

Reservations, fees: Reservations are not accepted. Sites are $10 per night, $5 per night for an additional vehicle. There is a 14-day stay limit. Senior discount available. Open mid-May–late September.

Directions: From Salem on I-5, take Exit 253 to Highway 22. Turn east and drive 25 miles to Elkhorn Road (North Fork Road). Turn left (northeast) and drive nine miles to the campground on the left.

Contact: Bureau of Land Management, Salem

District Office, 1717 Fabry Rd. SE, Salem, OR 97306, 503/375-5646, fax 503/375-5622, website: www.or.blm.gov/salem.

18 JOHN NEAL MEMORIAL PARK

Rating: 6

On the North Santiam River.

Map 8.4, grid b4, page 489

This camp is set on the banks of the North Santiam River, offering good boating and trout fishing possibilities. Other recreation options include exploring lakes and trails in the adjacent national forest land or visiting Silver Falls State Park.

Campsites, facilities: There are 40 sites for tents or self-contained RVs, and 14 sites can be reserved as a group area. Restrooms, garbage bins, and drinking water are available. Recreational facilities include a boat ramp, a playground, horseshoes, a barbecue, and a recreation field. Ice and a grocery store are within one mile. Leashed pets are permitted.

Reservations, fees: Reservations are not accepted. Sites are $11 per night. Senior discount available. Reservations available for the group site ($50 reservation fee); $100 per night. Major credit cards accepted for reservations. Open May–October, weather permitting.

Directions: From Salem, drive east on Highway 22 for about 20 miles to Highway 226. Turn right and drive south for two miles to Lyons and John Neal Park Road. Turn east and drive a short distance to the campground on the left.

Contact: Linn County Parks Department, 3010 Ferry St. SW, Albany, OR 97322, 541/967-3917, fax 541/924-6915, website: www.co.linn.or.us.

19 YELLOWBOTTOM

Rating: 7

On Quartzville Creek.

Map 8.4, grid d5, page 489

Out-of-town visitors always miss this campground across the road from Quartzville Creek.

It's nestled under a canopy of old-growth forest. The Rhododendron Trail, which is just under a mile, provides a challenging hike through forest and patches of rhododendrons. Some folks pan for gold here. Though primitive, the camp is ideal for a quiet getaway weekend.

Campsites, facilities: There are 21 sites for tents or RVs up to 28 feet long; 10 are drive-through. Picnic tables, garbage bins, and fire grills are provided. Drinking water and vault toilets are available. Firewood is available for purchase. Some facilities are wheelchair accessible. Leashed pets are permitted. There is a camp host.

Reservations, fees: Reservations are not accepted. Sites are $8 per night, with a 14-day stay limit, $5 per night for an additional vehicle. Senior discount available. Open mid-May–late September.

Directions: From Albany, drive east on U.S. 20 for about 35 miles (through Sweet Home) to Quartzville Road. Turn left (northeast) on Quartzville Road and drive 24 miles to the campground on the left.

Contact: Bureau of Land Management, Salem District, 1717 Fabry Rd. SE, Salem, OR 97306, 503/375-5646, fax 503/375-5622.

20 WATERLOO COUNTY CAMPGROUND

Rating: 8

On the South Santiam River.

Map 8.4, grid e2, page 489

This campground features more than a mile of South Santiam River frontage. Swimming, fishing, picnicking, and field sports are options here. Small boats with trolling motors are the only boats usable here.

Campsites, facilities: There are 121 sites for tents or RVs; 101 have partial hookups. Drinking water, fire pits, and picnic tables are provided. Restrooms with showers are available. Boat ramps and a playground are in the surrounding day-use area. A small grocery store is within one mile. Leashed pets are permitted.

Reservations, fees: Reservations accepted ($11 reservation fee). Sites are $13–16 per night; there is a $5 fee for one additional vehicle. Senior discounts are available. Major credit cards accepted for reservations. Open year-round.
Directions: From Albany, drive east on U.S. 20 for about 20 miles through Lebanon to the Waterloo exit. Turn north at the Waterloo exit and drive approximately two miles to the camp on the right. The camp is on the south side of the South Santiam River.
Contact: Linn County Parks Department, 3010 Ferry St. SW, Albany, OR 97322, 541/967-3917, fax 541/924-6915, website: www.co.linn.or.us.

21 WHITCOMB CREEK COUNTY PARK

Rating: 8

On Green Peter Reservoir.
Map 8.4, grid e4, page 489
This camp is set on the north shore of Green Peter Reservoir in a wooded area with lots of ferns, which gives it a rainforest feel. Recreation options include swimming, sailing, hiking, and picnicking. Two boat ramps are on the reservoir about a mile from camp.
Campsites, facilities: There are 39 sites for tents or RVs and one group area for up to 100 people. Picnic tables are provided. Drinking water is available to haul; vault toilets and garbage bins are available. Facilities are within 15 miles. Leashed pets are permitted.
Reservations, fees: Reservations are not accepted for family sites; $11 per night. Senior discount available. Reservations required for the group site ($50 reservation fee); $100 per night. Major credit cards accepted for reservations. Open April–October.
Directions: From Albany, drive east on U.S. 20 for about 35 miles (through Lebanon and Sweet Home) to the Quartzville Road exit (near Foster Reservoir). Turn north on Quartzville Road and drive 10 miles to the campground.
Contact: Linn County Parks Department, 3010

Ferry St. SW, Albany, OR 97322, 541/967-3917, fax 541/924-6915, website: www.co.linn.or.us.

22 SUNNYSIDE COUNTY PARK

Rating: 8

On Foster Reservoir.
Map 8.4, grid e4, page 489
This is Linn County's most popular park. Recreation options include boating, fishing, waterskiing, and swimming. A golf course is within 15 miles.
Campsites, facilities: There are 165 sites for tents or RVs. Electricity and drinking water are available at 133 sites; 27 sites are reserved for groups, who must take a minimum of eight sites, with a maximum of eight people per site. Drinking water, flush toilets, showers, an RV dump station, picnic areas, volleyball courts, a boat ramp, and moorage are available. Firewood can be obtained for a fee. Additional facilities are within two miles. Leashed pets are permitted.
Reservations, fees: Reservations accepted ($11 reservation fee), $13–16 per night, $5 for one additional vehicle. Reservations accepted for the group site ($50 reservation fee). Senior discounts are available. Open April–October.
Directions: From Albany, drive east on U.S. 20 for about 35 miles (through Lebanon and Sweet Home) to the Quartzville Road exit (near Foster Reservoir). Turn north on Quartzville Road and drive one mile to the campground on the right. The camp is on the south side of Foster Reservoir.
Contact: Linn County Parks Department, 3010 Ferry St. SW, Albany, OR 97322, 541/967-3917, fax 541/924-0202, website: www.co.linn.or.us.

23 CASCADIA STATE PARK

Rating: 7

On the Santiam River.
Map 8.4, grid e5, page 489
The highlight of this 258-acre park is Soda

Creek Falls, with a fun three-quarter-mile hike to reach it. The park is set along the banks of the Santiam River. A newer trail ushers you through Douglas fir trees along the river, a good place to fish and swim. It's a great spot for a more intimate getaway for hikers, and also for reunions and meets for families, Boy Scouts, and other groups.

Campsites, facilities: There are 25 primitive sites for tents or self-contained RVs up to 35 feet long and two group areas for tents. Picnic tables, garbage bins, and fire grills are provided. Drinking water, vault toilets, firewood, and ice are available. Some facilities are wheelchair accessible. Leashed pets are permitted.

Reservations, fees: Reservations accepted for group areas only at 503/854-3406. Sites are $7–12 per night, $5 per night for an additional vehicle, and $5 per person for hike-in/bike-in sites. Group sites are $60 for up to 25 people and $2.40 for each additional person. Major credit cards accepted. Open March–October, weather permitting.

Directions: From Albany, drive east on U.S. 20 for 40 miles to the park on the left (14 miles east of the town of Sweet Home).

Contact: Cascadia State Park, P.O. Box 736, Cascadia, OR 97329, 800/551-6949 or 541/367-6021.

24 WHITTAKER CREEK

Rating: 7

Near the Siuslaw River.
Map 8.5, grid b5, page 490

This campground is home to one of the area's premier salmon spawning grounds, where annual runs of chinook, coho salmon, and steelhead can be viewed. The Old Growth Ridge Trail is accessible from the campground. This moderately difficult trail ascends 1,000 feet above the Siuslaw River through a stand of old-growth Douglas fir. Fishing is for trout and crayfish.

Campsites, facilities: There are 31 sites for tents or RVs up to 35 feet long. Picnic tables and fire pits are provided. A camp host is on-site, and drinking water, vault toilets, garbage bins, boat ramp, a swimming beach, a playground, and a picnic shelter are available. Leashed pets are permitted. Some facilities are wheelchair accessible.

Reservations, fees: Reservations are not accepted. Sites are $8 per night, with a charge of $5 per each additional vehicle. Senior discount available. Open mid-May–mid-October, weather permitting.

Directions: From Eugene, drive west on Highway 126 for 33 miles to Siuslaw River Road. Turn left (south) and drive two miles to the campground on the right.

Contact: Bureau of Land Management, Eugene District Office, 2890 Chad Dr., P.O. Box 10226, Eugene, OR 97440-2226, 541/683-6600, fax 541/683-6981.

25 CLAY CREEK

Rating: 7

Near the Siuslaw River.
Map 8.5, grid b5, page 490

Clay Creek Trail, a two-mile loop, takes you to a ridge overlooking the river valley and is well worth the walk. Fishing for trout and crayfish is popular. Sites are situated in a forest of cedars, Douglas fir, and maple trees. The campground gets a medium amount of use.

Campsites, facilities: There are 21 sites for tents or RVs up to 35 feet long. Picnic tables and fire pits are provided. Drinking water, vault toilets, garbage bins, a swimming beach with changing rooms, a softball field, horseshoe pits, a playground, and two group picnic shelters with fireplaces are available. There is a camp host. Leashed pets are permitted. Some facilities are wheelchair accessible.

Reservations, fees: Reservations are not accepted. Sites are $8 per night, with a charge of $5 per each additional vehicle. Senior discount available. Open mid-May–mid-October, weather permitting.

Directions: From Eugene, drive west on Highway 126 for 33 miles to Siuslaw River Road. Turn left (south) and drive 9.7 miles to Siuslaw River Access Road. Bear left and continue six miles to the campground on the right.

Contact: Bureau of Land Management, Eugene District Office, 2890 Chad Dr., P.O. Box 10226, Eugene, OR 97440-2226, 541/683-6600, fax 541/683-6981.

26 KOA SHERWOOD FOREST

Rating: 5

Near Eugene.

Map 8.5, grid a8, page 490

Seven miles south of Eugene, this KOA provides an easy-to-reach layover for RV travelers heading up and down on I-5. Nearby recreational facilities include a golf course and tennis courts.

Campsites, facilities: There are 20 tent sites, 100 sites for RVs of any length, and three cabins. Electricity, drinking water, sewer hookups, and picnic tables are provided. Flush toilets, showers, an RV dump station, a recreation hall, a store, a laundry room, ice, a playground, and a swimming pool are available. Bottled gas and a café are within one mile. Leashed pets are permitted.

Reservations, fees: Reservations at 800/541-4110. Sites are $21–26 per night, $2 per person for more than two people. Major credit cards accepted. Open year-round.

Directions: From Eugene, drive south on I-5 for seven miles to the Creswell exit. Take that exit and turn west on Oregon Avenue and drive one-half block to the campground at 298 East Oregon Avenue.

Contact: KOA Sherwood Forest, 298 E. Oregon Ave., Creswell, OR 97426, 541/895-4110, fax 541/895-5037, website: www.koa.com.

27 PASS CREEK COUNTY PARK

Rating: 7

Near Cottage Grove.

Map 8.5, grid c7, page 490

This decent layover spot for travelers on I-5 is situated in a wooded, hilly area and features many shaded sites. Mountain views give the park scenic value. There is a covered pavilion and gazebo with barbecue grills for get-togethers. You can find fishing and other water activities 11 miles away; history buffs can look for a covered bridge eight miles away. There are no other campgrounds in the immediate area, so if it's late and you need a place to stay, grab this one.

Campsites, facilities: There are 30 tent sites and 30 sites for RVs up to 30 feet long. Electricity, drinking water, sewer hookups, and picnic tables are provided. Flush toilets, showers, and a playground are available. A store, a café, and ice are within one mile. Leashed pets are permitted.

Reservations, fees: Reservations are not accepted. Sites are $11–14 per night, $3 for additional vehicle unless towed. Senior discount available for Douglas County residents. Major credit cards accepted. Open year-round.

Directions: On I-5, drive to Exit 163 (between Roseburg and Eugene). Take Exit 163 and turn west on Curtain Park Road. Drive west (under the freeway) for a very short distance to the park entrance.

Contact: Pass Creek County Park, 201 Curtin Park Rd., P.O. Box 81, Curtin, OR 97428, 541/942-3281, website: www.co.douglas.or.us/parks.

28 COTTAGE GROVE LAKE/ PINE MEADOWS

Rating: 6

On Cottage Grove Reservoir.

Map 8.5, grid c8, page 490

This campground is surrounded by a varied landscape—marshland, grassland, and forest—

near the banks of Cottage Grove Reservoir. Boating, fishing, water-skiing, and swimming are among the recreation options. It's an easy hop from I-5.

Campsites, facilities: There are 92 sites for tents or RVs of any length, with some drive-through sites. Drinking water, picnic tables, garbage bins, and fire rings are provided. Flush toilets, showers, an RV dump station, a children's play area, an amphitheater, interpretive displays, and a swimming area are available. A boat dock, launching facilities, and a small store are nearby. Leashed pets are permitted.

Reservations, fees: Reservations at 877/444-6777 or www.ReserveUsa.com ($9 reservation fee). Sites are $14 per night, $4 per night for an additional vehicle. Senior discount available. Open mid-May–mid-September.

Directions: From Eugene, drive south on I-5 past Cottage Grove to Exit 172. Take that exit to London Road and drive south for 4.5 miles to Reservoir Road. Turn left and drive three miles to the camp entrance on the right.

Contact: U.S. Army Corps of Engineers, Recreation Information, Cottage Grove, OR 97424, 541/942-8657 or 541/942-5631, fax 541/942-1305, website: www.nwp.usace.army.mil.

29 COTTAGE GROVE LAKE/PRIMITIVE

Rating: 6

On Cottage Grove Reservoir.
Map 8.5, grid c8, page 490

This campground on Cottage Grove Reservoir is open to boating, fishing, water-skiing, and swimming. See the description of neighboring Pine Meadows for more information.

Campsites, facilities: There are 15 primitive sites for tents, or small, self-contained RVs. Picnic tables, vault toilets, drinking water, garbage bins, and fire rings are provided. Boat docks, launching facilities, and a mini-market are nearby. Leashed pets are permitted.

Reservations, fees: Reservations at 877/444-

6777 or www.ReserveUsa.com ($9 reservation fee). Sites are $8 per night, $4 per night for an additional vehicle. Senior discount available. Open late May–early September.

Directions: From Eugene, drive south on I-5 past Cottage Grove to Exit 172. Take that exit to London Road and drive south for 4.5 miles to Reservoir Road. Turn left and drive three miles to the camp entrance.

Contact: U.S. Army Corps of Engineers, Recreation Information, Cottage Grove, OR 97424, 541/942-8657 or 541/942-5631, fax 541/942-1305, website: www.nwp.usace.army.mil.

30 CASCARA CAMPGROUND

Rating: 7

Fall Creek Reservoir State Recreation Area.
Map 8.6, grid a2, page 491

Campsites are set back and across the road from the reservoir, but you still get a lake view. Most of these spacious sites have Douglas fir and white fir tree cover. Water recreation is the primary activity here. Personal watercraft and water-skiing are allowed. The lake level drops in August, and water temperatures are ideal for summer swimming.

Campsites, facilities: There are five walk-in sites for tents and 42 sites for RVs; no pull-through sites. Picnic tables, garbage service, and fire grills are provided. Drinking water, vault toilets, a pay phone, and firewood are available, and there is a camp host. A boat launch, dock, and swimming area are also available. Leashed pets are permitted.

Reservations, fees: Reservations are not accepted. Sites are $11 per night, plus $5 for each additional vehicle. Major credit cards accepted. Open May–September.

Directions: From south Eugene on I-5, take Exit 188 to Highway 58. Drive 11 miles south to Lowell and Pioneer Street (at the covered bridge). Turn left and drive less than one-quarter mile to West Boundary Road. Turn left and drive one block to Lowell Jasper Road. Turn right and drive 1.5 miles to Unity and Place Road. Turn right and drive about one mile to a fork with North Shore Road (Big Fall Creek Road). Bear left onto Big Fall Creek Road and drive about eight miles to the head of Fall Creek Reservoir and Peninsula Road (Forest Road 6250). Turn right and drive one-half mile to the campground.

Contact: Oregon State Parks, Southern Willamette Management Unit, 541/937-1173, 800/551-6949, website: www.Oregonstate parks.org.

31 DEXTER SHORES RV PARK

🛶 🚐 🏠 👫 🚐 ⛰️

Rating: 7

Near Dexter Point Reservoir.

Map 8.6, grid a2, page 491

If you're driving on I-5, this RV park is well worth the 15-minute drive out of Springfield. It's across the street from Dexter Point Reservoir, where fishing and boating are permitted. Nearby Dexter and Fall Creek Lakes offer swimming, sailing, windsurfing, and water-skiing. There are three authentic Sioux teepees on the property in the summer and three cabins.

Campsites, facilities: There are five tent sites and 56 sites for RVs up to 40 feet in length, three teepees, and three one-bedroom cabins. Electricity, drinking water, sewer, cable TV and telephone hookups, picnic tables, and fire pits are provided. Flush toilets, showers, an RV dump station, firewood, a laundry room, and a playground are available. Bottled gas, a café, a restaurant, and ice are within one mile. Boat docks and launching facilities are nearby. Leashed pets permitted. No pets or smoking in vacation rentals.

Reservations, fees: Reservations at 866/558-9777. Sites are $16–26 per night; teepees are $25–35 per night; $3–7 per person for more than two people; $1 per pet per night. No pets in teepees or cabins. Open year-round.

Directions: From south Eugene on I-5, drive to Exit 188A and Highway 58. Take Highway

58 east and drive 11.5 miles to Lost Creek Road. Turn right (south) and drive to Dexter Road. Turn left (in front of the café) and drive east for one-half block to the park on the right.

Contact: Dexter Shores RV Park, P.O. Box 70, Dexter, OR 97431, 541/937-3711, fax 541/937-1724, website:dextershoresrvpark.com.

32 BAKER BAY COUNTY PARK

🥾 🚲 🛶 🛶 🚣 🐕 ♿ 🚐 ⛰️

Rating: 6

On Dorena Lake.

Map 8.6, grid b1, page 491

This campground is set along the shore of Dorena Lake, where fishing, sailing, water-skiing, canoeing, swimming, and boating are among the recreation options. Row River Trail follows part of the lake for a hike or bike ride, and there are covered bridges in the area. For golf, head to Cottage Grove.

Campsites, facilities: There are 49 sites for tents or self-contained RVs up to 35 feet long, plus two group sites for up to 25 people per group. Picnic tables and fire grills are provided. Drinking water, flush toilets, coin-operated showers, firewood, garbage bins, and an RV dump station are available. Some facilities are wheelchair accessible. A concession stand with ice is in the park. A store is within two miles. Boat docks and launching facilities are nearby, with seasonal on-shore facilities for catamarans. Leashed pets are permitted.

Reservations, fees: Reservations are not accepted for family sites. Single sites are $12 per night, $5 for an additional vehicle. Reservations required for group sites ($40 deposit) at 541/942-7669; $40 per night. Open mid-April–mid-October.

Directions: From Eugene, drive south on I-5 for 22 miles to Cottage Grove and Exit 174 (Dorena Lake exit). Take that exit to Row Road and drive east for 4.4 miles (the road becomes Shore View Drive). Bear right and drive 2.8 miles to the campground entrance on the left.

Contact: Baker Bay Park, 35635 Shore View

Dr., Dorena, OR 97434, 541/942-7669, website: www.co.lane.or.us/parks.

33 SCHWARZ PARK

Rating: 7

On Dorena Lake.

Map 8.6, grid b1, page 491

This large campground is set below Dorena Lake on the Row River, where fishing, swimming, boating, and water-skiing are among the recreation options. Note that chances of rain are high May–mid-June and that there is a posted warning for consumption of fish from Dorena Lake. The Row River Trail parallels Dorena Lake's north shoreline for 6.2 miles. This paved trail is excellent for walking, bike riding, and shoreline access.

Campsites, facilities: There are 72 sites for RVs of any length and six group sites. Drinking water, garbage bins, picnic tables, and fire rings are provided. Flush toilets, showers, and an RV dump station are available. Boat-launching facilities are on the lake about two miles upstream. Three sites are wheelchair accessible. Leashed pets are permitted.

Reservations, fees: Reservations at 877/444-6777 or website: www.ReserveUsa.com. Sites are $10 per night; group sites are $90 per night; an additional vehicle is $4 per night. Senior discount available. Open late April–late September.

Directions: From Eugene, drive south on I-5 for 22 miles to Cottage Grove and Exit 174. Take that exit to Shoreview Drive and continue (past Row Road) four miles east to the campground entrance.

Contact: U.S. Army Corps of Engineers, Recreation Information, Cottage Grove, OR 97424, 541/942-1418 or 541/942-5631, fax 541/942-1305.

BOB RACE

Chapter 9
The Columbia River Gorge
and Mount Hood

Chapter 9—
The Columbia River Gorge and Mount Hood

The Columbia River area is at once a living history lesson, a geological wonder, and a recreation paradise. The waterway is probably best known as the route the Lewis and Clark expedition followed two centuries ago. It's also famous for carving out a deep gorge through the Cascade Range that divides Oregon. And nearby Mount Hood and its surrounding national forest and many lakes provide almost unlimited opportunities for camping, hiking, and fishing.

The Columbia spans hundreds of square miles and is linked to a watershed that in turn is connected to the Snake River, which covers thousands of square miles. Interstate 84 provides a major route along the southern shore of the Columbia, but the river view is not what you will remember. After you depart the traffic of the Portland area, driving west to east, you will pass along the wooded foothills of the Cascade Range to your south. When you pass Hood River, the world suddenly changes. The trees disappear. In their place are rolling grasslands that seem to extend for as far as you can see. It is often hot and dry here, with strong winds blowing straight down the river.

However, the entire time you are within the realm of Mount Hood. At 11,239 feet, Hood is a beautiful mountain, shaped like a diamond, its flanks supporting many stellar destinations with campsites and small lakes set in forest. Snowmelt feeds many major rivers as well as numerous smaller streams, which roll down Mount Hood in every direction.

The transformation of the Gorge-area landscape from forest to grasslands to high desert is quick and striking. Particularly remarkable is how the Deschutes River has cut a path through the desert bluffs. And while the Deschutes is one of Oregon's better steelhead streams, unless you're fishing, you are more likely encounter a desert chukar on a rock perch than anything water-bound.

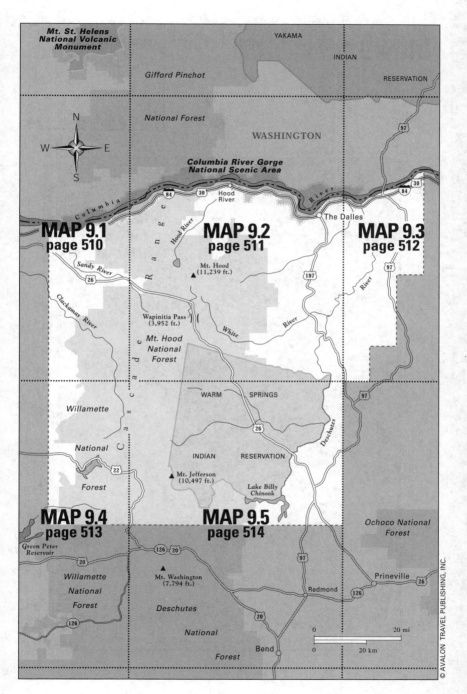

Map 9.1

Campgrounds 1–19
Pages 515–522

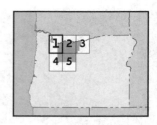

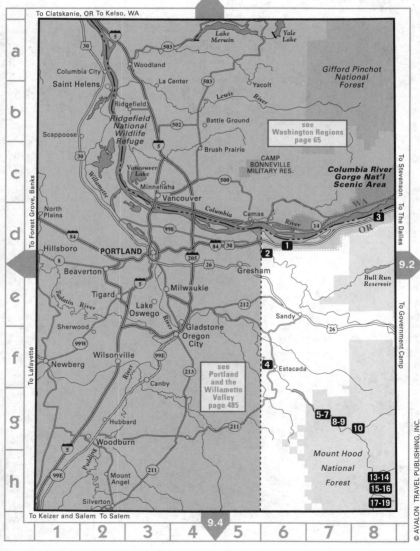

To Clatskanie, OR To Kelso, WA

Lake Merwin
Yale Lake

Woodland

Columbia City
Saint Helens

La Center

Yacolt

Gifford Pinchot National Forest

Ridgefield

Lewis River

Scappoose

Ridgefield National Wildlife Refuge

Battle Ground

Brush Prairie

see Washington Regions page 65

North Plains

Vancouver Lake

Minnehaha

Vancouver

CAMP BONNEVILLE MILITARY RES.

Columbia River Gorge Nat'l Scenic Area

To Stevenson

To The Dalles

Columbia River

Camas

To Forest Grove, Banks

HILLSBORO

PORTLAND

Gresham

Bull Run Reservoir

Beaverton

Tualatin River

Tigard

Milwaukie

Lake Oswego

Sandy

To Government Camp

Sherwood

Gladstone
Oregon City

Newberg

Wilsonville

Estacada

To Lafayette

Canby

see Portland and the Willamette Valley page 485

5-7
8-9
10

Hubbard

Mount Hood National Forest

Woodburn

13-14
15-16
17-19

Mount Angel

Silverton

© AVALON TRAVEL PUBLISHING, INC.

To Keizer and Salem To Salem

Map 9.2

Campgrounds 20–71
Pages 522–544

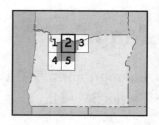

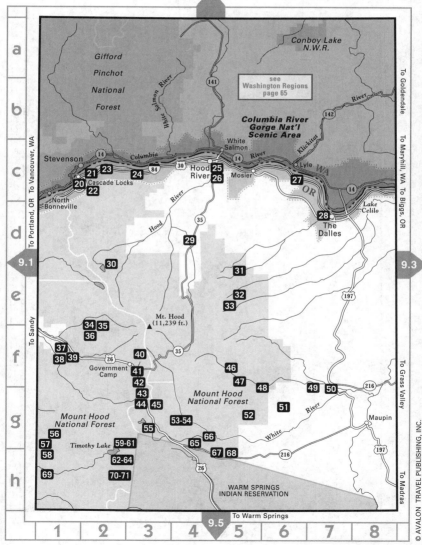

Map 9.3

Campgrounds 72–74
Pages 544–545

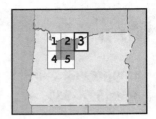

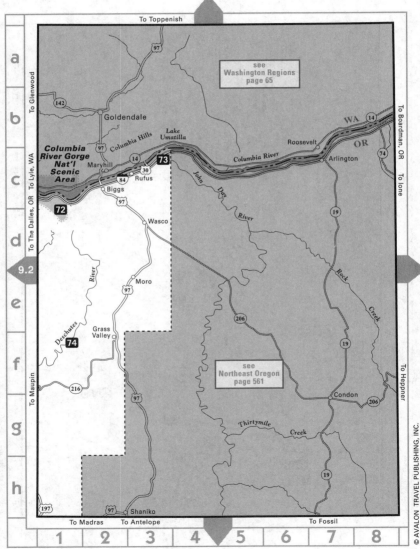

Map 9.4

Campgrounds 75–84
Pages 546–549

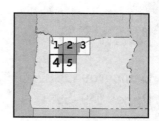

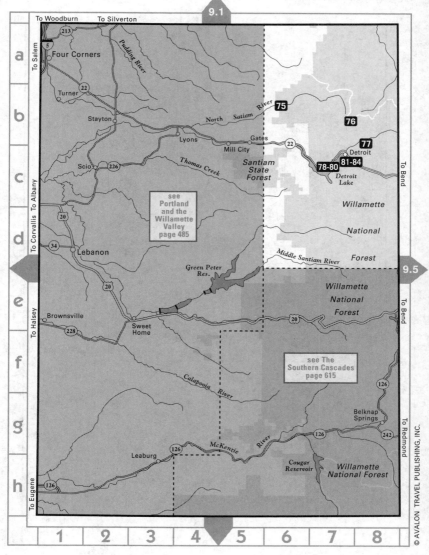

To Woodburn To Silverton

9.1

To Salem

213

5

Four Corners

Pudding River

a

Turner

22

b

Stayton

North Santiam River

Lyons

Mill City

Gates

22

75

76

77

Detroit

81-84

78-80

Santiam
State
Forest

Detroit
Lake

Scio

226

Thomas Creek

To Bend

To Corvallis To Albany

c

Willamette

see
Portland
and the
Willamette
Valley
page 485

National

20

34

d

Lebanon

Forest

Middle Santiam River

9.5

Green Peter
Res.

Willamette

20

National

To Halsey

Brownsville

e

Forest

To Bend

228

Sweet
Home

20

f

Calapooia River

see The
Southern Cascades
page 615

126

Belknap
Springs

126

g

McKenzie River

126

242

To Redmond

Leaburg

126

Cougar
Reservoir

Willamette
National Forest

To Eugene

h

126

1   2   3   4   5   6   7   8

© AVALON TRAVEL PUBLISHING, INC.

Map 9.5

Campgrounds 85–104
Pages 549–558

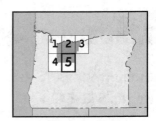

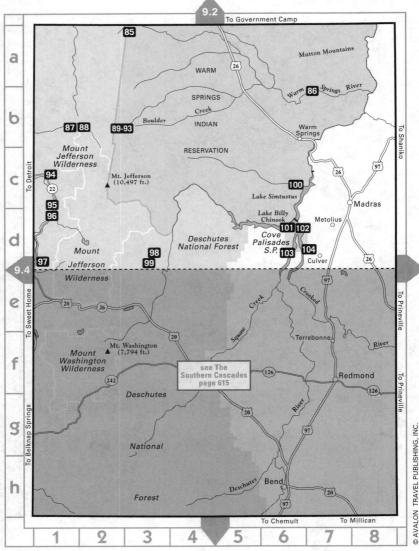

◼CROWN POINT RV PARK

Rating: 6

Near the Columbia River.

Map 9.1, grid d6, page 510

This little park is located near the Columbia River along scenic U.S. 30. Nearby Crown Point State Park is open during the day and offers views of the Columbia River Gorge and the historic Vista House, a memorial built in 1918 to honor Oregon's pioneers. Multnomah Falls offers another possible side trip.

Campsites, facilities: There are five tent sites and 21 sites for RVs of any length. Electricity, drinking water, and picnic tables are provided. Flush toilets, bottled gas, an RV dump station, coin-operated showers, a beauty shop, and a laundry room are available. A store and ice are within walking distance. Leashed pets are permitted.

Reservations, fees: Reservations accepted. Sites are $15–24 per night. Senior discount available. Open year-round.

Directions: From Portland on I-84 eastbound, drive 16 miles to Exit 22 and Corbett. Take that exit and turn right on Corbett Hill Road. Drive 1.5 miles to a Y intersection with East Historic Columbia River Highway. Bear left and drive one-quarter mile to the park on the right.

Note: The recommended route has a 10 percent grade for 1.5 miles. An alternate route: from Portland on I-84 eastbound, drive to Exit 18/Lewis and Clark State Park. Take that exit to East Historic Columbia River Highway and drive seven miles to the park on the right.

Contact: Crown Point RV Park, 37000 E. Historic Columbia River Hwy., Corbett, OR 97019, 503/695-5207, fax 503/695-3217.

◼OXBOW REGIONAL PARK

Rating: 7

On the Sandy River.

Map 9.1, grid e6, page 510

This 1,000-acre park along the Sandy River, a short distance from the Columbia River Gorge, is a designated natural preservation area. Fishing, swimming, and nonmotorized boating are permitted here.

Campsites, facilities: There are 67 sites for tents or RVs up to 35 feet long. Picnic tables are provided. Drinking water, flush and vault toilets, coin-operated showers, firewood, barbecues, and a playground are available. Boat-launching facilities are nearby. Gates lock at sunset and open at 6:30 A.M. No pets are permitted.

Reservations, fees: Reservations are not accepted. Sites are $10–13 per night, $4 per extra vehicle, and park entrance fee of $3 per vehicle. Open year-round, but subject to periodic closure; call for current status.

Directions: From Portland on I-84, drive to Exit 17. Turn south on Highway 257 and drive three miles to Division Street. Turn left and drive seven miles to the park.

Contact: Oxbow Regional Park, 3010 S.E. Oxbow Pkwy., Gresham, OR 97080, 503/663-4708. The park is managed by Metro-Region Parks and Green Spaces.

◼AINSWORTH STATE PARK

Rating: 8

Along the Columbia River Gorge.

Map 9.1, grid d8, page 510

This state park is set along the scenic Columbia River Gorge, home to the world's greatest concentration of high waterfalls, including famous Multnomah Falls. From the Nesmith Point Trail, enjoy a great view of St. Peter's Dome. A two-mile section of the Columbia River Gorge Trail connects this park with John Yeon State Park, which is open during the day. Anglers should check out the Bonneville Fish Hatchery.

Campsites, facilities: There are 45 sites with full hookups for RVs up to 60 feet long, and walk-in sites. Picnic tables and fire grills are provided. Drinking water, flush toilets, showers, garbage bins, an RV dump station, and firewood are available. Leashed pets are permitted.

Reservations, fees: Reservations are not accepted. Sites are $13–18 per night, $7 per extra vehicle, and $5 per person per night for walk-in sites. Major credit cards accepted. Open March–October, weather permitting.

Directions: From Portland on I-84 eastbound, drive 37 miles to Exit 35. Turn southwest on the Columbia River Scenic Highway and continue a short distance to the park. An alternate route is to take the historic Columbia River Highway, a designated scenic highway, all the way from Portland (37 miles).

Contact: Columbia River Gorge District, Oregon State Parks, P.O. Box 100, Corbett, OR 97019, 800/551-6949 or 503/695-2301.

4 MILO MCIVER STATE PARK

Rating: 7

On the Clackamas River.
Map 9.1, grid f6, page 510

Though only 45 minutes from Portland, this park is far enough off the beaten track to provide a feeling of separation from the metropolitan area. It's set along the banks of the Clackamas River and has a boat ramp. Trails for hiking are available, and a 4.5-mile equestrian trail is also accessible. A fish hatchery is a nearby point of interest. Every April, 300 actors participate in a Civil War re-enactment here.

Campsites, facilities: There are nine primitive tent sites and 44 sites with water and electrical hookups for RVs up to 50 feet long, one hiker/biker site, and three group tent areas. Picnic tables and fire grills are provided. Drinking water, garbage bins, flush toilets, an RV dump station, showers, picnic shelters, and firewood are available. Most facilities are wheelchair accessible. Boat-launching facilities and Frisbee golf are nearby. Group facilities are available. Leashed pets are permitted.

Reservations, fees: Reservations at 800/452-5687 or website: www.OregonStateParks.org ($7 reservation fee). Sites are $10–16 per night, $7 per extra vehicle, and group sites are $60 per night. Major credit cards accepted. Open mid-March–October.

Directions: From Portland, drive east on U.S. 26 from Gresham 11 miles to Sandy and Highway 211. Turn right (south) and drive six miles to a junction. Turn south (still Highway 211) and drive five miles to the park entrance road on the right.

Contact: Milo McIver State Park, 24101 South Entrance Rd., Estacada, OR 97023, 503/630-7150 or 800/551-6949.

5 PROMONTORY

Rating: 7

On North Fork Reservoir.
Map 9.1, grid g7, page 510

This Portland General Electric camp on North Fork Reservoir is part of a large recreation area and park. The water is calm and ideal for boating, and the trout fishing is excellent. This reservoir is actually a dammed-up overflow on the Clackamas River. A trail travels along about one mile of the lake shoreline.

Campsites, facilities: There are 47 sites for tents or RVs up to 35 feet long, one group site for up to 35 people, and two yurts. There are no RV hookups. Restrooms, garbage bins, showers, limited groceries, ice, a playground, horseshoes, covered picnic shelters with sinks and electric stoves, and snacks are available. A fish-cleaning station, a fishing pier, a children's fishing pond, a boat ramp, a dock, and boat rentals are also on-site. Some facilities, including restrooms, some sites, the boat ramp, and the fishing pier, are wheelchair accessible. Leashed pets are permitted.

Reservations, fees: Reservations at 503/630-7229. Sites are $14.50 per night, $20 per night for a yurt. Open mid-May–September.

Directions: From Portland, drive east on U.S. 26 from Gresham 11 miles to Sandy and Highway 211. Turn right (south) and drive six miles to a junction. Turn south (still Highway 211) and drive six miles to Estacada. Continue south on Highway 224 and drive seven miles to the campground on the right. The route is well signed.

Contact: Portland General Electric, 121 S.W. Salmon St., P.O. Box 4438, Portland, OR 97204, 503/464-8515, fax 503/464-2944, website: www.portlandgeneral.com/parks.

6 LAZY BEND

Rating: 8

On the Clackamas River in Mount Hood National Forest.

Map 9.1, grid g7, page 510

This campground is set at 800 feet elevation along the banks of the Clackamas River near the large North Fork Reservoir. It's far enough off the highway to provide a secluded, primitive feeling, though it fills quickly on weekends and holidays. There's only catch-and-release fishing in the Clackamas.

Campsites, facilities: There are 21 sites for tents or RVs up to 16 feet long. Picnic tables, garbage service, and fireplaces are provided. Drinking water and flush toilets are available. Leashed pets are permitted.

Reservations, fees: Reservations at 877/444-6777 or website: www.ReserveUsa.com ($9 reservation fee). Sites are $12 per night, $6 per extra vehicle. Senior discount available. Open late April–Labor Day.

Directions: From Portland, drive east on U.S. 26 from Gresham 11 miles to Sandy and Highway 211. Turn right (south) and drive six miles to a junction. Turn south (still Highway 211) and drive six miles to Estacada. Continue south on Highway 224 and drive 10.5 miles to the campground on the right.

Contact: Mount Hood National Forest, Clackamas River Ranger District, 595 N.W. Industrial Way, Estacada, OR 97023, 503/630-6861, fax 503/630-2299.

7 ARMSTRONG

Rating: 5

On the Clackamas River in Mount Hood National Forest.

Map 9.1, grid g7, page 510

This campground is set at an elevation of 900 feet along the banks of the Clackamas River and offers good fishing access. Fishing is catch-and-release only.

Campsites, facilities: There are 12 sites for tents or RVs up to 16 feet long. Picnic tables and fire rings are provided. Vault toilets and drinking water are available. Garbage service is available in the summer only. Some facilities are wheelchair accessible. Leashed pets are permitted.

Reservations, fees: Reservations at 877/444-6777 or website: www.ReserveUsa.com ($9 reservation fee). Sites are $12 per night, $6 per extra vehicle. Senior discount available. Open year-round, with limited winter services.

Directions: From Portland, drive east on U.S. 26 from Gresham 11 miles to Sandy and Highway 211. Turn right (south) and drive six miles to a junction. Turn south (still Highway 211) and drive six miles to Estacada. Continue south on Highway 224 and drive 15 miles to the campground on the right.

Contact: Mount Hood National Forest, Clackamas River Ranger District, 595 N.W. Industrial Way, Estacada, OR 97023, 503/630-6861, fax 503/630-2299.

8 CARTER BRIDGE

Rating: 5

On the Clackamas River in Mount Hood National Forest.

Map 9.1, grid g7, page 510

This small, flat campground is popular with anglers. The Clackamas River flows along one end, and the other end borders the highway, with the attendant traffic noise.

Campsites, facilities: There are 15 sites for tents or RVs up to 28 feet long. Picnic tables and fire pits are provided. Drinking water, vault toilets, and garbage bins are available. Some facilities are wheelchair accessible. Leashed pets are permitted.

Reservations, fees: Reservations at 877/444-6777 or website: www.ReserveUsa.com ($9 reservation fee). Sites are $10 per night, $5 per extra vehicle. Senior discount available. Open late May–early September, weather permitting.

Directions: From Portland, drive east on U.S. 26 from Gresham 11 miles to Sandy and Highway 211. Turn right (south) and drive six miles to a junction. Turn south (still Highway 211) and drive six miles to Estacada. Continue south on Highway 224 and drive 15.2 miles to the campground on the left.

Contact: Mount Hood National Forest, Clackamas River Ranger District, 595 N.W. Industrial Way, Estacada, OR 97023, 503/630-6861, fax 503/630-2299.

9 LOCKABY

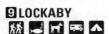

Rating: 6

On the Clackamas River in Mount Hood National Forest.

Map 9.1, grid g7, page 510

This campground is set at an elevation of 900 feet along the banks of the Clackamas River, next to Armstrong. Fishing in the Clackamas River is catch-and-release only.

Campsites, facilities: There are 30 sites for tents or RVs up to 16 feet long. Picnic tables, fireplaces, drinking water, garbage service, and vault toilets are available. Leashed pets are permitted.

Reservations, fees: Reservations at 877/444-6777 or website: www.ReserveUsa.com ($9 reservation fee). Sites are $6 per night, $3 per extra vehicle. Senior discount available. Open late May–early September.

Directions: From Portland, drive east on U.S. 26 from Gresham 11 miles to Sandy and High-

way 211. Turn right (south) and drive six miles to a junction. Turn south (still Highway 211) and drive six miles to Estacada. Continue south on Highway 224 and drive 15.3 miles to the campground on the left.

Contact: Mount Hood National Forest, Clackamas River Ranger District, Estacada Ranger Station, 595 N.W. Industrial Way, Estacada, OR 97023, 503/630-6861, fax 503/630-2299.

10 ROARING RIVER

Rating: 8

On the Roaring River in Mount Hood National Forest.

Map 9.1, grid h8, page 510

This campground, set among old-growth cedars at the confluence of the Roaring and Clackamas Rivers at an elevation of 1,000 feet, has access to the Dry Ridge Trail. The trail starts in camp, and it's a butt-kicker of an uphill climb. Several other trails into the adjacent roadless area are accessible from camp. See a U.S. Forest Service map for details.

Campsites, facilities: There are 19 sites for tents or RVs up to 16 feet long. Picnic tables, garbage service, fireplaces, drinking water, and vault toilets are available. Leashed pets are permitted.

Reservations, fees: Reservations at 877/444-6777 or website: www.ReserveUsa.com ($9 reservation fee). Sites are $12 per night, $6 per extra vehicle. Senior discount available. Open mid-May–mid-September.

Directions: From Portland, drive east on U.S. 26 from Gresham 11 miles to Sandy and Highway 211. Turn right (south) and drive six miles to a junction. Turn south (still Highway 211) and drive six miles to Estacada and Highway 224. Bear south on Highway 224 and drive 18 miles to the campground on the left.

Contact: Mount Hood National Forest, Clackamas River Ranger District, 595 N.W. Industrial Way, Estacada, OR 97023, 503/630-6861, fax 503/630-2299.

11 SUNSTRIP

Rating: 3

On the Clackamas River in Mount Hood National Forest.
Map 9.1, grid h8, page 510

This campground on the banks of the Clackamas River offers fishing and rafting access. One of several camps along the Highway 224 corridor, Sunstrip is a favorite with rafting enthusiasts and can fill up quickly on weekends. Note: This campground, squeezed between the river and the highway and traversed by power lines, may be a turn-off for those wanting another kind of experience.

Campsites, facilities: There are nine sites for tents or RVs up to 18 feet long. Picnic tables, garbage service, fireplaces, drinking water, and vault toilets are available. Leashed pets are permitted.

Reservations, fees: Reservations at 877/444-6777 or website: www.ReserveUsa.com ($9 reservation fee). Sites are $12 per night, $6 per extra vehicle. Senior discount available. Open year-round, with limited winter services.

Directions: From Portland, drive east on U.S. 26 from Gresham 11 miles to Sandy and Highway 211. Turn right (south) and drive six miles to a junction. Turn south (still Highway 211) and drive six miles to Estacada and Highway 224. Bear south on Highway 224 and drive 19 miles to the campground.

Contact: Mount Hood National Forest, Clackamas River Ranger District, 595 N.W. Industrial Way, Estacada, OR 97023, 503/630-6861, fax 503/630-2299.

12 RAINBOW

Rating: 6

On the Oak Grove Fork of the Clackamas River in Mount Hood National Forest.
Map 9.1, grid h8, page 510

This campground is set at an elevation of 1,400 feet along the banks of the Oak Grove Fork

of the Clackamas River, not far from where it empties into the Clackamas River. The camp is less than one-quarter mile from Ripplebrook Campground.

Campsites, facilities: There are 17 sites for tents or RVs up to 16 feet long. There is no drinking water. Garbage service is provided during the summer. Fire grills and picnic tables are provided. Vault toilets are available. Leashed pets are permitted.

Reservations, fees: Reservations at 877/444-6777 or website: www.ReserveUsa.com ($9 reservation fee). Sites are $10 per night, $5 per extra vehicle. Senior discount available. Open year-round, with limited winter services.

Directions: From Portland, drive east on U.S. 26 from Gresham 11 miles to Sandy and Highway 211. Turn right (south) and drive six miles to a junction. Turn south (still Highway 211) and drive six miles to Estacada and Highway 224. Bear south on Highway 224 and drive 27 miles in national forest (the road becomes Forest Road 46). Continue south and drive about 100 yards to the campground on the right.

Contact: Mount Hood National Forest, Clackamas River Ranger District, 595 N.W. Industrial Way, Estacada, OR 97023, 503/630-6861, fax 503/630-2299.

13 INDIAN HENRY

Rating: 8

On the Clackamas River in Mount Hood National Forest.
Map 9.1, grid h8, page 510

One of the most popular campgrounds in the Clackamas River Ranger District, Indian Henry sits along the banks of the Clackamas River at an elevation of 1,250 feet and has a wheelchair-accessible trail. Group campsites and an amphitheater are available. The nearby Clackamas River Trail has fishing access.

Campsites, facilities: There are 86 sites for tents or RVs up to 22 feet long and eight group tent sites. Picnic tables, garbage service, and fire grills are provided. Flush toilets, a sanitary dump station, and drinking water are available. Some facilities are wheelchair accessible. Leashed pets are permitted.

Reservations, fees: Reservations at 877/444-6777 or website: www.ReserveUsa.com ($9 reservation fee). Sites are $12 per night, $6 per extra vehicle; group sites are $35 per night. Senior discount available. Call for group site rates. Open late May–early September.

Directions: From Portland, drive east on U.S. 26 from Gresham 11 miles to Sandy and Highway 211. Turn right (south) and drive six miles to a junction. Turn south (still Highway 211) and drive six miles to Estacada and Highway 224. Bear south on Highway 224 and drive 23 miles to Forest Road 4620. Turn right and drive one-half mile southeast to the campground on the left.

Contact: Mount Hood National Forest, Clackamas River Ranger District, 595 N.W. Industrial Way, Estacada, OR 97023, 503/630-6861, fax 503/630-2299.

14 RIPPLEBROOK

Rating: 7

On the Oak Grove Fork of the Clackamas River in Mount Hood National Forest.
Map 9.1, grid h8, page 510

Shaded sites with river views are a highlight at this campground along the banks of the Oak Grove Fork of the Clackamas River, where anglers are limited to artificial lures and catch-and-release only. Note that the road to this camp was closed for two years in the late 1990s, and only recently have campers begun to return.

Campsites, facilities: There are 13 sites for RVs up to 16 feet long. Picnic tables, garbage service, and fire grills are provided. Vault toilets are available, but there is no drinking water. Leashed pets are permitted; horses are not allowed in the campground.

Reservations, fees: Reservations at 877/444-6777 or website: www.ReserveUsa.com ($9 reservation fee). Sites are $10 per night, $5 per extra vehicle. Senior discount available. Open late April–late September.

Directions: From Portland, drive east on U.S. 26 from Gresham 11 miles to Sandy and Highway 211. Turn right (south) and drive six miles to a junction. Turn south (still Highway 211) and drive six miles to Estacada and Highway 224. Bear south on Highway 224 and drive 26.5 miles to the campground entrance on the left.

Contact: Mount Hood National Forest, Clackamas River Ranger District, 595 N.W. Industrial Way, Estacada, OR 97023, 503/630-6861, fax 503/630-2299.

15 ALDER FLAT HIKE-IN

Rating: 9

On the Clackamas River in Mount Hood National Forest.
Map 9.1, grid h8, page 510

This secluded hike-in campground is set along the banks of the Clackamas River in old-growth forest. If you want peace and quiet and don't mind a short walk to get it, this is the spot. Be sure to pack out whatever you bring in and remember that fishing in the Clackamas River is catch-and-release only.

Campsites, facilities: There are six tent sites at this hike-in campground. Picnic tables and fire grills are provided. There is no drinking water, no toilet, and no garbage service; pack out all garbage. Leashed pets are permitted.

Reservations, fees: Reservations are not accepted. There is no fee for camping. Open year-round.

Directions: From Portland, drive east on U.S. 26 from Gresham 11 miles to Sandy and Highway 211. Turn right (south) and drive six miles to a junction. Turn south (still Highway 211) and drive six miles to Estacada and Highway 224. Bear south on Highway 224 and drive 26 miles to the Ripplebrook Ranger Station. Parking for the camp is about one-half mile west

of the ranger station at the Alder Flat Trailhead. Hike one mile to the campground.
Contact: Mount Hood National Forest, Clackamas River Ranger District, 595 N.W. Industrial Way, Estacada, OR 97023, 503/630-6861, fax 503/630-2299.

16 RIVERSIDE

Rating: 8

On the Clackamas River in Mount Hood National Forest.

Map 9.1, grid h8, page 510

The banks of the Clackamas River are home to this campground (elevation 1,400 feet). A trail worth hiking leaves the camp and follows the river for four miles north. Fishing is another option here, and several old forest roads in the vicinity make excellent mountain biking trails.

Campsites, facilities: There are 16 sites for tents or RVs up to 22 feet long. Picnic tables, garbage service, and fire grills are provided. Vault toilets and drinking water are available. Leashed pets are permitted; no horses are allowed in the campground.

Reservations, fees: Reservations at 877/444-6777 or website: www.ReserveUsa.com ($9 reservation fee). Sites are $12 per night, $6 per extra vehicle. Senior discount available. Open mid-May–late September.

Directions: From Portland, drive east on U.S. 26 from Gresham 11 miles to Sandy and Highway 211. Turn right (south) and drive six miles to a junction. Turn south (still Highway 211) and drive six miles to Estacada and Highway 224. Bear south on Highway 224 and drive 27 miles and into national forest (Highway 224 becomes Forest Road 46). Continue 2.5 miles south on Forest Road 46 to the campground on the right.

Contact: Mount Hood National Forest, Clackamas River Ranger District, 595 N.W. Industrial Way, Estacada, OR 97023, 503/630-6861, fax 503/630-2299.

17 RIVERFORD

Rating: 4

On the Clackamas and Collawash Rivers in Mount Hood National Forest.

Map 9.1, grid h8, page 510

This campground, just a two-minute walk from the confluence of the Clackamas and Collawash Rivers, offers access to good fishing. Otherwise, it's small, and the sites provide little privacy. It is set at an elevation of 1,500 feet.

Campsites, facilities: There are 10 sites for tents. Picnic tables and fire grills are provided. Vault toilets are available. Garbage service is provided in the summer. There is no drinking water at the campground; water is available at nearby Two Rivers Picnic Area. Leashed pets are permitted.

Reservations, fees: Reservations are not accepted. Sites are $10 per night, $5 per extra vehicle. Senior discount available. Open year-round, with limited winter services.

Directions: From Portland, drive east on U.S. 26 from Gresham 11 miles to Sandy and Highway 211. Turn right (south) and drive six miles to a junction. Turn south (still Highway 211) and drive six miles to Estacada and Highway 224. Bear south on Highway 224 and drive 27 miles in national forest (the road becomes Forest Road 46). Continue south on Forest Road 46 for 3.5 miles to the campground on the right.

Contact: Mount Hood National Forest, Clackamas River Ranger District, 595 N.W. Industrial Way, Estacada, OR 97023, 503/630-6861, fax 503/630-2299.

18 RAAB

Rating: 7

On the Collawash River in Mount Hood National Forest.

Map 9.1, grid h8, page 510

This camp is set at an elevation of 1,500 feet along the banks of the Collawash River, about a mile from its confluence with the Clackamas River. Raab gets moderate use, but it's usually quiet and has a nice, secluded atmosphere with lots of privacy among the sites.

Campsites, facilities: There are 27 sites for tents or RVs up to 22 feet long. Picnic tables, garbage service, and fire grills are provided. Vault toilets are available. There is no drinking water in the campground; water is available one mile away at Two Rivers Picnic Area. Leashed pets are permitted.

Reservations, fees: Reservations at 877/444-6777 or website: www.ReserveUsa.com ($9 reservation fee). Sites are $10 per night, $5 per extra vehicle. Senior discount available. Open late May–early September.

Directions: From Portland, drive east on U.S. 26 from Gresham 11 miles to Sandy and Highway 211. Turn right (south) and drive six miles to a junction. Turn south (still Highway 211) and drive six miles to Estacada and Highway 224. Bear south on Highway 224 and drive 27 miles in national forest (the road becomes Forest Road 46). Continue south on Forest Road 46 for 2.5 miles to Forest Road 63. Turn right and drive 1.5 miles to the campground on the right.

Contact: Mount Hood National Forest, Clackamas River Ranger District, 595 N.W. Industrial Way, Estacada, OR 97023, 503/630-6861, fax 503/630-2299.

19 KINGFISHER

Rating: 7

On the Hot Springs Fork of the Collawash River in Mount Hood National Forest.

Map 9.1, grid h8, page 510

This pretty campground, set at an elevation of 1,250 feet among old-growth forest, is situated along the banks of the Hot Springs Fork of the Collawash River. It's about three miles from Bagby Hot Springs, a U.S. Forest Service day-use area. The hot springs are an easy 1.5-mile hike from the day-use area. The camp provides fishing access.

Campsites, facilities: There are 23 sites for tents or RVs up to 16 feet long. Picnic tables and fireplaces are provided. Garbage service is provided during the summer. Vault toilets and drinking water are available. Leashed pets are permitted.

Reservations, fees: Reservations at 877/444-6777 or website: www.ReserveUsa.com ($9 reservation fee). Sites are $12 per night, $6 per extra vehicle. Senior discount available. Open year-round, with limited winter facilities.

Directions: From Portland, drive east on U.S. 26 from Gresham 11 miles to Sandy and Highway 211. Turn right (south) and drive six miles to a junction. Turn south (still Highway 211) and drive six miles to Estacada and Highway 224. Bear south on Highway 224 and drive 27 miles in national forest (the road becomes Forest Road 46). Continue south on Forest Road 46 for 3.5 miles to Forest Road 63. Turn right and drive three miles to Forest Road 70. Turn right again and drive one mile to the campground on the left.

Contact: Mount Hood National Forest, Clackamas River Ranger District, 595 N.W. Industrial Way, Estacada, OR 97023, 503/630-6861, fax 503/630-2299.

20 EAGLE CREEK

Rating: 8

Near the Columbia Wilderness in Mount Hood National Forest.

Map 9.2, grid c1, page 511

Eagle Creek is the oldest Forest Service Camp in America. Set at 400 feet elevation among old-growth Douglas fir and hemlock, it makes a good base camp for a hiking trip. The Eagle Creek Trail leaves the campground and goes 13 miles to Wahtum Lake, where it intersects with the Pacific Crest Trail. A primitive campground sits at the 7.5-mile point. The upper seven miles of the trail pass through the Hatfield Wilderness.

Campsites, facilities: There are 20 sites for tents

or RVs up to 22 feet long and one group site. Picnic tables and fire grills are provided. Drinking water, garbage bins, and flush toilets are available. Boat docks and launching facilities are nearby on the Columbia River. Leashed pets are permitted.

Reservations, fees: Reservations are not accepted. Sites are $10 per night, $5 per extra vehicle. Senior discount available. Reservations required for groups. Open mid-May–October.

Directions: From Portland, drive east on I-84 for 40 miles to Bonneville. Continue east for two miles to the campground.

Contact: Columbia River Gorge National Scenic Area, 902 Wasco Ave., Suite 200, Hood River, OR 97031, 541/386-2333, fax 541/386-1916.

21 CASCADE LOCKS MARINE PARK

Rating: 8

In Cascade Locks.
Map 9.2, grid c2, page 511

This public riverfront park covers 200 acres and offers a museum and boat rides. The salmon fishing is excellent here. Stern-wheeler dinner cruises are available. A new bike-in provides a recreation option, along with nearby hiking trails and tennis courts.

Campsites, facilities: There are 35 sites, some with partial hookups, for tents or RVs of any length. Picnic tables are provided. Drinking water, flush toilets, an RV dump station, showers, boat docks, launching facilities, and a playground are available. Bottled gas, a store, a café, a coin-operated laundry, and ice are within one mile. Leashed pets are permitted.

Reservations, fees: Reservations are not accepted. Sites are $15–25 per night. Open year-round, with limited winter facilities.

Directions: From Portland, drive east on I-84 for 44 miles to Cascade Locks. Take Exit 44 to Wanapa Street and drive one-half mile to the sign for the park on the left. Turn left and drive to the park (well signed).

Contact: Cascade Locks Marine Park, P.O. Box 307, 355 Wanapa St., Cascade Locks, OR 97014, 541/374-8619, fax 541/374-8428. Campground managed by Port of Cascade Locks.

22 KOA CASCADE LOCKS

Rating: 5

Near the Columbia River.
Map 9.2, grid c2, page 511

This KOA is a good layover spot for RVers touring the Columbia River corridor. The campground offers level, shaded RV sites and grassy tent sites. Nearby recreation options include bike trails, hiking trails, and tennis courts. The 200-acre Cascade Locks Marine Park is close by and offers everything from museums to boat trips.

Campsites, facilities: There are 78 sites for tents or RVs of any length, nine cabins, and two cottages. Electricity, drinking water, sewer hookups, and picnic tables are provided. Flush toilets, bottled gas, an RV dump station, showers, firewood, a hot tub, cable TV hookups, modem access, a recreation hall, a store, a laundry room, ice, a playground, and a heated swimming pool are available. A café is within one mile. Leashed pets are permitted.

Reservations, fees: Reservations at 800/562-8698. Sites are $20–28 per night, $3–4 per person for more than two people. Major credit cards accepted. Open February–November.

Directions: From Portland, drive east on I-84 for 44 miles to Cascade Locks and Exit 44. Turn east on Forest Lane and drive one mile to the campground.

Contact: KOA Cascade Locks, 841 N.W. Forest Ln., Cascade Locks, OR 97014, 541/374-8668, website: www.koa.com.

23 HERMAN CREEK HORSE CAMP

Rating: 5

Near the Pacific Crest Trail in Mount Hood National Forest.

Map 9.2, grid c2, page 511

This rustic campground with spacious sites sits at 1,000 feet elevation and is about one-half mile from Herman Creek, not far from the Pacific Crest Trail. This area, separated from Washington by the Columbia River, is particularly beautiful. There are many recreation options here, including biking, hiking, fishing, and boat trips.

Campsites, facilities: There are seven sites for tents or RVs up to 24 feet long. Drinking water, garbage bins, fire grills, and picnic tables are provided. Stock handling facilities are available. An RV dump station, showers, a store, a café, a coin laundry, and ice are nearby. Leashed pets are permitted.

Reservations, fees: Reservations are not accepted. Sites are $8 per night, $5 per extra vehicle. Senior discount available. Open mid-May–October.

Directions: From Portland, drive east on I-84 for 44 miles to Cascade Locks and Exit 44. Take that exit and drive straight ahead to the frontage road (Wanapa Street). Continue 1.5 miles (the road becomes Herman Creek Road) to the campground on the right.

Contact: Columbia River Gorge National Scenic Area, 902 Wasco Ave., Suite 200, Hood River, OR 97031, 541/386-2333, fax 541/386-1916.

24 WYETH

Rating: 5

On Gordon Creek in Mount Hood National Forest.

Map 9.2, grid c2, page 511

Wyeth makes a good layover spot for Columbia River corridor cruisers. The camp is set at 400 feet elevation along Gordon Creek, near the Columbia River. See the description of Herman Creek Horse Camp for recreation details.

Campsites, facilities: There are 16 sites for tents or RVs up to 32 feet long and three group sites. Fire grills and picnic tables are provided. Drinking water and flush toilets are available. Leashed pets are permitted.

Reservations, fees: Reservations are not accepted. Sites are $10 per night, $5 per extra vehicle. Senior discount available. Open mid-May–October.

Directions: From Portland, drive east on I-84 for 44 miles to Cascade Locks. Continue east on I-84 for seven miles to Wyeth and Exit 51. Turn right and drive one-quarter mile to the campground entrance.

Contact: Columbia River Gorge National Scenic Area, 902 Wasco Ave., Suite 200, Hood River, OR 97031, 541/386-2333, fax 541/386-1916.

25 VIENTO STATE PARK

Rating: 8

Along the Columbia River Gorge.

Map 9.2, grid c4, page 511

This park along the Columbia River Gorge offers scenic hiking trails and some of the best windsurfing in the Gorge. Just 12 miles to the east, old U.S. 30 skirts the Columbia River, offering a picturesque drive. Viento has a day-use picnic area right next to a babbling creek. Look for weekend interpretive programs during the summer. There are several other day-use state parks along I-84 just west of Viento, including Wygant, Vinzenz Lausmann, and Seneca Fouts. All offer quality hiking trails and scenic views.

Campsites, facilities: There are 17 tent sites and 58 sites with water and electrical hookups for RVs up to 30 feet long, with some sites accessible for RVs up to 40 feet long. Picnic tables and fire grills are provided. Drinking water, garbage bins, flush toilets, showers, firewood, and a playground are available. Leashed pets are permitted.

Reservations, fees: Reservations are not accepted. Sites are $13–16 per night, $7 per extra vehicle. Major credit cards accepted. Open March–October, weather permitting.

Directions: From Portland, drive east on I-84 for 56 miles to Exit 56 (eight miles west of Hood River). Take Exit 56 and drive to the park entrance. The park is set on both sides of I-84.

Contact: Columbia River Gorge District, Oregon State Parks, P.O. Box 126, Hood River, OR 97031, 541/374-8811 or 800/551-6949.

26 TUCKER COUNTY PARK

Rating: 6

On the Hood River.

Map 9.2, grid c4, page 511

This county park along the banks of the Hood River is just far enough out of the way to be missed by most of the tourist traffic. Many people who choose this county park come for the windsurfing. Other recreation opportunities include trout fishing, rafting, and kayaking.

Campsites, facilities: There are 80 tent sites and 13 sites for tents or RVs up to 30 feet long. Picnic tables and fire rings are provided. Electricity, drinking water, flush toilets, showers, firewood, and a playground are available. A store, a café, coin-operated laundry facilities, and ice are within two miles. Leashed pets are permitted. Most facilities are wheelchair accessible.

Reservations, fees: Reservations are not accepted. Sites are $13–14 per night, $6 per extra tent, and $2 per extra vehicle. Open April–October.

Directions: From Portland, turn east on I-84 and drive about 65 miles to the town of Hood River and Exit 62. Take the exit and drive east on Cascade Street and continue to 13th Street (first light). Turn right (south) and drive through and out of town; 13th Street becomes Tucker Road and then Dee Highway (Highway 281).

Follow the signs to Parkdale. The park is four miles out of town on the right.

Contact: Hood River County Parks, 918 18th St., Hood River, OR 97031, 541/387-6889, fax 541/386-6325.

27 MEMALOOSE STATE PARK

Rating: 7

In the Columbia River Gorge.

Map 9.2, grid c6, page 511

This park borrows its name from nearby Memaloose Island, which ancient Native Americans used as a sacred burial ground. Set along the hottest part of the scenic Columbia River Gorge, it makes a prime layover spot for campers cruising the Oregon-Washington border. Nature programs and interpretive events are also held here. This popular camp receives a good deal of traffic, so plan on arriving early to claim a spot even if you have a reservation.

Campsites, facilities: There are 67 tent sites and 43 sites with full hookups for RVs up to 60 feet long. Picnic tables and fire grills are provided. Drinking water, garbage bins, flush toilets, an RV dump station, showers, and firewood are available. Leashed pets are permitted.

Reservations, fees: Reservations at 800/452-5687 or website: www.OregonStateParks.org ($7 reservation fee). Sites are $13–20 per night, $7 per extra vehicle. Major credit cards accepted. Open mid-March–late October.

Directions: This park is accessible only to westbound traffic on I-84. From The Dalles, drive west on I-84 for 11 miles to the signed turnoff. (The park is about 75 miles east of Portland.)

Contact: Columbia River Gorge District, Oregon State Parks, P.O. Box 100, Corbett, OR 97019, 541/478-3008 or 800/551-6949.

28 LONE PINE RV PARK

Rating: 7

Near the Columbia River.

Map 9.2, grid d7, page 511

This private park isn't far from the Columbia River, where fishing, boating, and swimming are options. The area gets hot weather and occasional winds shooting through the river canyon during summer. Nearby recreation possibilities include an 18-hole golf course and tennis courts.

Campsites, facilities: There are 22 drive-through sites for RVs of any length. Electricity, drinking water, and sewer hookups are provided. Flush toilets, showers, a café, a laundry room, ice, and a playground are available. Bottled gas and an RV dump station are within one mile. Boat docks and launching facilities are nearby. Leashed pets are permitted.

Reservations, fees: Reservations accepted. Sites are $22–25 per night. Open mid-April–September.

Directions: From Portland, turn east on I-84 and drive about 90 miles to The Dalles and Exit 87. Take Exit 87 to U.S. 197 and drive less than one-quarter mile to the park.

Contact: Lone Pine RV Park, 335 U.S. 197, The Dalles, OR 97058, 541/506-3755.

29 KINNICKKINNICK

Rating: 5

On Laurence Lake in Mount Hood National Forest.

Map 9.2, grid d4, page 511

The campground sits on a peninsula that juts into Laurence Lake. Only nonmotorized boats are allowed on this lake. Campsite privacy varies because of the fairly sparse tree cover. More than half of the sites are a short walk from your vehicle.

Campsites, facilities: There are 20 sites for tents or RVs up to 16 feet long. No drinking water

is available, but picnic tables and fire rings with fire grills are provided. Vault toilets, garbage bins, and a boat ramp are available. Some sites are wheelchair accessible. Leashed pets are permitted.

Reservations, fees: Reservations are not accepted. Sites are $10 per night. Senior discount available. Open May–September, weather permitting.

Directions: From Portland, drive 62 miles west on I-84 to the city of Hood River. Take Exit 64 and drive about 14 miles south on Highway 35 to the town of Mount Hood and Cooper Spur Road. Turn right and drive three miles to Parkdale and Clear Creek Road. Turn left (south) and drive three miles to the Laurence Lake turnoff. Turn right on Forest Road 2840 (Laurence Lake Road) and drive four miles to the campground on the right.

Contact: Mount Hood National Forest, Hood River Ranger District, 6780 Hwy. 35, Mount Hood, OR 97041, 541/352-6002, fax 541/352-7365.

30 LOST LAKE

Rating: 9

On Lost Lake, Mount Hood National Forest, Hood River District.

Map 9.2, grid e2, page 511

Only nonmotorized boats are allowed on this clear, 240-acre lake set against the Cascade Range. The campground is nestled in an old-growth forest of cedar, Douglas fir, and hemlock trees at 3,200 feet elevation. Many sites have a lake view, and the campground affords a great view of Mount Hood. Significant improvements to this campground were completed in late 1999.

Campsites, facilities: There are 125 sites for tents or RVs up to 32 feet long, and there is one large, separate group site. A horse camp with a corral is also available. Picnic tables and fire rings with grills are provided. Drinking water, vault toilets, garbage containers, a dump station, and a covered picnic shelter are available. Cabins, a grocery store, showers, beach picnic areas, a boat launch, and boat rentals are nearby. Many sites are wheelchair accessible, and there is barrier-free boating and fishing, as well as 3.5 miles of barrier-free trails. Leashed pets are permitted.

Reservations, fees: Reservations are not accepted. Sites are $15–20 per night, with an additional $5 per extra vehicle. Major credit cards accepted. Reservations required for the group site at 541/386-6366; $40 per night. Senior discount available. Open mid-May–mid-October, weather permitting.

Directions: From Portland, drive 62 miles east on I-84 to the city of Hood River. Take Exit 62/Westcliff exit to Cascade Road and drive east on Cascade Road to 13th Street. Turn right on 13th Street and drive through Hood River Heights. The road turns into Dee Highway. Continue seven miles, then turn right onto Lost Lake Road (Forest Road 13). Continue seven miles to the campground.

Contact: Mount Hood National Forest, Hood River Ranger District, 6780 Hwy. 35, Mount Hood, OR 97041, 541/352-6002, fax 541/352-7365.

31 KNEBAL SPRINGS

Rating: 6

Near Knebal Springs in Mount Hood National Forest.
Map 9.2, grid e5, page 511

This spot is in a semi-primitive area near Knebal Springs, an ephemeral water source. The Knebal Springs Trail begins at the campground. A nice, level family bike trail is available here. Another trail from the camp provides access to a network of trails in the area. A U.S. Forest Service map is advised.

Campsites, facilities: There are eight sites for tents or RVs up to 22 feet long. Drinking water, picnic tables, and fire grills are provided. Vault toilets and horse loading and tending facilities are available. Leashed pets are permitted. All garbage must be packed out.

Reservations, fees: Reservations are not accepted. Northwest Forest Pass ($5 daily fee or $30 annual fee per parked vehicle) is required. Open June–early October, weather permitting.

Directions: From Portland, turn east on I-84 and drive about 90 miles to Exit 87. Take Exit 87 and turn south on U.S. 197; drive 13 miles to Dufur and Dufur Valley Road. Turn right on Dufur Valley Road and drive west for 12 miles to Forest Road 44. Continue west on Forest Road 44 for four miles to Forest Road 4430. Turn north and drive four miles to Forest Road 1720. Turn southwest and drive one mile to the campground.

Contact: Mount Hood National Forest, Barlow Ranger District, 780 N.E. Court St., Dufur, OR 97021, 541/467-2291, fax 541/467-2271.

32 EIGHTMILE CROSSING

Rating: 7

On Eightmile Creek in Mount Hood National Forest.
Map 9.2, grid e5, page 511

This campground is set at an elevation of 4,200 feet along Eightmile Creek. Although pretty and shaded, with sites scattered along the banks of the creek, it gets relatively little camping pressure. From the day-use area you have access to a nice hiking trail that runs along Eightmile Creek. In addition, a three-quarter-mile wheelchair-accessible trail links Eightmile Campground to Lower Crossing Campground. The fishing can be good here, so bring your gear.

Campsites, facilities: There are 24 sites for tents or RVs up to 30 feet long. No drinking water is available, and all garbage must be packed out. Picnic tables and fire grills are provided. Vault toilets are available. Leashed pets are permitted.

Reservations, fees: Reservations are not accepted. Northwest Forest Pass ($5 daily fee or $30 annual fee per parked vehicle) is required. Open June–mid-October.

Directions: From Portland, turn east on I-84 and drive about 90 miles to Exit 87. Take Exit 87 and turn south on U.S. 197; drive 13 miles to Dufur and Dufur Valley Road. Turn right on Dufur Valley Road and drive west for 12 miles to Forest Road 44. Continue west on Forest Road 44 for four miles to Forest Road 4430. Turn right and drive a short distance to the campground.

Contact: Mount Hood National Forest, Barlow Ranger District, 780 N.E. Court St., Dufur, OR 97021, 541/467-2291, fax 541/467-2271.

33 PEBBLE FORD

Rating: 6

In Mount Hood National Forest.

Map 9.2, grid e5, page 511

This is just a little camping spot by the side of a gravel forest road. Primitive and quiet, it's an alternative to the better-known Eightmile Crossing. There are some quality hiking trails in the area if you're willing to drive two or three miles.

Campsites, facilities: There are three sites for tents or RVs up to 16 feet long. Picnic tables and fire grills are provided. Vault toilets are available. There is no drinking water. Leashed pets are permitted.

Reservations, fees: Reservations are not accepted. Northwest Forest Pass ($5 daily fee or $30 annual fee per parked vehicle) is required. Senior discount available. Open July–early October.

Directions: From Portland, turn east on I-84 and drive about 90 miles to Exit 87. Take Exit 87 and turn south on U.S. 197; drive 13 miles to Dufur and Dufur Valley Road. Turn right on Dufur Valley Road and drive west for 12 miles to Forest Road 44. Continue west on Forest Road 44 for five miles to Forest Road 130. Turn left (south) and drive a short distance to the campground on the left.

Contact: Mount Hood National Forest, Barlow Ranger District, 780 N.E. Court St., Dufur, OR 97021, 541/467-2291, fax 541/467-2271.

34 MCNEIL

Rating: 5

On the Clear Fork of the Sandy River in Mount Hood National Forest.

Map 9.2, grid e2, page 511

This campground is set at an elevation of 2,040 feet in Old Maid Flat, a special geological area along the Clear Fork of the Sandy River. There's a good view of Mount Hood from the campground entrance. Several trails nearby provide access to the wilderness backcountry. See a U.S. Forest Service map for details.

Campsites, facilities: There are 34 sites for tents or RVs up to 22 feet long. Picnic tables and vault toilets are provided. There is no drinking water. Leashed pets are permitted.

Reservations, fees: Reservations are not accepted. Sites are $10 per night, $5 per extra vehicle. Senior discount available. Open May–late September.

Directions: From Portland, drive 40 miles east on U.S. 26 to Zigzag. Turn left on County Road 18/East Lolo Pass Road and drive 4.5 miles to Forest Road 1825. Turn right on Forest Road 1825, drive less than one mile, bear right onto a bridge to stay on Forest Road 1825, and drive one-quarter mile to the campground on the left.

Contact: Mount Hood National Forest, Zigzag Ranger District, Mount Hood Information Center, 65000 E. Hwy. 26, Welches, OR 97067, 503/622-7674, fax 503/622-7625.

35 RILEY HORSE CAMP

Rating: 6

Near the Clear Fork of the Sandy River in Mount Hood National Forest.

Map 9.2, grid e2, page 511

Riley Horse Camp is close to McNeil and offers the same opportunities, except Riley provides stock facilities and is reserved for horse camping only on holidays. Secluded in an area of Douglas fir and lodgepole pine at 2,100 feet elevation, Riley is a popular base camp for horse packing trips.

Campsites, facilities: There are 14 sites for tents or RVs up to 16 feet long. Drinking water, fire grills, vault toilets, and picnic tables are provided. Facilities for horses are available. Leashed pets are permitted.

Reservations, fees: Reservations at 877/444-6777 or website: www.ReserveUsa.com ($9 reservation fee). Sites are $12 per night, $6 per extra vehicle. Senior discount available. Open May–late September.

Directions: From Portland, drive 40 miles east on U.S. 26 to Zigzag. Turn right (northeast) on County Road 18/East Lolo Pass Road and drive 4.5 miles to Forest Road 1825. Turn right and drive one-half mile to Forest Road 380. Turn right and drive 100 yards to the camp.

Contact: Mount Hood National Forest, Zigzag Ranger District, Mount Hood Information Center, 65000 E. Hwy. 26, Welches, OR 97067, 503/622-7674, fax 503/622-7625.

36 LOST CREEK

Rating: 8

On Lost Creek in Mount Hood National Forest.

Map 9.2, grid f2, page 511

This campground near McNeil and Riley has some of the same opportunities. Set in a cool, lush area on a creek at 2,600 feet elevation, it's barrier-free and offers an interpretive nature trail about one mile long as well as a wheelchair-accessible fishing pier.

Campsites, facilities: There are five walk-in sites for tents and nine sites for RVs up to 22 feet long. Some facilities are wheelchair accessible. Drinking water, garbage service, fire grills, vault toilets, and picnic tables are provided. Leashed pets are permitted.

Reservations, fees: Reservations at 877/444-6777 or website: www.ReserveUsa.com ($9 reservation fee). Sites are $12 for a single site, $24 for a double site, and $6 per extra vehi-

cle. Senior discount available. Open May–late September.

Directions: From Portland, drive 40 miles east on U.S. 26 to Zigzag. Turn north on County Road 18/East Lolo Pass Road and drive 4.5 miles to Forest Road 1825. Turn right and drive two miles to a fork. Bear right and drive one-quarter mile to the campground on the right.

Contact: Mount Hood National Forest, Zigzag Ranger District, Mount Hood Information Center, 65000 E. Hwy. 26, Welches, OR 97067, 503/622-7674, fax 503/622-7625.

37 TOLL GATE

Rating: 8

On the Zigzag River in Mount Hood National Forest.

Map 9.2, grid f1, page 511

This shady campground along the banks of the Zigzag River near Rhododendron is extremely popular, and finding a site on a summer weekend can be next to impossible. Luckily you can get a reservation. There are numerous hiking trails in the area. The nearest one leads east for several miles along the river. The campground features a historic Civilian Conservation Corps shelter from the 1930s, which can be used by campers.

Campsites, facilities: There are 14 tent sites and nine sites for RVs up to 16 feet long. Picnic tables and fire grills are provided. Drinking water, garbage service, and pit toilets are available. Leashed pets are permitted.

Reservations, fees: Reservations at 877/444-6777 or website: www.ReserveUsa.com ($9 reservation fee). Single sites are $12–14 per night; double sites are $24 per night; $6 per extra vehicle. Senior discount available. Open late May–late September.

Directions: From Portland, drive east on U.S. 26 for 40 miles to Zigzag. Continue 2.5 miles southeast on U.S. 26 to the campground entrance.

Contact: Mount Hood National Forest, Zigzag Ranger District, Mount Hood Information Center, 65000 E. Hwy. 26, Welches, OR 97067, 503/622-7674, fax 503/622-7625.

38 GREEN CANYON

Rating: 8

On the Salmon River in Mount Hood National Forest.

Map 9.2, grid f1, page 511

Few out-of-towners know about this winner. But the locals do, and they keep the place hopping in the summer. The camp sits at 1,600 feet elevation along the banks of the Salmon River. A long trail cuts through the area and parallels the river, passing through a magnificent old-growth forest. See a U.S. Forest Service map for details.

Campsites, facilities: There are 15 sites for tents or RVs up to 22 feet long. Picnic tables, garbage service, and fire grills are provided. Pit toilets are available. Drinking water is intermittently available. A store, a café, and ice are within five miles. Some facilities are wheelchair accessible. Leashed pets are permitted.

Reservations, fees: Reservations are not accepted. Sites are $12–14 per night, $6 per extra vehicle. Senior discount available. Open May–late September.

Directions: From Portland, drive east on U.S. 26 for 39 miles to Forest Road 2618 (Salmon River Road) near Zigzag. Turn right and drive 4.5 miles to the campground on the right.

Contact: Mount Hood National Forest, Zigzag Ranger District, Mount Hood Information Center, 65000 E. Hwy. 26, Welches, OR 97067, 503/622-7674, fax 503/622-7625.

39 CAMP CREEK   7-4-07

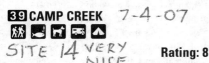

SITE 14 VERY NICE

Rating: 8

Near the Zigzag River in Mount Hood National Forest.

Map 9.2, grid f1, page 511

This campground is set at 2,200 feet elevation along Camp Creek, not far from the Zigzag River. It looks similar to Toll Gate, but larger and farther from the road. A hiking trail runs through camp and along the river; another one leads south to Still Creek. This campground, along with Toll Gate to the west, is very popular and you'll probably need a reservation.

Campsites, facilities: There are 24 sites for tents or RVs up to 22 feet long. Drinking water, garbage bins, fire grills, and picnic tables are provided. Vault toilets are available. Leashed pets are permitted.

Reservations, fees: Reservations at 877/444-6777 or website: www.ReserveUsa.com ($9 reservation fee). Sites are $12–14 per night, $12 for a double site, and $6 per extra vehicle. Senior discount available. Open late May–late September.

Directions: From Portland, drive east on U.S. 26 for 40 miles to Zigzag. Continue southeast on U.S. 26 for about four miles to the camp on the right.

Contact: Mount Hood National Forest, Zigzag Ranger District, Mount Hood Information Center, 65000 E. Hwy. 26, Welches, OR 97067, 503/622-7674, fax 503/622-7625.

40 ALPINE

Rating: 8

Near the Pacific Crest Trail in Mount Hood National Forest.

Map 9.2, grid f3, page 511

This small campground is set on the south slopes of Mount Hood (5,400 feet elevation), one mile from the Timberline Ski Area lodge. It can get quite crowded here on weekends. If you can bear with some traffic noise, you'll be rewarded with big trees, a mountain feel, and year-round skiing and snowboarding less than one mile away. The Pacific Crest Trail is accessible from the Timberline Lodge. Be sure to come prepared for very cold nights.

Campsites, facilities: There are 16 tent sites. Drinking water, fire grills, vault toilets, garbage service, and picnic tables are provided. Leashed pets are permitted.

Reservations, fees: Reservations are not accepted. Sites are $12 per night, $6 per extra

vehicle. Senior discount available. Open July–late September.

Directions: From Portland, drive east on U.S. 26 for 55 miles to the small town of Government Camp. Continue east for one mile to Timberline Road (Forest Road 173). Turn left and drive 4.5 miles to the campground on the left.

Contact: Mount Hood National Forest, Zigzag Ranger District, 65000 E. Hwy. 26, Welches, OR 97067, 503/622-7674, fax 503/622-3163.

41 STILL CREEK

Rating: 6

On Still Creek in Mount Hood National Forest.

Map 9.2, grid f3, page 511

This primitive camp , shaded primarily by fir and hemlock, sits along Still Creek where the creek pours off Mount Hood's south slope. Adjacent to Summit Meadows and site of a pioneer gravesite from the Oregon Trail days, it's a great place for mountain views, sunsets, and wildlife. Anglers should bring along their rods: The fishing in Still Creek can be excellent. The camp sits at 3,600 feet elevation.

Campsites, facilities: There are 27 sites for tents or self-contained RVs up to 16 feet long. Picnic tables, garbage service, and fire grills are provided. Pit toilets and drinking water are available. Leashed pets are permitted.

Reservations, fees: Reservations at 877/444-6777 or website: www.ReserveUsa.com ($9 reservation fee). Sites are $12 per night, $6 per extra vehicle. Senior discount available. Open mid-June–late September.

Directions: From Portland, drive 55 miles east on U.S. 26 to Government Camp. Continue east on U.S. 26 for one mile to Forest Road 2650. Turn right and drive south for 500 yards to the campground.

Contact: Mount Hood National Forest, Zigzag Ranger District, Mount Hood Information Center, 65000 E. Hwy. 26, Welches, OR 97067, 503/622-7674, fax 503/622-7625.

42 GRINDSTONE

Rating: 7

Near Barlow Creek in Mount Hood National Forest.

Map 9.2, grid f3, page 511

This tiny campground, set at 3,400 feet elevation in a meadow along Barlow Creek, is a little-known and little-used spot. You won't find much out here but wind, water, and trees—but sometimes that's all you need. High-clearance vehicles recommended. This camp was a site first used by the pioneers.

Campsites, facilities: There are three primitive sites for tents. Picnic tables and fire grills are provided. Vault toilets are available, but there is no drinking water and no garbage service; pack out all garbage. Leashed pets are permitted.

Reservations, fees: Reservations are not accepted. Northwest Forest Pass ($5 daily fee or $30 annual fee per parked vehicle) is required. Senior discount available. Open May–September.

Directions: From Portland, turn east on U.S. 26 and drive 57 miles (just past the town of Government Camp) to the junction with Highway 35. Turn right (southeast) on U.S. 26 and drive 4.5 miles to Forest Road 3530. Turn right and drive two miles to the campground on the right.

Contact: Mount Hood National Forest, Hood River Ranger District, 6780 Hwy. 35, Mount Hood, OR 97041, 541/352-6002, fax 541/352-7365.

43 DEVIL'S HALF ACRE MEADOW

Rating: 8

On Barlow Creek in Mount Hood National Forest.

Map 9.2, grid g3, page 511

On a site used by the pioneers, this campground is set a few miles upstream from Grindstone Campground on Barlow Creek. Several hiking trails close to camp, including the Pacific Crest Trail, provide access to small lakes in the area. There are many historic points of interest in the vicinity. High-clearance vehicles recommended. The camp is at 3,600 feet elevation.

Campsites, facilities: There are five sites for tents or RVs up to 16 feet long. Picnic tables and fire grills are provided. Firewood and pit toilets are available, but there is no drinking water and no garbage service; pack out all garbage. Leashed pets are permitted.

Reservations, fees: Reservations are not accepted. Northwest Forest Pass ($5 daily fee or $30 annual fee per parked vehicle) is required. Senior discount available. Open May–October.

Directions: From Portland, turn east on U.S. 26 and drive 57 miles (just past the town of Government Camp) to the junction with Highway 35. Turn right (southeast) on U.S. 26 and drive 4.5 miles to Forest Road 3530. Turn southeast and drive one mile to the campground.

Contact: Mount Hood National Forest, Hood River Ranger District, 6780 Hwy. 35, Mount Hood, OR 97041, 541/352-6002, fax 541/352-7365.

44 TRILLIUM LAKE

Rating: 9

On Trillium Lake in Mount Hood National Forest.

Map 9.2, grid g3, page 511

This campground is set at 3,600 feet elevation along the shores of Trillium Lake, which is about one-half mile long and one-quarter mile wide. Fishing is good in the evening here, and the nearby boat ramp makes this an ideal camp for anglers. The lake is great for canoes, rafts, and small rowboats. Trillium Lake is an extremely popular vacation destination, so expect plenty of company. Reservations highly recommended.

Campsites, facilities: There are 55 sites for tents or RVs up to 40 feet long. Picnic tables and fire grills are provided. Pit toilets and drinking water are available. Some sites are wheelchair accessible. Boat docks and launching facilities are available on the lake, but no motors are allowed. Leashed pets are permitted.

Reservations, fees: Reservations at 877/444-6777 or website: www.ReserveUsa.com ($9 reservation fee). Sites are $12–14 per night; double sites are $24 per night; $6 per extra vehicle. Senior discount available. Open late May–late September.

Directions: From Portland, drive east on U.S. 26 for 55 miles to the small town of Government Camp. Continue east on U.S. 26 for 1.5 miles to Forest Road 2656. Turn right and drive 1.3 miles to the campground on the right.

Contact: Mount Hood National Forest, Zigzag Ranger District, Mount Hood Information Center, 65000 E. Hwy. 26, Welches, OR 97067, 503/622-7674, fax 503/622-7625.

45 FROG LAKE

Rating: 6

Near the Pacific Crest Trail in Mount Hood National Forest.

Map 9.2, grid g3, page 511

This classic spot in the Cascade Range is situated on the shore of little Frog Lake (more of a pond than a lake), at an elevation of 3,800 feet and a short distance from the Pacific Crest Trail. Several other trails lead to nearby lakes. Clear Lake, to the south, provides a possible day trip and offers more recreation options.

Campsites, facilities: There are 33 sites for tents or RVs up to 22 feet long. Drinking water, garbage bins, and picnic tables are provided. Vault toilets and firewood are available. Boat-launching facilities are nearby. No motorized boats are allowed. Leashed pets are permitted. Some barrier-free facilities are available.

Reservations, fees: Reservations at 877/444-6777 or website: www.ReserveUsa.com ($9 reservation fee). Sites are $12 per night, $6 per extra vehicle. Senior discount available. Open mid-June–mid-September.

Directions: From Portland, drive east on U.S. 26 for 57 miles to the junction with Highway 35 (two miles past Government Camp). Turn right (southeast) on U.S. 26 and drive seven miles to Forest Road 2610. Turn southeast and drive one-half mile to the campground.

Contact: Mount Hood National Forest, Hood River Ranger District, 6780 Hwy. 35, Mount Hood, OR 97041, 541/352-6002, fax 541/352-7365.

46 BADGER LAKE

Rating: 8

On Badger Lake in Mount Hood National Forest.

Map 9.2, grid f5, page 511

This campground is set at an elevation of 4,400 feet, along the shore of Badger Lake. Non-motorized boating is permitted if you can manage to get a boat in here over the rough roads. No trailers are allowed on campground roads. The camp is adjacent to the Badger Creek Wilderness, and numerous trails provide access to the backcountry. Badger Creek Trail heads out of camp, northeast along Badger Creek for several miles.

Campsites, facilities: There are four sites for tents only, accessible only by high-clearance vehicles. Picnic tables and fire grills are provided. Vault toilets are available. There is no drinking water and all garbage must be packed out. Leashed pets are permitted.

Reservations, fees: Reservations are not accepted. Northwest Forest Pass ($5 daily fee or $30 annual fee per parked vehicle) is required. Open July–early October.

Directions: From Portland, drive east on I-84

for 65 miles to Hood River, Exit 64 and Highway 35. Turn south and drive 37 miles to Forest Road 48. Turn left and drive 16 miles to Forest Road 4860. Turn left (north) and drive eight miles to Forest Road 140. Bear right and drive four miles to the lake. The last two miles on this primitive road require a high-clearance vehicle.

Contact: Mount Hood National Forest, Barlow Ranger District, 780 N.E. Court St., Dufur, OR 97021, 541/467-2291, fax 541/467-2271.

47 BONNEY MEADOW

Rating: 9

In Mount Hood National Forest.

Map 9.2, grid g5, page 511

This primitive campground is on the east side of the Cascade Range at an elevation of 4,800 feet. As a result, there is little water in the area, and also very few people, so you're liable to have the place all to yourself. Bonney Meadow Trail leaves from the campground and travels 1.5 miles up to a group of small lakes. This trail provides great mountain views. See a U.S. Forest Service map for details.

Campsites, facilities: There are eight sites for tents or RVs up to 16 feet long. Picnic tables and fire grills are provided. Vault toilets are available. There is no drinking water. Leashed pets are permitted.

Reservations, fees: Reservations are not accepted. Northwest Forest Pass ($5 daily fee or $30 annual fee per parked vehicle) is required. Senior discount available. Open July–early October.

Directions: From Portland, turn east on I-84 and drive 65 miles to the town of Hood River, Exit 64 and Highway 35. Turn south on Highway 35 and drive 37 miles to Forest Road 48. Turn left and drive 14 miles to Forest Road 4890. Turn left and drive four miles north to Forest Road 4891. Turn right and drive a short distance to the campground.

Contact: Mount Hood National Forest, Barlow

Ranger District, 780 N.E. Court St., Dufur, OR 97021, 541/467-2291, fax 541/467-2271.

48 BONNEY CROSSING

Rating: 7

On Badger Creek in Mount Hood National Forest.

Map 9.2, grid g5, page 511

This campground at 2,200 feet elevation along Badger Creek is the trailhead for the Badger Creek Trail, which provides access to the Badger Creek Wilderness. The camp gets fairly light use and is usually very quiet. Fishing is available in the creek and is usually pretty good. Horse campers are welcome here.

Campsites, facilities: There are eight sites for tents or RVs up to 16 feet long. Picnic tables and fire grills are provided. Vault toilets are available. Stock facilities include horse corrals. There is no drinking water. Leashed pets are permitted. Pack out all garbage.

Reservations, fees: Reservations are not accepted. Northwest Forest Pass ($5 daily fee or $30 annual fee per parked vehicle) is required. Open mid-April–mid-October.

Directions: From The Dalles, drive south on U.S. 197 for 32 miles to Tygh Valley. Take the Tygh Valley exit to Tygh Valley Road. Turn west and drive one-quarter mile to Wamic Market Road (County Road 226). Turn right (west) and drive eight miles to Wamic. Continue through Wamic and drive seven miles to Forest Road 4810. Bear right and drive three miles to Forest Road 4811. Turn right and drive two miles to a junction with Forest Road 2710. Turn right and drive three miles to the campground on the right.

Contact: Mount Hood National Forest, Barlow Ranger District, 780 N.E. Court St., Dufur, OR 97021, 541/467-2291, fax 541/467-2271.

49 PINE HOLLOW LAKESIDE RESORT

Rating: 8

On Pine Hollow Reservoir.

Map 9.2, grid g7, page 511

This resort on the shore of Pine Hollow Reservoir is the best game in town for RV campers, with some shaded lakefront sites and scenic views. Year-round fishing, boating, swimming, and water-skiing are some recreation options here.

Campsites, facilities: There are 35 tent sites, 75 sites for RVs, and 10 cabins. Electricity, drinking water, and picnic tables are provided. Flush toilets, bottled gas, an RV dump station, showers, firewood, a store, a café, a laundry room, and ice are available. Boat docks, launching facilities, and rentals are nearby. Leashed pets are permitted.

Reservations, fees: Reservations accepted. Sites are $17–24 per night, $2 per person for more than two people, $2 per extra vehicle, and $2 per pet per night. Major credit cards accepted. Open mid-March–October.

Directions: From Portland, turn east on I-84 and drive 91 miles to The Dalles, Exit 87, and Highway 197. Turn south and drive 31 miles to Tygh Valley and Wamic Market Road. Turn west and drive 4.5 miles to Ross Road. Turn north and drive 3.5 miles to the campground.

Contact: Pine Hollow Lakeside Resort, 34 N. Mariposa Dr., Wamic, OR 97063, 541/544-2271, website: www.pinehollowlakeside.com.

50 WASCO COUNTY FAIRGROUNDS

Rating: 6

Near Badger Creek.

Map 9.2, grid g7, page 511

This county campground is set near the confluence of Badger and Tygh Creeks. Hiking trails, marked bike trails, and tennis courts are nearby.

Campsites, facilities: There are 50 tent sites and 100 drive-through sites for RVs of any length. Electricity, drinking water, and picnic tables are provided. Flush toilets, a dump station, garbage bins, and coin-operated showers are available. Two community kitchens are available for a fee. A store, a café, and ice are within one mile. Leashed pets are permitted. Some facilities are wheelchair accessible. Horse facilities, including stalls and an arena, are available.

Reservations, fees: Reservations are not accepted for family sites. Sites are $10–12 per night, $3 per extra vehicle. Group reservations available. Open May–October.

Directions: From Portland, turn east on I-84 and drive 91 miles to The Dalles, Exit 87, and Highway 197. Turn south and drive 31 miles to Tygh Valley and Main Street. Turn right at Main Street and drive two blocks to Fairgrounds Road. Turn right and drive one mile to the fairgrounds on the right.

Contact: Wasco County, 81849 Fairgrounds Rd., Tygh Valley, OR 97063, 541/483-2288.

51 ROCK CREEK RESERVOIR

Rating: 7

On Rock Creek Reservoir in Mount Hood National Forest.

Map 9.2, grid g6, page 511

Fishing is excellent, and the environment is perfect for canoes or rafts at this campground along the shore of Rock Creek Reservoir. Enjoy views of Mount Hood from the day-use area. No hiking trails are in the immediate vicinity, but there are many old forest roads that are ideal for walking or mountain biking. The camp sits at 2,200 feet elevation.

Campsites, facilities: There are 33 sites for tents or RVs up to 18 feet long. Picnic tables, garbage service, and fire grills are provided. Vault toilets, drinking water, and firewood are available. Some of the facilities are wheelchair accessible. There are boat docks nearby, but

no motorboats are allowed on the reservoir. Leashed pets are permitted.

Reservations, fees: Reservations at 877/444-6777 or website: www.ReserveUsa.com ($9 reservation fee). Sites are $12–14 per night. Senior discount available. Open mid-April–early October.

Directions: From Portland, turn east on I-84 and drive 91 miles to The Dalles, Exit 87, and Highway 197. Turn south and drive 31 miles to Tygh Valley and Wamic Market Road. Turn right and drive west for six miles to Forest Road 48. Turn west and drive one mile to Forest Road 4820. Turn west and drive a short distance to the campground.

Contact: Mount Hood National Forest, Barlow Ranger District, 780 N.E. Court St., Dufur, OR 97021, 541/467-2291, fax 541/467-2271.

52 FOREST CREEK

Rating: 6

On Forest Creek in Mount Hood National Forest.

Map 9.2, grid g5, page 511

The elevation here is 3,000 feet. This very old camp is set along Forest Creek on the original Barlow Trail was once used by early settlers. Shaded by old-growth Douglas fir and ponderosa pine forest, you'll find solitude here. See a U.S. Forest Service map for specific roads and trails.

Campsites, facilities: There are eight sites for tents or RVs up to 16 feet long. No drinking water is available. Picnic tables and fire grills are provided. Vault toilets are available. Leashed pets are permitted. Pack out all garbage.

Reservations, fees: Reservations are not accepted. Northwest Forest Pass ($5 daily fee or $30 annual fee per parked vehicle) is required. Open July–early October.

Directions: From Portland, turn east on I-84 and drive 91 miles to The Dalles, Exit 87, and Highway 197. Turn south and drive 31 miles to Tygh Valley and Wamic Market Road. Turn right and drive west for six miles to Forest Road 48. Continue west and drive 12.5 miles southwest to Forest Road 4885. Turn left and drive one mile to Forest Road 3530. Turn left to the campground.

Contact: Mount Hood National Forest, Barlow Ranger District, 780 N.E. Court St., Dufur, OR 97021, 541/467-2291, fax 541/467-2271.

53 BARLOW CREEK

Rating: 7

On Barlow Creek in Mount Hood National Forest.

Map 9.2, grid g4, page 511

One of several primitive U.S. Forest Service camps in the immediate vicinity, this campground is set along Barlow Creek at an elevation of 3,100 feet. It is on Old Barlow Road, which was the wagon trail for early settlers in this area. There may not be much to do in these parts, but you sure can't beat the price. If this campground is full, Barlow Crossing Campground is one mile southeast on Forest Road 3530.

Campsites, facilities: There are five sites for tents. Picnic tables and fire grills are provided. Vault toilets are available, but there is no drinking water and no garbage service; pack out all garbage. Leashed pets are permitted.

Reservations, fees: Reservations are not accepted. Northwest Forest Pass ($5 daily fee or $30 annual fee per parked vehicle) is required. Senior discount available. Open May–September.

Directions: From Portland, drive east on U.S. 26 for 57 miles to the junction with Highway 35 (two miles past Government Camp). Turn right (southeast) on U.S. 26 and drive 12 miles to Forest Road 43. Turn left and drive five miles to Forest Road 3530. Turn left (north) and drive 1.5 miles to the campground on the left.

Contact: Mount Hood National Forest, Hood River Ranger District, 6780 Hwy. 35, Mount Hood, OR 97041, 541/352-6002, fax 541/352-7365.

54 WHITE RIVER STATION

Rating: 9

On the White River in Mount Hood National Forest.

Map 9.2, grid g4, page 511

This tiny campground is set along the White River at an elevation of 3,000 feet. It is on Old Barlow Road, an original wagon trail used by early settlers. One of several small, secluded camps in the area, White River Station is quiet and private, but with poor fishing prospects.

Campsites, facilities: There are five sites for tents or RVs up to 32 feet long. Picnic tables and fire grills are provided. Vault toilets are available, but there is no drinking water and no garbage service; pack out all garbage. Leashed pets are permitted.

Reservations, fees: Reservations are not accepted. Northwest Forest Pass ($5 daily fee or $30 annual fee per parked vehicle) is required. Open May–September.

Directions: From Portland, drive east on U.S. 26 for 57 miles to the junction with Highway 35 (two miles past Government Camp). Turn left on Highway 35 and drive two miles east to Forest Road 48. Turn right (south) and drive nine miles southeast to Forest Road 43. Turn right and drive one-quarter mile to Forest Road 3530. Turn left and drive 1.5 miles to the campground on the left.

Contact: Mount Hood National Forest, Barlow Ranger District, 780 N.E. Court St., Dufur, OR 97021, 541/467-2291, fax 541/467-2271.

55 CLEAR LAKE

Rating: 4

Near the Pacific Crest Trail in Mount Hood National Forest.

Map 9.2, grid g3, page 511

This campground is located along the shore of Clear Lake, a spot favored by anglers, swimmers, and windsurfers, but as a reservoir, it is subject to water-level fluctuations. This wooded camp features shady sites and is set at 3,600 feet elevation. The camp sometimes gets noisy from the revels of the party set. If you want quiet, this camp is probably not for you. A nearby trail heads north from the lake and provides access to the Pacific Crest Trail and Frog Lake, both good recreation options.

Campsites, facilities: There are 28 sites for tents or RVs up to 32 feet long. Picnic tables, fire grills, drinking water, garbage bins, firewood, and vault toilets are available. Some facilities are wheelchair accessible. Boat-launching facilities are nearby and motorboats are allowed, but the speed limit is 10 mph. Leashed pets are permitted.

Reservations, fees: Reservations at 877/444-6777 or website: www.ReserveUsa.com ($9 reservation fee). Sites are $12 per night, $6 per extra vehicle. Senior discount available. Open late May–early September.

Directions: From Portland, drive east on U.S. 26 for 57 miles to the junction with Highway 35 (two miles past Government Camp). Turn right (southeast) on U.S. 26 and drive nine miles to Forest Road 2630. Turn south and drive one mile to the campground on the right.

Contact: Mount Hood National Forest, Hood River Ranger District, 6780 Hwy. 35, Mount Hood, OR 97041, 541/352-6002, fax 541/352-7365.

56 HIDEAWAY LAKE

Rating: 9

Near the Rock Lakes Basin in Mount Hood National Forest.
Map 9.2, grid h1, page 511

This jewel of a spot features a small, deep lake where nonmotorized boats are allowed—but they must be carried about 100 yards to the lake. The campsites are separate and scattered around the shore. At the north end of the lake, an 8.5-mile loop trail goes past a number of lakes in the Rock Lakes Basin, all of which

support populations of rainbow and brook trout. If you don't want to make the whole trip in a day, you can camp overnight at Serene Lake. See a U.S. Forest Service map for information.

Campsites, facilities: There are nine sites for tents or small RVs up to 16 feet long. Picnic tables and fire grills are provided. Pit toilets are available. There is no drinking water. Leashed pets are permitted.

Reservations, fees: Reservations are not accepted. Sites are $10 per night, $5 per extra vehicle. Open mid-June–late September, weather permitting.

Directions: From Portland, drive east on U.S. 26 from Gresham 11 miles to Sandy and Highway 211. Turn right (south) and drive six miles to a junction. Turn south (still Highway 211) and drive six miles to Estacada and Highway 224. Bear south on Highway 224 and drive 27 miles to Forest Road 57. Turn east and drive 7.5 miles to Forest Road 58. Turn left and drive three miles north to Forest Road 5830. Turn left (northwest) and drive 5.5 miles to the campground on the left.

Contact: Mount Hood National Forest, Clackamas River Ranger District, 595 N.W. Industrial Way, Estacada, OR 97023, 503/630-6861, fax 503/630-2299.

57 HIGH ROCK SPRINGS

Rating: 7

Near the Rock Lakes Basin in Mount Hood National Forest.
Map 9.2, grid g1, page 511

This small, remote campground is set within two miles of Stet Mountain at an elevation of 5,200 feet. A half-mile climb earns a tremendous view of the surrounding area, including Mount Hood. About four miles east of the camp, trails lead to some of the fishing lakes in the Rock Lakes Basin. In August and September, ripe huckleberries are yours for the picking.

Campsites, facilities: There are six tent sites. Picnic tables and fire grills are provided. Drinking water and a pit toilet are available. Garbage must be packed out. Leashed pets are permitted.

Reservations, fees: Reservations are not accepted. There is no fee for camping. Open mid-June–late September, weather permitting.

Directions: From Portland, drive east on U.S. 26 from Gresham 11 miles to Sandy and Highway 211. Turn right (south) and drive six miles to a junction. Turn south (still Highway 211) and drive six miles to Estacada and Highway 224. Bear south on Highway 224 and drive 27 miles to Forest Road 57. Turn east and drive 7.5 miles to Forest Road 58. Turn left and drive nine miles to Forest Road 58-190. Turn left and drive 1.5 miles to the campground.

Contact: Mount Hood National Forest, Clackamas River Ranger District, 595 N.W. Industrial Way, Estacada, OR 97023, 503/630-6861, fax 503/630-2299.

58 LAKE HARRIET

Rating: 5

On Lake Harriet in Mount Hood National Forest.

Map 9.2, grid g1, page 511

Formed by a dam on the Oak Grove Fork of the Clackamas River, this little lake is a popular spot during the summer. Rowboats and boats with small motors are permitted, but only nonmotorized boats are encouraged. The lake is stocked regularly and can provide good fishing for a variety of trout, including brown, brook, rainbow, and cutthroat. Anglers often stand shoulder to shoulder in summer.

Campsites, facilities: There are 13 sites for tents or RVs up to 30 feet long. Picnic tables and fire grills are provided. Drinking water and vault toilets are available. Garbage service is provided in the summer. Some facilities are wheelchair accessible. A fishing pier and boat-

launching facilities are on the lake. Leashed pets are permitted.

Reservations, fees: Reservations at 877/444-6777 or website: www.ReserveUsa.com ($9 reservation fee). Sites are $12 per night, $6 per extra vehicle. Senior discount available. Open year-round, with limited winter services.

Directions: From Portland, drive east on U.S. 26 from Gresham 11 miles to Sandy and Highway 211. Turn right (south) and drive six miles to a junction. Turn south (still Highway 211) and drive six miles to Estacada and Highway 224. Bear south on Highway 224 and drive 27 miles to Forest Road 57. Turn east and drive 7.5 miles to Forest Road 58. Turn left and drive 7.5 miles to Forest Road 4630. Turn left and drive two miles to the campground on the left.

Contact: Mount Hood National Forest, Clackamas River Ranger District, 595 N.W. Industrial Way, Estacada, OR 97023, 503/630-6861, fax 503/630-2299.

59 GONE CREEK

Rating: 8

On Timothy Lake in Mount Hood National Forest.

Map 9.2, grid h2, page 511

This campground, set along the south shore of Timothy Lake at 3,200 feet elevation, is one of four camps at the lake. Timothy Lake provides good fishing for brook trout, cutthroat trout, rainbow trout, and kokanee salmon. Boats with motors are allowed, but a 10-mph speed limit keeps it quiet. Several trails in the area—including the Pacific Crest Trail—provide access to several small mountain lakes.

Campsites, facilities: There are 45 sites for tents or RVs up to 31 feet long. Drinking water, fire grills, garbage service, and picnic tables are provided. Vault toilets and firewood are available. A boat ramp is nearby. Leashed pets are permitted.

Reservations, fees: Reservations at 877/444-6777 or website: www.ReserveUsa.com ($9 reservation fee). Sites are $12–14 per night, $6 per extra vehicle. Senior discount available. Open mid-May–mid-September.

Directions: From Portland, turn east on U.S. 26 and drive 57 miles (just past the town of Government Camp) to the junction with Highway 35. Turn southeast on U.S. 26 and drive 15 miles to Forest Road 42 (Skyline Road). Turn right and drive eight miles to Forest Road 57. Turn right and drive one mile west to the campground on the right.

Contact: Mount Hood National Forest, Zigzag Ranger District, Mount Hood Information Center, 65000 E. Hwy. 26, Welches, OR 97067, 503/622-7674, fax 503/622-7625.

60 OAK FORK

Rating: 8

On Timothy Lake in Mount Hood National Forest.

Map 9.2, grid h2, page 511

This forested camp is set in heavy timber and bear grass along the south shore of Timothy Lake, just east of Hoodview and Gone Creek campgrounds. Refer to these camps for more details.

Campsites, facilities: There are 47 sites for tents or RVs up to 32 feet long. Picnic tables and fire grills are provided. Drinking water, firewood, and vault toilets are available. A boat ramp and launching facilities are nearby; the speed limit on the lake is 10 mph. Leashed pets are permitted.

Reservations, fees: Reservations at 877/444-6777 or website: www.ReserveUsa.com ($9 reservation fee). Sites are $12–14 per night, $6 per extra vehicle. Senior discount available. Open June–mid-September.

Directions: From Portland, turn east on U.S. 26 and drive 57 miles (just past the town of Government Camp) to the junction with Highway 35. Turn southeast on U.S. 26 and drive 15 miles to Forest Road 42 (Skyline Road). Turn right and drive eight miles to Forest Road

57. Turn right and drive three miles to the camp on the right.

Contact: Mount Hood National Forest, Zigzag Ranger District, Mount Hood Information Center, 65000 E. Hwy. 26, Welches, OR 97067, 503/622-7674, fax 503/622-7625.

61 PINE POINT

Rating: 8

On Timothy Lake in Mount Hood National Forest.

Map 9.2, grid h2, page 511

One of five camps on Timothy Lake, this spot sits at an elevation of 3,200 feet on the southwest shore and has lake access and more open vegetation than the other Timothy Lake campgrounds. The trail that leads around the lake and to the Pacific Crest Trail passes along this campground. See the description of Gone Creek for boating and fishing details.

Campsites, facilities: There are 25 sites for tents or RVs up to 31 feet long (10 single sites, 10 double sites, and five group sites). Picnic tables, garbage service, and fire grills are provided. Drinking water, firewood, a wheelchair-accessible fishing pier, and vault toilets are available. A boat ramp and launching facilities are nearby; the speed limit on the lake is 10 mph. Leashed pets are permitted.

Reservations, fees: Reservations at 877/444-6777 or website: www.ReserveUsa.com ($9 reservation fee). Sites are $12–14 per night, $24 for a double site, and $6 per extra vehicle; group sites are $36 per night. Senior discount available. Open late May–mid-September.

Directions: From Portland, turn east on U.S. 26 and drive 57 miles (just past the town of Government Camp) to the junction with Highway 35. Turn southeast on U.S. 26 and drive 15 miles to Forest Road 42 (Skyline Road). Turn right and drive eight miles to Forest Road 57. Turn right and drive four miles to the park on the right.

Contact: Mount Hood National Forest, Zigzag Ranger District, Mount Hood Information Center, 65000 E. Hwy. 26, Welches, OR 97067, 503/622-7674, fax 503/622-7625.

62 HOODVIEW

Rating: 9

On Timothy Lake in Mount Hood National Forest.

Map 9.2, grid h2, page 511

Here's another camp along the south shore of Timothy Lake; this one is set at 3,200 feet elevation. A trail out of camp branches south for a few miles, and if followed to the east, eventually leads to the Pacific Crest Trail. See the description of Gone Creek for boating and fishing information.

Campsites, facilities: There are 43 sites for tents or RVs up to 31 feet long. Picnic tables, garbage service, and fire grills are provided. Drinking water, firewood, and vault toilets are available. A boat ramp is nearby and motorized boats are allowed but are limited to a speed of 10 mph. Leashed pets are permitted.

Reservations, fees: Reservations at 877/444-6777 or website: www.ReserveUsa.com ($9 reservation fee). Sites are $12–14 per night, $6 per extra vehicle. Senior discount available. Open mid-May–mid-September.

Directions: From Portland, turn east on U.S. 26 and drive 57 miles (just past the town of Government Camp) to the junction with Highway 35. Turn southeast on U.S. 26 and drive 15 miles to Forest Road 42 (Skyline Road). Turn right and drive eight miles to Forest Road 57. Turn right and drive three miles to the campground on the right.

Contact: Mount Hood National Forest, Zigzag Ranger District, Mount Hood Information Center, 65000 E. Hwy. 26, Welches, OR 97067, 503/622-7674, fax 503/622-7625.

63 MEDITATION POINT WALK-IN/BOAT-IN

Rating: 9

On Timothy Lake in Mount Hood National Forest.

Map 9.2, grid h2, page 511

Accessible only by foot or boat, this remote and rustic camp sits at 3,200 feet elevation and offers the most secluded location along Timothy Lake. It's the only campground on the north shore of the lake, which means you'll get a quieter, less crowded environment, though you'll have to bring your own water. The lake has a 10-mph speed limit for boaters. Timothy Lake Trail makes a 14-mile loop around the lake.

Campsites, facilities: There are four boat-in or walk-in tent sites. Picnic tables and fire grills are provided. Vault toilets are available. There is no drinking water, and garbage must be packed out. Boat docks and launching facilities are nearby. Leashed pets are permitted.

Reservations, fees: Reservations are not accepted. There is no fee for camping. Open late May–mid-September.

Directions: From Portland, drive east on U.S. 26 and drive 57 miles to the junction with Highway 35 (two miles past Government Camp). Turn right (southeast) on U.S. 26 and continue for 15 miles to Forest Road 42/Skyline Road. Turn right and drive eight miles south to Forest Road 57. Turn right and drive five miles to Pine Point Campground. Park and hike one mile or take a boat to the north shore of the lake.

Contact: Mount Hood National Forest, Zigzag Ranger District, 65000 E. Hwy. 26, Welches, OR 97067, 503/622-7674, fax 503/622-3163.

64 LITTLE CRATER

Rating: 5

On Little Crater Lake in Mount Hood National Forest.

Map 9.2, grid h2, page 511

Little Crater campground is set at 3,200 feet elevation next to Crater Creek and scenic Little Crater Lake. This camp is popular with hunters in the fall. Both the drinking water and the lake water flow from an artesian well, and the water is numbingly cold. The Pacific Crest Trail is located near camp, providing hiking trail access. Fishing is poor at Little Crater Lake. It is about a mile to Little Timothy Lake lies about a mile away; note the 10-mph speed limit for boats. Bring your mosquito repellent; you'll need it.

Campsites, facilities: There are 16 sites for tents or RVs up to 22 feet long. Picnic tables, garbage bins, and fire grills are provided. Vault toilets, firewood, and drinking water are available. Leashed pets are permitted.

Reservations, fees: Reservations at 877/444-6777 or website: www.ReserveUsa.com ($9 reservation fee). Sites are $12 per night, $6 per extra vehicle. Senior discount available. Open June–mid-September.

Directions: From Portland, drive east on U.S. 26 for 57 miles to the junction with Highway 35 (two miles past Government Camp). Turn right (southeast) on U.S. 26 and drive 15 miles to Forest Road 42 (Skyline Road). Turn right and drive about six miles to Forest Road 58. Turn right and drive about 2.5 miles to the campground on the left.

Contact: Mount Hood National Forest, Zigzag Ranger District, Mount Hood Information Center, 65000 E. Hwy. 26, Welches, OR 97067, 503/622-7674, fax 503/622-7625.

65 CLEAR CREEK CROSSING

Rating: 7

On Clear Creek in Mount Hood National Forest.

Map 9.2, grid g4, page 511

This secluded, little-known spot is set along the banks of Clear Creek at an elevation of 3,600 feet. Clear Creek Trail, a very pretty walk, begins at the campground. Fishing and hiking are two recreation options here.

Campsites, facilities: There are seven sites for tents or RVs up to 16 feet long. Picnic tables and fire grills are provided. Vault toilets are available. There is no drinking water, and all garbage must be packed out. Leashed pets are permitted.

Reservations, fees: Reservations are not accepted. Northwest Forest Pass ($5 daily fee or $30 annual fee per parked vehicle) is required. Open May–September.

Directions: From Portland, drive east on U.S. 26 for 55 miles to Government Camp. Continue three miles to a junction, turn right on U.S. 26, and drive south for 12 miles to Highway 216. Turn left (east) on Highway 216 and drive seven miles to Forest Road 2130. Turn left (north) on Forest Road 2130 and drive three miles to the campground.

Contact: Mount Hood National Forest, Barlow Ranger District, 780 N.E. Court St., Dufur, OR 97021, 541/467-2291, fax 541/467-2271.

66 KEEPS MILL

Rating: 9

On Clear Creek in Mount Hood National Forest.

Map 9.2, grid g4, page 511

This small, pretty campground is situated at the confluence of Clear Creek and the White River. No RVs are permitted. The elevation is 2,600 feet. Many hiking trails, some with awesome views of the White River Canyon, crisscross the area, but be warned: These are butt-kicking canyon climbs.

Campsites, facilities: There are five sites for tents only. The road to the campground is not good for trailers. Picnic tables and fire grills are provided. Vault toilets are available. There is no drinking water. Leashed pets are permitted.

Reservations, fees: Reservations are not accepted. Northwest Forest Pass ($5 daily fee or $30 annual fee per parked vehicle) is required. Open May–September.

Directions: From Portland, drive east on U.S. 26 for 55 miles to Government Camp. Continue three miles to a junction, turn right on U.S. 26, and drive south for 12 miles to Highway 216. Turn left (east) on Highway 216 and drive three miles to Forest Road 2120. Turn left (north) on Forest Road 2120 and drive three miles to the campground.

Contact: Mount Hood National Forest, Barlow Ranger District, 780 N.E. Court St., Dufur, OR 97021, 541/467-2291, fax 541/467-2271.

67 BEAR SPRINGS

Rating: 6

On Indian Creek in Mount Hood National Forest.

Map 9.2, grid h5, page 511

This campground is set along the banks of Indian Creek on the border of the Warm Springs Indian Reservation. The Bear Springs Work Center is near the camp, and rangers will be happy to supply maps and answer your questions about the area. The camp features both secluded and open sites set in old-growth forest.

Campsites, facilities: There are 21 sites for tents or RVs up to 32 feet long. Drinking water, fire grills, garbage bins, and picnic tables are provided. Vault toilets and firewood are available. Leashed pets are permitted.

Reservations, fees: Reservations are not accepted. Sites are $10 per night and $6 for each

additional vehicle. Senior discount available. Open June–September.

Directions: From Portland, drive east on U.S. 26 for 55 miles to Government Camp. Continue three miles to a junction, turn right on U.S. 26, and drive south for 12 miles to Highway 216. Turn left (east) on Highway 216 and drive five miles to Reservation Road. Turn right (east) on Reservation Road and look for the campground on the right.

Contact: Mount Hood National Forest, Barlow Ranger District, 780 N.E. Court St., Dufur, OR 97021, 541/467-2291, fax 541/467-2271.

68 MCCUBBINS GULCH

Rating: 5

In Mount Hood National Forest.

Map 9.2, grid h5, page 511

This small, primitive camp sits alongside a small creek and offers decent fishing and OHV recreation. A 40-mile network of OHV trails runs through the surrounding forest, with access right from camp. So, though out of the way, this camp gets heavy use; claim a spot early in the day. To the south is the Warm Springs Indian Reservation; do not trespass, as large fines are assessed to those prosecuted. Bear Springs provides a nearby camping alternative.

Campsites, facilities: There are 18 sites for tents and RVs up to 25 feet long. Picnic tables and fire grills are provided. Vault toilets are available. There is no drinking water and all garbage must be packed out. Leashed pets are permitted.

Reservations, fees: Reservations are not accepted. Northwest Forest Pass ($5 daily fee or $30 annual fee per parked vehicle) is required. Open May–September.

Directions: From Portland, drive east on U.S. 26 for 55 miles to Government Camp. Continue three miles to a junction, turn right on U.S. 26, and drive south for 12 miles to Highway 216. Turn left (east) on Highway 216 and drive six miles to Forest Road 2110. Take a sharp left and drive 1.5 miles to the campground entrance on the right.

Contact: Mount Hood National Forest, Barlow Ranger District, 780 N.E. Court St., Dufur, OR 97021, 541/467-2291, fax 541/467-2271.

69 SHELLROCK CREEK

Rating: 6

On Shellrock Creek in Mount Hood National Forest.

Map 9.2, grid h1, page 511

Used primarily as an overflow area for Lake Harriet campground, this quiet, little campground is set at an elevation of 2,200 feet at a nice spot on Shellrock Creek. Small trout can be caught here, but remember that on the Clackamas River it's catch-and-release only. Obtain a U.S. Forest Service map for details on the backcountry roads and trails.

Campsites, facilities: There are eight sites for tents or RVs up to 16 feet long. Picnic tables and fire grills are provided. Garbage service is provided during the summer. Vault toilets are available. There is no drinking water. Leashed pets are permitted.

Reservations, fees: Reservations are not accepted. Sites are $10 per night, $5 per extra vehicle. Senior discount available. Open year-round, with limited winter services.

Directions: From Portland, drive east on U.S. 26 from Gresham 11 miles to Sandy and Highway 211. Turn right (south) and drive six miles to a junction. Turn south (still Highway 211) and drive six miles to Estacada and Highway 224. Bear south on Highway 224 and drive 27 miles in national forest (the road becomes Forest Road 46) to Forest Road 57. Turn left (east) and drive 7.5 miles to Forest Road 58. Turn left and drive north one mile to the campground on the left.

Contact: Mount Hood National Forest, Clackamas River Ranger District Estacada Ranger Station, 595 N.W. Industrial Way, Estacada, OR 97023, 503/630-6861, fax 503/630-2299.

70 JOE GRAHAM HORSE CAMP

Rating: 8

Near Clackamas Lake in Mount Hood National Forest.

Map 9.2, grid h2, page 511

Named for a forest ranger, this campground sits at 3,250 feet elevation among majestic Douglas fir and hemlock, just north of tiny Clackamas Lake. It's one of two campgrounds in the area that allows horses; see the description of Clackamas Lake for additional information. Timothy Lake (the setting for the Gone Creek, Hoodview, Oak Fork, Pine Point, and Meditation Point camps) provides a nearby alternative to the northwest. The Pacific Crest Trail is just east of camp.

Campsites, facilities: There are 14 sites for tents, horse trailers, or RVs up to 28 feet long; 11 have corrals and two have hitching rails. Picnic tables, hitching posts, garbage service, and fire grills are provided. Drinking water, vault toilets, and firewood are available. Leashed pets are permitted.

Reservations, fees: Reservations at 877/444-6777 or website: www.ReserveUsa.com ($9 reservation fee). Sites are $12 per night, $6 per extra vehicle. Senior discount available. Open mid-May–mid-September.

Directions: From Portland, turn east on U.S. 26 for 57 miles (just past the town of Government Camp) to the junction with Highway 35. Turn southeast on U.S. 26 and drive 15 miles to Forest Road 42 (Skyline Road). Turn right and drive eight miles to the campground on the left.

Contact: Mount Hood National Forest, Zigzag Ranger District, Mount Hood Information Center, 65000 E. Hwy. 26, Welches, OR 97067, 503/622-7674, fax 503/622-7625.

7.1 CLACKAMAS LAKE

🏃 🛶 🚗 🎣 🚐 ⛺

Rating: 7

Near the Clackamas River in Mount Hood
National Forest.

Map 9.2, grid h2, page 511

This camp, set at 3,400 feet elevation, is a
good place to go to escape the hordes of people at the lakeside sites in neighboring camps.
The Pacific Crest Trail passes nearby, and
Timothy Lake requires little more than a one-
mile hike from camp. See the description of
Gone Creek for information on Timothy
Lake. This is a popular spot for campers with
horses.

Campsites, facilities: There are 46 sites for
tents, trailers, horse trailers, or RVs up to 16
feet long. Some sites have hitch rails and horses are permitted at the first 19 sites. Drinking
water, garbage service, fire grills, and picnic
tables are provided. Vault toilets and firewood
are available. Boat docks and launching facilities are nearby at Timothy Lake, but only nonmotorized boats are allowed. Leashed pets are
permitted.

Reservations, fees: Reservations accepted for
some sites ($8.65 reservation fee). Sites are
$12 per night, $6 per extra vehicle. Senior discount available. Open June–mid-September.

Directions: From Portland, turn east on U.S.
26 and drive 57 miles (just past the town of
Government Camp) to the junction with
Highway 35. Turn southeast on U.S. 26 and
drive 15 miles to Forest Road 42 (Skyline
Road). Turn right and drive eight miles to
Forest Road 57. Continue 500 feet (on Forest Road 42) past the Clackamas Lake Historic Ranger Station to Forest Road 4270.
Turn left and drive one-half mile to the campground on the left.

Contact: Mount Hood National Forest, Zigzag
Ranger District, Mount Hood Information
Center, 65000 E. Hwy. 26, Welches, OR 97067,
503/622-7674, fax 503/622-7625.

7.2 DESCHUTES RIVER STATE RECREATION AREA

🏃 🚲 🛶 🚗 🎣 🚐 ⛺

Rating: 7

On the Deschutes River.

Map 9.3, grid c1, page 512

This tree-shaded park along the Deschutes
River in the Deschutes Canyon offers bicycling
and hiking trails and good steelhead fishing in
season. The Atiyeh Deschutes River Trail at
river level is a favorite jaunt for hikers; be sure
to look for the basket-like hanging nests of the
orioles. A small day-use state park called Heritage Landing, which has a boat ramp and restroom facilities, is located across the river. The
U.S. Army Corps of Engineers offers a free
train ride and tour of the dam at The Dalles
during the summer. Good rafting is a bonus
here. For 25 miles upstream, the river is mostly inaccessible by car. Many fishermen launch
boats here and then go upstream to steelhead
fishing grounds. Note that boat fishing is not
allowed here; you must wade into the river or
fish from shore.

Campsites, facilities: There are 35 primitive
sites for tents or self-contained RVs up to 30
feet long, 34 sites with electrical hookups, and
one covered camper wagon. There is also a
group area for RVs and tents. Picnic tables
and fire grills are provided. Drinking water,
garbage bins, and flush toilets are available.
Leashed pets are permitted.

Reservations, fees: Reservations at 800/452-5687
or website: www.OregonStateParks.org ($7 reser-
vation fee). Sites are $13–19 per night, $5 per
extra vehicle; the covered wagon is $27 per night.
Major credit cards accepted. Open year-round,
with limited services November–March.

Directions: From Portland, turn east on I-84
and drive about 90 miles to The Dalles. Continue east on I-84 for 12 miles to Exit 97, turn
right, and drive 50 feet to Biggs-Rufus Highway. Turn left and drive about one mile, cross
the Deschutes River, and turn right to the
campground entrance.

Contact: Deschutes River State Recreation Area, 89600 Biggs-Rufus Hwy., Wasco, OR 97065, 541/739-2322 or 800/452-5687.

73 LE PAGE PARK

Rating: 6

On the John Day River.

Map 9.3, grid c3, page 512

One half of the campsites are adjacent to the John Day River and the other half are on the other side of the road at this partially shaded campground. The John Day River feeds into the Columbia just one-eighth mile north of the campground. Rattlesnakes are occasionally seen in the area, but are not abundant. Anglers come for the smallmouth bass and catfish during the summer. The day-use area has a swimming beach, a lawn, a boat launch, and boat docks. There are several other campgrounds nearby.

Campsites, facilities: There are five tent sites and 22 partial hookup sites for tents or RVs up to 40 feet long. Picnic tables and fire pits are provided. Drinking water and electricity, restrooms with flush toilets, sinks, and hot showers are available. A boat ramp, docks, a dump station, and garbage containers are also available. Food and laundry services are available five miles away in the town of Rufus. Leashed pets are permitted.

Reservations, fees: Reservations at 877/444-6777 or website: www.ReserveUsa.com ($9 reservation fee). Sites are $10–16 per night, $3 per extra vehicle. Senior discount available. Open April–October.

Directions: From Portland on I-84, drive east 120 miles (30 miles past The Dalles) to Exit 114, the John Day River Recreation Area. The campground is just off I-84.

Contact: Army Corps of Engineers, Portland District, P.O. Box 2946, Portland, OR 97208-2946, 503/808-5150, fax 503/808-4515.

74 BEAVERTAIL

Rating: 6

On the Deschutes River.

Map 9.3, grid f1, page 512

This isolated campground is set at an elevation of 2,900 feet along the banks of the Deschutes River, one of the classic steelhead streams in the Pacific Northwest. The camp provides fishing and rafting options. The open landscape affords canyon views. This is my favorite put-in spot for a drift boat for fishing float trips on the Deschutes. I've made the trip from Beavertail to the mouth of the Deschutes, ideal in four days, camping at BLM boat-in sites along the river and fly-fishing for steelhead. A boating pass is required to float the river. There are 12 other BLM campgrounds along upper and lower Deschutes River Road. The hardest part is getting used to the freight trains that rumble through the canyon at night.

Campsites, facilities: There are 17 sites for tents or RVs up to 30 feet long and two group sites for up to 24 people. Picnic tables, garbage bins, and fire grills are provided. Drinking water and vault toilets are available. Some facilities are wheelchair accessible. Boat-launching facilities are nearby. Leashed pets are permitted.

Reservations, fees: Reservations are not accepted. Sites are $8–12 per night, with a 14-day stay limit. Senior discount available. Group site is $25 per night. Open year-round.

Directions: From Portland, drive east on U.S. 84 to The Dalles and Highway 197. Turn south and drive to Maupin. Continue through Maupin, cross the bridge, and within a mile look for Deschutes River Road on your left. Turn left on Deschutes River Road and drive 21 miles northeast to the campground.

Contact: Bureau of Land Management, Prineville District, 3050 N.E. 3rd St., Prineville, OR 97754, 541/416-6700, fax 541/416-6798.

75 SHADY COVE

Rating: 7

On the Little North Santiam River in Willamette National Forest.

Map 9.4, grid b6, page 513

This campground is on the Little North Santiam River in the recently designated Opal Creek Scenic Recreation Area. Little North Santiam Trail runs adjacent to the campground.

Campsites, facilities: There are 12 sites for tents or self-contained RVs up to 16 feet long. Picnic tables, garbage service (summer only), fire grills, and vault toilets are available. There is no drinking water. Leashed pets are permitted.

Reservations, fees: Reservations are not accepted. Sites are $5–10 per night, $3 per extra vehicle. Senior discount available. Open year-round, weather permitting.

Directions: From Salem on I-5, take Exit 253 to Highway 22. Turn east and drive 23 miles to Mehama and North Fork Road (Marion County Road). Turn left and drive 17 miles northeast to the fork. Bear right on Forest Road 2207 and continue for two miles to the campground on the right.

Contact: Willamette National Forest, Detroit Ranger District, HC 73, P.O. Box 320, Mill City, OR 97360, 503/854-3366, fax 503/854-4239.

76 ELK LAKE

Rating: 9

Near Bull of the Woods Wilderness.

Map 9.4, grid b8, page 513

This remote and primitive campground is set on the shore of Elk Lake, where boating, fishing and swimming can be quite good in the summer. Wildflower blooms can be beautiful in the nearby meadows. Several trails in the area provide access to the Bull of the Woods Wilderness (operated by Mount Hood National Forest) and the newly designated Opal Creek Wilderness. The campground also offers beautiful views of Battle Ax Mountain.

Campsites, facilities: There are 14 primitive tent sites. No drinking water is available. Garbage must be packed out. Primitive boat-launching facilities are available. Leashed pets are permitted.

Reservations, fees: Reservations are not accepted. There is no fee for camping. Open July–mid-September.

Directions: From Salem on I-5, take Exit 253, turn east on Highway 22, and drive 52 miles to Detroit. Turn left on Forest Road 46/Breitenbush Road and drive 4.5 miles to Forest Road 4696/Elk Lake Road. Turn left and drive less than one mile to Forest Road 4697. Turn left and drive 9.5 miles to the campground on the left. The road is extremely rough for the last two miles. High-clearance vehicles recommended.

Contact: Willamette National Forest, Detroit Ranger District, HC 73, P.O. Box 320, Mill City, OR 97360, 503/854-3366, fax 503/854-4239.

77 HUMBUG

Rating: 9

On the Breitenbush River in Willamette National Forest.

Map 9.4, grid b8, page 513

Fishing and hiking are popular at this campground along the banks of the Breitenbush River, about four miles from where it empties into Detroit Lake. The lake offers many other recreation opportunities. The Humbug Flat Trailhead is behind Sites 9 and 10, and a scenic stroll through an old-growth forest follows the Breitenbush River. The rhododendrons put on a spectacular show from May–July.

Campsites, facilities: There are 21 sites for tents or RVs up to 22 feet long. Picnic tables, garbage service (summer only), fire grills, drinking water, and vault toilets are available. Leashed pets are permitted.

Reservations, fees: Reservations are not accepted. Sites are $10 per night, $5 per extra vehicle. Senior discount available. Open year-round, weather permitting, with limited winter facilities.

Directions: From Salem on I-5, take Exit 253, turn east on Highway 22, and drive 52 miles to Detroit. Turn left on Forest Road 46/Breitenbush Road and drive five miles northeast to the campground on the right.

Contact: Willamette National Forest, Detroit Ranger District, HC 73, P.O. Box 320, Mill City, OR 97360, 503/854-3366, fax 503/854-4239.

78 DETROIT LAKE STATE PARK

Rating: 7

On Detroit Lake.

Map 9.4, grid c7, page 513

This campground is set at 1,600 feet elevation along the shore of Detroit Lake, which is 400 feet deep, nine miles long, and has more than 32 miles of shoreline. The park offers a fishing dock and a moorage area, and a boat ramp and bathhouse are available nearby at the Mongold Day Use Area. The lake is crowded on the opening day of trout season in late April because it's heavily stocked.

Campsites, facilities: There are 132 tent sites, 179 sites with full or partial hookups for RVs up to 60 feet long, and 82 boat slips. Drinking water, garbage bins, fire grills, and picnic tables are provided. Flush toilets, showers, two playgrounds, swimming areas, a store, a visitor center, and firewood are available. Two boat docks and launching facilities are nearby. Leashed pets are permitted.

Reservations, fees: Reservations at 800/452-5687 or website: www.OregonStateParks.org ($7 reservation fee). Sites are $17–22 per night, $7 per extra vehicle. Boating moor-

age is $7 per night. Major credit cards accepted. Open March–November, weather permitting.

Directions: From Salem, drive east on Highway 22 for 50 miles to the park entrance on the right (located two miles west of Detroit).

Contact: Detroit Lake State Park, P.O. Box 549, Detroit, OR 97342, 503/854-3346.

79 PIETY ISLAND BOAT-IN

Rating: 10

On Detroit Lake in Willamette National Forest.

Map 9.4, grid c7, page 513

This island gets crowded and has a reputation for sometimes attracting rowdy groups. Other campgrounds along the shore have drinking water. Piety Island Trail climbs 1.5 miles to the top of the island. You'll find great vistas on this island.

Campsites, facilities: There are 12 tent sites on this island campground, which is accessible by boat only. Picnic tables and fire grills are provided. Pit toilets are available, but there is no drinking water, and all garbage must be packed out. Boat docks, launching facilities, and rentals are nearby. Leashed pets are permitted.

Reservations, fees: Reservations are not accepted. There is no fee for camping. Open May–late September.

Directions: From Salem, drive east on Highway 22 for 45 miles to Detroit Lake. Continue east on Highway 22 along the north side of the lake to the boat ramp (a boat ramp is three miles west of the town of Detroit). Launch your boat and head southeast to the island in the middle of the lake. The campground is on the east side of the island.

Contact: Willamette National Forest, Detroit Ranger District, HC 73, Box 320, Mill City, OR 97360, 503/854-3366, fax 503/854-4239.

80 SOUTHSHORE

Rating: 9

On Detroit Lake in Willamette National Forest.

Map 9.4, grid c7, page 513

This popular camp is set along the south shore of Detroit Lake, where fishing, swimming, and water-skiing are some of the recreation options. The Stahlman Point Trailhead is about one-half mile from camp. There's a day-use area for picnicking and swimming. The views of the lake and surrounding mountains are outstanding.

Campsites, facilities: There are eight walk-in tent sites and 24 sites for tents or RVs up to 22 feet long. Fire grills, garbage service, and picnic tables are provided. Vault toilets and drinking water are available. Boat-launching facilities are nearby at a day-use area. Leashed pets are permitted.

Reservations, fees: Reservations are not accepted. Sites are $12 for single site, $24 for double site, and $5 per extra vehicle. Open mid-April–late September, with a gate preventing access during the off-season.

Directions: From Salem, drive east on Highway 22 for 52 miles to Detroit. Continue southeast on Highway 22 for 2.5 miles to Forest Road 10 (Blowout Road). Turn right and drive four miles to the campground on the right.

Contact: Willamette National Forest, Detroit Ranger District, HC 73, Box 320, Mill City, OR 97360, 503/854-3366, fax 503/854-4239.

81 COVE CREEK

Rating: 10

On Detroit Lake in Willamette National Forest.

Map 9.4, grid c7, page 513

See the description of Southshore and Hoover for recreation options.

Campsites, facilities: There are 63 sites for tents or RVs and one group site for up to 70 people. Picnic tables, garbage service, and fire rings are provided. Drinking water, restrooms with flush toilets and coin-operated showers, garbage bins, and a boat ramp are available. Some facilities are wheelchair accessible. Leashed pets are permitted.

Reservations, fees: Reservations are not accepted for family sites; $16 per night, $32 for double sites, and $5 per extra vehicle. Reservations for the group site at 877/444-6777 or website: www.ReserveUsa.com ($9 reservation fee); $150 per night. Senior discount available. Open late May–late September.

Directions: From Salem, drive east on Highway 22 for 52 miles to Detroit. Continue southeast on Highway 22 for 2.5 miles to Forest Road 10 (Blowout Road). Turn right and drive three miles to the campground on the right.

Contact: Willamette National Forest, Detroit Ranger District, HC 73, Box 320, Mill City, OR 97360, 503/854-3366, fax 503/854-4239.

82 HOOVER

Rating: 9

On Detroit Lake in Willamette National Forest.

Map 9.4, grid c7, page 513

This campground is along the eastern arm of Detroit Lake, near the mouth of the Santiam River. It features a wheelchair-accessible fishing area and nature trail. You're likely to see osprey fishing during the day, a truly special sight. See the description of Southshore for other recreation options.

Campsites, facilities: There are 37 sites for tents or RVs up to 32 feet long. Picnic tables, garbage service, and fire grills are provided. Flush toilets and drinking water are available. Some facilities are wheelchair accessible. Boat docks and launching facilities are nearby. Leashed pets are permitted.

Reservations, fees: Reservations are not ac-

cepted. Sites are $12 for a single site per night, $24 for a double site, and $5 per extra vehicle. Senior discount available. Open mid-April–late September; a gate prevents access in the off-season.

Directions: From Salem, drive east on Highway 22 for 52 miles to Detroit. Continue southeast on Highway 22 for 2.5 miles to Forest Road 10 (Blowout Road). Turn right and drive one mile to the campground on the right.

Contact: Willamette National Forest, Detroit Ranger District, HC 73, Box 320, Mill City, OR 97360, 503/854-3366, fax 503/854-4239.

83 UPPER ARM

Rating: 7

On Detroit Lake in Willamette National Forest.

Map 9.4, grid c8, page 513

This little campground is set along the shore of the narrow upper arm of Detroit Lake, close to where the Breitenbush River empties into it. The smallest and most primitive camp in the area, it features a large day-use area.

Campsites, facilities: There are five tent sites. Fire grills and picnic tables are provided. Pit toilets and garbage service (summer only) are available. There is no drinking water. Boat docks, launching facilities, and rentals are nearby. Leashed pets are permitted.

Reservations, fees: Reservations are not accepted. There is no fee for camping. Open year-round.

Directions: From Salem, drive east on Highway 22 for 52 miles to Detroit and Forest Road 46 (Breitenbush Road). Turn left and drive one mile northeast to the campground on the left.

Contact: Willamette National Forest, Detroit Ranger District, HC 73, Box 320, Mill City, OR 97360, 503/854-3366, fax 503/854-4239.

84 HOOVER GROUP CAMP

Rating: 9

On Detroit Lake in Willamette National Forest.

Map 9.4, grid c8, page 513

This is a perfect spot for a family reunion or club trip. Detroit Lake offers a myriad of activities, including hiking, fishing, swimming, and boating, just to name a few. The campground has nice, open sites and direct access to the lake. See descriptions of Hoover and Southshore Campgrounds.

Campsites, facilities: There are nine sites for tents or RVs up to 15 feet long. This is a group camp that will accommodate up to 70 people. Drinking water and picnic tables are provided. Vault toilets and a group picnic shelter are available. Boat docks, launching facilities, and rentals are nearby. Leashed pets are permitted.

Reservations, fees: Reservations at 877/444-6777 or website: www.ReserveUsa.com ($9 reservation fee); $120 per night, with a two-night minimum for weekend reservations. Open mid-April–late September.

Directions: From Salem, drive east on Highway 22 for 52 miles to Detroit. Continue southeast on Highway 22 for 2.5 miles to Forest Road 10 (Blowout Road). Turn right and drive one-half mile to the campground on the right.

Contact: Willamette National Forest, Detroit Ranger District, HC 73, Box 320, Mill City, OR 97360, 503/854-3366, fax 503/854-4239.

85 SUMMIT LAKE

Rating: 6

On Summit Lake in Mount Hood National Forest.

Map 9.5, grid a3, page 514

This idyllic camp is set in a remote area along the western slopes of the Cascade Range at an elevation of 4,200 feet. On the shore of little Summit Lake, the camp is primitive but a jewel.

It's a perfect alternative to the more crowded camps at Timothy Lake, and you have access to all the same recreation options by driving just a short distance north.

Campsites, facilities: There are six tent sites. Fire grills, garbage service, and picnic tables are provided. Vault toilets and drinking water are available. There is no drinking water. Nonmotorized boats are allowed. Leashed pets are permitted.

Reservations, fees: Reservations are not accepted. Sites are $8 per night. Senior discount available. Open late May–September, weather permitting.

Directions: From Portland, turn east on U.S. 26 and drive 57 miles (just past the town of Government Camp) to the junction with Highway 35. Turn southeast on U.S. 26 and drive 15 miles to Forest Road 42 (Skyline Road). Turn right and drive 12 miles south to Forest Road 141 (a dirt road). Turn right and drive west about one mile to the campground on the left.

Contact: Mount Hood National Forest, Zigzag Ranger District, Mount Hood Information Center, 65000 E. Hwy. 26, Welches, OR 97067, 503/622-7674, fax 503/622-7625.

86 KAH-NEE-TA RESORT

Rating: 7

On the Warm Springs Indian Reservation.
Map 9.5, grid b7, page 514

This resort features a stellar-rated, full-concept spa, with the bonus of a nearby casino. It is also the only public camp on the east side of the Warm Springs Indian Reservation; there are no other camps within 30 miles. The Warm Springs River runs nearby. Recreation options in the area include an 18-hole golf course, miniature golf, biking and hiking trails, a riding stable, and tennis courts.

Campsites, facilities: There are 50 drive-through sites for RVs of any length. Electricity, drinking water, cable TV, and sewer hookups are provided. Flush toilets, bottled gas, an RV dump station, showers, a concession stand, laundry facilities, ice, a playground, a spa with a therapist, mineral baths, and an Olympic-sized, spring-fed swimming pool with a 140-foot water slide are available. Some facilities are wheelchair accessible. Leashed pets are permitted, but some areas are restricted.

Reservations, fees: Reservations at 800/554-4786. Sites are $38 per night for three people; two-night minimum on weekends, three-night minimum on holiday weekends. Major credit cards accepted. Open year-round.

Directions: From Portland, turn east on U.S. 26 and drive about 105 miles to Warm Springs and Agency Hot Springs Road on the left. Turn left and drive 11 miles northeast to Kah-Nee-Ta and the resort on the right.

Contact: Kah-Nee-Ta Resort, P.O. Box 1240, Warm Springs, OR 97761, 541/553-1112, website: www.kah-neetaresort.com.

87 CLEATER BEND

Rating: 8

Near the Breitenbush River in Willamette National Forest.
Map 9.5, grid b1, page 514

Creek views and pretty, shaded sites are the highlights of this camp on the banks of the Breitenbush River. The camp is one-quarter mile from Breitenbush; see the description of Breitenbush for area details.

Campsites, facilities: There are nine sites for tents or RVs up to 16 feet long. Picnic tables, garbage service (summer only), fire grills, drinking water, and vault toilets are available. Leashed pets are permitted.

Reservations, fees: Reservations are not accepted. Sites are $10 per night, $5 per extra vehicle. Senior discount available. Open year-round, weather permitting.

Directions: From Salem on I-5, take Exit 253, turn east on Highway 22, and drive 50 miles to Detroit. Turn left on Forest Road 46/Breitenbush Road and drive nine miles to the campground on the right.

Contact: Willamette National Forest, Detroit Ranger District, HC 73, Box 320, Mill City, OR 97360, 503/854-3366, fax 503/854-4239.

88 BREITENBUSH

Rating: 8

On the Breitenbush River in Willamette National Forest.

Map 9.5, grid b1, page 514

There is fishing access at this campground along the Breitenbush River. Nearby recreation options include the South Breitenbush Gorge National Recreation Trail, three miles away, and Breitenbush Hot Springs, just over a mile away. If this campground is crowded, try nearby Cleater Bend.

Campsites, facilities: There are 29 sites for tents or RVs up to 22 feet long (longer trailers may be difficult to park and turn). Picnic tables, garbage service (summer only), and fire grills are provided. Drinking water and vault toilets are available. Leashed pets are permitted.

Reservations, fees: Reservations are not accepted. Sites are $10 per night for a single site, $20 per night for a double site, and $5 per extra vehicle. Senior discount available. Open year-round, weather permitting, with limited winter facilities.

Directions: From Salem on I-5, take Exit 253, turn east on Highway 22, and drive 50 miles to Detroit. Turn left (north) on Forest Road 46/Breitenbush Road and drive 10 miles to the campground on the right.

Contact: Willamette National Forest, Detroit Ranger District, HC 73, Box 320, Mill City, OR 97360, 503/854-3366, fax 503/854-4239.

89 LOWER LAKE

Rating: 7

Near Olallie Lake in Mount Hood National Forest.

Map 9.5, grid b2, page 514

This sunny, open campground is set at an elevation of 4,600 feet about three-quarters of a mile from Lower Lake, a small, deep lake that's perfect for fishing and swimming. The camp is less than a mile from Olallie Lake and near a network of trails that provide access to other nearby lakes. It's advisable to obtain a U.S. Forest Service map that details the backcountry roads and trails.

Campsites, facilities: There are eight walk-in tent sites. Picnic tables and fire grills are provided. Pit toilets and garbage service are available. There is no drinking water. Boat docks, launching facilities, and rentals are nearby at Olallie Lake. Leashed pets are permitted.

Reservations, fees: Reservations are not accepted. Sites are $8 per night, $4 per extra vehicle. Senior discount available. Open mid-June–late September.

Directions: From Portland, drive east on U.S. 26 from Gresham 11 miles to Sandy and Highway 211. Turn right (south) and drive six miles to a junction. Turn south (still Highway 211) and drive six miles to Estacada and Highway 224. Bear south on Highway 224 and drive 27 miles in national forest (the road becomes Forest Road 46). Continue south on Forest Road 46 for 20 miles to Forest Road 4690. Turn left on Forest Road 4690 and drive southeast for 8.2 miles to Forest Road 4220. Turn right (south) and drive about 4.5 miles of rough road to the campground on the right.

Contact: Mount Hood National Forest, Clackamas River Ranger District, 595 N.W. Industrial Way, Estacada, OR 97023, 503/630-6861, fax 503/630-2299.

90 CAMP TEN

Rating: 9

On Olallie Lake in Mount Hood National Forest.

Map 9.5, grid b2, page 514

Here's a camp along the shore of Olallie Lake, a popular area. Camp Ten is set at an elevation of 5,000 feet on the western shore in the midst of the Olallie Lake Scenic Area, which is home to a number of pristine mountain lakes and a network of hiking trails. See a U.S. Forest Service map for trail locations. Boats without motors—including canoes, kayaks, and rafts—are permitted on the lake.

Campsites, facilities: There are 10 sites for tents or RVs up to 16 feet long. Picnic tables, garbage service, and fire grills are provided. Pit toilets are available. There is no drinking water. Boat docks, launching facilities, boat rentals, and a store that sells fishing tackle and other supplies are nearby. Leashed pets are permitted.

Reservations, fees: Reservations are not accepted. Sites are $8 per night, $4 per extra vehicle. Senior discount available. Open mid-June–late September, weather permitting.

Directions: From Portland, drive east on U.S. 26 from Gresham 11 miles to Sandy and Highway 211. Turn right (south) and drive six miles to a junction. Turn south (still Highway 211) and drive six miles to Estacada and Highway 224. Bear south on Highway 224 and drive 27 miles in national forest (the road becomes Forest Road 46). Continue south on Forest Road 46 for 20 miles to Forest Road 4690. Turn left on Forest Road 4690 and drive southeast for 8.2 miles to Forest Road 4220. Turn right (south) and drive about six miles of rough road to the campground.

Contact: Mount Hood National Forest, Clackamas River Ranger District, 595 N.W. Industrial Way, Estacada, OR 97023, 503/630-6861, fax 503/630-2299.

91 PAUL DENNIS

Rating: 10

On Olallie Lake in Mount Hood National Forest.

Map 9.5, grid b2, page 514

This campground is set at an elevation of 5,000 feet along the north shore of Olallie Lake. From here you can see the reflection of Mt. Jefferson (10,497 feet). Boats with motors are not permitted on the lake. A trail from camp

leads to Nep-Te-Pa Lake, Monon Lake, and Long Lake, which lies just east of the border of the Warm Springs Indian Reservation. It's advisable to obtain a U.S. Forest Service map.

Campsites, facilities: There are 17 sites for tents or small campers up to 16 feet long (trailers not recommended) and three hike-in tent sites. Picnic tables, garbage service, and fire grills are provided. Pit toilets are available. There is no drinking water. A store and ice are nearby. Boat docks, launching facilities, and rentals are on Olallie Lake. Leashed pets are permitted.

Reservations, fees: Reservations at 503/557-1010 or website: www.olallielake.com. Sites are $12 per night, $4.50 per extra vehicle. Open mid-June–late September.

Directions: From Portland, drive east on U.S. 26 from Gresham 11 miles to Sandy and Highway 211. Turn right (south) and drive six miles to a junction. Turn south (still Highway 211) and drive six miles to Estacada and Highway 224. Bear south on Highway 224 and drive 27 miles in national forest (the road becomes Forest Road 46). Continue south on Forest Road 46 for 20 miles to Forest Road 4690. Turn left and drive southeast for 8.2 miles to Forest Road 4220. Turn right (south) and drive 6.2 miles to Forest Road 4220-170. Turn left and drive one-eighth mile to the campground.

Contact: Mount Hood National Forest, Clackamas River Ranger District, 595 N.W. Industrial Way, Estacada, OR 97023, 503/630-6861, fax 503/630-2299.

92 PENINSULA

Rating: 10

On Olallie Lake in Mount Hood National Forest.

Map 9.5, grid b2, page 514

Peninsula, the largest of several campgrounds along Olallie Lake, is set at an elevation of 4,900 feet on the south shore. An amphitheater is located near camp, and during the summer rangers present campfire programs. Boats without motors are permitted on the lake. Nearby trails lead to a number of smaller lakes in the area. See the description of Paul Dennis for details.

Campsites, facilities: There are 35 sites for tents or RVs up to 24 feet long and six walk-in tent sites. Picnic tables, garbage service, and fire grills are provided. Vault toilets are available. There is no drinking water. Some facilities are wheelchair accessible. Boat docks, launching facilities, and rentals are nearby. Leashed pets are permitted.

Reservations, fees: Reservations at 503/557-1010 or website: www.olallielake.com. Sites are $10 per night, $6 per extra vehicle, and $6 for walk-in sites. Senior discount available. Open mid-June–late September.

Directions: From Portland, drive east on U.S. 26 from Gresham 11 miles to Sandy and Highway 211. Turn right (south) and drive six miles to a junction. Turn south (still Highway 211) and drive six miles to Estacada and Highway 224. Bear south on Highway 224 and drive 27 miles in national forest (the road becomes Forest Road 46). Continue south on Forest Road 46 for 20 miles to Forest Road 4690. Turn left and drive southeast for 8.2 miles to Forest Road 4220. Turn right (south) and drive 6.5 miles of rough road to the campground.

Contact: Mount Hood National Forest, Clackamas River Ranger District, 595 N.W. Industrial Way, Estacada, OR 97023, 503/630-6861, fax 503/630-2299.

93 OLALLIE MEADOWS

Rating: 8

Near Olallie Lake in Mount Hood National Forest.
Map 9.5, grid b3, page 514

This campground is set at 4,500 feet along a large and peaceful alpine meadow about three miles from Olallie Lake. The Pacific Crest Trail passes very close to camp. See the description of Paul Dennis for area details.

Campsites, facilities: There are seven sites for tents or RVs up to 16 feet long. Picnic tables, garbage service, and fire grills are provided. Pit toilets are available. There is no drinking water. Boat docks, launching facilities, and rentals are about three miles away on Olallie Lake. Leashed pets are permitted.

Reservations, fees: Reservations are not accepted. Sites are $8 per night, $4 per extra vehicle. Senior discount available. Open mid-June–late September.

Directions: From Portland, drive east on U.S. 26 from Gresham 11 miles to Sandy and Highway 211. Turn right (south) and drive six miles to a junction. Turn south (still Highway 211) and drive six miles to Estacada and Highway 224. Bear south on Highway 224 and drive 27 miles in national forest (the road becomes Forest Road 46). Continue south on Forest Road 46 for 20 miles to Forest Road 4690. Turn left and drive southeast for 8.2 miles to Forest Road 4220. Turn right (south) and drive 1.5 miles to the campground on the left.

Contact: Mount Hood National Forest, Clackamas River Ranger District, 595 N.W. Industrial Way, Estacada, OR 97023, 503/630-6861, fax 503/630-2299.

94 WHISPERING FALLS

Rating: 10

On the North Santiam River near Detroit Lake in Willamette National Forest.
Map 9.5, grid c1, page 514

This popular campground sits on the banks of the North Santiam River, where you can fish. If the campsites at Detroit Lake are crowded, this camp provides a more secluded option, and it's only about a 10-minute drive from the lake. Ospreys sometimes nest near the campground.

Campsites, facilities: There are 16 sites for tents or RVs up to 22 feet long. Picnic tables, garbage service, and fire grills are provided. Drinking water and flush toilets are available. Leashed pets are permitted.

Reservations, fees: Reservations are not accepted. Sites are $10 per night, $5 per extra vehicle. Senior discount available. Open mid-April–late September; a gate prevents access in the off-season.

Directions: From Salem, drive east on Highway 22 for 50 miles to Detroit. Continue east on Highway 22 for eight miles to the campground on the right.

Contact: Willamette National Forest, Detroit Ranger District, HC 73, Box 320, Mill City, OR 97360, 503/854-3366, fax 503/854-4239.

95 RIVERSIDE

Rating: 7

On the North Santiam River in Willamette National Forest.

Map 9.5, grid c1, page 514

This campground is set at an elevation of 2,400 feet along the banks of the North Santiam River, where the fishing can be good. A point of interest, the Marion Forks Fish Hatchery and interpretive site lies just 2.5 miles south. Other day-trip options include the Mt. Jefferson Wilderness, directly to the east in Willamette National Forest, and Minto Mountain Trail, three miles to the east.

Campsites, facilities: There are 37 sites for tents or RVs up to 21 feet long. Picnic tables and fire grills are provided. Drinking water and pit toilets are available. Leashed pets are permitted.

Reservations, fees: Reservations are not accepted. Sites are $10 per night, $5 per extra vehicle. Senior discount available. Open late April–late September; a gate prevents access during the off-season.

Directions: From Salem, drive east on Highway 22 for 50 miles to Detroit. Continue southeast on Highway 22 for 14 miles to the campground on the right.

Contact: Willamette National Forest, Detroit Ranger District, HC 73, Box 320, Mill City, OR 97360, 503/854-3366, fax 503/854-4239.

96 MARION FORKS

Rating: 8

On the Santiam River in Willamette National Forest.

Map 9.5, grid d1, page 514

This campground is situated along Marion Creek, adjacent to the Marion Forks Fish Hatchery. A U.S. Forest Service guard station and a restaurant are across Highway 22. The area boasts some quality hiking trails; the nearest is Independence Rock Trail, one-quarter mile north of the campground.

Campsites, facilities: There are 15 sites for tents or RVs up to 22 feet long. Picnic tables, fire grills, and garbage containers are provided. Pit toilets and drinking water are available. Leashed pets are permitted.

Reservations, fees: Reservations are not accepted. Sites are $10 per night, $5 per extra vehicle. Senior discount available. Open year-round, weather permitting, with no winter services.

Directions: From Salem, drive east on Highway 22 for 50 miles to Detroit. Continue southeast on Highway 22 for 16 miles to the campground on the left.

Contact: Willamette National Forest, Detroit Ranger District, HC 73, Box 320, Mill City, OR 97360, 503/854-3366, fax 503/854-4239.

97 BIG MEADOWS HORSE CAMP

Rating: 10

Near Mt. Jefferson Wilderness in Willamette National Forest.

Map 9.5, grid d1, page 514

Built by the U.S. Forest Service with the support of a horse club, this camp is used heavily by equestrians riding into the Big Meadows area and the adjacent Mt. Jefferson Wilderness. If you're not a horse lover, you may want to stick with Riverside or Marion Forks.

Campsites, facilities: There are nine sites for

tents or RVs. Picnic tables, garbage service, fire grills, and enclosed four-horse corrals are provided at each site. Drinking water and vault toilets are available. Leashed pets are permitted.

Reservations, fees: Reservations are not accepted. Sites are $12 per night, $5 per extra vehicle. Senior discount available. Open mid-April–mid-September, weather permitting.

Directions: From Salem, drive east on Highway 22 for 50 miles to Detroit. Continue southeast on Highway 22 for 27 miles to Big Meadows Road (Forest Road 2267). Turn left and drive one mile to Forest Road 2257. Turn left and drive one-half mile to the campground on the left.

Contact: Willamette National Forest, Detroit Ranger District, HC 73, Box 320, Mill City, OR 97360, 503/854-3366, fax 503/854-4239.

98 SHEEP SPRINGS HORSE CAMP

Rating: 7

Near the Mt. Jefferson Wilderness in Deschutes National Forest.

Map 9.5, grid d3, page 514

This well-shaded equestrian camp with privacy screening between sites is near the trailhead for the Metolius-Windigo Horse Trail, which heads northeast into the Mt. Jefferson Wilderness and south to Black Butte. Contact the U.S. Forest Service for details and maps of the backcountry. The camp is set at an elevation of 3,200 feet.

Campsites, facilities: There are 11 sites for tents or RVs up to 30 feet long. Drinking water and fire grills are provided. Vault toilets and box stalls for horses are available.

Reservations, fees: Reservations at 877/444-6777 or website: www.ReserveUsa.com ($9 reservation fee). Sites are $12 per night, $6 per extra vehicle. Senior discount available. Open late May–mid-October.

Directions: From Albany, drive east on U.S. 20 for 87 miles to the sign for Jack Lake (lo-

cated one mile east of Suttle Lake) and Suttle-Sherman Road. Turn left on Forest Road 12 and drive eight miles to Forest Road 1260. Turn left and drive 1.5 miles to Forest Road 1260-200. Turn right and drive 1.5 miles to the campground on the right.

Contact: Deschutes National Forest, Sisters Ranger District, P.O. Box 249, Sisters, OR 97759, 541/549-7700, fax 541/549-7746.

99 JACK CREEK

Rating: 5

Near Mt. Jefferson Wilderness in Deschutes National Forest.

Map 9.5, grid d3, page 514

A more primitive alternative to the other camps in the area, this campground sits along the banks of Jack Creek in an open setting among ponderosa pine. To protect the bull trout habitat, no fishing is permitted here.

Campsites, facilities: There is an area for dispersed tent, trailer, or RV camping with access to some picnic tables and fire grills. Vault toilets are available. There is no drinking water, and all garbage must be packed out. Leashed pets are permitted.

Reservations, fees: Reservations are not accepted. There is no fee for camping. Open mid-April–mid-October.

Directions: From Albany, drive east on U.S. 20 for 87 miles to the sign for Jack Lake (located one mile east of Suttle Lake) and Suttle-Sherman Road. Turn left on Forest Road 12 and drive five miles to Forest Road 1230. Turn left and drive three-quarters of a mile to Forest Road 1232. Turn left and drive one-quarter mile to the campground on the left.

Contact: Deschutes National Forest, Sisters Ranger District, P.O. Box 249, Sisters, OR 97759, 541/549-7700, fax 541/549-7746.

100 PELTON

Rating: 8

On Lake Simtustus in Deschutes
National Forest.

Map 9.5, grid c6, page 514

This campground claims one-half mile of shoreline along the north side of Lake Simtustus. Campsites here are shaded with juniper in an area of rolling hills and sagebrush. One section of the lake is accessible for water-skiing and personal watercraft. Simtustus is a trophy fishing lake for kokanee and rainbow, brown, and bull trout. Cove Palisades State Park, about 15 miles south, provides additional recreational opportunities. Watch for osprey and bald and golden eagles.

Campsites, facilities: There are 75 sites, 30 with partial hook-ups, for tents or RVs up to 40 feet long, one group site for up to 50 people, and two yurts. Drinking water, picnic tables, garbage service, and fire grills are provided. Restrooms, a restaurant, snack bar, small store, gasoline, and a picnic shelter with sinks and electric stoves are available. Also, a full-service marina with boat rentals, a boat launch, boat dock, fishing pier, swimming beach, volleyball courts, horseshoe pits, and a playground are available. Leashed pets are permitted.

Reservations, fees: Reservations at 541/475-0517. Sites are $14.50–20 per night; the group site is $65 per night; yurts are $20 per night. Major credit cards accepted. Open mid-April–October.

Directions: From Portland, drive south on U.S. 26 for 108 miles to the town of Warm Springs. Continue south two miles to Pelton Dam Road. Turn right and drive three miles to the campground on the right.

Contact: Portland General Electric, 121 S.W. Salmon St., P.O. Box 4438, Portland, OR 97204, 503/464-8515, fax 503/464-2944, website: www.portlandgeneral.com/parks.

101 PERRY SOUTH

Rating: 6

On Lake Billy Chinook in Deschutes
National Forest.

Map 9.5, grid d6, page 514

This campground is set near the shore of the Metolius arm of Lake Billy Chinook. The lake can get very crowded and noisy; it attracts powerboat/water-ski enthusiasts. See the description of KOA Madras/Culver (in this chapter) and Crooked River Ranch RV Park (see the Southern Cascades chapter) for recreation details. The lake borders the Warm Springs Indian Reservation.

Campsites, facilities: There are four tent sites and 59 sites for tents or RVs up to 40 feet long. Picnic tables, garbage service, and fire grills are provided. Drinking water, vault toilets, a fish-cleaning station, boat docks, and launching facilities are available. Some facilities are wheelchair accessible. Leashed pets are permitted.

Reservations, fees: Reservations are not accepted. Sites are $12–14 per night, $6–7 per extra vehicle. Senior discount available. Open May–September.

Directions: From Bend, drive north on U.S. 97 to Redmond, then continue north for 15 miles to the Culver Highway. Take the Culver Highway north to Culver, and continue two miles to Gem Lane. Turn left and drive two miles to Frazier Drive. Turn left and drive a short distance to Peck Road. Turn right and drive through Cove Palisades State Park to Jordan Road at the shore of Lake Billy Chinook. Turn left on Jordan Road and drive about 10 miles (over the bridge) to County Road 64. Continue (bearing left) and drive about eight miles to the campground entrance on the left (on the upper end of the Metolius Fork of Lake Billy Chinook).

Contact: Deschutes National Forest, Sisters Ranger District, P.O. Box 249, Sisters, OR 97759, 541/549-7700, fax 541/549-7746.

102 MONTY

Rating: 5

On the Metolius River in Deschutes
National Forest.

Map 9.5, grid d6, page 514

Trout fishing can be good at this remote campground along the banks of the Metolius River,
near where it empties into Lake Billy Chinook.
The camp gets light use. Warm Springs Indian Reservation is across the river.

Campsites, facilities: There are 20 sites for tents
or RVs up to 22 feet long. Picnic tables, garbage
service, and fire grills are provided. Firewood
and vault toilets are available. There is no drinking water. Boat docks and launching facilities
are nearby at Perry South. Leashed pets are
permitted.

Reservations, fees: Reservations are not accepted. Sites are $10 per night, $5 per extra
vehicle. Senior discount available. Open
May–September.

Directions: From Bend, drive north on U.S.
97 to Redmond and continue north for 15
miles to the Culver Highway. Take the Culver Highway north to Culver and continue
two miles to Gem Lane. Turn left and drive
two miles to Frazier Drive. Turn left and
drive a short distance to Peck Road. Turn
right and drive through Cove Palisades State
Park to Jordan Road at the shore of Lake
Billy Chinook. Turn left on Jordan Road and
drive about 10 miles (over the bridge) to
County Road 64. Turn left and drive about
13 miles to the campground entrance (on the
Metolius River above the headwaters of Lake
Billy Chinook). The last five miles are very
rough.

Contact: Deschutes National Forest, Sisters
Ranger District, P.O. Box 249, Sisters, OR
97759, 541/549-7700, fax 541/549-7746.

103 COVE PALISADES STATE PARK

Rating: 7

On Lake Billy Chinook.

Map 9.5, grid d6, page 514

This park is a mile away from the shore of
Lake Billy Chinook, where some lakeshore
cabins are available. Here in Oregon's high
desert region, the weather is sunny and warm
in the summer and chilly but generally mild
in the winter. Towering cliffs surround the
lake and about 10 miles of hiking trails crisscross the area. Two popular special events
are held here annually: Lake Billy Chinook
Day in September and the Eagle Watch in
February.

Campsites, facilities: There are 94 tent sites,
178 sites with full or partial hookups for RVs
up to 60 feet long, three cabins, and a group
area. Picnic tables and fire grills are provided. Drinking water, garbage bins, flush
toilets, an RV dump station, showers, firewood, a store, a restaurant, and ice are available. Some facilities are wheelchair accessible.
Boat docks, launching facilities, a marina,
and boat rentals are nearby. Leashed pets
are permitted.

Reservations, fees: Reservations at 800/452-
5687 or website: www.OregonStateParks.org
($7 reservation fee). Sites are $16–20 per night;
cabins are $65 per night; the group area is $60
per night; $7 per extra vehicle. Major credit
cards accepted. Open year-round.

Directions: From Bend, drive north on U.S.
97 for 13 miles to Redmond and continue
north for 15 miles to the Culver Highway.
Take the Culver Highway north to Culver and
continue two miles to Gem Lane. Turn left
and drive two miles to Frazier Drive. Turn
left and drive a short distance to Peck Road.
Turn right and drive to the park entrance.

Contact: Cove Palisades State Park, 7300 Jordan Rd., Culver, OR 97734, 800/551-6949 or
541/546-3412.

104 KOA MADRAS/CULVER

Rating: 6

Near Lake Billy Chinook.

Map 9.5, grid d7, page 514

This campground has a relaxing atmosphere, with some mountain views. It is set about three miles from Lake Billy Chinook, a steep-sided reservoir formed where the Crooked River, Metolius River, Deschutes River, and Squaw Creek all merge. Like much of the country east of the Cascades, this is a high desert area.

Campsites, facilities: There are 31 tent sites and 68 drive-through sites for RVs of any length. Electricity, drinking water, sewer hookups, and picnic tables are provided. Flush toilets, bottled gas, an RV dump station, showers, firewood, a recreation hall, a store, a laundry room, ice, a playground, and a swimming pool are available. Boat docks and launching facilities are nearby. Leashed pets are permitted.

Reservations, fees: Reservations at 800/562-1992. Sites are $19–30 per night, $2–4 per person for more than two people. Major credit cards accepted. Open year-round.

Directions: From Madras, drive south on U.S. 97 for nine miles to Jericho Lane. Turn east and drive one-half mile to the campground.

Contact: KOA Madras/Culver, S.W. Jericho Ln., Culver, OR 97734, 541/546-3046, fax 541/546-7972, website: www.koa.com.

COURTESY OF OREGON TOURISM COMMISSION

Chapter 10
Northeastern Oregon

Chapter 10—Northeastern Oregon

It might be difficult to believe that there are many places left in America that are little known and little traveled. Yet that is how it is in northeast Oregon. Even longtime residents often overlook this area of the Oregon (the same is true with the southeast portion of the state, detailed in Chapter 12). With its high desert abutting craggy Blue Mountains, it just doesn't look like the archetypal Oregon.

In this corner of the state you'll find Wallowa-Whitman National Forest and little-known sections of Umatilla, Malheur, and Ochoco National Forests. Idaho, the Snake River and the Hells Canyon National Recreation Area border this region to the east. My favorite destinations are the Wallowa Mountains and the Eagle Cap Wilderness, a wildlife paradise with deer, elk, bear, mountain lion, and bighorn sheep.

This region covers a huge swatch of land, most of it explored by few. But those few have learned to love for its unique qualities. Among the highlights are the John Day River and its headwaters, the Strawberry Mountain Wilderness in Malheur National Forest, and various sections of the linked John Day Fossil Beds National Monument. One of the prettiest spots in northeast Oregon is Wallowa Lake State Park, where 9,000-foot snowcapped mountains surround a pristine lake on three sides.

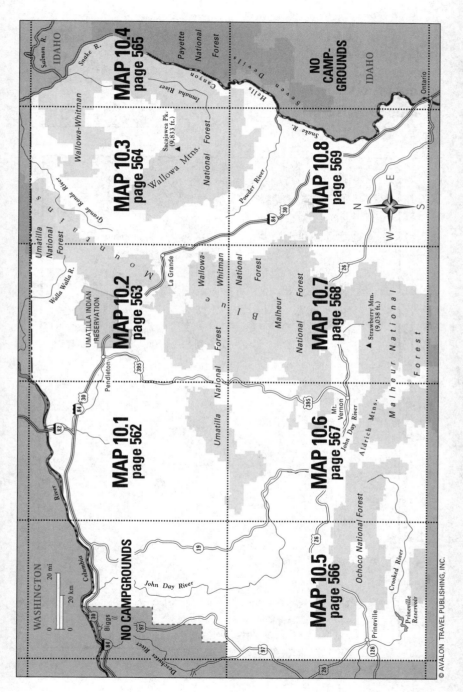

MAP 10.4
page 565

MAP 10.3
page 564

MAP 10.8
page 569

NO CAMP-
GROUNDS

IDAHO

Salmon R.

Snake R.

IDAHO

Payette National Forest

Wallowa-Whitman

Imnaha River

Seven Devils

Hells

Canyon

Snake R.

Ontario

Sacajawea Pk.
(9,833 ft.)

Wallowa Mtns.

National Forest

Powder River

Grande Ronde River

Umatilla National Forest

Walla Walla R.

MAP 10.2
page 563

La Grande

Wallowa-Whitman National Forest

Malheur National Forest

UMATILLA INDIAN RESERVATION

Pendleton

MAP 10.7
page 568

Strawberry Mtn.
(9,038 ft.)

Umatilla National Forest

Malheur National Forest

N
W   E
S

84   30

30

26

395

395

MAP 10.1
page 562

River

82

84 30

97 39 Biggs

WASHINGTON

20 mi

20 km

Columbia

NO CAMPGROUNDS

John Day River

19

MAP 10.6
page 567

Mt. Vernon

John Day River

Aldrich Mtns.

MAP 10.5
page 566

26

Ochoco National Forest

Crooked River

Prineville

Prineville Reservoir

126

97

26

Deschutes River

© AVALON TRAVEL PUBLISHING, INC.

Map 10.1

Campgrounds 1–6
Pages 570–572

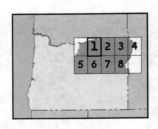

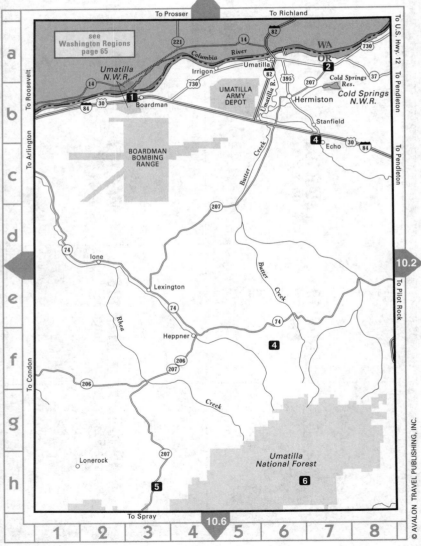

Map 10.2

Campgrounds 7–23
Pages 572–578

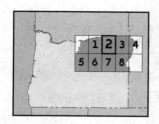

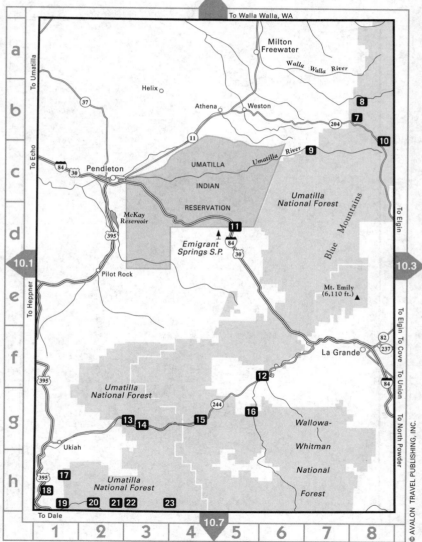

Map 10.3

Campgrounds 24–39
Pages 579–585

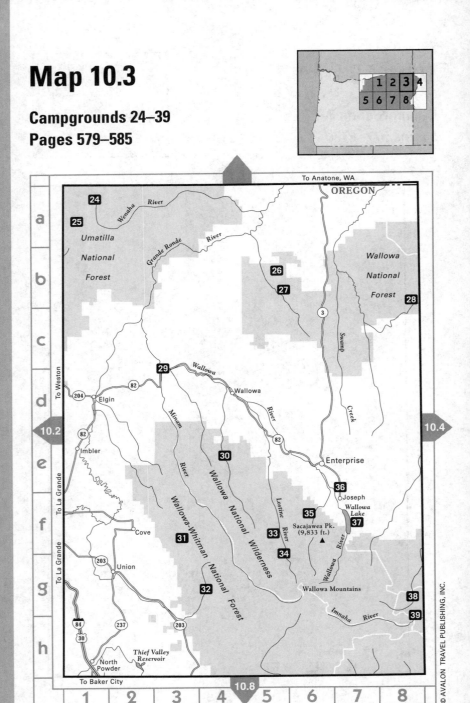

To Anatone, WA
OREGON

24

25

Wenaha River

Umatilla

National

Forest

Grande Ronde River

Wallowa

26

27

National

Forest

28

3

Swamp

Creek

29

Wallowa

82

204

To Weston

Elgin

Wallowa

River

82

Minam River

30

Enterprise

36

Joseph

Wallowa

Lake

37

82

Imbler

Wallowa National Wilderness

Lostine River

35

Sacajawea Pk.

(9,833 ft.)

To La Grande

Cove

31

33

34

Wallowa River

203

Union

Wallowa-Whitman National Forest

32

Wallowa Mountains

38

To La Grande

Imnaha River

39

84

30

237

203

Thief Valley

Reservoir

North

Powder

To Baker City

© AVALON TRAVEL PUBLISHING, INC.

Map 10.4

Campgrounds 40–46
Pages 585–587

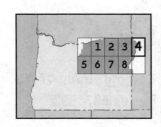

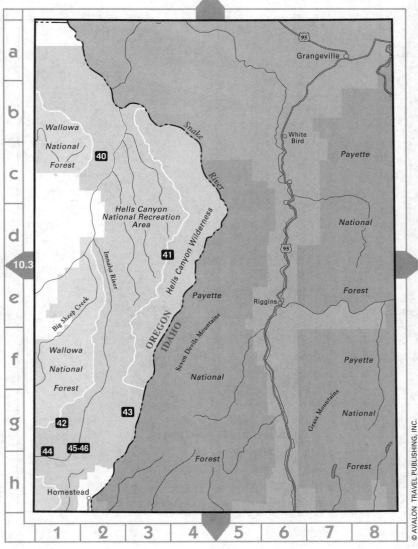

Grangeville

Wallowa

National

Forest

40

Snake

River

White
Bird

Payette

Hells Canyon
National Recreation
Area

Hells Canyon Wilderness

National

41

Imnaha River

95

Payette

Big Sheep Creek

Riggins

Forest

OREGON
IDAHO

Seven Devils Mountains

Wallowa

National

Forest

National

Payette

42

43

Grass Mountains

National

44 **45-46**

Forest

Forest

Homestead

10.3

© AVALON TRAVEL PUBLISHING, INC.

Map 10.5

Campgrounds 47–59
Pages 587–592

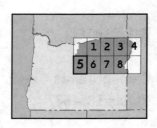

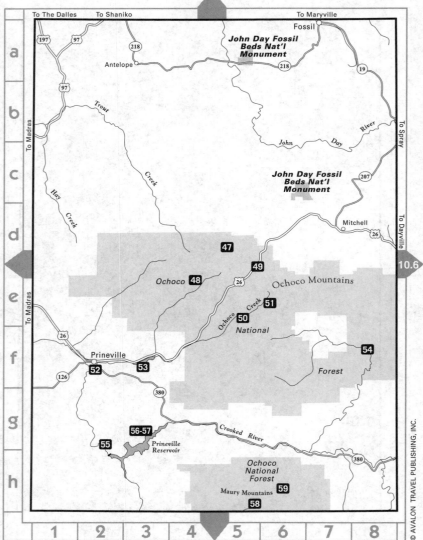

© AVALON TRAVEL PUBLISHING, INC.

Map 10.6

Campgrounds 60–66
Pages 592–595

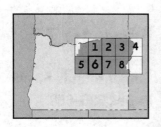

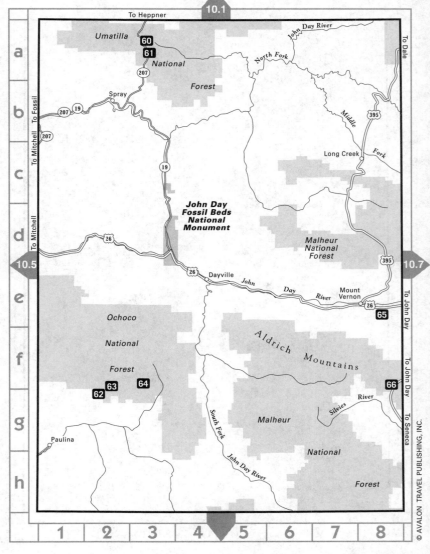

Map 10.7

Campgrounds 67–99
Pages 595–608

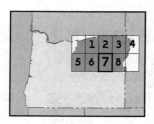

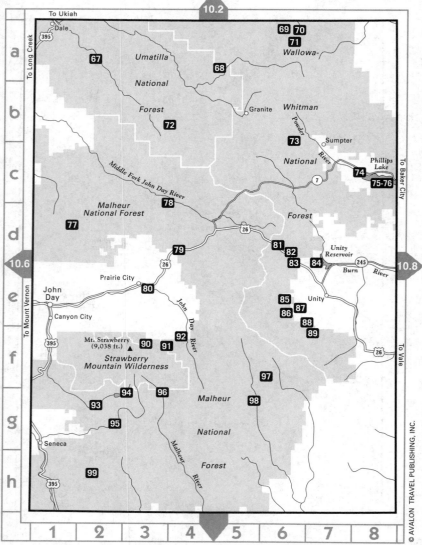

To Ukiah

Dale
395
To Long Creek

a 67
Umatilla

69 70
71
Wallowa-

68

b
National

Forest

72
Granite

Whitman

73
Sumpter

National

Phillips Lake
River
Powder

c
Middle Fork John Day River
74
75-76

Malheur
National Forest
78

Forest

d 77
26
79
81 82
Unity Reservoir
83 84
245
Burn
River

10.6
26
To Mount Vernon

e
Prairie City
80
John Day
Canyon City
85
86 87
Unity
88
89

10.8

f 395
Mt. Strawberry
(9,038 ft.)
90 91
92
John Day River
Strawberry Mountain Wilderness
97
26
To Vale

98

g
93
94
96
Malheur

95
National

Seneca
Forest

h 99
395
Malheur River

© AVALON TRAVEL PUBLISHING, INC.

10.2

Map 10.8

Campgrounds 100–109
Pages 608–611

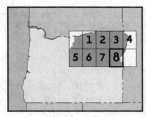

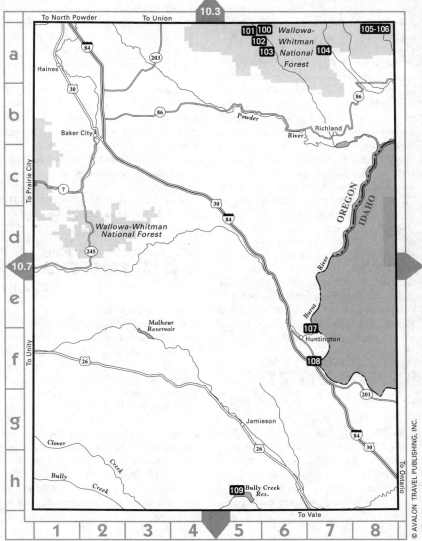

■ BOARDMAN MARINA PARK

🚲 🏊 🎣 � 🐕 🚐 ⛺

Rating: 7

On the Columbia River.
Map 10.1, grid b3, page 562

This campground is set near the Columbia River among maple, sycamore, and linden trees. In addition to fishing for bass, walleye, and crappie, nearby recreation options include a golf course, a marina, and tennis courts.

Campsites, facilities: There are 63 sites for tents or RVs of any length. Electricity, drinking water, and sewer hookups are available. Flush toilets, showers, fire grills, an RV dump station, garbage bins, coin-operated laundry facilities, a day-use area with picnic shelters, a pay phone, firewood for sale and a boat dock are available. A boat marina, gasoline, propane, ice, and a grocery store are available within one mile. Leashed pets are permitted.

Reservations, fees: Reservations at 888/481-7217 or website: www.visitboardman.com. Tent sites are $10 per night; RV sites are $20 per night; $2 per night for a third vehicle. Senior discount available. Open year-round.

Directions: From Portland on I-84 eastbound, drive 164 miles to Boardman and Exit 164. Take that exit and turn left (north) on Main Street. Drive one-half mile to the park on the left

Contact: Boardman Marina Park, No. 1 West Marine Dr., P.O. Box 8, Boardman, OR 97818, 541/481-7217, fax 541/481-2828.

■ HAT ROCK CAMPGROUND

🥾 🚲 🏊 🎣 🚐 🐕 🚐 ⛺

Rating: 7

Near the Columbia River.
Map 10.1, grid a7, page 562

This campground is not far from Hat Rock State Park, a day-use area with a boat launch along the banks of the Columbia River. The campground itself is very pretty, with lots of trees, and offers close access to the river and fishing.

Campsites, facilities: There are eight tent sites and 60 sites for RVs of any length, 30 with full and 30 with partial hookups. Electricity, drinking water, sewer hookups, and picnic tables are provided. Flush toilets, an RV dump station, showers, a store, a café, a laundry room, a swimming pool, and ice are available. Boat docks and launching facilities are nearby. Leashed pets are permitted.

Reservations, fees: Reservations at 541/567-4188 or 541/567-0917. Sites are $16 per night, $8 per night on Tuesdays and Wednesdays, and $2 per person for more than two people. Open year-round.

Directions: From Portland, drive east on U.S. 84 for roughly 170 miles past Boardman to the junction of U.S. 84 and U.S. 730. Turn northeast on U.S. 730 and drive 18 miles to the junction with I-82. Continue east on U.S. 730 for one mile to the state park access road. Turn left (north) and drive one-half mile to the park on the left.

Contact: Hat Rock Campground, 82280 Hat Rock Rd., Hermiston, OR 97838, 541/567-4188, or the Hat Rock Store, 541/567-0917.

■ FORT HENRIETTA RV PARK

🥾 🚲 🏊 🎣 🐕 ♿ 🚐 ⛺

Rating: 7

On the Umatilla River.
Map 10.1, grid c7, page 562

This park, located in the historic community of Echo, sits along the Umatilla River. The river provides some good trout fishing. The park provides a quiet, pleasant layover spot for travelers cruising I-84.

Campsites, facilities: There are seven sites, including some with full hookups and cable TV, for RVs and an area for dispersed tent camping. Drinking water, restrooms, showers, and an RV dump station are available. Some of the facilities are wheelchair accessible. The camp is within walking distance of two restaurants. Licensed, leashed pets are permitted.

Reservations, fees: Reservations are not accepted. Sites are $10–18 per night, $2 per person for more than two people. Open year-round.

Directions: From Pendleton, drive west on I-84 to Exit 188 and the Echo Highway. Take the exit, turn southeast, and drive one mile; cross the railroad tracks and drive to Dupont Street. Turn south and drive three-tenths of a mile to Main Street. Turn west and drive one block to the park on the left.

Contact: Echo City Hall, P.O. Box 9, Echo, OR 97826, 541/376-8411, fax 541/376-8218.

4 CUTSFORTH FOREST PARK

Rating: 8

On Willow Creek.

Map 10.1, grid f6, page 562

This county park is secluded and private. It's set beside a small, wheelchair-accessible pond in a quiet, wooded area. Trout fishing is available in the stocked ponds. Three of the campsites have corrals available. See the description of Anson Wright Memorial Park for details on the area.

Campsites, facilities: There are 35 sites for tents or RVs up to 30 feet long, including 22 sites with full hookups. Restrooms, showers, horseshoes, firewood, ice, and a playground are available. A large building with kitchen facilities is available for rent by groups. Some facilities are wheelchair accessible. Supplies are available in Heppner (22 miles away). Leashed pets are permitted.

Reservations, fees: Reservations at 541/989-9500. Sites are $6–12 per night, $2 per extra vehicle, and $5 for horse corrals. Open May 5–November 20, weather permitting.

Directions: From Pendleton on I-84, drive west for 27 miles to Exit 182 and Highway 207 (Heppner Highway). Turn south and drive 32 miles to Lexington and Highway 74. Turn left (southeast) on Highway 74 and drive 10 miles to Heppner. Continue south on Highway 207

for one-half mile to Willow Creek Road. Turn left on Willow Creek Road and drive 23 miles to the park.

Contact: Morrow County Public Works, P.O. Box 428, Lexington, OR 97839, 541/989-9500, fax 541/989-8352, website: www.heppner.net/parks/index.html.

5 ANSON WRIGHT MEMORIAL PARK

Rating: 7

On Rock Creek.

Map 10.1, grid h3, page 562

Set among wooded hills along a small stream, this county park offers visitors prime trout fishing in several stocked ponds as well as hiking opportunities. One of the fishing ponds is wheelchair accessible. Attractions in the area include the Pendleton Mills, Emigrant Springs State Park, Hardman Ghost Town (10 miles away), and the Columbia River. There's also a nearby opal mine.

Campsites, facilities: There are 34 sites for tents or RVs up to 30 feet long, including 24 sites with full hookups. Restrooms, showers, a barbecue, firewood, ice, and a playground are provided. Some facilities are wheelchair accessible. Leashed pets are permitted.

Reservations, fees: Reservations at 541/989-9500, $6–12 per night, $2 for additional vehicle. Open late spring–early fall.

Directions: From Pendleton, drive west on I-84 for 27 miles to Exit 182 and Highway 207 (Heppner Highway). Turn south and drive 32 miles to Lexington and Highway 74. Turn left (south) and drive 10 miles to Heppner. Continue south on Highway 207 for 11 miles to Ruggs and a fork. Bear left at the fork (still Highway 207) and drive 12 miles to the park on the right.

Contact: Morrow County Public Works, P.O. Box 428, Lexington, OR 97839, 541/989-9500, fax 541/989-8352, website: www.heppner.net/parks/index.html.

6 DIVIDE WELL

Rating: 5

In Umatilla National Forest.
Map 10.1, grid h7, page 562

This is a primitive campground, but it is busy in the summer, even occasionally used for reunions. Set at 4,700 feet elevation, it can serve as a good base camp for a hunting trip. Mule deer and Rocky Mountain elk can be spotted in the surrounding ponderosa pine and fir forest. Potamus Point Scenic Overlook, offering a spectacular view of the John Day River drainage, is 11 miles south of the camp on Forest Road 5316.

Campsites, facilities: There are 11 primitive tent sites and three primitive group sites. Picnic tables and a vault toilet are provided, but there is no drinking water. Pack out all garbage. Leashed pets are permitted.

Reservations, fees: Reservations are not accepted. There is no fee for camping. Open March–November.

Directions: From Pendleton, drive south on U.S. 395 for 48 miles to Ukiah and Highway 244. Turn right (the road becomes Forest Road 53) and drive west on Forest Road 53 for about 14 miles to Forest Road 5327. Turn south and drive seven miles to the campground. A U.S. Forest Service map is recommended.

Contact: Umatilla National Forest, North Fork John Day Ranger District, P.O. Box 158, Ukiah, OR 97880, 541/427-3231, fax 541/276-5026.

7 TARGET MEADOWS

Rating: 6

Near the South Fork of the Walla Walla River in Umatilla National Forest.
Map 10.2, grid b8, page 563

This quiet campground with shady sites and a sunny meadow is set at 4,800 feet elevation and is adjacent to the Burnt Cabin Trailhead, which leads to the South Fork of the Walla Walla River. An old military site can be viewed here.

Campsites, facilities: There are 19 sites for tents or RVs. Drinking water, picnic tables, and fire grills are provided. Garbage bins and vault toilets are available. Leashed pets are permitted.

Reservations, fees: Reservations are not accepted. Sites are $10 per night, $5 per night for an additional vehicle. Senior discount available. Open mid-June–mid-November, weather permitting.

Directions: From Pendleton, drive north on Highway 11 for 16 miles to Highway 204 near Weston. Turn east on Highway 204 and drive 17.5 miles to Forest Road 64. Turn left and drive one-half mile to Forest Road 6401. Turn left (north) and drive two miles to Road 6401-050. Turn right (north) and drive one-half mile to the camp.

Contact: Umatilla National Forest, Walla Walla Ranger District, 1415 W. Rose St., Walla Walla, WA 99362, 509/522-6290, fax 509/522-6000.

8 WOODWARD

Rating: 7

Near Langdon Lake in Umatilla National Forest.
Map 10.2, grid b8, page 563

Nestled among the trees at an elevation of 4,950 feet, with some privacy screening between campsites, this popular campground has a view of Langdon Lake (though campers do not have access to the private lake). A flat trail circles the camp.

Campsites, facilities: There are 18 sites for tents or RVs. Drinking water, picnic tables, garbage bins, fire grills, and wheelchair-accessible vault toilets are provided. A picnic shelter is available. Leashed pets are permitted.

Reservations, fees: Reservations are not accepted. Sites are $10 per night, $5 per night for an additional vehicle. Open mid-June–mid-September.

Directions: From Pendleton on I-84, turn north on Highway 11 and drive approximately 27 miles to Weston and Highway 204. Turn east on Highway 204 and drive 17 miles to the campground along the highway (near Langdon Lake).
Contact: Umatilla National Forest, Walla Walla Ranger District, 1415 W. Rose St., Walla Walla, WA 99362, 509/525-6290, fax 509/522-6000.

9 UMATILLA FORKS

Rating: 3

Along the Umatilla River in Umatilla National Forest.

Map 10.2, grid c7, page 563

From mid- to late summer, it can get very warm at this camp. Set in a canyon between the South and North Forks of the Umatilla River, it has some tree cover, but little privacy between sites. It sits at an elevation of 2,400 feet. Fishing (catch-and-release only) and hiking in the North Fork Umatilla Wilderness are popular nearby activities from early spring to late fall.
Campsites, facilities: There are nine tent sites and five sites that can accommodate tents or RVs. Drinking water, picnic tables, fire grills, and vault toilets are provided. No garbage service provided. Leashed pets are permitted.
Reservations, fees: Reservations are not accepted. Sites are $5 per night, $5 per night for additional vehicle. Senior discount available. Open April–October.
Directions: From Pendleton, drive north on Highway 11 for about 25 miles to Athena and Pambrun Road. Turn right on Pambrun Road and drive five miles to Spring Hollow Road. Turn left on Spring Hollow Road (it becomes Thorn Hollow Road) and drive about 6.5 miles to Bingham Road (River Road). Turn left on Bingham Road (River Road), cross the railroad tracks, and follow signs for about five miles to Gibbon. Cross the railroad tracks at Gibbon and continue on Bingham Road (it becomes Forest Road 32) about 11 miles to the campground on the right.

Contact: Umatilla National Forest, Walla Walla Ranger District, 1415 W. Rose St., Walla Walla, WA 99362, 509/522-6290, fax 509/522-6000.

10 WOODLAND

Rating: 4

In Umatilla National Forest.

Map 10.2, grid c8, page 563

This primitive camp with easy highway access— and related road noise—can be a perfect spot for I-84 cruisers looking for a short detour. Both shaded and sunny sites are available. It is popular with hunters during the fall. See a U.S. Forest Service map for details about the recreation options within driving distance.
Campsites, facilities: There are six sites for tents or RVs. Picnic tables, fire grills, and vault toilets are provided, but there is no drinking water. No garbage facilities are provided, so campers must pack out their own trash. Leashed pets are permitted.
Reservations, fees: Reservations are not accepted. Sites are $5 per night. Open mid-June–mid-November, weather permitting.
Directions: From Pendleton, drive north on Highway 11 for 16 miles to Highway 204 near Weston. Turn east on Highway 204 and drive 23 miles. The campground is just off the highway on the left.
Contact: Umatilla National Forest, Walla Walla Ranger District, 1415 W. Rose St., Walla Walla, WA 99362, 509/522-6290, fax 509/522-6000.

11 EMIGRANT SPRINGS STATE HERITAGE AREA

Rating: 7

Near the Umatilla Indian Reservation.

Map 10.2, grid d5, page 563

Perched near the summit of the Blue Mountains, Emigrant Springs provides an opportunity to explore a popular pioneer stopover along the Oregon Trail. The park is nestled in an old-growth forest, lush with flora and teeming with native wildlife. You can explore nearby attractions, such as the Blue Mountain Crossing Oregon Trail interpretive park or the Pendleton Woolen Mills and underground tours.

Campsites, facilities: There are 33 tent sites, 18 sites with full hookups for RVs up to 60 feet long, a designated horse camp, and eight cabins. Picnic tables and fire grills are provided. Drinking water, garbage bins, flush toilets, showers, firewood, a laundry room, some horse facilities, a community building with a kitchen, a basketball court, an amphitheater, and a baseball field are available. Leashed pets are permitted.

Reservations, fees: Reservations at 800/452-5687 or website: www.oregonstateparks.org ($7 reservation fee). Sites are $15–17 per night, cabins $20–35 per night, and horse campsites are $15 per night and $1.50 per horse; $7 per night per extra vehicle. Major credit cards accepted. Open year-round for cabins and four tent sites. Full operations are open mid-April–October.

Directions: From Pendleton, drive southeast on I-84 for 26 miles to Exit 234. Take that exit to Old Oregon Trail Road (frontage road) and drive one-half mile to the park on the right.

Contact: Emigrant Springs State Heritage Area, P.O. Box 85, Meacham, OR 97859, 541/983-2277.

12 BIRD TRACK SPRINGS

Rating: 7

Near the Grande Ronde River in Wallowa-Whitman National Forest.

Map 10.2, grid f5, page 563

Set at an elevation of 3,100 feet about a five-minute walk from the Grande Ronde River, this campground has open, spacious sites right off the highway. The surrounding woods are primarily Douglas and white fir. The Bird Track Springs Interpretive Springs Trail provides a hiking option.

Campsites, facilities: There are 16 sites for tents.

Picnic tables, garbage service (summer only), and fire rings are provided. Drinking water and wheelchair-accessible vault toilets are available. A camp host is on-site. Leashed pets are permitted.

Reservations, fees: Reservations are not accepted. Sites are $8 per night. Senior discount available. Open mid-May–November, weather permitting.

Directions: From Pendleton, drive southeast on U.S. 84 for 42 miles to Highway 244. Turn southwest and drive 13 miles to the campground on the left.

Contact: Wallowa-Whitman National Forest, La-Grande Ranger District, 3502 Hwy. 30, La-Grande, OR 97850, 541/963-7186, fax 541/962-8580.

13 LANE CREEK

Rating: 4

On Camas Creek in Umatilla National Forest.

Map 10.2, grid g2, page 563

This campground is set at 3,850 feet elevation along Camas Creek and Lane Creek, just inside the forest boundary, and provides easy access to all the amenities of town. It's a popular stop for overnighters passing through. Some of the sites close to the highway get traffic noise. Highlights include hot springs (privately owned) and good hunting and fishing. A U.S. Forest Service map details the back roads.

Campsites, facilities: There are eight sites for tents or RVs up to 45 feet long and one group site. Picnic tables, garbage bins, and fire grills are provided. Vault toilets are available. No drinking water is provided. Leashed pets are permitted.

Reservations, fees: Reservations are not accepted. Sites are $5 per night, $10 for the group site. Senior discount available. Open May–November.

Directions: From Pendleton, drive south on U.S. 395 for 50 miles to Ukiah and Highway 244. Turn east on Highway 244 and drive nine miles to the campground.

Contact: Umatilla National Forest, North Fork John Day Ranger District, P.O. Box 158, Ukiah, OR 97880, 541/427-3231, fax 541/276-5026.

14 BEAR WALLOW CREEK

Rating: 5

On Bear Wallow Creek in Umatilla National Forest.

Map 10.2, grid g3, page 563

Set near the confluence of Bear Wallow and Camus Creeks at an elevation of 3,900 feet, this camp is one of three off Highway 244. The others are Lane Creek and Frazier. Quiet and primitive, the camp is used primarily in the summer. A three-quarter-mile interpretive trail highlighting the steelhead habitat meanders next to Bear Wallow Creek. The trail is wheelchair accessible.

Campsites, facilities: There are eight sites for tents or RVs up to 30 feet long and one group site. No drinking water is available, and garbage bins are provided in the summer only. Picnic tables and fire grills are provided. Vault toilets are available. Some facilities are wheelchair accessible. Leashed pets are permitted.

Reservations, fees: Reservations are not accepted. Sites are $5 per night, with a 14-day stay limit; the group site is $10 per night. Senior discount available. Open March–November.

Directions: From Pendleton, drive south on U.S. 395 for 50 miles to Ukiah and Highway 244. Turn east on Highway 244 and drive 10 miles to the camp.

Contact: Umatilla National Forest, North Fork John Day Ranger District, P.O. Box 158, Ukiah, OR 97880, 541/427-3231, fax 541/276-5026.

15 FRAZIER

Rating: 5

On Frazier Creek in Umatilla National Forest.

Map 10.2, grid g4, page 563

This campground, set at 4,300 feet elevation along the banks of Frazier Creek, is a popu-

lar hunting area that also has some fishing. It's advisable to obtain a map of Umatilla National Forest. With nearly 100 miles of ATV and motorcycle trails at the nearby Winom-Frazier Off-Highway-Vehicle Complex, this camp is popular in the summer with the ATV crowd. On weekends, it's not a good spot for the traditional camper looking for quiet and solitude. Lehman Hot Springs, one mile away, provides a side-trip option.

Campsites, facilities: There are 18 sites for tents or RVs up to 30 feet long and some group sites. Picnic tables, fire grills, a picnic shelter, and vault toilets are available. Drinking water and garbage bins are available only in summer. Some facilities are wheelchair accessible. An ATV loading ramp is available. Leashed pets are permitted.

Reservations, fees: Reservations are not accepted. Sites are $5 per night; group sites are $10 per night. Senior discount available. Open May–November.

Directions: From Pendleton, drive south on U.S. 395 for 50 miles to Ukiah and Highway 244. Turn east on Highway 244 and drive 18 miles to Forest Road 5226. Turn south and drive one-half mile to the campground.

Contact: Umatilla National Forest, North Fork John Day Ranger District, P.O. Box 158, Ukiah, OR 97880, 541/427-3231, fax 541/276-5026.

16 SPOOL CART

Rating: 6

On the Grande Ronde River in Wallowa-Whitman National Forest.

Map 10.2, grid g5, page 563

This campground, set at 3,500 feet elevation on the banks of the Grande Ronde River, gets its name from the large cable spools that were left on a cart here for some years. The sites are fully wheelchair accessible. Hilgard Junction State Park to the north provides numerous recreation options, and the Oregon Trail Interpretive Park is nearby. This camp

Chapter 10 • Northeastern Oregon   575

is popular with hunters in the fall. It's advisable to obtain a map of Wallowa-Whitman National Forest, which details the back roads and other side trips.

Campsites, facilities: There are 16 sites for tents or RVs up to 22 feet long. Picnic tables and fire grills are provided. Firewood and vault toilets are available. There is no drinking water, and all garbage must be packed out. Leashed pets are permitted.

Reservations, fees: Reservations are not accepted. Sites are $8 per night. Senior discount available. Open late May–late November.

Directions: From Pendleton, drive southeast on U.S. 84 for 42 miles to Highway 244. Turn southwest and drive 13 miles to Forest Road 51. Turn south and drive seven miles to the campground on the right.

Contact: Wallowa-Whitman National Forest, LaGrande Ranger District, 3502 Hwy. 30, LaGrande, OR 97850, 541/963-7186, fax 541/962-8580.

17 DRIFT FENCE

Rating: 5

Near Ross Springs in Umatilla National Forest.

Map 10.2, grid h1, page 563

Get this: It's not marked on the Umatilla National Forest Map. Hunting is a highlight at this campground with some elk and deer in the area. The camp, set at 4,250 feet elevation, is adjacent to Blue Mountain National Forest Scenic Byway. The Bridge Creek Interpretive Trail, three miles northwest of the campground off Forest Road 52, leads to a beautiful view of open meadow with various wildflowers and wildlife. Elk may be seen roaming in the Bridge Creek area.

Campsites, facilities: There are six sites for tents or RVs up to 16 feet long. There is no drinking water, and all garbage must be packed out. A vault toilet and picnic tables are available. Leashed pets are permitted.

Reservations, fees: Reservations are not accepted. There is no fee for camping. Open May–November.

Directions: From Pendleton, drive south on U.S. 395 for 50 miles to Highway 244. Turn east on Highway 244 and drive one mile to Ukiah and Forest Road 52. Turn south on Forest Road 52 and drive eight miles to the campground on the right.

Contact: Umatilla National Forest, North Fork John Day Ranger District, P.O. Box 158, Ukiah, OR 97880, 541/427-3231, fax 541/276-5026.

18 UKIAH-DALE FOREST STATE SCENIC CORRIDOR

Rating: 7

Near the North Fork of the John Day River.

Map 10.2, grid h1, page 563

Fishing is a prime activity at this Camas Creek campground, set at an elevation of 3,140 feet near the banks of the North Fork of the John Day River. It's a good layover for visitors cruising U.S. 395 looking for a spot for the night. Emigrant Springs State Park near Pendleton is a possible side trip.

Campsites, facilities: There are 28 primitive sites for tents or self-contained RVs up to 50 feet long. Picnic tables and fire pits are provided. Drinking water, firewood, and flush toilets are available. Leashed pets are permitted.

Reservations, fees: Reservations are not accepted. Sites are $10 per night, $7 per additional vehicle. Open mid-April–late October.

Directions: From Pendleton, drive south on U.S. 395 for 50 miles to Highway 244 (near Ukiah). Continue south on U.S. 395 for three miles to the park.

Contact: Emigrant Springs State Heritage Area, P.O. Box 85, Meacham, OR 97859, 800/551-6949, or Emigrant Springs State Park, 541/983-2277.

19 TOLLBRIDGE

Rating: 4

On the North Fork of the John Day River in Umatilla National Forest.

Map 10.2, grid h1, page 563

This small, secluded campground (elevation 3,800 feet) lies at the confluence of Desolation Creek and the North Fork of the John Day River and is adjacent to the Bridge Creek Wildlife Area. It can be beautiful or ugly, depending upon which direction you look. It's dusty in the summer, and there's sparse tree cover. Hunting and fishing are two options here. Look for the geological interpretive sign in the camp.

Campsites, facilities: There are seven sites for tents or RVs up to 31 feet long. Picnic tables and fire grills are provided. Drinking water and a vault toilet are available, but all garbage must be packed out. Leashed pets are permitted.

Reservations, fees: Reservations are not accepted. Sites are $5 per night, with a 14-day stay limit. Senior discount available. Open May–November.

Directions: From Pendleton, drive south on U.S. 395 for 50 miles to the intersection with Highway 244. Continue south on U.S. 395 for 18 miles to Forest Road 55 (one mile north of Dale). Turn left and drive one-half mile southeast to Forest Road 10 and the campground access road. Drive a short distance to the campground.

Contact: Umatilla National Forest, North Fork John Day Ranger District, P.O. Box 158, Ukiah, OR 97880, 541/427-3231, fax 541/276-5026.

20 GOLD DREDGE CAMP

Rating: 7

On the North Fork of the John Day River in Umatilla National Forest.

Map 10.2, grid h2, page 563

Hunting and fishing are among the recreation possibilities at this campground along the banks of the North Fork of the John Day River, a federally certified Wild and Scenic River. Dredge tailings from old mining activity are visible from the camp. By traveling to the end of Forest Road 5506, you have access to a trail that heads into the adjacent North Fork John Day Wilderness.

Campsites, facilities: There are six sites for tents or RVs. No drinking water or fire grills are provided, but vault toilets and picnic tables are available. All garbage must be packed out. Leashed pets are permitted.

Reservations, fees: Reservations are not accepted. There is no fee for camping. Open May–November.

Directions: From Pendleton, drive south on U.S. 395 for 62 miles to Forest Road 55 (one mile north of Dale). Turn left and drive six miles to the crossroads. Continue east on Forest Road 5506 for 2.5 miles to the campground. Note: The last two miles of road are very rough.

Contact: Umatilla National Forest, North Fork John Day Ranger District, P.O. Box 158, Ukiah, OR 97880, 541/427-3231, fax 541/276-5026.

21 DRIFTWOOD

Rating: 6

On the North Fork of the John Day River in Umatilla National Forest.

Map 10.2, grid h2, page 563

This tiny campground with ponderosa pine and Douglas fir cover sits on the banks of the North Fork of the John Day River at an elevation of 3,855 feet. Recreational opportunities include hunting, fishing, swimming, rafting, and float tubing. Driftwood is similar to Gold Dredge Campground.

Campsites, facilities: There are five sites for tents or RVs. Fire grills and picnic tables are provided. A vault toilet is available. No drinking water is available. All garbage must be packed out. Leashed pets are permitted.

Reservations, fees: Reservations are not accepted. There is no fee for camping. Open March–November.

Directions: From Pendleton, drive south on U.S. 395 for 62 miles to Forest Road 55 (one mile north of Dale; it's easier to find if you know the marker, Texas Bar Road). Turn left and drive six miles to the crossroads. Continue east on Forest Road 5506 for one mile to the campground. Note: The last two miles of road are very rough.

Contact: Umatilla National Forest, North Fork John Day Ranger District, P.O. Box 158, Ukiah, OR 97880, 541/427-3231, fax 541/276-5026.

22 ORIENTAL CREEK

Rating: 4

On the North Fork of the John Day River in Umatilla National Forest.

Map 10.2, grid h3, page 563

This campground is set in a stand of mixed conifer at 3,500 feet elevation along the banks of the North Fork of the John Day River and is popular with horse campers. Evidence of old mining activity is visible here. Nearby trails provide access to the North Fork John Day Wilderness. Hunting and fishing are two possible activities here. No motorbikes are permitted in the wilderness area. Be advised that the road into this campground is rough and narrow in places.

Campsites, facilities: There are seven primitive tent sites. Pit toilets and picnic tables are available, but there is no drinking water. All garbage must be packed out. One toilet is wheelchair accessible. Leashed pets are permitted.

Reservations, fees: Reservations are not accepted. There is no fee for camping. Open May–November.

Directions: From Pendleton, drive south on U.S. 395 for 62 miles to Forest Road 55 (one mile north of Dale; it's easier to find if you know the marker, Texas Bar Road). Turn left and drive six miles to the crossroads. Continue east on Forest Road 5506 for six miles to

the campground. This road is rough and not recommended for trailers.

Contact: Umatilla National Forest, North Fork John Day Ranger District, P.O. Box 158, Ukiah, OR 97880, 541/427-3231, fax 541/276-5026.

23 WINOM CREEK

Rating: 2

On Winom Creek in Umatilla National Forest.

Map 10.2, grid h4, page 563

This campground has access to the Winom-Frazier ATV Trail Complex, 140 miles of ATV trails of varying difficulty. It was developed in the late 1980s for ATV enthusiasts. Check the campground bulletin boards for detailed maps of the terrain. The camp is also near the North Fork John Day Wilderness. Note that a fire during the 1990s burned part of the campground and surrounding area, but with the arrival of the new century, it is beginning to green up again.

Campsites, facilities: There are five sites for tents or RVs and three group sites. Picnic tables and fire rings are provided. Vault toilets and an ATV loading ramp are available. There is no drinking water, and garbage must be packed out. Two of the group sites have picnic shelters. Some facilities are wheelchair accessible.

Reservations, fees: Reservations are not accepted. There is no fee for camping. Open May–November, weather permitting.

Directions: From Pendleton, drive south on U.S. 395 for 50 miles to Highway 244. Turn east on Highway 244 and drive one mile to Ukiah and Forest Road 52. Turn south on Forest Road 52 and drive 20 miles to Forest Road 440. Turn right and drive one mile to the campground on the right. The last mile of the access road is narrow and steep.

Contact: Umatilla National Forest, North Fork John Day Ranger District, P.O. Box 158, Ukiah, OR 97880, 541/427-3231, fax 541/276-5026.

24 MOTTET

Rating: 6

Near the South Fork of the Walla Walla River in Umatilla National Forest.
Map 10.3, grid a1, page 564

This campground is set at 5,200 feet elevation along a ridge top in a heavily timbered forest. A trailhead leads down to the South Fork of the Walla Walla River. Far from the beaten path, it's quite primitive and relatively unknown, so you're almost guaranteed privacy.

Campsites, facilities: There is one site for tents and five sites for RVs. Picnic tables and fire grills are provided. Spring water and vault toilets are available. Trash must be packed out; no garbage facilities are provided. Leashed pets are permitted.

Reservations, fees: Reservations are not accepted. Sites are $5 per night. Senior discount available. Open late June–November, weather permitting.

Directions: From Pendleton, drive north on Highway 11 for 16 miles to Highway 204 near Weston. Turn east on Highway 204 and drive 17.5 miles to Forest Road 64. Turn left and drive about 15 miles on Forest Road 64 to Forest Road 6403. Turn left and drive about two miles to the campground on the left. The road is rough for the last 1.5 miles.

Contact: Umatilla National Forest, Walla Walla Ranger District, 1415 W. Rose St., Walla Walla, WA 99362, 509/522-6290, fax 509/522-6000.

25 JUBILEE LAKE

Rating: 8

On Jubilee Lake in Umatilla National Forest.
Map 10.3, grid a1, page 564

This campground along the shore of 90-acre Jubilee Lake (elevation 4,800 feet) is a good area for swimming, fishing, and hiking. The largest and most popular campground in Umatilla National Forest, it fills up on weekends and

holidays. Nonmotorized boats are permitted. A 2.8-mile trail loops around the lake and provides different levels of accessibility for people with disabilities. Fishing access is available along the trail.

Campsites, facilities: There are four sites for tents and 47 sites for tents or RVs up to 27 feet long, with some drive-through sites. Picnic tables and fire grills are provided. Drinking water, firewood, four picnic areas, and flush toilets are available. Some facilities are barrier-free. Boat docks and launching facilities are nearby. Leashed pets are permitted. Garbage service is provided during the summer.

Reservations, fees: Reservations are not accepted. Sites are $14 per night, plus $5 for each additional vehicle. Senior discount available. Open mid-June–mid-October.

Directions: From Pendleton, drive north on Highway 11 for 16 miles to Highway 204 near Weston. Turn east on Highway 204 and drive 17.5 miles to Forest Road 64. Turn left and drive 12 miles northeast to Forest Road 250. Turn south and drive less than one-half mile to the camp.

Contact: Umatilla National Forest, Walla Walla Ranger District, 1415 W. Rose St., Walla Walla, WA 99362, 509/522-6290, fax 509/522-6000.

26 DOUGHERTY SPRINGS

Rating: 5

Near Dougherty Springs in Wallowa-Whitman National Forest.
Map 10.3, grid b5, page 564

This wooded, primitive campground (elevation 5,100 feet) adjacent to Dougherty Springs is one in a series of remote camps set near natural springs. This camp is in an open area with sparse Douglas and white fir. Deer, elk, birds, and small mammals can be seen in the area. Hells Canyon National Recreation Area to the east provides many recreation options.

Campsites, facilities: There are 12 sites for tents or RVs up to 22 feet long. Picnic tables and fire grills are provided. Vault toilets are available, but there is no drinking water, and all garbage must be packed out. Leashed pets are permitted.

Reservations, fees: Reservations are not accepted. There is no fee for camping. Open June–late November.

Directions: From LaGrande, drive northeast on Highway 82 for 62 miles to Enterprise and Highway 3. Turn north on Highway 3 and drive 15 miles to Forest Road 46. Turn northeast and drive 30 miles to the campground.

Contact: Hells Canyon National Recreation Area, Wallowa Mountains Visitor Center, 88401 Hwy. 82, Enterprise, OR 97828, 541/426-5546.

27 COYOTE

Rating: 4

Near Coyote Springs in Wallowa-Whitman National Forest.

Map 10.3, grid b5, page 564

This campground, set at 4,800 feet elevation and adjacent to Coyote Springs, is the largest of the three primitive camps in the vicinity, offering open sites and privacy.

Campsites, facilities: There are 12 sites for tents or RVs up to 22 feet long. Picnic tables and fire grills are provided. Vault toilets are available, but there is no drinking water, and all garbage must be packed out. A spring is within one-quarter mile. Leashed pets are permitted.

Reservations, fees: Reservations are not accepted. There is no fee for camping. Open mid-May–December.

Directions: From LaGrande, drive northeast on Highway 82 for 62 miles to Enterprise and Highway 3. Turn north on Highway 3 and drive 15 miles to Forest Road 46. Turn northeast and drive 25 miles to the campground.

Contact: Wallowa-Whitman National Forest, Wallowa Valley Ranger District, Wallowa Mountains Visitor Center, 88401 Hwy. 82, Enterprise, OR 97828, 541/426-5546.

28 VIGNE

Rating: 5

On Chesnimnus Creek in Wallowa-Whitman National Forest.

Map 10.3, grid b8, page 564

This campground, set at 3,500 feet elevation along the banks of Chesnimus Creek, has pretty riverside sites shaded by Douglas and white fir. Fishing, along with exploring a few of the many hiking trails in the area, is a recreation possibility here. See a U.S. Forest Service map for details.

Campsites, facilities: There are seven sites for tents or RVs up to 22 feet long. Picnic tables and fire grills are provided. Drinking water and vault toilets are available. All garbage must be packed out. Leashed pets are permitted.

Reservations, fees: Reservations are not accepted. Sites are $5 per night. Senior discount available. Open mid-April–late November.

Directions: From LaGrande, drive northeast on Highway 82 for 62 miles to Enterprise and Highway 3. Turn north on Highway 3 and drive 15 miles to Forest Road 46. Turn northeast and drive 10 miles to Forest Road 4625. Turn east and drive 10 miles to the campground.

Contact: Wallowa-Whitman National Forest, Wallowa Valley Ranger District, Wallowa Mountains Visitor Center, 88401 Hwy. 82, Enterprise, OR 97828, 541/426-5546.

29 MINAM STATE PARK

Rating: 7

Near the Grande Ronde River.

Map 10.3, grid c3, page 564

In a remote, steep valley, this park has a landscape dominated by large pine trees. The Wallowa River flows through the park and is noted for its fishing and rafting, especially for spring and fall steelhead fishing. Wildlife is abundant, including deer, elk, bear, cougar, and occasionally, mountain sheep downriver. The park is small and pretty, well worth the detour off I-84 necessary to get here.

Campsites, facilities: There are 12 primitive sites for tents or self-contained RVs up to 71 feet long. Picnic tables and fire grills are provided. Drinking water is available May 1–October 15. Garbage bins and vault toilets are available. Raft rentals are available nearby. Leashed pets are permitted.

Reservations, fees: Reservations are not accepted. Sites are $7–10 per night, $7 per night for an additional vehicle. Open year-round.

Directions: From LaGrande, drive northeast on Highway 82 for 18 miles to Elgin, then continue 14 miles to the park entrance road. Turn left (north) and drive two miles to the park.

Contact: Wallowa Lake State Park, 72214 Marina Ln., Joseph, OR 97846, 541/432-8855 or 800/551-6949.

30 BOUNDARY

Rating: 6

Near the Eagle Cap Wilderness in Wallowa-Whitman National Forest.
Map 10.3, grid e4, page 564

This pretty and primitive campground is set 100 yards from the banks of Bear Creek at 3,600 feet elevation and is heavily wooded with tamarack, Douglas, red, and white fir. Nearby trails provide access to the Eagle Cap Wilderness. This is another in a series of little-known, primitive sites in the area.

Campsites, facilities: There are eight primitive tent sites. Picnic tables and fire rings are provided. Vault toilets are available. There is no drinking water and all garbage must be packed out. Leashed pets are permitted.

Reservations, fees: Reservations are not accepted. There is no fee for camping. Open mid-June–November.

Directions: From LaGrande, drive north on Highway 82 for 46 miles to Wallowa and Forest Road 8250. Turn south and drive eight miles to Forest Road 8250-040. Turn

south and drive three-quarters of a mile to the camp.

Contact: Wallowa-Whitman National Forest, Eagle Cap Ranger District, Wallowa Mountains Visitor Center, 88401 Hwy. 82, Enterprise, OR 97828, 541/426-5546.

31 MOSS SPRINGS

Rating: 7

Near the Eagle Cap Wilderness in Wallowa-Whitman National Forest.
Map 10.3, grid f3, page 564

At 5,400 feet elevation, this campground has good views of the Grande Ronde Valley. A trailhead at this camp provides access to the Eagle Cap Wilderness, a good jump-off point for a multi-day backpacking trip. Obtain a map of Wallowa-Whitman National Forest for detailed trail information. This camp is also a popular spot with horse packers. A loading ramp is provided. The Bieshears OHV Trail and the Mt. Fanny Mountain Bike Trail are just north of the camp.

Campsites, facilities: There are 12 sites for tents and RVs. Picnic tables and fire grills are provided. No drinking water is provided, but water is available for stock. Horse facilities and wheelchair-accessible vault toilets are available. All garbage must be packed out. A camp host is on-site. Leashed pets are permitted.

Reservations, fees: Reservations are not accepted. Sites are $8 per night. Senior discount available. Open June–mid-October.

Directions: From LaGrande, drive east on Highway 237 for 15 miles to Cove and County Road 237. Turn southeast and drive 1.5 miles to Forest Road 6220. Turn east and drive eight miles to the camp entrance. The last 9.5 miles are on a steep gravel road.

Contact: Wallowa-Whitman National Forest, LaGrande Ranger District, 3502 Hwy. 30, LaGrande, OR 97850, 541/963-7186, fax 541/962-8580.

32 NORTH FORK CATHERINE CREEK

🏃 🚴 ⛵ 🐴 ⛺ 🚐

Rating: 5

Near the Eagle Cap Wilderness in Wallowa-Whitman National Forest.

Map 10.3, grid g4, page 564

This campground along the North Fork of Catherine Creek is near a trailhead that provides access to various lakes and streams in the Eagle Cap Wilderness. The elevation here is 4,400 feet. The camp makes a good starting point for a hiking trip. It's popular with hunters in the fall. A U.S. Forest Service map details the possibilities.

Campsites, facilities: There are six sites for tents or small, self-contained RVs. Picnic tables and fire grills are provided. Drinking water and vault toilets are available. All garbage must be packed out. Leashed pets are permitted.

Reservations, fees: Reservations are not accepted. There is no fee for camping. Open June–late October.

Directions: From LaGrande, drive southeast on Highway 203 for 14 miles to Union. Continue southeast on Highway 203 for 10 miles to Forest Road 7785. Turn east and drive four miles east on Forest Road 7785 to a fork. Bear left at the fork (still on 7785) and drive 3.5 miles northeast to the camp.

Contact: Wallowa-Whitman National Forest, LaGrande Ranger District, 3502 Hwy. 30, LaGrande, OR 97850, 541/963-7186, fax 541/962-8580.

33 SHADY

🏃 ⛵ 🐴 🚐 ⛺

Rating: 6

On the Lostine River in Wallowa-Whitman National Forest.

Map 10.3, grid f5, page 564

This campground, set along the banks of the Lostine River at an elevation of 5,400 feet, is close to trails that provide access to the Eagle Cap Wilderness, a beautiful and pristine area that's perfect for an extended backpacking trip.

The camp has wooded as well as meadow areas. Mountain sheep can sometimes be spotted.

Campsites, facilities: There are 12 sites for tents or RVs up to 16 feet long. Vault toilets are available, but there is no drinking water, and all garbage must be packed out. Picnic tables and fire grills are provided. Leashed pets are permitted.

Reservations, fees: Reservations are not accepted. There is no fee for camping. Open mid-June–November.

Directions: From LaGrande, turn north on Highway 82 and drive 52 miles to Lostine and Forest Road 8210. Turn south and drive 15 miles to the campground.

Contact: Wallowa-Whitman National Forest, Eagle Cap Ranger District Wallowa Mountains Visitor Center, 88401 Hwy. 82, Enterprise, OR 97828, 541/426-5546.

34 TWO PAN

🏃 ⛵ 🐴 ⛺ 🚐

Rating: 6

On the Lostine River in Wallowa-Whitman National Forest.

Map 10.3, grid g5, page 564

This campground lies at the end of a forest road on the banks of the Lostine River. Adjacent trails provide access to numerous lakes and streams in the Eagle Cap Wilderness. At 5,600 feet elevation, this camp is a prime jump-off spot for a multi-day wilderness adventure. Another campground option is Williamson, seven miles north on Forest Road 8210.

Campsites, facilities: There are eight sites for tents or small, self-contained RVs. Vault toilets are available, but there is no drinking water, and all garbage must be packed out. Picnic tables and fire grills are provided. Leashed pets are permitted.

Reservations, fees: Reservations are not accepted. There is no fee for camping. Open mid-June–November.

Directions: From LaGrande, turn north on

Highway 82 and drive 52 miles to Lostine and Forest Road 8210. Turn south and drive 17 miles to the campground.

Contact: Wallowa-Whitman National Forest, Eagle Cap Ranger District; Wallowa Mountains Visitor Center, 88401 Hwy. 82, Enterprise, OR 97828, 541/426-5546.

35 HURRICANE CREEK

Rating: 5

Near the Eagle Cap Wilderness in Wallowa-Whitman National Forest.

Map 10.3, grid f6, page 564

This campground, set along Hurricane Creek at an elevation of 5,000 feet, is on the edge of the Eagle Cap Wilderness and is a good place to begin a backcountry backpacking trip. There is no access for RVs, providing more of a wilderness environment. Obtaining maps of the area from the ranger district is essential.

Campsites, facilities: There are eight tent sites. Picnic tables and fire grills are provided. Firewood and vault toilets are available, but there is no drinking water, and all garbage must be packed out. Leashed pets are permitted.

Reservations, fees: Reservations are not accepted. The fee is $5 per night. Open mid-June–late October.

Directions: From LaGrande, turn north on Highway 82 and drive 62 miles to Enterprise and Hurricane Creek Road. Turn south on Hurricane Creek Road and drive five miles to Hurricane Grange Hall and Forest Road 8205; bear right (off the paved road) and drive two miles to the campground.

Contact: Wallowa-Whitman National Forest, Eagle Cap Ranger District, Wallowa Mountains Visitor Center, 88401 Hwy. 82, Enterprise, OR 97828, 541/426-5546.

36 MOUNTAIN VIEW MOTEL AND RV PARK

Rating: 3

Near Wallowa Lake.

Map 10.3, grid f7, page 564

This park is centrally located for exploring the greater Wallowa Lake area. Enjoy views of the Seven Devils Mountains and of the Eagle Cap Wilderness from here. Nearby recreational facilities include a golf course, hiking trails, bike paths, and a riding stable. Fishing and jet boating are also nearby options. This park is under new ownership and considerable improvements were made in late 2001.

Campsites, facilities: There are 30 sites, including three drive-through, for RVs of any length, a few tent sites, and nine cabins. Electricity, drinking water, sewer hookups, and picnic tables are provided at eight sites. Flush toilets and showers are available. Bottled gas, a store, a café, and a coin laundry are within two miles. Leashed pets are permitted.

Reservations, fees: Reservations accepted. RV sites are $20 per night; tent sites are $15 per night; $2 per person for more than two people. Major credit cards accepted. Open year-round.

Directions: From LaGrande, turn north on Highway 82 and drive 62 miles to Enterprise and the junction with Highway 3. Continue south on Highway 82 for four miles to the campground (1.5 miles north of Joseph).

Contact: Mountain View Motel and RV Park, 83450 Joseph Hwy., Joseph, OR 97846, 866/262-9891 or 541/432-2982 (phone or fax).

37 WALLOWA LAKE STATE PARK

Rating: 8

On Wallowa Lake.

Map 10.3, grid f7, page 564

Surrounded on three sides by 9,000-foot, snow-capped mountains and large, clear Wallowa

Lake, this area is popular for fishing and boating recreation, including water-skiing and para sailing. You can also enjoy hiking, horseback riding, bumper boats, canoeing, miniature golf, or a tram ride up 4,000 feet to a mountaintop. A nearby artist community makes world-class bronze castings and tours are available. This is also the gateway to Hells Canyon, the deepest gorge in North America. Other highlights include a pretty one-mile nature trail and trailheads that provide access into the Eagle Cap Wilderness. A marina is nearby for boaters and anglers. Picnicking, swimming, and wildlife viewing are a few of the other activities available to visitors.

Campsites, facilities: There are 89 tent sites, 121 full-hookup sites for RVs up to 90 feet long, some hiker/biker sites, three group tent areas, two yurts, and one deluxe cabin. Electricity, drinking water, sewer hookups, and picnic tables are provided. Garbage bins, flush toilets, an RV dump station, showers, and firewood are available. A store, a café, and ice are within one mile. Some facilities are wheelchair accessible. Boat docks, launching facilities, and rentals are nearby. Leashed pets are permitted.

Reservations, fees: Reservations at 800/452-5687 or website: www.OregonStateParks.org ($6 reservation fee). Sites are $11–20 per night; hiker/biker sites are $4 per night; group areas are $60 per night; yurts are $29 per night; the deluxe cabin is $55–75 per night; an additional vehicle is $7 per night. Major credit cards accepted. Open year-round.

Directions: From LaGrande, turn north on Highway 82 and drive 62 miles to Enterprise and the junction with Highway 3. Continue south on Highway 82 to Joseph. Continue for six miles to the south shore of the lake and the campground.

Contact: Wallowa Lake State Park, 72214 Marina Ln., Joseph, OR 97846, 541/432-4185.

38 LICK CREEK

Rating: 7

On Lick Creek in Wallowa-Whitman National Forest.

Map 10.3, grid g8, page 564

This campground is set at an elevation of 5,400 feet in park-like surroundings along the banks of Lick Creek in Hells Canyon National Recreation Area. It is secluded and pretty. Tall Douglas fir, white fir, tamarack, and lodgepole pine are interspersed throughout the campground, providing habitat for some of the birds and small mammals you might see.

Campsites, facilities: There are seven tent sites and five sites for RVs up to 30 feet long. Picnic tables and fire grills are provided. Vault toilets are available, but there is no drinking water, and garbage must be packed out. Leashed pets are permitted.

Reservations, fees: Reservations are not accepted. Sites are $5 per night. Senior discount available. Open mid-June–late November.

Directions: From LaGrande, turn north on Highway 82 and drive 62 miles to Enterprise and the junction with Highway 3. Continue south on Highway 82 to Joseph and Highway 350. Turn east and drive 7.5 miles to Forest Road 39. Turn south and drive 15 miles to the campground.

Contact: Hells Canyon National Recreation Area, Wallowa Mountains Visitor Center, 88401 Hwy. 82, Enterprise, OR 97828, 541/426-5546.

39 OLLOKOT

Rating: 5

On the Imnaha River in Wallowa-Whitman National Forest.

Map 10.3, grid c3, page 564

This campground sits on the banks of the Imnaha River in Hells Canyon National Recreation Area at an elevation of 4,000 feet. It's named for Chief Joseph's brother, a member of the Nez Perce tribe. For those seeking a little more solitude, this could be the spot.

Campsites, facilities: There are 12 sites for tents or RVs up to 30 feet long. Picnic tables and fire grills are provided. Drinking water and vault toilets are available, but all garbage must be packed out. Leashed pets are permitted.

Reservations, fees: Reservations are not accepted. Sites are $5 per night. Senior discount available. Open June–late November.

Directions: From I-84 at LaGrande, turn north on Highway 82 and drive 62 miles to Enterprise. Continue six miles south to Joseph, and then drive eight miles east on Highway 350. Turn south on Forest Road 39 and drive 30 miles to the campground.

Contact: Hells Canyon National Recreation Area, Wallowa Mountains Visitor Center, 88401 Hwy. 82, Enterprise, OR 97828, 541/426-5546.

40 BUCKHORN
Rating: 8

Near Buckhorn Overlook in Wallowa-Whitman National Forest.

Map 10.4, grid c2, page 565

Set at 5,200 feet elevation and adjacent to Buckhorn Springs, this small, primitive, and obscure camp gets little use. The elevation provides a spectacular view of the Imnaha River drainage from the nearby Buckhorn Lookout (not from campsites).

Campsites, facilities: There are six sites for tents or small, self-contained RVs. Picnic tables and fire grills are provided. Vault toilets are available, but there is no drinking water and all garbage must be packed out. Leashed pets are permitted.

Reservations, fees: Reservations are not accepted. There is no fee for camping. Open June–late November.

Directions: From LaGrande, drive northeast on Highway 82 for 62 miles to Enterprise. Continue east for three miles on Highway 82 to County Road 772. Turn north and drive 32 miles to a junction at Thomason Meadows. Continue straight on Forest Road 46 for 10 miles to Forest Road 780. Turn right and drive one-quarter mile to the campground.

Contact: Hells Canyon National Recreation Area, Wallowa Mountains Visitor Center, 88401 Hwy. 82, Enterprise, OR 97828, 541/426-5546.

41 SADDLE CREEK
Rating: 8

Near the Hells Canyon Wilderness in Wallowa-Whitman National Forest.

Map 10.4, grid d3, page 565

This campground is set at 6,800 feet elevation in a wooded environment on a ridge between two canyons, providing excellent views of the Seven Devils Mountains. Nearby trails provide access to Saddle Creek and Hells Canyon National Recreation Area. Note that a fire here left its mark on the area.

Campsites, facilities: There are seven sites for tents. Picnic tables and fire grills are provided. Vault toilets are available, but there is no drinking water and all garbage must be packed out. Leashed pets are permitted. Note: RVs and trailers are not recommended on the access road.

Reservations, fees: Reservations are not accepted. There is no fee for camping. Open July–mid-November.

Directions: From LaGrande, turn north on Highway 82 and drive 62 miles to Enterprise and the junction of Highway 3. At the junction bear south on Highway 82 and drive six miles to Joseph and Highway 350. Turn east on Highway 350 and drive 30 miles to the small town of Imnaha and Forest Road 4240. Drive straight up the hill on Forest Road 4240 and continue 19 miles to the campground.

Contact: Hells Canyon National Recreation Area, Wallowa Mountains Visitor Center, 88401 Hwy. 82, Enterprise, OR 97828, 541/426-5546.

42 BLACKHORSE

Rating: 7

On the Imnaha River in Wallowa-Whitman National Forest.

Map 10.4, grid g1, page 565

This campground along the banks of the Imnaha River in Hells Canyon National Recreation Area is located in a secluded section of Wallowa-Whitman National Forest at an elevation of 4,000 feet.

Campsites, facilities: There are 16 sites for tents or RVs up to 30 feet long. Picnic tables and fire grills are provided. Drinking water and vault toilets are available, but all garbage must be packed out. Leashed pets are permitted.

Reservations, fees: Reservations are not accepted. Sites are $5 per night. Senior discount available. Open June–late November.

Directions: From I-84 at LaGrande, turn north on Highway 82 and drive 62 miles to Enterprise. Continue six miles south to Joseph and then drive eight miles east on Highway 350. Turn south on Forest Road 39 and drive 29 miles to the campground.

Contact: Hells Canyon National Recreation Area, Wallowa Mountains Visitor Center, 88401 Hwy. 82, Enterprise, OR 97828, 541/426-5546.

43 LAKE FORK

Rating: 6

On Lake Fork Creek in Wallowa-Whitman National Forest.

Map 10.4, grid g2, page 565

This little campground (at 3,200 feet elevation) along the banks of Lake Fork Creek is tucked away off the main road and makes an ideal jumping-off point for a backpacking trip. A trail from camp follows the creek west for about 10 miles to Fish Lake, then continues to several smaller lakes.

Campsites, facilities: There are 10 sites for tents or RVs up to 22 feet long. Picnic tables and fire grills are provided. Drinking water and vault toilets are available, but all garbage must be packed out. Leashed pets are permitted.

Reservations, fees: Reservations are not accepted. Sites are $5 per night. Senior discount available. Open June–late November.

Directions: From Baker City, drive east on Highway 86 for 82 miles to Forest Road 39. Turn north and drive eight miles to the campground entrance road on the left.

Contact: Hells Canyon National Recreation Area, Wallowa Mountains Visitor Center, 88401 Hwy. 82, Enterprise, OR 97828, 541/426-5546.

44 HIDDEN

Rating: 6

On the Imnaha River in Wallowa-Whitman National Forest.

Map 10.4, grid h1, page 565

River views and spacious sites can be found at this campground in a pretty spot along the banks of the Imnaha River in the Hells Canyon National Recreation Area. It's essential to obtain a map of Wallowa-Whitman National Forest that details back roads and hiking trails. If full, Coverdale Campground is an option just four miles northeast on Forest Road 3960.

Campsites, facilities: There are 10 tent sites and three sites for tents or small, self-contained RVs. Picnic tables and fire grills are provided. Drinking water, firewood, and vault toilets are available, but all garbage must be packed out. Leashed pets are permitted.

Reservations, fees: Reservations are not accepted. Sites are $5 per night. Senior discount available. Open June–late November.

Directions: From LaGrande, drive east on Highway 82 for 62 miles to Enterprise. Continue six miles south to Joseph and Highway 350. Turn east and drive eight miles to Wallowa Mountain Loop Road (Forest Road 39). Turn south and drive 30 miles to Forest Road 3960. Turn right (southwest) and drive seven miles to the campground.

Contact: Hells Canyon National Recreation Area, Wallowa Mountains Visitor Center, 88401 Hwy. 82, Enterprise, OR 97828, 541/426-5546.

45 EVERGREEN

Rating: 6

On the Imnaha River in Wallowa-Whitman National Forest.

Map 10.4, grid h1, page 565

This campground can be found along the banks of the Imnaha River in Hells Canyon National Recreation Area. One of seven camps in the vicinity, it is popular with hunters in the fall.

Campsites, facilities: This is a group campsite for tents or RVs up to 31 feet long. Vault toilets are available, but there is no drinking water, and all garbage must be packed out. Picnic tables and fire grills are provided. Leashed pets are permitted.

Reservations, fees: Reservations are not accepted. There is no fee for camping. Open June–late November.

Directions: From LaGrande, turn north on Highway 82 and drive 62 miles to Enterprise and the junction with Highway 3. Continue on Highway 82 for six miles to Joseph and Highway 350. Turn east on Highway 350 and drive eight miles to Forest Road 39. Turn south and drive about 30 miles to Forest Road 3960. Turn right and drive seven miles to the campground.

Contact: Hells Canyon National Recreation Area, Wallowa Mountains Visitor Center, 88401 Hwy. 82, Enterprise, OR 97828, 541/426-5546.

46 INDIAN CROSSING

Rating: 6

On the Imnaha River in Wallowa-Whitman National Forest.

Map 10.4, grid h1, page 565

This campground is set at an elevation of 4,500 feet and is more developed than nearby Evergreen and Hidden Campgrounds. A trailhead

for the Eagle Cap Wilderness is near this camp. Obtain a U.S. Forest Service map for side-trip possibilities.

Campsites, facilities: There are 14 sites for tents or RVs up to 30 feet long. Drinking water, picnic tables, and fire grills are provided, but all garbage must be packed out. Vault toilets and horse facilities are available. Leashed pets are permitted.

Reservations, fees: Reservations are not accepted. Sites are $5 per night. Senior discount available. Open June–late November.

Directions: From LaGrande, turn north on Highway 82 and drive 62 miles to Enterprise and the junction with Highway 3. Continue on Highway 82 for six miles to Joseph and Highway 350. Turn east on Highway 350 and drive eight miles to Forest Road 39. Turn south and drive about 30 miles to Forest Road 3960. Turn right and drive 10 miles to the campground at the end of the road.

Contact: Hells Canyon National Recreation Area, Wallowa Mountains Visitor Center, 88401 Hwy. 82, Enterprise, OR 97828, 541/426-5546.

47 WHISTLER

Rating: 7

In Ochoco National Forest.

Map 10.5, grid d5, page 566

Whistler is a trailhead camp for the Wildcat Trail, which heads into the Mill Creek Wilderness. The area is extremely popular with rock hounds, who search for thunder eggs, jasper, and agates (digging is forbidden in wilderness areas, however). Though primitive, this pretty camp in a conifer forest guarantees quiet and privacy.

Campsites, facilities: There is a large area for dispersed tent camping. A picnic table and a vault toilet are provided. There is no drinking water, and garbage must be packed out. Horses are welcome. Leashed pets are permitted.

Reservations, fees: Reservations are not accepted. There is no fee for camping. Open late May–late October.

Directions: From Prineville, drive east on U.S. 26 for about 30 miles to Forest Road 27 (just east of Bandit Spring State Rest Area, near Ochoco Pass). Turn left on Forest Road 27 and drive nine miles to the campground entrance on the left.

Contact: Ochoco National Forest, Lookout Mountain Ranger District, P.O. Box 490, Prineville, OR 97754, 541/416-6500, fax 541/416-6695.

48 WILDCAT

Rating: 4

On the East Fork of Mill Creek in Ochoco National Forest.

Map 10.5, grid e3, page 566

This quiet, cool campground, surrounded by conifer forest, is set at an elevation of 3,799 feet in a canyon. Situated along the East Fork of Mill Creek, the camp is near the Twin Pillars Trailhead, which provides access into the Mill Creek Wilderness. Stein's Pillar and Twin Pillars, popular rock-climbing spots, are nearby. Ochoco Lake and Ochoco Lake State Park to the south provide side-trip possibilities.

Campsites, facilities: There are 17 sites for tents or RVs up to 30 feet long. Picnic tables and fire grills are provided. Drinking water and vault toilets are available, but garbage must be packed out. Leashed pets are permitted.

Reservations, fees: Reservations are not accepted. Sites are $8 per night, plus $3 for each additional vehicle. Senior discount available. Open mid-April–late October.

Directions: From Prineville, drive east on U.S. 26 for nine miles to Mill Creek Road (Forest Road 33). Turn left on Mill Creek Road and drive about 10 miles to the campground

Contact: Ochoco National Forest, Lookout Mountain Ranger District, P.O. Box 490, Prineville, OR 97754, 541/416-6500, fax 541/416-6695.

49 OCHOCO DIVIDE

Rating: 5

In Ochoco National Forest.

Map 10.5, grid e5, page 566

This camp is set at an elevation of 4,700 feet amid an old-growth stand of ponderosa pine just off scenic U.S. 26. An unused forest road on the far side of the campground provides an easy stretch walk after a long day of driving. Most visitors arrive late in the day and leave early in the morning, so the area is normally quiet during the day. Marks Creek is nearby and the Bandit Springs Rest Stop, one mile west, is the jumping-off point for a network of trails.

Campsites, facilities: There are 28 sites for tents or RVs up to 30 feet long, with a separate area with walk-in and bike-in sites. Picnic tables and fire pits are provided. Drinking water, garbage bins, and vault toilets are available. Some facilities are wheelchair accessible. Leashed pets are permitted.

Reservations, fees: Reservations are not accepted. Sites are $10 per night, $5 per night for an additional vehicle. Senior discount available. Open late May–mid-November, weather permitting.

Directions: From Prineville, drive east on U.S. 26 for 30 miles to the campground at the summit of Ochoco Pass.

Contact: Ochoco National Forest, Lookout Mountain Ranger District, P.O. Box 490, Prineville, OR 97754, 541/416-6500, fax 541/416-6695.

50 OCHOCO FOREST CAMP

Rating: 4

In Ochoco National Forest.

Map 10.5, grid e5, page 566

Campsites here are set at an elevation of 4,000 feet along Ochoco Creek in a lush setting of ponderosa pine and aspen. Fishing for rainbow trout is fair. A large group picnic area with a beautiful log shelter, perfect for weddings, family reunions, and other group events, is available for reservation. The nearby Lookout Mountain Trail provides access to the Lookout Mountain Recreation Area, 15,000 acres without roads. But hey, the truth is: don't expect privacy and solitude at this campground.

Campsites, facilities: There are six sites for tents or RVs up to 24 feet long. Picnic tables and fire rings are provided. Drinking water, garbage bins, and vault toilets are available. Some facilities are wheelchair accessible. Boat-launching facilities are nearby (only electric motors are allowed). Leashed pets are permitted.

Reservations, fees: Reservations are not accepted. Sites are $10 per night, $5 per night for an additional vehicle. Senior discount available. Open mid-May–November, weather permitting.

Directions: From Prineville, drive east on U.S. 26 for 16.5 miles to County Road 23. Turn right on County Road 23 and drive nine miles (County Road 23 becomes Forest Road 42) to the campground, across from the Ochoco Ranger Station.

Contact: Ochoco National Forest, Lookout Mountain Ranger District, P.O. Box 490, Prineville, OR 97754, 541/416-6500, fax 541/416-6695.

51 WALTON LAKE

Rating: 7

On Walton Lake in Ochoco National Forest.
Map 10.5, grid e5, page 566

This campground sits among old-growth ponderosa pine and mountain meadows along the shore of small Walton Lake, where fishing and swimming are popular; only nonmotorized boats or those with electric motors are allowed. Hikers can explore a nearby trail that leads south to Round Mountain. The lake is stocked with rainbow trout and the fishing can range

from middle-of-the-road fair right up to down-right excellent.

Campsites, facilities: There are 30 sites for tents or RVs up to 31 feet long and one group site. Picnic tables, garbage bins, and fire grills are provided. Drinking water and vault toilets are available. Some facilities are wheelchair accessible. Boat-launching facilities are nearby (only electric motors are allowed). Leashed pets are permitted.

Reservations, fees: Reservations are not accepted for family sites. Sites are $10–12 per night, $7 per night for an additional vehicle. Senior discount available. Reservations for the group site required at 877/444-6777 or website: www.ReserveUsa.com ($9 reservation fee); $25 per night. Open June–late September.

Directions: From Prineville, drive east on U.S. 26 for 16.5 miles to County Road 23. Turn right (northeast) and drive nine miles (County Road 23 becomes Forest Road 42) to the Ochoco Ranger Station and Forest Road 22. Drive north on Forest Road 22 for seven miles to the campground.

Contact: Ochoco National Forest, Big Summit Ranger District, 348855 Ochoco Ranger District, Prineville, OR 97754-9612, 541/416-6645.

52 CROOK COUNTY RV PARK

Rating: 6

Near the Crooked River.
Map 10.5, grid f2, page 566

This campground is in a landscaped and grassy area near the Crooked River, where fly-fishing is popular. The camp is set right next to the Crook County Fairgrounds, which, in season, offers horse races, rodeos, and expositions.

Campsites, facilities: There are 81 sites for tents or RVs up to 70 feet long, all with full hookups. There are also two cabins. Electricity, drinking water, and picnic tables are provided. Flush toilets, an RV dump station, cable TV, vending machines, and showers are available. A small store, a restaurant, laundry facilities, ice, and propane are available within one mile. Some facilities are wheelchair accessible. Leashed pets are permitted.

Reservations, fees: Reservations at 800/609-2599; $9 per night for tent sites, $20–22 for RVs, and $1 per extra vehicle. Weekly and monthly rates are available. Cabins are $25 per night. Open year-round.

Directions: From Redmond, drive east on Highway 126 for 18 miles to Prineville (Highway 126 becomes 3rd Street). Turn east on 3rd Street and drive to Main Street. Turn right on Main Street and drive about one-half mile south to the campground on the left, next to the fairgrounds.

Contact: Crook County RV Park, 1040 S. Main St., Prineville, OR 97754, 541/447-2599, fax 541/416-9022.

53 OCHOCO LAKE

Rating: 6

On Ochoco Lake.

Map 10.5, grid f3, page 566

This is one of the nicer camps along U.S. 26 in eastern Oregon. The state park is located on the shore adjacent to Ochoco Lake, where boating and fishing are popular pastimes. Some quality hiking trails can be found in the area.

Campsites, facilities: There are 22 primitive sites for tents or self-contained RVs up to 30 feet long and a special area for hikers and bicyclists. Picnic tables, garbage bins, and fire grills are provided. Drinking water, firewood, hot showers, and flush toilets are available. Boat-launching facilities are nearby. Leashed pets are permitted.

Reservations, fees: Reservations are not accepted. Sites are $14 per night, $4 per person hike-in/bike-in sites, and $7 per extra vehicle. Open April–October, weather permitting.

Directions: From Prineville, drive east on U.S. 26 for seven miles to the park entrance on the right.

Contact: Crook County Parks and Recreation,

398 N.E. Fairview St., Prineville, OR 97754, 541/447-1209, fax 541/447-9894.

54 DEEP CREEK

Rating: 5

On the North Fork of the Crooked River in Ochoco National Forest.

Map 10.5, grid f8, page 566

This small camp on the edge of high desert gets little use, but it's in a nice spot—the confluence of Deep Creek and the North Fork of the Crooked River. Highlights include pretty, shady sites and river access. Fishing is possible here.

Campsites, facilities: There are six sites for tents or RVs up to 22 feet long. Picnic tables and fire grills are provided. Drinking water and vault toilets are available. Garbage must be packed out. Leashed pets are permitted.

Reservations, fees: Reservations are not accepted. Sites are $8 per night, $3 per additional vehicle. Senior discount available. Open June–mid-October.

Directions: From Prineville, drive east on U.S. 26 for 16.5 miles to County Route 23. Turn right (northeast) and drive 8.5 miles (it becomes Forest Road 42). Continue east on Forest Road 42 for 23.5 miles to the campground.

Contact: Ochoco National Forest, Lookout Mountain Ranger District, P.O. Box 490, Prineville, OR 97754, 541/416-6500, fax 541/416-6695.

55 CHIMNEY ROCK

Rating: 6

On the Crooked River.

Map 10.5, grid g2, page 566

This well-spaced campground is a favorite for picnicking and wildlife viewing. The Chimney Rock Trailhead, just across the highway, is the jump-off point for the 1.7-mile, moderately difficult hike to Chimney Rock. There are numerous scenic overlooks along the trail, and wildlife sightings are common. The elevation here is 3,000 feet. Chimney Rock Campground is one of eight BLM camps along a six-mile stretch of Highway 27.

Campsites, facilities: There are 20 sites for tents or RVs of any length. Drinking water and picnic tables are provided. Vault toilets and garbage bins are available. Wheelchair-accessible toilets, tables, and a fishing dock are also available. Leashed pets are permitted.

Reservations, fees: Reservations are not accepted. Sites are $8 per night, $2 per night for an additional vehicle. Senior discount available. Open year-round.

Directions: In Prineville, drive south on Highway 27 for 16.4 miles to the campground.

Contact: Bureau of Land Management, Prineville District, 3050 N.E. 3rd St., Prineville, OR 97754, 541/416-6700, fax 541/416-6798.

56 PRINEVILLE RESERVOIR STATE PARK

Rating: 7

On Prineville Reservoir.
Map 10.5, grid g3, page 566

This state park is set along the shore of Prineville Reservoir, which formed with the damming of the Crooked River. Swimming, boating, fishing, and water-skiing are among the activities here. The nearby boat docks and ramp are a bonus. The reservoir supports rainbow and cutthroat trout, small and largemouth bass, catfish, and crappie. You can even ice fish in the winter. This is one of two campgrounds on the lake; the other is Prineville Reservoir Resort (RVs only).

Campsites, facilities: There are 25 tent sites, 75 sites with partial hookups for RVs up to 40 feet long, two rustic cabins, and three deluxe cabins. Electricity, drinking water, sewer hookups, garbage bins, and picnic tables are provided. Flush toilets, showers, and firewood are available. Boat docks and launching facilities are nearby. Leashed pets are permitted.

Reservations, fees: Reservations at 800/452-5687 or website: www.OregonStateParks.org ($7 reservation fee). Sites are $12–20 per night; cabins are $35–55 per night. Major credit cards accepted. Open year-round.

Directions: From Prineville, drive east on U.S. 26 for one mile to Combs Flat Road. Turn right (south) and drive one mile to Juniper Canyon Road. Turn right (south) and drive 18 miles to the campground.

Contact: Prineville Reservoir State Park, 19020 S.E. Parkland Dr., Prineville, OR 97754, 541/447-4363 or 800/551-6949.

57 PRINEVILLE RESERVOIR RESORT

Rating: 6

On Prineville Reservoir.
Map 10.5, grid g3, page 566

This resort sits on the shore of Prineville Reservoir in the high desert, a good spot for water sports and fishing. The mostly shaded sites are a combination of dirt and gravel. The camp features easy access to the reservoir and some colorful rock formations to check out.

Campsites, facilities: There are 70 sites, including four drive-through, for tents or RVs of any length, seven motel rooms, and one primitive cabin. Electricity, drinking water, fire pits, and picnic tables are provided. Flush toilets, bottled gas, an RV dump station, showers, firewood, a store, a café, and ice are available. A full-service marina, a boat ramp, and boat rentals, including personal watercraft, are onsite. Leashed pets are permitted.

Reservations, fees: Reservations at 541/447-7468. Sites are $14–20 per night. A pet deposit of $25 is required. Open mid-March–mid-October, weather permitting.

Directions: From Prineville, drive east on U.S. 26 for one mile to Combs Flat Road. Turn right (south) and drive one mile to Juniper Canyon Road. Turn right (south) and drive 18 miles to the campground.

Contact: Prineville Reservoir Resort, 19600 S.E. Juniper Canyon Rd., Prineville, OR 97754, 541/447-7468 (phone or fax).

58 ANTELOPE FLAT RESERVOIR

Rating: 6

On Antelope Flat Reservoir in Ochoco National Forest.

Map 10.5, grid h5, page 566

This pretty spot is situated along the west shore of Antelope Flat Reservoir. The campground sits amid ponderosa pine and juniper on the edge of the high desert at an elevation of 4,600 feet. It features wide sites and easy access to the lake. Trout fishing can be good in the spring, and boating with motors is permitted. This is also a good lake for canoes.

Campsites, facilities: There are 25 sites for tents or RVs up to 30 feet long. Picnic tables and fire grills are provided. Drinking water and vault toilets are available, but all garbage must be packed out. Boat-launching facilities are nearby. Leashed pets are permitted.

Reservations, fees: Reservations are not accepted. Sites are $8 per night, plus $3 for each additional vehicle. Senior discount available. Open early May–late October.

Directions: From Prineville, drive southeast on Combs Flat Road (Paulina Highway) for 30 miles to Forest Road 17 (Antelope Reservoir Junction). Turn right on Forest Road 17 and drive about 10 miles to Forest Road 1700-600. Drive a quarter mile on Forest Road 1700-600 to the campground.

Contact: Ochoco National Forest, Lookout Mountain Ranger District, P.O. Box 490, Prineville, OR 97754, 541/416-6500, fax 541/416-6695.

59 WILEY FLAT

Rating: 3

On Wiley Creek in Ochoco National Forest.

Map 10.5, grid h6, page 566

This campground is set along Wiley Creek in a nice, hidden spot with minimal crowds and is popular with hunters. A map of Ochoco National Forest details nearby access roads. For a good gut-thumping hike, take the trip to Tower Point Lookout. It's one mile north of the camp—and a 1,000-foot climb straight up.

Campsites, facilities: There are five sites for tents or RVs up to 30 feet long. Picnic tables and fire grills are provided. Vault toilets are available, but there is no drinking water, and all garbage must be packed out. Leashed pets are permitted.

Reservations, fees: Reservations are not accepted. There is no fee for camping. Open mid-June–late October.

Directions: From Prineville, drive southeast on the Paulina Highway (Combs Flat Road) for 34 miles to Forest Road 16. Turn right (southeast) and drive 10 miles to Forest Road 1600-400. Turn right (west) and drive one mile to the camp.

Contact: Ochoco National Forest, Lookout Mountain Ranger District, P.O. Box 490, Prineville, OR 97754, 541/416-6500, fax 541/416-6695.

60 BULL PRAIRIE

Rating: 8

On Bull Prairie Lake in Umatilla National Forest.

Map 10.6, grid a3, page 567

This campground is set along the shore of Bull Prairie Lake, a 24-acre lake at 4,000 feet elevation. Boating (no motors permitted), swimming, fishing, and hunting are some of the options here. A hiking trail circles the lake. This spot attracts little attention from out-of-towners, yet it offers plenty of recreation opportunities, making it an ideal vacation destination for many.

Campsites, facilities: There are 28 sites for tents or RVs up to 31 feet long. Picnic tables and fire grills are provided. Drinking water, an RV dump station, garbage bins (summer only), firewood, and vault toilets are available. Boat docks, launching facilities, and a wheelchair-accessible boat ramp are on-site. Leashed pets are permitted.

Reservations, fees: Reservations are not accepted. Sites are $12 per night, $5 per night for additional vehicle. Senior discount available. Open May–October.

Directions: From Heppner, drive south on Highway 207 for roughly 35 miles to the national forest boundary and continue four miles to Forest Road 2039 (paved). Turn left and drive three miles northeast to the campground on the right.

Contact: Umatilla National Forest, Heppner Ranger District, P.O. Box 7, Heppner, OR 97836, 541/676-9187, fax 541/676-2105.

61 FAIRVIEW

Rating: 5

Near Bull Prairie Lake in Umatilla National Forest.
Map 10.6, grid a3, page 567

This small, rugged, and primitive campground near Mahogany Butte and adjacent to Fairview Springs is known by very few people. Primarily, hunters use it as a base camp. In a remote area at 4,300 feet elevation, it's very easy to miss—and not even marked on maps for the Umatilla National Forest. Bull Prairie Lake is only four miles away.

Campsites, facilities: There are five sites for RVs up to 16 feet long. Picnic tables and fire grills are provided. Firewood and vault toilets are available. There is no drinking water and all garbage must be packed out. Boat docks and launching facilities are nearby at Bull Prairie Lake. Leashed pets are permitted.

Reservations, fees: Reservations are not accepted. There is no fee for camping. Open May–late October.

Directions: From Heppner, drive south on Highway 207 for roughly 35 miles to the national forest boundary. Continue four miles to Forest Road 2039 (the turnoff for Bull Prairie Lake). Continue on Highway 207 for one mile to Forest Road 400 (if you pass through an immediate series of hairpin turns, you have gone too far). Turn west and drive 500 yards to the campground.

Contact: Umatilla National Forest, Heppner Ranger District, P.O. Box 7, Heppner, OR 97836, 541/676-9187, fax 541/676-2105.

62 WOLF CREEK

Rating: 5

On Wolf Creek in Ochoco National Forest.
Map 10.6, grid g2, page 567

This campground is set along the banks of Wolf Creek, a nice trout stream that runs through Ochoco National Forest. A quality spot, it features some excellent hiking trails to the northeast in the Black Canyon Wilderness.

Campsites, facilities: There are 12 sites for tents or RVs up to 22 feet long. Picnic tables and fire grills are provided, but there is no drinking water, and all garbage must be packed out. Vault toilets are available. Leashed pets are permitted.

Reservations, fees: Reservations are not accepted. Sites are $6 per night, with a 14-day stay limit, and $3 per night for an additional vehicle. Senior discount available. Open May–early November.

Directions: From Prineville, drive southeast on Combs Flat Road (Paulina Highway) for 55 miles to Paulina. Continue east for 3.5 miles to County Road 112. Turn left (north) and drive 6.5 miles to Forest Road 42. Turn north and drive 1.5 miles to the campground.

Contact: Ochoco National Forest, Paulina Ranger District, 7803 Beaver Creek Rd., Paulina, OR 97751, 541/477-6900, fax 541/477-6949.

63 SUGAR CREEK

🚶 🏊 🐕 ♿ 🚐 🏕️

Rating: 6

On Sugar Creek in Ochoco National Forest.
Map 10.6, grid f2, page 567

This small, quiet, and remote campground sits on the banks of Sugar Creek. It is set at an elevation of 4,000 feet. A three-quarter-mile trail loops along the creek. The camp also offers a covered group shelter in the day-use area and a wheelchair-accessible trail. Because of the presence of bald eagles, there may be seasonal closures on land access in the area. Be sure to check posted notices.

Campsites, facilities: There are 17 sites for tents or RVs up to 21 feet long. Picnic tables, garbage bins, and fire grills are provided. Drinking water, a picnic shelter, and vault toilets are available. Some facilities are wheelchair accessible. Leashed pets are permitted.

Reservations, fees: Reservations are not accepted. Sites are $8 per night, with a 14-day stay limit, and $3 per night for an additional vehicle. Senior discount available. Open June–early November.

Directions: From Prineville, drive southeast on Combs Flat Road (Paulina Highway) for 55 miles to Paulina. Continue east and drive 3.5 miles to a fork with County Road 112. Bear left at the fork onto County Road 112 and drive 7.5 miles to Forest Road 58. Continue on Forest Road 58 for 2.25 miles to the campground on the right.

Contact: Ochoco National Forest, Paulina Ranger District, 7803 Beaver Creek Rd., Paulina, OR 97751, 541/477-6900, fax 541/477-6949.

64 FRAZIER

🚶 🚵 ❄️ 🐕 🚐 🏕️

Rating: 4

On Frazier Creek in Ochoco National Forest.
Map 10.6, grid f3, page 567

This small, remote, and little-used camp is located at an elevation of 4,300 feet. The land-scape is open, grassy, and sprinkled with a few large trees. Some dirt roads adjacent to the camp are good for mountain biking in summer and cross-country skiing and snowmobiling in winter. The camp, with its meadow setting, is popular for reunions during the holidays.

Campsites, facilities: There are six sites for tents or RVs up to 21 feet long. Picnic tables and fire grills are provided. Vault toilets are available. There is no drinking water and all garbage must be packed out. Leashed pets are permitted.

Reservations, fees: Reservations are not accepted. There is no fee for camping. The stay limit is 14 days. Open June–early November.

Directions: From Prineville, drive southeast on Combs Flat Road (Paulina Highway) for 55 miles to Paulina. Continue east and drive 3.5 miles to a fork with County Road 112. Bear left at the fork onto County Road 112 and drive 2.5 miles to County Road 135. Turn right (east) and drive 10 miles to Forest Road 58. Turn right and drive six miles to Forest Road 58-500. Turn left and drive two miles to the campground.

Contact: Ochoco National Forest, Paulina Ranger District, 7803 Beaver Creek Rd., Paulina, OR 97751, 541/477-6900, fax 541/477-6949.

65 CLYDE HOLLIDAY STATE RECREATION SITE

🚶 🚴 🛶 🐕 🚐 🏕️

Rating: 7

Near the John Day River.
Map 10.6, grid e8, page 567

Think of this campground as an oasis. Its tall, willowy cottonwood trees provide shade and serenity, giving you that private, secluded feeling. It borders the John Day River, and you're as likely to have wildlife neighbors as human ones; Rocky Mountain elk and mule deer are frequent visitors. You might also see steelhead rushing upriver to spawn.

Campsites, facilities: There are 31 sites for RVs

up to 60 feet long, a hiker/biker tent area, and two teepees. Electricity, picnic tables, and fire grills are provided. Drinking water, firewood, an RV dump station, showers, and flush toilets are available. Leashed pets are permitted.

Reservations, fees: Reservations are not accepted. Sites are $16 per night, $4 per person per night for hike-in/bike-in sites, $28 per night for teepees, and $7 per night for an additional vehicle. The campground is open March–November, weather permitting.

Directions: From John Day, drive west on U.S. 26 for six miles to the park on the left.

Contact: Clyde Holliday State Recreation Site, P.O. Box 10, Mt. Vernon, OR 97865, 541/932-4453 or 800/551-6949.

66 STARR

Rating: 4

On Starr Ridge in Malheur National Forest.
Map 10.6, grid f8, page 567

A good layover spot for travelers on U.S. 395, Starr happens to be adjacent to Starr Ski Bowl, which is popular in winter for skiing and sledding. The camp itself doesn't offer much in the way of recreation, but to the northeast is the Strawberry Mountain Wilderness, which has a number of trails, lakes, and streams. The camp sits at an elevation of 5,100 feet.

Campsites, facilities: There are eight sites for tents or RVs up to 25 feet long. Picnic tables and fire grills are provided. Vault toilets are available. There is no drinking water, and all garbage must be packed out. Some facilities are wheelchair accessible. Leashed pets are permitted.

Reservations, fees: Reservations are not accepted. Sites are $4 per night, $2 per night for an additional vehicle. Senior discount available. Open early May–November.

Directions: From John Day, drive south on U.S. 395 for 15 miles to the campground.

Contact: Malheur National Forest, Blue Mountain Ranger District, P.O. Box 909, John Day, OR 97845, 541/575-3000, fax 541/575-3001.

67 WELCH CREEK

Rating: 5

On Desolation Creek in Umatilla National Forest.
Map 10.7, grid a2, page 568

This primitive camp is on the banks of Desolation Creek. Road noise may be a problem for some, and there's little privacy among sites. The camp features trail access to the Desolation Area, both for non-motorized and motorized traffic. Hunting and fishing are popular here.

Campsites, facilities: There are six primitive sites for tents or small RVs. Picnic tables and fire rings are provided. A vault toilet is available. No drinking water. All garbage must be packed out. Leashed pets are permitted.

Reservations, fees: Reservations are not accepted; sites are $5 per night. Senior discount available. Open late May–November.

Directions: From Pendleton, drive south on U.S. 395 for 62 miles to Forest Road 55 (one mile north of Dale; it's easier to find if you know the marker, Texas Bar Road). Turn left and drive one mile to Forest Road 10. Turn right and drive 13 miles to the campground.

Contact: Umatilla National Forest, North Fork John Day Ranger District, P.O. Box 158, Ukiah, OR 97880, 541/427-3231, fax 541/276-5026.

68 NORTH FORK JOHN DAY

Rating: 6

On the North Fork of the John Day River in Umatilla National Forest.
Map 10.7, grid a4, page 568

This campground is set in a conifer stand along the banks of the North Fork of the John Day River and makes an ideal base camp for a wilderness backpacking trip. In the fall, it has a great view of salmon spawning in the river. A horse-handling area is also available for wilderness users. Trails from camp lead into the North Fork John Day Wilderness. The camp is set at an elevation of 5,200 feet at the intersection of Elkhorn and Blue Mountain National Forest Scenic Byways. No motorbikes are permitted in the wilderness.

Campsites, facilities: There are 15 sites for tents or RVs up to 22 feet long and two additional tent-only sites. Picnic tables and fire rings are provided. Vault toilets are available. There is no drinking water. All garbage must be packed out. Leashed pets are permitted.

Reservations, fees: Reservations are not accepted. Sites are $5 per night, with a 14-day stay limit. Senior discount available. Open June–November. For trailhead use only, a Northwest Forest Pass ($5 daily fee or $30 annual fee per parked vehicle) is required.

Directions: From Pendleton, drive south on U.S. 395 for 50 miles to Highway 244. Turn east on Highway 244 and drive one mile to Ukiah and Forest Road 52. Turn south on Forest Road 52 and drive 36 miles to the campground.

Contact: Umatilla National Forest, North Fork John Day Ranger District, P.O. Box 158, Ukiah, OR 97880, 541/427-3231, fax 541/276-5026.

69 ANTHONY LAKES

Rating: 10

On Anthony Lake in Wallowa-Whitman National Forest.

Map 10.7, grid a6, page 568

This campground is set at 7,100 feet elevation, adjacent to Anthony Lake, where boating without motors is permitted. Sites are wooded, providing good screening between them. Alas, mosquitoes are often in particular abundance. Several smaller lakes within two miles by car or trail are ideal for trout fishing from a raft, float tube, or canoe. Sometimes mountain goats can be seen from the Elkhorn Crest Trail, which begins near here. Weekends and holidays are full.

Campsites, facilities: There are 37 sites for tents or RVs up to 22 feet long and one group site.

Drinking water, fire grills, garbage bins (summer only), and picnic tables are provided. Vault toilets are available. Some facilities are wheelchair accessible. Boat-launching facilities are nearby. Leashed pets are permitted.

Reservations, fees: Reservations are not accepted for family sites; $8 per night, $5 per extra vehicle. Senior discount available. Group reservations required at 541/894-2505; $30–75 per night. Open July–late September.

Directions: From Baker City on I-84, turn north on U.S. 30. Drive north for 10 miles to Haines and County Road 1146 (signed for Anthony Lakes Ski Resort). Turn left on County Road 1146 and drive 20 miles (the road becomes Forest Road 73) to the campground on the left.

Contact: Wallowa-Whitman National Forest, Baker Ranger District, 3165 10th St., Baker City, OR 97814, 541/523-4476, fax 541/523-1965.

70 GRANDE RONDE LAKE

Rating: 8

On Grande Ronde Lake in Wallowa-Whitman National Forest.

Map 10.7, grid a6, page 568

This campground sits amid Douglas and white fir at an elevation of 6,800 feet along the shore of Grande Ronde Lake, a small lake where the trout fishing can be good. Mountain goats are sometimes seen in the area. Several trails lie to the south, near Anthony Lake. A map of Wallowa-Whitman National Forest details the possibilities.

Campsites, facilities: There are eight sites for tents or RVs up to 16 feet long. Picnic tables and fire grills are provided. Drinking water and vault toilets are available, but garbage must be packed out. Boat docks and launching facilities are nearby. Leashed pets are permitted.

Reservations, fees: Reservations are not accepted. Sites are $8 per night, $4 per extra vehicle. Senior discount available. Open July–mid-September.

Directions: Drive on I-84 to Baker City and U.S. 30. Turn north on U.S. 30 and drive for 10 miles to Haines and County Road 1146 (signed for Anthony Lakes Ski Resort). Turn left on County Road 1146 and drive 20 miles (the road becomes Forest Road 73) to the campground on the right.

Contact: Wallowa-Whitman National Forest, Baker Ranger District, 3165 10th St., Baker City, OR 97814, 541/523-4476, fax 541/523-1965; concessionaire, Recreation Resource Management, 541/894-2505.

71 MUD LAKE

Rating: 7

On Mud Lake in Wallowa-Whitman National Forest.
Map 10.7, grid a6, page 568

This campground is situated in fir forest on the shore of small Mud Lake, where the trout fishing can be fairly good. Mud Lake is shallow and more marshy than muddy. Set at an elevation of 7,100 feet, the campground is tiny and pleasant, with lots of vegetation and relatively little use. Bring your mosquito repellent.

Campsites, facilities: There are three tent sites and five sites for RVs up to 16 feet long. Picnic tables and fire grills are provided. Drinking water and vault toilets are available, but all garbage must be packed out. Boat docks and launching facilities are nearby at Anthony Lake. Leashed pets are permitted.

Reservations, fees: Reservations are not accepted. Sites are $8 per night, $4 per extra vehicle. Senior discount available. Open July–mid-September.

Directions: Drive on I-84 to Baker City and U.S. 30. Turn north on U.S. 30 and drive for 10 miles to Haines and County Road 1146 (signed for Anthony Lakes Ski Resort). Turn left on County Road 1146 and drive 21 miles (the road becomes Forest Road 73) to the campground on the right.

Contact: Wallowa-Whitman National Forest,

Baker Ranger District, 3165 10th St., Baker City, OR 97814, 541/523-4476, fax 541/523-1965; concessionaire, Recreation Resource Management, 541/894-2505.

72 OLIVE LAKE

Rating: 9

On Olive Lake in Umatilla National Forest.
Map 10.7, grid b4, page 568

This campground is set at 6,100 feet along the shore of Olive Lake, between two sections of the North Fork John Day Wilderness. Dammed to hold an increased volume of water, the glacial lake is a beautiful tint of blue. Motorized boats are allowed, but water-skiing is prohibited. Fishing is fair for kokanee salmon and cutthroat, rainbow, and brook trout. Sections of the old wooden pipeline for the historic Fremont Powerhouse can still be seen. Nearby trails provide access to the wilderness; motorbikes and mountain bikes are not permitted there. The old mining town of Granite is 12 miles east of camp.

Campsites, facilities: There are 28 sites for tents or RVs up to 31 feet long (four sites available for RVs up to 45 feet long) and two groups sites. Vault toilets are available, but there is no drinking water and garbage must be packed out. Picnic tables and fire grills are provided. Boat docks, launching facilities, and two picnic areas are available. Leashed pets are permitted.

Reservations, fees: Reservations are not accepted. Sites are $5 per night, with a 14-day stay limit; $10 for a group camp. Senior discount available. Open June–mid-October, weather permitting.

Directions: From Pendleton, drive south on U.S. 395 for 62 miles to Forest Road 55 (one mile north of Dale). Turn right and drive one-half mile to Forest Road 10. Turn right on Forest Road 10 and drive 26 miles to the campground on the right.

Contact: Umatilla National Forest, North Fork

John Day Ranger District, P.O. Box 158, Ukiah, OR 97880, 541/427-3231, fax 541/276-5026.

73 MCCULLY FORKS

Rating: 5

On McCully Creek in Wallowa-Whitman National Forest.

Map 10.7, grid b6, page 568

Here's an easy-access campground that's tiny, free, and primitive. It's set at 4,600 feet elevation along the banks of McCully Creek. Wedged between highway and mountains, it gets moderately heavy use and is often full on weekends. Note that highway noise can be audible. Sites are wooded with alder and cottonwood.

Campsites, facilities: There are six tent sites. Picnic tables and fire grills are provided. Vault toilets are available. There is no drinking water and all garbage must be packed out. Leashed pets are permitted.

Reservations, fees: Reservations are not accepted. There is no fee for camping. Open late May–late October.

Directions: From Baker City, drive southwest on Highway 7 for 29 miles (bear west at Salisbury) to Sumpter. Continue three miles past Sumpter (the road becomes Forest Road 24) to the campground.

Contact: Wallowa-Whitman National Forest, Baker Ranger District, 3165 10th St., Baker City, OR 97814, 541/523-4476, fax 541/523-1965.

74 UNION CREEK

Rating: 8

On Phillips Lake in Wallowa-Whitman National Forest.

Map 10.7, grid c8, page 568

This campground along the north shore of Phillips Lake is easy to reach, yet missed by most I-84 travelers. It's the largest of three camps on the lake and the only one with drinking water. An old narrow-gauge railroad has been restored and runs up the valley from McEwen Depot (six miles from the campground) to Sumpter (10 miles away). Visit Sumpter to see an old dredge.

Campsites, facilities: There are 58 sites for tents or RVs up to 32 feet long. Electricity, drinking water, sewer hookups, garbage bins (summer only), and picnic tables are provided. Flush toilets, an RV dump station, firewood, and ice are available. There is a small concession stand for packaged goods and fishing tackle. Some facilities are wheelchair accessible. Boat docks and launching facilities are adjacent to the campground. Leashed pets are permitted.

Reservations, fees: Reservations are not accepted for family sites; $11–20 per night, $5 per extra vehicle. Senior discount available. Group reservations required at 541/894-2505. Open from mid-April–mid-September.

Directions: From Baker City, drive southwest on Highway 7 for 20 miles to the campground.

Contact: Wallowa-Whitman National Forest, Baker Ranger District, 3165 10th St., Baker City, OR 97814, 541/523-4476, fax 541/523-1965; concessionaire, Recreation Resource Management, 541/894-2505.

75 SOUTHWEST SHORE

Rating: 7

On Phillips Lake in Wallowa-Whitman National Forest.

Map 10.7, grid c8, page 568

This campground is set at 4,120 feet elevation along the south shore of Phillips Lake, a four-mile-long reservoir created by the Mason Dam on the Powder River. It's one of two primitive camps on the lake. The boat ramp is usable only when water is high in the reservoir. An old narrow-gauge railroad runs out of McEwen Depot. See the description of Union Creek.

Campsites, facilities: There are 18 sites for tents or RVs up to 24 feet long. Fire grills and vault toilets are available. There is no drinking water, and all garbage must be packed out. A boat ramp is adjacent to the campground. Leashed pets are permitted.

Reservations, fees: Reservations are not accepted. Sites are $8 per night, $4 per extra vehicle. Senior discount available. Open from May–mid-November.

Directions: From Baker City, drive southwest on Highway 7 for 24 miles (just past Phillips Lake) to Hudspeth Lane (County Road 667). Turn south on Hudspeth Lane and drive two miles to Forest Road 2220. Turn southeast and drive 2.5 miles to the campground.

Contact: Wallowa-Whitman National Forest, Baker Ranger District, 3165 10th St., Baker City, OR 97814, 541/523-4476, fax 541/523-1965; concessionaire, Recreation Resource Management, 541/894-2505.

76 MILLERS LANE

Rating: 7

On Phillips Lake in Wallowa-Whitman National Forest.

Map 10.7, grid c8, page 568

This small campground is situated at an elevation of 4,120 feet along the south shore of Phillips Lake, a long, narrow reservoir and the largest in the region. Millers Lane is one of two primitive camps on the lake. An old narrow-gauge railroad runs out of McEwen Depot. See the description of Union Creek.

Campsites, facilities: There are seven sites for tents or RVs up to 20 feet long. Picnic tables and fire grills are provided. Firewood and vault toilets are available. There is no drinking water, and all garbage must be packed out. A boat ramp is at Southwest Shore. Leashed pets are permitted.

Reservations, fees: Reservations are not accepted. There is no fee for camping. Open from May–mid-November.

Directions: From Baker City, drive southwest on Highway 7 for 24 miles (just past Phillips Lake) to Hudspeth Lane (County Road 667).

Turn south on Hudspeth Lane and drive two miles to Forest Road 2220. Turn southeast and drive 3.5 miles to the campground.

Contact: Wallowa-Whitman National Forest, Baker Ranger District, 3165 10th St., Baker City, OR 97814, 541/523-4476, fax 541/523-1965; concessionaire, Recreation Resource Management, 541/894-2505.

77 MAGONE LAKE

Rating: 8

On Magone Lake in Malheur National Forest.

Map 10.7, grid d1, page 568

This campground is set along the shore of little Magone Lake at an elevation of 5,100 feet. A 1.8-mile trail rings the lake, and the section extending from the beach area to the campground (about a quarter mile) is barrier-free. A half-mile trail leads to Magone Slide, an unusual geological formation. Swimming, fishing, sailing, and canoeing are some of the popular activities at this lake. Easy-access bike trails can be found within a quarter mile of the campground.

Campsites, facilities: There are three sites for tents and 18 sites for RVs up to 40 feet long; four are drive-through sites. There is a separate group camping site designed for 10 families and a picnic shelter that can accommodate 50–100 people. Picnic tables and fire grills are provided. Drinking water, composting toilets, a boat ramp, and a beach area are available. Some facilities are wheelchair accessible. Boat docks and launching facilities are nearby. Leashed pets are permitted.

Reservations, fees: Reservations are not accepted for family sites; $10 per night, $2.50 per extra vehicle. Senior discount available. Reservations required for the group site and group picnic shelter at 541/820-3863; $60 per night for group sites. Open May–November, weather permitting.

Directions: From John Day, drive east on U.S.

26 for eight miles to County Road 18. Turn north and drive 10 miles to Forest Road 3620. Turn left (west) on Forest Road 3620 and drive 1.5 miles to Forest Road 3618. Turn right (northwest) and drive 1.5 miles to the campground.

Contact: Malheur National Forest, Blue Mountain Ranger District, P.O. Box 909, John Day, OR 97845, 541/575-3000, fax 541/575-3001.

78 MIDDLE FORK

Rating: 6

On the Middle Fork of the John Day River in Malheur National Forest.

Map 10.7, grid c4, page 568

Scattered along the banks of the Middle Fork of the John Day River at 4,100 feet elevation, these rustic campsites are easy to reach off a paved road. Besides wildlife watching and berry picking, the main activity at this camp is fishing, so bring along your fly rod, and pinch down your barbs for catch-and-release. The John Day is a state scenic waterway.

Campsites, facilities: There are 10 sites for tents or RVs up to 30 feet long. Picnic tables and fire grills are provided. Vault toilets are available. There is no drinking water, and all garbage must be packed out. Some facilities are wheelchair accessible. Leashed pets are permitted.

Reservations, fees: Reservations are not accepted. Sites are $5 per night, $2.50 per night for an additional vehicle. Senior discount available. Open May–November, weather permitting.

Directions: From John Day, drive northeast on U.S. 26 for 28 miles to Highway 7. Turn left (north) and drive one mile to County Road 20. Turn left and drive five miles to the campground on the left.

Contact: Malheur National Forest, Blue Mountain Ranger District, P.O. Box 909, John Day, OR 97845, 541/575-3000, fax 541/575-3001.

79 DIXIE

Rating: 5

Near Dixie Summit in Malheur National Forest.

Map 10.7, grid d4, page 568

This campground is set at Dixie Summit (elevation 5,300 feet) near Bridge Creek, where you can toss in a fishing line. The camp is just off U.S. 26, close enough to provide easy access. It draws overnighters, but otherwise gets light use. The Sumpter Valley Railroad interpretive site is one mile west on U.S. 26.

Campsites, facilities: There are 11 sites for tents or RVs up to 30 feet long. Picnic tables, vault toilets, and fire grills are provided. Drinking water is available, but all garbage must be packed out. A store, a café, gas, and ice are available within six miles. Some facilities are wheelchair accessible. Leashed pets are permitted.

Reservations, fees: Reservations are not accepted. Sites are $5 per night, $2.50 per night for an additional vehicle. Senior discount available. Open May–November, weather permitting.

Directions: From John Day, drive northeast on U.S. 26 for 24 miles to Forest Road 365. Turn left and drive one-quarter mile to the campground.

Contact: Malheur National Forest, Blue Mountain Ranger District, P.O. Box 909, John Day, OR 97845, 541/575-3000, fax 541/575-3001.

80 DEPOT PARK

Rating: 6

On the John Day River.

Map 10.7, grid e3, page 568

This urban park on grassy flatlands provides access to the John Day River, a good trout fishing spot. The camp is a more developed alternative to the many U.S. Forest Service campgrounds in the area. Depot Park features a historic rail depot on the premises as well as a related museum. Nearby attractions include the Strawberry Mountain Wilderness (prime hiking trails) and Clyde Holliday State Recreation Site.

Campsites, facilities: There are 20 sites for tents or RVs up to 35 feet long. Restrooms, showers, an RV dump station, a gazebo, a picnic area, and a public phone are provided. Leashed pets are permitted.

Reservations, fees: Reservations are not accepted. Sites are $11–16 per night. Open May–November, weather permitting.

Directions: From John Day, drive east on U.S. 26 for 13 miles to Prairie City and the junction of U.S. 26 and Main Street. Turn right (south) on Main Street and drive one-half mile to the park (well signed).

Contact: Prairie City Hall, P.O. Box 370, Prairie City, OR 97869, 541/820-3605.

81 WETMORE

Rating: 7

On the Middle Fork of the Burnt River in Wallowa-Whitman National Forest.
Map 10.7, grid d6, page 568

This campground, set at an elevation of 4,320 feet near the Middle Fork of the Burnt River, makes a nice base camp for a fishing or hiking trip. The stream can provide good trout fishing. Trails are detailed on a map of Wallowa-Whitman National Forest. In addition, an excellent half-mile, wheelchair-accessible trail passes through old-growth forest. Watch for bald eagles.

Campsites, facilities: There are 16 sites for tents or RVs up to 28 feet long. Picnic tables and fire grills are provided. Drinking water, firewood, and vault toilets are available, but all garbage must be packed out. Some facilities are wheelchair accessible. Leashed pets are permitted.

Reservations, fees: Reservations are not accepted. Sites are $5 per night. Senior discount available. Open late May–mid-September.

Directions: From John Day, drive east on U.S.

26 for 29 miles to Austin Junction. Continue east on U.S. 26 for 10 miles to the campground.

Contact: Wallowa-Whitman National Forest, Unity Ranger District, 214 Main St., P.O. Box 39, Unity, OR 97884, 541/446-3351, fax 541/523-1479.

82 OREGON

Rating: 6

Near Austin Junction in Wallowa-Whitman National Forest.
Map 10.7, grid d6, page 568

This campground at 4,880 feet elevation is just off U.S. 26 and is the staging area for ATV enthusiasts; several ATV trails crisscross the area. The camp is surrounded by hillside, Douglas fir, white fir, and tamarack. Bald eagles nest in the area.

Campsites, facilities: There are 11 sites for tents or RVs up to 28 feet long. Picnic tables and fire grills are provided. Drinking water and vault toilets are available, but garbage must be packed out. Leashed pets are permitted.

Reservations, fees: Reservations are not accepted. Sites are $5 per night. Senior discount available. Open May–mid-September.

Directions: From John Day, drive east on U.S. 26 for 29 miles to Austin Junction. Continue east for 20 miles to the campground.

Contact: Wallowa-Whitman National Forest, Unity Ranger District, 214 Main St., P.O. Box 39, Unity, OR 97884, 541/446-3351, fax 541/523-1479.

83 YELLOW PINE

Rating: 7

Near Middle Fork Burnt River.
Map 10.7, grid d6, page 568

Highlights of this camp include easy access and good recreation potential. The camp offers a number of hiking trails; one half-mile-long, wheelchair-accessible trail connects to the Wetmore Campground. Yellow Pine is similar to Oregon Campground, but larger. Keep an eye out for bald eagles in this area.

Campsites, facilities: There are 21 sites for tents or RVs up to 28 feet long. Picnic tables and fire grills are provided. Drinking water, an RV dump station, and vault toilets are available, but all garbage must be packed out. Leashed pets are permitted.

Reservations, fees: Reservations are not accepted. Sites are $5 per night. Senior discount available. Open late May–mid-September.

Directions: From John Day, drive east on U.S. 26 for 29 miles to Austin Junction. Continue east for 21 miles to the campground.

Contact: Wallowa-Whitman National Forest, Unity Ranger District, 214 Main St., P.O. Box 39, Unity, OR 97884, 541/446-3351, fax 541/523-1479.

84 UNITY LAKE STATE RECREATION SITE

Rating: 7

On Unity Reservoir.
Map 10.7, grid d7, page 568

This camp, set along the east shore of Unity Reservoir, is a popular spot in good weather. Campers can choose from hiking, swimming, boating, fishing, picnicking, or enjoying the scenic views. Set in the high desert, this grassy park provides a contrast to the sagebrush and cheat grass of the bordering land.

Campsites, facilities: There are 35 sites with water and electrical hookups for tents or RVs of any length, a separate area for hikers and bicyclists, and two teepees. Picnic tables, garbage bins, and fire grills are provided. Drinking water, flush toilets, showers, an RV dump station, and firewood are available. Some facilities are wheelchair accessible. Boat docks and launching facilities are nearby. Leashed pets are permitted.

Reservations, fees: Reservations are not accepted. Sites are $13–15 per night, $4 per person for hike-in/bike-in sites, $27 per night for

teepees, and $7 per night for an additional vehicle. Open mid-April–late October.

Directions: From John Day, drive east on U.S. 26 for 50 miles to Highway 245. Turn left (north) on Highway 245 and drive three miles to the park on the left.

Contact: Clyde Holliday State Recreation Site, P.O. Box 10, Mt. Vernon, OR 97820, 541/932-4453 or 800/551-6949.

85 MAMMOTH SPRINGS

Rating: 4

On the South Fork of the Burnt River in Wallowa-Whitman National Forest.
Map 10.7, grid e6, page 568

The South Fork of the Burnt River is a nice trout creek with, according to the local ranger, "good evening bites for anglers who know how to sneak-fish." The camp is private and scenic. Popular with hunters in the fall, it's set in brush and Douglas firs. By the way, the hot springs consist of a spot the size of a washtub, not large enough for human use. Maybe a Lemurian could fit in.

Campsites, facilities: There is a dispersed camping area for tents or RVs up to 28 feet long. Picnic tables and fire grills are provided. Vault toilets are available. No drinking water. Leashed pets are permitted. Pack out all garbage.

Reservations, fees: Reservations are not accepted. There is no fee for camping. Open May–mid-September.

Directions: From John Day, drive east on U.S. 26 for 49 miles to Unity and County Road 600. Turn right on County Road 600 and drive west for six miles (the road becomes Forest Road 6005/South Fork Road). Continue past the forest boundary for two miles to a Y with Forest Road 2640. Bear right (west) and drive one-half mile to the camp.

Contact: Wallowa-Whitman National Forest, Unity Ranger District, 214 Main St., P.O. Box 39, Unity, OR 97884, 541/446-3351, fax 541/523-1479.

86 SOUTH FORK

Rating: 5

On the South Fork of the Burnt River in Wallowa-Whitman National Forest.

Map 10.7, grid e6, page 568

This campground is set at an elevation of 4,400 feet along the banks of the South Fork of the Burnt River, a nice trout creek with good evening bites for anglers who know how to sneak-fish. A gem of a spot, it offers drinking water, privacy, and scenery—all for free.

Campsites, facilities: There are 14 sites for tents or RVs up to 28 feet long. Picnic tables and fire grills are provided. Drinking water and vault toilets are available, but all garbage must be packed out. Leashed pets are permitted.

Reservations, fees: Reservations are not accepted. There is no fee for camping. Open late May–mid-September.

Directions: From John Day, drive east on U.S. 26 for 49 miles to Unity and County Road 600. Turn right on County Road 600 and drive west for six miles (the road becomes Forest Road 6005/South Fork Road). Continue past the forest boundary for one mile to the campground on the left.

Contact: Wallowa-Whitman National Forest, Unity Ranger District, 214 Main St., P.O. Box 39, Unity, OR 97884, 541/446-3351, fax 541/523-1479.

87 STEVENS CREEK

Rating: 5

On the South Fork of the Burnt River in Wallowa-Whitman National Forest.

Map 10.7, grid e6, page 568

This campground along the banks of the South Fork of the Burnt River provides an alternative to the other small camps along the river. The trout fishing is often good here. It is set at an elevation of 4,480 feet. See the description of South Fork for more information.

Campsites, facilities: There is one group area for up to six tents or RVs of any length. Picnic tables and fire grills are provided, but there is no drinking water, and all garbage must be packed out. Vault toilets are available. Leashed pets are permitted.

Reservations, fees: Reservations are not accepted. There is no fee for camping. Open late May–mid-September.

Directions: From John Day, drive east on U.S. 26 for 49 miles to Unity and County Road 600. Turn right on County Road 600 and drive west for six miles (the road becomes Forest Road 6005/South Fork Road). Continue past the forest boundary for two miles to the campground on the right.

Contact: Wallowa-Whitman National Forest, Unity Ranger District, 214 Main St., P.O. Box 39, Unity, OR 97884, 541/446-3351, fax 541/523-1479.

88 LONG CREEK

Rating: 4

On Long Creek Reservoir in Wallowa-Whitman National Forest.

Map 10.7, grid f6, page 568

This small, little-known campground set at 4,430 feet elevation boasts good trout fishing in Long Creek Reservoir. Several nearby campgrounds, including Mammoth Springs, Eldorado, and Elk Creek, have similar surroundings and facilities.

Campsites, facilities: There is a dispersed camping area for tents or RVs up to 28 feet long. Picnic tables and fire grills are provided. A vault toilet is available, but there is no drinking water, and all garbage must be packed out. Leashed pets are permitted.

Reservations, fees: Reservations are not accepted. There is no fee for camping. Open May–mid-September.

Directions: From John Day, drive east on U.S. 26 for 49 miles to Unity, then continue for one mile to Forest Road 1680 (West Camp Creek

Road). Turn right (south) and drive seven miles to the access road on the left for Long Creek Reservoir and campground. Turn left and drive three miles to the campground.

Contact: Wallowa-Whitman National Forest, Unity Ranger District, 214 Main St., P.O. Box 39, Unity, OR 97884, 541/446-3351, fax 541/523-1479.

89 ELDORADO

Rating: 5

On East Camp Creek in Wallowa-Whitman National Forest.

Map 10.7, grid f6, page 568

Trout fishing at East Camp Creek in spring and early summer is a draw here. The campground is also convenient for fishing at Murray Reservoir. Eldorado sits at an elevation of 4,600 feet.

Campsites, facilities: There are six sites for tents or RVs up to 28 feet long. Picnic tables and fire grills are provided. Vault toilets are available, but there is no drinking water, and all garbage must be packed out. Leashed pets are permitted.

Reservations, fees: Reservations are not accepted. There is no fee for camping. Open May–mid-September.

Directions: From John Day, drive east on U.S. 26 for 49 miles to Unity, then continue 10 miles to Forest Road 16 (well signed, on the right). Turn right (south) and drive three miles to the campground on the left.

Contact: Wallowa-Whitman National Forest, Unity Ranger District, 214 Main St., P.O. Box 39, Unity, OR 97884, 541/446-3351, fax 541/523-1479.

90 STRAWBERRY

Rating: 7

On Strawberry Creek in Malheur National Forest.

Map 10.7, grid f5, page 568

This campground is set along the banks of Strawberry Creek at 5,700 feet elevation. Nearby trails provide access to the Strawberry Mountain Wilderness, Strawberry Lake, and Strawberry Falls. This pretty area features a variety of hiking and hunting options. Fishing in Strawberry Creek is another possibility.

Campsites, facilities: There are 11 sites for tents. Picnic tables and fire grills are provided. Drinking water and wheelchair-accessible vault toilets are available. Leashed pets are permitted. Pack out all garbage.

Reservations, fees: Reservations are not accepted. Sites are $6 per night, $3 per night for an additional vehicle. Senior discount available. Open June–mid-October.

Directions: From John Day, drive east on U.S. 26 for 13 miles to Prairie City and County Road 62. Turn right (southeast) and drive one-half mile to County Road 60. Turn right and drive south on County Road 60 for 8.5 miles (County Road 60 becomes Forest Road 6001). Continue 2.5 miles to the campground.

Contact: Malheur National Forest, Prairie City Ranger District, P.O. Box 337, Prairie City, OR 97869, 541/820-3311, fax 541/820-3838.

91 LITTLE CRANE

Rating: 5

On Little Crane Creek in Malheur National Forest.

Map 10.7, grid f4, page 568

Small, primitive, quiet, and private all describe this camp along the banks of Little Crane Creek at an elevation of 5,500 feet. The creek provides good trout fishing (only artificial bait and artificial lures are allowed). There are also some nice hiking trails in the area, the closest one at the North Fork of the Malheur River, about 10 miles away.

Campsites, facilities: There are four tent and trailer sites. Picnic tables and fire grills are provided. Vault toilets are available. There is no drinking water, and all garbage must be packed out. Leashed pets are permitted.

Reservations, fees: Reservations are not accepted. There is no fee for camping. Open June–mid-November.

Directions: From John Day, drive east on U.S. 26 for 13 miles to Prairie City and County Road 62. Turn right and drive 8.5 miles to Forest Road 13. Turn left and drive 16 miles to Forest Road 16. Turn right and drive 5.5 miles south to the campground.

Contact: Malheur National Forest, Prairie City Ranger District, P.O. Box 337, Prairie City, OR 97869, 541/820-3311, fax 541/820-3838.

92 TROUT FARM

Rating: 6

Near Prairie City in Malheur National Forest.

Map 10.7, grid f4, page 568

This campground (4,900 feet elevation) is situated on the Upper John Day River, which provides good trout fishing with easy access for people who don't wish to travel off paved roads. A picnic shelter is available for family picnics, and a small pond at the campground has a wheelchair-accessible trail.

Campsites, facilities: There are six sites for tents or RVs up to 21 feet long. Picnic tables and fire grills are provided. Drinking water and wheelchair-accessible vault toilets are available, but all garbage must be packed out. Leashed pets are permitted.

Reservations, fees: Reservations are not accepted. Sites are $6 per night, $3 per extra vehicle. Senior discount available. Open June–mid-October.

Directions: From John Day, drive east on U.S. 26 for 13 miles to Prairie City and County Road 62. Turn right and drive 15 miles to the campground entrance on the right.

Contact: Malheur National Forest, Prairie City Ranger District, P.O. Box 337, Prairie City, OR 97869, 541/820-3311, fax 541/820-3838.

93 WICKIUP

Rating: 5

On Wickiup Creek in Malheur National Forest.

Map 10.7, grid g2, page 568

This campground sits along the forks of Wickiup Creek and Canyon Creek at a historic site with many original Civilian Conservation Corps structures still in place. There is limited fishing in the creek. To the north are many trails that lead into the Strawberry Mountain Wilderness.

Campsites, facilities: There are eight sites for tents or RVs up to 25 feet long. Picnic tables and fire grills are provided. Vault toilet and horse corrals are available. No drinking water is available and all garbage must be packed out. Some facilities are wheelchair accessible. Leashed pets are permitted.

Reservations, fees: No reservation; no fee. Open early May–November.

Directions: From John Day, drive south on U.S. 395 for 10 miles to Forest Road 15. Turn southeast and drive eight miles to the campground.

Contact: Malheur National Forest, Blue Mountain Ranger District, P.O. Box 909, John Day, OR 97845, 541/575-3000, fax 541/575-3001.

94 CANYON MEADOWS

Rating: 5

On Canyon Meadows Reservoir in Malheur National Forest.

Map 10.7, grid g2, page 568

This campground is set on the shore of Canyon Meadows Reservoir, where nonmotorized boating, plus swimming, sailing, fishing, and hiking, are recreation options. However, this reservoir dries up by the Fourth of July because of a leak in the dam. Several hiking trails nearby lead north into the Strawberry Mountain Wilderness.

Campsites, facilities: There are 14 sites for tents or RVs up to 25 feet long. Picnic tables and fire grills are provided. Vault toilets are available. No drinking water is available and all garbage must be packed out. Some facilities are wheelchair accessible. Leashed pets are permitted.

Reservations, fees: Reservations are not accepted. There is no fee. Open mid-May–late October.

Directions: From John Day, drive south on U.S. 395 for 10 miles to Forest Road 15. Turn left and drive nine miles southeast to Forest Road 1520. Turn left and drive five miles to the campground.

Contact: Malheur National Forest, Blue Mountain Ranger District, P.O. Box 909, John Day, OR 97845, 541/575-3000, fax 541/575-3001.

95 PARISH CABIN

Rating: 6

On Little Bear Creek in Malheur National Forest.

Map 10.7, grid g2, page 568

This campground along the banks of Little Bear Creek (elevation of 4,900 feet) is in a pretty spot that's not heavily used. The creek offers limited fishing. The road is paved all the way to the campground. This campground is popular with groups of families and hunters in season.

Campsites, facilities: There are 16 sites for tents or RVs up to 32 feet long. Picnic tables and fire grills are provided. Drinking water, vault toilets, and horse facilities are available. Leashed pets are permitted. All garbage must be packed out. Some facilities are wheelchair accessible. Leashed pets are permitted.

Reservations, fees: Reservations are not accepted. Sites are $6 per night, $3 per extra vehicle. Senior discount available. Open mid-May–late November.

Directions: From John Day, drive south on U.S. 395 for 10 miles to Forest Road 15. Turn

left and drive 16 miles southeast to Forest Road 16. Turn right onto Forest Road 16 and drive a short distance to the campground on the right.

Contact: Malheur National Forest, Blue Mountain Ranger District, P.O. Box 909, John Day, OR 97845, 541/575-3000, fax 541/575-3001.

96 BIG CREEK

Rating: 6

Near the Strawberry Mountain Wilderness in Malheur National Forest.

Map 10.7, grid g3, page 568

This campground is set at an elevation of 5,100 feet along the banks of Big Creek. Nearby forest roads provide access to the Strawberry Mountain Wilderness. Other recreation options include fishing and mountain biking. Note that fishing is restricted to the use of artificial lures with a single, barbless hook. In the appropriate seasons, elk, bear, coyote, and deer are hunted here.

Campsites, facilities: There are 15 sites for tents or RVs up to 16 feet long. Picnic tables and fire grills are provided. Drinking water and wheelchair-accessible vault toilets are available. All garbage must be packed out. Leashed pets are permitted.

Reservations, fees: Reservations are not accepted. Sites are $5 per night, $2.50 per night for an additional vehicle. Senior discount available. Open mid-May–mid-November.

Directions: From John Day, drive east on U.S. 26 for 13 miles to Prairie City and County Road 62. Turn right and drive 24 miles to Forest Road 16. Turn right and drive six miles to Forest Road 815. Turn right and drive one-half mile to the campground on the right.

Contact: Malheur National Forest, Prairie City Ranger District, P.O. Box 337, Prairie City, OR 97869, 541/820-3311, fax 541/820-3838.

97 ELK CREEK

Rating: 8

On Elk Creek in Malheur National Forest.
Map 10.7, grid f6, page 568

This tiny, pretty camp at the confluence of the North and South Forks of Elk Creek (elevation 5,000 feet) has lots of hunting and fishing opportunities. The camp gets light use, except during the hunting season. North Fork Malheur is an alternate camp in the area.

Campsites, facilities: There are five tent sites. Picnic tables and fire grills are provided. Vault toilets are available. There is no drinking water and all garbage must be packed out. Leashed pets are permitted.

Reservations, fees: Reservations are not accepted. There is no fee for camping. Open mid-May–mid-November.

Directions: From John Day, drive east on U.S. 26 for 13 miles to Prairie City and County Road 62. Turn right (southeast) on County Road 62 and drive 8.5 miles to Forest Road 13. Turn left and drive 16 miles to Forest Road 16. Turn right and drive 1.5 miles south to the campground.

Contact: Malheur National Forest, Prairie City Ranger District, P.O. Box 337, Prairie City, OR 97869, 541/820-3311, fax 541/820-3838.

98 NORTH FORK MALHEUR

Rating: 7

On the North Fork of the Malheur River in Malheur National Forest.
Map 10.7, grid g5, page 568

This secluded campground sits at an elevation of 4,700 feet along the banks of the North Fork of the Malheur River, a designated Wild and Scenic River. Hiking trails and dirt roads provide additional access to the river and backcountry streams. It's essential to obtain a U.S. Forest Service map. Good fishing, hunting, and mountain biking opportunities

abound in the area. Fishing is restricted to the use of artificial lures with a single, barbless hook.

Campsites, facilities: There are five sites for tents or small, self-contained RVs. Picnic tables and fire grills are provided. Vault toilets are available. There is no drinking water, and all garbage must be packed out. Leashed pets are permitted.

Reservations, fees: Reservations are not accepted. There is no fee for camping. Open mid-May–mid-November.

Directions: From John Day, drive east on U.S. 26 for 13 miles to Prairie City and County Road 62. Turn right and drive 8.5 miles to Forest Road 13. Turn left and drive 16 miles to Forest Road 16. Turn right and drive two miles south to a fork with Forest Road 1675. Take the left fork to Forest Road 1675 and drive two miles to the camp on the right.

Contact: Malheur National Forest, Prairie City Ranger District, P.O. Box 337, Prairie City, OR 97869, 541/820-3311, fax 541/820-3838.

99 ROCK SPRINGS FOREST CAMP

Rating: 5

At Rock Springs in Malheur National Forest.
Map 10.7, grid h2, page 568

If you want to camp in a big forest filled with the scent of ponderosa pines, this camp is for you. This primitive camp also has a sprinkling of pretty aspens and several little springs. In fact, it's located right on Rock Springs, with Cave Spring, Sunshine Spring, and House Creek Spring within a few miles. Do not count on the springs for drinking water, however, without a water filter. The elevation is 4,800 feet.

Campsites, facilities: There are eight sites for tents or RVs up to 20 feet long. Picnic tables and fire grills are provided. Vault toilets are available. There is no drinking water. Garbage must be packed out. Leashed pets are permitted.

Reservations, fees: Reservations are not accepted. There is no fee for camping. Open late May–mid-October.

Directions: From Burns, drive north on U.S. 395 for 30 miles to Van-Silvies Highway (County Road 73). Turn right on Van-Silvies Highway (which turns into Forest Road 17) and drive four miles to Forest Road 054. Turn right (south) and drive three-quarters of a mile to the camp on the left.

Contact: Malheur National Forest, Emigrant Creek Ranger District, 265 Hwy. 20 S, Hines, OR 97738, 541/573-4300, fax 541/573-4398.

100 EAGLE FORKS

Rating: 6

On Eagle Creek in Wallowa-Whitman National Forest.

Map 10.8, grid a6, page 569

This campground, set at 3,000 feet elevation, is at the confluence of Little Eagle Creek and Eagle Creek. A trail follows the creek northwest for several miles, making for a prime day hike, yet the spot attracts few people. It's quite pretty as well and perfect for a weekend getaway or an extended layover.

Campsites, facilities: There are seven tent sites and five sites for RVs up to 21 feet long. Picnic tables and fire grills are provided. Drinking water and vault toilets are available, but all garbage must be packed out. Leashed pets are permitted.

Reservations, fees: Reservations are not accepted. There is no fee for camping. Open June–late October.

Directions: From Baker City, drive east on Highway 86 for 36 miles to Richland. Turn north on Eagle Creek Road and drive to Newbridge; continue on Forest Road 7735 for seven miles to the campground entrance on the left.

Contact: Wallowa-Whitman National Forest, Pine Ranger District, 38470 Pinetown Ln., Halfway, OR 97834, 541/742-7511, fax 541/742-6705.

101 WEST EAGLE MEADOW

Rating: 7

Near West Eagle Creek in Wallowa-Whitman National Forest.

Map 10.8, grid a6, page 569

This campground in a big, open meadow is set at 5,200 feet elevation about a five-minute walk from West Eagle Creek. The West Eagle Trail starts at the campground, providing access to the Eagle Cap Wilderness and offering a good opportunity to observe wildlife. The adjacent meadow fills with wildflowers in the summer. For those with horses, there are new stock facilities with water available in a separate, adjacent campground .

Campsites, facilities: There are 24 sites for tents. There is an adjacent campground for those with horses with six sites. Picnic tables, garbage service (summer only), and fire rings are provided. There is no drinking water. Vault toilets are available. Stock facilities include water, corrals, hitching rails, and a nearby loading ramp. Some facilities are wheelchair accessible. Leashed pets are permitted.

Reservations, fees: Reservations are not accepted. There is no fee for camping. Open mid-June–late October.

Directions: From Baker City, drive north on I-84 for six miles to Highway 203. Turn east and drive 17 miles to the town of Medical Springs and Forest Road 67. Turn on Forest Road 67 and drive 15.5 miles (across Eagle Creek) to Forest Road 77. Turn left and drive 20 miles to the campground on the left.

Contact: Wallowa-Whitman National Forest, LaGrande Ranger District, 3502 Hwy. 30, LaGrande, OR 97850, 541/963-7186, fax 541/962-8580.

102 TWO COLOR

Rating: 6

On Eagle Creek in Wallowa-Whitman National Forest.

Map 10.8, grid a6, page 569

This campground is set at 4,800 feet elevation along the banks of Eagle Creek, about a mile north of Tamarack. Another option for campers is nearby Boulder Park campground, three miles northeast on Forest Road 7755.

Campsites, facilities: There are 14 sites for tents and six sites for RVs up to 22 feet long. Picnic tables and fire grills are provided. Drinking water and vault toilets are available, but garbage must be packed out. Leashed pets are permitted.

Reservations, fees: Reservations are not accepted. The fee is $5 per night. Senior discount available. Open mid-June–late October.

Directions: From Baker City, drive north on I-84 for six miles to Highway 203. Turn east on Highway 203 and drive 17 miles to Medical Springs and Big Springs Road (Forest Road 67). Turn left on Forest Road 67 and drive 15.5 miles (staying on Forest Road 67 at all Y junctions) to Forest Road 77. Turn left and drive one-quarter mile to the camp.

Contact: Wallowa-Whitman National Forest, LaGrande Ranger District, 3502 Hwy. 30, LaGrande, OR 97850, 541/963-7186, fax 541/962-8580.

103 TAMARACK

Rating: 5

On Eagle Creek in Wallowa-Whitman National Forest.

Map 10.8, grid a6, page 569

On the banks of Eagle Creek in a beautiful area with lush vegetation and abundant wildlife, this camp (4,600 feet elevation) is a good spot for a fishing and hiking trip in a remote setting.

Campsites, facilities: There are 12 tent sites and 12 sites for RVs up to 22 feet long. Picnic tables and fire grills are provided. Drinking water and vault toilets are available, but all garbage must be packed out. Leashed pets are permitted.

Reservations, fees: Reservations are not accepted. The fee is $5 per night. Senior discount available. Open June–late October.

Directions: From Baker City, drive north on I-84 for six miles to Highway 203. Turn east on Highway 203 and drive 17 miles to Medical Springs and Big Springs Road (Forest Road 67). Turn left on Forest Road 67 and drive 15.5 miles (staying on Forest Road 67 at all Y junctions) to Forest Road 77. Turn right and drive one-quarter mile to the camp.

Contact: Wallowa-Whitman National Forest, Pine Ranger District, 38470 Pinetown Ln., Halfway, OR 97834, 541/742-7511, fax 541/742-6705.

104 MCBRIDE

Rating: 6

On Brooks Ditch in Wallowa-Whitman National Forest.

Map 10.8, grid a7, page 569

This campground is set along the banks of Brooks Ditch at an elevation of 4,800 feet. It is little used, primitive, and obscure. Though not particularly scenic, it will work as a quick, free layover spot.

Campsites, facilities: There are 11 tent sites and eight sites for RVs up to 16 feet long. Picnic tables and fire grills are provided. Drinking water and vault toilets are available, but all garbage must be packed out. Leashed pets are permitted.

Reservations, fees: Reservations are not accepted. The fee is $5 per night. Senior discount available. Open mid-May–late October.

Directions: From Baker City, drive east on Highway 86 for 52 miles to Halfway. Turn northwest on Highway 413 and drive six miles to Forest Road 7710. Turn west and drive 2.5 miles to the campground.

Contact: Wallowa-Whitman National Forest, Pine

Ranger District, 38470 Pinetown Ln., Halfway, OR 97834, 541/742-7511, fax 541/742-6705.

105 TWIN LAKES

Rating: 6

Near Twin Lakes in Wallowa-Whitman National Forest.
Map 10.8, grid a8, page 569

This campground is nestled between the little Twin Lakes at 6,500 feet elevation. Both lakes offer excellent fishing. Nearby trails provide access to backcountry lakes and streams. See a U.S. Forest Service map for details. Another campground option is Fish Lake, about six miles south on Forest Road 66.

Campsites, facilities: There are six tent sites. Picnic tables and fire grills are provided. Firewood and vault toilets are available, but there is no drinking water, and all garbage must be packed out. Leashed pets are permitted.

Reservations, fees: Reservations are not accepted. The fee is $5 per night. Senior discount available. Open July–mid-September.

Directions: From Baker City on I-84, turn east on Highway 86 and drive 52 miles to Halfway and County Road 733. Turn north on County Road 733 and drive five miles north to Fish Lake Road (Forest Road 66). Turn north and drive 24 miles to the campground.

Contact: Hells Canyon National Recreation Area, Wallowa Mountains Visitor Center, 88401 Hwy. 82, Enterprise, OR 97828, 541/426-5546; or Pine Ranger District, Wallowa-Whitman National Forest, 38470 Pinetown Lane, Halfway, OR 97834, 541/742-7511.

106 FISH LAKE

Rating: 6

On Fish Lake in Wallowa-Whitman National Forest.
Map 10.8, grid a8, page 569

This pretty, well-forested camp with comfort-able sites along the shore of Fish Lake makes a good base for a fishing trip. Side-trip options include hiking on nearby trails that lead to mountain streams. It sits at an elevation of 6,600 feet.

Campsites, facilities: There are 10 tent sites and five sites for RVs up to 22 feet long. Picnic tables and fire grills are provided. Drinking water and vault toilets are available. Boat-launching facilities are nearby. Leashed pets are permitted. Garbage must be packed out.

Reservations, fees: Reservations are not accepted. Sites are $5 per night. Senior discount available. Open mid-June–late October.

Directions: From Baker City, drive north on I-84 for four miles to Highway 86. Turn east on Highway 86 and drive 52 miles to Halfway and County Road 733. Turn north on County Road 733 and drive five miles to Forest Road 66. Continue north on Forest Road 66 for 18.5 miles to the campground on the left.

Contact: Wallowa-Whitman National Forest, Pine Ranger District, 38470 Pinetown Ln., Halfway, OR 97834, 541/742-7511, fax 541/742-6705.

107 SPRING RECREATION SITE

Rating: 5

On the Snake River.
Map 10.8, grid f7, page 569

One of two camps in or near Huntington, this campground sits along the banks of the Snake River Reservoir. A more developed alternative, Farewell Bend State Recreation Area offers showers and all the other luxuries a camper could want. Fishing is popular at this reservoir.

Campsites, facilities: There are 35 sites for tents or RVs of any length. Picnic tables, garbage service, and fire grills are provided. Drinking water (summer only), an RV dump station, and vault toilets are available. Boat-launching facilities and a fish-cleaning station are on-site. Leashed pets are permitted.

Reservations, fees: Reservations are not accepted. Sites are $5 per night per vehicle, with a 14-day stay limit. Senior discount available. Open from March–October and some off-season weekends.

Directions: From Ontario (near the Oregon/Idaho border), drive northwest on I-84 for 28 miles to Huntington and Snake River Road. Turn northeast on Snake River Road and drive five miles to the campground.

Contact: Bureau of Land Management, Baker City Office, 3165 10th St., Baker City, OR 97814, 541/523-1256, fax 541/523-1965.

108 FAREWELL BEND STATE RECREATION AREA

Rating: 7

On the Snake River.
Map 10.8, grid f7, page 569

This campground offers a desert experience on the banks of the Snake River's Brownlee Reservoir. Situated along the Oregon Trail, it offers historic interpretive displays and an evening interpretive program at the amphitheater. Among the amenities are horseshoe pits, basketball hoops, and a sand volleyball court.

Campsites, facilities: There are 45 primitive tent sites and 91 sites with partial hookups for RVs up to 56 feet long. There are also four teepees, two cabins, two covered camper wagons, and two group tent areas. Drinking water, garbage bins, barbecues, and picnic tables are provided. Flush toilets, an RV dump station, showers, and firewood are available. Boat-launching facilities are nearby. Leashed pets are permitted.

Reservations, fees: Reservations at 800/452-5687 or website: ww.OregonStateParks.org; $12–18 per night. Teepees or covered wagons are $27 a night, and cabins are $35 per night. There is a $7 per night fee for an additional vehicle. Major credit cards accepted. Open year-round, with limited winter facilities.

Directions: From Ontario (near the Oregon/Idaho border), drive northwest on I-84 for 21 miles

to Exit 353 and the park entrance on the right side of the road.

Contact: Farewell Bend State Recreation Area, 23751 Old Hwy. 30, Huntington, OR 97907, 541/869-2365 or 800/551-6949.

109 BULLY CREEK PARK

Rating: 7

On Bully Creek Reservoir.
Map 10.8, grid h5, page 569

The reservoir is set in a kind of high desert area with sagebrush and poplar trees for shade. People come here to swim, boat, water-ski, and fish (mostly for warm-water fish, such as crappie and large and smallmouth bass). You can bike on the gravel roads. It's beautiful if you like the desert, and the sunsets are worth the trip. The primitive setting is home to deer, jackrabbits, squirrels, and many birds. The elevation is 2,300 feet. No monthly rentals are permitted here, a big plus for overnighters.

Campsites, facilities: There are 33 double sites for tents or RVs up to 30 feet in length. There are also three group sites. Electricity, picnic tables, and fire pits are provided. Drinking water, flush toilets, showers, ice, garbage bins, a dump station, and a boat ramp and dock are available. A restaurant, a café, groceries, a small store, gasoline, bottled gas, charcoal, and a coin-operated laundry are within 10 miles. Bring your own firewood. Leashed pets are permitted.

Reservations, fees: Reservations accepted ($10 deposit). Sites are $10 per sleeping unit per night. Open April–mid-November, weather permitting.

Directions: From Ontario (near the Oregon/Idaho border), drive west on U.S. 20/26 for 12 miles to Vale and Graham Boulevard. Turn northwest on Graham Boulevard and drive five miles to Bully Creek Road. Turn left (west) and drive three miles to Bully Creek Park.

Contact: Bully Creek Park, 2475 Bully Creek Rd., Vale, OR 97918, 541/473-2969, fax 541/473-9462.

Chapter 11
The Southern Cascades

Chapter 11—The Southern Cascades

This region of Oregon is famous for one of its lakes, but it holds many fantastic recreation secrets. The crown jewel is Crater Lake, of course, and visitors come from all over the world to see its vast cobalt-blue waters within the clifflike walls. The lake's Rim Drive is one of those trips that everybody should have on their life's to-do list.

Beyond the lake, though, you'll find stellar camping, hiking, and fishing spots. The best among them are neighboring Mount Washington Wilderness and Three Sisters Wilderness in Willamette National Forest, accessible via a beautiful drive on the McKenzie River Highway (Highway 126) east from Eugene and Springfield. Many ideal trailhead camps are detailed in this chapter for these areas.

But wait, there's more. Wickiup Reservoir, Crane Prairie, and Waldo Lake provide camping, boating, and good fishing. Wickiup, in turn, feeds into the headwaters of the Deschutes River, a prime steelhead locale. The Umpqua and Rogue National Forests offer some great water-sport destinations, including the headwaters of the North Umpqua, one of the prettiest rivers in North America; Diamond Lake; and the headwaters of the Rogue River. Upper Klamath Lake and the Klamath Basin are the number-one wintering areas in America for bald eagles. Klamath Lake also provides a chance to catch huge but elusive trout; same with the nearby Williamson River out of Chiloquin. All of this is but a small sampling of one of Oregon's best regions for adventure.

This region is all the more special for me because it evokes powerful personal memories. One of these is of a time at Hills Creek Reservoir southeast of Eugene. My canoe flipped on a cold winter day and I almost drowned after 20 minutes in the icy water. After I'd gone down for the count twice, my brother Bob jumped in, swam out, grabbed the front of the flipped canoe, and towed me to shore. Then, once ashore, he kept me awake, preventing me from lapsing into a coma from hypothermia.

Thanks, Bob.

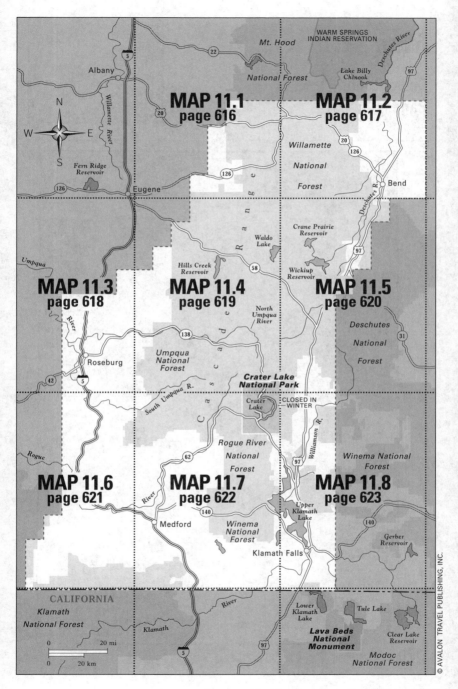

Map 11.1

Campgrounds 1–18
Pages 624–631

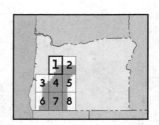

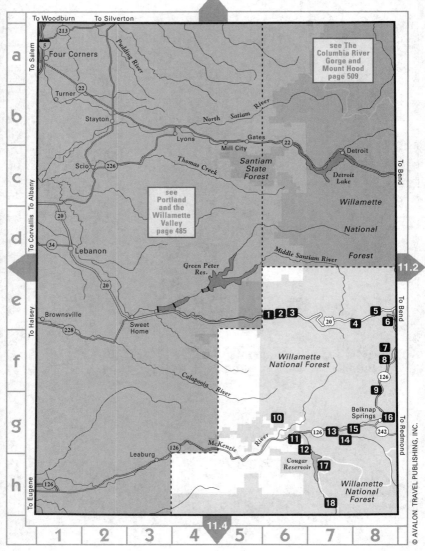

To Woodburn   To Silverton

see The
Columbia River
Gorge and
Mount Hood
page 509

To Salem

213

5

Four Corners

Padding River

a

Turner

22

b

Stayton

North Santiam River

Gates

Lyons

Mill City

22

Detroit

Scio

226

Thomas Creek

Santiam
State
Forest

Detroit
Lake

Willamette

c

20

see
Portland
and the
Willamette
Valley
page 485

National

To Corvallis   To Albany

34

d

Lebanon

Middle Santiam River

Forest

Green Peter
Res.

11.2

20

To Bend

Brownsville

e

228

Sweet
Home

1 2 3

20

4

5

6

To Bend

To Halsey

Willamette
National Forest

7

8

f

Calapooia River

126

9

Belknap
Springs

16

10

126

13

15

To Redmond

g

11

12

14

242

Leaburg

126

McKenzie River

Cougar
Reservoir

17

To Eugene

126

Willamette
National
Forest

h

18

1   2   3   4   11.4 5   6   7   8

© AVALON TRAVEL PUBLISHING, INC.

Map 11.2

Campgrounds 19–53
Pages 631–644

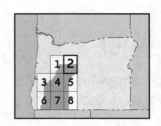

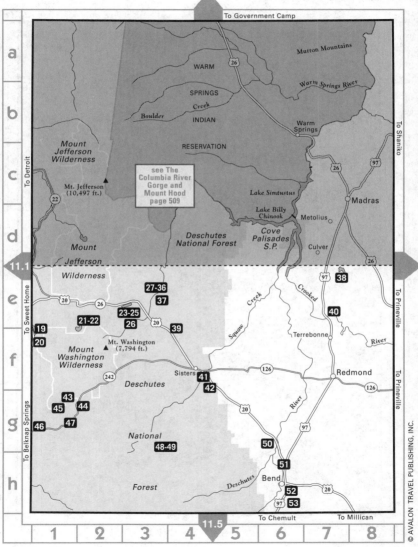

Map 11.3

Campgrounds 54–58
Pages 644–646

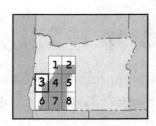

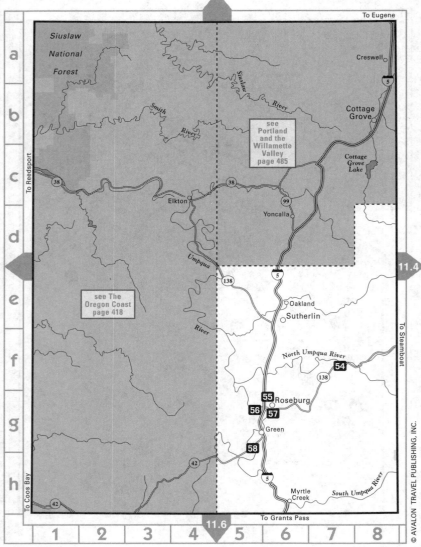

To Eugene

Siuslaw

National

Forest

Creswell

Cottage
Grove

Cottage
Grove
Lake

see
Portland
and the
Willamette
Valley
page 485

Smith

River

Siuslaw

River

To Reedsport

38

38

Elkton

99

Yoncalla

Umpqua

138

5

11.4

see The
Oregon Coast
page 418

River

Oakland

Sutherlin

To Steamboat

North Umpqua River

54

138

55 Roseburg

56

57

Green

58

To Coos Bay

42

42

5

Myrtle
Creek

South Umpqua River

11.6

To Grants Pass

1 2 3 4 5 6 7 8

a b c d e f g h

© AVALON TRAVEL PUBLISHING, INC.

Map 11.4

Campgrounds 59–114
Pages 646–669

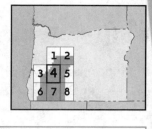

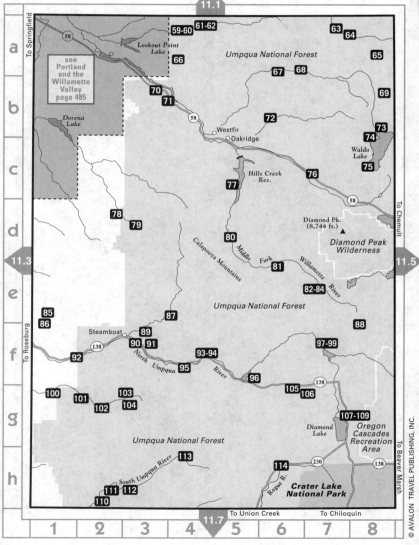

To Springfield

To Chemult

To Roseburg

To Beaver Marsh

To Union Creek

To Chiloquin

Lookout Point Lake

see Portland and the Willamette Valley page 485

Umpqua National Forest

Dorena Lake

Westfir
Oakridge

Hills Creek Res.

Waldo Lake

Diamond Pk. (8,744 ft.)

Diamond Peak Wilderness

Calapooya Mountains

Middle Fork

Willamette River

Umpqua National Forest

Steamboat

North Umpqua River

Umpqua National Forest

South Umpqua River

Diamond Lake

Oregon Cascades Recreation Area

Rogue R.

Crater Lake National Park

© AVALON TRAVEL PUBLISHING, INC.

Map 11.5

Campgrounds 115–169
Pages 669–691

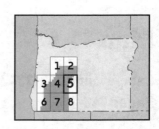

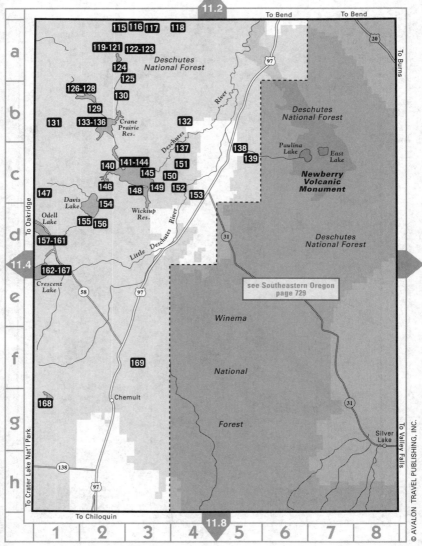

Map 11.6

Campgrounds 170–192
Pages 691–699

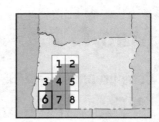

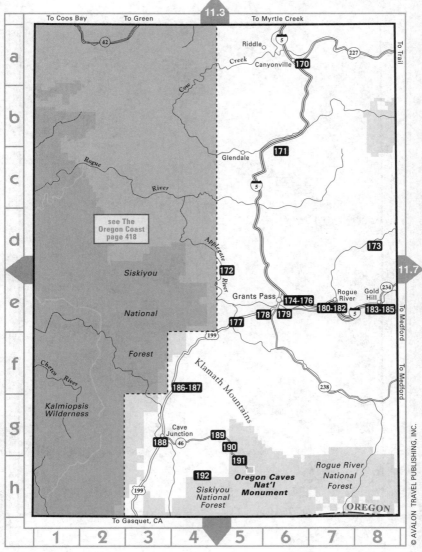

Map 11.7

Campgrounds 193–248
Pages 700–722

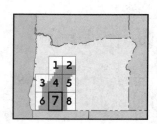

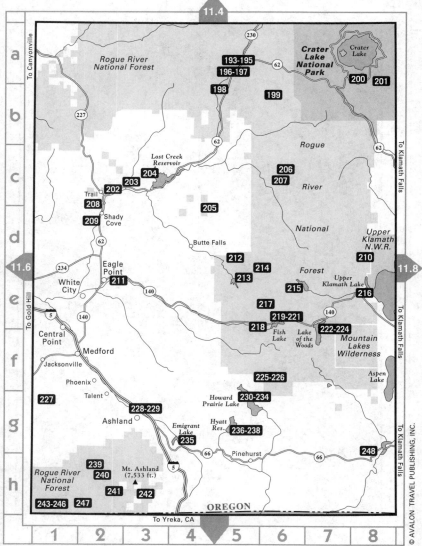

11.4

11.6

11.8

To Canyonville

Rogue River
National Forest

227

Lost Creek
Reservoir

202 203 204

Trail
208

209
Shady
Cove

62

234

Eagle
Point

White
City

211

140

140

Central
Point

Medford

Jacksonville

Phoenix

Talent

227

Ashland

228-229

Emigrant
Lake
235

To Gold Hill

Rogue River
National
Forest

239
240

241

243-246 247

Mt. Ashland
(7,533 ft.)

242

230

62

193-195
196-197

198

199

Crater
Lake
National
Park

Crater
Lake

200 201

Rogue

206
207

205

River

National

Butte Falls

212

213 214

215

Forest

Upper
Klamath
N.W.R.

210

Upper
Klamath Lake

216

217

219-221

218
Fish
Lake

Lake
of the
Woods

222-224

Mountain
Lakes
Wilderness

Aspen
Lake

225-226

230-234

Howard
Prairie Lake

Hyatt
Res.
236-238

66
Pinehurst

66

248

OREGON

To Yreka, CA

To Klamath Falls

To Klamath Falls

© AVALON TRAVEL PUBLISHING, INC.

Map 11.8

Campgrounds 249–258
Pages 722–726

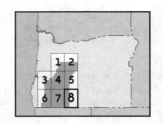

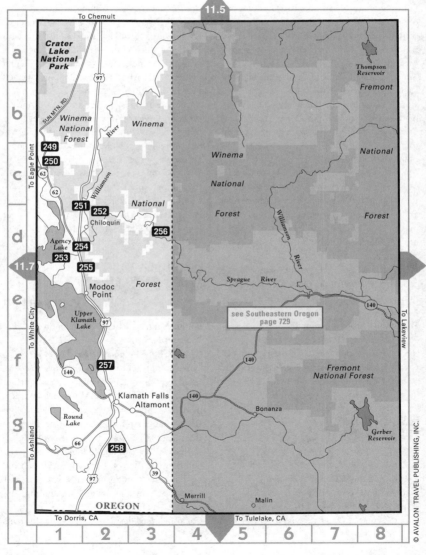

1 TROUT CREEK

Rating: 8

On the South Santiam River in Willamette National Forest.

Map 11.1, grid e6, page 616

This campground is set along the banks of the South Santiam River, about seven miles east of Cascadia. Fishing and swimming are some of the recreation possibilities here. There is a historic shelter and the remains of stonework from the era of the Civilian Conservation Corps. The Trout Creek Trail, just across the highway, leads into the Menagerie Wilderness. The Long Ranch Elk Viewing Area is immediately west of the campground, and at the Trout Creek Trailhead you'll also find a short trail leading to an elk-viewing platform. Nearby is the Old Santiam Wagon Road.

Campsites, facilities: There are 24 sites for tents or RVs up to 22 feet long, including three sites for any length RV. Picnic tables, garbage bins, and fire grills are provided. Drinking water and vault toilets are available. Some facilities are wheelchair accessible. Leashed pets are permitted.

Reservations, fees: Reservations are not accepted. Sites are $10 per night, $5 per extra vehicle. Senior discount available. Open May–October.

Directions: From Albany, drive east on U.S. 20 for 45 miles (19 miles past Sweet Home) to the campground entrance on the right.

Contact: Willamette National Forest, Sweet Home Ranger District, 3225 U.S. 20, Sweet Home, OR 97386, 541/367-5168, fax 541/367-9221.

2 YUKWAH

Rating: 7

On the Santiam River in Willamette National Forest.

Map 11.1, grid e6, page 616

Yukwah campground is set in a second-growth Douglas fir forest on the banks of the Santiam River. The camp is one-quarter mile east of Trout Creek Campground and offers the same recreation possibilities. The camp features a half-mile, compacted-surface interpretive trail that's barrier-free.

Campsites, facilities: There are 19 sites for tents or RVs of any length, including a deluxe group site for four or five families and three large RVs. Picnic tables, garbage bins, and fire grills are provided. Drinking water, vault toilets, a large picnic area, and a fishing platform are available. Some facilities, including a fishing platform, are wheelchair accessible. Leashed pets are permitted.

Reservations, fees: Reservations are not accepted. Sites are $10 per night, $5 per extra vehicle. The deluxe site is $20 per night. Senior discount available. Open May–October.

Directions: From Albany, drive east on U.S. 20 for 45 miles (19 miles past Sweet Home) to the campground.

Contact: Willamette National Forest, Sweet Home Ranger District, 3225 U.S. 20, Sweet Home, OR 97386, 541/367-5168, fax 541/367-9221.

3 FERNVIEW

Rating: 7

On the Santiam River in Willamette National Forest.

Map 11.1, grid e6, page 616

This campground is set high above the confluence of Boulder Creek and the Santiam River, just south of the Menagerie Wilderness. A stepped walkway leads down to the river. Just across U.S. 20 lies the Rooster Rock Trail, which leads to—where else?—Rooster Rock, the site of an old lookout tower. The Old Santiam Wagon Road runs through the back of the campground. The camp is best suited for tent and small RV camping; the sites are small.

Campsites, facilities: There are 11 sites for tents

or RVs up to 22 feet long. Picnic tables, garbage bins, and fire grills are provided. Drinking water and vault toilets are available. Some facilities are wheelchair accessible. Leashed pets are permitted.

Reservations, fees: Reservations are not accepted. Sites are $10 per night, $5 per extra vehicle. Senior discount available. Open May–September.

Directions: From Albany drive east on U.S. 20 for 49 miles (23 miles past Sweet Home) to the campground entrance on the right.

Contact: Willamette National Forest, Sweet Home Ranger District, 3225 U.S. 20, Sweet Home, OR 97386, 541/367-5168, fax 541/367-9221.

4 HOUSE ROCK

Rating: 8

On the Santiam River in Willamette National Forest.

Map 11.1, grid e8, page 616

This campground is set at the confluence of Sheep Creek and the South Santiam River. Botany students come here from long distances to see firsthand many uncommon and spectacular specimens of plant life. The camp is set in the midst of an old-growth forest and is surrounded by huge, majestic Douglas fir. Trout fishing can be good, particularly during summer evenings. History buffs should explore the short loop trail out of camp, which passes by House Rock, a historic shelter for Native Americans, and continues to the historic Old Santiam Wagon Road.

Campsites, facilities: There are 17 sites for tents or RVs up to 22 feet long. Picnic tables, garbage bins, and fire grills are provided. Vault toilets and drinking water are available. Some facilities are wheelchair accessible. Leashed pets are permitted.

Reservations, fees: Reservations are not accepted. Sites are $10 per night, $5 per extra vehicle. Open May–October.

Directions: From Albany drive east on U.S. 20 for 52.5 miles (26.5 miles past Sweet Home) to Squaw Creek Road (Forest Road 2044). Turn right and drive a short distance to the campground.

Contact: Willamette National Forest, Sweet Home Ranger District, 3225 U.S. 20, Sweet Home, OR 97386, 541/367-5168, fax 541/367-9221.

5 LOST PRAIRIE

Rating: 7

On Hackleman Creek in Willamette National Forest.

Map 11.1, grid e8, page 616

This campground is set along the banks of Hackleman Creek at 3,200 feet elevation in an area of fir, spruce, and Douglas fir. Three excellent hiking trails can be found within five miles of the camp: Hackleman Old-Growth Grove, Cone Peak, and Iron Mountain. The latter two offer spectacular wildflower viewing in the late spring and early summer. This camp provides an alternative to nearby Fish Lake.

Campsites, facilities: There are eight tent sites and two sites for RVs up to 22 feet long. Picnic tables, garbage bins, and fire grills are provided. Drinking water and vault toilets are available. Some facilities are wheelchair accessible. Leashed pets are permitted.

Reservations, fees: Reservations are not accepted. Sites are $10 per night, $5 per extra vehicle. Senior discount available. Open mid-May–October, weather permitting.

Directions: From Albany, drive east on U.S. 20 for 63 miles to the camp on the right.

Contact: Willamette National Forest, Sweet Home Ranger District, 3225 U.S. 20, Sweet Home, OR 97386, 541/367-5168, fax 541/367-9221.

6 FISH LAKE
🏃 🏊 🎣 � 🏕

Rating: 7

Near Clear Lake in Willamette National Forest.

Map 11.1, grid e8, page 616

This campground (3,200 feet elevation) sits on the shore of Fish Lake, though the "lake" usually dries up by the middle of the summer. Interpretive information is set up at the guard station nearby. Across the road, a trail follows the Old Santiam Wagon Road, and you can also find the northern trailhead for the McKenzie River National Recreation Trail. The Clear Lake picnic area is two miles south off Highway 126.

Campsites, facilities: There are eight sites for tents or RVs up to 16 feet long. Picnic tables, garbage service, and fire grills are provided. Drinking water and vault toilets are available. Leashed pets are permitted.

Reservations, fees: Reservations are not accepted. Sites are $6 per night, $3 per extra vehicle. Senior discount available. Open late May–early September.

Directions: From Eugene, drive east on Highway 126 for 47 miles to the town of McKenzie Bridge. Continue on Highway 126 for 23 miles to the campground entrance road on the left. Turn left and drive 100 yards to the campground.

Contact: Willamette National Forest, McKenzie Ranger District, 57600 McKenzie Hwy., McKenzie Bridge, OR 97413, 541/822-3381, fax 541/822-7254.

7 LAKES END BOAT-IN
🏊 🏊 🚣 🎣 🏕

Rating: 9

On Smith Reservoir in Willamette National Forest.

Map 11.1, grid f8, page 616

This secluded boat-in campground is set along the shore of the headwaters of Smith Reservoir, a long narrow lake. You'll find no cars and no traffic. The trout fishing in this reservoir can be exceptional; note the 10-mph speed limit. The campground is split into two areas, providing camping opportunities on Smith Creek or on the reservoir.

Campsites, facilities: There are 17 boat-in tent sites. Picnic tables and fire grills are provided. Pit toilets are available, but there is no drinking water, and all garbage must be packed out. Boat docks are nearby. Leashed pets are permitted.

Reservations, fees: Reservations are not accepted. There is no fee for camping. Open late April–late September.

Directions: From Eugene, drive east on Highway 126 for 47 miles to the town of McKenzie Bridge. Continue on Highway 126 for 13 miles to the signed turnoff for Lakes End at the north end of Trailbridge Reservoir. Turn left on Forest Road 1477 and drive a short distance; then bear left and continue (past Trailbridge Campground) for one-half mile to Forest Road 730 (Smith Reservoir Road). Continue three miles to the boat launch.

Contact: Willamette National Forest, McKenzie Ranger District, 57600 McKenzie Hwy., McKenzie Bridge, OR 97413, 541/822-3381, fax 541/822-7254.

8 TRAILBRIDGE
🏃 🏊 🚣 🚤 🐕 � 🏕

Rating: 6

On Trailbridge Reservoir in Willamette National Forest.

Map 11.1, grid f8, page 616

This campground is set along the shore of Trailbridge Reservoir, where recreation options include boating, fishing, and hiking. Highway 126 east of McKenzie Bridge is a designated scenic route, providing a pleasant trip to the camp and making Trailbridge an exceptional spot for car campers. For a good side trip, take the beautiful 40-minute drive east to the little town of Sisters. From this camp there is access to the McKenzie River National Recreation Trail.

Campsites, facilities: There are 28 sites for tents and 100-plus sites for RVs up to 45 feet long, with unlimited RV space at Trailbridge Flats. Picnic tables, garbage service, and fire grills are provided. Drinking water and vault and flush toilets are available. Boat ramps are nearby. Leashed pets are permitted.

Reservations, fees: Reservations are not accepted. Sites are $6 per night, $3 per extra vehicle. Senior discount available. Open late April–late September.

Directions: From Eugene, drive east on Highway 126 for 47 miles to the town of McKenzie Bridge. Continue on Highway 126 for 13 miles to the signed turnoff for Trailbridge Reservoir. Turn left on Forest Road 1477 and drive a short distance; then bear left and continue one-quarter mile to the campground.

Contact: Willamette National Forest, McKenzie Ranger District, 57600 McKenzie Hwy., McKenzie Bridge, OR 97413, 541/822-3381, fax 541/822-7254.

9 OLALLIE

Rating: 7

On the McKenzie River in Willamette National Forest.

Map 11.1, grid g8, page 616

This campground (2,000 feet elevation) along the banks of the McKenzie River offers opportunities for boating, fishing, and hiking. Other bonuses include easy access from Highway 126. Fishing for rainbow trout usually is good. The campground is two miles southwest of Trailbridge Reservoir off Highway 126.

Campsites, facilities: There are 17 sites for tents or RVs up to 30 feet long. Picnic tables, garbage service, and fire grills are provided. Vault toilets and drinking water are available. A boat launch is nearby (nonmotorized boats only). Leashed pets are permitted.

Reservations, fees: Reservations at 877/444-6777 or website: www.ReserveUsa.com ($9 reservation fee). Sites are $10 per night, $5 per

extra vehicle. Open mid-April–September, weather permitting.

Directions: From Eugene, drive east on Highway 126 for 47 miles to the town of McKenzie Bridge. Continue on Highway 126 for 11 miles to the campground on the left.

Contact: Willamette National Forest, McKenzie Ranger District, 57600 McKenzie Hwy., McKenzie Bridge, OR 97413, 541/822-3381, fax 541/822-7254.

10 MONA

Rating: 8

Near Blue River Reservoir in Willamette National Forest.

Map 11.1, grid g6, page 616

This forested campground is set along the shore of Blue River Reservoir, close to where the Blue River joins it. A boat ramp is located across the river from the campground. After launching a boat, campers can ground it near the campsite. This camp is extremely popular when the reservoir is full. Lookout Campground (next to the boat launch at Blue River Reservoir) is another option if this camp is full.

Campsites, facilities: There are 23 sites for tents or RVs up to 21 feet long. Picnic tables, garbage bins, and fire grills are provided. Drinking water and flush toilets are available. Some facilities are wheelchair accessible. Leashed pets are permitted.

Reservations, fees: Reservations are not accepted. The fee is $12 per night, $20 per night for double sites, and $6 per extra vehicle. Senior discount available. Open mid-April–late September.

Directions: From Eugene, drive east on Highway 126 for 41 miles to Blue River. Continue east on Highway 126 for three miles to Forest Road 15. Turn north and drive three miles to the campground.

Contact: Willamette National Forest, McKenzie River Ranger District, Blue River Forest

Service Center, P.O. Box 199, Blue River, OR 97413, 541/822-3317, fax 541/822-1255.

11 PATIO RV PARK

Rating: 7

Near the South Fork of the McKenzie River.
Map 11.1, grid g6, page 616

This RV park is situated near the banks of the South Fork of the McKenzie River, not far from Cougar Lake, which offers opportunities for fishing, swimming, and water-skiing. Nearby recreation options include a golf course, hiking trails, and bike paths.

Campsites, facilities: There are 60 sites for RVs of any length in this adult-only RV park. Electricity, drinking water, sewer hookups, and picnic tables are provided. Flush toilets, ice, showers, firewood, a recreation hall, video rentals, full group kitchen facilities, cable TV, and a laundry room are available. A store and a café are within two miles. Leashed pets are permitted.

Reservations, fees: Reservations at 800/650-0290. Sites are $22–24 per night, $2 per person for more than two people. Senior discount available. Open year-round, weather permitting.

Directions: From Eugene, drive east on Highway 126 for 37 miles to the town of Blue River. Continue east on Highway 126 for six miles to McKenzie River Drive. Turn east and drive two miles to the park on the right.

Contact: Patio RV Park, 55636 McKenzie River Dr., Blue River, OR 97413, 541/822-3596, fax 541/822-8392, website: http://hometown.aol.com/thepatio.

12 DELTA

Rating: 8

On the McKenzie River in Willamette National Forest.
Map 11.1, grid g6, page 616

This popular campground sits along the banks of the McKenzie River. This spot is heavily forested, primarily with old-growth Douglas fir. The Delta Old Growth Nature Trail, a half-mile wheelchair-accessible interpretive trail, is adjacent to the campground. The camp also features an amphitheater. Nearby are Blue River and Cougar Reservoirs (seven and five miles away, respectively), both of which offer trout fishing, water-skiing, and swimming.

Campsites, facilities: There are 38 sites for tents or RVs up to 21 feet long. Picnic tables, garbage bins, and fire grills are provided. Drinking water and vault toilets are available. Some facilities are wheelchair accessible. Leashed pets are permitted.

Reservations, fees: Reservations are not accepted. The fee is $12 per night, $20 per night for a double site, and $6 per extra vehicle. Senior discount available. Open mid-May–late September.

Directions: From Eugene, drive east on Highway 126 for 37 miles to the town of Blue River. Continue east on Highway 126 for five miles to Forest Road 19 (Aufderheide Scenic Byway). Turn right (south) and drive one-quarter mile to Forest Road 400. Turn right and drive one mile to the campground.

Contact: Willamette National Forest, McKenzie River Ranger District, Blue River Forest Service Center, P.O. Box 199, Blue River, OR 97413, 541/822-3317, fax 541/822-1255.

13 MCKENZIE BRIDGE

Rating: 8

On the McKenzie River in Willamette National Forest.
Map 11.1, grid g7, page 616

This campground (1,400 feet elevation) is set along the banks of the McKenzie River, one mile from the town of McKenzie Bridge. This stretch of river provides good evening fly-fishing for trout during the summer.

Campsites, facilities: There are 20 sites for tents or RVs up to 35 feet long. Picnic tables, garbage service, and fire rings are provided. Vault toilets and drinking water are available. A grocery store, gasoline, restaurants, and a pay phone are available within one mile. Leashed pets are permitted. Only nonmotorized boats are permitted.

Reservations, fees: Reservations at 877/444-6777 or website: www.ReserveUsa.com ($9 reservation fee). Sites are $10 per night, $6 per extra vehicle. Senior discount available. Open late April–early September.

Directions: From Eugene, drive east on Highway 126 for 46 miles to the campground entrance on the right (one mile west of the town of McKenzie Bridge).

Contact: Willamette National Forest, McKenzie Ranger District, 57600 McKenzie Hwy., McKenzie Bridge, OR 97413, 541/822-3381, fax 541/822-7254.

14 HORSE CREEK GROUP CAMP

Rating: 9

On Horse Creek in Willamette National Forest.

Map 11.1, grid g7, page 616

This campground reserved for groups is set on the banks of Horse Creek near the town of McKenzie Bridge. In spite of the name, no horse camping is permitted. Fishing is catch-and-release only. The camp sits at 1,400 feet elevation.

Campsites, facilities: This is a group site with 21 sites for tents or RVs up to 35 feet long. Picnic tables, garbage service, and fire grills are provided. Drinking water and vault toilets are available. Leashed pets are permitted.

Reservations, fees: Reservations at 877/444-6777 or website: www.ReserveUsa.com ($9 reservation fee); $40 per night for up to 49 people, $60 per night for 50–100 people. Open late April–October.

Directions: From Eugene, drive east on Highway 126 for 47 miles to the town of McKenzie Bridge and Horse Creek Road. Turn right (south) on Horse Creek Road and drive three miles to the campground on the left.

Contact: Willamette National Forest, McKen-

zie Ranger District, 57600 McKenzie Hwy., McKenzie Bridge, OR 97413, 541/822-3381, fax 541/822-7254.

15 PARADISE

Rating: 9

On the McKenzie River in Willamette National Forest.

Map 11.1, grid g7, page 616

This campground (1,600 feet elevation) along the banks of the McKenzie River may be right off the highway, but it offers a rustic, streamside setting with access to the McKenzie River National Recreation Trail. Trout fishing can be good here.

Campsites, facilities: There are 64 sites for tents or RVs up to 40 feet long. Picnic tables, garbage service, and fire rings are provided. Flush, vault, and pit toilets, drinking water, a boat ramp, and firewood are available. Leashed pets are permitted.

Reservations, fees: Reservations at 877/444-6777 or website: www.ReserveUsa.com ($9 reservation fee); $14 per night, $7 per extra vehicle, and double sites are $25 per night. Senior discount available. Open late April–mid-October.

Directions: From Eugene, drive east on Highway 126 for 47 miles to the town of McKenzie Bridge. Continue east on Highway 126 for 3.5 miles to the campground on the left.

Contact: Willamette National Forest, McKenzie Ranger District, 57600 McKenzie Hwy., McKenzie Bridge, OR 97413, 541/822-3381, fax 541/822-7254.

16 BELKNAP HOT SPRINGS RESORT

Rating: 9

On the McKenzie River.

Map 11.1, grid h7, page 616

This beautiful park has been featured on at least one magazine cover. It's in a wooded, mountainous area on the McKenzie River. Trout fishing can be excellent here. If you're looking for hiking opportunities, check out the Three Sisters and Mt. Washington Wilderness Areas, both accessible by driving west of Sisters on Highway 242. Exceptionally scenic and pristine expanses of forest, they are well worth exploring. The Pacific Crest Trail runs north and south through both wilderness areas.

Campsites, facilities: There are 15 sites for tents, 42 sites with electrical and water hookups, some with sewer hookups, for RVs of any length, a lodge with 18 rooms, and six cabins. Drinking water, restrooms, showers, an RV dump station, and a public phone are provided. Recreational facilities include a hot-spring fed swimming pool, a recreation field, and a recreation hall. Some facilities are wheelchair accessible. Leashed pets are permitted at the campground and in three of the cabins. Pets are not permitted in the other cabins and lodge rooms.

Reservations, fees: Reservations at 541/822-3512; $19–20 per night, $7 per person for more than two people. Open year-round.

Directions: From Eugene, drive east on Highway 126 for 56 miles to Belknap Spring Road. Turn left and drive one-half mile. The road dead-ends at the lodge.

Contact: Belknap Hot Springs Resort, P.O. Box 2001, 59296 Belknap Springs Rd., McKenzie Bridge, OR 97413, 541/822-3512, fax 541/822-3327.

17 SLIDE CREEK

Rating: 6

On Cougar Reservoir in Willamette National Forest.

Map 11.1, grid g8, page 616

This campground sits on a hillside overlooking Cougar Reservoir, which covers about 1,300 acres, has a paved boat landing, and offers opportunities for fishing, swimming, and water-skiing. This pretty lakeside camp is quite popular,

so plan to arrive early on weekends. If the camp is full, Cougar Crossing (off Road 19) and Sunnyside (off Road 500) are nearby alternatives.

Campsites, facilities: There are 16 sites for tents or RVs. Picnic tables, garbage bins, and fire grills are provided. Drinking water and vault toilets are available. A boat ramp is available. Leashed pets are permitted.

Reservations, fees: Reservations are not accepted. The fee is $12 per night, $6 for extra vehicle, and $20 for double site. Senior discount available. Open mid-May–mid-September.

Directions: From Eugene, drive east on Highway 126 for 41 miles to the town of Blue River. Continue east on Highway 126 for five miles to Aufderheide Scenic Byway. Turn right (south) and drive 11 miles (along the west shore of Cougar Reservoir, crossing the reservoir bridge) to Eastside Road (Forest Road 500). Turn left and drive 1.5 miles northeast to the campground set on the southeast shore of the lake.

Contact: Willamette National Forest, McKenzie River Ranger District, Blue River Forest Service Center, P.O. Box 199, Blue River, OR 97413, 541/822-3317, fax 541/822-1255.

18 FRENCH PETE

Rating: 8

On the South Fork of the McKenzie River in Willamette National Forest.

Map 11.1, grid h7, page 616

This quiet, wooded campground is set on the banks of the South Fork of the McKenzie River and French Pete Creek. Fishing is catch-and-release only. A trail across the road from the campground provides access to the Three Sisters Wilderness. French Pete is only two miles from Cougar Reservoir, and the camp attracts campers wanting to use Cougar Reservoir facilities. Two more primitive camps (Homestead and Frissell Crossing) are located a few miles southeast on the same road.

Campsites, facilities: There are 17 sites for

tents or RVs. Picnic tables, garbage containers, and fire grills are provided. Drinking water and vault toilets are available. Some facilities are wheelchair accessible. Leashed pets are permitted.

Reservations, fees: Reservations are not accepted. The fee is $12 per night, $6 for extra vehicle, and $20 for double site. Senior discount available. Open mid-May–mid-September.

Directions: From Eugene, drive east on Highway 126 for 41 miles to the town of Blue River. Continue east on Highway 126 for five miles to Forest Road 19 (Aufderheide Scenic Byway). Turn right (south) and drive 12 miles to the campground.

Contact: Willamette National Forest, McKenzie River Ranger District, Blue River Forest Service Center, P.O. Box 199, Blue River, OR 97413, 541/822-3317, fax 541/822-1255.

19 COLDWATER COVE

Rating: 10

On Clear Lake in Willamette National Forest.

Map 11.2, grid f1, page 617

This campground sits at 3,000 feet elevation on the south shore of Clear Lake, a spring-fed lake formed by a natural lava dam and the source of the McKenzie River. No motors are permitted on the lake, making it ideal for anglers in rowboats or canoes. The northern section of the McKenzie River National Recreation Trail passes by the camp.

Campsites, facilities: There are 35 sites for tents or RVs up to 30 feet long. Picnic tables, garbage service, and fire grills are provided. Drinking water and vault toilets are available. Some facilities are wheelchair accessible. Boat docks, launching facilities, rowboats, a store, a café, and cabin rentals are available nearby at Clear Lake Resort. Leashed pets are permitted.

Reservations, fees: Reservations at 877/444-6777 or website: www.ReserveUsa.com ($9 reservation fee). Sites are $14 per night, $7 per

extra vehicle. Senior discount available. Open late May–early October.

Directions: From Eugene, drive east on Highway 126 for 47 miles to the town of McKenzie Bridge. Continue on Highway 126 for 14 miles to Forest Road 770. Turn right (east) and drive to the campground.

Contact: Willamette National Forest, McKenzie Ranger District, 57600 McKenzie Hwy., McKenzie Bridge, OR 97413, 541/822-3381, fax 541/822-7254.

20 ICE CAP

Rating: 9

On Carmen Reservoir in Willamette National Forest.

Map 11.2, grid f1, page 617

This campground (3,000 feet elevation) is set on a hill above Carmen Reservoir, which was created by a dam on the McKenzie River. The McKenzie River National Recreation Trail passes by the camp, and Koosah Falls and Sahalie Falls are nearby. Clear Lake, a popular local vacation destination, is two miles away.

Campsites, facilities: There are 11 tent sites and 11 sites for tents or RVs up to 16 feet long. Picnic tables, garbage service, and fire grills are provided. Drinking water and flush toilets, boat-launching facilities, and boat rentals are about two miles away at Clear Lake Resort. Only nonmotorized boats are allowed on Carmen Reservoir. Leashed pets are permitted.

Reservations, fees: Reservations are not accepted. Sites are $12 per night, $6 per extra vehicle. Senior discount available. Open mid-May–mid-September.

Directions: From Eugene, drive east on Highway 126 for 47 miles to the town of McKenzie Bridge. Continue on Highway 126 for 19 miles to the campground entrance road on the left. Turn left and drive 200 yards to the campground.

Contact: Willamette National Forest, McKenzie Ranger District, 57600 McKenzie Hwy., McKenzie Bridge, OR 97413, 541/822-3381, fax 541/822-7254.

21 BIG LAKE
Rating: 9

On Big Lake in Willamette National Forest.
Map 11.2, grid e1, page 617

This jewel of a spot on the north shore of Big Lake at 4,650 feet elevation offers a host of activities, including fishing, swimming, water-skiing, and hiking. Big Lake has heavy motorized boat use. One of the better hikes is the five-mile wilderness loop trail (Patjens Lakes Trail) that heads out from the south shore of the lake and cuts past a few small lakes before returning. There's a great view of Mt. Washington from the lake. The Pacific Crest Trail is only one-half mile away.

Campsites, facilities: There are 49 sites for tents or RVs up to 16 feet long. Picnic tables, garbage service, and fire grills are provided. Drinking water and vault and flush toilets are available. Boat ramps and launching facilities are nearby. Leashed pets are permitted.

Reservations, fees: Reservations at 877/444-6777 or website: www.ReserveUsa.com ($9 reservation fee). Sites are $14 per night, $7 per extra vehicle. Senior discount available. Open mid-June–early October.

Directions: From Eugene, drive east on Highway 126 for 47 miles to the town of McKenzie Bridge. Continue northeast on Highway 126 for 40 miles to Big Lake Road (Forest Road 2690). Turn right and drive three miles to the campground on the left.

Contact: Willamette National Forest, McKenzie Ranger District, 57600 McKenzie Hwy., McKenzie Bridge, OR 97413, 541/822-3381, fax 541/822-7254.

22 BIG LAKE WEST WALK-IN
Rating: 9

On Big Lake in Willamette National Forest.
Map 11.2, grid e1, page 617

This spot, located west of the Big Lake Campground at an elevation of 4,650 feet, has many of the same attractions, but the walk-in sites offer some seclusion and quiet. The Mt. Washington Wilderness and Patjens Lake access trails can be reached from here. See the description of Big Lake Campground.

Campsites, facilities: There are 11 walk-in sites (only 200 feet from the road). Fire pits, garbage service, and picnic tables are provided. Drinking water and vault toilets are available. Leashed pets permitted.

Reservations, fees: Reservations are not accepted. Sites are $18 per night, $9 per extra vehicle, and double sites are $33 per night. Open late May–early October.

Directions: From Eugene, drive east on Highway 126 for 47 miles to the town of McKenzie Bridge. Continue northeast on Highway 126 for 40 miles to Big Lake Road (Forest Road 2690). Turn right and drive four miles to the campground entrance on the left.

Contact: Willamette National Forest, McKenzie Ranger District, 57600 McKenzie Hwy., McKenzie Bridge, OR 97413, 541/822-3381, fax 541/822-7254.

23 SOUTH SHORE

Rating: 6

On Suttle Lake in Deschutes National Forest.
Map 11.2, grid e3, page 617

This campground is at 3,500 feet elevation on the south shore of Suttle Lake, where water-skiing is permitted. A hiking trail winds around the lake. Other popular activities include fishing and windsurfing. The camp often fills up on weekends and holidays; reserve early. Quite a few dead trees have recently been removed, so the campground is now more open and spacious.

Campsites, facilities: There are 38 sites for tents or RVs up to 40 feet long. Picnic tables, garbage service, and fire grills are provided. Drinking water and vault toilets are available. A fish-cleaning station, boat docks, launching facilities, and rentals are nearby. Leashed pets are permitted.

Reservations, fees: Reservations at 877/444-6777 or website: www.ReserveUsa.com ($9 reservation fee). Sites are $12 per night, $6 per extra vehicle. Senior discount available. Open mid-April–late September.

Directions: From Albany, drive east on U.S. 20 to the junction with Highway 126. Continue east on Highway 126 for 12 miles to Forest Road 2070 (Suttle Lake). Turn right and proceed a short distance to the campground.

Contact: Deschutes National Forest, Sisters Ranger District, P.O. Box 249, Sisters, OR 97759, 541/549-7700, fax 541/549-7746.

24 LINK CREEK

Rating: 6

On Suttle Lake in Deschutes National Forest.

Map 11.2, grid e3, page 617

This campground (elevation 3,450 feet) is set at the west end of Suttle Lake. The high-speed boating area is on this end of the lake, making it a popular spot with water-skiers. See the description of South Shore for recreation details.

Campsites, facilities: There are 33 sites for tents or RVs up to 40 feet long. Picnic tables, garbage service, and fire grills are provided. Drinking water and vault toilets are available. Boat docks, launching facilities, and rentals are nearby. Leashed pets are permitted.

Reservations, fees: Reservations at 877/444-6777 or website: www.ReserveUsa.com ($9 reservation fee). Sites are $12 per night, $6 per

extra vehicle. Senior discount available. Open mid-April–mid-October.

Directions: From Albany, drive east on U.S. 20 for 74 miles to the junction of U.S. 20 and Highway 126. Continue east on Highway 126 for 12 miles to Forest Road 2070 (Suttle Lake). Turn right and drive a short distance to the campground.

Contact: Deschutes National Forest, Sisters Ranger District, P.O. Box 249, Sisters, OR 97759, 541/549-7700, fax 541/549-7746.

25 BLUE BAY

Rating: 7

On Suttle Lake in Deschutes National Forest.

Map 11.2, grid e3, page 617

This campground is situated along the south shore of Suttle Lake, the low-speed end of the lake. It's a quieter campground, with more tree cover than South Shore or Link Creek. See the description of South Shore for recreation details.

Campsites, facilities: There are 25 sites for tents or RVs up to 30 feet long. Picnic tables, garbage service, and fire grills are provided. Drinking water and vault toilets are available. A fish-cleaning station, boat docks, launching facilities, and rentals are nearby. Leashed pets are permitted.

Reservations, fees: Reservations at 877/444-6777 or website: www.ReserveUsa.com ($9 reservation fee). Sites are $12 per night, $6 per extra vehicle. Senior discount available. Open mid-April–mid-October.

Directions: From Albany, drive east on U.S. 20 for 74 miles to the junction of U.S. 20 and Highway 126. Continue east on Highway 126 for 12 miles to Forest Road 2070 (Suttle Lake). Turn right and drive a short distance to the campground.

Contact: Deschutes National Forest, Sisters Ranger District, P.O. Box 249, Sisters, OR 97759, 541/549-7700, fax 541/549-7746.

26 SCOUT LAKE GROUP

Rating: 5

On Scout Lake in Deschutes National Forest.

Map 11.2, grid e3, page 617

This campground with a mix of sunny and shady sites lies about one-half mile from Suttle Lake and is a good spot for swimming and hiking. The camp is available for groups of up to 100 campers; reservations are required.

Campsites, facilities: There are 10 group sites for 12-18 people per site with tents or RVs up to 40 feet long. Picnic tables, garbage service, and fire grills are provided. Vault toilets and drinking water are available. Also available are a picnic shelter, volleyball court, and horseshoe pits. Leashed pets are permitted in the campground only (not in the day-use area).

Reservations, fees: Reservations at 877/444-6777 or website: www.ReserveUsa.com ($9 reservation fee). Sites are $25 per night. Open mid-April-mid-September.

Directions: From Eugene, drive east on Highway 126 for 74 miles to the junction of U.S. 20 and Highway 126. Continue east on Highway 126 for 12 miles to Forest Road 2070 (Suttle Lake). Turn right and drive to Forest Road 2066. Turn left and drive less than one mile to the campground.

Contact: Deschutes National Forest, Sisters Ranger District, P.O. Box 249, Sisters, OR 97759, 541/549-7700, fax 541/549-7746.

27 CAMP SHERMAN

Rating: 6

On the Metolius River in Deschutes National Forest.

Map 11.2, grid e3, page 617

Camp Sherman is set at an elevation of 2,950 feet along the banks of the Metolius River, where you can fish for wild trout. This place is for expert fly anglers seeking a quality fishing experience. It's advisable to obtain a map of the Deschutes National Forest that details back roads, trails, and streams. Camp Sherman is one of five camps in the immediate area.

Campsites, facilities: There are 15 sites for tents or RVs up to 40 feet long. Picnic tables, garbage service, and fire grills are provided. Vault toilets, a picnic shelter, and drinking water are available. Leashed pets are permitted.

Reservations, fees: Reservations are not accepted. Sites are $12 per night, $6 per extra vehicle. Senior discount available. Open April-mid-October.

Directions: From Albany, drive east on U.S. 20 for 87 miles (near Black Butte) to the sign for Camp Sherman and Forest Road 14. Turn left on Forest Road 14 and drive five miles to Camp Sherman, the store, and Forest Road 900. Turn left on Forest Road 900 and drive one-half mile to the campground on the left.

Contact: Deschutes National Forest, Sisters Ranger District, P.O. Box 249, Sisters, OR 97759, 541/549-7700, fax 541/549-7746.

28 ALLINGHAM

Rating: 5

On the Metolius River in Deschutes National Forest.

Map 11.2, grid e3, page 617

One of five camps in the immediate area, Allingham sits along the banks of the Metolius River. See the description of Camp Sherman for area details.

Campsites, facilities: There are 10 sites for tents or RVs up to 40 feet long. Picnic tables, garbage service, and fire grills are provided. Vault toilets and drinking water are available. An RV dump station is nearby. Leashed pets are permitted.

Reservations, fees: Reservations are not accepted. Sites are $12 per night, $6 per extra vehicle. Senior discount available. Open April-mid-October.

Directions: From Albany, drive east on U.S.

20 for 87 miles (near Black Butte) to the sign for Camp Sherman and Forest Road 14. Turn left on Forest Road 14 and drive five miles to Camp Sherman, the store, and Forest Road 900. Turn left on Forest Road 900 and drive one mile to the campground on the left.

Contact: Deschutes National Forest, Sisters Ranger District, P.O. Box 249, Sisters, OR 97759, 541/549-7700, fax 541/549-7746.

29 BLACK BUTTE RESORT MOTEL AND RV PARK

Rating: 6

Near the Metolius River.

Map 11.2, grid e3, page 617

This RV park offers a choice of graveled or grassy sites in a clean, scenic environment. See the description of Camp Sherman for more area information.

Campsites, facilities: There are 30 sites with full hookups and 11 sites with partial hookups for RVs of any length. Electricity, drinking water, sewer hookups, and picnic tables are provided. Flush toilets, showers, firewood, and a laundry room are available. Bottled gas, an RV dump station, a store, a café, and ice are within one block. Leashed pets are permitted.

Reservations, fees: Reservations encouraged. Sites are $19–23 per night, $3 per person for more than two people. Senior discount available. Open year-round.

Directions: From Albany, drive east on U.S. 20 for 87 miles (near Black Butte) to the sign for Camp Sherman. Turn north on Forest Road 1419 and drive 4.5 miles to a stop sign and the camp access road. Turn right and drive one-half mile to the campground on the right.

Contact: Black Butte Resort and RV Park, 25635 S.W. Forest Service Rd. 1419, Camp Sherman, OR 97730, 877/595-6514 or 541/595-6514, fax 541/595-5971, website: www.black-butte-resort.com.

30 PINE REST

Rating: 5

On the Metolius River in Deschutes National Forest.

Map 11.2, grid e3, page 617

This campground is set at an elevation of 2,900 feet along the banks of the Metolius River. See the description of Camp Sherman for more information.

Campsites, facilities: There are eight tent sites. Picnic tables, garbage service, and fire grills are provided. Vault toilets, a picnic shelter, and drinking water are available. Leashed pets are permitted.

Reservations, fees: Reservations are not accepted. Sites are $12 per night, $6 per extra vehicle. Senior discount available. Open April–mid-October.

Directions: From Albany, drive east on U.S. 20 for 87 miles (near Black Butte) to the sign for Camp Sherman and Forest Road 14. Turn left on Forest Road 14 and drive five miles to Camp Sherman, the store, and Forest Road 900. Turn left on Forest Road 900 and drive two miles to the campground on the left.

Contact: Deschutes National Forest, Sisters Ranger District, P.O. Box 249, Sisters, OR 97759, 541/549-7700, fax 541/549-7746.

31 GORGE

Rating: 5

On the Metolius River in Deschutes National Forest.

Map 11.2, grid e3, page 617

Here is another of the camps set along the banks of the Metolius River. This one is more open, with less vegetation than many of the others. It is set at an elevation of 2,900 feet. See the description of Camp Sherman for more details.

Campsites, facilities: There are 18 sites for tents or RVs up to 22 feet long. A few of the sites can accommodate RVs up to 40 feet long. Picnic tables, garbage service, and fire grills are provided. Vault toilets and drinking water are available. Leashed pets are permitted.

Reservations, fees: Reservations are not accepted. Sites are $12 per night, $6 per extra vehicle. Senior discount available. Open April–mid-October.

Directions: From Albany, drive east on U.S. 20 for 87 miles (near Black Butte) to the sign for Camp Sherman and Forest Road 14. Turn left on Forest Road 14 and drive five miles to Camp Sherman, the store, and Forest Road 900. Turn left on Forest Road 900 and drive 2.5 miles to the campground on the left.

Contact: Deschutes National Forest, Sisters Ranger District, P.O. Box 249, Sisters, OR 97759, 541/549-7700, fax 541/549-7746.

32 SMILING RIVER

Rating: 5

On the Metolius River in Deschutes National Forest.

Map 11.2, grid e3, page 617

Here's another camp along the banks of the Metolius River. It's set at an elevation of 2,900 feet. See the description of Camp Sherman for more details.

Campsites, facilities: There are 37 sites for tents or RVs up to 30 feet long. A few sites can accommodate RVs up to 40 feet in length. Picnic tables, garbage service, and fire grills are provided. Vault toilets and drinking water are available. Leashed pets are permitted.

Reservations, fees: Reservations are not accepted. Sites are $12 per night, $6 per extra vehicle. Senior discount available. Open May–mid-October.

Directions: From Albany, drive east on U.S. 20 for 87 miles (near Black Butte) to the sign for Camp Sherman and Forest Road 14. Turn left on Forest Road 14 and drive five miles to Camp Sherman, the store, and Forest Road

900. Turn left on Forest Road 900 and drive one mile to the campground on the left.

Contact: Deschutes National Forest, Sisters Ranger District, P.O. Box 249, Sisters, OR 97759, 541/549-7700, fax 541/549-7746.

33 ALLEN SPRINGS

Rating: 7

On the Metolius River in Deschutes National Forest.

Map 11.2, grid e3, page 617

This shady campground is set in a conifer forest along the banks of the Metolius River, where fishing and hiking can be good. For an interesting side trip, head to the Wizard Falls Fish Hatchery about a mile away.

Campsites, facilities: There are three tent sites and 12 sites for tents or RVs up to 22 feet long. Picnic tables, garbage service, and fire grills are provided. Vault toilets and drinking water are available. A store, a café, and ice are within five miles. Leashed pets are permitted.

Reservations, fees: Reservations are not accepted. Sites are $12 per night, $6 per extra vehicle. Senior discount available. Open April–mid-October.

Directions: From Albany, drive east on U.S. 20 for 87 miles (near Black Butte) to the sign for Camp Sherman and Forest Road 14. Turn left on Forest Road 14 and drive about nine miles to the campground on the left.

Contact: Deschutes National Forest, Sisters Ranger District, P.O. Box 249, Sisters, OR 97759, 541/549-7700, fax 541/549-7746.

34 LOWER BRIDGE

Rating: 6

On the Metolius River in Deschutes National Forest.

Map 11.2, grid e3, page 617

This campground is set along the banks of

the Metolius River. See the description of Camp Sherman for details about the area. This camp is similar to Pioneer Ford, but with less vegetation.

Campsites, facilities: There are 12 sites for tents or RVs up to 22 feet long. Picnic tables, garbage service, and fire grills are provided. Vault toilets and drinking water are available. Leashed pets are permitted.

Reservations, fees: Reservations are not accepted. Sites are $12 per night, $6 per extra vehicle. Senior discount available. Open April–mid-October.

Directions: From Albany, drive east on U.S. 20 for 87 miles (near Black Butte) to the sign for Camp Sherman and Forest Road 14. Turn left on Forest Road 14 and drive 12 miles to the campground on the left.

Contact: Deschutes National Forest, Sisters Ranger District, P.O. Box 249, Sisters, OR 97759, 541/549-7700, fax 541/549-7746.

35 PIONEER FORD

Rating: 7

On the Metolius River in Deschutes National Forest.

Map 11.2, grid e3, page 617

This quiet and serene wooded campground is set along the banks of the Metolius River and features grassy sites. See the description of Camp Sherman for recreation options.

Campsites, facilities: There are two tent sites and 18 sites for tents or RVs up to 40 feet long. Drinking water, garbage service, and fire grills are provided. Vault toilets, a barrier-free picnic shelter, and firewood are available. Leashed pets are permitted.

Reservations, fees: Reservations are not accepted. Sites are $12 per night, $6 per extra vehicle. Senior discount available. Open April–September.

Directions: From Albany, drive east on U.S. 20 for 87 miles (near Black Butte) to the sign for Camp Sherman and Forest Road 14. Turn

left on Forest Road 14 and drive 11 miles to the campground on the left.

Contact: Deschutes National Forest, Sisters Ranger District, P.O. Box 249, Sisters, OR 97759, 541/549-7700, fax 541/549-7746.

36 COLD SPRINGS RESORT AND RV PARK

Rating: 7

On the Metolius River.

Map 11.2, grid e3, page 617

This pretty, wooded RV park on the Metolius River is world-famous for its fly-fishing and features an acre of riverfront lawn. Nearby recreation options include a golf course, swimming, boating, water-skiing, windsurfing, hiking and biking trails, a riding stable, and tennis courts. Winter activities vary from alpine and Nordic skiing to sledding, snowmobiling, and winter camping. A private bridge leads from the resort to Camp Sherman; the towns of Sisters and Bend are nearby (15 miles and 35 miles, respectively).

Campsites, facilities: There are 45 sites with full hookups for RVs of any length, plus five cabins on the river. Fire pits, picnic tables, and patios are provided. Restrooms, showers, laundry facilities, firewood, and a riverfront picnic facility are available. Bottled gas, a store with groceries, fishing and sport supplies, a café, a coin-operated laundry, a post office, and ice are within one-quarter mile. Leashed pets are permitted.

Reservations, fees: Reservations accepted. Sites are $20–22 per night, $2 per person for more than two people, and $1 per pet per night. Open year-round.

Directions: From Albany, drive east on U.S. 20 for 87 miles (near Black Butte) to the sign for Camp Sherman. Turn north and drive about five miles to the stop sign. Turn right at the stop sign and drive about 300 feet to Cold Springs Resort Lane. Turn right and drive through the forest and the meadow, crossing Cold Springs Creek, to the resort.

Contact: Cold Springs Resort and RV Park, 25615 Cold Springs Resort Ln., Camp Sherman, OR 97730, 541/595-6271, fax 541/595-1400, website: www.coldsprings-resort.com.

37 RIVERSIDE WALK-IN

Rating: 7

On the Metolius River in Deschutes National Forest.

Map 11.2, grid e3, page 617

This campground is set 100 yards back from the banks of the Metolius River, less than a mile from Metolius Springs at the base of Black Butte. Because it's a tent-only campground and just far enough off the highway to be missed by most other people, it stays very quiet; you'll find plenty of solitude here. After parking along the road, you must walk to the campsites, carrying your gear in the process.

Campsites, facilities: There are 16 tent sites. Picnic tables and fire grills are provided. Vault toilets, garbage service, and drinking water are available. Leashed pets are permitted.

Reservations, fees: Reservations are not accepted. Sites are $10 per night, $5 per extra vehicle. Senior discount available. Open mid-April–September.

Directions: From Albany, drive east on U.S. 20 for 87 miles to the sign for Camp Sherman and Forest Road 14. Turn left and drive five miles to Forest Road 800. Turn left and drive a short distance to the campground.

Contact: Deschutes National Forest, Sisters Ranger District, P.O. Box 249, Sisters, OR 97759, 541/549-7700, fax 541/549-7746.

38 HAYSTACK RESERVOIR

Rating: 5

On Haystack Reservoir in Crooked River National Grassland.

Map 11.2, grid e7, page 617

This campground can be found in the high desert along the shore of Haystack Reservoir, a bright spot in an expansive desert landscape. The camps feature a moderate amount of privacy, as well as views of nearby Mt. Jefferson. Haystack Lake receives a moderate number of people who boat, water-ski, swim, or fish. The camping and fishing crowds are also rated as moderate.

Campsites, facilities: There are 23 sites for tents or RVs up to 22 feet long. Picnic tables and fire grills are provided. Vault toilets and drinking water are available. A store, a café, and ice are within five miles. Boat docks, launching facilities, and rentals are nearby. Leashed pets are permitted.

Reservations, fees: Reservations are not accepted. Sites are $8 per night, $3 per extra vehicle. Open mid-May–September.

Directions: From Madras, drive south on U.S. 97 for nine miles to County Road 100. Turn southeast and drive three miles to Forest Road 96. Turn north and drive one-half mile to the campground.

Contact: Crooked River National Grassland, 813 S.W. Hwy. 97, Madras, OR 97741, 541/475-9272 or 541/416-6640, fax 541/416-6694.

39 KOA SISTERS/BEND

Rating: 7

On Branchwater Lake.

Map 11.2, grid f4, page 617

This park is located amid wooded mountains outside of Sisters at an elevation of 3,200 feet. Branchwater Lake offers swimming and good trout fishing. See the description of Belknap Springs Lodge for information about the surrounding area.

Campsites, facilities: There are 64 sites for tents or RVs and three cabins. Drinking water, air-conditioning, electric heat, cable TV, restrooms, showers, an RV dump station, security, a public phone, a laundry room, limited groceries, ice, snacks, RV supplies, LP gas, and a barbecue are available. Recreational facilities include a sports field, a playground, a game room, horseshoes, a spa, and a heated swimming pool. Some facilities are wheelchair accessible. Leashed pets are permitted.

Reservations, fees: Reservations at 800/562-0363. Sites are $20–40 per night, $2–4 per person for more than two people. Open late March–November, weather permitting.

Directions: From Eugene, drive east on Highway 126 to its junction with U.S. 20. Turn east and drive 26 miles to Sisters. Continue southeast on U.S. 20 for three miles to the park on the right side of the highway.

Contact: KOA Sisters/Bend, 67667 Hwy. 20 W, Bend, OR 97701, 541/549-3021, fax 541/549-8144, website: www.koa.com.

40 CROOKED RIVER RANCH RV PARK

Rating: 6

Near Smith Rock State Park.

Map 11.2, grid f7, page 617

Spectacular wildlife abounds in this area. This campground is a short distance from Smith Rock State Park, which contains unusual, colorful volcanic formations overlooking the Crooked River Canyon. Lake Billy Chinook to the north is a good spot for water-skiing and fishing for bass and panfish. The park has a basketball court and a softball field; nearby recreation options include fishing, golf, and tennis. One of Oregon's nicest golf courses is nearby.

Campsites, facilities: There are 40 tent sites and 88 sites for RVs of any length; 15 are drive-through sites. Electricity, drinking water, and sewer hookups are provided. Flush toilets, an RV dump station, cable TV, showers, a store, a café, laundry facilities, ice, a playground, and a swimming pool are available. Leashed pets are permitted.

Reservations, fees: Reservations at 800/841-0563. Sites are $14–23 per night. Senior discount available. Major credit cards accepted. Open mid-March–late October.

Directions: From Redmond, drive north on U.S. 97 for six miles to Lower Bridge Way. Turn west on Lower Bridge Way at Terrebonne and drive to 43rd Street. Turn right and drive seven miles (the road names changes to Chinook, then to Clubhouse Road) to Hays Lane. Turn right on Hays Lane and drive one-quarter mile to the park.

Contact: Crooked River Ranch RV Park, P.O. Box 1448, Crooked River Ranch, OR 97760, 800/841-0563 or 541/923-1441, website: www.crookedriverranch.com.

41 INDIAN FORD

Rating: 4

On Indian Ford Creek in Deschutes National Forest.

Map 11.2, grid f4, page 617

This campground is on the banks of Indian Ford Creek at an elevation of 3,250 feet. There's a lot of traffic noise from U.S. 20. The camp is used primarily by overnighters on their way to the town of Sisters. The campground is sprinkled with aspen trees, and great bird-watching opportunities are available.

Campsites, facilities: There are 25 sites for tents or RVs up to 40 feet long. Picnic tables, garbage service, and fire grills are provided. Vault toilets are available. There is no drinking water. Leashed pets are permitted.

Reservations, fees: Reservations are not accepted. Sites are $8 per night, $4 per extra vehicle. Senior discount available. Open May–mid-October.

Directions: From Albany, drive east on U.S. 20 to the junction with Highway 126. Continue east on Highway 126 and drive 21 miles to the campground on the left.

Contact: Deschutes National Forest, Sisters Ranger District, P.O. Box 249, Sisters, OR 97759, 541/549-7700, fax 541/549-7746.

42 COLD SPRINGS

🛏️ 🚐 ⛺

Rating: 7

In Deschutes National Forest.

Map 11.2, grid f4, page 617

This wooded campground is set at 3,400 feet elevation at the source of a small creek. It's just far enough off the main drag to be missed by many campers. Spring and early summer are the times for great bird-watching in the area's abundant aspen.

Campsites, facilities: There are 23 sites for tents or RVs up to 40 feet long. Picnic tables, fire grills, and garbage service are provided. Vault toilets and drinking water are available. Leashed pets are permitted.

Reservations, fees: Reservations are not accepted. Sites are $12 per night, $6 per extra vehicle. Senior discount available. Open May–September.

Directions: From Albany, drive east on U.S. 20 to the junction with Highway 126. Continue east on Highway 126 and drive 26 miles to Sisters and Highway 242. Turn right and drive 4.2 miles to the campground on the right.

Contact: Deschutes National Forest, Sisters Ranger District, P.O. Box 249, Sisters, OR 97759, 541/549-7700, fax 541/549-7746.

43 SCOTT LAKE WALK-IN

🧗 🚣 🛶 🚤 🛏️ ⛺

Rating: 10

On Scott Lake in Willamette National Forest.

Map 11.2, grid g1, page 617

This campground, set around Scott Lake at an elevation of 4,680 feet, offers hike-in sites (only about an eighth of a mile from the road). Only nonmotorized boats are allowed on the lake. Trails leading out of the camp provide access to several small lakes in the Mt. Washington Wilderness. This camp provides great views of the Three Sisters Mountains. Mosquitoes are heavy during the spring and early summer.

Campsites, facilities: There are 12 walk-in tent sites. Picnic tables are provided. Vault toilets are available, but there is no drinking water, and garbage must be packed out. Leashed pets are permitted.

Reservations, fees: Reservations are not accepted. There is no fee for camping. Open late June–early October.

Directions: From Eugene, drive east on Highway 126 for 54 miles to the junction with Highway 242 (part of the Santiam Scenic Byway). Turn right (east) on Highway 242 and drive 14.5 miles to Forest Road 260. Turn left and drive to the campground. Note: Highway 242 is spectacularly scenic, but it's also very narrow, winding, and steep; not recommended for RVs or trailers. The maximum vehicle length is 35 feet.

Contact: Willamette National Forest, McKenzie Ranger District, 57600 McKenzie Hwy., McKenzie Bridge, OR 97413, 541/822-3381, fax 541/822-7254.

44 LAVA CAMP LAKE

🧗 🚣 🛏️ 🚐 ⛺

Rating: 4

Near the Pacific Crest Trail in Deschutes National Forest.

Map 11.2, grid g2, page 617

This campground is set at an elevation of 5,200 feet among subalpine fir in the McKenzie Pass, not far from the Pacific Crest Trail. A number of trails provide other hiking possibilities. A map of Deschutes National Forest details back roads, trails, and streams. Fishing is allowed, but don't expect to catch anything. Perhaps that is why this campground gets such light use.

Campsites, facilities: There are 10 sites for tents or RVs up to 22 feet long. Picnic tables and fire grills are provided. Pit toilets are available. There is no drinking water, and all garbage must be packed out. Leashed pets are permitted.

Reservations, fees: Reservations are not accepted. There is no fee for camping. Open June–September, weather permitting.

Directions: From Eugene, drive east on Highway 126 for 47 miles to the town of McKenzie Bridge. Continue east on Highway 126 for five miles to Highway 242. Turn right (east) and drive 14.6 miles on Highway 242 to the campground entrance. Note: Highway 242 is spectacularly scenic, but also very narrow, winding, and steep. RVs and trailers are discouraged (a 35-foot length limit is in effect).

Contact: Deschutes National Forest, Sisters Ranger District, P.O. Box 249, Sisters, OR 97759, 541/549-7700, fax 541/549-7746.

45 WHISPERING PINE HORSE CAMP

Rating: 5

Near the Trout Creek Swamp in Deschutes National Forest.

Map 11.2, grid g1, page 617

This wooded campground (elevation 4,400 feet) near Trout Creek Swamp is pretty, isolated, and private. Be sure to bring your own water. It's set up as a horse camp with corrals. Although generally not crowded, the camp is gaining in popularity, and groups of horse users occasionally fill it up. Hikers, beware: You'll be sharing the trails with horses.

Campsites, facilities: There are nine primitive sites for tents or RVs. Picnic tables, garbage service, and fire grills are provided. Pit toilets are available. There is no drinking water. Leashed pets are permitted.

Reservations, fees: Reservations are not accepted. Sites are $10 per night, $5 per extra vehicle. Senior discount available. Open June–mid-October.

Directions: From Eugene, drive east on Highway 126 for 47 miles to the town of McKenzie Bridge. Continue east on Highway 126 for five miles to Highway 242. Turn right (east) and drive six miles on Highway 242 to Forest Road 1018. Turn left and drive four miles to the campground entrance. Note:

Highway 242 is spectacularly scenic, but also very narrow, winding, and steep. RVs and trailers are discouraged (a 35-foot length limit is in effect).

Contact: Deschutes National Forest, Sisters Ranger District, P.O. Box 249, Sisters, OR 97759, 541/549-7700, fax 541/549-7746.

46 LIMBERLOST

Rating: 9

On Lost Creek in Willamette National Forest.

Map 11.2, grid g1, page 617

This secluded campground is set at 1,800 feet elevation along Lost Creek, about two miles from where it empties into the McKenzie River. Relatively unknown, the camp gets light use; it makes a good base camp for a trout-fishing trip.

Campsites, facilities: There are two sites for tents and 10 sites for tents or small RVs up to 16 feet long. Picnic tables, garbage service, and fire grills are provided. Vault toilets are available, but there is no drinking water. Leashed pets are permitted.

Reservations, fees: Reservations are not accepted. Sites are $8 per night, $4 per extra vehicle. Senior discount available. Open mid-April–mid-September.

Directions: From Eugene, drive east on Highway 126 for 47 miles to the town of McKenzie Bridge. Continue east on Highway 126 for five miles to Highway 242. Turn right (east) and drive 1.5 miles on Highway 242 to the camp. Note: Highway 242 is spectacularly scenic, but also very narrow, winding, and steep. RVs and trailers are discouraged (a 35-foot length limit is in effect).

Contact: Willamette National Forest, McKenzie Ranger District, 57600 McKenzie Hwy., McKenzie Bridge, OR 97413, 541/822-3381, fax 541/822-7254.

47 ALDER SPRINGS

Rating: 7

In Willamette National Forest.
Map 11.2, grid g1, page 617
This remote campground (at 3,600 feet elevation) features good hiking possibilities, including access to the Linton Lake Trail. This three-mile hike leads to Linton Lake, where fishing is available. The Three Sisters Wilderness is just south of the highway.

Campsites, facilities: There are six tent sites. No drinking water is available, and all garbage must be packed out. Picnic tables and fire grills are provided. Vault toilets are available. Leashed pets are permitted.

Reservations, fees: Reservations are not accepted. There is no fee for camping. Open late May–late September, weather permitting.

Directions: From Eugene, drive east on Highway 126 for 47 miles to the town of McKenzie Bridge. Continue east on Highway 126 for five miles to Highway 242. Turn right (east) and drive 10 miles on Highway 242 to the campground on the left. Note: Highway 242 is spectacularly scenic, but also very narrow, winding, and steep. RVs and trailers are discouraged (a 35-foot length limit is in effect).

Contact: Willamette National Forest, McKenzie Ranger District, 57600 McKenzie Hwy., McKenzie Bridge, OR 97413, 541/822-3381, fax 541/822-7254.

48 DRIFTWOOD

Rating: 9

On Three Creeks Lake in Deschutes National Forest.
Map 11.2, grid g3, page 617
This wooded campground at an elevation of 6,600 feet is often blocked by snowdrifts until July Fourth. At this high elevation, the views of Tam McArthur Rim are spectacular. Al-

though located on the lakeshore and hidden from outsiders, the area can get very crowded. The campground is full most weekends from July Fourth to Labor Day. Some of the recreation options include fishing, swimming, hiking, and nonmotorized boating.

Campsites, facilities: There are 17 tent sites and five sites for tents or RVs up to 16 feet long. Picnic tables, garbage service, and fire grills are provided. Pit toilets are available. There is no drinking water. Boats with motors are not allowed. Leashed pets are permitted.

Reservations, fees: Reservations are not accepted. Sites are $10 per night, $5 per extra vehicle. Senior discount available. Open mid-June–mid-September, weather permitting.

Directions: From Eugene, drive east on Highway 126 to its junction with U.S. 20. Turn east and drive 26 miles to Sisters and Forest Road 16. Turn right and drive 16.4 miles to the campground.

Contact: Deschutes National Forest, Sisters Ranger District, P.O. Box 249, Sisters, OR 97759, 541/549-7700, fax 541/549-7746.

49 THREE CREEKS LAKE

Rating: 8

On Three Creeks Lake in Deschutes National Forest.
Map 11.2, grid g3, page 617
This wooded campground is set along the south shore of Three Creeks Lake in a pretty spot at 6,600 feet elevation. Fishing, swimming, hiking, and nonmotorized boating are the highlights. Also see the description of Driftwood.

Campsites, facilities: There are 10 sites for tents or RVs up to 25 feet long. Picnic tables, garbage service, and fire grills are provided. Vault toilets are available. There is no drinking water. Boats with motors are not allowed. Leashed pets are permitted.

Reservations, fees: Reservations are not accepted. Sites are $10 per night, $5 per extra

vehicle. Open mid-June–mid-October, weather permitting.

Directions: From Eugene, drive east on Highway 126 to its junction with Highway 20. Turn east and drive 26 miles to Sisters and Forest Road 16. Turn right and drive 17 miles to the campground.

Contact: Deschutes National Forest, Sisters Ranger District, P.O. Box 249, Sisters, OR 97759, 541/549-7700, fax 541/549-7746.

50 TUMALO STATE PARK

Rating: 7

On the Deschutes River.

Map 11.2, grid g6, page 617

Trout fishing can be good at this camp along the banks of the Deschutes River, just five miles from Bend. Mount Bachelor is just up the road and provides plenty of winter recreation opportunities. The swimming area is generally safe and a good spot for children. Rafting is also an option here. See the description of Bend Keystone RV Park for more recreation information.

Campsites, facilities: There are 61 sites for tents, 21 sites with full hookups for RVs up to 44 feet long, a special camping area for hikers and bicyclists, eight yurts, and a group area for tent camping. Electricity, drinking water, sewer hookups, fire grills, and picnic tables are provided. Flush toilets, showers, firewood, and a playground are available. A store, a café, and ice are within one mile. Leashed pets are permitted.

Reservations, fees: Reservations at 800/452-5687 or website: www.OregonStateParks.org ($7 reservation fee). Sites are $13–19 per night, $4 per night for hikers/bikers, $29 per night for yurts, $64 per night for the group area, and $7 per extra vehicle. Major credit cards accepted. Open year-round.

Directions: From Bend, drive north on U.S. 97 for two miles to U.S. 20 West. Turn northwest and drive five miles to Tumalo Junction.

Turn left at Tumalo Junction onto Cook Avenue, and drive one mile to the campground.

Contact: High Desert Management Unit, 62976 O. B. Riley Rd., Bend, OR 97701, 800/551-6949 or 541/388-6055, reservations 800/452-5687.

51 BEND KAMPGROUND

Rating: 5

Near Bend.

Map 11.2, grid h6, page 617

Recreation options near this camp include a golf course, hiking trails, bike paths, and tennis courts. See the description of Bend Keystone RV Park for additional recreation information.

Campsites, facilities: There are 40 tent sites and 74 sites for RVs of any length; 40 are drive-through sites. Drinking water and picnic tables are provided. Electricity, sewer hookups, flush toilets, showers, a laundry room, a store, a deli, ice, firewood, a playground, a swimming pool, a recreation room, bottled gas, and an RV dump station are available. Leashed pets are permitted.

Reservations, fees: Reservations at 800/713-5333. Sites are $18–28 per night, $2–3 per person for more than two people, and $4 per extra vehicle. Major credit cards accepted. Open year-round.

Directions: In Bend, drive north on U.S. 97 for two miles to the park entrance road.

Contact: Bend Kampground, 63615 N. U.S. 97, Bend, OR 97701, 541/382-7738, fax 541/382-3149.

52 SCANDIA RV AND MOBILE PARK

Rating: 5

Near the Deschutes River.

Map 11.2, grid h6, page 617

This park near the Deschutes River is close

to a golf course, a stable, bike paths, and tennis courts.

Campsites, facilities: There are 60 sites for tents or RVs of any length; seven are drive-through sites. Electricity, drinking water, picnic tables, cable TV, and sewer hookups are provided. Flush toilets, showers, and a laundry room are available. Bottled gas, an RV dump station, a store, a café, and ice are within one mile. Leashed pets are permitted.

Reservations, fees: Reservations at 541/382-6206. Sites are $22 per night, $2 per person for more than two people. Major credit cards accepted. Open year-round.

Directions: In Bend, drive south on U.S. 97 for one-half mile to the park entrance.

Contact: Scandia RV and Mobile Park, 61415 S. U.S. 97, Bend, OR 97702, 541/382-6206, fax 541/382-4087.

53 CROWN VILLA RV RESORT

Rating: 6

Near Bend.
Map 11.2, grid h6, page 617

This RV park offers large and landscaped grassy sites. Nearby recreation options include horseback riding and golf.

Campsites, facilities: There are 124 sites for RVs of any length; 106 have full hookups, and 24 have partial hookups. Electricity, drinking water, sewer hookups, picnic tables, flush toilets, showers, cable TV, a laundry room, bottled gas, ice, an RV dump station, and a playground are available. A store and a café are within one mile. Leashed pets are permitted.

Reservations, fees: Reservations accepted. Sites are $35–45 per night, $2.50 per person for more than two people. Senior discount available. Major credit cards accepted. Open year-round.

Directions: From Bend, drive south on U.S. 97 for two miles to Brosterhous Road. Turn east and drive to the park.

Contact: Crown Villa RV Resort, 60801 Brosterhous Rd., Bend, OR 97702, 541/388-1131.

54 WHISTLER'S BEND

Rating: 7

On the North Umpqua River.
Map 11.3, grid f7, page 618

This Douglas County park along the banks of the North Umpqua River is an idyllic spot because it gets little pressure from outsiders, yet is just a 20-minute drive from I-5. Two boat ramps accommodate boaters, and fishing is a plus. A wildlife reserve provides habitat for deer.

Campsites, facilities: There are 23 sites for tents or RVs up to 35 feet long and two yurts. Group camping is available. Picnic tables and fire grills are provided. Drinking water, flush toilets, showers, a playground, and launching facilities are available. Leashed pets are permitted.

Reservations, fees: Reservations are not accepted for tent or RV sites; $10 per night, $3 per extra vehicle. Reservations for yurts or group camps at 541/440-4500; yurts $28 per night; $40 for the group camp for up to 25 people, $70 for 26–50 people, and $100 for 51 or more people. Senior discount available for Douglas County residents. Major credit cards accepted. Open year-round.

Directions: From Roseburg, drive east on Highway 138 for 12 miles to Whistler's Bend Park Road (well signed). Turn left and drive two miles to the end of the road and the park entrance.

Contact: Whistler's Bend, 2828 Whistlers Park Rd., Roseburg, OR 97470, 541/673-4863, website: www.co.douglas.or.us/parks.

55 JOHN P. AMACHER COUNTY PARK

Rating: 6

On the Umpqua River.
Map 11.3, grid g6, page 618

This prime layover spot for I-5 RV cruisers is

in a wooded Douglas County park, set along the banks of the North Umpqua River. An 18-hole golf course and tennis courts are close by. Riding stables are within a 20-minute drive, and Winchester Dam is within one-quarter mile. The camp was renovated in 2001.

Campsites, facilities: There are 10 sites for tents and 20 sites with full or partial hookups for RVs up to 30 feet long; 11 are drive-through sites. Electricity, drinking water, sewer hookups, and picnic tables are provided. Flush toilets, showers, a gazebo, and a playground are available. Bottled gas, a store, a café, a coin-operated laundry, and ice are within one mile. Boat-launching facilities are available. Some facilities are wheelchair accessible. Leashed pets are permitted.

Reservations, fees: Reservations are not accepted. Sites are $11–14 per night, $3 per extra vehicle. Senior discount available for residents of Douglas County. Open year-round.

Directions: From Roseburg, drive five miles north on I-5 to Exit 129. Take that exit and drive south on Old Highway 99 for one-quarter mile to the park on the right (just across Winchester Bridge).

Contact: John P. Amacher County Park, P.O. Box 800, Winchester, OR 97495, 541/672-4901 or 541/440-4500, fax 541/440-6248, website: www.co.douglas.or.us/parks.

56 TWIN RIVERS VACATION PARK

Rating: 6

Near the Umpqua River.
Map 11.3, grid g5, page 618

This wooded campground near the Umpqua River is the only camp in Roseburg with tent and RV sites. It features large shaded pull-through sites and more than 100 kinds of trees on the property. Nearby recreation options include a golf course, a county park, and bike paths.

Campsites, facilities: There are 72 sites for RVs of any length; 35 are drive-through with

full hookups. Electricity, drinking water, cable TV, sewer hookups, and picnic tables are provided. Flush toilets, bottled gas, showers, firewood, a store, a laundry room, ice, and a playground are available. Boat-launching facilities are nearby. Leashed pets are permitted.

Reservations, fees: Reservations accepted. Sites are $18–28 per night, $2 per person for more than two people. Major credit cards accepted. Open year-round.

Directions: In Roseburg on I-5, take Exit 125 to Garden Valley Road. Drive west for five miles (over the river) to Old Garden Valley Road. Turn left and drive 1.5 miles to River Forks Road. Turn left and drive to the entrance to the park.

Contact: Twin Rivers Vacation Park, 433 River Forks Rd., Roseburg, OR 97470, 541/673-3811.

57 DOUGLAS COUNTY FAIRGROUNDS RV PARK

Rating: 8

On the South Umpqua River.
Map 11.3, grid g6, page 618

This 74-acre county park is very easily accessible off the highway. Nearby Umpqua River, one of Oregon's prettiest rivers, often has good fishing in season. A golf course, bike paths, and tennis courts are nearby. Horse stalls and a boat ramp are available at the nearby fairgrounds. The campground fills up the third weekend in March during the annual fiddlers' convention.

Campsites, facilities: There are 50 sites with partial hookups for tents or RVs of any length. Tent camping is limited to two nights. Electricity, drinking water, and picnic tables are provided. Flush toilets, an RV dump station, showers, and a dump station are available. A store, a café, a coin-operated laundry, and ice are within one mile. Some facilities are wheelchair accessible. Leashed pets are permitted.

Reservations, fees: Reservations are not accepted. Sites are $20 per night, with a 14-day stay limit. Open year-round, except one week in August during the county fair. Phone ahead to confirm current status.

Directions: From I-5 in Roseburg, take Exit 123 and drive south under the freeway to Frear Street. Turn right and enter the park.

Contact: Douglas County Fairgrounds & Speedway, 2110 S.W. Frear St., Roseburg, OR 97470, 541/957-7010, fax 541/440-6023.

58 WILDLIFE SAFARI RV PARK

Rating: 6

Near Roseburg.
Map 11.3, grid g5, page 618

This park is part of the Wildlife Safari Park in Winston (near Roseburg), which offers a walk-through petting zoo. Nearby recreation options include an 18-hole golf course, hiking trails, and marked bike trails.

Campsites, facilities: There are 18 drive-through sites for self-contained RVs. Electricity and a café are available. There is no drinking water. A gift shop is within one-half mile. Leashed pets are permitted.

Reservations, fees: Reservations are not accepted. Sites are $8–10 per night. The campground is closed in the winter.

Directions: From Roseburg, drive south on I-5 for five miles to Exit 119 and Highway 42. Take Highway 42 southwest for three miles to Looking Glass Road (just before reaching Winston). Turn right and drive one block to Safari Road. Turn right and enter the park.

Contact: Wildlife Safari RV Park, 1291 Safari Rd., P.O. Box 1600, Winston, OR 97496, 541/679-6761 or 800/355-4848, fax 541/679-9210, website: www.maserith.com/safari.

59 DOLLY VARDEN

Rating: 6

On Fall Creek in Willamette National Forest.
Map 11.4, grid a4, page 619

This pretty campground is adjacent to Fall Creek and is at the lower trailhead for the scenic, 13.7-mile Fall Creek National Recreation Trail, which follows the creek and varies between 960 and 1,385 feet in elevation. This campground gets moderate to heavy use. It is set on the inlet stream for Fall Creek Reservoir.

Campsites, facilities: There are three sites for tents and two sites for tents or RVs up to 16 feet long. Picnic tables, garbage service, and fire grills are provided. Vault toilets are available. There is no drinking water. Leashed pets are permitted.

Reservations, fees: Reservations are not accepted. Sites are $8 per night, $4 per extra vehicle. Senior discount available. Open May–mid-September.

Directions: From south Eugene on I-5, take Exit 188 to Highway 58. Drive 11 miles south to Lowell and Pioneer Street (at the covered bridge). Turn left and drive less than one-quarter mile to West Boundary Road. Turn left and drive one block to Lowell Jasper Road. Turn right and drive 1.5 miles to Unity and Place Road. Turn right and drive about one mile to a fork with North Shore Road. Bear left onto North Shore Road (Big Fall Creek Road) and drive about 10 miles (the road becomes Forest Road 18) to the campground on the left.

Contact: Willamette National Forest, Middle Fork Ranger District, Lowell Service Center, 60 Pioneer St., Lowell, OR 97452, 541/937-2129, fax 541/937-2032.

60 BIG POOL

Rating: 6

On Fall Creek in Willamette National Forest.
Map 11.4, grid a4, page 619
This campground along Fall Creek at about 1,000 feet elevation is quiet, secluded, and primitive. The scenic Fall Creek National Recreation Trail passes the camp on the other side of the creek. See the description of Dolly Varden for more details on the area.

Campsites, facilities: There are three tent sites and two sites for tents or RVs up to 16 feet long. Picnic tables, garbage containers, and fire grills are provided. Vault toilets are available. There is no drinking water. Leashed pets are permitted.

Reservations, fees: Reservations are not accepted. Sites are $10 per night, $5 per extra vehicle. Senior discount available. Open May–mid-September.

Directions: From south Eugene on I-5, take Exit 188 to Highway 58. Drive 11 miles south to Lowell and Pioneer Street (at the covered bridge). Turn left and drive less than one-quarter mile to West Boundary Road. Turn left and drive one block to Lowell Jasper Road. Turn right and drive 1.5 miles to Unity and Place Road. Turn right and drive about one mile to a fork with North Shore Road. Bear left onto North Shore Road (Big Fall Creek Road) and drive about 12 miles (the road becomes Forest Road 18) to the campground on the right.

Contact: Willamette National Forest, Middle Fork Ranger District, Lowell Service Center, 60 Pioneer St., Lowell, OR 97452, 541/937-2129, fax 541/937-2032.

61 BEDROCK

Rating: 6

On Fall Creek in Willamette National Forest.
Map 11.4, grid a4, page 619
This campground along the banks of Fall Creek is one of the access points for the scenic Fall Creek National Recreation Trail, which in turn offers access to Jones Trail, a six-mile uphill climb. See the description of Dolly Varden for trail information.

Campsites, facilities: There are 20 sites for tents or RVs up to 22 feet long. Picnic tables, garbage service, and fire grills are provided. Vault toilets and drinking water are available. Leashed pets are permitted.

Reservations, fees: Reservations are not accepted. Sites are $10 per night, $5 per extra vehicle. Senior discount available. Open May–late October.

Directions: From south Eugene on I-5, take Exit 188 to Highway 58. Drive 11 miles south to Lowell and Pioneer Street (at the covered bridge). Turn left and drive less than one-quarter mile to West Boundary Road. Turn left and drive one block to Lowell Jasper Road. Turn right and drive 1.5 miles to Unity and Place Road. Turn right and drive about one mile to a fork with North Shore Road. Bear left onto North Shore Road (Big Fall Creek Road) and drive about 14 miles (the road becomes Forest Road 18) to the campground on the left.

Contact: Willamette National Forest, Middle Fork Ranger District, Lowell Service Center, 60 Pioneer St., Lowell, OR 97452, 541/937-2129, fax 541/937-2032.

62 PUMA CREEK

Rating: 6

On Fall Creek in Willamette National Forest.
Map 11.4, grid a4, page 619
This campground is set along the banks of Fall Creek, across from the Fall Creek National Recreation Trail. It's one of four camps in the immediate area. See the description of Dolly Varden for more information.

Campsites, facilities: There are 11 sites for tents or RVs up to 16 feet long. Picnic tables, garbage containers, and fire grills are provided. Vault toilets and drinking water are available. Leashed pets are permitted.

Reservations, fees: Reservations are not accepted. Sites are $10 per night, $5 per extra vehicle. Senior discount available. Open May–early October.

Directions: From I-5 south of Eugene, take Exit 188 to Highway 58. Drive about 11 miles to Lowell. Turn left at Pioneer Street (at the covered bridge), drive two-tenths of a mile and turn left on West Boundary Road. Drive one block and turn right at Lowell Jasper Road. Drive 1.5 miles to Place Road and turn right. Drive about one mile to a fork and bear left onto North Shore Road (Big Fall Creek Road). Drive about 16 miles (the road becomes Forest Road 18) to the campground on the left.

Contact: Willamette National Forest, Middle Fork Ranger District, Lowell Service Center, 60 Pioneer St., Lowell, OR 97452, 541/937-2129, fax 541/937-2032.

63 HOMESTEAD

Rating: 8

On the South Fork of the McKenzie River in Willamette National Forest.

Map 11.4, grid a7, page 619

This quiet little campground is set among the trees along the banks of the South Fork of the McKenzie River. It's primitive, little known, and free. Nearby Frissell Crossing has water available from a hand pump.

Campsites, facilities: There are eight sites for tents or RVs. Picnic tables and fire grills are provided. Vault toilets are available, but there is no drinking water. All garbage must be packed out. Leashed pets are permitted.

Reservations, fees: Reservations are not accepted. There is no fee for camping. Open year-round.

Directions: From Eugene, drive east on Highway 126 for 41 miles to Blue River. Continue east on Highway 126 for five miles to Forest Road 19 (Aufderheide Scenic Byway). Turn south on Forest Road 19 and drive 17 miles to the camp.

Contact: Willamette National Forest, McKenzie River Ranger District, Blue River Forest

Service Center, P.O. Box 199, Blue River, OR 97413, 541/822-3317, fax 541/822-1255.

64 FRISSELL CROSSING

Rating: 8

Near the Three Sisters Wilderness in Willamette National Forest.

Map 11.4, grid a7, page 619

This campground (elevation 2,800 feet) sits on the banks of the South Fork of the McKenzie River, adjacent to a trailhead that provides access to the backcountry of the Three Sisters Wilderness. Frissell Crossing is the only camp in the immediate area that has drinking water. If you're looking for solitude, this place should be heaven to you. Homestead provides a free, primitive alternative.

Campsites, facilities: There are 12 sites for tents or RVs. Picnic tables, garbage bins, and fire grills are provided. Drinking water and vault toilets are available. Leashed pets are permitted.

Reservations, fees: Reservations are not accepted. Sites are $10 per night, $5 per extra vehicle. Senior discount available. Open mid-May–mid-September.

Directions: From Eugene, drive east on Highway 126 for 37 miles to Blue River. Continue east on Highway 126 for five miles to Forest Road 19 (Aufderheide Scenic Byway). Turn south and drive 23 miles to the camp.

Contact: Willamette National Forest, McKenzie River Ranger District, Blue River Forest Service Center, P.O. Box 199, Blue River, OR 97413, 541/822-3317, fax 541/822-1255.

65 BOX CANYON HORSE CAMP

Rating: 4

Near Chucksney Mountain in Willamette National Forest.

Map 11.4, grid a8, page 619

Only 80 miles from Eugene, this secluded campground with sparse tree cover offers wilderness trails, including the Chucksney Mountain Trail, Crossing-Way Trail, and Grasshopper Trail. It's a good base camp for a backpacking trip.

Campsites, facilities: There are 11 sites for tents or RVs that allow horse and rider to camp close together. Picnic tables, fire grills, stock water, and corrals are provided. A manure disposal site and vault toilets are available. There is no drinking water and all garbage must be packed out. Leashed pets are permitted.

Reservations, fees: Reservations are not accepted. There is no fee for camping. Open year-round, weather permitting.

Directions: From Eugene, drive east on Highway 126 for 41 miles to Blue River. Continue east on Highway 126 for five miles to Forest Road 19 (Aufderheide Scenic Byway). Turn south and drive 30 miles to the camp.

Contact: Willamette National Forest, McKenzie River Ranger District, Blue River Forest Service Center, P.O. Box 199, Blue River, OR 97413, 541/822-3317, fax 541/822-1255.

66 WINBERRY

Rating: 6

On Winberry Creek in Willamette National Forest.

Map 11.4, grid a4, page 619

This campground is on Winberry Creek in a tree-shaded area. The closest hiking option is Station Butte Trail, just downstream from the campground on Forest Road 1802-150. Be cautious—poison oak grows at the top of the butte.

Campsites, facilities: There are five sites for tents and two sites for RVs up to 16 feet long. Picnic tables, garbage service, and fire grills are provided. Drinking water, vault toilets, and A-frame shelters are available. Leashed pets are permitted.

Reservations, fees: Reservations are not accepted. Sites are $6–8 per night, $3 per extra vehicle. Senior discount available. Open late May–mid-September.

Directions: From south Eugene on I-5, take Exit 188 to Highway 58. Drive 11 miles south to Lowell and Pioneer Street (at the covered bridge). Turn left and drive less than one-quarter mile to West Boundary Road. Turn left and drive one block to Lowell Jasper Road. Turn right and drive 1.5 miles to Unity and Place Road. Turn right and drive about one mile to a fork with Winberry Road. Bear right and drive six miles (the road becomes Forest Road 1802). Continue 3.5 miles to the campground.

Contact: Willamette National Forest, Middle Fork Ranger District, Lowell Service Center, 60 Pioneer St., Lowell, OR 97452, 541/937-2129, fax 541/937-2032.

67 BLAIR LAKE WALK-IN

Rating: 6

On Blair Lake in Willamette National Forest.

Map 11.4, grid b6, page 619

If you're looking for a pristine alpine, lakeside setting, you'll find it here. The lake, set at 4,800 feet elevation, is small (only 35 acres) and shallow (20 feet). It supports a population of brook and rainbow trout and is stocked in the summer. The surrounding meadows and woods are well known for their wide range of wildflowers and huckleberries.

Campsites, facilities: There are seven walk-in tent sites. Picnic tables and garbage bins are provided. Drinking water, fire rings, and a pit toilet are available. Leashed pets are permitted.

Reservations, fees: Reservations are not accepted. Sites are $6 per night, $3 per extra vehicle. Senior discount available. Open June–mid-October, weather permitting.

Directions: From south Eugene on I-5, take Exit 188 to Highway 58. Drive 35 miles southeast on Highway 58 to Oakridge. Turn left at the signal to downtown and Salmon Creek Road. Turn east and drive nine miles (it becomes Forest

Road 24) to Forest Road 1934. Turn left and drive eight miles to Forest Road 733. Turn right and continue for less than one mile to the campground.

Contact: Willamette National Forest, Middle Fork Ranger District, 46375 Hwy. 58, Westfir, OR 97492, 541/782-2283, fax 541/782-5306.

68 KIAHANIE

Rating: 5

On the West Fork of the Willamette River in Willamette National Forest.

Map 11.4, grid a7, page 619

This is one heck of a spot for fly-fishing (the only kind allowed). This remote campground is set at 2,200 feet elevation along the North Fork of the Willamette River, a designated Wild and Scenic River. If you want beauty and quiet among enormous Douglas fir trees, you came to the right place. An even more remote campground, Box Canyon Horse Camp, is farther north on Forest Road 19.

Campsites, facilities: There are 19 sites for tents or RVs up to 24 feet long. Picnic tables, garbage bins, a recycling center, and fire rings are provided. Drinking water and vault toilets are available. Leashed pets are permitted.

Reservations, fees: Reservations are not accepted. Sites are $10 per night, $5 per extra vehicle. Open late May–September.

Directions: From south Eugene on I-5, take Exit 188 to Highway 58. Drive 31 miles southeast on Highway 58 to Westfir. Take the Westfir exit and drive two miles to Westfir and the junction with Aufderheide Scenic Byway (Forest Road 19). Bear left (northeast) and drive 19 miles to the campground.

Contact: Willamette National Forest, Middle Fork Ranger District, 46375 Hwy. 58, Westfir, OR 97492, 541/782-2283, fax 541/782-5306.

69 SKOOKUM CREEK

Rating: 7

Near the Three Sisters Wilderness in Willamette National Forest.

Map 11.4, grid b8, page 619

Skookum Creek is a popular starting point for backcountry fishing, hiking, or horseback riding. The Erma Bell Lakes Trail, a portal into the Three Sisters Wilderness, begins here. This trail is maintained for wheelchair accessibility, though it is challenging.

Campsites, facilities: There are eight walk-in tent sites, two of which are wheelchair accessible. Picnic tables and fire rings are provided. Drinking water, hitching rails, and pit toilets are available. All garbage must be packed out. Leashed pets are permitted.

Reservations, fees: Reservations are not accepted. Sites are $6 per night, $3 per extra vehicle. Senior discount available. Open mid-May–September, weather permitting.

Directions: From Eugene, drive east on Highway 126 for 37 miles to Blue River. Continue east for five miles to Forest Road 19 (Aufderheide Scenic Byway). Turn right and drive 35 miles south to Forest Road 1957. Turn left (south) and drive four miles to the campground.

Contact: Willamette National Forest, Middle Fork Ranger District, 46375 Hwy. 58, Westfir, OR 97492, 541/782-2283, fax 541/782-5306.

70 BLACK CANYON

Rating: 7

On the Middle Fork of the Willamette River in Willamette National Forest.

Map 11.4, grid b3, page 619

This campground is set along the banks of the Middle Fork of the Willamette River, not far above Lookout Point Reservoir, where fishing and boating are available. The camp is pretty and wooded and has comfortable sites. Within the camp is a one-mile-long nature trail with interpretive signs. The amphitheater stages weekend programs in July and August. You will hear train noise from the other side of the river.

Campsites, facilities: There are 72 sites for tents or RVs up to 22 feet long. Picnic tables, garbage service, and fire grills are provided. Drinking water, vault toilets, and firewood are available. An RV dump station, a café, and a coin-operated laundry are within six miles. Some facilities are wheelchair accessible. Launching facilities are nearby at the south end of Lookout Point Reservoir. Leashed pets are permitted.

Reservations, fees: Reservations are not accepted. Sites are $12–20 per night, $6 per extra vehicle. Open May–late October.

Directions: From south Eugene on I-5, take Exit 188 to Highway 58. Drive southeast on Highway 58 for 27 miles to the camp on the left (six miles west of Oakridge).

Contact: Willamette National Forest, Middle Fork Ranger District, Lowell Service Center, 60 Pioneer St., Lowell, OR 97452, 541/937-2129, fax 541/937-2032.

71 SHADY DELL GROUP CAMP

Rating: 5

On the Middle Fork of the Willamette River in Willamette National Forest.

Map 11.4, grid b3, page 619

This camp is rented only to groups. It is set near the Middle Fork of the Willamette River, across from Lookout Point Reservoir, a long, narrow lake adjacent to Highway 58. Noteworthy here is a stand of old-growth cedars.

Campsites, facilities: There is a group site for tents or RVs up to 15 feet long. Picnic tables, garbage service, and fire grills are provided. Drinking water and vault toilets are available. An RV dump station, a café, and a coin-operated laundry are available within five miles. Some facilities are wheelchair accessible. Leashed pets are permitted.

Reservations, fees: Reservations required at

541/822-3799; $40 per night. Open May–late October.

Directions: From south Eugene on I-5, take Exit 188 to Highway 58. Drive southeast on Highway 58 for 32 miles (five miles west of Oakridge) to the camp on the right.

Contact: Willamette National Forest, Middle Fork Ranger District, Lowell Service Center, 60 Pioneer St., Lowell, OR 97452, 541/937-2129, fax 541/937-2032.

72 SALMON CREEK FALLS

Rating: 8

On Salmon Creek in Willamette National Forest.

Map 11.4, grid b6, page 619

This pretty campground sits in a lush, old-growth forest, right along Salmon Creek. The rocky gorge area creates two small but beautiful waterfalls and several deep pools in the clear, blue-green waters. Springtime brings a full range of wildflowers and wild thimbleberries; hazelnuts abound in the summer. This area is a popular recreation spot.

Campsites, facilities: There are 14 sites for tents or RVs up to 24 feet long. Picnic tables, garbage bins, and fire grills are provided. Drinking water and vault toilets are available. A store, a café, a coin-operated laundry, and ice are available within five miles. Leashed pets are permitted.

Reservations, fees: Reservations are not accepted. Sites are $12 per night, $6 per extra vehicle. Senior discount available. Open late April–September.

Directions: From south Eugene on I-5, take Exit 188 to Highway 58. Drive southeast on Highway 58 for 35 miles to Oakridge and the signal light for downtown. Turn left on Crestview Street and drive one-quarter mile to 1st Street. Turn right and drive six miles (the road becomes Forest Road 24, then Salmon Creek Road) to the campground entrance on the right.

Contact: Willamette National Forest, Middle Fork Ranger District, 46375 Hwy. 58, Westfir, OR 97492, 541/782-2283, fax 541/782-5306.

73 NORTH WALDO

Rating: 10

On Waldo Lake in Willamette National Forest.

Map 11.4, grid b8, page 619

This camp, at an elevation of 5,400 feet, is the most popular of the Waldo Lake campgrounds. The drier environment supports fewer mosquitoes, but they can still be plentiful in season. The boat launch is deeper than the others on the lake, making it more accommodating for large sailboats. North Waldo is also a popular starting point to many wilderness trails and lakes, most notably the Rigdon, Wahanna, and Torrey Lakes. Waldo Lake has the special distinction of being one of the three purest lakes in the world. Of those three lakes, two are in Oregon (the other is Crater Lake), and the third is in Siberia. Amphitheater programs are presented here on weekends from late July to Labor Day.

Campsites, facilities: There are 58 sites for tents or RVs up to 30 feet long. Picnic tables, garbage bins, a recycle center, and fire rings are provided. Drinking water, vault and flush toilets, a swimming area, and an amphitheater are available. Boat-launching facilities are available. Leashed pets are permitted.

Reservations, fees: Reservations are not accepted. Sites are $10–12 per night, $5 per extra vehicle. Senior discount available. Northwest Forest Pass ($5 daily fee or $30 annual fee per parked vehicle) is required at the nearby boat launch and trailheads. Open July–September, weather permitting.

Directions: From Eugene, drive south on I-5 for four miles to Exit 188 and Highway 58. Turn southeast and drive about 60 miles southeast to Waldo Lake Road (Forest Road 5897). Turn left and drive north on Waldo Lake Road

for 14 miles to Forest Road 5898. Turn left and drive about two miles to the campground at the northeast end of Waldo Lake.

Contact: Willamette National Forest, Middle Fork Ranger District, 46375 Hwy. 58, Westfir, OR 97492, 541/782-2283, fax 541/782-5306.

74 ISLET

Rating: 10

On Waldo Lake in Willamette National Forest.

Map 11.4, grid c8, page 619

You'll find sandy beaches and an interpretive sign at this campground at the north end of Waldo Lake. The winds blow consistently every afternoon. A picnic table placed strategically on the rock jetty provides a great spot to enjoy a sunset. A one-mile shoreline trail stretches between Islet and North Waldo Campground. Bring your mosquito repellent June–August; you'll need it. For more information, see North Waldo.

Campsites, facilities: There are 55 sites for tents or RVs up to 30 feet long. Picnic tables, garbage bins, a recycling center, and fire rings are provided. Drinking water and vault toilets are available. Boat-launching facilities are available. Leashed pets are permitted.

Reservations, fees: Reservations are not accepted. Sites are $12 per night, $6 per extra vehicle. Double sites are $20 per night. Senior discount available. Northwest Forest Pass ($5 daily fee or $30 annual fee per parked vehicle) is required at the nearby boat launch and trailheads. Open July–September, weather permitting.

Directions: From Eugene, drive south on I-5 for four miles to Exit 188 and Highway 58. Turn southeast and drive about 60 miles southeast to Waldo Lake Road (Forest Road 5897). Turn left and drive north on Waldo Lake Road for 14 miles to Forest Road 5898. Turn left and continue 1.5 miles to the campground at the northeast end of Waldo Lake.

Contact: Willamette National Forest, Middle Fork Ranger District, 46375 Hwy. 58, Westfir, OR 97492, 541/782-2283, fax 541/782-5306.

75 SHADOW BAY

Rating: 10

On Waldo Lake in Willamette National Forest.

Map 11.4, grid c8, page 619

This campground is situated on a large bay at the south end of Waldo Lake. It has a considerably wetter environment than either North Waldo or Islet, supporting a more diverse and prolific ground cover as well as more mosquitoes. The camp receives considerably lighter use than North Waldo. You have access to the Shore Line Trail and then the Waldo Lake Trail from here. The boating speed limit is 10 mph for all of Waldo Lake.

Campsites, facilities: There are 92 sites for tents or RVs up to 24 feet long. Picnic tables, garbage bins, a recycle center, and fire grills are provided. Drinking water and vault and flush toilets are available. Boat-launching facilities are nearby. Leashed pets are permitted.

Reservations, fees: Reservations are not accepted. Sites are $12 per night, $6 per extra vehicle. Senior discount available. Northwest Forest Pass ($5 daily fee or $30 annual fee per parked vehicle) is required at the nearby boat launch and trailheads. Open July–September, weather permitting.

Directions: From Eugene, drive south on I-5 for four miles to Exit 188 and Highway 58. Turn southeast and drive about 60 miles southeast to Waldo Lake Road (Forest Road 5897). Turn left on Waldo Lake Road and drive north for 6.5 miles to the Shadow Bay turnoff. Turn left and drive on Forest Road 5896 to the campground at the south end of Waldo Lake.

Contact: Willamette National Forest, Middle Fork Ranger District, 46375 Hwy. 58, Westfir, OR 97492, 541/782-2283, fax 541/782-5306.

76 BLUE POOL

Rating: 4

On Salt Creek in Willamette National Forest.

Map 11.4, grid c7, page 619

This campground is situated in an old-growth forest alongside Salt Creek at 1,900 feet elevation. The camp features a large picnic area along the creek with picnic tables, a large grassy area, and fire stoves built in the 1930s by the Civilian Conservation Corps. One-half mile east of the campground on Highway 58 is McCredie Hot Springs. This spot is undeveloped, without any facilities. Exercise caution when using the hot springs; they can be very hot.

Campsites, facilities: There are 24 sites for tents or RVs up to 18 feet long. Picnic tables, garbage bins, a recycle center, and fire rings are provided. Drinking water and pit and flush toilets are available. Leashed pets are permitted.

Reservations, fees: Reservations are not accepted. Sites are $10 per night, $5 per extra vehicle. Senior discount available. Open mid-May–mid-September.

Directions: From Eugene, drive south on I-5 for four miles to Exit 188 and Highway 58. Turn southeast and drive 35 miles to Oakridge. Continue east on Highway 58 for 10 miles to the campground.

Contact: Willamette National Forest, Middle Fork Ranger District, 46375 Hwy. 58, Westfir, OR 97492, 541/782-2283, fax 541/782-5306.

77 PACKARD CREEK

Rating: 6

On Hills Creek Reservoir in Willamette National Forest.

Map 11.4, grid c5, page 619

Situated on a large flat beside Hills Creek Reservoir, this campground is extremely popular with families and fills up on weekends and holidays. The mix of vegetation in the campground includes an abundance of poison oak. The speed limit around the swimming area and boat ramp is 5 mph.

Campsites, facilities: There are 33 sites for tents or RVs up to 30 feet long. Picnic tables, garbage bins, and fire rings are provided. Drinking water, vault toilets, and firewood are available. Some facilities are wheelchair accessible. Fishing and boat docks, boat-launching facilities, a roped swimming area, a picnic shelter, and an amphitheater are available. Some sites have their own docks. Leashed pets are permitted.

Reservations, fees: Reservations are not accepted. The fee is $12 per night, $20 per night for double sites, and $6 per extra vehicle. Senior discount available. Open mid-April–mid-September.

Directions: From Eugene, drive south on I-5 for four miles to Exit 188 and Highway 58. Turn southeast and drive 35 miles to Oakridge. Continue east on Highway 58 for two miles to Kitson Springs Road. Turn right and drive one-half mile to Forest Road 21. Turn right and continue six miles to the campground.

Contact: Willamette National Forest, Middle Fork Ranger District, 46375 Hwy. 58, Westfir, OR 97492, 541/782-2283, fax 541/782-5306.

78 SHARPS CREEK

Rating: 5

On Sharps Creek.
Map 11.4, grid d2, page 619

Like nearby Rujada, this camp on the banks of Sharps Creek is just far enough off the beaten path to be missed by most campers. It's quiet, primitive, and remote, and fishing, swimming, and gold-panning are popular activities in the day-use area.

Campsites, facilities: There are 10 sites for tents or RVs up to 30 feet long. Picnic tables and fire pits are provided. Drinking water, vault toilets, and firewood are available. A camp host is here in summer. Some facilities are wheelchair accessible. Leashed pets are permitted.

Reservations, fees: Reservations are not accepted. Sites are $5 per night, with a 14-day stay limit; $3 per extra vehicle. Senior discount available. Open mid-May–mid-October, weather permitting.

Directions: From Eugene, drive south on I-5 to Cottage Grove and Exit 174. Take that exit and drive east on Row River Road for 18 miles to Sharps Creek Road. Turn south and drive four miles to the campground.

Contact: Bureau of Land Management, 2890 Chad Dr., Eugene District, P.O. Box 10226, Eugene, OR 97408, 541/683-6600, fax 541/683-6981.

79 RUJADA

Rating: 7

On Layng Creek in Umpqua National Forest.
Map 11.4, grid d3, page 619

This campground is situated on a river terrace on the banks of Layng Creek, right at the national forest border. The Swordfern Trail follows Layng Creek through a beautiful forest within a lush fern grotto. There is a fair swimming hole near the campground. Those with patience and persistence can fish in the creek. By continuing east on Forest Road 17, you reach a trailhead that leads one-half mile to beautiful Spirit Falls, a spectacular 60-foot waterfall. A bit farther east is another easy trail, which leads to Moon Falls, even more awe-inspiring at 125 feet. Another campground option is Cedar Creek, about six miles southeast on Brice Creek Road (County Road 2470).

Campsites, facilities: There are 11 sites for tents or RVs up to 22 feet long. Picnic tables, garbage bins, and fire pits are provided. Flush toilets, drinking water, and a softball field are available. Some facilities are wheelchair accessible. Leashed pets are permitted.

Reservations, fees: Reservations are not accepted for camping; reservations accepted for large groups for day-use. Sites are $7 per night, $3 per extra vehicle. Senior discount available. Open late May–late September.

Directions: From Eugene, drive south on I-5 to Cottage Grove and Exit 174. Take that exit and drive east on Row River Road for 19 miles to Layng Creek Road (Forest Road 17). Turn left and drive two miles to the campground on the right.

Contact: Umpqua National Forest, Cottage Grove Ranger District, 78405 Cedar Park Rd., Cottage Grove, OR 97424, 541/767-5000, fax 541/767-5075.

80 SAND PRAIRIE

Rating: 6

On the Willamette River in Willamette National Forest.

Map 11.4, grid d5, page 619

Situated at 1,600 feet elevation in a mixed stand of Douglas fir, western hemlock, cedar, dogwood, and hazelnut, this campground provides easy access to the Middle Fork of the Willamette River. An access road leads to the south (upstream) end of the Hills Creek Reservoir. The 27-mile Middle Fork Trail begins at the south end of the campground. Fishing is good here; you can expect to catch large-scale suckers, rainbows, and cutthroat trout in the Middle Fork.

Campsites, facilities: There are 20 sites for tents or RVs up to 22 feet long. Picnic tables, garbage bins, and fire rings are provided. Vault and flush toilets, a group picnic area, and drinking water are available. Some facilities are wheelchair accessible. A boat launch is nearby on Hills Creek Reservoir. Leashed pets are permitted.

Reservations, fees: Reservations are not accepted. Sites are $12 per night, $6 per extra vehicle. Senior discount available. Open May–September.

Directions: From Eugene, drive south on I-5 for four miles to Exit 188 and Highway 58.

Turn southeast and drive 35 miles to Oakridge. Continue east on Highway 58 for two miles to Kitson Springs Road. Turn right and drive one-half mile to Forest Road 21. Turn right and continue 11 miles to the campground.

Contact: Willamette National Forest, Middle Fork Ranger District, 46375 Hwy. 58, Westfir, OR 97492, 541/782-2283, fax 541/782-5306.

81 SACANDAGA

Rating: 5

On the Willamette River in Willamette National Forest.

Map 11.4, grid e6, page 619

This campground sits along the Middle Fork of the Willamette River, where a segment of the historic Oregon Central Military Wagon Road is visible. Two trails from the campground access the Willamette River, and the Middle Fork Trail is in close proximity. Also, a short trail leads to a viewpoint with a bench, great for a short break. This campground gets low use and the sites are well separated by vegetation. Count on solitude here. The elevation is 2,400 feet.

Campsites, facilities: There are 16 sites for tents or RVs up to 24 feet long. Picnic tables and fire rings are provided. Drinking water, vault toilets, and firewood are available. Leashed pets are permitted.

Reservations, fees: Reservations are not accepted. Sites are $6 per night, $3 per extra vehicle. Senior discount available. Open mid-April–mid-November, weather permitting.

Directions: From Eugene, drive south on I-5 for four miles to Exit 188 and Highway 58. Turn southeast and drive 35 miles to Oakridge. Continue east on Highway 58 for two miles to Kitson Springs Road. Turn right and drive one-half mile to Forest Road 21. Turn right and drive 24 miles to the campground.

Contact: Willamette National Forest, Middle Fork Ranger District, 46375 Hwy. 58, Westfir, OR 97492, 541/782-2283, fax 541/782-5306.

82 CAMPERS FLAT

Rating: 5

On the Willamette River in Willamette National Forest.

Map 11.4, grid e7, page 619

This pretty but small campground is located on a small flat adjacent to the Middle Fork of the Willamette River. The river drowns out the sound of traffic from the road right next to the campground. There is an interpretive sign about the Oregon Central Military Wagon Road in the campground. The camp provides easy access to the water's edge—and the fishing is good. Young's Rock Trailhead, very popular with mountain bikers, is across the road from the campground entrance.

Campsites, facilities: There are five sites for tents or RVs up to 21 feet long. Picnic tables, garbage bins, and fire grills are provided. Drinking water, vault toilets, and firewood are available. Leashed pets are permitted.

Reservations, fees: Reservations are not accepted. Sites are $10 per night, $5 per extra vehicle. Open mid-April–September.

Directions: From Eugene, drive south on I-5 for five miles to Exit 188 and Highway 58. Turn east and drive 35 miles to the town of Oakridge. From Oakridge, continue east on Highway 58 about two miles to Kitson Springs Road. Turn right and drive one-half mile to Forest Road 21. Turn right and drive 19 miles to the campground.

Contact: Willamette National Forest, Middle Fork Ranger District, 46375 Hwy. 58, Westfir, OR 97492, 541/782-2283, fax 541/782-5306.

83 SECRET

Rating: 5

On the Willamette River in Willamette National Forest.

Map 11.4, grid e7, page 619

This small campground, set on the Middle Fork of the Willamette River, gets regular use from local know-hows. The tree cover is scant, but there is adequate vegetation to buffer the campsites from the nearby road noise. Fishing the Middle Fork Willamette is generally fair.

Campsites, facilities: There are six sites for tents or RVs up to 15 feet long. Picnic tables, garbage bins, and fire rings are provided. Vault toilets are available, but there is no drinking water. Leashed pets are permitted.

Reservations, fees: Reservations are not accepted. Sites are $8 per night, $4 per extra vehicle. Senior discount available. Open mid-April–September.

Directions: From Eugene, drive south on I-5 for five miles to Exit 188 and Highway 58. Turn east and drive 35 miles to the town of Oakridge. From Oakridge, continue east on Highway 58 about two miles to Kitson Springs Road. Turn right and drive one-half mile to Forest Road 21. Turn right and drive 19 miles to the campground.

Contact: Willamette National Forest, Middle Fork Ranger District, 46375 Hwy. 58, Westfir, OR 97492, 541/782-2283, fax 541/782-5306.

84 INDIGO SPRINGS

Rating: 5

Near the Willamette River in Willamette National Forest.

Map 11.4, grid e7, page 619

This small, semi-open campground sits at 2,800 feet elevation in a stand of old-growth Douglas fir. A nearby 250-foot walk leads to the origin of this cold water spring. A remnant of the historic Oregon Central Military Wagon Road passes near the campground, with an interpretive sign explaining it.

Campsites, facilities: There are three sites for tents or RVs up to 16 feet long. Picnic tables and fire grills are provided. Vault toilets and firewood are available. There is no drinking water. Leashed pets are permitted.

Reservations, fees: Reservations are not ac-

cepted. There is no fee for camping. Open mid-April–mid-November, weather permitting.
Directions: From Eugene, drive south on I-5 for five miles to Exit 188 and Highway 58. Turn east and drive 35 miles to the town of Oakridge. From Oakridge, continue east on Highway 58 about two miles to Kitson Springs Road. Turn right and drive one-half mile to Forest Road 21. Turn right and drive 27 miles to the campground.
Contact: Willamette National Forest, Middle Fork Ranger District, 46375 Hwy. 58, Westfir, OR 97492, 541/782-2283, fax 541/782-5306.

85 ROCK CREEK

Rating: 8

On Rock Creek.
Map 11.4, grid e1, page 619
Since we started roaming around the state 20 years ago, we've noticed that this campground on the banks of Rock Creek in a relatively obscure spot has been considerably improved by the BLM. It's not well known, either, so you're likely to have privacy as a bonus. No fishing is allowed in Rock Creek.
Campsites, facilities: There are 17 sites for tents or RVs up to 40 feet long. Picnic tables and fire grills are provided. A camp host is on-site, and vault toilets, drinking water, a pavilion, and firewood are available. Leashed pets are permitted.
Reservations, fees: Reservations are not accepted. Sites are $8 per night, with a 14-day stay limit; $3 per extra vehicle. Senior discount available. Open mid-May–mid-October.
Directions: From Roseburg, drive east on Highway 138 for 22 miles to Rock Creek Road. Turn right (north) and drive seven miles to the campground on the right.
Contact: Bureau of Land Management, Roseburg District, 777 N.W. Garden Valley Blvd., Roseburg, OR 97470, 541/440-4930, fax 541/440-4948, website: www.or.blm.gov/roseburg.

86 MILLPOND

Rating: 8

On Rock Creek.
Map 11.4, grid e1, page 619
Rock Creek flows past Millpond and empties into the North Umpqua River five miles downstream. Just below this confluence is the Rock Creek Fish Hatchery, which is open year-round to visitors, with free access. This campground along the banks of Rock Creek is the first camp you'll see along Rock Creek Road, which accounts for its relative popularity in this area. Like Rock Creek Campground, it's primitive and remote. No fishing is allowed in Rock Creek. Note that a new campground called White Pine is planned just down the road, with construction beginning in 2002.
Campsites, facilities: There are 12 sites for tents or RVs up to 40 feet long. Picnic tables, garbage service, and fire grills are provided. A camp host is on-site, and flush and vault toilets, drinking water, firewood, a ball field, a playground, and a pavilion (with 24 picnic tables, sinks, electricity, and fireplaces) are available. Some facilities are wheelchair accessible. Leashed pets are permitted.
Reservations, fees: Reservations are not accepted. Sites are $8 per night, with a 14-day stay limit; $3 per extra vehicle. Senior discount available. Open mid-May–mid-October.
Directions: From Roseburg, drive east on Highway 138 for 22 miles to Rock Creek Road. Turn right (north) and drive five miles to the campground on the right.
Contact: Bureau of Land Management, Roseburg District, 777 N.W. Garden Valley Blvd., Roseburg, OR 97470, 541/440-4930, fax 541/440-4948, website: www.or.blm.gov/roseburg.

87 STEAMBOAT FALLS

Rating: 8

On Steamboat Creek in Umpqua National Forest.

Map 11.4, grid e4, page 619

This Steamboat Creek campground boasts some excellent scenery at beautiful Steamboat Falls, which features a fish ladder that provides passage for steelhead and salmon on their upstream migration. No fishing is permitted in Steamboat Creek. Other nearby camping options are Island and Canton Creek.

Campsites, facilities: There are 10 sites for tents or RVs up to 24 feet long. Picnic tables, garbage bins, vault toilets, and fire grills are provided. There is no drinking water. Leashed pets are permitted.

Reservations, fees: Reservations are not accepted. Sites are $6 per night, $3 per extra vehicles. Senior discount available. Open year-round, with no fee November-late May.

Directions: From Roseburg on I-5, take Exit 120 to Highway 138. Drive east on Highway 138 to Steamboat and Forest Road 38. Turn left on Forest Road 38 (Steamboat Creek Road) and drive six miles to a fork with Forest Road 3810. Bear right and drive one mile to the campground.

Contact: Umpqua National Forest, North Umpqua Ranger District, 18782 North Umpqua Hwy., Glide, OR 97443, 541/496-3532, fax 541/496-3534.

88 TIMPANOGAS

Rating: 8

On Timpanogas Lake in Willamette National Forest.

Map 11.4, grid e8, page 619

At 5,200 feet elevation, this campground is situated in a stand of silver, grand, and noble fir. Timpanogas Lake is the headwaters of the Middle Fork Willamette River. Only nonmotorized boating is permitted. Fishing in the lake is often very good for cutthroat and brook trout. The Timpanogas Basin offers 23 miles of hiking trails, with a bonus of excellent views of Diamond Peak, Sawtooth, and Cowhorn Mountains. Warning: Time it wrong and the mosquitoes will eat you alive if you forget your insect repellent.

Campsites, facilities: There are 10 sites for tents or RVs up to 24 feet long. Picnic tables, garbage bins, and fire rings are provided. Drinking water, vault toilets, and firewood are available. Boat docks are nearby, but no boats with motors are allowed. Leashed pets are permitted.

Reservations, fees: Reservations are not accepted. Sites are $8 per night, $4 per extra vehicle. Senior discount available. Open mid-June–mid-October, weather permitting.

Directions: From Eugene, drive south on I-5 for five miles to Exit 188 and Highway 58. Turn east and drive 35 miles to the town of Oakridge. Continue east on Highway 58 for two miles to Kitson Springs Road. Turn right and drive one-half mile to Forest Road 21. Turn right and drive 32 miles to Forest Road 2154. Turn left and drive about 10 miles to the campground.

Contact: Willamette National Forest, Middle Fork Ranger District, 46375 Hwy. 58, Westfir, OR 97492, 541/782-2283, fax 541/782-5306.

89 SCAREDMAN

Rating: 6

On Canton Creek.

Map 11.4, grid f3, page 619

This small campground along the banks of Canton Creek is virtually unknown to out-of-towners. Set in an old-growth forest, this private and secluded camp offers a chance to swim in the creek. Scaredman gets its name from an old legend that says some early settlers camped here, heard a pack of hungry wolves, and then ran off, scared to death. One of the few free camps left in the region, it was considerably improved in 2001 with larger sites, new vault toilets, and revegetation. Even though fishing is closed on Canton Creek and all Steamboat drainages, the North Umpqua River 3.5 miles downstream offers fly-fishing for steelhead or salmon.

Campsites, facilities: There are nine sites for tents or RVs up to 25 feet long. Picnic tables, garbage service, and fire grills are provided. Vault toilets are available and there is a camp host. Some facilities are wheelchair accessible. There is no drinking water. Leashed pets are permitted.

Reservations, fees: Reservations are not accepted. There is no fee for camping. The stay limit is 14 days. Open year-round.

Directions: From Roseburg, drive east on Highway 138 for 40 miles to Steamboat Creek Road. Turn left (north) and drive one-half mile to Canton Creek Road. Turn left (north) and drive three miles to the campground.

Contact: Bureau of Land Management, Roseburg District, 777 N.W. Garden Valley Blvd., Roseburg, OR 97470, 541/440-4930, fax 541/440-4948.

90 ISLAND

Rating: 8

On the Umpqua River in Umpqua National Forest.

Map 11.4, grid f3, page 619

The North Umpqua is one of Oregon's most beautiful rivers, and this scenic campground is set along its banks at a spot popular for both rafting and steelhead fishing. Note: fly-fishing only and with a 20-inch minimum size limit. A hiking trail that leads east and west along the river is accessible a short drive to the west. See a U.S. Forest Service map for details.

Campsites, facilities: There are seven sites for tents or RVs up to 24 feet long. Picnic tables, garbage bins, and fire grills are provided. Some facilities are wheelchair accessible.

There is no drinking water. Leashed pets are permitted.

Reservations, fees: Reservations are not accepted. Sites are $7 per night, $3 per extra vehicle. Senior discount available. Open year-round.

Directions: From Roseburg, drive east on Highway 138 for 40 miles (just past Steamboat). The campground is along the highway.

Contact: Umpqua National Forest, North Umpqua Ranger District, 18782 North Umpqua Hwy., Glide, OR 97443, 541/496-3532, fax 541/496-3534.

91 CANTON CREEK

Rating: 8

Near the North Umpqua River in Umpqua National Forest.

Map 11.4, grid f3, page 619

This campground (1,195 feet elevation) is set at the confluence of Canton and Steamboat Creeks, less than a mile from the North Umpqua River, and gets little overnight use—but lots of day swimmers come here in July and August. No fishing is permitted on Steamboat or Canton Creeks because they are spawning areas for steelhead and salmon. Steamboat Falls is six miles north on Forest Road 38. See the description of Steamboat Falls for other area details.

Campsites, facilities: There are five sites for tents or RVs up to 22 feet long. Picnic tables, garbage bins, and fire grills are provided. Drinking water, a covered picnic gazebo, and flush toilets are available. Leashed pets are permitted.

Reservations, fees: Reservations are not accepted. Sites are $7 per night, $3 per extra vehicle. Senior discount available. Open mid-May–mid-October.

Directions: From Roseburg, drive east on Highway 138 for 39 miles to Steamboat and Forest Road 38 (Steamboat Creek Road). Turn left and drive one-quarter mile to the campground.

Contact: Umpqua National Forest, North Umpqua Ranger District, 18782 North Umpqua Hwy., Glide, OR 97443, 541/496-3532, fax 541/496-3534.

92 SUSAN CREEK

Rating: 9

On the North Umpqua River.
Map 11.4, grid f1, page 619

This popular and pretty campground is set along the banks of the North Umpqua Wild and Scenic River. This pretty setting features plenty of trees and river access. Highlights include two barrier-free trails, one traveling one-half mile to the day-use area. From there, a hike of about three-quarters of a mile leads to the 50-foot Susan Creek Falls. Another four-tenths of a mile up the trail are the Susan Creek Indian Mounds. These moss-covered rocks are believed to be a spiritual site and are visited by Native Americans in search of guardian spirit visions. This area also boasts an excellent osprey interpretive site with a viewing platform along the river.

Campsites, facilities: There are 31 sites for RVs up to 35 feet long. Picnic tables, garbage service, and fire grills are provided. Flush toilets, drinking water, showers, and firewood are available, and there is a camp host. Some facilities and trails are wheelchair accessible. Leashed pets are permitted.

Reservations, fees: Reservations are not accepted. Sites are $11 per night, with a 14-day stay limit; $3 per extra vehicle. Senior discount available. Open early May–late October.

Directions: From Roseburg, drive east on Highway 138 for 29.5 miles to the campground (turnoff well signed).

Contact: Bureau of Land Management, Roseburg District, N.W. 777 Garden Valley Blvd., Roseburg, OR 97470, 541/440-4930, fax 541/440-4948, website: www.or.blm.gov/roseburg.

93 EAGLE ROCK

Rating: 9

On the North Umpqua River in Umpqua National Forest.
Map 11.4, grid f4, page 619

This camp is set next to the North Umpqua River and adjacent to the Boulder Creek Wilderness. It is named after Eagle Rock, which, along with Rattlesnake Rock, towers above the campground. The camp offers outstanding views of these unusual rock formations. It gets moderate use, even heavy on weekends. The camp sits at 1,676 feet elevation near Boulder Flat, a major launch point for rafting. Fishing here is restricted to the use of artificial lures with a single barbless hook.

Campsites, facilities: There are 23 sites for tents or RVs up to 30 feet long. Picnic tables and fire grills are provided. Vault toilets and garbage bins are available. There is no drinking water. A store, propane, and ice are within five miles. Some facilities are wheelchair accessible. Leashed pets are permitted.

Reservations, fees: Reservations are not accepted. Sites are $8 per night, $3 per extra vehicle. Senior discount available. Open mid-May–mid-September.

Directions: From Roseburg, drive east on Highway 138 for 53 miles to the campground on the left.

Contact: Umpqua National Forest, North Umpqua Ranger District, 18782 North Umpqua Hwy., Glide, OR 97443, 541/496-3532, fax 541/496-3534.

94 BOULDER FLAT

Rating: 8

On the North Umpqua River in Umpqua National Forest.
Map 11.4, grid f4, page 619

This campground is set along the banks of the North Umpqua River at the confluence with

Boulder Creek. There's good trout fishing here (fly-fishing only) and outstanding scenery. The camp sits at a major launching point for white-water rafting. Across the river from the campground, a trail follows Boulder Creek north for 10.5 miles through the Boulder Creek Wilderness, a climb in elevation from 2,000 to 5,400 feet. It's a good thumper for backpackers. Access to the trail is at Soda Springs Dam, two miles east of the camp. A little over a mile to the east you can see some huge, dramatic pillars of volcanic rock, colored with lichen.

Campsites, facilities: There are 11 sites for tents or RVs up to 24 feet long. Picnic tables, garbage bins, and fire grills are provided. Vault toilets are available. There is no drinking water. A store, propane, and ice are within five miles. A raft launch is on-site. Leashed pets are permitted.

Reservations, fees: Reservations are not accepted. Sites are $7 per night, $3 per extra vehicle. Senior discount available. Open year-round.

Directions: From Roseburg, drive east on Highway 138 for 54 miles to the campground on the left.

Contact: Umpqua National Forest, North Umpqua Ranger District, 18782 North Umpqua Hwy., Glide, OR 97443, 541/496-3532, fax 541/496-3534.

95 HORSESHOE BEND

Rating: 8

On the Umpqua River in Umpqua National Forest.

Map 11.4, grid f4, page 619

This campground, set at an elevation of 1,300 feet, is in the middle of a big bend in the North Umpqua River. This spot is a major launching point for white-water rafting. Fly-fishing is popular here.

Campsites, facilities: There are 24 sites for tents or RVs up to 35 feet long and one group site for up to 70 people. Picnic tables, fire grills, garbage bins, drinking water, and flush toilets are provided. A coin-operated laundry, a store,

gas, and propane are available one mile east. Some facilities are wheelchair accessible. Raft-launching facilities are nearby. Leashed pets are permitted.

Reservations, fees: Reservations are not accepted for family sites; $11 per night, $3 per extra vehicle. Senior discount available. Reservations required for the group site at 541/496-3532; $70 per night. Open mid-May–late September.

Directions: From Roseburg on I-5, take Exit 120. Drive east on Highway 138 for 47 miles to Forest Road 4750. Turn right and drive south a short distance to the campground.

Contact: Umpqua National Forest, North Umpqua Ranger District, 18782 North Umpqua Hwy., Glide, OR 97443, 541/496-3532, fax 541/496-3534.

96 TOKETEE LAKE

Rating: 7

On Toketee Lake in Umpqua National Forest.

Map 11.4, grid f5, page 619

This campground is located just north of Toketee Lake and is set at an elevation of 2,200 feet. The North Umpqua River Trail passes near camp and continues east along the river for many miles. Diehard hikers can also take the trail west, where it meanders for a while before heading north near the Boulder Creek Wilderness. Toketee Lake, an 80-acre reservoir, offers a good population of brown and rainbow trout and many recreation options. A worthwhile point of interest is Toketee Falls, just west of the lake turnoff. Another is Umpqua Hot Springs, a few miles northeast of the camp. The area sustains a wide variety of wildlife; you might see otter, beaver, great blue heron, kingfishers, a variety of ducks and geese, and bald eagles in fall and winter.

Campsites, facilities: There are 32 sites for tents or RVs up to 22 feet long and one group site for up to 30 people. Picnic tables, garbage bins, and fire grills are provided. Vault toilets are available, but there is no drinking water. Boat docks and launching facilities are nearby. Leashed pets are permitted.

Reservations, fees: Reservations are not accepted for family sites; $6 per night, $2 per extra vehicle. Reservations required for the group site at 541/498-2531; $15 per night. Open year-round.

Directions: From Roseburg, drive east on Highway 138 for 60 miles to Forest Road 34. Turn north and drive one mile to the campground on the right.

Contact: Umpqua National Forest, Diamond Lake Ranger District, 2020 Toketee Ranger Station Rd., Idleyld Park, OR 97447, 541/498-2531, fax 541/498-2515.

97 EAST LEMOLO

Rating: 8

On Lemolo Lake in Umpqua National Forest.
Map 11.4, grid f7, page 619

This campground is on the southeastern shore of Lemolo Lake, where boating and fishing are some of the recreation possibilities. Boats with motors are allowed. The North Umpqua River and its adjacent trail lie just beyond the north shore of the lake. If you hike for two miles northwest of the lake, you can reach spectacular Lemolo Falls. Large German brown trout, a wild, native fish, can be taken on troll and fly. Lemolo Lake also provides fishing for kokanee, brook trout, and a sprinkling of rainbow trout.

Campsites, facilities: There are 15 sites for tents or small RVs up to 22 feet long. No drinking water is available. Picnic tables, garbage bins, and fire rings are provided. Vault toilets are available. Boat docks, launching facilities, and rentals are nearby. Leashed pets are permitted.

Reservations, fees: Reservations are not accepted. Sites are $6 per night, $2 per extra vehicle. Senior discount available. Open mid-May–late October.

Directions: From Roseburg, drive east on Highway 138 for 74 miles to Forest Road 2610 (three miles east of Clearwater Falls). Turn north and drive three miles to Forest Road 2610-400. Turn right and drive two miles to Forest Road 2610-430. Turn left and drive a short distance to the campground at the end of the road.

Contact: Umpqua National Forest, Diamond Lake Ranger District, 2020 Toketee Ranger Station Rd., Idleyld Park, OR 97447, 541/498-2531, fax 541/498-2515.

98 POOLE CREEK

Rating: 8

On Lemolo Lake in Umpqua National Forest.
Map 11.4, grid f7, page 619

This campground on the western shore of Lemolo Lake isn't far from Lemolo Lake Resort, which is open for recreation year-round. The camp is just south of the mouth of Poole Creek in a lodgepole pine, mountain hemlock, and Shasta red fir forest. This is by far the most popular U.S. Forest Service camp at the lake, especially with water-skiers, who are allowed to ski in designated areas of the lake. See the description of East Lemolo for more information.

Campsites, facilities: There are 59 sites for tents or RVs up to 30 feet long and a group site for up to 60 people. Picnic tables and fire grills are provided. Drinking water and vault toilets are available. A grocery store, restaurant, lounge, boat docks, launching facilities, and rentals are nearby. Leashed pets are permitted.

Reservations, fees: Reservations at 877/444-6777 or website: www.ReserveUsa.com ($9 reservation fee); $9–12 per night, $3 per extra vehicle. Senior discount available. Open late April–late October.

Directions: From Roseburg, drive east on Highway 138 for 72 miles to Forest Road 2610 (Bird's Point Road). Turn north and drive four miles to the signed turnoff for the campground entrance on the right.

Contact: Umpqua National Forest, Diamond Lake Ranger District, 2020 Toketee Ranger Station Rd., Idleyld Park, OR 97447, 541/498-2531, fax 541/498-2515.

99 INLET

Rating: 5

On Lemolo Lake in Umpqua National Forest.

Map 11.4, grid f7, page 619

This campground sits on the eastern inlet of Lemolo Lake, hidden in the deep, green, and quiet forest where the North Umpqua River rushes into Lemolo Reservoir. The lake exceeds 100 feet in depth in some spots. The camp is just across the road from the North Umpqua River Trail, which is routed east into the Oregon Cascades Recreation Area and the Mt. Thielsen Wilderness. See the description of East Lemolo for more recreation details.

Campsites, facilities: There are 14 sites for tents or RVs up to 22 feet long. Vault toilets are available, but there is no drinking water. Picnic tables, garbage bins, and fire grills are provided. Boat docks, launching facilities, rentals, a restaurant, a lounge, groceries, and a gas station are available nearby. Leashed pets are permitted.

Reservations, fees: Reservations are not accepted. Sites are $6 per night, $2 per extra vehicle. Senior discount available. Open mid-May–late October.

Directions: From Roseburg, drive east on Highway 138 for 74 miles to Forest Road 2610. Turn north and drive three miles to Forest Road 2610-400. Turn east and drive three miles to the campground.

Contact: Umpqua National Forest, Diamond Lake Ranger District, 2020 Toketee Ranger Station Rd., Idleyld Park, OR 97447, 541/498-2531, fax 541/498-2515.

100 WOLF CREEK

Rating: 6

On the Little River in Umpqua National Forest.

Map 11.4, grid g1, page 619

This pretty Little River camp is located at the entrance to the national forest, near the Wolf Creek Civilian Conservation Center. It is set at an elevation of 1,100 feet, with easy access to civilization. This camp has abundant wildflowers in the spring. If you want to get deeper into the Cascades, Hemlock Lake and Lake of the Woods are about 21 and 15 miles east, respectively.

Campsites, facilities: There are eight sites for tents or RVs up to 30 feet long and one group site for up to 130 people. A covered pavilion for groups, 14 tables, and stone fireplaces are available. Picnic tables, fire grills, garbage bins, horseshoe pits, a softball field, and a volleyball court are provided. Flush toilets and drinking water are available. Some facilities are wheelchair accessible. Leashed pets are permitted.

Reservations, fees: Reservations are not accepted for family sites; $8 per night, $3 per extra vehicle. Senior discount available. Reservations required for the group site at 541/496-3532; $80 per night. Open mid-May–September.

Directions: From Roseburg on I-5, take Exit 120. Drive east on Highway 138 for 18 miles to Glide and County Road 17. Turn southeast and drive 12 miles (the road becomes Little River Road) to the campground.

Contact: Umpqua National Forest, North Umpqua Ranger District, 18782 North Umpqua Hwy., Glide, OR 97443, 541/496-3532, fax 541/496-3534.

101 COOLWATER

Rating: 6

On the Little River in Umpqua National Forest.

Map 11.4, grid g2, page 619

This campground along the banks of the Little River gets moderate use. It is set at 1,300 feet elevation and features a pretty forest setting with some scenic hiking trails nearby. Overhang Trail is within one-half mile of the campground. Fishing and swimming are also options here. Scenic Grotto Falls can be reached by traveling north on Forest Road 2703 (across the road from the camp). Near the falls, you'll find Emile Grove, home of a thicket of old-growth Douglas firs and the huge "Bill Taft Tree," named after the former president.

Campsites, facilities: There are seven sites for tents or RVs up to 24 feet long. Picnic tables and fire grills are provided. Vault toilets and drinking water are available. Leashed pets are permitted.

Reservations, fees: Reservations are not accepted. Sites are $5 per night; $3 per extra vehicle. Senior discount available. Open year-round.

Directions: From Roseburg on I-5, take Exit 120. Drive east on Highway 138 for 18 miles to Glide and County Road 17. Turn southeast and drive 15.5 miles (the road becomes Little River Road) to the campground on the right.

Contact: Umpqua National Forest, North Umpqua Ranger District, 18782 North Umpqua Hwy., Glide, OR 97443, 541/496-3532, fax 541/496-3534.

102 WHITE CREEK

Rating: 6

On the Little River in Umpqua National Forest.

Map 11.4, grid g2, page 619

Hiking and fishing are two of the recreation options at this campground set at the confluence of White Creek and the Little River. There is a sandy beach on shallow Little River. See the description of Coolwater for other details about the area.

Campsites, facilities: There are four sites for tents or RVs up to 30 feet long. Picnic tables, fire grills, and garbage bins are provided. Vault toilets are available. There is no drinking water. Leashed pets are permitted.

Reservations, fees: Reservations are not accepted. Sites are $5 per night (with no fee November–May 20), $3 per extra vehicle. Senior discount available. Open year-round.

Directions: From Roseburg on I-5, take Exit 120. Drive east on Highway 138 for 18 miles to Glide and County Road 17. Turn southeast and drive 17 miles (the road becomes Little River Road) to Forest Road 2792 (Red Butte Road). Bear right and drive one-quarter mile to the campground on the left.

Contact: Umpqua National Forest, North Umpqua Ranger District, 18782 North Umpqua Hwy., Glide, OR 97443, 541/496-3532, fax 541/496-3534.

103 LAKE IN THE WOODS

Rating: 7

On Lake in the Woods in Umpqua National Forest.

Map 11.4, grid g3, page 619

The shore of little Lake in the Woods is the setting of this camp, which makes a nice home base for several good hikes. One of them leaves the camp and heads south for about three miles to the Hemlock Lake Campground. Two other nearby trails provide short, scenic hikes to either Hemlock Falls or Yakso Falls. The campground is set at 3,200 feet elevation. There is a man-made, four-acre lake, eight feet at its deepest point. Boats without motors are allowed.

Campsites, facilities: There are 11 sites for tents or RVs up to 35 feet long. Picnic tables, fire grills, and garbage bins are provided. Flush toilets are available. There is no drinking water. Leashed pets are permitted.

Reservations, fees: Reservations are not accepted. Sites are $8 per night, $3 per extra vehicle. Senior discount available. Open June–late October.

Directions: From Roseburg on I-5, take Exit 120. Drive east on Highway 138 for 18 miles to Glide and County Road 17. Turn southeast and drive 16.5 miles (the road becomes Little River Road) to Forest Road 27. Continue 11 miles to the campground. The last seven miles are gravel.

Contact: Umpqua National Forest, North Umpqua Ranger District, 18782 North Umpqua Hwy., Glide, OR 97443, 541/496-3532, fax 541/496-3534.

104 HEMLOCK LAKE

Rating: 8

On Hemlock Lake in Umpqua National Forest.
Map 11.4, grid g3, page 619

This is a little-known jewel of a spot. For starters, it's set along the shore of Hemlock Lake at 4,400 feet elevation. There is a 28-acre, man-made reservoir that is 33 feet at its deepest point. An eight-mile loop trail called the Yellow Jacket Loop is just south of the campground. Another trail leaves camp and heads north for about three miles to the Lake of the Woods Campground. From there, it's just a short hike to either Hemlock Falls or Yakso Falls, both spectacularly scenic.

Campsites, facilities: There are 13 sites for tents or RVs up to 35 feet long. Picnic tables, fire grills, and garbage bins are provided. Vault toilets are available, but there is no drinking water. Boat docks and launching facilities are nearby. No motors are allowed on the lake. Leashed pets are permitted.

Reservations, fees: Reservations are not accepted. Sites are $7 per night (with no fee November–May 20), $3 per extra vehicle. Senior

discount available. Open year-round, weather permitting.

Directions: From Roseburg on I-5, take Exit 120. Drive east on Highway 138 for 18 miles to Glide and County Road 17. Turn southeast and drive 32 miles to the campground.

Contact: Umpqua National Forest, North Umpqua Ranger District, 18782 North Umpqua Hwy., Glide, OR 97443, 541/496-3532, fax 541/496-3534.

105 WHITEHORSE FALLS

Rating: 8

On the Clearwater River in Umpqua National Forest.
Map 11.4, grid g6, page 619

This campground sits along the Clearwater River, one of the coldest streams in Umpqua National Forest. Even though the camp is adjacent to the highway, the setting is primitive. It is shaded by old-growth Douglas fir and is set at an elevation of 3,790 feet. Pretty Clearwater Falls, a few miles east, makes for a good side trip. Other recreation options include fishing and hiking.

Campsites, facilities: There are five tent sites. Picnic tables, fire grills, and garbage bins are provided. Vault toilets are available, but there is no drinking water. Leashed pets are permitted.

Reservations, fees: Reservations are not accepted. Sites are $6 per night, $2 per extra vehicle. Senior discount available. Open June–late October.

Directions: From Roseburg on I-5, take Exit 120. Drive east on Highway 138 for 67 miles (before reaching the Lemolo Lake turnoff) to the campground.

Contact: Umpqua National Forest, Diamond Lake Ranger District, 2020 Toketee Ranger Station Rd., Idleyld Park, OR 97447, 541/498-2531, fax 541/498-2515.

106 CLEARWATER FALLS

Rating: 8

On the Clearwater River in Umpqua National Forest.

Map 11.4, grid g7, page 619

The main attraction at this campground along the banks of the Clearwater River is the cascading section of stream called Clearwater Falls. The camp sits at an elevation of 4,100 feet. See the description of Whitehorse Falls for area details. Two miles from the main campground is another camping area with eight more sites that include picnic tables and fire rings.

Campsites, facilities: There are nine sites for tents or self-contained RVs up to 30 feet long. Picnic tables, fire grills, and garbage bins are provided. Vault toilets are available, but there is no drinking water. Leashed pets are permitted.

Reservations, fees: Reservations are not accepted. Sites are $6 per night, $2 per extra vehicle. Senior discount available. Open mid-May–late October.

Directions: From Roseburg on I-5, take Exit 120 for Highway 138. Drive east on Highway 138 for 70 miles to a signed turn for Clearwater Falls. Turn right and drive one mile to the campground.

Contact: Umpqua National Forest, Diamond Lake Ranger District, 2020 Toketee Ranger Station Rd., Idleyld Park, OR 97447, 541/498-2531, fax 541/498-2515.

107 BROKEN ARROW

Rating: 6

On Diamond Lake in Umpqua National Forest.

Map 11.4, grid g7, page 619

This campground sits at 5,190 feet elevation near the south shore of Diamond Lake, the largest natural lake in Umpqua National Forest. Set back from the lake, it is surrounded by lodgepole pine and features views of Mt. Bailey and Mt. Thielsen.

Boating, fishing, swimming, hiking, and bicycling keep visitors busy here. Concerns over the size of the trout have initiated a trout-planting program of one- and two-pound rainbow trout. Diamond Lake is adjacent to the Mt. Thielsen Wilderness, Crater Lake National Park, and Mt. Bailey, all of which offer a variety of recreation opportunities year-round. Diamond Lake is quite popular with anglers because of its good trout trolling, particularly in early summer.

Campsites, facilities: There are 117 sites for tents or RVs up to 35 feet long and group sites for 40–104 people. Picnic tables, fire grills, and garbage bins are provided. Flush toilets, showers, an RV dump station, and drinking water are available. Some facilities are wheelchair accessible. Boat docks, launching facilities, and rentals are nearby. Leashed pets are permitted.

Reservations, fees: Reservations are not accepted for family sites; $9–12 per night, $3 per extra vehicle. Senior discount available. Reservations required for the group site at 877/444-6777 or website: www.ReserveUsa.com ($9 reservation fee); $45–110 per night. Open late May–mid-September.

Directions: From Roseburg on I-5, take Exit 120. Drive east on Highway 138 for 80 miles to Diamond Lake Loop (Forest Road 4795). Turn right and drive a short distance to the junction with the loop road. Turn south and drive four miles (along the east shore) to the campground at the southern end of the lake.

Contact: Umpqua National Forest, Diamond Lake Ranger District, 2020 Toketee Ranger Station Rd., Idleyld Park, OR 97447, 541/498-2531, fax 541/498-2515.

108 THIELSEN VIEW

Rating: 7

On Diamond Lake in Umpqua National Forest.

Map 11.4, grid g7, page 619

This campground sits along the west shore of Diamond Lake in the shadow of majestic Mt.

Bailey. There is a beautiful view of Mt. Thielsen from here. See the description of Broken Arrow for information on recreation opportunities.

Campsites, facilities: There are 60 sites for tents or RVs up to 30 feet long. Picnic tables, fire grills, and garbage bins are provided. Drinking water and vault toilets are available. Some facilities are wheelchair accessible. Boat docks, launching facilities, and rentals are nearby. Leashed pets are permitted.

Reservations, fees: Reservations are not accepted. Sites are $9–12 per night, $3 per extra vehicle. Senior discount available. Open late May–late September.

Directions: From Roseburg on I-5, take Exit 120. Drive east on Highway 138 for 80 miles to Diamond Lake Loop (Forest Road 4795). Turn right and drive a short distance to the junction with the loop road. Continue on the loop road and drive four miles to the campground on the left.

Contact: Umpqua National Forest, Diamond Lake Ranger District, 2020 Toketee Ranger Station Rd., Idleyld Park, OR 97447, 541/498-2531, fax 541/498-2515.

109 DIAMOND LAKE

Rating: 9

On Diamond Lake in Umpqua National Forest.

Map 11.4, grid g8, page 619

This extremely popular camp along the east shore of Diamond Lake has all the luxuries: flush toilets, showers, and drinking water. There are campfire programs every Friday and Saturday night in the summer. See the description of Broken Arrow for recreation information.

Campsites, facilities: There are 238 sites for tents or RVs up to 45 feet long. Picnic tables, garbage bins, and fire grills are provided. Flush toilets, showers, drinking water, an RV dump station, firewood, and an amphitheater are available. Boat docks, launching facilities,

boat rentals, and a fish-cleaning station are nearby. Leashed pets are permitted.

Reservations, fees: Reservations at 877/444-6777 or website: www.ReserveUsa.com ($9 reservation fee); $10–20 per night, $5 per extra vehicle. Senior discount available. Open late April–late October.

Directions: From Roseburg on I-5, take Exit 120. Drive east on Highway 138 for 80 miles to Diamond Lake Loop (Forest Road 4795). Turn right and drive a short distance to the junction with a loop road. Turn south and drive two miles (along the east shore) to the campground on the right.

Contact: Umpqua National Forest, Diamond Lake Ranger District, 2020 Toketee Ranger Station Rd., Idleyld Park, OR 97447, 541/498-2531, fax 541/498-2515.

110 BOULDER CREEK

Rating: 4

On the South Umpqua River in Umpqua National Forest.

Map 11.4, grid h2, page 619

This campground is on the banks of the South Umpqua River near Boulder Creek. No fishing is allowed here. It is set at 1,400 feet elevation. See the description of Dumont Creek for information on the area.

Campsites, facilities: There are 12 sites for tents or RVs up to 25 feet long. Picnic tables, fire grills, and garbage bins are provided. Vault toilets are available, but there is no drinking water. Leashed pets are permitted.

Reservations, fees: Reservations are not accepted. There is no fee for camping. Open late May–late October.

Directions: At Canyonville on I-5, take Exit 99 to County Road 1. Drive east on County Road 1 for 25 miles to Tiller and County Road 46. Turn left and drive six miles northeast (County Road 46 turns into South Umpqua Road/Forest Road 28). Continue northeast and drive seven miles to the camp.

Contact: Umpqua National Forest, Tiller Ranger District, 27812 Tiller Trail Hwy., Tiller, OR 97484, 541/825-3201, fax 541/825-3259.

111 DUMONT CREEK

Rating: 4

On the South Umpqua River in Umpqua National Forest.

Map 11.4, grid h2, page 619

The future of this camp is in a state of flux. It was closed in 2002 because trees here have root rot and an environmental study to determine the cause is underway. Depending on the results, this campground could be reopened or closed permanently. Call for status. It is set at 1,300 feet elevation along the banks of the South Umpqua River, just above the mouth of Dumont Creek. Quiet, primitive, and remote, it gets moderate to heavy use. A short trail leads to a small beach on the river. No fishing is allowed at this camp, and there is no trailer turnaround here. Boulder Creek, just a few miles east, provides a camping alternative. A good side trip is nearby South Umpqua Falls, a beautiful, wide waterfall featuring a fish ladder and a platform so you can watch the fish struggle upstream.

Campsites, facilities: There are five sites for tents or RVs up to 16 feet long. Picnic tables, fire grills, and garbage bins are provided. Vault toilets are available, but there is no drinking water. Leashed pets are permitted.

Reservations, fees: Reservations are not accepted. There is no fee for camping. Open year-round.

Directions: At Canyonville on I-5, take Exit 99 to County Road 1. Drive east on County Road 1 for 25 miles to Tiller and County Road 46. Turn left and drive six miles northeast (County Road 46 turns into South Umpqua Road/Forest Road 28). Continue northeast and drive 5.5 miles to the camp.

Contact: Umpqua National Forest, Tiller Ranger District, 27812 Tiller Trail Hwy., Tiller, OR 97484, 541/825-3201, fax 541/825-3259.

112 COVER

Rating: 4

On Jackson Creek in Umpqua National Forest.

Map 11.4, grid h2, page 619

If you want quiet, this camp set at 1,700 feet elevation along the banks of Jackson Creek is the right place, since hardly anyone knows about it. Cover gets light use during the summer. During the fall hunting season, however, it is known to fill. If you head east to Forest Road 68 and follow the road south, you'll have access to a major trail into the Rogue-Umpqua Divide Wilderness. Be sure not to miss the world's largest sugar pine tree, a few miles west of camp. No fishing is allowed here.

Campsites, facilities: There are seven sites for tents or RVs up to 22 feet long. Picnic tables, fire grills, and garbage bins are provided. Vault toilets are available, but there is no drinking water. Leashed pets are permitted.

Reservations, fees: Reservations are not accepted. There is no fee for camping. Open year-round.

Directions: At Canyonville on I-5, take Exit 99 to County Road 1. Drive east on County Road 1 for 25 miles to Tiller and County Road 46. Turn left and drive five miles to Forest Road 29 (Jackson Creek Road). Turn right and drive east for 12 miles to the campground on the right.

Contact: Umpqua National Forest, Tiller Ranger District, 27812 Tiller Trail Hwy., Tiller, OR 97484, 541/825-3201, fax 541/825-3259.

113 CAMP COMFORT

Rating: 6

On the South Umpqua River in Umpqua National Forest.

Map 11.4, grid h3, page 619

This campground is set near the upper South Umpqua River, deep in the Umpqua National Forest, at an elevation of 2,000 feet. Large old-growth cedars shade the campsites. No fishing is permitted. A good side trip is visiting South Umpqua Falls (you will pass the access point while driving to this camp). Nearby trailheads (see map of Umpqua National Forest) provide access to Rogue-Umpqua Divide Wilderness. By the way, those familiar with this camp might remember a rain shelter. It's gone now, having burned down.

Campsites, facilities: There are five sites for tents or RVs up to 22 feet long. Picnic tables, fire grills, and garbage bins are provided. A wheelchair-accessible vault toilet is available. There is no drinking water. Leashed pets are permitted.

Reservations, fees: Reservations are not accepted. There is no fee for camping. Open year-round.

Directions: At Canyonville on I-5, take Exit 99 to County Road 1. Drive east on County Road 1 for 25 miles to Tiller and County Road 46. Turn left and drive six miles northeast (County Road 46 turns into South Umpqua Road/Forest Road 28). Continue northeast and drive 18 miles to the camp on the right.

Contact: Umpqua National Forest, Tiller Ranger District, 27812 Tiller Trail Hwy., Tiller, OR 97484, 541/825-3201, fax 541/825-3259.

114 HAMAKER

Rating: 8

Near the Upper Rogue River in Rogue River National Forest.

Map 11.4, grid h6, page 619

Set at 4,000 feet elevation near the Upper Rogue River, Hamaker is a beautiful little spot high in a mountain meadow. Wildflowers and wildlife abound in the spring and early summer. One of the least-used camps in the area, it's a prime camp for Crater Lake visitors.

Campsites, facilities: There are 10 sites for tents or RVs up to 30 feet long. Picnic tables, fire grills, garbage service, and stoves are provid-

ed. Drinking water and vault toilets are available. Firewood is available for purchase. Leashed pets are permitted.

Reservations, fees: Reservations are not accepted. Sites are $8 per night, $4 per extra vehicle a night. Senior discount available. Open late May–late October.

Directions: From Medford, drive northeast on Highway 62 for 57 miles (just past Union Creek) to Highway 230. Turn left (north) and drive 11 miles to a junction with Forest Road 6530. Continue on Forest Road 6530 for one-half mile to Forest Road 6530-900. Turn right and drive one-half mile to the campground on the right.

Contact: Rogue River National Forest, Prospect Ranger district, 47201 Hwy. 62, Prospect, OR 97536, 541/560-3400, fax 541/560-3444.

115 QUINN MEADOW HORSE CAMP

Rating: 8

Near Quinn Creek in the Deschutes National Forest.

Map 11.5, grid a2, page 620

This scenic campground is open only to horse camping and gets high use. The Elk-Devil's Trail and Wickiup Plains Trail offer access to the Three Sisters Wilderness. There's also a horse route to Devil's Lake via Katsuk Trail. The camp sits at an elevation of 5,100 feet.

Campsites, facilities: There are 24 sites for tents or RVs up to 30 feet long. Picnic tables, fire rings, and horse corrals are provided. Drinking water, vault toilets, and garbage bins are available. Some facilities are wheelchair accessible. Leashed pets are permitted.

Reservations, fees: Reservations required at 877/444-6777 or website: www.ReserveUsa.com ($9 reservation fee). Two-horse corral sites are $12 and four-horse sites are $16; $10 for each additional RV and $5 per extra vehicle. Senior discount available. Open late June–September, weather permitting.

Directions: From Bend, drive southwest on Cascades Lakes Highway (also called Century Drive Highway and County Road 46) for 31.2 miles to the campground entrance.

Contact: Deschutes National Forest, Bend-Fort Rock Ranger District, 1230 N.E. 3rd St., Suite A-262, Bend, OR 97701, 541/383-4000, fax 541/383-4700.

116 DEVIL'S LAKE WALK-IN

Rating: 8

On Devil's Lake in Deschutes National Forest.

Map 11.5, grid a2, page 620

This walk-in campground is set along the shore of a scenic alpine lake with aqua-jade water and fishing access. Devil's Lake, set at 5,500 feet, is a popular rafting and canoeing spot, and several trailheads lead from the lake into the wilderness. The Elk-Devil's Trail and Wickiup Plains Trail offer access to the Three Sisters Wilderness. There's also a horse route to Quinn Meadow Horse Camp via Katsuk Trail.

Campsites, facilities: There are nine walk-in tent sites. Picnic tables and fire grills are provided. Vault toilets are available. There is no drinking water, and all garbage must be packed out. Leashed pets are permitted.

Reservations, fees: Reservations are not accepted. Northwest Forest Pass ($5 daily fee or $30 annual fee per parked vehicle) is required. Open July–September, weather permitting.

Directions: From Bend, drive southwest on Cascades Lakes Highway (Century Drive Highway, which becomes County Road 46) for 28.7 miles to the parking area. Walk 200 yards to the campground.

Contact: Deschutes National Forest, Bend-Fort Rock Ranger District, 1230 N.E. 3rd St., Suite A-262, Bend, OR 97701, 541/383-4000, fax 541/383-4700.

117 SODA CREEK

Rating: 5

Near Sparks Lake in Deschutes National Forest.

Map 11.5, grid a2, page 620

This campground, nestled between two meadows in a pastoral setting, is on the road to Sparks Lake. Boating—particularly canoeing—is ideal at Sparks Lake, about a two-mile drive away. Also at Sparks Lake, a loop trail hugs the shore; about one-half mile of it is paved and barrier-free. Only fly-fishing is permitted. The camp sits at 5,450 feet elevation.

Campsites, facilities: There are 10 sites for tents or RVs up to 22 feet long. Picnic tables and fire grills are provided. Vault toilets are available. There is no drinking water and all garbage must be packed out. Leashed pets are permitted.

Reservations, fees: Reservations are not accepted. Northwest Forest Pass ($5 daily fee or $30 annual fee per parked vehicle) is required. Senior discount available. Open July–October, weather permitting.

Directions: From Bend, drive southwest on Cascades Lakes Highway (also called Century Drive Highway and County Road 46) for 26.2 miles to Forest Road 400 (at sign for Sparks Lake). Turn left (east) and drive 100 yards to the campground.

Contact: Deschutes National Forest, Bend-Fort Rock Ranger District, 1230 N.E. 3rd St., Suite A-262, Bend, OR 97701, 541/383-4000, fax 541/383-4700.

118 TODD LAKE HIKE-IN

Rating: 8

Near Todd Lake in Deschutes National Forest.

Map 11.5, grid a2, page 620

This is a trailhead camp, with a trail access point here for hikers and horses to the Three

Sisters Wilderness. One of numerous camps in the area that offer a pristine mountain experience yet can be reached by car, small Todd Lake campground is set one-half mile from the shore of an alpine lake at 6,150 feet elevation. It's popular for canoeing and offers great views. No bikes or horses are allowed on the trail around the lake.

Campsites, facilities: There are 11 hike-in tent sites. Picnic tables and fire grills are provided. Vault toilets are available. There is no drinking water, and all garbage must be packed out. Leashed pets are permitted.

Reservations, fees: Reservations are not accepted. Northwest Forest Pass ($5 daily fee or $30 annual fee per parked vehicle) is required. Open July–October, weather permitting.

Directions: From Bend, drive southwest on Cascades Lakes Highway (also called Century Drive Highway and County Road 46) for 24 miles to Forest Road 370. Turn right (north) and drive one-half mile to the parking area. Hike one-half mile to the campground.

Contact: Deschutes National Forest, Bend-Fort Rock Ranger District, 1230 N.E. 3rd St., Suite A-262, Bend, OR 97701, 541/383-4000, fax 541/383-4700.

119 POINT

Rating: 8

On Elk Lake in Deschutes National Forest.
Map 11.5, grid a2, page 620

This campground is situated along the shore of Elk Lake at an elevation of 4,900 feet. Fishing for kokanee salmon, rainbow trout, and brown trout can be good; hiking is another option. Swimming and water sports are popular during warm weather.

Campsites, facilities: There are 10 sites for tents or RVs up to 22 feet long. Picnic tables, garbage service, and fire grills are provided. Vault toilets and drinking water are available. Boat docks and launching facilities are on-site. Boat rentals, a store, a restaurant, gas, and propane are at Elk Lake Resort, one mile away. Leashed pets are permitted.

Reservations, fees: Reservations are not accepted. Sites are $10 per night, $5 per extra vehicle, and $10 for an additional RV. Senior discount available. Open late May–late September, weather permitting.

Directions: From Bend, drive southwest on Cascades Lakes Highway (Century Drive Highway, which becomes County Road 46) for 34 miles to the campground on the left.

Contact: Deschutes National Forest, Bend-Fort Rock Ranger District, 1230 N.E. 3rd St., Suite A-262, Bend, OR 97701, 541/383-4000, fax 541/383-4700.

120 ELK LAKE

Rating: 8

On Elk Lake in Deschutes National Forest.
Map 11.5, grid a2, page 620

This campground hugs the shore of Elk Lake at 4,900 feet elevation. It is adjacent to Elk Lake Resort, which has boat rentals, a store, a restaurant, gas, and propane. Elk Lake is popular for windsurfing and sailing. See the description of Point for recreation options.

Campsites, facilities: There are 23 sites for tents or RVs up to 22 feet long. Picnic tables, garbage service, and fire grills are provided. Vault toilets and drinking water are available. Boat-launching facilities are on-site. Boat rentals can be obtained nearby. Leashed pets are permitted.

Reservations, fees: Reservations are not accepted. Sites are $10 per night, $5 per extra vehicle, and $10 per extra RV. Senior discount available. Open June–September, weather permitting.

Directions: From Bend, drive southwest on Cascades Lakes Highway (Century Drive Highway, which becomes County Road 46) and drive 33.1 miles to the campground at the north end of Elk Lake.

Contact: Deschutes National Forest, Bend-Fort

Rock Ranger District, 1230 N.E. 3rd St., Suite A-262, Bend, OR 97701, 541/383-4000, fax 541/383-4700.

121 LITTLE FAWN

🚶 🏊 🛶 🚤 🏕 🦌 🚐 ⛺

Rating: 5

On Elk Lake in Deschutes National Forest.

Map 11.5, grid a2, page 620

Choose between sites on the water's edge or nestled in the forest at this campground along the eastern shore of Elk Lake. Afternoon winds are common here, making this a popular spot for sailing and windsurfing. A play area for children can be found at one of the lake's inlets. See the description of Point for recreation options. Little Fawn Group Camp is just beyond Little Fawn campground. The camp sits at 4,900 feet elevation.

Campsites, facilities: There are 20 sites for tents or RVs up to 22 feet long and one group site that can accommodate up to 60 campers. Picnic tables, garbage service, drinking water, and fire grills are provided. Vault toilets are available. Boat-launching facilities and rentals are on-site. Leashed pets are permitted.

Reservations, fees: Reservations are not accepted for family sites; $8 per night, $5 per extra vehicle. Reservations for the group site required at 877/444-6777 or website: www .ReserveUsa.com ($9 reservation fee); $70 per night. Open June–September, weather permitting.

Directions: From Bend, drive southwest on Cascades Lakes Highway (Century Drive Highway, which becomes County Road 46) and drive 35.5 miles to Forest Road 4625. Turn left (east) and drive 1.7 miles to the campground.

Contact: Deschutes National Forest, Bend-Fort Rock Ranger District, 1230 N.E. 3rd St., Suite A-262, Bend, OR 97701, 541/383-4000, fax 541/383-4700.

122 MALLARD MARSH

🚶 🏊 🚐 🏕 🚐 ⛺

Rating: 8

On Hosmer Lake in Deschutes National Forest.

Map 11.5, grid a2, page 620

This quiet campground is located on the shore of Hosmer Lake, elevation 5,000 feet. The lake is stocked with brown trout and Atlantic salmon and reserved for catch-and-release fly-fishing only. You'll get a pristine, quality fishing experience here. The lake is ideal for canoeing. Nonmotorized boats only.

Campsites, facilities: There are 15 sites for tents or RVs up to 22 feet long. Picnic tables, garbage service, and vault toilets are provided. No drinking water is available. Boat-launching facilities are nearby. Leashed pets are permitted.

Reservations, fees: Reservations are not accepted. Sites are $5 per night per extra vehicle. Senior discount available. Open late May–late September.

Directions: From Bend, drive southwest on Cascades Lakes Highway (Century Drive Highway, which becomes County Road 46) and drive 35.5 miles to Forest Road 4625. Turn left (southeast) and drive 1.3 miles to the camp.

Contact: Deschutes National Forest, Bend-Fort Rock Ranger District, 1230 N.E. 3rd St., Suite A-262, Bend, OR 97701, 541/383-4000, fax 541/383-4700.

123 SOUTH

🚶 🏊 🏕 🚐 ⛺

Rating: 8

On Hosmer Lake in Deschutes National Forest.

Map 11.5, grid a3, page 620

This campground is located along the shore of Hosmer Lake, adjacent to Mallard Marsh. See the description of Mallard Marsh for recreation details.

Campsites, facilities: There are 23 sites for tents or RVs up to 22 feet long. Picnic tables, garbage service, and fire grills are provided. Vault toilets and boat launch facilities are available. No drinking water is provided. Leashed pets are permitted.

Reservations, fees: Reservations are not accepted. Sites are $5 per night per extra vehicle. Senior discount available. Open late May–late September, weather permitting.

Directions: From Bend, drive southwest on Cascades Lakes Highway (Century Drive Highway, which becomes County Road 46) and drive 35.5 miles to Forest Road 4625. Turn left (east) and drive 1.2 miles to the campground on the right.

Contact: Deschutes National Forest, Bend-Fort Rock Ranger District, 1230 N.E. 3rd St., Suite A-262, Bend, OR 97701, 541/383-4000, fax 541/383-4700.

124 LAVA LAKE

Rating: 10

On Lava Lake in Deschutes National Forest.
Map 11.5, grid a2, page 620

This well-designed campground sits on the shore of pretty Lava Lake at 4,750 feet elevation. Mount Bachelor and the Three Sisters are in the background, making a classic picture. Boating and fishing are popular here. A bonus is nearby Lava Lake Resort, which has showers, laundry facilities, an RV dump station, a store, gasoline, and propane.

Campsites, facilities: There are 43 sites for tents or RVs up to 28 feet long. Picnic tables, garbage service, and fire grills are provided. Vault toilets, drinking water, and a fish-cleaning station are available. Some facilities are wheelchair accessible. Boat docks and launching facilities are on-site. Boat rentals are nearby. Leashed pets are permitted.

Reservations, fees: Reservations are not accepted. Sites are $10 per night, $5 per extra vehicle, and $10 per extra RV. Senior discount available. Open mid-April–October, weather permitting.

Directions: From Bend, drive southwest on Cascades Lakes Highway (Century Drive Highway, which becomes County Road 46) and drive 38.4 miles to Forest Road 4600-500. Turn left (east) and drive one mile to the campground.

Contact: Deschutes National Forest, Bend-Fort Rock Ranger District, 1230 N.E. 3rd St., Suite A-262, Bend, OR 97701, 541/383-4000, fax 541/383-4700.

125 LITTLE LAVA LAKE

Rating: 8

On Little Lava Lake in Deschutes National Forest.
Map 11.5, grid b3, page 620

Boating, fishing, swimming, and hiking are some of the recreation options here. This lake feeds into the Deschutes River. Some sites are lakeside and some are riverside. The elevation is 4,750 feet.

Campsites, facilities: There are 12 sites for tents or RVs up to 22 feet long. Picnic tables, garbage service, and fire grills are provided. Vault toilets and drinking water are available. A boat launch, docks, and rentals are nearby. Launching facilities are on-site. Leashed pets are permitted.

Reservations, fees: Reservations are not accepted. Sites are $5 per night per extra vehicle. Senior discount available. Open May–late September, weather permitting.

Directions: From Bend, drive southwest on Cascades Lakes Highway (Century Drive Highway, which becomes County Road 46) and drive 38.4 miles to Forest Road 4600-500. Turn left (east) and drive seven-tenths of a mile to Forest Road 4600-520. Continue east for four-tenths of a mile to the campground.

Contact: Deschutes National Forest, Bend-Fort Rock Ranger District, 1230 N.E. 3rd St., Suite A-262, Bend, OR 97701, 541/383-4000, fax 541/383-4700.

126 WEST CULTUS HIKE-IN/ BOAT-IN

Rating: 5

On Cultus Lake in Deschutes National Forest.

Map 11.5, grid b1, page 620

This campground set at 4,700 feet elevation along the west shore of Cultus Lake is accessible by boat or trail only. It's about three miles by trail from the parking area to the campground. The lake is a good spot for water-skiing, fishing, and swimming. Trails branch out from the campground and provide access to numerous small backcountry lakes. Drinking water and boat-launching facilities are available at Cultus Lake.

Campsites, facilities: There are 12 boat-in or hike-in tent sites. Picnic tables and fire grills are provided. Vault toilets are available. There is no drinking water, and all garbage must be packed out. Boat docks are available on-site; boat rentals are at Cultus Lake Resort. Leashed pets are permitted.

Reservations, fees: Reservations are not accepted. Northwest Forest Pass ($5 daily fee or $30 annual fee per parked vehicle) is required. Open June–late September, weather permitting.

Directions: From Bend, drive southwest on Cascades Lakes Highway (Century Drive Highway, which becomes County Road 46) and drive 46 miles to Forest Road 4635. Turn right (west) and drive two miles to the parking area. Boat in or hike in about three miles to the west end of the lake.

Contact: Deschutes National Forest, Bend-Fort Rock Ranger District, 1230 N.E. 3rd St., Suite A-262, Bend, OR 97701, 541/383-4000, fax 541/383-4700.

127 CULTUS LAKE

Rating: 7

On Cultus Lake in Deschutes National Forest.

Map 11.5, grid b2, page 620

This camp along the east shore of Cultus Lake is set at 4,700 feet elevation. It is a popular spot for windsurfing, water-skiing, swimming, fishing, and hiking. It fills up early on weekends and holidays.

Campsites, facilities: There are 54 sites for tents or RVs up to 30 feet long. Picnic tables, garbage service, and fire grills are provided. Drinking water and vault toilets are available. Boat docks and launching facilities are on-site. Boat rentals are nearby. A restaurant, gasoline, and cabins are available at Cultus Lake Resort nearby. Leashed pets are permitted.

Reservations, fees: Reservations are not accepted. Sites are $10 per night, $5 per extra vehicle, and $10 per extra RV. Senior discount available. Open June–October.

Directions: From Bend, drive southwest on Cascades Lakes Highway (Century Drive Highway, which becomes County Road 46) and drive 46 miles to Forest Road 4635. Turn right (west) and drive two miles to the campground.

Contact: Deschutes National Forest, Bend-Fort Rock Ranger District, 1230 N.E. 3rd St., Suite A-262, Bend, OR 97701, 541/383-4000, fax 541/383-4700.

128 CULTUS CORRAL HORSE CAMP

Rating: 3

Near Cultus Lake in Deschutes National Forest.

Map 11.5, grid b1, page 620

Check for status before planning a trip to this horse camp. It could be closed in 2003 or 2004 because of a road access detour. It is set at 4,450 feet elevation, about one mile from Cultus Lake, in a stand of lodgepole pine. Many trees have been removed because of disease. Several nearby trails provide access to back-country lakes. This is a good overflow campground for Quinn Meadow Horse Camp.

Campsites, facilities: There are 11 sites for tents or RVs of any length. Picnic tables, garbage service, fire grills, and four-horse corrals are provided. Drinking water and vault toilets are available. Leashed pets are permitted.

Reservations, fees: Reservations are not accepted. Sites are $5 per night per extra vehicle. Senior discount available. Open June–October.

Directions: From Bend, drive southwest on Cascades Lakes Highway (Century Drive Highway, which becomes County Road 46) and drive 46 miles to Forest Road 4635. Turn right (west) and drive one mile to Forest Road 4630. Turn right and drive 1.5 miles to the campground on the right.

Contact: Deschutes National Forest, Bend-Fort Rock Ranger District, 1230 N.E. 3rd St., Suite A-262, Bend, OR 97701, 541/383-4000, fax 541/383-4700.

129 LITTLE CULTUS LAKE

Rating: 7

On Little Cultus Lake in Deschutes National Forest.

Map 11.5, grid b2, page 620

This campground is set near the shore of Little Cultus Lake at an elevation of 4,800 feet. It's a popular spot for swimming, fishing, boating (10 mph speed limit), and hiking. Nearby trails offer access to numerous backcountry lakes, and the Pacific Crest Trail passes about six miles west of the camp.

Campsites, facilities: There are 20 sites for tents or RVs up to 22 feet long. Picnic tables, garbage service, and fire grills are provided. Drinking water, vault toilets, and a boat launch are available. Leashed pets are permitted.

Reservations, fees: Reservations are not ac-

cepted. Sites are $5 per night, $5 for extra vehicles. Senior discount available. Open late May–late September, weather permitting.

Directions: From Bend, drive southwest on Cascades Lakes Highway (Century Drive Highway, which becomes County Road 46) and drive 46 miles to Forest Road 4635. Turn right (west) and drive two miles to Forest Road 4630. Turn left (south) and drive 1.7 miles to Forest Road 4636. Turn right (west) and drive one mile to the campground.

Contact: Deschutes National Forest, Bend-Fort Rock Ranger District, 1230 N.E. 3rd St., Suite A-262, Bend, OR 97701, 541/383-4000, fax 541/383-4700.

130 DESCHUTES BRIDGE

Rating: 5

On the Upper Deschutes River in the Deschutes National Forest.

Map 11.5, grid b3, page 620

This wooded campground is on the banks of the Deschutes River in a beautiful, green spot. It's set at 4,650 feet elevation. Fishing is often difficult and is restricted to artificial lures with a single barbless hook.

Campsites, facilities: There are 12 sites for tents or RVs up to 22 feet long. Picnic tables, garbage service, and fire grills are provided. Drinking water and vault toilets are available. Leashed pets are permitted.

Reservations, fees: Reservations are not accepted. Sites are $5 per night per extra vehicle. Senior discount available. Open June–October.

Directions: From Bend, drive southwest on Cascades Lakes Highway (Century Drive Highway, which becomes County Road 46) and drive 41.1 miles to the campground on the left (just past the Deschutes River Bridge).

Contact: Deschutes National Forest, Bend-Fort Rock Ranger District, 1230 N.E. 3rd St., Suite A-262, Bend, OR 97701, 541/383-4000, fax 541/383-4700.

131 IRISH AND TAYLOR

Rating: 7

Near Irish and Taylor Lakes in Deschutes National Forest.

Map 11.5, grid b1, page 620

Little known and beautiful, this remote campground is set between two small lakes about a mile from the Pacific Crest Trail. Other nearby trails provide access into the Three Sisters Wilderness. A four-wheel-drive with high clearance is recommended for access. The camp sits at 5,550 feet elevation.

Campsites, facilities: There are six tent sites. Picnic tables and fire grills are provided. Vault toilets are available. There is no drinking water. Leashed pets are permitted.

Reservations, fees: Reservations are not accepted. Northwest Forest Pass ($5 daily fee or $30 annual fee per parked vehicle) is required. Open mid-June–mid-September.

Directions: From Bend, drive southwest on Cascades Lakes Highway (Century Drive Highway, which becomes County Road 46) and drive 46 miles to Forest Road 4635. Turn right (west) on Forest Road 4635 and drive a short distance to Forest Road 4630. Turn south and drive 1.7 miles to Forest Road 4636. Turn west and drive 6.4 miles to the campground. A high-clearance vehicle is needed for the last four miles.

Contact: Deschutes National Forest, Bend-Fort Rock Ranger District, 1230 N.E. 3rd St., Suite A-262, Bend, OR 97701, 541/383-4000, fax 541/383-4700.

132 FALL RIVER

Rating: 5

On the Fall River in Deschutes National Forest.

Map 11.5, grid b4, page 620

This campground is on the Fall River, where fishing is restricted to fly-fishing only. Check the regulations for other restrictions. Fall River is beautiful, crystal clear, and cold. Fall River Trail meanders along the river for 3.5 miles and is open for bicycling. The elevation is 4,300 feet.

Campsites, facilities: There are 10 sites for tents or RVs up to 22 feet long. Picnic tables, garbage service, and fire grills are provided. Vault toilets are available. There is no drinking water. Leashed pets are permitted.

Reservations, fees: Reservations are not accepted. Sites are $5 per night per extra vehicle. Senior discount available. Open mid-April–October, weather permitting.

Directions: From Bend, drive south on U.S. 97 for 17.3 miles to Forest Road 42. Turn right (southwest) and drive 12.2 miles to the campground.

Contact: Deschutes National Forest, Bend-Fort Rock Ranger District, 1230 N.E. 3rd St., Suite A-262, Bend, OR 97701, 541/383-4000, fax 541/383-4700.

133 COW MEADOW

Rating: 6

On Crane Prairie Reservoir in Deschutes National Forest.

Map 11.5, grid b2, page 620

This campground is set near the north end of Crane Prairie Reservoir and near the Deschutes River. It's a pretty spot, great for fly-fishing and bird-watching, and the price is right. The elevation is 4,450 feet.

Campsites, facilities: There are 21 sites for tents or RVs up to 22 feet long. Picnic tables, garbage service, and fire grills are provided. Vault toilets are available. There is no drinking water. A boat launch for small boats is available nearby. Leashed pets are permitted.

Reservations, fees: Reservations are not accepted. Sites are $5 per night per extra vehicle. Open May–mid-October.

Directions: From Bend, drive southwest on Cascades Lakes Highway (Century Drive

Highway, which becomes County Road 46) for 44.7 miles to Forest Road 40. Turn left (east) on Forest Road 40 and drive four-tenths of a mile to Forest Road 4000-970. Turn right (south) and drive two miles to the campground on the right.

Contact: Deschutes National Forest, Bend-Fort Rock Ranger District, 1230 N.E. 3rd St., Suite A-262, Bend, OR 97701, 541/383-4000, fax 541/383-4700.

134 CRANE PRAIRIE

Rating: 6

On Crane Prairie Reservoir in Deschutes National Forest.
Map 11.5, grid b2, page 620

This campground along the north shore of Crane Prairie Reservoir is a good spot for fishing and boating. World-renowned for rainbow trout fishing, this reservoir is also popular for bass fishing.

Campsites, facilities: There are six sites for tents and 140 sites for RVs. Picnic tables, garbage service, and fire grills are provided. Drinking water and vault toilets are available. Some facilities are wheelchair accessible. Boat docks, launching facilities, and a fish-cleaning station are available on-site. Boat rentals, showers, gas, and laundry facilities are nearby. Leashed pets are permitted.

Reservations, fees: Reservations are not accepted. Sites are $10–12 per night, $5 per extra vehicle, and $10 per extra RV. Senior discount available. Open April 20–October, weather permitting.

Directions: From Bend, drive south on U.S. 97 for 26.8 miles to Wickiup Junction and County Road 43. Turn right (west) on County Road 43 and drive 11 miles to Forest Road 42. Continue west on Forest Road 42 for 5.4 miles to Forest Road 4270. Turn right (north) and drive 4.2 miles to the campground on the left.

Contact: Deschutes National Forest, Bend-Fort Rock Ranger District, 1230 N.E. 3rd St., Suite

A-262, Bend, OR 97701, 541/383-4000, fax 541/383-4700.

135 QUINN RIVER

Rating: 5

On Crane Prairie Reservoir in Deschutes National Forest.
Map 11.5, grid b2, page 620

This campground is set along the western shore of Crane Prairie Reservoir, a popular spot for anglers and a great spot for bird-watching. A separate, large parking lot is available for boats and trailers. Boat speed is limited to 10 mph here. The elevation is 4,450 feet.

Campsites, facilities: There are 41 sites for tents or RVs up to 30 feet long. Picnic tables, garbage service, and fire grills are provided. Drinking water and vault toilets are available. Some facilities are wheelchair accessible. Boat launch facilities are available. Leashed pets are permitted.

Reservations, fees: Reservations are not accepted. Sites are $10 per night, $5 per extra vehicle, and $10 per extra RV. Senior discount available. Open late April–mid-October.

Directions: From Bend, drive southwest on Cascade Lakes Highway (Century Drive Highway, which becomes County Road 46) and drive 48 miles to the campground.

Contact: Deschutes National Forest, Bend-Fort Rock Ranger District, 1230 N.E. 3rd St., Suite A-262, Bend, OR 97701, 541/383-4000, fax 541/383-4700.

136 ROCK CREEK

Rating: 5

On Crane Prairie Reservoir in Deschutes National Forest.
Map 11.5, grid b2, page 620

This campground is set along the west shore of Crane Prairie Reservoir. See the description of Quinn River. The elevation is 4,450 feet.

Campsites, facilities: There are 31 sites for tents or RVs up to 22 feet long. Picnic tables, garbage service, and fire grills are provided. Drinking water, a fish-cleaning station, and vault toilets are available. Some facilities are wheelchair accessible. Boat docks and launching facilities are on-site. Leashed pets are permitted.

Reservations, fees: Reservations are not accepted. Sites are $10 per night, $5 per extra vehicle, and $10 per extra RV. Senior discount available. Open mid-April–October, weather permitting.

Directions: From Bend, drive southwest on Cascade Lakes Highway (Century Drive Highway, which becomes County Road 46) for 48.8 miles to the campground.

Contact: Deschutes National Forest, Bend-Fort Rock Ranger District, 1230 N.E. 3rd St., Suite A-262, Bend, OR 97701, 541/383-4000, fax 541/383-4700.

137 BIG RIVER

Rating: 4

On the Deschutes River in Deschutes National Forest.

Map 11.5, grid c4, page 620

This is a good spot. Located between the banks of the Deschutes River and the road, it has easy access and is popular as an overnight camp. Rafting, fishing, and motorized boating are permitted.

Campsites, facilities: There are two tent sites and nine sites for tents or RVs up to 22 feet long. There is also one group site that can accommodate up to 60 people. Picnic tables, garbage service, and fire grills are provided. Vault toilets are available. There is no drinking water. Some facilities are wheelchair accessible. Boat-launching facilities are on-site. Leashed pets are permitted.

Reservations, fees: Reservations are not accepted. Individual sites are $5 per night per extra vehicle. Senior discount available. Open April–September.

Directions: From Bend, drive south on U.S.

97 for 17.3 miles to Forest Road 42. Turn right (west) and drive 7.9 miles to the campground.

Contact: Deschutes National Forest, Bend-Fort Rock Ranger District, 1230 N.E. 3rd St., Suite A-262, Bend, OR 97701, 541/383-4000, fax 541/383-4700.

138 PRAIRIE

Rating: 4

On Paulina Creek in Deschutes National Forest.

Map 11.5, grid c5, page 620

Here's another good overnight campground that is quiet and private. This camp along the banks of Paulina Creek is set about one-half mile from the trailhead for the Peter Skene Ogden National Recreation Trail. The elevation is 4,300 feet.

Campsites, facilities: There are 16 sites for tents or RVs up to 30 feet long. Picnic tables, garbage service, and fire grills are provided. Drinking water, firewood, and vault toilets are available. Leashed pets are permitted.

Reservations, fees: Reservations are not accepted. Sites are $10 per night, $5 per extra vehicle, and $10 per extra RV. Senior discount available. Open mid-May–October, weather permitting.

Directions: From Bend, drive south on U.S. 97 for 23.5 miles to County Road 21 (Paulina/East Lake Road). Turn left (east) and drive 3.1 miles to the campground.

Contact: Deschutes National Forest, Bend-Fort Rock Ranger District, 1230 N.E. 3rd St., Suite A-262, Bend, OR 97701, 541/383-4000, fax 541/383-4700.

139 MCKAY CROSSING

Rating: 6

On Paulina Creek in Deschutes National Forest.

Map 11.5, grid c5, page 620

This pleasant little campground is set along the banks of Paulina Creek. An outstanding site for bird-watching, it sits at an elevation of 4,300 feet. The nearby Peter Skene Ogden National Recreation Trail travels east for six miles to Paulina Lake (also reachable by car). This spot is the gateway to Newberry National Volcanic Monument, about 10 miles east on County Road 21.

Campsites, facilities: There are 16 sites for tents or RVs up to 22 feet long. Picnic tables, garbage service, and fire grills are provided. Vault toilets are available. There is no drinking water. Leashed pets are permitted.

Reservations, fees: Reservations are not accepted. Sites are $5 per night, $5 per extra vehicle per night. Senior discount available. Open June–late October.

Directions: From Bend, drive south on U.S. 97 for 23.5 miles to County Road 21 (Paulina/East Lake Road). Turn left (east) and drive 3.2 miles to Forest Road 2120. Continue east for 2.7 miles to the campground.

Contact: Deschutes National Forest, Bend-Fort Rock Ranger District, 1230 N.E. 3rd St., Suite A-262, Bend, OR 97701, 541/383-4000, fax 541/383-4700.

140 SHEEP BRIDGE

Rating: 3

Near Wickiup Reservoir in Deschutes National Forest.

Map 11.5, grid c2, page 620

This campground is set along the north Deschutes River Channel of Wickiup Reservoir in an open, treeless area that has minimal privacy and is dusty in summer. Dispersed sites here are popular with group campers. The elevation is 4,350 feet.

Campsites, facilities: There are 18 sites for tents or RVs of any length. Picnic tables, garbage service, and fire grills are provided. Drinking water, vault toilets, boat-launching facilities, and a picnic area are available. Leashed pets are permitted.

Reservations, fees: Reservations are not ac-

cepted. Sites are $5 per night per extra vehicle. Senior discount available. Open April–October, weather permitting.

Directions: From Bend, drive south on U.S. 97 for 26.8 miles to Wickiup Junction. Turn right (west) on County Road 43 and drive 11 miles to Forest Road 42. Continue 4.6 miles west on Forest Road 42 to Forest Road 4260. Turn left (south) and drive three-quarters of a mile to the campground on the right.

Contact: Deschutes National Forest, Bend-Fort Rock Ranger District, 1230 N.E. 3rd St., Suite A-262, Bend, OR 97701, 541/383-4000, fax 541/383-4700.

141 NORTH TWIN LAKE

Rating: 6

On North Twin Lake in Deschutes National Forest.

Map 11.5, grid c3, page 620

This campground on the shore of North Twin Lake is a popular weekend spot for families. Although small and fairly primitive, it has lake access and a pretty setting. Only nonmotorized boats are permitted. The elevation is 4,350 feet.

Campsites, facilities: There are 19 sites for tents or RVs up to 22 feet long. Picnic tables and fire grills are provided. Vault toilets are available. There is no drinking water. Boat-launching facilities are on-site. Leashed pets are permitted.

Reservations, fees: Reservations are not accepted. Sites are $5 per night per extra vehicle. Senior discount available. Open June–late September, weather permitting.

Directions: From Bend, drive southwest on Cascade Lakes Highway (Century Drive Highway, which becomes County Road 46) for 52 miles and drive past Crane Prairie Reservoir to Forest Road 42. Turn east and drive four miles to Forest Road 4260. Turn right (south) and drive one-quarter mile to the campground.

Contact: Deschutes National Forest, Bend-Fort

Rock Ranger District, 1230 N.E. 3rd St., Suite A-262, Bend, OR 97701, 541/383-4000, fax 541/383-4700.

142 TWIN LAKES RESORT

Rating: 8

On Twin Lakes.

Map 11.5, grid c3, page 620

This resort is a popular family vacation destination with a full-service marina and all the amenities, including beach areas. Recreational activities vary from hiking to fishing, swimming, and boating on Wickiup Reservoir. Nearby South Twin Lake is popular with paddleboaters and kayakers. It's stocked with rainbow trout. See the description of West South Twin and South Twin Lake.

Campsites, facilities: There are 22 full-hookup sites for RVs of any length. There are also 14 cabins. Restrooms, showers, an RV dump station, a public telephone, a laundry room, a store, a full-service restaurant, ice, snacks, some RV supplies, LP gas, gasoline, and a barbecue are available. A boat ramp, rentals, and a dock are provided; no motors are permitted on South Twin Lake. Leashed pets are permitted.

Reservations, fees: Reservations are recommended. Sites are $28 per night, $8 per person for more than two people, $10 per pet per night, and cabins are $60–145 per night. Major credit cards accepted. Open late April–mid-October.

Directions: From Bend, drive south on U.S. 97 for 26.8 miles to Wickiup Junction. Turn right (west) on County Road 43 and drive 11 miles to Forest Road 42. Continue 4.6 miles west on Forest Road 42 to Forest Road 4260. Turn left (south) and drive two miles to the resort.

Contact: Twin Lakes Resort, 11200 S. Century Drive, P.O. Box 3550, Sunriver, OR 97707, 541/593-6526, fax 541/410-4688, website: www.twinlakesresortoregon.com.

143 SOUTH TWIN LAKE

Rating: 6

On South Twin Lake in Deschutes National Forest.

Map 11.5, grid c3, page 620

This campground is on the shore of South Twin Lake, a popular spot for swimming, fishing, and boating (nonmotorized only). See the description of West South Twin. The elevation is 4,350 feet.

Campsites, facilities: There are 24 sites for tents or RVs up to 22 feet long. Picnic tables, garbage service, and fire grills are provided. Drinking water and vault and flush toilets are available. Some facilities are wheelchair accessible. Boat-launching facilities (small boats only), boat rentals, showers, and laundry facilities are nearby. Leashed pets are permitted.

Reservations, fees: Reservations are not accepted. Sites are $12 per night, $5 per extra vehicle, and $12 per extra RV. Senior discount available. Open mid-April–October, weather permitting.

Directions: From Bend, drive south on U.S. 97 for 26.8 miles to Wickiup Junction. Turn right (west) on County Road 43 and drive 11 miles to Forest Road 42. Continue west on Forest Road 42 for 4.6 miles to Forest Road 4260. Turn left (south) and drive two miles to the campground on the left.

Contact: Deschutes National Forest, Bend-Fort Rock Ranger District, 1230 N.E. 3rd St., Suite A-262, Bend, OR 97701, 541/383-4000, fax 541/383-4700.

144 WEST SOUTH TWIN

Rating: 4

On South Twin Lake in Deschutes National Forest.

Map 11.5, grid c3, page 620

A major access point to the Wickiup Reservoir, this camp is set on South Twin Lake adjacent to the reservoir. It's a popular angling spot with very good kokanee salmon fishing. Twin Lakes Resort is adjacent to West South Twin. The elevation is 4,350 feet.

Campsites, facilities: There are 24 sites for RVs up to 22 feet long. Picnic tables, garbage service, and fire grills are provided. Drinking water and flush toilets are available. Boat-launching facilities are on-site, and boat rentals, a restaurant, showers, a coin-operated laundry, gas, propane, cabins, and a store are nearby. Leashed pets are permitted.

Reservations, fees: Reservations are not accepted. Sites are $10 per night, $5 per extra vehicle, and $10 per extra RV. Senior discount available. Open mid-May–mid-October, weather permitting.

Directions: From Bend, drive southwest on Cascade Lakes Highway (Century Drive Highway, which becomes County Road 46) for 52 miles (past Crane Prairie Reservoir) to Forest Road 42. Turn east and drive four miles to Forest Road 4260. Turn right (south) and drive one-quarter mile to the campground.

Contact: Deschutes National Forest, Bend-Fort Rock Ranger District, 1230 N.E. 3rd St., Suite A-262, Bend, OR 97701, 541/383-4000, fax 541/383-4700.

145 GULL POINT

Rating: 5

On Wickiup Reservoir in Deschutes National Forest.

Map 11.5, grid c3, page 620

This campground sits in an open ponderosa stand on the north shore of Wickiup Reservoir. You'll find good fishing for kokanee salmon here. About two miles from West South Twin Campground, Gull Point is the most popular campground on Wickiup Reservoir.

Campsites, facilities: There are 79 sites for tents or RVs up to 30 feet long. There are also two sites available for groups of up to 25 people. Picnic tables, garbage service, and fire grills

are provided. Drinking water, an RV dump station, and flush and vault toilets are available. Some facilities are wheelchair accessible. Boat-launching facilities and fish-cleaning stations are on-site. Leashed pets are permitted.

Reservations, fees: Reservations are not accepted. The fee is $10 per night, $5 per extra vehicle, and $10 per extra RV. Senior discount available. Reservations required for the group sites at 541/382-9443; $40 per night. Open mid-April–October, weather permitting.

Directions: From Bend, drive south on U.S. 97 for about 26.8 miles to County Road 43 (three miles north of LaPine). Turn west on County Road 43 and drive 11 miles to Forest Road 42. Turn west on Forest Road 42 and drive 4.6 miles to Forest Road 4260. Turn left (south) and drive three miles to the campground on the right.

Contact: Deschutes National Forest, Bend-Fort Rock Ranger District, 1230 N.E. 3rd St., Suite A-262, Bend, OR 97701, 541/383-4000, fax 541/383-4700.

146 NORTH DAVIS CREEK

Rating: 4

On North Davis Creek in Deschutes National Forest.

Map 11.5, grid c2, page 620

This remote, secluded campground is set along a western channel that feeds into Wickiup Reservoir. It receives little use and can be used as an overflow camp if campsites are filled at Wickiup. In late summer, the reservoir level tends to drop. Fishing for brown and rainbow trout as well as kokanee salmon is good here. The elevation is 4,350 feet.

Campsites, facilities: There are 15 sites for tents or RVs up to 22 feet long. Picnic tables, garbage service, and fire grills are provided. Drinking water and vault toilets are available. Boat-launching facilities are on-site. Leashed pets are permitted.

Reservations, fees: Reservations are not accepted.

Sites are $8 per night, $5 for each additional vehicle, and $8 per extra RV. Senior discount available. Open May–late October.

Directions: From Bend, drive southwest on Cascade Lake Highway (Highway 46/Forest Road 46) for 56.2 miles to the campground on the left.

Contact: Deschutes National Forest, Bend-Fort Rock Ranger District, 1230 N.E. 3rd St., Suite A-262, Bend, OR 97701, 541/383-4000, fax 541/383-4700.

147 GOLD LAKE

Rating: 8

On Gold Lake in Willamette National Forest.
Map 11.5, grid c1, page 620

This campground wins the popularity contest for high use. Although motors are not allowed on this small lake (100 acres, 25 feet deep), rafts and rowboats provide excellent fishing access. A primitive log shelter built in the early 1940s provides a dry picnic area. In the spring and summer, this area abounds with wildflowers and huckleberries. The Gold Lake Bog is another special attraction where one can often see deer, elk, and smaller wildlife.

Campsites, facilities: There are 25 sites for tents or RVs up to 22 feet long. Picnic tables, garbage bins, and fire grills are provided. Drinking water and vault toilets are available. Boat docks and launching facilities are nearby. Leashed pets are permitted.

Reservations, fees: Reservations are not accepted. Sites are $12 per night, $6 per extra vehicle. Senior discount available. Open June–September, weather permitting.

Directions: From Eugene, drive south on I-5 for five miles to Exit 188 and Highway 58. Turn east and drive 35 miles to the town of Oakridge. From Oakridge, continue east on Highway 58 for 28 miles to Gold Lake Road (Forest Road 500). Turn left (north) and drive two miles to the campground on the right.

Contact: Willamette National Forest, Middle Fork Ranger District, 46375 Hwy. 58, Westfir, OR 97492, 541/782-2283, fax 541/782-5306.

148 RESERVOIR

Rating: 4

On Wickiup Reservoir in Deschutes National Forest.
Map 11.5, grid c3, page 620

This campground is set along the south shore of Wickiup Reservoir, where the kokanee salmon fishing is good. The camp is best in early summer, before the lake level drops. This campground gets little use, so you won't find crowds here. The elevation is 4,350 feet.

Campsites, facilities: There are 28 sites for tents or RVs up to 22 feet long. Picnic tables, garbage service, and fire grills are provided. Boat-launching facilities and vault toilets are available, but there is no drinking water. Leashed pets are permitted.

Reservations, fees: Reservations are not accepted. Sites are $5 per night per extra vehicle. Senior discount available. Open May–late October, weather permitting.

Directions: From Bend, drive southwest on Cascade Lakes Highway (Century Drive Highway, which becomes County Road 46) for 57.8 miles to Forest Road 44. Turn left (east) and drive 1.7 miles to the campground.

Contact: Deschutes National Forest, Bend-Fort Rock Ranger District, 1230 N.E. 3rd St., Suite A-262, Bend, OR 97701, 541/383-4000, fax 541/383-4700.

149 WICKIUP BUTTE

Rating: 4

On Wickiup Reservoir in Deschutes National Forest.
Map 11.5, grid c3, page 620

This campground is set at 4,350 feet elevation along the southeast shore of Wickiup Reservoir, where kokanee salmon fishing is good during the early summer. Wickiup Butte is more remote than the other campgrounds on Wickiup Reservoir.

Campsites, facilities: There are eight sites for tents or RVs up to 22 feet long. Picnic tables, garbage service, and fire grills are provided. Vault toilets are available. There is no drinking water. Boat-launching facilities are nearby. Leashed pets are permitted.

Reservations, fees: Reservations are not accepted. Sites are $5 per night per extra vehicle. Senior discount available. Open May–late October, weather permitting.

Directions: From Bend, drive south on U.S. 97 for 26.8 miles to Wickiup Junction. Turn right (west) on County Road 43 and drive 10.4 miles to Forest Road 4380. Turn left (south) and drive 3.6 miles to Forest Road 4260. Turn left (east) and drive three miles to the campground.

Contact: Deschutes National Forest, Bend-Fort Rock Ranger District, 1230 N.E. 3rd St., Suite A-262, Bend, OR 97701, 541/383-4000, fax 541/383-4700.

150 BULL BEND

Rating: 5

On the Deschutes River in Deschutes National Forest.

Map 11.5, grid c3, page 620

This campground is located on the inside of a major bend in the Deschutes River at 4,300 feet elevation. For a mini-float trip, start at the upstream end of camp, float around the bend, and then take out at the downstream end of camp. This is a low-use getaway spot.

Campsites, facilities: There are 12 sites for tents or RVs. Picnic tables, garbage service, fire grills, vault toilets, and boat-launching facilities are available. There is no drinking water. Leashed pets are permitted.

Reservations, fees: Reservations are not accepted. Sites are $5 per night per extra vehi-

cle. Senior discount available. Open April–September, weather permitting.

Directions: From Bend, drive south on U.S. 97 for 26.8 miles to Wickiup Junction. Turn right (west) on County Road 43 and drive eight miles to Forest Road 4370. Turn left (south) and drive 1.5 miles to the campground.

Contact: Deschutes National Forest, Bend-Fort Rock Ranger District, 1230 N.E. 3rd St., Suite A-262, Bend, OR 97701, 541/383-4000, fax 541/383-4700.

151 PRINGLE FALLS

Rating: 4

On the Deschutes River in Deschutes National Forest.

Map 11.5, grid c4, page 620

This campground is set along the Deschutes River and is less than a mile from Pringle Falls. The camp gets light use and is pretty and serene.

Campsites, facilities: There are six sites for tents or RVs up to 22 feet long. Picnic tables, garbage service, and fire grills are provided. Vault toilets are available. There is no drinking water. Leashed pets are permitted.

Reservations, fees: Reservations are not accepted. Sites are $5 per night per extra vehicle. Senior discount available. Open April–September, weather permitting.

Directions: From Bend, drive south on U.S. 97 for 26.8 miles to Wickiup Junction. Turn right (west) on County Road 43 and drive 7.4 miles to Forest Road 4330-500. Turn north (right) and drive one mile to the campground.

Contact: Deschutes National Forest, Bend-Fort Rock Ranger District, 1230 N.E. 3rd St., Suite A-262, Bend, OR 97701, 541/383-4000, fax 541/383-4700.

152 LAPINE STATE PARK
🛶 ❄ ♿ 🚙 ⛺

Rating: 7

On the Deschutes River.
Map 11.5, grid c4, page 620
This clean, quiet campground sits next to a twisting, cold river brimming with trout, a nearby legendary fly-fishing spot, and a giant tree. Be sure to visit Oregon's "Big Tree," the largest ponderosa pine in the state. The camp is set in a subalpine pine forest, and you just might see an eagle or red-tailed hawk grabbing breakfast right in front of you. Many high mountain lakes are in proximity, as is snow-skiing in the winter.

Campsites, facilities: There are 141 sites, including 92 with full hookups and 49 with partial hookups, for tents or self-contained RVs up to 85 feet long. There are also five cabins and three yurts. Picnic tables and fire grills are provided. Drinking water, restrooms with flush toilets and showers, garbage bins, a dump station, and firewood are available. Leashed pets are permitted.

Reservations, fees: Reservations at 800/452-5687 or website: www.OregonStateParks.org ($7 reservation fee). Sites are $13–15 per night, $7 per extra vehicle. Yurts are $27 per night, and cabins are $35 per night. Major credit cards accepted. Open year-round.

Directions: From Bend, turn south on U.S. 97 and drive 23 miles to State Recreation Road. Turn right and drive four miles to the park.

Contact: LaPine State Park, Oregon State Parks, 15800 State Recreation Rd., LaPine, OR 97739, 800/551-6949 or 541/536-2071.

153 HIDDEN PINES RV PARK
🚲 🛶 🛶 🚙 🐕 ♿ ⛺

Rating: 7

Near the Little Deschutes River.
Map 11.5, grid c4, page 620
So you think you've come far enough, eh? If you want a spot in a privately run RV park two miles from the bank of the Little Deschutes River, you've found it. Within a 30-minute drive are two reservoirs, four lakes, and a golf course. The nearby town of LaPine is the gateway to the Newberry National Volcanic Monument.

Campsites, facilities: There are six tent sites and 25 sites for RVs up to 40 feet long; 16 are pull-through sites. Electricity, drinking water, cable TV, sewer hookups (19 sites only), and picnic tables are provided. Flush toilets, an RV dump station, showers, a laundry room, RV supplies, LP gas, a community fire ring with firewood, and ice are available. The full-service community of LaPine is about five miles away. Leashed pets are allowed with restrictions; call first.

Reservations, fees: Reservations accepted. Sites are $17.50–22.50 per night, $2.50 per person for more than two people. Major credit cards accepted. Open year-round.

Directions: From Bend, drive south on U.S. 97 for 24 miles to Wickiup Junction and Milepost 165 and County Road 43/Burgess Road (lighted). Turn right (west) on County Road 43 (Burgess Road) and drive 2.4 miles to Pine Forest Road. Turn left and drive seven-tenths of a mile to Wright Avenue. Turn left and drive one block to the campground.

Contact: Hidden Pines RV Park, 52158 Elderberry Ln., LaPine, OR 97739, 541/536-2265 (phone or fax).

154 LAVA FLOW
🛶 🚙 ♿ 🚙 ⛺

Rating: 8

On Davis Lake in Deschutes National Forest.
Map 11.5, grid c2, page 620
This campground is set in old-growth forest along the northeast shore of Davis Lake, a very shallow lake formed by lava flow. The water level fluctuates here, and this campground can sometimes be closed in summer. There's good duck hunting during the fall. Fishing can be decent, but only fly-fishing is allowed. Boat speed is limited to 10 mph.

Campsites, facilities: There is a dispersed camping area for 12 tents or RVs up to 22 feet long. Picnic tables and fire grills are provided. Vault toilets and firewood (to be gathered from the surrounding area) are available. There is no drinking water, and all garbage must be packed out. A boat launch is nearby. Leashed pets are permitted.

Reservations, fees: Reservations are not accepted. There is no fee for camping. Open September–December, weather permitting.

Directions: From Eugene, drive south on I-5 for five miles to Exit 188 and Highway 58. Turn east on Highway 58 and drive 86 miles to County Road 61. Turn left and drive three miles to Forest Road 46. Turn left and drive 7.7 miles to Forest Road 850. Turn left and drive 1.8 miles to the campground.

Contact: Deschutes National Forest, Crescent Ranger District, P.O. Box 208, Crescent, OR 97733, 541/433-3200, fax 541/433-3224.

155 WEST DAVIS LAKE

Rating: 9

On Davis Lake in Deschutes National Forest.
Map 11.5, grid d2, page 620
This campground on the south shore of Davis Lake features spacious sites and easy access to the water. Only fly-fishing is permitted, and the boat speed limit is 10 mph. See notes for East Davis Lake.

Campsites, facilities: There are 21 sites for tents or RVs up to 22 feet long. Picnic tables, garbage service, and fire grills are provided. Drinking water, vault toilets, and firewood (to be gathered from the surrounding area) are available. A boat launch is on-site. Leashed pets are permitted.

Reservations, fees: Reservations are not accepted. Sites are $8 per night, $4 per extra vehicle. Senior discount available. Open May–late October, weather permitting.

Directions: From Eugene, drive south on I-5 for five miles to Exit 188 and Highway 58.

Turn east and drive 73 miles to County Road 61. Turn left (east) and drive three miles to Forest Road 46. Turn left and drive three miles north to Forest Road 4660. Turn left and drive three miles to Forest Road 4669. Turn right and drive 1.5 miles to the campground.

Contact: Deschutes National Forest, Crescent Ranger District, P.O. Box 208, Crescent, OR 97733, 541/433-3200, fax 541/433-3224.

156 EAST DAVIS LAKE

Rating: 9

On Davis Lake in Deschutes National Forest.
Map 11.5, grid d2, page 620
This campground is nestled in the lodgepole pines along the south shore of Davis Lake. Recreation options include fly-fishing, boating (speed limit 10 mph), and hiking. Leeches prevent swimming here. Bald eagles and sandhill cranes are frequently seen.

Campsites, facilities: There are 33 sites for tents or RVs up to 22 feet long. Picnic tables, garbage service, fire grills, drinking water, and vault toilets are provided. Firewood may be gathered from the surrounding area. Primitive boat-launching facilities are available on-site. Leashed pets are permitted.

Reservations, fees: Reservations are not accepted. Sites are $8 per night, $4 per extra vehicle. Senior discount available. Open May–late October, weather permitting.

Directions: From Eugene, drive south on I-5 for five miles to Exit 188 and Highway 58. Turn east and drive 73 miles to County Road 61. Turn left (east) and drive three miles to Forest Road 46. Turn left and drive 7.7 miles to Forest Road 850. Turn left and drive one-quarter mile to Forest Road 855. Turn left and drive two miles to the campground.

Contact: Deschutes National Forest, Crescent Ranger District, P.O. Box 208, Crescent, OR 97733, 541/433-3200, fax 541/433-3224.

157 TRAPPER CREEK

🏃 🏊 🎣 🛶 🐕 🚐 ⛺

Rating: 8

On Odell Lake in Deschutes National Forest.
Map 11.5, grid d1, page 620
The west end of Odell Lake is the setting for this camp. Boat docks and rentals are nearby at the Shelter Cove Resort. One of Oregon's prime fisheries for kokanee salmon and mackinaw (lake trout), this lake also has some huge brown trout.

Campsites, facilities: There are 32 sites for tents or RVs up to 22 feet long. Picnic tables, garbage service, and fire grills are provided. Drinking water, vault toilets, and a boat launch are available. Firewood may be gathered from the surrounding area. A store, a coin-operated laundry, and ice are within one mile. Leashed pets are permitted.

Reservations, fees: Reservations are not accepted. Sites are $10–12 per night, $5 per extra vehicle. Senior discount available. Open June–September, weather permitting.

Directions: From Eugene, drive south on I-5 for five miles to Exit 188 and Highway 58. Turn east and drive 61 miles to the turnoff for Odell Lake and Forest Road 5810. Turn right on Forest Road 5810 and drive 1.9 miles to the campground on the left.

Contact: Deschutes National Forest, Crescent Ranger District, P.O. Box 208, Crescent, OR 97733, 541/433-3200, fax 541/433-3224.

158 SHELTER COVE RESORT

🏃 🚴 🏊 🎣 🛶 🐕 🚐 ⛺

Rating: 9

On Odell Lake.
Map 11.5, grid d1, page 620
This private resort along the north shore of Odell Lake is set at the base of the Diamond Peak Wilderness and offers opportunities for hiking, fishing, and swimming. The cabins sit right on the lakefront. A general store and tackle shop are available.

Campsites, facilities: There are 18 tent sites, 54 drive-through sites for RVs up to 40 feet long, and 12 cabins. Electricity and picnic tables are provided. Drinking water, flush toilets, showers, a store, laundry facilities, and ice are available. Boat docks, launching facilities, and boat rentals are on-site. Leashed pets are permitted.

Reservations, fees: Reservations at 800/647-2729; $12–21 per night. Open year-round.

Directions: From Eugene, drive south on I-5 for five miles to Exit 188 and Highway 58. Turn east and drive 61 miles to the turnoff for Odell Lake and West Odell Lake Road. Take that road and drive south for 1.8 miles to the camp.

Contact: Shelter Cove Resort, West Odell Lake Rd., Hwy. 58, P.O. Box 52, Crescent Lake, OR 97425, 541/433-2548, website: www.shelter coveresort.com.

159 ODELL CREEK

🏃 🏊 🎣 🛶 🐕 🚐 ⛺

Rating: 9

On Odell Lake in Deschutes National Forest.
Map 11.5, grid d1, page 620
You can fish, swim, and hike at this campground (4,800 feet elevation) along the east shore of Odell Lake. A trail from the nearby Crater Buttes trailhead leads southwest into the Diamond Peak Wilderness and provides access to several small lakes in the backcountry. Another trail follows the north shore of the lake. Boat docks, launching facilities, and rentals are nearby at the Odell Lake Lodge and Resort, adjacent to the campground. Windy afternoons are common here.

Campsites, facilities: There are 21 sites for tents or RVs up to 22 feet long. Picnic tables, garbage service, and fire grills are provided. Drinking water and vault toilets are available. Firewood may be gathered from the surrounding area. Leashed pets are permitted.

Reservations, fees: Reservations are not accepted. Sites are $10 per night, $5 per extra

vehicle. Senior discount available. Open mid-May–late September, weather permitting.
Directions: From Eugene, drive south on I-5 for five miles to Exit 188 and Highway 58. Turn east and drive 68 miles to Odell Lake and Forest Road 680 (at the east end of the lake). Turn right on Forest Road 680 and drive 400 yards to the campground on the right.
Contact: Deschutes National Forest, Crescent Ranger District, P.O. Box 208, Crescent, OR 97733, 541/433-3200, fax 541/433-3224.

160 SUNSET COVE
Rating: 8

On Odell Lake in Deschutes National Forest.
Map 11.5, grid d1, page 620

This campground is set on the northeast shore of Odell Lake. Boat docks and rentals are available nearby at Odell Lake Lodge and Resort. Campsites are surrounded by large Douglas fir and some white pine. The camp backs up to the highway; expect to hear the noise.
Campsites, facilities: There are 20 sites for tents or RVs up to 22 feet long. Picnic tables and fire grills are provided. Drinking water, vault toilets, a barrier-free boat launch and day-use area, and fish-cleaning facilities are available. Firewood may be gathered from the surrounding area. Leashed pets are permitted.
Reservations, fees: Reservations are not accepted. Sites are $10 per night, $5 per extra vehicle. Senior discount available. Open mid-May–mid-October, weather permitting.
Directions: From Eugene, drive south on I-5 for five miles to Exit 188 and Highway 58. Turn east and drive 67 miles to the campground on the right.
Contact: Deschutes National Forest, Crescent Ranger District, P.O. Box 208, Crescent, OR 97733, 541/433-3200, fax 541/433-3224.

161 PRINCESS CREEK
Rating: 9

On Odell Lake in Deschutes National Forest.
Map 11.5, grid d1, page 620

This wooded campground is on the northeast shore of Odell Lake, but it backs up to the highway; expect traffic noise. See the description of Odell Creek for recreation details. Boat docks and rentals are available nearby at the Shelter Cove Resort.
Campsites, facilities: There are 46 sites for tents or RVs up to 22 feet long. Picnic tables and fire grills are provided. Drinking water, vault toilets, and boat-launching facilities are available. Firewood may be gathered from the surrounding area. Showers, a store, coin-operated laundry facilities, and ice are within five miles. Leashed pets are permitted.
Reservations, fees: Reservations are not accepted. Sites are $10–12 per night, $5 per extra vehicle. Senior discount available. Open mid-May–September, weather permitting.
Directions: From Eugene, drive south on I-5 for five miles to Exit 188 and Highway 58. Turn east and drive 64 miles to the campground on the right.
Contact: Deschutes National Forest, Crescent Ranger District, P.O. Box 208, Crescent, OR 97733, 541/433-3200, fax 541/433-3224.

162 SIMAX GROUP CAMP
Rating: 8

On Crescent Lake in Deschutes National Forest.
Map 11.5, grid e1, page 620

This camp is set at an elevation of 4,850 feet on Crescent Lake and provides trails to day-use beaches. Fishing is variable year to year and is usually better earlier in the season. A boat launch is available at Crescent Lake, about two miles away. See neighboring Crescent Lake for more details.

Campsites, facilities: There are three group campsites for 30–40 campers each. Drinking water, tent pads, flush toilets, showers, picnic tables, garbage service, fireplaces, and a group shelter (with an electrical outlet) that accommodates 50 campers are available. Tents must be placed on tent pads. Some facilities are wheelchair accessible. Leashed pets are permitted.

Reservations, fees: Reservations at 877/444-6777 or website: www.ReserveUsa.com ($9 reservation fee). Rates are $65 per night for Site A (the most accessible) and $85 per night for Sites B and C. Site B is the most difficult to reach and only tents are advised; Site C is best for RVs. The group shelter fee is $25 per day. The campground is generally open from Memorial Day through Labor Day, weather permitting.

Directions: From Eugene, drive south on I-5 for five miles to Exit 188 and Highway 58. Turn east and drive 70 miles to Crescent Lake Highway (Forest Road 50). Turn right and drive two miles to Forest Road 6005. Turn left and drive one mile to the campground on the right.

Contact: Deschutes National Forest, Crescent Ranger District, P.O. Box 208, Crescent, OR 97733, 541/433-3200, fax 541/433-3224.

163 CRESCENT LAKE

Rating: 8

On Crescent Lake in Deschutes National Forest.

Map 11.5, grid e1, page 620

This campground is set along the north shore of Crescent Lake, and it is often windy here in the afternoon. Boat docks, launching facilities, and rentals are nearby at Crescent Lake Resort, adjacent to the campground. A trail from camp heads into the Diamond Peak Wilderness and also branches north to Odell Lake.

Campsites, facilities: There are 47 sites for tents or RVs up to 35 feet long. Picnic tables, garbage service, and fire grills are provided. Drinking water, vault toilets, and boat-launching facilities are available. Firewood may be gathered from the surrounding area. Leashed pets are permitted.

Reservations, fees: Reservations are not accepted. Sites are $10–12 per night, $5 per extra vehicle. Senior discount available. Open mid-May–late October, weather permitting.

Directions: From Eugene, drive south on I-5 for five miles to Exit 188 and Highway 58. Turn east and drive 70 miles to Crescent Lake Highway (Forest Road 60). Turn right (west) and drive 2.2 miles southwest. Bear right to remain on Forest Road 60, and drive another one-quarter mile to the campground on the left.

Contact: Deschutes National Forest, Crescent Ranger District, P.O. Box 208, Crescent, OR 97733, 541/433-3200, fax 541/433-3224.

164 SPRING

Rating: 8

On Crescent Lake in Deschutes National Forest.

Map 11.5, grid e1, page 620

This campground is set in a lodgepole pine forest on the southern shore of Crescent Lake. Sites are open and some are on the lake with Diamond Peak views. See Contorta Point for more information. The camp is at an elevation of 4,850 feet.

Campsites, facilities: There are 68 sites for tents or RVs up to 22 feet long. Picnic tables, garbage service, and fire grills are provided. Drinking water, vault toilets, boat-launching facilities, and firewood (to be gathered from the surrounding area) are available. Leashed pets are permitted.

Reservations, fees: Reservations are not accepted. Sites are $10–12 per night, $5 per extra vehicle. Senior discount available. Open June–September, weather permitting.

Directions: From Eugene, drive south on I-5 for five miles to Exit 188 and Highway 58. Turn east and drive 70 miles to Crescent Lake Highway (Forest Road 60). Turn right and drive eight miles west to the campground entrance road on the left. Turn left and drive one mile to the campground.

Contact: Deschutes National Forest, Crescent Ranger District, P.O. Box 208, Crescent, OR 97733, 541/433-3200, fax 541/433-3224.

165 CONTORTA POINT

Rating: 8

On Crescent Lake in Deschutes National Forest.

Map 11.5, grid e1, page 620

This campground (4,850 feet elevation) is set on the southern shore of Crescent Lake, where swimming, boating, and water-skiing are among the summer pastimes. A number of trails from the nearby Windy-Oldenburg Trailhead provide access to lakes in the Oregon Cascades Recreation Area. Motorized vehicles are restricted to open roads only.

Campsites, facilities: There are about 15 sites in an area for dispersed camping for tents or RVs up to 22 feet long. There is no drinking water, and all garbage must be packed out. Picnic tables and vault toilets are provided. Boat docks and launching facilities are three miles away at Spring Campground. Leashed pets are permitted.

Reservations, fees: Reservations are not accepted. There is no fee for camping. Open May–late October, weather permitting.

Directions: From Eugene, drive south on I-5 for five miles to Exit 188 and Highway 58. Turn east and drive 70 miles to Crescent Lake Highway (Forest Road 60). Turn right and drive 9.9 miles to Forest Road 280. Turn left and drive one mile to the campground.

Contact: Deschutes National Forest, Crescent Ranger District, P.O. Box 208, Crescent, OR 97733, 541/433-3200, fax 541/433-3224.

166 WHITEFISH HORSE CAMP

Rating: 5

On Whitefish Creek in Deschutes National Forest.

Map 11.5, grid e1, page 620

This just might be the best horse camp in the state. Horse camping only is allowed here, and manure removal is required. High lines are not allowed; horses must be kept in stalls. On Whitefish Creek at the west end of Crescent Lake, this campground is set in lodgepole pine and has shaded sites. Although located in a flat area across the road from the lake, the campground has no lake view. Moderately to heavily used, it has access to about 100 miles of trail, leading to Diamond Peak Wilderness, the Oregon Cascades Recreation Area, many high mountain lakes, and the Metolius-Windigo National Recreation Trail. The camp sits at 4,850 feet elevation.

Campsites, facilities: There are 17 sites for tents or RVs up to 40 feet long. Picnic tables, horse corrals, and fire rings are provided. Drinking water and garbage bins are available in the summer only. Vault toilets are available. Firewood may be gathered from the surrounding area. Leashed pets are permitted.

Reservations, fees: Reservations at 877/444-6777 or website: www.ReserveUsa.com ($9 reservation fee). Sites are $10 per night for two stalls, $12 per night for four stalls, and $5 per extra vehicle. Open May–November, weather permitting.

Directions: From Eugene, drive south on I-5 for five miles to Exit 188 and Highway 58. Turn east and drive 70 miles to Crescent Lake Highway (Forest Road 60). Turn right (west) and drive 2.2 miles southwest. Stay to the right to remain on Forest Road 60, and drive six miles to the campground on the right.

Contact: Deschutes National Forest, Crescent Ranger District, P.O. Box 208, Crescent, OR 97733, 541/433-3200, fax 541/433-3224.

167 CRESCENT CREEK

Rating: 7

On Crescent Creek in Deschutes National Forest.

Map 11.5, grid e1, page 620

One of the Cascade's classic hidden campgrounds, Crescent Creek camp sits along the banks of its namesake at 4,500 feet elevation. The buzzwords here are pretty, developed, and private. Hunters are the primary users of this campground, mainly in the fall. Otherwise, it gets light use. There's some highway noise here, and even if you can't hear it, traffic is visible from some sites.

Campsites, facilities: There are 10 sites for tents or RVs up to 22 feet long. Picnic tables, garbage service, and fire grills are provided. Drinking water and vault toilets are available. Firewood may be gathered from the surrounding area. Leashed pets are permitted.

Reservations, fees: Reservations are not accepted. Sites are $8 per night, $4 per extra vehicle. Senior discount available. Open May–late October, weather permitting.

Directions: From Eugene, drive south on I-5 for five miles to Exit 188 and Highway 58. Turn east and drive 73 miles to County Road 61. Turn left (east) and drive three miles to the campground on the right.

Contact: Deschutes National Forest, Crescent Ranger District, P.O. Box 208, Crescent, OR 97733, 541/433-3200, fax 541/433-3224.

168 DIGIT POINT

Rating: 7

On Miller Lake in Winema National Forest.

Map 11.5, grid g1, page 620

This campground is set in lodgepole forest at 5,600 feet elevation on the shore of Miller Lake, a popular spot for boating, fishing, and swimming. Nearby trails provide access to the Mt. Thielsen Wilderness and the Pacific Crest Trail.

Campsites, facilities: There are 64 sites for tents or RVs up to 30 feet long. Picnic tables, garbage bins, and fire grills are provided. Drinking water, an RV dump station, and flush toilets are available. Boat docks and launching facilities are nearby. Leashed pets are permitted.

Reservations, fees: Reservations are not accepted. Sites are $8 per night, $4 per extra vehicle. Senior discount available. Open Memorial Day–mid-October.

Directions: From Eugene, drive southeast on Highway 58 for 86 miles to U.S. 97. Turn south and drive seven miles to Forest Road 9772 (one mile north of Chemult). Turn right and drive 12 miles west to the campground.

Contact: Winema National Forest, Chemult Ranger District, P.O. Box 150, Chemult, OR 97731, 541/365-7001, fax 541/365-7019.

169 CORRAL SPRING

Rating: 4

In Winema National Forest.

Map 11.5, grid f3, page 620

This flat campground with no water source is located next to Corral Spring at 4,900 feet elevation. The main attraction is solitude; it's primitive, remote, and quiet. The landscape features stands of lodgepole pine, interspersed by several small meadows.

Campsites, facilities: There are six sites for tents or RVs up to 34 feet long. Picnic tables, garbage bins, and fire grills are provided. Vault toilets are available, but there is no drinking water. A store, a café, a coin-operated laundry, and ice are within five miles. Leashed pets are permitted.

Reservations, fees: Reservations are not accepted. There is no fee for camping. Open mid-May–late October.

Directions: From Eugene, drive southeast on Highway 58 for 86 miles to U.S. 97. Turn south and drive 6.5 miles to Forest Road 9774 (2.5 miles north of Chemult). Turn right and drive two miles west to the campground.

Contact: Winema National Forest, Chemult Ranger District, P.O. Box 150, Chemult, OR 97731, 541/365-7001, fax 541/365-7019.

170 CHARLES V. STANTON PARK

Rating: 7

On the South Umpqua River.
Map 11.6, grid a6, page 621

This campground, set along the banks of the South Umpqua River, is an all-season spot with a nice beach for swimming in the summer, good steelhead fishing in the winter, and wild grape picking in the fall.

Campsites, facilities: There are 20 tent sites, 20 sites for RVs up to 30 feet long, and one group area for tents or RVs. Electricity, sewer hookups, and picnic tables are provided. Drinking water, flush toilets, showers, a dump station, a pavilion, and a playground are available. Bottled gas, a store, a café, a coin-operated laundry, and ice are within one mile. Leashed pets are permitted.

Reservations, fees: Reservations are not accepted for family sites; $13–19 per night. Senior discount available for county residents. Major credit cards accepted. Group reservations required ($10 reservation fee) at 541/440-4500; $160 per night. Open year-round.

Directions: Depending on your heading on I-5, there are two routes to reach this campground. In Canyonville northbound on I-5, take Exit 99 and drive one mile north on the frontage road to the campground on the right. Otherwise: In Canyonville southbound on I-5, take Exit 101 and drive one mile south on the frontage road to the campground on the left.

Contact: Charles V. Stanton Park, Douglas County Parks, 1540 Stanton Park Rd., Canyonville, OR 97417, 541/839-4483, fax 541/440-4500, website: www.co.douglas.or.us/parks.

171 MEADOW WOOD RV PARK

Rating: 6

In Glendale.
Map 11.6, grid c6, page 621

Meadow Wood is a good option for RVers looking for a camping spot along I-5. It features 80 wooded acres and all the amenities. Nearby attractions include a ghost town, gold panning, and Wolf Creek Tavern.

Campsites, facilities: There are 25 tent sites and 34 drive-through sites for RVs of any length; 23 sites have full hookups. Electricity, drinking water, and picnic tables are provided. Flush toilets, bottled gas, an RV dump station, showers, firewood, a store, a laundry room, ice, a playground, and a heated swimming pool are available. Leashed pets are permitted.

Reservations, fees: Reservations at 800/606-1274. Sites are $13–19 per night, $2 per person for more than two people. Senior discount available. Major credit cards accepted. Monthly rentals available. Open year-round.

Directions: Depending on your heading on I-5, there are two routes to reach this campground. From Roseburg, drive south on I-5 to Exit 86 (near Glendale). Take that exit and drive south on the frontage road for three miles to Barton Road. Turn east and drive one-quarter mile to Autumn Lane. Turn south on Autumn Lane and drive three-quarters of a mile to the park. Otherwise: From Grants Pass, drive north on I-5 to Exit 83 (near Glendale) and drive east for one-quarter mile to Autumn Lane. Turn south on Autumn Lane and drive three-quarters of a mile to the park.

Contact: Meadow Wood RV Park, 869 Autumn Ln., Glendale, OR 97442, 800/606-1274 or 541/832-3114, fax 541/832-2454, website: www.meadow-woodrvpark.com.

172 INDIAN MARY PARK

Rating: 9

On the Rogue River.

Map 11.6, grid d5, page 621

This park is the crown jewel of the Josephine County parks. Set right on the Rogue River at an elevation of 900–1,000 feet, the park sports hiking trails, a picnic shelter for 150 people, swimming (unsupervised), fishing, disc golf (Frisbee golf), and a historic mining town nearby. Rogue River is famous for its rafting, which can be done commercially or on your own.

Campsites, facilities: There are 34 sites for tents, 68 sites for RVs of up to 40 feet (44 are full hookup, 14 are partial), and two yurts. Picnic tables and fire pits are provided. Drinking water, restrooms with flush toilets and coin-operated showers, a barrier-free campsite and restroom, garbage bins, a dump station, a boat ramp, a playground, ice, and firewood are available. A store and café are seven miles away, and a laundry is 16 miles away. Leashed pets are permitted.

Reservations, fees: Reservations at 541/474-5285. Sites are $13–20 per night, $5 for a third vehicle, and $28 for a yurt per night with a $28 refundable cleaning deposit. Open year-round.

Directions: From Grants Pass, drive north on I-5 for 3.5 miles to Exit 61 (Merlin-Galice Road). Take that exit and drive northwest for 10 miles to Indian Mary Park on the right.

Contact: Josephine County Parks, 125 Ringuette St., Grants Pass, OR 97527, 541/474-5285, fax 541/474-5288, website: www.co.josephine.or.us /parks/index.htm.

173 ELDERBERRY FLAT

Rating: 7

On West Fork Evans Creek.

Map 11.6, grid d8, page 621

Virtually unknown, this campground on the banks of Evans Creek is only about a 30-minute drive from I-5. Small and primitive, it has access to swimming holes along the creek. ATV/motorcycle trails originate from this area. No fishing is allowed in the creek.

Campsites, facilities: There are nine primitive tent sites. Picnic tables and fire grills are provided. Vault toilets and garbage service are available, but there is no drinking water. Some facilities are wheelchair accessible. Leashed pets are permitted.

Reservations, fees: Reservations are not accepted. There is no fee for camping. There is a 14-day stay limit. Open mid-April–mid-November.

Directions: From Grants Pass, drive south on I-5 for 10 miles to the Rogue River exit. Take that exit, turn right on Depot Street, and drive to Pine Street. Turn left and drive 18 miles (it becomes East Evans Creek Road) to West Fork Evans Creek Road. Turn left and drive nine miles to the campground.

Contact: Bureau of Land Management, Medford District, 3040 Biddle Rd., Medford, OR 97504, 541/618-2200, fax 541/618-2400, website: www.or.blm.gov/medfoRoad.

174 WHITE HORSE

Rating: 9

On the Rogue River.

Map 11.6, grid e6, page 621

This pleasant county park on the banks of the Rogue River is one of several parks in the Grants Pass area that provide opportunities for trout fishing, hiking, and boating. Wildlife Images, a wildlife rehabilitation center, is nearby. Possible side trips include Oregon Caves, Kerby Museum, and Crater Lake National Park (two hours away).

Campsites, facilities: There are 42 sites for tents or RVs, including eight with full hookups, one group site for 12–18 people, and one yurt. Drinking water and picnic tables are provided. Restrooms, coin-operated showers, a public phone, fire grills, horseshoes, a reservable picnic shelter, and a playground are available. Leashed pets are permitted.

Reservations, fees: Reservations at 541/474-5285. Sites are $12–19 per night, $5 for a third vehicle; $28 for a yurt per night with a $28 refundable cleaning deposit. Open year-round, but only to self-contained RVs in the winter.

Directions: In Grants Pass on I-5, take Exit 58 to 6th Street. Drive south on 6th Street to G Street. Turn west and drive seven miles (the road becomes Upper River Road, then Lower River Road). The park is on the left at 7600 Lower River Road.

Contact: Josephine County Parks, 125 Ringuette St., Grants Pass, OR 97527, 541/474-5285, fax 541/474-5288, website: www.co.josephine.or.us /parks/index.htm.

175 GRANTS PASS OVERNITERS

Rating: 6

Near Grants Pass.
Map 11.6, grid e6, page 621
This wooded park, set in a rural area just outside Grants Pass, is mostly shaded. Several other campgrounds are in the area. Don't let the name mislead you; whereas several spaces are reserved for overnighters, there are many monthly rentals at the park.

Campsites, facilities: There are eight tent sites and 26 drive-through sites for RVs of any length. Electricity, drinking water, sewer hookups, and picnic tables are provided. Flush toilets, showers, a laundry room, and a swimming pool are available. A store is within one mile. Leashed pets are permitted.

Reservations, fees: Reservations accepted. Sites are $12–18 per night, $1 per person for more than two people. Open year-round.

Directions: From Grants Pass, drive north on I-5 for three miles to Exit 61 and bear right to a stop sign and Highland Avenue. Turn left and drive a very short distance to the campground on the right.

Contact: Grants Pass Overniters, 5941 Highland Ave., Grants Pass, OR 97526, 541/479-7289.

176 RIVER PARK RV RESORT

Rating: 6

On the Rogue River.
Map 11.6, grid e6, page 621
This park has a quiet, serene riverfront setting, yet it is close to all the conveniences of a small city. Highlights here include 700 feet of Rogue River frontage for trout fishing and swimming. It's one of several parks in the immediate area.

Campsites, facilities: There are three tent sites and 47 sites for RVs. Cable TV, restrooms, showers, an RV dump station, a public phone, laundry facilities, and ice are available. Leashed pets are permitted.

Reservations, fees: Reservations at 800/677-8857. Sites are $25 per night, $3 per person for more than two people. Major credit cards accepted. Open year-round.

Directions: In Grants Pass on I-5, take Exit 55 west to Highway 199. Drive west two miles to Parkdale. Turn left on Parkdale and drive one block to Highway 99. Turn left on Highway 99 and drive two miles to the park on the left.

Contact: River Park RV Resort, 2956 Rogue River Hwy., Grants Pass, OR 97527, 800/677-8857 or 541/479-0046, fax 541/471-1448, website: www.riverparkrvresort.com.

177 GRANTS PASS/REDWOOD HIGHWAY KOA

Rating: 8

Near Grants Pass.
Map 11.6, grid e5, page 621
This KOA campground along a stream in the hills outside of Grants Pass attracts bird-watchers. It also makes a perfect layover spot for travelers who want to get away from the highway for a while. For an interesting side trip,

drive south down scenic U.S. 199 to Cave Junction or Illinois River State Park.

Campsites, facilities: There are 40 sites for tents or RVs, one cabin, and on RV rental. Restrooms, showers, drinking water, an RV dump station, security, a public phone, a laundry room, limited groceries, ice, RV supplies, LP gas, and a barbecue are available. There are also a recreation hall, a playground, and a recreation field. Leashed pets are permitted.

Reservations, fees: Reservations at 800/562-7556. Sites are $21–30 per night, $2–3 per person for more than two people. Major credit cards accepted. Open year-round.

Directions: In Grants Pass on I-5, take the U.S. 199 exit. Turn southwest on U.S. 199 and drive 14.5 miles to the campground on the right (at Milepost 14.5).

Contact: Grants Pass/ Redwood Highway KOA, 13370 Redwood Hwy., Wilderville, OR 97543, 541/476-6508, website: www.koa.com.

178 SCHROEDER

Rating: 9

On the Rogue River.

Map 11.6, grid e5, page 621

Trout fishing, swimming, and boating are among the possibilities at this camp along the Rogue River. Just a short jog off the highway, it makes an excellent layover for I-5 travelers. It's not a highly publicized camp, so many tourists pass by it in favor of the more commercial camps in the area. The park is set close to Hellgate Excursions, which provides jet-boat trips on the Rogue River. Tennis courts are close by, and horse rentals are available within a 10-minute drive.

Campsites, facilities: There are 22 tent sites and 28 sites, three with partial hookups, for RVs, and two yurts. Restrooms, coin-operated showers, and a public phone are available. Recreational facilities include horseshoes, a recreation field, a barbecue, a playground, and

a boat ramp. Some facilities are wheelchair accessible. Leashed pets are permitted.

Reservations, fees: Reservations at 541/474-5285. Sites are $13–20 per night, $5 for a third vehicle. Major credit cards accepted. Open year-round.

Directions: In Grants Pass on I-5, take Exit 58 to U.S. 199. Drive west on U.S. 199 for four miles to the campground.

Contact: Josephine County Parks, 125 Ringuette St., Grants Pass, OR 97527, 541/474-5285, fax 541/474-5288, website: www.co.josephine.or.us /parks/index.htm.

179 ROGUE VALLEY OVERNITERS

Rating: 5

Near the Rogue River.

Map 11.6, grid e6, page 621

This park is just off the freeway in Grants Pass, the jumping-off point for trips down the Rogue River. The summer heat in this part of Oregon can surprise visitors in late June and early July. This is a nice, comfortable park with shade trees.

Campsites, facilities: There are 110 sites for tents or self-contained RVs; 26 are drive-through sites. Electricity, drinking water, cable TV, and sewer hookups are provided. Flush toilets, an RV dump station, showers, and a laundry room are available. Bottled gas, a store, a café, and ice are available within one mile. Leashed pets are permitted.

Reservations, fees: Reservations accepted. Sites are $20–22 per night, $2 per person for more than two people. Senior discount available. Open year-round.

Directions: In Grants Pass on I-5, take Exit 58 to 6th Street. Drive south on 6th Street for one-quarter mile to the park on the right.

Contact: Rogue Valley Overniters, 1806 N.W. 6th St., Grants Pass, OR 97526, 541/479-2208.

180 CIRCLE W RV PARK

Rating: 6

On the Rogue River.

Map 11.6, grid e7, page 621

This campground along the Rogue River is close to chartered boat trips down the Rogue and a golf course. Fishing and swimming access are available from the campground. No tents are permitted here.

Campsites, facilities: There are 25 sites for RVs of any length; four are drive-through sites. Electricity, drinking water, sewer hookups, and picnic tables are provided. Flush toilets, an RV dump station, showers, a laundry room, and ice are available. A boat dock is nearby. Leashed pets are permitted.

Reservations, fees: Reservations accepted. Sites are $22 per night, $1.50 per person for more than two people. Open year-round.

Directions: From Grants Pass, drive south on I-5 for 10 miles to Exit 48 at Rogue River. Take that exit west (over the bridge) to Highway 99. Turn right and drive west one mile to the camp.

Contact: Circle W RV Park, 8110 Rogue River Hwy., Grants Pass, OR 97527, 541/582-1686.

181 HAVE A NICE DAY CAMPGROUND

Rating: 6

On the Rogue River.

Map 11.6, grid e7, page 621

This campground with grassy, shaded sites is set along the Rogue River, where fishing, swimming, and boating are options. It has nice river views.

Campsites, facilities: There are 22 sites for tents or RVs and 18 for RVs only, including some sites that are drive-through and some with sewer hook-ups. Electricity, drinking water, and picnic tables are provided. Flush toilets, an RV dump station, showers, a laundry room, and a playground are available. A store and a café are within two miles. Boat docks and launching facilities are nearby. Leashed pets are permitted.

Reservations, fees: Reservations accepted. Sites are $17 per night, $1.50 per person for more than two people. Monthly rentals available. Open year-round, weather permitting, with limited winter facilities.

Directions: From Grants Pass, drive south on I-5 for seven miles to Exit 48 at Rogue River. Take that exit and drive west over the bridge to Highway 99. Turn right (downriver) and drive west for 2.5 miles to the campground (on both sides of the road).

Contact: Have a Nice Day Campground, 7275 Rogue River Hwy., Grants Pass, OR 97527, 541/582-1421.

182 RIVERFRONT RV PARK

Rating: 6

On the Rogue River.

Map 11.6, grid e7, page 621

This spot is convenient to good fishing, swimming, and boating on the Rogue River. Many of these large sites face the river. This park features a round driveway, so there is no backing up. No tents are permitted here, and some sites are rented for the entire summer season.

Campsites, facilities: There are 22 sites, 19 with full hookups and three with partial hookups, for RVs of any length. Electricity, drinking water, sewer and cable TV hookups, and picnic tables are provided. Flush toilets, an RV dump station, showers, a laundry room, and ice are available. Bottled gas, a store, and a café are within two miles. Fishing docks, boat docks, and launching facilities are nearby. Small leashed pets are permitted.

Reservations, fees: Reservations accepted. Sites are $20 per night, $2.50 per person for more than two people. Monthly rates available. Open year-round.

Directions: From Grants Pass, drive south on I-5 for seven miles to Exit 48 and Highway 99.

Take that exit, bear west on Highway 99, and drive two miles to the park on the right.
Contact: Riverfront RV Park, 7060 Rogue River Hwy., Grants Pass, OR 97527, 541/582-0985.

183 LAZY ACRES RV & MOTEL

Rating: 6

On the Rogue River.
Map 11.6, grid e8, page 621
This wooded campground on the Rogue River may be a bit less scenic than KOA Gold n' Rogue, but its evergreen, maple, and birch trees still make this a beautiful spot. The camp also offers the same recreation options. No tent camping is permitted.

Campsites, facilities: There are 68 sites with full hookups for RVs of any length and a 6-unit motel. Electricity, drinking water, sewer hookups, and picnic tables are provided. Flush toilets, bottled gas, cable TV, a dump station, a playground, and a laundry room are available. Boat docks are nearby. Leashed pets are permitted.

Reservations, fees: Reservations accepted. Sites are $20 per night, $2 per person for more than two people. Major credit cards accepted. Monthly rates available. Open year-round.

Directions: From Medford, drive north on I-5 for 18 miles to the South Gold Hill exit. Take that exit and drive one-quarter mile north to 2nd Avenue. Turn west and drive 1.2 miles to the campground on the left.

Contact: Lazy Acres RV, 1550 2nd Ave., Gold Hill, OR 97525, 541/855-7000.

184 VALLEY OF THE ROGUE STATE PARK

Rating: 7

On the Rogue River.
Map 11.6, grid e8, page 621
With easy highway access, this popular spot along the banks of the Rogue River often fills to near capacity during the summer. Recre-ation options include fishing and boating. This spot makes a good base camp for taking in the Rogue Valley and surrounding attractions: Crater Lake National Park, Oregon Caves National Monument, historic Jacksonville, Ashland's Shakespeare Festival, or the Britt Music Festival.

Campsites, facilities: There are 21 sites for tents or self-contained RVs and 146 sites with full or partial hookups for RVs up to 75 feet long. Three group tent areas for up to 25 people each and six yurts are available. Picnic tables and fire grills are provided. Flush toilets, drinking water, garbage bins, an RV dump station, showers, firewood, two laundry rooms, a meeting hall, and playgrounds are available. A restaurant is nearby. Some facilities are wheelchair accessible. Boat-launching facilities are nearby. Leashed pets are permitted.

Reservations, fees: Reservations at 800/452-5687 or website: www.OregonStateParks.org ($7 reservation fee). Sites are $12–18 per night. Group areas are $60 per area, yurts are $27 per night, and extra vehicles are $7 per night. Open year-round. Major credit cards accepted.

Directions: From Grants Pass, drive south on I-5 for 12 miles to Exit 45B. Take that exit, turn right, and drive one mile to the park on the right.

Contact: Valley of the Rogue State Park, 3792 N. River Rd., Gold Hill, OR 97525, 541/582-1118.

185 KOA GOLD N' ROGUE

Rating: 6

On the Rogue River.
Map 11.6, grid e8, page 621
This campground is set a half mile from the Rogue River, with a golf course, bike paths, and the Oregon Vortex in the vicinity. It's one of the many camps between Gold Hill and Grants Pass.

Campsites, facilities: There are 53 sites, 27

drive-through, for RVs of any length, 12 tent sites, and four cabins. Electricity, drinking water, sewer hookups, and picnic tables are provided. Flush toilets, bottled gas, an RV dump station, showers, firewood, a store, a laundry room, ice, a playground, and a swimming pool are available. A café is within one mile, and boat-launching facilities are within five miles. Leashed pets are permitted.

Reservations, fees: Reservations at 800/562-7608. Sites are $21–28 per night, $2 per person for more than two people. Major credit cards accepted. Open year-round.

Directions: From Medford, drive north on I-5 for 10 miles to South Gold Hill and Exit 40. Take that exit, turn right, and drive one-quarter mile to Blackwell Road. Turn right (on a paved road) and drive one-quarter mile to the park.

Contact: KOA Gold n' Rogue, 12297 Blackwell Rd., Gold Hill, OR 97525, 541/855-7710, website: www.koa.com.

186 LAKE SELMAC

Rating: 9

On Lake Selmac.

Map 11.6, grid f4, page 621

Nestled in a wooded, mountainous area, this 300-acre park offers swimming, hiking, boating, sailing, and good trout fishing on beautiful Lake Selmac. There are seasonal hosts and an assistant park ranger on-site.

Campsites, facilities: There are 81 sites for tents or RVs up to 32 feet long and two yurts. Drinking water and picnic tables are provided. Facilities include restrooms, coin-operated showers, an RV dump station, a public phone, snacks, a barbecue, horseshoes, a playground, a recreation field, two boat ramps, and a dock. Some facilities are wheelchair accessible. Leashed pets are permitted.

Reservations, fees: Reservations at 541/474-5285. Sites are $13–20 per night, $5 for a third vehicle, and $28 per night for a yurt plus a $28

refundable deposit. Open year-round, with limited winter service.

Directions: In Grants Pass on I-5, take the U.S. 199 exit. Turn southwest on U.S. 199 and drive for 23 miles to Selma and the Lake Selmac exit (Lakeshore Drive). Turn left (east) and drive two miles to the lake and the campground entrance.

Contact: Josephine County Parks, 125 Ringuette St., Grants Pass, OR 97527, 541/474-5285, fax 541/474-5288, website: www.co.josephine.or.us /parks/index.htm.

187 LAKE SELMAC RESORT

Rating: 7

On Lake Selmac.

Map 11.6, grid f4, page 621

This resort is set along the shore of Lake Selmac. Fishing is great for largemouth bass (the state record has been set here three times). Trout, crappie, bluegill, and catfish are also catchable here. There is a 5-mph speed limit on the lake. A trail circles the lake, and hikers, bikers, and horses are welcome. A golf course is about six miles away. Oregon Caves National Monument, about 30 miles away, makes a good side trip.

Campsites, facilities: There are 29 sites for tents or RVs of any length. Electricity, drinking water, fire rings, and picnic tables are provided. Flush toilets, showers, firewood, a store, a café, a laundry room, ice, and a playground are available. Boat docks and launching facilities are nearby, and rentals are on-site. Horseback riding trails are available in the summer. Leashed pets are permitted. Corrals are available for horse campers.

Reservations, fees: Reservations accepted. Sites are $17–19 per night. Major credit cards accepted. Open year-round, with limited winter facilities.

Directions: In Grants Pass on I-5, take the U.S. 199 exit. Turn southwest on U.S. 199 and drive 23 miles to Selma and the Lake Selmac exit

(Lakeshore Drive). Turn left (east) and drive 2.5 miles to the lake and the resort on the left.
Contact: Lake Selmac Resort, 2700 Lakeshore Dr., Selma, OR 97538, 541/597-2277, website: www.lakeselmacresort.com.

188 TOWN AND COUNTRY RV PARK

Rating: 7

On the Illinois River.

Map 11.6, grid g3, page 621

This park on the Illinois River provides good opportunities for swimming and boating (no motors are permitted). Nearby side trips include Oregon Caves National Monument (21 miles) and Grants Pass (31 miles). Crescent City is 50 miles away. Note that a majority of the campground is taken by monthly rentals, with the remainder available for overnighters.

Campsites, facilities: There are 51 sites for tents or RVs. Cable TV, showers, restrooms, an RV dump station, a public phone, a laundry room, and ice are available. Horseshoe pits, a clubhouse, and a playground are also provided. Leashed pets are permitted.

Reservations, fees: Reservations recommended. Sites are $16.50 for two people per night, $2 per additional person per night. Monthly rates available. Senior discount available. Open year-round.

Directions: In Grants Pass on I-5, take Exit 55 for U.S. 199. Bear southwest on U.S. 199 for 30 miles to Cave Junction and the campground.

Contact: Town and Country RV Park, 28288 Redwood Hwy., Cave Junction, OR 97523; tel./fax 541/592-2656.

189 COUNTRY HILLS RESORT

Rating: 7

Near Oregon Caves National Monument.

Map 11.6, grid g5, page 621

Lots of sites at this wooded camp border Sucker Creek, a popular spot for swimming. Lake Selmac and Oregon Caves National Monument provide nearby side-trip options.

Campsites, facilities: There are 12 tent sites and 20 sites for RVs of any length; two are drive-through sites. There are also six cabins and a 5-unit motel. Picnic tables are provided. Flush toilets, showers, drinking water, electricity, firewood, a small store, a laundry room, a motel, an ice cream parlor, an outdoor café, and ice are available. Leashed pets are permitted.

Reservations, fees: Reservations accepted. Tent sites are $15 per night; RV sites are $19 per night. Major credit cards accepted. Open year-round.

Directions: In Grants Pass on I-5, take Exit 55 for U.S. 199. Bear southwest on U.S. 199 for 30 miles to Cave Junction and Highway 46. Turn east on Highway 46 and drive eight miles to the campground on the right.

Contact: Country Hills Resort, 7901 Caves Hwy., Cave Junction, OR 97523, 541/592-3406, fax 541/592-3406.

190 GRAYBACK

Rating: 7

Near Oregon Caves National Monument in Siskiyou National Forest.

Map 11.6, grid g5, page 621

This wooded campground at an elevation of 2,000 feet along the banks of Sucker Creek has sites with ample shade and is a good choice if you're planning to visit Oregon Caves National Monument, about 10 miles away. The camp, set in a grove of old-growth firs, is a prime place for bird-watching. A half-mile barrier-free trail cuts through the camp.

Campsites, facilities: There are 37 sites for tents or RVs up to 22 feet long; one site has a full hookup. Picnic tables, garbage bins, and fire grills are provided. Flush toilets and drinking water are available. Some facilities are wheelchair accessible. Leashed pets are permitted.

Reservations, fees: Some sites can be reserved at 541/592-3311. Sites are $15 per night, $5 per extra vehicle. Senior discount available. Open May–October.

Directions: In Grants Pass on I-5, take Exit 55 for U.S. 199. Bear southwest on U.S. 199 for 30 miles to Cave Junction and Highway 46. Turn east on Highway 46 and drive 12 miles to the campground.

Contact: Siskiyou National Forest, Illinois Valley Ranger District, P.O. Box 389, Cave Junction, OR 97523, 541/592-4000, fax 541/592-4010.

191 CAVE CREEK

Rating: 7

Near Oregon Caves National Monument in Siskiyou National Forest.

Map 11.6, grid h5, page 621

No campground is closer to Oregon Caves National Monument than this U.S. Forest Service camp, a mere four miles away. There is even a two-mile trail out of camp that leads directly to the caves. The camp, at an elevation of 2,500 feet, lies in a grove of old-growth timber along the banks of Cave Creek, a small stream with some trout fishing opportunities (catch-and-release only). The sites are shaded, and an abundance of wildlife can be spotted in the area. Hiking opportunities abound.

Campsites, facilities: There are 18 tent sites. Drinking water, garbage bins, vault toilets, and picnic tables are provided. Showers are within eight miles. Leashed pets are permitted.

Reservations, fees: Some sites can be reserved at 541/592-3311. Sites are $12 per night, $5 per extra vehicle. Senior discount available. Open mid-May–mid-September.

Directions: In Grants Pass on I-5, take Exit 55 for U.S. 199. Bear southwest on U.S. 199 for 30 miles to Cave Junction and Highway 46. Turn east on Highway 46 and drive 16 miles to Forest Road 4032. Turn right and drive south for one mile to the campground.

Contact: Siskiyou National Forest, Illinois Valley Ranger District, P.O. Box 389, Cave Junction, OR 97523, 541/592-4000, fax 541/592-4010.

192 BOLAN LAKE

Rating: 9

On Bolan Lake in Siskiyou National Forest.

Map 11.6, grid h5, page 621

Very few out-of-towners know about this camp with pretty, shaded sites along the shore of 15-acre Bolan Lake. The lake is stocked with trout, and the fishing can be good. Only nonmotorized boats are allowed. A trail from the lake leads up to a fire lookout and ties into miles of other trails, including the Bolan Lake Trail. This spot is truly a bird-watcher's paradise, with a variety of species to view. The camp is set at 5,500 feet elevation.

Campsites, facilities: There are 12 sites for tents or RVs up to 16 feet long. Picnic tables and fire grills are provided. Vault toilets and firewood are available, but there is no drinking water, and all garbage must be packed out. Leashed pets are permitted.

Reservations, fees: Reservations are not accepted. Sites are $5 per night. Senior discount available. Open July–October.

Directions: From Grants Pass, drive south on U.S. 199 for 30 miles to Cave Junction and Rockydale Road (County Road 5560). Turn southeast on Rockydale Road and drive eight miles to County Road 5828 (also called Waldo Road and Happy Camp Road). Turn southeast and drive 14 miles to Forest Road 4812. Turn east and drive four miles to Forest Road 4812-040. Turn south and drive two miles to the campground. This access road is very narrow and rough. Large RVs are strongly discouraged.

Contact: Siskiyou National Forest, Illinois Valley Ranger District, P.O. Box 389, Cave Junction, OR 97523, 541/592-4000, fax 541/592-4010.

193 FAREWELL BEND

🏃 🛶 🐕 ♿ 🚐 ⛺

Rating: 7

On the Upper Rogue River in Rogue River National Forest.

Map 11.7, grid a5, page 622

This extremely popular campground is set at an elevation of 3,400 feet along the banks of the Upper Rogue River near the Rogue River Gorge. A quarter-mile barrier-free trail leads from camp to the Rogue Gorge Viewpoint and is definitely worth the trip. The Upper Rogue River Trail passes near camp. This spot attracts a lot of the campers visiting Crater Lake. See description of Union Creek.

Campsites, facilities: There are 61 sites for tents or RVs up to 40 feet long. Picnic tables, fire grills, and fire rings are provided. Drinking water, firewood for purchase, and flush toilets are available. Some facilities are wheelchair accessible. Leashed pets are permitted.

Reservations, fees: Reservations are not accepted. Sites are $12 per night, $6 per extra vehicle a night. Senior discount available. Open late May–late October.

Directions: From Medford, drive northeast on Highway 62 for 59 miles (near Union Creek) to the campground on the left.

Contact: Rogue River National Forest, Prospect Ranger District, 47201 Hwy. 62, Prospect, OR 97536, 541/560-3400, fax 541/560-3444.

194 UNION CREEK

🏃 🛶 🐕 ♿ 🚐 ⛺

Rating: 8

Near the Upper Rogue River in Rogue River National Forest.

Map 11.7, grid a5, page 622

One of the most popular camps in the district, this spot is more developed than the nearby camps of Mill Creek, River Bridge, and Natural Bridge. It's set at 3,200 feet elevation along the banks of Union Creek, where the creek joins the Upper Rogue River. The Upper Rogue River Trail passes near camp. Interpretive programs are offered in the summer, and a convenience store and a restaurant are within walking distance. A private riding stable is less than one mile away.

Campsites, facilities: There are 78 sites for tents or RVs up to 30 feet long. Picnic tables, garbage service, and fire grills are provided. Drinking water and vault toilets are available. Firewood is available for purchase. A store and a restaurant are within walking distance. At least one toilet and one site are wheelchair accessible. Leashed pets are permitted.

Reservations, fees: Reservations are not accepted. Sites are $10 per night, $4 per second vehicle per night. Senior discount available. Open mid-May–mid-October.

Directions: From Medford, drive northeast on Highway 62 for 56 miles (near Union Creek) to the campground on the left.

Contact: Rogue River National Forest, Prospect Ranger District, 47201 Hwy. 62, Prospect, OR 97536, 541/560-3400, fax 541/560-3444.

195 NATURAL BRIDGE

🏃 🛶 🐕 ♿ 🚐 ⛺

Rating: 8

On the Upper Rogue River Trail in Rogue River National Forest.

Map 11.7, grid a5, page 622

Expect lots of company in midsummer at this popular camp, which sits at an elevation of 3,200 feet, where the Upper Rogue River runs underground. The Upper Rogue River Trail passes by the camp and follows the river for many miles to the Pacific Crest Trail in Crater Lake National Park. There is an interpretive area and a spectacular geological viewpoint adjacent to the camp. A quarter-mile, barrier-free trail is also available.

Campsites, facilities: There are 17 sites for tents or RVs up to 30 feet long. Picnic tables, garbage service, and fire grills are provided. Vault toilets are available, but there is no drinking water.

One toilet and one site are wheelchair accessible. Leashed pets are permitted.

Reservations, fees: Reservations are not accepted. Sites are $3 per night, $2.50 per extra vehicle. Senior discount available. Open early May–early November.

Directions: From Medford, drive northeast on Highway 62 for 54 miles (near Union Creek) to Forest Road 300. Turn left and drive one mile west to the campground on the right.

Contact: Rogue River National Forest, Prospect Ranger District, 47201 Hwy. 62, Prospect, OR 97536, 541/560-3400, fax 541/560-3444.

196 ABBOTT CREEK

Rating: 8

On Abbott and Woodruff Creeks in Rogue River National Forest.

Map 11.7, grid a5, page 622

Set at an elevation of 3,100 feet, at the confluence of Abbott and Woodruff Creeks about two miles from the Upper Rogue River, this camp is a better choice for visitors with children than some of the others along the Rogue River. Abbott Creek is small and tame compared to the roaring Rogue. The kids probably still won't be tempted to dip their toes, however, because the water usually runs at a body-numbing 42 degrees, even in the summer.

Campsites, facilities: There are 25 sites for tents or RVs up to 20 feet long. Picnic tables, garbage service, and fire grills are provided. Drinking water and vault toilets are available. Firewood is available for purchase. Leashed pets are permitted.

Reservations, fees: Reservations are not accepted. Sites are $8 per night, $4 per extra vehicle a night. Senior discount available. Open late May–late October.

Directions: From Medford, drive northeast on Highway 62 for 47 miles (near Union Creek) to Forest Road 68. Turn left and drive 3.5 miles west to the campground on the left.

Contact: Rogue River National Forest, Prospect

Ranger District, 47201 Hwy. 62, Prospect, OR 97536, 541/560-3400, fax 541/560-3444.

197 MILL CREEK

Rating: 7

Near the Upper Rogue River in Rogue River National Forest.

Map 11.7, grid a5, page 622

This campground (elevation of 2,800 feet) along the banks of Mill Creek, about two miles from the Upper Rogue River, features beautiful, private sites and heavy vegetation. One in a series of remote, primitive camps near Highway 62 missed by out-of-towners, this camp is an excellent choice for tenters.

Campsites, facilities: There are eight sites for tents. Picnic tables, garbage service, and fire grills are provided. Vault toilets are available. There is no drinking water. Leashed pets are permitted.

Reservations, fees: Reservations are not accepted. Sites are $5 per night, $2.50 per extra vehicle. Senior discount available. Open April–November.

Directions: From Medford, drive north on Highway 62 for 47 miles (near Union Creek) to Forest Road 30. Turn right (southeast) and drive one mile to the campground on the right.

Contact: Rogue River National Forest, Prospect Ranger District, 47201 Hwy. 62, Prospect, OR 97536, 541/560-3400, fax 541/560-3444.

198 RIVER BRIDGE

Rating: 7

On the Upper Rogue River in Rogue River National Forest.

Map 11.7, grid b5, page 622

This campground, situated at 2,900 feet elevation along the banks of the Upper Rogue River, is particularly scenic, with secluded sites and river views. This is a calmer part of the Wild and Scenic Upper Rogue River, but swimming and rafting are not recommended. The Upper Rogue River Trail passes by the camp and follows the river for many miles to the Pacific Crest Trail in Crater Lake National Park.

Campsites, facilities: There are six sites for tents. Picnic tables, garbage service, and fireplaces are provided. Vault toilets are available. There is no drinking water. Leashed pets are permitted.

Reservations, fees: Reservations are not accepted. Sites are $5 per night, $2.50 per extra vehicle. Senior discount available. Open April–November, weather permitting.

Directions: From Medford, drive northeast on Highway 62 (Crater Lake Highway) for 42 miles (before reaching Union Creek) to Forest Road 6210. Turn left and drive one mile north to the campground on the left.

Contact: Rogue River National Forest, Prospect Ranger District, 47201 Hwy. 62, Prospect, OR 97536, 541/560-3400, fax 541/560-3444.

199 HUCKLEBERRY MOUNTAIN

Rating: 6

Near Crater Lake National Park in Rogue River National Forest.

Map 11.7, grid b6, page 622

Here's a hideaway for Crater Lake visitors. The camp is located at the site of an old 1930s Civilian Conservation Corps camp, and an ATV trail runs through and next to the campground. Set at an elevation of 5,400 feet, this camp, about 15 miles from the entrance to Crater Lake National Park, really does get overlooked by highway travelers, so you have a good shot at privacy.

Campsites, facilities: There are 25 primitive sites for tents or RVs up to 26 feet long. Picnic tables and fireplaces are provided. Drinking water and vault toilets are available, but all garbage must be packed out. Leashed pets are permitted.

Reservations, fees: Reservations are not ac-

cepted. There is no fee for camping. Open June–late October.

Directions: From Medford, drive north on Highway 62 for 52 miles (near Union Creek) to Forest Road 60. Turn south and drive 12 miles to the campground on the right.

Note: The access road is quite rough; large RVs are not recommended.

Contact: Rogue River National Forest, Prospect Ranger District, 47201 Hwy. 62, Prospect, OR 97536, 541/560-3400, fax 541/560-3444.

200 MAZAMA

Rating: 6

Near the Pacific Crest Trail in Crater Lake National Park.

Map 11.7, grid a8, page 622

One of two campgrounds at Crater Lake—the other being Lost Creek—this camp sits at 6,000 feet elevation and is known for cold nights, even in late June and early September. I once got caught in a snowstorm here at the opening in mid-June. A nearby store is a great convenience. The Pacific Crest Trail passes near the camp, but the only trail access down to Crater Lake is at Cleetwood Cove. Note that winter access to the park is from the west only on Highway 62 to Rim Village.

Campsites, facilities: There are 213 sites for tents or RVs up to 32 feet long. Picnic tables, fire grills, and garbage bins are provided. Drinking water, flush toilets, an RV dump station, coin-operated showers, a laundry room, gas pumps, a mini-mart, firewood, and ice are available. Some facilities are wheelchair accessible. Leashed pets are permitted on paved roads only.

Reservations, fees: Reservations are not accepted. Sites are $15–19 per night, plus a $10 park entrance fee per vehicle and $3.50 per person for more than two people. Senior discount available. Open late June–early October.

Directions: From I-5 at Medford, turn east on Highway 62 and drive 72 miles into Crater Lake

National Park and to Annie Springs junction. Turn left and drive to the national park entrance kiosk. Just beyond the kiosk, turn right to the campground and Mazama store entrance.

Contact: Crater Lake National Park, P.O. Box 7, Crater lake, OR 97604, 541/594-3000.

201 LOST CREEK

Rating: 6

Near the Crater Lake Pinnacles in Crater Lake National Park.
Map 11.7, grid b8, page 622

In good weather this is a prime spot in Crater Lake National Park; you avoid most of the crowd on Rim Drive. This campground is located near little Lost Creek and the Pinnacles, a series of spires. The only trail access down to Crater Lake is at Cleetwood Cove. This campground is set in a lodgepole pine forest and is more private than Mazama Campground. There are paved roads in the campground and there is a possibility (hint, hint) that a black bear could visit your campsite. Follow all bear precautions described in the Camping Tips section of this book.

Campsites, facilities: There are 16 sites for tents. Picnic tables and fire grills are provided. Drinking water, flush toilets, and garbage bins are available. Leashed pets are permitted on paved roads only.

Reservations, fees: Reservations are not accepted. Sites are $10 per night, plus a $10 park entrance fee per vehicle and $3.50 per person for more than two people. Senior discount available. Open mid-July–mid-September, weather permitting.

Directions: From I-5 at Medford, turn east on Highway 62 and drive 72 miles into Crater Lake National Park and to Annie Springs junction. Turn left and drive to the junction with Rim Drive. Turn right and drive east on Rim Drive to Pinnacles Road Junction. Turn right on Pinnacles Road and drive five miles to the campground.

Contact: Crater Lake National Park, P.O. Box 7, Crater Lake, OR 97604, 541/594-3000.

202 BEAR MOUNTAIN RV PARK

Rating: 7

On the Rogue River.
Map 11.7, grid c2, page 622

This campground is set in an open, grassy area on the Rogue River about six miles from Lost Creek Lake, where boat ramps and picnic areas are available for day use. The campsites are spacious and shaded.

Campsites, facilities: There are some tent sites and 37 drive-through sites for RVs of any length; 30 have full hookups and seven have partial hookups. Electricity, drinking water, sewer hookups, and picnic tables are provided. Flush toilets, bottled gas, an RV dump station, showers, a laundry room, ice, and a playground are available. A store and a café are within one mile. Boat docks and launching facilities are nearby. Leashed pets are permitted.

Reservations, fees: Reservations at 541/878-2400 (from Oregon) or 800/586-2327 (from outside Oregon). Sites are $14–18 per night, $2 per person for more than two people. Major credit cards accepted. Open year-round.

Directions: From Medford, drive northeast on Highway 62 to the junction with Highway 227. Continue east on Highway 62 for 2.5 more miles to the campground.

Contact: Bear Mountain RV Park, 27301 Hwy. 62, Trail, OR 97541, 541/878-2400.

203 ROGUE ELK CAMPGROUND

Rating: 8

On the Rogue River east of the city of Trail.
Map 11.7, grid c3, page 622

Set right on the Rogue River at an elevation of 1,476 feet, the park has hiking trails, creek swimming (unsupervised), fishing, rafting, a Douglas fir forest, and wildlife. The forest is very beautiful here. Lost Creek Lake on Highway 62 makes a good side trip.

Campsites, facilities: There are 37 sites for tents or RVs of up to 25 feet long; 15 are partial hookups. Picnic tables and fire pits are provided. Drinking water, restrooms with flush toilets and coin-operated showers, garbage bins, a dump station, a soft drink machine, a boat ramp, and a playground are available. Some facilities are wheelchair accessible. A café, a mini-mart, ice, laundry facilities, and firewood are available within three miles. Leashed pets are permitted.

Reservations, fees: Reservations are not accepted. Family sites are $16–18 per night, $6 for a third vehicle, and $1 per pet per night. Senior discount available. Open mid-April–mid-October.

Directions: From Medford, take Exit 30 for the Crater Lake Highway (Highway 62) and drive northeast on Highway 62 for 29 miles to the park entrance (well signed).

Contact: Jackson County Parks, 400 Antelope Rd., White City, OR 97503, 541/774-8183, fax 541/774-6320; www.jacksoncountyparks.com.

204 JOSEPH H. STEWART STATE PARK

Rating: 7

On Lost Creek Reservoir.
Map 11.7, grid c3, page 622

This state park is on the shore of Lost Creek Reservoir, a lake with a marina, a beach, and boat rentals. Home to eight miles of hiking and biking trails, the park is about 40 miles from Crater Lake National Park and makes an excellent jumping-off point for an exploration of southern Oregon.

Campsites, facilities: There are 151 sites with partial hookups (water and electricity) for tents or self-contained RVs, including some sites for RVs up to 80 feet long, and 50 sites for tents or self-contained RVs, and two group tent areas. Picnic tables and fire grills are provided. Flush

toilets, garbage bins, drinking water, an RV dump station, showers, firewood, and a playground are available. Boat rentals and launching facilities are nearby. Leashed pets are permitted.

Reservations, fees: Reservations are not accepted. Sites are $14–15 per night, $7 per extra vehicle. Reservations for the group site at 800/452-5687 or website: www.OregonStateParks.org ($7 reservation fee); $60 per night. Major credit cards accepted. Open mid-April–late October.

Directions: From Medford, drive northeast on Highway 62 for 34 miles to the Lost Creek Reservoir and the campground on the left.

Contact: Joseph H. Stewart State Park, 35251 Hwy. 62, Trail, OR 97541, 800/551-6949 or 541/560-3334.

205 WHISKEY SPRINGS

Rating: 9

Near Burre Falls in Rogue River National Forest.
Map 11.7, grid c5, page 622

This campground at Whiskey Springs, near Fourbit Ford Campground, is one of the larger, more developed backwoods U.S. Forest Service camps in the area. A one-mile, wheelchair-accessible nature trail passes nearby. You can see beaver dams and woodpeckers here. The camp is set at 3,200 feet elevation.

Campsites, facilities: There are 34 sites for tents or RVs up to 30 feet long. Picnic tables, garbage service, and fire grills are provided. Drinking water and vault toilets are available. Firewood is available for purchase. Boat docks, launching facilities, and rentals are within 1.5 miles. Some facilities are wheelchair accessible. Leashed pets are permitted.

Reservations, fees: Reservations are not accepted. Sites are $8 per night, $4 per extra vehicle a night. Senior discount available. Open late May–September.

Directions: From Medford, drive northeast on

Highway 62 for 16 miles to the Butte Falls Highway. Turn right and drive east for 16 miles to the town of Butte Falls. Continue southeast on Butte Falls Highway for nine miles to Forest Road 3065. Turn left on Forest Road 3065 and drive 300 yards to the campground on the left.
Contact: Rogue River National Forest, Butte Falls Ranger District, 800 Laurel St., P.O. Box 227, Butte Falls, OR 97522, 541/865-2700, fax 541/865-2795.

206 IMNAHA

Rating: 7

Near the Sky Lakes Wilderness in Rogue River National Forest.
Map 11.7, grid c6, page 622
This campground along Imnaha Creek at an elevation of 3,800 feet makes a good base camp for a wilderness trip. Trailheads at the ends of the nearby forest roads lead east into the Sky Lakes Wilderness; there are also two, shorter interpretive trails.
Campsites, facilities: There are four sites for tents. Picnic tables, garbage service, and fire grills are provided. Drinking water and vault toilets are available. A furnished cabin is also available. Leashed pets are permitted.
Reservations, fees: Reservations are not accepted for tent sites. Sites are $5 per night, $2.50 per extra vehicle. Reservations required at 541/865-2700 for the cabin; $40 per night. Senior discount available. Open mid-June–mid-November.
Directions: From Medford, drive northeast on Highway 62 for about 35 miles to Prospect and Mill Creek Drive. Turn right and drive one mile to County Road 992/Butte Falls Prospect Highway. Turn right and drive 2.5 miles to Forest Road 37. Turn left and drive 10 miles east to the campground.
Contact: Rogue River National Forest, Butte Falls Ranger District, 800 Laurel St., P.O. Box 227, Butte Falls, OR 97522, 541/865-2700, fax 541/865-2795.

207 SOUTH FORK

Rating: 7

On the South Rogue River in Rogue River National Forest.
Map 11.7, grid c6, page 622
This campground is set at an elevation of 4,000 feet along the South Rogue River. To the east, trails at the ends of the nearby forest roads provide access to the Sky Lakes Wilderness. The Southfork Trail, across the road from the campground, has a good biking trail in one direction and a hiking trail in the other. A map of Rogue River National Forest details all back roads, trails, and waters.
Campsites, facilities: There are two sites for tents and four sites for tents or RVs up to 15 feet long. Picnic tables, drinking water, garbage service, and fire grills are provided. Vault toilets are available. Leashed pets are permitted.
Reservations, fees: Reservations are not accepted. Sites are $3 per night, $1.50 per extra vehicle. Senior discount available. Open mid-June–mid-November.
Directions: From Medford, drive northeast on Highway 62 for 16 miles to Butte Falls Highway. Turn right and drive 16 miles east to the town of Butte Falls. Continue one mile past Butte Falls to County Road 992 (Butte Falls Prospect Highway) and drive nine miles to Forest Road 34. Turn right and drive 8.5 miles to the campground on the right.
Contact: Rogue River National Forest, Butte Falls Ranger District, 800 Laurel St., P.O. Box 227, Butte Falls, OR 97522, 541/865-2700, fax 541/865-2795.

208 FLY CASTERS RV PARK

Rating: 6

On the Rogue River.
Map 11.7, grid d2, page 622
This spot along the banks of the Rogue River is a good base camp for RVers who want to

fish or hike. The county park, located across the river in Shady Cove, offers picnic facilities and a boat ramp. Lost Creek Lake is about a 15-minute drive northeast. No tent camping is permitted at this park. Note that about half of the sites are taken by long-term rentals.

Campsites, facilities: There are 47 sites for RVs of any length; two are drive-through sites. Electricity, drinking water, sewer hookups, and picnic tables are provided. Flush toilets, bottled gas, showers, cable, a clubhouse, and a laundry room are available. A store, a café, and ice are within one mile. Boat-launching facilities are nearby. Leashed pets are permitted.

Reservations, fees: Reservations accepted. Sites are $17–34 per night, $1 per person for more than two people. Major credit cards accepted. Monthly rates available. Open year-round.

Directions: From Medford, drive northeast on Highway 62 for 23 miles to the campground on the right (it is 2.7 miles south of the junction of Highways 62 and 227).

Contact: Fly-Casters RV Park, 21655 Crater Lake Hwy., P.O. Box 699, Shady Cove, OR 97539, 541/878-2749, fax 541/878-2742.

209 SHADY TRAILS RV PARK AND CAMP

Rating: 7

On the Rogue River.
Map 11.7, grid d2, page 622

This grassy park with many shaded sites is set along the banks of the Rogue River in a wooded, mountainous area. Recreation options include fishing on the Rogue River and exploring Casey State Park.

Campsites, facilities: There are 10 tent sites and 49 sites for RVs of any length. Electricity, drinking water, sewer hookups, and picnic tables are provided. Flush toilets, cable TV, bottled gas, an RV dump station, showers, a store, ice, and a playground are available. A

café is within one mile. Boat-launching facilities are nearby. Leashed pets are permitted.

Reservations, fees: Reservations accepted. RV sites are $22–26 per night and tent sites are $14 per night; $2 per night for each additional person. Major credit cards accepted. Senior discount available. Open year-round.

Directions: From I-5 at Medford, drive northeast on Highway 62 for 23 miles to the campground.

Contact: Shady Trails RV Park and Camp, 1 Meadow Ln., Shady Cove, OR 97539, 541/878-2206.

210 ODESSA

Rating: 4

Near Klamath Lake in Winema National Forest.
Map 11.7, grid d8, page 622

This campground is set at an elevation of 4,100 feet along Odessa Creek, near the shore of Upper Klamath Lake. The lake is the main attraction, with fishing the main activity. The lake can provide excellent fishing for rainbow trout on both flies and Rapalas. Boating is also popular. Campsites sit in among scattered mixed conifers and native brush.

Campsites, facilities: There are five tent sites. Picnic tables, garbage bins, and fire grills are provided. Vault toilets are available, but there is no drinking water. Leashed pets are permitted.

Reservations, fees: Reservations are not accepted. There is no fee for camping. Open year-round, weather permitting.

Directions: From Klamath Falls, drive north on Highway 140 about 18 miles to Forest Road 3639. Turn northeast and drive one mile to the campground.

Contact: Winema National Forest, Klamath Ranger District, 1936 California Ave., Klamath Falls, OR 97601, 541/885-3400, fax 541/885-3452.

211 MEDFORD OAKS RV PARK

Rating: 6

Near Eagle Point.
Map 11.7, grid e2, page 622

This park is in a quiet, rural setting among the trees. Just a short hop off I-5, it's an excellent choice for travelers heading south to California. The campground is located along the shore of a pond that provides good fishing.

Campsites, facilities: There are 60 sites for tents or RVs of any length and three cabins. Restrooms, showers, an RV dump station, a public phone, a laundry room, limited groceries, ice, RV supplies, and LP gas are available. Recreational facilities include a seasonal, heated swimming pool, movies, horseshoe pits, table tennis, a recreation field for baseball and volleyball, and a playground. Call for pet policy.

Reservations, fees: Reservations are recommended. Sites are $17–30 per night. Group rates are available. Major credit cards accepted. Open year-round.

Directions: From Medford, drive northeast on Highway 62 for five miles to Exit 30 and Highway 140. Turn east on Highway 140 and drive 6.8 miles to the campground on the left.

Contact: Medford Oaks RV Park, 7049 Hwy. 140, Eagle Point, OR 97524, 541/826-5103, fax 541/826-5984, website: www.medfordoaks.com.

212 FOURBIT FORD

Rating: 6

On Fourbit Creek in Rogue River National Forest.
Map 11.7, grid d5, page 622

This campground, set at an elevation of 3,200 feet along Fourbit Creek, is one in a series of hidden spots tucked away near County Road 821.

Campsites, facilities: There are seven sites for tents. Picnic tables, garbage service, and fire grills are provided. Drinking water and vault toilets are available. A store, a café, and ice are within five miles. Boat docks, launching facilities, and rentals are nearby. Leashed pets are permitted.

Reservations, fees: Reservations are not accepted. Sites are $8 per night, $4 per extra vehicle per night. Open late May–late September.

Directions: From Medford, drive northeast on Highway 62 for 16 miles to Butte Falls Highway. Turn right and drive 16 miles east to the town of Butte Falls and County Road 821. Turn left and drive nine miles southeast to Forest Road 3065. Turn left and drive one mile to the campground on the left.

Contact: Rogue River National Forest, Butte Falls Ranger District, 800 Laurel St., P.O. Box 227, Butte Falls, OR 97522, 541/865-2700, fax 541/865-2795.

213 WILLOW LAKE RESORT

Rating: 9

On Willow Lake.
Map 11.7, grid e5, page 622

This campground is set on the shore of Willow Lake. A hiking trail starts near camp.

Campsites, facilities: There are 29 tent sites, 20 drive-through sites with full hookups for RVs, and 17 sites with electricity and water for RVs. There are also four cabins for up to six people each. Picnic tables and fire rings are provided. Flush toilets, an RV dump station, coin-operated showers, and firewood are available. Leashed pets are permitted.

Reservations, fees: Reservations accepted for groups and cabins only. Sites are $16–20 per night, $1 per pet per night. Major credit cards accepted. Senior discount available. Open mid-March–October.

Directions: From Medford, drive northeast on Highway 62 for 15 miles to Butte Falls Highway. Turn east and drive 25 miles to Willow Lake Road. Turn south and drive two miles to the campground.

Contact: Jackson County Parks, 400 Antelope Rd., White City, OR 97503, 541/774-8183, fax 541/774-6320, website: JacksonCountyParks.com.

214 PARKER MEADOWS

Rating: 7

On Parker Meadow in Rogue River National Forest.

Map 11.7, grid e6, page 622

Fantastic views of nearby Mt. McLoughlin are among the highlights of this rustic camp set at 5,000 feet elevation in a beautiful meadow. Trailheads at the ends of the forest roads lead into the Sky Lakes Wilderness. Parker Meadows is a nice spot, complete with water and lots of privacy between sites. Except during hunting season in the fall, this camp does not get much use.

Campsites, facilities: There are three sites for tents and five sites for tents or RVs up to 15 feet long. Picnic tables, garbage service, and fire grills are provided. Drinking water and vault toilets are available. Leashed pets are permitted.

Reservations, fees: Reservations are not accepted. Sites are $3 per night, $1.50 per extra vehicle. Senior discount available. Open mid-June–late October.

Directions: From Medford, drive northeast on Highway 62 for 16 miles to Butte Falls Highway. Turn right and drive 16 miles east to the town of Butte Falls and County Road 821. Turn left and drive 10 miles southeast to Forest Road 37. Turn left and drive 11 miles to the campground on the left.

Contact: Rogue River National Forest, Butte Falls Ranger District, 800 Laurel St., P.O. Box 227, Butte Falls, OR 97522, 541/865-2700, fax 541/865-2795.

215 FOURMILE LAKE

Rating: 8

At Fourmile Lake in Winema National Forest.

Map 11.7, grid e6, page 622

This beautiful spot is the only camp on the shore of Fourmile Lake. Several nearby trails provide access to the Sky Lakes Wilderness. The Pacific Crest Trail passes about two miles from camp. Primitive and with lots of solitude, it attracts a calm and quiet crowd. Afternoon winds can be a problem, and in the evening, if the wind isn't blowing, the mosquitoes often arrive. This campground is near the foot of Mt. McLoughlin (9,495 feet). There is no view of Mt. McLoughlin from the campground, though. Go to the lake for a good view.

Campsites, facilities: There are 25 sites for tents or RVs up to 22 feet long. Picnic tables, garbage bins, and fire grills are provided. Drinking water and vault toilets are available. Leashed pets are permitted.

Reservations, fees: Reservations are not accepted. Sites are $10 per night, $5 per extra vehicle. Senior discount available. Open June–late September.

Directions: From Medford, drive northeast on Highway 62 for five miles to Exit 30 and Highway 140. Turn east on Highway 140 and drive approximately 40 miles to Forest Road 3661. Turn north and drive six miles to the campground.

Contact: Winema National Forest, Klamath Ranger District, 1936 California Ave., Klamath Falls, OR 97601, 541/885-3400, fax 541/885-3452.

216 ROCKY POINT RESORT

Rating: 7

On Upper Klamath Lake.

Map 11.7, grid e8, page 622

Rocky Point Resort, at the Upper Klamath Wildlife Refuge, boasts 10 miles of canoe trails, with opportunities for fishing, boating, and canoeing.

Campsites, facilities: There are 28 sites, some drive-through, with partial or full hookups for RVs, four tent sites, four cabins, and motel rooms. Picnic tables are provided. Restrooms, drinking water, flush toilets, showers, firewood, a store, a laundry room, ice, a marina with boat gas, and boat and canoe rentals are available. There is a free boat launch and game area. A restaurant and lounge overlook the lake. Leashed pets are permitted.

Reservations, fees: Reservations accepted. Sites are $14–21 per night, $2 per person for more than two people, and $1 per pet per night. Major credit cards accepted. Open April–November.

Directions: From Klamath Falls, drive northeast on Highway 140 for about 25 miles to Rocky Point Road. Turn north and drive three miles to the campground.

Contact: Rocky Point Resort, 28121 Rocky Point Rd., Klamath Falls, OR 97601, 541/356-2287, fax 541/356-2222, website: www.rocky pointoregon.com.

217 WILLOW PRAIRIE & EQUESTRIAN CAMP

Rating: 7

Near Fish Lake in Rogue River National Forest.

Map 11.7, grid e6, page 622

There are two campgrounds here, including one for equestrian campers. This spot is located near the origin of the west branch of Willow Creek and next to a beaver swamp and several large ponds that attract sandhill cranes, ducks, geese, elk, and deer. A number of riding trails pass nearby. A map of Rogue River National Forest details the back roads and can help you get here. Fish Lake is four miles south.

Campsites, facilities: There are 10 sites for tents or RVs up to 15 feet long, one primitive cabin with cots, and an equestrian campground. Pic-

nic tables and fire grills are provided. Drinking water, vault toilets, garbage service. The equestrian camp has 10 sites for tents or small RVs, two stock water troughs, and horse corrals. A store, a café, and ice are within five miles. Boat docks, launching facilities, and rentals are nearby. A camp host is on-site. Leashed pets are permitted.

Reservations, fees: Reservations are not accepted for tent and RV sites; $6 per night, $3 per extra vehicle. Reservations required for equestrian camp and cabin at 541/865-2700. Senior discount available. Open late May–late October.

Directions: From Medford, drive northeast on Highway 62 for five miles to Exit 30 and Highway 140. Turn east on Highway 140 and drive 31.5 miles to Forest Road 37. Turn left and drive north 1.5 miles to Forest Road 3738. Turn left and drive one mile west to Forest Road 3735. Turn left and drive 100 yards to the campground. For the equestrian camp, continue for one-quarter mile to the campground entrance.

Contact: Rogue River National Forest, Butte Falls Ranger District, 800 Laurel St., Butte Falls, OR 97522, 541/865-2700, fax 541/865-2795.

218 NORTH FORK

Rating: 7

Near Fish Lake in Rogue River National Forest.

Map 11.7, grid e6, page 622

Here is a small, pretty campground with easy access from the highway and proximity to Fish Lake. Situated on the North Fork of Little Butte Creek at an elevation of 4,500 feet, it's fairly popular, so reserve your spot early. Excellent fly-fishing can be found along the Fish Lake Trail, which leads directly out of camp.

Campsites, facilities: There are six tent sites and three sites for RVs up to 24 feet long. Picnic tables and fire grills are provided. All garbage must be packed out. Vault toilets and drinking water are available. Boat docks, launching facilities, and rentals are nearby. Some facilities are wheelchair accessible, including a barrier-free vault toilet. Leashed pets are permitted.

Reservations, fees: Reservations are not accepted. Sites are $8 per night, $4 per extra vehicle. Senior discount available. Open early May–mid-November.

Directions: From Medford, drive northeast on Highway 62 for five miles to Exit 30 and Highway 140. Turn east on Highway 140 and drive 31.5 miles to Forest Road 37. Turn south and drive one-half mile to the campground.

Contact: Rogue River National Forest, Ashland Ranger District, 645 Washington St., Ashland, OR 97520, 541/482-3333, fax 541/858-2402.

219 FISH LAKE

Rating: 8

On Fish Lake in Rogue River National Forest.
Map 11.7, grid e6, page 622

Bikes can be rented here by the hour or by the day, a nice bonus. Same with boats. Add it up: Boating, fishing, hiking, and bicycling are among the recreation options at this campground on the north shore of Fish Lake. Easy one-mile access to the Pacific Crest Trail is also available. If this campground is full, Doe Point and Fish Lake Resort are nearby.

Campsites, facilities: There are 19 sites for tents or RVs up to 32 feet long and two walk-in sites for tents. There is one wheelchair-accessible site. Picnic tables, fire grills, and garbage bins are provided. Drinking water, showers, flush toilets, an RV dump station, a wheelchair-accessible picnic shelter, a store, a café, and ice are available. Firewood is available for purchase. Boat docks, launching facilities, and rentals are nearby. Leashed pets are permitted.

Reservations, fees: Reservations are not accepted for family sites. Sites are $12 per night, $6 per extra vehicle a night. Reservations for the group site required at 800/416-6992. Senior discount available. Open mid-May–mid-October, weather permitting.

Directions: From Medford, drive northeast on Highway 62 for five miles to Exit 30 and Highway 140. Turn east on Highway 140 and drive 30 miles to the campground on the right.

Contact: Rogue River National Forest, Ashland Ranger District, 645 Washington St., Ashland, OR 97520, 541/482-3333, fax 541/858-2402.

220 DOE POINT

Rating: 8

On Fish Lake in Rogue River National Forest.
Map 11.7, grid e6, page 622

This campground (at 4,600 feet elevation) sits along the north shore of Fish Lake, nearly adjacent to Fish Lake Campground. Doe Point is slightly preferable because of its dense vegetation, offering shaded, quiet, well-screened sites. Privacy, rare at many campgrounds, can be found here. Recreation options include boating, fishing, hiking, and biking, plus an easy one-mile access trail to the Pacific Crest Trail.

Campsites, facilities: There are five walk-in tent sites and 25 sites for tents or RVs up to 32 feet long. Picnic tables and fire grills are provided. Drinking water, garbage service, flush toilets, a store, a café, and ice are available. Firewood is available for purchase. Boat docks, launching facilities, boat rentals, showers, and an RV dump station are nearby. Leashed pets are permitted.

Reservations, fees: Reservations are not accepted. Sites are $12 per night, $6 per extra vehicle. Senior discount available. Open mid-May–late September.

Directions: From Medford, drive northeast on Highway 62 for five miles to Exit 30 and Highway 140. Turn east on Highway 140 and drive 30 miles to the campground on the right.

Contact: Rogue River National Forest, Ashland Ranger District, 645 Washington St., Ashland, OR 97520, 541/482-3333, fax 541/858-2402.

221 FISH LAKE RESORT

Rating: 7

On Fish Lake.
Map 11.7, grid e6, page 622

This resort along Fish Lake is privately operated under permit by the U.S. Forest Service and offers a resort-type feel, catering primarily to families. Hiking, bicycling, fishing, and boating are some of the activities here. This is the largest and most developed of the three camps at Fish Lake. Cozy cabins are available for rent. Boat speed on the lake is limited to 10 mph.

Campsites, facilities: There are six tent sites and 45 sites for RVs up to 30 feet long, plus 11 cabins. Electricity, drinking water, sewer hookups, garbage bins, and picnic tables are provided. Flush toilets, bottled gas, an RV dump station, showers, a recreation hall, a store, a café, a laundry room, ice, boat docks, boat rentals, and launching facilities are available. Leashed pets are permitted.

Reservations, fees: Reservations at 541/949-8500. Sites are $17–23 per night. Major credit cards accepted. Open May–October, weather permitting.

Directions: From Medford, drive northeast on Highway 62 for five miles to Exit 30 and Highway 140. Turn east on Highway 140 and drive 30 miles to Fish Lake Road. Turn right (south) and drive one-half mile to the campground on the left.

Contact: Fish Lake Resort, P.O. Box 990, Eagle Point, OR 97524, 541/949-8500.

222 LAKE OF THE WOODS RESORT

Rating: 9

On Lake of the Woods.
Map 11.7, grid f7, page 622

On beautiful Lake of the Woods, this resort offers fishing (four kinds of trout, catfish, and bass) and boating in a secluded forest setting.

It's on one of the most beautiful lakes in the Cascade Mountains, surrounded by tall pine trees. A family-oriented campground, it has all the amenities. In the winter, snowmobiling and cross-country skiing are popular (you can rent equipment at the resort). Attractions in the area include the Mountain Lakes Wilderness and the Pacific Crest Trail.

Campsites, facilities: There are 27 sites for tents or RVs up to 35 feet long, plus eight cabins that can accommodate one–six people. Restrooms, showers, an RV dump station, a public phone, a laundry room, ice, snacks, a restaurant, a lounge, and LP gas bottles are available. There are also a boat ramp, a dock, a marina, boat and mountain bike rentals, and a barbecue. Leashed pets are permitted.

Reservations, fees: Reservations are not accepted for family sites. Sites are $16–20 per night and double sites are $32 per night; $4 per extra vehicle, $5 per pet per night. Reservations for groups required at 541/949-8300. Open year-round, weather permitting.

Directions: In Medford on I-5, take Exit 14 to Highway 66. Drive east for less than a mile to Dead Indian Memorial Road. Turn left (east) and drive 40 miles to Lake of the Woods Road. Turn north and drive less than one-half mile to the resort.

Contact: Lake of the Woods Resort, 950 Harriman Rte., Klamath Falls, OR 97601, 541/949-8300, fax 541/949-8229, website: www.lakeof thewoodsresort.com.

223 ASPEN POINT

Rating: 8

On Lake of the Woods in Winema National Forest.
Map 11.7, grid f7, page 622

This campground (at 5,000 feet elevation) is near the north shore of Lake of the Woods, adjacent to Lake of the Woods Resort. It's heavily timbered with old-growth fir and has a great view of Mt. McLoughlin (9,495 feet).

A hiking trail just north of camp leads north for several miles, wandering around Fourmile Lake and extending into the Sky Lakes Wilderness. Other trails nearby head into the Mountain Lakes Wilderness. Fishing, swimming, boating, and water-skiing are among the activities here. Note that of the 60 campsites, 20 are available by reservation, the rest are first-come, first-served.

Campsites, facilities: There are 60 sites for tents or RVs up to 55 feet long. Picnic tables, garbage bins, and fire grills are provided. Drinking water, an RV dump station, and flush toilets are available. Boat docks, launching facilities, and rentals are nearby. Leashed pets are permitted.

Reservations, fees: Reservations at 877/444-6777 or website: www.ReserveUsa.com ($9 reservation fee). Sites are $13 per night, $6 per extra vehicle. Senior discount available. Open late May–late September.

Directions: In Medford on I-5, take Exit 14 to Highway 66. Drive east for less than a mile to Dead Indian Memorial Road. Turn left (east) and drive 40 miles to Lake of the Woods. Continue along the east shore to the campground turnoff on the left.

Contact: Winema National Forest, Klamath Ranger District, 1936 California Ave., Klamath Falls, OR 97601, 541/885-3400, fax 541/885-3452.

224 SUNSET

Rating: 8

Near Lake of the Woods in Winema National Forest.

Map 11.7, grid f7, page 622

This campground (at 5,000 feet elevation) near the eastern shore of Lake of the Woods is fully developed and offers a myriad of recreation options. It's popular for both fishing and boating. Of the 67 sites, 20 are available by reservation.

Campsites, facilities: There are 67 sites for tents or RVs up to 55 feet long. Picnic tables, garbage bins, and fire grills are provided. Drinking water and flush toilets are available. Some facilities are wheelchair accessible. Boat docks, launching facilities, and rentals are nearby. Leashed pets are permitted.

Reservations, fees: Reservations at 877/444-6777 or website: www.ReserveUsa.com ($9 reservation fee). Sites are $13 per night, $6 per extra vehicle. Senior discount available. Open June–mid-September.

Directions: In Medford on I-5, take Exit 14 to Highway 66. Drive east for less than a mile to Dead Indian Memorial Road. Turn left (east) and drive 40 miles to Lake of the Woods. Continue along the east shore to Forest Road 3738. Turn west and drive one-half mile to the camp.

Contact: Winema National Forest, Klamath Ranger District, 1936 California Ave., Klamath Falls, OR 97601, 541/885-3400, fax 541/885-3452.

225 DALEY CREEK

Rating: 6

On Daley Creek in Rogue River National Forest.

Map 11.7, grid f6, page 622

This campground (at 4,500 feet elevation) along the banks of Daley Creek among old-growth Douglas and white fir is a primitive and free alternative to some of the more developed spots in the area. The camp sits near the confluence of Beaver Dam and Daley Creeks. The Beaver Dam Trail heads right out of camp, running along the creek. Fishing can be decent downstream from here.

Campsites, facilities: There are three tent sites and three sites for RVs up to 18 feet long. Picnic tables, garbage bins, and fire grills are provided, but there is no drinking water. Some facilities are wheelchair accessible, including two campsites and a barrier-free vault toilet. Leashed pets are permitted.

Reservations, fees: Reservations are not accepted.

Sites are $5 per night, $2 per extra vehicle. Senior discount available. Open early May–mid-November.

Directions: In Ashland on I-5, take Exit 14 to Highway 66. Drive east for less than a mile to Dead Indian Memorial Road. Turn left (east) and drive 22 miles to Forest Road 37. Turn north and drive 1.5 miles to the campground.

Contact: Rogue River National Forest, Ashland Ranger District, 645 Washington St., Ashland, OR 97520, 541/482-3333, fax 541/858-2402.

226 BEAVER DAM

Rating: 5

On Beaver Dam Creek in Rogue River National Forest.

Map 11.7, grid f6, page 622

This campground sits at an elevation of 4,500 feet along Beaver Dam Creek. Look for beaver dams. There's not much screening between sites, but it's a pretty, rustic, and quiet spot, with unusual vegetation along the creek for botany fans. The trailhead for the Beaver Dam Trail is also here. The camp is adjacent to Daley Creek Campground.

Campsites, facilities: There are two primitive tent sites and two sites for RVs up to 16 feet long. Picnic tables, garbage bins, and fire grills are provided. Vault toilets are available, but there is no drinking water. Leashed pets are permitted.

Reservations, fees: Reservations are not accepted. Sites are $5 per night, $2 per extra vehicle. Senior discount available. Open early May–early November.

Directions: In Medford on I-5, take Exit 14 to Highway 66. Drive east for less than a mile to Dead Indian Memorial Road. Turn left (east) and drive 22 miles to Forest Road 37. Turn left (north) and drive 1.5 miles to the campground.

Contact: Rogue River National Forest, Ashland Ranger District, 645 Washington St., Ashland, OR 97520, 541/482-3333, fax 541/858-2402.

227 CANTRALL-BUCKLEY PARK & GROUP CAMP

Rating: 8

On the Applegate River.

Map 11.7, grid g1, page 622

This county park outside of Medford offers pleasant, shady sites in a wooded setting. The Applegate River, which has good trout fishing, runs nearby.

Campsites, facilities: There are 25 sites for tents or self-contained RVs up to 25 feet long and one group area for up to 60–100 people. Picnic tables and fire pits are provided. Drinking water, restrooms, coin-operated showers, and a public phone are available. Recreational facilities include horseshoes, a playground, and a recreation field. Leashed pets are permitted.

Reservations, fees: Reservations are not accepted. Sites are $10 per night, $1 per pet per night. Senior discount available. Reservations for the group site required at 541/774-8183. Major credit cards accepted with reservations only. Open year-round.

Directions: In Medford on I-5, take the Jacksonville exit to the Jacksonville Highway. Drive west on the Jacksonville Highway (Highway 238) for seven miles to Jacksonsville. Bear left on Highway 238 and drive to Hamilton Road. Turn south on Hamilton Road and drive to Cantrall Road. Turn right on Cantrall and drive to the campground.

Contact: Jackson County Parks, 400 Antelope Rd., White City, OR 97503, 541/774-8183, fax 541/774-6320, website: www.jacksoncounty parks.com.

228 THE WELLSPRINGS

Rating: 5

Near Ashland.

Map 11.7, grid g3, page 622

Hey, massages are free here. After getting this book done, we'll take two. This wooded campground has mineral hot springs that empty into a swimming pool, not a hot pool (76 degrees). Hot mineral baths are available in private rooms. Swimming and sauna are also available for a fee. This is an old Indian birthing ground. Nearby recreation options include a golf course, hiking trails, a bike path, and tennis courts. Boating, fishing, and water-skiing are within 10 miles. Some may remember this campground under its former name, Jackson Hot Springs.

Campsites, facilities: There are 30 tent sites, 20 drive-through sites for RVs of any length, and three teepees. Electricity, drinking water, sewer hookups, and picnic tables are provided. Flush toilets, showers, a laundry room, ice, and a swimming pool are available. Bottled gas is within one mile. Pets are permitted with deposit.

Reservations, fees: Reservations are not accepted. Sites are $16–20 per night, $4 per person for more than two people, and $25 per teepee per night for up to three people. Major credit cards accepted. Open year-round.

Directions: From Ashland, drive north on I-5 to Exit 19. Take that exit and drive west for one-quarter mile to the stoplight at Highway 99. Turn right and drive 500 feet to the campground.

Contact: The WellSprings, 2253 Hwy. 99 N, Ashland, OR 97520, 541/482-3776, fax 541/488-3590.

229 GLENYAN CAMPGROUND OF ASHLAND

Rating: 7

Near Emigrant Lake.
Map 11.7, grid g3, page 622

This campground within seven miles of Ashland offers shady sites near Emigrant Lake. Recreation options in the area include a golf course, hiking trails, a bike path, and tennis courts. It's an easy jump from I-5 at Ashland.

Campsites, facilities: There are 68 sites for tents or RVs of any length; 12 have full and 38 have partial hookups. Electricity, drinking water, sewer

hookups, and picnic tables are provided. Flush toilets, bottled gas, an RV dump station, showers, firewood, a recreation hall, a store, a laundry room, ice, a playground, and a swimming pool are available. Leashed pets are permitted.

Reservations, fees: Reservations at 877/453-6926. Sites are $18.50–23 per night, $2 per person for more than two people. Major credit cards accepted. Senior discount available. Open year-round.

Directions: From Ashland, drive east on Highway 66 for 3.5 miles to the campground on the right.

Contact: Glenyan Campground of Ashland, 5310 Hwy. 66, Ashland, OR 97520, 541/488-1785, website: www.glenyancampground.com.

230 HOWARD PRAIRIE LAKE RESORT

Rating: 7

On Howard Prairie Lake.
Map 11.7, grid g5, page 622

This wooded campground is located along the shore of Howard Prairie Lake, where hiking, swimming, fishing, and boating are among the recreation options. This is one of the largest campgrounds in more than 100 miles.

Campsites, facilities: There are 300 sites for tents or RVs of any length and 20 furnished RV rentals. Electricity, drinking water, sewer hookups, 24-hour security, and picnic tables are provided. Flush toilets, bottled gas, an RV dump station, showers, firewood, a store, a café, a laundry room, boat docks, boat rentals, moorage, and launching facilities are available. Leashed pets are permitted.

Reservations, fees: Reservations are not accepted. Sites are $17–21 per night, $5 per person for more than two people. Major credit cards accepted. Open mid-April–October.

Directions: In Ashland on I-5, take Exit 14 to Highway 66. Drive east for less than a mile to Dead Indian Memorial Road. Turn left (east) and drive 17 miles to Howard Prairie Road. Turn right (south) and drive two miles to the reservoir.

Contact: Howard Prairie Lake Resort, 3249 Hyatt Prairie Rd., Ashland, OR 97520, 541/482-1979, fax 541/488-7485, website: www.howard-prairieresort.com.

231 LILY GLEN CAMPGROUND

Rating: 6

Near Howard Prairie Lake.
Map 11.7, grid g5, page 622

Set along the shore of Howard Prairie Lake, this horse camp is a secluded, primitive getaway. Trout fishing is available. Tubb Springs Wayside State Park and the nearby Rogue River National Forest are possible side trips. There is also nearby access to the Pacific Crest Trail.

Campsites, facilities: There are 26 sites for tents or self-contained RVs and two group sites for 60–100 people. Picnic tables, drinking water, vault toilets, individual corrals, and a large barn are available. Some facilities are wheelchair accessible. Leashed pets are permitted.

Reservations, fees: Reservations are not accepted for family sites. Sites are $14–16 per night, $1 per pet per night. Group reservations at 541/774-8183; $75–125 per night. Major credit cards accepted for reservations. Senior discount available. Open year-round, with limited winter services.

Directions: In Ashland on I-5, take Exit 14 to Highway 66. Drive east for less than a mile to Dead Indian Memorial Road. Turn left (east) and drive 21 miles to the campground.

Contact: Jackson County Parks, 400 Antelope Rd., White City, OR 97503, 541/774-8183, fax 541/774-6320, website: www.jacksoncounty parks.com.

232 GRIZZLY

Rating: 7

Near Howard Prairie Lake.
Map 11.7, grid g5, page 622

One of a series of three county campgrounds at Howard Prairie Lake, Grizzly features well-spaced campsites amid a forest and lake setting. The lake level is known to fluctuate, and in low-water years, this camp is subject to being shut down. It gets moderate use. The elevation is 4,550 feet.

Campsites, facilities: There are 21 sites with no hookups for tents or RVs. Picnic tables and fire rings are provided. Drinking water, vault toilets, and garbage bins are available. Some facilities are wheelchair accessible. A boat ramp is nearby. A store, café, laundry facilities, and boat rentals are available within two miles. Leashed pets are permitted.

Reservations, fees: Reservations are not accepted. Sites are $14 per night for the first two vehicles, $1 per pet per night. Senior discount available. Open mid-April–October.

Directions: In Ashland on I-5, take Exit 14 to Highway 66. Drive east for less than a mile to Dead Indian Memorial Road. Turn left (east) and drive 17 miles to Howard Prairie Road. Turn right (south) and drive eight miles to Howard Prairie Dam Road. Turn left (east) and drive one-quarter mile to the campground.

Contact: Jackson County Parks, 400 Antelope Rd., White City, OR 97503, 541/774-8183, fax 541/774-6320, website: www.jacksoncounty parks.com.

233 WILLOW POINT

Rating: 7

Near Howard Prairie Lake.
Map 11.7, grid g5, page 622

Willow Point is the most popular of the three county campgrounds on Howard Prairie Lake. Similar to Grizzly, it offers flat tent sites in an area well covered by trees.

Campsites, facilities: There are 40 sites for tents or self-contained RVs and one group site for up to 100 people. Picnic tables and fire rings are provided. Drinking water, vault toilets, and garbage bins are available. Some facilities are wheelchair accessible. A boat ramp is nearby. A store, a café, laundry facilities, and boat rentals are available within four miles. Leashed pets are permitted.

Reservations, fees: Reservations are not accepted for family sites. Sites are $14–16 per night, $1 per pet per night. Group reservations at 541/774-8183; $150 per night. Major credit cards accepted for reservations. Senior discount available. Open mid-April–October.

Directions: In Ashland on I-5, take Exit 14 to Highway 66. Drive east for less than a mile to Dead Indian Memorial Road. Turn left (east) and drive 17 miles to Howard Prairie Road. Turn right (south) and drive three miles to the reservoir.

Contact: Jackson County Parks, 400 Antelope Rd., White City, OR 97503, 541/774-8183, fax 541/774-6320, website: www.jacksoncounty parks.com.

234 KLUM LANDING

Rating: 7

Near Howard Prairie Lake.

Map 11.7, grid g5, page 622

Klum Landing is one of three county campgrounds on Howard Prairie Lake. The others are Grizzly and Lookout Point. A bonus at this one is that coin-operated showers are available.

Campsites, facilities: There are 30 sites for tents or self-contained RVs. Picnic tables and fire rings are provided. Drinking water, garbage bins, and restrooms with flush toilets and showers are available. Some facilities are wheelchair accessible. A boat ramp is nearby. A store, a café, laundry facilities, and boat rentals are available at Howard Prairie Lake Resort. Leashed pets are permitted.

Reservations, fees: Reservations are not accepted. Sites are $16 per night, $1 per pet per night. Senior discount available. Open mid-April–October.

Directions: In Ashland on I-5, take Exit 14 to Highway 66. Drive east for less than a mile to Dead Indian Memorial Road. Turn left (east) and drive 17 miles to Howard Prairie Road. Turn right (south) and drive eight miles

to Howard Prairie Dam Road. Turn left (east) and drive one mile to the campground.

Contact: Jackson County Parks, 400 Antelope Rd., White City, OR 97503, 541/774-8183, fax 541/774-6320, website: www.jacksoncounty parks.com.

235 EMIGRANT CAMPGROUND

Rating: 8

On Emigrant Lake.

Map 11.7, grid g4, page 622

This camp is nestled among the trees above Emigrant Lake, a well-known recreational area. Activities at this park include swimming, hiking, boating, water-skiing, and fishing. There are also two super water slides. The park has its own swimming cove (unsupervised). Side-trip possibilities include exploring nearby Mt. Ashland, where a ski area operates in the winter, and visiting the world-renowned Shakespeare Festival in Ashland as well as historic Jacksonville and the Britt Music Festival.

Campsites, facilities: There are 42 sites for tents or self-contained RVs, 32 sites with full hookups for RVs, an overflow area, and one group camp area for up to 75 people. Restrooms, coin-operated showers, an RV dump station, a public phone, snacks in summer, and a barbecue are available. A group picnic and barbecue area is also available. Recreational facilities include horseshoe pits, volleyball, and a recreation field. Two boat ramps are provided. Some facilities are wheelchair accessible. Laundry and food facilities are within six miles. Pets are permitted in designated areas only.

Reservations, fees: Reservations for RV sites and the group site at 541/774-8183; RV and family sites are $16–20 per night, the group site is $100 per night. Major credit cards accepted for reservations. Senior discount available. Open mid-April–October.

Directions: From Ashland, drive east on Highway 66 for five miles to the campground.

Contact: Jackson County Parks, 400 Antelope Rd., White City, OR 97503, 541/774-8183, fax 541/774-6320, website: www.jacksoncountyparks.com.

236 HYATT LAKE

Rating: 8

On Hyatt Lake.
Map 11.7, grid g5, page 622

This campground is situated on the south end of Hyatt Reservoir, which has six miles of shoreline. Fishing is good for brook and rainbow trout and smallmouth bass. Another campground option is Wildcat, about two miles north, with 12 semi-primitive sites. The boat speed limit here is 10 mph.

Campsites, facilities: There are 47 sites for tents or RVs up to 40 feet in length, one horse campsite, one group site, and a few walk-in tent sites. Picnic tables and fire grills are provided. Drinking water, flush toilets, showers, garbage service, an RV dump station, a group kitchen, a fish-cleaning station, a day-use area, athletic fields, a playground, horseshoe pits, and two boat ramps are available. Some facilities are wheelchair accessible. Leashed pets are permitted.

Reservations, fees: Reservations are not accepted. Sites are $12–15 per night, $3 per extra vehicle, with a 14-day stay limit. Campsites with horse facilities are $10 per night; the group site is $45 per night. Sites at nearby primitive Wildcat Campground are $7 per night. Senior discount available. Open late April–October, weather permitting.

Directions: From Ashland, drive east on Highway 66 for 17 miles to East Hyatt Lake Road. Turn north and drive three miles to the campground entrance on the left.

Contact: Bureau of Land Management, Medford District, 3040 Biddle Rd., Medford, OR 97504, 541/618-2200, fax 541/618-2400, website: www.or.blm.gov/medfoRoad.

237 HYATT LAKE RESORT

Rating: 7

On Hyatt Lake.
Map 11.7, grid g5, page 622

This campground is set along the shore of Hyatt Lake, just west of the dam, where hiking and fishing are some of the recreation options. This is a scaled-down alternative to the resort at adjacent Howard Prairie Lake. The Pacific Crest Trail is just half a mile away.

Campsites, facilities: There are 13 no-hookup and 22 full-hookup sites for RVs of any length, including four drive-through sites. There are also four cabins with no kitchen facilities; each sleeps four. Electricity (10 sites have 50-amp), drinking water, sewer hookups, and picnic tables are provided. Flush toilets, an RV dump station, showers, a store, a laundry room, ice, and boat rentals are available. Boat docks and launching facilities are on the resort property. Leashed pets are permitted.

Reservations, fees: Reservations accepted. Sites are $15–20 per night, $5 per extra tent or vehicle. Major credit cards accepted. Open April–October.

Directions: From Ashland, drive east on Highway 66 for 17 miles to East Hyatt Lake Road. Turn north and drive three miles to Hyatt Prairie Road. Turn left and drive one mile to the resort.

Contact: Hyatt Lake Resort, 7979 Hyatt Prairie Rd., Ashland, OR 97520, 541/482-3331, website: www.hyattlake.resort.com.

238 CAMPER'S COVE

Rating: 7

On Hyatt Lake.
Map 11.7, grid g5, page 622

This campground is set about 400 feet from the shore of Hyatt Lake, with the Pacific Crest Trail passing about a mile away. It is in a cove east of the dam. No tents are permitted here.

Campsites, facilities: There are 23 sites, seven drive-through, for RVs up to 30 feet long. Picnic tables are provided. Electricity, drinking water, sewer hookups, flush toilets, showers, firewood, a store, a café, a bar, a lounge, and ice are available. Boat docks are nearby. Leashed pets are permitted.

Reservations, fees: Reservations accepted. Sites are $18 per night, $1 per person for more than two people. Major credit cards accepted. Open year-round.

Directions: From Ashland drive east on Highway 66 for 17 miles to East Hyatt Lake Road. Turn north and drive three miles to Hyatt Prairie Road. Turn right and drive 2.5 miles (over the dam) to the resort.

Contact: Camper's Cove, 7900 Hyatt Prairie Rd., Ashland, OR 97520, 541/482-1201, website: www.camperscove.com.

239 JACKSON

Rating: 7

On the Applegate River in Rogue River National Forest.

Map 11.7, grid h2, page 622

This camp is nestled in an old mining area at 1,700 feet elevation. Situated between the Applegate River and the road, under a canopy of ponderosa pine, it features a swimming hole and good trout fishing. Mine tailings can be seen from the camp. Trailers and large RVs are not advised.

Campsites, facilities: There are 10 sites for tents. Picnic tables and fire rings are provided. Drinking water (summer only), garbage service (summer only), and flush toilets are available. Leashed pets are permitted. Some facilities are wheelchair accessible.

Reservations, fees: Reservations are not accepted. Sites are $8 per night, $4 per extra vehicle. Senior discount available. Open year-round, with limited winter services.

Directions: In Medford on I-5, take the Jacksonville exit to the Jacksonville Highway. Drive west on the Jacksonville Highway (Highway 238) for seven miles to Jacksonville. Bear left on Highway 238 and drive eight miles to the town of Ruch and Upper Applegate Road (County Road 10). Turn left and drive 10 miles to the campground on the right (this camp is directly across from Flumet Flat Campground).

Contact: Rogue River National Forest, Applegate Ranger District, 6941 Upper Applegate Rd., Jacksonville, OR 97530, 541/899-1812, fax 541/899-3888.

240 BEAVER SULPHUR GROUP

Rating: 7

On Beaver Creek in Rogue River National Forest.

Map 11.7, grid h2, page 622

This group camp is well hidden along the banks of Beaver Creek. It is set at an elevation of 2,100 feet and situated in an area with mixed tree cover, including maple, live oak, and tall Douglas fir. The camp is about nine miles from Applegate Reservoir, features pretty, shaded sites, and offers easy access to the creek. Some recreational mining is done here; a permit can be obtained at the ranger station. Groups are provided a key from the ranger station to access the site after paying the campground fee.

Campsites, facilities: There is one group site for up to 100 people. Picnic tables and fire grills are provided. Vault toilets, garbage bins (summer only), and drinking water are available. Some facilities are wheelchair accessible. Leashed pets are permitted.

Reservations, fees: Reservations required at 541/899-1812; $50 per night. Open May–November.

Directions: In Medford on I-5, take the Jacksonville exit to the Jacksonville Highway. Drive west on the Jacksonville Highway (Highway 238) for seven miles to Jacksonville. Bear left on Highway 238 and drive eight miles to the town of Ruch and Upper Applegate Road (County Road 10). Turn left (south) and drive

9.5 miles to Forest Road 20. Continue three miles to the campground.

Contact: Rogue River National Forest, Applegate Ranger District, 6941 Upper Applegate Rd., Jacksonville, OR 97530, 541/899-1812, fax 541/899-3888.

241 WRANGLE

Rating: 10

Near the Pacific Crest Trail in Rogue River National Forest.

Map 11.7, grid h2, page 622

This campground is set at the headwaters of Glade Creek in the Siskiyou Mountains at an elevation of 6,400 feet. The Pacific Crest Trail passes near camp. Dutchman Peak Lookout, built in the late 1920s and featured in the National Historic Register, is within five miles. This lovely campground, in a beautiful, high country setting, boasts huge Shasta red firs and views of the Siskiyou Mountains. Wrangle is along the Scenic Siskiyou Loop driving tour.

Campsites, facilities: There are five sites for tents. Picnic tables and fire grills are provided. The availability of drinking water is intermittent. All garbage must be packed out. Vault toilets and a community kitchen are available. Leashed pets are permitted.

Reservations, fees: Reservations are not accepted. There is no fee for camping. Open early June–late October, weather permitting.

Directions: In Ashland on I-5, take the Jacksonville exit. Drive east on the Jacksonville Highway to Jacksonville and Highway 238. Bear left on Highway 238 and drive eight miles to the town of Ruch and County Road 10 (Upper Applegate Road). Turn left and drive 9.5 miles to Forest Road 20. Turn left and drive 21 miles to Forest Road 2030. Continue one mile on Forest Road 2030 to the campground.

Contact: Rogue River National Forest, Applegate District, 6941 Upper Applegate Rd., Jacksonville, OR 97530, 541/899-1812, fax 541/899-3888.

242 MOUNT ASHLAND

Rating: 8

On the Pacific Crest Trail in Klamath National Forest.

Map 11.7, grid h3, page 622

Set at 6,600 feet elevation along the Pacific Crest Trail, this beautiful camp is heavily wooded and has abundant wildlife. On a clear day, enjoy great lookouts from nearby Siskiyou Peak, particularly to the south, where California's 14,162-foot Mt. Shasta is an awesome sight. Mount Ashland Ski Resort is one mile west of the campground.

Campsites, facilities: There are nine sites for tents or RVs up to 15 feet long, with extremely limited space for RVs. Picnic tables and fire grills are provided. Vault toilets are available. There is no drinking water. All garbage must be packed out. Leashed pets are permitted.

Reservations, fees: Reservations are not accepted. There is no fee for camping. Open May–late October, weather permitting.

Directions: From Ashland, drive south on I-5 for 12 miles to Mount Ashland Ski Park Road (County Road 993). Turn west and drive 10 miles (the road becomes Forest Road 20) to the campground.

Contact: Klamath National Forest, Scott and Salmon Rivers Ranger District, 11263 N. Hwy. 3, Fort Jones, CA 96032, 530/468-5351, fax 530/468-1290.

243 HART-TISH RECREATION AREA WALK-IN

Rating: 7

On Applegate Reservoir, Rogue River National Forest.

Map 11.7, grid h1, page 622

This concessionaire-managed campground on Applegate Lake has shaded sites and a great view of the lake. Bald eagles and osprey nest in the area, and it's a treat to watch them fish.

A nearby boat launch and boat rentals are available. The walk-in sites are only 200 yards from the parking area.

Campsites, facilities: There are five walk-in tent sites and eight RV parking lot sites. Picnic tables and fire pits are provided. Drinking water, flush toilets, garbage bins, firewood, a mini-mart, and wheelchair facilities (a restroom, one site, and a barrier-free loading ramp) are available. Leashed pets are permitted.

Reservations, fees: Reservations are not accepted for family sites. Sites are $10 per night, $5 per extra vehicle. This campground can be reserved as a group site; reservations required at 541/899-1812. Open Memorial Day–September.

Directions: In Medford on I-5, take the Jacksonville exit to the Jacksonville Highway. Drive west on the Jacksonville Highway (Highway 238) for seven miles to Jacksonville. Bear left on Highway 238 and drive eight miles to the town of Ruch and Upper Applegate Road (County Road 10). Turn left (south) and drive 15.5 miles to the campground.

Contact: Rogue River National Forest, Applegate Ranger District, 6941 Upper Applegate Rd., Jacksonville, OR 97530, 541/899-1812, fax 541/899-3888.

244 WATKINS

🏃 🚲 🏊 🛶 ⛴ 🐕 ♿ ⛺

Rating: 6

On Applegate Reservoir in Rogue River National Forest.

Map 11.7, grid h1, page 622

On the southwest shore of Applegate Reservoir at an elevation of 2,000 feet, this campground, like Carberry Walk-In and French Gulch, is small and quite primitive—yet pretty—and offers all the same recreation options. Few campers know about this spot, so it usually doesn't fill up quickly. There are good views of the lake and the surrounding Siskiyou Mountains.

Campsites, facilities: There are 14 walk-in sites

for tents. Picnic tables, drinking water, garbage bins, and fire grills are provided. Vault toilets and firewood are available. Boat docks and launching facilities are within two miles. Some facilities are wheelchair accessible. Leashed pets are permitted.

Reservations, fees: Reservations are not accepted. Sites are $8 per night, $4 per extra vehicle. Senior discount available. Open May–September.

Directions: In Medford on I-5, take the Jacksonville exit to the Jacksonville Highway. Drive west on the Jacksonville Highway (Highway 238) for seven miles to Jacksonville. Bear left on Highway 238 and drive eight miles to the town of Ruch and Upper Applegate Road (County Road 10). Turn left (south) and drive 17 miles to the campground.

Contact: Rogue River National Forest, Applegate Ranger District, 6941 Upper Applegate Rd., Jacksonville, OR 97530, 541/899-1812, fax 541/899-3888.

245 LATGAWA COVE BOAT-IN

🏃 🚲 🏊 🛶 ⛴ 🐕 ⛺

Rating: 5

On Applegate Reservoir, Rogue River National Forest.

Map 11.7, grid h1, page 622

Because of ongoing problems regarding funding priorities in the U.S. National Forest, this campground may be closed in summer of 2003. Call before planning a visit. The elevation of this lake is 2,000 feet. Latgawa Cove has semi-primitive lakeshore campsites with tree cover providing shade. A mountain bike trail runs through the campground. The water level fluctuates, sometimes preventing boat access. Several boat launches can be used to reach this campground and the other boat-in campgrounds on Applegate Lake: Harr Point and Typsu Tyee, both with similar amenities as Latgawa and within three miles of each other by boat.

Campsites, facilities: There are five boat-in sites. No drinking water is available, but picnic tables and fire rings are provided. Pit toilets are available. Pack out all garbage. Leashed pets are permitted.

Reservations, fees: Reservations are not accepted. There is no fee for camping. Open year-round.

Directions: In Medford on I-5, take the Jacksonville exit to the Jacksonville Highway. Drive west on Jacksonville Highway (Highway 238) for seven miles to Jacksonville. Bear left on Highway 238 and drive eight miles to the town of Ruch and Upper Applegate Road (County Road 10). Turn left and drive 15 miles to Forest Road 1075. Turn right and drive 1.5 miles to the parking area for French Gulch Campground and the boat ramp. Boat-in to Latgawa Cove Campground.

Contact: Rogue River National Forest, Applegate Ranger District, 6941 Upper Applegate Rd., Jacksonville, OR 97530, 541/899-1812, fax 541/899-3888.

246 CARBERRY WALK-IN

Rating: 5

Near Applegate Reservoir in Rogue River National Forest.

Map 11.7, grid h1, page 622

You'll find recreational opportunities aplenty, including fishing, boating, hiking, mountain biking, and swimming, at this campground on Cougar Creek near the southwest shore of Applegate Reservoir. Dense forest covers the campsites, providing much-needed shade. This camp is similar to French Gulch and Watkins Walk-in.

Campsites, facilities: There are 10 walk-in sites for tents. Space is available in the parking lot for RVs. Picnic tables and fire grills are provided. Vault toilets and drinking water are available. Boat docks and launching facilities are within two miles. Leashed pets are permitted. Some facilities are wheelchair accessible.

Reservations, fees: Reservations are not accepted. Sites are $8 per night, $4 per extra vehicle. Senior discount available. Open year-round,

weather permitting, with limited services and no fee in winter.

Directions: In Medford on I-5, take the Jacksonville exit to the Jacksonville Highway. Drive west on the Jacksonville Highway (Highway 238) for seven miles to Jacksonville. Bear left on Highway 238 and drive eight miles to the town of Ruch and Upper Applegate Road (County Road 10). Turn left (south) and drive 18 miles to the campground parking area. A short walk is required.

Contact: Rogue River National Forest, Applegate Ranger District, 6941 Upper Applegate Rd., Jacksonville, OR 97530, 541/899-1812, fax 541/899-3888.

247 SQUAW LAKE HIKE-IN

Rating: 10

On Squaw Lake in Rogue River National Forest.

Map 11.7, grid h1, page 622

"Paradise Found" should be the name here. Numerous trails crisscross the area around this camp on the shore of spectacular Squaw Lake (3,000 feet elevation). The setting is more intimate than that of larger Applegate Reservoir to the west. This spot has a mix of developed and primitive sites and is also more popular. In fact, it's the only campground in the district that requires reservations. This area attracts the canoe/kayak crowd. Be sure to call ahead for a space. Campers with disabilities are welcome, but arrangements should be made in advance with the local U.S. Forest Service office.

Campsites, facilities: There are 17 walk-in sites for tents and two family group sites that can accommodate up to 10 people each. Picnic tables, garbage bins (summer only), and fire grills are provided. Vault toilets are available. Drinking water is available at one end of the camp during the summer only. Some facilities are wheelchair accessible. Leashed pets are permitted.

Reservations, fees: Reservations required during the summer at 541/899-1812. Sites are $10 per night; group sites are $20 per night. Senior discount available. Open year-round, with limited winter services.

Directions: In Medford on I-5, take the Jacksonville exit to the Jacksonville Highway. Drive west on the Jacksonville Highway (Highway 238) for seven miles to Jacksonville. Bear left on Highway 238 and drive eight miles to the town of Ruch and Upper Applegate Road (County Road 10). Turn left (south) and drive 15 miles to Forest Road 1075. Continue eight miles to Squaw Lake and the trailhead. Hike one mile to the campsites.

Contact: Rogue River National Forest, Applegate Ranger District, 6941 Upper Applegate Rd., Jacksonville, OR 97530, 541/899-1812, fax 541/899-3888.

248 TOPSY

Rating: 7

On the Upper Klamath River.
Map 11.7, grid h8, page 622

This campground is on Boyle Reservoir near the Upper Klamath River, a good spot for trout fishing and a top river for rafters (experts only, or non-experts with professional licensed guides). There are Class IV and V rapids about four miles southwest at Caldera, Satan's Gate, and Hells Corner. I flipped at Caldera and ended up swimming for it, finally getting out at an eddy. Luckily, I was wearing a dry suit and the best lifejacket available, perfect fitting, which saved my butt. The area is good for mountain biking, too.

Campsites, facilities: There are 13 sites for RVs up to 40 feet long. Picnic tables and fire grills are provided. Drinking water, vault toilets, garbage service, and an RV dump station are available. Some facilities are wheelchair accessible. Boat-launching facilities are nearby. A camp host is on-site. Leashed pets are permitted.

Reservations, fees: Reservations are not accepted. Sites are $7 per night, $4 per extra vehicle, with a 14-day stay limit. Senior discount available. Open mid-May–mid-September.

Directions: From Klamath Falls, drive west on Highway 66 for 20 miles to Topsy Road. Turn south on Topsy Road and drive 1.5 miles to the campground on the right.

Contact: Bureau of Land Management, Klamath Falls Resource Area, 2795 Anderson Ave., Building 25, Klamath Falls, OR 97603, 541/883-6916, fax 541/884-2097.

249 JACKSON F. KIMBALL STATE PARK

Rating: 7

On the Wood River.
Map 11.8, grid c1, page 623

This primitive state campground at the headwaters of the Wood River is another nice spot just far enough off the main drag to remain a secret. Wood River offers fine fishing that's accessible from the park by canoe. A walking trail leads from the campground to a clear spring bubbling from a rocky hillside.

Campsites, facilities: There are 10 primitive sites for tents or self-contained RVs up to 45 feet long. Picnic tables, fire grills, and garbage bins are provided. Vault toilets are available. There is no drinking water. Leashed pets are permitted.

Reservations, fees: Reservations are not accepted. Sites are $7 per night, $7 per extra vehicle. Open mid-April–late October.

Directions: From Klamath Falls, drive north on U.S. 97 for 21 miles to Highway 62. Turn northwest on Highway 62 and drive 10 miles to Highway 232 (near Fort Klamath). Turn north and drive three miles to the campground.

Contact: Jackson F. Kimball State Park, c/o Collier Memorial State Park, 46000 Hwy. 97 N, Chiloquin, OR 97624, 800/551-6949 or 541/783-2471. This park is managed by Collier Memorial State Park.

250 CRATER LAKE RESORT

Rating: 6

On the Wood River.

Map 11.8, grid c1, page 623

This campground, set among huge pine trees, is on the banks of the beautiful, crystal-clear Fort Creek, just outside Fort Klamath, the site of numerous military campaigns against the Modoc Indians in the late 1800s.

Campsites, facilities: There are 23 sites, 11 with full hookups and 12 with partial hookups, for RVs of any length, some tent sites, nine cabins, one teepee, and one log cabin. Electricity, drinking water, sewer hookups, and picnic tables are provided. Flush toilets, showers, a recreation hall, and a laundry room are available. Bottled gas, a store, a café, and ice are within one mile. Leashed pets are permitted.

Reservations, fees: Reservations accepted. Sites are $16–22 per night, $2 per person for more than two people, and $2 per pet per night. Open mid-April–mid-October.

Directions: From Klamath Falls, drive north on U.S. 97 for 21 miles to Highway 62. Bear left on Highway 62 and drive 12.5 miles north to the campground (just before reaching Fort Klamath).

Contact: Crater Lake Resort, P.O. Box 457, Fort Klamath, OR 97626, 541/381-2349, website: www.craterlakeresort.com.

251 COLLIER MEMORIAL STATE PARK

Rating: 7

On the Williamson River.

Map 11.8, grid c2, page 623

This campground is set at the confluence of Spring Creek and the Williamson River, both of which are superior trout streams. A nature trail is also available. The park features a pioneer village and one of the state's finer logging museums. Movies about old-time logging and other activities are shown on weekend nights during the summer.

Campsites, facilities: There are 18 sites for tents or self-contained RVs and 50 sites with full hookups for RVs up to 60 feet long. Picnic tables, fire grills, garbage bins, and drinking water are provided. Flush toilets, an RV dump station, showers, firewood, a laundry room, a playground, and a day-use hitching area are available. Some facilities are wheelchair accessible. Leashed pets are permitted.

Reservations, fees: Reservations are not accepted. Sites are $15–18 per night, $7 per extra vehicle. Major credit cards accepted. Open April–late October, weather permitting.

Directions: From Klamath Falls, drive north on U.S. 97 for 28 miles to the park on the left (well signed).

Contact: Collier Memorial State Park, 46000 Hwy. 97 N, Chiloquin, OR 97624, 800/551-6949 or 541/783-2471.

252 WILLIAMSON RIVER

Rating: 6

Near Collier Memorial State Park in Winema National Forest.

Map 11.8, grid d2, page 623

Another great little spot is discovered, this one at 4,200 feet elevation, with excellent trout fishing along the banks of the Williamson River. Although accessible to a world-famous fly-fishing river, the camp does not get high use. Mosquitoes are numerous in spring and early summer, which can drive people away. A map of Winema National Forest details the back roads and trails. Collier Memorial State Park provides a nearby side-trip option.

Campsites, facilities: There are three tent sites and seven sites for RVs up to 30 feet long. Picnic tables, garbage bins, and fire grills are provided. Drinking water and vault toilets are available. Some facilities are wheelchair accessible. A restaurant is within five miles. Leashed pets are permitted.

Reservations, fees: Reservations are not accepted. Sites are $6 per night, $2 per extra vehicle. Senior discount available. Open mid-May–late November 25, weather permitting.
Directions: From Klamath Falls, drive north on U.S. 97 for 30 miles to Chiloquin. Continue north on U.S. 97 for 5.5 miles to Forest Road 9730 on the right. Turn northeast and drive one mile to the campground.
Contact: Winema National Forest, Klamath Ranger District, 1936 California Ave., Klamath Falls, OR 97601, 541/885-3400, fax 541/885-3452.

253 AGENCY LAKE RESORT

Rating: 5

On Agency Lake.
Map 11.8, grid d1, page 623
This campground is on Agency Lake in an open, grassy area with some shaded sites. It has more than 700 feet of lakefront property, offering world-class trout fishing. Look across the lake and watch the sun set on the Cascades. See the description of Rocky Point Resort for more information.
Campsites, facilities: There are 15 tent sites and 25 sites for RVs of any length, three cabins, and one rental trailer. Electricity, drinking water, sewer hookups, and picnic tables are provided. Flush toilets, showers, a general store, ice, boat docks, launching facilities, and marine gas are available. Leashed pets are permitted.
Reservations, fees: Reservations accepted. Sites are $8–16 per night. Open year-round, weather permitting.
Directions: From Klamath Falls, drive north on U.S. 97 for 17 miles to Modoc Point Road. Turn left (north) and drive about 10 miles to the campground on the left.
Contact: Agency Lake Resort, 37000 Modoc Point Rd., Chiloquin, OR 97624, 541/783-2489.

254 WALT'S COZY CAMP

Rating: 7

On the Williamson River.
Map 11.8, grid d1, page 623
This heavily treed campground, across the highway from the Williamson River near Collier Memorial State Park, is one of three camps in the immediate area. For a more remote setting, head east to Potter's Trailer Park (in this chapter) or Head of the River (in the Southeast Oregon chapter). The Williamson River has excellent trout fishing. And by the way, the "Walt" who started this place is still here, providing friendly advice as he has for years.
Campsites, facilities: There are 20 tent sites and 34 sites for RVs of any length; six are drive-through sites. Electricity, drinking water, sewer hookups, and picnic tables are provided. Flush toilets, showers, firewood, a laundry room, and ice are available. A café is available within one-quarter mile and a store is available in Chiloquin. Leashed pets are permitted.
Reservations, fees: Reservations accepted. Sites are $12–14 per night, $1 per person for more than two people. Open April–mid-October, weather permitting.
Directions: From Klamath Falls, drive north on U.S. 97 for 24 miles to Chiloquin Junction. Continue north for one-quarter mile to the campground (adjacent to the Chiloquin Ranger Station) on the left.
Contact: Walt's Cozy Camp, 38400 Hwy. 97, P.O. Box 243, Chiloquin, OR 97624, 541/783-2537.

255 WATERWHEEL CAMPGROUND

Rating: 6

On the Williamson River.
Map 11.8, grid d2, page 623
This rural campground right on the Williamson River is close to hiking trails. Fishing can be

excellent here, with a boat ramp and fishing tackle right at the camp.

Campsites, facilities: There are six tent sites and 28 sites for RVs of any length; 22 are drive-through sites. Electricity, drinking water, sewer hookups, and picnic tables are provided. Flush toilets, bottled gas, an RV dump station, showers, firewood, a store, a laundry room, ice, and a playground are available. A café is within one mile. Boat docks and launching facilities are nearby. Leashed pets are permitted.

Reservations, fees: Reservations accepted. Sites are $16–23 per night, $1.50 per person for more than two people. Major credit cards accepted. Open year-round, weather permitting.

Directions: From Klamath Falls, drive north on U.S. 97 for 20 miles to the campground (one-quarter mile south of the junction of U.S. 97 and Highway 62).

Contact: Waterwheel Campground, 200 Williamson River Dr., Chiloquin, OR 97624, 541/783-2738.

256 POTTER'S PARK

Rating: 6

On the Sprague River.
Map 11.8, grid d3, page 623

This park on a bluff overlooking the river is in a wooded setting and bordered by the Sprague River and the Winema National Forest. For the most part, the area east of Klamath Lake doesn't get much attention. But if you want to check out a relatively close spot that's out in remote country, try Head of the River (in the Southeast Oregon chapter).

Campsites, facilities: There are 17 tent sites and 23 full-hookup sites for RVs of any length. Electricity, drinking water, sewer hookups, and picnic tables are provided. Flush toilets, showers, firewood, a convenience store, a café, a tavern, a laundry room, a telephone, and ice are available. Leashed pets are permitted.

Reservations, fees: Reservations accepted. Sites are $13.50–15 per night, $2.50–5 per person for more than two people. Monthly rates available. Open year-round, with limited winter facilities.

Directions: From Klamath Falls, drive north on U.S. 97 for 27 miles to Chiloquin and Sprague River Highway. Turn east on Sprague River Highway and drive 12 miles to the resort.

Contact: Potter's Trailer Park, 11700 Sprague River Rd., Chiloquin, OR 97624, 541/783-2253.

257 OREGON 8 MOTEL AND RV PARK

Rating: 6

On Upper Klamath Lake.
Map 11.8, grid f2, page 623

This campground, surrounded by mountains, big rocks, and trees, is near Hanks Marsh on the southeast shore of Upper Klamath Lake, within 50 miles of Crater Lake. Nearby recreation options include a golf course, bike paths, and a marina.

Campsites, facilities: There are 10 tent sites and 29 drive-through sites for RVs of any length. Electricity, drinking water, cable TV, sewer hookups, and picnic tables are provided. Flush toilets, showers, a recreation hall, a laundry room, ice, and a swimming pool are available. Bottled gas, a store, and a café are within one mile. Leashed pets are permitted.

Reservations, fees: Reservations accepted. Tent sites are $15 per night and RV sites are $21–27 per night; $2 per person for more than two people, $1 per pet per night. Major credit cards accepted. Senior discount available. Open year-round, with limited winter facilities.

Directions: From Klamath Falls, drive north on U.S. 97 for 3.5 miles to the campground on the right.

Contact: Oregon 8 Motel and RV Park, 5225 Hwy. 97 N, Klamath Falls, OR 97601, 541/883-3431.

258 TINGLEY LAKE ESTATES

Rating: 7

On Tingley Lake.

Map 11.8, grid h2, page 623

This privately-operated RV park provides a layover for travelers crossing the Oregon border on U.S. 97. You can see California's Mt. Shasta from this park right on the lake. All sites have a view of Tingley Lake, which has opportunities for bass fishing, boating, and swimming. Note that about half of the 16 sites at this park are booked for the entire summer season. A nice bonus: Free use of rowboats and canoes is included with the price.

Campsites, facilities: There are six tent sites and 10 sites for RVs of any length; three have full and seven have partial hookups. Electric- ity, drinking water, sewer hookups, and picnic tables are provided. Telephone and cable TV hookups, flush toilets, showers, boat docks, and a playground are available. A store, a café, and ice are within two miles. Leashed pets are permitted.

Reservations, fees: Reservations accepted. Sites are $15–18 per night, $2 per person for more than two people. Monthly rates available. Open year-round, weather permitting, with limited winter services.

Directions: From Klamath Falls, drive southwest on U.S. 97 for seven miles to Old Midland Road. Turn east and drive two miles to Tingley Lane. Turn right (south) and drive one-half mile to the park.

Contact: Tingley Lake Estates, 11800 Tingley Ln., Klamath Falls, OR 97603, tel./fax 541/882-8386.

Chapter 12
Southeastern Oregon

Chapter 12—Southeastern Oregon

Some people think that southeastern Oregon is one big chunk of nothing. They are only half right. True, this high-desert region is dry and foreboding, with many miles between camps in several areas. However, because this part of Oregon is so undervisited, often you'll have vast areas of great land all to yourself.

Among the southeast's highlights are the Newberry Volcanic Monument, with East and Paulina Lakes set within its craters; Paulina is one of the best lakes for a chance to catch big brown trout in the Western United States. Other great spots include trailhead camps that provide access to Gearhart Mountain Wilderness in Fremont National Forest, and camps at Steens Mountain Recreation Lands. Here are also some of the most remote drive-to campgrounds in Oregon, particularly in underused Ochoco and Malheur National Forests, as well as the launch point for one of the best canoe trips, the Owyhee River. This watershed is like nothing most have ever seen. It looks like a miniature Grand Canyon, with steep, orange walls and the river cutting a circuitous route through the desert. I have paddled a canoe through most of it, lucking into a permit from its most remote stretches below the Jarbridge Mountains in Nevada through Idaho and then into Oregon.

Be aware, though, if you tour this area of Oregon, keep an eye on your gas tank and be alert about how far you are from the coming night's campground. You can cover a hellacious number of miles between either a chance for gas and a camp.

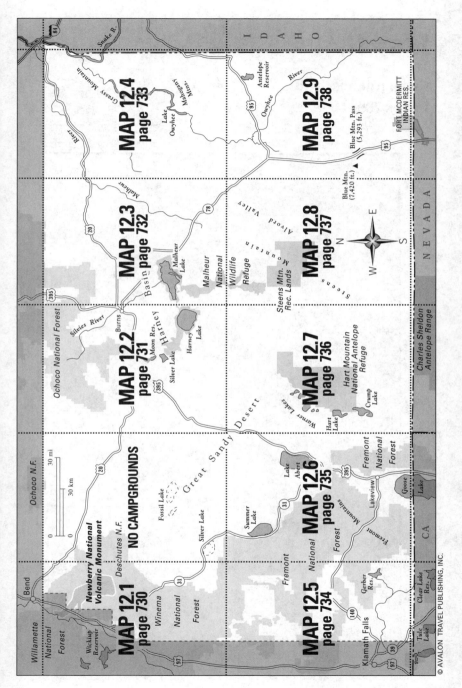

MAP 12.1
page 730

MAP 12.2
page 731

MAP 12.3
Basin page 732

MAP 12.4
page 733

MAP 12.5
page 734

MAP 12.6
page 735

MAP 12.7
page 736

MAP 12.8
page 737

MAP 12.9
page 738

NO CAMPGROUNDS

© AVALON TRAVEL PUBLISHING, INC.

Chapter 12 • Southeastern Oregon   729

Map 12.1

Campgrounds 1–10
Pages 739–742

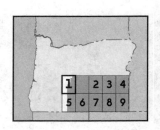

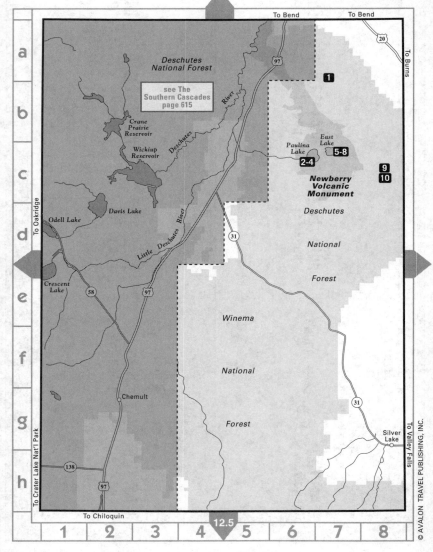

Map 12.2

Campgrounds 11–15
Pages 743–744

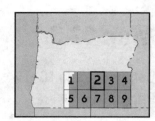

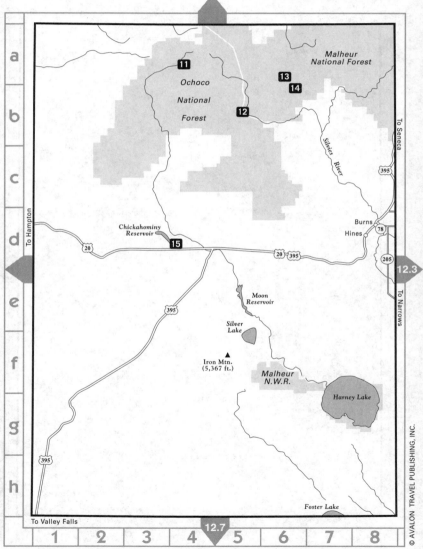

a

b

c

To Hampton

d

e

f

g

h

Malheur
National Forest

11

Ochoco

National

Forest

13
14

12

Silvies River

To Seneca

395

Burns

Hines

78

To Narrows

12.3

205

15
Chickahominy
Reservoir

20

20 395

395

Moon
Reservoir

Silver
Lake

▲
Iron Mtn.
(5,367 ft.)

Malheur
N.W.R.

Harney Lake

395

395

Foster Lake

To Valley Falls

12.7

1   2   3   4   5   6   7   8

© AVALON TRAVEL PUBLISHING, INC.

Map 12.3

Campgrounds 16–19
Pages 745–746

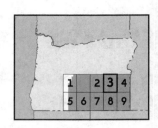

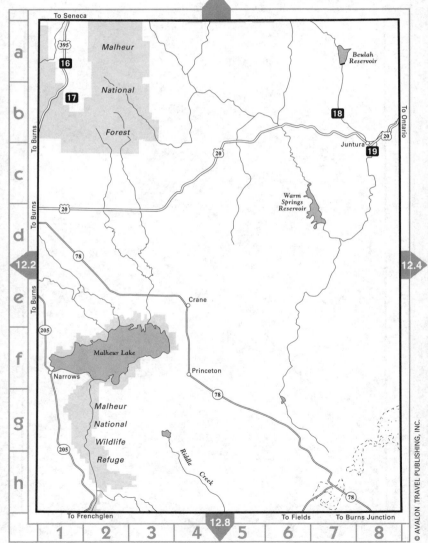

To Seneca

Malheur

National

Forest

16

17

18

19

Beulah Reservoir

Juntura

To Ontario

To Burns

To Burns

Warm Springs Reservoir

To Burns

12.2

12.4

Crane

Princeton

Narrows

Malheur Lake

Malheur

National

Wildlife

Refuge

Riddle Creek

To Frenchglen

12.8

To Fields

To Burns Junction

© AVALON TRAVEL PUBLISHING, INC.

Map 12.4

Campgrounds 20–24
Pages 746–748

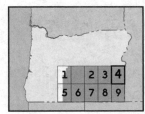

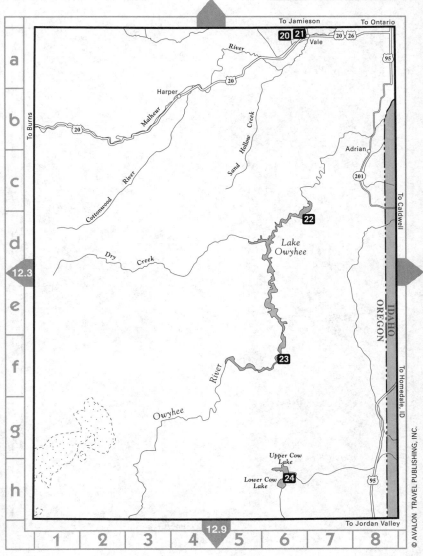

Map 12.5

Campgrounds 25–29
Pages 748–750

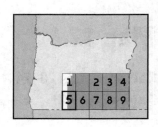

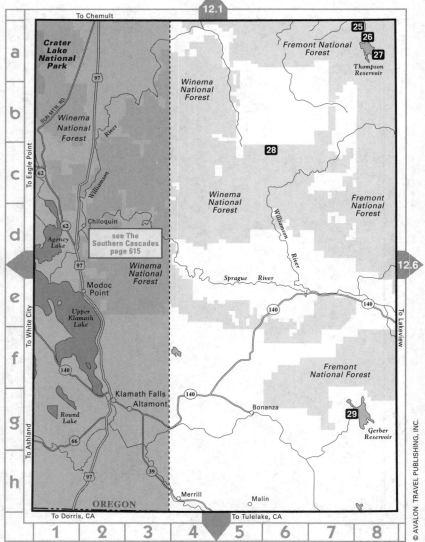

© AVALON TRAVEL PUBLISHING, INC.

Map 12.6

Campgrounds 30–46
Pages 750–757

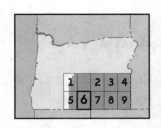

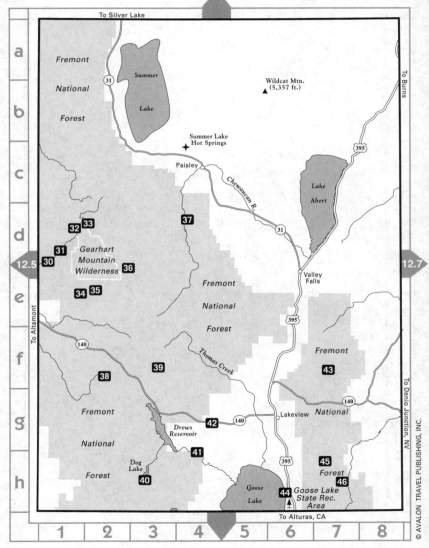

To Silver Lake

Fremont

National

Forest

31

Summer

Lake

Wildcat Mtn.
▲ (5,357 ft.)

To Burns

Summer Lake
✦ Hot Springs

Paisley

Chewaucan R.

395

Lake
Abert

a

b

c

d

e

f

g

h

32 33

31

30

Gearhart
Mountain
Wilderness

34 35

36

37

31

Valley
Falls

395

Fremont

National

Forest

Fremont

12.5

12.7

To Altamont

140

Thomas Creek

38

39

43

To Denio Junction, NV

140

Fremont

National

42

140

Lakeview

Drews
Reservoir

41

395

45

Forest

46

Fremont

National

Dog
Lake

40

Forest

Goose
Lake

44 Goose Lake
State Rec.
Area

To Alturas, CA

1   2   3   4   5   6   7   8

© AVALON TRAVEL PUBLISHING, INC.

Map 12.7

Campgrounds 47–48
Page 757

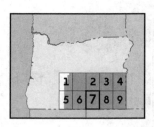

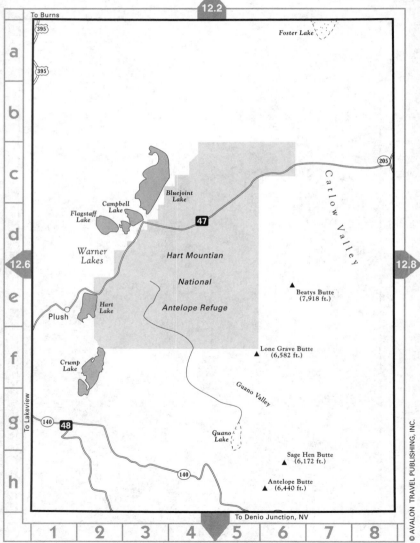

To Burns
395
395

Foster Lake

a

b

c

Bluejoint Lake

Campbell Lake

Flagstaff Lake

Catlow Valley

205

47

d

Warner Lakes

Hart Mountian

12.6

12.8

National

Beatys Butte (7,918 ft.)

e

Hart Lake

Antelope Refuge

Plush

Lone Grave Butte (6,582 ft.)

f

Crump Lake

Guano Valley

To Lakeview

140

48

g

Guano Lake

Sage Hen Butte (6,172 ft.)

140

Antelope Butte (6,440 ft.)

h

To Denio Junction, NV

12.2

1   2   3   4   5   6   7   8

© AVALON TRAVEL PUBLISHING, INC.

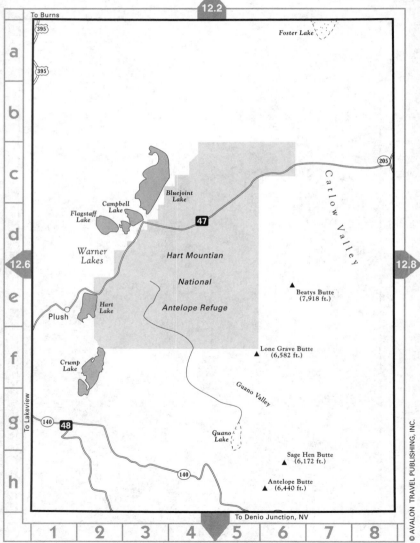

Map 12.8

Campgrounds 49–55
Pages 758–760

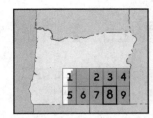

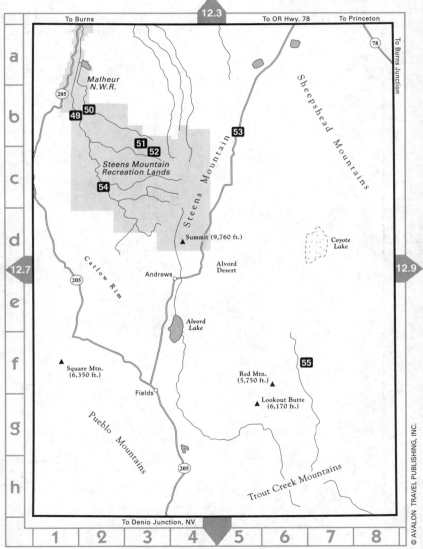

To Burns

12.3

To OR Hwy. 78   To Princeton

To Burns Junction

78

Malheur
N.W.R.

205

49 50

51

52

Steens Mountain
Recreation Lands

54

Steens Mountain

53

Sheepshead Mountains

Coyote
Lake

Summit (9,760 ft.)

Catlow Rim

205

Andrews

Alvord
Desert

Alvord
Lake

Square Mtn.
(6,350 ft.)

Fields

Red Mtn.
(5,750 ft.)

55

Lookout Butte
(6,170 ft.)

Pueblo Mountains

205

Trout Creek Mountains

12.7

12.9

© AVALON TRAVEL PUBLISHING, INC.

To Denio Junction, NV

Map 12.9

Campgrounds 56–57
Pages 760–761

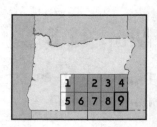

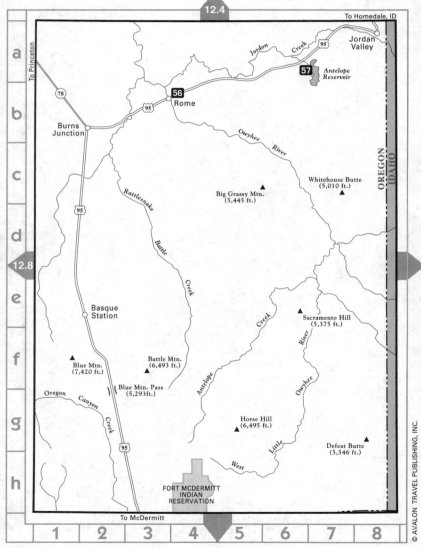

12.4

To Homedale, ID

a
To Princeton

Jordon Creek

95

Jordan Valley

57 Antelope Reservoir

78

95

56
Rome

b

Burns Junction

Owyhee River

Whitehouse Butte (5,010 ft.)

95

Rattlesnake

c

Big Grassy Mtn. (5,445 ft.)

OREGON IDAHO

Battle Creek

d

12.8

Basque Station

Creek

e

Sacramento Hill (5,375 ft.)

River

Blue Mtn. (7,420 ft.)

Battle Mtn. (6,493 ft.)

f

Oregon Canyon Creek

Blue Mtn. Pass (5,293ft.)

Antelope

Owyhee

95

Horse Hill (6,495 ft.)

g

Little

Defeat Butte (5,546 ft.)

West

h

FORT McDERMITT INDIAN RESERVATION

To McDermitt

© AVALON TRAVEL PUBLISHING, INC.

1   2   3   4   5   6   7   8

1 SWAMP WELLS HORSE CAMP

🚶 🐎 🚐 ⛺

Rating: 3

Near the Arnold Ice Caves in Deschutes National Forest.

Map 12.1, grid a7, page 730

If you look at the map, this campground may appear to be quite remote, but it's actually in an area that is less than 30 minutes from Bend. Set at an elevation of 5,450 feet, this area is a good place for horseback riding; trails heading south reenter the forested areas. The system of lava tubes at the nearby Arnold Ice Caves is fun to explore; bring a flashlight, bicycle helmet, and knee pads. A U.S. Forest Service map details trail options. You don't need a horse to enjoy this spot.

Campsites, facilities: There are six primitive sites for tents or RVs up to 22 feet long. Picnic tables and fire grills are provided. There are vault toilets, but no drinking water, and all garbage must be packed out. Leashed pets are permitted.

Reservations, fees: Reservations are not accepted. There is no fee for camping. Open April–late November.

Directions: From Bend, drive south on U.S. 97 for four miles to Forest Road 18. Turn southeast and drive 5.4 miles to Forest Road 1810. Turn right (south) and drive 5.8 miles to Forest Road 1816. Turn left (east) and drive three miles to the campground.

Contact: Deschutes National Forest, Bend-Fort Rock Ranger District, 1230 N.E. 3rd St., Suite A-262, Bend, OR 97701, 541/383-4000, fax 541/383-4700.

2 PAULINA LAKE

🚶 ≈ 🚣 🎣 🐎 ♿ 🚐

Rating: 8

On Paulina Lake in Deschutes National Forest.

Map 12.1, grid c6, page 730

This campground (6,350 feet elevation) is set along the south shore of Paulina Lake and within the Newberry National Volcanic Monument. The lake itself sits in a volcanic crater. Nearby trails provide access to the remains of volcanic activity, including craters and obsidian flows. My longtime friend Guy Carl caught the state's record brown trout here, right after I'd written a story about his unique method of using giant Rapala and Rebel bass lures for giant browns. The boat speed limit is 10 mph. The camp is adjacent to Paulina Lake Resort. The recreation options here include boating, sailing, fishing, and hiking. Note that food-raiding bears are common at all the campgrounds in the Newberry Caldera area, and that all food must be kept out of reach. Do not store food in vehicles.

Campsites, facilities: There are 69 sites for RVs up to 30 feet long. Picnic tables, garbage service, and fire grills are provided. Flush and vault toilets, showers, and a coin-operated laundry are within five miles. Drinking water is available. Some facilities are wheelchair accessible. Boat docks, launching facilities, boat rentals, a small store, a restaurant, cabins, gas, and propane are within five miles. The Newberry RV dump station is nearby. Leashed pets are permitted.

Reservations, fees: Reservations are not accepted. Sites are $10–12 per vehicle per night for the first two vehicles, $5 for each additional vehicle. Senior discount available. Open late May–late October.

Directions: From Bend, drive south on U.S. 97 for 23.5 miles to County Road 21 (Paulina/East Lake Road). Turn left (east) and drive 12.9 miles to the campground.

Contact: Deschutes National Forest, Bend-Fort Rock Ranger District, 1230 N.E. 3rd St., Suite A-262, Bend, OR 97701, 541/383-4000, fax 541/383-4700.

3 CHIEF PAULINA HORSE CAMP

Rating: 4

On Paulina Lake in Deschutes National Forest.

Map 12.1, grid c6, page 730

This campground is set at an elevation of 6,400 feet, about one-quarter mile from the south shore of Paulina Lake. Horse trails and a vista point are close by. See the description of Paulina Lake for additional recreation information.

Campsites, facilities: There are 14 sites for tents or RVs up to 30 feet long. Picnic tables, garbage service, and fire grills are provided. Vault toilets are available, but there is no drinking water. Boat docks and rentals are nearby. Leashed pets are permitted.

Reservations, fees: Reservations are not accepted. Sites are $12 per night, $5 per additional vehicle. Senior discount available. Open late May–late October, weather permitting.

Directions: From Bend, drive south on U.S. 97 for 23.5 miles to County Road 21 (Paulina/East Lake Road). Turn left (east) and drive 14 miles to the campground.

Contact: Deschutes National Forest, Bend-Fort Rock Ranger District, 1230 N.E. 3rd St., Suite A-262, Bend, OR 97701, 541/383-4000, fax 541/383-4700.

4 LITTLE CRATER

Rating: 8

Near Paulina Lake in Deschutes National Forest.

Map 12.1, grid c7, page 730

This campground is set at 6,350 feet elevation near the east shore of Paulina Lake in Newberry National Volcanic Monument, a caldera. This camp is very popular. See the description of Paulina Lake for more information.

Campsites, facilities: There are 50 sites for tents or RVs up to 30 feet long. Picnic tables, garbage service, and fire grills are provided. Drinking water and vault toilets are available. Boat docks and launching facilities are on-site, and boat rentals are nearby. Some facilities are wheelchair accessible. Leashed pets are permitted.

Reservations, fees: Reservations are not accepted. Sites are $14 per vehicle per night for the first two vehicles, plus $5 per additional vehicle. Senior discount available. Parking at the trailhead at the campground requires a Northwest Forest Pass ($5 daily fee or $30 annual fee per parked vehicle). Open late May–late October.

Directions: From Bend, drive south on U.S. 97 for 23.5 miles to County Road 21 (Paulina/East Lake Road). Turn left (east) and drive 14.5 miles to Forest Road 2110. Turn left (north) and drive one-half mile to the campground.

Contact: Deschutes National Forest, Bend-Fort Rock Ranger District, 1230 N.E. 3rd St., Suite A-262, Bend, OR 97701, 541/383-4000, fax 541/383-4700.

5 CINDER HILL

Rating: 7

On East Lake in Deschutes National Forest.

Map 12.1, grid c7, page 730

The campground is situated along the northeast shore of East Lake at an elevation of 6,400 feet. Located within the Newberry National Volcanic Monument, Cinder Hill makes a good base camp for area activities. Boating, fishing, and hiking are among the recreation options here. Boat speed is limited to 10 mph.

Campsites, facilities: There are 110 sites for tents or RVs up to 30 feet long. Picnic tables, garbage service, and fire grills are provided. Drinking water and flush and vault toilets are available. Boat docks and launching facilities are on-site, and boat rentals, a store, a restaurant, showers, a coin-operated laundry, and cabins are nearby at East Lake Resort. Some facilities are wheelchair accessible. Leashed pets are permitted.

Reservations, fees: Reservations are not accepted. Sites are $10–12 per vehicle per night for the first two vehicles, plus $5 per additional vehicle. Parking at the trailhead at the campground requires a Northwest Forest Pass ($5 daily fee or $30 annual fee per parked vehicle). Senior discount available. Open late May–late October.

Directions: From Bend, drive south on U.S. 97 for 23.5 miles to County Road 21 (Paulina/East Lake Road). Turn left (east) and drive 17.6 miles to Forest Road 2110-700. Turn left (north) and drive one-half mile to the campground.

Contact: Deschutes National Forest, Bend-Fort Rock Ranger District, 1230 N.E. 3rd St., Suite A-262, Bend, OR 97701, 541/383-4000, fax 541/383-4700.

6 EAST LAKE

Rating: 8

On East Lake in Deschutes National Forest.
Map 12.1, grid c7, page 730

This campground is set along the south shore of East Lake at an elevation of 6,400 feet. Boating and fishing are popular here, and hiking trails provide access to signs of former volcanic activity in the area. East Lake Campground is similar to Cinder Hill, but smaller. Boat speed is limited to 10 mph.

Campsites, facilities: There are 29 sites for tents or RVs up to 30 feet long. Picnic tables, garbage service, and fire grills are provided. Drinking water and flush and vault toilets are available. Some facilities are wheelchair accessible. Boat docks, launching facilities, and rentals are nearby. Leashed pets are permitted.

Reservations, fees: Reservations are not accepted. Sites are $10–12 per vehicle per night for the first two vehicles, plus $5 per additional

vehicle. Senior discount available. Open late May–late October.

Directions: From Bend, drive south on U.S. 97 for 23.5 miles to County Road 21 (Paulina/East Lake Road). Turn left (east) and drive 16.6 miles to the campground.

Contact: Deschutes National Forest, Bend-Fort Rock Ranger District, 1230 N.E. 3rd St., Suite A-262, Bend, OR 97701, 541/383-4000, fax 541/383-4700.

7 HOT SPRINGS

Rating: 5

Near East Lake in Deschutes National Forest.
Map 12.1, grid c7, page 730

Don't be fooled by the name. There are no hot springs at this campsite. It lies across the road from East Lake at 6,400 feet elevation. It's a good tent camping spot if you want to be near East Lake but farther away from RVs. See the description of East Lake for additional recreation information.

Campsites, facilities: There are 52 sites for tents or RVs up to 30 feet long. Picnic tables, garbage service, and fire grills are provided. Drinking water and vault toilets are available. Boat docks, launching facilities, and rentals are nearby. Leashed pets are permitted.

Reservations, fees: Reservations are not accepted. Sites are $7 per vehicle per night for the first two vehicles, plus $5 per additional vehicle. Senior discount available. Open late May–late October.

Directions: From Bend, drive south on U.S. 97 for 23.5 miles to County Road 21 (Paulina/East Lake Road). Turn left (east) and drive 17.2 miles to the campground.

Contact: Deschutes National Forest, Bend-Fort Rock Ranger District, 1230 N.E. 3rd St., Suite A-262, Bend, OR 97701, 541/383-4000, fax 541/383-4700.

8 EAST LAKE RESORT AND RV PARK

Rating: 7

On East Lake.

Map 12.1, grid c7, page 730

This resort offers shaded sites in a wooded, mountainous setting on the east shore of East Lake. Opportunities for fishing, boating, and swimming abound.

Campsites, facilities: There are 38 sites for tents or RVs up to 36 feet in length and 16 cabins. Electricity, drinking water, and picnic tables are provided. Flush toilets, bottled gas, showers, barbecues, cabins, firewood, a store, a café, a laundry room, ice, boat-launching facilities, boat rentals, and a playground are available. A dump station is on-site. Leashed pets are permitted.

Reservations, fees: Reservations accepted. Sites are $15 per night. Open mid-May–mid-October, weather permitting.

Directions: From Bend, drive south on U.S. 97 for 23.5 miles to County Road 21 (Paulina/East Lake Road). Turn left (east) and drive 22 miles to the campground at the end of the road.

Contact: East Lake Resort and RV Park, P.O. Box 95, La Pine, OR 97739, 541/536-2230, website: www.eastlakeresort.com.

9 CHINA HAT

Rating: 3

In Deschutes National Forest.

Map 12.1, grid c8, page 730

This remote campground is set at 5,100 feet elevation in a rugged, primitive area. There is direct trail access here to the East Fort Rock OHV Trail System. Hunters use China Hat as a base camp in the fall, but it is a summer base camp for off-road motorcyclists.

Campsites, facilities: There are 14 sites for tents or RVs up to 30 feet long. Picnic tables and fire grills are provided. Vault toilets are available. There is no drinking water, and all garbage must be packed out. Leashed pets are permitted.

Reservations, fees: Reservations are not accepted. There is no fee for camping. Open May–late October, weather permitting.

Directions: From Bend, drive south on U.S. 97 for 29.6 miles to Forest Road 22. Turn left (east) and drive 26.4 miles to Forest Road 18. Turn left (north) and drive 5.9 miles to the campground on the left.

Contact: Deschutes National Forest, Bend-Fort Rock Ranger District, 1230 N.E. 3rd St., Suite A-262, Bend, OR 97701, 541/383-4000, fax 541/383-4700.

10 CABIN LAKE

Rating: 3

In Deschutes National Forest.

Map 12.1, grid c8, page 730

This remote campground set at 4,500 feet elevation is adjacent to a bird blind that's more than 80 years old—it's a great place to watch birds. Primitive and secluded with sparse tree cover, this spot receives little use even in the busy summer months.

Campsites, facilities: There are 14 sites for tents or RVs up to 30 feet long. Picnic tables and fire grills are provided. Vault toilets and drinking water are available. All garbage must be packed out. Leashed pets are permitted.

Reservations, fees: Reservations are not accepted. There is no fee for camping. Open mid-May–late October.

Directions: From Bend, drive south on U.S. 97 for 29.6 miles to Forest Road 22. Turn left (east) and drive 26.4 miles to Forest Road 18. Turn left (north) and drive six miles to the campground on the left.

Contact: Deschutes National Forest, Bend-Fort Rock Ranger District, 1230 N.E. 3rd St., Suite A-262, Bend, OR 97701, 541/383-4000, fax 541/383-4700.

11 DELINTMENT LAKE

Rating: 7

On Delintment Lake in Malheur National Forest.

Map 12.2, grid a3, page 731

This very pretty, forested camp is set along the shore of Delintment Lake. Originally a beaver pond, the lake was gradually developed to its current size of 57 acres. It is now pretty and blue and is stocked with trout, providing good bank and boat fishing. Here's an insider's note: Rainbow trout here average 12–18 inches.

Campsites, facilities: There are 29 sites for tents or RVs up to 30 feet long. Picnic tables and fire grills are provided. Drinking water, a group picnic area on the lake with tables and grills, and vault toilets are available. All garbage must be packed out. Some facilities are wheelchair accessible. Launching facilities are in the campground. Leashed pets are permitted.

Reservations, fees: Reservations are not accepted. Sites are $7–10 per night, $3 per night for an additional vehicle. Senior discount available. Open May–October.

Directions: From Burns, drive southwest on U.S. 20 for three miles to County Road 127. Turn right (northwest) and drive about 18 miles to Forest Road 41. Turn left on Forest Road 41 and drive about 35 miles (staying on Forest Road 41 at all junctions, paved all the way) to the campground at the lake.

Contact: Malheur National Forest, Emigrant Creek Ranger District, 265 Hwy. 20 S, Hines, OR 97738, 541/573-4300, fax 541/573-4398.

12 EMIGRANT

Rating: 4

Near Emigrant Creek in Malheur National Forest.

Map 12.2, grid b5, page 731

You'll get peace and quiet here because this spot is usually uncrowded. One of two camps in the immediate area, it is set at an elevation of 5,200 feet in Malheur National Forest, in a meadow near Emigrant Creek. There's good fly-fishing here in the spring and early summer. Falls camp, two miles away, is busier but has drinking water. Several nearby backcountry dirt roads are good for mountain biking. See a U.S. Forest Service map for details.

Campsites, facilities: There are six sites for tents or RVs up to 30 feet long. Picnic tables and fire grills are provided, but there is no drinking water, and all garbage must be packed out. Vault toilets are available. Some facilities are wheelchair accessible. Leashed pets are permitted. Drinking water is available nearby at Falls.

Reservations, fees: Reservations are not accepted. Sites are $5 per night, $3 per night for an additional vehicle, except for towed vehicles. Senior discount available. Open May–October.

Directions: From Burns, drive southwest on U.S. 20 for three miles to County Road 127. Turn right (northwest) and drive 25 miles (passing Forest Road 41 on the left) to Forest Road 43 and the junction for Allison Guard Station, Delintment Lake, and Paulina. Turn left on Forest Road 43 and drive 9.75 miles to Forest Road 4340. Turn left and drive on Forest Road 4340-050 to the campground.

Contact: Malheur National Forest, Emigrant Creek Ranger District, 265 Hwy. 20 S, Hines, OR 97738, 541/573-4300, fax 541/573-4398.

13 YELLOWJACKET

Rating: 8

On Yellowjacket Lake in Malheur National Forest.

Map 12.2, grid a6, page 731

This campground (elevation 4,800 feet) in the ponderosa pines is set along the shore of Yellowjacket Lake, where fishing for rainbow trout can be very good in the summer. Boats without motors are encouraged. The camp is quiet and uncrowded.

Campsites, facilities: There are 20 sites for tents or RVs up to 22 feet long. Picnic tables, drinking water, and pit and vault toilets are available, but all garbage must be packed out. A boat launch is nearby. Leashed pets are permitted.

Reservations, fees: Reservations are not accepted. Sites are $7 per night, $3 per night for an additional vehicle, except for towed vehicles. Senior discount available. Open late May–October, weather permitting.

Directions: From Burns, drive southwest on U.S. 20 for three miles to County Road 127. Turn right (northwest) and drive 32 miles to Forest Road 37. Turn right and drive three miles to Forest Road 3745. Turn right and drive one mile to the campground on the right.

Contact: Malheur National Forest, Emigrant Creek Ranger District, 265 Hwy. 20 S, Hines, OR 97738, 541/573-4300, fax 541/573-4398.

14 FALLS

Rating: 5

Near Emigrant Creek in Malheur National Forest.

Map 12.2, grid b6, page 731

Falls camp is set in a beautiful meadow next to Emigrant Creek and is surrounded by ponderosa pine forests. This campground is a great place to see wildflowers in the early summer. A short trail leads to a small waterfall on the creek, from which the camp gets its name. Fly-fishing and mountain biking are good here, as well as at nearby Emigrant, set two miles down the road. The elevation is 5,200 feet.

Campsites, facilities: There are seven sites for tents or RVs up to 30 feet long. Picnic tables and fire grills are provided. Drinking water and vault toilets are available. Garbage must be packed out. Some facilities are wheelchair accessible. Leashed pets are permitted.

Reservations, fees: Reservations are not accepted. Sites are $7 per night, $3 per night for an additional vehicle, except for towed

vehicles. Senior discount available. Open May–October.

Directions: From Burns, drive southwest on U.S. 20 for three miles to County Road 127. Turn right (northwest) and drive 25 miles (passing Forest Road 41 on the left) to Forest Road 43 and the junction for Allison Guard Station, Delintment Lake, and Paulina. Turn left on Forest Road 43 and drive eight miles to the campground on the left.

Contact: Malheur National Forest, Emigrant Creek Ranger District, 265 Hwy. 20 S, Hines, OR 97738, 541/573-4300, fax 541/573-4398.

15 CHICKAHOMINY RESERVOIR

Rating: 4

On Chickahominy Reservoir.

Map 12.2, grid d4, page 731

While a good spot for group camping, this camp is set in the high desert with no shade. Weather conditions can be extreme, so come prepared. The camp is used primarily as an overnight stop for travelers driving through the area. Boats with motors are allowed on the reservoir. There is a new access road on the northwest side of the reservoir for day use. The nearest services are eight miles east (via U.S. 20) in Riley.

Campsites, facilities: There are 28 sites for tents or RVs up to 35 feet long. Picnic tables, garbage bins, and fire grills are provided. Drinking water and vault toilets are available. A fish-cleaning station is available nearby. Some facilities are wheelchair accessible. Leashed pets are permitted.

Reservations, fees: Reservations are not accepted. Sites are $6 per night per vehicle, with a stay limit of 14 days. Open April–October, weather permitting.

Directions: From Burns, drive west on U.S. 20 for 30 miles to the campground on the right.

Contact: Bureau of Land Management, Burns District, 28910 Hwy. 20 W, Hines, OR 97738, 541/573-4400, fax 541/573-4411, website: www.or.blm.gov/burns.

16 JOAQUIN MILLER HORSE CAMP

Rating: 5

In Malheur National Forest.
Map 12.3, grid a1, page 732

Campsites are spread out and there's a fair amount of privacy at this camp set among mature ponderosa pine and adjacent to a meadow. Expect some highway noise. Lots of old logging roads are available for walking, biking, and horseback riding. The camp gets low use; and while it caters to horse campers, all are welcome. Campers with horses are strongly advised to arrive early before weekends to claim the campsites set nearest to the corrals.

Campsites, facilities: There are 18 sites for tents or RVs up to 28 feet long. Picnic tables and fire rings are provided. Drinking water and vault toilets are available. All garbage must be packed out. Stock facilities include four corrals and hitching rails. Leashed pets are permitted.

Reservations, fees: Reservations are not accepted. There is no fee for camping. Open mid-May–November, weather permitting.

Directions: From Burns, drive north on U.S. 395 for 19 miles to the campground on the left (this turnoff is easy to miss; watch for a very small green sign on the right that says, Joaquin Miller Horse Camp).

Contact: Malheur National Forest, Emigrant Creek Ranger District, 265 Hwy. 20 S, Hines, OR 97738, 541/573-4300, fax 541/573-4398.

17 IDLEWILD

Rating: 8

In Devine Canyon in Malheur National Forest.
Map 12.3, grid b1, page 732

This campground is set at an elevation of 5,300 feet in Devine Canyon, a designated Sno-Park in the winter that's popular with locals for snowmobiling and cross-country skiing. Several hiking and biking trailheads start here, including the Divine Summit Interpretive Loop Trail and the Idlewild Loop Trail. Since it provides easy access and a pretty setting, it's also a popular spot for visitors traveling up U.S. 395 and in need of a stopover. Bird-watching for white-headed woodpeckers and goshawks is popular. Expect to hear some highway noise. But the ponderosa pine forest and area trails are so beautiful that this area can feel divine, even if Devine Canyon and neighboring Devine Ridge are spelled after the guy who named the place in the good old days when nobody worried about spelling.

Campsites, facilities: There are 26 sites for tents and five sites for RVs up to 30 feet long. Picnic tables, fire grills, and picnic areas are provided. Drinking water, a group shelter, and vault toilets are available. All garbage must be packed out. Some facilities are wheelchair accessible. Leashed pets are permitted.

Reservations, fees: Reservations are not accepted. Sites are $7 per night, $3 per night for an additional vehicle, except for towed vehicles. Senior discount available. Open late May–mid-October.

Directions: From Burns, drive north on U.S. 395 for 17 miles to the campground on the right.

Contact: Malheur National Forest, Emigrant Creek Ranger District, 265 Hwy. 20 S, Hines, OR 97738, 541/573-4300, fax 541/573-4398.

18 CHUKAR PARK

Rating: 7

Near the North Fork of the Malheur River.
Map 12.3, grid b7, page 732

This campground is set along the banks of the North Fork of the Malheur River. The general area provides habitat for chukar, an upland game bird species. Hunting can be good in season during the fall, but requires much hiking in rugged terrain. Trout fishing is also popular here. BLM asks that visitors please respect the surrounding private property.

Campsites, facilities: There are 18 sites for tents or RVs up to 28 feet long. Picnic tables, fire grills, and garbage services are provided. Drinking water (May–October only) and vault toilets are available. Leashed pets are permitted.

Reservations, fees: Reservations are not accepted. Sites are $5 per night per vehicle, with a 14-day stay limit. Senior discount available. Open year-round, with limited winter facilities.

Directions: From Burns, drive north on U.S. 395 for three miles to U.S. 20. Turn east and drive 55 miles to Juntura and Beulah Reservoir Road. Turn northwest and drive six miles to the campground.

Contact: Bureau of Land Management, Vale District, 100 Oregon St., Vale, OR 97918-9630, 541/473-3144, fax 541/473-6213.

19 OASIS MOTEL & RV PARK

Rating: 6

In Juntura.
Map 12.3, grid c8, page 732

One of the only camps in the area, this well-maintained RV park is close to Chukar Park. See the description of Chukar Park for more details.

Campsites, facilities: There are 22 sites, including eight drive-through, for RVs of any length, one cabin, and nine motel rooms. Electricity, drinking water, and sewer hookups are provided. Flush toilets, showers, a café, and ice are available. Leashed pets are permitted.

Reservations, fees: Reservations are not accepted. Sites are $16 per night. Open year-round.

Directions: From Burns, drive north on U.S. 395 for three miles to U.S. 20. Turn east and drive 55 miles to Juntura. The park is in Juntura (a very small town) along U.S. 20.

Contact: Oasis Motel & RV Park, P.O. Box 277, Juntura, OR 97911, 541/277-3605, fax 541/277-3312.

20 PROSPECTOR RV PARK

Rating: 5

In Vale.
Map 12.4, grid a6, page 733

Prospector is one of two RV parks (Westerner RV Park is the other) for travelers in the Vale area. For tents, this one is more comfortable, featuring a specifically designated wooded and grassy area. It claims to be a fishing and hunting paradise, and it even has a game bird cleaning room. It is set on the historical Oregon Trail.

Campsites, facilities: There are 10 tent sites and 28 drive-through sites for RVs of any length, plus a separate area for tents. Picnic tables are provided. Flush toilets, bottled gas, an RV dump station, showers, a laundry room, and ice are available. A store and a café are within one mile. Leashed pets are permitted.

Reservations, fees: Reservations accepted. Sites are $20 per RV, $8 per person per night, and $2–5 per person for more than two people. Senior discount available. Major credit cards accepted. Open year-round.

Directions: From Ontario (near the Oregon/Idaho border), drive west on U.S. 20/26 for 12 miles to Vale and U.S. 26. Turn north on U.S. 26 and drive one-half mile to Hope Street. Turn east and drive one block east to the park on the left.

Contact: Prospector RV Park, 511 N. 11th St. E, Vale, OR 97918, 541/473-3879, fax 541/473-2338.

21 WESTERNER MOTEL & RV PARK

Rating: 5

On Willow Creek.
Map 12.4, grid a6, page 733

This campground on the banks of Willow Creek provides a good layover spot for travelers heading to or from Idaho on U.S. 20/26. See the description of Prospector RV Park for more information.

Campsites, facilities: There are 10 sites for tents or RVs of any length and 14 motel rooms. Electricity, drinking water, cable TV, sewer hookups, and picnic tables are provided. Flush toilets, showers, a laundry room, and ice are available. Bottled gas, a store, a café, and a swimming pool are within two blocks. Leashed pets are permitted.

Reservations, fees: Reservations accepted. Sites are $10 per night, $1 per person for more than two people. Open year-round.

Directions: From Ontario (near the Oregon/Idaho border), drive west on U.S. 20/26 for 12 miles to Vale and to the junction of U.S. 26. The campground is on the left at the junction of U.S. 20 and U.S. 26.

Contact: Westerner Motel & RV Park, 317 A St. E, Vale, OR 97918, 541/473-3947.

22 LAKE OWYHEE STATE PARK

🏊 🎣 🚤 🐕 🚐 🏕️

Rating: 7

On Owyhee Lake.

Map 12.4, grid d7, page 733

This state park is set along the shore of 53-mile-long Owyhee Lake, a good lake for water-skiing in the day and fishing for warm-water species in the morning and evening. Owyhee is famous for its superb bass fishing. The place even has floating restrooms. Other highlights include views of unusual geological formations and huge rock pinnacles from the park. Bighorn sheep, pronghorn antelope, golden eagles, coyotes, mule deer, wild horses, and mountain lions live around here.

Campsites, facilities: There are seven sites for tents or self-contained RVs and 33 sites with water and electrical hookups for RVs up to 55 feet long. There are also two teepees. Drinking water, garbage bins, picnic tables, and fire grills are provided. Flush toilets, an RV dump station, and showers are available. Boat docks and launching facilities are available nearby. Leashed pets are permitted.

Reservations, fees: Reservations accepted for teepees only ($6 reservation fee) at 800/452-5687, website: www.oregonstateparks.org. Sites are $14–15 per night; teepees are $27 per night; $7 per night for an additional vehicle. Open mid-April–October.

Directions: From Ontario (near the Oregon/Idaho border), drive south on U.S. 20/26 for six miles to the Nyssa exit. Turn south and drive eight miles to Nyssa and Highway 201. Turn southeast on Highway 201 and drive eight miles to Owyhee. Turn east and drive about 20 miles to road's end and the entrance to the park.

Contact: Lake Owyhee State Park, 3012 Island Ave., 800/551-6949 or 541/339-2331.

23 LESLIE GULCH-SLOCUM CREEK

🚶 🎣 🚤 🐕 🚐 🏕️

Rating: 6

On Owyhee Lake.

Map 12.4, grid f6, page 733

This campground sits on the eastern shore of Owyhee Lake, not far from the Oregon/Idaho border. Warm-water fishing, water-skiing, and hiking are among the recreation options in this high desert area. Lake Owyhee State Park provides the other nearby recreation destination.

Campsites, facilities: There are 10 undeveloped sites for tents or RVs up to 20 feet long. Picnic tables and garbage service are provided. Vault toilets are available. There is no drinking water. Boat-launching facilities are available on-site. Leashed pets are permitted.

Reservations, fees: Reservations are not accepted. There is no fee for camping. The campground is open from mid-March–mid-November.

Directions: From U.S. 95 where it crosses the Idaho/Oregon border, drive north for five miles to McBride Creek Road. Turn west and drive 10 miles to Leslie Gulch Road. Turn left (west) and drive 15 miles to the campground.

Contact: Bureau of Land Management, Vale District, 100 Oregon St., Vale, OR 97918-9630, 541/473-3144, fax 541/473-6213.

24 COW LAKES

Rating: 6

Near Cow Lakes.
Map 12.4, grid h6, page 733

This little-used campground is adjacent to an old lava flow. The lake is shallow and murky, which makes fishing popular here. The campsites are open and treeless, and the road is rutted and rough in places.

Campsites, facilities: There are 10 sites for tents or small RVs. Picnic tables and fire rings are provided. Vault toilets and a boat ramp are available. No drinking water is available, and all garbage must be packed out. Leashed pets are permitted.

Reservations, fees: Reservations are not accepted. There is no fee for camping. Open year-round, weather permitting.

Directions: From Burns Junction, drive east on U.S. 95 for 30 miles to Danner Loop Road. Turn left (north) and drive 14 miles (past Danner) to Cow Lakes and the campground.

Contact: Bureau of Land Management, Vale District, 100 Oregon St., Vale, OR 97918-9630, 541/473-3144, fax 541/473-6213.

25 SILVER CREEK MARSH

Rating: 4

Near Silver Creek in Fremont National Forest.
Map 12.5, grid a8, page 734

A trailhead and terminus for segments of the National Recreational Trail are located at this small, quiet, and primitive camp that gets little attention. It's a short walk to the creek, a popular fishing spot. The camp is also set close to a wildlife area boundary.

Campsites, facilities: There are 17 tent sites. Picnic tables and fire grills are provided. Drinking water, vault toilets, and hitching rails and corrals for horses are available. Firewood is available nearby. All garbage must be packed out. Leashed pets are permitted.

Reservations, fees: Reservations are not accepted. There is no fee for camping. Open May–mid-November.

Directions: From Bend, drive south on U.S. 97 for 32 miles to Highway 31. Turn southeast on Highway 31 and drive 48 miles to County Road 4-11 (one mile west of the town of Silver Lake). Turn right and drive six miles (the road becomes Forest Road 27). Continue south for five miles to the campground entrance road on the left.

Contact: Fremont National Forest, Silver Lake Ranger District, P.O. Box 129, Hwy. 31, Silver Lake, OR 97638, 541/576-2107, fax 541/576-7587.

26 THOMPSON RESERVOIR

Rating: 3

On Thompson Reservoir in Fremont National Forest.
Map 12.5, grid a8, page 734

Located on the north shore of Thompson Reservoir among black-bark ponderosa pines the height of telephone poles, this simple and pretty camp features shaded sites close to the water. This area is popular for fishing and boating. See the description of East Bay. Water in the reservoir fluctuates and sometimes dries up altogether in late summer.

Campsites, facilities: There are 19 sites for tents or RVs up to 22 feet long, plus a separate group camping area. Picnic tables and fire grills are provided. Drinking water and vault toilets are available, but all garbage must be packed out. Boat-launching facilities are nearby. Leashed pets are permitted.

Reservations, fees: Reservations are not accepted. There is no fee for camping. Open May–mid-November.

Directions: From Bend, drive south on U.S. 97 for 32 miles to Highway 31. Turn southeast on Highway 31 and drive 48 miles to County Road 4-11 (one mile west of the town of Silver Lake). Turn right and drive six miles (the road becomes Forest Road 27) and continue south for nine miles to the campground entrance road. Turn left and drive one mile to the camp.

Contact: Fremont National Forest, Silver Lake Ranger District, P.O. Box 129, Hwy. 31, Silver Lake, OR 97638, 541/576-2107, fax 541/576-7587.

27 EAST BAY

Rating: 3

On Thompson Reservoir in Fremont National Forest.

This campground on the east shore of Thompson Reservoir has paved roads, but it's still a long way from home, so be sure to bring all of your supplies with you. A day-use area is adjacent to the camp. Silver Creek Marsh Campground provides an even more primitive setting along a stream.

Campsites, facilities: There are 17 sites, including two drive-through, for tents or RVs. Picnic tables, garbage bins, and fire grills are provided. Drinking water, vault toilets, and a fishing pier are available. Some facilities are wheelchair accessible. Boat-launching facilities are nearby. Leashed pets are permitted.

Reservations, fees: Reservations are not accepted. Sites are $8 per night, $5 per extra vehicle. Senior discount available. Open May–mid-November.

Directions: From Bend, drive south on U.S. 97 for 32 miles to Highway 31. Turn southeast on Highway 31 and drive 49 miles to Silver Lake. Continue east a short distance on Highway 31 to Forest Road 28. Turn right on Forest Road 28 and drive 13 miles to Forest Road 014. Turn right on Forest Road 014 and drive two miles to the campground.

Contact: Fremont National Forest, Silver Lake Ranger District, P.O. Box 129, Hwy. 31, Silver Lake, OR 97638, 541/576-2107, fax 541/576-7587.

28 HEAD OF THE RIVER

Rating: 8

On the Williamson River in Winema National Forest.
Map 12.5, grid c6, page 734
Almost nobody knows about this small, extremely remote spot on the edge of a meadow in the lodgepole and ponderosa pine, though hunters use it in the fall. The only camp for miles around, it's set at 4,500 feet elevation along the Williamson River headwaters, where you can actually see the beginning of the river bubbling up from underground springs.

Campsites, facilities: There are five sites for tents or RVs up to 30 feet long. Picnic tables, garbage bins, and fire pits are provided. Vault toilets are available. There is no drinking water. Leashed pets are permitted.

Reservations, fees: Reservations are not accepted. There is no fee for camping. Open from Memorial Day weekend through late November.

Directions: From Klamath Falls, drive north on U.S. 97 for 30 miles to Chiloquin and Sprague River Highway. Turn east on Sprague River Highway and drive five miles to Williamson River Road. Turn northeast and drive 20 miles to Forest Road 4648. Turn north on Forest Road 4648 and drive one-half mile to the campground.

Contact: Winema National Forest, Klamath Ranger District, 1936 California Ave., Klamath Falls, OR 97601, 541/885-3400, fax 541/885-3452.

29 GERBER RESERVOIR

Rating: 6

On Gerber Reservoir.
Map 12.5, grid g7, page 734
This camp can be found at an elevation of 4,800 feet alongside the west shore of Gerber Reservoir (10 mph boat speed limit). Off the beaten path, Gerber attracts mainly locals.

Recreation options include swimming, fishing, boating, and hiking.

Campsites, facilities: There are 50 sites for tents or RVs up to 30 feet long. Picnic tables and fire grills are provided. Drinking water, firewood, an RV dump station, vault toilets, a boat ramp, a boat dock, launching facilities, and a fish-cleaning station are available. Some facilities are wheelchair accessible. Leashed pets are permitted.

Reservations, fees: Reservations are not accepted. Sites are $7 per night, $4 per night for additional vehicle. Senior discount available. Open year-round, with drinking water and services available May–mid-September.

Directions: From Klamath Falls, drive east on Highway 140 for 16 miles to Dairy and Highway 70. Turn south on Highway 70 and drive seven miles to Bonanza and East Langell Valley Road. Turn east on East Langell Valley Road and drive 11 miles to Gerber Road. Turn left on Gerber Road and drive eight miles to the campground on the right.

Contact: Bureau of Land Management, Klamath Falls Resource Area, 2795 Anderson Ave,, Building 25, Klamath Falls, OR 97603, 541/883-6916, fax 541/884-2097, website: www.or .blm.gov/lakeview.

30 LEE THOMAS

Rating: 6

Near the North Fork of the Sprague River in Fremont National Forest.
Map 12.6, grid d1, page 735

This camp is set near the trailhead that provides access to the Dead Horse Rim Trail. Nestled along the North Fork of the Sprague River in the interior of Fremont National Forest, this small, cozy camp is a genuine hideaway, with all the necessities provided. It is set in a meadow at an elevation of 6,306 feet. Like Sandhill Crossing Campground, two miles downstream, this camp is popular with fishermen and hunters in the fall.

Campsites, facilities: There are eight sites for tents or RVs up to 16 feet long. Picnic tables and fire grills are provided. Drinking water and vault toilets are available. All garbage must be packed out. Leashed pets are permitted.

Reservations, fees: Reservations are not accepted. There is no fee for camping. Open June–late October.

Directions: From Lakeview, drive north on U.S. 395 for 23 miles to Highway 31. Turn northwest and drive 22 miles to Paisley. Continue on Highway 31 for one-half mile to Mill Street. Turn west on Mill Street and drive 20 miles (the road becomes Forest Road 33) and continue to the T intersection with Forest Road 28. Turn right and drive 11 miles to Forest Road 3411. Turn left and drive five miles to the campground.

Contact: Fremont National Forest, Paisley Ranger District, P.O. Box 67, Paisley, OR 97636, 541/943-3114, fax 541/943-4479.

31 SANDHILL CROSSING

Rating: 6

On the North Fork of the Sprague River in Fremont National Forest.
Map 12.6, grid d1, page 735

If you're looking for a combination of beauty and solitude, you've found it. This camp is set at 6,306 feet elevation on the banks of the designated Wild and Scenic North Fork Sprague River, where fishing is superior. Although a low-use camp, it is popular with anglers and hunters in the fall. A nearby trailhead leads into the Gearheart Wilderness.

Campsites, facilities: There are five sites for tents or RVs; some are drive-through sites. Picnic tables, fire grills, vault toilets, and drinking water are provided. All garbage must be packed out. Leashed pets are permitted.

Reservations, fees: Reservations are not accepted. There is no fee for camping. Open June–October.

Directions: From Lakeview, drive north on

U.S. 395 for 23 miles to Highway 31. Turn northwest and drive 22 miles to Paisley. Continue on Highway 31 for one-half mile to Mill Street. Turn west on Mill Street and drive 20 miles (the road becomes Forest Road 33); continue to the T intersection with Forest Road 28. Turn right and drive 11 miles to Forest Road 3411. Turn left and drive eight miles to the campground.

Contact: Fremont National Forest, Paisley Ranger District, P.O. Box 67, Paisley, OR 97636, 541/943-3114, fax 541/943-4479.

32 DEAD HORSE LAKE

Rating: 9

On Dead Horse Lake in Fremont National Forest.

Map 12.6, grid d1, page 735

The shore of Dead Horse Lake is home to this camp (at 7,372 feet elevation). It generally fills on most weekends and holidays. A hiking trail winds around the perimeter of the lake, hooking up with other trails along the way. One original Civilian Conservation Corps canoe, a relic of the 1930s, remains in the lake. Good side trips are nearby in Fremont National Forest. See description of Campbell Lake.

Campsites, facilities: There are nine sites for tents or self-contained RVs up to 16 feet long and a separate area with seven sites for group camping. Picnic tables and fire grills are provided. Drinking water and vault toilets are available, but all garbage must be packed out. A boat launch is nearby. Boats with electric motors are permitted, but gas motors are prohibited. All garbage must be packed out. Leashed pets are permitted.

Reservations, fees: Reservations are not accepted. There is no fee for camping. Open July–October.

Directions: From Lakeview, drive north on U.S. 395 for 23 miles to Highway 31. Turn northwest and drive 22 miles to Paisley. Continue on Highway 31 for one-half mile to Mill

Street. Turn west on Mill Street and drive 20 miles (the road becomes Forest Road 033); continue to the T intersection with Forest Road 28. Turn right and drive 11 miles (watch for the turn to Campbell-Dead Horse Lakes) to Forest Road 033. Turn left and drive three miles (gravel road) to the campground.

Contact: Fremont National Forest, Paisley Ranger District, P.O. Box 67, Paisley, OR 97636, 541/943-3114, fax 541/943-4479.

33 CAMPBELL LAKE

Rating: 9

On Campbell Lake in Fremont National Forest.

Map 12.6, grid d2, page 735

This campground on the pebbled shore of Campbell Lake is located near Dead Horse Lake Campground. These high-elevation, crystal-clear lakes were formed during the glacier period. Evidence of the past glacial nature of this area can be found on the nearby Lakes Trail system. Both camps are very busy, filling most weekends in July and August. No boats with gas motors are permitted on Campbell Lake. Good side trips are available in Fremont National Forest. A U.S. Forest Service map details the back roads.

Campsites, facilities: There are 21 sites for tents or RVs up to 16 feet long. Picnic tables and fire grills are provided. Drinking water and vault toilets are available. A boat launch is adjacent to the camp. Boats with electric motors are permitted, but gas motors are prohibited. All garbage must be packed out. Leashed pets are permitted.

Reservations, fees: Reservations are not accepted. There is no fee for camping. Open July–late October.

Directions: From Lakeview, drive north on U.S. 395 for 23 miles to Highway 31. Turn northwest and drive 22 miles to Paisley. Continue on Highway 31 for one-half mile to Mill Street. Turn west on Mill Street and drive 20

miles (the road becomes Forest Road 33) and continue to the T intersection with Forest Road 28. Turn right and drive eight miles to Forest Road 033. Turn left and drive two miles to the campground.

Contact: Fremont National Forest, Paisley Ranger District, P.O. Box 67, Paisley, OR 97636, 541/943-3114, fax 541/943-4479.

34 CORRAL CREEK

Rating: 4

Near the Gearhart Mountain Wilderness in Fremont National Forest.

Map 12.6, grid e1, page 735

Set along Corral Creek, this camp is adjacent to a trailhead that provides access into the Gearhart Mountain Wilderness, making it a prime base camp for a backpacking trip. Access is also available from camp to the Palisade Rocks, a worthwhile side trip. Another option is Quartz Mountain Snowpark, which is 14 miles east of the campground. The elevation is 6,000 feet.

Campsites, facilities: There are six sites for tents or RVs up to 16 feet long. Picnic tables and fire grills are provided. Vault toilets are available. There is no drinking water, and all garbage must be packed out. Stock facilities include hitching posts, stalls, and corrals. Leashed pets are permitted.

Reservations, fees: Reservations are not accepted. There is no fee for camping. Open mid-May–late October.

Directions: From Klamath Falls, drive east on Highway 140 for 53 miles to the town of Bly. Continue east on Highway 140 for another 13 miles to Forest Road 3660. Turn left and drive 13 miles to Forest Road 34. Turn right and drive about one-eighth mile to Forest Road 012 and continue to the campground.

Contact: Fremont National Forest, Bly Ranger District, P.O. Box 25, Bly, OR 97622, 541/353-2427, fax 541/353-2750.

35 DAIRY POINT

Rating: 6

On Dairy Creek in Fremont National Forest.

Map 12.6, grid e2, page 735

This campground, elevation 5,200 feet, is situated next to the Dairy Creek Bridge in a stand of ponderosa pine and white fir at the edge of a large and open meadow. The setting is beautiful and peaceful, with a towering backdrop of mountains. In the spring, wildflowers are a sight to behold; bird-watching can also be excellent this time of year. Fishing and inner tubing are popular activities at Dairy Creek. Warning: This campground is suitable for large groups and is often full on holidays and most weekends.

Campsites, facilities: There are four sites for tents or small, self-contained RVs. Picnic tables, fire grills, a vault toilet, and drinking water are provided. All garbage must be packed out. Leashed pets are permitted.

Reservations, fees: Reservations are not accepted. There is no fee for camping. Open mid-May–October.

Directions: From Lakeview, drive north on U.S. 395 for 23 miles to Highway 31. Turn northwest and drive 22 miles to Paisley. Continue on Highway 31 for one-half mile to Mill Street. Turn west on Mill Street and drive 20 miles (the road becomes Forest Road 33); continue to the T intersection with Forest Road 28. Turn left and drive two miles (crossing the Dairy Creek Bridge) to Forest Road 3428. Turn left and drive to the campground (just past the intersection on the left).

Contact: Fremont National Forest, Paisley Ranger District, P.O. Box 67, Paisley, OR 97636, 541/943-3114, fax 541/943-4479.

36 HAPPY CAMP

Rating: 6

On Dairy Creek in Fremont National Forest.
Map 12.6, grid e2, page 735

Here's a pleasant spot with open sites along Dairy Creek, though only one site is close to the water. The camp features some old Depression-era Civilian Conservation Corps shelters, preserved in their original state. There are three 1930s-era picnic shelters. Horseshoe pits are provided. Fishing is available here for rainbow trout, though the creek is no longer stocked. The camp sits at 5,289 feet elevation.

Campsites, facilities: There are nine sites for tents or RVs up to 16 feet long. Picnic tables and fire grills are provided. Vault toilets are available, but there is no drinking water. All garbage must be packed out. Leashed pets are permitted.

Reservations, fees: Reservations are not accepted. There is no fee for camping. Open mid-May–late October.

Directions: From Lakeview, drive north on U.S. 395 for 23 miles to Highway 31. Turn northwest and drive 22 miles to Paisley. Continue on Highway 31 for one-half mile to Mill Street. Turn west on Mill Street and drive 20 miles (the road becomes Forest Road 33); continue to the T intersection with Forest Road 28. Turn left and drive two miles (just before Dairy Creek) to Forest Road 047. Turn right and drive two miles to the campground on the left.

Contact: Fremont National Forest, Paisley Ranger District, P.O. Box 67, Paisley, OR 97636, 541/943-3114, fax 541/943-4479.

37 MARSTER SPRING

Rating: 6

On the Chewaucan River in Fremont National Forest.
Map 12.6, grid d4, page 735

This pretty campground is set at an elevation of 4,845 feet on the banks of the Chewau-

can River, a good fishing area. The largest of several popular camps in this river corridor, Marster Spring sits right on the river among ponderosa pine trees, yet is close to the town of Paisley. The Fremont National Recreation Trail is accessible at the Chewaucan Crossing Trailhead, one-quarter mile to the south.

Campsites, facilities: There are 11 sites for tents or RVs up to 22 feet long. Picnic tables and fire grills are provided. Drinking water and vault toilets are available. Leashed pets are permitted.

Reservations, fees: Reservations are not accepted. There is no fee for camping. Open May–October.

Directions: From Lakeview, drive north on U.S. 395 for 23 miles to Highway 31. Turn northwest and drive 22 miles to Paisley. Continue on Highway 31 for one-half mile to Mill Street. Turn west on Mill Street and drive seven miles (the road becomes Forest Road 33) to the campground on the left.

Contact: Fremont National Forest, Paisley Ranger District, P.O. Box 67, Paisley, OR 97636, 541/943-3114, fax 541/943-4479.

38 LOFTON RESERVOIR

Rating: 6

On Lofton Reservoir in Fremont National Forest.
Map 12.6, grid f2, page 735

This remote campground sits on the shore of Lofton Reservoir, a small lake that can provide the best trout fishing in this region. Other nearby lakes are accessible by forest roads. This area marks the beginning of the Great Basin, a high-desert area that extends to Idaho. A large fire burned much of the surrounding forest about 20 years ago, making this campground an oasis of sorts.

Campsites, facilities: There are 26 sites for tents or RVs up to 22 feet long. Picnic tables and fire grills are provided. Vault toilets are available. No drinking water is available. Garbage must be packed out. Boat docks and launching facilities are nearby. Leashed pets are permitted.

Reservations, fees: Reservations are not accepted. There is no fee for camping. Open mid-May–late October.

Directions: From Klamath Falls, drive east on Highway 140 for 54 miles to Bly. Continue east on Highway 140 for 13 miles to Forest Road 3715. Turn right and drive seven miles to Forest Road 013. Turn left on Forest Road 013 and drive one mile to the campground.

Contact: Fremont National Forest, Bly Ranger District, P.O. Box 25, Bly, OR 97622, 541/353-2427, fax 541/353-2750.

39 COTTONWOOD RECREATION AREA

Rating: 6

On Cottonwood Meadow Lake in Fremont National Forest.

Map 12.6, grid f3, page 735

This campground along the shore of little Cottonwood Meadow Lake is one of the better spots in the vicinity for fishing and hiking. Boats with electric motors are allowed on the lake, but gas motors are prohibited. Three hiking trails wind around the lake, and facilities for horses include hitching posts, feeders, water, and corrals. The camp is set at an elevation of 6,130 feet in a forested setting with aspen and many huge ponderosa pines.

Campsites, facilities: There are 21 sites for tents or small RVs. Picnic tables and fire grills are provided. Drinking water and vault toilets are available, but all garbage must be packed out. Boat docks are nearby. Electric motors are allowed, but gasoline motors are prohibited on the lake. The boating speed limit is 5 mph. Leashed pets are permitted.

Reservations, fees: Reservations are not accepted. There is no fee for camping. Open early June–mid-October.

Directions: From Lakeview, drive west on Highway 140 for 24 miles to Forest Road 3870. Turn right and drive about 10 miles to the campground.

Contact: Fremont National Forest, Lakeview Ranger District, 18049 Hwy. 395, Lakeview, OR 97630, 541/947-3334, fax 541/947-6375.

40 DOG LAKE

Rating: 5

On Dog Lake in Fremont National Forest.

Map 12.6, grid h3, page 735

This campground is located on the west shore of Dog Lake at an elevation of 5,100 feet. Fishing and boats with motors are permitted, though speeds are limited to 5 mph. Dog Lake provides a popular fishery for bass, perch, and crappie. Native Americans named the lake for its resemblance in shape to the hind leg of a dog. Prospects for seeing waterfowl and eagles are good.

Campsites, facilities: There are eight sites for tents or RVs up to 16 feet long. Drinking water, picnic tables, and fire grills are provided. Vault toilets are available. Garbage must be packed out. A boat launch is nearby. Leashed pets are permitted.

Reservations, fees: Reservations are not accepted. There is no fee for camping. Open mid-April–mid-October.

Directions: From Lakeview, drive west on Highway 140 for seven miles to County Road 1-13. Turn left on County Road 1-13 and drive four miles to County Road 1-11D (Dog Lake Road). Turn right and drive four miles (the road becomes Forest Road 4017) into national forest. Continue on Forest Road 4017 for 12 miles (two miles past Drew Reservoir) to Dog Lake and the campground entrance on the left.

Contact: Fremont National Forest, Lakeview Ranger District, 18049 Hwy. 395, Lakeview, OR 97630, 541/947-3334, fax 541/947-6375.

41 DREWS CREEK

Rating: 9

Near Lakeview in Fremont National Forest.
Map 12.6, grid h4, page 735
This is an exceptionally beautiful campground, set along Drews Creek at 4,900 feet elevation. Gorgeous, wild roses grow near the creek, and several unmarked trails lead to nearby hills where campers can enjoy scenic views. A great spot for a family trip, Drews Creek features horseshoe pits, an area for baseball, and a large group barbecue, making it equally popular with group campers. Fishing is available in nearby Dog Lake, which also provides facilities for boating. Water-skiing is another option at Drews Reservoir, two miles to the west.

Campsites, facilities: There are five sites for tents or RVs. Picnic tables, fire grills, vault toilets, and drinking water are provided. All garbage must be packed out. Leashed pets are permitted.

Reservations, fees: Reservations are not accepted. There is no fee for camping. Open early June–mid-October.

Directions: From Lakeview, drive west on Highway 140 for 10 miles to County Road 1-13. Turn left and drive four miles to County Road 1-11D. Turn right and drive six miles (the road will become Forest Road 4017) to the bridge that provides access to the campground.

Contact: Fremont National Forest, Lakeview Ranger District, 18049 Hwy. 395, Lakeview, OR 97630, 541/947-3334, fax 541/947-6375.

42 JUNIPERS RESERVOIR RV RESORT

Rating: 6

On Junipers Reservoir.
Map 12.6, grid g4, page 735
This resort on an 8,000-acre cattle ranch is situated in a designated Oregon Wildlife Viewing Area, and campers may catch glimpses of seldom-seen species. Many nature-walking trails meander through the park, and guests can also take driving tours. Fishing for catfish and trout can be good, and because it is a private lake, no fishing license is required. The summer climate is mild and pleasant. Antelope and elk can be spotted in this area.

Campsites, facilities: There are 15 tent sites and 40 sites for RVs of any length. Drinking water, restrooms, showers, an RV dump station, a public phone, modem access, a laundry room, and ice are available. Recreational facilities include a recreation hall, a volleyball court, and horseshoe pits. Some of the facilities are wheelchair accessible. Leashed pets are permitted.

Reservations, fees: Reservations are recommended. Sites are $18–24 per night. Senior discount available. Open May–mid-October.

Directions: From Lakeview, drive west on Highway 140 for 10 miles to the resort (at Milepost 86.5) on the right.

Contact: Junipers Reservoir RV Resort, 91029 Hwy. 140 W, Lakeview, OR 97630, 541/947-2050, website: www.junipersrv.com.

43 MUD CREEK

Rating: 4

On Mud Creek in Fremont National Forest.
Map 12.6, grid f7, page 735
This remote and quiet camp (at 6,600 feet elevation) is set in an isolated stand of lodgepole pines along the banks of Mud Creek. Drake Peak (8,405 feet elevation) is nearby. There are no other camps in the immediate vicinity. Fishing in Mud Creek is surprisingly good.

Campsites, facilities: There are seven sites for tents or RVs up to 16 feet long. Drinking water, picnic tables, fire grills, and vault toilets are available. Leashed pets are permitted.

Reservations, fees: Reservations are not

accepted. There is no fee for camping. Open June–mid-October.

Directions: From Lakeview, drive five miles north on U.S. 395 to Highway 140. Turn right on Highway 140 and drive eight miles to Forest Road 3615. Turn left and drive seven miles to the campground.

Contact: Fremont National Forest, Lakeview Ranger District, 18049 Hwy. 395, Lakeview, OR 97630, 541/947-3334, fax 541/947-6375.

44 GOOSE LAKE STATE PARK

Rating: 7

On Goose Lake.

Map 12.6, grid h6, page 735

This park is situated on the east shore of unusual Goose Lake, which lies half in Oregon and half in California. Waterfowl from the Pacific flyway frequent this out-of-the-way spot. It is home to many species of birds and other wildlife, including a large herd of mule deer that spends much of the time in the campground. When the lake is full, canoes and personal watercraft are popular here.

Campsites, facilities: There are 48 sites with partial hookups (water and electricity) for tents or RVs up to 50 feet long. Picnic tables, fire grills, garbage bins, and drinking water are provided. Flush toilets, showers, an RV dump station, a telephone, and firewood are available. Boat-launching facilities are nearby. Leashed pets are permitted.

Reservations, fees: Reservations are not accepted. Sites are $12 per night, $5 per night for an additional vehicle. Open from mid-April–late October.

Directions: From Lakeview, drive south on U.S. 395 for 14 miles to the California border and Stateline Road. Turn right (west) and drive one mile to the campground.

Contact: Goose Lake State Park, P.O. Box 207, New Pine Creek, OR 97635, 800/551-6949 or 541/947-3111.

45 WILLOW CREEK

Rating: 4

Near Willow Creek in Fremont National Forest.

Map 12.6, grid h7, page 735

This campground (at 5,800 feet elevation) is situated among tall pines and quaking aspen not far from the banks of Willow Creek. Among the secluded campsites, wildflowers bloom in the spring. The campground is set in a canyon, with campsites along the creek. A hiking trail offers access to the Crane Mountain Trail and a nearby dirt road heads north to Burnt Creek. Pick up a U.S. Forest Service map that details the back roads.

Campsites, facilities: There are eight sites for tents or RVs up to 22 feet long. Picnic tables and fire grills are provided. There is no drinking water, and all garbage must be packed out. Vault toilets are available. Leashed pets are permitted.

Reservations, fees: Reservations are not accepted. There is no fee for camping. Open June–mid-October.

Directions: From Lakeview, drive five miles north on U.S. 395 to Highway 140. Turn right (east) on Highway 140 and drive seven miles to Forest Road 3915. Turn right and drive nine miles to Forest Road 4011. Turn right and drive one mile to the campground.

Contact: Fremont National Forest, Lakeview Ranger District, 18049 Hwy. 395, Lakeview, OR 97630, 541/947-3334, fax 541/947-6375.

46 DEEP CREEK

Rating: 8

On Deep Creek in Fremont National Forest.

Map 12.6, grid h7, page 735

Shaded by huge ponderosa pines and cottonwoods and set on the banks of Deep Creek, this pretty, little-used campground is the place if you're after privacy. Magnificent spring wildflowers are a highlight here. The camp sits at an elevation of 5,600 feet.

Campsites, facilities: There are two sites for tents and four sites for RVs up to 22 feet long. Picnic tables and fire grills are provided. Vault toilets are available. There is no drinking water, and all garbage must be packed out. Leashed pets are permitted.

Reservations, fees: Reservations are not accepted. There is no fee for camping. Open June–mid-October.

Directions: From Lakeview, drive five miles north on U.S. 395 to Highway 140. Turn right (east) on Highway 140 and drive six miles to Forest Road 3915. Turn right on Forest Road 3915 and drive 14 miles to Deep Creek and the campground entrance road on the right (Forest Road 4015). Turn right and drive one mile to the campground.

Contact: Fremont National Forest, Lakeview Ranger District, 18049 Hwy. 395, Lakeview, OR 97630, 541/947-3334, fax 541/947-6375.

47 HART MOUNTAIN ANTELOPE REFUGE

Rating: 6

Near Adel.
Map 12.7, grid d4, page 736
One of the few campgrounds managed by the U.S. Fish and Wildlife Service, this unusual refuge features canyons and hot springs in a high desert area. There is no drinking water at the campground, but it can be obtained at the headquarters, which you pass on the way in. Some of Oregon's largest antelope herds roam this large area. The nearest place for supplies is in the town of Plush.

Campsites, facilities: There are 12 primitive sites for tents or RVs up to 20 feet long. Pit toilets are provided, but there is no drinking water. Garbage must be packed out. Leashed pets are permitted.

Reservations, fees: Reservations are not accepted. There is no fee for camping. Open

from May–November, with limited facilities in the winter.

Directions: From Lakeview, drive north on U.S. 395 for five miles to Highway 140. Turn east on Highway 140 and drive 28 miles to Adel and the Plush-Hart Mountain Cutoff. Turn left (signed for Hart Antelope Refuge) and drive north for 43 miles (first paved, then gravel) to the refuge headquarters. Continue four miles to the campground (the road is often impassable in the winter).

Contact: Hart Mountain National Antelope Refuge, P.O. Box 111, Lakeview, OR 97630, 541/947-3315, fax 541/947-4414, website: www.fws.gov.

48 ADEL STORE AND RV PARK

Rating: 5

In Adel.
Map 12.7, grid g1, page 736
This remote park is the only game in town, so you'd better grab it while you can. Recreation options in the area include hang gliding, rockhounding, or visiting Hart Mountain National Antelope Refuge, 40 miles north of Adel.

Campsites, facilities: There are eight sites for RVs of any length. Electricity, drinking water, and sewer hookups are provided. A store, a small café, and ice are available. Leashed pets are permitted.

Reservations, fees: Reservations accepted. Sites are $15 per night. Open year-round.

Directions: From Lakeview, drive five miles north on U.S. 395 to Highway 140. Turn right (east) on Highway 140 and drive 28 miles to Adel (a very small town). The RV park is in town along Highway 140 on the right.

Contact: Adel Store and RV Park, P.O. Box 58, Adel, OR 97620, 541/947-3850.

49 STEENS MOUNTAIN RESORT

Rating: 9

On the Blitzen River.
Map 12.8, grid b1, page 737

The self-proclaimed "gateway to the Steens Mountains," this resort is bordered by the Malheur National Wildlife Refuge on three sides, and it has great views. The mile-high mountain and surrounding gorges make an excellent photo opportunity. Hiking and hunting are other possibilities in the area. Fishing is available on the Blitzen River, with easy access from the camp.

Campsites, facilities: There are 99 sites for tents or RVs, plus nine cabins and one rental home. Drinking water, restrooms, showers, an RV dump station, a public phone, laundry facilities, and ice are available. Leashed pets are permitted.

Reservations, fees: Reservations at 800/542-3765. Sites are $12–20 per night, $5 per person for more than two people. Open year-round.

Directions: From Burns, drive east on Highway 78 for two miles to Highway 205. Turn south on Highway 205 and drive 59 miles to Frenchglen and Steens Mountain Road. Turn east and drive three miles to the resort on the right.

Contact: Steens Mountain Resort, North Loop Road, Frenchglen, OR 97736, 541/493-2415.

50 PAGE SPRINGS

Rating: 7

Near Malheur National Wildlife Refuge.
Map 12.8, grid b2, page 737

This campground is adjacent to the Malheur National Wildlife Refuge. The Frenchglen Hotel (three miles away) is administered by the state parks department and offers overnight accommodations and meals. Activities include hiking on the area trails, plus bird-watching, fishing, hunting, and sight-seeing.

Campsites, facilities: There are 36 sites for tents or RVs up to 35 feet long. Picnic tables, garbage service, and fire grills are provided. Drinking water and vault toilets are available. Some facilities are wheelchair accessible. A day-use area with a shelter is available nearby. Leashed pets are permitted.

Reservations, fees: Reservations are not accepted. Sites are $8 per vehicle per night, with a 14-day stay limit. Senior discount available. Open year-round.

Directions: From Burns, drive east on Highway 78 for two miles to Highway 205. Turn south on Highway 205 and drive 60 miles to Frenchglen and Steens Mountain Loop Road. Turn east and drive three miles to the campground.

Contact: Bureau of Land Management, Burns District, 28910 Hwy. 20 W, Hines, OR 97738, 541/573-4400, fax 541/573-4411.

51 FISH LAKE

Rating: 8

On Fish Lake.
Map 12.8, grid c3, page 737

The shore of Fish Lake is the setting for this primitive but pretty camp. Set among the aspens at 7,400 feet elevation, it can make an excellent weekend-getaway spot for sight-seeing. Trout fishing is an option, made easier by the boat ramp near camp.

Campsites, facilities: There are 23 sites for tents or RVs up to 35 feet long. Picnic tables, garbage bins, and fire grills are provided. Drinking water and vault toilets are available. Boat-launching facilities are nearby (nonmotorized boats only). Some facilities are wheelchair accessible. Leashed pets are permitted.

Reservations, fees: Reservations are not accepted. Sites are $8 per vehicle per night, with a 14-day stay limit. Senior discount available. Open from June–October, weather permitting.

Directions: From Burns, drive east on Highway 78 for two miles to Highway 205. Turn south on Highway 205 and drive 60 miles to

Frenchglen and Steens Mountain Loop Road. Turn east and drive 20 miles to the campground. **Contact:** Bureau of Land Management, Burns District, 28910 Hwy. 20 W, Hines, OR 97738, 541/573-4400, fax 541/573-4411.

52 JACKMAN PARK

Rating: 8

Near Malheur National Wildlife Refuge.
Map 12.8, grid c3, page 737
One of four camps in the area, Jackman Park is set at 7,800 feet elevation in the eastern Oregon desert. Fish Lake is 2.5 miles away. This scenic campground, with its aspen and willow trees, is known as one of the best places in the fall to view the golden aspen leaves on Steens Mountain. Trailers and RVs are not recommended on the access road.
Campsites, facilities: There are six primitive sites for tents. Picnic tables and fire rings are provided. Drinking water and pit toilets are available. Leashed pets are permitted.
Reservations, fees: Reservations are not accepted. Sites are $6 per vehicle a night, with a 14-day stay limit. Senior discount available. Open from July–late October, weather permitting.
Directions: From Burns, drive east on Highway 78 for two miles to Highway 205. Turn south on Highway 205 and drive 60 miles to Frenchglen and Steens Mountain Loop Road. Turn east and drive 22 miles to the campground
Contact: Bureau of Land Management, Burns District, 28910 Hwy. 20 W, Hines, OR 97738, 541/573-4400, fax 541/573-4411.

53 MANN LAKE

Rating: 8

On Mann Lake.
Map 12.8, grid b5, page 737
Mann Lake has two small boat ramps and a 10 horsepower limit on motors. Fishing, including wintertime ice fishing, and wildlife viewing are popular here. Weather can be extreme. The campground sits at the base of Steens Mountains and is open, with sagebrush and no trees. The scenic, high desert camp is mainly used as a fishing camp; please respect private property on parcels of land next to the lake. Fishing can be very good for cutthroat trout. Nearby Alvord Desert is also an attraction.
Campsites, facilities: There are dispersed sites for tents or RVs of up to 35 feet long; there are open areas on each side of the lake. No drinking water is available. Some facilities are wheelchair accessible. Garbage must be packed out. Leashed pets are permitted.
Reservations, fees: Reservations are not accepted. There is no fee for camping. Open year-round.
Directions: From Burns, drive southeast on Highway 78 for 65 miles to Fields/Denio Road (Folly Farm Road). Turn right (south) and drive 22 miles to the campground at Mann Lake.
Contact: Bureau of Land Management, Burns District, 28910 Hwy. 20 W, Hines, OR 97738, 541/573-4400, fax 541/573-4411.

54 SOUTH STEENS

Rating: 6

Steens Mountain Wilderness.
Map 12.8, grid c2, page 737
This campground is set on the edge of the Steens Mountain Wilderness. The area features deep, glacier-carved gorges, volcanic uplifts, stunning scenery, and a rare chance to see elk and bighorn sheep. Redband trout fishing is a mile away at Donner und Blitzen River and its tributaries, a new reserve. This campground is also good for horse campers, providing them with a separate area from the other campers. Trails are accessible from the campground.
Campsites, facilities: There are 36 sites for tents or RVs of up to 35 feet long; 15 of the

sites are designated for horse campers. Picnic tables, hitching posts, and fire grills are provided. Drinking water and vault toilets are available. Some facilities are wheelchair accessible. Leashed pets are permitted.

Reservations, fees: Reservations are not accepted. There is a 14-day stay limit. Sites are $6 per vehicle per night. Senior discount available. Open May–October, weather permitting.

Directions: From Burns, drive east on Highway 78 for two miles to Highway 205. Turn south on Highway 205 and drive 60 miles to Frenchglen. Continue south on Highway 205 for 10 miles to Steens South Loop Road. Turn left (east) and drive 18 miles to the campground on the right.

Contact: Bureau of Land Management, Burns District, 28910 Hwy. 20 W, Hines, OR 97738, 541/573-4400, fax 541/573-4411.

55 WILLOW CREEK HOT SPRINGS

Rating: 7

Near Whitehorse Butte.
Map 12.8, grid f7, page 737

This campground can be difficult to find, and only the adventurous should attempt this trip. A very small campground with no privacy, it features campsites about 100 feet from the hot springs, which are two connected smaller pools. Despite being out of the way, it still attracts travelers from far and away. The surrounding scenery is rocky hills, not a flat expanse.

Campsites, facilities: There are four sites for tents or small RVs. Fire rings are provided. Vault toilets are available. No drinking water is available, and all garbage must be packed out. Leashed pets are permitted.

Reservations, fees: Reservations are not accepted. There is no fee for camping. Open year-round, weather permitting.

Directions: From Burns, drive southeast on Highway 78 for 105 miles to Burns Junction and U.S. 95. Turn right (south) on U.S. 95 and drive 20 miles to Whitehorse Road. Turn right

(southwest) and drive 21 miles (passing Whitehorse Ranch); continue for 2.5 miles to a fork (look for the telephone pole). Bear left and drive two miles to the campground.

Contact: Bureau of Land Management, Vale District, 100 Oregon St., Vale, OR 97918-9630, 541/473-3144, fax 541/473-6213.

56 ROME LAUNCH

Rating: 6

On the Owyhee River.
Map 12.9, grid b3, page 738

This campground is used mainly by people rafting the Owyhee River and overnighters passing through. A few cottonwood trees and sagebrush live in this campground. There are some farms and ranches in the area. Campsites are adjacent to the Owyhee River. I have canoed most of the Owyhee from the headwaters in Nevada below the Jarbidge Mountains all the way through Idaho and into Oregon, and I would rate this river as one of the top canoeing destinations in North America. The Owyhee Canyon is quite dramatic, like a miniature Grand Canyon. Rome Launch is also a good wildlife-viewing area; mountain lions and bobcats have been spotted. Note: No motorized boats are allowed on the river.

Campsites, facilities: There are five sites for tents or small RVs. Picnic tables and fire rings are provided. Drinking water, vault toilets, and a boat launch are available. No firewood is available, and all garbage must be packed out. Leashed pets are permitted.

Reservations, fees: Reservations are not accepted. There is no fee for camping. Open March–November, weather permitting.

Directions: From Burns Junction, drive east on U.S. 95 for 15 miles to Jordan Valley and the signed turnoff for the Owyhee River and BLM-Rome boat launch. Turn south and drive one-quarter mile to the campground.

Contact: Bureau of Land Management, Vale

District, 100 Oregon St., Vale, OR 97918-9630, 541/473-3144, fax 541/473-6213.

57 ANTELOPE RESERVOIR

Rating: 3

On the Antelope Reservoir.

Map 12.9, grid a6, page 738

Water levels fluctuate at this shallow lake and it can dry up. An open area on a slope above the reservoir, the camp has no tree cover. Be prepared for extreme weather. The campground gets little use, except during the hunting season.

Campsites, facilities: There are four sites for tents or small RVs. Picnic tables and fire rings are provided. Vault toilets and boat access are available. No drinking water is available and all garbage must be packed out. Leashed pets are permitted.

Reservations, fees: Reservations are not accepted. There is no fee for camping. Open year-round, weather permitting.

Directions: From Burns Junction, drive east on U.S. 95 for 36 miles to the signed turnoff for Antelope Reservoir. Turn south and drive one mile to the campground on the left.

Contact: Bureau of Land Management, Vale District, 100 Oregon St., Vale, OR 97918-9630, 541/473-3144, fax 541/473-6213.

Resource Guide

Resource Guide

NATIONAL FORESTS

The Forest Service provides many secluded camps and allows camping anywhere except where it is specifically prohibited. If you ever want to clear the cobwebs from your head and get away from it all, this is the way to go.

Many Forest Service campgrounds are remote and have no drinking water. You usually don't need to check in or make reservations, and sometimes there is no fee. At many Forest Service campgrounds that provide drinking water, the camping fee is often only a few dollars, with payment made on the honor system. Because most of these camps are in mountain areas, they are subject to winter closure due to snow or mud.

Dogs are permitted in national forest with no extra charge. Always carry documentation of current vaccinations.

Northwest Forest Pass

A Northwest Forest Pass is required for certain activities in some Washington and Oregon national forests and at some national parks. The pass is required for parking at participating trailheads, rustic camping areas, boat launches, picnic areas, and visitor centers.

Daily passes cost $5 per vehicle; annual passes are $30 per vehicle. You can buy Northwest Forest Passes at national forest offices and dozens of retail outlets and online vendors. Holders of Golden Age and Golden Access (not Golden Eagle) cards can buy the Northwest Forest Pass at a 50 percent discount at national forest offices only, or at retail outlets for the retail price. Major credit cards are accepted at most retail and online outlets, but not at forest service offices.

More information about the Northwest Forest Pass program, including a listing of retail and online vendors, can be obtained at the following websites; www.fs.fed.us/r6/feedemo/ or www.naturenw.org

National Forest Reservations

Some of the more popular camps, and most of the group camps, are on a reservation system. Reservations can be made up to 240 days in advance and up to 360 days in advance for groups. To reserve a site, call 877/444-6777 or visit the website: www.reserveusa.com. The reservation fee is usually $9 for a campsite in a national forest, but group site reservation fees are higher. Major credit cards are accepted. Holders of Golden Age or Golden Access passports receive a 50 percent discount for campground fees, except for group sites.

National Forest Maps

National Forest maps are among the best you can get for the price. They detail all backcountry streams, lakes, hiking trails, and logging roads for access. They usually cost $8 and can be obtained in person at forest service offices. Maps can also be purchased through Nature of the Northwest, an interpretive center, by telephone at 503/872-2750 or by website: www.naturenw.org.

Forest Service Information

Forest Service personnel are most helpful for obtaining camping or hiking trail information. Unless you are buying a map or Northwest Forest Pass, it is advisable to call to get the best service. For specific information on a national forest, contract the following offices:

OREGON
USDA Forest Service
Pacific Northwest Region 6
333 SW First Ave.
P.O. Box 3623
Portland, OR 97208-3623
503/808-2651
website: www.fs.fed.us/r6

Deschutes National Forest
1645 Highway 20 East
Bend, OR 97701
541/383-5300
fax: 541/383-5531
website: www.fs.fed.us/r6/centraloregon

Fremont National Forest
1301 South G St.
Lakeview, OR 97630
541/947-2151
fax: 541/947-6399
website: www.fs.fed.us/r6/fremont

Malheur National Forest
431 Patterson Bridge Road
P.O. Box 909
John Day, OR 97845
541/575-3000
fax: 541/575-3001
website: www.fs.fed.us/r6/malheur

Mount Hood National Forest
16400 Champion Way
Sandy, OR 97055
503/668-1700 or 503/622-7674
website: www.fs.fed.us/r6/mthood

Ochoco National Forest
3160 N.E. Third Street, PO Box 490
Prineville, OR 97754
541/416-6500
fax: 541/416-6695
website: www.fs.fed.us/r6/centraloregon

Rogue River National Forest
333 W. Eighth St.
P.O. Box 520
Medford, OR 97501-0209
541/858-2200
fax: 54/858-2220
website: www.fs.fed.us/r6/rogue

Siskiyou National Forest
333 W. Eighth St.
Medford, OR 97503
541/858-2200
fax: 541/858-2220

Siuslaw National Forest
4077 S.W. Research Way
P.O. Box 1148
Corvallis, OR 97330
541/750-7000
fax: 541/750-7234
website: www.fs.fed.us/r6/siuslaw

Umatilla National Forest
2517 S.W. Hailey Ave.
Pendleton, OR 97801
541/278-3716
fax: 541/278-3730
website: www.fs.fed.us/r6/uma

Umpqua National Forest
2900 N.W. Stewart Parkway
P.O. Box 1008
Roseburg, OR 97470
541/672-6601
fax: 541/957-3495

website: www.fs.fed.us/r6/umpqua
Wallowa-Whitman National Forest
1550 Dewey Ave.
P.O. Box 907
Baker City, OR 97814
541/523-6391
fax: 541/523-1315
website: www.fs.fed.us/r6/w-w

Willamette National Forest
Federal Building
211 E Seventh Ave.
P.O. Box 10607
Eugene, OR 97440
541/225-6300
fax: 531/225-6223
website: www.fs.fed.us/r6/willamette

Winema National Forest
2819 Dahlia St.
Klamath Falls, OR 97601
541/883-6714
fax: 541/883-6709
website: www.fs.fed.us/r6/winema

WASHINGTON
Colville National Forest
765 South Main St.
Colville, WA 99114
509/684-7000
fax: 509/684-7280
website: www.fs.fed.us/r6/colville
Gifford Pinchot National Forest
10600 N.E. 51st Circle
Vancouver, WA 98682
360/891-5000
fax: 360/891-5045
website: www.fs.fed.us/r6/gpnf

Mount Baker-Snoqualmie National Forest
21905 64th Ave. West
Mountlake Terrace, WA 98043
425/775-9702 or 800/627-0062
fax: 425/744-3255
website: www.fs.fed.us/r6/mbs

Okanogan and Wenatchee National Forests
215 Melody Lane
Wenatchee, WA 98801-5933
509/662-4335
fax: 509/662-4368
website: www.fs.fed.us/r6/okanogan

Olympic National Forest
1835 Black Lake Blvd. S.W.
Olympia, WA 98512-5623
360/959-2402
fax: 360/956-2330
website: www.fs.fed.us/r6/olympic

NATIONAL PARKS

The national parks in Oregon and Washington are natural wonders, ranging from the breathtaking Crater Lake National Park to the often fog-bound Olympic National Park to the spectacular Mount Rainier National Park. Reservations are available at some of the campgrounds at these parks and recreation areas. Various discounts are available for holders of Golden Age and Golden Access passports, including a 50 percent reduction of camping fees (group camps not included).

For information about each of the national parks in Oregon and Washington, contact the parks directly at the following telephone numbers or addresses:

Pacific West Region
One Jackson Center
1111 Jackson St., Suite 700
Oakland, CA 94607
510/817-1300
website: www.nps.gov

OREGON

Columbia River Gorge National Scenic Area
902 Wasco Ave., Suite 200
Hood River, OR 97031
541/386-2333
fax: 541/386-1916
website: www.fs.fed.us/r6/columbia

Crater Lake National Park
P.O. Box 7
Crater Lake, OR 97604
541/594-3100
fax: 541/594-3010
website: www.nps.gov/crla

Crooked River National Grassland
813 S.W. Highway 97
Madras, OR 97741
541/475-9272
fax: 541/416-6694
website: www.fs.fed.us/r6/centraloregon

Hells Canyon National Recreation Area
88401 Highway 82
Enterprise, OR 97828
541/426-5546 or 541/426-4978
fax: 541/426-5522
website: www.fs.fed.us/r6/w-w/henra.htm

Oregon Dunes National Recreation Area
855 U.S. Highway 101
Reedsport, OR 97467
541/271-3611
fax: 541/271-6019
website: www.fs.fed.us/r6/siuslaw /oregondunes

WASHINGTON

Lake Roosevelt National Recreation Area
1008 Crest Dr.
Coulee Dam, WA 99116-1259
509/633-9441 or (509/738-6266
fax: 509/633-9332
website: www.nps.gov/laro

Mount Rainier National Park
Tahoma Woods, Star Route
Ashford, WA 98304-9751
360/569-2211
fax: 360/569-2170
website: www.nps.gov/mora

Mount St. Helens National Volcanic Monument
42218 N.E. Yale Bridge Road
Amboy, WA 98601
360/247-3900
fax: 360/247-3901
website: www.fs.fed.us/r6/gpnf

Olympic National Park
1835 Black Lake Blvd. SW
Olympia, WA 98512-5623
360/956-2402
fax: 360/956-2330
website: www.fs.fed.us/r6/olympic

STATE PARKS

The Oregon and Washington State Parks systems provide many popular camping spots. Reservations are often a necessity during the summer months. The camps include drive-in numbered sites, tens spaces, and picnic tables, with showers and bathrooms provided nearby. Although some parks are well known, there are still some little-known gems in the state parks systems where campers can get seclusion, even in the summer months.

Oregon

Oregon now sponsors a central reservation system. Reservations can be made for many Oregon state parks through Reservations Northwest at 800/452-5687. Online reservations for Oregon State Parks can be made through the website: www.oregonstateparks.org. A nonrefundable reservation fee of $6 is charged for a campsite, and the reservation fee for group sites is higher. Major credit cards are accepted for reservations, and credit cards are accepted at some of the parks during the summer. Under this system, reservations can be made throughout the year, up to nine months in advance.

General information regarding Oregon State Parks can be obtained by calling 800/551-6949 or accessing the website: www.oregonstateparks.org. For more information, contact: Oregon Parks and Recreation Department, 1115 Commercial St. N.E., Salem, OR 97301-1002.

Washington

More than 50 of the state park campgrounds are on a reservation system, and campsites can be booked up to nine months in advance at these parks. Reservations can be made by telephone at 888/CAMPOUT (888/226-7688) or online at website: www.parks.wa.gov/reservations. The reservation number is open from 7 a.m. to 8 p.m. (Pacific Standard Time) almost every day of the year. Major credit cards are accepted for reservations, and credit cards are accepted at some of the parks during the summer. A $7 reservation fee is charged for a campsite, and the reservation fee for group sites is higher. Discounts are available for pass holders of disabled, limited-income, off-season senior citizen and disabled veterans status.

General information regarding Washington State Parks can be obtained by telephoning 360/902-8844 or accessing the website: www.parks.wa.gov. For more information, contact: Washington State Parks and Recreation Commission, 7150 Cleanwater Lane, P.O. Box 42650, Olympia, WA 98504-2650.

BUREAU OF LAND MANAGEMENT

Most of the BLM campgrounds are primitive and in remote areas. Often, there is no fee charged for camping. Holders of Golden Age or Golden Access passports receive a 50 percent discount, except for group camps, at BLM fee campgrounds.

Oregon State Office
3333 W. First Ave.
P.O. Box 2965
Portland, OR 97208
503/808-6002
fax: 503/808-6308
website: www.or.blm.gov

Burns District
28910 Highway 20 West
Hines, OR 97738
541/573-4400
fax: 541/573-4411
website: www.or.blm.gov/burns

Coos Bay District
1300 Airport Ln.
North Bend, OR 97459
541/756-0100 or 888/809-0839
fax: 541/751-4303
website: www.or.blm.gov/coosbay

Eugene District
2890 Chad Dr.
P.O. Box 10226
Eugene, OR 97440-2226
541/683-6600 or 888/442-3061
fax: 541/683-6981
website: www.edo.or.blm.gov

Lakeview District
1301 South G St.
Lakeview, OR 97630
541/947-2177
fax: 541/947-6399
website: www.or.blm.gov/lakeview

Medford District
3040 Biddle Road
Medford, OR 97504
541/618-2200
fax: 541/618-2400
website: www.or.blm.gov/medford

Prineville District
3050 NE Third St.
P.O. Box 550
Prineville, OR 97754
541/416-6700
fax: 541/416-6798
website: www.or.blm.gov/prineville

Roseburg District
777 N.W. Garden Valley Blvd.
Roseburg, OR 97470
541/440-4930
fax: 541/440-4948
website: www.or.blm.gov/roseburg

Salem District
1717 Fabry Road S.E.
Salem, OR 97306
503/375-5646
fax: 503/375-5622
website: www.or.blm.gov/salem

Vale District
100 Oregon St.
Vale, OR 97918-9630
531/473-3144
fax: 541/473-6213
website: www.or.blm.gov/vale

U.S. ARMY CORPS OF ENGINEERS

Some of the family camps and most of the group camps operated by the U.S. Army Corps of Engineers are on a reservation system. Reservations can be made up to 240 days in advance and up to 360 days in advance for groups. To reserve a site, call 877/444-6777 or visit the website: www.reserveusa.com. The reservation fee is usually $9 for a campsite, but group site reservation fees are higher. Major credit cards are accepted. Holders of Golden Age or Golden Access passports receive a 50 percent discount for campground fees, except for group sites.

Portland District
333 SW First Ave.
P.O. Box 2946
Portland, OR 97208-2946
503/808-5150
fax: 503/808-4515
website: www.nwp.usace.army.mil

Walla Walla District
201 North Third Ave.
Walla Walla, WA 99362-1876
509/527-7700
fax: 509/527-7800
website: www.nww.usace.army.mil

DEPARTMENT OF NATURAL RESOURCES

The Department of Natural Resources manages more than five million acres of public land in Washington. All of it is managed under the concept of "multiple use," designed to provide the greatest number of recreational opportunities while still protecting natural resources.

The campgrounds in these areas are among the most primitive, remote, and least known of the camps listed in the book. The campsites are usually free, and you are asked to remove all litter and trash from the area, leaving only your footprints behind. Due to budget cutbacks, some of these campgrounds have been closed in recent years; expect more closures in the future.

In addition to maps of the area it manages, the Department of Natural Resources also has state forest maps, U.S. Geological Survey maps, and U.S. Army Corps of Engineers maps. For information about map sales, contact DNR Photo and Map Sales at 360/902-1234.

For more information, contact the Department of Natural Resources at its state or regional address:

State of Washington
1111 Washington St. S.E.
P.O. Box 47000
Olympia, WA 98504-7000
360/902-1000 or 800/527-3305
fax: 360/902-1775
website: www.wa.gov/dnr

Central Region
1405 Rush Road
Chehalis, WA 98532-8763
360/748-2383
fax: 360/748-2387

Northeast Region
225 S. Silke Road
P.O. Box 190
Colville, WA 99114-0190
509/684-7474
fax: (509) 684-7484

Northwest Region
919 N. Township St.
Sedro-Woolley, WA 98284-9384
360/856-3500
fax: 360/856-2150

Olympic Region
411 Tillicum Ln.
Forks, WA 98331-9271
360/374-6131
fax: 360/374-5446

South Puget Sound Region
950 Farman Ave. North
Enumclaw, WA 98022-9282
360/825-1631
fax: 360/825-1672

Southeast Region
713 Bowers Road
Ellensburg, WA 98926-9301
509/925-8510
fax: 509/925-8522

Southwest Region
601 Bond Road
P.O. Box 280
Castle Rock, WA 98611-0280
360/577-2025
fax: 360/274-4196

Oregon Department of Forestry
2600 State St.
Salem, OR 97310
503/945-7200
fax: 503/945-7212
website: www.odf.state.or.us

Tillamook State Forest
Forest Grove District
801 Gales Creek Road
Forest Grove, OR 97116
503/357-2191
fax: 503/357-4548
website: www.odf.state.or.us/tsf

Tillamook State Forest
Tillamook District
4907 E. Third St.
Tillamook, OR 97141-2999
503/842-2545
fax: 503/842-3143
website: www.odf.state.or.us/tsf

OTHER VALUABLE RESOURCES

Nature of the Northwest Information Center
800 NE Oregon St., Suite 177
Portland, OR 97232
503/872-2750
fax: 503/731-4066
website: www.naturenw.org

Oregon Department of Transportation
800/977-ODOT (6368) or 503/588-2941
website: www.odot.state.or.us

Tacoma Power
3628 S. 35th St.
P.O. Box 11007
Tacoma, WA 98411
253/502-8000
website: tacomapower.com

U.S. Geological Survey
Branch of Information Services
P.O. Box 25286
Federal Center
Denver, CO 80225
303/202-4700 or 888/ASK-USGS (888/275-8747)
website: http://earthexplorer.usgs.gov

Acknowledgments

The following state and federal resource experts provided critical information and galley reviews regarding changes in reservations, fees, directions, and recreational opportunities. We are extremely grateful for their timely help and expert advice:

U. S. Forest Service

Daniel Harkenrider, Columbia River Gorge National Scenic Area
Barbara Smith, Crooked River National Grassland, Haystack Reservoir
Tina Smith, Deschutes National Forest, Crescent Ranger District
Bob Henning, Deschutes National Forest, Sisters Ranger District
Theresa Whitmire, Fremont National Forest, Bly Ranger District
Barry Schullanberger, Fremont National Forest, Lakeview Ranger District
Annette Montgomery, Fremont National Forest, Paisley Ranger District
Doug Ehran, Fremont National Forest, Silver Lake Ranger District
Charlie Krauss, Klamath National Forest, Scott River Ranger District
Amanda Vonwiller, Malheur National Forest
Shannon Winegar and Tracie Lieuallan, Malheur National Forest, Blue Mountain
   Ranger District
Joan Suther, Malheur National Forest, Emigrant Creek Ranger District
Carole Holly, Malheur National Forest, Prairie City Ranger District
Christine Hunt, Mt. Hood National Forest, Barlow Ranger District
Glenda Woodcock, Mt. Hood National Forest, Clackamas River Ranger District
Doug Jones, Mt. Hood National Forest, Hood River Ranger District
Fran Lanagan, Mt. Hood National Forest, Zigzag Ranger District
Linda Rock, Ochoco National Forest
John Zapell, Oregon Dunes National Recreation Area
John McKelligott, Rogue River National Forest, Applegate Ranger District
Bryce Leppek, Rogue River National Forest, Ashland Ranger District
Newell Schooler, Rogue River National Forest, Butte Falls and Prospect Ranger Districts
Linda Elfman, Siskiyou National Forest, Chetco Ranger District
Judith McHugh, Siskiyou National Forest, Galice and Illinois Valley Ranger Districts
Theresa Miller, Siskiyou National Forest, Gold Beach Ranger District
Reenay Stinson, Siskiyou National Forest, Powers Ranger District
Kathy Bailey, Siuslaw National Forest, Hebo Ranger District
John Zapell, Siuslaw National Forest, Mapleton Ranger District
Roxanne Lechner, Siuslaw National Forest, Waldport Ranger District
Sheri Gregory, Umatilla National Forest, Heppner Ranger District
Karen Kendall, Umatilla National Forest, North Fork John Day Ranger District
Jeff Bloom, Umatilla National Forest, Walla Walla Ranger District
Cindy Pack, Umpqua National Forest, Cottage Grove Ranger District
Terry Klingenberg, Umpqua National Forest, Diamond Lake Ranger District
Wayne Brady, Umpqua National Forest, North Umpqua Ranger District
Lori Depew, Umpqua National Forest, Tiller Ranger District
Angelica Johnson, Wallowa-Whitman National Forest

Tom Smit, Wallowa-Whitman National Forest, Pine Ranger District
Betty Duncan, Wallow-Whitman National Forest, Unity Ranger District
Rick Thompson, Wallowa-Whitman National Forest
Rick Ley, Willamette National Forest, Blue River Ranger District
Ray Crist, Willamette National Forest, Detroit Ranger District
Dave Graham, Willamette National Forest, McKenzie Ranger District
Sherri Jensen, Willamette National Forest, Middle Fork Ranger District
Lupe Wilson, Willamette National Forest, Sweet Home Ranger District
Jeanie Sheehan, Winema National Forest
The publicity-shy staffs at Wallowa Mountains Visitor Center at Wallowa-Whitman National
    Forest, Eagle Cap, and Wallowa Valley Ranger Districts, Hells Canyon National
    Recreation Area
Nan Berger, Colville National Forest, Newport Ranger District
Dortha Sattler, Colville National Forest, Republic Ranger District
Leon Beam, Colville National Forest, Sullivan Lake Ranger District
George McNicholl, Colville National Forest, Three Rivers Ranger District
Diana Baxter, Colville National Forest, Three Rivers Ranger District, Colville Office
Jack Thorne, Gifford Pinchot National Forest, Cowlitz Ranger District
Ross Bluestone, Gifford Pinchot National Forest, Mount Adams Ranger District
Tom Linde, Gifford Pinchot National Forest, Mount Adams Ranger District, Wind River
    Work Center
Theresa Newton, Gifford Pinchot National Forest, Mount St. Helens National
    Volcanic Monument
Diane Holz and Diane Boyd, Mt. Baker-Snoqualmie National Forest, Darrington
    Ranger District
Eli Warren, Mt. Baker-Snoqualmie National Forest, Mount Baker Ranger District
Kelly Redfield, Mt. Baker-Snoqualmie National Forest, North Bend Ranger District
Pam Young, Mt. Baker-Snoqualmie National Forest, Skykomish Ranger District
Mary Coughlin, Mt. Baker-Snoqualmie National Forest, White River Ranger District
Margie Peterson, Okanogan and Wenatchee National Forests, Chelan Ranger District
Mike Ames, Okanogan and Wenatchee National Forests, Cle Elum Ranger District
Les Julian, Okanogan and Wenatchee National Forests, Entiat Ranger District
Susan Peterson, Okanogan and Wenatchee National Forests, Lake Wenatchee Ranger District
Robin Wanner, Okanogan and Wenatchee National Forests, Leavenworth Ranger District
Patricia Boley and Kathy Corrigan, Okanogan and Wenatchee National Forests, Methow
    Valley Visitor Center
Mikel Davis, Okanogan and Wenatchee National Forests, Naches Ranger District
Howard Christensen, Okanogan and Wenatchee National Forests, Tonasket Ranger District
Susan Graham, Olympic National Forest, Hood Canal Ranger District
Molly Erickson, Olympic National Forest, Pacific Ranger District
Steve Ricketts, Olympic National Forest, Quilcene Ranger District
Pete Erben and Daniel Hull, Olympic National Forest, Quinault Ranger District
Monte Fujishin, Umatilla National Forest, Pomeroy Ranger District
U.S. Army Corps of Engineers
Rich Hess, Portland District
Barbara Logston, Walla Walla District

U.S. Army Corps of Engineers
Terry Green, Portland Ranger District

Bureau of Land Management
Fred McDonald and Evelyn Treiman, Burns District
Nancy Zepf, Coos Bay District
Doug Huntington, Eugene District
Grant Wiedenbach, Lakeview District
Jim Leffman, Medford District
Charlie Moon, Prineville District
Chuck White, Roseburg District
Tina Tyler, Salem District
Tom Christensen and Bob Alward, Vale District
Staff, Baker City Office

National Parks
Raven Balderas, Crater Lake National Park
Lynne Brougher, Lake Roosevelt National Recreation Area
Steve Harvey and Patty Wold, Mount Rainier National Park
Joyce Brown and Nancy Holman, North Cascades National Park
Kathy Steichen and Maurie Sprague, Olympic National Park

National Wildlife Refuge
Tori Nunn, Hart Mountain National Antelope Refuge

Oregon State Parks
Debbie Lund, Ainsworth State Park
Greg Pelton, Beachside State Park
Patty Green, Beverly Beach State Park
Frank Arnold, Bullards Beach State Park
Pat Bry, Cape Blanco State Park and Humbug State Park
Brian Wais, Cape Lookout State Park
Bonnie Lee, Cascadia State Park
Sven Anderson, Cascara Campground
Jeff Powell, Champoeg State Heritage Area
Dennis Bradley, Clyde Holliday State Park and Unity Lake State Recreation Area
Barb Lakey, Collier Memorial State Park and Jackson F. Kimball State Park
Melanie Collins, Devil's Lake State Park
Bob Spratt, Deschutes River State Recreation Area
Mike Kuihuis, Detroit Lake State Park
Irene Fitzpatrick, Emigrant Springs State Heritage Area and Ukiah-Dale State Recreation Site
Bill Myers, Farewell Bend State Recreation Area
Macy Yates, Fort Stevens State Park
Wally Conklin, Goose Lake State Park
Fawn Gates, Jessie M. Honeyman Memorial State Park
Kelli Leiby, Joseph H. Stewart State Park

Ben Cox, Lake Owyhee State Park
Sue Gravin, LaPine State Park
Wanda Powell, Loeb State Park
Heidi Hansberger, Memaloose State Park
Eric Timmons, Milo McIver State Park
Randy Diestler, Minam State Park and Wallowa Lake State Park
Marsha Staben, Nehalem Bay State Park and Oswald West State Park
Arliss Perkins, Prineville Reservoir State Park
John Martin, Saddle Mountain State Park
Paul Lucas, Silver Falls State Park
Melanie Whisler, South Beach State Park
Celia Sheridan, Sunset Bay State Park
Lee Allen, Umpqua Lighthouse State Park
Diane McClay, Viento State Park
Donna Wilson, Valley of the Rogue State Park
Loretta Munsterman, William M. Tugman State Park

Oregon State Forest
Randy Peterson, Tillamook State Forest, Forest Grove District
Clyde Zeller, Tillamook State Forest, Tillamook District

Washington State Parks
Thuy Luu-Beams, Public Information Officer
Judy Sabin, Eastern Region Office
Billy Hoppe, San Juan Marine Area
John Clayton, Bogachiel State Park
Kay Keck, Spencer Spit State Park
Teri Ockwell, Central Ferry State Park
Andy Kallinen, Horsethief Lake State Park
John Scarola, Maryhill State Park
Mike Sternback, Sun Lakes State Park
Tom Poplawski, Steamboat Rock State Park
George Eidson, Daroga State Park
Rick Lewis, Pearrygin State Park
Rob Wilson, Lincoln Rock State Park
Matt Morrison, Wenatchee Confluence State Park
Jack Hartt, Riverside State Park
Robert Meyer, Birch Bay State Park
Barb Buman, Moran State Park
Kevin Kratochvil, Rasar State Park
Steve Shively, Fort Worden State Park
Bob Fisher, Fort Ebey State Park
Greg John, Bay View State Park
Brian Hageman and Josh Lancaster, Deception Pass State Park
Tom Riggs, Illahee State Park
Eric Plunkett, Beacon Rock State Park

John Ernster, Paradise Point State Park
Aaron Tritto, Kopachuck State Park
Janet Shonk, Jarrell Cove State Park
Dave Rush, Rainbow Falls State Park
Pam Ripp, Lewis and Clark State Park
Seth Mason-Todd, Millersylvania State Park
Terry Carlton, Ocean City State Park
JoAnne Gardner, Twin Harbors State Park
Tracy Zuern, Fort Canby State Park
State Department of Natural Resources
Sarah Thirtyacre, Darrell Fields, and Bud Clark, Central Region
Andrew Spenbeck, Northeast Region
Stan Kurowski, Northwest Region
Elena Kuo-Harrison, Olympic Region
Jon Byerly and Walt Pulliam, South Puget Sound Region
Jim Munroe, Southeast Region
Kris Aanzerud and Dee Becker, Southwest Region

Other

Paul Rehse and Gary Rinta, Tacoma Power
Bob Reynolds, Whitman County
Michelle Brooks, City of Entiat
Joe Miller, Snohomish County
Connie Thomas, City of Omak
Peggy Reifsnyder, City of Coulee City
Paul Wilson, Pend Oreille County
Lee Reynolds, City of Chelan
Scott Green, Skagit County
Cathy Mulhall, Chelan County
Rosemary Morrison, City of Oak Harbor
Valora Mendum, City of Anacortes
Bill Karruf, Snohomish County Parks
Laura Eastman, City of Auburn
Galin Downing, Clallam County

Index

YZ

Notes

Notes

Notes

Notes